ABS Tax Service

Tax Preparation Made Simple

By:
Mary W. Adams, E.A.

Edited By:
D. Blake
Linda Williams
Stella Steele

AuthorHouse™
1663 Liberty Drive
Bloomington, IN 47403
www.authorhouse.com
Phone: 1 (800) 839-8640

Published by AuthorHouse   07/07/2015

ISBN: 978-1-4670-4275-8 (sc)
ISBN: 978-1-4670-4273-4 (e)

Library of Congress Control Number: 2011917298

Print information available on the last page.

This book is printed on acid-free paper.

Table of Contents

Part I

Chapter 1 – The Basics 1-1

A Brief History of Taxation 1-1

The Tax Forms 1-6

A Brief Introduction to the Form 1040 1-16

Required Retention of Records 1-17

Assembly 1-17

How to File 1-18

Accounting Periods 1-18

Accounting Methods 1-18

Due Dates 1-21

Calculations 1-21

Chapter Review 1-22

Chapter 2 – Filing Status and Exemptions 2-1

Filing Status 2-1

Standard Deduction 2-7

Personal Exemptions 2-12

Dependent Exemptions 2-12

Qualifying Child 2-13

Qualifying Relative 2-23

Chapter Review 2-27

Exercise 2-29

Chapter 3 – Income 3-1

Line 7 – Wages, salaries, tips, etc 3-1

Lines 8a-9b Interest and Dividend Income 3-7

Line 10 – Taxable refunds, credits, or offsets of state and local income taxes 3-8

Line 11 – Alimony Received 3-8

Line 12 – Business income or (loss) 3-9

Line 13 – Capital gain or (loss) 3-9

Line 14 – Other gains or (losses) 3-9

Lines 15a and 15b – IRA distributions 3-9

Lines 16a and 16b – Pensions and annuities 3-9

Line 17 – Rental Real Estate, Royalties, Partnerships, S Corporations, etc. 3-9

Line 18 – Farm income or (loss) 3-9

Line 19 – Unemployment compensation 3-10

Lines 20a and 20b – Social security benefits 3-10

Line 21 – Other income 3-10

Let's tackle our first tax return.. 3-10

Chapter Review 3-17

Exercise 3-18

Chapter 4 – Tips and Other Income **4-1**

Tip Income 4-1

Interest Income 4-5

Dividends.. 4-11

Other Income 4-16

Chapter Review 4-18

Exercise 4-19

Chapter 5 – Credits, Part I.. **5-1**

Earned Income Credit... 5-1

Schedule EIC 5-9

Disallowance of Earned Income Credit in a Prior Year.................................... 5-9

Due Diligence 5-13

How much EIC are they entitled to receive?... 5-19

Child Tax Credit 5-30

Additional Child Tax Credit 5-34

Chapter Review 5-38

Exercise 5-39

Chapter 6 – Credits, Part II... **6-1**

Credit for Child and Dependent Care Expenses... 6-1

Credit for the Elderly or the Disabled... 6-11

Education Credits 6-14

Foreign Tax Credit... 6-17

Retirement Savings Contribution Credit 6-21

Residential Energy Credits 6-23

The Remaining Nonrefundable Credits 6-26

Excess Social Security and Tier 1 Railroad Tax Withheld................................ 6-26

The Remaining Refundable Credits... 6-27

Chapter Review 6-28

Exercise 6-29

Chapter 7 – Individual Retirement Arrangements (IRAs).................................. **7-1**

Contributions to a Traditional IRA.. 7-1

Traditional IRA Distributions 7-7

Contributions to a Roth IRA... 7-9

Roth IRA Distributions 7-15

SIMPLE IRA... 7-15

Chapter Review 7-18

Exercise 7-19

Chapter 8 – Retirement Income **8-1**

Pensions and Annuities 8-1

Railroad Retirement Benefits 8-12

Social Security Benefits 8-13

Chapter Review 8-17

Exercise 8-18

Chapter 9 – Adjustments to Income **9-1**

Educator Expense 9-1

Certain Business expenses of Reservists, Performing Artists, and Fee-Basis Governmental
Officials 9-1

Health Savings Accounts 9-3

Moving Expenses 9-4

Self Employment Adjustments 9-7

Penalty on Early Withdrawal of Savings 9-7

Alimony Paid 9-7

IRA Deduction 9-7

Student Loan Interest Deduction 9-7

Tuition and Fees Deduction 9-10

Domestic Production Activities Deduction 9-10

Chapter Review 9-13

Exercise 9-14

Chapter 10 – Affordable Health Care **10-1**

Minimum Essential Coverage 10-1

Exemptions 10-6

Individual Shared Responsibility Payment 10-13

Premium Tax Credit 10-22

Chapter Review 10-39

Exercise 10-41

Part II

Chapter 11 – Itemized Deductions **11-1**

Medical and Dental Expenses 11-1

Taxes Paid 11-6

Interest Paid 11-10

Charitable Contributions 11-12

Casualty and Theft Loss 11-15

Job Expenses and Certain Miscellaneous Deductions 11-19

Other Miscellaneous Deductions 11-19

Chapter Review 11-20

Exercise 11-21

Chapter 12 – Employee Business Expenses **12-1**

Travel Expenses 12-1

Meals 12-2

Entertainment 12-5

Gifts 12-7

Transportation 12-7

Business Use of Home 12-8

Reimbursements 12-11

Recordkeeping 12-12

Form 2106 12-14

Chapter Review 12-21

Exercise 12-22

Chapter 13 – Depreciation, Part I **13-1**

Depreciable Property 13-1

Types of Property 13-2

Basis 13-2

Which Depreciation to Use 13-3

Learning to Depreciate Step-By-Step 13-4

Prior Depreciation 13-12

Chapter Review 13-17

Exercise 13-18

Chapter 14 – Depreciation, Part II **14-1**

Form 4562 14-1

Chapter 1 Revisited 14-13

Sale of Depreciable Property 14-13

Chapter Review...14-16

Exercise 14-17

Chapter 15 – Self Employment Income **15-1**

Self Employed Taxpayers 15-1

Schedule C...15-2

Form 8829 15-8

Schedule SE 15-9

Chapter Review...15-15

Exercise 15-16

Chapter 16 – Rental and Royalty Income **16-1**

Rental Income 16-1

Royalty Income 16-1

Schedule E...16-1

Rental Income Belonging on a Schedule C 16-5

Personal Use of Rental Property...16-5

Vacation Home..16-5

Rental Not for Profit...16-6

Other Income Reported on the Schedule E 16-6

Chapter Review...16-8

Exercise 16-9

Chapter 17 – Capital Gains and Losses **17-1**

Capital Assets 17-1

Basis 17-2

Holding Period..17-4

Form 8949..17-5

Schedule D...17-6

Sale of a Main Home..17-16

Net Investment Income Tax 17-16

Comprehensive Example 17-18

Chapter Review...17-26

Exercise 17-27

Chapter 18 – AMT, Kiddie Tax, Underpayments, and Estimates....................**18-1**

Alternative Minimum Tax (AMT)..18-1

Kiddie Tax 18-10

Underpayment Penalty..18-17

Estimated Tax 18-20

Chapter Review...18-23

Exercise 18-24

Chapter 19 – Other Tax Topics...**19-1**

Amendments..19-1

Injured Spouse...19-8

Innocent Spouse..19-8

Household Employment Taxes..19-12

Extensions..19-12

Tax Preparers 19-16

Penalties 19-16

Electronic Filing..19-17

Chapter Review..19-21

Exercise 19-22

Appendix A – Tax Tables **A-1**

Appendix B – Earned Income Credit Tables **B-1**

Appendix C – Optional Sales Tax Tables **C-1**

Appendix D – Depreciation Tables..**D-1**

Appendix E – Schedule C Business Codes **E-1**

Appendix F - Answer Guide...**F-1**

Introduction

So, you would like to learn how to prepare tax returns. Maybe, you're looking for a new career or you just want to know more about your own tax return. This course will help you!

In this book, you will learn how to prepare a basic tax return. As you read through each chapter, you will learn the tax laws, and see them in practice in examples. At the end of each chapter, there will be an exercise so you can apply the knowledge you have gained in that chapter, because the best way to learn is through practice.

Note: For the more experienced tax preparer you will notice that we ignore credits, deductions, and penalties in the tax problems until we cover them in the text.

As you move through this course, you will not only learn how to prepare a basic return, but you will also be introduced to some of the more involved aspects of taxation. At the end of the book, in Appendix F, you will find the answers to the Chapter Review Questions and Exercises that are included at the end of each chapter. You can find the Forms and Schedules needed on the IRS website at www.IRS.gov. Don't worry, if you read the chapters and do the exercises, you'll do fine.

Good Luck!

Chapter 1 – The Basics

A Brief History of Taxation

Did you ever wonder how income taxes got started? Well, you're not alone. The first tax created for our great nation was created after the Revolutionary War. It was an excise tax placed on whiskey. After that, there were tariffs and taxes placed on different services and goods. These were placed whenever the nation was faced with war or national crisis.

In 1862, President Abraham Lincoln and Congress passed *The Revenue Act of 1862*. This was the first Federal Tax Law and was used to ease the burden of the Civil War debts. *The Revenue Act of 1862* created the Bureau of Internal Revenue.

The Revenue Act of 1862 was repealed 10 years later and declared unconstitutional in 1895. In 1913, Congress reinstated federal income tax under the 16th Amendment. The 16th Amendment gave Congress the authority to levy income tax. The following 4 pages show a tax return from 1864.

In 1950, the Internal Revenue Service was created. Over the years, tax laws have changed and because of these changes and the complexities of them, a need to protect and help taxpayers has arisen. The rest, as they say, is history…

(24.)

_____

INCOME TAX: 1864

By the sixth section of the Act of July 1, 1863, it is made the duty of any person liable to the income tax, on or before the first Monday of May in each year, to make a list or return of the amount of his annual income to the assistant assessor of the district in which he or she resides.

Every person who shall fail to make such return by the day specified, will be liable to be assessed by the assessor according to the best information which he can obtain; and in such case the assessor will add fifty per centum to the amount of the items of such list.

Every person who shall deliver to an assessor any false or fraudulent list or statement, with intent to evade the valuation of his income, is subject to a fine of five hundred dollars; and in such case the list will be made out by the assessor or assistant assessor, and from the valuation so made there can be no appeal.

As it is not impossible that certain changes in the rates of income tax may be adopted by the present Congress, the rate to which any income is liable cannot now be stated. The proposed changes, however, will not affect the principles upon which the return is to be made.

In no case, whatever may be the rate of tax to which an income is liable, is a higher rate than 1½ per cent to be assessed upon that portion of income derived from interest upon notes, bonds, or other securities of the United States. In order to give full effect to this provision, it is directed that when income is derived partly from these and partly from other sources, the $600 and other allowances made by law shall be deducted, as far as possible, from that portion of income derived from other sources.

When a married woman is entitled to an income which is secured to her own use, free from any control of her husband, the return should be made in her own name, and the assessment will be made separate from that assessed against her husband. Where a husband and wife live together, and their taxable incomes are in excess of $600, they will be entitled to but one deduction of $600 — that being the average fixed by law as an estimated commutation for the expense of maintaining a family. Where they live apart, by divorce or under contract of separation, they will be each entitled to a deduction of $600.

Guardians and trustees, whether such trustees are so by virtue of their office as executors, administrators, or other fiduciary capacity, are required to make return of the income belonging to minors or other persons which may be held by them in trust; and the income tax will be assessed upon the amount returned, after deducting such sums as are exempted by law: Provided, That the exemption of six hundred dollars shall not be allowed on account of any minor or other beneficiary of a trust, except upon the statement of the guardian or trustee, made under oath, that the minor or beneficiary has no other income from which the said amount of six hundred dollars may be exempted and deducted. Every fatherless child who is possessed of an income in his own right is entitled to the exemption.

On the following pages will be found detailed statements to assist in making out returns.

DETAILED STATEMENT OF SOURCES OF INCOME AND THE AMOUNT DERIVED FROM EACH, DURING THE YEAR 1863.

☞ *Gross Amounts must be stated.* ☜	AMOUNTS.	
1. Income of a resident in the United States from profits on any trade, business, or vocation, or any interest therein, wherever carried on		
2. From rents, or the use of real estate		
3. From interest on notes, bonds, mortgages, or other personal securities, not those of the United States		
4. From interest on notes, bonds, or other securities of the United States		
5. From interest or dividends on any bonds or other evidences of indebtedness of any railroad company or corporation		
6. From interest or dividends on stock, capital, or deposits in any bank, trust company, or savings institution, insurance or railroad company, or corporation		
7. From interest on bonds or dividends on stock, shares or property in gas, bridge, canal, turnpike, express, telegraph, steamboat, ferry-boat, or manufacturing company or corporation, or from the business usually done thereby . . .		
8. From property, securities, or stocks owned in the United States by a citizen thereof residing abroad, not in the employment of the Government of the United States		
9. From salary other than as an officer or employee of the United States		
10. From salary as an officer or employee of the United States		
11. From farms or plantations, including all products and profits		
12. From advertisements		
13. From all sources not herein enumerated		
TOTAL		

DETAILED STATEMENT OF DEDUCTIONS AUTHORIZED TO BE MADE

	AMOUNTS.	
1. Expenses necessarily incurred and paid in carrying on any trade, business, or vocation, such as rent of store, clerk hire, insurance, fuel, freight, etc. . .		
2. Amount actually paid by a property owner for necessary repairs, insurance, and interest on incumbrances upon his property		
3. Amount paid by a farmer or planter for—		
(a) Hired labor, including the subsistence of the laborers		
(b) Necessary repairs upon his farm or plantation		
(c) Insurance, and interest on incumbrances upon his farm or plantation . . .		
4. Other national, state, and local taxes assessed and paid for the year 1863, and not elsewhere included		
5. Amount actually paid for rent of the dwelling-house or estate occupied as a residence		
6. Exempted by law, (except in the case of a citizen of the United States residing abroad,) $600	600	00
7. Income from interest or dividends on stock, capital, or deposits in any bank, trust company, or savings institution, insurance, or railroad company, from which 3 per cent thereon was withheld by the officers thereof		
8. Income from interest on bonds, or other evidences of indebtedness of any railroad company or corporation, from which 3 per cent thereon was withheld by the officers thereof		
9. Salaries of officers, or payments to persons in the civil, military, naval, or other service of the United States, in excess of $600		
10. Income from advertisements, on which 3 per cent was paid		
TOTAL		

I hereby certify that the following is a true and faithful statement of the gains, profits, or income of .... of .... in the County of ...., and State of ...., whether derived from any kind of property, rents, interest, dividends, salary, or from any profession, trade, employment, or vocation, or from any other source whatever, from the 1st day of January to the 31st day of December, 1863, both days inclusive, and subject to an Income Tax under the excise laws of the United States:

	RATE.	AMOUNT.	AMOUNT OF TAX.
Income subject to	3 percent.		
De. subject to	per cent.		
Income derived from interest upon notes, bonds, or other securities of the United States, subject to	1½ per cent.		
Income from property in the United States owned by a citizen thereof residing abroad, subject to .	per cent.		
Income exceeding upon a portion of which a tax of 3 per cent has already been paid, subject to .	per cent.		
TOTAL			

(Signed)

Dated at .... **this** .... **day**

of ...., 1864.

Sworn and subscribed before me, this .... **day**

of ...., 1864.

_____

Assistant Assessor.

1-5

The Tax Forms

Every tax return must have one of these four forms:

- Form 1040EZ
- Form 1040A
- Form 1040
- Form 1040NR

1040NR

The first form we'll discuss is the 1040NR (Illustration 1-1). A resident alien will file a tax return following the same rules as a U.S. citizen. If the taxpayer is a nonresident alien with U.S. source income, they will be required to file a Form 1040NR. This form will not be covered any further in this course.

Illustration 1-1

Form **1040NR**

Department of the Treasury
Internal Revenue Service

U.S. Nonresident Alien Income Tax Return

▶ Information about Form 1040NR and its separate instructions is at *www.irs.gov/form1040nr*.

For the year January 1–December 31, 2014, or other tax year
beginning _____ , 2014, and ending _____ , 20 ____

OMB No. 1545-0074

2014

	Your first name and initial	Last name	Identifying number (see instructions)

Please print or type

Present home address (number, street, and apt. no., or rural route). If you have a P.O. box, see instructions.

Check if: ☐ Individual ☐ Estate or Trust

City, town or post office, state, and ZIP code. If you have a foreign address, also complete spaces below (see instructions).

Foreign country name	Foreign province/state/county	Foreign postal code

Filing Status

Check only one box.

- 1 ☐ Single resident of Canada or Mexico or single U.S. national
- 2 ☐ Other single nonresident alien
- 3 ☐ Married resident of Canada or Mexico or married U.S. national
- 4 ☐ Married resident of South Korea
- 5 ☐ Other married nonresident alien
- 6 ☐ Qualifying widow(er) with dependent child (see instructions)

If you checked box 3 or 4 above, enter the information below.

(i) Spouse's first name and initial	(ii) Spouse's last name	(iii) Spouse's identifying number

Exemptions

If more than four dependents, see instructions.

7a ☐ **Yourself.** If someone can claim you as a dependent, **do not** check box 7a . . . .

b ☐ **Spouse.** Check box 7b only if you checked box 3 or 4 above **and** your spouse **did not** have any U.S. gross income . . . .

c Dependents: (see instructions)

(1) First name Last name	(2) Dependent's identifying number	(3) Dependent's relationship to you	(4) ✔ if qualifying child for child tax credit (see instr.)
			☐
			☐
			☐
			☐

Boxes checked on 7a and 7b _____
No. of children on 7c who:
• lived with you _____
• did not live with you due to divorce or separation (see instructions) _____
Dependents on 7c not entered above _____

d Total number of exemptions claimed . . . .

Add numbers on lines above ▶ ☐

Income Effectively Connected With U.S. Trade/ Business

Attach Form(s) W-2, 1042-S, SSA-1042S, RRB-1042S, and 8288-A here. Also attach Form(s) 1099-R if tax was withheld.

8	Wages, salaries, tips, etc. Attach Form(s) W-2	**8**	
9a	**Taxable** interest	**9a**	
b	**Tax-exempt** interest. **Do not** include on line 9a	**9b**	
10a	Ordinary dividends	**10a**	
b	Qualified dividends (see instructions)	**10b**	
11	Taxable refunds, credits, or offsets of state and local income taxes (see instructions) . .	**11**	
12	Scholarship and fellowship grants. Attach Form(s) 1042-S or required statement (see instructions)	**12**	
13	Business income or (loss). Attach Schedule C or C-EZ (Form 1040)	**13**	
14	Capital gain or (loss). Attach Schedule D (Form 1040) if required. If not required, check here ☐	**14**	
15	Other gains or (losses). Attach Form 4797	**15**	
16a	IRA distributions . .	16a _____	**16b** Taxable amount (see instructions)	**16b**	
17a	Pensions and annuities	17a _____	**17b** Taxable amount (see instructions)	**17b**	
18	Rental real estate, royalties, partnerships, trusts, etc. Attach Schedule E (Form 1040) . .	**18**	
19	Farm income or (loss). Attach Schedule F (Form 1040)	**19**	
20	Unemployment compensation	**20**	
21	Other income. List type and amount (see instructions) _____	**21**	
22	Total income exempt by a treaty from page 5, Schedule OI, Item L (1)(e) **22** ____		
23	Combine the amounts in the far right column for lines 8 through 21. This is your **total effectively connected income** . . . . ▶	**23**	

Adjusted Gross Income

24	Educator expenses (see instructions)	**24**	
25	Health savings account deduction. Attach Form 8889 . . .	**25**	
26	Moving expenses. Attach Form 3903	**26**	
27	Deductible part of self-employment tax. Attach Schedule SE (Form 1040)	**27**	
28	Self-employed SEP, SIMPLE, and qualified plans	**28**	
29	Self-employed health insurance deduction (see instructions)	**29**	
30	Penalty on early withdrawal of savings	**30**	
31	Scholarship and fellowship grants excluded	**31**	
32	IRA deduction (see instructions)	**32**	
33	Student loan interest deduction (see instructions) . . .	**33**	
34	Domestic production activities deduction. Attach Form 8903 .	**34**	
35	Add lines 24 through 34	**35**	
36	Subtract line 35 from line 23. This is your **adjusted gross income** . . . . . . ▶	**36**	

For Disclosure, Privacy Act, and Paperwork Reduction Act Notice, see instructions.

Cat. No. 11364D

Form **1040NR** (2014)

Illustration 1-1 continued

Form 1040NR (2014)

Page **2**

Tax and Credits	37 Amount from line 36 (adjusted gross income)	37	
	38 **Itemized deductions** from page 3, Schedule A, line 15	38	
	39 Subtract line 38 from line 37	39	
	40 Exemptions (see instructions)	40	
	41 **Taxable income.** Subtract line 40 from line 39. If line 40 is more than line 39, enter -0-	41	
	42 **Tax** (see instructions). Check if any tax is from: **a** ☐ Form(s) 8814 **b** ☐ Form 4972	42	
	43 **Alternative minimum tax** (see instructions). Attach Form 6251	43	
	44 Excess advance premium tax credit repayment. Attach Form 8962	44	
	45 Add lines 42, 43 and 44 . . . . ▶	45	
	46 Foreign tax credit. Attach Form 1116 if required	46	
	47 Credit for child and dependent care expenses. Attach Form 2441	47	
	48 Retirement savings contributions credit. Attach Form 8880 .	48	
	49 Child tax credit. Attach Schedule 8812, if required	49	
	50 Residential energy credits. Attach Form 5695	50	
	51 Other credits from Form: **a** ☐ 3800 **b** ☐ 8801 **c** ☐	51	
	52 Add lines 46 through 51. These are your **total credits**	52	
	53 Subtract line 52 from line 45. If line 52 is more than line 45, enter -0- . . . . . ▶	53	
Other Taxes	54 Tax on income not effectively connected with a U.S. trade or business from page 4, Schedule NEC, line 15	54	
	55 Self-employment tax. Attach Schedule SE (Form 1040)	55	
	56 Unreported social security and Medicare tax from Form: **a** ☐ 4137 **b** ☐ 8919	56	
	57 Additional tax on IRAs, other qualified retirement plans, etc. Attach Form 5329 if required	57	
	58 Transportation tax (see instructions)	58	
	59a Household employment taxes from Schedule H (Form 1040)	59a	
	b First-time homebuyer credit repayment. Attach Form 5405 if required	59b	
	60 Taxes from: **a** ☐ Form 8959 **b** ☐ Instructions; enter code(s) _____	60	
	61 Add lines 53 through 60. This is your **total tax** . . . . ▶	61	
Payments	62 Federal income tax withheld from:		
	a Form(s) W-2 and 1099	62a	
	b Form(s) 8805	62b	
	c Form(s) 8288-A	62c	
	d Form(s) 1042-S	62d	
	63 2014 estimated tax payments and amount applied from 2013 return	63	
	64 Additional child tax credit. Attach Schedule 8812	64	
	65 Net premium tax credit. Attach Form 8962	65	
	66 Amount paid with request for extension to file (see instructions) .	66	
	67 Excess social security and tier 1 RRTA tax withheld (see instructions)	67	
	68 Credit for federal tax paid on fuels. Attach Form 4136 . . .	68	
	69 Credits from Form: **a** ☐ 2439 **b** ☐ Reserved **c** ☐ Reserved **d** ☐	69	
	70 Credit for amount paid with Form 1040-C	70	
	71 Add lines 62a through 70. These are your **total payments** . . . . ▶	71	
Refund Direct deposit? See instructions.	72 If line 71 is more than line 61, subtract line 61 from line 71. This is the amount you **overpaid**	72	
	73a Amount of line 72 you want **refunded to you.** If Form 8888 is attached, check here . ▶ ☐	73a	
	b Routing number ☐☐☐☐☐☐☐☐☐ ▶ **c** Type: ☐ Checking ☐ Savings		
	d Account number ☐☐☐☐☐☐☐☐☐☐☐☐☐☐☐☐☐		
	e If you want your refund check mailed to an address outside the United States not shown on page 1, enter it here. _____		
	74 Amount of line 72 you want **applied to your 2015 estimated tax** ▶	74	
Amount You Owe	75 **Amount you owe.** Subtract line 71 from line 61. For details on how to pay, see instructions ▶	75	
	76 Estimated tax penalty (see instructions)	76	

Third Party Designee	Do you want to allow another person to discuss this return with the IRS (see instructions)? ☐ **Yes.** Complete below. ☐ **No**
	Designee's name ▶ Phone no. ▶ Personal identification number (PIN) ▶ ☐☐☐☐☐

Sign Here Keep a copy of this return for your records.	Under penalties of perjury, I declare that I have examined this return and accompanying schedules and statements, and to the best of my knowledge and belief, they are true, correct, and complete. Declaration of preparer (other than taxpayer) is based on all information of which preparer has any knowledge.
	Your signature ▶ Date Your occupation in the United States If the IRS sent you an Identity Protection PIN, enter it here (see inst.) ☐☐☐☐☐☐

Paid Preparer Use Only	Print/Type preparer's name Preparer's signature Date Check ☐ if self-employed PTIN
	Firm's name ▶ Firm's EIN ▶
	Firm's address ▶ Phone no.

Form **1040NR** (2014)

You will be introduced to the remaining 3 forms; however you will use the Form 1040 for this course. The 1040 is the most involved of the 3 forms. Once you learn how to use it, you will be able to use both the 1040EZ and the 1040A.

Form 1040EZ

The 1040EZ (Illustration 1-2) is the simplest of the 3 forms. It can be used if:

- The filing status is Single or Married Filing Joint.
- The taxpayer (and/or spouse if Married Filing Joint) were under age 65 and not blind at the end of the tax year.
- The taxpayer (and/or spouse if Married Filing Joint) does not claim any dependents.
- The taxpayer (and/or spouse if Married Filing Joint) has taxable income of less than $100,000.
- The taxpayer's (and/or spouse's if Married Filing Joint) only income is wages, salaries, tips, unemployment compensation, Alaska Permanent Fund dividends, taxable scholarship and fellowship grants, and taxable interest of $1,500 or less.
- If tips are earned, they are included in boxes 5 and 7 of Form W-2 and the taxpayer (and spouse if Married Filing Joint) does not have any unreported tip income.
- The taxpayer (and/or spouse if Married Filing Joint) does not claim any adjustments to income.
- The taxpayer (and spouse if Married Filing Joint) does not claim any credits other than Earned Income Credit.
- The taxpayer (and/or spouse if Married Filing Joint) does not owe any household employment taxes.
- The taxpayer (and/or spouse if Married Filing Joint) does not itemize deductions.
- The taxpayer (and/or spouse if Married Filing Joint) is not a debtor in a Chapter 11 bankruptcy case filed after October 16, 2005.
- Advance payments of the Premium Tax Credit were not made for the taxpayer, spouse, or any individual the taxpayer enrolled in coverage for whom no one else is claiming the personal exemption.

Form 1040A

The 1040A (Illustration 1-3) can be used if:

- The taxpayer's (and/or spouse's if Married Filing Joint) only income is from wages, salaries, tips, IRA distributions, pensions and annuities, taxable social security and railroad retirement benefits, taxable scholarship and fellowship grants, interest, ordinary dividends, capital gain distributions, Alaska Permanent Fund Dividends, and unemployment compensation.
- The only adjustments to the taxpayer's (and/or spouse's if Married Filing Joint) income are Educator expenses, an IRA deduction, a Student loan interest deduction, and the Tuition and fees deduction.
- The taxpayer's (and/or spouse's if Married Filing Joint) taxable income is less than $100,000.
- The taxpayer (and/or spouse if Married Filing Joint) does not itemize.

- The taxpayer's (and/or spouse's if Married Filing Joint) only taxes are from the tax table, Alternative minimum tax, recapture of an education credit, tax from Form 8615, qualified dividend and capital gain tax worksheet, and excess Premium Tax Credit repayments.
- The only credits the taxpayer (and/or spouse if Married Filing Joint) claims are credit for child and dependent care, credit for the elderly or the disabled, child tax credit, additional child tax credit, the education credits, the retirement savings contributions credit, the earned income credit, and Premium Tax Credit.
- The taxpayer (and/or spouse if Married Filing Joint) did not have alternative minimum tax adjustment on stock you acquired from the exercise of an incentive stock option.

Form 1040

If they cannot use Form 1040EZ or Form 1040A, the Form 1040 must be used (Illustration 1-4).

Illustration 1-2

Department of the Treasury—Internal Revenue Service

Form 1040EZ

Income Tax Return for Single and Joint Filers With No Dependents (99) **2014**

OMB No. 1545-0074

Your first name and initial	Last name

Your social security number

If a joint return, spouse's first name and initial	Last name

Spouse's social security number

Home address (number and street). If you have a P.O. box, see instructions. Apt. no.

▲ Make sure the SSN(s) above are correct.

City, town or post office, state, and ZIP code. If you have a foreign address, also complete spaces below (see instructions).

Presidential Election Campaign
Check here if you, or your spouse if filing jointly, want $3 to go to this fund. Checking a box below will not change your tax or refund. ☐ You ☐ Spouse

Foreign country name	Foreign province/state/county	Foreign postal code

Income

Attach Form(s) W-2 here.

Enclose, but do not attach, any payment.

1	Wages, salaries, and tips. This should be shown in box 1 of your Form(s) W-2. Attach your Form(s) W-2.	1
2	Taxable interest. If the total is over $1,500, you cannot use Form 1040EZ.	2
3	Unemployment compensation and Alaska Permanent Fund dividends (see instructions).	3
4	Add lines 1, 2, and 3. This is your **adjusted gross income.**	4
5	If someone can claim you (or your spouse if a joint return) as a dependent, check the applicable box(es) below and enter the amount from the worksheet on back. ☐ You ☐ Spouse If no one can claim you (or your spouse if a joint return), enter $10,150 if **single;** $20,300 if **married filing jointly.** See back for explanation.	5
6	Subtract line 5 from line 4. If line 5 is larger than line 4, enter -0-. This is your **taxable income.** ▶	6

Payments, Credits, and Tax

7	Federal income tax withheld from Form(s) W-2 and 1099.	7
8a	**Earned income credit (EIC)** (see instructions)	8a
b	Nontaxable combat pay election. 8b	
9	Add lines 7 and 8a. These are your **total payments and credits.** ▶	9
10	**Tax.** Use the amount on **line 6 above** to find your tax in the tax table in the instructions. Then, enter the tax from the table on this line.	10
11	Health care: individual responsibility (see instructions) Full-year coverage ☐	11
12	Add lines 10 and 11. This is your **total tax.**	12

Refund

Have it directly deposited! See instructions and fill in 13b, 13c, and 13d, or Form 8888.

13a	If line 9 is larger than line 12, subtract line 12 from line 9. This is your **refund.** If Form 8888 is attached, check here ▶ ☐	13a
▶ b	Routing number ▶ c Type: ☐ Checking ☐ Savings	
▶ d	Account number	

Amount You Owe

14	If line 12 is larger than line 9, subtract line 9 from line 12. This is the **amount you owe.** For details on how to pay, see instructions. ▶	14

Third Party Designee

Do you want to allow another person to discuss this return with the IRS (see instructions)? ☐ **Yes.** Complete below. ☐ **No**

Designee's name ▶	Phone no. ▶	Personal identification number (PIN) ▶

Sign Here

Joint return? See instructions.

Keep a copy for your records.

Under penalties of perjury, I declare that I have examined this return and, to the best of my knowledge and belief, it is true, correct, and accurately lists all amounts and sources of income I received during the tax year. Declaration of preparer (other than the taxpayer) is based on all information of which the preparer has any knowledge.

Your signature	Date	Your occupation	Daytime phone number
Spouse's signature. If a joint return, **both** must sign.	Date	Spouse's occupation	If the IRS sent you an Identity Protection PIN, enter it here (see inst.)

Paid Preparer Use Only

Print/Type preparer's name	Preparer's signature	Date	Check ☐ if self-employed	PTIN
Firm's name ▶			Firm's EIN ▶	
Firm's address ▶			Phone no.	

For Disclosure, Privacy Act, and Paperwork Reduction Act Notice, see instructions. Cat. No. 11329W Form **1040EZ** (2014)

Illustration 1-3

Form
1040A

Department of the Treasury—Internal Revenue Service

U.S. Individual Income Tax Return (99) **2014** IRS Use Only—Do not write or staple in this space.

OMB No. 1545-0074

Your first name and initial	Last name

Your social security number

If a joint return, spouse's first name and initial	Last name

Spouse's social security number

Home address (number and street). If you have a P.O. box, see instructions.	Apt. no.

▲ Make sure the SSN(s) above and on line 6c are correct.

City, town or post office, state, and ZIP code. If you have a foreign address, also complete spaces below (see instructions).

Presidential Election Campaign
Check here if you, or your spouse if filing jointly, want $3 to go to this fund. Checking a box below will not change your tax or refund. ☐ You ☐ Spouse

Foreign country name	Foreign province/state/county	Foreign postal code

Filing status
Check only one box.

1 ☐ Single
2 ☐ Married filing jointly (even if only one had income)
3 ☐ Married filing separately. Enter spouse's SSN above and full name here. ▶
4 ☐ Head of household (with qualifying person). (See instructions.) If the qualifying person is a child but not your dependent, enter this child's name here. ▶
5 ☐ Qualifying widow(er) with dependent child (see instructions)

Exemptions

If more than six dependents, see instructions.

6a ☐ **Yourself.** If someone can claim you as a dependent, **do not** check box 6a.

b ☐ **Spouse**

c **Dependents:**

(1) First name Last name	(2) Dependent's social security number	(3) Dependent's relationship to you	(4) ✓ if child under age 17 qualifying for child tax credit (see instructions)
			☐
			☐
			☐
			☐
			☐
			☐

Boxes checked on 6a and 6b ____
No. of children on 6c who:
• lived with you ____
• did not live with you due to divorce or separation (see instructions) ____
Dependents on 6c not entered above ____
Add numbers on lines above ▶ ____

d Total number of exemptions claimed.

Income

Attach Form(s) W-2 here. Also attach Form(s) 1099-R if tax was withheld.

If you did not get a W-2, see instructions.

7 Wages, salaries, tips, etc. Attach Form(s) W-2. **7**

8a **Taxable** interest. Attach Schedule B if required. **8a**
b **Tax-exempt** interest. **Do not** include on line 8a. **8b**

9a Ordinary dividends. Attach Schedule B if required. **9a**
b Qualified dividends (see instructions). **9b**

10 Capital gain distributions (see instructions). **10**

11a IRA distributions. **11a**   **11b** Taxable amount (see instructions). **11b**

12a Pensions and annuities. **12a**   **12b** Taxable amount (see instructions). **12b**

13 Unemployment compensation and Alaska Permanent Fund dividends. **13**

14a Social security benefits. **14a**   **14b** Taxable amount (see instructions). **14b**

15 Add lines 7 through 14b (far right column). This is your **total income.** ▶ **15**

Adjusted gross income

16 Educator expenses (see instructions). **16**

17 IRA deduction (see instructions). **17**

18 Student loan interest deduction (see instructions). **18**

19 Tuition and fees. Attach Form 8917. **19**

20 Add lines 16 through 19. These are your **total adjustments.** **20**

21 Subtract line 20 from line 15. This is your **adjusted gross income.** ▶ **21**

For Disclosure, Privacy Act, and Paperwork Reduction Act Notice, see separate instructions. Cat. No. 11327A Form **1040A** (2014)

Illustration 1-3 continued

Tax, credits, and payments	22	Enter the amount from line 21 (adjusted gross income).	22	
	23a	Check if: ☐ **You** were born before January 2, 1950, ☐ Blind ☐ **Spouse** was born before January 2, 1950, ☐ Blind } **Total boxes checked ▶** 23a		
	b	If you are married filing separately and your spouse itemizes deductions, check here ▶ 23b ☐		

Standard Deduction for—

• People who check any box on line 23a or 23b **or** who can be claimed as a dependent, see instructions.

• All others:

Single or Married filing separately, $6,200

Married filing jointly or Qualifying widow(er), $12,400

Head of household, $9,100

24	Enter your **standard deduction**.		24	
25	Subtract line 24 from line 22. If line 24 is more than line 22, enter -0-.		25	
26	**Exemptions.** Multiply $3,950 by the number on line 6d.		26	
27	Subtract line 26 from line 25. If line 26 is more than line 25, enter -0-. This is your **taxable income.**		▶ 27	
28	**Tax,** including any alternative minimum tax (see instructions).	28		
29	Excess advance premium tax credit repayment. Attach Form 8962.	29		
30	Add lines 28 and 29.		30	
31	Credit for child and dependent care expenses. Attach Form 2441.	31		
32	Credit for the elderly or the disabled. Attach Schedule R.	32		
33	Education credits from Form 8863, line 19.	33		
34	Retirement savings contributions credit. Attach Form 8880.	34		
35	Child tax credit. Attach Schedule 8812, if required.	35		
36	Add lines 31 through 35. These are your **total credits.**		36	
37	Subtract line 36 from line 30. If line 36 is more than line 30, enter -0-.		37	
38	Health care: individual responsibility (see instructions). Full-year coverage ☐		38	
39	Add line 37 and line 38. This is your **total tax.**		39	

	40	Federal income tax withheld from Forms W-2 and 1099.	40	
If you have a qualifying child, attach Schedule EIC.	41	2014 estimated tax payments and amount applied from 2013 return.	41	
	42a	**Earned income credit (EIC).**	42a	
	b	Nontaxable combat pay election. 42b		
	43	Additional child tax credit. Attach Schedule 8812.	43	
	44	American opportunity credit from Form 8863, line 8.	44	
	45	Net premium tax credit. Attach Form 8962.	45	
	46	Add lines 40, 41, 42a, 43, 44, and 45. These are your **total payments.** ▶	46	

Refund	47	If line 46 is more than line 39, subtract line 39 from line 46. This is the amount you **overpaid.**	47	
Direct deposit? See instructions and fill in 48b, 48c, and 48d or Form 8888.	48a	Amount of line 47 you want **refunded to you.** If Form 8888 is attached, check here ▶ ☐ 48a		
	▶ b	Routing number ☐☐☐☐☐☐☐☐☐ ▶ c Type: ☐ Checking ☐ Savings		
	▶ d	Account number ☐☐☐☐☐☐☐☐☐☐☐☐☐☐☐☐☐		
	49	Amount of line 47 you want **applied to your 2015 estimated tax.**	49	

Amount you owe	50	**Amount you owe.** Subtract line 46 from line 39. For details on how to pay, see instructions. ▶	50	
	51	Estimated tax penalty (see instructions).	51	

Third party designee	Do you want to allow another person to discuss this return with the IRS (see instructions)? ☐ **Yes.** Complete the following. ☐ **No** Designee's name ▶ Phone no. ▶ Personal identification number (PIN) ▶ ☐☐☐☐☐

Sign here

Joint return? See instructions. Keep a copy for your records.

Under penalties of perjury, I declare that I have examined this return and accompanying schedules and statements, and to the best of my knowledge and belief, they are true, correct, and accurately list all amounts and sources of income I received during the tax year. Declaration of preparer (other than the taxpayer) is based on all information of which the preparer has any knowledge.

Your signature	Date	Your occupation	Daytime phone number
Spouse's signature. If a joint return, **both** must sign.	Date	Spouse's occupation	If the IRS sent you an Identity Protection PIN, enter it here (see inst.) ☐☐☐☐☐☐

Paid preparer use only

Print/type preparer's name	Preparer's signature	Date	Check ▶ ☐ if self-employed	PTIN
Firm's name ▶			Firm's EIN ▶	
Firm's address ▶			Phone no.	

Form **1040A** (2014)

Illustration 1-4

Form **1040** Department of the Treasury—Internal Revenue Service (99)
U.S. Individual Income Tax Return **2014** OMB No. 1545-0074 IRS Use Only—Do not write or staple in this space.

For the year Jan. 1–Dec. 31, 2014, or other tax year beginning _____, 2014, ending _____, 20____ See separate instructions.

Your first name and initial	Last name		Your social security number

If a joint return, spouse's first name and initial	Last name		Spouse's social security number

Home address (number and street). If you have a P.O. box, see instructions. | Apt. no.

▲ Make sure the SSN(s) above and on line 6c are correct.

City, town or post office, state, and ZIP code. If you have a foreign address, also complete spaces below (see instructions).

Presidential Election Campaign
Check here if you, or your spouse if filing jointly, want $3 to go to this fund. Checking a box below will not change your tax or refund. ☐ You ☐ Spouse

Foreign country name | Foreign province/state/county | Foreign postal code

Filing Status

Check only one box.

1 ☐ Single
2 ☐ Married filing jointly (even if only one had income)
3 ☐ Married filing separately. Enter spouse's SSN above and full name here. ▶
4 ☐ Head of household (with qualifying person). (See instructions.) If the qualifying person is a child but not your dependent, enter this child's name here. ▶
5 ☐ Qualifying widow(er) with dependent child

Exemptions

6a ☐ **Yourself.** If someone can claim you as a dependent, **do not** check box 6a . . . . .
b ☐ **Spouse** . . . .

c Dependents:

(1) First name Last name	(2) Dependent's social security number	(3) Dependent's relationship to you	(4) ✓ if child under age 17 qualifying for child tax credit (see instructions)
			☐
			☐
			☐
			☐

If more than four dependents, see instructions and check here ▶ ☐

d Total number of exemptions claimed . . . .

Boxes checked on 6a and 6b ____
No. of children on 6c who:
• lived with you ____
• did not live with you due to divorce or separation (see instructions) ____
Dependents on 6c not entered above ____
Add numbers on lines above ▶ ____

Income

Attach Form(s) W-2 here. Also attach Forms W-2G and 1099-R if tax was withheld.

If you did not get a W-2, see instructions.

7 Wages, salaries, tips, etc. Attach Form(s) W-2 . . . . | 7 |
8a **Taxable** interest. Attach Schedule B if required . . . . | 8a |
b **Tax-exempt** interest. **Do not** include on line 8a . . . | 8b |
9a Ordinary dividends. Attach Schedule B if required . . . . | 9a |
b Qualified dividends . . . . | 9b |
10 Taxable refunds, credits, or offsets of state and local income taxes . . . . . | 10 |
11 Alimony received . . . . | 11 |
12 Business income or (loss). Attach Schedule C or C-EZ . . . . | 12 |
13 Capital gain or (loss). Attach Schedule D if required. If not required, check here ▶ ☐ | 13 |
14 Other gains or (losses). Attach Form 4797 . . . . | 14 |
15a IRA distributions . | 15a | b Taxable amount . . . | 15b |
16a Pensions and annuities | 16a | b Taxable amount . . . | 16b |
17 Rental real estate, royalties, partnerships, S corporations, trusts, etc. Attach Schedule E | 17 |
18 Farm income or (loss). Attach Schedule F . . . . | 18 |
19 Unemployment compensation . . . . | 19 |
20a Social security benefits | 20a | b Taxable amount . . . | 20b |
21 Other income. List type and amount _____ | 21 |
22 Combine the amounts in the far right column for lines 7 through 21. This is your **total income** ▶ | 22 |

Adjusted Gross Income

23 Educator expenses . . . . | 23 |
24 Certain business expenses of reservists, performing artists, and fee-basis government officials. Attach Form 2106 or 2106-EZ | 24 |
25 Health savings account deduction. Attach Form 8889 . | 25 |
26 Moving expenses. Attach Form 3903 . . . . . . | 26 |
27 Deductible part of self-employment tax. Attach Schedule SE . | 27 |
28 Self-employed SEP, SIMPLE, and qualified plans . | 28 |
29 Self-employed health insurance deduction . . . . | 29 |
30 Penalty on early withdrawal of savings . . . . . . | 30 |
31a Alimony paid b Recipient's SSN ▶ _____ | 31a |
32 IRA deduction . . . . | 32 |
33 Student loan interest deduction . . . . . . | 33 |
34 Tuition and fees. Attach Form 8917 . . . . . . | 34 |
35 Domestic production activities deduction. Attach Form 8903 | 35 |
36 Add lines 23 through 35 . . . . | 36 |
37 Subtract line 36 from line 22. This is your **adjusted gross income** . . . . . ▶ | 37 |

For Disclosure, Privacy Act, and Paperwork Reduction Act Notice, see separate instructions. Cat. No. 11320B Form **1040** (2014)

Illustration 1-4 continued

Tax and Credits	38	Amount from line 37 (adjusted gross income)	38	

39a	Check if: ☐ **You** were born before January 2, 1950, ☐ Blind. ☐ **Spouse** was born before January 2, 1950, ☐ Blind. } Total boxes checked ▶ 39a	
b	If your spouse itemizes on a separate return or you were a dual-status alien, check here▶ 39b☐	

Standard Deduction for—
- **People who check any box on line 39a or 39b or who can be claimed as a dependent, see instructions.**
- **All others:**

Single or Married filing separately, $6,200

Married filing jointly or Qualifying widow(er), $12,400

Head of household, $9,100

40	**Itemized deductions** (from Schedule A) **or** your **standard deduction** (see left margin) . .	40
41	Subtract line 40 from line 38	41
42	**Exemptions.** If line 38 is $152,525 or less, multiply $3,950 by the number on line 6d. Otherwise, see instructions	42
43	**Taxable income.** Subtract line 42 from line 41. If line 42 is more than line 41, enter -0- . .	43
44	**Tax** (see instructions). Check if any from: **a** ☐ Form(s) 8814 **b** ☐ Form 4972 **c** ☐ _____	44
45	**Alternative minimum tax** (see instructions). Attach Form 6251	45
46	Excess advance premium tax credit repayment. Attach Form 8962	46
47	Add lines 44, 45, and 46 . . . . ▶	47

48	Foreign tax credit. Attach Form 1116 if required	48	
49	Credit for child and dependent care expenses. Attach Form 2441	49	
50	Education credits from Form 8863, line 19	50	
51	Retirement savings contributions credit. Attach Form 8880	51	
52	Child tax credit. Attach Schedule 8812, if required . . .	52	
53	Residential energy credits. Attach Form 5695	53	
54	Other credits from Form: **a** ☐ 3800 **b** ☐ 8801 **c** ☐	54	

55	Add lines 48 through 54. These are your **total credits**	55
56	Subtract line 55 from line 47. If line 55 is more than line 47, enter -0- . . . . ▶	56

Other Taxes

57	Self-employment tax. Attach Schedule SE	57
58	Unreported social security and Medicare tax from Form: **a** ☐ 4137 **b** ☐ 8919	58
59	Additional tax on IRAs, other qualified retirement plans, etc. Attach Form 5329 if required	59
60a	Household employment taxes from Schedule H	60a
b	First-time homebuyer credit repayment. Attach Form 5405 if required	60b
61	Health care: individual responsibility (see instructions) Full-year coverage ☐ . .	61
62	Taxes from: **a** ☐ Form 8959 **b** ☐ Form 8960 **c** ☐ Instructions; enter code(s) _____	62
63	Add lines 56 through 62. This is your **total tax** . . . . ▶	63

Payments

If you have a qualifying child, attach Schedule EIC.

64	Federal income tax withheld from Forms W-2 and 1099 . .	64	
65	2014 estimated tax payments and amount applied from 2013 return	65	
66a	**Earned income credit (EIC)**	66a	
b	Nontaxable combat pay election 66b		
67	Additional child tax credit. Attach Schedule 8812 . . .	67	
68	American opportunity credit from Form 8863, line 8 . . .	68	
69	Net premium tax credit. Attach Form 8962	69	
70	Amount paid with request for extension to file	70	
71	Excess social security and tier 1 RRTA tax withheld . . .	71	
72	Credit for federal tax on fuels. Attach Form 4136 . . .	72	
73	Credits from Form: **a** ☐ 2439 **b** ☐ Reserved **c** ☐ Reserved **d** ☐	73	

74	Add lines 64, 65, 66a, and 67 through 73. These are your **total payments** . . . . . ▶	74

Refund

Direct deposit? See instructions.

75	If line 74 is more than line 63, subtract line 63 from line 74. This is the amount you **overpaid**	75
76a	Amount of line 75 you want **refunded to you.** If Form 8888 is attached, check here . ▶ ☐	76a
▶ b	Routing number _____ ▶ c Type: ☐ Checking ☐ Savings	
▶ d	Account number _____	
77	Amount of line 75 you want **applied to your 2015 estimated tax** ▶ 77	

Amount You Owe

78	**Amount you owe.** Subtract line 74 from line 63. For details on how to pay, see instructions ▶	78
79	Estimated tax penalty (see instructions) 79	

Third Party Designee

Do you want to allow another person to discuss this return with the IRS (see instructions)?   ☐ **Yes.** Complete below.   ☐ **No**

Designee's name ▶	Phone no. ▶	Personal identification number (PIN) ▶

Sign Here

Joint return? See instructions.
Keep a copy for your records.

Under penalties of perjury, I declare that I have examined this return and accompanying schedules and statements, and to the best of my knowledge and belief, they are true, correct, and complete. Declaration of preparer (other than taxpayer) is based on all information of which preparer has any knowledge.

Your signature	Date	Your occupation	Daytime phone number
Spouse's signature. If a joint return, **both** must sign.	Date	Spouse's occupation	If the IRS sent you an Identity Protection PIN, enter it here (see inst.)

Paid Preparer Use Only

Print/Type preparer's name	Preparer's signature	Date	Check ☐ if self-employed	PTIN
Firm's name ▶			Firm's EIN ▶	
Firm's address ▶			Phone no.	

A Brief Introduction to the Form 1040

Use the Form 1040 in Illustration 1-4 to follow along as we learn the different parts of the tax return.

Name, Address, and SSN

The first part of preparing a tax return is the heading. The name and address of the taxpayer (and spouse if MFJ[1]) are entered here. Next to the name and address, you must enter the taxpayer's (and spouse's if MFJ or MFS[2]) social security number. Make sure the name and social security number match what is on the social security card. If it is incorrect, it will delay the tax return.

Note: One of the most common errors for tax preparers is to assume both the taxpayer and spouse have the same last name. When dealing with a married couple, always double check to see if the wife has changed her last name with the Social Security Administration.

The Presidential Election Campaign fund is a fund set up to help pay for Presidential election campaigns. The more help the candidates receive from this fund, the less they have to rely on large contributions from individuals and groups. Marking the box on the tax return gives $3.00 to this fund. It will not change your tax or lessen your refund.

Filing Status and Exemptions

We will cover this section in the next chapter.

Income

This section is pretty self-explanatory. We'll enter the income for the taxpayer (and the spouse if MFJ) here. The different types of income will be covered in more detail throughout the book.

Adjustments to Income

The IRS allows certain adjustments to the income. These amounts are deducted from the income, which will decrease the gross income. The different adjustments will be covered in depth throughout the text.

Taxes and Credits

This section is where the standard deduction or itemized deductions and the exemptions are deducted to arrive at the taxable income. The tax is calculated on the taxable amount. Then, any nonrefundable credits for which the taxpayer (and spouse if MFJ) is eligible are deducted from the tax. We will cover all of these items as we move through the book.

Other Taxes

Any of the extra taxes assessed on the taxpayer (and spouse if MFJ) will be added in this section. The different taxes will be explained further throughout the text.

Payments

---

[1] MFJ is the abbreviation for Married Filing Joint. This will be used throughout the text.
[2] MFS is the abbreviation for Married Filing Separately. This will be used throughout the text.

Any payments the taxpayer (and spouse if MFJ) made, and any refundable credits to which the taxpayer is entitled, are entered here. These will also be covered in depth throughout the text.

Refund/ Amount You Owe

If the payments are more than the tax liability, the taxpayer will be due a refund. If the tax liability is more than the payments, the taxpayer will have a balance due with his or her return.

Third Party Designee

If the taxpayer wants to allow the IRS to discuss the tax return with a third party (friend, family member, or tax preparer), he or she may check the yes box and complete the information. This will allow the IRS to call the designee to answer any questions and:

- Give information that is missing from your return,
- Call the IRS for information about the processing of your return and status of your refund or payments,
- Receive copies of notices or transcripts related to your return, upon request, and
- Respond to certain IRS notices about math errors, offsets, and return preparation.

The authorization will last until the due date of the <u>next</u> tax return. For the 2014 tax return, the Third Party Designee will expire on April 15th, 2016.

Signature

The taxpayer (and spouse if MFJ) will sign their tax return. If a paid preparer prepares the return, he or she must sign and put their preparer tax identification number (PTIN) on the return. As of the 2010 filing season, the IRS began requiring that paid tax preparers apply for a PTIN before preparing any federal returns. The PTIN can be obtained by going to the IRS website (www.IRS.gov) or filing a Form W-12, IRS Paid Preparer Tax Identification Number. The fine for not signing or providing an identification number on a tax return is $50 per return, up to $25,000.

Required Retention of Records

A return and any supporting documents should be kept for the statute of limitations by the taxpayer. This is usually 3 years from the date the return is filed or the date the tax was paid, whichever is later. A paid tax preparer must keep copies of the return or maintain a list of clients for 3 years following the close of the return period in which the tax return was presented to the taxpayer for signature. The return period for this purpose is the 12 month period ending July 1st. Failure to do so will result in a fine of $50 per return, up to $25,000 per year.

> **Note:** A paid preparer must always furnish the client with a copy of the return that is filed. Failure to furnish the copy will also result in a penalty of $50 per return, up to $25,000 per year.

Assembly

Assembling the tax return can seem pretty confusing; especially when you're faced with some of the more difficult returns that have multiple forms and schedules to attach. Assembly is actually easy if you follow the simple rules: The Form 1040 (whichever version) is always first. The other forms and schedules are attached using sequence numbers, always shown in the top right corner (Illustration 1-5). These will be attached behind the Form 1040 in sequential order. Any worksheets used in preparing the return are not filed with the IRS.

Illustration 1-5 shows the Schedule A and Form 8863. Notice that the sequence number on the Schedule A (07), is lower than the sequence number on Form 8863 (50). Schedule A will be attached in front of the Form 8863.

How to File

A tax return may be filed one of two ways. It may be filed by mail or electronically filed. To file by mail, the return will be mailed to the filing center listed in the 1040, 1040A, or 1040EZ instruction booklet.

To electronically file the return, the taxpayer can file online through an IRS accepted online service which may charge a fee, or they may file electronically through a tax preparer. This will be covered further in the second half of the course.

Accounting Periods

There are two different accounting periods:

Calendar year – this is the 12 month period from January 1st through December 31st. This is the period used by most taxpayers.

Fiscal year – A 12 month period that ends on the last day of any month other than December.

The taxpayer will choose their accounting period when they file their first tax return. In order to change it, the IRS must generally give permission.

Accounting Methods

The accounting method is the way the taxpayer accounts for their income or expenses. Most taxpayers choose either the cash or accrual accounting methods.

Cash method – Counting income when it is constructively received and expenses when paid. Constructive receipt is when it becomes available to the taxpayer whether it is actually in their hand or not. For example, the taxpayer counts a paycheck when it is made available or placed in the mail to the taxpayer, not when the taxpayer goes to pick it up or retrieves it from their mail box.

Garnished wages – If the taxpayer has wages that an employer garnishes to pay a debt, the taxpayer constructively receives them when they would have been received had they not been garnished.

Accrual method – Counting income when earned and expenses when accrued.

The accounting method is chosen when the first return is filed. After that, the taxpayer must obtain permission from the IRS to change it.

Illustration 1-5

SCHEDULE A (Form 1040) Department of the Treasury Internal Revenue Service (99)	**Itemized Deductions** ▶ Information about Schedule A and its separate instructions is at *www.irs.gov/schedulea*. ▶ **Attach to Form 1040.**	OMB No. 1545-0074 20**14** Attachment Sequence No. **07**

Name(s) shown on Form 1040	Your social security number

Medical and Dental Expenses		**Caution.** Do not include expenses reimbursed or paid by others.		
	1	Medical and dental expenses (see instructions)	1	
	2	Enter amount from Form 1040, line 38 **2**		
	3	Multiply line 2 by 10% (.10). But if either you or your spouse was born before January 2, 1950, multiply line 2 by 7.5% (.075) instead	3	
	4	Subtract line 3 from line 1. If line 3 is more than line 1, enter -0-		4
Taxes You Paid	5	State and local **(check only one box):** a ☐ Income taxes, **or** b ☐ General sales taxes }	5	
	6	Real estate taxes (see instructions)	6	
	7	Personal property taxes	7	
	8	Other taxes. List type and amount ▶ ------------------------------	8	
	9	Add lines 5 through 8		9
Interest You Paid **Note.** Your mortgage interest deduction may be limited (see instructions).	10	Home mortgage interest and points reported to you on Form 1098	10	
	11	Home mortgage interest not reported to you on Form 1098. If paid to the person from whom you bought the home, see instructions and show that person's name, identifying no., and address ▶ ------------------------------	11	
	12	Points not reported to you on Form 1098. See instructions for special rules	12	
	13	Mortgage insurance premiums (see instructions)	13	
	14	Investment interest. Attach Form 4952 if required. (See instructions.)	14	
	15	Add lines 10 through 14		15
Gifts to Charity If you made a gift and got a benefit for it, see instructions.	16	Gifts by cash or check. If you made any gift of $250 or more, see instructions	16	
	17	Other than by cash or check. If any gift of $250 or more, see instructions. You **must** attach Form 8283 if over $500 . . .	17	
	18	Carryover from prior year	18	
	19	Add lines 16 through 18		19
Casualty and Theft Losses	20	Casualty or theft loss(es). Attach Form 4684. (See instructions.)		20
Job Expenses and Certain Miscellaneous Deductions	21	Unreimbursed employee expenses—job travel, union dues, job education, etc. Attach Form 2106 or 2106-EZ if required. (See instructions.) ▶ ------------------------------	21	
	22	Tax preparation fees	22	
	23	Other expenses—investment, safe deposit box, etc. List type and amount ▶ ------------------------------	23	
	24	Add lines 21 through 23	24	
	25	Enter amount from Form 1040, line 38 **25**		
	26	Multiply line 25 by 2% (.02)	26	
	27	Subtract line 26 from line 24. If line 26 is more than line 24, enter -0-		27
Other Miscellaneous Deductions	28	Other—from list in instructions. List type and amount ▶ ------------------------------		28
Total Itemized Deductions	29	Is Form 1040, line 38, over $152,525? ☐ **No.** Your deduction is not limited. Add the amounts in the far right column for lines 4 through 28. Also, enter this amount on Form 1040, line 40. } ☐ **Yes.** Your deduction may be limited. See the Itemized Deductions Worksheet in the instructions to figure the amount to enter.		29
	30	If you elect to itemize deductions even though they are less than your standard deduction, check here . . . . ▶ ☐		

For Paperwork Reduction Act Notice, see Form 1040 instructions.   Cat. No. 17145C   Schedule A (Form 1040) 2014

Illustration 1-5 continued

Form **8863**

Department of the Treasury
Internal Revenue Service (99)

Education Credits
(American Opportunity and Lifetime Learning Credits)

▶ Attach to Form 1040 or Form 1040A.
▶ Information about Form 8863 and its separate instructions is at *www.irs.gov/form8863*.

OMB No. 1545-0074

20**14**

Attachment
Sequence No. **50**

Name(s) shown on return

Your social security number

⚠ **CAUTION**

Complete a separate Part III on page 2 for each student for whom you are claiming either credit before you complete Parts I and II.

Part I	**Refundable American Opportunity Credit**		
1	After completing Part III for each student, enter the total of all amounts from all Parts III, line 30 .	**1**	
2	Enter: $180,000 if married filing jointly; $90,000 if single, head of household, or qualifying widow(er)	**2**	
3	Enter the amount from Form 1040, line 38, or Form 1040A, line 22. If you are filing Form 2555, 2555-EZ, or 4563, or you are excluding income from Puerto Rico, see Pub. 970 for the amount to enter	**3**	
4	Subtract line 3 from line 2. If zero or less, **stop**; you cannot take any education credit	**4**	
5	Enter: $20,000 if married filing jointly; $10,000 if single, head of household, or qualifying widow(er)	**5**	
6	If line 4 is: • Equal to or more than line 5, enter 1.000 on line 6 . . . . • Less than line 5, divide line 4 by line 5. Enter the result as a decimal (rounded to at least three places)	**6**	.
7	Multiply line 1 by line 6. **Caution:** If you were under age 24 at the end of the year **and** meet the conditions described in the instructions, you **cannot** take the refundable American opportunity credit; skip line 8, enter the amount from line 7 on line 9, and check this box . . . . ▶ ☐	**7**	
8	**Refundable American opportunity credit.** Multiply line 7 by 40% (.40). Enter the amount here and on Form 1040, line 68, or Form 1040A, line 44. Then go to line 9 below.	**8**	
Part II	**Nonrefundable Education Credits**		
9	Subtract line 8 from line 7. Enter here and on line 2 of the Credit Limit Worksheet (see instructions)	**9**	
10	After completing Part III for each student, enter the total of all amounts from all Parts III, line 31. If zero, skip lines 11 through 17, enter -0- on line 18, and go to line 19	**10**	
11	Enter the smaller of line 10 or $10,000	**11**	
12	Multiply line 11 by 20% (.20)	**12**	
13	Enter: $128,000 if married filing jointly; $64,000 if single, head of household, or qualifying widow(er)	**13**	
14	Enter the amount from Form 1040, line 38, or Form 1040A, line 22. If you are filing Form 2555, 2555-EZ, or 4563, or you are excluding income from Puerto Rico, see Pub. 970 for the amount to enter	**14**	
15	Subtract line 14 from line 13. If zero or less, skip lines 16 and 17, enter -0- on line 18, and go to line 19	**15**	
16	Enter: $20,000 if married filing jointly; $10,000 if single, head of household, or qualifying widow(er)	**16**	
17	If line 15 is: • Equal to or more than line 16, enter 1.000 on line 17 and go to line 18 • Less than line 16, divide line 15 by line 16. Enter the result as a decimal (rounded to at least three places)	**17**	.
18	Multiply line 12 by line 17. Enter here and on line 1 of the Credit Limit Worksheet (see instructions) ▶	**18**	
19	**Nonrefundable education credits.** Enter the amount from line 7 of the Credit Limit Worksheet (see instructions) here and on Form 1040, line 50, or Form 1040A, line 33	**19**	

For Paperwork Reduction Act Notice, see your tax return instructions.　　Cat. No. 25379M　　Form **8863** (2014)

- They paid more than half the cost of keeping up the home for the tax year.
- The spouse did not live in the home during the last six months of the year.
- The home is the main home for his or her child, stepchild, or eligible foster child for more than half the year and the child can be claimed as a dependent.

   *Exception: This test can be met if the only reason the taxpayer cannot claim the child as a dependent is if the noncustodial parent can claim the child under the rules for Children of Divorced or Separated Parents (discussed later in the chapter).

Cost of Keeping up a Home

Costs included in keeping up a home are rent, mortgage interest, utilities, upkeep, repairs, real estate taxes, food eaten in the home, etc. If the taxpayer receives any assistance, this must be included in the total cost, but not in the amount paid by taxpayer. Do not include personal costs such as clothing, medical expenses, transportation, etc., in the cost of keeping up the home. See the worksheet in Illustration 2-1.

Example: Mary Smith lives in the house with her dependent son, Timmy. Her expenses are as follows:

Rent	$650 per month
Utilities	$225 per month
Groceries	$2400 for the year

Her parents wanted to help Mary out, so they paid for all of her groceries for the year. As you can see in Illustration 2-2, Mary paid more than half of the cost of keeping up her home for the year.

¹Table 2-1

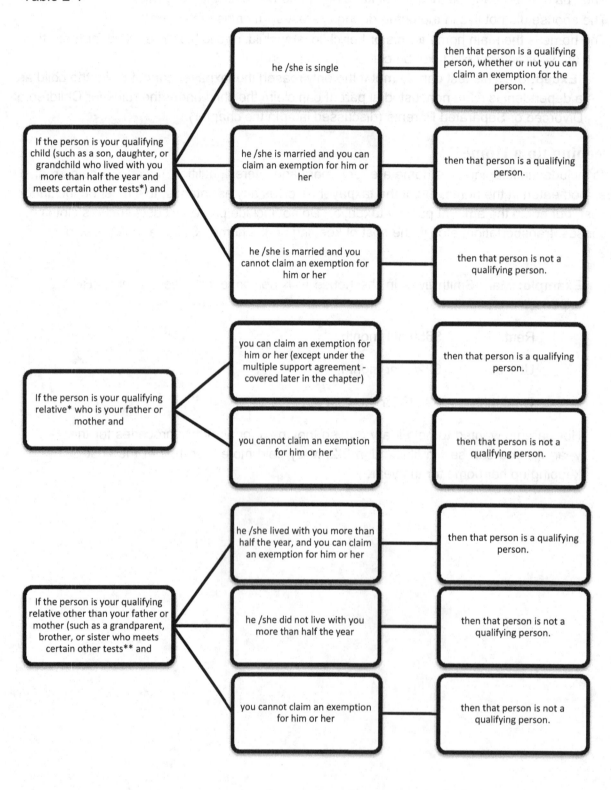

If the person is your qualifying child (such as a son, daughter, or grandchild who lived with you more than half the year and meets certain other tests*) and

- he /she is single → then that person is a qualifying person, whether or not you can claim an exemption for the person.
- he /she is married and you can claim an exemption for him or her → then that person is a qualifying person.
- he /she is married and you cannot claim an exemption for him or her → then that person is not a qualifying person.

If the person is your qualifying relative* who is your father or mother and

- you can claim an exemption for him or her (except under the multiple support agreement - covered later in the chapter) → then that person is a qualifying person.
- you cannot claim an exemption for him or her → then that person is not a qualifying person.

If the person is your qualifying relative other than your father or mother (such as a grandparent, brother, or sister who meets certain other tests** and

- he /she lived with you more than half the year, and you can claim an exemption for him or her → then that person is a qualifying person.
- he /she did not live with you more than half the year → then that person is not a qualifying person.
- you cannot claim an exemption for him or her → then that person is not a qualifying person.

---

¹ Exceptions: *The terms qualifying relative and qualifying child are defined later in this chapter.
**A person who is your qualifying relative only because of the "member of the household" test is not a qualifying person.

Illustration 2-1

Cost of Keeping Up a Home	Amount you Paid	Total Cost
Property taxes	$	$
Mortgage Interest Expense		
Rent		
Utility Charges		
Upkeep and repairs		
Property insurance		
Food consumed on the premises		
Other household expenses		
Totals	$	$
Minus Total amount you paid		( )
Amount others paid		$

If the amount you paid is more than the amount others paid, you pay more than half the cost of keeping up the home.

Illustration 2-2

Cost of Keeping Up a Home	Amount you Paid	Total Cost
Property taxes	$	$
Mortgage Interest Expense		
Rent	7,800	7,800
Utility Charges	2,700	2,700
Upkeep and repairs		
Property insurance		
Food consumed on the premises		2,400
Other household expenses		
Totals	$ 10,500	$ 12,900
Minus Total amount you paid		(10,500)
Amount others paid		$ 2,400
If the amount you paid is more than the amount others paid, you pay more than half the cost of keeping up the home.		

Qualifying Widow(er)

A taxpayer may use qualifying widow(er) for the two years following a spouse's death if:

- He/she was eligible to file a MFJ return in the year the spouse died.
- He/she did not remarry by the end of the tax year.
- He/she has a child that qualifies as a dependent.
- He/she is paying more than half the cost of keeping up a home in which they live with a qualifying child.

Filing Status Examples

Example: Bill and Betty are married with a dependent child and lived together the entire year. They qualify for MFJ status. They may also file MFS if they choose.

Example: Bill and Betty are married with a dependent child. Bill moved out in May and did not help Betty with any expenses. Betty paid more than half the cost of maintaining the household. If they don't file MFJ, Bill must file MFS, but Betty may file HH.

Example: The scenario is the same as the previous example, but Bill moves back in for the month of September as he and Betty try to work things out. He moves back out at the end of September. Betty and Bill must file MFS, because Bill lived there at some point during the last 6 months of the year, unless they file MFJ.

Example: Bill and Betty are married with a dependent child. Bill dies during the tax year. Betty may file MFJ this year. She may then file QW for the next 2 years as long as she still has her dependent child.

Standard Deduction

The Standard Deduction is an amount that can be deducted from your income to reduce the income on which you are taxed. The taxpayer may generally use Itemized Deductions instead of the Standard Deduction if it results in a bigger deduction. Itemizing involves keeping receipts for things such as medical expenses, mortgage interest, taxes, etc. Some taxpayers are not eligible for the standard deduction. In that case, they will be required to use Itemized Deductions. Itemizing will be covered further in Chapter 9. The Standard Deduction amount depends on your filing status along with some other factors (Illustration 2-3).

Taxpayers not eligible for the standard deduction:

- The filing status is MFS and the spouse itemizes.
- Filing for a short tax year because of a change in the accounting period.

Additional Standard Deduction

Some taxpayers (and their spouses if MFJ) may be eligible for an additional Standard Deduction amount if:

- the taxpayer (and/or spouse if MFJ) is age 65 or older at the end of the tax year (They are considered 65 on the day before their 65th birthday.) or
- the taxpayer (and/or spouse if MFJ) is totally or partly blind on the last day of the tax year.

The additional Standard Deduction amounts are $1,200 for each instance if MFJ, QW, or MFS; and $1,550 for each instance if S or HH (Illustration 2-5).

Partly Blind

The taxpayer (and/or spouse if MFJ) is partly blind if:

- they cannot see better than 20/200 in the better eye with glasses or contact lenses or
- their field of vision is not more than 20 degrees.

If the taxpayer's (and/or spouse's if MFJ) vision can be corrected by contact lenses that can be worn only briefly due to pain, infection, or ulcers, he or she may still claim the additional Standard Deduction. In order to get the additional Standard Deduction in this instance, the taxpayer (and/or spouse if MFJ) must get a certified statement from a doctor that state these facts. The statement must also say that the eye condition will never improve beyond these limits.

Example: Jim and Mary are Married Filing Jointly. Jim is 67 and Mary is 62. Neither is blind. Their Standard Deduction would be $13,600.

Example: Jim and Mary are Married Filing Jointly. Jim is 67 and Mary is 62 and blind. Their Standard Deduction is $14,800.

Standard Deduction for Dependents

The Standard Deduction for someone that can be claimed as a dependent on someone else's tax return is the greater of:

- their earned income plus $350 not to exceed the Single Standard Deduction of $6,200, or
- $1,000

The Standard deduction worksheet may be used to calculate the dependent's Standard Deduction (Illustration 2-4).

Example: Tom is 16 and can be claimed as a dependent on his parents' tax return. He had $2,000 in wages and $500 in interest income. His Standard Deduction would be $2,350 ($2,000 earned income + $350).

Example: Same scenario as previous example except he had $2,000 interest income and $500 wages. His Standard Deduction would be $1,000 ($500 + $350 = $850 which is less than $1,000).

Example: Same scenario except Tom has $6,000 wages and interest income of $500. His Standard Deduction would be $6,200 ($6000 + $350 = $6,350 which is more than the Single Standard Deduction).

Illustration 2-3

Standard Deduction for Most People 2014

Filing Status	Amount
Married Filing Jointly or Qualifying Widow(er)	$12,400
Single	6,200
Head of Household	9,100
Married Filing Separately	6,200

Illustration 2-4

Standard Deduction Worksheet for Dependents—Line 40   *Keep for Your Records*

Use this worksheet **only** if someone can claim you, or your spouse if filing jointly, as a dependent.

1.	Is your **earned income*** more than $650?	
	☐ **Yes.** Add $350 to your earned income. Enter the total	⎫
	☐ **No.** Enter $1,000	⎬ .... **1.** _____
2.	Enter the amount shown below for your filing status.	
	• Single or married filing separately—$6,200	⎫
	• Married filing jointly or qualifying widow(er)—$12,400	⎬ .... **2.** _____
	• Head of household—$9,100	⎭
3.	**Standard deduction.**	
	a. Enter the **smaller** of line 1 or line 2. If born after January 1, 1950, and not blind, **stop here** and enter this amount on Form 1040, line 40. Otherwise, go to line 3b .... **3a.** _____	
	b. If born before January 2, 1950, or blind, multiply the number on Form 1040, line 39a, by $1,200 ($1,550 if single or head of household) .... **3b.** _____	
	c. Add lines 3a and 3b. Enter the total here and on Form 1040, line 40 .... **3c.** _____	

* *Earned income includes wages, salaries, tips, professional fees, and other compensation received for personal services you performed. It also includes any taxable scholarship or fellowship grant. Generally, your earned income is the total of the amount(s) you reported on Form 1040, lines 7, 12, and 18, minus the amount, if any, on line 27.*

Illustration 2-5

Standard Deduction for People Born Before January 2nd, 1960 and/or Blind

2014

Are You...	Married Filing Joint Filing Status and Qualifying Widow(er)	Amount
65 or older? If yes, check box. ☐	If one box is checked	$13,600
	If two boxes are checked	14,800
Totally or Partially Blind? If yes, check box. ☐	If three boxes are checked	16,000
	If four boxes are checked	17,200
	Single	**Amount**
Is Your Spouse...	If one box is checked	7,700
65 or older? If yes, check box. ☐	If two boxes are checked	9,300
	Head of Household	**Amount**
	If one box is checked	10,650
Totally or Partially Blind? If yes, check box. ☐	If two boxes are checked	12,200
	Married filing Separately	**Amount**
	If one box is checked	7,400
	If two boxes are checked	8,600
	If three boxes are checked*	9,800
	If four boxes are checked*	11,000

*and you can claim your spouse's exemption

Exemptions

There are two types of exemptions: personal and dependent. The amount of each exemption is $3,950, but will be reduced if the taxpayer's AGI is more than the following amounts:

- $152,525 if Married Filing Separately,
- $254,200 if Single,
- $279,650 if Head of Household, or
- $305,000 if Married Filing Joint or Qualifying Widow(er).

If the taxpayer's AGI is above the applicable amount, a Deduction for Exemptions worksheet (Illustration 2-6) will be used.

Illustration 2-6

Deduction for Exemptions Worksheet—Line 42   *Keep for Your Records*

1.	Is the amount on Form 1040, line 38, more than the amount shown on line 4 below for your filing status?
	☐ **No.** (STOP) Multiply $3,950 by the total number of exemptions claimed on Form 1040, line 6d, and enter the result on line 42.
	☐ **Yes.** **Continue.**
2.	Multiply $3,950 by the total number of exemptions claimed on Form 1040, line 6d .... **2.** _____
3.	Enter the amount from Form 1040, line 38 .... **3.** _____
4.	Enter the amount shown below for your filing status.
	• Single —$254,200
	• Married filing jointly or qualifying widow(er)—$305,050 .... **4.**
	• Married filing separately—$152,525
	• Head of household—$279,650
5.	Subtract line 4 from line 3. If the result is more than $122,500 ($61,250 if married filing separately), (STOP) Enter -0- on line 42 .... **5.** _____
6.	Divide line 5 by $2,500 ($1,250 if married filing separately). If the result is not a whole number, increase it to the next higher whole number (for example, increase .00004 to 1) .... **6.** _____
7.	Multiply line 6 by 2% (.02) and enter the result as a decimal .... **7.** _____
8.	Multiply line 2 by line 7 .... **8.** _____
9.	**Deduction for exemptions.** Subtract line 8 from line 2. Enter the result here and on Form 1040, line 42 .... **9.** _____

Personal Exemptions

Each individual claimed on a tax return is allowed one exemption. A personal exemption is allowed for the taxpayer and/or the spouse. The only time a taxpayer and/or the spouse is not allowed the personal exemption is if they can be claimed as dependents on someone else's tax return. It does not matter if they are claimed, they are not allowed to claim their own exemption if they <u>can</u> be claimed by someone else.

A personal exemption is claimed for a spouse. A spouse can never be claimed as a dependent on the taxpayer's return. The personal exemption for the spouse is taken on a Married Filing Joint return even if the spouse had no income. An exemption for the spouse can be taken on a Married Filing Separate return if the spouse has no income and cannot be claimed as a dependent on someone else's return (as stated on pg. 2-1).

Dependent Exemption

The taxpayer can claim one exemption for each person they can claim as a dependent. A dependent can be either a

- Qualifying child or
- Qualifying relative.

There are qualifications that have to be satisfied to determine if the person is a qualifying child or a qualifying relative. The qualifications are summarized in Illustration 2-12 on page 2-26. These three tests must be met for both:

- Dependent Taxpayer Test
- Joint Return Test
- Citizen or Resident Test

Dependent Taxpayer Test

If the taxpayer (or spouse if MFJ) can be claimed as a dependent by anyone else, they may not claim any dependents.

Joint Return Test

Generally, a married individual filing a joint return cannot be claimed as a dependent on someone else's return. The exception to this rule is if the dependent and the dependent's spouse have no tax liability and are only filing to receive a refund of taxes paid.

Citizen or Resident Test

A person cannot be claimed as a dependent unless that person is a U.S. citizen, U.S. resident alien, U.S. national, or a resident of Canada or Mexico for some part of the year. The exception to this rule is for an adopted child who is not a U.S. citizen. If the child is adopted by a U.S. citizen or U.S.

national and lives as a member of the household for the entire year, the child meets the qualification for this test.

Child's place of residence

Children are usually citizens or residents of the country of their parents. If one of the parents is a U.S. citizen when the child is born, the test is met, even if the other parent is a nonresident alien and the child is born in a foreign country.

Qualifying Child

To qualify as a qualifying child, five additional tests must be met:

- Relationship
- Age
- Residency
- Support
- Special test for qualifying child of more than one person

Relationship Test

The child must be

- The taxpayer's son, daughter, stepchild, eligible foster child, or a descendent of any of them, or
- The taxpayer's brother, sister, half brother, half sister, step brother, step sister, or a descendent of any of them.

An adopted child includes a child lawfully placed with you for legal adoption. An eligible foster child is one placed with you by an authorized placement agency or by judgment, decree, or other order of any court of competent jurisdiction.

> **Example:** Anita wants to claim her daughter as a dependent. She meets the relationship test.

> **Example:** Robert's girlfriend and her son lived with Robert all year. The girlfriend's son does not meet the relationship test for Robert to claim him as a qualifying child.

Age Test

The child must be

- Under 19 at the end of the tax year and younger than the taxpayer (or spouse if MFJ),
- Under 24 and a full time student and younger than the taxpayer (or spouse if MFJ), or
- Permanently and totally disabled at any time during the year regardless of age.

Child must be younger than the taxpayer (or spouse if MFJ)

To be the qualifying child, a child who is not permanently and totally disabled must be younger than the taxpayer. However, if the taxpayer is Married Filing Jointly, the child must be younger than the taxpayer or spouse but does not have to be younger than both.

Full time student

A student enrolled for the number of hours or courses the school considers to be full time.

Student

A student must have been enrolled for some part of each of 5 calendar months during the year as:

- A full time student at a school that has a regular teaching staff, a course of study, and a regularly enrolled student body or
- A student taking a full time, on-farm training course, given by a school described above, or by a state, county, or local government agency.

Note: The five months do not have to be consecutive.

School

An elementary school, junior and senior high school, college, university, technical, trade, or mechanical school. A student who works on a "co-op" job in private industry as a part of a school's regular course of classroom and practical training is considered a full time student.

Note: On the job training course, correspondence school, or a school offering courses only through the internet does not count.

Permanently and Totally Disabled

The child is permanently and totally disabled if both of the following apply:

- They cannot engage in any substantial gainful activity because of a physical or mental condition.
- A doctor determines the condition has lasted or can be expected to last continuously for at least one year or can lead to death.

Example: Anita's daughter is 20 and a full time student. She qualifies under the age test.

Example: Bob and Joanne have a son that is 19. He graduated in 2013 and plans to start college in August of 2014. He does not pass the age test. However, if he started college and completed the year he will have been a student for 5 months and will be a qualifying child if all of the other tests are met.

Residency Test

The child must have lived with the taxpayer for more than half of the year. The child is considered to have lived with the taxpayer if either the taxpayer or child was temporarily absent due to reasons such as illness, education, business, vacation, or military service. The exceptions to the residency test are for the death or birth of a child, kidnapped children, and children of divorced or separated parents.

Death or Birth of a Child

A child who was born or died during the year meets the residency test if the child lived with the taxpayer for more than half of the time the child was alive. If, during the tax year, the child was born alive but died a short time later (even if the child lived for only a moment), the child meets the residency test. There must be proof of a live birth shown by an official document such as a birth certificate. An exemption cannot be claimed for a stillborn child.

Kidnapped Child

A kidnapped child meets the residency test if both of the following statements are true:

- The child is presumed by law enforcement authorities to have been kidnapped by someone who is not a member of the taxpayer's family or the child's family and
- in the year the kidnapping occurred the child lived with the taxpayer for more than half of the part of the year before the date of the kidnapping.

This test is considered met for all years until the child is returned or the earlier of:

- the year there is a determination that the child is dead or
- the year the child would have reached age 18.

Children of Divorced or Separated Parents

To determine this test, you must know the definition of a custodial parent and a noncustodial parent.

Custodial Parent

The parent with whom the child lived for the greater part of the year.

Noncustodial Parent

The other parent.

Generally for the residency test, the child is the qualifying child of the custodial parent. However, a child can be the qualifying child of the noncustodial parent if all four of the following statements are true:

- The parents:
  - are divorced or legally separated under a decree of divorce or separate maintenance,
  - are separated under a written separation agreement, or
  - lived apart at all times during the last 6 months of the year.
- The child received over half of his or her support for the year from the parents.
- The child is in the custody of one or both parents for more than half of the year.
- A decree of divorce or separate maintenance or written separation agreement provides that the noncustodial parent can claim the child for the tax year, depending on when the divorce or separation occurred, or the custodial parent signs a Form 8332 (Release of Claim to

Exemption for Child of Divorced or Separated Parents, Illustration 2-7) or similar statement that he will not claim the child as a dependent for the year.

> **Note:** The exemption can be released for 1 year, for a number of specified years, or for all future years, as specified in the declaration.

Post-1984 and Pre-2009 Divorce Decree or Separation Agreement

If the divorce decree or separation agreement went into effect after 1984 and before 2009, the noncustodial parent may be able to attach certain pages from the divorce decree agreement instead of the Form 8332.

Post-2008 Divorce Decree or Separation Agreement

Beginning with 2009 tax returns, the noncustodial parent cannot attach pages from the decree or agreement instead of Form 8332, if the decree or agreement went into effect after 2008. The noncustodial parent will have to attach Form 8332 or a similar statement signed by the custodial parent whose only purpose is to release a claim to exemption.

The special rule for divorced or separated parents also applies to parents who were never married.

> **Example:** Anita's daughter lived with her all year except a summer vacation she took with her class to Europe for a month. She qualifies under the residency test.

> **Example:** Andy and Sara became divorced in March of 2013. Their daughter, Vicki, lived with Sara all year and received all of her support from her parents. The divorce decree provides that Andy may claim Vicki for the even years and Sara will claim her for the odd years. In 2013, Andy claimed Vicki as a dependent. In 2014, Sara can claim the dependency exemption. **Note:** A Form 8332 is required to be attached to Andy's return for the years he is able to claim Vicki.

Support

For the Qualifying Child test, a child cannot have provided more than half of his or her own support for the year. This includes social security payments received in the name of the child. Use the dependency support worksheet (Illustration 2-8) to determine if the taxpayer meets this test.

Household Expenses

This section is to calculate expenses solely for the maintenance of the household. Mortgage interest and real estate taxes are not entered in this section. Instead, use the fair rental value of the home. The fair rental value is what a stranger would be willing to pay to rent your home. If the house belongs to the person supported, enter the fair rental value here, but also enter it under funds belonging to the person supported.

Expenses for the person supported

This is where the total support provided for the person is calculated, no matter who provided it. Support includes necessities required for health and living as well as expenses for recreation and

Illustration 2-7

Form **8332**
(Rev. January 2010)
Department of the Treasury
Internal Revenue Service

Release/Revocation of Release of Claim to Exemption for Child by Custodial Parent

▶ Attach a separate form for each child.

OMB No. 1545-0074

Attachment
Sequence No. **115**

Name of noncustodial parent

Noncustodial parent's
social security number (SSN) ▶

Part I   Release of Claim to Exemption for Current Year

I agree not to claim an exemption for _____
                                                        Name of child

for the tax year 20____ .

_____
Signature of custodial parent releasing claim to exemption

_____
Custodial parent's SSN

_____
Date

Note. If you choose not to claim an exemption for this child for future tax years, also complete Part II.

Part II   Release of Claim to Exemption for Future Years (If completed, see **Noncustodial Parent** on page 2.)

I agree not to claim an exemption for _____
                                                        Name of child

for the tax year(s)_____
                         (Specify. See instructions.)

_____
Signature of custodial parent releasing claim to exemption

_____
Custodial parent's SSN

_____
Date

Part III   Revocation of Release of Claim to Exemption for Future Year(s)

I revoke the release of claim to an exemption for _____
                                                                    Name of child

for the tax year(s)_____
                         (Specify. See instructions.)

_____
Signature of custodial parent revoking the release of claim to exemption

_____
Custodial parent's SSN

_____
Date

General Instructions
What's New

Post-2008 decree or agreement. If the divorce decree or separation agreement went into effect after 2008, the noncustodial parent cannot attach certain pages from the decree or agreement instead of Form 8332. See *Release of claim to exemption* below.

Definition of custodial parent. New rules apply to determine who is the custodial parent and the noncustodial parent. See *Custodial Parent and Noncustodial Parent* on this page.

Purpose of Form

If you are the custodial parent, you can use this form to do the following.

• Release a claim to exemption for your child so that the noncustodial parent can claim an exemption for the child.

• Revoke a previous release of claim to exemption for your child.

Release of claim to exemption. This release of the exemption will also allow the noncustodial parent to claim the child tax credit and the additional child tax credit (if either applies). Complete this form (or sign a similar statement containing the same

information required by this form) and give it to the noncustodial parent. The noncustodial parent must attach this form or similar statement to his or her tax return each year the exemption is claimed. Use Part I to release a claim to the exemption for the current year. Use Part II if you choose to release a claim to exemption for any future year(s).

Note. If the decree or agreement went into effect after 1984 and before 2009, you can attach certain pages from the decree or agreement instead of Form 8332, provided that these pages are substantially similar to Form 8332. See *Post-1984 and pre-2009 decree or agreement* on page 2.

Revocation of release of claim to exemption. Use Part III to revoke a previous release of claim to an exemption. The revocation will be effective no earlier than the tax year following the year in which you provide the noncustodial parent with a copy of the revocation or make a reasonable effort to provide the noncustodial parent with a copy of the revocation. Therefore, if you revoked a release on Form 8332 and provided a copy of the form to the noncustodial parent in 2010, the earliest tax year the revocation can be effective is 2011. You must attach a copy of the revocation to your tax return each year the exemption is claimed as a result of the revocation. You must also keep for your records a copy of the revocation and evidence

of delivery of the notice to the noncustodial parent, or of reasonable efforts to provide actual notice.

Custodial Parent and Noncustodial Parent

The custodial parent is generally the parent with whom the child lived for the greater number of nights during the year. The noncustodial parent is the other parent. If the child was with each parent for an equal number of nights, the custodial parent is the parent with the higher adjusted gross income. For details and an exception for a parent who works at night, see Pub. 501.

Exemption for a Dependent Child

A dependent is either a qualifying child or a qualifying relative. See your tax return instruction booklet for the definition of these terms. Generally, a child of divorced or separated parents will be a qualifying child of the custodial parent. However, if the special rule on page 2 applies, then the child will be treated as the qualifying child or qualifying relative of the noncustodial parent for purposes of the dependency exemption, the child tax credit, and the additional child tax credit.

For Paperwork Reduction Act Notice, see back of form.   Cat. No. 13910F   Form **8332** (Rev. 1-2010)

pleasure. It can be expenses for birthday parties, presents, school field trips, summer camps, and sports. It also includes anything from medical and dental bills, insurance premiums, car payments, and even dependent care expenses. However, life insurance premiums, taxes paid, and funeral expenses are not included.

Funds belonging to the person supported

This includes any income the person receives during the year, for example: wages, social security benefits, and interest income. Notice that any amount that was put into savings and other accounts during the year, and remained there, are subtracted along with any that remained in the accounts. Any money borrowed during the year in the person's name is money that person used to provide their own support. If the money borrowed is a student loan, remember to include the tuition and school related expenses under the "expenses for the person supported". Scholarships and fellowships for a full time student are not included here.

Example: Jim lived in the house with his dad, Gary. Jim is 18 years old, still in school, and has a part time job. He made $6,000 in 2014. Gary wants to know if he can claim Jim on his 2013 tax return. Gary's household bills are as follows:

Rent	$450 per month
Power bill	130 per month
Phone bill	70 per month
Water bill	25 per month
Groceries	95 per week

Gary purchased a car for Jim for $3,000 and bought a stereo system for Jim's birthday for $250. Jim spent the following on himself.

Gas	$ 20 per week
Auto insurance	70 per month
New clothes	400
School books	250

Jim also opened a savings account in March and put $100 in every month. He didn't make any withdrawals (Illustration 2-9). Using the dependent support worksheet, Jim didn't provide over half of his own support. Therefore, Gary can claim Jim on his tax return.

Special Test for Qualifying Child of more than one Person

Sometimes, a child meets the relationship, age, residency, and support tests to be a qualifying child of more than one person. However, only one person may claim the child on their tax return. The person that claims the child will receive the following tax benefits (if otherwise eligible).

- The child's exemption
- The child tax credit

- Head of Household Filing Status
- Credit for child and dependent care expenses
- Exclusion for dependent care benefits
- Earned Income Credit

If the child is a qualifying child of more than one person, they can choose who gets to claim the child. The benefits listed above cannot be divided; whoever claims the child receives the benefits. If they cannot agree and more than one person claims the child, the IRS will use the tie-breaker rule (Illustration 2-10).

> **Note:** If there is more than one child who qualifies for more than one person, they can divide the children. For example, you have two children that qualify for both you and your mom. You may each claim a child.

Illustration 2-8

Dependency Support Worksheet

Household Expenses	Funds belonging to the person supported
1. Rent paid or fair rental value	17. Income received during the year (taxable and nontaxable)
2. Food consumed in the home	18. Amounts borrowed by the person supported during the year
3. Utilities	19. Amount in savings and other account at the beginning of the year
4. Repairs on the house	20. If home belongs to the person supported, enter the fair rental value of the home here.
5. Total household expense, add lines 1 through 4.	21. Add lines 17 through 20
6. Number of people living in the house	22. Amount in savings and other accounts at the end of the year
7. Divide line 5 by line 6. This is the amount of household expenses for each person in the house.	23. Subtract line 22 from line 21. This is the amount the person supported provided toward their own support.
Expenses for the person supported	**Qualifying child support test**
8. Amount from line 7 above	24. Enter the amount from line 16.
9. Clothing	25. Multiply line 24 by 50%.
10. Education	26. Enter the amount from line 23.
11. Out of pocket medical and dental expenses	27. Is line 26 less than line 25? If yes, they meet the support test to be a qualifying child.
12. Travel and recreation	**Qualifying relative support test**
13. Transportation	28. Enter the amount from line 23.
14. Capital expenditures, for example: tv's, cars, furniture, etc	29. Enter the amount provided by anyone other than the taxpayer.
15. Other expenses	30. Add lines 28 and 29.
16. Add lines 8 through 16. These are the total expenses for the person supported.	31. Is line 30 less than line 25? If yes, they meet the support test to be a qualifying relative.

Illustration 2-9

Dependency Support Worksheet

Household Expenses		Funds belonging to the person supported	
1. Rent paid or fair rental value	5400	17. Income received during the year (taxable and nontaxable)	6000
2. Food consumed in the home	4940	18. Amounts borrowed by the person supported during the year	
3. Utilities	2700	19. Amount in savings and other account at the beginning of the year	
4. Repairs on the house		20. If home belongs to the person supported, enter the fair rental value of the home here.	
5. Total household expense, add lines 1 through 4.	13040	21. Add lines 17 through 20	6000
6. Number of people living in the house	2	22. Amount in savings and other accounts at the end of the year	1000
7. Divide line 5 by line 6. This is the amount of household expenses for each person in the house.	6520	23. Subtract line 22 from line 21. This is the amount the person supported provided toward their own support.	5000
Expenses for the person supported		**Qualifying child support test**	
8. Amount from line 7 above	6520	24. Enter the amount from line 16.	12300
9. Clothing	400	25. Multiply line 24 by 50%.	6150
10. Education	250	26. Enter the amount from line 23.	5000
11. Out of pocket medical and dental expenses		27. Is line 26 less than line 25? If yes, they meet the support test to be a qualifying child.	yes
12. Travel and recreation		**Qualifying relative support test**	
13. Transportation	1880	28. Enter the amount from line 23.	
14. Capital expenditures, for example: tv's, cars, furniture, etc	3250	29. Enter the amount provided by anyone other than the taxpayer.	
15. Other expenses		30. Add lines 28 and 29.	
16. Add lines 8 through 16. These are the total expenses for the person supported.	12300	31. Is line 30 less than line 25? If yes, they meet the support test to be a qualifying relative.	

Illustration 2-10

Tie-Breaker Rule

If more than one person files a return claiming the same qualifying child and ….	THEN the child will be treated as the qualifying child of the…
only one of the persons is the child's parent.	parent.
two of the persons are parents of the child and they do not file a joint return together,	parent with whom the child lived for the longer period of time during the year.
two of the persons are parents of the child, they do not file a joint return together, and the child lived with each parent the same amount of time during the year.	parent with the higher adjusted gross income (AGI).
none of the persons are the child's parent,	person with the highest AGI.
a parent can claim the child as a qualifying child but no parent does so.	Person with the highest AGI, only if the person's AGI is higher than the highest AGI of any of the child's parent who can claim the child.

Example: You and your son live with your mother all year. You earn $9,000 of wages and your mom earns $25,000 for the year. You can let your mother claim the child.

Example: Same scenario as previous example, but you and your mom both claim your son. Using the tie-breaker rules, you will be the only one allowed to claim him because you are his parent.

Example: Same scenario, except you have two children. Your mom can claim one and you can claim the other.

Example: Tom and Betty are married and have a daughter, Sara. Tom moved out at the end of August, 2014. Sara lived with him in September and half of October. Then, she moved back in with Betty for the rest of October, November, and December. If Betty and Tom cannot agree on who will claim Sara and they both do, Betty will get her because Sara lived with her longer.

Example: Same scenario as above, except Tom didn't move out until January of this year. He lived in the house with Betty and Sara for all of 2014. Betty and Tom file Married Filing Separately. They can choose who will claim Sara. If they both do, the IRS will give her to the one with the highest AGI.

Example: Joanne and her 22 year old daughter, Tiffany, live in the same house. Joanne made $40,000 in wages in 2014 and Tiffany made $18,000. Tiffany's niece (Joanne's granddaughter), Cindy, lived with them all year. They can choose which one will claim her. If they both do, Joanne will get Cindy's exemption along with any other benefits she is entitled to because she has the highest AGI.

them all year. They can choose which one will claim her. If they both do, Joanne will get Cindy's exemption along with any other benefits she is entitled to because she has the highest AGI.

Qualifying Relative

If someone doesn't meet all of the tests to be a qualifying child, they may still be a qualifying relative. There are four tests for a qualifying relative:

- Not a qualifying child test
- Member of the household or relationship test
- Gross income test
- Support test

Not a Qualifying Child Test

There are two parts to this test: The person must not be a qualifying child of the taxpayer or anyone else. First, if the person meets the test to be the taxpayer's qualifying child, the taxpayer will receive more tax benefits than if the person was their qualifying relative (this will be demonstrated throughout the course). Second, remember each person only gets one exemption, so if they're the qualifying child of anyone else, the taxpayer will not be able to claim them.

Member of the Household or Relationship Test

Again, this test has two parts. We are going to cover the relationship test first. If the person is related to the taxpayer in any of the following ways, they do not have to live with the taxpayer all year to qualify:

- Their child, stepchild, eligible foster child, or a descendant of any of them.
- Their brother, sister, half-brother, half-sister, stepbrother, stepsister, or a child of any of them.
- Their father, mother, grandparent, or other direct ancestor (not a foster parent).
- Their stepfather or stepmother.
- A brother or sister of their father or mother.
- Their son-in-law, daughter-in-law, father-in-law, mother-in-law, brother-in-law, or sister-in-law. **Note:** Any relationship established by marriage is not ended by divorce.

If the person is not related to the taxpayer in any of those ways, then they must have lived with the taxpayer as a member of the household.

Gross Income Test

The person's gross income must be less than $3,950 for 2014.

Gross Income

All income in the form of money, property, and services that is not exempt from tax. Different types of gross income include, but are not limited to:

- In a manufacturing, or mineral business, gross income is the net sales minus cost of goods sold plus other income for the business.
- Gross income from rental property. Do not deduct any expenses.
- A partner's share of the partnership's gross income
- Taxable unemployment compensation.

Items not included for the gross income test are:

- Tax exempt income including social security.
- Scholarships for a degree candidate that is used to pay for tuition, fees, supplies, books, and equipment required for particular courses.
- Income for services performed at a sheltered workshop by someone who is permanently and totally disabled, if the availability of medical care is the reason they are there. A sheltered workshop is a school that provides special instruction or training designed to alleviate the disability of the individual and is operated by certain tax-exempt organizations, or by a state, a U.S. possession, a political subdivision, of a state or possession, the United States, or the District of Columbia.

Support Test

The support test for a qualifying relative is different than that of a qualifying child. The support test for the qualifying relative is that the taxpayer must have provided over half of the support of the person. In this test, any assistance provided by the government (for example, welfare and food stamps) that is used for support is support provided by someone else. This makes it a more difficult test to pass. Also, foster care payments from an agency are considered support provided by the agency. Again, the dependency support worksheet (Illustration 2-8) is useful in determining if this test is met.

Multiple Support Agreement

If two or more people provided over half of the support and would have been able to claim the person as a dependent except for the support test, they may still qualify under the multiple support agreement. Any one of them that provided over 10% of the support may be able to claim the exemption. In order to do this, the others who also provided over 10% must sign a statement (Form 2120, Illustration 2-11) agreeing not to claim the exemption. If everyone cannot agree on who will claim the exemption, no one will be able to. Remember, they must still pass all of the other tests, including the relationship or member of the household test.

> **Example:** Jill's children provided 70% of her support. She provided the other 30% with her social security benefits. Her son, John, provided 25%; her daughter, Catherine provided 35%; her other son, Jimmy, provided 7%; and her other daughter, Linda, provided the other 3%. Either John or Catherine may claim Jill because they both provided over 10%. The other one must agree and sign Form 2120.

> **Example:** 55% of Deborah's support is provided by her two cousins, Jerry and Jack. Jerry provided 30% and Jack provided 25%. Deborah's son, Martin, provided the other 45%. She lives by herself. No one may claim her exemption

because Jerry and Jack did not qualify under the relationship test and they provided over 50% of her support.

Illustration 2-11

Form 2120
(Rev. October 2005)
Department of the Treasury
Internal Revenue Service

Multiple Support Declaration

▶ **Attach to Form 1040 or Form 1040A.**

OMB No. 1545-0074

Attachment
Sequence No. **114**

Name(s) shown on return

Your social security number

During the calendar year ...., the eligible persons listed below each paid over 10% of the support of:

Name of your qualifying relative

I have a signed statement from each eligible person waiving his or her right to claim this person as a dependent for any tax year that began in the above calendar year.

Eligible person's name

Social security number

Address (number, street, apt. no., city, state, and ZIP code)

Eligible person's name

Social security number

Address (number, street, apt. no., city, state, and ZIP code)

Eligible person's name

Social security number

Address (number, street, apt. no., city, state, and ZIP code)

Eligible person's name

Social security number

Address (number, street, apt. no., city, state, and ZIP code)

Instructions

What's New

The rules for multiple support agreements still apply to claiming an exemption for a qualifying relative, but they no longer apply to claiming an exemption for a qualifying child. For the definitions of "qualifying relative" and "qualifying child," see your tax return instruction booklet.

Purpose of Form

Use Form 2120 to:

● Identify each other eligible person (see below) who paid over 10% of the support of your qualifying relative whom you are claiming as a dependent, and

● Indicate that you have a signed statement from each other eligible person waiving his or her right to claim that person as a dependent.

An eligible person is someone who could have claimed a person as a dependent except that he or she did not pay over half of that person's support.

If there are more than four other eligible persons, attach a statement to your return with the required information.

Claiming a Qualifying Relative

Generally, to claim a person as a qualifying relative, you must pay over half of that person's support. However, even if you did not meet this support test, you may be able to claim him or her as a dependent if all five of the following apply.

1. You and one or more other eligible person(s) (see above) together paid over half of that person's support.

2. You paid over 10% of the support.

3. No one alone paid over half of that person's support.

4. The other dependency tests are met. See *Step 4, Is Your Qualifying Relative Your Dependent?* in the Form 1040 or Form 1040A instructions.

5. Each other eligible person who paid over 10% of the support agrees not to claim that person as a dependent by giving you a signed statement. See *Signed Statement* on this page.

Note. To find out what is included in support, see Pub. 501, Exemptions, Standard Deduction, and Filing Information.

Signed Statement

You must have received, from each other eligible person listed above, a signed statement waiving his or her right to claim the person as a dependent for the calendar year indicated on this form. The statement must include:

● The calendar year the waiver applies to,

● The name of your qualifying relative the eligible person helped to support, and

● The eligible person's name, address, and social security number.

Do not file the signed statement with your return. But you must keep it for your records and be prepared to furnish it and any other information necessary to show that you qualify to claim the person as your dependent.

Additional Information

See Pub. 501 for details.

Paperwork Reduction Act Notice. We ask for the information on this form to carry out the Internal Revenue laws of the United States. You are required to give us the information. We need it to ensure that you are complying with these laws and to allow us to figure and collect the right amount of tax.

You are not required to provide the information requested on a form that is subject to the Paperwork Reduction Act unless the form displays a valid OMB control number. Books or records relating to a form or its instructions must be retained as long as their contents may become material in the administration of any Internal Revenue law. Generally, tax returns and return information are confidential, as required by Internal Revenue Code section 6103.

The average time and expenses required to complete and file this form will vary depending on individual circumstances. For the estimated averages, see the instructions for your income tax return.

If you have suggestions for making this form simpler, we would be happy to hear from you. See the instructions for your income tax return.

Cat. No. 11712F

Form **2120** (Rev. 10-2005)

Illustration 2-12

Dependency Rule Summary

The three rules for both the Qualifying Dependent and the Qualifying Relative Test are:

- Dependent Taxpayer Test – You (or your spouse if MFJ) cannot be a dependent of someone else.
- Joint Return Test – You cannot claim someone who files a joint return unless it is only a claim for a refund and there would be no tax liability.
- Citizen or Resident Test – The person must be a U.S. citizen, U.S. resident alien, U.S. national, or a resident of Canada or Mexico for some part of the year.

Qualifying Dependent Test

Relationship Test

The child must be your son, daughter, stepchild, eligible foster child, brother, sister, half brother, half sister, stepbrother, stepsister, or a descendant of any of them.

Age Test

The child must be either under age 19 at the end of the year and younger than you, under 24 and a full time student at the end of the year and younger than you, or permanently and totally disabled.

Residency Test

The child must have lived with you for more than half of the year.

Support Test

The child must not have provided more than half of his or her own support for the year.

Qualifying Child of more than one person

If the child is the qualifying child of more than one person, you must be the one entitled to claim them.

Qualifying Relative Test

Not a Qualifying Child Test

The person cannot be your qualifying child or the qualifying child of anyone else.

Member of the Household or Relationship Test

The person must be either related to you in one of the ways stated earlier in the text, or they must have lived with you as a member of the household for the entire year. **Note:** The relationship test for Qualifying Relative is different from the test for Qualifying Child.

Gross Income Test

The person's gross income for the year must be less than $3,800.

Support Test

You must have provided over half of the person's total support.

Chapter Review

(1) What are the five filing statuses?

(2) On what day of the year is the marital status determined?

(3) When can a Married Filing Separate taxpayer claim an exemption for his or her spouse?

(4) What are the four qualifications for married but unmarried for tax purposes?

(5) What are the two reasons a taxpayer may get an additional standard deduction for tax year 2014?

(6) What is the standard deduction for a dependent?

(7) What is the exemption amount for 2014?

(8) What are the three tests that apply for both the qualifying child and the qualifying relative?

(9) What are the five qualifying child tests?

(10) What is a Custodial parent?

(11) What is a noncustodial parent?

(12) What are the four qualifying relative tests?

Exercise

Jerry lives in the house with his mom, Lucy. Jerry is 19, a full time student in college, and made $8,000 working a part time job. Lucy wants to know if she can claim Jerry on her tax return. Her household expenses are:

Mortgage payment	$950 per month
Real estate taxes	553
Utilities	345 per month
Leaky faucet in the wall	350
Groceries	425 per month

The fair rental value of her home is $850 per month. The following expenses are for Jerry:

Clothes	$850
School books and supplies	345
Car payment	225 per month
Auto insurance	85 per month
Christmas gifts	350
Birthday gifts	425
Football expenses	1,030

He, also, had tuition expense of $3,000. He had a scholarship that paid for the rest of the tuition. He spent about $200 per month going out on the weekends. Use the dependency support worksheet to find out if Lucy can claim Jerry.

Chapter 3 – Income

Income can be received in the form of money, property, or services. Income received falls into one of two categories: taxable or nontaxable. Because the IRS cannot cover all types of income and whether it's taxable or nontaxable, all income is taxable unless it is specifically exempt by law. Income that is taxable must be included on the tax return. Income that is nontaxable may still be included on the return, but it won't be taxed. We will cover different types of income in this chapter, as well as how to prepare a simple tax return. A Form 1040 is shown in Illustration 3-1.

Form 1040, Line 7 – Wages, salaries, tips, etc.

Employee Compensation

Employee compensation is what you receive in payment for personal services performed for an employer. It can include wages salaries, commissions, fees, and tips as well as fringe benefits and stock options. Employee compensation will be reported on a Form W-2 (Illustration 3-2).

Form W-2 must be furnished to the employees of a company by January 31st. There are five copies of the W-2. Copy A must be sent to the Social Security Administration by the employer. Copies B, C, and 2 are sent to the employee. Copy B will be filed with the Federal tax return. Copy 2 will be filed with the state return if required. Copy C is to be retained by the employee for their records. Copy D is kept by the employer. We will go over the W-2 briefly in this chapter. However, some of it may not be clear just yet. As we proceed in the course, it will all become clearer.

Illustration 3-1

Form **1040**	Department of the Treasury—Internal Revenue Service (99) **U.S. Individual Income Tax Return**	**2014**	OMB No. 1545-0074	IRS Use Only—Do not write or staple in this space.

For the year Jan. 1–Dec. 31, 2014, or other tax year beginning _____ , 2014, ending _____ , 20 ___ See separate instructions.

Your first name and initial	Last name		Your social security number
If a joint return, spouse's first name and initial	Last name		Spouse's social security number

Home address (number and street). If you have a P.O. box, see instructions. | Apt. no.

▲ Make sure the SSN(s) above and on line 6c are correct.

City, town or post office, state, and ZIP code. If you have a foreign address, also complete spaces below (see instructions).

Presidential Election Campaign
Check here if you, or your spouse if filing jointly, want $3 to go to this fund. Checking a box below will not change your tax or refund. ☐ You ☐ Spouse

Foreign country name	Foreign province/state/county	Foreign postal code

Filing Status

Check only one box.

1 ☐ Single
2 ☐ Married filing jointly (even if only one had income)
3 ☐ Married filing separately. Enter spouse's SSN above and full name here. ▶
4 ☐ Head of household (with qualifying person). (See instructions.) If the qualifying person is a child but not your dependent, enter this child's name here. ▶
5 ☐ Qualifying widow(er) with dependent child

Exemptions

6a ☐ **Yourself.** If someone can claim you as a dependent, **do not** check box 6a . . . . . .
b ☐ **Spouse** . . . .

c **Dependents:**

(1) First name Last name	(2) Dependent's social security number	(3) Dependent's relationship to you	(4) ✓ if child under age 17 qualifying for child tax credit (see instructions)
			☐
			☐
			☐
			☐

If more than four dependents, see instructions and check here ▶ ☐

Boxes checked on 6a and 6b
No. of children on 6c who:
• lived with you
• did not live with you due to divorce or separation (see instructions)
Dependents on 6c not entered above
Add numbers on lines above ▶

d Total number of exemptions claimed . . . .

Income

Attach Form(s) W-2 here. Also attach Forms W-2G and 1099-R if tax was withheld.

If you did not get a W-2, see instructions.

7	Wages, salaries, tips, etc. Attach Form(s) W-2	7	
8a	**Taxable** interest. Attach Schedule B if required	8a	
b	**Tax-exempt** interest. **Do not** include on line 8a . . .	8b	
9a	Ordinary dividends. Attach Schedule B if required	9a	
b	Qualified dividends	9b	
10	Taxable refunds, credits, or offsets of state and local income taxes	10	
11	Alimony received	11	
12	Business income or (loss). Attach Schedule C or C-EZ	12	
13	Capital gain or (loss). Attach Schedule D if required. If not required, check here ▶ ☐	13	
14	Other gains or (losses). Attach Form 4797	14	
15a	IRA distributions .	15a	b Taxable amount . . .	15b	
16a	Pensions and annuities	16a	b Taxable amount . . .	16b	
17	Rental real estate, royalties, partnerships, S corporations, trusts, etc. Attach Schedule E	17	
18	Farm income or (loss). Attach Schedule F	18	
19	Unemployment compensation	19	
20a	Social security benefits	20a	b Taxable amount . . .	20b	
21	Other income. List type and amount _____	21	
22	Combine the amounts in the far right column for lines 7 through 21. This is your **total income** ▶	22	

Adjusted Gross Income

23	Educator expenses	23	
24	Certain business expenses of reservists, performing artists, and fee-basis government officials. Attach Form 2106 or 2106-EZ	24	
25	Health savings account deduction. Attach Form 8889 .	25	
26	Moving expenses. Attach Form 3903	26	
27	Deductible part of self-employment tax. Attach Schedule SE .	27	
28	Self-employed SEP, SIMPLE, and qualified plans . .	28	
29	Self-employed health insurance deduction	29	
30	Penalty on early withdrawal of savings	30	
31a	Alimony paid b Recipient's SSN ▶ _____	31a	
32	IRA deduction	32	
33	Student loan interest deduction	33	
34	Tuition and fees. Attach Form 8917	34	
35	Domestic production activities deduction. Attach Form 8903	35	
36	Add lines 23 through 35	36	
37	Subtract line 36 from line 22. This is your **adjusted gross income** . . . . . ▶	37	

For Disclosure, Privacy Act, and Paperwork Reduction Act Notice, see separate instructions.   Cat. No. 11320B   Form **1040** (2014)

Illustration 3-1 continued

Form 1040 (2014)   Page **2**

Tax and Credits	38	Amount from line 37 (adjusted gross income)	38	
	39a	Check if: ☐ **You** were born before January 2, 1950, ☐ Blind. ☐ **Spouse** was born before January 2, 1950, ☐ Blind. **Total boxes checked ▶ 39a**		
	b	If your spouse itemizes on a separate return or you were a dual-status alien, check here ▶ 39b ☐		
Standard Deduction for— • People who check any box on line 39a or 39b **or** who can be claimed as a dependent, see instructions. • All others: Single or Married filing separately, $6,200 Married filing jointly or Qualifying widow(er), $12,400 Head of household, $9,100	40	**Itemized deductions** (from Schedule A) **or** your **standard deduction** (see left margin) . .	40	
	41	Subtract line 40 from line 38	41	
	42	**Exemptions.** If line 38 is $152,525 or less, multiply $3,950 by the number on line 6d. Otherwise, see instructions	42	
	43	**Taxable income.** Subtract line 42 from line 41. If line 42 is more than line 41, enter -0- . .	43	
	44	**Tax** (see instructions). Check if any from: **a** ☐ Form(s) 8814 **b** ☐ Form 4972 **c** ☐	44	
	45	**Alternative minimum tax** (see instructions). Attach Form 6251	45	
	46	Excess advance premium tax credit repayment. Attach Form 8962	46	
	47	Add lines 44, 45, and 46 . . . . ▶	47	
	48	Foreign tax credit. Attach Form 1116 if required	48		
	49	Credit for child and dependent care expenses. Attach Form 2441	49		
	50	Education credits from Form 8863, line 19	50		
	51	Retirement savings contributions credit. Attach Form 8880	51		
	52	Child tax credit. Attach Schedule 8812, if required . . .	52		
	53	Residential energy credits. Attach Form 5695	53		
	54	Other credits from Form: **a** ☐ 3800 **b** ☐ 8801 **c** ☐	54		
	55	Add lines 48 through 54. These are your **total credits**	55	
	56	Subtract line 55 from line 47. If line 55 is more than line 47, enter -0- . . . . . . ▶	56	
Other Taxes	57	Self-employment tax. Attach Schedule SE	57	
	58	Unreported social security and Medicare tax from Form: **a** ☐ 4137 **b** ☐ 8919 . .	58	
	59	Additional tax on IRAs, other qualified retirement plans, etc. Attach Form 5329 if required . .	59	
	60a	Household employment taxes from Schedule H	60a	
	b	First-time homebuyer credit repayment. Attach Form 5405 if required	60b	
	61	Health care: individual responsibility (see instructions) Full-year coverage ☐	61	
	62	Taxes from: **a** ☐ Form 8959 **b** ☐ Form 8960 **c** ☐ Instructions; enter code(s)	62	
	63	Add lines 56 through 62. This is your **total tax** . . . . ▶	63	
Payments If you have a qualifying child, attach Schedule EIC.	64	Federal income tax withheld from Forms W-2 and 1099 . .	64		
	65	2014 estimated tax payments and amount applied from 2013 return	65		
	66a	**Earned income credit (EIC)**	66a		
	b	Nontaxable combat pay election	66b			
	67	Additional child tax credit. Attach Schedule 8812	67		
	68	American opportunity credit from Form 8863, line 8 . . .	68		
	69	Net premium tax credit. Attach Form 8962	69		
	70	Amount paid with request for extension to file	70		
	71	Excess social security and tier 1 RRTA tax withheld . . .	71		
	72	Credit for federal tax on fuels. Attach Form 4136	72		
	73	Credits from Form: **a** ☐ 2439 **b** ☐ Reserved **c** ☐ Reserved **d** ☐	73		
	74	Add lines 64, 65, 66a, and 67 through 73. These are your **total payments** . . . . . ▶	74	
Refund Direct deposit? See instructions.	75	If line 74 is more than line 63, subtract line 63 from line 74. This is the amount you **overpaid**	75	
	76a	Amount of line 75 you want **refunded to you.** If Form 8888 is attached, check here . ▶ ☐	76a	
	▶ b	Routing number ☐☐☐☐☐☐☐☐☐ ▶ c Type: ☐ Checking ☐ Savings		
	▶ d	Account number ☐☐☐☐☐☐☐☐☐☐☐☐☐☐☐☐☐		
	77	Amount of line 75 you want **applied to your 2015 estimated tax ▶**	77		
Amount You Owe	78	**Amount you owe.** Subtract line 74 from line 63. For details on how to pay, see instructions ▶	78	
	79	Estimated tax penalty (see instructions)	79		

Third Party Designee

Do you want to allow another person to discuss this return with the IRS (see instructions)? ☐ **Yes.** Complete below. ☐ **No**

Designee's name ▶	Phone no. ▶	Personal identification number (PIN) ▶
		☐☐☐☐☐

Sign Here

Joint return? See instructions. Keep a copy for your records.

Under penalties of perjury, I declare that I have examined this return and accompanying schedules and statements, and to the best of my knowledge and belief, they are true, correct, and complete. Declaration of preparer (other than taxpayer) is based on all information of which preparer has any knowledge.

Your signature	Date	Your occupation	Daytime phone number
Spouse's signature. If a joint return, **both** must sign.	Date	Spouse's occupation	If the IRS sent you an Identity Protection PIN, enter it here (see inst.) ☐☐☐☐☐☐

Paid Preparer Use Only

Print/Type preparer's name	Preparer's signature	Date	Check ☐ if self-employed	PTIN
Firm's name ▶			Firm's EIN ▶	
Firm's address ▶			Phone no.	

www.irs.gov/form1040   Form **1040** (2014)

Illustration 3-1

	a Employee's social security number		OMB No. 1545-0008	Safe, accurate, FAST! Use	IRS e~file	Visit the IRS website at www.irs.gov/efile

b Employer identification number (EIN)	**1** Wages, tips, other compensation	**2** Federal income tax withheld
c Employer's name, address, and ZIP code	**3** Social security wages	**4** Social security tax withheld
	5 Medicare wages and tips	**6** Medicare tax withheld
	7 Social security tips	**8** Allocated tips
d Control number	**9**	**10** Dependent care benefits
e Employee's first name and initial Last name Suff.	**11** Nonqualified plans	**12a** See instructions for box 12
	13 Statutory employee ☐ Retirement plan ☐ Third-party sick pay ☐	**12b**
	14 Other	**12c**
		12d
f Employee's address and ZIP code		

15 State Employer's state ID number	**16** State wages, tips, etc.	**17** State income tax	**18** Local wages, tips, etc.	**19** Local income tax	**20** Locality name

Form **W-2** Wage and Tax Statement   **2014**   Department of the Treasury—Internal Revenue Service

Copy B—To Be Filed With Employee's FEDERAL Tax Return.
This information is being furnished to the Internal Revenue Service.

Box a – Employee's Social Security number.

Box b – Employer Identification number (EIN). The employer must have one of these if they have employees.

Box c – Employer's name, address, and zip code are entered here.

Box d – This box is for the employer's convenience. It has nothing to do with the tax preparation.

Boxes e and f – The employee's name and address are entered here.

Box 1 Wages, tips, other compensation – This box is where the total taxable compensation is reported. This amount includes wages, tips reported, and noncash payments. This amount does not include amounts paid into deferred compensation plans.

> **Deferred Compensation Plan**
> Compensation that is being earned but not received. The compensation is not taxed until it is actually received at a later date. For example pension plans, profit sharing plans, and stock options.

Box 2 Federal income tax withheld – The total federal income tax withheld from the employee's compensation for the year.

Box 3 Social security wages – The total wages subject to social security tax. The maximum amount of wages that are subject to social security tax for 2013 is $113,700.

Box 4 Social security tax withheld – The amount of social security tax withheld from the employee's wages at a rate of 6.2%. This is half of the social security tax required. The employer pays in the other half.

Box 5 Medicare wages and tips – The wages and tips subject to Medicare tax.

Box 6 Medicare tax withheld – The amount of Medicare tax withheld at a rate of 1.45%. This is half of the Medicare tax required. The employer pays in the other half.

Box 7 Social security tips – Tips reported to the employer that are subject to social security tax. The social security tax on the tips will be included in Box 4. These tips will also be included in Box 1.

Box 8 Allocated tips – Tips that the employer allocated to the employee. This amount must be added to the Box 1 amount and reported on the Form 1040, line 7. A Form 4137 also must be filed. We'll learn about the Form 4137 and tip income in Chapter 4.

Box 10 Dependent care benefits – These are the total dependent benefits paid or incurred by the employer.

Box 11 Nonqualified Plans – This is the amount contributed to a nonqualified plan. A nonqualified plan is a plan that doesn't qualify for any tax benefits under the tax code. The employees also may not be protected by law from losing money on the plan. This amount will be included in Box 1.

Box 12 Codes –

- **A** Uncollected Social security or RRTA tax on tips. These could not be collected because the employee did not have enough funds from which to deduct them.
- **B** Uncollected Medicare tax on tips. The employee did not have enough funds from which to deduct these.
- **C** Taxable cost of group-term life insurance over $50,000.
- **D-H involves retirement plans.** These will be discussed further, later in the course.
  - **D** Elective deferrals under section 401(k) cash or deferred arrangement plan.
  - **E** Elective deferrals under section 403(b) salary reduction agreement.
  - **F** Elective deferrals under a section 408(k)(6) salary reduction SEP.
  - **G** Elective deferrals and employer contributions (including nonelective deferrals) to any governmental or nongovernmental section 457(b) deferred compensation plan.
  - **H** Elective deferrals under section 501(c)(18)(D) tax-exempt organization plan.
- **J** Nontaxable sick pay. Any sick pay that was paid by a third party from a plan that the employee contributed to.
- **K** 20% excess tax on golden parachute payments. This only applies to certain key corporate employees.
- **L** Substantiated employee business expense reimbursements. This code is for reimbursements under the per diem method or mileage allowance that were in excess of the amount treated as substantiated by the IRS. Only the amount substantiated will go here. The rest will be included in boxes 1, 3, and 5.
- **M** Uncollected Social security or RRTA tax on the taxable cost of group term life insurance over $50,000 (for former employees).
- **N** Uncollected Medicare tax on the taxable cost of group term life insurance over $50,000 (for former employees).
- **P** Excludable moving expense reimbursements paid directly to the employee. This amount is not included in income.
- **Q** Nontaxable Combat Pay. This is for the military.
- **R** Employer Contributions to an Archer MSA (Medical Savings Account). If any portion of this is taxable it will be included in box 1.
- **S** Employee salary reduction contributions under a section 408(p) SIMPLE.
- **T** Adoption Benefits. These are adoption benefits provided by the employer. These are nontaxable up to a certain amount. We will cover this later in the course.
- **V** Income from the exercise of nonstatutory stock options. This will be included in boxes 1, 3, and 5.
- **W** Employer contributions to a Health Savings Account (HSA).
- **Y** Deferrals under a section 409A nonqualified deferred compensation plan.
- **Z** Income under section 409A in a nonqualified deferred compensation plan. This will be subject to an additional 20% tax.
- **AA** Designated Roth contributions under a section 401(k) plan.
- **BB** Designated Roth contributions under a section 403(b) salary reduction agreement.
- **DD** Cost of employer-sponsored health coverage (nontaxable).
- **EE** Designated Roth contributions under a governmental Section 457(b) plan [but not contributions under a tax-exempt organization Section 457(b) plan].

Box 13 Checkboxes

- **Statutory Employee** – This box will be checked for an employee whose earnings are subject to social security and Medicare tax withholding but are not subject to federal income tax withholding. That does not mean they are not subject to federal income tax. A statutory employee will file a Schedule C to report the income and any expenses. The definition of a statutory employee is a worker who is an independent contractor under the common-law rules but is treated by statute as an employee. This can include full-time life insurance salespersons, full-time traveling salespersons and drivers who distribute meat, vegetables, fruit, or bakery products.
- **Retirement Plan** – This box will be checked if the employee was an active participant in a
  - Qualified pension, profit-sharing, or stock-bonus plan described in section 401(a).
  - An annuity plan described in section 403(a).
  - An annuity contract or custodial account described in section 403(b).
  - A simplified employee pension (SEP) plan described in section 408(k).
  - A SIMPLE retirement account described in section 408(p).
  - A trust described in section 501(c)(18)/
  - A plan for federal, state, or local government employees or by an agency or instrument ability thereof (other than a section 457 (b) plan.
- **Third-party sick pay** – This will be marked if the income is sick pay payments made by a third party.

Box 14 Other – In this box the employer may enter other information for the employee's benefits such as union dues, uniform payments, health insurance premiums, etc.

Boxes 15 through 20 – State and local income tax information. These boxes are used to report state and local income and tax information. These will be used to file the state tax returns.

The Form W-2 and Tax Preparation

When preparing a tax return, the information from the W-2 must be entered on the tax return exactly as it appears. If the taxpayer feels there is an error on the W-2, they must get a corrected one from their employer. They may not report only what they think "it should be" on the tax return. The W-2 they receive from their employer is what the employer filed with the IRS. The amount in Box 1 will be reported on line 7 of the Form 1040. The amount in box 2 of the W-2 will be reported on line 64 of the Form 1040 (Illustration 3-1).

Form 1040, Lines 8a-9b – Interest and Dividend Income

Interest is the charge for the use of borrowed money. Most interest income is taxable when earned. If a taxpayer received taxable interest of $10 or more from one payer, they are required to send a form 1099-INT. Dividends are distributions of money, stock, or other property paid to the taxpayer by a corporation. The taxpayer will receive a 1099-DIV showing the dividends received during the year. We will cover this in depth in the next chapter.

Form 1040, Line 10 – Taxable refunds, credits, or offsets of state and local income taxes

If the taxpayer took a deduction in a prior year for state and local income tax paid and received a refund of those taxes paid in the current tax year, the taxpayer must include that refund in their income on the tax return. We will cover this in the chapter on Itemized Deductions.

Form 1040, Line 11 – Alimony Received

Alimony received is taxable in the year it is received. Alimony is a payment to or for a spouse or former spouse under a divorce or separation instrument. It does not include voluntary payments that are not made under a divorce or separation instrument. To qualify as alimony, the payment must be:

- Paid in cash
- Not designated as not alimony
- To be discontinued upon the death of the recipient spouse
- Paid under decree of divorce or separation while the spouses are living apart.

The following payments are not alimony:

- Child support
- Noncash property settlements
- Payments that are the spouse's part of community income
- Payments to keep up the payer's property, or
- Use of the payer's property.

Child support

Child support is never taxable to the recipient. In most agreements, child support will be specifically designated as such. Payments not specifically designated to be child support may still be considered to be child support. These payments are reduced either

- On the happening of a contingency relating to the child or
- At a time that can be clearly associated with the contingency.

The contingency can be becoming employed, dying, leaving the household, leaving school, marrying, or reaching a specified age or income level.

If both alimony and child support payments are received, child support is always considered to be received first. This means that if the payments have fallen behind, alimony is the amount left over after the child support is caught up.

Example: Bill is required to pay Sarah $3,000 alimony per year and $1,500 child support per year. Bill lost his job in October and only made payments totaling $2,800 for the year. The first $1,500 is considered child support and Sarah must report only $1,300 as alimony.

Form 1040, Line 12 – Business income or (loss)

If the taxpayer operates a business or acts as an independent contractor, a Schedule C is required to report income and expenses. The net income will be carried to this line on the Form 1040. We will cover this further in a later chapter.

Form 1040, Line 13 – Capital gain or (loss)

Capital gains and losses occur when a capital asset is sold. In most cases, the taxpayer will be taxed on the difference between the basis of the asset and the sales price. This will be reported on a Schedule D. We will discuss this in a later chapter.

Form 1040, Line 14 – Other gains or (losses)

These occur when you sell property used in a trade or business. We will discuss this in a later chapter.

Form 1040, Lines 15a and 15b – IRA distributions

An Individual Retirement Arrangement is a personal savings plan used to set aside money for retirement. There are many tax benefits involved. This line is to report the distributions of any of these funds. This will be covered in depth later in the course.

Form 1040, Lines 16a and 16b – Pensions and annuities

This line is for pensions, annuities, and other retirement distributions. This will also be covered later.

Form 1040, Line 17 – Rental Real Estate, Royalties, Partnerships, S Corporations, etc.

This line is to report any Schedule E income. The Schedule E is for income or loss from rental real estate, royalties, partnerships, S corporations, estates, trusts, and residual interests in Real Estate Mortgage Investment Conduits (REMICs). I know this is getting repetitive, but I promise we will cover all of this during the course.

Form 1040, Line 18 – Farm income or (loss)

Farm income or loss will be reported on a Schedule F. This is beyond the scope of this course.

Form 1040, Line 19 – Unemployment compensation

When a taxpayer is out of work, they may qualify for unemployment compensation from the government. Unemployment compensation received is taxable. If the taxpayer received an overpayment during the year and had to repay it, subtract it form the total before reporting it on line 19. Enter "repaid" and the amount overpaid on the dotted line next to line 19. If the taxpayer received an overpayment during a prior year and repaid it during this year, additional research will be required. Generally federal tax is not withheld. If the taxpayer would like to have the tax withheld, they may file a Form W-4V with the payer.

Form 1040, Lines 20a and 20b – Social security benefits

Contrary to many beliefs, Social security benefits may be taxable. The taxability depends on the filing status and income level of the taxpayer. Up to 85% of the benefits could be taxable. We will discuss the requirements and guidelines in a later chapter.

Form 1040, Line 21 – Other income

This line will cover many different types of income. We will discuss these in the next chapter.

Let's tackle our first tax return!

Now we are going to learn step-by-step how to file a simple tax return. There are two important tips that will make preparing a tax return much easier. First of all, experience the flow of the tax form. As you are preparing a Form 1040, start at the top and work your way down. It will be very tempting to skip around as you get to all of the reporting documents, but that will make it easier to forget some of the information. You should work the return line by line. At this point though, if we haven't covered it yet, you may skip over it. Secondly, and most importantly, read the lines. If you read the lines, the return will almost prepare itself.

Situation: Benny and Martha Stevens were married all year. Benny's social security number is 012-34-5678 and his birth date is April 14th, 1955. Martha's social security number is   023-45-6789 and her birth date is October 17th, 1957. Benny is a salesperson and Martha is a bookkeeper. They would both like to designate $3 to go to the presidential election campaign fund. They have an 18 year old son, Ryan. His birth date is January 14, 1997 and he is a full-time student in high school. His Social security number is 223-45-6788. Their W-2's are on the following page. Get out a Form 1040 and let's do this together. As you get to each step, complete it. You will find the completed return in Illustration 3-4.

Step 1: First, we are going to fill in the heading on the Form 1040. Remember, that's the name and address of the tax return.

Step 2: The filing status: What filing statuses may Benny and Martha use? What filing status should Benny and Martha file? Benny and Martha may file Married Filing Joint or Married Filing Separately. Usually, Married Filing Joint is more beneficial for the taxpayer.

Step 3: Exemptions. How many exemptions do they have? What about Ryan? Can they claim his dependency exemption? Remember the dependency tests. Dependency tests:

- Dependent taxpayer test: Can anyone else claim either Benny or Martha on their return?
- Joint return test: Can Ryan file a joint return?
- Citizen or resident test: Is Ryan a U.S. citizen, U.S. resident alien, U.S. national, or a resident of Canada or Mexico?
- Qualifying Child Test:
    - Relationship: Does Ryan meet the relationship test?
    - Age: Is Ryan under 19 or under 24 and a full time student?
    - Residency: Did Ryan live with Benny and Martha over half the year?
    - Support: Did Ryan provide over half of his own support?
    - Special test for qualifying child of more than one person: Does not apply to Ryan.

Step 4: How much income do Benny and Martha have? Where is it reported on the tax return? Notice lines 8a through 21 do not apply to the Stevens. Follow the directions for line 22.

Step 5: Finish page 1. We have not learned about adjustments yet, so just skip over those lines and look at line 37.

Step 6: Lines 38-42. Read the lines very carefully. They will tell you what to do.

Step 7: Lines 43 & 44. Finding the taxable income.

Step 8: Reading the tax tables (Illustration 3-3).

Notice the first column. It is under the
"At least". That means it could be that amount or over. The second column is "But less than". That means it cannot be that amount, it has to be less than that amount.

If you had taxable income of $32,300 and you are Single your tax would be $4,395.
If you had taxable income of $32,350 and you are Single, your tax would be $4,403.
If you had taxable income of $32,349 though and you are Single, your tax would be $4,395. The same taxable income, but with Married filing jointly would have different taxes.
Income of $32,300 = tax of $3,941
Income of $32,350 = tax of $3,949
Income of $32,349 = tax of $3,941

Check the tax table in the Appendix to find the correct tax for the Stevens. Lines 47 through 63 can be completed by just reading the lines.

Step 9 Lines 64 through 78. Remember, the federal tax withheld from the W-2's is entered on line 64. From that point reading the lines will tell you how to finish the tax return.

Step 10 Finish the tax return. Don't forget to sign it!

Illustration 3-3

If line 43 (taxable income) is—		And you are—			
At least	But less than	Single	Married filing jointly *	Married filing separately	Head of a household
		Your tax is—			

30,000

At least	But less than	Single	Married filing jointly *	Married filing separately	Head of a household
30,000	30,050	4,050	3,596	4,050	3,856
30,050	30,100	4,058	3,604	4,058	3,864
30,100	30,150	4,065	3,611	4,065	3,871
30,150	30,200	4,073	3,619	4,073	3,879
30,200	30,250	4,080	3,626	4,080	3,886
30,250	30,300	4,088	3,634	4,088	3,894
30,300	30,350	4,095	3,641	4,095	3,901
30,350	30,400	4,103	3,649	4,103	3,909
30,400	30,450	4,110	3,656	4,110	3,916
30,450	30,500	4,118	3,664	4,118	3,924
30,500	30,550	4,125	3,671	4,125	3,931
30,550	30,600	4,133	3,679	4,133	3,939
30,600	30,650	4,140	3,686	4,140	3,946
30,650	30,700	4,148	3,694	4,148	3,954
30,700	30,750	4,155	3,701	4,155	3,961
30,750	30,800	4,163	3,709	4,163	3,969
30,800	30,850	4,170	3,716	4,170	3,976
30,850	30,900	4,178	3,724	4,178	3,984
30,900	30,950	4,185	3,731	4,185	3,991
30,950	31,000	4,193	3,739	4,193	3,999

31,000

At least	But less than	Single	Married filing jointly *	Married filing separately	Head of a household
31,000	31,050	4,200	3,746	4,200	4,006
31,050	31,100	4,208	3,754	4,208	4,014
31,100	31,150	4,215	3,761	4,215	4,021
31,150	31,200	4,223	3,769	4,223	4,029
31,200	31,250	4,230	3,776	4,230	4,036
31,250	31,300	4,238	3,784	4,238	4,044
31,300	31,350	4,245	3,791	4,245	4,051
31,350	31,400	4,253	3,799	4,253	4,059
31,400	31,450	4,260	3,806	4,260	4,066
31,450	31,500	4,268	3,814	4,268	4,074
31,500	31,550	4,275	3,821	4,275	4,081
31,550	31,600	4,283	3,829	4,283	4,089
31,600	31,650	4,290	3,836	4,290	4,096
31,650	31,700	4,298	3,844	4,298	4,104
31,700	31,750	4,305	3,851	4,305	4,111
31,750	31,800	4,313	3,859	4,313	4,119
31,800	31,850	4,320	3,866	4,320	4,126
31,850	31,900	4,328	3,874	4,328	4,134
31,900	31,950	4,335	3,881	4,335	4,141
31,950	32,000	4,343	3,889	4,343	4,149

32,000

At least	But less than	Single	Married filing jointly *	Married filing separately	Head of a household
32,000	32,050	4,350	3,896	4,350	4,156
32,050	32,100	4,358	3,904	4,358	4,164
32,100	32,150	4,365	3,911	4,365	4,171
32,150	32,200	4,373	3,919	4,373	4,179
32,200	32,250	4,380	3,926	4,380	4,186
32,250	32,300	4,388	3,934	4,388	4,194
32,300	32,350	4,395	3,941	4,395	4,201
32,350	32,400	4,403	3,949	4,403	4,209
32,400	32,450	4,410	3,956	4,410	4,216
32,450	32,500	4,418	3,964	4,418	4,224
32,500	32,550	4,425	3,971	4,425	4,231
32,550	32,600	4,433	3,979	4,433	4,239
32,600	32,650	4,440	3,986	4,440	4,246
32,650	32,700	4,448	3,994	4,448	4,254
32,700	32,750	4,455	4,001	4,455	4,261
32,750	32,800	4,463	4,009	4,463	4,269
32,800	32,850	4,470	4,016	4,470	4,276
32,850	32,900	4,478	4,024	4,478	4,284
32,900	32,950	4,485	4,031	4,485	4,291
32,950	33,000	4,493	4,039	4,493	4,299

33,000

At least	But less than	Single	Married filing jointly *	Married filing separately	Head of a household
33,000	33,050	4,500	4,046	4,500	4,306
33,050	33,100	4,508	4,054	4,508	4,314
33,100	33,150	4,515	4,061	4,515	4,321
33,150	33,200	4,523	4,069	4,523	4,329
33,200	33,250	4,530	4,076	4,530	4,336
33,250	33,300	4,538	4,084	4,538	4,344
33,300	33,350	4,545	4,091	4,545	4,351
33,350	33,400	4,553	4,099	4,553	4,359
33,400	33,450	4,560	4,106	4,560	4,366
33,450	33,500	4,568	4,114	4,568	4,374
33,500	33,550	4,575	4,121	4,575	4,381
33,550	33,600	4,583	4,129	4,583	4,389
33,600	33,650	4,590	4,136	4,590	4,396
33,650	33,700	4,598	4,144	4,598	4,404
33,700	33,750	4,605	4,151	4,605	4,411
33,750	33,800	4,613	4,159	4,613	4,419
33,800	33,850	4,620	4,166	4,620	4,426
33,850	33,900	4,628	4,174	4,628	4,434
33,900	33,950	4,635	4,181	4,635	4,441
33,950	34,000	4,643	4,189	4,643	4,449

34,000

At least	But less than	Single	Married filing jointly *	Married filing separately	Head of a household
34,000	34,050	4,650	4,196	4,650	4,456
34,050	34,100	4,658	4,204	4,658	4,464
34,100	34,150	4,665	4,211	4,665	4,471
34,150	34,200	4,673	4,219	4,673	4,479
34,200	34,250	4,680	4,226	4,680	4,486
34,250	34,300	4,688	4,234	4,688	4,494
34,300	34,350	4,695	4,241	4,695	4,501
34,350	34,400	4,703	4,249	4,703	4,509
34,400	34,450	4,710	4,256	4,710	4,516
34,450	34,500	4,718	4,264	4,718	4,524
34,500	34,550	4,725	4,271	4,725	4,531
34,550	34,600	4,733	4,279	4,733	4,539
34,600	34,650	4,740	4,286	4,740	4,546
34,650	34,700	4,748	4,294	4,748	4,554
34,700	34,750	4,755	4,301	4,755	4,561
34,750	34,800	4,763	4,309	4,763	4,569
34,800	34,850	4,770	4,316	4,770	4,576
34,850	34,900	4,778	4,324	4,778	4,584
34,900	34,950	4,785	4,331	4,785	4,591
34,950	35,000	4,793	4,339	4,793	4,599

35,000

At least	But less than	Single	Married filing jointly *	Married filing separately	Head of a household
35,000	35,050	4,800	4,346	4,800	4,606
35,050	35,100	4,808	4,354	4,808	4,614
35,100	35,150	4,815	4,361	4,815	4,621
35,150	35,200	4,823	4,369	4,823	4,629
35,200	35,250	4,830	4,376	4,830	4,636
35,250	35,300	4,838	4,384	4,838	4,644
35,300	35,350	4,845	4,391	4,845	4,651
35,350	35,400	4,853	4,399	4,853	4,659
35,400	35,450	4,860	4,406	4,860	4,666
35,450	35,500	4,868	4,414	4,868	4,674
35,500	35,550	4,875	4,421	4,875	4,681
35,550	35,600	4,883	4,429	4,883	4,689
35,600	35,650	4,890	4,436	4,890	4,696
35,650	35,700	4,898	4,444	4,898	4,704
35,700	35,750	4,905	4,451	4,905	4,711
35,750	35,800	4,913	4,459	4,913	4,719
35,800	35,850	4,920	4,466	4,920	4,726
35,850	35,900	4,928	4,474	4,928	4,734
35,900	35,950	4,935	4,481	4,935	4,741
35,950	36,000	4,943	4,489	4,943	4,749

36,000

At least	But less than	Single	Married filing jointly *	Married filing separately	Head of a household
36,000	36,050	4,950	4,496	4,950	4,756
36,050	36,100	4,958	4,504	4,958	4,764
36,100	36,150	4,965	4,511	4,965	4,771
36,150	36,200	4,973	4,519	4,973	4,779
36,200	36,250	4,980	4,526	4,980	4,786
36,250	36,300	4,988	4,534	4,988	4,794
36,300	36,350	4,995	4,541	4,995	4,801
36,350	36,400	5,003	4,549	5,003	4,809
36,400	36,450	5,010	4,556	5,010	4,816
36,450	36,500	5,018	4,564	5,018	4,824
36,500	36,550	5,025	4,571	5,025	4,831
36,550	36,600	5,033	4,579	5,033	4,839
36,600	36,650	5,040	4,586	5,040	4,846
36,650	36,700	5,048	4,594	5,048	4,854
36,700	36,750	5,055	4,601	5,055	4,861
36,750	36,800	5,063	4,609	5,063	4,869
36,800	36,850	5,070	4,616	5,070	4,876
36,850	36,900	5,078	4,624	5,078	4,884
36,900	36,950	5,088	4,631	5,088	4,891
36,950	37,000	5,100	4,639	5,100	4,899

37,000

At least	But less than	Single	Married filing jointly *	Married filing separately	Head of a household
37,000	37,050	5,113	4,646	5,113	4,906
37,050	37,100	5,125	4,654	5,125	4,914
37,100	37,150	5,138	4,661	5,138	4,921
37,150	37,200	5,150	4,669	5,150	4,929
37,200	37,250	5,163	4,676	5,163	4,936
37,250	37,300	5,175	4,684	5,175	4,944
37,300	37,350	5,188	4,691	5,188	4,951
37,350	37,400	5,200	4,699	5,200	4,959
37,400	37,450	5,213	4,706	5,213	4,966
37,450	37,500	5,225	4,714	5,225	4,974
37,500	37,550	5,238	4,721	5,238	4,981
37,550	37,600	5,250	4,729	5,250	4,989
37,600	37,650	5,263	4,736	5,263	4,996
37,650	37,700	5,275	4,744	5,275	5,004
37,700	37,750	5,288	4,751	5,288	5,011
37,750	37,800	5,300	4,759	5,300	5,019
37,800	37,850	5,313	4,766	5,313	5,026
37,850	37,900	5,325	4,774	5,325	5,034
37,900	37,950	5,338	4,781	5,338	5,041
37,950	38,000	5,350	4,789	5,350	5,049

38,000

At least	But less than	Single	Married filing jointly *	Married filing separately	Head of a household
38,000	38,050	5,363	4,796	5,363	5,056
38,050	38,100	5,375	4,804	5,375	5,064
38,100	38,150	5,388	4,811	5,388	5,071
38,150	38,200	5,400	4,819	5,400	5,079
38,200	38,250	5,413	4,826	5,413	5,086
38,250	38,300	5,425	4,834	5,425	5,094
38,300	38,350	5,438	4,841	5,438	5,101
38,350	38,400	5,450	4,849	5,450	5,109
38,400	38,450	5,463	4,856	5,463	5,116
38,450	38,500	5,475	4,864	5,475	5,124
38,500	38,550	5,488	4,871	5,488	5,131
38,550	38,600	5,500	4,879	5,500	5,139
38,600	38,650	5,513	4,886	5,513	5,146
38,650	38,700	5,525	4,894	5,525	5,154
38,700	38,750	5,538	4,901	5,538	5,161
38,750	38,800	5,550	4,909	5,550	5,169
38,800	38,850	5,563	4,916	5,563	5,176
38,850	38,900	5,575	4,924	5,575	5,184
38,900	38,950	5,588	4,931	5,588	5,191
38,950	39,000	5,600	4,939	5,600	5,199

(Continued)

* This column must also be used by a qualifying widow(er).

Form 1040

Department of the Treasury—Internal Revenue Service (99)

U.S. Individual Income Tax Return 2014 OMB No. 1545-0074 IRS Use Only—Do not write or staple in this space.

For the year Jan. 1–Dec. 31, 2014, or other tax year beginning _____ , 2014, ending _____ , 20 ___ See separate instructions.

Your first name and initial	Last name	Your social security number
Benny	Stevens	0 1 2 3 4 5 6 7 8
If a joint return, spouse's first name and initial	Last name	Spouse's social security number
Martha	Stevens	0 2 3 4 5 6 7 8 9

Home address (number and street). If you have a P.O. box, see instructions. | Apt. no.

23 Hubb St.

▲ Make sure the SSN(s) above and on line 6c are correct.

City, town or post office, state, and ZIP code. If you have a foreign address, also complete spaces below (see instructions).

Your City, Your State, Your Zip Code

Presidential Election Campaign
Check here if you, or your spouse if filing jointly, want $3 to go to this fund. Checking a box below will not change your tax or refund. ☑ You ☑ Spouse

Foreign country name	Foreign province/state/county	Foreign postal code

Filing Status

Check only one box.

1. ☐ Single
2. ☑ Married filing jointly (even if only one had income)
3. ☐ Married filing separately. Enter spouse's SSN above and full name here. ▶
4. ☐ Head of household (with qualifying person). (See instructions.) If the qualifying person is a child but not your dependent, enter this child's name here. ▶
5. ☐ Qualifying widow(er) with dependent child

Exemptions

6a ☑ **Yourself.** If someone can claim you as a dependent, **do not** check box 6a . . . . .
b ☑ **Spouse** . . . .

c **Dependents:**		(2) Dependent's social security number	(3) Dependent's relationship to you	(4) ✓ if child under age 17 qualifying for child tax credit (see instructions)
(1) First name Last name				
Ryan Stevens		2 2 3 4 5 6 7 8 9	Son	☐
				☐
				☐
				☐

If more than four dependents, see instructions and check here ▶ ☐

Boxes checked on 6a and 6b **2**
No. of children on 6c who:
• lived with you **1**
• did not live with you due to divorce or separation (see instructions) ___
Dependents on 6c not entered above ___
Add numbers on lines above ▶ **3**

d Total number of exemptions claimed . . . .

Income

Attach Form(s) W-2 here. Also attach Forms W-2G and 1099-R if tax was withheld.

If you did not get a W-2, see instructions.

7	Wages, salaries, tips, etc. Attach Form(s) W-2	7	64,018	00
8a	**Taxable** interest. Attach Schedule B if required	8a		
b	**Tax-exempt** interest. **Do not** include on line 8a . .	8b		
9a	Ordinary dividends. Attach Schedule B if required	9a		
b	Qualified dividends	9b		
10	Taxable refunds, credits, or offsets of state and local income taxes	10		
11	Alimony received	11		
12	Business income or (loss). Attach Schedule C or C-EZ	12		
13	Capital gain or (loss). Attach Schedule D if required. If not required, check here ▶ ☐	13		
14	Other gains or (losses). Attach Form 4797	14		
15a	IRA distributions . 15a	b Taxable amount . . .	15b		
16a	Pensions and annuities 16a	b Taxable amount . . .	16b		
17	Rental real estate, royalties, partnerships, S corporations, trusts, etc. Attach Schedule E	17		
18	Farm income or (loss). Attach Schedule F	18		
19	Unemployment compensation	19		
20a	Social security benefits 20a	b Taxable amount . . .	20b		
21	Other income. List type and amount _____	21		
22	Combine the amounts in the far right column for lines 7 through 21. This is your **total income** ▶	22	64,018	00

Adjusted Gross Income

23	Educator expenses	23		
24	Certain business expenses of reservists, performing artists, and fee-basis government officials. Attach Form 2106 or 2106-EZ	24		
25	Health savings account deduction. Attach Form 8889 .	25		
26	Moving expenses. Attach Form 3903	26		
27	Deductible part of self-employment tax. Attach Schedule SE .	27		
28	Self-employed SEP, SIMPLE, and qualified plans .	28		
29	Self-employed health insurance deduction .	29		
30	Penalty on early withdrawal of savings	30		
31a	Alimony paid b Recipient's SSN ▶	31a		
32	IRA deduction	32		
33	Student loan interest deduction	33		
34	Tuition and fees. Attach Form 8917	34		
35	Domestic production activities deduction. Attach Form 8903	35		
36	Add lines 23 through 35	36		
37	Subtract line 36 from line 22. This is your **adjusted gross income** . . . . . ▶	37	64,018	00

For Disclosure, Privacy Act, and Paperwork Reduction Act Notice, see separate instructions. Cat. No. 11320B Form **1040** (2014)

Tax and Credits

38	Amount from line 37 (adjusted gross income)	38	64,018	00
39a	Check if: ☐ **You** were born before January 2, 1950, ☐ Blind. ☐ **Spouse** was born before January 2, 1950, ☐ Blind. } Total boxes checked ▶ 39a			
b	If your spouse itemizes on a separate return or you were a dual-status alien, check here▶ 39b☐			

Standard Deduction for—
- People who check any box on line 39a or 39b **or** who can be claimed as a dependent, see instructions.
- All others:

Single or Married filing separately, $6,200

Married filing jointly or Qualifying widow(er), $12,400

Head of household, $9,100

40	**Itemized deductions** (from Schedule A) **or** your **standard deduction** (see left margin)	40	12,400	00
41	Subtract line 40 from line 38	41	51,618	00
42	**Exemptions.** If line 38 is $152,525 or less, multiply $3,950 by the number on line 6d. Otherwise, see instructions	42	11,850	00
43	**Taxable income.** Subtract line 42 from line 41. If line 42 is more than line 41, enter -0-	43	39,768	00
44	**Tax** (see instructions). Check if any from: **a** ☐ Form(s) 8814 **b** ☐ Form 4972 **c** ☐ _____	44	5,059	00
45	**Alternative minimum tax** (see instructions). Attach Form 6251	45		
46	Excess advance premium tax credit repayment. Attach Form 8962	46		
47	Add lines 44, 45, and 46 ▶	47	5,059	00
48	Foreign tax credit. Attach Form 1116 if required	48		
49	Credit for child and dependent care expenses. Attach Form 2441	49		
50	Education credits from Form 8863, line 19	50		
51	Retirement savings contributions credit. Attach Form 8880	51		
52	Child tax credit. Attach Schedule 8812, if required	52		
53	Residential energy credits. Attach Form 5695	53		
54	Other credits from Form: **a** ☐ 3800 **b** ☐ 8801 **c** ☐	54		
55	Add lines 48 through 54. These are your **total credits**	55		
56	Subtract line 55 from line 47. If line 55 is more than line 47, enter -0- ▶	56	5,059	00

Other Taxes

57	Self-employment tax. Attach Schedule SE	57		
58	Unreported social security and Medicare tax from Form: **a** ☐ 4137 **b** ☐ 8919	58		
59	Additional tax on IRAs, other qualified retirement plans, etc. Attach Form 5329 if required	59		
60a	Household employment taxes from Schedule H	60a		
b	First-time homebuyer credit repayment. Attach Form 5405 if required	60b		
61	Health care: individual responsibility (see instructions)　Full-year coverage ☐	61		
62	Taxes from: **a** ☐ Form 8959 **b** ☐ Form 8960 **c** ☐ Instructions; enter code(s)	62		
63	Add lines 56 through 62. This is your **total tax** ▶	63	5,059	00

Payments

If you have a qualifying child, attach Schedule EIC.

64	Federal income tax withheld from Forms W-2 and 1099	64	8,487	00		
65	2014 estimated tax payments and amount applied from 2013 return	65				
66a	**Earned income credit (EIC)**	66a				
b	Nontaxable combat pay election	66b				
67	Additional child tax credit. Attach Schedule 8812	67				
68	American opportunity credit from Form 8863, line 8	68				
69	Net premium tax credit. Attach Form 8962	69				
70	Amount paid with request for extension to file	70				
71	Excess social security and tier 1 RRTA tax withheld	71				
72	Credit for federal tax on fuels. Attach Form 4136	72				
73	Credits from Form: **a** ☐ 2439 **b** ☐ Reserved **c** ☐ Reserved **d** ☐	73				
74	Add lines 64, 65, 66a, and 67 through 73. These are your **total payments** ▶	74	8,487	00		

Refund

Direct deposit? See instructions.

75	If line 74 is more than line 63, subtract line 63 from line 74. This is the amount you **overpaid**	75	3,428	00
76a	Amount of line 75 you want **refunded to you.** If Form 8888 is attached, check here ▶ ☐	76a	3,428	00
▶ b	Routing number _____ ▶c Type: ☐ Checking ☐ Savings			
▶ d	Account number _____			
77	Amount of line 75 you want **applied to your 2015 estimated tax** ▶ 77			

Amount You Owe

78	**Amount you owe.** Subtract line 74 from line 63. For details on how to pay, see instructions ▶	78		
79	Estimated tax penalty (see instructions) 79			

Third Party Designee

Do you want to allow another person to discuss this return with the IRS (see instructions)? ☐ **Yes.** Complete below. ☐ **No**

Designee's name ▶ _____　Phone no. ▶ _____　Personal identification number (PIN) ▶ ☐☐☐☐☐

Sign Here

Joint return? See instructions.
Keep a copy for your records.

Under penalties of perjury, I declare that I have examined this return and accompanying schedules and statements, and to the best of my knowledge and belief, they are true, correct, and complete. Declaration of preparer (other than taxpayer) is based on all information of which preparer has any knowledge.

Your signature	Date	Your occupation	Daytime phone number
		Salesperson	(555)555-5555
Spouse's signature. If a joint return, **both** must sign.	Date	Spouse's occupation	If the IRS sent you an Identity Protection PIN, enter it here (see inst.)
		Bookkeeper	☐☐☐☐☐☐

Paid Preparer Use Only

Print/Type preparer's name	Preparer's signature	Date	Check ☐ if self-employed	PTIN
Jane Doe				P00000000
Firm's name ▶ My Tax Service			Firm's EIN ▶	63-9999999
Firm's address ▶ 100 Main St., Your City, Your State, Your Zip Code			Phone no.	(555)555-1111

Chapter Review

1) What is employee compensation?

2) On what line of the tax return is the amount in Box 1 of the W-2's entered?

3) On what line of the tax return is the amount in Box 2 of the W-2's entered?

4) How many copies are there of the Form W-2?

5) Is alimony received taxable?

6) Is child support received taxable?

7) On what line of the Form 1040 is taxable unemployment compensation entered?

8) What is reported on Form 1099-INT?

9) What is reported on Form 1099-DIV?

Exercise

Prepare a tax return for the Mark and Beverly Jones. Mark's social security number is 098-76-5432 and his birth date is March 1st, 1973. He is a supervisor. Beverly's social security number is 023-45-9876 and her birth date is January 8th, 1972. She is a teacher. Neither wants to designate $3 to go to the presidential campaign fund. They have one daughter, Catherine Smith. Catherine's social security number is 345-67-4321 and her birth date is June 6th, 1996. She is a full-time student. Their W-2's follow. Beverly received $500 in child support for Catherine.

Form W-2 (First)

Visit the IRS website at www.irs.gov/efile

a Employee's social security number		
098-76-5432		

OMB No. 1545-0008

b Employer identification number (EIN)	1 Wages, tips, other compensation	2 Federal income tax withheld
63-3456765	46,786.00	5,298.00

c Employer's name, address, and ZIP code	3 Social security wages	4 Social security tax withheld
Harris Auto Sales 344 First St. Your City, Your State, Your Zip Code	46,786.00	2,900.73
	5 Medicare wages and tips	6 Medicare tax withheld
	46,786.00	678.40
	7 Social security tips	8 Allocated tips

d Control number	9	10 Dependent care benefits

e Employee's first name and initial Last name Suff.	11 Nonqualified plans	12a See instructions for box 12
	13 Statutory employee ☐ Retirement plan ☐ Third-party sick pay ☐	12b
Mark Jones 877 Oak Ave. Your City, Your State, Your Zip Code	14 Other	12c
		12d

f Employee's address and ZIP code

15 State	Employer's state ID number	16 State wages, tips, etc.	17 State income tax	18 Local wages, tips, etc.	19 Local income tax	20 Locality name
YS	77786543	46,786.00	1,871.44			

Form **W-2** Wage and Tax Statement   **2014**   Department of the Treasury—Internal Revenue Service

Copy B—To Be Filed With Employee's FEDERAL Tax Return.
This information is being furnished to the Internal Revenue Service.

Form W-2 (Second)

Visit the IRS website at www.irs.gov/efile

a Employee's social security number		
023-45-9876		

OMB No. 1545-0008

b Employer identification number (EIN)	1 Wages, tips, other compensation	2 Federal income tax withheld
63-1234567	36,777.00	4,045.47

c Employer's name, address, and ZIP code	3 Social security wages	4 Social security tax withheld
ABC Learning Center 43 Alphabet Way Your City, Your State, Your Zip Code	36,777.00	2,280.17
	5 Medicare wages and tips	6 Medicare tax withheld
	36,777.00	533.27
	7 Social security tips	8 Allocated tips

d Control number	9	10 Dependent care benefits

e Employee's first name and initial Last name Suff.	11 Nonqualified plans	12a See instructions for box 12
	13 Statutory employee ☐ Retirement plan ☐ Third-party sick pay ☐	12b
Beverly Jones 877 Oak Ave Your City, Your State, Your Zip Code	14 Other	12c
		12d

f Employee's address and ZIP code

15 State	Employer's state ID number	16 State wages, tips, etc.	17 State income tax	18 Local wages, tips, etc.	19 Local income tax	20 Locality name
YS	00066543	36,777.00	1,122.00			

Form **W-2** Wage and Tax Statement   **2014**   Department of the Treasury—Internal Revenue Service

Copy B—To Be Filed With Employee's FEDERAL Tax Return.
This information is being furnished to the Internal Revenue Service.

Chapter 4 – Tips and Other Income

Tip Income

Tips are received in many industries. To how many people have you given tips? Have you ever thought of them being taxable to the recipient? Tips are not only subject to federal income tax, but if the taxpayer receives over $20 a month, tips are also subject to social security and Medicare tax.

The employee that receives the tips should report them to their employer. Then, the employer will withhold the correct amount of income tax, Medicare, and social security. The employee is required to report tips to the employer if they received $20 or over in any month. If the taxpayer worked for more than one employer in a month, the $20 limit applies separately to each employer. They must report the tips received in that month by the 10th day of the following month. They should be included in the taxpayer's Form W-2.

If the employee does not report tips of $20 or more in a month, they must file a Form 4137 (Illustration 4-1). The Form 4137 will tell the employee how much social security and Medicare tax they must pay with their tax return. They may also be penalized 50% of the Medicare and social security tax due on those tips. If the employee received a Form W-2 with an amount in Box 8 (allocated tips), they must file a Form 4137 for this also.

Form 4137

Line 1: Column a – Enter the name of the employer to whom the taxpayer did not report the tips. Column b – Enter the employer identification number for that employer. Column c – Enter all tips the taxpayer received while working for that employer. These include tips that were or were not reported and allocated tips. Column d – Enter the tips that were reported to the employer.

Line 2: This is the total tips received in the tax year. Total the amounts on line 1, column c.

Line 3: This is the total tips that the taxpayer reported to their employer. Total the amounts on line 1, column d.

Line 4: Subtract line 3 from line 2. This is the amount of tips the taxpayer received but did not report to their employer. This amount must be included on line 7 of the Form 1040.

Line 5: Enter the amount of tips that were not required to be reported to the employer because they were less than $20 in a month. These are not subject to Medicare or social security tax.

Line 6: Subtract line 5 from line 4. These are the tips subject to Medicare tax.

Line 7: This is the maximum amount of income that is subject to social security tax. For 2013 it is 113,700.

Line 8: Enter the amount of social security wages and tip income from Boxes 3 and 7 of Forms W-2. This is the amount of income the taxpayer has that has already been subject to social security tax.

Illustration 4-1

Form **4137**	**Social Security and Medicare Tax on Unreported Tip Income**	OMB No. 1545-0074
Department of the Treasury Internal Revenue Service (99)	▶ Information about Form 4137 and its instructions is at *www.irs.gov/form4137*. ▶ **Attach to Form 1040, Form 1040NR, Form 1040NR-EZ, Form 1040-SS, or Form 1040-PR.**	**20**14 Attachment Sequence No. **24**

Name of person who received tips. If married, complete a separate Form 4137 for each spouse with unreported tips. | **Social security number**

1	(a) Name of employer to whom you were required to, but did not report all your tips (see instructions)	(b) Employer identification number (see instructions)	(c) Total cash and charge tips you received (including unreported tips) (see instructions)	(d) Total cash and charge tips you reported to your employer
A				
B				
C				
D				
E				

2	Total cash and charge tips you **received** in 2014. Add the amounts from line 1, column (c)	2		
3	Total cash and charge tips you **reported** to your employer(s) in 2014. Add the amounts from line 1, column (d)	3	
4	Subtract line 3 from line 2. This amount is income you **must** include in the total on Form 1040, line 7; Form 1040NR, line 8; or Form 1040NR-EZ, line 3	4	
5	Cash and charge tips you received but did not report to your employer because the total was less than $20 in a calendar month (see instructions)	5	
6	Unreported tips subject to Medicare tax. Subtract line 5 from line 4	6	
7	Maximum amount of wages (including tips) subject to social security tax	7	117,000 00	
8	Total social security wages and social security tips (total of boxes 3 and 7 shown on your Form(s) W-2) and railroad retirement (RRTA) compensation (subject to 6.2% rate) (see instructions)	8		
9	Subtract line 8 from line 7. If line 8 is more than line 7, enter -0-	9	
10	Unreported tips subject to social security tax. Enter the **smaller** of line 6 or line 9. If you received tips as a federal, state, or local government employee (see instructions)	10	
11	Multiply line 10 by .062 (social security tax rate)	11	
12	Multiply line 6 by .0145 (Medicare tax rate).	12	
13	Add lines 11 and 12. Enter the result here and on Form 1040, line 58; Form 1040NR, line 56; or Form 1040NR-EZ, line 16 (Form 1040-SS and 1040-PR filers, see instructions.) . . .	13	

Line 9: Subtract line 8 from line 7. This is the amount of income that can still be subject to social security tax. If line 8 is more that line 7, enter 0. The taxpayer has already paid the maximum amount and the tips are not subject to social security tax.

Line 10: Enter the smaller of line 8 or line 9. These are the tips that are subject to social security tax.

Line 11: Multiply line 10 by 6.2% (.062). This is the social security tax rate.

Line 12: Multiply line 6 by 1.45% (.0145). This is the Medicare tax rate.

Line 13: Add lines 11 and 12. Enter here and on Form 1040, line 58.

> **Example:** Lisa Bentley works at Larry's Steakhouse. She forgot to report February's tips of $452 and July's tips of $665. She was not required to report April's tips of $18. Her W-2 follows.
>
> Illustration 4-2 shows Form 4137 and Form 1040, lines 7 and 58. She had to include all of the unreported tips in her income and enter on line 7 of the 1040. She had to pay social security and Medicare taxes on $1,117. The additional tax is entered on line 58 of the 1040.

a Employee's social security number 223-34-3344	OMB No. 1545-0008	Safe, accurate, FAST! Use IRS e-file	Visit the IRS website at www.irs.gov/efile

b Employer identification number (EIN) 63-0096876	1 Wages, tips, other compensation 16,450.00	2 Federal income tax withheld 2,234.00
c Employer's name, address, and ZIP code	3 Social security wages 11,959.00	4 Social security tax withheld 1,019.90
Larry's Steakhouse 500 Angus Lane Your City, Your State, Your Zip Code	5 Medicare wages and tips 16,450.00	6 Medicare tax withheld 238.53
	7 Social security tips 4,491.00	8 Allocated tips
d Control number	9	10 Dependent care benefits
e Employee's first name and initial Last name Suff.	11 Nonqualified plans	12a See instructions for box 12
Lisa Bentley 298 Pine St. Your City, Your State, Your Zip Code	13 Statutory employee ☐ Retirement plan ☐ Third-party sick pay ☐	12b
	14 Other	12c
		12d
f Employee's address and ZIP code		

15 State	Employer's state ID number	16 State wages, tips, etc.	17 State income tax	18 Local wages, tips, etc.	19 Local income tax	20 Locality name
YS	002899767	16,450.00	549.00			

Form **W-2** Wage and Tax Statement   **2014**   Department of the Treasury—Internal Revenue Service

Copy B—To Be Filed With Employee's FEDERAL Tax Return.
This information is being furnished to the Internal Revenue Service.

Illustration 4-2

Form **4137**		**Social Security and Medicare Tax on Unreported Tip Income**		OMB No. 1545-0074
Department of the Treasury Internal Revenue Service (99)		▶ Information about Form 4137 and its instructions is at *www.irs.gov/form4137.* ▶ **Attach to Form 1040, Form 1040NR, Form 1040NR-EZ, Form 1040-SS, or Form 1040-PR.**		**2014** Attachment Sequence No. **24**

Name of person who received tips. If married, complete a separate Form 4137 for each spouse with unreported tips.

Lisa Bentley

Social security number

223-34-3344

1	(a) Name of employer to whom you were required to, but did not report all your tips (see instructions)	(b) Employer identification number (see instructions)	(c) Total cash and charge tips you received (including unreported tips) (see instructions)		(d) Total cash and charge tips you reported to your employer	
A	Larry's Steakhouse	63-0096876	5,626	00	4,491	00
B						
C						
D						
E						

2	Total cash and charge tips you **received** in 2014. Add the amounts from line 1, column (c)	**2**	5,626	00		
3	Total cash and charge tips you **reported** to your employer(s) in 2014. Add the amounts from line 1, column (d)	**3**			4,491	00
4	Subtract line 3 from line 2. This amount is income you **must** include in the total on Form 1040, line 7; Form 1040NR, line 8; or Form 1040NR-EZ, line 3	**4**			1,135	00
5	Cash and charge tips you received but did not report to your employer because the total was less than $20 in a calendar month (see instructions)	**5**			18	00
6	Unreported tips subject to Medicare tax. Subtract line 5 from line 4	**6**			1,117	00
7	Maximum amount of wages (including tips) subject to social security tax	**7**	117,000	00		
8	Total social security wages and social security tips (total of boxes 3 and 7 shown on your Form(s) W-2) and railroad retirement (RRTA) compensation (subject to 6.2% rate) (see instructions)	**8**	16,450	00		
9	Subtract line 8 from line 7. If line 8 is more than line 7, enter -0-	**9**			100,550	00
10	Unreported tips subject to social security tax. Enter the **smaller** of line 6 or line 9. If you received tips as a federal, state, or local government employee (see instructions)	**10**			1,117	00
11	Multiply line 10 by .062 (social security tax rate)	**11**			69	00
12	Multiply line 6 by .0145 (Medicare tax rate).	**12**			16	00
13	Add lines 11 and 12. Enter the result here and on Form 1040, line 58; Form 1040NR, line 56; or Form 1040NR-EZ, line 16 (Form 1040-SS and 1040-PR filers, see instructions.) . . .	**13**			85	00

Income	7	Wages, salaries, tips, etc. Attach Form(s) W-2	**7**	17,585	00
	8a	**Taxable** interest. Attach Schedule B if required	**8a**		

Other Taxes	57	Self-employment tax. Attach Schedule SE	**57**		
	58	Unreported social security and Medicare tax from Form: **a** ☑ 4137 **b** ☐ 8919 . .	**58**	85	00
	59	Additional tax on IRAs, other qualified retirement plans, etc. Attach Form 5329 if required . .	**59**		

Interest Income

Interest is money paid for the use of money. The taxpayer can receive interest from many different sources, including interest on a bank account, interest on a personal loan, and interest on insurance policies. In this section we will discuss the different types of interest income and how they are treated.

Schedule B, Part I, Interest

A Schedule B (Illustration 4-3) is required to report interest income if the taxpayer received over $1,500 of taxable interest, has a seller-financed mortgage, Nominee interest, Accrued interest, Original Issue Discount, Amortizable Bond Premiums, or if the taxpayer is claiming the exclusion of interest from a series EE or I U.S. savings bonds issued after 1989 used for education purposes. Otherwise, the interest income can be directly reported on Form 1040, line 8a and b.

Line 1: Report all of the taxable interest on this line. Also, include series EE and I US savings bond interest.

Line 2: Total all of the amounts listed on line 1.

Line 3: If any of the series EE and I U.S. savings bond interest is excluded, a Form 8815 must be filed and the amount of excluded interest will be carried to this line.

Line 4: Total interest. Total the amounts and enter that total here and on Form 1040, line 8a.

Generally, interest is taxable when constructively received. For example, when interest is credited to the taxpayer's savings account, the taxpayer may not withdraw it. Even though it is not withdrawn, it is available. Therefore, the interest is taxable.

Seller-Financed Mortgage

If the taxpayer sells his home to a buyer and finances the home for the buyer, they have a seller-financed mortgage. The taxpayer must report the buyer's name, address, social security number and any interest received. The taxpayer must also provide the buyer with their name, address, and social security number so the buyer may deduct the mortgage interest on the Schedule A.

Nominee Interest

Nominee interest is interest that is in the taxpayer's name, but the interest actually belongs to someone else. This must be entered on line 1 of the Schedule B, regardless of whether the taxpayer distributed the interest income to someone else. Below the last line of interest income listed on line 1 of the Schedule B, total the amounts. Under the subtotal, enter "Nominee Distribution" and show the interest amount received as a nominee. Subtract this amount and enter the result on line 2.

Illustration 4-3

| SCHEDULE B
(Form 1040A or 1040)

Department of the Treasury
Internal Revenue Service (99) | Interest and Ordinary Dividends

▶ Attach to Form 1040A or 1040.
▶ Information about Schedule B and its instructions is at *www.lrs.gov/scheduleb*. | OMB No. 1545-0074
2014
Attachment
Sequence No. 08 |

Name(s) shown on return   Your social security number

Part I

Interest

(See instructions on back and the instructions for Form 1040A, or Form 1040, line 8a.)

Note. If you received a Form 1099-INT, Form 1099-OID, or substitute statement from a brokerage firm, list the firm's name as the payer and enter the total interest shown on that form.

1 List name of payer. If any interest is from a seller-financed mortgage and the buyer used the property as a personal residence, see instructions on back and list this interest first. Also, show that buyer's social security number and address ▶

         Amount

1

2 Add the amounts on line 1 . . . . **2**

3 Excludable interest on series EE and I U.S. savings bonds issued after 1989. Attach Form 8815 . . . . **3**

4 Subtract line 3 from line 2. Enter the result here and on Form 1040A, or Form 1040, line 8a . . . . ▶ **4**

Note. If line 4 is over $1,500, you must complete Part III.

Part II

Ordinary Dividends

(See instructions on back and the instructions for Form 1040A, or Form 1040, line 9a.)

Note. If you received a Form 1099-DIV or substitute statement from a brokerage firm, list the firm's name as the payer and enter the ordinary dividends shown on that form.

5 List name of payer ▶

         Amount

5

6 Add the amounts on line 5. Enter the total here and on Form 1040A, or Form 1040, line 9a . . . . ▶ **6**

Note. If line 6 is over $1,500, you must complete Part III.

Part III

Foreign Accounts and Trusts

(See instructions on back.)

You must complete this part if you **(a)** had over $1,500 of taxable interest or ordinary dividends; **(b)** had a foreign account; or **(c)** received a distribution from, or were a grantor of, or a transferor to, a foreign trust.

                     Yes | **No**

7a At any time during 2014, did you have a financial interest in or signature authority over a financial account (such as a bank account, securities account, or brokerage account) located in a foreign country? See instructions . . . .

If "Yes," are you required to file FinCEN Form 114, Report of Foreign Bank and Financial Accounts (FBAR), to report that financial interest or signature authority? See FinCEN Form 114 and its instructions for filing requirements and exceptions to those requirements . . . . . .

b If you are required to file FinCEN Form 114, enter the name of the foreign country where the financial account is located ▶

8 During 2014, did you receive a distribution from, or were you the grantor of, or transferor to, a foreign trust? If "Yes," you may have to file Form 3520. See instructions on back . . . . . .

For Paperwork Reduction Act Notice, see your tax return instructions. Cat. No. 17146N Schedule B (Form 1040A or 1040) 2014

Accrued Interest

When the taxpayer buys bonds from a seller between interest payment dates and pays the accrued interest to the seller, the interest is taxable to the seller. Follow the same guidelines as reporting nominee interest, but identify the amount to be subtracted as "Accrued Interest".

Original Issue Discount and

These items are beyond the scope of this course and will have to be researched if encountered.

Excludable Interest on Series EE and I U.S. Savings Bonds Issued After 1989

Part or all of the interest earned on Series EE and I bonds may be excludable if used to pay higher education expenses. A Form 8815 must be attached to the return (Illustration 4-4). To qualify:

- The bonds must have been issued after 1989.

- The purchaser must have been at least 24 years old on the purchase date.

- The bond must be issued in the taxpayer's name as sole owner or in the taxpayer's and spouse's name as co-owners.

- Qualified higher education expenses must have been paid in the same year for the taxpayer, the spouse, or their dependent.

Qualified higher education expenses – Tuition and fees required for the taxpayer, spouse, or dependent to attend an eligible educational institution. They may also be contributions to a qualified state tuition program or an educational IRA.

Other Types of Interest

Let's discuss a few other types of interest income. Illustration 4-5 deals with many other types of interest and whether they are taxable or not.

U.S. Treasury Obligations

Treasury Bills are purchased at an amount less than the face value. When they mature they are worth the face value. They mature in 1 year or less. The difference between the purchase price and the face value is considered interest income and is taxable at maturity. Treasury Notes and Bonds have a maturity period of longer than 1 year. Generally, interest is paid every 6 months and is taxable when paid. Interest income on U.S. Treasury obligations is not taxable to any state by federal law.

Municipal Bonds

Municipal Bonds are obligations of state and local governments. They are usually sold to create revenue for capital improvement projects. Municipal Bond interest is not taxable to the federal government. However, it is taxable in some states.

Illustration 4-4

Form **8815**

Department of the Treasury
Internal Revenue Service (99)

Exclusion of Interest From Series EE and I
U.S. Savings Bonds Issued After 1989
(For Filers With Qualified Higher Education Expenses)
▶ Information about Form 8815 and its instructions is at *www.irs.gov/form8815.*
▶ Attach to Form 1040 or Form 1040A.

OMB No. 1545-0074

2014

Attachment
Sequence No. **167**

Name(s) shown on return | Your social security number

1

(a) Name of person (you, your spouse, or your dependent) who was enrolled at or attended an eligible educational institution	(b) Name and address of eligible educational institution

If you need more space, attach a statement.

2	Enter the total qualified higher education expenses you paid in 2014 for the person(s) listed in column (a) of line 1. See the instructions to find out which expenses qualify	**2**		
3	Enter the total of any nontaxable educational benefits (such as nontaxable scholarship or fellowship grants) received for 2014 for the person(s) listed in column (a) of line 1 (see instructions)	**3**		
4	Subtract line 3 from line 2. If zero or less, **stop.** You **cannot** take the exclusion	**4**		
5	Enter the total proceeds (principal and interest) from all series EE and I U.S. savings bonds **issued after 1989** that you **cashed during 2014**	**5**		
6	Enter the interest included on line 5 (see instructions)	**6**		
7	If line 4 is equal to or more than line 5, enter "1.000." If line 4 is less than line 5, divide line 4 by line 5. Enter the result as a decimal (rounded to at least three places)	**7**	×	.
8	Multiply line 6 by line 7	**8**		
9	Enter your modified adjusted gross income (see instructions)	**9**		
	Note: *If line 9 is $91,000 or more if single or head of household, or $143,950 or more if married filing jointly or qualifying widow(er) with dependent child,* **stop.** *You* **cannot** *take the exclusion.*			
10	Enter: $76,000 if single or head of household; $113,950 if married filing jointly or qualifying widow(er) with dependent child	**10**		
11	Subtract line 10 from line 9. If zero or less, skip line 12, enter -0- on line 13, and go to line 14	**11**		
12	Divide line 11 by $15,000 if single or head of household; $30,000 if married filing jointly or qualifying widow(er) with dependent child. Enter the result as a decimal (rounded to at least three places)	**12**	×	.
13	Multiply line 8 by line 12	**13**		
14	**Excludable savings bond interest.** Subtract line 13 from line 8. Enter the result here and on Schedule B (Form 1040A or 1040), line 3 . . . . ▶	**14**		

For Paperwork Reduction Act Notice, see your tax return instructions. Cat. No. 10822S Form **8815** (2014)

Dividends That Are Actually Interest

Some distributions that are reported as dividends are actually interest income. Income from deposit or share accounts from the following sources must be reported as interest income.

- Cooperative banks,

- Credit unions,

- Domestic building and loan associations,

- Domestic savings and loan associations,

- Federal savings and loan associations,

- Mutual savings banks.

Illustration 4-5

Type of Interest Income	Source	Taxable	When
Certificate of Deposits	Banks	Yes	As earned
Checking/Savings Accounts	Banks	Yes	As earned
Exempt Interest Dividends	Mutual Funds	No	--------------
Gifts for Opening Accounts	Banks	Yes	As received
Installment Sales	Buyer	Yes	As received
Insurance Dividends Left on Deposit	Insurance Companies	Yes	As earned
Interest on Tax Refunds	U.S./State/Local Governments	Yes	As received
Municipal Bonds	State/Local Governments	No	--------------
Personal Loans	Borrower	Yes	As received
Roth IRAs	Banks/Financial Institutions	No	--------------
Series E, EE, and I Bonds	U.S. Treasury	Yes	At maturity, unless taxpayer elects to be taxed as earned
		No	If proceeds are used to pay qualified higher education expenses.
Series H or HH Bonds	U.S. Treasury	Yes	As earned
Traditional IRAs	Banks/Financial Institutions	Yes	As withdrawn
Treasury Bills	U.S. Treasury	Yes	At maturity
Treasury Notes and Bonds	U.S. Treasury	Yes	As earned

Note: These rules do not apply to state tax laws.

Form 1099-INT

A Form 1099-INT is required to be filed by the payer of the interest if the interest income is $10 or more. If the taxpayer receives taxable interest of less than $10 and a Form 1099-INT was not filed, the interest is still taxable and must be reported on the tax return.

Box 1 – Interest income: This box shows taxable interest paid to the taxpayer during the year.

Box 2 – Early withdrawal penalty: In time savings accounts, if some interest or principal is forfeited due to early withdrawal, the amount forfeited is in this box. This amount may be taken as an adjustment to income, which we will cover later.

Box 3 – Interest on U.S. Savings Bonds and Treasury obligations: Interest from U.S. savings bonds and Treasury obligations is entered here. This interest is not included in the amount in Box 1.

Box 4 – Federal income tax withheld: Tax isn't generally withheld from interest income. However, if the taxpayer did not furnish their social security number or taxpayer identification number, the income is subject to backup withholding of 28%.

Box 5 – Investment expenses: This is the taxpayer's share of investment expense from a real estate mortgage investment conduit (REMIC). This amount may be deducted on a Schedule A. If this is encountered, additional research may be required.

Box 6 – Foreign tax paid: This is any foreign tax that is withheld from the interest income. This amount can be used as either a credit or a deduction. We will explore both of these options later in the course.

Box 7 – Foreign country or U.S. possession: The Foreign country or U.S. to which the foreign tax was paid.

Box 8 – Tax-exempt interest: Tax exempt interest paid to the taxpayer is entered here. This amount is reported on the Form 1040, line 8b.

Box 9 – Specified private activity bond interest: This is any tax exempt interest subject to alternative minimum tax. If this is encountered, additional research may be required.

Box 10 – Market discount: If the taxpayer owns a covered security and made an election to include the market discount in income as it accrues, that amount is entered here. If this is encountered, additional research may be required.

Box 11 – Bond premium: If the taxpayer owns a covered security, the amount of premium amortization for the year is entered here, unless the taxpayer made an election to not amortize the bond premium. In that case, the net amount of interest will be reported in boxes 1, 3, 8, or 9, whichever is applicable. Additional research may be required.

☐ CORRECTED (if checked)

PAYER'S name, street address, city or town, state or province, country, ZIP or foreign postal code, and telephone no.	Payer's RTN (optional)	OMB No. 1545-0112	
		20**14**	**Interest Income**
	1 Interest income $	Form **1099-INT**	
	2 Early withdrawal penalty $		**Copy B**
PAYER'S federal identification number RECIPIENT'S identification number			**For Recipient**
	3 Interest on U.S. Savings Bonds and Treas. obligations $		
RECIPIENT'S name	**4** Federal income tax withheld $	**5** Investment expenses $	This is important tax information and is being furnished to the Internal Revenue Service. If you are required to file a return, a negligence penalty or other sanction may be imposed on you if this income is taxable and the IRS determines that it has not been reported.
Street address (including apt. no.)	**6** Foreign tax paid $	**7** Foreign country or U.S. possession	
City or town, state or province, country, and ZIP or foreign postal code	**8** Tax-exempt interest $	**9** Specified private activity bond interest $	
	10 Market discount $	**11** Bond premium $	
Account number (see instructions)	**12** Tax-exempt bond CUSIP no.	**13** State **14** State identification no.	**15** State tax withheld $ $

Form **1099-INT**   (keep for your records)   www.irs.gov/form1099int   Department of the Treasury - Internal Revenue Service

Dividends

Shareholders are people who own stock in a corporation. Dividends, which represent the shareholder's portion of the corporation's earnings, are paid to these shareholders. Dividends may also be paid from a partnership, an estate, a trust, or an association that is taxed as a corporation.

Types of Dividends

Ordinary dividends are the most common type of dividend distribution. Ordinary dividends paid are taxed as ordinary income. Generally, unless stated otherwise, dividends paid are ordinary dividends.

Qualified Dividends

Qualified dividends are dividends that are subject to the capital gains tax rate. This tax rate is 0% for taxpayers whose regular tax rate is 10% or 15%; 15% for taxpayers whose regular tax rate is greater than 15%, but less than 39.6%; and 20% for taxpayers whose regular tax rate is 39.6% To qualify all of the following requirements must be met:

- The dividends must have been paid by a U.S. corporation or a qualified foreign corporation.

- The dividends are not:

  o Capital gain distributions

- Dividends paid on deposits with mutual savings banks, cooperative banks, credit unions, U.S. building and loan associations, federal savings and loan associations, and similar financial institutions. (Report these amounts as interest income.)
- Dividends from a corporation that is a tax-exempt organization or farmer's cooperative during the corporation's tax year in which the dividends were paid or during the corporation's previous tax year.
- Dividends paid by a corporation on employer securities which are held on the date of record by an employee ownership plan (ESOP) maintained by that corporation.
- Dividends on any share of stock to the extent that you are obligated (whether under a short sale or otherwise) to make related payments for positions in substantially similar or related property.
- Payments in lieu of dividends, but only if you know or have reason to know that the payments are not qualified dividends.
- Payments shown in Form 1099-DIV, box 1b, from a foreign corporation to the extent you know or have reason to know the payments are not qualified dividends.

- The taxpayer meets the holding period.

Qualified Foreign Corporation

A qualified foreign corporation must meet at least one of the following conditions:

- The corporation is incorporated in a U.S. possession.
- The corporation is eligible for the benefits of a comprehensive income tax treaty, as shown on the next page, with the United States that the Treasury Department determines is satisfactory for this purpose and that includes an exchange of information program.

Income Tax Treaties

Australia	Indonesia	Poland
Austria	Ireland	Portugal
Bangladesh	Israel	Romania
Barbados	Italy	Russian Federation
Belgium	Jamaica	Slovak Republic
Bulgaria	Japan	Slovenia
Canada	Kazakhstan	South Africa
China	Korea, South	Spain
Cyprus	Latvia	Sri Lanka
Czech Republic	Lithuania	Sweden
Denmark	Luxembourg	Switzerland
Egypt	Malta	Thailand
Estonia	Mexico	Trinidad
Finland	Morocco	Tobago
France	Netherlands	Tunisia
Germany	New Zealand	Turkey
Greece	Norway	Ukraine
Hungary	Pakistan	United Kingdom
Iceland	Philippines	Venezuela
India		

- The corporation does not meet either of the conditions above, but the stock for which the dividend is paid is readily tradable on an established securities market in the United States.

Exception: A corporation is not a qualified foreign corporation if it is a passive foreign investment company during its tax year in which the dividends are paid or during its previous tax year.

Holding Period

To determine the holding period you have to know what the ex-dividend date is. Dividends from corporations are paid to the shareholders on a certain date. The next day is the ex-dividend date. The taxpayer must have held the stock for more than 60 days during the 121 day period that begins before the ex-dividend date. When counting the days, include the day the taxpayer disposed of the stock, but not the day the stock was acquired.

Exception: If the stock is preferred the dividends must have been held for more than 90 days during the 181 day period that begins 90 days before the ex-dividend date.

Capital Gain Distributions

Capital Gain distributions are paid by mutual funds, regulated investment companies, and real estate investment trusts. These are treated as long term and subject to the capital gains tax rate as discussed earlier. These will be discussed further in the second half of the course.

Nondividend Distributions

A nondividend distribution is a return of capital or investment. When the taxpayer purchases the stock, they are investing a certain amount in the stock. When they receive a nondividend distribution, it is a return of the investment the taxpayer originally put in. The distribution is not taxable, but reduces the taxpayer's investment (basis) in the stock. When the taxpayer's investment is completely recovered, the distributions become taxable. We will cover the basis of stock further in the second half of the course.

Reinvested Dividends

If the taxpayer chooses, they may reinvest the dividends distributed. This means that they will purchase additional stock with the dividends they earned. These dividends are still taxable to the taxpayer, but the reinvested dividends add to the basis of the additional stock purchased. It is important that the taxpayer keep all of this information so the basis may be determined when the stock is sold.

Schedule B, Part II, Ordinary Dividends

A Schedule B (Illustration 4-3) is required if the taxpayer has over $1,500 of ordinary dividends or the taxpayer received nominee dividends. Otherwise, the ordinary dividends can be reported directly on Form 1040, line 9a.

Line 5: List all of the ordinary dividends received on this line.

Line 6: Total all of the amounts listed on line 5.

Form 1099-DIV

A Form 1099-DIV is required if one payer pays dividends of $10 or more to one person. One is also required if the foreign tax or federal income tax was withheld or the payee was paid $600 or more as part of a liquidation.

Box 1a – Total ordinary dividends: This is the total ordinary dividends paid by the company issuing the 1099-DIV.

Box 1b – Qualified dividends: This is the portion of box 1a that is qualified and will be eligible for the capital gains tax rate.

Box 2a – Total capital gain distributions: This is the total capital gain distribution paid to the taxpayer.

Box 2b – Unrecaptured Sec. 1250 gain: This is the taxpayer's share of a gain on certain business real estate. This will be covered further in the second half of the course.

Box 2c – Section 1202 gain: This is the gain on Section 1202 property which is certain qualified small business stock. This is beyond the scope of the course and additional research needs to be done if encountered.

Box 2d – Collectibles (28%) gain: This is a gain that is from the sale of certain collectibles and is subject to a 28% tax rate. This will be covered further in the second half.

Box 3 – Nondividend distributions: This is a return of capital and will not be taxable until the taxpayer's basis is recovered.

Box 4 – Federal income tax withheld: The amount of federal income tax withheld from the dividends.

Box 5 – Investment Expenses: This amount is the taxpayer's share of a nonpublicly offered regulated investment company's expenses. This amount may be taken as an itemized deduction.

Box 6 – Foreign tax paid: This amount is the foreign tax withheld and paid on the dividends and other distributions.

Box 7 – Foreign country or U.S. possession: The foreign country or possession to which the foreign tax was paid.

Box 8 – Cash liquidation distributions & Box 9 – Noncash liquidation distributions: These are the distributions from a corporation that is completely or partially liquidating. Treatment of these distributions is beyond the scope of this course.

Box 10 – Exempt-interest dividends: The amount of tax exempt interest dividends from a mutual fund or other regulated investment company paid to the taxpayer is entered in this box. This amount is reported on Form 1040, line 8b as tax exempt interest.

Box 11 – Specified private activity bond interest dividends: This is the amount of exempt interest dividends subject to alternative minimum tax. Additional research may be required if this is encountered.

□ CORRECTED (if checked)

PAYER'S name, street address, city or town, state or province, country, ZIP or foreign postal code, and telephone no.		1a Total ordinary dividends $	OMB No. 1545-0110 2014 Form **1099-DIV**	**Dividends and Distributions**
		1b Qualified dividends $		
		2a Total capital gain distr. $	2b Unrecap. Sec. 1250 gain $	**Copy B** **For Recipient**
PAYER'S federal identification number	RECIPIENT'S identification number	2c Section 1202 gain $	2d Collectibles (28%) gain $	
RECIPIENT'S name		3 Nondividend distributions $	4 Federal income tax withheld $	This is important tax information and is being furnished to the Internal Revenue Service. If you are required to file a return, a negligence penalty or other sanction may be imposed on you if this income is taxable and the IRS determines that it has not been reported.
Street address (including apt. no.)			5 Investment expenses $	
		6 Foreign tax paid $	7 Foreign country or U.S. possession	
City or town, state or province, country, and ZIP or foreign postal code		8 Cash liquidation distributions $	9 Noncash liquidation distributions $	
		10 Exempt-interest dividends $	11 Specified private activity bond interest dividends $	
Account number (see instructions)		12 State	13 State identification no.	14 State tax withheld $
				$

Form **1099-DIV**   (keep for your records)   www.irs.gov/form1099div   Department of the Treasury - Internal Revenue Service

4-15

Schedule B, Part III, Foreign Accounts and Trusts

This section must be completed if the taxpayer (Illustration 4-3):

- Had over $1,500 of taxable interest or ordinary dividends,
- Had a foreign account, or
- Received a distribution from, or were a grantor of, or a transferor to, a foreign trust.

Type of income	If you file Form 1040, report on...
Taxable interest that totals $1,500 or less	Line 8a (You may need to file Schedule B as well)
Taxable interest that totals more than $1,500	Line 8a; also use Schedule B.
Savings bond interest you will exclude because of higher education expenses	Schedule B; also use Form 8815
Ordinary dividends that total $1,500 or less	Line 9a (You may need to file Schedule B as well.)
Ordinary dividends that total more than $1,500	Line 9a; also use Schedule B
Qualified Dividends (if you do not have to file Schedule D)	Line 9b; also use the Qualified Dividends and Capital Gain Tax Worksheet
Qualified dividends (if you have to file Schedule D)	Line 9b; also use the Qualified Dividends and Capital Gain Tax Worksheet or the Schedule D Tax Worksheet

This illustration is an easy research tool while learning where the interest and dividend income should be reported.

Other Income

Line 21 of the Form 1040 is the "other income" line. The Form 1040 instructions say to use line 21 to report any income not reported elsewhere on your return or other schedules. Enlightening, isn't it? We will cover some of the different types of income that can be included on this line as well as some types of nontaxable income. Remember, if you don't know for sure that it's nontaxable income, do some research.

Examples of line 21 income:

- Gambling Winnings – These must be included in income in the year they were won. Winnings from lotteries and raffles are included in this category. If the winnings are not cash, the taxpayer must include the fair market value of the property. If the taxpayer wins a state lottery that is paid in yearly installments, the taxpayer must include the annual payments and any interest earned on the unpaid installments. Gambling losses are deductible up to the amount of the gambling winnings. These are deducted on a Schedule A. We will discuss this further in that chapter.

Sometimes, depending on the type of winnings and amount, the taxpayer might receive a Form W-2G. This will show the amount of gambling winnings and any tax taken out of them. Include the winnings on Form 1040, line 21 and the taxes withheld on Form 1040, line 61.

- Gifts and Inheritances – Generally, gifts and inheritances are not taxable to the recipient. If the property later produces income, however, that income will be taxable.

- Bribes – Any bribes are taxable to the recipient and must be included in income.

- Illegal Income – Illegal income such as income from selling drugs or extortion is taxable. Include on Form 1040, line 21 unless it is self-employment income. This will be reported on a Schedule C.

- Kickbacks – This must also be included in taxable income.

- Prizes and awards – Cash prizes and awards are taxable and reported on Form 1040, line 21. The fair market value of goods or services received is also reported on Form 1040, line 21.

- Jury Duty – Jury duty pay is included in income. If the taxpayer is being paid by their employer and has to give the jury duty pay to the employer, they can take it as an adjustment to income on Form 1040, line 36. Write "Jury Pay" on the dotted line next to line 36.

- Activity Not for Profit – If the taxpayer is involved in something, but does not expect to make a profit from it, the income is entered on line 21. An example of this is hobby income. The expenses up to the amount of the income can be deducted on the Schedule A. We will discuss this further in a later chapter.

- Compensatory Damages – If the taxpayer receives compensation for lost wages, this amount is included on Form 1040, line 21 in other income. **Note:** Do not include in income compensatory damages for personal physical injury or personal physical sickness.

Nontaxable income

As stated earlier, income is taxable unless it is specifically exempt by law. Some types of nontaxable income are welfare benefits, workers compensation, and life insurance proceeds paid because of the death of the insured person. A federal tax refund is also not taxable on the federal tax return.

Some scholarships and fellowships are not taxable if certain requirements are met. These requirements are:

- The student must be a degree candidate.
- The funds must be used to pay the tuition and fees to enroll at or attend an educational institution, or
- Fees, books, supplies, and equipment required for courses at the educational institution.

Amounts used for room and board are not excludable from income and are taxable to the recipient.

Chapter Review

1) How much tip income may a taxpayer make per month without having to report it to the employer?

2) What is the penalty for a taxpayer who was required to report the tip income to their employer but did not?

3) In what situations is a Schedule B required to be filed?

4) What requirements must the taxpayer meet to be able to exclude series EE and I U.S. savings bond interest?

5) What is the difference between ordinary dividends and qualified dividends?

6) What is a nondividend distribution and how is it taxed?

7) Name three types of taxable "other income".

8) Are scholarships and fellowships taxable?

Exercise

Prepare a tax return for Hank and Hilary Lee. Hank's social security number is 767-89-1212 and his birth date is May 31, 1978. Hank is a manager. Hilary's social security number is 434-55-3322 and her birth date is February 17th, 1975. Hilary is a server. They both would like $3 to go to the presidential campaign fund. Hilary works at a restaurant and usually reports the tips to her employer as required. However, in July she forgot to report $87. In November she received $14 that she was not required to report. Their reporting documents follow.

☐ CORRECTED (if checked)

PAYER'S name, street address, city or town, state or province, country, ZIP or foreign postal code, and telephone no. First National Bank 2300 Financial Way Your City, Your State, Your Zip Code	Payer's RTN (optional)	OMB No. 1545-0112	
	1 Interest income $ 1,676.22	20**14** Form **1099-INT**	**Interest Income**
	2 Early withdrawal penalty $		**Copy B**
PAYER'S federal identification number | RECIPIENT'S identification number 63-1111110 | 434-55-3322	**3** Interest on U.S. Savings Bonds and Treas. obligations $		**For Recipient**
RECIPIENT'S name Hank Lee	**4** Federal income tax withheld $	**5** Investment expenses $	This is important tax information and is being furnished to the Internal Revenue Service. If you are required to file a return, a negligence penalty or other sanction may be imposed on you if this income is taxable and the IRS determines that it has not been reported.
Street address (including apt. no.) 99 Juice St.	**6** Foreign tax paid $	**7** Foreign country or U.S. possession	
City or town, state or province, country, and ZIP or foreign postal code Your City, Your State, Your Zip Code	**8** Tax-exempt interest $	**9** Specified private activity bond interest $	
	10 Market discount $	**11** Bond premium $	
Account number (see instructions)	**12** Tax-exempt bond CUSIP no.	**13** State | **14** State identification no.	**15** State tax withheld $ $

Form **1099-INT**   (keep for your records)   www.irs.gov/form1099int   Department of the Treasury - Internal Revenue Service

W-2 Form 1

a Employee's social security number		Safe, accurate, FAST! Use		Visit the IRS website at www.irs.gov/efile
767-89-1212	OMB No. 1545-0008	IRS e-file		

b Employer identification number (EIN)	1 Wages, tips, other compensation	2 Federal income tax withheld
63-8887766	32,230.00	3,889.00

c Employer's name, address, and ZIP code	3 Social security wages	4 Social security tax withheld
Grocery's R Us	32,200.00	1,998.26
200 Fruit Lane	5 Medicare wages and tips	6 Medicare tax withheld
Your City, Your State, Your Zip Code	32,200.00	467.34
	7 Social security tips	8 Allocated tips

d Control number	9	10 Dependent care benefits

e Employee's first name and initial Last name Suff.	11 Nonqualified plans	12a See instructions for box 12
	13 Statutory employee / Retirement plan / Third-party sick pay	12b
Hank Lee		
99 Juice St	14 Other	12c
Your City, Your State, Your Zip Code		
		12d

f Employee's address and ZIP code

15 State	Employer's state ID number	16 State wages, tips, etc.	17 State income tax	18 Local wages, tips, etc.	19 Local income tax	20 Locality name
YS	688976544	32,230.00	1,156.00			

Form W-2 Wage and Tax Statement 2014   Department of the Treasury—Internal Revenue Service

Copy B—To Be Filed With Employee's FEDERAL Tax Return.
This information is being furnished to the Internal Revenue Service.

W-2 Form 2

a Employee's social security number		Safe, accurate, FAST! Use		Visit the IRS website at www.irs.gov/efile
434-55-3322	OMB No. 1545-0008	IRS e-file		

b Employer identification number (EIN)	1 Wages, tips, other compensation	2 Federal income tax withheld
63-8853766	16,780.00	1,198.00

c Employer's name, address, and ZIP code	3 Social security wages	4 Social security tax withheld
Mom's Home Cooking	14,465.00	1,040.00
124 Yummy Blvd.	5 Medicare wages and tips	6 Medicare tax withheld
Your City, Your State, Your Zip Code	16,780.00	243.31
	7 Social security tips	8 Allocated tips
	2,315.00	

d Control number	9	10 Dependent care benefits

e Employee's first name and initial Last name Suff.	11 Nonqualified plans	12a See instructions for box 12
	13 Statutory employee / Retirement plan / Third-party sick pay	12b
Hilary Lee		
99 Juice St.	14 Other	12c
Your City, Your State, Your Zip Code		
		12d

f Employee's address and ZIP code

15 State	Employer's state ID number	16 State wages, tips, etc.	17 State income tax	18 Local wages, tips, etc.	19 Local income tax	20 Locality name
YS	77676776	16,780.00	879.00			

Form W-2 Wage and Tax Statement 2014   Department of the Treasury—Internal Revenue Service

Copy B—To Be Filed With Employee's FEDERAL Tax Return.
This information is being furnished to the Internal Revenue Service.

☐ CORRECTED (if checked)

PAYER'S name, street address, city or town, state or province, country, ZIP or foreign postal code, and telephone no. Brighton Financial Services 777 Money Way Your City, Your State, Your Zip Code	**1a** Total ordinary dividends $ 2,898.00	OMB No. 1545-0110 20**14** Form **1099-DIV**	**Dividends and Distributions**
	1b Qualified dividends $		**Copy B** **For Recipient**
	2a Total capital gain distr. $	**2b** Unrecap. Sec. 1250 gain $	
PAYER'S federal identification number RECIPIENT'S identification number 63-0000010 767-89-1212	**2c** Section 1202 gain $	**2d** Collectibles (28%) gain $	
RECIPIENT'S name Hank and Hilary Lee	**3** Nondividend distributions $	**4** Federal income tax withheld $	This is important tax information and is being furnished to the Internal Revenue Service. If you are required to file a return, a negligence penalty or other sanction may be imposed on you if this income is taxable and the IRS determines that it has not been reported.
		5 Investment expenses $	
Street address (including apt. no.) 99 Juice St.	**6** Foreign tax paid $	**7** Foreign country or U.S. possession	
City or town, state or province, country, and ZIP or foreign postal code Your City, Your State, Your Zip Code	**8** Cash liquidation distributions $	**9** Noncash liquidation distributions $	
	10 Exempt-interest dividends $	**11** Specified private activity bond interest dividends $	
Account number (see instructions)	**12** State **13** State identification no. --------------	**14** State tax withheld $ ------------- $	

Form **1099-DIV**   (keep for your records)   www.irs.gov/form1099div   Department of the Treasury - Internal Revenue Service

---

☐ CORRECTED (if checked)

PAYER'S name, street address, city or town, state or province, country, ZIP or foreign postal code, and telephone no. Your State Unemployment Agency 150 Grand Ave. Your City, Your State, Your Zip Code	**1** Unemployment compensation $ 2,893.27	OMB No. 1545-0120 20**14** Form **1099-G**	**Certain Government Payments**
	2 State or local income tax refunds, credits, or offsets $		
PAYER'S federal identification number RECIPIENT'S identification number 63-0000001 434-55-3322	**3** Box 2 amount is for tax year	**4** Federal income tax withheld $ 289.33	**Copy B** **For Recipient**
RECIPIENT'S name Hilary Lee	**5** RTAA payments $	**6** Taxable grants $	This is important tax information and is being furnished to the Internal Revenue Service. If you are required to file a return, a negligence penalty or other sanction may be imposed on you if this income is taxable and the IRS determines that it has not been reported.
	7 Agriculture payments $	**8** If checked, box 2 is trade or business income ▶ ☐	
Street address (including apt. no.) 99 Juice St.	**9** Market gain $		
City or town, state or province, country, and ZIP or foreign postal code Your City, Your State, Your Zip Code	**10a** State **10b** State identification no.	**11** State income tax withheld $	
Account number (see instructions)	--------------	------------- $	

Form **1099-G**   (keep for your records)   www.irs.gov/form1099g   Department of the Treasury - Internal Revenue Service

Chapter 5 – Credits, Part I

A credit is a deduction that can reduce the tax liability dollar for dollar. There are two types of credits: refundable and nonrefundable.

A nonrefundable credit cannot reduce the tax liability below zero. Notice lines 48 through 54 on page 2 of the Form 1040 (Illustration 5-1). These are all nonrefundable credits. See the instructions on line 56? Subtract line 55 from line 47. If line 55 is more than line 47, enter 0. That is because if any of these amounts are more than the tax liability, the excess is not refunded to the taxpayer.

A refundable credit is added to the tax payments made. If the total is more than the tax liability, then the excess is refunded to the taxpayer. Lines 66 through 69 and lines 71 through 73 are the refundable credits. Notice line 74 adds the credits and tax payments together. Line 75 gives directions to subtract the tax liability from the payments and the rest is refunded to the taxpayer.

The credits we are going to cover in this chapter are Earned Income credit, child tax credit and additional child tax credit. These are the most commonly used credits.

Earned Income Credit

Earned Income Credit (EIC) is a refundable credit for certain people who work and have adjusted gross income under $46,997 ($52,427 if Married Filing Joint) for 2013. In order to receive EIC, the taxpayer must file a tax return even if they are not required to file. We will go over the requirements to qualify for EIC and how to compute the amount of EIC the taxpayer is eligible to receive.

Earned Income

The first requirement is that the taxpayer must have earned income. Unearned income will not qualify for EIC. Unearned income is income that comes from investments and other sources unrelated to employment services, for example dividends, interest, and retirement income. In order to have earned income, the taxpayer must work. A married couple filing a joint tax return may qualify even if only one spouse has earned income. Earned income includes the following types of income: wages, salaries, tips, and other taxable employee pay; net earnings from self-employment; and gross income received as a statutory employee.

Wages, salaries, tips, and other taxable employee pay

These types of income only qualify as earned income if they are taxable. These amounts should be included in box 1 of the W-2's. Nontaxable employee pay, such as certain dependent care benefits and adoption benefits, do not qualify. However, nontaxable combat pay is the exception. The taxpayer can choose to use their nontaxable combat pay to calculate the Earned Income Credit if it would be more beneficial. The nontaxable combat pay should be included on the W-2, box 12, identified with code Q.

Net earnings from self-employment

The taxpayer may have net earnings from self-employment if they own their own business or they are a member of a religious order or a minister.

Illustration 5-1

Tax and Credits		Amount from line 37 (adjusted gross income)	**38**	
	39a	Check if: ☐ **You** were born before January 2, 1950, ☐ Blind. ☐ **Spouse** was born before January 2, 1950, ☐ Blind. **Total boxes checked ▶ 39a**		
	b	If your spouse itemizes on a separate return or you were a dual-status alien, check here ▶ 39b ☐		
Standard Deduction for— • People who check any box on line 39a or 39b **or** who can be claimed as a dependent, see instructions. • All others: Single or Married filing separately, $6,200 Married filing jointly or Qualifying widow(er), $12,400 Head of household, $9,100	**40**	Itemized deductions (from Schedule A) **or** your **standard deduction** (see left margin)	**40**	
	41	Subtract line 40 from line 38	**41**	
	42	**Exemptions.** If line 38 is $152,525 or less, multiply $3,950 by the number on line 6d. Otherwise, see instructions	**42**	
	43	**Taxable income.** Subtract line 42 from line 41. If line 42 is more than line 41, enter -0-	**43**	
	44	**Tax** (see instructions). Check if any from: **a** ☐ Form(s) 8814 **b** ☐ Form 4972 **c** ☐	**44**	
	45	**Alternative minimum tax** (see instructions). Attach Form 6251	**45**	
	46	Excess advance premium tax credit repayment. Attach Form 8962	**46**	
	47	Add lines 44, 45, and 46 ▶	**47**	
	48	Foreign tax credit. Attach Form 1116 if required	**48**	
	49	Credit for child and dependent care expenses. Attach Form 2441	**49**	
	50	Education credits from Form 8863, line 19	**50**	
	51	Retirement savings contributions credit. Attach Form 8880	**51**	
	52	Child tax credit. Attach Schedule 8812, if required	**52**	
	53	Residential energy credits. Attach Form 5695	**53**	
	54	Other credits from Form: **a** ☐ 3800 **b** ☐ 8801 **c** ☐	**54**	
	55	Add lines 48 through 54. These are your **total credits**	**55**	
	56	Subtract line 55 from line 47. If line 55 is more than line 47, enter -0- ▶	**56**	
Other Taxes	**57**	Self-employment tax. Attach Schedule SE	**57**	
	58	Unreported social security and Medicare tax from Form: **a** ☐ 4137 **b** ☐ 8919	**58**	
	59	Additional tax on IRAs, other qualified retirement plans, etc. Attach Form 5329 if required	**59**	
	60a	Household employment taxes from Schedule H	**60a**	
	b	First-time homebuyer credit repayment. Attach Form 5405 if required	**60b**	
	61	Health care: individual responsibility (see instructions) Full-year coverage ☐	**61**	
	62	Taxes from: **a** ☐ Form 8959 **b** ☐ Form 8960 **c** ☐ Instructions; enter code(s)	**62**	
	63	Add lines 56 through 62. This is your **total tax** ▶	**63**	
Payments If you have a qualifying child, attach Schedule EIC.	**64**	Federal income tax withheld from Forms W-2 and 1099	**64**	
	65	2014 estimated tax payments and amount applied from 2013 return	**65**	
	66a	**Earned income credit (EIC)**	**66a**	
	b	Nontaxable combat pay election **66b**		
	67	Additional child tax credit. Attach Schedule 8812	**67**	
	68	American opportunity credit from Form 8863, line 8	**68**	
	69	Net premium tax credit. Attach Form 8962	**69**	
	70	Amount paid with request for extension to file	**70**	
	71	Excess social security and tier 1 RRTA tax withheld	**71**	
	72	Credit for federal tax on fuels. Attach Form 4136	**72**	
	73	Credits from Form: **a** ☐ 2439 **b** Reserved **c** Reserved **d** ☐	**73**	
	74	Add lines 64, 65, 66a, and 67 through 73. These are your **total payments** ▶	**74**	
Refund Direct deposit? See instructions.	**75**	If line 74 is more than line 63, subtract line 63 from line 74. This is the amount you **overpaid**	**75**	
	76a	Amount of line 75 you want **refunded to you.** If Form 8888 is attached, check here ▶ ☐	**76a**	
	b	Routing number ▶ **c** Type: ☐ Checking ☐ Savings		
	d	Account number		
	77	Amount of line 75 you want **applied to your 2015 estimated tax** ▶ 77		
Amount You Owe	**78**	**Amount you owe.** Subtract line 74 from line 63. For details on how to pay, see instructions ▶	**78**	
	79	Estimated tax penalty (see instructions) 79		

Third Party Designee

Do you want to allow another person to discuss this return with the IRS (see instructions)? ☐ **Yes.** Complete below. ☐ **No**

Designee's name ▶ | Phone no. ▶ | Personal identification number (PIN) ▶

Sign Here

Joint return? See instructions. Keep a copy for your records.

Under penalties of perjury, I declare that I have examined this return and accompanying schedules and statements, and to the best of my knowledge and belief, they are true, correct, and complete. Declaration of preparer (other than taxpayer) is based on all information of which preparer has any knowledge.

Your signature | Date | Your occupation | Daytime phone number

Spouse's signature. If a joint return, **both** must sign. | Date | Spouse's occupation | If the IRS sent you an Identity Protection PIN, enter it here (see inst.)

Paid Preparer Use Only

Print/Type preparer's name | Preparer's signature | Date | Check ☐ if self-employed | PTIN

Firm's name ▶ | Firm's EIN ▶

Firm's address ▶ | Phone no.

Gross income received as a statutory employee

As discussed in Chapter 2, a statutory employee will have box 13, the statutory employee box, of the W-2 checked. They will take their expenses on a Schedule C.

Earned Income Credit Rules

In order for the taxpayer to receive Earned Income Credit, they must meet several eligibility tests. These tests are outlined in Illustration 5-2 and explained below.

Rules for Everyone

The rules in this section will apply to everyone claiming EIC, whether or not they have any dependents.

The taxpayer must have a valid social security number.

The taxpayer (and spouse if MFJ) must have a valid social security number to qualify for EIC. If the social security card says "Not valid for employment" they do not qualify. Any qualifying children must also have a valid social security number unless the child was born and died during the year. See the residency test for more information on this situation.

The filing status cannot be Married Filing Separately.

The filing status on the return cannot be Married Filing Separately. If the taxpayer is married they generally must file Married Filing Jointly. If the spouse did not live with the taxpayer at any time during the last 6 months of the year they may qualify for married but considered unmarried for tax purposes as explained in chapter 2. If they meet the qualifications and are able to file Head of Household, they can still qualify for Earned Income Credit.

The taxpayer cannot file Form 2555 or Form 2555-EZ.

Form 2555 and Form 2555-EZ are used to exclude foreign income from the tax return or, to deduct or exclude a foreign housing amount. These forms are beyond the scope of this course. Publication 54 will give you more information on this topic.

The taxpayer's investment income cannot be more than $3,350.

The taxpayer does not qualify for EIC unless their investment income is $3,350 or less. Investment income includes income such as taxable and tax-exempt interest, dividends, net capital gains, net rent and royalty income, and passive activity income.

The taxpayer (and spouse if MFJ) cannot be the qualifying child of another person.

They are the qualifying child of another person if all of the following apply:

- They are that person's son, daughter, stepchild, or foster child. Or they are that person's brother, sister, half brother, half sister, stepbrother, or stepsister (or the child or grandchild of that person's brother, sister, half brother, half sister, stepbrother, or stepsister).
- At the end of the year they were under age 19, or under age 24 and a student, or any age if they were permanently and totally disabled at any time during the year.
- They lived with that person in the United States for more than half of the year.

If the taxpayer (and spouse if MFJ) is the qualifying child of another person, the taxpayer (and spouse if MFJ) may not qualify for EIC even if the other person does not claim EIC.

Illustration 5-2

Earned Income Credit Rules

Rules for everyone

- The taxpayer must have a valid social security number.

- The filing status cannot be Married Filing Separately.

- The taxpayer cannot file Form 2555 or Form 2555- EZ.

- The taxpayer's investment income cannot be more than $3,350.

- The taxpayer (and spouse if MFJ) cannot be the qualifying child of another person.

Rules if you have a qualifying child.

- The taxpayer's AGI must be less than:
  - •$46,997 ($52,427 if MFJ) if they have three or more qualfiying children
  - •$43,756 ($49,186 if MFJ) if they have two qualifying children
  - •$38,511 ($43,941 if MFJ) if they have one qualifying child

- The qualifying child must meet the relationship test.

- The qualifying child must meet the age test.

- The qualifying child must meet the residency test.

- The qualifying child cannot be the qualifying child of more than one person.

Rules if you do not have a qualifying child

- The taxpayer's AGI must be less than $14,590 ($20,020 if MFJ).

- The taxpayer must be at least age 25 but under age 65.

- The taxpayer cannot be a dependent of another.

- The taxpayer must have lived in the United States over half of the year.

Rules if you have a qualifying child

If the taxpayer has one or more qualifying children these rules will apply to them. If they do not have any qualifying children and meet all of the above tests, skip this section and see the *Rules if you do not have a qualifying child* later.

The taxpayer's AGI

If the taxpayer has one qualifying child, their AGI must be less than $38,511 ($43,941 if MFJ). If the taxpayer has two qualifying children, their AGI must be less than $43,756 ($49,186 if MFJ).If the taxpayer has three or more qualifying children, the AGI must be less than $46,997 ($52,427 if MFJ). The AGI is found on line 38 of the Form 1040. If the taxpayer's AGI is equal to or more than the limit, they will not qualify for EIC.

The qualifying child must meet the relationship test.

Remember, in Chapter 2 we covered the tests to determine if someone can be claimed as a dependent? Under the qualifying child test was the relationship test. The requirements are the same. The child must be

- The taxpayer's son, daughter, stepchild, eligible foster child, or a descendent of any of them, or
- The taxpayer's brother, sister, half brother, half sister, step brother, step sister, or a descendent of any of them.

An adopted child includes a child lawfully placed with you for legal adoption. An eligible foster child is one placed with you by an authorized placement agency or by judgment, decree, or other order of any court of competent jurisdiction.

The qualifying child must meet the age test.

Again, this test repeats the age test for the qualifying child dependency test.

The child must be

- Under 19 at the end of the tax year and younger than the taxpayer (or spouse if filing jointly,
- Under 24 and a full time student and younger than the taxpayer (or spouse if filing jointly, or
- Permanently and totally disabled at any time during the year.

Full time student

A student enrolled for the number of hours or courses the school considers to be full time.

Student

A student must have been enrolled for some part of each of 5 calendar months during the year as:

- A full time student at a school that has a regular teaching staff, a course of study, and a regularly enrolled student body or
- A student taking a full time, on-farm training course, given by a school described above, or by a state, county, or local government agency.

Note: The five months do not have to be consecutive.

School

An elementary school, junior and senior high school, college, university, or technical, trade, or mechanical school. A student who works on a "co-op" job in private industry as a part of a school's regular course of classroom and practical training are considered full time students. **Note:** On the job training course, correspondence school, or a school offering courses only through the internet does not count.

Permanently and Totally Disabled

The child is permanently and totally disabled if both of the following apply:

- They cannot engage in any substantial gainful activity because of a physical or mental condition.
- A doctor determines the condition has lasted or can be expected to last continuously for at least one year or can lead to death.

The qualifying child must meet the residency test.

The child must have lived with the taxpayer in the United States for more than half of the tax year. In this case, United States means the 50 states and the District of Columbia. It does not include Puerto Rico or U.S. possessions.

Exception for Military personnel stationed outside the United States – U.S. military personnel stationed outside the United States on extended active duty are considered to live in the United States during that duty period for purposes of the EIC. Extended active duty means the taxpayer is called or ordered to duty for an indefinite period or for a period of more than 90 days. Once they begin serving their extended active duty, they are still considered to have been on extended active duty even if they do not serve more than 90 days.

The child is considered to have lived with the taxpayer if one or the other was temporarily absent due to reasons such as illness, education, business, vacation, or military service. The exceptions to the residency test are for the death or birth of a child, kidnapped children, and children of divorced or separated parents.

Death or Birth of a Child

A child who was born or died during the year meets the residency test if the child lived with the taxpayer for more than half of the time the child was alive. If, during the tax year, the child was born alive but died a short time later (even if the child lived for only a moment), the child meets the residency test. There must be proof of a live birth shown by an official document such as a birth certificate. An exemption or Earned Income Credit cannot be claimed for a stillborn child.

Kidnapped Child

A kidnapped child meets the residency test if both of the following statements are true:

- The child is presumed by law enforcement authorities to have been kidnapped by someone who is not a member of the taxpayer's family or the child's family and
- In the year the kidnapping occurred the child lived with the taxpayer for more than half of the part of the year before the date of the kidnapping.

This test is considered met for all years until the child is returned or the earlier of:

- The year there is a determination that the child is dead or
- The year the child would have reached age 18.

The qualifying child cannot be the qualifying child of more than one person.

Sometimes, a child meets the relationship, age, residency, and support tests to be a qualifying child of more than one person. However, only one person may claim the child on their tax return. The person that claims the child will receive the following tax benefits (if otherwise eligible).

- The child's exemption
- The child tax credit
- Head of Household Filing Status
- Credit for child and dependent care expenses
- Exclusion for dependent care benefits
- Earned Income Credit

If the child is a qualifying child of more than one person, and one person is the parent, the other person may only claim the child if their AGI is higher than that of the parent. Otherwise, they can choose who gets to claim the child. The benefits listed above cannot be divided; whoever claims the child receives the benefits. If they cannot agree and more than one person claims the child, the IRS will use the tie-breaker rule (Illustration 5-3).

Note: If there is more than one child who qualifies for more than one person, they can divide the children. For example, you have two children that qualify for both you and your mom. You may each claim a child.

Illustration 5-3

If more than one person files a return claiming the same qualifying child and ….	THEN the child will be treated as the qualifying child of the…
only one of the persons is the child's parent.	parent.
two of the persons are parents of the child and they do not file a joint return together,	parent with whom the child lived for the longer period of time during the year.
two of the persons are parents of the child, they do not file a joint return together, and the child lived with each parent the same amount of time during the year.	parent with the higher adjusted gross income (AGI).
none of the persons are the child's parent,	person with the highest AGI.
a parent can claim the child as a qualifying child but no parent does so.	Person with the highest AGI, but only if that person's AGI is higher than the highest AGI of any of the child's parent who can claim the child.

Children of Divorced or Separated Parents

This was covered in Chapter 2. The rule is not the same for Earned Income Credit as it is for the dependency exemption. We will cover the rule for the dependency exemption again here and then go over what the difference is.

To determine this test, you must know the definition of a custodial parent and a noncustodial parent.

Custodial Parent

The parent with whom the child lived for the greater part of the year.

Noncustodial parent

The other parent.

Generally for the residency test, the child is the qualifying child of the custodial parent. However, a child can be the qualifying child of the noncustodial parent if all four of the following statements are true:

- The parents:
  - Are divorced or legally separated under a decree of divorce or separate maintenance,
  - Are separated under a written separation agreement, or
  - Lived apart at all times during the last 6 months of the year.
- The child received over half of his or her support for the year from the parents.
- The child is in the custody of one or both parents for more than half of the year.
- A decree of divorce or separate maintenance or written separation agreement provides that the noncustodial parent can claim the child for the tax year or the custodial parent signs a Form 8332 (Release of Claim to Exemption for Child of Divorced or Separated Parents) or similar statement that he will not claim the child as a dependent for the year. **Note:** The exemption can be released for 1 year, for a number of specified years, or for all future years, as specified in the declaration.

The special rule for divorced or separated parents also applies to parents who were never married.

How this rule applies to Earned Income Credit: If the noncustodial parent claims the exemption for the child, they do not qualify for Earned Income Credit because they do not meet the residency test. If the custodial parent otherwise qualifies for EIC, they may claim Earned Income Credit for that child.

Following are some examples to illustrate this rule.

Example: Joanne and her 22 year old daughter, Tiffany, live in the same house. Joanne made $40,000 in wages in 2013 and Tiffany made $18,000. Tiffany's niece (Joanne's granddaughter), Cindy, lived with them all year. They can choose which one will claim her. If they both do, Joanne will get Cindy's exemption along with any other benefits she is entitled to because she has the highest AGI. However, because Joanne's AGI is above the limit allowed for EIC, she does not qualify for that benefit. If Joanne's AGI was within the limit and she otherwise qualified for the EIC, she would receive that benefit along with the exemption.

Example: Tom and Betty are divorced. Their son, Jeremiah, lives with Betty. Their divorce decree states that Tom may claim the exemption for Jeremiah for the odd years. Because he is not the custodial parent, though, he does not qualify for EIC. Betty may claim EIC for Jeremiah if she is otherwise eligible.

Rules if you do not have a qualifying child

These rules apply only to taxpayer's who do not have any qualifying children.

The taxpayer's AGI

The taxpayer's AGI must be less than $14,590 ($20,020 if MFJ). The AGI is found on line 38 of the Form 1040.

The taxpayer must be at least age 25 but under age 65.

The taxpayer must be at least 25 or over and 64 or under at the end of the tax year. If the taxpayer is filing a Married Filing Joint tax return, only one spouse has to meet the age test. It does not matter which one.

The taxpayer cannot be a dependent of another.

If the taxpayer qualifies as the dependent of another person, the taxpayer does not qualify for EIC. It does not matter whether or not the other person does claim the taxpayer as a dependent. If the other person is eligible, the taxpayer cannot claim EIC.

The taxpayer must have lived in the United States over half of the year.

The taxpayer's home must have been in the United States for more than half of the year. The United States means the 50 states and the District of Columbia. It does not include Puerto Rico or U.S. possessions.

Exception for Military personnel stationed outside the U.S. – U.S. military personnel stationed outside the United States on extended active duty are considered to live in the United States during that duty period for purposes of the EIC. Extended active duty means the taxpayer is called or ordered to duty for an indefinite period or for a period of more than 90 days. Once the taxpayer begins serving their extended active duty, they are still considered to have been on extended active duty even if they do not serve more than 90 days.

Schedule EIC

If the taxpayer has one or more qualifying children and qualifies for the Earned Income Credit, they must attach a completed Schedule EIC (Illustration 5-4) to the tax return. Not doing so may result in a longer processing time or disallowance of the EIC. A taxpayer without qualifying children, who is receiving EIC, is not required to attach the Schedule EIC to their tax return.

Disallowance of Earned Income Credit in a Prior Year

If the taxpayer's EIC was disallowed in a prior year they may be required to file an additional form to claim EIC on the current tax return. If they claimed EIC for any year after 1996 and the EIC was disallowed or reduced for any reason other than a math or clerical error, they will have to file a Form 8862 (Illustration 5-5) to claim EIC for this year unless:

- They filed Form 8862 in a later year and the EIC for that later year was allowed and the EIC has not been reduced or disallowed again for any reason other than a math or clerical error or

- They are taking EIC without a qualifying child for the current year and the only reason their EIC was reduced or disallowed in the earlier year was because the IRS determined that a child listed on Schedule EIC was not their qualifying child.

If the IRS determines that the EIC claim was due to reckless or intentional disregard of the EIC rules, the taxpayer will not be allowed to claim EIC for 2 years after the determination. If the IRS determines that the EIC claim was due to fraud, the taxpayer will not be allowed to claim EIC for 10 years following the determination.

Illustration 5-4

SCHEDULE EIC (Form 1040A or 1040)	**Earned Income Credit** Qualifying Child Information	OMB No. 1545-0074 **2014**
Department of the Treasury Internal Revenue Service (99)	▶ Complete and attach to Form 1040A or 1040 only if you have a qualifying child. ▶ Information about Schedule EIC (Form 1040A or 1040) and its instructions is at *www.irs.gov/scheduleeic*.	Attachment Sequence No. **43**

Name(s) shown on return	Your social security number

Before you begin:
- See the instructions for Form 1040A, lines 42a and 42b, or Form 1040, lines 66a and 66b, to make sure that (a) you can take the EIC, and (b) you have a qualifying child.
- Be sure the child's name on line 1 and social security number (SSN) on line 2 agree with the child's social security card. Otherwise, at the time we process your return, we may reduce or disallow your EIC. If the name or SSN on the child's social security card is not correct, call the Social Security Administration at 1-800-772-1213.

⚠ CAUTION
- *If you take the EIC even though you are not eligible, you may not be allowed to take the credit for up to 10 years. See the instructions for details.*
- *It will take us longer to process your return and issue your refund if you do not fill in all lines that apply for each qualifying child.*

Qualifying Child Information	Child 1		Child 2		Child 3	
1 Child's name If you have more than three qualifying children, you have to list only three to get the maximum credit.	First name	Last name	First name	Last name	First name	Last name
2 Child's SSN The child must have an SSN as defined in the instructions for Form 1040A, lines 42a and 42b, or Form 1040, lines 66a and 66b, unless the child was born and died in 2014. If your child was born and died in 2014 and did not have an SSN, enter "Died" on this line and attach a copy of the child's birth certificate, death certificate, or hospital medical records.						
3 Child's year of birth	Year ____ ____ ____ ____ *If born after 1995 and the child is younger than you (or your spouse, if filing jointly), skip lines 4a and 4b; go to line 5.*		Year ____ ____ ____ ____ *If born after 1995 and the child is younger than you (or your spouse, if filing jointly), skip lines 4a and 4b; go to line 5.*		Year ____ ____ ____ ____ *If born after 1995 and the child is younger than you (or your spouse, if filing jointly), skip lines 4a and 4b; go to line 5.*	
4 a Was the child under age 24 at the end of 2014, a student, and younger than you (or your spouse, if filing jointly)?	☐ **Yes.** *Go to line 5.*	☐ **No.** *Go to line 4b.*	☐ **Yes.** *Go to line 5.*	☐ **No.** *Go to line 4b.*	☐ **Yes.** *Go to line 5.*	☐ **No.** *Go to line 4b.*
b Was the child permanently and totally disabled during any part of 2014?	☐ **Yes.** *Go to line 5.*	☐ **No.** The child is not a qualifying child.	☐ **Yes.** *Go to line 5.*	☐ **No.** The child is not a qualifying child.	☐ **Yes.** *Go to line 5.*	☐ **No.** The child is not a qualifying child.
5 Child's relationship to you (for example, son, daughter, grandchild, niece, nephew, foster child, etc.)						
6 Number of months child lived with you in the United States during 2014 • If the child lived with you for more than half of 2014 but less than 7 months, enter "7." • If the child was born or died in 2014 and your home was the child's home for more than half the time he or she was alive during 2014, enter "12."	____ months *Do not enter more than 12 months.*		____ months *Do not enter more than 12 months.*		____ months *Do not enter more than 12 months.*	

For Paperwork Reduction Act Notice, see your tax return instructions.   Cat. No. 13339M   Schedule EIC (Form 1040A or 1040) 2014

Illustration 5-5

Form 8862
(Rev. December 2012)
Department of the Treasury
Internal Revenue Service

Information To Claim Earned Income Credit After Disallowance
▶ Attach to your tax return.
▶ Information about Form 8862 and its instructions is at *www.irs.gov/form8862*.

OMB No. 1545-0074

Attachment
Sequence No. **43A**

Name(s) shown on return   Your social security number

Before you begin: ✓ See your tax return instructions or **Pub. 596**, Earned Income Credit (EIC), for the year for which you are filing this form to make sure you can take the earned income credit (EIC) **and** to find out who is a qualifying child.

✓ If you have a qualifying child, complete **Schedule EIC** before you fill in this form.

✓ **Do not** file this form if you are taking the EIC without a qualifying child **and** the only reason your EIC was reduced or disallowed in the earlier year was because it was determined that a child listed on **Schedule EIC** was not your qualifying child.

Part I	**All Filers**

1   Enter the year for which you are filing this form (for example, 2012) . . . . ▶ ☐☐☐☐

2   If the **only** reason your EIC was reduced or disallowed in the earlier year was because you incorrectly reported your earned income or investment income, check "Yes." Otherwise, check "No" . . . . ▶ ☐ **Yes** ☐ **No**
Caution. If you checked "Yes," **stop. Do not** fill in the rest of this form. But you must attach it to your tax return to take the EIC. If you checked "No," continue.

3   Could you (or your spouse if filing jointly) be claimed as a qualifying child of another taxpayer for the year shown on line 1? See the instructions before answering . . . . ▶ ☐ **Yes** ☐ **No**
Caution. If you checked "Yes," **stop.** You cannot take the EIC. If you checked "No," continue.

Part II	**Filers With a Qualifying Child or Children**

Note. Child 1, Child 2, and **Child 3** are the same children you listed as Child 1, Child 2, and Child 3 on **Schedule EIC** for the year shown on line 1 above.

4   Enter the **number of days** each child lived with you in the United States during the year shown on line 1 above:
a   **Child 1** ▶ ☐☐☐   b   **Child 2** ▶ ☐☐☐   c   **Child 3** ▶ ☐☐☐
Caution. If you entered less than **183** (184 if the year on line 1 is a leap year) for any child, you cannot take the EIC based on that child, unless the special rule for a child who was born or died during the year shown on line 1 applies. See the instructions.

5   If your child was born or died during the year shown on line 1, enter the month and day the child was born and/or died. Otherwise, skip this line.
a   **Child 1** ▶ **(1)** Month and day of birth (MM/DD) ▶ ☐☐/☐☐   **(2)** Month and day of death (MM/DD) ▶ ☐☐/☐☐
b   **Child 2** ▶ **(1)** Month and day of birth (MM/DD) ▶ ☐☐/☐☐   **(2)** Month and day of death (MM/DD) ▶ ☐☐/☐☐
c   **Child 3** ▶ **(1)** Month and day of birth (MM/DD) ▶ ☐☐/☐☐   **(2)** Month and day of death (MM/DD) ▶ ☐☐/☐☐

6   Enter the address where you and the child lived together during the year shown on line 1. If you lived with the child at more than one address during the year, attach a list of the addresses where you lived:
a   **Child 1** ▶ Number and street
                City or town, state, and ZIP code
b   **Child 2** ▶ **If same as shown for child 1, check this box.** ▶ ☐ Otherwise, enter below:
                Number and street
                City or town, state, and ZIP code
c   **Child 3** ▶ **If same as shown for child 1, check this box.** ▶ ☐ **Or if same as shown for child 2 (and this is different from address shown for child 1), check this box.** ▶ ☐ Otherwise, enter below:
                Number and street
                City or town, state, and ZIP code

7   Did any other person (except your spouse, if filing jointly, and your dependents under age 19) live with child 1, child 2, or child 3 for more than half the year shown on line 1? . . . . ▶ ☐ **Yes** ☐ **No**
If "Yes," enter that person's name and relationship to the child below. If more than one other person lived with the child for more than half the year, attach a list of each person's name and relationship to the child:
a   **Other person living with child 1:**   Name
                                        Relationship to child 1
b   **Other person living with child 2:**   **If same as shown for child 1, check this box.** ▶ ☐ Otherwise, enter below:
                                        Name
                                        Relationship to child 2
c   **Other person living with child 3:**   **If same as shown for child 1, check this box.** ▶ ☐ **Or if same as shown for child 2 (and this is different from the person living with child 1), check this box.** ▶ ☐
                                        Otherwise, enter below:
                                        Name
                                        Relationship to child 3

Caution. The IRS may ask you to provide additional information to verify your eligibility to claim the EIC.

For Paperwork Reduction Act Notice, see page 3.   Cat. No. 25145E   Form **8862** (Rev. 12-2012)

Due Diligence

Paid preparers must practice due diligence when preparing tax returns, especially returns with EIC. Below is a due diligence checklist provided by the IRS.

Requirement	Description
1. Completion of Eligibility checklist	• Complete Form 8867, Paid Preparer's Earned Income Credit Checklist, to make sure you consider all EITC eligibility criteria for each claim you prepare. • Complete checklist based on information provided by your client(s). • For EITC returns or claims for refund filed electronically, submit Form 8867 to the IRS electronically with the return. • For EITC returns or claims for refund not filed electronically, attach the completed form to any paper return you prepare and send to the IRS. • For EITC returns or claims for refund you prepare but do not submit directly to the IRS, provide the completed Form 8867 to your client to send with the filed tax return or claim for refund.
2. Computation of the Credit	• Keep the EIC worksheet or an equivalent that demonstrates how the EIC was computed
3. Knowledge	• Not know or have reason to know any information used to determine your client's eligibility for, or the amount of EITC is incorrect, inconsistent or incomplete. • Make additional inquiries if a reasonable and well-informed tax return preparer would know the information is incomplete, inconsistent or incorrect • Know the law and use your knowledge of the law to ensure you are asking your client the right questions to get all relevant facts. • Document any additional questions you ask and your client's answer at the time of the interview.

4. Record Retention	• Keep a copy of the Form 8867 and the EIC worksheet.
	• Keep a record of all additional questions you asked your client to comply with your due diligence requirements and your client's answers to those questions.
	• Keep copies of any documents your client gives you that you relied on to determine eligibility for, or the amount of the EITC.
	• Verify the identity of the person giving you the return information and keep a record of who provided the information and when you got it.
	• Keep your records in either paper or electronic format but make sure you can produce them if the IRS asks for them.
	• Keep these records for 3 years from the latest date of the following that apply:
	  ▪ The original due date of the tax return (this does not include any extension of time for filing.), or
	  ▪ If you electronically file the return or claim for refund and sign it as the return preparer, the date the tax return or claim for refund is filed, or
	  ▪ If the return or claim for refund is not filed electronically and you sign it as the return preparer, the date you present the tax return or claim for refund to your client for signature, or
	  ▪ If you prepare part of the return or claim for refund and another preparer completes and signs the return or claim for refund, you must keep the part of the return you were responsible to complete for 3 years from the date you submit it to the signing tax return preparer.

The items on this list are fairly self-explanatory, but let's discuss the Form 8867 (Illustration 5-6). The Form 8867 is the Paid Preparer's Earned Income Credit Checklist. The Form 8867 must be completed by the paid preparer and filed with the return. If the items on this list are not completed, it could result in a penalty to the paid preparer of $500 per instance.

Illustration 5-6

<table>
<tr><td>Form **8867**</td><td rowspan="2">**Paid Preparer's Earned Income Credit Checklist**
▶ To be completed by preparer and filed with Form 1040, 1040A, or 1040EZ.
▶ Information about Form 8867 and its separate instructions is at *www.irs.gov/form8867*.</td><td>OMB No. 1545-1629
20**14**</td></tr>
<tr><td>Department of the Treasury
Internal Revenue Service</td><td>Attachment
Sequence No. **177**</td></tr>
</table>

Taxpayer name(s) shown on return	Taxpayer's social security number

For the definitions of **Qualifying Child** and **Earned Income**, see **Pub. 596**.

Part I	All Taxpayers

1 Enter preparer's name and PTIN ▶ _____

2 Is the taxpayer's filing status married filing separately? . . . . ☐ Yes ☐ No

> ▶ If you checked **"Yes"** on line 2, **stop;** the taxpayer **cannot** take the EIC. Otherwise, continue.

3 Does the taxpayer (and the taxpayer's spouse if filing jointly) have a social security number (SSN) that allows him or her to work and is valid for EIC purposes? See the instructions before answering . . . . ☐ Yes ☐ No

> ▶ If you checked **"No"** on line 3, **stop;** the taxpayer **cannot** take the EIC. Otherwise, continue.

4 Is the taxpayer (or the taxpayer's spouse if filing jointly) filing Form 2555 or 2555-EZ (relating to the exclusion of foreign earned income)? . . . . ☐ Yes ☐ No

> ▶ If you checked **"Yes"** on line 4, **stop;** the taxpayer **cannot** take the EIC. Otherwise, continue.

5a Was the taxpayer (or the taxpayer's spouse) a nonresident alien for any part of 2014? . . . . . ☐ Yes ☐ No

> ▶ If you checked **"Yes"** on line 5a, go to line 5b. Otherwise, skip line 5b and go to line 6.

b Is the taxpayer's filing status married filing jointly? . . . . ☐ Yes ☐ No

> ▶ If you checked **"Yes"** on line 5a and **"No"** on line 5b, **stop;** the taxpayer **cannot** take the EIC. Otherwise, continue.

6 Is the taxpayer's **investment income** more than $3,350? See the instructions before answering. ☐ Yes ☐ No

> ▶ If you checked **"Yes"** on line 6, **stop;** the taxpayer **cannot** take the EIC. Otherwise, continue.

7 Could the taxpayer be a **qualifying child** of another person for 2014? If the taxpayer's filing status is married filing jointly, check **"No."** Otherwise, see instructions before answering . . . . . . ☐ Yes ☐ No

> ▶ If you checked **"Yes"** on line 7, **stop;** the taxpayer **cannot** take the EIC. Otherwise, go to Part II or Part III, whichever applies.

For Paperwork Reduction Act Notice, see separate instructions.　　　　Cat. No. 26142H　　　　Form **8867** (2014)

Illustration 5-6 continued

Part II	Taxpayers With a Child	Child 1	Child 2	Child 3

Caution. If there is more than one child, complete lines 8 through 14 for one child before going to the next column.

8 Child's name . . . .

9 Is the child the taxpayer's son, daughter, stepchild, foster child, brother, sister, stepbrother, stepsister, half brother, half sister, or a descendant of any of them?

	Child 1	Child 2	Child 3
9	☐ Yes ☐ No	☐ Yes ☐ No	☐ Yes ☐ No

10 Was the child unmarried at the end of 2014?
If the child was married at the end of 2014, see the instructions before answering . . . .

	Child 1	Child 2	Child 3
10	☐ Yes ☐ No	☐ Yes ☐ No	☐ Yes ☐ No

11 Did the child live with the taxpayer in the United States for over half of 2014? See the instructions before answering . . . .

	Child 1	Child 2	Child 3
11	☐ Yes ☐ No	☐ Yes ☐ No	☐ Yes ☐ No

12 Was the child (at the end of 2014)—

• Under age 19 and younger than the taxpayer (or the taxpayer's spouse, if the taxpayer files jointly),

• Under age 24, a student (defined in the instructions), and younger than the taxpayer (or the taxpayer's spouse, if the taxpayer files jointly), or

• Any age and permanently and totally disabled? . . . .

	Child 1	Child 2	Child 3
12	☐ Yes ☐ No	☐ Yes ☐ No	☐ Yes ☐ No

▶ If you checked **"Yes"** on lines 9, 10, 11, **and** 12, the child is the taxpayer's qualifying child; go to line 13a. If you checked **"No"** on line 9, 10, 11, **or** 12, the child is not the taxpayer's qualifying child; see the instructions for line 12.

13a Do you or the taxpayer know of another person who could check **"Yes"** on lines 9, 10, 11, **and** 12 for the child? (If the only other person is the taxpayer's spouse, see the instructions before answering.) . . . .

	Child 1	Child 2	Child 3
13a	☐ Yes ☐ No	☐ Yes ☐ No	☐ Yes ☐ No

▶ If you checked **"No"** on line 13a, go to line 14. Otherwise, go to line 13b.

b Enter the child's relationship to the other person(s) . . . .

c Under the tiebreaker rules, is the child treated as the taxpayer's qualifying child? See the instructions before answering . . . .

	Child 1	Child 2	Child 3
13c	☐ Yes ☐ No ☐ Don't know	☐ Yes ☐ No ☐ Don't know	☐ Yes ☐ No ☐ Don't know

▶ If you checked **"Yes"** on line 13c, go to line 14. If you checked **"No,"** the taxpayer **cannot** take the EIC based on this child and cannot take the EIC for taxpayers who do not have a qualifying child. If there is more than one child, see the **Note** at the bottom of this page. If you checked **"Don't know,"** explain to the taxpayer that, under the tiebreaker rules, the taxpayer's EIC and other tax benefits may be disallowed. Then, if the taxpayer wants to take the EIC based on this child, complete lines 14 and 15. If not, and there are no other qualifying children, the taxpayer cannot take the EIC, including the EIC for taxpayers without a qualifying child; do not complete Part III. If there is more than one child, see the **Note** at the bottom of this page.

14 Does the qualifying child have an SSN that allows him or her to work and is valid for EIC purposes? See the instructions before answering . . . .

	Child 1	Child 2	Child 3
14	☐ Yes ☐ No	☐ Yes ☐ No	☐ Yes ☐ No

▶ If you checked **"No"** on line 14, the taxpayer **cannot** take the EIC based on this child and cannot take the EIC available to taxpayers without a qualifying child. If there is more than one child, see the **Note** at the bottom of this page. If you checked "Yes" on line 14, continue.

15 Are the taxpayer's **earned income** and **adjusted gross income** each less than the limit that applies to the taxpayer for 2014? See instructions . .

☐ Yes ☐ No

▶ If you checked **"No"** on line 15, **stop;** the taxpayer **cannot** take the EIC. If you checked **"Yes"** on line 15, the taxpayer can take the EIC. Complete **Schedule EIC** and attach it to the taxpayer's return. If there are two or three qualifying children with valid SSNs, list them on Schedule EIC in the same order as they are listed here. If the taxpayer's EIC was reduced or disallowed for a year after 1996, see Pub. 596 to see if **Form 8862** must be filed. Go to line 20.

Note. If there is more than one child, complete lines 8 through 14 for the other child(ren) (but for no more than three qualifying children).

Illustration 5-6 continued

Part III	Taxpayers Without a Qualifying Child

16 Was the taxpayer's main home, and the main home of the taxpayer's spouse if filing jointly, in the United States for more than half the year? (Military personnel on extended active duty outside the United States are considered to be living in the United States during that duty period.) See the instructions before answering. ☐ Yes ☐ No

▶ If you checked **"No"** on line 16, **stop;** the taxpayer **cannot** take the EIC. Otherwise, continue.

17 Was the taxpayer, or the taxpayer's spouse if filing jointly, at least age 25 but under age 65 at the end of 2014? See the instructions before answering . . . . ☐ Yes ☐ No

▶ If you checked **"No"** on line 17, **stop;** the taxpayer **cannot** take the EIC. Otherwise, continue.

18 Is the taxpayer eligible to be claimed as a dependent on anyone else's federal income tax return for 2014? If the taxpayer's filing status is married filing jointly, check **"No"**. . . . . ☐ Yes ☐ No

▶ If you checked **"Yes"** on line 18, **stop;** the taxpayer **cannot** take the EIC. Otherwise, continue.

19 Are the taxpayer's **earned income** and **adjusted gross income** each less than the limit that applies to the taxpayer for 2014? See instructions . . . . ☐ Yes ☐ No

▶ If you checked **"No"** on line 19, **stop;** the taxpayer **cannot** take the EIC. If you checked **"Yes"** on line 19, the taxpayer can take the EIC. If the taxpayer's EIC was reduced or disallowed for a year after 1996, see Pub. 596 to find out if **Form 8862** must be filed. Go to line 20.

Part IV	Due Diligence Requirements

20 Did you complete Form 8867 based on current information provided by the taxpayer or reasonably obtained by you? . . . . ☐ Yes ☐ No

21 Did you complete the EIC worksheet found in the Form 1040, 1040A, or 1040EZ instructions (or your own worksheet that provides the same information as the 1040, 1040A, or 1040EZ worksheet)? . . ☐ Yes ☐ No

22 If any qualifying child was not the taxpayer's son or daughter, do you know or did you ask why the parents were not claiming the child? . . . . ☐ Yes ☐ No ☐ Does not apply

23 If the answer to question 13a is **"Yes"** (indicating that the child lived for more than half the year with someone else who could claim the child for the EIC), did you explain the tiebreaker rules and possible consequences of another person claiming your client's qualifying child? . . . . . . ☐ Yes ☐ No ☐ Does not apply

24 Did you ask this taxpayer any additional questions that are necessary to meet your knowledge requirement? See the instructions before answering . . . . ☐ Yes ☐ No ☐ Does not apply

To comply with the EIC knowledge requirement, you must not know or have reason to know that any information you used to determine the taxpayer's eligibility for, and the amount of, the EIC is incorrect. You may not ignore the implications of information furnished to you or known by you, and you must make reasonable inquiries if the information furnished to you appears to be incorrect, inconsistent, or incomplete. At the time you make these inquiries, you must document in your files the inquiries you made and the taxpayer's responses.

25 Did you document (a) the taxpayer's answer to question 22 (if applicable), (b) whether you explained the tiebreaker rules to the taxpayer and any additional information you got from the taxpayer as a result, and (c) any additional questions you asked and the taxpayer's answers? . . . . ☐ Yes ☐ No ☐ Does not apply

▶ You have complied with all the due diligence requirements if you:
1. Completed the actions described on lines 20 and 21 and checked **"Yes"** on those lines,
2. Completed the actions described on lines 22, 23, 24, and 25 (if they apply) and checked **"Yes"** (or **"Does not apply"**) on those lines,
3. Submit Form 8867 in the manner required, **and**
4. Keep all five of the following records for 3 years from the latest of the dates specified in the instructions under *Document Retention*:

    a. Form 8867,
    b. The EIC worksheet(s) or your own worksheet(s),
    c. Copies of any taxpayer documents you relied on to determine eligibility for or amount of EIC,
    d. A record of how, when, and from whom the information used to prepare the form and worksheet(s) was obtained, and
    e. A record of any additional questions you asked and your client's answers.

▶ You have not complied with all the due diligence requirements if you checked **"No"** on line 20, 21, 22, 23, 24, or 25. You may have to pay a $500 penalty for each failure to comply.

Form **8867** (2014)

Illustration 5-6 continued

Part V	Documents Provided to You

26   Identify below any document that the taxpayer provided to you and that you relied on to determine the taxpayer's EIC eligibility. Check all that apply. **Keep a copy of any documents you relied on.** See the instructions before answering. If there is no qualifying child, check box a. If there is no disabled child, check box o.

Residency of Qualifying Child(ren)

☐ a   No qualifying child
☐ b   School records or statement
☐ c   Landlord or property management statement
☐ d   Health care provider statement
☐ e   Medical records
☐ f   Child care provider records
☐ g   Placement agency statement
☐ h   Social service records or statement

☐ i   Place of worship statement
☐ j   Indian tribal official statement
☐ k   Employer statement
☐ l   Other (specify) ▼
_____
_____
_____

☐ m   Did not rely on any documents, but made notes in file
☐ n   Did not rely on any documents

Disability of Qualifying Child(ren)

☐ o   No disabled child
☐ p   Doctor statement
☐ q   Other health care provider statement
☐ r   Social services agency or program statement

☐ s   Other (specify) ▼
_____
_____

☐ t   Did not rely on any documents, but made notes in file
☐ u   Did not rely on any documents

27   If a Schedule C is included with this return, identify below the information that the taxpayer provided to you and that you relied on to prepare the Schedule C. Check all that apply. **Keep a copy of any documents you relied on.** See the instructions before answering. If there is no Schedule C, check box a.

Documents or Other Information

☐ a   No Schedule C
☐ b   Business license
☐ c   Forms 1099
☐ d   Records of gross receipts provided by taxpayer
☐ e   Taxpayer summary of income
☐ f   Records of expenses provided by taxpayer
☐ g   Taxpayer summary of expenses

☐ h   Bank statements
☐ i   Reconstruction of income and expenses
☐ j   Other (specify) ▼
_____
_____

☐ k   Did not rely on any documents, but made notes in file
☐ l   Did not rely on any documents

Form **8867** (2014)

How Much EIC are they entitled to receive?

Once you have determined that the taxpayer is entitled to EIC, filled out Schedule EIC, and satisfied the due diligence requirements, you need to determine how much EIC the taxpayer is entitled to receive. The Earned Income Credit worksheet (Illustration 5-7) will help.

Line 1: Enter the amount from Form 1040, line 7.

Line 2: Taxable Scholarship or Fellowship grant not reported on a W-2. Enter that amount here only if it was included in the line 7 amount on the Form 1040.

Line 3: Amount received for work performed while an inmate in a penal institution. These amounts do not qualify as earned income for the purposes of Earned Income Credit.

Line 4: Amount received as a pension or annuity from a nonqualified deferred compensation plan or a nongovernmental sec. 457 plan. Enter these amounts only if they were included on Form 1040, line 7.

Line 5: Add lines 2, 3, and 4.

Line 6: Subtract line 5 from line 1.

Line 7: Nontaxable Combat Pay. A taxpayer with nontaxable combat pay can elect to include it in their earned income if it would result in them receiving more EIC. If it would result in them receiving less, they can choose to leave it out. It is beneficial to calculate the EIC both ways and determine which way would result in the bigger refund.

Line 8: Add lines 6 and 7.

Line 9: If the taxpayer receives any of their income from self-employment or as a statutory employee, they must complete lines 10-18. If they do not, line 8 is their total earned income. Go to line 19.

Line 10: If the taxpayer is filing a Schedule SE, enter the amount from the Schedule SE, Section A, line 3 (total self-employment and farming income), or Section B, line 3 (total self-employment and farming income, as well as income for Ministers and members of religious orders), whichever applies. If the taxpayer has self-employment income, but is not required to file a Schedule SE, go to line 15. If the taxpayer is a statutory employee, go to line 18.

Line 11: Enter any amounts from Schedule SE, Section B, line 4b and line 5a. If Section B does not apply, enter 0.

Line 12: Combine lines 10 and 11.

Line 13: Enter the amount from Schedule SE, Section A, line 6 or Section B, line 13, whichever applies. This is the amount of the deduction allowed for one-half of the self-employment tax. We will cover this in a later chapter.

Line 14: Subtract line 13 from line 12. If the lines 15 and 18 do not apply to the taxpayer, enter this amount on line 17 and go to line 19.

Illustration 5-7

Earned Income Credit Worksheet

1.	Enter the amount from Form 1040, Line 7.	1.
2.	Taxable Scholarship or Fellowship grant not reported on a W-2, if included on line 7, Form 10...................................... _____	
3.	Amount received for work performed while an inmate in a penal institution (enter "PRI" and the amount subtracted on the dotted line next to Form 1040, line 7), if included on line 7.. _____	
4.	Amount received as a pension or annuity from a nonqualified deferred compensation plan or a nongovernmental Sec. 457 plan. (Enter "DFC" and amount subtracted on the dotted line next to Form 1040, line 7), if included on line 7................... _____	
5.	Add lines 2, 3, and 4.	5.
6.	Subtract line 5 from line 1.	6.
7.	Nontaxable Combat pay if the election is made to use it. You will have to complete two worksheets: one with the combat pay and one without. Use the one that will result in the most EIC.	7.
8.	Add lines 6 and 7.	8.
9.	If the taxpayer had any income from self-employment or was a statutory employee, complete lines 10 –18. If not skip lines 10 –18 and go to line 19.	
10.	If the taxpayer is filing a Schedule SE, enter the amount from Schedule SE, Section A, line 3 or Section B, line 3, whichever applies. If the taxpayer is not filing a Schedule SE, skip lines 10 –14 and go to line 15. If the taxpayer is a statutory employee, go to line 18.	10.
11.	Enter any amounts from Schedule SE, Section B, line 4b, and line 5a.	11.
12.	Combine lines 10 and 11.	12.
13.	Enter the amount from Schedule SE, Section A, line 6 or Section B, line 13.	13.
14.	Subtract line 13 from line 12. If lines 15 and 18 do not apply, enter this amount on line 17 and go to line 19.	14.
15.	If the taxpayer is not required to file a Schedule SE because the net earnings were less than $400, enter amount from Schedule F, line 36, and from farm partnerships, Schedule K-1 (Form 1065), box 14, code A.	15.
16.	Enter any net profit or (loss) from Schedule C, line 31; Schedule C-EZ, line 3, Schedule K-1, box 14, code A (other than farming); and Schedule K-1, box 9, code J1.	16.
17.	Combine lines 14, 15, and 16.	17.
18.	If the taxpayer is a statutory employee, enter the amount from Schedule C, line 1, or Schedule C-EZ, line 1 that the taxpayer is filing as a statutory employee.	18.
19.	Add lines 8, 17, and 18. This is the earned income.	19.
20.	Look up the amount on line 19 above in the EIC Table to find the credit. If the amount is 0, stop. The taxpayer does not qualify for the credit.	20.
21.	Enter the amount from Form 1040, line 38. If the amount on line 21 is the same as the amount on line 19, stop and enter the amount from line 20 on line 66a of the Form 1040. This is the taxpayer's Earned Income Credit. If not, go to line 22.	21.
22.	Is the amount on line 21 less than: • $8,150 ($13,550 if MFJ) if the taxpayer has no qualifying children? • $17,850 ($23,300 if MFJ) if the taxpayer has one or more qualifying children? If the answer is yes, stop and enter the amount from line 21 on the Form 1040, line 66a. If the answer is no, look up the amount from line 21 in the EIC Table to find the credit and go to line 23.	22.
23.	Look at the amounts on line 20 and 22. Enter the smaller amount here and on Form 1040, line 66a.	23.

Line 15: If the taxpayer is not required to file a Schedule SE because the net earnings were less than $400, enter amount from Schedule F (Profit or Loss from Farming), line 36, and from farm partnerships, Schedule K-1 (Form 1065), box 14, code A.

Line 16: Enter any net profit or (loss) from Schedule C, line 31; Schedule C-EZ, line 3, Schedule K-1, box 14, code A (other than farming); and Schedule K-1, box 9, code J1.

Line 17: Combine lines 14, 15, and 16.

Line 18: If the taxpayer is a statutory employee, enter the amount from Schedule C, line 1 or Schedule C-EZ, line 1 that the taxpayer is filing as a statutory employee.

Line 19: Add lines 8, 17, and 18. This is the total earned income.

Line 20: Look up the amount on line 19 above in the EIC Table (Illustration 5-9) to find the credit. If the amount is 0, stop. The taxpayer does not qualify for the credit. Looking up amounts in the EIC table is pretty much the same as using the tax tables. You have to know how many qualifying children the taxpayer has, if any. You also have to know the filing status. The complete EIC tables are located in the appendix.

Line 21: Enter the amount from Form 1040, line 38. This is the Adjusted Gross Income. If the amount on line 21 is the same as the amount on line 19, stop and enter the amount from line 20 on line 66a of the Form 1040. This is the taxpayer's Earned Income Credit. If it is not the same, go to line 22.

Line 22: Is the amount on line 21 (AGI) less than:

- $8,150 ($13,550 if MFJ) if the taxpayer has no qualifying children?
- $17,850 ($23,300 if MFJ) if the taxpayer has one or more qualifying children?

If the answer is yes, stop and enter the amount from line 21 on the Form 1040, line 66a. This is the taxpayer's Earned Income Credit. If the answer is no, look up the amount from line 21 in the EIC Table to find the credit and go to line 23. Illustration 5-8 shows a page from the EIC Table. The entire table is in Appendix B.

Line 23: Look at the amounts on lines 20 and 22. Enter the smaller amount here and on the Form 1040, line 66a. This is the amount of the taxpayer's Earned Income Credit.

Comprehensive Earned Income Credit Example: Elizabeth Jeffreys (444-55-6666) is Single and her birth date is September 1st, 1985. She cannot be claimed on anyone else's tax return. Her daughter, Alicia Jeffreys (222-33-4444), lived with her in the United States all year. Her birth date is October 20th, 2012. No one else can claim Alicia on their tax return. Elizabeth only has 1 Form W-2 and the amount in box 1 is $14,998. She has no other income. First, let's do the Form 8867 to make sure she's eligible to receive Earned Income Credit (Illustration 5-9). Then, we'll complete the EIC worksheet to determine how much she'll receive (Illustration 5-10). After we've done that, we fill out the Schedule EIC to file with the Form 1040 (page 2 only shown in Illustration 5-11).

Illustration 5-8

Earned Income Credit (EIC) Table - Continued
(Caution. This is **not** a tax table.)

If the amount you are looking up from the worksheet is—		Single, head of household, or qualifying widow(er) and the number of children you have is—				Married filing jointly and the number of children you have is—			
At least	But less than	0	1	2	3	0	1	2	3
		Your credit is—				Your credit is—			
12,800	12,850	135	3,305	5,130	5,771	496	3,305	5,130	5,771
12,850	12,900	131	3,305	5,150	5,794	496	3,305	5,150	5,794
12,900	12,950	127	3,305	5,170	5,816	496	3,305	5,170	5,816
12,950	13,000	124	3,305	5,190	5,839	496	3,305	5,190	5,839
13,000	13,050	120	3,305	5,210	5,861	496	3,305	5,210	5,861
13,050	13,100	116	3,305	5,230	5,884	496	3,305	5,230	5,884
13,100	13,150	112	3,305	5,250	5,906	496	3,305	5,250	5,906
13,150	13,200	108	3,305	5,270	5,929	496	3,305	5,270	5,929
13,200	13,250	104	3,305	5,290	5,951	496	3,305	5,290	5,951
13,250	13,300	101	3,305	5,310	5,974	496	3,305	5,310	5,974
13,300	13,350	97	3,305	5,330	5,996	496	3,305	5,330	5,996
13,350	13,400	93	3,305	5,350	6,019	496	3,305	5,350	6,019
13,400	13,450	89	3,305	5,370	6,041	496	3,305	5,370	6,041
13,450	13,500	85	3,305	5,390	6,064	496	3,305	5,390	6,064
13,500	13,550	81	3,305	5,410	6,086	496	3,305	5,410	6,086
13,550	13,600	78	3,305	5,430	6,109	493	3,305	5,430	6,109
13,600	13,650	74	3,305	5,450	6,131	489	3,305	5,450	6,131
13,650	13,700	70	3,305	5,460	6,143	485	3,305	5,460	6,143
13,700	13,750	66	3,305	5,460	6,143	482	3,305	5,460	6,143
13,750	13,800	62	3,305	5,460	6,143	478	3,305	5,460	6,143
13,800	13,850	59	3,305	5,460	6,143	474	3,305	5,460	6,143
13,850	13,900	55	3,305	5,460	6,143	470	3,305	5,460	6,143
13,900	13,950	51	3,305	5,460	6,143	466	3,305	5,460	6,143
13,950	14,000	47	3,305	5,460	6,143	462	3,305	5,460	6,143
14,000	14,050	43	3,305	5,460	6,143	459	3,305	5,460	6,143
14,050	14,100	39	3,305	5,460	6,143	455	3,305	5,460	6,143
14,100	14,150	36	3,305	5,460	6,143	451	3,305	5,460	6,143
14,150	14,200	32	3,305	5,460	6,143	447	3,305	5,460	6,143
14,200	14,250	28	3,305	5,460	6,143	443	3,305	5,460	6,143
14,250	14,300	24	3,305	5,460	6,143	439	3,305	5,460	6,143
14,300	14,350	20	3,305	5,460	6,143	436	3,305	5,460	6,143
14,350	14,400	16	3,305	5,460	6,143	432	3,305	5,460	6,143
14,400	14,450	13	3,305	5,460	6,143	428	3,305	5,460	6,143
14,450	14,500	9	3,305	5,460	6,143	424	3,305	5,460	6,143
14,500	14,550	5	3,305	5,460	6,143	420	3,305	5,460	6,143
14,550	14,600	*	3,305	5,460	6,143	417	3,305	5,460	6,143
14,600	14,650	0	3,305	5,460	6,143	413	3,305	5,460	6,143
14,650	14,700	0	3,305	5,460	6,143	409	3,305	5,460	6,143
14,700	14,750	0	3,305	5,460	6,143	405	3,305	5,460	6,143
14,750	14,800	0	3,305	5,460	6,143	401	3,305	5,460	6,143
14,800	14,850	0	3,305	5,460	6,143	397	3,305	5,460	6,143
14,850	14,900	0	3,305	5,460	6,143	394	3,305	5,460	6,143
14,900	14,950	0	3,305	5,460	6,143	390	3,305	5,460	6,143
14,950	15,000	0	3,305	5,460	6,143	386	3,305	5,460	6,143
15,000	15,050	0	3,305	5,460	6,143	382	3,305	5,460	6,143
15,050	15,100	0	3,305	5,460	6,143	378	3,305	5,460	6,143
15,100	15,150	0	3,305	5,460	6,143	374	3,305	5,460	6,143
15,150	15,200	0	3,305	5,460	6,143	371	3,305	5,460	6,143
15,200	15,250	0	3,305	5,460	6,143	367	3,305	5,460	6,143
15,250	15,300	0	3,305	5,460	6,143	363	3,305	5,460	6,143
15,300	15,350	0	3,305	5,460	6,143	359	3,305	5,460	6,143
15,350	15,400	0	3,305	5,460	6,143	355	3,305	5,460	6,143
15,400	15,450	0	3,305	5,460	6,143	352	3,305	5,460	6,143
15,450	15,500	0	3,305	5,460	6,143	348	3,305	5,460	6,143
15,500	15,550	0	3,305	5,460	6,143	344	3,305	5,460	6,143
15,550	15,600	0	3,305	5,460	6,143	340	3,305	5,460	6,143
15,600	15,650	0	3,305	5,460	6,143	336	3,305	5,460	6,143
15,650	15,700	0	3,305	5,460	6,143	332	3,305	5,460	6,143
15,700	15,750	0	3,305	5,460	6,143	329	3,305	5,460	6,143
15,750	15,800	0	3,305	5,460	6,143	325	3,305	5,460	6,143
15,800	15,850	0	3,305	5,460	6,143	321	3,305	5,460	6,143
15,850	15,900	0	3,305	5,460	6,143	317	3,305	5,460	6,143
15,900	15,950	0	3,305	5,460	6,143	313	3,305	5,460	6,143
15,950	16,000	0	3,305	5,460	6,143	309	3,305	5,460	6,143
16,000	16,050	0	3,305	5,460	6,143	306	3,305	5,460	6,143
16,050	16,100	0	3,305	5,460	6,143	302	3,305	5,460	6,143
16,100	16,150	0	3,305	5,460	6,143	298	3,305	5,460	6,143
16,150	16,200	0	3,305	5,460	6,143	294	3,305	5,460	6,143
16,200	16,250	0	3,305	5,460	6,143	290	3,305	5,460	6,143
16,250	16,300	0	3,305	5,460	6,143	286	3,305	5,460	6,143
16,300	16,350	0	3,305	5,460	6,143	283	3,305	5,460	6,143
16,350	16,400	0	3,305	5,460	6,143	279	3,305	5,460	6,143
16,400	16,450	0	3,305	5,460	6,143	275	3,305	5,460	6,143
16,450	16,500	0	3,305	5,460	6,143	271	3,305	5,460	6,143
16,500	16,550	0	3,305	5,460	6,143	267	3,305	5,460	6,143
16,550	16,600	0	3,305	5,460	6,143	264	3,305	5,460	6,143
16,600	16,650	0	3,305	5,460	6,143	260	3,305	5,460	6,143
16,650	16,700	0	3,305	5,460	6,143	256	3,305	5,460	6,143
16,700	16,750	0	3,305	5,460	6,143	252	3,305	5,460	6,143
16,750	16,800	0	3,305	5,460	6,143	248	3,305	5,460	6,143
16,800	16,850	0	3,305	5,460	6,143	244	3,305	5,460	6,143
16,850	16,900	0	3,305	5,460	6,143	241	3,305	5,460	6,143
16,900	16,950	0	3,305	5,460	6,143	237	3,305	5,460	6,143
16,950	17,000	0	3,305	5,460	6,143	233	3,305	5,460	6,143
17,000	17,050	0	3,305	5,460	6,143	229	3,305	5,460	6,143
17,050	17,100	0	3,305	5,460	6,143	225	3,305	5,460	6,143
17,100	17,150	0	3,305	5,460	6,143	221	3,305	5,460	6,143
17,150	17,200	0	3,305	5,460	6,143	218	3,305	5,460	6,143
17,200	17,250	0	3,305	5,460	6,143	214	3,305	5,460	6,143
17,250	17,300	0	3,305	5,460	6,143	210	3,305	5,460	6,143
17,300	17,350	0	3,305	5,460	6,143	206	3,305	5,460	6,143
17,350	17,400	0	3,305	5,460	6,143	202	3,305	5,460	6,143
17,400	17,450	0	3,305	5,460	6,143	199	3,305	5,460	6,143
17,450	17,500	0	3,305	5,460	6,143	195	3,305	5,460	6,143
17,500	17,550	0	3,305	5,460	6,143	191	3,305	5,460	6,143
17,550	17,600	0	3,305	5,460	6,143	187	3,305	5,460	6,143
17,600	17,650	0	3,305	5,460	6,143	183	3,305	5,460	6,143
17,650	17,700	0	3,305	5,460	6,143	179	3,305	5,460	6,143
17,700	17,750	0	3,305	5,460	6,143	176	3,305	5,460	6,143
17,750	17,800	0	3,305	5,460	6,143	172	3,305	5,460	6,143
17,800	17,850	0	3,305	5,460	6,143	168	3,305	5,460	6,143
17,850	17,900	0	3,298	5,451	6,133	164	3,305	5,460	6,143
17,900	17,950	0	3,290	5,440	6,122	160	3,305	5,460	6,143
17,950	18,000	0	3,282	5,429	6,112	156	3,305	5,460	6,143
18,000	18,050	0	3,274	5,419	6,101	153	3,305	5,460	6,143
18,050	18,100	0	3,266	5,408	6,091	149	3,305	5,460	6,143
18,100	18,150	0	3,258	5,398	6,080	145	3,305	5,460	6,143
18,150	18,200	0	3,250	5,387	6,070	141	3,305	5,460	6,143
18,200	18,250	0	3,242	5,377	6,059	137	3,305	5,460	6,143
18,250	18,300	0	3,234	5,366	6,049	133	3,305	5,460	6,143
18,300	18,350	0	3,226	5,356	6,038	130	3,305	5,460	6,143
18,350	18,400	0	3,218	5,345	6,028	126	3,305	5,460	6,143
18,400	18,450	0	3,210	5,335	6,017	122	3,305	5,460	6,143
18,450	18,500	0	3,202	5,324	6,007	118	3,305	5,460	6,143
18,500	18,550	0	3,194	5,314	5,996	114	3,305	5,460	6,143
18,550	18,600	0	3,186	5,303	5,986	111	3,305	5,460	6,143
18,600	18,650	0	3,178	5,293	5,975	107	3,305	5,460	6,143
18,650	18,700	0	3,170	5,282	5,965	103	3,305	5,460	6,143
18,700	18,750	0	3,162	5,272	5,954	99	3,305	5,460	6,143
18,750	18,800	0	3,154	5,261	5,943	95	3,305	5,460	6,143
18,800	18,850	0	3,146	5,250	5,933	91	3,305	5,460	6,143
18,850	18,900	0	3,138	5,240	5,922	88	3,305	5,460	6,143
18,900	18,950	0	3,130	5,229	5,912	84	3,305	5,460	6,143
18,950	19,000	0	3,122	5,219	5,901	80	3,305	5,460	6,143
19,000	19,050	0	3,114	5,208	5,891	76	3,305	5,460	6,143
19,050	19,100	0	3,106	5,198	5,880	72	3,305	5,460	6,143
19,100	19,150	0	3,098	5,187	5,870	68	3,305	5,460	6,143
19,150	19,200	0	3,090	5,177	5,859	65	3,305	5,460	6,143

* If the amount you are looking up from the worksheet is at least $14,550 but less than $14,590, and you have no qualifying children, your credit is $2. If the amount you are looking up from the worksheet is $14,590 or more, and you have no qualifying children, you cannot take the credit.

Illustration 5-9

<table>
<tr><td rowspan="2">Form **8867**
Department of the Treasury
Internal Revenue Service</td><td colspan="2">**Paid Preparer's Earned Income Credit Checklist**
▶ To be completed by preparer and filed with Form 1040, 1040A, or 1040EZ.
▶ Information about Form 8867 and its separate instructions is at *www.irs.gov/form8867.*</td><td>OMB No. 1545-1629
20**14**
Attachment
Sequence No. **177**</td></tr>
</table>

Taxpayer name(s) shown on return	Taxpayer's social security number
Elizabeth Jeffreys	444-55-6666

For the definitions of **Qualifying Child** and **Earned Income**, see **Pub. 596**.

Part I	All Taxpayers

1 Enter preparer's name and PTIN ▶ Jane Doe P00000000

2 Is the taxpayer's filing status married filing separately? . . . . ☐ Yes ☑ No

   ▶ If you checked **"Yes"** on line 2, **stop;** the taxpayer **cannot** take the EIC. Otherwise, continue.

3 Does the taxpayer (and the taxpayer's spouse if filing jointly) have a social security number (SSN) that allows him or her to work and is valid for EIC purposes? See the instructions before answering . . . . ☑ Yes ☐ No

   ▶ If you checked **"No"** on line 3, **stop;** the taxpayer **cannot** take the EIC. Otherwise, continue.

4 Is the taxpayer (or the taxpayer's spouse if filing jointly) filing Form 2555 or 2555-EZ (relating to the exclusion of foreign earned income)? . . . . ☐ Yes ☑ No

   ▶ If you checked **"Yes"** on line 4, **stop;** the taxpayer **cannot** take the EIC. Otherwise, continue.

5a Was the taxpayer (or the taxpayer's spouse) a nonresident alien for any part of 2014? . . . . . ☐ Yes ☑ No

   ▶ If you checked **"Yes"** on line 5a, go to line 5b. Otherwise, skip line 5b and go to line 6.

b Is the taxpayer's filing status married filing jointly? . . . . ☐ Yes ☑ No

   ▶ If you checked **"Yes"** on line 5a and **"No"** on line 5b, **stop;** the taxpayer **cannot** take the EIC. Otherwise, continue.

6 Is the taxpayer's **investment income** more than $3,350? See the instructions before answering. ☐ Yes ☑ No

   ▶ If you checked **"Yes"** on line 6, **stop;** the taxpayer **cannot** take the EIC. Otherwise, continue.

7 Could the taxpayer be a **qualifying child** of another person for 2014? If the taxpayer's filing status is married filing jointly, check **"No."** Otherwise, see instructions before answering . . . . ☐ Yes ☑ No

   ▶ If you checked **"Yes"** on line 7, **stop;** the taxpayer **cannot** take the EIC. Otherwise, go to Part II or Part III, whichever applies.

For Paperwork Reduction Act Notice, see separate instructions.　　　　Cat. No. 26142H　　　　Form **8867** (2014)

Illustration 5-9 continued

Part II	Taxpayers With a Child	Child 1	Child 2	Child 3
	Caution. If there is more than one child, complete lines 8 through 14 for one child before going to the next column.			
8	Child's name	Alicia		
9	Is the child the taxpayer's son, daughter, stepchild, foster child, brother, sister, stepbrother, stepsister, half brother, half sister, or a descendant of any of them?	☑ Yes ☐ No	☐ Yes ☐ No	☐ Yes ☐ No
10	Was the child unmarried at the end of 2014? If the child was married at the end of 2014, see the instructions before answering	☑ Yes ☐ No	☐ Yes ☐ No	☐ Yes ☐ No
11	Did the child live with the taxpayer in the United States for over half of 2014? See the instructions before answering	☑ Yes ☐ No	☐ Yes ☐ No	☐ Yes ☐ No
12	Was the child (at the end of 2014)— • Under age 19 and younger than the taxpayer (or the taxpayer's spouse, if the taxpayer files jointly), • Under age 24, a student (defined in the instructions), and younger than the taxpayer (or the taxpayer's spouse, if the taxpayer files jointly), or • Any age and permanently and totally disabled? . . . . ▶ If you checked **"Yes"** on lines 9, 10, 11, **and** 12, the child is the taxpayer's qualifying child; go to line 13a. If you checked **"No"** on line 9, 10, 11, **or** 12, the child is not the taxpayer's qualifying child; see the instructions for line 12.	☑ Yes ☐ No	☐ Yes ☐ No	☐ Yes ☐ No
13a	Do you or the taxpayer know of another person who could check **"Yes"** on lines 9, 10, 11, **and** 12 for the child? (If the only other person is the taxpayer's spouse, see the instructions before answering.) . . . . ▶ If you checked **"No"** on line 13a, go to line 14. Otherwise, go to line 13b.	☐ Yes ☑ No	☐ Yes ☐ No	☐ Yes ☐ No
b	Enter the child's relationship to the other person(s)			
c	Under the tiebreaker rules, is the child treated as the taxpayer's qualifying child? See the instructions before answering . . . . ▶ If you checked **"Yes"** on line 13c, go to line 14. If you checked **"No,"** the taxpayer **cannot** take the EIC based on this child and cannot take the EIC for taxpayers who do not have a qualifying child. If there is more than one child, see the **Note** at the bottom of this page. If you checked **"Don't know,"** explain to the taxpayer that, under the tiebreaker rules, the taxpayer's EIC and other tax benefits may be disallowed. Then, if the taxpayer wants to take the EIC based on this child, complete lines 14 and 15. If not, and there are no other qualifying children, the taxpayer cannot take the EIC, including the EIC for taxpayers without a qualifying child; do not complete Part III. If there is more than one child, see the **Note** at the bottom of this page.	☐ Yes ☐ No ☐ Don't know	☐ Yes ☐ No ☐ Don't know	☐ Yes ☐ No ☐ Don't know
14	Does the qualifying child have an SSN that allows him or her to work and is valid for EIC purposes? See the instructions before answering . . . . ▶ If you checked **"No"** on line 14, the taxpayer **cannot** take the EIC based on this child and cannot take the EIC available to taxpayers without a qualifying child. If there is more than one child, see the **Note** at the bottom of this page. If you checked "Yes" on line 14, continue.	☑ Yes ☐ No	☐ Yes ☐ No	☐ Yes ☐ No
15	Are the taxpayer's **earned income** and **adjusted gross income** each less than the limit that applies to the taxpayer for 2014? See instructions . . ▶ If you checked **"No"** on line 15, **stop;** the taxpayer **cannot** take the EIC. If you checked **"Yes"** on line 15, the taxpayer can take the EIC. Complete **Schedule EIC** and attach it to the taxpayer's return. If there are two or three qualifying children with valid SSNs, list them on Schedule EIC in the same order as they are listed here. If the taxpayer's EIC was reduced or disallowed for a year after 1996, see Pub. 596 to see if **Form 8862** must be filed. Go to line 20.		☑ Yes ☐ No	

Note. If there is more than one child, complete lines 8 through 14 for the other child(ren) (but for no more than three qualifying children).

Illustration 5-9 continued

Part III   Taxpayers Without a Qualifying Child

16   Was the taxpayer's main home, and the main home of the taxpayer's spouse if filing jointly, in the United States for more than half the year? (Military personnel on extended active duty outside the United States are considered to be living in the United States during that duty period.) See the instructions before answering.   ☐ Yes   ☐ No

> ▶ If you checked **"No"** on line 16, **stop;** the taxpayer **cannot** take the EIC. Otherwise, continue.

17   Was the taxpayer, or the taxpayer's spouse if filing jointly, at least age 25 but under age 65 at the end of 2014? See the instructions before answering .   ☐ Yes   ☐ No

> ▶ If you checked **"No"** on line 17, **stop;** the taxpayer **cannot** take the EIC. Otherwise, continue.

18   Is the taxpayer eligible to be claimed as a dependent on anyone else's federal income tax return for 2014? If the taxpayer's filing status is married filing jointly, check **"No"** .   ☐ Yes   ☐ No

> ▶ If you checked **"Yes"** on line 18, **stop;** the taxpayer **cannot** take the EIC. Otherwise, continue.

19   Are the taxpayer's **earned income** and **adjusted gross income** each less than the limit that applies to the taxpayer for 2014? See instructions .   ☐ Yes   ☐ No

> ▶ If you checked **"No"** on line 19, **stop;** the taxpayer **cannot** take the EIC. If you checked **"Yes"** on line 19, the taxpayer can take the EIC. If the taxpayer's EIC was reduced or disallowed for a year after 1996, see Pub. 596 to find out if **Form 8862** must be filed. Go to line 20.

Part IV   Due Diligence Requirements

20   Did you complete Form 8867 based on current information provided by the taxpayer or reasonably obtained by you? .   ☑ Yes   ☐ No

21   Did you complete the EIC worksheet found in the Form 1040, 1040A, or 1040EZ instructions (or your own worksheet that provides the same information as the 1040, 1040A, or 1040EZ worksheet)? .   ☑ Yes   ☐ No

22   If any qualifying child was not the taxpayer's son or daughter, do you know or did you ask why the parents were not claiming the child? .   ☐ Yes   ☐ No   ☑ Does not apply

23   If the answer to question 13a is **"Yes"** (indicating that the child lived for more than half the year with someone else who could claim the child for the EIC), did you explain the tiebreaker rules and possible consequences of another person claiming your client's qualifying child? .   ☐ Yes   ☐ No   ☑ Does not apply

24   Did you ask this taxpayer any additional questions that are necessary to meet your knowledge requirement? See the instructions before answering .   ☐ Yes   ☐ No   ☑ Does not apply

> **To comply with the EIC knowledge requirement, you must not know or have reason to know that any information you used to determine the taxpayer's eligibility for, and the amount of, the EIC is incorrect. You may not ignore the implications of information furnished to you or known by you, and you must make reasonable inquiries if the information furnished to you appears to be incorrect, inconsistent, or incomplete. At the time you make these inquiries, you must document in your files the inquiries you made and the taxpayer's responses.**

25   Did you document (a) the taxpayer's answer to question 22 (if applicable), (b) whether you explained the tiebreaker rules to the taxpayer and any additional information you got from the taxpayer as a result, and (c) any additional questions you asked and the taxpayer's answers? .   ☐ Yes   ☐ No   ☑ Does not apply

> ▶ You have complied with all the due diligence requirements if you:
>   1. Completed the actions described on lines 20 and 21 and checked **"Yes"** on those lines,
>   2. Completed the actions described on lines 22, 23, 24, and 25 (if they apply) and checked **"Yes"** (or **"Does not apply"**) on those lines,
>   3. Submit Form 8867 in the manner required, **and**
>   4. Keep all five of the following records for 3 years from the latest of the dates specified in the instructions under *Document Retention*:
>
>   a. Form 8867,
>   b. The EIC worksheet(s) or your own worksheet(s),
>   c. Copies of any taxpayer documents you relied on to determine eligibility for or amount of EIC,
>   d. A record of how, when, and from whom the information used to prepare the form and worksheet(s) was obtained, and
>   e. A record of any additional questions you asked and your client's answers.
>
> ▶ You have not complied with all the due diligence requirements if you checked **"No"** on line 20, 21, 22, 23, 24, or 25. You may have to pay a $500 penalty for each failure to comply.

Illustration 5-9 continued

Part V	Documents Provided to You

26 Identify below any document that the taxpayer provided to you and that you relied on to determine the taxpayer's EIC eligibility. Check all that apply. **Keep a copy of any documents you relied on.** See the instructions before answering. If there is no qualifying child, check box a. If there is no disabled child, check box o.

Residency of Qualifying Child(ren)

☐ a No qualifying child	☐ i Place of worship statement
☐ b School records or statement	☐ j Indian tribal official statement
☐ c Landlord or property management statement	☐ k Employer statement
☐ d Health care provider statement	☐ l Other (specify) ▼
☐ e Medical records	_____
☐ f Child care provider records	_____
☐ g Placement agency statement	
☐ h Social service records or statement	☐ m Did not rely on any documents, but made notes in file
	☑ n Did not rely on any documents

Disability of Qualifying Child(ren)

☐ o No disabled child	☐ s Other (specify) ▼
☐ p Doctor statement	_____
☐ q Other health care provider statement	_____
☐ r Social services agency or program statement	☐ t Did not rely on any documents, but made notes in file
	☐ u Did not rely on any documents

27 If a Schedule C is included with this return, identify below the information that the taxpayer provided to you and that you relied on to prepare the Schedule C. Check all that apply. **Keep a copy of any documents you relied on.** See the instructions before answering. If there is no Schedule C, check box a.

Documents or Other Information

☐ a No Schedule C	☐ h Bank statements
☐ b Business license	☐ i Reconstruction of income and expenses
☐ c Forms 1099	☐ j Other (specify) ▼
☐ d Records of gross receipts provided by taxpayer	_____
☐ e Taxpayer summary of income	_____
☐ f Records of expenses provided by taxpayer	☐ k Did not rely on any documents, but made notes in file
☐ g Taxpayer summary of expenses	☐ l Did not rely on any documents

Form **8867** (2014)

Illustration 5-10

Earned Income Credit Worksheet

1.	Enter the amount from Form 1040, Line 7.	1.	14,998
2.	Taxable Scholarship or Fellowship grant not reported on a W-2, if included on line 7, Form 1040 .... _____		
3.	Amount received for work performed while an inmate in a penal institution (enter "PRI" and the amount subtracted on the dotted line next to Form 1040, line 7), if included on line 7............... _____		
4.	Amount received as a pension or annuity from a nonqualified deferred compensation plan or a nongovernmental Sec. 457 plan. (Enter "DFC" and amount subtracted on the dotted line next to Form 1040, line 7), if included on line 7............................ _____		
5.	Add lines 2, 3, and 4.	5.	
6	Subtract line 5 from line 1.	6.	14,998
7.	Nontaxable Combat pay if the election is made to use it. You will have to complete two worksheets: one with the combat pay and one without. Use the one that will result in the most EIC.	7.	
8.	Add lines 6 and 7.	8.	14,998
9.	If the taxpayer had any income from self-employment or was a statutory employee, complete lines 10 –18. If not skip lines 10 –18 and go to line 19.		
10.	**If the taxpayer is filing a Schedule SE**, enter the amount from Schedule SE, Section A, line 3 or Section B, line 3, whichever applies. If the taxpayer is not filing a Schedule SE, skip lines 10 –14 and go to line 15. If the taxpayer is a statutory employee, go to line 18.	10.	
11.	Enter any amounts from Schedule SE, Section B, line 4b, and line 5a.	11.	
12.	Combine lines 10 and 11.	12.	
13.	Enter the amount from Schedule SE, Section A, line 6 or Section B, line 13.	13.	
14.	Subtract line 13 from line 12. If lines 15 and 18 do not apply, enter this amount on line 17 and go to line 19.	14.	
15.	**If the taxpayer is not required to file a Schedule SE because the net earnings were less than $400,** enter amount from Schedule F, line 36, and from farm partnerships, Schedule K-1 (Form 1065), box 14, code A.	15.	
16.	Enter any net profit or (loss) from Schedule C, line 31; Schedule C-EZ, line 3, Schedule K-1, box 14, code A (other than farming); and Schedule K-1, box 9, code J1.	16.	
17.	Combine lines 14, 15, and 16.	17.	
18.	**If the taxpayer is a statutory employee**, enter the amount from Schedule C, line 1, or Schedule C-EZ, line 1 that the taxpayer is filing as a statutory employee.	18.	
19.	Add lines 8, 17, and 18. This is the earned income.	19.	14,998
20.	Look up the amount on line 19 above in the EIC Table to find the credit. If the amount is 0, stop. The taxpayer does not qualify for the credit.	20.	3,305
21.	Enter the amount from Form 1040, line 38. If the amount on line 21 is the same as the amount on line 19, stop and enter the amount from line 20 on line 66a of the Form 1040. This is the taxpayer's Earned Income Credit. If not, go to line 22.	21.	14,998
22.	Is the amount on line 21 less than: • $8,150 ($13,550 if MFJ) if the taxpayer has no qualifying children? • $17,850 ($23,300 if MFJ) if the taxpayer has one or more qualifying children? **If the answer is yes**, stop and enter the amount from line 21 on the Form 1040, line 66a. **If the answer is no,** look up the amount from line 21 in the EIC Table to find the credit and go to line 23.	22.	
23.	Look at the amounts on line 20 and 22. Enter the smaller amount here and on Form 1040, line 66a.	23.	

Illustration 5-11

SCHEDULE EIC
(Form 1040A or 1040)

Department of the Treasury
Internal Revenue Service (99)

Earned Income Credit
Qualifying Child Information

1040A
1040

EIC

► Complete and attach to Form 1040A or 1040 only if you have a qualifying child.

► Information about Schedule EIC (Form 1040A or 1040) and its instructions is at www.irs.gov/scheduleeic.

OMB No. 1545-0074

20**14**

Attachment
Sequence No. **43**

Name(s) shown on return

Elizabeth Jeffreys

Your social security number

444-55-6666

Before you begin:
- See the instructions for Form 1040A, lines 42a and 42b, or Form 1040, lines 66a and 66b, to make sure that **(a)** you can take the EIC, and **(b)** you have a qualifying child.
- Be sure the child's name on line 1 and social security number (SSN) on line 2 agree with the child's social security card. Otherwise, at the time we process your return, we may reduce or disallow your EIC. If the name or SSN on the child's social security card is not correct, call the Social Security Administration at 1-800-772-1213.

CAUTION

- *If you take the EIC even though you are not eligible, you may not be allowed to take the credit for up to 10 years. See the instructions for details.*
- *It will take us longer to process your return and issue your refund if you do not fill in all lines that apply for each qualifying child.*

Qualifying Child Information	Child 1	Child 2	Child 3
1 Child's name If you have more than three qualifying children, you have to list only three to get the maximum credit.	First name Last name Alicia Jeffreys	First name Last name	First name Last name
2 Child's SSN The child must have an SSN as defined in the instructions for Form 1040A, lines 42a and 42b, or Form 1040, lines 66a and 66b, unless the child was born and died in 2014. If your child was born and died in 2014 and did not have an SSN, enter "Died" on this line and attach a copy of the child's birth certificate, death certificate, or hospital medical records.	223-33-4444		
3 Child's year of birth	Year 2 0 1 2 *If born after 1995 and the child is younger than you (or your spouse, if filing jointly), skip lines 4a and 4b; go to line 5.*	Year ___ ___ ___ ___ *If born after 1995 and the child is younger than you (or your spouse, if filing jointly), skip lines 4a and 4b; go to line 5.*	Year ___ ___ ___ ___ *If born after 1995 and the child is younger than you (or your spouse, if filing jointly), skip lines 4a and 4b; go to line 5.*
4 a Was the child under age 24 at the end of 2014, a student, and younger than you (or your spouse, if filing jointly)?	☑ Yes. ☐ No. *Go to line 5.* *Go to line 4b.*	☐ Yes. ☐ No. *Go to line 5.* *Go to line 4b.*	☐ Yes. ☐ No. *Go to line 5.* *Go to line 4b.*
b Was the child permanently and totally disabled during any part of 2014?	☐ Yes. ☐ No. *Go to line 5.* The child is not a qualifying child.	☐ Yes. ☐ No. *Go to line 5.* The child is not a qualifying child.	☐ Yes. ☐ No. *Go to line 5.* The child is not a qualifying child.
5 Child's relationship to you (for example, son, daughter, grandchild, niece, nephew, foster child, etc.)	Daughter		
6 Number of months child lived with you in the United States during 2014 • If the child lived with you for more than half of 2014 but less than 7 months, enter "7." • If the child was born or died in 2014 and your home was the child's home for more than half the time he or she was alive during 2014, enter "12."	___12___ months *Do not enter more than 12 months.*	_____ months *Do not enter more than 12 months.*	_____ months *Do not enter more than 12 months.*

For Paperwork Reduction Act Notice, see your tax return instructions.

Cat. No. 13339M

Schedule EIC (Form 1040A or 1040) 2014

Illustration 5-11 continued

Tax and Credits	38	Amount from line 37 (adjusted gross income)	38	14,998	00
	39a	Check if: ☐ **You** were born before January 2, 1950, ☐ Blind. ☐ **Spouse** was born before January 2, 1950, ☐ Blind. Total boxes checked ▶ 39a			
	b	If your spouse itemizes on a separate return or you were a dual-status alien, check here▶ 39b☐			
Standard Deduction for— • People who check any box on line 39a or 39b **or** who can be claimed as a dependent, see instructions. • All others: Single or Married filing separately, $6,200 Married filing jointly or Qualifying widow(er), $12,400 Head of household, $9,100	40	**Itemized deductions** (from Schedule A) **or** your **standard deduction** (see left margin)	40	9,100	00
	41	Subtract line 40 from line 38	41	5,898	00
	42	**Exemptions.** If line 38 is $152,525 or less, multiply $3,950 by the number on line 6d. Otherwise, see instructions	42	7,900	00
	43	**Taxable income.** Subtract line 42 from line 41. If line 42 is more than line 41, enter -0-	43	0	00
	44	**Tax** (see instructions). Check if any from: **a** ☐ Form(s) 8814 **b** ☐ Form 4972 **c** ☐ ____	44		
	45	**Alternative minimum tax** (see instructions). Attach Form 6251	45		
	46	Excess advance premium tax credit repayment. Attach Form 8962	46		
	47	Add lines 44, 45, and 46 ▶	47	0	00
	48	Foreign tax credit. Attach Form 1116 if required			
	49	Credit for child and dependent care expenses. Attach Form 2441			
	50	Education credits from Form 8863, line 19			
	51	Retirement savings contributions credit. Attach Form 8880			
	52	Child tax credit. Attach Schedule 8812, if required			
	53	Residential energy credits. Attach Form 5695			
	54	Other credits from Form: **a** ☐ 3800 **b** ☐ 8801 **c** ☐			
	55	Add lines 48 through 54. These are your **total credits**	55		
	56	Subtract line 55 from line 47. If line 55 is more than line 47, enter -0- ▶	56	0	00
Other Taxes	57	Self-employment tax. Attach Schedule SE	57		
	58	Unreported social security and Medicare tax from Form: **a** ☐ 4137 **b** ☐ 8919	58		
	59	Additional tax on IRAs, other qualified retirement plans, etc. Attach Form 5329 if required	59		
	60a	Household employment taxes from Schedule H	60a		
	b	First-time homebuyer credit repayment. Attach Form 5405 if required	60b		
	61	Health care: individual responsibility (see instructions) Full-year coverage ☐	61		
	62	Taxes from: **a** ☐ Form 8959 **b** ☐ Form 8960 **c** ☐ Instructions; enter code(s)	62		
	63	Add lines 56 through 62. This is your **total tax** ▶	63	0	00
Payments If you have a qualifying child, attach Schedule EIC.	64	Federal income tax withheld from Forms W-2 and 1099			
	65	2014 estimated tax payments and amount applied from 2013 return			
	66a	**Earned income credit (EIC)**		3,305	00
	b	Nontaxable combat pay election 66b			
	67	Additional child tax credit. Attach Schedule 8812			
	68	American opportunity credit from Form 8863, line 8			
	69	Net premium tax credit. Attach Form 8962			
	70	Amount paid with request for extension to file			
	71	Excess social security and tier 1 RRTA tax withheld			
	72	Credit for federal tax on fuels. Attach Form 4136			
	73	Credits from Form: **a** ☐ 2439 **b** ☐ Reserved **c** ☐ Reserved **d** ☐			
	74	Add lines 64, 65, 66a, and 67 through 73. These are your **total payments** ▶	74	3,305	00
Refund Direct deposit? See instructions.	75	If line 74 is more than line 63, subtract line 63 from line 74. This is the amount you **overpaid**	75	3,305	00
	76a	Amount of line 75 you want **refunded to you.** If Form 8888 is attached, check here ▶ ☐	76a	3,305	00
	b	Routing number | | | | | | | | | ▶c Type: ☐ Checking ☐ Savings			
	d	Account number			
	77	Amount of line 75 you want **applied to your 2015 estimated tax** ▶ 77			
Amount You Owe	78	**Amount you owe.** Subtract line 74 from line 63. For details on how to pay, see instructions ▶	78		
	79	Estimated tax penalty (see instructions) 79			

Third Party Designee

Do you want to allow another person to discuss this return with the IRS (see instructions)? ☐ **Yes.** Complete below. ☐ **No**

Designee's name ▶	Phone no. ▶	Personal identification number (PIN) ▶	

Sign Here

Joint return? See instructions. Keep a copy for your records.

Under penalties of perjury, I declare that I have examined this return and accompanying schedules and statements, and to the best of my knowledge and belief, they are true, correct, and complete. Declaration of preparer (other than taxpayer) is based on all information of which preparer has any knowledge.

Your signature	Date	Your occupation Manager	Daytime phone number (555)555-5555
Spouse's signature. If a joint return, **both** must sign.	Date	Spouse's occupation	If the IRS sent you an Identity Protection PIN, enter it here (see inst.)

Paid Preparer Use Only

Print/Type preparer's name Jane Doe	Preparer's signature	Date	Check ☐ if self-employed	PTIN P00000000
Firm's name ▶ My Tax Service			Firm's EIN ▶	63-0000000
Firm's address ▶ 100 Main St., Your City, Your State, Your Zip Code			Phone no.	(555)555-1111

www.irs.gov/form1040

Form **1040** (2014)

Child Tax Credit

Child Tax Credit is a credit given to taxpayers who have qualifying children under the age of 17. There are two types of credits; Child Tax Credit and Additional Child Tax Credit. It is important to keep the two different credits separate. One is nonrefundable while the other is a refundable credit. We'll discuss the Child Tax Credit first.

The Child Tax Credit is a nonrefundable credit which means the credit cannot be more than the tax liability. The Child Tax Credit can be up to $1,000 per qualifying child. To be a qualifying child for Child Tax Credit, the child must:

- Be the taxpayer's son, daughter, stepchild, foster child, brother, sister, stepbrother, stepsister, or a descendant of any of them (for example, your grandchild, niece, or nephew),
- Be under the age of 17 at the end of the tax year,
- Not provide over half of his or her own support for the tax year,
- Have lived with the taxpayer for more than half of the tax year, and
- Be a U.S. citizen, a U.S. national, or a U.S. resident alien. If the child is adopted (lawfully placed with the taxpayer for legal adoption) by a U.S. citizen or a U.S. national and that child lived with the taxpayer as a member of the household in 2013, that child qualifies.

If the taxpayer has a qualifying child for Child Tax Credit, they must mark the box on line 6c of the Form 1040.

Qualifying child of more than one person

We've discussed the rules for a qualifying child of more than one person. In the case of Child Tax Credit, whoever claims the exemption for the child, claims the Child Tax Credit.

Children of divorced or separated parents

If the noncustodial parent is eligible to claim the exemption for the child, the noncustodial parent will also be eligible to claim the Child Tax Credit.

AGI phase out

The Child Tax Credit begins to phase out when the income reaches certain levels:

- $110,000 for Married Filing Jointly
- $75,000 for Single, Head of Household, and Qualifying Widow(er)
- $55,000 for Married Filing Separately

If the taxpayer's income is above the amount that applies, they may have to use the Child Tax Credit worksheet in the IRS Publication 972. Pub. 972 will need to be used if the income is over the amount above and one of the following applies:

- The taxpayer is claiming any of the following credits:
    - Adoption Credit
    - Residential energy credit
    - Mortgage interest credit
    - District of Columbia first-time homebuyer credit
- The taxpayer is excluding income from Puerto Rico or filing one of the following forms:

o   Form 2555 or 2555-EZ (relating to foreign earned income)
o   Form 4563 (exclusion of income for residents of American Samoa).

Child Tax Credit Worksheet

If none of the above applies to the taxpayer, the Child Tax Credit worksheet found in the Form 1040 instructions, page 47 (Illustration 5-12) may be used. The Child Tax Credit will then be carried to Form 1040, line 52.

Illustration 5-12

2014 Child Tax Credit Worksheet—Line 52

Keep for Your Records

1. To be a qualifying child for the child tax credit, the child must be your dependent, **under age 17** at the end of 2014, and meet all the conditions in Steps 1 through 3 in the instructions for line 6c. Make sure you checked the box on Form 1040, line 6c, column (4), for each qualifying child.

2. If you do not have a qualifying child, you cannot claim the child tax credit.

3. If your qualifying child has an ITIN instead of an SSN, file Schedule 8812.

4. Do **not** use this worksheet, but use Pub. 972 instead, if:

   a. You are claiming the adoption credit, mortgage interest credit, District of Columbia first-time homebuyer credit, or residential energy efficient property credit,

   b. You are excluding income from Puerto Rico, or

   c. You are filing Form 2555, 2555-EZ, or 4563.

Part 1

1. Number of qualifying children: _____ × $1,000. Enter the result.

   1 ☐

2. Enter the amount from Form 1040, line 38.

   2 ☐

3. Enter the amount shown below for your filing status.

   ● Married filing jointly — $110,000

   ● Single, head of household, or qualifying widow(er) — $75,000

   ● Married filing separately — $55,000

   3 ☐

4. Is the amount on line 2 more than the amount on line 3?

   ☐ **No.** Leave line 4 blank. Enter -0- on line 5, and go to line 6.

   ☐ **Yes.** Subtract line 3 from line 2.
   If the result is not a multiple of $1,000, increase it to the next multiple of $1,000. For example, increase $425 to $1,000, increase $1,025 to $2,000, etc.

   4 ☐

5. Multiply the amount on line 4 by 5% (.05). Enter the result.

   5 ☐

6. Is the amount on line 1 more than the amount on line 5?

   ☐ **No.** (STOP)
   You cannot take the child tax credit on Form 1040, line 52. You also cannot take the additional child tax credit on Form 1040, line 67. Complete the rest of your Form 1040.

   ☐ **Yes.** Subtract line 5 from line 1. Enter the result. *Go to Part 2.*

   6 ☐

Illustration 5-12 continued

2014 Form 1040—Line 52

| **2014 Child Tax Credit Worksheet**—*Continued* | *Keep for Your Records* |

Before you begin Part 2: √ Figure the amount of any credits you are claiming on Form 5695, Part II; Form 8910; Form 8936; or Schedule R.

Part 2	7.	Enter the amount from Form 1040, line 47.	**7**	

8. Add any amounts from:

Form 1040, line 48	
Form 1040, line 49	+
Form 1040, line 50	+
Form 1040, line 51	+
Form 5695, line 30	+
Form 8910, line 15	+
Form 8936, line 23	+
Schedule R, line 22	+

Enter the total. **8** |

9. Are the amounts on lines 7 and 8 the same?

☐ **Yes.** (STOP)
You cannot take this credit because there is no tax to reduce. However, you may be able to take the **additional child tax credit.** See the **TIP** below.

☐ **No.** Subtract line 8 from line 7.

9 |

10. Is the amount on line 6 more than the amount on line 9?

☐ **Yes.** Enter the amount from line 9.
Also, you may be able to take the **additional child tax credit.** See the **TIP** below.

☐ **No.** Enter the amount from line 6.

} **This is your child tax credit.**

10 |

Enter this amount on Form 1040, line 52.

1040

TIP — You may be able to take the **additional child tax credit** on Form 1040, line 67, if you answered "Yes" on line 9 **or** line 10 above.

● First, complete your Form 1040 through lines 66a and 66b.

● Then, use Schedule 8812 to figure any additional child tax credit.

Additional Child Tax Credit

As opposed to the Child Tax Credit, the Additional Child Tax Credit is a refundable credit. Remember, this means that it is treated as a payment and may result in a refund. It is important to keep in mind that these are two separate credits. The taxpayer may qualify for the Additional Child Tax Credit if they qualified for the Child Tax Credit, but did not receive the full amount from line 1 of the Child Tax Credit worksheet. To receive the Additional Child Tax Credit, Schedule 8812 (Illustration 5-13) must be completed and attached to the tax return. The following lines require additional explanation:

Part I: Part I should only be completed if the taxpayer's qualifying dependent has an ITIN instead of a SSN. An individual Taxpayer Identification Number (ITIN) is for a nonresident or resident alien who is not eligible to receive a Social Security Number. An ITIN is issued for tax purposes only.

Line 1: Enter the amount from line 6 of the Child Tax Credit Worksheet. If the taxpayer was required to use the worksheet in Pub 972, enter the amount from line 8 of that worksheet.

Line 2: Enter the amount from Form 1040, line 52. This is the amount of Child Tax Credit claimed on the tax return.

Line 4a: Enter the total earned income. Earned income for purposes of the Additional Child Tax Credit is generally the same as earned income for EIC purposes. However, nontaxable combat pay is always included in the earned income for the purpose of the Additional Child Tax Credit. If the taxpayer is not self-employed or filing Schedule SE, C, or C-EZ, the earned income is line 7 of the Form 1040 minus the following items if they were included in the line 7 amount:

- Taxable scholarship or fellowship grant not reported on a Form W-2.
- Amount received for work performed while an inmate in a penal institution.
- Amount received as a pension or annuity from a nonqualified deferred compensation plan or a nongovernmental section 457 plan.
- Amount from Form 2555, line 43, or Form 2555-EZ, line 18.
- Medicaid waiver payment the taxpayer excluded from income.

If the taxpayer is self-employed or is filing Schedule SE, C, or C-EZ, complete the worksheet found in Publication 972, page 8 (Illustration 5-14).

Line 4b: Enter the amount of nontaxable combat pay. This should be reported on the Form W-2, box 12, code Q.

Once the amount of Additional Child Tax Credit the taxpayer will receive is determined, it will be entered on Form 1040, line 67.

Illustration 5-13

SCHEDULE 8812
(Form 1040A or 1040)

Child Tax Credit

▶ Attach to Form 1040, Form 1040A, or Form 1040NR.
▶ Information about Schedule 8812 and its separate instructions is at
www.irs.gov/schedule8812.

1040
1040A
1040NR
8812

OMB No. 1545-0074

2014

Attachment
Sequence No. 47

Department of the Treasury
Internal Revenue Service (99)

Name(s) shown on return

Your social security number

Part I | **Filers Who Have Certain Child Dependent(s) with an ITIN (Individual Taxpayer Identification Number)**

⚠ **CAUTION**

Complete this part only for each dependent who has an ITIN and for whom you are claiming the child tax credit.
If your dependent is not a qualifying child for the credit, you cannot include that dependent in the calculation of this credit.

Answer the following questions for each dependent listed on Form 1040, line 6c; Form 1040A, line 6c; or Form 1040NR, line 7c, who has an ITIN (Individual Taxpayer Identification Number) and that you indicated is a qualifying child for the child tax credit by checking column (4) for that dependent.

A For the first dependent identified with an ITIN and listed as a qualifying child for the child tax credit, did this child meet the substantial presence test? See separate instructions.

☐ Yes   ☐ No

B For the second dependent identified with an ITIN and listed as a qualifying child for the child tax credit, did this child meet the substantial presence test? See separate instructions.

☐ Yes   ☐ No

C For the third dependent identified with an ITIN and listed as a qualifying child for the child tax credit, did this child meet the substantial presence test? See separate instructions.

☐ Yes   ☐ No

D For the fourth dependent identified with an ITIN and listed as a qualifying child for the child tax credit, did this child meet the substantial presence test? See separate instructions.

☐ Yes   ☐ No

Note. If you have more than four dependents identified with an ITIN and listed as a qualifying child for the child tax credit, see the instructions and check here . . . . ▶ ☐

Part II | **Additional Child Tax Credit Filers**

1 **1040 filers:** Enter the amount from line 6 of your Child Tax Credit Worksheet (see the Instructions for Form 1040, line 52).

1040A filers: Enter the amount from line 6 of your Child Tax Credit Worksheet (see the Instructions for Form 1040A, line 35).

1040NR filers: Enter the amount from line 6 of your Child Tax Credit Worksheet (see the Instructions for Form 1040NR, line 49).

If you used Pub. 972, enter the amount from line 8 of the Child Tax Credit Worksheet in the publication.

1		

2 Enter the amount from Form 1040, line 52; Form 1040A, line 35; or Form 1040NR, line 49 . . . . . | **2** |

3 Subtract line 2 from line 1. If zero, **stop;** you cannot take this credit . . . . | **3** |

4a Earned income (see separate instructions) **4a**

b Nontaxable combat pay (see separate instructions) **4b**

5 Is the amount on line 4a more than $3,000?
☐ **No.** Leave line 5 blank and enter -0- on line 6.
☐ **Yes.** Subtract $3,000 from the amount on line 4a. Enter the result . . . **5**

6 Multiply the amount on line 5 by 15% (.15) and enter the result . . . . | **6** |

Next. Do you have three or more qualifying children?
☐ **No.** If line 6 is zero, stop; you cannot take this credit. Otherwise, skip Part III and enter the **smaller** of line 3 or line 6 on line 13.
☐ **Yes.** If line 6 is equal to or more than line 3, skip Part III and enter the amount from line 3 on line 13. Otherwise, go to line 7.

For Paperwork Reduction Act Notice, see your tax return instructions.   Cat. No. 59761M   Schedule 8812 (Form 1040A or 1040) 2014

Illustration 5-13 continued

Part III	Certain Filers Who Have Three or More Qualifying Children					
7	Withheld social security, Medicare, and Additional Medicare taxes from Form(s) W-2, boxes 4 and 6. If married filing jointly, include your spouse's amounts with yours. If your employer withheld or you paid Additional Medicare Tax or tier 1 RRTA taxes, see separate instructions	**7**				
8	**1040 filers:** Enter the total of the amounts from Form 1040, lines 27 and 58, plus any taxes that you identified using code "UT" and entered on line 62. **1040A filers:** Enter -0-. **1040NR filers:** Enter the total of the amounts from Form 1040NR, lines 27 and 56, plus any taxes that you identified using code "UT" and entered on line 60.	**8**				
9	Add lines 7 and 8	**9**				
10	**1040 filers:** Enter the total of the amounts from Form 1040, lines 66a and 71. **1040A filers:** Enter the total of the amount from Form 1040A, line 42a, plus any excess social security and tier 1 RRTA taxes withheld that you entered to the left of line 46 (see separate instructions). **1040NR filers:** Enter the amount from Form 1040NR, line 67.	**10**				
11	Subtract line 10 from line 9. If zero or less, enter -0-				**11**	
12	Enter the **larger** of line 6 or line 11				**12**	
	Next, enter the **smaller** of line 3 or line 12 on line 13.					
Part IV	Additional Child Tax Credit					
13	**This is your additional child tax credit**				**13**	

1040
1040A
1040NR

Enter this amount on Form 1040, line 67, Form 1040A, line 43, or Form 1040NR, line 64.

Illustration 5-14

1040 and 1040NR Filers — Earned Income Worksheet
(for line 2 of the Line 11 Worksheet or line 4a of Schedule
8812, Child Tax Credit)

Keep for Your Records

Before you begin:

✓ Use this worksheet only if you were sent here from the Line 11 Worksheet earlier in this publication or line 4a of Schedule 8812, Child Tax Credit.

✓ Disregard community property laws when figuring the amounts to enter on this worksheet.

✓ If married filing jointly, include your spouse's amounts with yours when completing this worksheet.

1.   a. Enter the amount from Form 1040, line 7, or Form 1040NR, line 8 . . . . **1a.** _____

    b. Enter the amount of any nontaxable combat pay received. Also enter this amount on Schedule 8812, line 4b. This amount should be shown in Form(s) W-2, box 12, with code Q. . . . . **1b.** _____

      Next, if you are filing Schedule C, C-EZ, F, or SE, or you received a Schedule K-1 (Form 1065 or Form 1065-B), go to line 2a. Otherwise, skip lines 2a through 2e and go to line 3.

2.   a. Enter any statutory employee income reported on line 1 of Schedule C or C-EZ . . . . **2a.** _____

    b. Enter any net profit or (loss) from Schedule C, line 31; Schedule C-EZ, line 3; Schedule K-1 (Form 1065), box 14, code A (other than farming); and Schedule K-1 (Form 1065-B), box 9, code J1.* Reduce any Schedule K-1 amounts as described in the instructions for completing Schedule SE in the Partner's Instructions for Schedule K-1. **Do not** include on this line any statutory employee income or any other amounts exempt from self-employment tax. Options and commodities dealers must add any gain or subtract any loss (in the normal course of dealing in or trading section 1256 contracts) from section 1256 contracts or related property . . . . **2b.** _____

    c. Enter any net farm profit or (loss) from Schedule F, line 34, and from farm partnerships, Schedule K-1 (Form 1065), box 14, code A.* Reduce any Schedule K-1 amounts as described in the instructions for completing Schedule SE in the Partner's Instructions for Schedule K-1. **Do not** include on this line any amounts exempt from self-employment tax . . . . **2c.** _____

    d. If you used the farm optional method to figure net earnings from self-employment, enter the amount from Schedule SE, Section B, line 15. Otherwise, skip this line and enter on line 2e the amount from line 2c . . . . **2d.** _____

    e. If line 2c is a profit, enter the **smaller** of line 2c or line 2d. If line 2c is a (loss), enter the (loss) from line 2c . . . . **2e.** _____

3. Combine lines 1a, 1b, 2a, 2b, and 2e. If zero or less, **stop.** Do not complete the rest of this worksheet. Instead, enter -0- on line 2 of the Line 11 Worksheet or line 4a of Schedule 8812, whichever applies . . . . **3.** _____

4. Enter any amount included on line 1a that is:

    a. A scholarship or fellowship grant not reported on Form W-2 . . . . **4a.** _____

    b. For work done while an inmate in a penal institution (enter "PRI" and this amount on the dotted line next to line 7 of Form 1040 or line 8 of Form 1040NR) . . . . **4b.** _____

    c. A pension or annuity from a nonqualified deferred compensation plan or a nongovernmental section 457 plan (enter "DFC" and this amount on the dotted line next to line 7 of Form 1040 or line 8 of Form 1040NR). This amount may be shown in box 11 of your Form W-2. If you received such an amount but box 11 is blank, contact your employer for the amount received as a pension or annuity . . . . **4c.** _____

    d. A Medicaid waiver payment you exclude from income (see the instructions for Form 1040, line 21, and Pub. 525 for information about these payments) . . . . **4d.** _____

5.   a. Enter any amount included on line 3 that is also included on Form 2555, line 43, or Form 2555-EZ, line 18. **Do not** include any amount that is also included on line 4a, 4b, 4c, or 4d above . . . . **5a.** _____

    b. Enter the portion, if any, of the amount from Form 2555, line 44 that you also included on Schedule E in partnership net income or (loss) or deducted on Form 1040, line 27, or Form 1040NR, line 27; Schedule C; Schedule C-EZ; or Schedule F. . . . . **5b.** _____

    c. Subtract line 5b from line 5a . . . . **5c.** _____

6. Enter the amount from Form 1040, line 27, or Form 1040NR, line 27 . . . . **6.** _____

7. Add lines 4a through 4d, 5c, and 6 . . . . **7.** _____

8. Subtract line 7 from line 3 . . . . **8.** _____

    • If you were sent here from the Line 11 Worksheet, enter this amount on line 2 of that worksheet.

    • If you were sent here from Schedule 8812, enter this amount on line 4a of that form.

*If you have any Schedule K-1 amounts and you are not required to file Schedule SE, complete the appropriate line(s) of Schedule SE, Section A. Put your name and social security number on Schedule SE and attach it to your return.

Chapter Review

1) What is a nonrefundable credit?

2) What is a refundable credit?

3) Ed and Erma are Married Filing Jointly. They have a son, Ethan. Ethan is 14 and lived with them all year. What is the most adjusted gross income they can have and still be eligible for the Earned Income Credit?

4) Mike and Julie are divorced. Steven, their son, lives with Mike all year. Julie gets to claim Steven's dependency exemption as stated in the divorce decree. If all other requirements are met, who will receive the EIC for Steven? The Child Tax Credit?

5) What is earned income?

6) What is the significance of earned income for the EIC?

7) What is the penalty for a tax preparer that does not meet the due diligence requirements?

8) What form must a preparer complete and file with the return in order to follow the due diligence requirements?

9) What is Form 8862 and when must it be filed?

10) Is Child Tax Credit refundable or nonrefundable? What about Additional Child Tax Credit?

Exercise

Jordan Smith (555-44-3333) and Judith Smith (888-77-6666) are married and have a daughter, Joanna (223-32-2232). Jordan's birth date is November 1st, 1988 and he is a mechanic. Judith's date of birth is January 14th, 1993 and she is a homemaker. Joanna's date of birth is July 2nd, 2013. Joanna lived with Jordan and Judith all year. Neither wants to give $3 to the presidential election campaign fund. Jordan's W-2 follows.

a Employee's social security number 555-44-3333	OMB No. 1545-0008	Safe, accurate, FAST! Use	IRS e-file	Visit the IRS website at www.irs.gov/efile

b Employer identification number (EIN) 63-8877654	**1** Wages, tips, other compensation 28,510.35 **2** Federal income tax withheld 3,053.31
c Employer's name, address, and ZIP code TLC Automotive Center 300 Oil St. Your City, Your State, Your Zip Code	**3** Social security wages 28,510.35 **4** Social security tax withheld 1,767.64
	5 Medicare wages and tips 28,510.35 **6** Medicare tax withheld 413
	7 Social security tips **8** Allocated tips
d Control number	**9** **10** Dependent care benefits
e Employee's first name and initial Last name Suff.	**11** Nonqualified plans **12a** See instructions for box 12
Jordan Smith 64 Miracle Blvd. Your City, Your State, Your Zip Code	**13** Statutory employee ☐ Retirement plan ☐ Third-party sick pay ☐ **12b**
	14 Other **12c**
	12d
f Employee's address and ZIP code	

15 State	Employer's state ID number	16 State wages, tips, etc.	17 State income tax	18 Local wages, tips, etc.	19 Local income tax	20 Locality name
YS	2899723	28,510.35	1,125.75			

Form **W-2** Wage and Tax Statement   **2014**   Department of the Treasury—Internal Revenue Service

Copy B—To Be Filed With Employee's FEDERAL Tax Return.
This information is being furnished to the Internal Revenue Service.

Chapter 6 – Credits, Part II

We've covered Earned Income Credit, Child Tax Credit, and Additional Child Tax Credit. Now we will cover the rest of the credits. First, let's go over the rest of the nonrefundable credits.

Credit for Child and Dependent Care Expenses

The tests to determine if a taxpayer is eligible to claim the credit are outlined below, followed by the explanations of these tests.

- The care must be for a qualifying person.
- The taxpayer (and spouse if married) must have earned income. (There is an exception for a student spouse or a spouse not able to care for him or herself.)
- The child and dependent care expenses must be paid so the taxpayer (and spouse if married) can work or look for work. (Again, an exception applies for students.)
- The payments must be paid to someone not claimed as a dependent on the taxpayer's return.
- The filing status must be Single, Head of Household, Qualifying Widow(er), or Married Filing Jointly.
- The care provider information must be included on the return.
- If excludable or deductible dependent care benefits were paid to the taxpayer (or spouse if married), the total amount of the benefits must be less than the limit for a qualifying person.

The care must be for a qualifying person. A qualifying person is:

- The taxpayer's qualifying child who is their dependent and who was under age 13 when the care was provided. If the qualifying child is a child of divorced or separated parents or parents living apart (as discussed in Chapter 2) and the noncustodial parent is able to claim the dependency exemption, that parent cannot claim the dependent care credit. However, the custodial parent can claim the credit if they meet all of the other requirements, even if not claiming the dependency exemption.
- The taxpayer's spouse who was physically or mentally not able to care for himself or herself and lived with you for more than half the year.
- A person who was physically or mentally not able to care for himself or herself, lived with the taxpayer for more than half the year, and either:
  - o Was the taxpayer's dependent, or
  - o Would have been their dependent except that:
    - He or she received gross income of $3,950 or more,
    - He or she filed a joint return, or
    - The taxpayer (or spouse if MFJ) could be claimed as a dependent on someone else's return.

The taxpayer (and spouse if married) must have earned income. Earned income includes wages, salaries, tips, other taxable employee compensation, and net earnings from self-employment. A net loss from self-employment reduces earned income. The taxpayer can also elect to add in their nontaxable combat pay if they choose. It doesn't matter if they made this election for EIC. They should compute the credit both ways and use whichever way results in the most credit. If both the taxpayer and spouse have nontaxable combat pay they may each make the election separately.

Exception for a student spouse or a spouse not able to care for self.
A spouse who is a full-time student or not able to care for himself or herself is treated as having earned income for every month or portion of a month the spouse is a student or disabled. If the taxpayer is claiming one qualifying person for the dependent care credit, the spouse's earned income is $250 per month or portion of a month. If the taxpayer is claiming two or more qualifying people, the spouse's earned income is $500 per month or portion of a month.

The child and dependent care expenses must be paid so the taxpayer (and spouse if married) can work or look for work. The expenses must be for the purpose of allowing the taxpayer (and spouse if married) to work. The work can be part-time or full-time. If the taxpayer is married, the taxpayer and spouse must be working or actively looking for work. Remember, if the expenses are so they can look for work but they don't find any, they will not be able to claim the credit unless they have earned income from another source or were a full time student.

Exception for a student spouse or a spouse not able to care for self.
The spouse is treated as working during any month they are a full-time student or was not able to care for him or herself.

The payments must be paid to someone not claimed as a dependent on the taxpayer's return. The taxpayer cannot include any amounts paid to:

- A dependent for whom the taxpayer (or spouse if married) can claim an exemption,
- The taxpayer's child who was under age 19 at the end of the year, even if they are not the taxpayer's dependent,
- A person who was the taxpayer's spouse any time during the year, or
- The parent of the qualifying child who is under age 13.

However, the taxpayer may include payments made to a relative that does not fall into the above categories even if the relative lived in the taxpayer's home.

The filing status must be Single, Head of Household, Qualifying Widow(er), or Married Filing Jointly. A taxpayer that is filing Married Filing Separately is not eligible for dependent care credit. They would only be eligible if they meet the requirements for *married but unmarried for tax purposes.*

The care provider information must be included on the return. In order to claim the dependent care credit the taxpayer must include the name, address, and identification number on the tax return. The identification number can be the employer identification number or the social security number, whichever applies. If the care provider is a tax-exempt organization, enter "Tax-Exempt" in place of the identification number. This information will be used by the IRS to match with the care provider's earnings. If the care provider refuses to give this information, attach a statement to the return explaining the refusal and what steps were taken to get the information.

If excludable or deductible dependent care benefits were paid to the taxpayer (or spouse if married), the total amount of benefits must be less than the limit for a qualifying person. Some employers provide dependent care benefits to their employees. Dependent care benefits include:

- Amounts the employer paid directly to the taxpayer or the care provider for the care of the taxpayer's qualifying person while the taxpayer works,
- The fair market value of care in a daycare facility provided or sponsored by the employer, and
- Pre-tax contributions you made under a dependent care flexible spending arrangement.

If the taxpayer receives dependent care benefits, page 2 of the Form 2441 (Illustration 6-2) must be completed. Employer provided dependent care benefits will be reported on Form W-2, box 10 (Illustration 6-1).

Qualifying Expenses

In order to claim the credit, the taxpayer must have qualifying dependent care expenses. The main purpose of the expense must be for the person's well-being and protection. Expenses for nursery school, pre-school, or similar programs for a child below the level of kindergarten qualify. Expenses for attending kindergarten or a higher grade do not qualify. After and before school care, however, does qualify.

Overnight camp is not considered a qualifying expense. Day camp expenses, however, do qualify. Transportation, provided by the care provider to transport the qualifying person from the home to the care provider's location, qualifies for the credit.

In-home care

Expenses for the in-home care of a qualifying individual do qualify for the dependent care credit. Incidental expenses such as cooking and minor house cleaning also qualify if they are incurred along with the care expenses. Keep in mind though that a taxpayer who pays a household worker wages of $1,900 or more for the year must pay the employer's share of social security and Medicare taxes. This will be done on a Schedule H which will be covered in the second half of the course.

Illustration 6-1

a Employee's social security number	OMB No. 1545-0008	Safe, accurate, FAST! Use IRS e-file	Visit the IRS website at www.irs.gov/efile
b Employer identification number (EIN)		1 Wages, tips, other compensation	2 Federal income tax withheld
c Employer's name, address, and ZIP code		3 Social security wages	4 Social security tax withheld
		5 Medicare wages and tips	6 Medicare tax withheld
		7 Social security tips	8 Allocated tips
d Control number		9	10 Dependent care benefits
e Employee's first name and initial Last name	Suff.	11 Nonqualified plans	12a See instructions for box 12 Code
		13 Statutory employee ☐ Retirement plan ☐ Third-party sick pay ☐	12b Code
		14 Other	12c Code
			12d Code
f Employee's address and ZIP code			

15 State Employer's state ID number	16 State wages, tips, etc.	17 State income tax	18 Local wages, tips, etc.	19 Local income tax	20 Locality name

Form **W-2** Wage and Tax Statement 2014 Department of the Treasury—Internal Revenue Service

Copy B—To Be Filed With Employee's FEDERAL Tax Return.
This information is being furnished to the Internal Revenue Service.

Form 2441

The Form 2441 (Illustration 6-2) must be filed to claim credit for child and dependent care expenses. It also must be filed if the taxpayer (or spouse if married) receives dependent care benefits.

Line 1: This line is where the taxpayer must identify the care provider. The total amount paid to each care provider is entered here also.

If the taxpayer received dependent care benefits, stop here and complete page 2 of the Form 2441.

Line 2: Enter the qualifying person's information and the amount paid for each on this line.

Line 3: Add the amounts on line 2, column c. The expenses for the child and dependent care credit are limited to $3,000 for one qualifying person and $6,000 for two or more. If the taxpayer had dependent care benefits and had to complete page 2, part III, enter the amount from line 31.

Line 4: This is where the amount of earned income of the taxpayer is entered.

Line 5: If the taxpayer is Married Filing Joint, the spouse's earned income is entered on this line. Remember if the spouse is disabled or a full-time student their earned income is $250 for each month they are disabled or a full-time student ($500 for more than one qualifying person). If the taxpayer is not married, enter the same amount here that was entered on line 4.

Line 10: Enter the amount from the Credit Limit Worksheet as found in the instructions for Form 2441:

Line 10
Credit Limit Worksheet

Complete this worksheet to figure the amount to enter on line 10.

1. Enter the amount from Form 1040, line 47; Form 1040A, line 28; or Form 1040NR, line 45 . . . . **1.** _____
2. Enter the amount from Form 1040, line 48; or Form 1040NR, line 46; Form 1040A filers enter -0- . . . . . **2.** _____
3. Subtract line 2 from line 1. Also enter this amount on Form 2441, line 10. But if zero or less, **stop**; you cannot take the credit . . . . **3.** _____

Line 12: Enter here the total amount of dependent care benefits received by the taxpayer.

Line 13: Some employer provided dependent care plans allow the employee to carry forward any unused amount from the prior year to be used during a grace period. Any of these amounts will be entered on this line.

Line 14: If any amount was included on line 14, that was forfeited (not received because the expense was not incurred) or carried forward to use during a grace period, enter that amount on this line.

Line 16: Enter the total expenses paid for the qualifying care on this line.

Line 18: Enter the taxpayer's earned income.

Line 19: If the taxpayer is Married Filing Joint, enter the spouse's earned income here. Remember the rule for a student spouse or a spouse that cannot care for him or herself. If the taxpayer is not Married Filing Joint, enter the same amount that's on line 18.

Line 22: Enter the amount that is included in line 12 that the taxpayer received from their sole proprietorship or partnership.

Line 24: If the taxpayer received dependent care benefits from their sole proprietorship or partnership, this amount would be deducted on the Schedule C, Schedule E, or Schedule F, whichever form applies.

Line 25: The amount on this line will be excluded from the taxable income.

Line 26: If there is an amount on this line, the taxpayer will be taxed on this part of the dependent care benefits received. This amount will be included on Form 1040, line 7. Enter "DCB" on the dotted line next to line 7.

Line 30: Complete Line 2 on the front of the form. Be sure the amount from line 32 (excluded dependent care benefits) are not included in the line 2 amount.

Line 31: These are the qualifying expenses that are eligible for the dependent care credit.

Illustration 6-2

Form 2441 — Child and Dependent Care Expenses

Form **2441**

Child and Dependent Care Expenses

▶ Attach to Form 1040, Form 1040A, or Form 1040NR.

▶ Information about Form 2441 and its separate instructions is at *www.irs.gov/form2441.*

Department of the Treasury
Internal Revenue Service (99)

OMB No. 1545-0074

20**14**

Attachment Sequence No. **21**

Name(s) shown on return

Your social security number

Part I — **Persons or Organizations Who Provided the Care**—You **must** complete this part.
(If you have more than two care providers, see the instructions.)

1	(a) Care provider's name	(b) Address (number, street, apt. no., city, state, and ZIP code)	(c) Identifying number (SSN or EIN)	(d) Amount paid (see instructions)

Did you receive **dependent care benefits?**
No ——▶ Complete only Part II below.
Yes ——▶ Complete Part III on the back next.

Caution. If the care was provided in your home, you may owe employment taxes. If you do, you cannot file Form 1040A. For details, see the instructions for Form 1040, line 60a, or Form 1040NR, line 59a.

Part II — **Credit for Child and Dependent Care Expenses**

2 Information about your **qualifying person(s).** If you have more than two qualifying persons, see the instructions.

(a) Qualifying person's name First	Last	(b) Qualifying person's social security number	(c) Qualified expenses you incurred and paid in 2014 for the person listed in column (a)

3 Add the amounts in column (c) of line 2. **Do not** enter more than $3,000 for one qualifying person or $6,000 for two or more persons. If you completed Part III, enter the amount from line 31 ... **3**

4 Enter your **earned income.** See instructions ... **4**

5 If married filing jointly, enter your spouse's earned income (if you or your spouse was a student or was disabled, see the instructions); **all others,** enter the amount from line 4 ... **5**

6 Enter the **smallest** of line 3, 4, or 5 ... **6**

7 Enter the amount from Form 1040, line 38; Form 1040A, line 22; or Form 1040NR, line 37. ... **7**

8 Enter on line 8 the decimal amount shown below that applies to the amount on line 7

If line 7 is: Over	But not over	Decimal amount is	If line 7 is: Over	But not over	Decimal amount is
$0	15,000	.35	$29,000	31,000	.27
15,000	17,000	.34	31,000	33,000	.26
17,000	19,000	.33	33,000	35,000	.25
19,000	21,000	.32	35,000	37,000	.24
21,000	23,000	.31	37,000	39,000	.23
23,000	25,000	.30	39,000	41,000	.22
25,000	27,000	.29	41,000	43,000	.21
27,000	29,000	.28	43,000	No limit	.20

8 X.

9 Multiply line 6 by the decimal amount on line 8. If you paid 2013 expenses in 2014, see the instructions ... **9**

10 Tax liability limit. Enter the amount from the Credit Limit Worksheet in the instructions. ... **10**

11 **Credit for child and dependent care expenses.** Enter the **smaller** of line 9 or line 10 here and on Form 1040, line 49; Form 1040A, line 31; or Form 1040NR, line 47 ... **11**

For Paperwork Reduction Act Notice, see your tax return instructions.

Cat. No. 11862M

Form **2441** (2014)

6-6

Illustration 6-2 continued

Part III	**Dependent Care Benefits**		
12	Enter the total amount of **dependent care benefits** you received in 2014. Amounts you received as an employee should be shown in box 10 of your Form(s) W-2. **Do not** include amounts reported as wages in box 1 of Form(s) W-2. If you were self-employed or a partner, include amounts you received under a dependent care assistance program from your sole proprietorship or partnership	**12**	
13	Enter the amount, if any, you carried over from 2013 and used in 2014 during the grace period. See instructions	**13**	
14	Enter the amount, if any, you forfeited or carried forward to 2015. See instructions . . .	**14** ( )
15	Combine lines 12 through 14. See instructions	**15**	
16	Enter the total amount of **qualified expenses** incurred in 2014 for the care of the **qualifying person(s)** . . . **16**		
17	Enter the **smaller** of line 15 or 16 . . . . **17**		
18	Enter your **earned income.** See instructions . . . **18**		
19	Enter the amount shown below that applies to you.		
	• If married filing jointly, enter your spouse's earned income (if you or your spouse was a student or was disabled, see the instructions for line 5). • If married filing separately, see instructions. • All others, enter the amount from line 18. } . . . **19**		
20	Enter the **smallest** of line 17, 18, or 19 . . . . . . **20**		
21	Enter $5,000 ($2,500 if married filing separately **and** you were required to enter your spouse's earned income on line 19). **21**		
22	Is any amount on line 12 from your sole proprietorship or partnership? (Form 1040A filers go to line 25.) ☐ **No.** Enter -0-. ☐ **Yes.** Enter the amount here	**22**	
23	Subtract line 22 from line 15 . . . . **23**		
24	**Deductible benefits.** Enter the **smallest** of line 20, 21, or 22. Also, include this amount on the appropriate line(s) of your return. See instructions	**24**	
25	**Excluded benefits. Form 1040 and 1040NR filers:** If you checked "No" on line 22, enter the smaller of line 20 or 21. Otherwise, subtract line 24 from the smaller of line 20 or line 21. If zero or less, enter -0-. **Form 1040A filers:** Enter the **smaller** of line 20 or line 21 . .	**25**	
26	**Taxable benefits. Form 1040 and 1040NR filers:** Subtract line 25 from line 23. If zero or less, enter -0-. Also, include this amount on Form 1040, line 7, or Form 1040NR, line 8. On the dotted line next to Form 1040, line 7, or Form 1040NR, line 8, enter "DCB." **Form 1040A filers:** Subtract line 25 from line 15. Also, include this amount on Form 1040A, line 7. In the space to the left of line 7, enter "DCB"	**26**	

To claim the child and dependent care
credit, complete lines 27 through 31 below.

27	Enter $3,000 ($6,000 if two or more qualifying persons)	**27**	
28	**Form 1040 and 1040NR filers:** Add lines 24 and 25. **Form 1040A filers:** Enter the amount from line 25	**28**	
29	Subtract line 28 from line 27. If zero or less, **stop.** You cannot take the credit. **Exception.** If you paid 2013 expenses in 2014, see the instructions for line 9	**29**	
30	Complete line 2 on the front of this form. **Do not** include in column (c) any benefits shown on line 28 above. Then, add the amounts in column (c) and enter the total here.	**30**	
31	Enter the **smaller** of line 29 or 30. Also, enter this amount on line 3 on the front of this form and complete lines 4 through 11	**31**	

Form **2441** (2014)

Example: Greg Gorman (232-32-2323) is single and has a son, Garth (554-45-4455). Garth is 9 years old. Greg paid Funtime Daycare $2,300 for Garth to attend their daycare in 2014. Funtime Daycare is located at 333 Kid Ave, Your City, Your State, Your Zip code. Their EIN number is 32-2223311. Greg's Form W-2 follows. Greg's AGI is $33,395 and his tax liability on the return is $1,809. Greg is eligible to receive $263 of Credit for Child and Dependent care expenses (Illustration 6-3).

a Employee's social security number 232-32-2323	OMB No. 1545-0008	Safe, accurate, FAST! Use	irs e~file	Visit the IRS website at www.irs.gov/efile

b Employer identification number (EIN) 63-9876543	1 Wages, tips, other compensation 39,395.00	2 Federal income tax withheld 3,122.00
c Employer's name, address, and ZIP code	3 Social security wages 39,395.00	4 Social security tax withheld 2,442.49
Mega Grocery 430 Potato Lane Your City, Your State, Your Zip Code	5 Medicare wages and tips 39,395.00	6 Medicare tax withheld 484.23
	7 Social security tips	8 Allocated tips
d Control number	9	10 Dependent care benefits 1,250.00
e Employee's first name and initial Last name Suff.	11 Nonqualified plans	12a See instructions for box 12
Greg Gorman 234 Shot St., Apt. 22 Your City, Your State, Your Zip Code	13 Statutory employee ☐ Retirement plan ☐ Third-party sick pay ☐	12b
	14 Other	12c
		12d
f Employee's address and ZIP code		

15 State YS	Employer's state ID number 639876543	16 State wages, tips, etc. 39,395.00	17 State income tax 595.00	18 Local wages, tips, etc.	19 Local income tax	20 Locality name

Form **W-2** Wage and Tax Statement   **2014**   Department of the Treasury—Internal Revenue Service

Copy B—To Be Filed With Employee's FEDERAL Tax Return.
This information is being furnished to the Internal Revenue Service.

Line 10

Credit Limit Worksheet

Complete this worksheet to figure the amount to enter on line 10.

1. Enter the amount from Form 1040, line 47; Form 1040A, line 28; or Form 1040NR, line 45 . . . .   1. _____1,809_____

2. Enter the amount from Form 1040, line 48; or Form 1040NR, line 46; Form 1040A filers enter -0- . . . . . .   2. _____0_____

3. Subtract line 2 from line 1. Also enter this amount on Form 2441, line 10. But if zero or less, **stop**; you cannot take the credit . . . .   3. _____1,809_____

Illustration 6-3

Form **2441**	**Child and Dependent Care Expenses**		OMB No. 1545-0074
Department of the Treasury Internal Revenue Service (99)	▶ Attach to Form 1040, Form 1040A, or Form 1040NR. ▶ Information about Form 2441 and its separate instructions is at *www.irs.gov/form2441*.	1040 1040A 1040NR 2441	20**14** Attachment Sequence No. **21**

Name(s) shown on return	Your social security number
Greg Gorman	232-32-2323

Part I **Persons or Organizations Who Provided the Care**—You **must** complete this part.
(If you have more than two care providers, see the instructions.)

1	**(a)** Care provider's name	**(b)** Address (number, street, apt. no., city, state, and ZIP code)	**(c)** Identifying number (SSN or EIN)	**(d)** Amount paid (see instructions)
	Funtime Daycare	333 Kid Ave., Your City, Your State, Your Zip Code	32-2223311	2,300 00

Did you receive **dependent care benefits?** — No ——▶ Complete only Part II below.
— Yes ——▶ Complete Part III on the back next.

Caution. If the care was provided in your home, you may owe employment taxes. If you do, you cannot file Form 1040A. For details, see the instructions for Form 1040, line 60a, or Form 1040NR, line 59a.

Part II **Credit for Child and Dependent Care Expenses**

2 Information about your **qualifying person(s)**. If you have more than two qualifying persons, see the instructions.

(a) Qualifying person's name		(b) Qualifying person's social security number	(c) **Qualified expenses** you incurred and paid in 2014 for the person listed in column (a)
First	Last		
Garth	Gorman	554-45-4455	1,050 00

3	Add the amounts in column (c) of line 2. **Do not** enter more than $3,000 for one qualifying person or $6,000 for two or more persons. If you completed Part III, enter the amount from line 31	**3**	1,050	00
4	Enter your **earned income.** See instructions	**4**	39,395	00
5	If married filing jointly, enter your spouse's earned income (if you or your spouse was a student or was disabled, see the instructions); **all others**, enter the amount from line 4 .	**5**	39,395	00
6	Enter the **smallest** of line 3, 4, or 5	**6**	1,050	00
7	Enter the amount from Form 1040, line 38; Form 1040A, line 22; or Form 1040NR, line 37.	**7**	33,395 00	

8 Enter on line 8 the decimal amount shown below that applies to the amount on line 7

If line 7 is:				If line 7 is:		
Over	But not over	Decimal amount is		Over	But not over	Decimal amount is
$0—	15,000	.35		$29,000—	31,000	.27
15,000—	17,000	.34		31,000—	33,000	.26
17,000—	19,000	.33		33,000—	35,000	.25
19,000—	21,000	.32		35,000—	37,000	.24
21,000—	23,000	.31		37,000—	39,000	.23
23,000—	25,000	.30		39,000—	41,000	.22
25,000—	27,000	.29		41,000—	43,000	.21
27,000—	29,000	.28		43,000—No limit		.20

8 X . 25

9	Multiply line 6 by the decimal amount on line 8. If you paid 2013 expenses in 2014, see the instructions	**9**	263	00
10	Tax liability limit. Enter the amount from the Credit Limit Worksheet in the instructions. **10** 1,809 00			
11	**Credit for child and dependent care expenses.** Enter the **smaller** of line 9 or line 10 here and on Form 1040, line 49; Form 1040A, line 31; or Form 1040NR, line 47	**11**	263	00

For Paperwork Reduction Act Notice, see your tax return instructions. Cat. No. 11862M Form **2441** (2014)

Illustration 6-3 continued

	Part III	**Dependent Care Benefits**			

12 Enter the total amount of **dependent care benefits** you received in 2014. Amounts you received as an employee should be shown in box 10 of your Form(s) W-2. **Do not** include amounts reported as wages in box 1 of Form(s) W-2. If you were self-employed or a partner, include amounts you received under a dependent care assistance program from your sole proprietorship or partnership . . . . **12** | 1,250 | 00

13 Enter the amount, if any, you carried over from 2013 and used in 2014 during the grace period. See instructions **13**

14 Enter the amount, if any, you forfeited or carried forward to 2015. See instructions . . . **14** (|)

15 Combine lines 12 through 14. See instructions . . . . **15** | 1,250 | 00

16 Enter the total amount of **qualified expenses** incurred in 2014 for the care of the **qualifying person(s)** . . . **16** | 2,300 | 00

17 Enter the **smaller** of line 15 or 16 . . . . . . **17** | 1,250 | 00

18 Enter your **earned income.** See instructions . . . . **18** | 39,395 | 00

19 Enter the amount shown below that applies to you.

- If married filing jointly, enter your spouse's earned income (if you or your spouse was a student or was disabled, see the instructions for line 5).
- If married filing separately, see instructions.
- All others, enter the amount from line 18.

19 | 39,395 | 00

20 Enter the **smallest** of line 17, 18, or 19 . . . . . . **20** | 1,250 | 00

21 Enter $5,000 ($2,500 if married filing separately **and** you were required to enter your spouse's earned income on line 19) . . . . **21** | 5,000 | 00

22 Is any amount on line 12 from your sole proprietorship or partnership? (Form 1040A filers go to line 25.)

☑ **No.** Enter -0-.

☐ **Yes.** Enter the amount here . . . . **22** | 0 | 00

23 Subtract line 22 from line 15 . . . . **23** | 1,250 | 00

24 **Deductible benefits.** Enter the **smallest** of line 20, 21, or 22. Also, include this amount on the appropriate line(s) of your return. See instructions . . . . **24** | 0 | 00

25 **Excluded benefits. Form 1040 and 1040NR filers:** If you checked "No" on line 22, enter the smaller of line 20 or 21. Otherwise, subtract line 24 from the smaller of line 20 or line 21. If zero or less, enter -0-. **Form 1040A filers:** Enter the **smaller** of line 20 or line 21 . . **25** | 1,250 | 00

26 **Taxable benefits. Form 1040 and 1040NR filers:** Subtract line 25 from line 23. If zero or less, enter -0-. Also, include this amount on Form 1040, line 7, or Form 1040NR, line 8. On the dotted line next to Form 1040, line 7, or Form 1040NR, line 8, enter "DCB." **Form 1040A filers:** Subtract line 25 from line 15. Also, include this amount on Form 1040A, line 7. In the space to the left of line 7, enter "DCB". . . . . **26** | 0 | 00

To claim the child and dependent care
credit, complete lines 27 through 31 below.

27 Enter $3,000 ($6,000 if two or more qualifying persons) . . . . **27** | 3,000 | 00

28 **Form 1040 and 1040NR filers:** Add lines 24 and 25. **Form 1040A filers:** Enter the amount from line 25 . . . . **28** | 1,250 | 00

29 Subtract line 28 from line 27. If zero or less, **stop.** You cannot take the credit. **Exception.** If you paid 2013 expenses in 2014, see the instructions for line 9 . . . . . **29** | 1,750 | 00

30 Complete line 2 on the front of this form. **Do not** include in column (c) any benefits shown on line 28 above. Then, add the amounts in column (c) and enter the total here. . . . . **30** | 1,050 | 00

31 Enter the **smaller** of line 29 or 30. Also, enter this amount on line 3 on the front of this form and complete lines 4 through 11 . . . . **31** | 1,050 | 00

Form **2441** (2014)

Credit for the Elderly or the Disabled

We are not going to spend much time on this credit as most taxpayers do not qualify for it. To claim this credit, mark box c on line 54 of Form 1040 and write Schedule R on the line next to box c. A Schedule R (Illustration 6-4) must then be completed and filed with the return. This credit is based on the taxpayer's filing status, age, and income. For a Married Filing Joint taxpayer, it is also based on the spouse's filing status, age, and income. To qualify for this credit, the taxpayer must be:

- Age 65 or older at the end of 2014, or
- Under age 65 at the end of 2014 and meet all of the following conditions:
    - The taxpayer was permanently and totally disabled on the date the taxpayer retired.
    - The taxpayer received taxable disability income for 2014.
    - The taxpayer had not reached mandatory retirement age on January 1st, 2014.
- Filing using a filing status other than Married Filing Separately.

The taxpayer's income limit must also be under the amounts in the following chart:

| If you are... | THEN you generally cannot take the credit if: | |
	The amount on Form 1040 line 38 is...	Or you received...
Single, head of household, or qualifying widow(er)	$17,500 or more	$5,000 or more of nontaxable social security or other nontaxable pensions, annuities, or disability income
Married filing jointly and only one spouse is eligible for the credit	$20,000 or more	$5,000 or more of nontaxable social security or other nontaxable pensions, annuities, or disability income
Married filing jointly and both spouses are eligible for the credit	$25,000 or more	$7,500 or more of nontaxable social security or other nontaxable pensions, annuities, or disability income
Married filing separately and you lived apart from your spouse for all of 2013	$12,500 or more	$3,750 or more of nontaxable social security or other nontaxable pensions, annuities, or disability income

Note: If the taxpayer files using the Married Filing Separately filing status and lived with the spouse at any time during 2014, the taxpayer does not qualify for the credit.

Illustration 6-4

Credit for the Elderly or the Disabled

▶ Complete and attach to Form 1040A or 1040.
▶ **Information about Schedule R and its separate instructions is at**
www.irs.gov/scheduler.

1040A
1040

R

OMB No. 1545-0074

20**14**

Attachment
Sequence No. **16**

Name(s) shown on Form 1040A or 1040

Your social security number

You may be able to take this credit and reduce your tax if by the end of 2014:

• You were age 65 or older　　**or**　　• You were under age 65, you retired on **permanent and total** disability, and
　　　　　　　　　　　　　　　　　　　　you received taxable disability income.

But you must also meet other tests. See instructions.

TIP In most cases, the IRS can figure the credit for you. See instructions.

Part I	**Check the Box for Your Filing Status and Age**	
If your filing status is:	**And by the end of 2014:**	**Check only one box:**

Single, Head of household, or Qualifying widow(er)	**1** You were 65 or older	**1**	☐
	2 You were under 65 and you retired on permanent and total disability . .	**2**	☐
Married filing jointly	**3** Both spouses were 65 or older	**3**	☐
	4 Both spouses were under 65, but only one spouse retired on permanent and total disability	**4**	☐
	5 Both spouses were under 65, and both retired on permanent and total disability	**5**	☐
	6 One spouse was 65 or older, and the other spouse was under 65 and retired on permanent and total disability	**6**	☐
	7 One spouse was 65 or older, and the other spouse was under 65 and **not** retired on permanent and total disability	**7**	☐
Married filing separately	**8** You were 65 or older and you lived apart from your spouse for all of 2014 .	**8**	☐
	9 You were under 65, you retired on permanent and total disability, and you lived apart from your spouse for all of 2014	**9**	☐

Did you check box 1, 3, 7, or 8?	── Yes ──▶	Skip Part II and complete Part III on the back.
	── No ──▶	Complete Parts II and III.

Part II	**Statement of Permanent and Total Disability** (Complete **only** if you checked box 2, 4, 5, 6, or 9 above.)

If: 1 You filed a physician's statement for this disability for 1983 or an earlier year, or you filed or got a statement for tax years after 1983 and your physician signed line B on the statement, **and**

2 Due to your continued disabled condition, you were unable to engage in any substantial gainful activity in 2014, check this box . . . . ▶ ☐

• If you checked this box, you do not have to get another statement for 2014.

• If you **did not** check this box, have your physician complete the statement in the instructions. You **must** keep the statement for your records.

For Paperwork Reduction Act Notice, see your tax return instructions.　　　Cat. No. 11359K　　　**Schedule R (Form 1040A or 1040) 2014**

Illustration 6-4 continued

Part III	Figure Your Credit

10 If you checked (in Part I):   **Enter:**

Box 1, 2, 4, or 7 . . . .$5,000 ⎫

Box 3, 5, or 6 . . . .$7,500 ⎬ **10**

Box 8 or 9 . . . .$3,750 ⎭

┌─────────────────────┐

│ **Did you check** │   **Yes** ──────▶ You **must** complete line 11.

│ **box 2, 4, 5, 6,** │

│ **or 9 in Part I?** │   **No** ──────▶ Enter the amount from line 10

└─────────────────────┘   on line 12 and go to line 13.

11 If you checked (in Part I):

• Box 6, add $5,000 to the taxable disability income of the
   spouse who was under age 65. Enter the total.   ⎫

• Box 2, 4, or 9, enter your taxable disability income.   ⎬ **11**

• Box 5, add your taxable disability income to your spouse's ⎭
   taxable disability income. Enter the total.

(TIP)   For more details on what to include on line 11, see *Figure Your Credit* in the instructions.

12 If you completed line 11, enter the **smaller** of line 10 or line 11. **All others,** enter the
amount from line 10 . . . . **12**

13 Enter the following pensions, annuities, or disability income that
you (and your spouse if filing jointly) received in 2014.

a Nontaxable part of social security benefits and nontaxable part
of railroad retirement benefits treated as social security (see
instructions). **13a**

b Nontaxable veterans' pensions and any other pension, annuity,
or disability benefit that is excluded from income under any
other provision of law (see instructions). **13b**

c Add lines 13a and 13b. (Even though these income items are
not taxable, they **must** be included here to figure your credit.) If
you did not receive any of the types of nontaxable income listed
on line 13a or 13b, enter -0- on line 13c **13c**

14 Enter the amount from Form 1040A, line
22, or Form 1040, line 38 . . . . . **14**

15 If you checked (in Part I):   **Enter:**

Box 1 or 2 . . . . . . $7,500 ⎫

Box 3, 4, 5, 6, or 7 . . . . $10,000 ⎬ **15**

Box 8 or 9 . . . . . . $5,000 ⎭

16 Subtract line 15 from line 14. If zero or
less, enter -0- **16**

17 Enter one-half of line 16 . . . . **17**

18 Add lines 13c and 17 . . . . **18**

19 Subtract line 18 from line 12. If zero or less, **stop;** you **cannot** take the credit. Otherwise,
go to line 20 . . . . **19**

20 Multiply line 19 by 15% (.15). **20**

21 Tax liability limit. Enter the amount from the Credit Limit Worksheet in the instructions . **21**

22 **Credit for the elderly or the disabled.** Enter the **smaller** of line 20 or line 21. Also enter
this amount on Form 1040A, line 32, or include on Form 1040, line 54 (check box **c** and
enter "Sch R" on the line next to that box) **22**

Education Credits

There are two different education credits: the American Opportunity credit and the Lifetime Learning credit. The American Opportunity credit is a nonrefundable and refundable credit. The Lifetime learning credit is nonrefundable. These credits are based on qualified education expenses paid to an eligible postsecondary educational institution.

Who is eligible for the credits

The credit may be taken for eligible education expenses paid on behalf of the taxpayer, the spouse, or a dependent claimed on the tax return. If the taxpayer or the spouse is a student and eligible for the credit and someone else pays the education expenses on behalf of the student, the expenses are treated as having been paid by the student. If the student can be claimed as a dependent on someone's tax return, the expenses are treated as having been paid by whoever claims the dependency exemption. If the eligible education expenses are paid with proceeds of a loan, those expenses qualify for the credit.

The taxpayer may not take the credits if any of the following apply:

- The taxpayer is claimed as a dependent on another person's tax return.
- The filing status of the taxpayer is Married Filing Separately.
- The adjusted gross income is one of the following:
  - $180,000 or more if MFJ, or $90,000 if S, HH, or QW, and the taxpayer is claiming the American opportunity credit.
  - $128,000 or more and the filing status is MFJ, and the taxpayer is claiming the Lifetime learning credit.
  - $64,000 or more and the filing status is S, HH, or QW, and the taxpayer is claiming the Lifetime learning credit.
- The taxpayer (or spouse if MFJ) was a nonresident alien for any part of the tax year and the nonresident alien did not elect to be treated as a resident alien.

Rules that apply to both Education credits

We need to discuss a few terms that will apply to both credits.

Qualified Education Expenses

Amounts paid in the tax year for tuition and fees required for the student's enrollment or attendance at an eligible educational institution. These amounts do not include:

- Room and board, insurance, medical expenses (including student health fees), transportation, or other similar personal, living, or family expenses.
- Course-related books, supplies, equipment, and nonacademic activities, except for fees required to be paid to the institution as a condition of enrollment or attendance if claiming the Lifetime learning credit.
- Any course or other education involving sports, games, or hobbies, or any noncredit course, unless such course or other education is part of the student's degree program (or if for the lifetime learning credit, helps the student acquire or improve job skills).

Note: To clarify the eligibility of the cost of course-related books: this is only eligible if the books are not only required to be purchased to attend a course, but also required to be purchased from the educational institution. Otherwise, they are not eligible education expenses for the Lifetime learning credit. However, if the taxpayer is claiming the American opportunity credit, qualified education expenses *do* include amounts spent on books, supplies, and equipment needed for a course of study, whether or not the materials are purchased from the educational institution as a condition of enrollment or attendance.

Tax-Free Educational Assistance

Tax-free educational assistance includes tax-free scholarships, Pell grants, or tax-free employer-provided educational assistance. Generally, the qualified education expenses must be reduced by any tax-free educational assistance the taxpayer received.

Coordination with Pell grants and other scholarships or fellowship grants.

If the student has a scholarship or fellowship grant that has terms allowing it to be used for expenses other than qualified education expenses, (for example, room and board), the taxpayer may choose to include part or all of the scholarship or grant in income to increases the education credit. Let's look at a couple of examples to help clarify this.

Example: Jennifer has a dependent daughter, Sue, who received a Pell grant in the amount of $5,000. The Pell grant may be used for expenses other than the qualified education expenses, according to its terms. She has qualified education expenses of $5,000 and she has $3,000 in room and board expenses. She used the Pell grant for the qualified education expenses and paid the room and board with a student loan. The Pell grant is tax-free education assistance because she used it for qualified education expenses. Also, because those qualified education expenses were paid with tax-free educational assistance, they do not qualify for the education credit.

Example: Let's look at the same example, except Sue used the Pell grant to pay her room and board. The remaining $2,000 was used to pay a portion of the qualified education expenses. Because $3,000 of the Pell grant was used to pay expenses other than qualified education expenses, that $3,000 will be included in Sue's income. Jennifer can use the $3,000 of qualified education expenses not paid with the Pell grant for the education credit because that amount was not paid with tax-free educational assistance.

Note: As long as Jennifer meets the requirements to claim Sue on her return, the education expenses are treated as having been paid by Jennifer. However, Sue will be the one to include the Pell grant money in her income. If she had no other income, the $3,000 does not meet the filing requirement for a dependent. Therefore, Sue will not be required to file a return to claim the $3,000.

Refunds of Qualified Education Expenses

If the taxpayer received a refund for qualified education expenses that were paid, reduce the qualified education expenses by the amount of the refund.

Prepaid Expenses

If the qualified education expenses paid during the tax year were for an academic period that begins during the first 3 months of the following year, those expenses are to be included in the qualified education expenses for the tax year.

Eligible Educational Institution

An eligible educational institution is any accredited public, nonprofit, or proprietary (private) college, university, vocational school, or other postsecondary institution. The institution must be able to participate in a student aid program administered by the Department of education.

American Opportunity Credit

For the American Opportunity Credit, the maximum credit is $2,500 per student and 40% of the credit is refundable. To qualify for the American Opportunity credit, all of the following qualifications must apply:

- As of the beginning of the tax year, the student had not completed the first 4 years of post-secondary education (generally, the freshman through senior years of college).
- The student was enrolled in 2014 in a program that leads to a degree, certificate, or other recognized educational credential.
- The student was taking at least one-half the normal full-time workload for his or her course of study for at least one academic period beginning in 2014.
- The student had not been convicted of a felony for possessing or distributing a controlled substance.

The American Opportunity credit equals 100% of the first $2,000 and 25% of the next $2,000 of qualified expenses paid for each eligible student.

Lifetime Learning Credit

The taxpayer is eligible to claim the lifetime learning credit if the taxpayer, spouse, or dependent attended an eligible educational institution and paid qualified education expenses for the tax year. The lifetime learning credit equals 20% of up to $10,000 of qualified expenses. The maximum credit allowed is $2,000 per return.

No Double Benefit

The American opportunity credit and Lifetime learning credit cannot be taken for the same student in the same tax year. As we move on through the course, we will cover other tax benefits allowed for qualifying education expenses. The taxpayer may not claim two educational tax benefits for the same student with the same qualifying education expenses for the same tax year.

Form 8863

To claim one of the Education credits a Form 8863 (Illustration 6-5) must be filed. First, Part III must be filled out. A separate Part III must be completed for each individual for whom the taxpayer is claiming either education credit. Use the Adjusted Qualified Education Expense Worksheet to calculate the amount to enter on lines 27 if claiming the American Opportunity Credit or 31 if claiming the Lifetime Learning Credit. Then Part I and Part II must be completed if the taxpayer is claiming the American Opportunity Credit. Only Part II must be completed if the taxpayer is claiming the Lifetime Learning Credit. The following Credit Limit Worksheet must be completed for Line 19 of the Form 8863.

Adjusted Qualified Education Expenses Worksheet

See *Qualified Education Expenses*, earlier, before completing.

Complete a separate worksheet for each student for each academic period beginning or treated as beginning (see below) in 2014 for which you paid (or are treated as having paid) qualified education expenses in 2014.

1. Total qualified education expenses paid for or on behalf of the student in 2014 for the academic period . . . . _____

2. Less adjustments:

    a. Tax-free educational assistance received in 2014 allocable to the academic period . . . . _____

    b. Tax-free educational assistance received in 2015 (and before you file your 2014 tax return) allocable to the academic period . . . _____

    c. Refunds of qualified education expenses paid in 2014 if the refund is received in 2014 or in 2015 before you file your 2014 tax return . . . . _____

3. Total adjustments (add lines 2a, 2b, and 2c) . . . . _____

4. Adjusted qualified education expenses. Subtract line 3 from line 1. If zero or less, enter -0- . . . . _____

Credit Limit Worksheet
Complete this worksheet to figure the amount to enter on line 19.

1. Enter the amount from Form 8863, line 18 . . . . **1.** _____

2. Enter the amount from Form 8863, line 9 . . . . **2.** _____

3. Add lines 1 and 2 . . . . **3.** _____

4. Enter the amount from:
    Form 1040, line 47; or
    Form 1040A, line 30 . . . . **4.** _____

5. Enter the total of your credits from either:
    Form 1040, lines 48 and 49,
    and Schedule R, line 22; or
    Form 1040A, lines 31 and 32 . . . . . . **5.** _____

6. Subtract line 5 from line 4 . . . . **6.** _____

7. Enter the smaller of line 3 or line 6 here and on Form 8863, line 19 . . . . **7.** _____

Foreign Tax Credit

If the taxpayer pays income taxes to a foreign country on federally taxable income, they may take the taxes paid or accrued as either a credit or an itemized deduction. Here, we will discuss the credit. To take the credit, Form 1116 (Illustration 6-6) should be filed. If all of the following conditions apply, a Form 1116 does not need to be filed. The credit can be entered directly on Form 1040, line 47.

- All of the foreign source gross income was passive income, which generally includes interest and dividends
- All of the foreign source gross income and the foreign tax paid on it were reported to you on a qualified payee statement, which includes Form 1099-INT and Form 1099-DIV.
- The total of the creditable foreign taxes was not more than $300 ($600 if MFJ).
- The taxpayer makes the election to file this way.

This is all we will cover of the foreign tax credit. If it is encountered, additional research will be required.

Illustration 6-5

Form **8863**

Department of the Treasury
Internal Revenue Service (99)

Education Credits
(American Opportunity and Lifetime Learning Credits)

► Attach to Form 1040 or Form 1040A.
► **Information about Form 8863 and its separate instructions is at** *www.irs.gov/form8863.*

OMB No. 1545-0074

2014

Attachment
Sequence No. **50**

Name(s) shown on return

Your social security number

> ⚠ **CAUTION** *Complete a separate Part III on page 2 for each student for whom you are claiming either credit before you complete Parts I and II.*

Part I	**Refundable American Opportunity Credit**

1 After completing Part III for each student, enter the total of all amounts from all Parts III, line 30   . | **1** |

2 Enter: $180,000 if married filing jointly; $90,000 if single, head of household, or qualifying widow(er) | **2** |

3 Enter the amount from Form 1040, line 38, or Form 1040A, line 22. If you are filing Form 2555, 2555-EZ, or 4563, or you are excluding income from Puerto Rico, see Pub. 970 for the amount to enter   .   .   .   . | **3** |

4 Subtract line 3 from line 2. If zero or less, **stop;** you cannot take any education credit   .   .   .   . | **4** |

5 Enter: $20,000 if married filing jointly; $10,000 if single, head of household, or qualifying widow(er)   .   .   .   . | **5** |

6 If line 4 is:
  • Equal to or more than line 5, enter 1.000 on line 6   .   .   .   .
  • Less than line 5, divide line 4 by line 5. Enter the result as a decimal (rounded to at least three places)   .   .   .   . | **6** |

7 Multiply line 1 by line 6. **Caution:** If you were under age 24 at the end of the year **and** meet the conditions described in the instructions, you **cannot** take the refundable American opportunity credit; skip line 8, enter the amount from line 7 on line 9, and check this box   .   .   .   .   ► ☐ | **7** |

8 **Refundable American opportunity credit.** Multiply line 7 by 40% (.40). Enter the amount here and on Form 1040, line 68, or Form 1040A, line 44. Then go to line 9 below.   .   .   .   . | **8** |

Part II	**Nonrefundable Education Credits**

9 Subtract line 8 from line 7. Enter here and on line 2 of the Credit Limit Worksheet (see instructions) | **9** |

10 After completing Part III for each student, enter the total of all amounts from all Parts III, line 31. If zero, skip lines 11 through 17, enter -0- on line 18, and go to line 19   .   .   .   .   . | **10** |

11 Enter the smaller of line 10 or $10,000   .   .   .   . | **11** |

12 Multiply line 11 by 20% (.20)   .   .   .   . | **12** |

13 Enter: $128,000 if married filing jointly; $64,000 if single, head of household, or qualifying widow(er)   .   .   .   . | **13** |

14 Enter the amount from Form 1040, line 38, or Form 1040A, line 22. If you are filing Form 2555, 2555-EZ, or 4563, or you are excluding income from Puerto Rico, see Pub. 970 for the amount to enter   .   .   .   .   . | **14** |

15 Subtract line 14 from line 13. If zero or less, skip lines 16 and 17, enter -0- on line 18, and go to line 19   .   .   .   . | **15** |

16 Enter: $20,000 if married filing jointly; $10,000 if single, head of household, or qualifying widow(er)   .   .   .   . | **16** |

17 If line 15 is:
  • Equal to or more than line 16, enter 1.000 on line 17 and go to line 18
  • Less than line 16, divide line 15 by line 16. Enter the result as a decimal (rounded to at least three places)   .   .   .   .   .   . | **17** |

18 Multiply line 12 by line 17. Enter here and on line 1 of the Credit Limit Worksheet (see instructions) ► | **18** |

19 **Nonrefundable education credits.** Enter the amount from line 7 of the Credit Limit Worksheet (see instructions) here and on Form 1040, line 50, or Form 1040A, line 33   .   .   .   . | **19** |

For Paperwork Reduction Act Notice, see your tax return instructions.   Cat. No. 25379M   Form **8863** (2014)

Illustration 6-5 continued

Name(s) shown on return	Your social security number

> ⚠️ **CAUTION**
> *Complete Part III for each student for whom you are claiming either the American opportunity credit or lifetime learning credit. Use additional copies of Page 2 as needed for each student.*

Part III **Student and Educational Institution Information**
See instructions.

20 Student name (as shown on page 1 of your tax return)

21 Student social security number (as shown on page 1 of your tax return)

22 Educational institution information (see instructions)

a. Name of first educational institution	**b.** Name of second educational institution (if any)
(1) Address. Number and street (or P.O. box). City, town or post office, state, and ZIP code. If a foreign address, see instructions.	**(1)** Address. Number and street (or P.O. box). City, town or post office, state, and ZIP code. If a foreign address, see instructions.
(2) Did the student receive Form 1098-T from this institution for 2014? ☐ Yes ☐ No	**(2)** Did the student receive Form 1098-T from this institution for 2014? ☐ Yes ☐ No
(3) Did the student receive Form 1098-T from this institution for 2013 with Box 2 filled in and Box 7 checked? ☐ Yes ☐ No	**(3)** Did the student receive Form 1098-T from this institution for 2013 with Box 2 filled in and Box 7 checked? ☐ Yes ☐ No
If you checked "No" in **both (2) and (3)**, skip **(4)**.	If you checked "No" in **both (2) and (3)**, skip **(4)**.
(4) If you checked "Yes" in **(2)** or **(3)**, enter the institution's federal identification number (from Form 1098-T).	**(4)** If you checked "Yes" in **(2)** or **(3)**, enter the institution's federal identification number (from Form 1098-T).

23 Has the Hope Scholarship Credit or American opportunity credit been claimed for this student for any 4 tax years before 2014?
☐ Yes — **Stop!** Go to line 31 for this student. ☐ No — Go to line 24.

24 Was the student enrolled at least half-time for at least one academic period that began or is treated as having begun in 2014 at an eligible educational institution in a program leading towards a postsecondary degree, certificate, or other recognized postsecondary educational credential? (see instructions)
☐ Yes — Go to line 25. ☐ No — **Stop!** Go to line 31 for this student.

25 Did the student complete the first 4 years of post-secondary education before 2014?
☐ Yes — **Stop!** Go to line 31 for this student. ☐ No — Go to line 26.

26 Was the student convicted, before the end of 2014, of a felony for possession or distribution of a controlled substance?
☐ Yes — **Stop!** Go to line 31 for this student. ☐ No — Complete lines 27 through 30 for this student.

> ⚠️ **CAUTION**
> *You **cannot** take the American opportunity credit and the lifetime learning credit for the **same student** in the same year. If you complete lines 27 through 30 for this student, do not complete line 31.*

American Opportunity Credit

27 Adjusted qualified education expenses (see instructions). **Do not enter more than $4,000**	**27**	
28 Subtract $2,000 from line 27. If zero or less, enter -0-.	**28**	
29 Multiply line 28 by 25% (.25)	**29**	
30 If line 28 is zero, enter the amount from line 27. Otherwise, add $2,000 to the amount on line 29 and enter the result. Skip line 31. Include the total of all amounts from all Parts III, line 30 on Part I, line 1.	**30**	

Lifetime Learning Credit

31 Adjusted qualified education expenses (see instructions). Include the total of all amounts from all Parts III, line 31, on Part II, line 10.	**31**	

Form **8863** (2014)

Illustration 6-6

Form 1116

Department of the Treasury
Internal Revenue Service (99)

Foreign Tax Credit

(Individual, Estate, or Trust)
▶ Attach to Form 1040, 1040NR, 1041, or 990-T.
▶ Information about Form 1116 and its separate instructions is at *www.irs.gov/form1116*.

OMB No. 1545-0121

2014

Attachment
Sequence No. **19**

Name | Identifying number as shown on page 1 of your tax return

Use a separate Form 1116 for each category of income listed below. See **Categories of Income** in the instructions. Check only one box on each Form 1116. Report all amounts in U.S. dollars except where specified in Part II below.

a ☐ Passive category income
b ☐ General category income
c ☐ Section 901(j) income
d ☐ Certain income re-sourced by treaty
e ☐ Lump-sum distributions

f Resident of (name of country) ▶

Note: *If you paid taxes to only one foreign country or U.S. possession, use column A in Part I and line A in Part II. If you paid taxes to* **more than one** *foreign country or U.S. possession, use a separate column and line for each country or possession.*

Part I — Taxable Income or Loss From Sources Outside the United States (for Category Checked Above)

		Foreign Country or U.S. Possession			Total (Add cols. A, B, and C.)
		A	B	C	
g	Enter the name of the foreign country or U.S. possession . . . . ▶				
1a	Gross income from sources within country shown above and of the type checked above (see instructions): _____ _____ _____				1a
b	Check if line 1a is compensation for personal services as an employee, your total compensation from all sources is $250,000 or more, and you used an alternative basis to determine its source (see instructions) . . ▶ ☐				
	Deductions and losses (*Caution: See instructions*):				
2	Expenses **definitely related** to the income on line 1a (attach statement)				
3	Pro rata share of other deductions **not definitely related:**				
a	Certain itemized deductions or standard deduction (see instructions)				
b	Other deductions (attach statement)				
c	Add lines 3a and 3b				
d	Gross foreign source income (see instructions) .				
e	Gross income from all sources (see instructions) .				
f	Divide line 3d by line 3e (see instructions) . . .				
g	Multiply line 3c by line 3f				
4	Pro rata share of interest expense (see instructions):				
a	Home mortgage interest (use the Worksheet for Home Mortgage Interest in the instructions) . .				
b	Other interest expense				
5	Losses from foreign sources				
6	Add lines 2, 3g, 4a, 4b, and 5				6
7	Subtract line 6 from line 1a. Enter the result here and on line 15, page 2 . . . . ▶				7

Part II — Foreign Taxes Paid or Accrued (see instructions)

Country	Credit is claimed for taxes (you must check one)		Foreign taxes paid or accrued								
			In foreign currency				In U.S. dollars				
	(h) ☐ Paid		Taxes withheld at source on:			(n) Other foreign taxes paid or accrued	Taxes withheld at source on:			(r) Other foreign taxes paid or accrued	(s) Total foreign taxes paid or accrued (add cols. (o) through (r))
	(i) ☐ Accrued										
	(j) Date paid or accrued	(k) Dividends	(l) Rents and royalties	(m) Interest		(o) Dividends	(p) Rents and royalties	(q) Interest			
A											
B											
C											
8	Add lines A through C, column (s). Enter the total here and on line 9, page 2 . . . . ▶									8	

For Paperwork Reduction Act Notice, see instructions.

Cat. No. 11440U

Form **1116** (2014)

Retirement Savings Contribution Credit

The Retirement Savings Contribution Credit (also known as Saver's Credit) was created to promote saving funds for retirement. This credit may be able to be taken if the taxpayer made contributions (other than rollover) to a traditional or Roth IRA, elective deferrals to a 401(k), 403(b), governmental 457, SEP, or SIMPLE plan, voluntary employee contributions to a qualified retirement plan as defined in section 4974(c), or contributions to a 501(c)(18)(D) plan.

If the person making the contributions was born after January 1, 1995 or claimed as a dependent on someone else's tax return, they may not take the credit. The credit may not be taken, also, if the person making the contributions was a student. They were a student if during any part of 5 calendar months they were enrolled as a full-time student at a school or they took a full-time, on-farm training course given by a school or a state, county, or local government agency.

The taxpayer may not take this credit if their AGI is more than:

- $30,000 and they are filing Single or Married Filing Separate.
- $45,000 and they are filing Head of Household.
- $60,000 and they are filing Married Filing Joint.

Form 8880

A Form 8880 (Illustration 6-7) must be filed to take the Retirement Savings Contribution Credit.

Lines 1 and 2: Enter the contributions made to the qualifying retirement plans on the line to which it applies.

Line 4: Any distributions made from the following plans after 2010 and before the due date of the tax return will be entered here. If the taxpayer is MFJ, add the amounts of both spouses together and enter the total amount in both columns.

- Traditional or Roth IRAs.
- 401(k), 403(b), governmental 457, 501(c)(18)(D), SEP, or SIMPLE plans.
- Qualified retirement plans as defined in section 4974(c) (including the federal Thrift Savings Plan).

Illustration 6-7

Form **8880**

Department of the Treasury
Internal Revenue Service

Credit for Qualified Retirement Savings Contributions

▶ Attach to Form 1040, Form 1040A, or Form 1040NR.
▶ Information about Form 8880 and its instructions is at *www.irs.gov/form8880*.

OMB No. 1545-0074

20**14**

Attachment
Sequence No. **54**

Name(s) shown on return

Your social security number

⚠ **CAUTION**

You **cannot** take this credit if **either** of the following applies.

- The amount on Form 1040, line 38; Form 1040A, line 22; or Form 1040NR, line 37 is more than $30,000 ($45,000 if head of household; $60,000 if married filing jointly).
- The person(s) who made the qualified contribution or elective deferral **(a)** was born after January 1, 1997, **(b)** is claimed as a dependent on someone else's 2014 tax return, or **(c)** was a **student** (see instructions).

		(a) You	(b) Your spouse
1	Traditional and Roth IRA contributions for 2014. **Do not** include rollover contributions **1**		
2	Elective deferrals to a 401(k) or other qualified employer plan, voluntary employee contributions, and 501(c)(18)(D) plan contributions for 2014 (see instructions) **2**		
3	Add lines 1 and 2 . . . . **3**		
4	Certain distributions received **after** 2011 and **before** the due date (including extensions) of your 2014 tax return (see instructions). If married filing jointly, include **both** spouses' amounts in **both** columns. See instructions for an exception **4**		
5	Subtract line 4 from line 3. If zero or less, enter -0- **5**		
6	In each column, enter the **smaller** of line 5 or $2,000 . . . . . **6**		
7	Add the amounts on line 6. If zero, **stop;** you cannot take this credit **7**		
8	Enter the amount from Form 1040, line 38*; Form 1040A, line 22; or Form 1040NR, line 37 . . . . **8**		

9   Enter the applicable decimal amount shown below:

If line 8 is—		And your filing status is—		
Over—	But not over—	Married filing jointly	Head of household	Single, Married filing separately, or Qualifying widow(er)
		Enter on line 9—		
---	$18,000	.5	.5	.5
$18,000	$19,500	.5	.5	.2
$19,500	$27,000	.5	.5	.1
$27,000	$29,250	.5	.2	.1
$29,250	$30,000	.5	.1	.1
$30,000	$36,000	.5	.1	.0
$36,000	$39,000	.2	.1	.0
$39,000	$45,000	.1	.1	.0
$45,000	$60,000	.1	.0	.0
$60,000	---	.0	.0	.0

9   X .

Note: *If line 9 is zero, **stop;** you cannot take this credit.*

10	Multiply line 7 by line 9 . . . . **10**	
11	Limitation based on tax liability. Enter the amount from the Credit Limit Worksheet in the instructions **11**	
12	**Credit for qualified retirement savings contributions.** Enter the **smaller** of line 10 or line 11 here and on Form 1040, line 51; Form 1040A, line 34; or Form 1040NR, line 48 . . . . **12**	

*See Pub. 590-A for the amount to enter if you are filing Form 2555, 2555-EZ, or 4563 or you are excluding income from Puerto Rico.

For Paperwork Reduction Act Notice, see your tax return instructions.   Cat. No. 33394D   Form **8880** (2014)

Residential Energy Credits

The Residential Energy Credits consist of the Nonbusiness energy property credit and Residential energy efficient property credit. Form 5695 (Illustration 6-8) must be used to claim either credit.

Residential Energy Efficient Property Credit

The taxpayer may be able to take a credit of 30% of their costs of qualified solar electric property, solar water heating property, small wind energy property, geothermal heat pump property, and fuel cell property. This credit includes labor costs properly allocable to the onsite preparation, assembly, or original installation of the property and for piping or wiring to interconnect such property to the home. The credit amounts for costs paid for qualified fuel cell property is limited to $500 for each one-half kilowatt of capacity of the property.

Nonbusiness Energy Property Credit

The Nonbusiness energy credit can be taken by the taxpayer if they made energy saving improvements to their home located in the United States during 2014. The credit is equal to 10% of the costs paid or incurred during the tax year for any qualified energy efficiency improvements and any residential energy property. The credit is limited as follows:

- A total combined credit limit of $500 for all tax years after 2005.
- A combined credit limit of $200 for windows for all tax years after 2005.
- A credit limit for residential energy property costs for 2014 of $50 for any advanced main air circulating fan; $150 for any qualified natural gas, propane, or oil furnace or hot water boiler; and $300 for any item of energy efficient building property.

Qualified energy efficiency improvements

The qualified energy efficiency must have been installed on or in the taxpayer's main home that they owned during 2014 located in the United States. The original use of the improvement must begin with the taxpayer and must be expected to remain in use at least 5 years. Qualified energy efficiency improvements are the following building envelope components:

- Insulation material or system that is specifically and primarily designed to reduce the heat loss or gain of a home when installed in or on such a home.

- Exterior windows (including certain storm windows and skylights), exterior doors, any metal roof with appropriate pigmented coatings, or asphalt roof with appropriate cooling granules that are specifically and primarily designed to reduce the heat gain of the taxpayer's home, and the roof meets or exceeds the Energy Star Program requirements in effect at the time of purchase or installment.

Note: Any amounts paid for the onsite preparation, assembly, or original installation of the property are not included in the credit.

Illustration 6-8

Form **5695**

Department of the Treasury
Internal Revenue Service

Residential Energy Credits

▶ **Information about Form 5695 and its separate instructions is at** *www.irs.gov/form5695*.
▶ **Attach to Form 1040 or Form 1040NR.**

OMB No. 1545-0074

2014

Attachment
Sequence No. **158**

Name(s) shown on return

Your social security number

Part I	**Residential Energy Efficient Property Credit** (See instructions before completing this part.)

Note. *Skip lines 1 through 11 if you only have a* **credit carryforward from 2013.**

1	Qualified solar electric property costs	**1**	
2	Qualified solar water heating property costs	**2**	
3	Qualified small wind energy property costs	**3**	
4	Qualified geothermal heat pump property costs	**4**	
5	Add lines 1 through 4	**5**	
6	Multiply line 5 by 30% (.30)	**6**	

7a Qualified fuel cell property. Was qualified fuel cell property installed on or in connection with your main home located in the United States? (See instructions) . . . . ▶ **7a** ☐ Yes ☐ No

Caution: *If you checked the "No" box, you cannot take a credit for qualified fuel cell property. Skip lines 7b through 11.*

b Print the complete address of the main home where you installed the fuel cell property.

Number and street   Unit No.

City, State, and ZIP code

8	Qualified fuel cell property costs	**8**	
9	Multiply line 8 by 30% (.30)	**9**	
10	Kilowatt capacity of property on line 8 above ▶ _____ . _____ x $1,000	**10**	
11	Enter the smaller of line 9 or line 10	**11**	
12	Credit carryforward from 2013. Enter the amount, if any, from your 2013 Form 5695, line 16 . .	**12**	
13	Add lines 6, 11, and 12	**13**	
14	Limitation based on tax liability. Enter the amount from the Residential Energy Efficient Property Credit Limit Worksheet (see instructions)	**14**	
15	**Residential energy efficient property credit.** Enter the smaller of line 13 or line 14. Also include this amount on Form 1040, line 53, or Form 1040NR, line 50	**15**	
16	Credit carryforward to 2015. If line 15 is less than line 13, subtract line 15 from line 13 . . . . **16**		

For Paperwork Reduction Act Notice, see your tax return instructions.   Cat. No. 13540P   Form **5695** (2014)

Illustration 6-8 continued

Part II	Nonbusiness Energy Property Credit

17a Were the qualified energy efficiency improvements or residential energy property costs for your main home located in the United States? (see instructions) . . . . ▶ | **17a** ☐ Yes ☐ No

Caution: *If you checked the "No" box, you cannot claim the nonbusiness energy property credit. Do not complete Part II.*

b Print the complete address of the main home where you made the qualifying improvements.
Caution: *You can only have one main home at a time.*

_____
Number and street   Unit No.

_____
City, State, and ZIP code

c Were any of these improvements related to the construction of this main home? . . . . . ▶ | **17c** ☐ Yes ☐ No

Caution: *If you checked the "Yes" box, you can only claim the nonbusiness energy property credit for qualifying improvements that were not related to the construction of the home. Do not include expenses related to the construction of your main home, even if the improvements were made after you moved into the home.*

18	Lifetime limitation. Enter the amount from the Lifetime Limitation Worksheet (see instructions) . .	**18**
19	Qualified energy efficiency improvements (original use must begin with you and the component must reasonably be expected to last for at least 5 years; do not include labor costs) (see instructions).	
a	Insulation material or system specifically and primarily designed to reduce heat loss or gain of your home that meets the prescriptive criteria established by the 2009 IECC	**19a**
b	Exterior doors that meet or exceed the Energy Star program requirements	**19b**
c	Metal or asphalt roof that meets or exceeds the Energy Star program requirements and has appropriate pigmented coatings or cooling granules which are specifically and primarily designed to reduce the heat gain of your home	**19c**
d	Exterior windows and skylights that meet or exceed the Energy Star program requirements	**19d**
e	Maximum amount of cost on which the credit can be figured	**19e** $2,000
f	If you claimed window expenses on your Form 5695 for 2006, 2007, 2009, 2010, 2011, 2012, or 2013, enter the amount from the Window Expense Worksheet (see instructions); otherwise enter -0-	**19f**
g	Subtract line 19f from line 19e. If zero or less, enter -0-	**19g**
h	Enter the smaller of line 19d or line 19g	**19h**
20	Add lines 19a, 19b, 19c, and 19h	**20**
21	Multiply line 20 by 10% (.10)	**21**
22	Residential energy property costs (must be placed in service by you; include labor costs for onsite preparation, assembly, and original installation) (see instructions).	
a	Energy-efficient building property. Do not enter more than **$300**	**22a**
b	Qualified natural gas, propane, or oil furnace or hot water boiler. Do not enter more than **$150** . .	**22b**
c	Advanced main air circulating fan used in a natural gas, propane, or oil furnace. Do not enter more than **$50**	**22c**
23	Add lines 22a through 22c	**23**
24	Add lines 21 and 23	**24**
25	Maximum credit amount. (If you jointly occupied the home, see instructions)	**25** $500
26	Enter the amount, if any, from line 18	**26**
27	Subtract line 26 from line 25. If zero or less, **stop;** you cannot take the nonbusiness energy property credit	**27**
28	Enter the smaller of line 24 or line 27	**28**
29	Limitation based on tax liability. Enter the amount from the Nonbusiness Energy Property Credit Limit Worksheet (see instructions)	**29**
30	**Nonbusiness energy property credit.** Enter the smaller of line 28 or line 29. Also include this amount on Form 1040, line 53, or Form 1040NR, line 50	**30**

Form **5695** (2014)

The Remaining Nonrefundable Credits

We have covered the most frequently used nonrefundable credits. Below, you will find a summary of the rest of the nonrefundable credits that can be claimed with the Form 1040. If you encounter any of these credits, additional research will be required.

- Mortgage interest credit – Form 1040, line 54. Form 8396 must be filed.
- District of Columbia first-time homebuyer credit – Form 1040, line 54. Form 8859 must be filed.
- Qualified plug-in electric drive motor vehicle credit – Form 1040, line 54. Form 8936 must be filed.
- Qualified electric vehicle credit – Form 1040, line 54. Form 8834 must be filed.
- General business credit – Form 1040, line 54. Form 3800 must be filed.
- Credit for prior year minimum tax – Form 1040, line 54. The taxpayer may claim this credit if alternative minimum tax was paid in a prior year. Form 8801 must be filed.
- Credit to holders of tax credit bonds – Form 1040, line 54. Form 8912 must be filed.
- Alternative motor vehicle credit – Form 1040, line 54. Form 8910 must be filed.
- Alternative fuel vehicle refueling property credit – Form 1040, line 54. Form 8911 must be filed.
- Adoption Credit – Form 1040, line 54. This credit may be claimed if the taxpayer paid expenses to adopt a child or adopted a special needs child and the adoption became final in the tax year. Form 8839 must be filed.

Now, we will discuss the rest of the refundable credits. Remember, these credits are treated as payments on the tax return.

Excess Social Security and Tier 1 Railroad Tax Withheld

If the taxpayer works for an employer, the employer is required to withhold social security tax unless the taxpayer is a railroad employee. In that case, the employer must withhold tier 1 railroad retirement tax. The maximum wages that are subject to social security or railroad retirement tier 1 taxes for 2014 are $117,000. The maximum social security or railroad retirement tier 1 taxes that should have been withheld are $7,254.00.

If the taxpayer worked for only one employer in 2014 and more than the maximum social security tax was withheld, the taxpayer must go back to the employer and have them adjust it. If the taxpayer worked for two or more employers in 2014 and more than the maximum social security tax was withheld, the taxpayer can take a credit for the excess amount on Form 1040, line 71. There is no Form that needs to be filed. The credit for the excess amount should be entered directly on the Form 1040.

The Remaining Refundable Credits

We have covered the most frequently used refundable credits. Below, you will find a summary of the rest of the refundable credits that can be claimed on Form 1040.

- Net Premium Tax Credit – This will be covered in Chapter 10.
- Undistributed Long Term Capital Gains – Form 1040, line 73. Form 2439 must be filed.
- Credit for Federal tax paid on fuels – Form 1040, line 72. Form 4136 must be filed.
- Health coverage tax credit – Form 1040, line 73. Form 8885 must be filed.

Chapter Review

1) What age must a child be under to be a qualifying person for the credit for child and dependent care expenses?

2) If the noncustodial parent is eligible to claim the exemption for a child, who is eligible to claim the credit for child and dependent care expenses?

3) How much earned income would be shown on the Form 2441, line 5 for a spouse that was a full-time student for 7 months of the year? The spouse earned no other income.

4) What information must the taxpayer have from the child care provider to claim child and dependent care credit?

5) What filing status is not eligible for the education credits?

6) What are the two types of education credits?

7) Betty paid $3,200 for tuition at State University for the year. She also paid $750 for room and board and she bought books from the University book store even though she was not required to. The books were $445 for the year. What amount are qualified education expenses if she takes the American Opportunity Credit? The Lifetime learning credit?

8) June finished her freshman year of college and started her sophomore year in 2014. If she meets all other requirements, which education credit may she claim?

9) Elizabeth is 20 and a full-time student. She only made $3,200 in 2014. She is filing a tax return to get back the taxes she paid in. Her parents are claiming her on their tax return. Who will receive the education credit for which she is eligible?

10) What are the maximum social security wages for 2014?

Exercise

1) Complete a Form 2441 for the Marrotts. Matt (SSN- 166-33-4444) and Mary (SSN- 322-66-4444) Marrott have a daughter, Miranda. Miranda attends the ABC Daycare. The information needed is below.

   Matt's earned income was $26,465 and Mary's was $12,200.

   Miranda's SSN is 321-54-9876 and her birth date is April 3rd, 2010.

   ABC Daycare is located at 544 Young One Lane, Your City, Your State, Your Zip code. Their EIN is 45-6654431. The Marrotts paid a total of $3,800 for their daughter attend to daycare in 2014.

   The amounts on page 2 of the Form 1040 are as follows:

   > **Line 38:** $38,665
   > **Line 40:** $12,400
   > **Line 41:** $26,265
   > **Line 42:** $11,850
   > **Line 43:** $14,415
   > **Line 44:** $ 1,443
   > **Line 47:** $ 1,443

2) Complete a Form 8863 for Mary Marrott from the above scenario. She attended two evening courses at State University. Her tuition was $4,335 and she bought books from the University book store for $753. She received a scholarship for her tuition in the amount of $2,000. She has not claimed the Hope credit or the American Opportunity credit for any 4 years.

☐ CORRECTED

FILER'S name, street address, city or town, state or province, country, ZIP or foreign postal code, and telephone number	1 Payments received for qualified tuition and related expenses	OMB No. 1545-1574	
State University 150 Grand Ave. Your City, Your State, Your Zip Code	$ 4,335.00	20**14**	**Tuition Statement**
	2 Amounts billed for qualified tuition and related expenses $	Form **1098-T**	
FILER'S federal identification no. 63-3321989	STUDENT'S social security number 322-66-4444	3 If this box is checked, your educational institution has changed its reporting method for 2014 ☐	**Copy B** **For Student**
STUDENT'S name Mary Marrott	4 Adjustments made for a prior year $	5 Scholarships or grants $ 2,000.00	This is important tax information and is being furnished to the Internal Revenue Service.
Street address (including apt. no.) 253 Main St.	6 Adjustments to scholarships or grants for a prior year	7 Checked if the amount in box 1 or 2 includes amounts for an academic period beginning January - March 2015 ▶ ☐	
City or town, state or province, country, and ZIP or foreign postal code Your City, Your State, Your Zip Code	$		
Service Provider/Acct. No. (see instr.)	8 Check if at least half-time student ☐	9 Checked if a graduate student . . . . ☐	10 Ins. contract reimb./refund $

Form **1098-T** (keep for your records) www.irs.gov/form1098t Department of the Treasury - Internal Revenue Service

Chapter 7 – Individual Retirement Arrangements (IRAs)

An Individual Retirement Arrangement (IRA) is an account in which a taxpayer can set aside amounts for future retirement. The amounts set aside may be deductible and the earnings are tax deferred. We will discuss the different types of IRAs and the tax advantages of them. In order to understand the tax advantages, we must first learn the terms *contribution* and *distribution*.

Contribution
When a taxpayer puts money into something. In this case that something would be an IRA.

Distribution
When a taxpayer withdraws money out of an account. In this case, an IRA.

Contributions to a Traditional IRA

A Traditional IRA is defined by the IRS as any IRA that is not a Roth IRA or Simple IRA. Depending on certain factors, contributions to a traditional IRA may be deductible. In order to contribute to a traditional IRA, a taxpayer (or spouse if MFJ) must have taxable compensation and be under age 70½ at the end of the tax year.

Let's look at the Traditional IRA worksheet (Illustration 7-1) and discuss the rules of contributing to a traditional IRA.

Modified AGI
The Modified Adjusted Gross Income is the total income from line 22 of the Form 1040 plus

- Any foreign earned income exclusion.
- Any foreign housing exclusion or deduction.
- Exclusion of qualified savings bond interest shown on Form 8815, for filers with qualified higher education expenses.
- Exclusion of employer-provided adoption benefits.

Minus any adjustments taken on the Form 1040, lines 23 through 31a.

The Modified AGI worksheet (Illustration 7-1) will help calculate the modified AGI.

Compensation
Lines 1 through 3 of the Traditional IRA Worksheet concern compensation. Generally, compensation is what is earned through working. Compensation includes:

- Wages, salaries, tips, professional fees, bonuses, and other amounts received for providing personal services.
- Commissions.

- Self-employment income minus deductible contributions made on taxpayer's behalf and the deduction allowed for one-half of the self-employment taxes. Do not subtract self-employment losses.
- Alimony and separate maintenance payments.
- Nontaxable combat pay.

Remember, the taxpayer (or spouse if MFJ) must have compensation to contribute to an IRA. A contribution may be made to a spousal IRA even if either the taxpayer or spouse has little or no compensation, a contribution may be made to a spousal IRA. In this case, the spouse with the greater compensation will complete the worksheet and determine how much they will contribute to an IRA. Then that spouse's compensation minus the IRA contributions will be added to the compensation of the spouse with the lesser compensation and entered on line 3 of the Traditional IRA Worksheet.

AGI Phase out

In some cases, the contribution to a traditional IRA may be partially deductible or not deductible at all. The deductibility of the contributions depend on whether the taxpayer (or spouse if MFJ) is covered by a retirement plan at work. A taxpayer is covered by a retirement plan at work if they are an active participant in one of the following plans:

- A qualified pension, profit-sharing, or stock-bonus plan described in section 401(a).
- An annuity plan described in section 403(a).
- An annuity contract or custodial account described in section 403(b).
- A simplified employee pension (SEP) plan described in 408(k).
- A SIMPLE retirement account described in section 409(p).
- A trust described in section 501(c)(18).
- A plan for federal, state or local government.

To make this easier to determine, the retirement box will be marked, in box 13 of the Form W-2 (Illustration 7-2).

If either the taxpayer or spouse, if MFJ, were covered by a retirement plan at work, their deductible IRA contribution may be limited based on their AGI. If neither the taxpayer nor the spouse, if MFJ, were covered the full amount will be deductible (up to the limit discussed later). Illustration 7-3 show the AGI phase out amounts.

Contribution Limit

When considering the contribution limit, keep in mind this is how much can be contributed to the traditional IRA, not how much can be deducted. The contribution limit is the smaller of the following amounts:

- $5,500 ($6,500 if age 50 or older), or
- The taxable compensation for the year.

Subtract contributions made to any other IRAs. The contribution also must be made before the taxpayer reaches 70½. Remember, this is the amount that can be contributed, not the amount that can be deducted as discussed under the AGI Phase out topic earlier. Any amount contributed over the contribution limit is an excess contribution and subject to a penalty.

Deductible Amount

Okay, now we know the contribution limits and the reasons the deductible amount may be limited. Let's discuss what happens next. The contribution limit is the limit that can be contributed. It does not matter how much can be deducted. Now, let's say your taxable compensation is $62,000 and you had no other income. You are single, age 35, and you made a $5,500 contribution into your traditional IRA. You are also covered by a retirement plan at work. Let's look at the worksheet (Illustration 7-4) while we discuss the results. The modified AGI and compensation amounts were easy to calculate (keep in mind that those two amounts may be different). Your *contribution* limit is the smaller of your taxable compensation or $5,500. Therefore, the contribution limit is $5,500. Now, we finish the worksheet to find out how much can be deducted. Due to the fact that you are covered by a retirement plan at work, you are single, and your income is over $60,000, we know that you may receive a partial deduction or none at all. This can be determined by using the Tables in Illustration 7-3. Through doing the worksheet, we find out you can only deduct $4,400 of the $5,500 contributed. This will go on line 32 of the Form 1040. You now have three choices: You may withdraw the additional $1,500 plus earnings by the due date of the return, you may leave the additional $1,100 in as a nondeductible contribution (discussed later in the chapter), or you may contribute the additional $1,100 to a Roth IRA.

Illustration 7-2

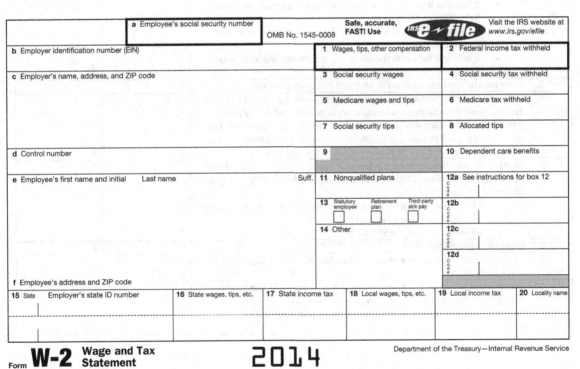

Illustration 7-1

Modified AGI

1.	Enter the amount from Form 1040, line 22.	1.
2.	Enter any amounts from Form 2555, lines 45 and 50, and Form 2555-EZ, line 18.	2.
3.	Enter any amounts from Form 8815, line 14.	3.
4.	Enter any amounts from Form 8839, line 26.	4.
5.	Add lines 1 through 5 and enter the total here.	5.
6.	Enter the sum of any amounts on Form 1040, lines 23 through 31a.	6.
7.	Subtract line 6 from line 5. **This is the modified AGI.**	7.

Traditional IRA Worksheet

		Taxpayer	Spouse
1.	Enter the total of the taxpayer's (and spouse's if MFJ) wages, salaries, tips, etc.; alimony and separate maintenance payments, and nontaxable combat pay.	1.	
2.	Enter any earned income the taxpayer (and spouse if MFJ) received as a self-employed individual or partner minus any deductions on Form 1040, lines 27 and 28.	2.	
3.	Add lines 1 and 2. If MFJ, enter the result in both columns. If the result is 0, stop here, the taxpayer may not make any IRA contributions	3.	3.
4.	• If the taxpayer (**and** spouse if MFJ) was not covered by a retirement plan at work and line 3 is over $5,500 ($6,500 If age 50 or older, they may take a full deduction. Enter $5,500($6,500 if age 50 or older) on line 7 and go to line 8. If line 3 is not over $5,500 ($6,500 if age 50 or older) enter the amount from line 3 on line 7 and go to line 8. • If the taxpayer is covered by a retirement plan at work and their filing status is S, HH, or MFS and the taxpayer did not live with spouse at all during the year, enter $70,000. • If MFJ and only one is covered by a retirement plan at work, enter $116,000 in the column of the one covered and $191,000 in the other column. • If MFJ and both are covered by a retirement plan at work, enter $116,000 in both columns. • If QW and the taxpayer is covered by a retirement plan at work, enter $116,000. • If MFS and lived with spouse at any time during the year, enter $10,000.	4.	4.
5.	Enter the amount from line7 in the Modified AGI worksheet above.	5.	5.
6.	Subtract line 5 from line 4. If 0 or less, the taxpayer cannot deduct any IRA contributions. If the taxpayer wants to contribute to a Roth IRA or make nondeductible traditional IRA contributions, go to the applicable worksheet on the next page. If this amount is $10,000 or more ($20,000 if MFJ or QW), enter $5,500 ($6,500 if age 50 or over) on line 7 and go to line 8.	6.	6.
7.	Multiply line 6 by the percentage below that applies to the taxpayer. If the result is not a multiple of $10, round it to the next highest multiple of $10. If the amount is less than $200, enter $200. • MFJ or QW and covered by a retirement plan at work, multiply by 27.5%(32.5% if age 50 or over). • All others, multiply by 55% (65% if age 50 or over).	7.	7.
8.	Enter the amount from line 3.	8.	8.
9.	Enter the contributions made or to be made. Not more than $5,500 ($6,500 if age 50 or over).	9.	9.
10.	Enter the smaller of lines 7, 8, and 9 here and on Form 1040, line 32. If line 9 is more than this amount, and the taxpayer will withdraw the excess and does not choose to make a Roth IRA or nondeductible contribution, stop here.	10.	10.

Illustration 7-3

If the taxpayer is covered by a retirement plan at work

Filing Status	Modified AGI	Deduction
Single or head of household	$60,000 or less.	Full deduction.
	More than $60,000 but less than $70,000.	A partial deduction.
	$70,000 or more.	No deduction.
Married filing jointly or qualifying widow(er)	$96,000 or less.	A full deduction.
	More than $96,000 but less than $116,000.	A partial deduction.
	$116,000 or more.	No deduction.
Married filing separately and lived with spouse at any time during the tax year.	Less than $10,000.	A partial deduction.
	$10,000 or more.	No deduction.
Married filing separately and did not live with spouse at any time during the tax year.	$60,000 or less.	Full deduction.
	More than $60,000 but less than $70,000	A partial deduction.
	$70,000 or more.	No deduction.

If the taxpayer is not covered by a retirement plan at work

Filing Status	Modified AGI	Deduction
Single, head of household, or qualifying widow(er).	Any amount.	A full deduction.
Married filing jointly with a spouse who is not covered by a plan at work.	Any amount.	A full deduction.
Married filing jointly with a spouse who is covered by a plan at work.	$181,000 or less	A full deduction.
	More than $181,000 but less than $191,000	A partial deduction.
	$191,000 or more.	No deduction.
Married filing separately and did not live with spouse at any time during the tax year or spouse was not covered by a retirement plan at work.	Any amount.	A full deduction.
Married filing separately, lived with spouse at any time during the tax year and spouse is covered by a plan at work.	Less than $10,000	A partial deduction.
	$10,000 or more.	No deduction.

Illustration 7-4

Modified AGI

1.	Enter the amount from Form 1040, line 22.	1.	62,000
2.	Enter any amounts from Form 2555, lines 45 and 50, and Form 2555-EZ, line 18.	2.	
3.	Enter any amounts from Form 8815, line 14.	3.	
4.	Enter any amounts from Form 8839, line 26.	4.	
5.	Add lines 1 through 5 and enter the total here.	5.	62,000
6.	Enter the sum of any amounts on Form 1040, lines 23 through 31a.	6.	
7.	Subtract line 6 from line 5. **This is the modified AGI.**	**7.**	62,000

Traditional IRA Worksheet

		Taxpayer	Spouse
1.	Enter the total of the taxpayer's (and spouse's if MFJ) wages, salaries, tips, etc.; alimony and separate maintenance payments, and nontaxable combat pay.	1. 62,000	
2.	Enter any earned income the taxpayer (and spouse if MFJ) received as a self-employed individual or partner minus any deductions on Form 1040, lines 27 and 28.	2.	
3.	Add lines 1 and 2. If MFJ, enter the result in both columns. If the result is 0, stop here, the taxpayer may not make any IRA contributions	3. 62,000	3.
4.	<ul><li>If the taxpayer (**and** spouse if MFJ) was not covered by a retirement plan at work and line 3 is over $5,500 ($6,500 If age 50 or older, they may take a full deduction. Enter $5,500($6,500 if age 50 or older) on line 7 and go to line 8. If line 3 is not over $5,500 ($6,500 if age 50 or older) enter the amount from line 3 on line 7 and go to line 8.</li><li>If the taxpayer is covered by a retirement plan at work and their filing status is S, HH, or MFS and the taxpayer did not live with spouse at all during the year, enter $70,000.</li><li>If MFJ and only one is covered by a retirement plan at work, enter $116,000 in the column of the one covered and $191,000 in the other column.</li><li>If MFJ and both are covered by a retirement plan at work, enter $116,000 in both columns.</li><li>If QW and the taxpayer is covered by a retirement plan at work, enter $116,000.</li><li>If MFS and lived with spouse at any time during the year, enter $10,000.</li></ul>	4. 70,000	4.
5.	Enter the amount from line7 in the Modified AGI worksheet above.	5. 62,000	5.
6.	Subtract line 5 from line 4. If 0 or less, the taxpayer cannot deduct any IRA contributions. If the taxpayer wants to contribute to a Roth IRA or make nondeductible traditional IRA contributions, go to the applicable worksheet on the next page. If this amount is $10,000 or more ($20,000 if MFJ or QW), enter $5,500 ($6,500 if age 50 or over) on line 7 and go to line 8.	6. 8,000	6.
7.	Multiply line 6 by the percentage below that applies to the taxpayer. If the result is not a multiple of $10, round it to the next highest multiple of $10. If the amount is less than $200, enter $200.<ul><li>MFJ or QW and covered by a retirement plan at work, multiply by 27.5% (32.5% if age 50 or over).</li><li>All others, multiply by 55% (65% if age 50 or over).</li></ul>	7. 4,400	7.
8.	Enter the amount from line 3.	8. 62,000	8.
9.	Enter the contributions made or to be made. Not more than $5,500 ($6,500 if age 50 or over).	9. 5,500	9.
10.	Enter the smaller of lines 7, 8, and 9 here and on Form 1040, line 32. If line 9 is more than this amount, and the taxpayer will withdraw the excess and does not choose to make a Roth IRA or nondeductible contribution, stop here.	10. 4,400	10.

Excess Contributions

We keep discussing the contribution limit, but what happens if the taxpayer contributes over this amount? If the taxpayer contributes an amount over the smaller of their taxable compensation or $5,500 ($6,500 if age 50 or older), they have an excess contribution. Also, if they contributed anything after they reached age 70½, that amount is an excess contribution. The taxpayer may withdraw the excess contribution and any earnings on that amount, before the due date of the tax return. If not, the taxpayer must pay 6% tax on the excess contribution and any earnings on that amount. This tax will be assessed every year the excess contribution remains in the account.

Traditional IRA Distributions

In this section we will cover the different types of traditional IRA distributions and the taxability of them.

Rollovers

A rollover is generally defined as a tax-free distribution to the taxpayer in cash or other assets from one retirement plan that the taxpayer contributes to another retirement plan. The taxpayer must generally make the rollover contribution within 60 days. If the taxpayer rolls over an amount into a traditional IRA, they may not deduct the amount. However, the rollover is not subject to the contribution limitations. If the taxpayer rolls over a traditional IRA into one of the following accounts, the transaction will be tax free.

- IRAs
- Qualified trusts
- Qualified employee annuity plans under section 403(a).
- Deferred compensation plans of state and local governments (section 457 plans).
- Tax-sheltered annuities (section 403(b) annuities)

Note: The amount rolled over tax free will generally become taxable when withdrawn from the account it was rolled over into.

Conversions

The taxpayer may withdraw some or all of the assets from a traditional IRA and reinvest them in a Roth IRA within 60 days. This action is called a conversion. The amount that is converted will be taxable to the extent it would have been taxable had it not been converted but the 10% early withdrawal penalty will not apply.

Required Minimum Distributions

A taxpayer that owns a traditional IRA must begin receiving distributions when they reach age 70½. They must keep receiving a minimum distribution for every year after that as long as there is a balance in the IRA. The required minimum distribution is based on age and some other factors. The IRS Publication 590 will help determine what the required minimum distribution for the taxpayer. If the taxpayer does not receive a required distribution after reaching age 70½, they may have to pay a 50% excise tax on the amount that should have been distributed. An amount rolled over may not qualify as a required minimum distribution.

The Taxability of Distributions

Generally, all traditional IRA distributions are taxable in the year received. However, remember, the taxpayer can make nondeductible contributions. Because the contribution is nondeductible, the taxpayer has paid taxes on the money contributed. Therefore, that amount adds to the basis (investment) of a traditional IRA and is not taxable when distributed. That part of the distribution is a return of the taxpayer's investment. If the taxpayer only makes deductible contributions his distribution will be fully taxable.

If the taxpayer makes a nondeductible contribution during the tax year, they must file a Form 8606 (Illustration 7-5) with their tax return to show their basis in the IRA. If they receive a distribution and ever made a nondeductible contribution, they must file a Form 8606 to show what part of the IRA is taxable.

Early Distributions

If the taxpayer receives a distribution before they have reached age 59½, they received an early distribution. Generally, early distributions are subject to a 10% additional tax that is assessed on any amount that is included in taxable income and is in addition to regular income tax.

There are several exceptions to the 10% additional tax penalty. The taxpayer may not have to pay an additional tax if one of the following situations applies:

- The taxpayer has unreimbursed medical expenses that are more than 10% of their adjusted gross income (7.5% of their adjusted gross income if the taxpayer or spouse was born before January 2, 1950).
- The distributions are not more than the cost of the taxpayer's medical insurance and all of the following conditions apply:
  - The taxpayer lost their job.
  - The taxpayer received unemployment compensation paid under any federal or state law for 12 consecutive weeks because of the loss of job.
  - The taxpayer received the distributions during the year unemployment was received or the following year.
  - The taxpayer received the distributions no later than 60 days after they were reemployed.
- The taxpayer is disabled.
- The taxpayer is the beneficiary of a deceased IRA owner.
- The taxpayer is receiving distributions in the form of an annuity.
- The distribution was not more than qualified higher education expenses.
- The distribution was to buy, build, or rebuild a first home. Generally, the taxpayer is a first time homebuyer if they had no present interest in a main home during the 2 year period ending on the acquisition of new home.
- The distribution is due to an IRS levy of the qualified plan.
- The distribution is a qualified reservist distribution.

If one of the exceptions apply, the taxpayer must file Form 5329 (Illustration 7-6) with their tax return.

Contributions to a Roth IRA

Contributions to a Roth IRA are similar to a traditional IRA except that contributions are not deductible and can be made after the taxpayer reaches age 70½. To be a Roth IRA, the account must be designated as a Roth IRA when it is set up. To be able to contribute to a Roth IRA, the taxpayer (or spouse if MFJ) must have taxable compensation and the modified AGI must be less than:

- $191,000 for married filing jointly or qualifying widow(er),
- $129,000 for single, head of household, or married filing separately and the taxpayer did not live with their spouse at any time during the year, and
- $10,000 for married filing separately and the taxpayer lived with their spouse at any time during the year.

Modified AGI

For purposes of the Roth IRA, the modified AGI begins with the modified AGI for traditional IRA purposes. Then, any conversion income is subtracted. These calculations are made on the Roth IRA Worksheet (Illustration 7-7).

Compensation

For purposes of the Roth IRA, compensation means the same as it does for traditional IRAs. This amount can be found on the Traditional IRA Worksheet, line 3 (Illustration 7-1).

AGI Phase out

With traditional IRAs, only the *deduction* is effected by the modified AGI. The taxpayer can still contribute as much as their contribution limit, no matter what their AGI is. With a Roth IRA, the *contribution* is effected by the modified AGI. Illustration 7-8 shows the effect of the modified AGI on Roth IRA contributions.

Illustration 7-5

<table>
<tr><td colspan="2">Form 8606</td><td>Nondeductible IRAs</td><td>OMB No. 1545-0074</td></tr>
<tr><td colspan="2">Department of the Treasury
Internal Revenue Service (99)</td><td>► Information about Form 8606 and its separate instructions is at www.irs.gov/form8606.
► Attach to Form 1040, Form 1040A, or Form 1040NR.</td><td>2014
Attachment
Sequence No. 48</td></tr>
</table>

Name. If married, file a separate form for each spouse required to file Form 8606. See instructions.	Your social security number

Fill in Your Address Only If You Are Filing This Form by Itself and Not With Your Tax Return ►

Home address (number and street, or P.O. box if mail is not delivered to your home)	Apt. no.

City, town or post office, state, and ZIP code. If you have a foreign address, also complete the spaces below.

Foreign country name	Foreign province/state/county	Foreign postal code

Part I — Nondeductible Contributions to Traditional IRAs and Distributions From Traditional, SEP, and SIMPLE IRAs

Complete this part only if one or more of the following apply.

- You made nondeductible contributions to a traditional IRA for 2014.
- You took distributions from a traditional, SEP, or SIMPLE IRA in 2014 **and** you made nondeductible contributions to a traditional IRA in 2014 or an earlier year. For this purpose, a distribution does not include a rollover, one-time distribution to fund an HSA, conversion, recharacterization, or return of certain contributions.
- You converted part, but not all, of your traditional, SEP, and SIMPLE IRAs to Roth IRAs in 2014 (excluding any portion you recharacterized) **and** you made nondeductible contributions to a traditional IRA in 2014 or an earlier year.

1	Enter your nondeductible contributions to traditional IRAs for 2014, including those made for 2014 from January 1, 2015, through April 15, 2015 (see instructions)	**1**	
2	Enter your total basis in traditional IRAs (see instructions)	**2**	
3	Add lines 1 and 2	**3**	

In 2014, did you take a distribution from traditional, SEP, or SIMPLE IRAs, or make a Roth IRA conversion?
— **No** ──► Enter the amount from line 3 on line 14. Do not complete the rest of Part I.
— **Yes** ──► Go to line 4.

4	Enter those contributions included on line 1 that were made from January 1, 2015, through April 15, 2015	**4**	
5	Subtract line 4 from line 3	**5**	
6	Enter the value of **all** your traditional, SEP, and SIMPLE IRAs as of December 31, 2014, plus any outstanding rollovers (see instructions) . .	**6**	
7	Enter your distributions from traditional, SEP, and SIMPLE IRAs in 2014. **Do not** include rollovers, a one-time distribution to fund an HSA, conversions to a Roth IRA, certain returned contributions, or recharacterizations of traditional IRA contributions (see instructions) .	**7**	
8	Enter the net amount you converted from traditional, SEP, and SIMPLE IRAs to Roth IRAs in 2014. **Do not** include amounts converted that you later recharacterized (see instructions). Also enter this amount on line 16 .	**8**	
9	Add lines 6, 7, and 8 . . . . **9**		
10	Divide line 5 by line 9. Enter the result as a decimal rounded to at least 3 places. If the result is 1.000 or more, enter "1.000"	**10** × .	
11	Multiply line 8 by line 10. This is the nontaxable portion of the amount you converted to Roth IRAs. Also enter this amount on line 17 . . .	**11**	
12	Multiply line 7 by line 10. This is the nontaxable portion of your distributions that you did not convert to a Roth IRA	**12**	
13	Add lines 11 and 12. This is the nontaxable portion of all your distributions	**13**	
14	Subtract line 13 from line 3. This is **your total basis in traditional IRAs for 2014 and earlier years**	**14**	
15	**Taxable amount.** Subtract line 12 from line 7. If more than zero, also include this amount on Form 1040, line 15b; Form 1040A, line 11b; or Form 1040NR, line 16b	**15**	

Note. You may be subject to an additional 10% tax on the amount on line 15 if you were under age 59½ at the time of the distribution (see instructions).

For Privacy Act and Paperwork Reduction Act Notice, see separate instructions.   Cat. No. 63966F   Form **8606** (2014)

Illustration 7-5 continued

Part II	2014 Conversions From Traditional, SEP, or SIMPLE IRAs to Roth IRAs

Complete this part if you converted part or all of your traditional, SEP, and SIMPLE IRAs to a Roth IRA in 2014 (excluding any portion you recharacterized).

16	If you completed Part I, enter the amount from line 8. Otherwise, enter the net amount you converted from traditional, SEP, and SIMPLE IRAs to Roth IRAs in 2014. **Do not** include amounts you later recharacterized back to traditional, SEP, or SIMPLE IRAs in 2014 or 2015 (see instructions)	16	
17	If you completed Part I, enter the amount from line 11. Otherwise, enter your basis in the amount on line 16 (see instructions)	17	
18	**Taxable amount.** Subtract line 17 from line 16. If more than zero, also include this amount on Form 1040, line 15b; Form 1040A, line 11b; or Form 1040NR, line 16b	18	

Part III	Distributions From Roth IRAs

Complete this part only if you took a distribution from a Roth IRA in 2014. For this purpose, a distribution does not include a rollover, one-time distribution to fund an HSA, recharacterization, or return of certain contributions (see instructions).

19	Enter your total nonqualified distributions from Roth IRAs In 2014, including any qualified first-time homebuyer distributions (see instructions)	19	
20	Qualified first-time homebuyer expenses (see instructions). **Do not** enter more than $10,000	20	
21	Subtract line 20 from line 19. If zero or less, enter -0-	21	
22	Enter your basis in Roth IRA contributions (see instructions). If line 21 is zero, **stop here**	22	
23	Subtract line 22 from line 21. If zero or less, enter -0- and skip lines 24 and 25. If more than zero, you may be subject to an additional tax (see instructions)	23	
24	Enter your basis in conversions from traditional, SEP, and SIMPLE IRAs and rollovers from qualified retirement plans to a Roth IRA (see instructions)	24	
25	**Taxable amount.** Subtract line 24 from line 23. If more than zero, also include this amount on Form 1040, line 15b; Form 1040A, line 11b; or Form 1040NR, line 16b	25	

Sign Here Only If You Are Filing This Form by Itself and Not With Your Tax Return

Under penalties of perjury, I declare that I have examined this form, including accompanying attachments, and to the best of my knowledge and belief, it is true, correct, and complete. Declaration of preparer (other than taxpayer) is based on all information of which preparer has any knowledge.

Your signature _____ Date _____

Paid Preparer Use Only

Print/Type preparer's name	Preparer's signature	Date	Check ☐ if self-employed	PTIN
Firm's name ▶			Firm's EIN ▶	
Firm's address ▶			Phone no.	

Form **8606** (2014)

Illustration 7-6

Form **5329**

Department of the Treasury
Internal Revenue Service (99)

Additional Taxes on Qualified Plans (Including IRAs) and Other Tax-Favored Accounts

► Attach to Form 1040 or Form 1040NR.
► Information about Form 5329 and its separate instructions is at *www.irs.gov/form5329.*

OMB No. 1545-0074

2014

Attachment
Sequence No. **29**

Name of individual subject to additional tax. If married filing jointly, see instructions.

Your social security number

Fill in Your Address Only If You Are Filing This Form by Itself and Not With Your Tax Return ►

Home address (number and street), or P.O. box if mail is not delivered to your home	Apt. no.

City, town or post office, state, and ZIP code. If you have a foreign address, also complete the spaces below (see instructions).

If this is an amended return, check here ► ☐

Foreign country name	Foreign province/state/county	Foreign postal code

If you **only** owe the additional 10% tax on early distributions, you may be able to report this tax directly on Form 1040, line 59, or Form 1040NR, line 57, without filing Form 5329. See the instructions for Form 1040, line 59, or for Form 1040NR, line 57.

Part I   Additional Tax on Early Distributions

Complete this part if you took a taxable distribution before you reached age 59½ from a qualified retirement plan (including an IRA) or modified endowment contract (unless you are reporting this tax directly on Form 1040 or Form 1040NR—see above). You may also have to complete this part to indicate that you qualify for an exception to the additional tax on early distributions or for certain Roth IRA distributions (see instructions).

1	Early distributions included in income. For Roth IRA distributions, see instructions	**1**	
2	Early distributions included on line 1 that are not subject to the additional tax (see instructions). Enter the appropriate exception number from the instructions: _____	**2**	
3	Amount subject to additional tax. Subtract line 2 from line 1	**3**	
4	**Additional tax.** Enter 10% (.10) of line 3. Include this amount on Form 1040, line 59, or Form 1040NR, line 57	**4**	

Caution: *If any part of the amount on line 3 was a distribution from a SIMPLE IRA, you may have to include 25% of that amount on line 4 instead of 10% (see instructions).*

Part II   Additional Tax on Certain Distributions From Education Accounts

Complete this part if you included an amount in income, on Form 1040 or Form 1040NR, line 21, from a Coverdell education savings account (ESA) or a qualified tuition program (QTP).

5	Distributions included in income from Coverdell ESAs and QTPs	**5**	
6	Distributions included on line 5 that are not subject to the additional tax (see instructions) . . .	**6**	
7	Amount subject to additional tax. Subtract line 6 from line 5	**7**	
8	**Additional tax.** Enter 10% (.10) of line 7. Include this amount on Form 1040, line 59, or Form 1040NR, line 57	**8**	

Part III   Additional Tax on Excess Contributions to Traditional IRAs

Complete this part if you contributed more to your traditional IRAs for 2014 than is allowable or you had an amount on line 17 of your 2013 Form 5329.

9	Enter your excess contributions from line 16 of your 2013 Form 5329 (see instructions). If zero, go to line 15		**9**	
10	If your traditional IRA contributions for 2014 are less than your maximum allowable contribution, see instructions. Otherwise, enter -0-	**10**		
11	2014 traditional IRA distributions included in income (see instructions) .	**11**		
12	2014 distributions of prior year excess contributions (see instructions) .	**12**		
13	Add lines 10, 11, and 12		**13**	
14	Prior year excess contributions. Subtract line 13 from line 9. If zero or less, enter -0-		**14**	
15	Excess contributions for 2014 (see instructions)		**15**	
16	Total excess contributions. Add lines 14 and 15		**16**	
17	**Additional tax.** Enter 6% (.06) of the **smaller** of line 16 **or** the value of your traditional IRAs on December 31, 2014 (including 2014 contributions made in 2015). Include this amount on Form 1040, line 59, or Form 1040NR, line 57 .		**17**	

Part IV   Additional Tax on Excess Contributions to Roth IRAs

Complete this part if you contributed more to your Roth IRAs for 2014 than is allowable or you had an amount on line 25 of your 2013 Form 5329.

18	Enter your excess contributions from line 24 of your 2013 Form 5329 (see instructions). If zero, go to line 23		**18**	
19	If your Roth IRA contributions for 2014 are less than your maximum allowable contribution, see instructions. Otherwise, enter -0-	**19**		
20	2014 distributions from your Roth IRAs (see instructions)	**20**		
21	Add lines 19 and 20		**21**	
22	Prior year excess contributions. Subtract line 21 from line 18. If zero or less, enter -0-		**22**	
23	Excess contributions for 2014 (see instructions)		**23**	
24	Total excess contributions. Add lines 22 and 23		**24**	
25	**Additional tax.** Enter 6% (.06) of the **smaller** of line 24 **or** the value of your Roth IRAs on December 31, 2014 (including 2014 contributions made in 2015). Include this amount on Form 1040, line 59, or Form 1040NR, line 57		**25**	

For Privacy Act and Paperwork Reduction Act Notice, see your tax return instructions.   Cat. No. 13329Q   Form **5329** (2014)

Illustration 7-7

Roth IRA Worksheet

		Taxpayer	Spouse
1.	Enter the amount from line 7 of the Modified AGI Worksheet. If MFJ, enter the amount in both columns.	1.	1.
2.	Enter any income resulting from the conversion of an IRA (other than Roth) to a Roth IRA. If MFJ, enter the amount in both columns.	2.	2.
3.	Subtract line 2 from line 1. If this amount is less than • $181,000 if MFJ or QW. • $114,000 if S, HH, or MFS and the taxpayer did not live with spouse at any time during the year. Enter $5,500 ($6,500 if age 50 or over) on line 12 and go to line 13.	3.	3.
4.	Enter • $181,000 if MFJ or QW. • $0 if MFS and the taxpayer lived with their spouse at any time during the year. • $114,000 for all others.	4.	4.
5.	Subtract line 4 from line 3. If 0 or less, the taxpayer cannot make a Roth IRA contribution. If they would like to make a nondeductible traditional IRA contribution, go to the Nondeductible IRA Contribution Worksheet.	5.	5.
6.	Enter • $10,000 if MFJ, QW, or MFS and the taxpayer lived with their spouse at any time during the year. • $15,000 for all others.	6.	6.
7.	Divide line 5 by line 6 and enter the result as a decimal (rounded to at least three places). If the result is 1.000 or more, enter 1.000.	7.	7.
8.	Enter $5,500 ($6,500 if age 50 or over).	8.	8.
9.	Enter the total wages, salaries, tips, etc.; alimony and separate maintenance payments, and nontaxable combat pay plus any earned income received as a self-employed individual or partner. If MFJ and one's income is less than their spouse's, complete this worksheet for the spouse with the greater income, then add both incomes together and subtract the amount of IRA contributions made by the spouse with the greater income and enter the result here for the spouse with the lesser income.. (If the Traditional IRA Worksheet has been completed, enter the amount from line 3 of that worksheet.)	9.	9.
10.	Enter the smaller of lines 8 or 9.	10.	10.
11.	Multiply the decimal on line 7 by the amount on line 10.	11.	11.
12.	Subtract line 11 from line 10. Round the result up to the nearest $10. If the result is less than $200, enter $200.	12.	12.
13.	Enter any amount from line 10 of the Traditional IRA Worksheet.	13.	13.
14.	Subtract line 13 from line 12.	14.	14.
15.	Enter the lesser of line 12 or line 14. This is the Roth IRA contribution limit.	15.	15.

Nondeductible IRA Contribution Worksheet

		Taxpayer	Spouse
1.	Enter the smaller of line 3 on the Traditional IRA Worksheet or $5,500 ($6,500 if age 50 or over).	1.	1.
2.	Enter the amount of line 10 or the Traditional IRA Worksheet.	2.	2.
3.	Enter the Roth IRA contribution made.	3.	3.
4.	Add lines 2 and 3.	4.	4.
5.	Subtract line 4 from line 1.This is the amount of nondeductible contributions that can be made.	5.	5.

Illustration 7-8

The Effect of Modified AGI on Roth IRA Contributions

Filing Status	Modified AGI	Contribution
Single or head of household.	Less than $114,000	Up to $5,500 ($6,500 if age 50 or older).
	At least $114,000 but less than $129,000.	Contribution will be limited.
	$129,000 or more.	No contribution.
Married filing jointly or qualifying widow(er).	Less than $181,000.	Up to $5,500 ($6,500 if age 50 or older).
	At least $181,000 but less than $191,000.	Contribution will be limited.
	$191,000 or more.	No contribution.
Married filing separately and lived with spouse at any time during the tax year.	Zero.	Up to $5,500 ($6,500 if age 50 or older).
	More than zero but less than $10,000.	Contribution will be limited.
	$10,000 or more.	No contribution.
Married filing separately and did not live with spouse at any time during the tax year.	Less than $114,000.	Up to $5,500 ($6,500 if age 50 or older).
	At least $114,000 but less than $129,000	Contribution will be limited.
	$129,000 or more.	No contribution.

Contribution Limit

The contribution limit for Roth IRA is generally the smaller of the following amounts:

- $5,500($6,500 if age 50 or older)
- The taxable compensation,

Subtract contributions made to any other IRAs. If the modified AGI is above the limits shown in Illustration 7-8, the contribution may be limited. Use the Roth IRA Worksheet (Illustration 7-7) to determine the contribution limit.

If the taxpayer contributes more than the limit, the amount over the limit is an excess contribution. The taxpayer can withdraw the excess contribution before the due date of the tax return. If not, the taxpayer must pay a 6% tax on the excess contribution for every year it stays in the account.

Example: Let's do another worksheet. You are single, age 35, and your taxable compensation is $117,000. You had no other income or deductions. You are not covered by a retirement plan at work. You would like to contribute $2,500 to your traditional IRA and $2,500 to your Roth IRA. Look at Illustration 7-9. You may contribute $2,500 to your traditional IRA by the due date of the return, and deduct it on your tax return because you were not covered by a retirement plan at work. However, because of your AGI, you may only contribute $1,900 to your Roth IRA.

Taxability of Distributions

With Roth IRAs there are no required minimum distributions. Qualified distributions from a Roth IRA are not taxable. To be a qualified distribution, the distribution must meet the following requirements:

- The distribution is made after the 5 year period beginning with the first taxable year for which a contribution was made to a Roth IRA, and
  Note: Conversions each have a separate 5 year holding period.
- The payment or distribution is:
  - Made on or after the date the taxpayer reaches age 59½,

- o Made because the taxpayer is disabled,
- o Made to a beneficiary or to their estate after their death, or
- o One that meets the first time homebuyer requirements up to a $10,000 lifetime limit.

Roth IRA Distributions

Distributions from Roth IRAs are treated differently from traditional IRAs because none of the contributions are taxable. We will discuss those differences.

Rollovers

Distributions from Roth IRAs can only be rolled over to other Roth IRA accounts. They may not be rolled over to any other types of accounts.

Conversions

The only conversions that can be made concerning Roth IRAs are converting from a traditional IRA to a Roth IRA. This was discussed in the section for traditional IRA distributions.

Early Distributions

The taxpayer may have to pay a 10% additional tax on early distributions if the distribution is not a qualified distribution. The taxpayer will not have to pay the 10% additional tax if one of the following exceptions applies:

- The taxpayer has reached age 59½.
- The taxpayer is disabled.
- The taxpayer is the beneficiary of a deceased IRA owner.
- The taxpayer uses the distribution to pay certain qualified first-time homebuyer amounts.
- The distributions are part of a series of substantially equal payments.
- The taxpayer has significant unreimbursed medical expenses.
- The taxpayer is paying medical insurance premiums after losing their job.
- The distributions are not more than the taxpayer's qualified higher education expenses.
- The distribution is due to an IRS levy of the qualified plan.
- The distribution is a qualified reservist distribution.

Rules on early distributions from conversions of Roth IRAs are beyond the scope of this course.

SIMPLE IRA

A SIMPLE plan is a tax-favored retirement plan that certain small employers (including self-employed individuals) can set up for the benefit of their employees. If you encounter a SIMPLE plan more research will be required. You can start with IRS Publication 560.

Illustration 7-9

Modified AGI

1.	Enter the amount from Form 1040, line 22.	1.	117,000
2.	Enter any amounts from Form 2555, lines 45 and 50, and Form 2555-EZ, line 18.	2.	
3.	Enter any amounts from Form 8815, line 14.	3.	
4.	Enter any amounts from Form 8839, line 26.	4.	
5.	Add lines 1 through 5 and enter the total here.	5.	117,000
6.	Enter the sum of any amounts on Form 1040, lines 23 through 31a.	6.	
7.	Subtract line 6 from line 5. **This is the modified AGI.**	7.	117,000

Traditional IRA Worksheet

		Taxpayer		Spouse
1.	Enter the total of the taxpayer's (and spouse's if MFJ) wages, salaries, tips, etc.; alimony and separate maintenance payments, and nontaxable combat pay.	1. 117,000		
2.	Enter any earned income the taxpayer (and spouse if MFJ) received as a self-employed individual or partner minus any deductions on Form 1040, lines 27 and 28.	2.		
3.	Add lines 1 and 2. If MFJ, enter the result in both columns. If the result is 0, stop here, the taxpayer may not make any IRA contributions	3. 117,000	3.	
4.	<ul><li>If the taxpayer (**and** spouse if MFJ) was not covered by a retirement plan at work and line 3 is over $5,500 ($6,500 If age 50 or older, they may take a full deduction. Enter $5,500($6,500 if age 50 or older) on line 7 and go to line 8. If line 3 is not over $5,500 ($6,500 if age 50 or older) enter the amount from line 3 on line 7 and go to line 8.</li><li>If the taxpayer is covered by a retirement plan at work and their filing status is S, HH, or MFS and the taxpayer did not live with spouse at all during the year, enter $70,000.</li><li>If MFJ and only one is covered by a retirement plan at work, enter $116,000 in the column of the one covered and $191,000 in the other column.</li><li>If MFJ and both are covered by a retirement plan at work, enter $116,000 in both columns.</li><li>If QW and the taxpayer is covered by a retirement plan at work, enter $116,000.</li><li>If MFS and lived with spouse at any time during the year, enter $10,000.</li></ul>	4.	4.	
5.	Enter the amount from line7 in the Modified AGI worksheet above.	5.	5.	
6.	Subtract line 5 from line 4. If 0 or less, the taxpayer cannot deduct any IRA contributions. If the taxpayer wants to contribute to a Roth IRA or make nondeductible traditional IRA contributions, go to the applicable worksheet on the next page. If this amount is $10,000 or more ($20,000 if MFJ or QW), enter $5,500 ($6,500 if age 50 or over) on line 7 and go to line 8.	6.	6.	
7.	Multiply line 6 by the percentage below that applies to the taxpayer. If the result is not a multiple of $10, round it to the next highest multiple of $10. If the amount is less than $200, enter $200.<ul><li>MFJ or QW and covered by a retirement plan at work, multiply by 27.5% (32.5% if age 50 or over).</li><li>All others, multiply by 55% (65% if age 50 or over).</li></ul>	7. 5,500	7.	
8.	Enter the amount from line 3.	8. 117,000	8.	
9.	Enter the contributions made or to be made. Not more than $5,500 ($6,500 if age 50 or over).	9. 2,500	9.	
10.	Enter the smaller of lines 7, 8, and 9 here and on Form 1040, line 32. If line 9 is more than this amount, and the taxpayer will withdraw the excess and does not choose to make a Roth IRA or nondeductible contribution, stop here.	10. 2,500	10.	

Illustration 7-9 continued

Roth IRA Worksheet

		Taxpayer		Spouse
1.	Enter the amount from line 7 of the Modified AGI Worksheet. If MFJ, enter the amount in both columns.	1.	117,000	1.
2.	Enter any income resulting from the conversion of an IRA (other than Roth) to a Roth IRA. If MFJ, enter the amount in both columns.	2.		2.
3.	Subtract line 2 from line 1. If this amount is less than • $181,000 if MFJ or QW. • $114,000 if S, HH, or MFS and the taxpayer did not live with spouse at any time during the year. Enter $5,500 ($6,500 if age 50 or over) on line 12 and go to line 13.	3.	117,000	3.
4.	Enter • $181,000 if MFJ or QW. • $0 if MFS and the taxpayer lived with their spouse at any time during the year. • $114,000 for all others.	4.	114,000	4.
5.	Subtract line 4 from line 3. If 0 or less, the taxpayer cannot make a Roth IRA contribution. If they would like to make a nondeductible traditional IRA contribution, go to the Nondeductible IRA Contribution Worksheet.	5.	3,000	5.
6.	Enter • $10,000 if MFJ, QW, or MFS and the taxpayer lived with their spouse at any time during the year. • $15,000 for all others.	6.	15,000	6.
7.	Divide line 5 by line 6 and enter the result as a decimal (rounded to at least three places). If the result is 1.000 or more, enter 1.000.	7.	0.2	7.
8.	Enter $5,500 ($6,500 if age 50 or over).	8.	5,500	8.
9.	Enter the total wages, salaries, tips, etc.; alimony and separate maintenance payments, and nontaxable combat pay plus any earned income received as a self-employed individual or partner. If MFJ and one's income is less than their spouse's, complete this worksheet for the spouse with the greater income, then add both incomes together and subtract the amount of IRA contributions made by the spouse with the greater income and enter the result here for the spouse with the lesser income.. (If the Traditional IRA Worksheet has been completed, enter the amount from line 3 of that worksheet.)	9.	117,000	9.
10.	Enter the smaller of lines 8 or 9.	10.	5,500	10.
11.	Multiply the decimal on line 7 by the amount on line 10.	11.	1,100	11.
12.	Subtract line 11 from line 10. Round the result up to the nearest $10. If the result is less than $200, enter $200.	12.	4,400	12.
13.	Enter any amount from line 10 of the Traditional IRA Worksheet.	13.	2,500	13.
14.	Subtract line 13 from line 12.	14.	1,900	14.
15.	Enter the lesser of line 12 or line 14. This is the Roth IRA contribution limit.	15.	1,900	15.

Nondeductible IRA Contribution Worksheet

		Taxpayer	Spouse
1.	Enter the smaller of line 3 on the Traditional IRA Worksheet or $5,500 ($6,500 if age 50 or over).	1.	1.
2.	Enter the amount of line 10 or the Traditional IRA Worksheet.	2.	2.
3.	Enter the Roth IRA contribution made.	3.	3.
4.	Add lines 2 and 3.	4.	4.
5.	Subtract line 4 from line 1.This is the amount of nondeductible contributions that can be made.	5.	5.

Chapter Review

1) What is a contribution?

2) What is a distribution?

3) When is a deductible contribution to a traditional IRA limited?

4) What is the contribution limit for a traditional IRA?

5) What is modified adjusted gross income for traditional IRA purposes?

6) How are excess contributions penalized?

7) When are traditional IRA distributions taxable?

8) When are Roth IRA contributions limited?

9) What is the contribution limit for a Roth IRA?

10) At what age are you required to make minimum distributions from a traditional IRA?

11) At what age are you required to make minimum distributions from a Roth IRA?

12) What is the additional tax penalty on early distributions?

Exercise

Prepare a tax return for Marian Monglow. She would like to contribute as much as is deductible to her traditional IRA. If she can't deduct the maximum, she would like to contribute what she can to her Roth IRA. Use the worksheets to find out what she can do. She is single and 32 years old. She is an accounts manager. Her Form W-2 is below.

a Employee's social security number 311-54-9876	OMB No. 1545-0008	Safe, accurate, FAST! Use	*IRS* e~file	Visit the IRS website at www.irs.gov/efile

	1 Wages, tips, other compensation 62,533.54	2 Federal income tax withheld 7,731.32
b Employer identification number (EIN) 87-8778765		
c Employer's name, address, and ZIP code	3 Social security wages 62,533.54	4 Social security tax withheld 3,877.08
Finances Rule 25 Dollar Ave. Your City, Your State, Your Zip Code	5 Medicare wages and tips 62,533.54	6 Medicare tax withheld 906.74
	7 Social security tips	8 Allocated tips
d Control number	9	10 Dependent care benefits
e Employee's first name and initial Last name Suff.	11 Nonqualified plans	12a See instructions for box 12
	13 Statutory employee ☐ Retirement plan ☐ Third-party sick pay ☐	12b
Marian Monglow 556 Willow Lane Your City, Your State, Your Zip Code	14 Other	12c
		12d
f Employee's address and ZIP code		

15 State	Employer's state ID number	16 State wages, tips, etc.	17 State income tax	18 Local wages, tips, etc.	19 Local income tax	20 Locality name
YS	631243659	62,533.54	1,862.45			

Form **W-2** Wage and Tax Statement   **2014**   Department of the Treasury—Internal Revenue Service

Copy B—To Be Filed With Employee's FEDERAL Tax Return.
This information is being furnished to the Internal Revenue Service.

Form 1099-INT — Interest Income (2014)

PAYER'S name, street address, city or town, state or province, country, ZIP or foreign postal code, and telephone no.	Payer's RTN (optional)	OMB No. 1545-0112
First National Bank 2300 Financial Way Your City, Your State, Your Zip Code	**1** Interest income $ 43.70 Form **1099-INT**	**20****14** Interest Income

PAYER'S federal identification number	RECIPIENT'S identification number	**2** Early withdrawal penalty $	Copy B
63-1111110	321-54-9876	**3** Interest on U.S. Savings Bonds and Treas. obligations $	For Recipient

RECIPIENT'S name		**4** Federal income tax withheld $	**5** Investment expenses $
Marian Monglow			
Street address (including apt. no.)		**6** Foreign tax paid $	**7** Foreign country or U.S. possession
556 Willow Lane			
City or town, state or province, country, and ZIP or foreign postal code		**8** Tax-exempt interest $	**9** Specified private activity bond interest $
Your City, Your State, Your Zip Code		**10** Market discount $	**11** Bond premium $

This is important tax information and is being furnished to the Internal Revenue Service. If you are required to file a return, a negligence penalty or other sanction may be imposed on you if this income is taxable and the IRS determines that it has not been reported.

Account number (see instructions)	**12** Tax-exempt bond CUSIP no.	**13** State	**14** State identification no.	**15** State tax withheld $ $

Form **1099-INT** (keep for your records) www.irs.gov/form1099int Department of the Treasury - Internal Revenue Service

Form 1099-DIV — Dividends and Distributions (2014)

PAYER'S name, street address, city or town, state or province, country, ZIP or foreign postal code, and telephone no.	**1a** Total ordinary dividends $ 67.23	OMB No. 1545-0110
Newton Financial Services 9125 Dinero St. Your City, Your State, Your Zip Code	**1b** Qualified dividends $ Form **1099-DIV**	**20****14** Dividends and Distributions

PAYER'S federal identification number	RECIPIENT'S identification number	**2a** Total capital gain distr. $	**2b** Unrecap. Sec. 1250 gain $
63-0000010	321-54-9876	**2c** Section 1202 gain $	**2d** Collectibles (28%) gain $

Copy B / For Recipient

RECIPIENT'S name		**3** Nondividend distributions $	**4** Federal income tax withheld $
Marian Monglow			**5** Investment expenses $
Street address (including apt. no.)		**6** Foreign tax paid $	**7** Foreign country or U.S. possession
556 Willow Lane			
City or town, state or province, country, and ZIP or foreign postal code		**8** Cash liquidation distributions $	**9** Noncash liquidation distributions $
Your City, Your State, Your Zip Code		**10** Exempt-interest dividends $	**11** Specified private activity bond interest dividends $

This is important tax information and is being furnished to the Internal Revenue Service. If you are required to file a return, a negligence penalty or other sanction may be imposed on you if this income is taxable and the IRS determines that it has not been reported.

Account number (see instructions)	**12** State	**13** State identification no.	**14** State tax withheld $ $

Form **1099-DIV** (keep for your records) www.irs.gov/form1099div Department of the Treasury - Internal Revenue Service

Chapter 8 – Retirement Income

Retirement income can be a very daunting topic, especially for the recipients. In this chapter we will discuss the different types of retirement income. We will also find out how to determine whether or not they are taxable.

Pensions and Annuities

Pensions – A pension is generally a series of definitely determinable payments made to the taxpayer after retiring from work. The payments are made regularly and are based on such factors as years of service and prior compensation.

Annuity – An annuity is a series of payments under a contract made at regular intervals over a period of more than one full year. They can either be fixed or variable.

Form 1099-R

Pensions and annuities are reported to the taxpayer on a Form 1099-R like the one shown below.

☐ CORRECTED (if checked)			
PAYER'S name, street address, city or town, state or province, country, and ZIP or foreign postal code	**1** Gross distribution $ **2a** Taxable amount $	OMB No. 1545-0119 20**14** Form **1099-R**	**Distributions From Pensions, Annuities, Retirement or Profit-Sharing Plans, IRAs, Insurance Contracts, etc.**
	2b Taxable amount not determined ☐	Total distribution ☐	**Copy B** **Report this income on your federal tax return. If this form shows federal income tax withheld in box 4, attach this copy to your return.**
PAYER'S federal identification number	RECIPIENT'S identification number	**3** Capital gain (included in box 2a) $	**4** Federal income tax withheld $
RECIPIENT'S name		**5** Employee contributions /Designated Roth contributions or insurance premiums $	**6** Net unrealized appreciation in employer's securities $
Street address (including apt. no.)		**7** Distribution code(s) ☐ IRA/ SEP/ SIMPLE ☐	**8** Other $ %	This information is being furnished to the Internal Revenue Service.
City or town, state or province, country, and ZIP or foreign postal code		**9a** Your percentage of total distribution %	**9b** Total employee contributions $
10 Amount allocable to IRR within 5 years $	**11** 1st year of desig. Roth contrib.	**12** State tax withheld $ $	**13** State/Payer's state no.	**14** State distribution $ $
Account number (see instructions)		**15** Local tax withheld $ $	**16** Name of locality	**17** Local distribution $ $

Form **1099-R**   www.irs.gov/form1099r   Department of the Treasury - Internal Revenue Service

Box 1 – The total distribution will be shown in this box.

Box 2a – The taxable portion of the distribution will be in this box. If this box is empty, the payer may not have enough information to determine how much of it is taxable.

Box 2b – If the first box is checked, the payer was unable to determine the taxable amount of the distribution. If the second box is checked, the distribution was a total distribution which closed out the account.

Box 3 – If a lump-sum distribution is received from a qualified plan, and the taxpayer was born before January 2, 1936 (or the taxpayer is the beneficiary of someone born before January 2, 1936), they may be able to treat the amount in this box as a capital gain distribution. If this situation is encountered, see the Form 4972 instructions.

Box 4 – Shows the federal income tax withheld from the distribution.

Box 5 – This box will generally show the taxpayer's after tax investment in the plan that is recovered tax free this year. It can also show the taxpayer's basis in a Roth IRA or premiums paid on commercial annuities or insurance contracts recovered tax free.

Box 6 – Net unrealized appreciation in employer's securities. This is beyond the scope of this course. If encountered, see IRS Publication 575.

Box 7 – Distribution codes:

- **1** – Early distribution, no known exception.
- **2** – Early distribution, exception applies.
- **3** – Disability.
- **4** – Death.
- **5** – Prohibited transaction.
- **6** – Section 1035 exchange (a tax-free exchange of life insurance,   annuity, or endowment contracts).
- **7** – Normal distribution.
- **8** – Excess contributions plus earnings/excess deferrals (and/or earnings) taxable in the tax year.
- **9** – Cost of current life insurance protection.
- **A** – May be eligible for 10-year tax option.
- **B** – Designated Roth account distribution.
- **D** – Annuity payments from nonqualified annuities that may be subject to tax under section 1411.
- **E** – Excess annual additions under section 415 and certain excess amounts under section 403(b) plans.
- **F** – Charitable gift annuity.
- **G** – Direct rollover to a qualified plan, a 403(b) plan, a governmental 457(b) plan, or an IRA.
- **H** – Direct rollover of a designated Roth account distribution to a Roth IRA.
- **J** – Early distribution from a Roth IRA, no known exception.
- **K** – Distribution of IRA assets without a readily available FMV.

- **L** – Loans treated as distributions.
- **N** – Recharacterized IRA contribution made for the current tax year and recharacterized in the current tax year.
- **P** – Excess contributions plus earnings/ excess deferrals taxable in the prior year.
- **Q** – Qualified distribution from a Roth IRA.
- **R** – Recharacterized IRA contribution made in the prior year and recharacterized in the current tax year.
- **S** – Early distribution from a SIMPLE IRA in first 2 years, no known exception.
- **T** – Roth IRA distribution, exception applies.
- **U** – Dividend distribution from ESOP under sec. 404(k).
- **W** – Charges or payments for purchasing qualified long-term care insurance contracts under combined arrangements.

Box 7 (continued) – If the IRA/SEP/SIMPLE box is checked, you have received a traditional IRA, SEP, or SIMPLE distribution.

Box 8 – If an annuity contract is received as part of the distribution, the value of the contract is shown here. It is not taxable when received and is not included in boxes 1 and 2a.

Box 9a – If more than one person received a total distribution, the percentage the taxpayer received is shown in this box.

Box 9b – For a life annuity from a qualified plan or from a 403(b) plan, an amount may be shown for the employee's total investment in the contract.

Boxes 10-15 – These boxes are attributable to state. Check the instructions for the state the taxpayer was a resident of or received the distribution from to determine what tax laws apply.

The Taxability of Pensions and Annuities

When a taxpayer takes a distribution of periodic payments from a pension or annuity, we sometimes have to be able to determine how much of it is taxable. Periodic payments are amounts paid at regular intervals for greater than one year. If any part of the distribution is a recovery of the taxpayer's cost (investment), that part will be recovered tax free. We will discuss how to calculate the taxable portion of a distribution in this section.

If the taxpayer has no cost in the plan, the distributions will be fully taxable. The taxpayer may not have a cost in the plan if they did not contribute anything to the plan, or only contributed pre-tax money. Also, if the taxpayer did contribute after tax dollars but has already recovered their cost in the plan in prior years, their distribution for this year will be fully taxable. In this case enter the amount of the distribution directly on line 16b of the Form 1040 and do not enter anything on line 16a.

If the taxpayer does have a cost in the plan, they must use one of two methods to figure the taxable portion: the Simplified Method or the General Rule. The first step in either of these is to determine what the taxpayer's cost in the plan is. The cost is any after tax contributions made by the taxpayer as well as any contributions the employer made that were taxable to the taxpayer. Any amounts already recovered tax-free in prior years must be deducted from the taxpayer's cost.

General Rule

The General Rule calculates the tax-free portion of each payment using the ratio of the cost of the contract to the total expected return. If the annuity starting date was before July 2, 1986, the General Rule may have been used. If the annuity starting date was after July 1, 1986, the General Rule had to be used if the pension or annuity payments are received from:

- A nonqualified plan (such as a private annuity, a purchased commercial annuity, or a nonqualified employee plan), or
- A qualified plan if you are age 75 or older on your annuity starting date and your annuity payments are guaranteed for at least 5 years.

If the starting date was after July 1, 1986 and before November 19, 1996, the taxpayer could choose to use the General Rule even if the above requirements don't apply. If the General Rule was used to begin with, it must be used for the plan until the cost is recovered. After November 18, 1996, the General Rule cannot be used unless the above requirements are met. The Simplified Method must be used. This is all of the information we will cover about the General Rule. More information can be found in the IRS Publication 939.

Simplified Method

The Simplified Method calculates the tax free part of each payment by dividing the total cost basis by the number of anticipated monthly payments. If it is paid over the life of the taxpayer, the number is taken from a table in the Simplified Method Worksheet (Illustration 8-1). If the plan is paid over a certain amount of time as specified in the contract, divide the cost of the plan by the specified number of payments.

The Simplified Method must be used if the starting date is after November 18, 1996, and both of the following conditions are met:
- The pension or annuity payments are from any of the following plans:
    - A qualified employee plan.
    - A qualified employee annuity.
    - A tax-sheltered annuity plan (403(b) plan).
- On the annuity starting date, at least one of the conditions apply:
    - The taxpayer is under age 75.
    - The taxpayer is entitled to less than 5 years of guaranteed payments.

To use the Simplified Method, the IRS provides a worksheet (Illustration 8-1). The first step to completing this worksheet is to understand the Tables 1 and 2 for line 3 of the worksheet. If the plan is payable for the taxpayer's life alone, Table 1 will be used. The first column in that table concerns the age at the starting date of the annuity. The second column is the number of payments anticipated if the annuity starting date begins before November 19, 1996. The third column is the number of payments anticipated if the annuity starting date is after November 18, 1996.

Table 2 is used if the annuity is payable for the lives of more than one annuitant. The first column is the combined ages of the plan owner and the survivor annuitant. The second column is the number of payments anticipated over the lives of both payees.

> **Example:** Bob is single. He is 67 and began receiving his annuity on January 1, 2014. He received 12 monthly payments of $600. He contributed $32,000 to his annuity with after tax money. See Illustration 8-2.

Illustration 8-1

Simplified Method Worksheet—Lines 16a and 16b   *Keep for Your Records*

Before you begin:	✓ If you are the beneficiary of a deceased employee or former employee who died **before** August 21, 1996, include any death benefit exclusion that you are entitled to (up to $5,000) in the amount entered on line 2 below.

More than one pension or annuity. If you had more than one partially taxable pension or annuity, figure the taxable part of each separately. Enter the total of the taxable parts on Form 1040, line 16b. Enter the total pension or annuity payments received in 2014 on Form 1040, line 16a.

1. Enter the total pension or annuity payments from Form 1099-R, box 1. Also, enter this amount on Form 1040, line 16a . . . . **1.** _____

2. Enter your cost in the plan at the annuity starting date . . . . **2.** _____
   Note. If you completed this worksheet last year, skip line 3 and enter the amount from line 4 of last year's worksheet on line 4 below (even if the amount of your pension or annuity has changed). Otherwise, go to line 3.

3. Enter the appropriate number from **Table 1** below. **But** if your annuity starting date was **after** 1997 **and** the payments are for your life and that of your beneficiary, enter the appropriate number from **Table 2** below . . . . **3.** _____

4. Divide line 2 by the number on line 3 . . . . **4.** _____

5. Multiply line 4 by the number of months for which this year's payments were made. If your annuity starting date was **before** 1987, skip lines 6 and 7 and enter this amount on line 8. Otherwise, go to line 6 . . . . **5.** _____

6. Enter the amount, if any, recovered tax free in years after 1986. If you completed this worksheet last year, enter the amount from line 10 of last year's worksheet . . . . **6.** _____

7. Subtract line 6 from line 2 . . . . **7.** _____

8. Enter the **smaller** of line 5 or line 7 . . . . **8.** _____

9. **Taxable amount.** Subtract line 8 from line 1. Enter the result, but not less than zero. Also, enter this amount on Form 1040, line 16b. If your Form 1099-R shows a larger amount, use the amount on this line instead of the amount from Form 1099-R. If you are a retired public safety officer, see *Insurance Premiums for Retired Public Safety Officers* before entering an amount on line 16b . . . . **9.** _____

10. Was your annuity starting date before 1987?
    ☐ **Yes.** (STOP) Do not complete the rest of this worksheet.

    ☐ **No.** Add lines 6 and 8. This is the **amount you have recovered tax free** through 2014. You will need this number if you need to fill out this worksheet next year . . . . **10.** _____

11. **Balance of cost to be recovered.** Subtract line 10 from line 2. If zero, you will not have to complete this worksheet next year. The payments you receive next year will generally be fully taxable . . . . **11.** _____

Table 1 for Line 3 Above

	AND your annuity starting date was—	
IF the age at annuity starting date was . . .	**before** November 19, 1996, enter on line 3 . . .	**after** November 18, 1996, enter on line 3 . . .
55 or under	300	360
56–60	260	310
61–65	240	260
66–70	170	210
71 or older	120	160

Table 2 for Line 3 Above

IF the combined ages at annuity starting date were . . .	**THEN enter on line 3 . . .**
110 or under	410
111–120	360
121–130	310
131–140	260
141 or older	210

Illustration 8-2

Simplified Method Worksheet—Lines 16a and 16b   *Keep for Your Records*

Before you begin: ✓ If you are the beneficiary of a deceased employee or former employee who died **before** August 21, 1996, include any death benefit exclusion that you are entitled to (up to $5,000) in the amount entered on line 2 below.	

More than one pension or annuity. If you had more than one partially taxable pension or annuity, figure the taxable part of each separately. Enter the total of the taxable parts on Form 1040, line 16b. Enter the total pension or annuity payments received in 2014 on Form 1040, line 16a.

1.	Enter the total pension or annuity payments from Form 1099-R, box 1. Also, enter this amount on Form 1040, line 16a	**1.**	7,200
2.	Enter your cost in the plan at the annuity starting date **2.** 32,000		
	Note. If you completed this worksheet last year, skip line 3 and enter the amount from line 4 of last year's worksheet on line 4 below (even if the amount of your pension or annuity has changed). Otherwise, go to line 3.		
3.	Enter the appropriate number from **Table 1** below. **But** if your annuity starting date was **after** 1997 **and** the payments are for your life and that of your beneficiary, enter the appropriate number from **Table 2** below **3.** 210		
4.	Divide line 2 by the number on line 3 . . . . **4.** 152.38		
5.	Multiply line 4 by the number of months for which this year's payments were made. If your annuity starting date was **before** 1987, skip lines 6 and 7 and enter this amount on line 8. Otherwise, go to line 6 . . . . **5.** 1,829		
6.	Enter the amount, if any, recovered tax free in years after 1986. If you completed this worksheet last year, enter the amount from line 10 of last year's worksheet . . . . . **6.**		
7.	Subtract line 6 from line 2 . . . . **7.** 32,000		
8.	Enter the **smaller** of line 5 or line 7	**8.**	1,829
9.	**Taxable amount.** Subtract line 8 from line 1. Enter the result, but not less than zero. Also, enter this amount on Form 1040, line 16b. If your Form 1099-R shows a larger amount, use the amount on this line instead of the amount from Form 1099-R. If you are a retired public safety officer, see *Insurance Premiums for Retired Public Safety Officers* before entering an amount on line 16b	**9.**	5,371
10.	Was your annuity starting date before 1987?		
	☐ **Yes.** (stop) Do not complete the rest of this worksheet.		
	■ **No.** Add lines 6 and 8. This is the **amount you have recovered tax free** through 2014. You will need this number if you need to fill out this worksheet next year . . . . **10.**		1,829
11.	**Balance of cost to be recovered.** Subtract line 10 from line 2. If zero, you will not have to complete this worksheet next year. The payments you receive next year will generally be fully taxable . . . . **11.**		30,171

Table 1 for Line 3 Above

	AND your annuity starting date was—	
IF the age at annuity starting date was . . .	**before** November 19, 1996, enter on line 3 . . .	**after** November 18, 1996, enter on line 3 . . .
55 or under	300	360
56–60	260	310
61–65	240	260
66–70	170	210
71 or older	120	160

Table 2 for Line 3 Above

IF the combined ages at annuity starting date were . . .	**THEN enter on line 3 . . .**
110 or under	410
111–120	360
121–130	310
131–140	260
141 or older	210

15a	IRA distributions .	**15a**			**b** Taxable amount . . .	**15b**		
16a	Pensions and annuities	**16a**	7,200	00	**b** Taxable amount . . .	**16b**	1,829	00
17	Rental real estate, royalties, partnerships, S corporations, trusts, etc. Attach Schedule E				**17**			

Early Distributions

Most distributions from qualified retirement plans and nonqualified annuity contracts received before age 59½ are considered early distributions and are subject to 10% additional tax. This additional tax only applies to the amount that is includable in income. Any part that is withdrawn tax-free, such as amounts that represent a return of the taxpayer's investment, are not subject to the additional tax.

If the payer knows there is an exception to the early distribution penalty, they will enter code "2", "3", or "4" in box 7 of the Form 1099-R. If they do not know of any exception to an early distribution, it will be represented as code "1" in box 7. If the taxpayer falls under one of the exceptions listed below, a Form 5329 (Illustration 8-3) must be filed with the tax return.

- Made as part of a series of substantially equal periodic payments for the life or joint lives of the taxpayer and designated beneficiary.
- Made because the taxpayer is permanently and totally disabled
- Made on or after the death of the plan participant or contract holder.
- A distribution from a qualified retirement plan after the separation from service in or after the year the taxpayer reaches age 55.
- A distribution from a qualified retirement plan to an alternative payee under a qualified domestic relations order.
- A distribution from a qualified retirement plan to the extent the taxpayer has medical expenses that would be deductible on Schedule A, whether or not the taxpayer is using itemized deductions for the tax year.
- A distribution from an employer plan under a written election that provides a specific schedule for distribution of the entire interest if, as of March 1, 1986, the taxpayer had separated from service and begun receiving payments under the election.
- A distribution from an employee stock ownership plan for dividends on employer securities held by the plan.
- A distribution from a qualified retirement plan due to an IRS levy of the plan.
- A distribution from elective deferral accounts under 401(k) or 403(b) plans, or similar arrangements, that are qualified reservist distributions.
- An IRA distribution made to unemployed individuals for health insurance premiums.
- An IRA distribution made for the payment of higher education expenses.
- An IRA distribution made for the purchase of a first home, up to $10,000.
- Distributions that are incorrectly indicated as early distributions by code 1, J, or S in box 7 of Form 1099-R. Any amount received after the taxpayer reached the age of 59½ is excluded from the penalty.
- Distributions from a section 457 plan, which are not rolled over from a qualified retirement plan.

Lump-Sum Distributions

A lump-sum distribution is the distribution or payment in a single tax year of a plan participant's entire balance from all of the employer's qualified plans of one kind. To qualify as a lump-sum distribution, the distribution must have been made for one of the following reasons:

Illustration 8-3

Form **5329**	**Additional Taxes on Qualified Plans (Including IRAs) and Other Tax-Favored Accounts**	OMB No. 1545-0074
Department of the Treasury Internal Revenue Service (99)	▶ **Attach to Form 1040 or Form 1040NR.** ▶ **Information about Form 5329 and its separate instructions is at** *www.irs.gov/form5329.*	20**14** Attachment Sequence No. **29**

Name of individual subject to additional tax. If married filing jointly, see instructions.		Your social security number

Fill in Your Address Only If You Are Filing This Form by Itself and Not With Your Tax Return ▶	Home address (number and street), or P.O. box if mail is not delivered to your home	Apt. no.
	City, town or post office, state, and ZIP code. If you have a foreign address, also complete the spaces below (see instructions).	If this is an amended return, check here ▶ ☐
	Foreign country name Foreign province/state/county	Foreign postal code

If you **only** owe the additional 10% tax on early distributions, you may be able to report this tax directly on Form 1040, line 59, or Form 1040NR, line 57, without filing Form 5329. See the instructions for Form 1040, line 59, or for Form 1040NR, line 57.

Part I **Additional Tax on Early Distributions**

Complete this part if you took a taxable distribution before you reached age 59½ from a qualified retirement plan (including an IRA) or modified endowment contract (unless you are reporting this tax directly on Form 1040 or Form 1040NR—see above). You may also have to complete this part to indicate that you qualify for an exception to the additional tax on early distributions or for certain Roth IRA distributions (see instructions).

1	Early distributions included in income. For Roth IRA distributions, see instructions	**1**	
2	Early distributions included on line 1 that are not subject to the additional tax (see instructions). Enter the appropriate exception number from the instructions: _____	**2**	
3	Amount subject to additional tax. Subtract line 2 from line 1	**3**	
4	**Additional tax.** Enter 10% (.10) of line 3. Include this amount on Form 1040, line 59, or Form 1040NR, line 57	**4**	
	Caution: *If any part of the amount on line 3 was a distribution from a SIMPLE IRA, you may have to include 25% of that amount on line 4 instead of 10% (see instructions).*		

Part II **Additional Tax on Certain Distributions From Education Accounts**

Complete this part if you included an amount in income, on Form 1040 or Form 1040NR, line 21, from a Coverdell education savings account (ESA) or a qualified tuition program (QTP).

5	Distributions included in income from Coverdell ESAs and QTPs	**5**	
6	Distributions included on line 5 that are not subject to the additional tax (see instructions) . . .	**6**	
7	Amount subject to additional tax. Subtract line 6 from line 5	**7**	
8	**Additional tax.** Enter 10% (.10) of line 7. Include this amount on Form 1040, line 59, or Form 1040NR, line 57	**8**	

Part III **Additional Tax on Excess Contributions to Traditional IRAs**

Complete this part if you contributed more to your traditional IRAs for 2014 than is allowable or you had an amount on line 17 of your 2013 Form 5329.

9	Enter your excess contributions from line 16 of your 2013 Form 5329 (see instructions). If zero, go to line 15		**9**	
10	If your traditional IRA contributions for 2014 are less than your maximum allowable contribution, see instructions. Otherwise, enter -0-	**10**		
11	2014 traditional IRA distributions included in income (see instructions) .	**11**		
12	2014 distributions of prior year excess contributions (see instructions) .	**12**		
13	Add lines 10, 11, and 12		**13**	
14	Prior year excess contributions. Subtract line 13 from line 9. If zero or less, enter -0-		**14**	
15	Excess contributions for 2014 (see instructions)		**15**	
16	Total excess contributions. Add lines 14 and 15		**16**	
17	**Additional tax.** Enter 6% (.06) of the **smaller** of line 16 **or** the value of your traditional IRAs on December 31, 2014 (including 2014 contributions made in 2015). Include this amount on Form 1040, line 59, or Form 1040NR, line 57 .		**17**	

Part IV **Additional Tax on Excess Contributions to Roth IRAs**

Complete this part if you contributed more to your Roth IRAs for 2014 than is allowable or you had an amount on line 25 of your 2013 Form 5329.

18	Enter your excess contributions from line 24 of your 2013 Form 5329 (see instructions). If zero, go to line 23		**18**	
19	If your Roth IRA contributions for 2014 are less than your maximum allowable contribution, see instructions. Otherwise, enter -0-	**19**		
20	2014 distributions from your Roth IRAs (see instructions)	**20**		
21	Add lines 19 and 20		**21**	
22	Prior year excess contributions. Subtract line 21 from line 18. If zero or less, enter -0-.		**22**	
23	Excess contributions for 2014 (see instructions)		**23**	
24	Total excess contributions. Add lines 22 and 23		**24**	
25	**Additional tax.** Enter 6% (.06) of the **smaller** of line 24 **or** the value of your Roth IRAs on December 31, 2014 (including 2014 contributions made in 2015). Include this amount on Form 1040, line 59, or Form 1040NR, line 57		**25**	

For Privacy Act and Paperwork Reduction Act Notice, see your tax return instructions.   Cat. No. 13329Q   Form **5329** (2014)

- The employee's or self-employed individual's death,
- The employee quit, retired, was laid off, or was fired,
- The self-employed individual has become totally and permanently disabled.

If the taxpayer receives a lump-sum distribution they have four options. The taxpayer may enter the total amount on Form 1040, line 16b and pay taxes on the entire amount. The taxpayer may, also, choose ten-year averaging, capital gain election, or rollover.

Ten-year averaging

Ten-year averaging allows the taxpayer to compute the tax as if the distribution was received over ten years. Although it is taxed as if it is received over ten years, the taxpayer will pay the tax on it in the year it is received. This plan can only be used if the plan participant was born before January 2, 1936 and it can only be used once for any plan participant. To choose the ten-year averaging, Form 4972 (Illustration 8-4) must be completed.

Example: Lenny Jones received a lump-sum distribution of $110,000. He was born October 15, 1934. He has never elected to use ten-year averaging before this year. We will complete Form 4972 (Illustration 8-4) for Mr. Jones. To complete line 24, we must use the tax rate schedule from the IRS instructions for Form 4972 (Illustration 8-6). The amount we need to figure the tax on is $11,000. The line states $1,297.70 plus 18% of the amount over $9,170:

$$11,000 - 9,170 = 1,830$$
$$1,830 * 18\% = 329.40$$
$$329.40 + 1,297.70 = 1,627.10$$

Once we multiply the $1,627 by 10, we get his tax liability of $16,270. If we had not used the ten-year averaging, and assuming he had no other income, his tax liability would have been $20,707.

$$\$110,000 - \$7,750 \ (stamdard\ deduction) - \$3,950 \ (exemption) = \$98,300 \ (taxable\ income)$$

Capital gain election

If the taxpayer has an amount in box 3 of Form 1099-R, that portion may be treated as a long term capital gain. This topic is beyond the scope of the course and may be researched further, if needed, in the Form 4972 instructions.

Rollover

The taxpayer may choose to roll over the distribution amount into another plan. The plan may be rolled over from a qualified retirement plan into another qualified retirement plan or a traditional IRA. This allows the taxpayer to defer tax on the distribution until withdrawn from the recipient account. If the distribution is rolled over into a traditional IRA, that contribution is not deductible. Any portion that is not rolled over (including taxes withheld) will be taxable to the taxpayer in the year of the rollover. The taxpayer must generally make the rollover within 60 days. The taxpayer can also choose to have it rolled over directly from one account to another through the financial institution.

Illustration 8-4

Form 4972

Department of the Treasury
Internal Revenue Service (99)

Tax on Lump-Sum Distributions
(From Qualified Plans of Participants Born Before January 2, 1936)
▶ Information about Form 4972 and its instructions is available at *www.irs.gov/form4972.*
▶ Attach to Form 1040, Form 1040NR, or Form 1041.

OMB No. 1545-0193

2014

Attachment
Sequence No. **28**

Name of recipient of distribution

Identifying number

Part I	Complete this part to see if you can use Form 4972		Yes	No
1	Was this a distribution of a plan participant's entire balance (excluding deductible voluntary employee contributions and certain forfeited amounts) from all of an employer's qualified plans of one kind (for example, pension, profit-sharing, or stock bonus)? If "No," **do not** use this form	1		
2	Did you roll over any part of the distribution? If "Yes," **do not** use this form	2		
3	Was this distribution paid to you as a beneficiary of a plan participant who was born before January 2, 1936?	3		
4	Were you **(a)** a plan participant who received this distribution, **(b)** born before January 2, 1936, **and (c)** a participant in the plan for at least 5 years before the year of the distribution? . . . . If you answered "No" to both questions 3 **and** 4, **do not** use this form.	4		
5a	Did you use Form 4972 after 1986 for a previous distribution from your own plan? If "Yes," **do not** use this form for a 2014 distribution from your own plan	5a		
b	If you are receiving this distribution as a beneficiary of a plan participant who died, did you use Form 4972 for a previous distribution received as a beneficiary of that participant after 1986? If "Yes," **do not** use this form for this distribution	5b		

Part II	Complete this part to choose the 20% capital gain election (see instructions)		
6	Capital gain part from Form 1099-R, box 3	6	
7	Multiply line 6 by 20% (.20) . . . . ▶	7	
	If you also choose to use Part III, go to line 8. Otherwise, include the amount from line 7 in the total on Form 1040, line 44; Form 1040NR, line 42; or Form 1041, Schedule G, line 1b.		

Part III	Complete this part to choose the 10-year tax option (see instructions)		
8	If you completed Part II, enter the amount from Form 1099-R, box 2a minus box 3. If you did not complete Part II, enter the amount from box 2a. Multiple recipients (and recipients who elect to include NUA in taxable income) see instructions	8	
9	Death benefit exclusion for a beneficiary of a plan participant who died before August 21, 1996 .	9	
10	Total taxable amount. Subtract line 9 from line 8	10	
11	Current actuarial value of annuity from Form 1099-R, box 8. If none, enter -0-	11	
12	Adjusted total taxable amount. Add lines 10 and 11. If this amount is $70,000 or more, **skip** lines 13 through 16, enter this amount on line 17, and go to line 18	12	
13	Multiply line 12 by 50% (.50), but **do not** enter more than $10,000 . . [13]		
14	Subtract $20,000 from line 12. If line 12 is $20,000 or less, enter -0- . . . . . . [14]		
15	Multiply line 14 by 20% (.20) . . . . [15]		
16	Minimum distribution allowance. Subtract line 15 from line 13	16	
17	Subtract line 16 from line 12	17	
18	Federal estate tax attributable to lump-sum distribution	18	
19	Subtract line 18 from line 17. If line 11 is zero, **skip** lines 20 through 22 and go to line 23 . . .	19	
20	Divide line 11 by line 12 and enter the result as a decimal (rounded to at least three places) . . . . [20] .		
21	Multiply line 16 by the decimal on line 20 . . . . [21]		
22	Subtract line 21 from line 11 . . . . [22]		
23	Multiply line 19 by 10% (.10)	23	
24	Tax on amount on line 23. Use the Tax Rate Schedule in the instructions	24	
25	Multiply line 24 by ten (10). If line 11 is zero, **skip** lines 26 through 28, enter this amount on line 29, and go to line 30	25	
26	Multiply line 22 by 10% (.10) . . . . [26]		
27	Tax on amount on line 26. Use the Tax Rate Schedule in the instructions . . . . [27]		
28	Multiply line 27 by ten (10)	28	
29	Subtract line 28 from line 25. Multiple recipients see instructions . . . . ▶	29	
30	**Tax on lump-sum distribution.** Add lines 7 and 29. Also include this amount in the total on Form 1040, line 44; Form 1040NR, line 42; or Form 1041, Schedule G, line 1b . . . . ▶	30	

For Paperwork Reduction Act Notice, see instructions.   Cat. No. 13187U   Form **4972** (2014)

Illustration 8-5

Form **4972**

Department of the Treasury
Internal Revenue Service (99)

Tax on Lump-Sum Distributions
(From Qualified Plans of Participants Born Before January 2, 1936)
▶ Information about Form 4972 and its instructions is available at *www.irs.gov/form4972.*
▶ **Attach to Form 1040, Form 1040NR, or Form 1041.**

OMB No. 1545-0193

20**14**

Attachment
Sequence No. **28**

Name of recipient of distribution	Identifying number
Lenny Jones	766-56-8775

	Part I	Complete this part to see if you can use Form 4972		**Yes**	**No**
1		Was this a distribution of a plan participant's entire balance (excluding deductible voluntary employee contributions and certain forfeited amounts) from all of an employer's qualified plans of one kind (for example, pension, profit-sharing, or stock bonus)? If "No," **do not** use this form	1	✓	
2		Did you roll over any part of the distribution? If "Yes," **do not** use this form	2		✓
3		Was this distribution paid to you as a beneficiary of a plan participant who was born before January 2, 1936?	3		✓
4		Were you **(a)** a plan participant who received this distribution, **(b)** born before January 2, 1936, **and (c)** a participant in the plan for at least 5 years before the year of the distribution?	4	✓	
		If you answered "No" to both questions 3 **and** 4, **do not** use this form.			
5a		Did you use Form 4972 after 1986 for a previous distribution from your own plan? If "Yes," **do not** use this form for a 2014 distribution from your own plan	5a		✓
	b	If you are receiving this distribution as a beneficiary of a plan participant who died, did you use Form 4972 for a previous distribution received as a beneficiary of that participant after 1986? If "Yes," **do not** use this form for this distribution	5b		✓

Part II	Complete this part to choose the 20% capital gain election (see instructions)			
6	Capital gain part from Form 1099-R, box 3	6		
7	Multiply line 6 by 20% (.20) ▶	7		
	If you also choose to use Part III, go to line 8. Otherwise, include the amount from line 7 in the total on Form 1040, line 44; Form 1040NR, line 42; or Form 1041, Schedule G, line 1b.			

Part III	Complete this part to choose the 10-year tax option (see instructions)				
8	If you completed Part II, enter the amount from Form 1099-R, box 2a minus box 3. If you did not complete Part II, enter the amount from box 2a. Multiple recipients (and recipients who elect to include NUA in taxable income) see instructions	8		110,000	00
9	Death benefit exclusion for a beneficiary of a plan participant who died before August 21, 1996	9			
10	Total taxable amount. Subtract line 9 from line 8	10		110,000	00
11	Current actuarial value of annuity from Form 1099-R, box 8. If none, enter -0-	11			
12	Adjusted total taxable amount. Add lines 10 and 11. If this amount is $70,000 or more, **skip** lines 13 through 16, enter this amount on line 17, and go to line 18	12		110,000	00
13	Multiply line 12 by 50% (.50), but **do not** enter more than $10,000	13			
14	Subtract $20,000 from line 12. If line 12 is $20,000 or less, enter -0-	14			
15	Multiply line 14 by 20% (.20)	15			
16	Minimum distribution allowance. Subtract line 15 from line 13	16			
17	Subtract line 16 from line 12	17		110,000	00
18	Federal estate tax attributable to lump-sum distribution	18			
19	Subtract line 18 from line 17. If line 11 is zero, **skip** lines 20 through 22 and go to line 23	19		110,000	00
20	Divide line 11 by line 12 and enter the result as a decimal (rounded to at least three places)	20	.		
21	Multiply line 16 by the decimal on line 20	21			
22	Subtract line 21 from line 11	22			
23	Multiply line 19 by 10% (.10)	23		11,000	00
24	Tax on amount on line 23. Use the Tax Rate Schedule in the instructions	24		1,627	00
25	Multiply line 24 by ten (10). If line 11 is zero, **skip** lines 26 through 28, enter this amount on line 29, and go to line 30	25		16,270	00
26	Multiply line 22 by 10% (.10)	26			
27	Tax on amount on line 26. Use the Tax Rate Schedule in the instructions	27			
28	Multiply line 27 by ten (10)	28			
29	Subtract line 28 from line 25. Multiple recipients see instructions ▶	29		16270	00
30	**Tax on lump-sum distribution.** Add lines 7 and 29. Also include this amount in the total on Form 1040, line 44; Form 1040NR, line 42; or Form 1041, Schedule G, line 1b ▶	30		16,270	00

For Paperwork Reduction Act Notice, see instructions.   Cat. No. 13187U   Form **4972** (2014)

Illustration 8-6

Tax Rate Schedule

If the amount on line 23 or 26 is:		Enter on line 24 or 27:	Of the amount over—
Over	But not over—		
$ 0	$ 1,190	- - - - - 11%	$ 0
1,190	2,270	$130.90 + 12%	1,190
2,270	4,530	260.50 + 14%	2,270
4,530	6,690	576.90 + 15%	4,530
6,690	9,170	900.90 + 16%	6,690
9,170	11,440	1,297.70 + 18%	9,170
11,440	13,710	1,706.30 + 20%	11,440
13,710	17,160	2,160.30 + 23%	13,710
17,160	22,880	2,953.80 + 26%	17,160
22,880	28,600	4,441.00 + 30%	22,880
28,600	34,320	6,157.00 + 34%	28,600
34,320	42,300	8,101.80 + 38%	34,320
42,300	57,190	11,134.20 + 42%	42,300
57,190	85,790	17,388.00 + 48%	57,190
85,790	- - - - -	31,116.00 + 50%	85,790

Disability pensions

A disability pension is received if the taxpayer retired on disability and has not yet reached retirement age. If the taxpayer receives disability payments from a plan paid for by the employer, the distribution must be included in income. If the disability payments are received before retirement age, they must be included on line 7 of Form 1040. Once the taxpayer reaches retirement age, the disability payments will be treated as retirement income and included on line 16b.

Railroad Retirement Benefits

Railroad Retirement Benefits are benefits paid under the Railroad Retirement Act. Railroad Retirement Benefits are paid in two categories. The first category is the tier 1 benefits that equal the social security benefits that a railroad employee or beneficiary would have been entitled to under the social security system. They are treated the same as social security benefits for tax purposes.

The second category is the remainder of tier 1 benefits and the tier 2 benefits. These benefits are treated as payments from a qualified employee plan. This allows for the tax-free treatment of employee contributions to the plan.

Social Security Benefits

Social Security Benefits include monthly retirement, survivor, and disability payments. They do not include supplemental survival income (SSI) benefits. Social security may be partially taxable depending on marital filing status and other income. If the taxpayer received social security benefits, they will have received a Form SSA-1099.

Box 3: Box 3 shows the total amount of benefits paid in the tax year. This is not the amount received or that will be used to figure if any of the benefits are taxable.

Description of Amount in Box 3: This will describe any adjustments made to the social security benefits. This includes any amounts paid for Medicare premiums, worker's compensation offset, and federal income tax withheld.

Box 5: This is the amount of net benefits paid in the tax year. This is the amount used to figure if any of the benefits are taxable.

FORM SSA-1099 – SOCIAL SECURITY BENEFIT STATEMENT

2014
- PART OF YOUR SOCIAL SECURITY BENEFITS SHOWN IN BOX 5 MAY BE TAXABLE INCOME.
- SEE THE REVERSE FOR MORE INFORMATION.

Box 1. Name		Box 2. Beneficiary's Social Security Number

Box 3. Benefits Paid in 2014	Box 4. Benefits Repaid to SSA in 2014	Box 5. Net Benefits for 2014 *(Box 3 minus Box 4)*

DESCRIPTION OF AMOUNT IN BOX 3	DESCRIPTION OF AMOUNT IN BOX 4

Box 6. Voluntary Federal Income Tax Withheld

Box 7. Address

Box 8. Claim Number *(Use this number if you need to contact SSA.)*

Form **SSA-1099-SM** (1-2015)   DO NOT RETURN THIS FORM TO SSA OR IRS

Taxability of Social Security Benefits

Up to 85% of the social security benefits may be taxable. To determine if any of the benefits are taxable, we must first determine the taxpayer's determining income. The determining income is one-half of the social security benefits plus all other income. If married filing joint, use both spouse's incomes. When determining all other income, do not take into account any exclusion for:

- Interest from qualified U.S. savings bonds,
- Employer-provide adoption benefits,
- Foreign earned income or housing, or
- Income earned by bona fide residents of American Samoa or Puerto Rico.

Once we have the amount of determining income, we must compare it with the base amount. If the income is over the base amount, the benefits may be partly taxable. The base amounts are as follows:

- $25,000 if single, head of household, or qualifying widow(er).
- $25,000 if married filing separately and lived apart from the spouse for all of the tax year.
- $32,000 if married filing joint.
- $0 if married filing separately and lived with the spouse at any time during the tax year.

Note: Benefits are taxable to whoever is the legal recipient. If a child receives social security, these benefits are not taxable to the parents. They must be added to any other income the child receives to determine if they are taxable.

Thankfully, the IRS has developed a worksheet (Illustration 8-7) to help determine if the social security benefits are taxable. To report the social security benefits on the tax return, the total benefits will be reported on line 20a of the Form 1040 and the taxable benefits will be reported on line 20b.

Example: Kenny McDonald is single and he received $18,223 of social security benefits. He also has pension income of $22,000. He received no other income for the tax year. (Illustration 8-8) His benefits will be reported as follows:

| 20a | Social security benefits | 20a | 18,223 | 00 | b Taxable amount . . . | 20b | 3,056 | 00 |

Illustration 8-7

Social Security Benefits Worksheet—Lines 20a and 20b

Keep for Your Records

Before you begin:	✓ Complete Form 1040, lines 21 and 23 through 32, if they apply to you.
	✓ Figure any write-in adjustments to be entered on the dotted line next to line 36 (see the instructions for line 36).
	✓ If you are married filing separately and you lived apart from your spouse for all of 2014, enter "D" to the right of the word "benefits" on line 20a. If you do not, you may get a math error notice from the IRS.
	✓ Be sure you have read the **Exception** in the line 20a and 20b instructions to see if you can use this worksheet instead of a publication to find out if any of your benefits are taxable.

1. Enter the total amount from **box 5** of **all** your **Forms SSA-1099** and **Forms RRB-1099.** Also, enter this amount on Form 1040, line 20a .... **1.** _____

2. Enter one-half of line 1 .... **2.** _____

3. Combine the amounts from Form 1040, lines 7, 8a, 9a, 10 through 14, 15b, 16b, 17 through 19, and 21 .... **3.** _____

4. Enter the amount, if any, from Form 1040, line 8b .... **4.** _____

5. Combine lines 2, 3, and 4 .... **5.** _____

6. Enter the total of the amounts from Form 1040, lines 23 through 32, plus any write-in adjustments you entered on the dotted line next to line 36 .... **6.** _____

7. Is the amount on line 6 less than the amount on line 5?

   ☐ **No.** 🛑 None of your social security benefits are taxable. Enter -0- on Form 1040, line 20b.

   ☐ **Yes.** Subtract line 6 from line 5 .... **7.** _____

8. If you are:
   - Married filing jointly, enter $32,000
   - Single, head of household, qualifying widow(er), or married filing separately and you **lived apart** from your spouse for all of 2014, enter $25,000

   - Married filing separately and you lived with your spouse at any time in 2014, skip lines 8 through 15; multiply line 7 by 85% (.85) and enter the result on line 16. Then go to line 17 } .... **8.** _____

9. Is the amount on line 8 less than the amount on line 7?

   ☐ **No.** 🛑 None of your social security benefits are taxable. Enter -0- on Form 1040, line 20b. If you are married filing separately and you **lived apart** from your spouse for all of 2014, be sure you entered "D" to the right of the word "benefits" on line 20a.

   ☐ **Yes.** Subtract line 8 from line 7 .... **9.** _____

10. Enter: $12,000 if married filing jointly; $9,000 if single, head of household, qualifying widow(er), or married filing separately and you **lived apart** from your spouse for all of 2014 .... **10.** _____

11. Subtract line 10 from line 9. If zero or less, enter -0- .... **11.** _____

12. Enter the **smaller** of line 9 or line 10 .... **12.** _____

13. Enter one-half of line 12 .... **13.** _____

14. Enter the **smaller** of line 2 or line 13 .... **14.** _____

15. Multiply line 11 by 85% (.85). If line 11 is zero, enter -0- .... **15.** _____

16. Add lines 14 and 15 .... **16.** _____

17. Multiply line 1 by 85% (.85) .... **17.** _____

18. **Taxable social security benefits.** Enter the **smaller** of line 16 or line 17. Also enter this amount on Form 1040, line 20b .... **18.** _____

TIP *If any of your benefits are taxable for 2014 **and** they include a lump-sum benefit payment that was for an earlier year, you may be able to reduce the taxable amount. See* Lump-Sum Election *in Pub. 915 for details.*

Illustration 8-8

Social Security Benefits Worksheet—Lines 20a and 20b

Keep for Your Records

Before you begin:	✓ Complete Form 1040, lines 21 and 23 through 32, if they apply to you.
	✓ Figure any write-in adjustments to be entered on the dotted line next to line 36 (see the instructions for line 36).
	✓ If you are married filing separately and you lived apart from your spouse for all of 2014, enter "D" to the right of the word "benefits" on line 20a. If you do not, you may get a math error notice from the IRS.
	✓ Be sure you have read the **Exception** in the line 20a and 20b instructions to see if you can use this worksheet instead of a publication to find out if any of your benefits are taxable.

1. Enter the total amount from **box 5** of **all** your **Forms SSA-1099** and **Forms RRB-1099.** Also, enter this amount on Form 1040, line 20a .... **1.** `18,223`

2. Enter one-half of line 1 . . . . **2.** `9,112`

3. Combine the amounts from Form 1040, lines 7, 8a, 9a, 10 through 14, 15b, 16b, 17 through 19, and 21 . . . . **3.** `22,000`

4. Enter the amount, if any, from Form 1040, line 8b . . . . **4.**

5. Combine lines 2, 3, and 4 . . . . **5.** `31,112`

6. Enter the total of the amounts from Form 1040, lines 23 through 32, plus any write-in adjustments you entered on the dotted line next to line 36 . . . . **6.**

7. Is the amount on line 6 less than the amount on line 5?

   ☐ **No.** 🛑 None of your social security benefits are taxable. Enter -0- on Form 1040, line 20b.

   ■ **Yes.** Subtract line 6 from line 5 . . . . **7.** `31,112`

8. If you are:
   - Married filing jointly, enter $32,000
   - Single, head of household, qualifying widow(er), or married filing separately and you **lived apart** from your spouse for all of 2014, enter $25,000
   - Married filing separately and you lived with your spouse at any time in 2014, skip lines 8 through 15; multiply line 7 by 85% (.85) and enter the result on line 16. Then go to line 17

   } . . . . **8.** `25,000`

9. Is the amount on line 8 less than the amount on line 7?

   ☐ **No.** 🛑 None of your social security benefits are taxable. Enter -0- on Form 1040, line 20b. If you are married filing separately and you **lived apart** from your spouse for all of 2014, be sure you entered "D" to the right of the word "benefits" on line 20a.

   ■ **Yes.** Subtract line 8 from line 7 . . . . **9.** `6,112`

10. Enter: $12,000 if married filing jointly; $9,000 if single, head of household, qualifying widow(er), or married filing separately and you **lived apart** from your spouse for all of 2014 . . . . **10.** `9,000`

11. Subtract line 10 from line 9. If zero or less, enter -0- . . . . **11.** `0`

12. Enter the **smaller** of line 9 or line 10 . . . . **12.** `6,112`

13. Enter one-half of line 12 . . . . **13.** `3,056`

14. Enter the **smaller** of line 2 or line 13 . . . . **14.** `3,056`

15. Multiply line 11 by 85% (.85). If line 11 is zero, enter -0- . . . . **15.** `0`

16. Add lines 14 and 15 . . . . **16.** `3,056`

17. Multiply line 1 by 85% (.85) . . . . **17.** `15,490`

18. **Taxable social security benefits.** Enter the **smaller** of line 16 or line 17. Also enter this amount on Form 1040, line 20b . . . . **18.** `3,056`

💡 **TIP** *If any of your benefits are taxable for 2014 **and** they include a lump-sum benefit payment that was for an earlier year, you may be able to reduce the taxable amount. See Lump-Sum Election in Pub. 915 for details.*

Chapter Review

1) Pensions and annuities are reported to the taxpayer on what form?

2) If the taxpayer has no cost in the pension plan will the distributions be taxable, nontaxable, or partly taxable?

3) If the taxpayer starts receiving partly taxable distributions from a qualified employee plan this year, what method will be used to determine the taxable amount?

4) What are periodic payments?

5) What is a lump-sum distribution?

6) What may the taxpayer do with a lump-sum distribution to totally defer the tax?

7) What is the maximum amount of social security distributions that may be taxable?

Exercise

Prepare a tax return for John Megginson. His SSN is 564-56-3676 and his birth date is January 2, 1934. He is single and has no dependents. He wishes to designate $3 to the presidential campaign fund. He worked part time for 3 months out of the year. His SSA-1099 reports that he received $16,221 of social security benefits. He had no tax withheld from them. His other reporting documents are below.

☐ CORRECTED (if checked)

PAYER'S name, street address, city or town, state or province, country, and ZIP or foreign postal code		**1** Gross distribution $ 32,778.09	OMB No. 1545-0119 **20**14	**Distributions From Pensions, Annuities, Retirement or Profit-Sharing Plans, IRAs, Insurance Contracts, etc.**
Provincial Retirement Planning 6664 Security Way Your City, Your State, Your Zip Code		**2a** Taxable amount $ 29,665.34	Form **1099-R**	
		2b Taxable amount not determined ☐	Total distribution ☐	**Copy B Report this income on your federal tax return. If this form shows federal income tax withheld in box 4, attach this copy to your return.**
PAYER'S federal identification number	RECIPIENT'S identification number	**3** Capital gain (included in box 2a) $	**4** Federal income tax withheld $ 3,466.50	
65-9876544	564-56-3676			
RECIPIENT'S name John Megginson		**5** Employee contributions /Designated Roth contributions or insurance premiums $ 3,112.75	**6** Net unrealized appreciation in employer's securities $	
Street address (including apt. no.) 7778 Happiness Circle		**7** Distribution code(s) 7	IRA/ SEP/ SIMPLE ☐	**8** Other $ %	This information is being furnished to the Internal Revenue Service.
City or town, state or province, country, and ZIP or foreign postal code Your City, Your State, Your Zip Code		**9a** Your percentage of total distribution %	**9b** Total employee contributions $	
10 Amount allocable to IRR within 5 years $	**11** 1st year of desig. Roth contrib.	**12** State tax withheld $ _ _ _ _ $	**13** State/Payer's state no.	**14** State distribution $ _ _ _ _ $
Account number (see instructions)		**15** Local tax withheld $ _ _ _ _ $	**16** Name of locality	**17** Local distribution $ _ _ _ _ $

Form **1099-R**   www.irs.gov/form1099r   Department of the Treasury - Internal Revenue Service

	a Employee's social security number 564-56-3676	OMB No. 1545-0008	Safe, accurate, FAST! Use	IRS *e~file*	Visit the IRS website at www.irs.gov/efile

b Employer identification number (EIN) 34-9358456	1 Wages, tips, other compensation 3,588.29	2 Federal income tax withheld 278.39
c Employer's name, address, and ZIP code Mary Beth's Fresh Market 453 Normal Way Your City, Your State, Your Zip Code	3 Social security wages 3,588.29	4 Social security tax withheld 222.47
	5 Medicare wages and tips 3,588.29	6 Medicare tax withheld 52.03
	7 Social security tips	8 Allocated tips
d Control number	9	10 Dependent care benefits
e Employee's first name and initial Last name Suff.	11 Nonqualified plans	12a See instructions for box 12
 John Megginson 778 Happiness Circle Your City, Your State, Your Zip Code	13 Statutory employee ☐ Retirement plan ☐ Third-party sick pay ☐	12b
	14 Other	12c
		12d
f Employee's address and ZIP code		

15 State	Employer's state ID number	16 State wages, tips, etc.	17 State income tax	18 Local wages, tips, etc.	19 Local income tax	20 Locality name
YS	39354463	3,588.29	53.51			

Form **W-2** Wage and Tax Statement   **2014**

Department of the Treasury—Internal Revenue Service

Copy B—To Be Filed With Employee's FEDERAL Tax Return.
This information is being furnished to the Internal Revenue Service.

Chapter 9 – Adjustments to Income

The IRS allows total income to be reduced by certain adjustments resulting in the adjusted gross income. On the Form 1040, the adjustments are on lines 23 through 35 (Illustration 9-1).

Educator Expense

Eligible educators may deduct up to $250 of qualified expenses they paid in 2013. If both the taxpayer and spouse are eligible educators and the filing status is married filing joint, they each may deduct expenses they paid up to the $250 maximum for a total deduction of $500. An eligible educator is a kindergarten through 12th grade teacher, instructor, counselor, principal, or aide who worked in a school. The eligible educator must have worked in the school for at least 900 hours during a school year.

Qualified expenses are ordinary and necessary expenses paid in connection with books, supplies, equipment, and other materials used in the classroom. These expenses also include computer equipment, software, and services. An ordinary expense is one that is common and accepted in the educational field. Necessary is helpful and appropriate for the profession of an educator. Keep in mind that an expense does not have to be required to be considered necessary.

The qualified expenses must be reduced by any of the following amounts:

- Excludable U.S. series EE and I savings bond interest from Form 8815.
- Nontaxable qualified tuition program earnings or distributions.
- Any nontaxable distribution of Coverdell education savings account earnings.
- Any reimbursements the taxpayer received for these expenses that were not reported to the taxpayer on Form W-2.

If the taxpayer has qualified expenses over the $250 allowed, the remainder may be deducted on the Schedule A as an employee business expense. This will be covered further in the next two chapters.

The educator expense will be entered directly on Form 1040, line 23.

Certain Business expenses of Reservists, Performing Artists, and Fee-Basis Government Officials

Most employee business expenses are deducted on the Schedule A, Itemized Deductions and therefore, only beneficial to the taxpayer if they have enough deductions to warrant itemizing. We will discuss this further in the next chapter. However, the IRS allows deductions for the following professions directly on the Form 1040.

- Certain business expenses of National Guard and reserve members who traveled more than 100 miles from home to perform services as a National Guard or reserve member.
- Performing-arts-related expenses as a qualified performing artist.
- Business expenses of fee-basis state or local government officials.

Illustration 9-1

Form 1040

Department of the Treasury—Internal Revenue Service (99)

U.S. Individual Income Tax Return **2014** OMB No. 1545-0074 | IRS Use Only—Do not write or staple in this space.

For the year Jan. 1–Dec. 31, 2014, or other tax year beginning , 2014, ending , 20 | See separate instructions.

Your first name and initial | Last name | Your social security number

If a joint return, spouse's first name and initial | Last name | Spouse's social security number

Home address (number and street). If you have a P.O. box, see instructions. | Apt. no. | ▲ **Make sure the SSN(s) above and on line 6c are correct.**

City, town or post office, state, and ZIP code. If you have a foreign address, also complete spaces below (see instructions).

Presidential Election Campaign
Check here if you, or your spouse if filing jointly, want $3 to go to this fund. Checking a box below will not change your tax or refund. ☐ You ☐ Spouse

Foreign country name | Foreign province/state/county | Foreign postal code

Filing Status	1 ☐ Single	4 ☐ Head of household (with qualifying person). (See instructions.) If the qualifying person is a child but not your dependent, enter this child's name here. ▶
	2 ☐ Married filing jointly (even if only one had income)	
Check only one box.	3 ☐ Married filing separately. Enter spouse's SSN above and full name here. ▶	5 ☐ Qualifying widow(er) with dependent child

Exemptions

6a ☐ **Yourself.** If someone can claim you as a dependent, **do not** check box 6a . . . . . .
b ☐ Spouse . . . .

c **Dependents:**

(1) First name Last name	(2) Dependent's social security number	(3) Dependent's relationship to you	(4) ✓ if child under age 17 qualifying for child tax credit (see instructions)
			☐
			☐
			☐
			☐

If more than four dependents, see instructions and check here ▶ ☐

Boxes checked on 6a and 6b
No. of children on 6c who:
• lived with you
• did not live with you due to divorce or separation (see instructions)
Dependents on 6c not entered above
Add numbers on lines above ▶

d Total number of exemptions claimed . . . .

Income

Attach Form(s) W-2 here. Also attach Forms W-2G and 1099-R if tax was withheld.

If you did not get a W-2, see instructions.

7	Wages, salaries, tips, etc. Attach Form(s) W-2	7	
8a	**Taxable** interest. Attach Schedule B if required	8a	
b	**Tax-exempt** interest. **Do not** include on line 8a . . .	8b			
9a	Ordinary dividends. Attach Schedule B if required	9a	
b	Qualified dividends	9b			
10	Taxable refunds, credits, or offsets of state and local income taxes	10	
11	Alimony received	11	
12	Business income or (loss). Attach Schedule C or C-EZ	12	
13	Capital gain or (loss). Attach Schedule D if required. If not required, check here ▶ ☐	13	
14	Other gains or (losses). Attach Form 4797	14	
15a	IRA distributions .	15a		b Taxable amount . . .	15b	
16a	Pensions and annuities	16a		b Taxable amount . . .	16b	
17	Rental real estate, royalties, partnerships, S corporations, trusts, etc. Attach Schedule E	17	
18	Farm income or (loss). Attach Schedule F	18	
19	Unemployment compensation	19	
20a	Social security benefits	20a		b Taxable amount . . .	20b	
21	Other income. List type and amount	21	
22	Combine the amounts in the far right column for lines 7 through 21. This is your **total income** ▶	22	

Adjusted Gross Income

23	Educator expenses	23			
24	Certain business expenses of reservists, performing artists, and fee-basis government officials. Attach Form 2106 or 2106-EZ	24			
25	Health savings account deduction. Attach Form 8889 .	25			
26	Moving expenses. Attach Form 3903	26			
27	Deductible part of self-employment tax. Attach Schedule SE .	27			
28	Self-employed SEP, SIMPLE, and qualified plans . .	28			
29	Self-employed health insurance deduction . .	29			
30	Penalty on early withdrawal of savings	30			
31a	Alimony paid b Recipient's SSN ▶	31a			
32	IRA deduction	32			
33	Student loan interest deduction	33			
34	Tuition and fees. Attach Form 8917	34			
35	Domestic production activities deduction. Attach Form 8903	35			
36	Add lines 23 through 35			36	
37	Subtract line 36 from line 22. This is your **adjusted gross income** . . . . ▶			37	

For Disclosure, Privacy Act, and Paperwork Reduction Act Notice, see separate instructions. Cat. No. 11320B Form **1040** (2014)

These expenses will first be deducted on a Form 2106 (discussed at length later in the course), then carried to the Form 1040, line 24.

Health Savings Accounts

A Health Savings Account (HSA) is an account set up exclusively for paying the qualified medical expenses of the account's beneficiary or their spouse or dependents. In order to contribute to an HSA, the taxpayer must be covered under a high deductible health plan (HDHP) and have no other coverage except insurance that provides benefits only for:

- Liabilities under workers' compensation laws, tort liabilities, or liabilities arising from the ownership or use of property,
- A specific disease or illness,
- A fixed amount per day (or other period) of hospitalization, or
- Coverage through insurance or otherwise for
    - Accidents,
    - Disability,
    - Dental care,
    - Vision care, or
    - Long-term care.

Also, if the taxpayer can be claimed as a dependent on another's tax return or is covered under Medicare, they may not contribute to an HSA. If the taxpayer is eligible, anyone may contribute to their HSA.

A high deductible health plan is a health plan that has a minimum annual deductible of $1,250 for self-only coverage or $2,500 for family coverage. The maximum annual out-of-pocket expenses must be $6,350 for self-only coverage or $12,700 for family coverage. If the plan uses network providers, the maximum annual out-of-pocket expenses are only for services within the network. Out-of-network expenses do not apply. An HDHP does not include a plan that is substantially for accidents, disability, dental care, vision care, or long-term care.

If distributions from an HSA are used to pay the qualified medical expenses of the beneficiary, spouse, or dependents, they are excludable from gross income. Any amount that is not used to pay qualified medical expenses is subject to an additional tax of 10%. Qualified medical expenses include any medical expenses that otherwise would be deductible on the Schedule A (we will cover this later in the course). Insurance premiums only qualify if they are for:

- Long-term care insurance,
- Health care continuation coverage (such as COBRA),
- Health care coverage while receiving unemployment compensation under federal or state law, or
- Medicare and other health care coverage if the taxpayer was 65 or older (other than premiums for a Medicare supplemental policy, such as Medigap).

If the taxpayer has eligible HSA contributions, a Form 8889 (Illustration 9-2) will be filed and the deductible contribution will be carried to Form 1040, line 25. If the taxpayer received a distribution from an HSA, a Form 8889 must be filed for that as well.

Moving Expenses

If the taxpayer moves to a new place of residence because they have a new principal workplace, their moving expenses may be deductible. The moving expenses are deductible for employees and the self employed. In order to deduct the moving expenses, the taxpayer must meet both the distance and time tests.

Distance Test

The new principal workplace must be at least 50 miles farther from the old home than the old workplace was. If the taxpayer does not have an old workplace, the new workplace must be at least 50 miles from the old home.

Time Test

If the taxpayer is an employee, they must work full time in the general area of the new workplace for at least 39 weeks during the first 12 months after moving. If the taxpayer is self-employed, they must work full time in the general area of the new workplace for at least 39 weeks during the first 12 months and a total of at least 78 weeks during the first 24 months after moving.

If the taxpayer expects to meet the time requirement, they may deduct the moving expenses in the year of the move. If they do not meet the time test later, they have two choices. They may amend their tax return for the year they claimed the moving deduction. Or if they would rather, in the year the taxpayer finds they do not meet the time requirement, they may include the amount of the deduction previously allowed in income.

Qualifying Moving Expenses

Qualifying moving expenses include the reasonable expenses of moving household goods and personal effects and of traveling from the old home to the new home. Reasonable expenses include the cost of lodging but not meals. All members of the household need not move at the same time, but can only deduct one trip per person. If the taxpayer uses their own vehicle they may deduct any out-of-pocket expenses for gas and oil, or mileage at a rate of 23.5 cents per mile for 2014. Moving expenses will be deducted on Form 3903 (Illustration 9-3) and then carried to Form 1040, line 26.

Illustration 9-2

Form 8889

Department of the Treasury
Internal Revenue Service

Health Savings Accounts (HSAs)

▶ Information about Form 8889 and its separate instructions is available at *www.irs.gov/form8889.*
▶ Attach to Form 1040 or Form 1040NR.

OMB No. 1545-0074

2014

Attachment
Sequence No. **53**

Name(s) shown on Form 1040 or Form 1040NR

Social security number of HSA beneficiary. If both spouses have HSAs, see instructions ▶

Before you begin: Complete Form 8853, Archer MSAs and Long-Term Care Insurance Contracts, if required.

Part I | **HSA Contributions and Deduction.** See the instructions before completing this part. If you are filing jointly and both you and your spouse each have separate HSAs, complete a separate Part I for each spouse.

1	Check the box to indicate your coverage under a high-deductible health plan (HDHP) during 2014 (see instructions). . . . . ▶	☐ Self-only ☐ Family	
2	HSA contributions you made for 2014 (or those made on your behalf), including those made from January 1, 2015, through April 15, 2015, that were for 2014. **Do not** include employer contributions, contributions through a cafeteria plan, or rollovers (see instructions)	**2**	
3	If you were under age 55 at the end of 2014, and on the first day of **every** month during 2014, you were, or were considered, an eligible individual with the **same** coverage, enter $3,300 ($6,550 for family coverage). **All others,** see the instructions for the amount to enter	**3**	
4	Enter the amount you and your employer contributed to your Archer MSAs for 2014 from Form 8853, lines 1 and 2. If you or your spouse had family coverage under an HDHP at any time during 2014, also include any amount contributed to your spouse's Archer MSAs	**4**	
5	Subtract line 4 from line 3. If zero or less, enter -0-	**5**	
6	Enter the amount from line 5. But if you and your spouse each have separate HSAs and had family coverage under an HDHP at any time during 2014, see the instructions for the amount to enter	**6**	
7	If you were age 55 or older at the end of 2014, married, and you or your spouse had family coverage under an HDHP at any time during 2014, enter your additional contribution amount (see instructions)	**7**	
8	Add lines 6 and 7	**8**	
9	Employer contributions made to your HSAs for 2014	**9**		
10	Qualified HSA funding distributions	**10**		
11	Add lines 9 and 10	**11**	
12	Subtract line 11 from line 8. If zero or less, enter -0-	**12**	
13	**HSA deduction.** Enter the **smaller** of line 2 or line 12 here and on Form 1040, line 25, or Form 1040NR, line 25	**13**	

Caution: *If line 2 is more than line 13, you may have to pay an additional tax (see instructions).*

Part II | **HSA Distributions.** If you are filing jointly and both you and your spouse each have separate HSAs, complete a separate Part II for each spouse.

14a	Total distributions you received in 2014 from all HSAs (see instructions)	**14a**	
b	Distributions included on line 14a that you rolled over to another HSA. Also include any excess contributions (and the earnings on those excess contributions) included on line 14a that were withdrawn by the due date of your return (see instructions)	**14b**	
c	Subtract line 14b from line 14a	**14c**	
15	Qualified medical expenses paid using HSA distributions (see instructions)	**15**	
16	**Taxable HSA distributions.** Subtract line 15 from line 14c. If zero or less, enter -0-. Also, include this amount in the total on Form 1040, line 21, or Form 1040NR, line 21. On the dotted line next to line 21, enter "HSA" and the amount	**16**	
17a	If any of the distributions included on line 16 meet any of the **Exceptions to the Additional 20% Tax** (see instructions), check here . . . . ▶ ☐		
b	**Additional 20% tax** (see instructions). Enter 20% (.20) of the distributions included on line 16 that are subject to the additional 20% tax. Also include this amount in the total on Form 1040, line 62, or Form 1040NR, line 60. On the dotted line next to Form 1040, line 62, or Form 1040NR, line 60, enter "HSA" and the amount	**17b**	

For Paperwork Reduction Act Notice, see your tax return instructions.

Cat. No. 37621P

Form **8889** (2014)

Illustration 9-2 continued

			Page **2**
Part III	**Income and Additional Tax for Failure To Maintain HDHP Coverage.** See the instructions before completing this part. If you are filing jointly and both you and your spouse each have separate HSAs, complete a separate Part III for each spouse.		

18	Last-month rule	**18**		
19	Qualified HSA funding distribution	**19**		
20	**Total income.** Add lines 18 and 19. Include this amount on Form 1040, line 21, or Form 1040NR, line 21. On the dotted line next to Form 1040, line 21, or Form 1040NR, line 21, enter "HSA" and the amount	**20**		
21	**Additional tax.** Multiply line 20 by 10% (.10). Include this amount in the total on Form 1040, line 62, or Form 1040NR, line 60. On the dotted line next to Form 1040, line 62, or Form 1040NR, line 60, enter "HDHP" and the amount	**21**		

Form **8889** (2014)

Illustration 9-3

Form **3903**	**Moving Expenses**	OMB No. 1545-0074
Department of the Treasury Internal Revenue Service (99)	▶ **Information about Form 3903 and its instructions is available at** *www.irs.gov/form3903.* ▶ **Attach to Form 1040 or Form 1040NR.**	20**14** Attachment Sequence No. **170**

Name(s) shown on return		**Your social security number**

Before you begin: ✓ See the **Distance Test** and **Time Test** in the instructions to find out if you can deduct your moving expenses.

                ✓ See **Members of the Armed Forces** in the instructions, if applicable.

1	Transportation and storage of household goods and personal effects (see instructions) . . .	**1**	
2	Travel (including lodging) from your old home to your new home (see instructions). **Do not** include the cost of meals	**2**	
3	Add lines 1 and 2	**3**	
4	Enter the total amount your employer paid you for the expenses listed on lines 1 and 2 that is **not** included in box 1 of your Form W-2 (wages). This amount should be shown in box 12 of your Form W-2 with code **P**	**4**	
5	Is line 3 **more than** line 4?		
	☐ **No.** You **cannot** deduct your moving expenses. If line 3 is less than line 4, subtract line 3 from line 4 and include the result on Form 1040, line 7, or Form 1040NR, line 8.		
	☐ **Yes.** Subtract line 4 from line 3. Enter the result here and on Form 1040, line 26, or Form 1040NR, line 26. This is your **moving expense deduction**	**5**	

For Paperwork Reduction Act Notice, see your tax return instructions.   Cat. No. 12490K   Form **3903** (2014)

Self Employment Adjustments

Lines 27, 28, and 29 of the Form 1040, concern deductions for the self-employed. We will cover these later in the course.

Penalty on Early Withdrawal of Savings

If the taxpayer withdraws a time deposit early, they may have forfeited some interest or principal. This amount will be reported in Box 2 of the Form 1099-INT (Illustration 9-4). This amount will be deducted on Form 1040, line 30.

Alimony Paid

We discussed what happens when someone receives alimony in a previous chapter. Now, we will discuss what happens for the person paying the alimony. If the alimony paid meets the requirements as stated in chapter 3, the payments are deductible for the payer. To deduct these payments, the social security number of the recipient must be reported as well as the amount on Form 1040, line 31.

IRA Deduction

The deductible IRA contribution (as discussed in chapter 7) will be reported on Form 1040, line 32.

Student Loan Interest Deduction

If the taxpayer (or spouse if MFJ) are in the process of paying back a student loan, up to $2,500 of the interest may be deductible. The deduction can be taken if the following requirements are met:

- The interest was paid during the tax year on a qualified student loan.
- The filing status is any status except married filing separately.
- The modified adjusted gross income is less than:
  - $80,000 if single, head of household, or qualifying widow(er) or
  - $160,000 if married filing jointly.
- The taxpayer (or spouse if MFJ) cannot be claimed as a dependent on someone else's return.

Qualified Student Loan

A qualified student loan is any loan that was taken out to pay the qualified higher education expenses for any of the following individuals:

- The taxpayer or spouse,
- Any person who was a dependent when the loan was taken out,
- Any person the taxpayer could have claimed as a dependent for the year the loan was taken out except that:
  - The person filed a joint return,

- The person had gross income that was equal to or more than the exemption amount for the year,
- The taxpayer, or spouse if filing jointly, could be claimed as a dependent on someone else's return.

The student loan cannot have been from a related person or a person who borrowed the proceeds under a qualified employer plan or a contract purchaser.

Qualified Higher Education Expenses

Qualified higher education expenses generally include tuition, fees, room and board, and related expenses such as books and supplies. The expenses must be for education in a degree, certificate, or similar program at an eligible educational institution. The expenses must be reduced by any of the following benefits:

- Employer-provided educational assistance benefits that are not included in box 1 of Forms W-2.
- Excludable U.S. series EE and I savings bond interest from Form 8815.
- Any nontaxable distribution of qualified tuition program earnings.
- Any nontaxable distribution of Coverdell education savings account earnings.
- Any scholarship, educational assistance allowance, or other payment (but not gifts, inheritances, etc.) excludable from income.

An eligible student is a person who was enrolled in a degree, certificate, or other program leading to a recognized educational credential at an eligible educational institution and carried at least half the normal full-time workload for the course of study being pursued.

If the taxpayer has eligible student loan interest, use the IRS worksheet (Illustration 9-5) and report the deductible amount on Form 1040, line 33.

Illustration 9-4

☐ CORRECTED (if checked)

PAYER'S name, street address, city or town, state or province, country, ZIP or foreign postal code, and telephone no.	Payer's RTN (optional)	OMB No. 1545-0112	
		20**14**	**Interest Income**
	1 Interest income		
	$	Form **1099-INT**	
	2 Early withdrawal penalty		**Copy B**
PAYER'S federal identification number / RECIPIENT'S identification number	$		**For Recipient**
	3 Interest on U.S. Savings Bonds and Treas. obligations		
	$		This is important tax information and is being furnished to the Internal Revenue Service. If you are required to file a return, a negligence penalty or other sanction may be imposed on you if this income is taxable and the IRS determines that it has not been reported.
RECIPIENT'S name	**4** Federal income tax withheld	**5** Investment expenses	
	$	$	
Street address (including apt. no.)	**6** Foreign tax paid	**7** Foreign country or U.S. possession	
	$		
City or town, state or province, country, and ZIP or foreign postal code	**8** Tax-exempt interest	**9** Specified private activity bond interest	
	$	$	
	10 Market discount	**11** Bond premium	
	$	$	
Account number (see instructions)	**12** Tax-exempt bond CUSIP no.	**13** State **14** State identification no.	**15** State tax withheld
			$
			$

Form **1099-INT**   (keep for your records)   www.irs.gov/form1099int   Department of the Treasury - Internal Revenue Service

Illustration 9-5

Student Loan Interest Deduction Worksheet—Line 33

Keep for Your Records

Before you begin:	✓ Figure any write-in adjustments to be entered on the dotted line next to line 36 (see the instructions for line 36).
	✓ Be sure you have read the **Exception** in the instructions for this line to see if you can use this worksheet instead of Pub. 970 to figure your deduction.

1. Enter the total interest you paid in 2014 on qualified student loans (see the instructions for line 33). **Do not** enter more than $2,500 . . . . **1.** _____

2. Enter the amount from Form 1040, line 22 . . . . **2.** _____

3. Enter the total of the amounts from Form 1040, lines 23 through 32, plus any write-in adjustments you entered on the dotted line next to line 36 . . . . **3.** _____

4. Subtract line 3 from line 2 . . . . **4.** _____

5. Enter the amount shown below for your filing status.

   • Single, head of household, or qualifying widow(er)—$65,000

   • Married filing jointly—$130,000   } . . . . **5.** _____

6. Is the amount on line 4 more than the amount on line 5?

   ☐ **No.**   Skip lines 6 and 7, enter -0- on line 8, and go to line 9.

   ☐ **Yes.**   Subtract line 5 from line 4 . . . . **6.** _____

7. Divide line 6 by $15,000 ($30,000 if married filing jointly). Enter the result as a decimal (rounded to at least three places). If the result is 1.000 or more, enter 1.000 . . . . **7.** . _____

8. Multiply line 1 by line 7 . . . . **8.** _____

9. **Student loan interest deduction.** Subtract line 8 from line 1. Enter the result here and on Form 1040, line 33. **Do not** include this amount in figuring any other deduction on your return (such as on Schedule A, C, E, etc.) . . . . **9.** _____

Tuition and Fees Deduction

A deduction for tuition and fees expenses may be taken for the taxpayer, spouse, or a dependent claimed on the tax return that was enrolled at or attending an eligible educational institution. The qualifying person must have either a high school diploma or a General Educational Development (GED) credential. Keep in mind, the tuition and fees deduction may not be taken if the American opportunity credit or lifetime learning credit is being claimed. The taxpayer should use whichever way is more beneficial.

The taxpayer may not claim the tuition and fees deduction if any of the following apply:

- The filing status is married filing separately.
- Another person can claim an exemption for the taxpayer as a dependent on their return.
- The modified adjusted gross income is more than $80,000 ($160,000 if MFJ).
- The taxpayer was a nonresident alien for any part of the year and did not elect to be treated as a resident alien for tax purposes.
- The taxpayer or anyone else claims the American Opportunity or Llifetime Learning credit in the tax year with respect to expenses of the student for whom the qualified education expenses were paid.

Qualified Education Expenses

Qualified education expenses include amounts paid during the tax year and the first three months of the following year. They are the tuition and fees required for the enrollment or attendance at an eligible educational institution. It doesn't matter if the fees were paid with borrowed funds. The qualified expenses do not include:

- Room and board, insurance, medical expenses, transportation, or similar personal, living, or family expenses.
- Course-related books, supplies, equipment, and nonacademic activities, except for fees required to be paid to the institution as a condition of enrollment or attendance.
- Any course or other education involving sports, games, or hobbies, or any noncredit course, unless such course or other education is part of the student's degree program.

Remember to reduce the qualified education expenses by the amount of any tax-free educational assistance and refunds of qualified education expenses as discussed in Chapter 6.

To claim the tuition and fees deduction, a Form 8917 (Illustration 9-6) must be filed and the deductible amount must be carried to Form 1040, line 34.

Domestic Production Activities Deduction

Up to 9% of qualified production activities income from the following activities may be deducted:

- Construction of real property performed in the United States.
- Engineering or architectural services performed in the United States for construction of real property in the United States.
- Any lease, rental, license, sale, exchange, or other disposition of:
  - Tangible personal property, computer software, and sound recordings that the taxpayer manufactured, produced, grew, or extracted in whole or in significant part in the United States,
  - Any qualified film produced, or
  - Electricity, natural gas, or potable water the taxpayer produced in the United States.

If this is encountered, additional research will be required.

Illustration 9-6

Form **8917**

Department of the Treasury
Internal Revenue Service

Tuition and Fees Deduction

▶ Attach to Form 1040 or Form 1040A.
▶ Information about Form 8917 and its instructions is at *www.irs.gov/form8917.*

OMB No. 1545-0074

20**14**

Attachment
Sequence No. **60**

Name(s) shown on return

Your social security number

⚠ **CAUTION**

*You **cannot** take both an education credit from Form 8863 and the tuition and fees deduction from this form for the **same student** for the same tax year.*

Before you begin:

✔ To see if you qualify for this deduction, see *Who Can Take the Deduction* in the instructions below.

✔ If you file Form 1040, figure any write-in adjustments to be entered on the dotted line next to Form 1040, line 36. See the 2014 Form 1040 instructions for line 36.

1

(a) Student's name (as shown on page 1 of your tax return)		(b) Student's social security number (as shown on page 1 of your tax return)	(c) Adjusted qualified expenses (see instructions)
First name	Last name		

2 Add the amounts on line 1, column (c), and enter the total **2**

3 Enter the amount from Form 1040, line 22, or Form 1040A, line 15 **3**

4 Enter the total from either:

• Form 1040, lines 23 through 33, plus any write-in adjustments entered on the dotted line next to Form 1040, line 36, **or**

• Form 1040A, lines 16 through 18. . . . . **4**

5 Subtract line 4 from line 3.* If the result is more than $80,000 ($160,000 if married filing jointly), **stop**; you cannot take the deduction for tuition and fees **5**

*If you are filing Form 2555, 2555-EZ, or 4563, or you are excluding income from Puerto Rico, see *Effect of the Amount of Your Income on the Amount of Your Deduction* in Pub. 970, chapter 6, to figure the amount to enter on line 5.

6 **Tuition and fees deduction.** Is the amount on line 5 more than $65,000 ($130,000 if married filing jointly)?

☐ **Yes.** Enter the smaller of line 2, or $2,000. ⎫
☐ **No.** Enter the smaller of line 2, or $4,000. ⎭ **6**

Also enter this amount on Form 1040, line 34, or Form 1040A, line 19.

For Paperwork Reduction Act Notice, see your tax return instructions.   Cat. No. 37728P   Form **8917** (2014)

Chapter Review

1) What is the maximum amount allowed for the educator expense deduction?

2) What kind of health plan must the taxpayer be covered under to be eligible to contribute to a HSA?

3) How much further must the taxpayer's new principal workplace be from the old home to qualify for the moving expense deduction?

4) What is the time requirement for an employee to qualify for the moving expense deduction?

5) Where will you find the amount of penalty on early withdrawal of savings?

6) What information is required to deduct alimony paid?

7) For whom can the student loan interest deduction be claimed?

8) Must the eligible person for the tuition and fees deduction have a high school diploma?

Exercise

Prepare a return for the Burrows.

Belinda and Byron Burrows are married and have two children, Beth and Brian. They are paying back a student loan for Byron and Belinda is a full-time student at college. She is in her junior year toward her Accounting degree. She has not been convicted of any felonies in the past. The required text books were $341.25. She purchased them from a local used book store. Neither wants to designate $3 for the presidential campaign fund. Their reporting documents are on the following pages.

Belinda's SSN is 354-57-3744 and her birth date is November 22, 1982.

Byron's SSN is 094-57-3570 and his birth date is April 11, 1979. Byron is a Sales Associate.

Beth's SSN is 662-54-8232 and her birth date is December 22, 1999.

Brian's SSN is 436-24-9433 and his birth date is January 13, 2006.

☐ CORRECTED (if checked)

RECIPIENT'S/LENDER'S name, address, city or town, state or province, country, ZIP or foreign postal code, and telephone number		OMB No. 1545-1576	
Student Financial Services 5534 Helpful Way Your City, Your State, Your Zip Code		2014 Form **1098-E**	**Student Loan Interest Statement**

RECIPIENT'S federal identification no. 44-6726262	BORROWER'S social security number 094-57-3570	**1** Student loan interest received by lender $ 2,331.21	**Copy B** **For Borrower**
BORROWER'S name Byron Burrows			This is important tax information and is being furnished to the Internal Revenue Service. If you are required to file a return, a negligence penalty or other sanction may be imposed on you if the IRS determines that an underpayment of tax results because you overstated a deduction for student loan interest.
Street address (including apt. no.) 55 Mammoth Ct.			
City or town, state or province, country, and ZIP or foreign postal code Your City, Your State, Your Zip Code			
Account number (see instructions)		**2** If checked, box 1 does **not** include loan origination fees and/or capitalized interest for loans made before September 1, 2004 . . . . ☐	

Form **1098-E**   (keep for your records)   www.irs.gov/form1098e   Department of the Treasury - Internal Revenue Service

---

☐ CORRECTED

FILER'S name, street address, city or town, state or province, country, ZIP or foreign postal code, and telephone number	**1** Payments received for qualified tuition and related expenses	OMB No. 1545-1574	
Sunny University 300 Sunshine Lane Your City, Your State, Your Zip Code	$ 3,444.56	2014	**Tuition Statement**
	2 Amounts billed for qualified tuition and related expenses $	Form **1098-T**	

FILER'S federal identification no. 67-7654891	STUDENT'S social security number 354-57-3744	**3** If this box is checked, your educational institution has changed its reporting method for 2014 ☐		**Copy B** **For Student**
STUDENT'S name Belinda Burrows		**4** Adjustments made for a prior year $	**5** Scholarships or grants $	This is important tax information and is being furnished to the Internal Revenue Service.
Street address (including apt. no.) 55 Mammoth Ct.		**6** Adjustments to scholarships or grants for a prior year $	**7** Checked if the amount in box 1 or 2 includes amounts for an academic period beginning January - March 2015 ▶ ☐	
City or town, state or province, country, and ZIP or foreign postal code Your City, Your State, Your Zip Code				
Service Provider/Acct. No. (see instr.)	**8** Check if at least half-time student ☑	**9** Checked if a graduate student . . . . ☐	**10** Ins. contract reimb./refund $	

Form **1098-T**   (keep for your records)   www.irs.gov/form1098t   Department of the Treasury - Internal Revenue Service

PAYER'S name, street address, city or town, state or province, country, ZIP or foreign postal code, and telephone no.	Payer's RTN (optional)	OMB No. 1545-0112	
First National Bank 2300 Financial Way Your City, Your State, Your Zip Code	**1** Interest income $ 1,442.50	20**14** Form **1099-INT**	**Interest Income**

PAYER'S federal identification number	RECIPIENT'S identification number	**2** Early withdrawal penalty $ 23.66	**Copy B**
63-2111111	354-57-3744	**3** Interest on U.S. Savings Bonds and Treas. obligations $	**For Recipient**

RECIPIENT'S name	**4** Federal income tax withheld $	**5** Investment expenses $	This is important tax information and is being furnished to the Internal Revenue Service. If you are required to file a return, a negligence penalty or other sanction may be imposed on you if this income is taxable and the IRS determines that it has not been reported.
Belinda Burrows			
Street address (including apt. no.) 55 Mammoth Ct.	**6** Foreign tax paid $	**7** Foreign country or U.S. possession	
City or town, state or province, country, and ZIP or foreign postal code Your City, Your State, Your Zip Code	**8** Tax-exempt interest $	**9** Specified private activity bond interest $	
	10 Market discount $	**11** Bond premium $	
Account number (see instructions)	**12** Tax-exempt bond CUSIP no.	**13** State **14** State identification no.	**15** State tax withheld $ $

Form **1099-INT**   (keep for your records)   www.irs.gov/form1099int   Department of the Treasury - Internal Revenue Service

a Employee's social security number 094-57-3570	OMB No. 1545-0008	Safe, accurate, **FAST! Use** IRS **e~file**	Visit the IRS website at www.irs.gov/efile

b Employer identification number (EIN) 87-8785566	**1** Wages, tips, other compensation 46,556.87	**2** Federal income tax withheld 4,443.77
c Employer's name, address, and ZIP code Shiny New Car Lot 6600 Gas Guzzler Blvd. Your City, Your State, Your Zip Code	**3** Social security wages 46,556.87	**4** Social security tax withheld 2,700.53
	5 Medicare wages and tips 46,556.87	**6** Medicare tax withheld 631.72
	7 Social security tips	**8** Allocated tips
d Control number	**9**	**10** Dependent care benefits
e Employee's first name and initial Last name Suff.	**11** Nonqualified plans	**12a** See instructions for box 12
	13 Statutory employee ☐ Retirement plan ☐ Third-party sick pay ☐	**12b**
Byron Burrows 55 Mammoth Ct. Your City, Your State, Your Zip Code	**14** Other	**12c**
		12d
f Employee's address and ZIP code		

15 State	Employer's state ID number	**16** State wages, tips, etc.	**17** State income tax	**18** Local wages, tips, etc.	**19** Local income tax	**20** Locality name
YS	349354563	46,556.87	1,307.07			

Form **W-2** Wage and Tax Statement   2014   Department of the Treasury—Internal Revenue Service

Copy B—To Be Filed With Employee's FEDERAL Tax Return.
This information is being furnished to the Internal Revenue Service.

Chapter 10 – Affordable Health Care

One of the first things you will need to know when your clients start coming in is if they have Minimum Essential Coverage. The Affordable Care Act states that the responsibility of having health insurance will now be shared by the Federal Government, the State Government, insurers, employers, and the individual taxpayers. The taxpayer and each member of their family must have either minimum essential coverage, have an exemption from the responsibility, or pay a shared responsibility payment when they file their 2014 federal tax return.

Minimum Essential Coverage

So first things first, what is Minimum Essential Coverage? In summary, Minimum Essential Coverage includes the following (See Illustration 10-1 for a more in depth list.):

- Health insurance coverage provided by their employer,
- Health insurance purchased through the Health Insurance Marketplace in the area where the taxpayer lives,
- Coverage provided under a government-sponsored program for which they are eligible (including Medicare, Medicaid, and health care programs for veterans),
- Health insurance purchased directly from an insurance company, and
- Other health insurance coverage that is recognized by the Department of Health & Human Services as minimum essential coverage.

Feeling overwhelmed yet? You're thinking, "How do I know whether my client has Minimum Essential Coverage?" The good news is the majority of your clients will be able to directly answer that question. Most people have Minimum Essential Coverage. If they have, or had an insurance policy that does not qualify as Minimum Essential Coverage, they should have been notified by the insurance company. If they have insurance, and are not sure whether their policy qualifies as Minimum Essential Coverage, they can contact their insurer.

Note: Beginning in 2016 for the 2015 filing season, the IRS will be requiring insurance companies and/or employers to meet reporting requirements to show who has Minimum Essential Coverage. Health insurance carriers will be required to file Form 1095B (Illustration 10-2) to the IRS and to policy holders. Employers subject to the shared responsibility provisions sponsoring self-insured group health plans will be required to file Form 1095C (Illustration 10-3) to the IRS and to policy holders.

Now that we have determined whether they have Minimum Essential coverage or not, what's the next step? We have to determine if they had it for every month of the year. The taxpayer is considered to have minimum essential coverage for the entire month as long as they have the coverage for at least one day during that month. So if Mr. Smith comes in and lets you know he was covered the entire year by his employer, then you will mark the box on Line 61 of the Form 1040, and you're done with the healthcare coverage part of the return.

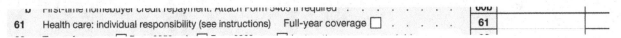

Illustration 10-1

The following qualifies as Minimum Essential Coverage

Employee sponsored coverage

- Employee coverage (including self-insured plans)
- COBRA coverage
- Retiree coverage

Individual health coverage

- Health insurance you purchase from an insurance company directly
- Health insurance you purchase through the Health Insurance Marketplace
- Health insurance provided through a student health plan
- Health coverage provided through a student health plan that is self-funded by a university (only for a plan year beginning on or before December 31, 2014, unless recognized as minimum essential coverage by the U.S. Department of Health and Human Services [HHS])

Coverage under government - sponsored programs

- Medicare Part A coverage
- Medicare Advantage plans
- Most Medicaid coverage
- Children's Health Insurance Propgram (CHIP)
- Most types of TRICARE coverage under chapter 55, title 10 of the United States Code
- Comprehensive health care programs offered by the Department of Veterans Affairs
- State high-risk health insurance pools (only for a plan year beginning on or before December 21, 2014, unless recognized as minimum essential coverage by the HHS)
- Health coverage provided to Peace Corps volunteers
- Department of Defense Nonappropriated Fund Health Benefits Program
- Refugee Medical Assistance

Illustration 10-1 continued

The following does not qualify as Minimum Essential Coverage

Certain coverage that may provide limited benefits

- •Coverage consisting soley of excepted benefits, such as:
  - •Stand-alone dental and vision insurance
  - •Accident or disability income insurance
  - •Workers' compensation insurance
- •Medicaid providing only family planning services*
- •Medicaid providing only tuberculosis-related services*
- •Medicaid providing only coverage limited to treatment of emergency medical conditions*
- •Pregnancy-related Medicaid coverage*
- •Medicaid coverage for the medically needy*
- •Section 1115 Medicaid demonstration projects*
- •Space available TRICARE coverage provided under chapter 55 of title 10 of the United States Code for individuals who are not eligible for TRICARE coverage for health services from private sector providers*
- •Line of duty TRICARE coverage provided under chapter 55 of title 10 of the United States Code*
- •AmeriCorps coverage for those serving in programs receiving AmeriCorps State and National grants
- •AfterCorps coverage purchased by returning members of the PeaceCorps

*These categories of coverage are generally not minimum essential coverage. However, to the extent that certain programs within these categories provide comprehensive coverage, the Secretary of HHS may recognize these programs as minimum essential coverage in the future. The IRS has announced relief from the shared responsibility payment for months in 2014 in which individuals are covered under any of these programs to the extent that they are not minimum essential coverage. Information will be made available later about how the income tax return will take account of coverage under one of these programs.

Illustration 10-2

Form **1095-B**

Department of the Treasury
Internal Revenue Service

Health Coverage

▶ Information about Form 1095-B and its separate instructions is at *www.irs.gov/form1095b.*

560115

OMB No. 1545-2252

2014

☐ VOID
☐ CORRECTED

Part I   Responsible Individual (Policy Holder)

1 Name of responsible individual

2 Social security number (SSN)

3 Date of birth (if SSN is not available)

4 Street address (including apartment no.)

5 City or town

6 State or province

7 Country and ZIP or foreign postal code

8 Enter letter identifying Origin of the Policy (see instructions for codes): . . . . . ▲

9 Small Business Health Options Program (SHOP) Marketplace identifier, if applicable

Part II   Employer Sponsored Coverage (If Line 8 is A or B, complete this part.)

10 Employer name

11 Employer identification number (EIN)

12 Street address (including room or suite no.)

13 City or town

14 State or province

15 Country and ZIP or foreign postal code

Part III   Issuer or Other Coverage Provider

16 Name

17 Employer identification number (EIN)

18 Contact telephone number

19 Street address (including room or suite no.)

20 City or town

21 State or province

22 Country and ZIP or foreign postal code

Part IV   Covered Individuals (Enter the information for each covered individual(s).

(a) Name of covered individual(s)	(b) SSN	(c) DOB (if SSN is not available)	(d) Covered all 12 months	(e) Months of coverage											
				Jan	Feb	Mar	Apr	May	Jun	Jul	Aug	Sep	Oct	Nov	Dec
23			☐	☐	☐	☐	☐	☐	☐	☐	☐	☐	☐	☐	☐
24			☐	☐	☐	☐	☐	☐	☐	☐	☐	☐	☐	☐	☐
25			☐	☐	☐	☐	☐	☐	☐	☐	☐	☐	☐	☐	☐
26			☐	☐	☐	☐	☐	☐	☐	☐	☐	☐	☐	☐	☐
27			☐	☐	☐	☐	☐	☐	☐	☐	☐	☐	☐	☐	☐
28			☐	☐	☐	☐	☐	☐	☐	☐	☐	☐	☐	☐	☐

For Privacy Act and Paperwork Reduction Act Notice, see separate instructions.

Cat. No. 60704B

Form **1095-B** (2014)

Illustration 10-3

600117

OMB No. 1545-2251

2014

☐ VOID
☐ CORRECTED

Form 1095-C

Department of the Treasury
Internal Revenue Service

Employer-Provided Health Insurance Offer and Coverage

▶ Information about Form 1095-C and its separate instructions is at *www.irs.gov/f1095c.*

Part I Employee

1 Name of employee

2 Social security number (SSN)

3 Street address (including apartment no.)

4 City or town

5 State or province

6 Country and ZIP or foreign postal code

Applicable Large Employer Member (Employer)

7 Name of employer

8 Employer identification number (EIN)

9 Street address (including room or suite no.)

10 Contact telephone number

11 City or town

12 State or province

13 Country and ZIP or foreign postal code

Part II Employee Offer and Coverage

	All 12 Months	Jan	Feb	Mar	Apr	May	June	July	Aug	Sept	Oct	Nov	Dec
14 Offer of Coverage (enter required code)													
15 Employee Share of Lowest Cost Monthly Premium, for Self-Only Minimum Value Coverage	$	$	$	$	$	$	$	$	$	$	$	$	$
16 Applicable Section 4980H Safe Harbor (enter code, if applicable)													

Part III Covered Individuals If Employer provided self-insured coverage, check the box and enter the information for each covered individual. ☐

				(e) Months of Coverage											
(a) Name of covered individual(s)	(b) SSN	(c) DOB (If SSN is not available)	(d) Covered all 12 months	Jan	Feb	Mar	Apr	May	June	July	Aug	Sept	Oct	Nov	Dec
17			☐	☐	☐	☐	☐	☐	☐	☐	☐	☐	☐	☐	☐
18			☐	☐	☐	☐	☐	☐	☐	☐	☐	☐	☐	☐	☐
19			☐	☐	☐	☐	☐	☐	☐	☐	☐	☐	☐	☐	☐
20			☐	☐	☐	☐	☐	☐	☐	☐	☐	☐	☐	☐	☐
21			☐	☐	☐	☐	☐	☐	☐	☐	☐	☐	☐	☐	☐
22			☐	☐	☐	☐	☐	☐	☐	☐	☐	☐	☐	☐	☐

For Privacy Act and Paperwork Reduction Act Notice, see separate instructions.

Cat. No. 60705M

Form **1095-C** (2014)

But they're not all going to be that easy, are they? Next, we are going to discuss exemptions and the penalty for not having coverage.

Exemptions

So now we have discovered that our client did not have Minimum Essential Coverage for some or all of the months in 2014, and may be subject to the Individual Shared Responsibility Payment on their 2014 tax return. Now, we will determine if they qualify for one of the exemptions to the payment. Some of the exemptions are obtained through the Marketplace while others are obtained by claiming them on their 2014 tax return.

Exemptions obtained only through the Marketplace

The following exemptions may only be claimed by the taxpayer applying for the exemption through the marketplace and receiving a certificate of exemption:

- Members of certain religious sects – The taxpayer is a member of a religious sect in existence since December 31, 1950, that is recognized by the Social Security Administration (SSA) as conscientiously opposed to accepting any insurance benefits, including Medicare and Social Security.
- The taxpayer qualifies for one of the following hardship exemptions:
  o They were homeless.
  o They were evicted in the past 6 months or were facing eviction or foreclosure.
  o They received a shut-off notice from a utility company.
  o They recently experienced domestic violence.
  o They recently experienced the death of a close family member.
  o They experienced a fire, flood, or other natural or human-caused disaster that caused substantial damage to their property.
  o They filed for bankruptcy in the last 6 months.
  o They had medical expenses they couldn't pay in the last 24 months which resulted in substantial debt.
  o They experienced unexpected increases in necessary expenses due to caring for an ill, disabled, or aging family member.
  o They expect to claim a child as a tax dependent who's been denied coverage in Medicaid and CHIP, and another person is required by court order to give medical support to the child. In this case, the exemption only applies to the child.
  o As a result of an eligibility appeals decision, they are eligible for enrollment in a qualified health plan through the Marketplace, lower costs on their monthly premiums, or cost-sharing reductions for a time period when they weren't enrolled in a qualified health plan through the marketplace.
  o They were determined ineligible for Medicaid because their state didn't expand eligibility for Medicaid under the Affordable Care Act.
  o Their individual plan was cancelled and they believe other Marketplace plans are unaffordable.
- They do not have affordable coverage based on their projected household income.
- They are an American Indian, Alaska Native, or a spouse or descendant who is eligible for services through an Indian health care provider.

Exemptions obtained only through the IRS.

The following exemptions may only be claimed on the tax return:

- Coverage is considered unaffordable – The amount they would have paid for employer-sponsored coverage or a bronze level health plan (depending on their circumstances) is more than 8% of their actual household income for the year as computed on their tax return.
- Short coverage gap – They went without coverage for less than three consecutive months during the year.
- Household income below the return filing threshold – Their household income is below the minimum threshold for filing a tax return.
- Certain noncitizens – They are neither a U.S. citizen, a U.S. national, nor an alien lawfully present in the U.S.
- The taxpayer qualifies for one of the following hardship exemptions –
  - Their gross income is below the filing threshold.
  - Two or more family members' aggregate cost of self-only employer-sponsored coverage exceeds 8% of household income, as does the cost of any available employer-sponsored coverage for the entire family.
  - The taxpayer purchased insurance through the Marketplace during the initial enrollment period but have a coverage gap at the beginning of 2014.

Exemptions that may be obtained either through the IRS or the Marketplace

The following exemptions may be claimed by the taxpayer applying through the Marketplace or by claiming it on their tax return.

- Members of a health care sharing ministry – The taxpayer is a member of a health care sharing ministry, which is an organization described in section 501(c)(3) whose members share a common set of ethical or religious beliefs and have shared medical expenses in accordance with those beliefs continuously since at least December 31, 1999.
- A member of Federally-recognized Indian Tribes – The taxpayer is a member of a federally-recognized Indian tribe.
- Incarceration – The taxpayer is in jail, prison, or similar penal institution or correctional facility after the disposition of charges.

Illustration 10-4

Form **8965**

Department of the Treasury
Internal Revenue Service

Health Coverage Exemptions

▶ Attach to Form 1040, Form 1040A, or Form 1040EZ.
▶ **Information about Form 8965 and its separate instructions is at** *www.irs.gov/form8965*.

OMB No. 1545-0074

20**14**

Attachment
Sequence No. **75**

Name as shown on return

Your social security number

Complete this form if you have a Marketplace-granted coverage exemption or you are claiming a coverage exemption on your return.

Part I | **Marketplace-Granted Coverage Exemptions for Individuals:** If you and/or a member of your tax household have an exemption granted by the Marketplace, complete Part I.

	a Name of Individual	b SSN	c Exemption Certificate Number
1			
2			
3			
4			
5			
6			

Part II | **Coverage Exemptions for Your Household Claimed on Your Return:**

7a Are you claiming an exemption because your household income is below the filing threshold? . . . . ☐ Yes ☐ No

b Are you claiming a hardship exemption because your gross income is below the filing threshold? . . . . ☐ Yes ☐ No

Part III | **Coverage Exemptions for Individuals Claimed on Your Return:** If you and/or a member of your tax household are claiming an exemption on your return, complete Part III.

	a Name of Individual	b SSN	c Exemption Type	d Full Year	e Jan	f Feb	g Mar	h Apr	i May	j June	k July	l Aug	m Sept	n Oct	o Nov	p Dec
8																
9																
10																
11																
12																
13																

For **Privacy Act and Paperwork Reduction Act Notice, see your tax return instructions.** Cat. No. 37787G Form **8965** (2014)

Claiming the Exemption

Form 8965, Part I

First of all, remember that we have to determine whether the taxpayer and each member of their family had Minimum Essential Coverage, or will receive an exemption, for each individual month of the tax year. If the taxpayer received the exemption through the marketplace then they will come to you with a certificate of exemption. Part I of Form 8965 (Illustration 10-4) will be used to show the exemption.

Form 8965, Part II

If the taxpayer qualifies for the exemption based on their gross income being below the filing threshold, and chooses to not file a tax return, they do not need to do anything to receive the exemption. It will be given automatically. However, if the taxpayer is filing to claim a refund and is claiming the exemption based on their household or gross income being below the filing threshold (see the following table), Part II of Form 8965 will be completed.

<u>Household income:</u> The adjusted gross income from the tax return plus any excludable foreign earned income and tax-exempt interest the taxpayer received during the taxable year. Household income also includes the incomes of all of their dependents who are required to file tax returns.

Filing Thresholds

Filing Status	Age	Must File a Return If Gross Income Exceeds
Single	Under 65	$10,150
	65 or older	$11,700
Head of Household	Under 65	$13,050
	65 or older	$14,600
Married Filing Jointly	Under 65 (both spouses)	$20,300
	65 or older (one spouse)	$21,500
	65 or older (both spouses)	$22,700
Married Filing Separately	Any age	$3,950
Qualifying Widow(er) with Dependent Children	Under 65	$16,350
	65 or older	$17,550

Form 8965, Part III

If the taxpayer qualifies for an exemption that can be claimed on the tax return, and they have not gone through the Healthcare Marketplace to obtain the exemption, Part III of the Form 8965 must be completed. Illustration 10-5 shows the exemption and codes. Complete a line for each individual for which the taxpayer is claiming the exemption.

Short coverage gap: A gap of coverage less than three consecutive months. If the taxpayer has a gap of three months or more, none of the months are treated as included in the short coverage gap exemption. If the taxpayer has more than one short coverage gap, the exemption only applies to the first one. Months not covered in the next tax year are not included in the previous year for purposes of the exemption, however months in the previous tax year are included in determining the exemption.

> **Example:** John had coverage January through November of 2014, but had no coverage December of 2014, and January and February of 2015. John will qualify for the exemption for 2014 because only December is considered. However for 2015, we will include December of 2014, as well as January and February of 2015, so he does not qualify for the short coverage gap because it was 3 months or greater.

> **Example:** The details are same as the above example. John had coverage beginning in March of 2015 but lost coverage again for July and August. He purchased coverage again in September and had it for September, October, and November. He did not have coverage for December. He qualifies for the exemption for the gap of July and August because that is his first short coverage gap. (Remember, January and February do not qualify.) He does not qualify for the exemption for the month of December, because that would be the second short coverage gap. Unless he qualifies for another exemption, he will be required to pay the Individual Shared Responsibility Payment for the months of January, February, and December.

Coverage considered unaffordable: The taxpayer can claim this exemption for any month the taxpayer's lowest cost coverage through an employer sponsored plan or through the Marketplace is more than 8% of the taxpayer's household income.

> **Example:** Jenny's household income is $55,000. Her cost of insurance premiums through her employer is $5,500. 8% of her income is $4,400 ($55,000 x 8%). She qualifies for the exemption.

Aggregate self-only coverage considered unaffordable: If this exemption applies for any month during the year, the taxpayer can claim the exemption for the entire year. This exemption applies if:

- The cost of each self-only plan through the employer for 2 or more members of the taxpayer's household does not exceed 8% of the household income when tested individually, and
- The cost of family coverage that the members of the taxpayer's household could enroll in through an employer exceeds 8% of household income, and
- The combined cost of the self-only coverage identified in the first condition exceeds 8% of household income.

> **Example:** Mark and Beth are married with no children. Mark's employer offers self only coverage for a cost of 5% of their household income and the cost of family coverage is 9% of their household income. Beth's employer provides self-only coverage for 4% of their household income and the cost of family coverage is 11% of their household income. The cost of family coverage is over 8% and

the combined cost of self-only coverage is 9% which also exceeds 8%, so they qualify for this exemption.

<u>Resident of a state that did not expand Medicaid</u>: If the taxpayer's household income is less than 138% of the Federal Poverty Line for their family size, and they resided in a state that did not expand their Medicaid coverage, they qualify for this exemption. **Note:** the states that did not expand their Medicaid coverage in 2014 are: Alabama, Alaska, Florida, Georgia, Idaho, Indiana, Kansas, Louisiana, Maine, Missouri, Mississippi, Montana, North Carolina, Nebraska, New Hampshire, Oklahoma, Pennsylvania, South Carolina, South Dakota, Tennessee, Texas, Utah, Virginia, Wyoming, and Wisconsin.

Note: Household income for this purpose is increased by the amount of any Social Security benefits not included in the gross income.

> **Example:** Henry's household income for 2014 was $24,500. He is single with 2 children and is a resident of Alabama. The Federal Poverty Line for his family size is $19,530. 138% of $19,530 is $26,951. His income is below 138% of the Federal Poverty Line and his state of residency did not expand their Medicaid coverage. He qualifies for this exemption.

Illustration 10-5

Types of Coverage Exemptions

Coverage Exemption	Granted by Marketplace	Claimed on tax return	Code for Exemption
Income below the filing threshold — Your gross income or your household income was less than your applicable minimum threshold for filing a tax return.		✓	No Code See Part II
Coverage considered unaffordable — The minimum amount you would have paid for premiums is more than 8% of your household income.		✓	A
Short coverage gap — You went without coverage for less than 3 consecutive months during the year.		✓	B
Citizens living abroad and certain noncitizens — You were: • A U.S. citizen or resident who spent at least 330 full days outside of the U.S. during a 12–month period; • A U.S. citizen who was a bona fide resident of a foreign country or U.S. territory; • A resident alien who was a citizen of a foreign country with which the U.S. has an income tax treaty with a nondiscrimination clause, and you were a bona fide resident of a foreign country for the tax year; or • Not a U.S. citizen, not a U.S. national, and not an individual lawfully present in the U.S. For more information about who is treated as lawfully present for purposes of this coverage exemption, visit healthcare.gov.		✓	C
Members of a health care sharing ministry — You were a member of a health care sharing ministry.	✓	✓	D
Members of Indian tribes — You were either a member of a Federally-recognized Indian tribe, including an Alaska Native Claims Settlement Act (ANCSA) Corporation Shareholder (regional or village), or you were otherwise eligible for services through an Indian health care provider or the Indian Health Service.	✓	✓	E
Incarceration — You were in a jail, prison, or similar penal institution or correctional facility after the disposition of charges.	✓	✓	F
Aggregate self-only coverage considered unaffordable — Two or more family members' aggregate cost of self-only employer-sponsored coverage was more than 8% of household income, as was the cost of any available employer-sponsored coverage for the entire family.		✓	G
Gap in coverage at the beginning of 2014 — You had a coverage gap at the beginning of 2014 but were either enrolled in, or were treated as having enrolled in, coverage through the Marketplace or outside of the Marketplace with an effective date on or before May 1, 2014.		✓	G
Gap in CHIP coverage — You applied for CHIP coverage during the initial open enrollment period and were found eligible for CHIP based on that application but had a coverage gap at the beginning of 2014.		✓	G
Resident of a state that did not expand Medicaid — Your household income was below 138% of the federal poverty line for your family size and at any time in 2014 you resided in a state that did not participate in the Medicaid expansion under the Affordable Care Act.		✓	G
Limited benefit Medicaid and TRICARE programs that are not minimum essential coverage — You were enrolled in certain types of Medicaid and TRICARE programs that are not minimum essential coverage. (Available only in 2014.)		✓	H
Employer coverage with non-calendar plan year beginning in 2013 — You were eligible, but did not purchase, coverage under an employer plan with a plan year that started in 2013 and ended in 2014. (Available only in 2014.)		✓	H
Members of certain religious sects — You are a member of a recognized religious sect.	✓		Need ECN See Part I
Determined ineligible for Medicaid in a state that did not expand Medicaid coverage — You were determined ineligible for Medicaid solely because the state in which you resided did not participate in Medicaid expansion under the Affordable Care Act.	✓		Need ECN See Part I
General hardship — You experienced a hardship that prevented you from obtaining coverage under a qualified health plan.	✓		Need ECN See Part I
Coverage considered unaffordable based on projected income — You did not have access to coverage that is considered affordable based on your projected household income.	✓		Need ECN See Part I
Unable to renew existing coverage — You were notified that your health insurance policy was not renewable and you considered the other plans available unaffordable.	✓		Need ECN See Part I
AmeriCorps coverage — You were engaged in service in AmeriCorps State and National, VISTA, or NCCC programs and were covered by short-term duration coverage or self-funded coverage provided by these programs.	✓		Need ECN See Part I

Individual Shared Responsibility Payment

First, to better understand the calculation of the Individual Shared Responsibility Payment, let's briefly discuss the different levels of coverage available in the Marketplace.

- Bronze – Pays about 60% of healthcare costs
- Silver – Pays about 70% of healthcare costs
- Gold – Pays about 80% of healthcare costs
- Platinum – Pays about 90% of healthcare costs
- Catastrophic – Available only to people under 30 or people with a hardship exemption. This plan will pay less than 60% of healthcare costs and is designed to protect the individual from very high medical costs.

The Individual Shared Responsibility Payment is the greater of a percentage of the taxpayer's household income or a flat dollar amount, but is capped at the national average premium for a bronze level health plan available through the Marketplace. The taxpayer will owe 1/12 of the annual payment for each month they or their dependents don't have either coverage or an exemption.

For 2014, the Individual Shared Responsibility Payment is the greater of:

- 1% of household income that is above the tax return filing threshold for their filing status, or
- The family's flat dollar amount which is $95 per adult and $47.50 per child (under 18 – based on the first day of each month), limited to a family maximum of $285.

This is capped at the cost of the national average premium for a bronze level health plan available through the Marketplace in 2014. For 2014, the annual national average premium for a bronze level health plan is $2,448 per individual ($204 per month) but $12,240 for a family with 5 or more members ($1,020 per month). The Shared Responsibility Payment worksheet, (Illustration 10-6), will be used to calculate the payment amount. The worksheets for the following example are shown in Illustrations 10-7 through 10-10.

Example 1: Jennifer and Sean are married with no children. Their household income is $36,000 and they had no coverage for all months of 2014. First, we will deduct the filing threshold for a Married Filing Joint couple: $36,000 - $20,300 = $15,700. Then we will multiply that by 1%: $15,700 x .01 = $157.00. The flat dollar amount for them is $190: $95 x 2 = $190. The greater of the two is $190. The cap, which is the cost of the national average premium for a bronze level health plan is $4,896: $2,448 x 2 = $4,896. Because $190 is less than the cap of $4,896, their Individual Shared Responsibility Payment is $190.

Example 2: Sarah and Donnie are married with one child. Their household income is $89,000 and they had coverage from January to March. We will have to calculate the penalty monthly to determine what their payment will be. First, we will deduct the filing threshold for a Married Filing Joint couple: $89,000 - $20,300 = $68,700. Then we will multiply that by 1%: $68,700 x .01 = $687.00. The flat dollar amount for them is $190: $95 x 2 + $47.50 = $237.50. The greater of the two is $687. The cap, which is the cost of the national average premium for a bronze level health plan is $7,344: $2,448 x 3 = $7,344. $687 is less than the cap of $7,344. The Individual Shared Responsibility payment is $57.25 per month: 1/12 of $687 is $57.25. They were not covered for 9 months, so their payment is $515: $57.25 x 9 = $515.25.

Example 3: John is single with no children. His household income is $134,000. He had no coverage during the year. First, deduct the filing threshold: $134,000 - $10,150 = $123,850. 1% of $123,850 is $1,238.50. The flat dollar amount for him is $95. The greater of the two is $1,238.50 which is less than the cap of $2,448. His Individual Shared Responsibility Payment is $1,239.

Example 4: James and Deborah have one child. Deborah has insurance through her job, but James and their child does not. Their household income is $68,000. First, deduct the filing threshold: $68,000 - $20,300 = $47,700. 1% of $47,400 is $474. The flat dollar amount would be $142.50: $95 + $47.50 = 142.50. The greater of the two is $474 which is less than the cap of $4,896: $2,448 x 2. Their Individual Shared Responsibility Payment is $474.

Illustration 10-6

Shared Responsibility Payment Worksheet

If you or another member of your tax household had neither minimum essential coverage nor a coverage exemption for any month during 2014, use the Shared Responsibility Payment Worksheet, below, to figure your shared responsibility payment. You will enter the amount from line 14 of the worksheet on Form 1040, line 61; Form 1040A, line 38; or Form 1040EZ, line 11.

Complete the monthly columns by placing "X's" in each month in which you or another member of your tax household had neither minimum essential coverage nor a coverage exemption.

Name	Jan	Feb	Mar	Apr	May	Jun	Jul	Aug	Sep	Oct	Nov	Dec
1. Total number of X's in a month. If 5 or more, enter 5												
2. Total number of X's in a month for individuals 18 or over*												
3. One-half the number of X's in a month for individuals under 18*												
4. Add lines 2 and 3 for each month												
5. Multiply line 4 by $95 for each month. If $285 or more, enter $285												

6. Sum of the monthly amounts entered on line 1 _____
7. Enter your household income (see *Household income*, earlier) _____
8. Enter your filing threshold (see *Filing Thresholds For Most People*, later) _____
9. Subtract line 8 from line 7 _____
10. Multiply line 9 by 1% (.01) _____
11. Is line 10 more than $285?
   ☐ **Yes.** Multiply line 10 by the number of months for which line 1 is more than zero
   ☐ **No.** Enter the amount from line 14 of the Flat Dollar Amount Worksheet } _____
12. Divide line 11 by 12.0 _____
13. Multiply line 6 by $204** _____
14. Enter the smaller of line 12 or line 13 here and on Form 1040, line 61; Form 1040A, line 38; or Form 1040EZ, line 11. This is your shared responsibility payment _____

*For purposes of figuring the shared responsibility payment, an individual is considered under 18 for an entire month if he or she did not turn 18 before the first day of the month. An individual turns 18 on the anniversary of the day the individual was born. For example, someone born on March 1, 1999, is considered age 18 on March 1, 2017, and, therefore, is not considered age 18 for purposes of the shared responsibility payment until April 2017.
**$204 is the 2014 national average premium for a bronze level health plan available through the Marketplace for one individual and should not be changed.

Illustration 10-6 continued

Flat Dollar Amount Worksheet

 Do not complete this worksheet unless the amount on line 10 of the Shared Responsibility Payment Worksheet is less than $285.

For each month, is the amount on line 5 of the Shared Responsibility Payment Worksheet less than the amount on line 10 of the Shared Responsibility Payment Worksheet?*	Yes	No
	Enter the amount from line 10	Enter the amount from line 5
1. January		
2. February		
3. March		
4. April		
5. May		
6. June		
7. July		
8. August		
9. September		
10. October		
11. November		
12. December		
13. Add the amounts in each column		
14. Add the amounts on line 13 of both columns. Enter the result on line 11 of the Shared Responsibility Payment Worksheet		

*If the amount on line 1 of the Shared Responsibility Payment Worksheet is -0- for any month, leave both columns of this worksheet blank for that month.

Filing Thresholds For Most People

If your filing status is:	And your age is:	Then you must file a tax return if your gross income is more than:
Single	Under 65	$10,150
	65 or older	$11,700
Head of Household	Under 65	$13,050
	65 or older	$14,600
Married Filing Jointly	Under 65 (both spouses)	$20,300
	65 or older (one spouse)	$21,500
	65 or older (both spouses)	$22,700
Married Filing Separately	Any age	$3,950
Qualifying Widow(er) with Dependent children	Under 65	$16,350
	65 or older	$17,550

 Gross income means all income you received in the form of money, goods, property, and services that is not exempt from tax, including any income from sources outside the United States or from the sale of your main home (even if you can exclude part or all of it). Include only the taxable part of social security benefits (Form 1040, line 20b; Form 1040A, line 14b). Also include gains, but not losses, reported on Form 8949 or Schedule D. Gross income from a business means, for example, the amount on Schedule C, line 7, or Schedule F, line 9. But, in figuring gross income, do not reduce your income by any losses, including any loss on Schedule C, line 7, or Schedule F, line 9.

Illustration 10-7

Shared Responsibility Payment Worksheet

If you or another member of your tax household had neither minimum essential coverage nor a coverage exemption for any month during 2014, use the Shared Responsibility Payment Worksheet, below, to figure your shared responsibility payment. You will enter the amount from line 14 of the worksheet on Form 1040, line 61; Form 1040A, line 38; or Form 1040EZ, line 11.

Complete the monthly columns by placing "X's" in each month in which you or another member of your tax household had neither minimum essential coverage nor a coverage exemption.

Name	Jan	Feb	Mar	Apr	May	Jun	Jul	Aug	Sep	Oct	Nov	Dec
Sean	✓	✓	✓	✓	✓	✓	✓	✓	✓	✓	✓	✓
Jennifer	✓	✓	✓	✓	✓	✓	✓	✓	✓	✓	✓	✓
1. Total number of X's in a month. If 5 or more, enter 5	2	2	2	2	2	2	2	2	2	2	2	2
2. Total number of X's in a month for individuals 18 or over*	2	2	2	2	2	2	2	2	2	2	2	2
3. One-half the number of X's in a month for individuals under 18*												
4. Add lines 2 and 3 for each month	2	2	2	2	2	2	2	2	2	2	2	2
5. Multiply line 4 by $95 for each month. If $285 or more, enter $285	190	190	190	190	190	190	190	190	190	190	190	190

6. Sum of the monthly amounts entered on line 1	24
7. Enter your household income (see _Household income_, earlier)	36,000
8. Enter your filing threshold (see _Filing Thresholds For Most People_, later)	20,300
9. Subtract line 8 from line 7	15,700
10. Multiply line 9 by 1% (.01)	157
11. Is line 10 more than $285?	
☐ **Yes.** Multiply line 10 by the number of months for which line 1 is more than zero ⎫ ...	2,280
☒ **No.** Enter the amount from line 14 of the Flat Dollar Amount Worksheet ⎭	
12. Divide line 11 by 12.0	190
13. Multiply line 6 by $204**	4,896
14. Enter the smaller of line 12 or line 13 here and on Form 1040, line 61; Form 1040A, line 38; or Form 1040EZ, line 11. This is your shared responsibility payment	190

*For purposes of figuring the shared responsibility payment, an individual is considered under 18 for an entire month if he or she did not turn 18 before the first day of the month. An individual turns 18 on the anniversary of the day the individual was born. For example, someone born on March 1, 1999, is considered age 18 on March 1, 2017, and, therefore, is not considered age 18 for purposes of the shared responsibility payment until April 2017.

**$204 is the 2014 national average premium for a bronze level health plan available through the Marketplace for one individual and should not be changed.

Illustration 10-7 continued

Flat Dollar Amount Worksheet

 Do not complete this worksheet unless the amount on line 10 of the <u>Shared Responsibility Payment Worksheet</u> is less than $285.

For each month, is the amount on line 5 of the Shared Responsibility Payment Worksheet less than the amount on line 10 of the Shared Responsibility Payment Worksheet?*	Yes	No
	Enter the amount from line 10	Enter the amount from line 5
1. January		190
2. February		190
3. March		190
4. April		190
5. May		190
6. June		190
7. July		190
8. August		190
9. September		190
10. October		190
11. November		190
12. December		190
13. Add the amounts in each column		2,280
14. Add the amounts on line 13 of both columns. Enter the result on line 11 of the Shared Responsibility Payment Worksheet		2,280

*If the amount on line 1 of the Shared Responsibility Payment Worksheet is -0- for any month, leave both columns of this worksheet blank for that month.

Filing Thresholds For Most People

If your filing status is:	And your age is:	Then you must file a tax return if your gross income is more than:
Single	Under 65	$10,150
	65 or older	$11,700
Head of Household	Under 65	$13,050
	65 or older	$14,600
Married Filing Jointly	Under 65 (both spouses)	$20,300
	65 or older (one spouse)	$21,500
	65 or older (both spouses)	$22,700
Married Filing Separately	Any age	$3,950
Qualifying Widow(er) with Dependent children	Under 65	$16,350
	65 or older	$17,550

 Gross income means all income you received in the form of money, goods, property, and services that is not exempt from tax, including any income from sources outside the United States or from the sale of your main home (even if you can exclude part or all of it). Include only the taxable part of social security benefits (Form 1040, line 20b; Form 1040A, line 14b). Also include gains, but not losses, reported on Form 8949 or Schedule D. Gross income from a business means, for example, the amount on Schedule C, line 7, or Schedule F, line 9. But, in figuring gross income, do not reduce your income by any losses, including any loss on Schedule C, line 7, or Schedule F, line 9.

Illustration 10-8

Shared Responsibility Payment Worksheet

If you or another member of your tax household had neither minimum essential coverage nor a coverage exemption for any month during 2014, use the Shared Responsibility Payment Worksheet, below, to figure your shared responsibility payment. You will enter the amount from line 14 of the worksheet on Form 1040, line 61; Form 1040A, line 38; or Form 1040EZ, line 11.

Complete the monthly columns by placing "X's" in each month in which you or another member of your tax household had neither minimum essential coverage nor a coverage exemption.

Name	Jan	Feb	Mar	Apr	May	Jun	Jul	Aug	Sep	Oct	Nov	Dec
Sarah				✓	✓	✓	✓	✓	✓	✓	✓	✓
Donnie				✓	✓	✓	✓	✓	✓	✓	✓	✓
Donnie Jr.				✓	✓	✓	✓	✓	✓	✓	✓	✓

	Jan	Feb	Mar	Apr	May	Jun	Jul	Aug	Sep	Oct	Nov	Dec
1. Total number of X's in a month. If 5 or more, enter 5	0	0	0	3	3	3	3	3	3	3	3	3
2. Total number of X's in a month for individuals 18 or over*	0	0	0	2	2	2	2	2	2	2	2	2
3. One-half the number of X's in a month for individuals under 18*	0	0	0	.5	.5	.5	.5	.5	.5	.5	.5	.5
4. Add lines 2 and 3 for each month	0	0	0	2.5	2.5	2.5	2.5	2.5	2.5	2.5	2.5	2.5
5. Multiply line 4 by $95 for each month. If $285 or more, enter $285	0	0	0	237.5	237.5	237.5	237.5	237.5	237.5	237.5	237.5	237.5

6. Sum of the monthly amounts entered on line 1	27
7. Enter your household income (see *Household income*, earlier)	89,000
8. Enter your filing threshold (see *Filing Thresholds For Most People*, later)	20,300
9. Subtract line 8 from line 7	68,700
10. Multiply line 9 by 1% (.01)	687
11. Is line 10 more than $285?	
■ **Yes.** Multiply line 10 by the number of months for which line 1 is more than zero	6,183
☐ **No.** Enter the amount from line 14 of the Flat Dollar Amount Worksheet	
12. Divide line 11 by 12.0	515
13. Multiply line 6 by $204**	5,508
14. Enter the smaller of line 12 or line 13 here and on Form 1040, line 61; Form 1040A, line 38; or Form 1040EZ, line 11. This is your shared responsibility payment	515

*For purposes of figuring the shared responsibility payment, an individual is considered under 18 for an entire month if he or she did not turn 18 before the first day of the month. An individual turns 18 on the anniversary of the day the individual was born. For example, someone born on March 1, 1999, is considered age 18 on March 1, 2017, and, therefore, is not considered age 18 for purposes of the shared responsibility payment until April 2017.

**$204 is the 2014 national average premium for a bronze level health plan available through the Marketplace for one individual and should not be changed.

Illustration 10-9

Shared Responsibility Payment Worksheet

If you or another member of your tax household had neither minimum essential coverage nor a coverage exemption for any month during 2014, use the Shared Responsibility Payment Worksheet, below, to figure your shared responsibility payment. You will enter the amount from line 14 of the worksheet on Form 1040, line 61; Form 1040A, line 38; or Form 1040EZ, line 11.

Complete the monthly columns by placing "X's" in each month in which you or another member of your tax household had neither minimum essential coverage nor a coverage exemption.

Name	Jan	Feb	Mar	Apr	May	Jun	Jul	Aug	Sep	Oct	Nov	Dec
John	✓	✓	✓	✓	✓	✓	✓	✓	✓	✓	✓	✓

	Jan	Feb	Mar	Apr	May	Jun	Jul	Aug	Sep	Oct	Nov	Dec
1. Total number of X's in a month. If 5 or more, enter 5	1	1	1	1	1	1	1	1	1	1	1	1
2. Total number of X's in a month for individuals 18 or over*	1	1	1	1	1	1	1	1	1	1	1	1
3. One-half the number of X's in a month for individuals under 18*												
4. Add lines 2 and 3 for each month	1	1	1	1	1	1	1	1	1	1	1	1
5. Multiply line 4 by $95 for each month. If $285 or more, enter $285	95	95	95	95	95	95	95	95	95	95	95	95

6. Sum of the monthly amounts entered on line 1	12
7. Enter your household income (see *Household income*, earlier)	134,000
8. Enter your filing threshold (see *Filing Thresholds For Most People*, later)	10,150
9. Subtract line 8 from line 7	123,850
10. Multiply line 9 by 1% (.01)	12,385
11. Is line 10 more than $285?	
☑ **Yes.** Multiply line 10 by the number of months for which line 1 is more than zero	
☐ **No.** Enter the amount from line 14 of the *Flat Dollar Amount Worksheet*	14,862
12. Divide line 11 by 12.0	1,239
13. Multiply line 6 by $204**	2,448
14. Enter the smaller of line 12 or line 13 here and on Form 1040, line 61; Form 1040A, line 38; or Form 1040EZ, line 11. This is your shared responsibility payment	1,239

*For purposes of figuring the shared responsibility payment, an individual is considered under 18 for an entire month if he or she did not turn 18 before the first day of the month. An individual turns 18 on the anniversary of the day the individual was born. For example, someone born on March 1, 1999, is considered age 18 on March 1, 2017, and, therefore, is not considered age 18 for purposes of the shared responsibility payment until April 2017.

**$204 is the 2014 national average premium for a bronze level health plan available through the Marketplace for one individual and should not be changed.

Illustration 10-10

Shared Responsibility Payment Worksheet

If you or another member of your tax household had neither minimum essential coverage nor a coverage exemption for any month during 2014, use the Shared Responsibility Payment Worksheet, below, to figure your shared responsibility payment. You will enter the amount from line 14 of the worksheet on Form 1040, line 61; Form 1040A, line 38; or Form 1040EZ, line 11.

Complete the monthly columns by placing "X's" in each month in which you or another member of your tax household had neither minimum essential coverage nor a coverage exemption.

Name	Jan	Feb	Mar	Apr	May	Jun	Jul	Aug	Sep	Oct	Nov	Dec
James	✓	✓	✓	✓	✓	✓	✓	✓	✓	✓	✓	✓
Deborah												
James Jr.	✓	✓	✓	✓	✓	✓	✓	✓	✓	✓	✓	✓

		Jan	Feb	Mar	Apr	May	Jun	Jul	Aug	Sep	Oct	Nov	Dec
1.	Total number of X's in a month. If 5 or more, enter 5	2	2	2	2	2	2	2	2	2	2	2	2
2.	Total number of X's in a month for individuals 18 or over*	1	1	1	1	1	1	1	1	1	1	1	1
3.	One-half the number of X's in a month for individuals under 18*	.5	.5	.5	.5	.5	.5	.5	.5	.5	.5	.5	.5
4.	Add lines 2 and 3 for each month	1.5	1.5	1.5	1.5	1.5	1.5	1.5	1.5	1.5	1.5	1.5	1.5
5.	Multiply line 4 by $95 for each month. If $285 or more, enter $285	142.5	142.5	142.5	142.5	142.5	142.5	142.5	142.5	142.5	142.5	142.5	142.5

6. Sum of the monthly amounts entered on line 1	24
7. Enter your household income (see *Household income*, earlier)	68,000
8. Enter your filing threshold (see *Filing Thresholds For Most People*, later)	20,300
9. Subtract line 8 from line 7	47,700
10. Multiply line 9 by 1% (.01)	477
11. Is line 10 more than $285?	
■ **Yes.** Multiply line 10 by the number of months for which line 1 is more than zero □ **No.** Enter the amount from line 14 of the Flat Dollar Amount Worksheet	5,724
12. Divide line 11 by 12.0	477
13. Multiply line 6 by $204**	4,896
14. Enter the smaller of line 12 or line 13 here and on Form 1040, line 61; Form 1040A, line 38; or Form 1040EZ, line 11. This is your shared responsibility payment	477

*For purposes of figuring the shared responsibility payment, an individual is considered under 18 for an entire month if he or she did not turn 18 before the first day of the month. An individual turns 18 on the anniversary of the day the individual was born. For example, someone born on March 1, 1999, is considered age 18 on March 1, 2017, and, therefore, is not considered age 18 for purposes of the shared responsibility payment until April 2017.

**$204 is the 2014 national average premium for a bronze level health plan available through the Marketplace for one individual and should not be changed.

Premium Tax Credit

Eligibility

The Premium Tax Credit is a refundable credit and is available if the taxpayer purchases their health insurance policy through the Marketplace and meets other requirements. The credit makes purchasing health insurance more affordable to people with moderate income. The taxpayer may get the credit in advance to help pay the monthly premiums or they may get the credit in a lump sum on their tax return. If the taxpayer qualifies for the credit, whether received in advance or not, they must file a tax return.

The taxpayer may be eligible for the credit if they meet all of the following:

- They purchase health coverage through the marketplace.
- They are within a certain income range.
- They are not able to get affordable coverage through an eligible employer plan that provides minimum value.
- They are not eligible for coverage through a government program, like Medicaid, Medicare, CHIP, or TRICARE.
- They do not file Married Filing Separate unless they qualify as a certain victim of domestic abuse and spousal abandonment.
- They cannot be claimed as a dependent by another person.

Income Requirement: In general, individuals and families whose household income for the year is between 100% and 400% of the federal poverty line for their family size. Household income for purposes of the Premium Tax Credit is the Modified AGI plus income of dependents required to file tax returns. Modified AGI is the AGI plus excluded foreign income, nontaxable social security (including Railroad Tier 1), plus tax exempt interest received or accrued during the tax year.

For purposes of the Premium Tax Credit, eligibility for a certain year is based on the most recently published poverty guidelines as of the first day of the annual enrollment period. As a result, the 2014 tax credit will be based on the 2013 guidelines, the 2015 tax credit will be based on the 2014 guidelines, etc.

2013 POVERTY GUIDELINES FOR THE 48 CONTIGUOUS STATES AND THE DISTRICT OF COLUMBIA

Persons in family/household	100% of the Federal Poverty Line	400% of the Federal Poverty Line
1	$11,490	$45,960
2	15,510	62,040
3	19,530	78,120
4	23,550	94,200
5	27,570	110,280
6	31,590	126,360
7	35,610	142,440
8	39,630	158,520
For families/households with more than 8 persons, add $4,020 for each additional person.		

2013 POVERTY GUIDELINES FOR ALASKA

Persons in family/household	100% of the Federal Poverty Line	400% of the Federal Poverty Line
1	$14,350	$57,400
2	19,380	77,520
3	24,410	97,640
4	29,440	117,760
5	34,470	137,880
6	39,500	158,000
7	44,530	178,120
8	49,560	198,240
For families/households with more than 8 persons, add $5,030 for each additional person.		

2013 POVERTY GUIDELINES FOR HAWAII

Persons in family/household	100% of the Federal Poverty Line	400% of the Federal Poverty Line
1	$13,230	$52,920
2	17,850	71,400
3	22,470	89,880
4	27,090	108,360
5	31,710	126,840
6	36,330	145,320
7	40,950	163,800
8	45,570	182,280
For families/households with more than 8 persons, add $4,620 for each additional person.		

Affordable Coverage: An employer-sponsored plan is affordable if the taxpayer's portion of the annual premium for self-only coverage does not exceed 9.5% of their household income. The affordability test only considers self-only coverage and does not take into account any additional cost for family coverage. If multiple plans are offered by the employer, the test applies to the lowest cost plan that meets the Minimum Essential Coverage.

Married Filing Separate: If the taxpayer files a Married Filing Separate tax return, they are not eligible for the Premium Tax Credit unless they are a victim of domestic abuse or abandonment. **Note:** This does not apply to a taxpayer that qualifies under "married but considered unmarried for tax purposes", as they will be filing using the Head of Household filing status. If the taxpayer files Married Filing Separate and is living apart from their spouse when the return is filed because they are a victim of domestic abuse, they will qualify for the Premium Tax Credit. Also, if the taxpayer is abandoned by their spouse and is unable to locate them after reasonable diligence, they will qualify for the Premium Tax Credit. Additional guidance will be released on this subject.

The Marketplace

When the taxpayer goes to the Marketplace to purchase their insurance coverage, they will provide information about the family composition and household income. The Marketplace will then determine if the taxpayer is eligible for the credit and estimate the amount. The taxpayer will then be able to choose whether they want to receive some or all of the credit in advance paid directly to the insurance company to be applied to the monthly premiums, or if they want to receive the full amount as a credit on their tax return.

If the taxpayer chooses to receive some or all in advance, they will be required to reconcile the amount on their tax return. If they did not receive the full amount for which they were eligible, they will receive the remainder on the tax return. If they received too much in advance, the difference, subject to certain caps (explained later), will be deducted from the taxpayer's refund or added to their balance due.

To prevent the advance credit from being less than the allowable credit, it is important for the taxpayer to notify the Marketplace of any changes in circumstances as soon as they happen. The following changes could affect the amount of the taxpayer's allowable credit:

- Increases or decreases in their household income.
- Marriage.
- Divorce.
- Birth or adoption of a child.
- Other changes to their household composition.
- Gaining or losing eligibility for government sponsored or employer sponsored health care coverage.

The Marketplace will be required to file a Form 1095-A (Illustration 10-11), to the IRS and any individual enrolled in an insurance plan through the Marketplace. The Form 1095-A will furnish the taxpayer with the information needed to claim or reconcile the Premium Tax Credit on the tax return. The Form 1095-A is required to be furnished on or before January 31, 2015 for the 2014 tax year.

Illustration 10-11

Form **1095-A**

Department of the Treasury
Internal Revenue Service

Health Insurance Marketplace Statement

▶ **Information about Form 1095-A and its separate instructions**
is at *www.irs.gov/form1095a.*

☐ CORRECTED

OMB No. 1545-2232

2014

Part I Recipient Information

1 Marketplace identifier	2 Marketplace-assigned policy number	3 Policy issuer's name	
4 Recipient's name		5 Recipient's SSN	6 Recipient's date of birth
7 Recipient's spouse's name		8 Recipient's spouse's SSN	9 Recipient's spouse's date of birth
10 Policy start date	11 Policy termination date	12 Street address (including apartment no.)	
13 City or town	14 State or province	15 Country and ZIP or foreign postal code	

Part II Coverage Household

	A. Covered Individual Name	B. Covered Individual SSN	C. Covered Individual Date of Birth	D. Covered Individual Start Date	E. Covered Individual Termination Date
16					
17					
18					
19					
20					

Part III Household Information

Month	A. Monthly Premium Amount	B. Monthly Premium Amount of Second Lowest Cost Silver Plan (SLCSP)	C. Monthly Advance Payment of Premium Tax Credit
21 January			
22 February			
23 March			
24 April			
25 May			
26 June			
27 July			
28 August			
29 September			
30 October			
31 November			
32 December			
33 **Annual Totals**			

For Privacy Act and Paperwork Reduction Act Notice, see separate instructions.   Cat. No. 60703Q   Form **1095-A** (2014)

Claiming the Credit

First, let's discuss how the amount of the credit is calculated. Then we will look at how it's reported on the tax return.

Step One: Determine the household income as a percentage of the Federal Poverty Line.

Divide the household income by the Federal Poverty Line amount for the family size.

2013 POVERTY GUIDELINES FOR THE 48 CONTIGUOUS STATES AND THE DISTRICT OF COLUMBIA	
Persons in family/household	100% of the Federal Poverty Line
1	$11,490
2	15,510
3	19,530
4	23,550
5	27,570
6	31,590
7	35,610
8	39,630
For families/households with more than 8 persons, add $4,020 for each additional person.	

Johnny has 2 children and a household income of $43,000. To find the household income as a percentage of the Federal Poverty Line, we will divide $43,000 by $19,530: $43,000 ÷ $19,530 = 2.20 *or* 220%

The household income as a percentage of the Federal Poverty Line for Johnny is 220%.

Rounding: Is the result is between 1.00 (100%) and 3.99 (399%)?

- Yes – Round up or down to the nearest whole percentage.
- No –
  - For any amount less than 1.00 (100%), round down to the nearest whole percentage.
  - For any amount between 3.99 (399%) and 4.00 (400%), round down to 3.99 (399%).
  - For any amount more than 4.00 (400%), but no more than 9.99 (999%), round up to the nearest whole percent.
  - For any amount more than 9.99 (999%), enter the result as 999%.

Step Two: Use the percentage to determine the Applicable Figure.

The table on the next page shows the Applicable Figures as determined by the percentage we calculated in the last step.

Johnny's household income as a percentage of the Federal Poverty Line is 220%, which gives him an Applicable Figure of 0.0700.

Applicable Figures

If the Income as Percentage of Poverty Line is...	The Applicable Figure is	If the Income as Percentage of Poverty Line is...	The Applicable Figure is	If the Income as Percentage of Poverty Line is...	The Applicable Figure is	If the Income as Percentage of Poverty Line is...	The Applicable Figure is	If the Income as Percentage of Poverty Line is...	The Applicable Figure is
Less than 133	0.0200	158	0.0437	184	0.0556	210	0.0665	236	0.0756
133	0.0300	159	0.0441	185	0.0561	211	0.0669	237	0.0760
134	0.0306	160	0.0446	186	0.0566	212	0.0672	238	0.0763
135	0.0312	161	0.0451	187	0.0570	213	0.0676	239	0.0767
136	0.0318	162	0.0455	188	0.0575	214	0.0679	240	0.0770
137	0.0324	163	0.0460	189	0.0579	215	0.0683	241	0.0774
138	0.0329	164	0.0464	190	0.0584	216	0.0686	242	0.0777
139	0.0335	165	0.0469	191	0.0589	217	0.0690	243	0.0781
140	0.0341	166	0.0474	192	0.0593	218	0.0693	244	0.0784
141	0.0347	167	0.0478	193	0.0598	219	0.0697	245	0.0788
142	0.0353	168	0.0483	194	0.0602	220	0.0700	246	0.0791
143	0.0359	169	0.0487	195	0.0607	221	0.0704	247	0.0795
144	0.0365	170	0.0492	196	0.0612	222	0.0707	248	0.0798
145	0.0371	171	0.0497	197	0.0616	223	0.0711	249	0.0802
146	0.0376	172	0.0501	198	0.0621	224	0.0714	250	0.0805
147	0.0382	173	0.0506	199	0.0625	225	0.0718	251	0.0808
148	0.0388	174	0.0510	200	0.0630	226	0.0721	252	0.0811
149	0.0394	175	0.0515	201	0.0634	227	0.0725	253	0.0814
150	0.0400	176	0.0520	202	0.0637	228	0.0728	254	0.0817
151	0.0405	177	0.0524	203	0.0641	229	0.0732	255	0.0820
152	0.0409	178	0.0529	204	0.0644	230	0.0735	256	0.0822
153	0.0414	179	0.0533	205	0.0648	231	0.0739	257	0.0825
154	0.0418	180	0.0538	206	0.0651	232	0.0742	258	0.0828
155	0.0423	181	0.0543	207	0.0655	233	0.0746	259	0.0831
156	0.0428	182	0.0547	208	0.0658	234	0.0749	260	0.0834
157	0.0432	183	0.0552	209	0.0662	235	0.0753	261	0.0837

If the Income as Percentage of Poverty Line is...	The Applicable Figure is	If the Income as Percentage of Poverty Line is...	The Applicable Figure is	If the Income as Percentage of Poverty Line is...	The Applicable Figure is	If the Income as Percentage of Poverty Line is...	The Applicable Figure is
262	0.0840	270	0.0863	278	0.0886	286	0.0909	294	0.0933
263	0.0843	271	0.0866	279	0.0889	287	0.0912	295	0.0936
264	0.0846	272	0.0869	280	0.0892	288	0.0915	296	0.0938
265	0.0849	273	0.0872	281	0.0895	289	0.0918	297	0.0941
266	0.0851	274	0.0875	282	0.0898	290	0.0921	298	0.0944
267	0.0854	275	0.0878	283	0.0901	291	0.0924	299	0.0947
268	0.0857	276	0.0880	284	0.0904	292	0.0927	More than 299	0.0950
269	0.0860	277	0.0883	285	0.0907	293	0.0930		

Step Three: Multiply the household income by the Applicable Figure.

When you multiply the household income by the Applicable Figure, the answer is the amount the taxpayer can afford to pay for insurance.

Johnny's household income is $43,000. We will multiply that amount by his Applicable Figure of 0.0700.

$$\$43,000 \times 0.0700 = \$3,010$$

Johnny can afford annual premiums of $3,010, or $250.93 per month ($3,010 ÷ 12).

Step Four: Subtract the affordable amount from the premium of the benchmark plan.

The benchmark plan is the second lowest cost silver plan (SLCSP). This is the maximum coverage the Marketplace will subsidize for the taxpayer. If the taxpayer purchases a plan above it, they are responsible for the difference in premium amounts. The Marketplace will give us this number on the Form 1095-A. The allowable Premium Tax Credit is the smaller of this amount or the premium amount of the policy Johnny purchased.

Johnny's benchmark plan premium is $7,900. He purchased a cheaper policy than this at $7,350 annually. $7,900 − $3,010 = $4,890. $4,890 is smaller than $7,350, so Johnny's Premium Tax Credit is $4,890. He can elect to receive that in advance to pay his premiums, or as a refundable credit on his tax return. If he chooses to receive it in advance, $407.50 ($4,890 ÷ 12) will go to his premium every month.

Form 8962

Thankfully, Form 8962 (Illustration 10-12) will calculate the Premium Tax Credit for us. We will also use Form 8962 to reconcile any advance Premium Tax Credit on the tax return. Let's do some examples to see how this form works.

Example 1: Bob and Sara have two children. Their household income is $58,000. Their benchmark plan as reported by the Marketplace is $13,500. They purchased a plan for an annual premium of $11,200. They had the same coverage for all of 2014 with no changes in monthly amounts. They did not elect to receive their Premium Tax Credit in advance. See Illustration 10-13.

for the completed Form 8962. The taxpayer will receive a refundable credit of $8,912. This amount is reported on Form 1040, line 69.

68	American opportunity credit from Form 8863, line 8 . . .	68		
69	Net premium tax credit. Attach Form 8962	69	8,912	
70	Amount paid with request for extension to file	70		

Illustration 10-12

Form **8962**	**Premium Tax Credit (PTC)**	OMB No. 1545-0074
Department of the Treasury Internal Revenue Service	▶ Attach to Form 1040, 1040A, or 1040NR. ▶ Information about Form 8962 and its separate instructions is at *www.irs.gov/form8962*.	**2014** Attachment Sequence No. **73**

Name shown on your return	Your social security number	Relief (see instructions) ☐

Part 1: Annual and Monthly Contribution Amount

1 Family Size: Enter the number of exemptions from Form 1040 or Form 1040A, line 6d, or Form 1040NR, line 7d . **1** [ ]

2a Modified AGI: Enter your modified AGI (see instructions) . . . . . **2a** [ ] **b** Enter total of your dependents' modified AGI (see instructions) . . . . . . **2b** [ ]

3 Household Income: Add the amounts on lines 2a and 2b . . . . **3** [ ]

4 Federal Poverty Line: Enter the federal poverty amount as determined by the family size on line 1 and the federal poverty table for your state of residence during the tax year (see instructions). Check the appropriate box for the federal poverty table used.   **a** ☐ Alaska   **b** ☐ Hawaii   **c** ☐ Other 48 states and DC   **4** [ ]

5 Household Income as a Percentage of Federal Poverty Line: Divide line 3 by line 4. Enter the result rounded to a whole percentage. (For example, for 1.542 enter the result as 154, for 1.549 enter as 155.) (See instructions for special rules.)   **5** [ ] %

6 Is the result entered on line 5 less than or equal to 400%? (See instructions if the result is less than 100%.)

☐ **Yes. Continue to line 7.**

☐ **No.** You are not eligible to receive PTC. If you received advance payment of PTC, see the instructions for how to report your Excess Advance PTC Repayment amount.

7 Applicable Figure: Using your line 5 percentage, locate your "applicable figure" on the table in the instructions . . **7** [ ]

8a Annual Contribution for Health Care: Multiply line 3 by line 7 . . . . . **8a** [ ] **b** Monthly Contribution for Health Care: Divide line 8a by 12. Round to whole dollar amount   **8b** [ ]

Part 2: Premium Tax Credit Claim and Reconciliation of Advance Payment of Premium Tax Credit

9 Did you share a policy with another taxpayer or get married during the year and want to use the alternative calculation? (see instructions)

☐ **Yes.** Skip to Part 4, Shared Policy Allocation, or Part 5, Alternative Calculation for Year of Marriage.   ☐ **No. Continue to line 10.**

10 Do all Forms 1095-A for your tax household include coverage for January through December with no changes in monthly amounts shown on lines 21–32, columns A and B?

☐ **Yes. Continue to line 11.** Compute your annual PTC. Skip lines 12–23 and continue to line 24.   ☐ **No. Continue to lines 12–23.** Compute your monthly PTC and continue to line 24.

Annual Calculation	A. Premium Amount (Form(s) 1095-A, line 33A)	B. Annual Premium Amount of SLCSP (Form(s) 1095-A, line 33B)	C. Annual Contribution Amount (Line 8a)	D. Annual Maximum Premium Assistance (Subtract C from B)	E. Annual Premium Tax Credit Allowed (Smaller of A or D)	F. Annual Advance Payment of PTC (Form(s) 1095-A, line 33C)
11 Annual Totals						

Monthly Calculation	A. Monthly Premium Amount (Form(s) 1095-A, lines 21–32, column A)	B. Monthly Premium Amount of SLCSP (Form(s) 1095-A, lines 21–32, column B)	C. Monthly Contribution Amount (Amount from line 8b or alternative marriage monthly contribution)	D. Monthly Maximum Premium Assistance (Subtract C from B)	E. Monthly Premium Tax Credit Allowed (Smaller of A or D)	F. Monthly Advance Payment of PTC (Form(s) 1095-A, lines 21–32, column C)
12 January						
13 February						
14 March						
15 April						
16 May						
17 June						
18 July						
19 August						
20 September						
21 October						
22 November						
23 December						

24 Total Premium Tax Credit: Enter the amount from line 11E or add lines 12E through 23E and enter the total here . **24** [ ]

25 Advance Payment of PTC: Enter the amount from line 11F or add lines 12F through 23F and enter the total here . **25** [ ]

26 Net Premium Tax Credit: If line 24 is greater than line 25, subtract line 25 from line 24. Enter the difference here and on Form 1040, line 69; Form 1040A, line 45; or Form 1040NR, line 65. If you elected the alternative calculation for marriage, enter zero. If line 24 equals line 25, enter zero. Stop here. If line 25 is greater than line 24, leave this line blank and continue to line 27 . **26** [ ]

Part 3: Repayment of Excess Advance Payment of the Premium Tax Credit

27 Excess Advance Payment of PTC: If line 25 is greater than line 24, subtract line 24 from line 25. Enter the difference here **27** [ ]

28 Repayment Limitation: Using the percentage on line 5 and your filing status, locate the repayment limitation amount in the instructions. Enter the amount here . . . . **28** [ ]

29 Excess Advance Premium Tax Credit Repayment: Enter the smaller of line 27 or line 28 here and on Form 1040, line 46; Form 1040A, line 29; or Form 1040NR, line 44 . . . . **29** [ ]

For Paperwork Reduction Act Notice, see your tax return instructions.   Cat. No. 37784Z   Form **8962** (2014)

Illustration 10-13

Form **8962**   **Premium Tax Credit (PTC)**   OMB No. 1545-0074

2014

Department of the Treasury
Internal Revenue Service

▶ Attach to Form 1040, 1040A, or 1040NR.
▶ Information about Form 8962 and its separate instructions is at *www.irs.gov/form8962*.

Attachment Sequence No. **73**

Name shown on your return	Your social security number	Relief (see instructions) ☐
Bob and Sara Jones	111-22-3333	

Part 1: Annual and Monthly Contribution Amount

1	Family Size: Enter the number of exemptions from Form 1040 or Form 1040A, line 6d, or Form 1040NR, line 7d .	**1**	4
2a	Modified AGI: Enter your modified AGI (see instructions) . . . . . **2a** 58,000 **b** Enter total of your dependents' modified AGI (see instructions)	**2b**	0
3	Household Income: Add the amounts on lines 2a and 2b	**3**	58,000
4	Federal Poverty Line: Enter the federal poverty amount as determined by the family size on line 1 and the federal poverty table for your state of residence during the tax year (see instructions). Check the appropriate box for the federal poverty table used. **a** ☐ Alaska **b** ☐ Hawaii **c** ☑ Other 48 states and DC	**4**	23,550
5	Household Income as a Percentage of Federal Poverty Line: Divide line 3 by line 4. Enter the result rounded to a whole percentage. (For example, for 1.542 enter the result as 154, for 1.549 enter as 155.) (See instructions for special rules.)	**5**	246 %
6	Is the result entered on line 5 less than or equal to 400%? (See instructions if the result is less than 100%.) ☑ **Yes. Continue to line 7.** ☐ **No.** You are not eligible to receive PTC. If you received advance payment of PTC, see the instructions for how to report your Excess Advance PTC Repayment amount.		
7	Applicable Figure: Using your line 5 percentage, locate your "applicable figure" on the table in the instructions . .	**7**	0.0791
8a	Annual Contribution for Health Care: Multiply line 3 by line 7 . . . . . **8a** 4,588 **b** Monthly Contribution for Health Care: Divide line 8a by 12. Round to whole dollar amount	**8b**	382

Part 2: Premium Tax Credit Claim and Reconciliation of Advance Payment of Premium Tax Credit

9 Did you share a policy with another taxpayer or get married during the year and want to use the alternative calculation? (see instructions)
☐ **Yes.** Skip to Part 4, Shared Policy Allocation, or Part 5, Alternative Calculation for Year of Marriage.   ☑ **No. Continue to line 10.**

10 Do all Forms 1095-A for your tax household include coverage for January through December with no changes in monthly amounts shown on lines 21–32, columns A and B?
☑ **Yes. Continue to line 11.** Compute your annual PTC. Skip lines 12–23 and continue to line 24.   ☐ **No. Continue to lines 12–23.** Compute your monthly PTC and continue to line 24.

Annual Calculation	A. Premium Amount (Form(s) 1095-A, line 33A)	B. Annual Premium Amount of SLCSP (Form(s) 1095-A, line 33B)	C. Annual Contribution Amount (Line 8a)	D. Annual Maximum Premium Assistance (Subtract C from B)	E. Annual Premium Tax Credit Allowed (Smaller of A or D)	F. Annual Advance Payment of PTC (Form(s) 1095-A, line 33C)
11 Annual Totals	11,200	13,500	4,588	8,912	8,912	0

Monthly Calculation	A. Monthly Premium Amount (Form(s) 1095-A, lines 21–32, column A)	B. Monthly Premium Amount of SLCSP (Form(s) 1095-A, lines 21–32, column B)	C. Monthly Contribution Amount (Amount from line 8b or alternative marriage monthly contribution)	D. Monthly Maximum Premium Assistance (Subtract C from B)	E. Monthly Premium Tax Credit Allowed (Smaller of A or D)	F. Monthly Advance Payment of PTC (Form(s) 1095-A, lines 21–32, column C)
12 January						
13 February						
14 March						
15 April						
16 May						
17 June						
18 July						
19 August						
20 September						
21 October						
22 November						
23 December						

24	Total Premium Tax Credit: Enter the amount from line 11E or add lines 12E through 23E and enter the total here .	**24**	8,912
25	Advance Payment of PTC: Enter the amount from line 11F or add lines 12F through 23F and enter the total here .	**25**	0
26	Net Premium Tax Credit: If line 24 is greater than line 25, subtract line 25 from line 24. Enter the difference here and on Form 1040, line 69; Form 1040A, line 45; or Form 1040NR, line 65. If you elected the alternative calculation for marriage, enter zero. If line 24 equals line 25, enter zero. Stop here. If line 25 is greater than line 24, leave this line blank and continue to line 27 .	**26**	8,912

Part 3: Repayment of Excess Advance Payment of the Premium Tax Credit

27	Excess Advance Payment of PTC: If line 25 is greater than line 24, subtract line 24 from line 25. Enter the difference here	**27**	
28	Repayment Limitation: Using the percentage on line 5 and your filing status, locate the repayment limitation amount in the instructions. Enter the amount here	**28**	
29	Excess Advance Premium Tax Credit Repayment: Enter the smaller of line 27 or line 28 here and on Form 1040, line 46; Form 1040A, line 29; or Form 1040NR, line 44	**29**	

For Paperwork Reduction Act Notice, see your tax return instructions.   Cat. No. 37784Z   Form **8962** (2014)

Example 2: Jason has one child. His household income is $27,000. The SLCSP as reported by the Marketplace is $6,800. He chose to receive his Premium Tax Credit in advance of $5,423. The annual premium amount for the plan he purchased was $7,100. His coverage was for the entire tax year of 2014 with no changes in coverage. See Illustration 10-14. Notice that the Premium Tax Credit will only allow for up to $6,800 in premium. Because Jason purchased a more expensive policy, he will have to cover the difference in premiums.

Reconciling the Premium Tax Credit

We discussed that the taxpayer should update their information on the Marketplace website, to keep from getting too much or too little advance Premium Tax Credit. But what happens if they don't? If the taxpayer was eligible for more credit than they received in advance, they will receive the additional amount on their tax return. If the taxpayer received more than they should have, they will be required to repay the additional amount, up to a certain limit, by adding it to their tax liability. This is why it is so important for the taxpayer to notify the Marketplace of any changes in their circumstances that will affect the Premium Tax Credit.

Repayment Limitation:

If the Household Income as a Percentage of the Federal Poverty Line (Form 8962, line 5)	The repayment limit is (Enter on Form 8962, line 28)	
	For a filing status of Single	For any other filing status
Less than 200%	$300	$600
At least 200% but less than 300%	$750	$1,500
At least 300% but less than 400%	$1,250	$2,500
400% or more	There is no limit (leave line 28 blank).	

Illustration 10-14

Form **8962**	**Premium Tax Credit (PTC)**	OMB No. 1545-0074
Department of the Treasury Internal Revenue Service	▶ Attach to Form 1040, 1040A, or 1040NR. ▶ Information about Form 8962 and its separate instructions is at *www.irs.gov/form8962.*	20**14** Attachment Sequence No. **73**

Name shown on your return	Your social security number	Relief (see instructions) ☐
Jason Jones	222-33-4444	

Part 1: Annual and Monthly Contribution Amount

1	Family Size: Enter the number of exemptions from Form 1040 or Form 1040A, line 6d, or Form 1040NR, line 7d .	**1**	2

2a Modified AGI: Enter your modified AGI (see instructions) . . . . . | **2a** | 27,000 | **b** Enter total of your dependents' modified AGI (see instructions) . . . . . . | **2b** |

3	Household Income: Add the amounts on lines 2a and 2b	**3**	27,000
4	Federal Poverty Line: Enter the federal poverty amount as determined by the family size on line 1 and the federal poverty table for your state of residence during the tax year (see instructions). Check the appropriate box for the federal poverty table used. **a** ☐ Alaska **b** ☐ Hawaii **c** ☑ Other 48 states and DC	**4**	15,510
5	Household Income as a Percentage of Federal Poverty Line: Divide line 3 by line 4. Enter the result rounded to a whole percentage. (For example, for 1.542 enter the result as 154, for 1.549 enter as 155.) (See instructions for special rules.)	**5**	174 %
6	Is the result entered on line 5 less than or equal to 400%? (See instructions if the result is less than 100%.) ☑ **Yes.** Continue to line 7. ☐ **No.** You are not eligible to receive PTC. If you received advance payment of PTC, see the instructions for how to report your Excess Advance PTC Repayment amount.		
7	Applicable Figure: Using your line 5 percentage, locate your "applicable figure" on the table in the instructions . .	**7**	0.0510

8a Annual Contribution for Health Care: Multiply line 3 by line 7 . . . . . | **8a** | 1,377 | **b** Monthly Contribution for Health Care: Divide line 8a by 12. Round to whole dollar amount | **8b** | 115 |

Part 2: Premium Tax Credit Claim and Reconciliation of Advance Payment of Premium Tax Credit

9	Did you share a policy with another taxpayer or get married during the year and want to use the alternative calculation? (see instructions) ☐ **Yes.** Skip to Part 4, Shared Policy Allocation, or Part 5, Alternative Calculation for Year of Marriage. ☑ **No.** Continue to line 10.
10	Do all Forms 1095-A for your tax household include coverage for January through December with no changes in monthly amounts shown on lines 21–32, columns A and B? ☑ **Yes.** Continue to line 11. Compute your annual PTC. Skip lines 12–23 and continue to line 24. ☐ **No.** Continue to lines 12–23. Compute your monthly PTC and continue to line 24.

Annual Calculation	A. Premium Amount (Form(s) 1095-A, line 33A)	B. Annual Premium Amount of SLCSP (Form(s) 1095-A, line 33B)	C. Annual Contribution Amount (Line 8a)	D. Annual Maximum Premium Assistance (Subtract C from B)	E. Annual Premium Tax Credit Allowed (Smaller of A or D)	F. Annual Advance Payment of PTC (Form(s) 1095-A, line 33C)
11 Annual Totals	7,100	6,800	1,377	5,423	5,423	5,423

Monthly Calculation	A. Monthly Premium Amount (Form(s) 1095-A, lines 21–32, column A)	B. Monthly Premium Amount of SLCSP (Form(s) 1095-A, lines 21–32, column B)	C. Monthly Contribution Amount (Amount from line 8b or alternative marriage monthly contribution)	D. Monthly Maximum Premium Assistance (Subtract C from B)	E. Monthly Premium Tax Credit Allowed (Smaller of A or D)	F. Monthly Advance Payment of PTC (Form(s) 1095-A, lines 21–32, column C)
12 January						
13 February						
14 March						
15 April						
16 May						
17 June						
18 July						
19 August						
20 September						
21 October						
22 November						
23 December						

24	Total Premium Tax Credit: Enter the amount from line 11E or add lines 12E through 23E and enter the total here .	**24**	5,423
25	Advance Payment of PTC: Enter the amount from line 11F or add lines 12F through 23F and enter the total here .	**25**	5,423
26	Net Premium Tax Credit: If line 24 is greater than line 25, subtract line 25 from line 24. Enter the difference here and on Form 1040, line 69; Form 1040A, line 45; or Form 1040NR, line 65. If you elected the alternative calculation for marriage, enter zero. If line 24 equals line 25, enter zero. Stop here. If line 25 is greater than line 24, leave this line blank and continue to line 27 .	**26**	0

Part 3: Repayment of Excess Advance Payment of the Premium Tax Credit

27	Excess Advance Payment of PTC: If line 25 is greater than line 24, subtract line 24 from line 25. Enter the difference here	**27**	
28	Repayment Limitation: Using the percentage on line 5 and your filing status, locate the repayment limitation amount in the instructions. Enter the amount here	**28**	
29	Excess Advance Premium Tax Credit Repayment: Enter the smaller of line 27 or line 28 here and on Form 1040, line 46; Form 1040A, line 29; or Form 1040NR, line 44	**29**	

For Paperwork Reduction Act Notice, see your tax return instructions.   Cat. No. 37784Z   Form **8962** (2014)

Let's revisit Johnny's situation. He did everything he was supposed to as far as going to the Marketplace and obtaining healthcare coverage. He elected to receive the Premium Tax Credit in advance. However, he received a raise during the year which increased his annual household income by $5,000. He did not go onto the Marketplace website and update his information.

He received $4,890 in Premium Tax Credit based on his estimated income. His income is $48,000 instead of $43,000. His Household Income as a Percentage of the Federal Poverty Line is 246%: $48,000 ÷ $19,530. The applicable figure is 0.0791 instead of 0.0700. The amount he can afford to pay is $3,797: $48,000 × 0.0791. His benchmark plan is $7,900, remember. The credit he is allowed is $4,103: $7,900 - $3,797. He received $4,890 in advance. That amount is $787 more than he was allowed. He is filing Head of Household so his repayment limit would be $1,500, which is more than $787. He will have to add the $787 to his 2014 tax liability.

Example 1: Beth is single with no children. She estimated her income to be $27,000 annually on the Marketplace. Her SLCSP is $5,900 (Form 1095-A, line 33B), and the advance Premium Tax Credit is $3,867 (Form 1095-A, line 33C). It turns out; her household income is actually $29,050 due to some overtime over the holidays. See Illustration 10-15.

44	Tax (see instructions). Check if any from: a ☐ Form(s) 8814 b ☐ Form 4972 c ☐ _____	44			
45	Alternative minimum tax (see instructions). Attach Form 6251	45			
46	Excess advance premium tax credit repayment. Attach Form 8962	46		137	00
47	Add lines 44, 45, and 46 . . . . ▶	47			

Example 2: Jim and Martha are married and have three children. When they purchased their insurance policy, only Jim had income and his estimated income was $49,000. They received advanced Premium Tax Credit of $10,908 (Form 1095-A, line 33C) to help them pay the premiums on their policy, which cost them $14,200 (Form 1095-A, line33A). Their SLCSP is $13,500 (Form 1095-A, line 33B). Martha became employed toward the end of the year and added an additional $15,000 to their household income. They forgot to update their information on the Marketplace. See Illustration 10-16.

44	Tax (see instructions). Check If any from: a ☐ Form(s) 8814 b ☐ Form 4972 c ☐ _____	44			
45	Alternative minimum tax (see instructions). Attach Form 6251	45			
46	Excess advance premium tax credit repayment. Attach Form 8962	46		1,500	00
47	Add lines 44, 45, and 46 . . . . ▶	47			

Illustration 10-15

Form **8962**

Department of the Treasury
Internal Revenue Service

Premium Tax Credit (PTC)

▶ Attach to Form 1010, 1040A, or 1040NR
▶ **Information about Form 8962 and its separate instructions is at www.irs.gov/form8962.**

OMB No. 1545-0074

2014

Attachment
Sequence No. **73**

Name shown on your return	Your social security number	Relief (see instructions) ☐
Beth Miller	444-55-6666	

Part 1: Annual and Monthly Contribution Amount

1	Family Size: Enter the number of exemptions from Form 1040 or Form 1040A, line 6d, or Form 1040NR, line 7d .	**1**	1
2a	Modified AGI: Enter your modified AGI (see instructions) . . . . . **2a** 29,050 **b** Enter total of your dependents' modified AGI (see instructions)	**2b**	
3	Household Income: Add the amounts on lines 2a and 2b	**3**	29,050
4	Federal Poverty Line: Enter the federal poverty amount as determined by the family size on line 1 and the federal poverty table for your state of residence during the tax year (see instructions). Check the appropriate box for the federal poverty table used. **a** ☐ Alaska **b** ☐ Hawaii **c** ☑ Other 48 states and DC	**4**	11,490
5	Household Income as a Percentage of Federal Poverty Line: Divide line 3 by line 4. Enter the result rounded to a whole percentage. (For example, for 1.542 enter the result as 154, for 1.549 enter as 155.) (See instructions for special rules.)	**5**	253 %
6	Is the result entered on line 5 less than or equal to 400%? (See instructions if the result is less than 100%.)		

☑ **Yes. Continue to line 7.**

☐ **No.** You are not eligible to receive PTC. If you received advance payment of PTC, see the instructions for how to report your Excess Advance PTC Repayment amount.

7	Applicable Figure: Using your line 5 percentage, locate your "applicable figure" on the table in the instructions . .	**7**	0.0814
8a	Annual Contribution for Health Care: Multiply line 3 by line 7 . . . . **8a** 2,365 **b** Monthly Contribution for Health Care: Divide line 8a by 12. Round to whole dollar amount	**8b**	197

Part 2: Premium Tax Credit Claim and Reconciliation of Advance Payment of Premium Tax Credit

9 Did you share a policy with another taxpayer or get married during the year and want to use the alternative calculation? (see instructions)

☐ **Yes.** Skip to Part 4, Shared Policy Allocation, or Part 5, Alternative Calculation for Year of Marriage. ☑ **No. Continue to line 10.**

10 Do all Forms 1095-A for your tax household include coverage for January through December with no changes in monthly amounts shown on lines 21–32, columns A and B?

☑ **Yes. Continue to line 11.** Compute your annual PTC. Skip lines 12–23 and continue to line 24. ☐ **No. Continue to lines 12–23.** Compute your monthly PTC and continue to line 24.

Annual Calculation	A. Premium Amount (Form(s) 1095-A, line 33A)	B. Annual Premium Amount of SLCSP (Form(s) 1095-A, line 33B)	C. Annual Contribution Amount (Line 8a)	D. Annual Maximum Premium Assistance (Subtract C from B)	E. Annual Premium Tax Credit Allowed (Smaller of A or D)	F. Annual Advance Payment of PTC (Form(s) 1095-A, line 33C)
11 Annual Totals	5,705	5,900	2,365	3,535	3,535	3,672

Monthly Calculation	A. Monthly Premium Amount (Form(s) 1095-A, lines 21–32, column A)	B. Monthly Premium Amount of SLCSP (Form(s) 1095-A, lines 21–32, column B)	C. Monthly Contribution Amount (Amount from line 8b or alternative marriage monthly contribution)	D. Monthly Maximum Premium Assistance (Subtract C from B)	E. Monthly Premium Tax Credit Allowed (Smaller of A or D)	F. Monthly Advance Payment of PTC (Form(s) 1095-A, lines 21–32, column C)
12 January						
13 February						
14 March						
15 April						
16 May						
17 June						
18 July						
19 August						
20 September						
21 October						
22 November						
23 December						

24	Total Premium Tax Credit: Enter the amount from line 11E or add lines 12E through 23E and enter the total here .	**24**	3,535
25	Advance Payment of PTC: Enter the amount from line 11F or add lines 12F through 23F and enter the total here .	**25**	3,672
26	Net Premium Tax Credit: If line 24 is greater than line 25, subtract line 25 from line 24. Enter the difference here and on Form 1040, line 69; Form 1040A, line 45; or Form 1040NR, line 65. If you elected the alternative calculation for marriage, enter zero. If line 24 equals line 25, enter zero. Stop here. If line 25 is greater than line 24, leave this line blank and continue to line 27 .	**26**	0

Part 3: Repayment of Excess Advance Payment of the Premium Tax Credit

27	Excess Advance Payment of PTC: If line 25 is greater than line 24, subtract line 24 from line 25. Enter the difference here	**27**	137
28	Repayment Limitation: Using the percentage on line 5 and your filing status, locate the repayment limitation amount in the instructions. Enter the amount here	**28**	750
29	Excess Advance Premium Tax Credit Repayment: Enter the smaller of line 27 or line 28 here and on Form 1040, line 46; Form 1040A, line 29; or Form 1040NR, line 44	**29**	137

For Paperwork Reduction Act Notice, see your tax return instructions.   Cat. No. 37784Z   Form **8962** (2014)

Illustration 10-16

Form **8962**	**Premium Tax Credit (PTC)**	OMB No. 1545-0074
Department of the Treasury Internal Revenue Service	▶ Attach to Form 1040, 1040A, or 1040NR. ▶ Information about Form 8962 and its separate instructions is at *www.irs.gov/form8962*.	**2014** Attachment Sequence No. **73**

Name shown on your return	Your social security number	Relief (see instructions) ☐
Jim and Martha Stevens	555-44-1111	

Part 1: Annual and Monthly Contribution Amount

1	Family Size: Enter the number of exemptions from Form 1040 or Form 1040A, line 6d, or Form 1040NR, line 7d .	**1**	5
2a	Modified AGI: Enter your modified AGI (see instructions) **2a**	64,000	**b** Enter total of your dependents' modified AGI (see instructions)	**2b**	
3	Household Income: Add the amounts on lines 2a and 2b	**3**	64,000
4	Federal Poverty Line: Enter the federal poverty amount as determined by the family size on line 1 and the federal poverty table for your state of residence during the tax year (see instructions). Check the appropriate box for the federal poverty table used. **a** ☐ Alaska **b** ☐ Hawaii **c** ☑ Other 48 states and DC	**4**	27,570
5	Household Income as a Percentage of Federal Poverty Line: Divide line 3 by line 4. Enter the result rounded to a whole percentage. (For example, for 1.542 enter the result as 154, for 1.549 enter as 155.) (See instructions for special rules.)	**5**	232 %
6	Is the result entered on line 5 less than or equal to 400%? (See instructions if the result is less than 100%.) ☑ **Yes. Continue to line 7.** ☐ **No.** You are not eligible to receive PTC. If you received advance payment of PTC, see the instructions for how to report your Excess Advance PTC Repayment amount.		
7	Applicable Figure: Using your line 5 percentage, locate your "applicable figure" on the table in the instructions . .	**7**	0.0742
8a	Annual Contribution for Health Care: Multiply line 3 by line 7 . . . . . **8a**	4,749	**b** Monthly Contribution for Health Care: Divide line 8a by 12. Round to whole dollar amount	**8b**	396

Part 2: Premium Tax Credit Claim and Reconciliation of Advance Payment of Premium Tax Credit

9	Did you share a policy with another taxpayer or get married during the year and want to use the alternative calculation? (see instructions) ☐ **Yes.** Skip to Part 4, Shared Policy Allocation, or Part 5, Alternative Calculation for Year of Marriage. ☑ **No. Continue to line 10.**
10	Do all Forms 1095-A for your tax household include coverage for January through December with no changes in monthly amounts shown on lines 21–32, columns A and B? ☑ **Yes. Continue to line 11.** Compute your annual PTC. Skip lines 12–23 and continue to line 24. ☐ **No. Continue to lines 12–23.** Compute your monthly PTC and continue to line 24.

Annual Calculation	**A.** Premium Amount (Form(s) 1095-A, line 33A)	**B.** Annual Premium Amount of SLCSP (Form(s) 1095-A, line 33B)	**C.** Annual Contribution Amount (Line 8a)	**D.** Annual Maximum Premium Assistance (Subtract C from B)	**E.** Annual Premium Tax Credit Allowed (Smaller of A or D)	**F.** Annual Advance Payment of PTC (Form(s) 1095-A, line 33C)
11 Annual Totals	14,200	13,500	4,749	8,751	8,751	10,908

Monthly Calculation	**A.** Monthly Premium Amount (Form(s) 1095-A, lines 21–32, column A)	**B.** Monthly Premium Amount of SLCSP (Form(s) 1095-A, lines 21–32, column B)	**C.** Monthly Contribution Amount (Amount from line 8b or alternative marriage monthly contribution)	**D.** Monthly Maximum Premium Assistance (Subtract C from B)	**E.** Monthly Premium Tax Credit Allowed (Smaller of A or D)	**F.** Monthly Advance Payment of PTC (Form(s) 1095-A, lines 21–32, column C)
12 January						
13 February						
14 March						
15 April						
16 May						
17 June						
18 July						
19 August						
20 September						
21 October						
22 November						
23 December						

24	Total Premium Tax Credit: Enter the amount from line 11E or add lines 12E through 23E and enter the total here .	**24**	8,751
25	Advance Payment of PTC: Enter the amount from line 11F or add lines 12F through 23F and enter the total here .	**25**	10,908
26	Net Premium Tax Credit: If line 24 is greater than line 25, subtract line 25 from line 24. Enter the difference here and on Form 1040, line 69; Form 1040A, line 45; or Form 1040NR, line 65. If you elected the alternative calculation for marriage, enter zero. If line 24 equals line 25, enter zero. Stop here. If line 25 is greater than line 24, leave this line blank and continue to line 27 .	**26**	0

Part 3: Repayment of Excess Advance Payment of the Premium Tax Credit

27	Excess Advance Payment of PTC: If line 25 is greater than line 24, subtract line 24 from line 25. Enter the difference here	**27**	2,157
28	Repayment Limitation: Using the percentage on line 5 and your filing status, locate the repayment limitation amount in the instructions. Enter the amount here	**28**	1,500
29	Excess Advance Premium Tax Credit Repayment: Enter the smaller of line 27 or line 28 here and on Form 1040, line 46; Form 1040A, line 29; or Form 1040NR, line 44	**29**	1,500

For Paperwork Reduction Act Notice, see your tax return instructions.   Cat. No. 37784Z   Form **8962** (2014)

Shared Policy Allocation

If the taxpayer is enrolled in a health insurance policy with a person not in their tax family, the taxpayer would have to allocate the amounts shown on the 1095A with the other person. The following situations may cause the taxpayer to do a shared policy allocation.

- Taxpayers who got divorced or legally separated during the tax year.
- A taxpayer who claims an exemption for an individual enrolled in another person's health insurance policy.
- A taxpayer enrolled in a policy with another individual who is being claimed on someone else's return.
- A taxpayer filing separately from their spouse.

If any of these situations are encountered, additional research may be required.

Chapter Review

1) If the taxpayer doesn't have Minimum Essential Coverage, what are the consequences?

2) In order for the taxpayer to be considered as having Minimum Essential Coverage for an entire month, they must have been covered for _____.

3) What form will the taxpayer file to claim an exemption to the Shared Responsibility Payment?

4) A gap in coverage of less than three months is what?

5) The Individual Shared Responsibility Payment is capped at the national average premium for what plan?

6) Is the Premium Tax Credit refundable or nonrefundable?

7) The taxpayer is required to file a return if they qualify for the _____.

8) Individuals and families qualify for the Premium Tax Credit if their income is between 100% and 400% of what?

9) What changes in circumstances should be reported to the Marketplace?

10) The taxpayer is not eligible for Premium Tax Credit if filing Married Filing Separately, unless what?

11) Employers subject to the shared responsibility provisions sponsoring self-insured group health plans will be required to file what form?

12) Health Coverage Exemptions can be claimed using what form?

13) What are the three hardship exemptions the taxpayer can obtain through the IRS?

14) Name the five different levels of coverage available through the Marketplace.

15) Using the answers to the previous question, what percentage of healthcare costs does each level pay?

Exercise

Calculate the Individual Shared Responsibility Payment for Clark and Catherine. Clark had insurance through his employer from January through March. Catherine did not have insurance any during the year. They have no children and qualify for no exemption. Their household income is $54,322.

Chapter 11 – Itemized Deductions

When filing a tax return, the taxpayer may either use the standard deduction for their filing status or use their itemized deductions. Generally, the taxpayer will use whichever will benefit them the most. Sometimes, however, the taxpayer may choose to use the standard deduction because they don't want to go to the trouble of gathering receipts together.

If the taxpayer and spouse file married filing separate tax returns and one of them itemizes, the other one must also itemize. They will not be allowed to use the standard deduction. However, if one of them qualifies for the married but unmarried for tax purposes and uses the head of household filing status, they may use either the standard deduction or itemized deductions regardless of what their spouse used.

If the taxpayer's AGI exceeds:

- $254,200 for Single,
- $305,050 for Married Filing Joint or Qualifying Widow(er),
- $279,650 for Head of Household, or
- $152,525 for Married Filing Separate,

The total itemized deductions may be reduced. Use the Itemized Deduction Worksheet (Illustration 11-2) to determine if the amount will be reduced and by how much.

To claim the itemized deductions, a Schedule A (Illustration 11-1) must be filed with the tax return. The amount of itemized deductions allowed will then be carried to Form 1040, line 40.

Medical and Dental Expenses

Medical and dental expenses paid are deductible on the Schedule A. The taxpayer may only deduct the medical and dental expenses that were paid during the tax year, regardless of when the services were provided. If the payment is made by check, the expenses are deductible when the check is mailed or hand delivered. If the payment is made by a credit card, the expenses are deductible when the credit card is charged.

Only include medical and dental expenses that were paid out-of-pocket. If they were paid by an insurance company, do not include those expenses, regardless of whether the payment was made directly to the service provider or to the taxpayer.

Only the part of the medical and dental expenses that exceed 10% of the adjusted gross income are deductible for most taxpayers If the taxpayer or spouse is 65 or older at the end of the tax year, they will be able to deduct the part of medical expenses that exceed 7.5% of their AGI. The total amount of the medical and dental expenses will be entered on the Schedule A, line 1. The 10% (or 7.5% if applicable) of the adjusted gross income calculation is made on lines 2 and 3 of Schedule A.

Illustration 11-1

SCHEDULE A **(Form 1040)**	**Itemized Deductions**	OMB No. 1545-0074
Department of the Treasury Internal Revenue Service (99)	► Information about Schedule A and its separate instructions is at *www.irs.gov/schedulea*. ► **Attach to Form 1040.**	2014 Attachment Sequence No. **07**

Name(s) shown on Form 1040   Your social security number

Medical and Dental Expenses	**Caution.** Do not include expenses reimbursed or paid by others. **1** Medical and dental expenses (see instructions) . . . . . . **1** **2** Enter amount from Form 1040, line 38 **2** **3** Multiply line 2 by 10% (.10). But if either you or your spouse was born before January 2, 1950, multiply line 2 by 7.5% (.075) instead **3** **4** Subtract line 3 from line 1. If line 3 is more than line 1, enter -0- . . .	**4**

**Taxes You
Paid**
	5 State and local **(check only one box):**
	  a ☐ Income taxes, **or** ⎫
	  b ☐ General sales taxes ⎭ **5**
	6 Real estate taxes (see instructions) **6**
	7 Personal property taxes **7**
	8 Other taxes. List type and amount ► _____
	_____ **8**
	9 Add lines 5 through 8 . . . .
		9

Interest You Paid **Note.** Your mortgage interest deduction may be limited (see instructions).	**10** Home mortgage interest and points reported to you on Form 1098 **10** **11** Home mortgage interest not reported to you on Form 1098. If paid to the person from whom you bought the home, see instructions and show that person's name, identifying no., and address ► _____ _____ **11** **12** Points not reported to you on Form 1098. See instructions for special rules . . . . **12** **13** Mortgage insurance premiums (see instructions) . . . . . **13** **14** Investment interest. Attach Form 4952 if required. (See instructions.) **14** **15** Add lines 10 through 14	**15**
Gifts to Charity If you made a gift and got a benefit for it, see instructions.	**16** Gifts by cash or check. If you made any gift of $250 or more, see instructions . . . . **16** **17** Other than by cash or check. If any gift of $250 or more, see instructions. You **must** attach Form 8283 if over $500 . . . **17** **18** Carryover from prior year . . . . **18** **19** Add lines 16 through 18	**19**
Casualty and Theft Losses	**20** Casualty or theft loss(es). Attach Form 4684. (See instructions.) . . .	**20**
Job Expenses and Certain Miscellaneous Deductions	**21** Unreimbursed employee expenses—job travel, union dues, job education, etc. Attach Form 2106 or 2106-EZ if required. (See instructions.) ► _____ **21** **22** Tax preparation fees . . . . **22** **23** Other expenses—investment, safe deposit box, etc. List type and amount ► _____ _____ **23** **24** Add lines 21 through 23 . . . . **24** **25** Enter amount from Form 1040, line 38 **25** **26** Multiply line 25 by 2% (.02) . . . . **26** **27** Subtract line 26 from line 24. If line 26 is more than line 24, enter -0-	**27**
Other Miscellaneous Deductions	**28** Other—from list in instructions. List type and amount ► _____ _____	**28**
Total Itemized Deductions	**29** Is Form 1040, line 38, over $152,525? ☐ **No.** Your deduction is not limited. Add the amounts in the far right column for lines 4 through 28. Also, enter this amount on Form 1040, line 40. ⎫ ☐ **Yes.** Your deduction may be limited. See the Itemized Deductions Worksheet in the instructions to figure the amount to enter. ⎭ **30** If you elect to itemize deductions even though they are less than your standard deduction, check here . . . . ► ☐	**29**

For Paperwork Reduction Act Notice, see Form 1040 instructions.   Cat. No. 17145C   Schedule A (Form 1040) 2014

Illustration 11-2

Itemized Deductions Worksheet—Line 29   *Keep for Your Records*

1. Enter the total of the amounts from Schedule A, lines 4, 9, 15, 19, 20, 27, and 28 . . . . **1.** _____

2. Enter the total of the amount from Schedule A, lines 4, 14, and 20, plus any gambling and casualty or theft losses
    included on line 28 . . . . **2.** _____

> ⚠ **CAUTION**   Be sure your total gambling and casualty or theft losses are clearly identified on
> the dotted lines next to line 28.

3. Is the amount on line 2 less than the amount on line 1?

    ☐ **No.** 🛑 Your deduction is not limited. Enter the amount from line 1 of this
    worksheet on Schedule A, line 29. **Do not** complete the rest of this worksheet.

    ☐ **Yes.** Subtract line 2 from line 1 . . . . **3.** _____

4. Multiply line 3 by 80% (.80) . . . . **4.** _____

5. Enter the amount from Form 1040, line 38 . . . . **5.** _____

6. Enter $305,050 if married filing jointly or qualifying widow(er); $279,650 if head of
    household; $254,200 if single; or $152,525 if married filing separately . . . . **6.** _____

7. Is the amount on line 6 less than the amount on line 5?

    ☐ **No.** 🛑 Your deduction is not limited. Enter the amount from line 1 of this
    worksheet on Schedule A, line 29. **Do not** complete the rest of this worksheet.

    ☐ **Yes.** Subtract line 6 from line 5 . . . . **7.** _____

8. Multiply line 7 by 3% (.03) . . . . **8.** _____

9. Enter the **smaller** of line 4 or line 8 . . . . **9.** _____

10. **Total itemized deductions.** Subtract line 9 from line 1. Enter the result here and on Schedule A, line 29 . . . . . . **10.** _____

Whose Medical Expenses are Deductible?

Generally, the taxpayer may include medical expenses paid for themselves, as well as expenses paid for someone who was their spouse or dependent either when the expenses were incurred or when the expenses were paid. If the taxpayer (or spouse if MFJ) can be claimed on someone else's return, they may still include any medical and dental expenses for someone they would have been able to claim if the taxpayer (or spouse if MFJ) was not able to be claimed on another's return.

If the taxpayer has a child that qualifies under the child of divorced or separated parents rule, the taxpayer can claim any medical and dental expenses they paid even if their spouse claims the dependency exemption.

What Medical Expenses are Deductible?

The IRS defines medical expenses as the costs of diagnosis, cure, mitigation, treatment, or prevention of disease, and the costs for treatments affecting any part or function of the body. They include the costs of equipment, supplies, and diagnostic devices needed for these purposes. Dental expenses are also included. The medical expenses must be primarily to alleviate or prevent a physical or mental defect or illness. Expenses that are merely beneficial to general health, such as vitamins or a vacation, are not included.

Following are some examples of deductible medical expenses. This is not an all-inclusive list. If an expense is encountered that you are not sure of, additional research may be required.

- Insurance premiums for medical and dental care (defined later).
- Prescription medicines or insulin.

- Acupuncturists, chiropractors, dentists, eye doctors, medical doctors, occupational therapists, osteopathic doctors, physical therapists, podiatrists, psychiatrists, psychoanalysts (medical care only), and psychologists.
- Medical examinations, X-ray and laboratory services, insulin treatment, and whirlpool baths the doctor ordered.
- Nursing help.
- Hospital care, clinic costs, and lab fees.
- Qualified long-term care services.
- The supplemental part of Medicare insurance (Medicare B).
- The premiums paid for Medicare part D insurance.
- A program to stop smoking and for prescription medicines to alleviate nicotine withdrawal.
- A weight-loss program as treatment for a specific disease (including obesity) diagnosed by a doctor.
- Medical treatment at a center for drug or alcohol addiction.
- Medical aids such as eyeglasses, contact lenses, hearing aids, braces, crutches, wheelchairs, and guide dogs, including the costs of maintaining them.
- Surgery to improve defective vision, such as laser eye surgery or radial keratotomy.
- Lodging expenses (but not meals) while away from home to receive medical care in a hospital or a medical care facility related to a hospital, provided there was no significant element of personal pleasure, recreation, or vacation in the travel. Do not deduct more than $50 a night for each person. The cost of someone traveling with the person receiving medical care can be included up to the limit.
- Ambulance service and other travel costs to get medical care. If the taxpayer used their own car, they can claim what they spent on gas and oil to go to and from the place they received care; or they can claim 23.5 cents per mile for 2014.

Following are some examples of medical expenses that are **not deductible**.

- The cost of diet food.
- Cosmetic surgery unless it was necessary to improve a deformity related to a congenital abnormality, an injury from an accident or trauma, or a disfiguring disease.
- Life insurance or income protection policies.
- The Medicare tax on the taxpayer's wages and tips or the Medicare tax paid as part of the self-employment tax.
- Nursing care for a healthy baby.
- Illegal operations or drugs.
- Imported drugs not approved by the U.S. Food and Drug Administration (FDA). This includes foreign-made versions of U.S. approved drugs manufactured without FDA approval.
- Nonprescription medicines (including nicotine gum and certain nicotine patches).
- Travel the taxpayer's doctor told them to take for a rest and a change.
- Funeral, burial, or cremation costs.

Health Insurance Premiums

Premiums paid for insurance policies that cover medical care are deductible as a medical expense. The coverage can include:

- Hospitalization, surgical fees, X-rays, etc.,
- Prescription drugs,
- Dental care,
- Replacement of lost or damaged contact lenses,
- Membership in an association that gives cooperative or so-called "free-choice" medical service, or group hospitalization and clinical care, or
- Qualified long-term care insurance contracts (subject to limitations as explained later).

Premiums for the following policies are not deductible:

- Life insurance policies,
- Policies providing payment for loss of earnings,
- Policies for loss of life, limb, sight, etc.,
- Policies that pay a guaranteed amount each week for a stated number of weeks if the taxpayer is hospitalized for sickness or injury,
- The part of the car insurance premiums that provide medical coverage for all person injured in or by the care because the part of the premium for the taxpayer, spouse, or dependents is not separately stated from the part of the premium for medical care for others, or
- Health or long-term care insurance if the taxpayer elected to pay these premiums with tax-free distributions from a retirement plan made directly to the insurance provider and these distributions would otherwise have been included in income.

For Insurance premiums to be deductible, the taxpayer must have paid them with "after tax" money. If the employer pays the premiums and doesn't include them in box 1 of the Form W-2, the premiums are not deductible. Also, if the taxpayer pays them with pre-tax money, they are not deductible.

Premiums paid for qualified long-term care insurance are deductible if the contract must:

- Be guaranteed renewable,
- Not provide for a cash surrender value or other money that can be paid, assigned, pledged, or borrowed,
- Provide that refunds, other than refunds on the death of the insured or complete surrender or cancellation of the contract, and dividends under the contract must be used only to reduce future premiums or increase future benefits, and
- Generally not pay or reimburse expenses incurred for services or items that would be reimbursed under Medicare, except where Medicare is a secondary payer, or the contract makes per diem or other periodic payments without regard to expenses.

The amount of qualified long-term care insurance premiums that is deductible is limited. The limits depend on the age of the contract holder and are for each person.

- Age 40 or under - $370
- Age 41 to 50 - $700
- Age 51 to 60 - $1,400
- Age 61 to 70 - $3,720
- Age 71 and over - $4,660

Capital Expenditures

If the taxpayer has special equipment installed in their home or modifies their home and the primary purpose is the medical care for them, their spouse, or their dependent, it qualifies as a deductible medical expense. If the improvement or modification does not increase the value of their home, the entire expense is deductible. If the improvement or modification does increase the value of their home, the difference between the actual expense and the value increase is deductible. Some improvements that are made to accommodate a home for a disabled person do not increase the value of the home and are entirely deductible. This includes, but is not limited to, widening doorways, constructing entrance and exit ramps, and adding handrails or grab bars.

Taxes Paid

Taxpayers are allowed deductions for some of the different taxes they paid during the year. The following taxes are **not deductible**:

- Federal income and excise taxes.
- Social security, Medicare, federal unemployment, and railroad retirement taxes.
- Custom duties.
- Federal estate and gift taxes.
- Certain state and local taxes, including tax on gasoline, car inspection fees, assessments for sidewalk or other improvements to the taxpayer's property, tax paid for someone else, and license fees.

Deductible State and Local Tax

The taxpayer may deduct either state and local income tax or state and local sales tax. They may not deduct both in the same year.

State and Local Income Tax

The following state and local income taxes are deductible:

- State and local income taxes withheld from the taxpayer's salary during the tax year.
- State and local income taxes paid during the tax year for a previous year. For example, if when the taxpayer filed their state tax return for 2013 (before April 15th, 2014) they were required to submit $50 with that return, that $50 will be deductible when paid (2014).
- State and local estimated tax payments made during the tax year.
- Mandatory contributions the taxpayer made to the California, New Jersey, or New York Nonoccupational Disability Benefit Fund, Rhode Island Temporary Disability Benefit Fund, or Washington State Supplemental Workmen's Compensation Fund.
- Mandatory contributions to the Alaska, New Jersey, or Pennsylvania state unemployment fund.

If the taxpayer receives a state or local tax refund in the current tax year and itemized deductions in the prior year, their refund may be taxable on the federal return. Complete the worksheet (Illustration 11-3) provided in the Form 1040 instructions to determine the taxable amount. Then, enter that amount on Form 1040, line 10.

State and Local General Sales Tax

Instead of deducting the state and local income tax, the taxpayer may choose to deduct the general sales tax on their return. The taxpayer may do this one of two ways. They may deduct the actual state and local general sales tax paid during the tax year, if the tax was the same as the general sales tax rate. This requires the taxpayer keep all receipts for the year. The taxpayer may choose, instead, to use the optional sales tax tables. (Illustration 11-4 shows a sample; the entire table can be found in the appendix.) To use the optional method, use the worksheet (Illustration 11-5) provided in the instructions for Schedule A. To use this method, the taxpayer will have to know the local general sales tax rate for their residence. With the optional method, the IRS allows a deduction of sales tax paid on specific items. On line 7 of the worksheet, enter any general sales tax paid on specified items, such as:

- A motor vehicle (including a car, motorcycle, motor home, recreational vehicle, sport utility vehicle, truck, van, and off-road vehicle). Also include any state and local general sales taxes paid for a leased motor vehicle. If the state sales tax rate on these items is higher than the general sales tax rate, only include the amount of tax the taxpayer would have paid at the general sales tax rate.
- An aircraft or boat, if the tax rate was the same as the general sales tax rate.
- A home (including a mobile home or prefabricated home), substantial addition to a home, or major renovation of a home, but only if the tax rate was the same as the general sales tax rate and any of the following applies.
    - The state or locality imposes a general sales tax directly on the sale of a home, or on the cost of a substantial addition or major renovation.
    - The taxpayer purchased the materials to build a home, to make a substantial addition, or to perform a major renovation and paid the sales tax directly.
    - Under the state law, the contractor is considered the taxpayer's agent in the construction of the home, substantial addition, or the performance of a major renovation. The contract must state that the contractor is authorized to act in the taxpayer's name, and must follow their direction on construction decisions.

Real Estate Taxes

This includes taxes paid on real estate that the taxpayer owns and does not use for business. The tax must be on the assessed value of the property to be deductible. Do not include any charges:

- For services to specific property or persons (for example, trash collection).
- For improvements that tend to increase the value of the property (for example, an assessment to build a sidewalk).

Personal Property Taxes

Deductible personal property taxes are the taxes that are based on the value of personal property and assessed on a yearly basis. For example, some states and localities base car registration on weight of vehicle. This is not deductible. Some base registration on the value of the vehicle. This is deductible.

Other taxes

We have discussed the credit for paying foreign tax. The tax paid can also be used as an itemized deduction. If the taxpayer chooses to use it as an itemized deduction, enter the amount on line 8 of the Schedule A.

Illustration 11-3

State and Local Income Tax Refund Worksheet—Line 10

Keep for Your Records

Before you begin: ✓ Be sure you have read the **Exception** in the instructions for this line to see if you can use this worksheet instead of Pub. 525 to figure if any of your refund is taxable.

1.	Enter the income tax refund from **Form(s) 1099-G** (or similar statement). But **do not** enter more than the amount of your state and local income taxes shown on your 2013 Schedule A, line 5	1.
2.	Enter your total itemized deductions from your 2013 Schedule A, line 29	2.

Note. If the filing status on your 2013 Form 1040 was married filing separately and your spouse itemized deductions in 2013, skip lines 3 through 5, enter the amount from line 2 on line 6, and go to line 7.

3.	Enter the amount shown below for the filing status claimed on your **2013** Form 1040.	
	• Single or married filing separately—$6,100 • Married filing jointly or qualifying widow(er)—$12,200 • Head of household—$8,950	3.
4.	Did you fill in line 39a on your 2013 Form 1040?	
	☐ **No.** Enter -0-.	
	☐ **Yes.** Multiply the number in the box on line 39a of your 2013 Form 1040 by $1,200 ($1,500 if your 2013 filing status was single or head of household).	4.
5.	Add lines 3 and 4	5.
6.	Is the amount on line 5 less than the amount on line 2?	
	☐ **No.** 🛑 None of your refund is taxable.	
	☐ **Yes.** Subtract line 5 from line 2	6.
7.	**Taxable part of your refund.** Enter the **smaller** of line 1 or line 6 here and on Form 1040, line 10	7.

Illustration 11-4

2014 Optional State Sales Tax Tables *(State Sales Tax Rate Shown Next to State Name)*

Income		Exemptions						Exemptions						Exemptions						
At least	But less than	1	2	3	4	5	Over 5	1	2	3	4	5	Over 5	1	2	3	4	5	Over 5	
		Alabama				1	4.0000%	Arizona			2	5.6000%		Arkansas			2	6.5000%		Cal
$0	$20,000	223	263	290	310	328	352	214	237	251	262	271	283	283	315	335	350	363	380	
$20,000	$30,000	329	387	426	456	481	517	364	403	428	446	462	482	460	513	546	572	592	620	
$30,000	$40,000	384	451	496	531	560	601	448	496	527	550	569	595	558	621	662	693	718	753	
$40,000	$50,000	431	505	556	595	628	673	524	580	616	644	666	696	644	718	765	801	830	869	
$50,000	$60,000	473	554	609	652	687	737	594	658	899	730	755	789	722	805	859	899	931	976	
$60,000	$70,000	510	598	657	703	741	795	658	729	775	809	837	875	794	886	945	989	1025	1074	
$70,000	$80,000	545	638	701	750	790	847	719	797	847	884	915	956	862	961	1025	1073	1112	1165	
$80,000	$90,000	577	675	742	793	836	896	777	861	915	955	988	1033	925	1032	1100	1152	1194	1251	
$90,000	$100,000	607	710	780	834	879	942	832	922	979	1023	1058	1106	985	1099	1172	1227	1272	1333	
$100,000	$120,000	647	757	831	888	936	1003	906	1004	1067	1115	1153	1206	1066	1189	1269	1328	1377	1443	1
$120,000	$140,000	699	817	896	958	1010	1082	1005	1114	1184	1237	1279	1338	1173	1309	1396	1462	1515	1588	1
$140,000	$160,000	747	873	957	1023	1078	1155	1099	1218	1295	1353	1399	1464	1274	1421	1516	1588	1646	1726	1
$160,000	$180,000	792	924	1013	1083	1141	1222	1187	1316	1399	1462	1512	1582	1368	1526	1628	1705	1768	1853	1
$180,000	$200,000	833	972	1066	1139	1200	1285	1272	1411	1499	1566	1621	1695	1457	1627	1736	1818	1884	1976	1
$200,000	$225,000	877	1023	1121	1198	1261	1351	1362	1510	1605	1677	1735	1815	1552	1732	1848	1936	2007	2104	1

Illustration 11-5

State and Local General Sales Tax Deduction Worksheet—Line 5b

Keep for Your Records

TIP *Instead of using this worksheet, you can find your deduction by using the Sales Tax Deduction Calculator at IRS.gov.*

Before you begin: See the instructions for line 1 of the worksheet if you:

      √ Lived in more than one state during 2014, or
      √ Had any **nontaxable** income in 2014.

1. Enter your **state** general sales taxes from the 2014 Optional State Sales Tax Table .... **1.** $ _____

   Next. If, for all of 2014, you lived only in Connecticut, the District of Columbia, Indiana, Kentucky, Maine, Maryland, Massachusetts, Michigan, New Jersey, or Rhode Island, skip lines 2 through 5, enter -0- on line 6, and go to line 7. Otherwise, go to line 2.

2. Did you live in Alaska, Arizona, Arkansas, Colorado, Georgia, Illinois, Louisiana, Missouri, New York, North Carolina, South Carolina, Tennessee, Utah, Virginia, or West Virginia in 2014?

   ☐ **No.** Enter -0-

   ☐ **Yes.** Enter your base **local** general sales taxes from the 2014 Optional Local Sales Tax Tables for Certain Local Jurisdictions

                                                             2. $ _____

3. Did your locality impose a **local** general sales tax in 2014? Residents of California and Nevada, see the instructions for line 3 of the worksheet.

   ☐ **No.** Skip lines 3 through 5, enter -0- on line 6, and go to line 7.

   ☐ **Yes.** Enter your **local** general sales tax rate, but omit the percentage sign. For example, if your local general sales tax rate was 2.5%, enter 2.5. If your local general sales tax rate changed or you lived in more than one locality in the same state during 2014, see the instructions for line 3 of the worksheet .... **3.** . _____

4. Did you enter -0- on line 2?

   ☐ **No.** Skip lines 4 and 5 and go to line 6.

   ☐ **Yes.** Enter your **state** general sales tax rate (shown in the table heading for your state), but omit the percentage sign. For example, if your state general sales tax rate is 6%, enter 6.0 .... **4.** . _____

5. Divide line 3 by line 4. Enter the result as a decimal (rounded to at least three places) .... **5.** . _____

6. Did you enter -0- on line 2?

   ☐ **No.** Multiply line 2 by line 3

   ☐ **Yes.** Multiply line 1 by line 5. If you lived in more than one locality in the same state during 2014, see the instructions for line 6 of the worksheet

                                                   6. $ _____

7. Enter your state and local general sales taxes paid on specified items, if any. See the instructions for line 7 of the worksheet .... **7.** $ _____

8. **Deduction for general sales taxes.** Add lines 1, 6, and 7. Enter the result here and the total from all your state and local general sales tax deduction worksheets, if you completed more than one, on Schedule A, line 5. Be sure to check **box b** on that line .... **8.** $ _____

Interest Paid

Interest Is what is paid for the use of borrowed money. The IRS allows a deduction for home mortgage interest and investment interest.

Home Mortgage Interest

Home mortgage interest is the interest on a loan secured by a home. In order for the interest to be deductible it must meet the following requirements:

- The taxpayer must be legally liable for the loan. The taxpayer may not deduct interest paid on someone else's mortgage if the taxpayer is not legally required to make the payments.
- The taxpayer and the lender must intend the loan to be repaid. There must be a debtor-creditor relationship.
- The mortgage must be a secured debt on a qualified home in which the taxpayer has an ownership interest.

Deductible mortgage interest can be on a main home or a second home. A home must provide basic living accommodations including sleeping space, toilet, and cooking facilities. A home can be a mobile home, boat, condominium, or other similar properties.

Some mortgage interest deductions may be limited. If the mortgage falls into one of the following three categories, the interest will be fully deductible:

- Mortgages taken out on or before October 13, 1987.
- Mortgages taken out after October 13, 1987 that were used to buy, build, or improve the home, but only if throughout the tax year, these mortgages plus any mortgage from the first category totaled $1 million or less ($500,000 if MFS).
- Mortgages taken out after October 13, 1987 that were for a purpose other than to buy, build, or improve the home, but only if throughout the tax year, these mortgages totaled $100,000 or less ($50,000 if MFS) and totaled no more than the fair market value of the home reduced by amounts that fall into the prior two categories.

Generally, mortgage interest is reported on a Form 1098 (Illustration 11-6).

If the taxpayer paid mortgage interest to an individual, they must include the amount of mortgage interest on Schedule A, line 11. The name, social security number, and the address of the recipient must be included on this line as well.

Points

Points are defined as certain charges paid, or treated as paid, by a borrower to obtain a home mortgage. Points are also called loan origination fees, maximum loan charges, loan discount, or discount points. Points may be deducted two different ways depending on the requirements met. They may be deductible in the year paid or ratably over the life of the loan. To be deducted in the year paid they must meet the following tests. If they meet these tests, however, the taxpayer may choose to deduct them in the year paid or over the life of the loan.

- The loan is secured by the main home.

- Paying points is an established business practice in the area where the loan is made.
- The points paid were not more than the points generally charged in that area.
- The taxpayer uses the cash method of accounting.
- The points were not paid in place of amounts that ordinarily are stated separately on the settlement statement, such as appraisal fees, inspection fees, title fees, attorney fees, and property taxes.
- The funds provided at or before closing by the taxpayer, plus any points the seller paid, were at least as much as the points charged. The funds the taxpayer provided do not have to have been applied to points.
- The loan is to buy or build the main home.
- The points were computed as a percentage of the principal amount of the mortgage.
- The amount is clearly shown on the settlement statement as points charged for the mortgage.

If the points <u>do not</u> meet the above requirements, the taxpayer may still be able to deduct the points ratably over the life of the loan. If the points <u>do</u> meet the above requirements, the taxpayer may choose to deduct their points ratably over the life of the loan. To deduct the points over the life of the loan, they must meet the following requirements:

- The taxpayer uses the cash method of accounting.
- The loan is secured by the main or second home.
- The loan period is not more than 30 years.
- If the loan period is more than 10 years, the terms of the loan is the same as other loans offered in the area for the same or longer period.
- Either the loan amount is $250,000 or less, or the number of points is not more than:
  - o 4 if the loan period is 15 years or less, or
  - o 6 if the loan period is more than 15 years.

Qualified Mortgage Insurance Premiums

If the taxpayer paid mortgage insurance premiums under a mortgage insurance contract issued after December 31, 2006, in connection with home acquisition debt that was secured by the first or second home, they may be deductible. These premiums will be found in box 4 of the Form 1098 (Illustration 11-6).

If the taxpayer's AGI is more than $100,000 ($50,000 if MFS), the deduction may be reduced or not allowed. The worksheet in the Schedule A instructions must be used to determine how much of a deduction will be allowed.

Investment Interest

Investment interest is interest paid on money borrowed that is allocable to property held for investment. Unless the investment interest meets the following three requirements, a Form 4952 (Illustration 11-7) must be attached.

- The investment interest expense is not more than the investment income from interest and ordinary dividends minus any qualified dividends.
- The taxpayer has no other deductible investment expenses.

- The taxpayer has no disallowed investment interest expense from 2012.

Charitable Contributions

A charitable contribution is defined as a donation or gift to, or for the use of, a qualified organization. It is voluntary and is made without getting, or expecting to get, anything of equal value. Qualified organizations are organizations that are religious, charitable, educational, scientific, or literary in purpose. To determine the qualification of the organization, the taxpayer can check with them. The organization should be able to provide verification of the charitable status. Also, the IRS Publication 78 provides a list of most qualified organizations.

Qualified organizations include:

- Churches, mosques, synagogues, temples, etc.,
- Boy Scouts, Boys and Girls Clubs, CARE, Girl Scouts, Goodwill Industries, Red Cross, Salvation Army, United Way, etc.,
- Veterans' and certain cultural groups.
- Nonprofit schools, hospitals, and organizations whose purpose is to find a cure for, or help people who have, arthritis, asthma, birth defects, cancer, cerebral palsy, cystic fibrosis, diabetes, heart disease, hemophilia, mental illness or retardation, multiple sclerosis, muscular dystrophy, tuberculosis, etc.,
- Federal, state, and local governments if the gifts are solely for public purposes.

The taxpayer may not deduct contributions to specific individuals. For example, someone in the community needs medical care and a fund has been set up in their name. Any contributions to that particular fund are not deductible. Instead, consider making the contribution to the medical facility at which the care will be provided.

Gifts by Cash or Check

Gifts made by cash or check to qualified organizations are deductible. The taxpayer must have records of any contributions. The records can be receipts from the organization, a canceled check, a credit card statement, or a bank record. If the taxpayer does not have a record of the contribution, they may not deduct it.

If the contribution to a qualified organization is $250 or more, a written acknowledgement must be provided from the organization. The acknowledgement must be received on or before the earlier of the date the return is filed or the due date of the return, including extensions, and it must include:

- The amount of cash contributed,
- Whether the qualified organization gave you any goods or services as a result of the contribution.
- A description and good faith estimate of the value of any goods or services described in the previous requirement, and
- A statement that the only benefit the taxpayer received was an intangible religious benefit. An intangible religious benefit is generally not sold in

commercial transactions outside a donative context. For example, an admission to a religious ceremony.

If the taxpayer receives any economic or financial benefit from the contribution, any part of the contribution attributable to the benefit is not deductible. For example, the cost of bingo or lottery tickets is not deductible (however, these may be deductible as a gambling loss, covered later).

Any out-of-pocket expenses the taxpayer incurs while giving services to a qualified organization are deductible as a cash contribution. These include uniforms that are required, the cost of transportation, and travel expenses. To be deductible, the expense must be:

- Unreimbursed,
- Directly connected with the services,
- Expenses the taxpayer had only because of the services given, and
- Not personal, living, or family expenses.

If the taxpayer used their own vehicle for transportation, they may deduct the cost of gas and oil directly related to the giving of services to the charitable organization. If they do not want to use the actual expenses, they may deduct 14 cents per mile.

Note: The value of time or services is not deductible.

Illustration 11-6

		☐ CORRECTED (if checked)		
RECIPIENT'S/LENDER'S name, street address, city or town, state or province, country, ZIP or foreign postal code, and telephone number		* **Caution:** *The amount shown may not be fully deductible by you. Limits based on the loan amount and the cost and value of the secured property may apply. Also, you may only deduct interest to the extent it was incurred by you, actually paid by you, and not reimbursed by another person.*	OMB No. 1545-0901 2014 Form **1098**	**Mortgage Interest Statement**
RECIPIENT'S federal identification no.	PAYER'S social security number	1 Mortgage interest received from payer(s)/borrower(s)* $		**Copy B** **For Payer/Borrower**
PAYER'S/BORROWER'S name		2 Points paid on purchase of principal residence $		The information in boxes 1, 2, 3, and 4 is important tax information and is being furnished to the Internal Revenue Service. If you are required to file a return, a negligence penalty or other sanction may be imposed on you if the IRS determines that an underpayment of tax results because you overstated a deduction for this mortgage interest or for these points or because you did not report this refund of interest on your return.
Street address (including apt. no.)		3 Refund of overpaid interest $		
City or town, state or province, country, and ZIP or foreign postal code		4		
Account number (see instructions)		5		

Form **1098**   (keep for your records)   www.irs.gov/form1098   Department of the Treasury - Internal Revenue Service

Illustration 11-7

Form **4952**

Department of the Treasury
Internal Revenue Service   (99)

Investment Interest Expense Deduction

▶ Information about Form 4952 and its instructions is at *www.irs.gov/form4952.*
▶ **Attach to your tax return.**

OMB No. 1545-0191

2014

Attachment
Sequence No. **51**

Name(s) shown on return	Identifying number

Part I	**Total Investment Interest Expense**			
1	Investment interest expense paid or accrued in 2014 (see instructions)	**1**		
2	Disallowed investment interest expense from 2013 Form 4952, line 7	**2**		
3	**Total investment interest expense.** Add lines 1 and 2	**3**		

Part II	**Net Investment Income**					
4a	Gross income from property held for investment (excluding any net gain from the disposition of property held for investment)	**4a**				
b	Qualified dividends included on line 4a	**4b**				
c	Subtract line 4b from line 4a			**4c**		
d	Net gain from the disposition of property held for investment	**4d**				
e	Enter the **smaller** of line 4d or your net capital gain from the disposition of property held for investment (see instructions)	**4e**				
f	Subtract line 4e from line 4d			**4f**		
g	Enter the amount from lines 4b and 4e that you elect to include in investment income (see instructions)			**4g**		
h	Investment income. Add lines 4c, 4f, and 4g			**4h**		
5	Investment expenses (see instructions)			**5**		
6	**Net investment income.** Subtract line 5 from line 4h. If zero or less, enter -0-			**6**		

Part III	**Investment Interest Expense Deduction**			
7	Disallowed investment interest expense to be carried forward to 2015. Subtract line 6 from line 3. If zero or less, enter -0-	**7**		
8	**Investment interest expense deduction.** Enter the **smaller** of line 3 or 6. See instructions	**8**		

For Paperwork Reduction Act Notice, see page 4.   Cat. No. 13177Y   Form **4952** (2014)

Other than Cash or Check Contributions

The contribution of property to a qualified charitable organization is deductible. If the property is used, such as clothing or furniture, the deduction will be the fair market value of the property. The fair market value would be what a willing buyer would be willing to pay for the property. To take the deduction for clothing or household items, the property must have been in good condition or better.

If the taxpayer is deducting more than $500 of other than cash or check contributions, a Form 8283 (Illustration 11-8) must be filed with the tax return. The Form 8283 must contain the following items:

- The organization's name and address,
- The property's value at the time of the gift,
- How the property's value was calculated,
- The cost or other basis of the property, and
- Any conditions attached to the gift.

Charitable contribution limitations

For some taxpayer's their charitable contribution may be limited. If the total contributions for the year are 20% or less of the adjusted gross income, the contribution is not limited. The total of all charitable contributions is limited to 50% of the adjusted gross income. Certain donations fall under a 30% or 20% limitation. If there is question as to whether a limit applies or not, additional research will be required.

If there were any limitations in a prior year, the excess may be used within 5 years or until it is used up. Any excess that is not used within 5 years will expire.

Casualty and Theft Losses

A casualty is the damage, destruction, or loss of property resulting from an identifiable event that is sudden, unexpected, or unusual. A sudden event is one that is swift, not gradual or progressive. An unexpected event is one that is ordinarily unanticipated and unintended. An unusual event is one that is not a day-to-day occurrence and that is not typical of the activity in which the taxpayer was engaged. Deductible casualty losses include car accidents, fires, floods, storms, and vandalism. Losses that are not deductible include accidental breaking of articles under normal conditions or losses caused by progressive deterioration. Progressive deterioration is a steadily operating cause or a normal process, rather than from a sudden event. Progressive deterioration includes termite or moth damage, the damage or destruction of trees by disease, insects, or worms, or the steady weakening of a building due to normal wind and weather conditions.

A theft is the taking and removing of money or property with the intent to deprive the owner of it. The taking of property must have been done with criminal intent. Theft includes blackmail, embezzlement, extortion, and robbery.

The casualty and theft loss is only deductible to the extent that the amount of each separate casualty or theft is more than $100, and the total amount of all losses are more than 10% of the AGI.

Form 4684 (Illustration 11-9) must be filed to claim a casualty and theft loss. Use a separate Form 4684 for each casualty or theft.

Line 1 – Enter the type, location, and date acquired for each property.

Line 2 – Enter the cost or other basis of the property. The other basis usually means the cost plus improvements.

Line 3 – Enter the amount of insurance received or expect to receive for the property. If the taxpayer is able to collect insurance, but chooses not to file the claim with the insurance company, any part of the loss that would have been covered is not deductible. In that case enter the amount that could have been recovered on this line.

Line 5 – Enter the fair market value of the property before the event.

Line 6 – Enter the fair market value of the property after the event. If the event is theft and the property is not recovered, enter 0 on this line.

Line 11 – Enter the smaller of the casualty or theft loss or $100. The $100 deduction applies to each event.

Line 17 – Enter 10% of the adjusted gross income. This amount will be subtracted from the total casualty and theft losses from all events. The amount over 10% of the AGI is the deductible casualty and theft loss and will be entered on Schedule A, line 20.

Note: If the casualty and theft loss is in a Presidential declared disaster area, the taxpayer can elect to deduct the loss in the tax year immediately prior to the tax year in which the disaster occurred, or in the year of the disaster.

Illustration 11-8

Form **8283**	**Noncash Charitable Contributions**	OMB No. 1545-0908
(Rev. December 2014) Department of the Treasury Internal Revenue Service	▶ Attach to your tax return if you claimed a total deduction of over $500 for all contributed property. ▶ Information about Form 8283 and its separate instructions is at *www.irs.gov/form8283*.	Attachment Sequence No. **155**

Name(s) shown on your income tax return	Identifying number

Note. Figure the amount of your contribution deduction before completing this form. See your tax return instructions.

Section A. Donated Property of $5,000 or Less and Publicly Traded Securities—List in this section **only** items (or groups of similar items) for which you claimed a deduction of $5,000 or less. Also list publicly traded securities even if the deduction is more than $5,000 (see instructions).

Part I   **Information on Donated Property**—If you need more space, attach a statement.

1	(a) Name and address of the donee organization	(b) If donated property is a vehicle (see instructions), check the box. Also enter the vehicle identification number (unless Form 1098-C is attached).	(c) Description of donated property (For a vehicle, enter the year, make, model, and mileage. For securities, enter the company name and the number of shares.)
A			
B			
C			
D			
E			

Note. If the amount you claimed as a deduction for an item is $500 or less, you do not have to complete columns (e), (f), and (g).

	(d) Date of the contribution	(e) Date acquired by donor (mo., yr.)	(f) How acquired by donor	(g) Donor's cost or adjusted basis	(h) Fair market value (see instructions)	(i) Method used to determine the fair market value
A						
B						
C						
D						
E						

Part II   **Partial Interests and Restricted Use Property**—Complete lines 2a through 2e if you gave less than an entire interest in a property listed in Part I. Complete lines 3a through 3c if conditions were placed on a contribution listed in Part I; also attach the required statement (see instructions).

2a   Enter the letter from Part I that identifies the property for which you gave less than an entire interest ▶ _____
If Part II applies to more than one property, attach a separate statement.

b   Total amount claimed as a deduction for the property listed in Part I: (1)   For this tax year   ▶ _____
  (2)   For any prior tax years   ▶ _____

c   Name and address of each organization to which any such contribution was made in a prior year (complete only if different from the donee organization above):

Name of charitable organization (donee)

_____

Address (number, street, and room or suite no.)

_____

City or town, state, and ZIP code

_____

d   For tangible property, enter the place where the property is located or kept ▶ _____

e   Name of any person, other than the donee organization, having actual possession of the property ▶ _____

		Yes	No
3a	Is there a restriction, either temporary or permanent, on the donee's right to use or dispose of the donated property?		
b	Did you give to anyone (other than the donee organization or another organization participating with the donee organization in cooperative fundraising) the right to the income from the donated property or to the possession of the property, including the right to vote donated securities, to acquire the property by purchase or otherwise, or to designate the person having such income, possession, or right to acquire?		
c	Is there a restriction limiting the donated property for a particular use?		

For Paperwork Reduction Act Notice, see separate instructions.   Cat. No. 62299J   Form **8283** (Rev. 12-2014)

Illustration 11-9

Form **4684**

Department of the Treasury
Internal Revenue Service

Casualties and Thefts

▶ Information about Form 4684 and its separate instructions is at *www.irs.gov/form4684.*
▶ **Attach to your tax return.**
▶ **Use a separate Form 4684 for each casualty or theft.**

OMB No. 1545-0177

2014

Attachment
Sequence No. **26**

Name(s) shown on tax return	Identifying number

SECTION A—Personal Use Property (Use this section to report casualties and thefts of property **not** used in a trade or business or for income-producing purposes.)

1 Description of properties (show type, location, and date acquired for each property). Use a separate line for each property lost or damaged from the same casualty or theft.

Property **A** _____

Property **B** _____

Property **C** _____

Property **D** _____

			Properties			
			A	B	C	D
2 Cost or other basis of each property	**2**					
3 Insurance or other reimbursement (whether or not you filed a claim) (see instructions)	**3**					
Note: *If line 2 is more than line 3, skip line 4.*						
4 Gain from casualty or theft. If line 3 is **more** than line 2, enter the difference here and skip lines 5 through 9 for that column. See instructions if line 3 includes insurance or other reimbursement you did not claim, or you received payment for your loss in a later tax year	**4**					
5 Fair market value **before** casualty or theft	**5**					
6 Fair market value **after** casualty or theft	**6**					
7 Subtract line 6 from line 5	**7**					
8 Enter the **smaller** of line 2 or line 7	**8**					
9 Subtract line 3 from line 8. If zero or less, enter -0-	**9**					

10 Casualty or theft loss. Add the amounts on line 9 in columns A through D	**10**	
11 Enter the **smaller** of line 10 or $100	**11**	
12 Subtract line 11 from line 10	**12**	
Caution: *Use only one Form 4684 for lines 13 through 18.*		
13 Add the amounts on line 12 of all Forms 4684	**13**	
14 Add the amounts on line 4 of all Forms 4684	**14**	
15 • If line 14 is **more** than line 13, enter the difference here and on Schedule D. **Do not** complete the rest of this section (see instructions). • If line 14 is **less** than line 13, enter -0- here and go to line 16. • If line 14 is **equal** to line 13, enter -0- here. **Do not** complete the rest of this section.	**15**	
16 If line 14 is **less** than line 13, enter the difference	**16**	
17 Enter 10% of your adjusted gross income from Form 1040, line 38, or Form 1040NR, line 37. Estates and trusts, see instructions	**17**	
18 Subtract line 17 from line 16. If zero or less, enter -0-. Also enter the result on Schedule A (Form 1040), line 20, or Form 1040NR, Schedule A, line 6. Estates and trusts, enter the result on the "Other deductions" line of your tax return	**18**	

For Paperwork Reduction Act Notice, see instructions.

Cat. No. 12997O

Form **4684** (2014)

Job Expenses and Certain Miscellaneous Deductions

Any expenses listed in this category are only deductible to the extent that they exceed 2% of the AGI. Unreimbursed employee expenses are total ordinary and necessary job expenses paid which the taxpayer was not reimbursed. These expenses will be covered in depth in the next half of the course.

The tax preparation fees paid during the tax year are deductible on line 22 of the Schedule A. This does include fees for electronic filing, but not fees related to refund anticipation loans or other similar products. Expenses that are deductible on line 23 are expenses related to the production or collection of taxable income such as:

- Certain legal and accounting fees,
- Investment fees,
- Safe deposit box fees, and
- Clerical help and office rent.

Other Miscellaneous Deductions

These miscellaneous deductions are deductible in full and are not subject to the 2% floor. Only the following expenses are deductible on this line:

- Gambling losses to the extent of winnings reported on Form 1040, line 21.
- Casualty and theft losses of income producing property.
- Loss from other activities from Schedule K-1.
- Federal estate tax on income in respect of a decedent.
- Amortizable bond premium on bonds acquired before October 23, 1986.
- Deduction for repayment of amounts under a claim of right if over $3,000. See Pub. 525 for more information.
- Certain unrecovered investment in a pension.
- Impairment-related work expenses of a disabled person.

Chapter Review

1) What floor are the medical expenses subject to?

2) What is the standard rate for medical mileage?

3) Joanne renews her car tag in November. She paid $78 in taxes and a tag fee of $29. What is her personal property tax deduction?

4) For how many houses may the taxpayer deduct mortgage interest?

5) Are loan origination fees deductible?

6) What is the standard mileage rate for volunteer mileage?

7) When is a Form 8283 needed?

8) Are gambling losses deductible?

9) What are the differences for claiming a casualty and theft loss in a federally declared disaster area?

Exercise

Prepare a Schedule A for Lloyd and Lynn Landon. Lloyd is 35 and Lynn is 32. Is it more beneficial for them to itemize or use the standard deduction?

Lloyd's SSN is 555-44-6666. Their AGI is $309,000.

Their expenses are as follows:

Doctor bills	$ 455
Medical Mileage	231
Dentist	$ 123
Prescriptions	$ 878
Glasses for Lloyd	$ 109
Vitamins	$ 78
Church tithes	$1,987
Credit card interest	$ 677
Salvation Army	$ 54
Real estate taxes	$ 544
State income taxes	$4,566
Mortgage interest	$9,987

They gave $599 to a fund for a local child to have a liver transplant. Lynn volunteers and believes her work is worth $25 per day. She volunteered 112 days this year. Her volunteer mileage was 344. She also had to buy uniforms to use for her volunteer work for $240.

Chapter 12 – Employee Business Expenses

At times, a taxpayer must pay their own expenses to correctly perform their job. If these expenses are not reimbursed by the employer, they are deductible for the taxpayer. Deductible employee business expenses must be ordinary and necessary. An ordinary expense is one that is common and accepted in the taxpayer's field of trade, business, or profession. A necessary expense is one that is helpful and appropriate for the taxpayer's business. An expense does not have to be required to be considered necessary.

In this chapter, we will discuss the different types of employee business expenses. We will also cover where they are reported on the tax return and what happens if the taxpayer is reimbursed by their employer.

Some employee business expenses may be claimed directly on Schedule A, line 21:

- Safety equipment, small tools, and supplies needed for the job.
- Uniforms required by the employer that are not suitable for ordinary wear.
- Protective clothing required in the work, such as hard hats, safety shoes, and glasses.
- Physical examinations required by the employer.
- Dues to professional organizations and chambers of commerce.
- Subscriptions to professional journals.
- Fees to employment agencies and other costs to look for a new job in the present occupation, even if the new job is not acquired.
- Certain educational expenses.

If the taxpayer is claiming any travel, transportation, meal, or entertainment expenses; or receives a reimbursement, a Form 2106 must be filed.

Travel Expenses

If the taxpayer has to temporarily travel away from their tax home to meet job requirements, those expenses may be deductible. The taxpayer is traveling away from home if:

- The taxpayer's duties require the taxpayer to be away from the general area of the tax home substantially longer than an ordinary day's work.
- The taxpayer needs to sleep or rest to meet the demands of work while away from home.

To meet the travel requirements, the taxpayer must be away from their "tax home". The taxpayer's tax home is the regular place of business or post of duty, regardless of where the home is maintained. If the taxpayer has more than one regular place of business, the tax home is determined by time, the level of business activity, and the income. If the taxpayer has no regular or main place of business because of the nature of work, the tax home is wherever the taxpayer regularly lives.

Some travel expenses are easy to ascertain; for example, business meetings, seminars, and research. However, sometimes it's not so easy to determine. If the taxpayer has a temporary assignment, the tax home remains at the location of the regular place of business. A temporary assignment is one that is realistically expected to last (and does last) for one year or less. If the assignment is indefinite, the location of the job or assignment becomes the new tax home and the travel expenses are not deductible. An assignment or job becomes indefinite if it is expected to last for more than one year (whether or not it actually lasts that long).

Sometimes, the taxpayer will travel to an assignment or job that is expected to last one year or less, but ends up taking longer than one year. The travel expenses for the time the job is expected to be temporary are deductible. Once the taxpayer realizes the job is going to last for longer than one year, the expenses stop being deductible.

Deductible Expenses

While traveling away from home on business, any ordinary and necessary expenses incurred will be deductible. The types of expenses that are deductible are shown in Illustration 12-1.

If the taxpayer's spouse or dependent travels along with the taxpayer on a business trip, the taxpayer cannot deduct the expenses of the spouse or dependent. If the taxpayer's employee or business associate travels with the taxpayer, those expenses are deductible if the employee or business associate:

- Has a bona fide business purpose for the travel and
- Would otherwise be allowed to deduct the travel expenses.

Bona fide business purpose – A bona fide business purpose exists if the taxpayer can prove a real business purpose for the individual's presence.

Meals

The cost of meals is deductible if:

- It is necessary for the taxpayer to stop for substantial sleep or rest to properly perform the duties while traveling away from home on business.
- The meal is business-related entertainment.

The meals cannot be lavish or extravagant to be deductible. The expense is not lavish or extravagant if it is reasonably based on the facts and circumstances.

Actual Cost

The taxpayer may use the actual cost of meals to calculate the deduction. The taxpayer must keep records of the actual cost to deduct this amount.

Illustration 12-1

Travel Expenses

If you have expenses for:	THEN you can deduct the cost of:
Transportation	Travel by airplane, train, bus, or car between your home and your business destination. If you were provided with a ticket or you are riding free as a result of frequent traveler or similar program, your cost is zero.
Taxi, commuter bus, and airport limousine	Fares for these and other types of transportation that take you between: <ul><li>The airport or station and your hotel, and</li><li>The hotel and the work location of your customers or clients, your business meeting place or your temporary work location.</li></ul>
Baggage and shipping	Sending baggage and sample or display material between your regular and temporary work locations.
Car	Operating and maintaining your car when traveling away from home on business. You can deduct actual expenses or the standard mileage rate, as well as business-related tolls and parking. If you rent a car while away from home on business, you can deduct only the business-use portion of the expense.
Lodging and meals	Your lodging and meals if your business trip is overnight or long enough that you need to stop for sleep or rest to properly perform your duties. Meals include the amounts you spend for food, beverages, taxes, and related tips. See *Meals* for additional rules and limits.
Cleaning	Dry cleaning and laundry.
Telephone	Business calls while on your business trip. This includes business communication by fax machine or other communication devices.
Tips	Tips you pay for any expenses in this chart.
Other	Other similar ordinary and necessary expenses related to your business travel. These expenses might include transportation to or from a business meal, public stenographer's fees, computer rental fees, and operating and maintaining a house trailer.

Standard Meal Allowance

Rather than use the actual cost method, the taxpayer may use the standard meal allowance. It allows the taxpayer to use a set amount for the daily meals and incidental expenses (M&IE). The incidental expenses are:

- Fees and tips given to porters, baggage carriers, bellhops, hotel maids, stewards, or stewardesses and others on ships, and hotel servants in foreign countries,
- Transportation between places of lodging or business and places where meals are taken, if suitable meals can be obtained at the temporary duty site, and
- Mailing costs associated with filing travel vouchers and payment of employer-sponsored charge card billings.

If the taxpayer did not incur any meal expenses, but did incur some of these incidental expenses, the standard amount for the incidental expense is $5 a day.

The standard meal allowance can either be an amount determined by where the taxpayer is traveling or the federal rate. The rates determined by the location can be found in IRS Pub. 1542. In this text, we will be using the federal M&IE rate which is $46 per day for travel within the United States for 2014.

Special rate for transportation workers
A transportation worker is someone who's work:

- Directly involves moving people or goods by airplane, barge, bus, ship, train, or truck, and
- Regularly requires the taxpayer to travel away from home and, during any single trip, usually involves travel to areas eligible for different standard meal allowance rates.

The special rate for a transportation worker is $59 per day for travel within the United States for 2014.

Limit

The deduction for meals is limited to 50% of the cost or standard meal allowance. If the taxpayer is subject to the Department of Transportation's "hours of service" limits, the deduction is limited to 80%. The individuals subject to the Department of Transportation's "hours of service" limit include:

- Certain air transportation workers (such as pilots, crew, dispatchers, mechanics, and control tower operators) who are under Federal Aviation Administration regulations.
- Interstate truck operators and bus drivers who are under Department of Transportation regulations.
- Certain railroad employees (such as engineers, conductors, train crews, dispatchers, and control operations personnel) who are under Federal Railroad Administration regulations.
- Merchant mariners who are under Coast Guard regulations and are off ship, in port awaiting sail.

Entertainment

For the taxpayer to be able to claim an entertainment expense, the expense must be ordinary and necessary and meet **one** of the following tests:

- Directly-related test
- Associated test

Directly Related

To be considered directly related the taxpayer must show that:

- The main purpose of the combined business and entertainment was the active conduct of business.
- The taxpayer did engage in business with the person during the entertainment period, and
- The taxpayer had more than a general expectation of getting income or some other specific business benefit at some future time.

Entertainment expenses in a situation where there is a substantial distraction are not considered directly related. Examples of situations where there are substantial distractions:

- A meeting or discussion at a nightclub, theater, or sporting event.
- A meeting or discussion during what is essentially a social gathering, such as a cocktail party.
- A meeting with a group that includes persons who are not business associates at places such as cocktail lounges, country clubs, golf clubs, athletic clubs, or vacation resorts.

Associated

To meet the associated test, the entertainment must be:

- Associated with the active conduct of the trade or business of the taxpayer and
- Directly before or after a substantial business discussion.

The entertainment expense may be to get new business or to encourage the continuation of an existing business relationship. For the discussion to be a substantial business discussion, the taxpayer must be able to show that they engaged in the discussion, meeting, negotiation, or other business transaction to get income or some other specific business benefit. If the entertainment and business discussion are held during the same day, the entertainment is considered held directly before or after the business discussion. Keep in mind that the entertainment expense does not have to meet both the associated and directly related tests. It only needs to meet one of the tests to be deductible.

Deductible Expenses

Illustration 12-2 shows what entertainment expenses are deductible. Entertainment expenses include any activity generally considered to provide entertainment, amusement, or recreation. These expenses include, but are not limited to, entertaining guests at the theater, at sporting events, at nightclubs, or at a sporting club.

Expenses that are **not deductible:**

- Membership in any club organized for:
  - Business,
  - Pleasure,
  - Recreation, or
  - Other social purpose.

- Dues paid to:
  - Country clubs,
  - Golf and athletic clubs,
  - Airline clubs,
  - Hotel clubs, and
  - Clubs operated to provide meals under circumstances generally considered to be conducive to business discussions.

Illustration 12-2

Entertainment Expenses

General Rule	You can deduct ordinary and necessary expenses to entertain a client, customer, or employee if the expenses meet the directly-related test or the associated test.
Definitions	<ul><li>Entertainment includes any activity generally considered to provide entertainment, amusement, or recreation, and includes meals provided to a customer or client.</li><li>An ordinary expense is one that is common and accepted in your field of business, trade, or profession.</li><li>A necessary expense is one that is helpful and appropriate.</li></ul>
Tests to be met	Directly-related test<ul><li>Entertainment took place in a clear business setting, or</li><li>The main purpose of entertainment was the active conduct of business, and you did engage in business with the person during the entertainment period, and you had more than a general expectation of getting income or some other specified business benefit.</li></ul>Associated test<ul><li>Entertainment is associated with your trade or business, and</li><li>Entertainment directly precedes or follows a substantial business discussion.</li></ul>
Other rules	<ul><li>You cannot deduct the cost of your meal as an entertainment expense if you are claiming the meal as a travel expense.</li><li>You cannot deduct expenses that are lavish or extravagant under the circumstances.</li><li>You generally can deduct only 50% of your unreimbursed entertainment expenses.</li></ul>

Gifts

In the course of the taxpayer's trade or business, the taxpayer may give gifts to clients or prospective clients. The taxpayer may deduct up to $25 for business gifts given to each person during the tax year. The costs of packaging, insuring, or mailing are not included in the $25 limit. The $25 limit does not apply if the item:

- Costs $4 or less and:
    - Has the taxpayer's name (or taxpayer's business's name) clearly and permanently imprinted on the gift, and
    - Is one of a number of identical items the taxpayer widely distributes. For example, pens, desk sets, and plastic bags.
- Is a sign, display rack, or other promotional material to be used on the business premises of the recipient.

Transportation

Transportation expenses are expenses of transportation by air, rail, bus, taxi, etc., and the cost of driving and maintaining the car. If the transportation expenses are incurred while traveling, they must be deducted as a travel expense. Deductible transportation expenses, first of all, do **not** include the expense of getting from the taxpayer's home to their regular workplace. These are commuting expenses and are never deductible. If the taxpayer has a second job, they may deduct the cost of getting from one workplace to the other. If the taxpayer has a temporary assignment or job, they may deduct the expense of getting from home to the temporary assignment or job as well as the cost of getting from the regular workplace to the temporary assignment or job. If the taxpayer visits clients or customers, goes to business meetings away from the workplace, or runs errands for the job, they may deduct the cost of transportation for these purposes. Illustration 12-3 shows when transportation expenses are deductible.

The cost of deductible transportation expense of air, rail, bus, or taxi is deductible. If the taxpayer is using their own vehicle, they may generally deduct the expenses one of two ways; actual auto expenses or standard mileage rate. In most cases, the method that will provide the biggest deduction can be used. However, if the taxpayer uses actual auto expenses the first year the vehicle is used for business purposes, actual auto expenses must always be used for that vehicle. If the taxpayer uses standard mileage in the first year, they can choose either the actual auto expenses or standard mileage in the later years. Any parking fees and tolls paid while incurring deductible transportation expenses are fully deductible with either method.

Actual Auto Expenses

The taxpayer may use the actual car expenses to claim their transportation expense deduction. Actual Expenses must be used if:

- The vehicle was used for hire,
- Five or more vehicles were used at the same time.

There are also many stipulations put on vehicles that have been depreciated. We will cover these stipulations in the Chapter 14.

Actual expenses include:

- Depreciation (This will be explained in the next chapter)
- Licenses
- Gas
- Lease Payments
- Insurance
- Garage Rent
- Registration Fees
- Repairs
- Tires

If the taxpayer uses their vehicle partly for business use and partly for personal use, they may only deduct the business portion of these expenses. To determine the business portion, the taxpayer must divide the business mileage by the total mileage the vehicle was driven for the year. That percentage will then be multiplied by the total of the above expenses.

Standard Mileage

The standard mileage rate varies from year to year and is generally adjusted for inflation. The standard mileage rate is 56 cents per mile for 2014.

Business Use of Home

If the taxpayer uses part of their home for business, they may be able to deduct otherwise nondeductible expenses in relation to the business use of home. To qualify to deduct expenses for the business use of home as an employee, the taxpayer must use part of the home _exclusively_ and _regularly_ as the principal place of business and for the convenience of the employer.

To satisfy the _exclusive_ use test, the taxpayer must use a specific area of the home only for the trade or business. The area the taxpayer uses for the trade or business cannot be used for any other reason. If the taxpayer does not meet the exclusive use test, they may not take a deduction for the business use of home.

Example: You have an extra room that you set up as a home office with a computer and desk. The computer is the only one in the house and your daughter uses it to surf the internet and do her homework on. The office does not satisfy the exclusive use test.

Exceptions: The storage of inventory or product samples and a daycare facility. These topics will be discussed in the chapter on Sole Proprietors.

To satisfy the _regular_ use test, the taxpayer must use a specific area of the home for business on a regular basis. If the taxpayer only uses it every now and then or on an infrequent basis, they do not meet the regular use test and may not deduct expenses for the business use of home.

Illustration 12-3

Transportation Expenses

Deductible if you have a regular or main job at another location.

Temporary work location

Always deductible

Never deductible

Always deductible

Home

Regular or Main Job

Never deductible on a day off from regular or main job.

Always deductible

Second job

Home: The place where you reside. Transportation expenses between your home and your main or regular place of work are personal commuting expenses.

Regular or main job: your principal place of business. If you have more than one job, you must determine which one is your regular or main job. Consider the time you spend at each, the activity you have at each, and the income you earn at each.

Temporary work location: A place where your work assignment is realistically expected to last (and does in fact last) one year or less. Unless you have a regular place of business, you can only deduct your transportation expenses to a temporary work location outside your metropolitan area.

Second job: If you regularly work at two or more places in one day, whether or not for the same employer, you can deduct your transportation expenses of getting from one workplace to another. You cannot deduct your transportation costs between your home and a second job on a day off from your main job.

Example: You set up a home office and use it exclusively for business, but you only use it when you cannot complete your work at your regular workplace. In the last 3 months, you've used it 4 times. You do not meet the regular use test.

To qualify as the principal place of business, the home must be the principal place of business for the taxpayer. The taxpayer may have more than one business location, but the home must be the principal place. To qualify as the principal place, the taxpayer must consider:

- The relative importance of the activities performed at each place where the business is conducted, and
- The amount of time spent at each place where the business is conducted.

If the taxpayer uses the home office exclusively and regularly for administrative or management activities of the trade or business, and the taxpayer has no other fixed location where substantial administrative or management activities of the trade or business, the home office will qualify as the principle place of business. Administrative activities include billing customers, keeping books, ordering supplies, setting up appointments, and forwarding orders or writing reports.

If the taxpayer has a separate structure, such as a garage or barn, they may deduct business use of home expenses if the area is used regularly and exclusively. It does not need to be the principal place of business to qualify.

Business Use of Home Worksheet

To claim the business use of home deduction as an employee, use a business use of home worksheet (Illustration 12-4) to figure the deduction.

Part 1 – Part of the home used for business

In this section, the area of the office is divided by the area of the entire home to calculate the percentage of the home used for business.

Line 4 – Gross income from business

Enter the total wages that are related to the business use of the home. The deduction for business use of home is limited to this amount.

Column a – Direct Expenses

Direct expenses are expenses only for the business part of the home. These expenses include painting and repairs only to the home office.

Column b – Indirect Expenses

Indirect expenses are expenses that relate to the entire home. These expenses include utilities, insurance, and rent. The indirect expenses will be multiplied by the percentage on line 3. The mortgage interest and real estate taxes will fall into this category. The taxpayer may not deduct the expense for the phone unless there is a second line used exclusively for business. Otherwise the taxpayer will only be able to deduct any long distance calls made for the business as a direct expense.

Note: The mortgage interest and real estate taxes are entered on this form for limitation purposes only. To maximize the taxpayer's deduction, the mortgage interest and real estate taxes should be deducted in full on the appropriate line of the Schedule A.

Part 3 – Depreciation
This will be covered in the next chapter.

Part 4 – Carryover of unallowed expenses to next year
If the taxpayer's business use of home expenses is limited due to their income, the expenses may be deductible in the next tax year.

Simplified Method

The taxpayer may elect to use the simplified method to calculate the business use of home. In this case, the calculation is made on a Simplified Method Worksheet (Illustration 12-5), and carried to the 2106. Generally, the simplified method of calculating the business use of home method is multiplying the area used regularly and exclusively for business, regularly for daycare, or regularly for storage of inventory or product samples, by $5.00. The area used to figure the deduction cannot exceed 300 square feet. Once this method is chosen in a taxable year, it may not change for that year. However, it may change from using the simplified method in one year to using the actual expense method in the next year, or vice-versa.

All of the use requirements needed for the Business Use of Home Worksheet must be also met for the simplified method. If the taxpayer used the Business Use of Home Worksheet in a prior year and had a carryover to the next year, they cannot claim the carryover using the simplified method. They will be carried over to the next year the taxpayer files the Business Use of Home Worksheet. Also, the depreciation of the home is not deducted using the simplified method. Therefore, the allowable depreciation deduction for any year the simplified method is used is deemed to be $0.

Note: Although depreciation is not deducted on the home, depreciation may still be claimed on other assets (for example: furniture or equipment) used in the qualified business use of the home.

Reimbursements

There are a few different methods that employers use to reimburse their employee's business expenses. If the employee report's their business expenses to the employer and the employer provides reimbursement that equals the expenses, the reimbursement is not included in income and the expenses are not deductible. The employee need not file a Form 2106.

If the employer does not require the employee to account for their expenses, but increases the employee's pay to cover any expenses the employee might incur, the reimbursement is included in box 1 of the Form W-2 and the taxpayer should file a Form 2106.

Sometimes the employer will provide reimbursement which exceeds the federal rate and will include the allowable amount in box 12 of the Form W-2 with code L. Any amount over the federal rate will be included in box 1 of the W-2. If the employee's expenses are in excess of the federal rate, the employee will file a Form 2106 and enter the reimbursement. If the reimbursement exceeds the deductible expenses, the excess amount must be included on Form 1040, line 7.

Rural Mail Carriers
Rural mail carriers are considered to have been reimbursed the equivalent amount to their transportation amount. Neither the reimbursement nor expenses are included on the tax return.

Recordkeeping

The taxpayer must have records to substantiate all expenses. To deduct travel expenses the taxpayer must keep receipts and records of the time, place, and the business purpose of the trip. If the taxpayer is using the standard meal allowance, they still must record the time, place and business purpose of the trip. If the taxpayer is claiming standard mileage, they must keep written records of the business mileage. If the taxpayer is claiming actual auto expenses, they must keep written records of the business mileage as well as receipts of gas, oil and any other expenses related to the business use of the vehicle. Entertainment expenses must be substantiated with receipts as well as who was present, where the entertainment occurred, and what the business purpose was.

Illustration 12-5

Simplified Method Worksheet

1. Enter the amount of the gross income limitation. See Instructions for the Simplified Method Worksheet .... 1. _____

2. Allowable square footage for the qualified business use. Do not enter more than 300 square feet. See Instructions for the Simplified Method Worksheet .... 2. _____

3. Simplified method amount
   a. Maximum allowable amount .... 3a. __$5___
   b. For daycare facilities not used exclusively for business, enter the decimal amount from the Daycare Facility Worksheet; otherwise, enter 1.0 .... 3b. _____
   c. Multiply line 3a by line 3b and enter result to 2 decimal places .... 3c. _____

4. Multiply line 2 by line 3c .... 4. _____

5. **Allowable expenses using the simplified method.** Enter the smaller of line 1 or line 4. If zero or less, enter -0-. See _Where To Deduct_, earlier, for where to enter this amount on your return .... 5. _____

6. **Carryover of unallowed expenses from 2013 that are not allowed in 2014.**
   a. Operating expenses. Enter the amount, if any, from your 2013 Worksheet To Figure the Deduction for Business Use of Your Home, line 40 .... 6a. _____
   b. Excess casualty losses and depreciation. Enter the amount, if any, from your 2013 Worksheet To Figure the Deduction for Business Use of Your Home, line 41 .... 6b. _____

Illustration 12-4

Worksheet To Figure the Deduction for Business Use of Your Home

PART 1—Part of Your Home Used for Business:

1) Area of home used for business . . . . 1) _____

2) Total area of home . . . . 2) _____

3) Percentage of home used for business (divide line 1 by line 2 and show result as percentage) . . . . . 3) _____ %

PART 2—Figure Your Allowable Deduction

4) Gross income from business (see instructions) . . . . 4) _____

	(a) Direct Expenses	(b) Indirect Expenses	
5) Casualty losses	5) _____	_____	**Enter lines**
6) Deductible mortgage interest and qualified mortgage insurance premiums	6) _____	_____	**5-7 in full** **here and**
7) Real estate taxes	7) _____	_____	**on**
8) Total of lines 5 through 7	8) _____	_____	**Schedule**

9) Multiply line 8, column (b), by line 3 . . . . 9) _____ **A.**

10) Add line 8, column (a), and line 9 . . . . 10) _____

11) Business expenses not from business use of home (see instructions) . . . . 11) _____

12) Add lines 10 and 11 . . . . 12) _____

13) Deduction limit. Subtract line 12 from line 4 . . . . 13) _____

14) Excess mortgage interest and qualified mortgage insurance premiums	14) _____	_____
15) Insurance	15) _____	_____
16) Rent	16) _____	_____
17) Repairs and maintenance	17) _____	_____
18) Utilities	18) _____	_____
19) Other expenses	19) _____	_____
20) Add lines 14 through 19	20) _____	_____

21) Multiply line 20, column (b) by line 3 . . . . 21) _____

22) Carryover of operating expenses from prior year (see instructions) . . . . 22) _____

23) Add line 20, column (a), line 21, and line 22 . . . . 23) _____

24) Allowable operating expenses. Enter the **smaller** of line 13 or line 23 . . . . 24) _____

25) Limit on excess casualty losses and depreciation. Subtract line 24 from line 13 . . . . 25) _____

26) Excess casualty losses (see instructions) . . . . 26) _____

27) Depreciation of your home from line 39 below . . . . 27) _____

28) Carryover of excess casualty losses and depreciation from prior year (see instructions) . . . . 28) _____

29) Add lines 26 through 28 . . . . 29) _____

30) Allowable excess casualty losses and depreciation. Enter the **smaller** of line 25 or line 29 . . . . 30) _____

31) Add lines 24 and 30 . . . . 31) _____

32) Casualty losses included on lines 10 and 30 (see instructions) . . . . 32) _____

33) Allowable expenses for business use of your home. (Subtract line 32 from line 31.) See instructions for where to enter on your return . . . . 33) _____

PART 3—Depreciation of Your Home

34) Smaller of adjusted basis or fair market value of home (see instructions) . . . . 34) _____

35) Basis of land . . . . 35) _____

36) Basis of building (subtract line 35 from line 34) . . . . 36) _____

37) Business basis of building (multiply line 36 by line 3) . . . . 37) _____

38) Depreciation percentage (from applicable table or method) . . . . 38) _____ %

39) Depreciation allowable (multiply line 37 by line 38) . . . . 39) _____

PART 4—Carryover of Unallowed Expenses to Next Year

40) Operating expenses. Subtract line 24 from line 23. If less than zero, enter -0- . . . . 40) _____

41) Excess casualty losses and depreciation. Subtract line 30 from line 29. If less than zero, enter -0- . . . . 41) _____

Form 2106

If the taxpayer has travel, transportation, meal, or entertainment expenses they must file a Form 2106 (Illustration 12-6). Remember the taxpayer may claim either the actual auto expense or the standard mileage but not both.

Example: Victor Peabody (344-25-6541) is in sales. His W-2 wages are $42,322. His AGI is $45,233. He has employee business expenses, including an office in the home. He doesn't have another office. His office is 125 square feet while his entire home is 1,650 square feet. His expenses are as follows:

- Utilities for the house $345 per month
- Repainted the office   193
- Real estate taxes   866
- Mortgage interest   5,449
- Insurance   1,253
- Personal property tax   82
- Charitable contributions   3,200

He has a 2006 Volkswagon that he placed into service on May 5, 2009. This year he put a total of 28,322 miles on his car. 10,826 of those miles were business. The Volkswagon is his only car and he keeps a calendar in his glove box in which he writes his daily mileage. He has no commuting mileage. He has paid $574 in parking fees throughout the year for his business.

Illustration 12-7 shows his completed Schedule A, Form 2106, and Business use of home worksheet. Please note that under normal circumstances, Mr. Peabody's house would be depreciated, but since we haven't covered that yet, it has been left off of this example.

Note: For this example, we will not be using the Simplified Method. However, under normal circumstances you will use whichever is more beneficial.

Illustration 12-6

Form **2106**

Department of the Treasury
Internal Revenue Service (99)

Employee Business Expenses

▶ Attach to Form 1040 or Form 1040NR.

▶ Information about Form 2106 and its separate instructions is available at *www.irs.gov/form2106.*

OMB No. 1545-0074

20**14**

Attachment
Sequence No. **129**

Your name	Occupation in which you incurred expenses	Social security number

Part I   Employee Business Expenses and Reimbursements

Step 1 Enter Your Expenses

			Column A Other Than Meals and Entertainment		Column B Meals and Entertainment	
1	Vehicle expense from line 22 or line 29. (Rural mail carriers: See instructions.)	1				
2	Parking fees, tolls, and transportation, including train, bus, etc., that **did not** involve overnight travel or commuting to and from work	2				
3	Travel expense while away from home overnight, including lodging, airplane, car rental, etc. **Do not** include meals and entertainment	3				
4	Business expenses not included on lines 1 through 3. **Do not** include meals and entertainment	4				
5	Meals and entertainment expenses (see instructions)	5				
6	**Total expenses.** In Column A, add lines 1 through 4 and enter the result. In Column B, enter the amount from line 5	6				

Note. *If you were not reimbursed for any expenses in Step 1, skip line 7 and enter the amount from line 6 on line 8.*

Step 2 Enter Reimbursements Received From Your Employer for Expenses Listed in Step 1

7	Enter reimbursements received from your employer that were **not** reported to you in box 1 of Form W-2. Include any reimbursements reported under code "L" in box 12 of your Form W-2 (see instructions).	7				

Step 3 Figure Expenses To Deduct on Schedule A (Form 1040 or Form 1040NR)

8	Subtract line 7 from line 6. If zero or less, enter -0-. However, if line 7 is greater than line 6 in Column A, report the excess as income on Form 1040, line 7 (or on Form 1040NR, line 8)	8				
	Note. *If both columns of line 8 are zero, you cannot deduct employee business expenses. Stop here and attach Form 2106 to your return.*					
9	In Column A, enter the amount from line 8. In Column B, multiply line 8 by 50% (.50). (Employees subject to Department of Transportation (DOT) hours of service limits: Multiply meal expenses incurred while away from home on business by 80% (.80) instead of 50%. For details, see instructions.)	9				
10	Add the amounts on line 9 of both columns and enter the total here. **Also, enter the total on Schedule A (Form 1040), line 21** (or on **Schedule A (Form 1040NR), line 7**). (Armed Forces reservists, qualified performing artists, fee-basis state or local government officials, and individuals with disabilities: See the instructions for special rules on where to enter the total.) ▶	10				

For Paperwork Reduction Act Notice, see your tax return instructions.   Cat. No. 11700N   Form **2106** (2014)

Illustration 12-6 continued

Part II	Vehicle Expenses			

Section A—General Information (You must complete this section if you are claiming vehicle expenses.)

			(a) Vehicle 1	**(b)** Vehicle 2
11	Enter the date the vehicle was placed in service	11	/ /	/ /
12	Total miles the vehicle was driven during 2014	12	miles	miles
13	Business miles included on line 12	13	miles	miles
14	Percent of business use. Divide line 13 by line 12	14	%	%
15	Average daily roundtrip commuting distance	15	miles	miles
16	Commuting miles included on line 12	16	miles	miles
17	Other miles. Add lines 13 and 16 and subtract the total from line 12	17	miles	miles
18	Was your vehicle available for personal use during off-duty hours?		☐ Yes ☐ No	
19	Do you (or your spouse) have another vehicle available for personal use?		☐ Yes ☐ No	
20	Do you have evidence to support your deduction?		☐ Yes ☐ No	
21	If "Yes," is the evidence written?		☐ Yes ☐ No	

Section B—Standard Mileage Rate (See the instructions for Part II to find out whether to complete this section or Section C.)

22	Multiply line 13 by 56¢ (.56). Enter the result here and on line 1	22	

Section C—Actual Expenses

			(a) Vehicle 1		**(b)** Vehicle 2	
23	Gasoline, oil, repairs, vehicle insurance, etc.	23				
24a	Vehicle rentals	24a				
b	Inclusion amount (see instructions)	24b				
c	Subtract line 24b from line 24a	24c				
25	Value of employer-provided vehicle (applies only if 100% of annual lease value was included on Form W-2—see instructions)	25				
26	Add lines 23, 24c, and 25	26				
27	Multiply line 26 by the percentage on line 14	27				
28	Depreciation (see instructions)	28				
29	Add lines 27 and 28. Enter total here and on line 1	29				

Section D—Depreciation of Vehicles (Use this section only if you owned the vehicle and are completing Section C for the vehicle.)

			(a) Vehicle 1		**(b)** Vehicle 2	
30	Enter cost or other basis (see instructions)	30				
31	Enter section 179 deduction (see instructions)	31				
32	Multiply line 30 by line 14 (see instructions if you claimed the section 179 deduction)	32				
33	Enter depreciation method and percentage (see instructions)	33				
34	Multiply line 32 by the percentage on line 33 (see instructions)	34				
35	Add lines 31 and 34	35				
36	Enter the applicable limit explained in the line 36 instructions	36				
37	Multiply line 36 by the percentage on line 14	37				
38	Enter the **smaller** of line 35 or line 37. If you skipped lines 36 and 37, enter the amount from line 35. Also enter this amount on line 28 above	38				

Form **2106** (2014)

Illustration 12-7

SCHEDULE A (Form 1040) Department of the Treasury Internal Revenue Service (99)	Itemized Deductions ▶ Information about Schedule A and its separate instructions is at *www.irs.gov/schedulea*. ▶ Attach to Form 1040.	OMB No. 1545-0074 20**14** Attachment Sequence No. **07**

Name(s) shown on Form 1040

Victor Peabody

Your social security number

344-25-6541

Medical and Dental Expenses		**Caution.** Do not include expenses reimbursed or paid by others.			
	1	Medical and dental expenses (see instructions)	1		
	2	Enter amount from Form 1040, line 38 ⌷2⌷			
	3	Multiply line 2 by 10% (.10). But if either you or your spouse was born before January 2, 1950, multiply line 2 by 7.5% (.075) instead	3		
	4	Subtract line 3 from line 1. If line 3 is more than line 1, enter -0-		4	
Taxes You Paid	5	State and local (**check only one box**): a ☑ Income taxes, **or** b ☐ General sales taxes	5	1,357 00	
	6	Real estate taxes (see instructions)	6	866 00	
	7	Personal property taxes	7	82 00	
	8	Other taxes. List type and amount ▶ _____	8		
	9	Add lines 5 through 8		9	2,305 00
Interest You Paid **Note.** Your mortgage interest deduction may be limited (see instructions).	10	Home mortgage interest and points reported to you on Form 1098	10	5,449 00	
	11	Home mortgage interest not reported to you on Form 1098. If paid to the person from whom you bought the home, see instructions and show that person's name, identifying no., and address ▶ _____	11		
	12	Points not reported to you on Form 1098. See instructions for special rules	12		
	13	Mortgage insurance premiums (see instructions)	13		
	14	Investment interest. Attach Form 4952 if required. (See instructions.)	14		
	15	Add lines 10 through 14		15	5,449 00
Gifts to Charity If you made a gift and got a benefit for it, see instructions.	16	Gifts by cash or check. If you made any gift of $250 or more, see instructions	16	3,200 00	
	17	Other than by cash or check. If any gift of $250 or more, see instructions. You **must** attach Form 8283 if over $500 . . .	17		
	18	Carryover from prior year	18		
	19	Add lines 16 through 18		19	3,200 00
Casualty and Theft Losses	20	Casualty or theft loss(es). Attach Form 4684. (See instructions.)		20	
Job Expenses and Certain Miscellaneous Deductions	21	Unreimbursed employee expenses—job travel, union dues, job education, etc. Attach Form 2106 or 2106-EZ if required. (See instructions.) ▶ Form 2106 _____	21	7,293 00	
	22	Tax preparation fees	22		
	23	Other expenses—investment, safe deposit box, etc. List type and amount ▶ _____	23		
	24	Add lines 21 through 23	24	7,293 00	
	25	Enter amount from Form 1040, line 38 ⌷25⌷ 45,233 00			
	26	Multiply line 25 by 2% (.02)	26	905 00	
	27	Subtract line 26 from line 24. If line 26 is more than line 24, enter -0-		27	6,334 00
Other Miscellaneous Deductions	28	Other—from list in instructions. List type and amount ▶ _____		28	
Total Itemized Deductions	29	Is Form 1040, line 38, over $152,525? ☑ **No.** Your deduction is not limited. Add the amounts in the far right column for lines 4 through 28. Also, enter this amount on Form 1040, line 40. ☐ **Yes.** Your deduction may be limited. See the Itemized Deductions Worksheet in the instructions to figure the amount to enter.		29	17,288 00
	30	If you elect to itemize deductions even though they are less than your standard deduction, check here . . . . ▶ ☐			

For Paperwork Reduction Act Notice, see Form 1040 instructions.   Cat. No. 17145C   Schedule A (Form 1040) 2014

Illustration 12-7 continued

Form **2106**	**Employee Business Expenses**	OMB No. 1545-0074
Department of the Treasury Internal Revenue Service (99)	▶ Attach to Form 1040 or Form 1040NR. ▶ Information about Form 2106 and its separate instructions is available at *www.irs.gov/form2106*.	20**14** Attachment Sequence No. **129**

Your name	Occupation in which you incurred expenses	Social security number
Victor Peabody	Sales	344 : 25 : 6541

Part I Employee Business Expenses and Reimbursements

Step 1 Enter Your Expenses

		Column A Other Than Meals and Entertainment		Column B Meals and Entertainment	
1	Vehicle expense from line 22 or line 29. (Rural mail carriers: See instructions.)	**1**	6,063 00		
2	Parking fees, tolls, and transportation, including train, bus, etc., that **did not** involve overnight travel or commuting to and from work	**2**	574 00		
3	Travel expense while away from home overnight, including lodging, airplane, car rental, etc. **Do not** include meals and entertainment	**3**			
4	Business expenses not included on lines 1 through 3. **Do not** include meals and entertainment	**4**	602 00		
5	Meals and entertainment expenses (see instructions)	**5**			
6	**Total expenses.** In Column A, add lines 1 through 4 and enter the result. In Column B, enter the amount from line 5	**6**	7,239 00		

Note. *If you were not reimbursed for any expenses in Step 1, skip line 7 and enter the amount from line 6 on line 8.*

Step 2 Enter Reimbursements Received From Your Employer for Expenses Listed in Step 1

7	Enter reimbursements received from your employer that were **not** reported to you in box 1 of Form W-2. Include any reimbursements reported under code "L" in box 12 of your Form W-2 (see instructions).	**7**			

Step 3 Figure Expenses To Deduct on Schedule A (Form 1040 or Form 1040NR)

8	Subtract line 7 from line 6. If zero or less, enter -0-. However, if line 7 is greater than line 6 in Column A, report the excess as income on Form 1040, line 7 (or on Form 1040NR, line 8)	**8**	7,239 00		
	Note. *If both columns of line 8 are zero, you cannot deduct employee business expenses. Stop here and attach Form 2106 to your return.*				
9	In Column A, enter the amount from line 8. In Column B, multiply line 8 by 50% (.50). (Employees subject to Department of Transportation (DOT) hours of service limits: Multiply meal expenses incurred while away from home on business by 80% (.80) instead of 50%. For details, see instructions.)	**9**	7,239 00		
10	Add the amounts on line 9 of both columns and enter the total here. **Also, enter the total on Schedule A (Form 1040), line 21** (or on **Schedule A (Form 1040NR), line 7**). (Armed Forces reservists, qualified performing artists, fee-basis state or local government officials, and individuals with disabilities: See the instructions for special rules on where to enter the total.) ▶	**10**		7,239	00

For Paperwork Reduction Act Notice, see your tax return instructions.   Cat. No. 11700N   Form **2106** (2014)

Illustration 12-7 continued

Form 2106 (2014)

Page **2**

Part II   Vehicle Expenses

Section A—General Information (You must complete this section if you are claiming vehicle expenses.)

			(a) Vehicle 1		**(b)** Vehicle 2
11	Enter the date the vehicle was placed in service	11	05 / 05 / 09		/ /
12	Total miles the vehicle was driven during 2014	12	28,322	miles	miles
13	Business miles included on line 12	13	10,826	miles	miles
14	Percent of business use. Divide line 13 by line 12	14	38.22	%	%
15	Average daily roundtrip commuting distance	15		miles	miles
16	Commuting miles included on line 12	16		miles	miles
17	Other miles. Add lines 13 and 16 and subtract the total from line 12	17	17,496	miles	miles
18	Was your vehicle available for personal use during off-duty hours?		☑ Yes ☐ No		
19	Do you (or your spouse) have another vehicle available for personal use?		☐ Yes ☑ No		
20	Do you have evidence to support your deduction?		☑ Yes ☐ No		
21	If "Yes," is the evidence written?		☑ Yes ☐ No		

Section B—Standard Mileage Rate (See the instructions for Part II to find out whether to complete this section or Section C.)

22	Multiply line 13 by 56¢ (.56). Enter the result here and on line 1	22	6,063	00

Section C—Actual Expenses

			(a) Vehicle 1	**(b)** Vehicle 2
23	Gasoline, oil, repairs, vehicle insurance, etc.	23		
24a	Vehicle rentals	24a		
b	Inclusion amount (see instructions)	24b		
c	Subtract line 24b from line 24a	24c		
25	Value of employer-provided vehicle (applies only if 100% of annual lease value was included on Form W-2—see instructions)	25		
26	Add lines 23, 24c, and 25	26		
27	Multiply line 26 by the percentage on line 14	27		
28	Depreciation (see instructions)	28		
29	Add lines 27 and 28. Enter total here and on line 1	29		

Section D—Depreciation of Vehicles (Use this section only if you owned the vehicle and are completing Section C for the vehicle.)

			(a) Vehicle 1	**(b)** Vehicle 2
30	Enter cost or other basis (see instructions)	30		
31	Enter section 179 deduction (see instructions)	31		
32	Multiply line 30 by line 14 (see instructions if you claimed the section 179 deduction)	32		
33	Enter depreciation method and percentage (see instructions)	33		
34	Multiply line 32 by the percentage on line 33 (see instructions)	34		
35	Add lines 31 and 34	35		
36	Enter the applicable limit explained in the line 36 instructions	36		
37	Multiply line 36 by the percentage on line 14	37		
38	Enter the **smaller** of line 35 or line 37. If you skipped lines 36 and 37, enter the amount from line 35. Also enter this amount on line 28 above	38		

Form **2106** (2014)

Illustration 12-7 continued

Worksheet To Figure the Deduction for Business Use of Your Home

PART 1—Part of Your Home Used for Business:
1) Area of home used for business .... 1)   125
2) Total area of home .... 2) 1,650
3) Percentage of home used for business (divide line 1 by line 2 and show result as percentage) ..... 3) 7.58 %

PART 2—Figure Your Allowable Deduction
4) Gross income from business (see instructions) .... 4) 42,322

	(a) Direct Expenses	(b) Indirect Expenses	
5) Casualty losses	5)		**Enter lines 5-7 in full here and on Schedule A.**
6) Deductible mortgage interest and qualified mortgage insurance premiums	6)	5,449	
7) Real estate taxes	7)	866	
8) Total of lines 5 through 7	8)	6,315	

9) Multiply line 8, column (b), by line 3 .... 9) 479
10) Add line 8, column (a), and line 9 .... 10) 479
11) Business expenses not from business use of home (see instructions) .... 11) 6,637
12) Add lines 10 and 11 .... 12) 7,116
13) Deduction limit. Subtract line 12 from line 4 .... 13) 35,206

	(a) Direct	(b) Indirect	
14) Excess mortgage interest and qualified mortgage insurance premiums	14)		
15) Insurance	15)	1,253	
16) Rent	16)		
17) Repairs and maintenance	17) 193		
18) Utilities	18)	4,140	
19) Other expenses	19)		
20) Add lines 14 through 19	20) 193	5,393	

21) Multiply line 20, column (b) by line 3 .... 21) 409
22) Carryover of operating expenses from prior year (see instructions) ...... 22)
23) Add line 20, column (a), line 21, and line 22 .... 23) 602
24) Allowable operating expenses. Enter the **smaller** of line 13 or line 23 ..... 24) 602
25) Limit on excess casualty losses and depreciation. Subtract line 24 from line 13 ..... 25) 34,604
26) Excess casualty losses (see instructions) .... 26)
27) Depreciation of your home from line 39 below .... 27)
28) Carryover of excess casualty losses and depreciation from prior year (see instructions) ..... 28)
29) Add lines 26 through 28 .... 29) 0
30) Allowable excess casualty losses and depreciation. Enter the **smaller** of line 25 or line 29 ..... 30) 0
31) Add lines 24 and 30 .... 31) 602
32) Casualty losses included on lines 10 and 30 (see instructions) ..... 32)
33) Allowable expenses for business use of your home. (Subtract line 32 from line 31.) See instructions for where to enter on your return ..... 33) 602

PART 3—Depreciation of Your Home
34) Smaller of adjusted basis or fair market value of home (see instructions) ..... 34)
35) Basis of land .... 35)
36) Basis of building (subtract line 35 from line 34) .... 36)
37) Business basis of building (multiply line 36 by line 3) .... 37)
38) Depreciation percentage (from applicable table or method) .... 38) %
39) Depreciation allowable (multiply line 37 by line 38) .... 39)

PART 4—Carryover of Unallowed Expenses to Next Year
40) Operating expenses. Subtract line 24 from line 23. If less than zero, enter -0- ..... 40)
41) Excess casualty losses and depreciation. Subtract line 30 from line 29. If less than zero, enter -0- ..... 41)

Chapter Review

1) What employee business expenses require the use of a Form 2106?

2) How long does a temporary assignment last?

3) Define bona fide business purpose.

4) What is the limitation on deductible meals?

5) What is the federal meal and incidental expense allowance?

6) How much of the federal allowance is for incidental expense?

7) What is the limitation for business gifts?

8) What is the standard mileage rate?

Exercise

Complete a Schedule A and a Form 2106 and a business use of home worksheet for Harry Henderson. Harry's SSN is 243-52-1656. He is in sales and his wages from that job are $35,300. His AGI is, also, $35,300. His employer does not reimburse him for any of his expenses. He had $1,553 withheld for state taxes. He donated $2,550 to his church and paid $23 in personal property taxes.

He owns a 2006 Ford Explorer. He placed it into service on March 1st of this year. He drove it for 26,540 miles this year. 21,100 miles were for business use. His regular place of employment is 2 miles from his home and he worked at that job 280 days. He would like to use the standard mileage. He paid $213 in tolls and $78 for parking. His Ford is his only car and he keeps a log book to record his mileage.

He has an office he uses regularly and exclusively for business. His office is 112 square feet. The area of his entire home is 1,600 square feet. He has no office at his workplace and his employer requires him to prepare invoices and make sales calls. His yearly expenses are as follows:

Paint for the office	$ 48
Electricity for the house	1,280
Expense for the only phone	780
Rent	4,800
Insurance	1,200

Harry was required to attend a conference in another state. His expenses for that were:

Airline	$ 670
Rental Car	190
Lodging	453
Meals	243

Chapter 13 – Depreciation, Part I

Depreciation is an annual deduction that allows a taxpayer to recover the cost or other basis of certain property over the life of the property. Different types of property require different methods of depreciation. This chapter will explain how to calculate the depreciable basis of the property, determine the class of the property, determine the method of depreciation, and calculate the depreciation.

Depreciable Property

To be depreciable property, the property must meet the following 4 requirements:
- It must be property the taxpayer owns.
- It must be used in the taxpayer's business or income-producing activity.
- It must have a determinable useful life.
- It must be expected to last more than one year.

It must be property the taxpayer owns.

The taxpayer must be the owner of the property. The taxpayer is considered the owner even if the property is subject to a debt. For example, the taxpayer purchased a house, but had to take a mortgage on it to be able to buy it. The taxpayer owns the house and can depreciate it if it meets the other requirements.

It must be used in the taxpayer's business or income-producing activity.

To be able to depreciate property, the taxpayer must use it in their business or in their income-producing activity. If the property is used to produce income, the income must be taxable. If the property is only partly used for the business or income-producing activity, depreciation can be taken only on that part of the property.

Inventory cannot be depreciated because it is held for the sale to customers. It is not actually used in the business.

It must have a determinable useful life.

The property must have a determinable useful life to be depreciable. This means that the property must wear out, decay, get used up, become obsolete, or lose its value from natural causes.

It must be expected to last more than one year.

The property must have a useful life of more than one year. If the property's useful life is one year or less, the taxpayer may deduct the entire cost of the property as a business expense.

Types of Property

Property falls into two categories: real and personal. Real property is also called real estate. It includes land, buildings, and their structural components. Land is never depreciable. If the taxpayer purchased real property which consisted of a building and land, the portion of the purchase price attributable to the land must be deducted from the total price before the property is depreciated.

Personal property is all other property. Personal property is not to be confused with personal-use property. Personal property falls into two categories: tangible and intangible. Tangible property has physical substance and its value is intrinsic. Intrinsic means the property has value in and of itself. Tangible property includes furniture, tools, and vehicles. Intangible property has no intrinsic value. The best example of intangible property is money in the form of bills. The bill itself is not worth anything because it is just made of paper. However, the bill gives the owner the right to purchase property and services, therefore it has value. Other intangible properties include insurance policies, stocks, and bonds.

Basis

The basis of purchased property is usually its cost plus any amounts paid for items such as sales tax, freight charges, and installation and testing fees. If the property has been held for personal use, but it's changed to use for a business or an income producing activity, the basis is lesser of the following:

- The fair market value (FMV) of the property on the date of the change in use.
- The original cost or other basis adjusted as follows:
  - Increased by the cost of any permanent improvements or additions and other costs that must be added to the basis.
  - Decreased by any deductions the taxpayer claimed for casualty and theft losses and other items that reduced the basis.

To find the depreciable basis of the property, some adjustments may have to be made. Any changes that incurred between the time the taxpayer acquired the property and placed it into service must be taken into account. Add in any amounts that are paid out to assist in the purchase of the property or retaining the property such as installing utility lines, paying legal fees for perfecting the title, or settling zoning issues. If improvements are made to the property prior to placing the property in service, add these amounts to the basis. If improvements are made to the property after the property has been placed in service, treat the improvement as a separate depreciable property.

As stated earlier, if the taxpayer purchased depreciable real property but the purchase price included the land the building was on, the amount attributable to the land must be subtracted to determine the depreciable basis.

Example: Sharon purchased an office building which included the ½ acre the building was on. She paid $150,000 for all of it. The purchase price included $100,000 for the building and $50,000 for the land. The depreciable basis of the building is $100,000 because land is never depreciable.

Which Depreciation to Use

Modified Accelerated Cost Recovery System (MACRS) must be used to depreciate most property. First, we will discuss the other types of depreciation, and then we will delve into MACRS.

Property Placed in Service Before 1987

If the property was placed in service before 1987, Accelerated Cost Recovery System must be used to depreciate it (except property placed in service after July 31, 1986 if MACRS was elected. If personal property was placed in service after 1986, but any of the following situations apply, ACRS must be used:

- The taxpayer or someone related to the taxpayer owned or used the property in 1986.
- The taxpayer acquired the property from a person who owned it in 1986 and as part of the transaction the user of the property did not change.
- The taxpayer leases the property to a person who owned or used the property in 1986.
- The taxpayer acquired the property in a transaction in which:
  - The user of the property did not change, and
  - The property was not MACRS property in the hands of the person from whom the taxpayer acquired it because of the prior 2 situations.

If the property falls into any of these categories and ACRS must be used, additional research will be required. Begin with IRS Pub. 534.

MACRS

MACRS consists of two depreciation systems. The General Depreciation System (GDS) is the one that will generally be used. Alternative Depreciation System (ADS) will be used if specifically required or elected. ADS is required for the following property:

- Listed property used 50% or less in a qualified business use. (We will discuss this later.)
- Any tangible property used predominantly outside the United States during the year.
- Any tax-exempt use property.
- Any tax-exempt bond-financed property.
- All property used predominantly in a farming business and placed in service in any tax year during which an election not to apply the uniform capitalization rules to certain farming costs is in effect.
- Any property imported from a foreign country for which an Executive Order is in effect because the country maintains trade restrictions or engages in other discriminatory acts.

Even if the property qualifies for GDS, the taxpayer may use ADS. This generally provides for a longer recovery period and while allowing a smaller deduction, the taxpayer may take the deduction for more years than is allowed under GDS. For the rest of this book, we will use GDS.

Learning to Depreciate Step-By-Step

There are many more intricacies to depreciation, but we will postpone them until we learn the basics of depreciation.

The First Step

The first step to depreciation is to determine the recovery period of the property. To find out the recovery period of personal property, we will use the table of MACRS/GDS Recovery Periods for Common Assets (Illustration 13-1) that appears in Pub. 946. (These tables are of the more commonly depreciated property. For a more detailed list see the tables in Appendix D and IRS Pub. 946.) The first thing we will do is find the property we are going to depreciate. What is the recovery period for an office desk? Notice it is under office furniture. The GDS Recovery Period is 7 years. Now, let's find the recovery period for a copy machine. We will find that under data handling equipment. The GDS Recovery Period is 5 years. Let's try one more. What is the recovery period for a car used for business purposes? This, we will find under transportation and the GDS Recovery Period is 5 years. Real property is easier to classify because it can fall into only two categories if placed in service in 1987 or later: nonresidential real property and residential rental property.

Nonresidential real property includes offices, stores, and other business structures. These properties have a recovery period of 39 years if placed into service after May 12, 1993. The recovery period for nonresidential real property placed into service before May 13, 1993 is 31.5 years.

Residential rental property includes buildings that are set up as residences that someone rents. Residential rental property has a recovery period of 27.5 years.

The Second Step

The second step to calculating depreciation is to find the correct MACRS table to use. To find the correct table, we must determine the method and convention of depreciation.

Convention

There are three different conventions: half- year, mid-quarter, and mid-month. Personal property falls into either half-year or mid-quarter. Generally, the half-year convention (HY) will be used. This means that for the first year the property is placed into service, it is depreciated for half of the year. Mid-quarter (MQ) convention is treated as having been placed in service in the middle of the quarter it's actually placed into service. Mid-quarter convention must be used if over 40%of the depreciable basis of all of the depreciable property placed into service during that year was placed into service during the last 3 months.

Example: Dianne purchased a desk, two chairs, and a filing cabinet to use for her business this year. She purchased the desk on January 5th for $250. She purchased the two chairs and the filing cabinet on November 1st. The chairs were $85 each and the filing cabinet was $150. The total depreciable basis of the property is $570 (250 + 85 + 85 + 150). The percentage of the basis that was placed into service during the last quarter is 56% (85 + 85 + 150 = 320; 320 ÷ 570 = 0.56). Dianne must use the mid-quarter convention to depreciate her property.

Illustration 13-1

MACRS/GDS Recovery Periods for Common Assets

Property Type	Recovery Period
Office Related	
• Office Furniture: Includes furniture and fixtures that are not a structural component of the building. Also, includes such assets as desks, files, safes, and communications equipment. Does not include communications equipment that is included in other classes.	7yrs
• Data Handling Equipment; except computers Includes only typewriters, calculators, adding and accounting machines, copiers, and duplicating equipment.	5yrs
• Information systems Includes computers and their peripheral equipment used in administering normal business transactions and the maintenance of business records, and their retrieval, and analysis.	5yrs
Transportation	
• Airplanes (noncommercial) and Helicopters	5yrs
• Automobiles, Taxis	5yrs
• Buses	5yrs
• Light General Purpose Trucks (less and 13,000 pounds)	5yrs
• Heavy General Purpose Trucks (13,000 pounds or more)	5yrs
• Tractor units for use over the road	3yrs
• Trailers and Trailer mounted containers	5yrs
Agricultural	
• Agricultural machinery and equipment Includes grain bins, and fences but no other land improvements, that are used in production of crops or plants, vines, and trees; livestock; the operation of farm dairies, nurseries, greenhouses, sod farms, mushroom cellars, cranberry bogs, apiaries and fur farms; the performance of agriculture, animal husbandry, and horticultural services.	7yrs
• Breeding or dairy cattle	5yrs
• Breeding or work horses (12 yrs old or less at the time placed in service)	7yrs
• Breeding or work horses (more than 12 yrs old at the time placed in service)	3yrs
• Breeding hogs	3yrs
• Breeding sheep and goats	5yrs
• Single purpose agricultural or horticultural structures	10yrs
Real Property	
• Residential rental property	27.5yrs
• Nonresidential real property placed in service on or after May 13, 1993.	39yrs
• Nonresidential real property placed in service before May 13, 1993.	31.5yrs
Other	
• Appliances, carpets, and furniture used in rental property	5yrs
• Personal property with no class life	7yrs

Real property requires the use of mid-month convention (MM). The property is treated as having been placed into service in the middle of the month it is actually placed into service.

Method

The different methods of depreciation are illustrated in Illustration 13-2. The methods are 150% declining balance, 200% declining balance, and straight line. The Straight Line method is the easiest to understand. When you find out what the recovery period of the property is, you can divide 100% by the number of years in the recovery period to get the yearly depreciation rates. Remember, under the half year convention you only take half of the depreciation in the first year. The straight line method table is shown in Illustration 13-3.

Example: The property you are depreciating is 5 year property using the Straight Line method. 100% ÷ 5 years = 20%. The depreciation deduction is 20% per year. The first year you will compute the depreciation deduction for only half of the year (20% ÷ 2) which is 10%. You will take the deduction of the other 10% in the final year.

The 150% declining balance method gives a greater deduction in the earlier years than does the straight line method. This method changes to the straight line method when the straight line method will give an equal or greater deduction (Don't worry, the table does this for us). The table is shown in Illustration 13-3.

Example: For five year property, the straight line method gives a deduction for 10% in the first year. Take 150% of the 10% deduction to arrive at the depreciation deduction for 150% declining balance. 10% x 150% = 15%. Note that the first year's deduction under the 150% declining balance method is 15%. In year two, 85% of the basis remains (100% of the basis – 15%). The depreciation deduction for year two is 85% x 20% (year 2 SL method depreciation rate) x 150% = 25.50%
Year three:
85% - 25.50% = 59.50%
59.50% x 20% x 150% = 17.85%

The 200% declining balance method works the same as the 150% declining balance method, but the taxpayer receives an even greater deduction at the beginning. This method also switches to the straight line method when the deduction is equal to or greater. This is the method most widely used because it gives a greater deduction in the earlier years. The table is shown in Illustration 13-3.

Example: For five year property the depreciation rate using the SL method is 10% the first year. 10% x 200% = 20% depreciation rate for year one using the 200% DB method.
Year two:
100% - 20% = 80%
80% x 20% x 200% = 32% depreciation rate for year two.
Year three:
80% - 32% = 48%
48% x 20% x 200% = 19.20% depreciation rate for year three.

For most personal property, the 200%DB (200% Declining Balance) will be used. Depreciating real property requires the SL (Straight Line) method. A comparison of the three methods is shown in Illustration 13-2.

Illustration 13-2

Depreciation Methods

Note: The declining balance method is abbreviated as DB and the straight line method is abbreviated as SL.		
Method	**Type of property**	**Benefit**
GDS using 200% DB	• Nonfarm 3-, 5- ,7-, and 10-year property	• Provides a greater deduction during the earlier recovery years. • Changes to SL when that method provides an equal to or greater deduction.
GDS using 150% DB	• All farm property (except real property). • All 15- and 20-year property (except qualified leasehold improvement property and qualified restaurant property placed in service before (January 1, 2010) • Nonfarm 3-, 5-, 7-, and 10-year property	• Provides a greater deduction during the earlier recovery years • Changes to SL when that method provides an equal to or greater deduction.
GDS using SL	• Nonresidential real property • Qualified leasehold improvement property placed in service before January 1, 2010. • Qualified restaurant property placed in service before January 1, 2010. • Residential rental property • Trees or vines bearing fruits or nuts • Water Utility property • All 3-, 5-, 7-, 10-, 15-, 20-year property	• Provides for equal yearly deductions (except for the first and last years)

Find the Correct Table

Some of the more common used tables are illustrated (Illustration 213-3) in the next few pages as well as in the appendix. Notice Table A is used for personal property that has a recovery period of 3, 5, or 7 years and is depreciated using the half-year convention and the 200%DB method. Table B is for personal property with a recovery period of 3, 5, or 7 years and is depreciated using the half-year convention and the 150%DB method. Table C is for personal property with a recovery period of 3, 5, or 7 years and is depreciated using the half-year convention and the SL method. Tables D through G are for properties with the same recovery periods, but property that must be depreciated using the mid-quarter convention. You will use whichever table is for the quarter the property you're looking up was placed in service.

Table H is for residential property. Table J is for nonresidential property placed in service before May 13, 1993. Table I is for nonresidential property that was placed in service on or after May 13, 1993. Notice the headings at the top of the table are for the recovery period of the property you are depreciating. The headings down the left side have to do with the year for which you are calculating the depreciation.

Illustration 13-3

Table A   **MACRS 3-year, 5-year, and 7-year property**

Half – Year Convention   **200%DB**

Year	Depreciation rate for recovery period		
	3-year	5-year	7-year
1	33.33%	20.00%	14.29%
2	44.45%	32.00%	24.49%
3	14.81%	19.20%	17.49%
4	7.41%	11.52%	12.49%
5		11.52%	8.93%
6		5.76%	8.92%
7			8.93%
8			4.46%

Table B   **MACRS 3-year, 5-year, and 7-year property**

Half – Year Convention   **150%DB**

Year	Depreciation rate for recovery period		
	3-year	5-year	7-year
1	25.00%	15.00%	10.71%
2	37.50%	25.50%	19.13%
3	25.00%	17.85%	15.03%
4	12.50%	16.66%	12.25%
5		16.66%	12.25%
6		8.33%	12.25%
7			12.25%
8			6.13%

Table C   **MACRS 3-year, 5-year, and 7-year property**

Half – Year Convention   **Straight Line**

Year	Depreciation rate for recovery period		
	3-year	5-year	7-year
1	16.67%	10.00%	7.14%
2	33.33%	20.00%	14.29%
3	33.33%	20.00%	14.29%
4	16.67%	20.00%	14.28%
5		20.00%	14.29%
6		10.00%	14.28%
7			14.29%
8			7.14%

Illustration 13-3 continued

Table D   **MACRS 3-year, 5-year, and 7-year property   200DB%**

Mid-Quarter Convention placed in Service in First Quarter

Year	Depreciation rate for recovery period		
	3-year	5-year	7-year
1	58.33%	35.00%	25.00%
2	27.78%	26.00%	21.43%
3	12.35%	15.60%	15.31%
4	1.54%	11.01%	10.93%
5		11.01%	8.75%
6		1.38%	8.74%
7			8.75%
8			1.09%

Table E

MACRS 3-year, 5-year, and 7-year property   200DB%

Mid-Quarter Convention placed in Service in Second Quarter

Year	Depreciation rate for recovery period		
	3-year	5-year	7-year
1	41.67%	25.00%	17.85%
2	38.89%	30.00%	23.47%
3	14.14%	18.00%	16.76%
4	5.30%	11.37%	11.97%
5		11.37%	8.87%
6		4.26%	8.87%
7			8.87%
8			3.34%

Table F

MACRS 3-year, 5-year, and 7-year property   200DB%

Mid-Quarter Convention placed in Service in Third Quarter

Year	Depreciation rate for recovery period		
	3-year	5-year	7-year
1	58.33%	35.00%	25.00%
2	27.78%	26.00%	21.43%
3	12.35%	15.60%	15.31%
4	1.54%	11.01%	10.93%
5		11.01%	8.75%
6		1.38%	8.74%
7			8.75%
8			1.09%

Illustration 13-3 continued

Table G

MACRS 3-year, 5-year, and 7-year property   200DB%
Mid-Quarter Convention placed in Service in Fourth Quarter

Year	Depreciation rate for recovery period		
	3-year	5-year	7-year
1	8.33%	5.00%	3.57%
2	61.11%	38.00%	27.55%
3	20.37%	22.80%	19.68%
4	10.19%	13.68%	14.06%
5		10.94%	10.04%
6		9.58%	8.73%
7			8.73%
8			7.64%

Table H

MACRS Residential Rental Property   Straight Line
Mid-Month Convention   27.5years

Year	Month Property was placed in service											
	1	2	3	4	5	6	7	8	9	10	11	12
1	3.485%	3.182%	2.879%	2.576%	2.273%	1.970%	1.667%	1.364%	1.061%	0.758%	0.455%	0.152%
2-9	3.636%	3.636%	3.636%	3.636%	3.636%	3.636%	3.636%	3.636%	3.636%	3.636%	3.636%	3.636%
10	3.637%	3.637%	3.637%	3.637%	3.637%	3.637%	3.636%	3.636%	3.636%	3.636%	3.636%	3.636%
11	3.636%	3.636%	3.636%	3.636%	3.636%	3.636%	3.637%	3.637%	3.637%	3.637%	3.637%	3.637%
12	3.637%	3.637%	3.637%	3.637%	3.637%	3.637%	3.636%	3.636%	3.636%	3.636%	3.636%	3.636%
13	3.636%	3.636%	3.636%	3.636%	3.636%	3.636%	3.637%	3.637%	3.637%	3.637%	3.637%	3.637%
14	3.637%	3.637%	3.637%	3.637%	3.637%	3.637%	3.636%	3.636%	3.636%	3.636%	3.636%	3.636%
15	3.636%	3.636%	3.636%	3.636%	3.636%	3.636%	3.637%	3.637%	3.637%	3.637%	3.637%	3.637%
16	3.637%	3.637%	3.637%	3.637%	3.637%	3.637%	3.636%	3.636%	3.636%	3.636%	3.636%	3.636%
17	3.636%	3.636%	3.636%	3.636%	3.636%	3.636%	3.637%	3.637%	3.637%	3.637%	3.637%	3.637%
18	3.637%	3.637%	3.637%	3.637%	3.637%	3.637%	3.636%	3.636%	3.636%	3.636%	3.636%	3.636%
19	3.636%	3.636%	3.636%	3.636%	3.636%	3.636%	3.637%	3.637%	3.637%	3.637%	3.637%	3.637%
20	3.637%	3.637%	3.637%	3.637%	3.637%	3.637%	3.636%	3.636%	3.636%	3.636%	3.636%	3.636%
21	3.636%	3.636%	3.636%	3.636%	3.636%	3.636%	3.637%	3.637%	3.637%	3.637%	3.637%	3.637%
22	3.637%	3.637%	3.637%	3.637%	3.637%	3.637%	3.636%	3.636%	3.636%	3.636%	3.636%	3.636%
23	3.636%	3.636%	3.636%	3.636%	3.636%	3.636%	3.637%	3.637%	3.637%	3.637%	3.637%	3.637%
24	3.637%	3.637%	3.637%	3.637%	3.637%	3.637%	3.636%	3.636%	3.636%	3.636%	3.636%	3.636%
25	3.636%	3.636%	3.636%	3.636%	3.636%	3.636%	3.637%	3.637%	3.637%	3.637%	3.637%	3.637%
26	3.637%	3.637%	3.637%	3.637%	3.637%	3.637%	3.636%	3.636%	3.636%	3.636%	3.636%	3.636%
27	3.636%	3.636%	3.636%	3.636%	3.636%	3.636%	3.637%	3.637%	3.637%	3.637%	3.637%	3.637%
28	1.97%	2.273%	2.576%	2.879%	3.182%	3.485%	3.636%	3.636%	3.636%	3.636%	3.636%	3.636%
29							0.152%	0.455%	0.758%	1.061%	1.364%	1.667%

Illustration 13-3 continued

Table I

MACRS Nonresidential Real Property — Straight Line — 39 years
Placed in service on or after May 13th, 1993 — Mid-Month Convention

Year	Month Property was placed in service											
	1	2	3	4	5	6	7	8	9	10	11	12
1	2.461%	2.247%	2.033%	1.819%	1.605%	1.391%	1.177%	0.963%	0.749%	0.535%	0.321%	0.107%
2-39	2.564%	2.564%	2.564%	2.564%	2.564%	2.564%	2.564%	2.564%	2.564%	2.564%	2.564%	2.564%
40	0.107%	0.321%	0.535%	0.749%	0.963%	1.177%	1.391%	1.605%	1.819%	2.033%	2.247%	2.461%

Table J

MACRS Nonresidential Real Property — Straight Line — 31.5 years
Placed in service before May 13th, 1993 — Mid-Month Convention

Year	Month Property was placed in service											
	1	2	3	4	5	6	7	8	9	10	11	12
1	3.042%	2.778%	2.513%	2.249%	1.984%	1.720%	1.455%	1.190%	0.926%	0.661%	0.397%	0.132%
2-7	3.175%	3.175%	3.175%	3.175%	3.175%	3.175%	3.175%	3.175%	3.175%	3.175%	3.175%	3.175%
8	3.175%	3.174%	3.175%	3.174%	3.175%	3.174%	3.175%	3.175%	3.175%	3.175%	3.175%	3.175%
9	3.174%	3.175%	3.174%	3.175%	3.174%	3.175%	3.174%	3.175%	3.174%	3.175%	3.174%	3.175%
10	3.175%	3.174%	3.175%	3.174%	3.175%	3.174%	3.175%	3.174%	3.175%	3.174%	3.175%	3.174%
11	3.174%	3.175%	3.174%	3.175%	3.174%	3.175%	3.174%	3.175%	3.174%	3.175%	3.174%	3.175%
12	3.175%	3.174%	3.175%	3.174%	3.175%	3.174%	3.175%	3.174%	3.175%	3.174%	3.175%	3.174%
13	3.174%	3.175%	3.174%	3.175%	3.174%	3.175%	3.174%	3.175%	3.174%	3.175%	3.174%	3.175%
14	3.175%	3.174%	3.175%	3.174%	3.175%	3.174%	3.175%	3.174%	3.175%	3.174%	3.175%	3.174%
15	3.174%	3.175%	3.174%	3.175%	3.174%	3.175%	3.174%	3.175%	3.174%	3.175%	3.174%	3.175%
16	3.175%	3.174%	3.175%	3.174%	3.175%	3.174%	3.175%	3.174%	3.175%	3.174%	3.175%	3.174%
17	3.174%	3.175%	3.174%	3.175%	3.174%	3.175%	3.174%	3.175%	3.174%	3.175%	3.174%	3.175%
18	3.175%	3.174%	3.175%	3.174%	3.175%	3.174%	3.175%	3.174%	3.175%	3.174%	3.175%	3.174%
19	3.174%	3.175%	3.174%	3.175%	3.174%	3.175%	3.174%	3.175%	3.174%	3.175%	3.174%	3.175%
20	3.175%	3.174%	3.175%	3.174%	3.175%	3.174%	3.175%	3.174%	3.175%	3.174%	3.175%	3.174%
21	3.174%	3.175%	3.174%	3.175%	3.174%	3.175%	3.174%	3.175%	3.174%	3.175%	3.174%	3.175%
22	3.175%	3.174%	3.175%	3.174%	3.175%	3.174%	3.175%	3.174%	3.175%	3.174%	3.175%	3.174%
23	3.174%	3.175%	3.174%	3.175%	3.174%	3.175%	3.174%	3.175%	3.174%	3.175%	3.174%	3.175%
24	3.175%	3.174%	3.175%	3.174%	3.175%	3.174%	3.175%	3.174%	3.175%	3.174%	3.175%	3.174%
25	3.174%	3.175%	3.174%	3.175%	3.174%	3.175%	3.174%	3.175%	3.174%	3.175%	3.174%	3.175%
26	3.175%	3.174%	3.175%	3.174%	3.175%	3.174%	3.175%	3.174%	3.175%	3.174%	3.175%	3.174%
27	3.174%	3.175%	3.174%	3.175%	3.174%	3.175%	3.174%	3.175%	3.174%	3.175%	3.174%	3.175%
28	3.175%	3.174%	3.175%	3.174%	3.175%	3.174%	3.175%	3.174%	3.175%	3.174%	3.175%	3.174%
29	3.174%	3.175%	3.174%	3.175%	3.174%	3.175%	3.174%	3.175%	3.174%	3.175%	3.174%	3.175%
30	3.175%	3.174%	3.175%	3.174%	3.175%	3.174%	3.175%	3.174%	3.175%	3.174%	3.175%	3.174%
31	3.174%	3.175%	3.174%	3.175%	3.174%	3.175%	3.174%	3.175%	3.174%	3.175%	3.174%	3.175%
32	1.720%	1.984%	2.249%	2.513%	2.778%	3.042%	3.175%	3.174%	3.175%	3.174%	3.175%	3.174%
33							0.132%	0.397%	0.661%	0.926%	1.190%	1.455%

Example: Edward has a business and has been depreciating a desk he placed in service on March 13, 2012. We can look up the recovery period and find that the desk is 7 year property. Using Table A, we look in the column for 7 year property. On the side, we find the number 3 because this is the 3rd year the property is being depreciated, with 2012 being the 1st, and 2013 being the 2nd. The percentage we will use to calculate the depreciation is 17.49%.

The Third Step

The third step is the actual calculation of the depreciation. Let's do this while we are filling out a depreciation worksheet (Illustration 13-4). Let's start with something fairly easy. How about a desk chair purchased on April 2, 2014 for $125? The first thing we'll do is enter the description of the property, the date placed in service, and the basis (Illustration 13-5).

Next, we will enter the business use. The desk chair is used in the office; therefore it is used 100% for business. We are going to ignore the Section 179 column until the next chapter.

The next column is basis for depreciation. Because we are using the property 100% and have no Section 179 deduction or Special allowance, the basis for depreciation is the same as the cost. The method for depreciation is 200%DB because it is personal property and the convention is half-year.

Now, we will look for the recovery period for the desk chair. It is listed under the asset class of office furniture, and the recovery period for that class is 7 years.

Finally, we will find the Rate % and calculate the depreciation. Table A is for 7 year property depreciation using the half-year convention. The percentage for the 1st year under 7 year property is 14.29%. Now, we multiply the basis for depreciation by the percentage, and end up with the depreciation deduction. ($125 x 14.29% = $18). The Depreciation for prior years will be 0 because she just placed it in service this year.

Note: Property can never be depreciated for an amount over its depreciable basis. Because of the rounding, there may be a case in which the last year of depreciation causes the total depreciation to be over the basis. In this case an adjustment should be made to the last year's depreciation deduction.

Prior Depreciation

If the taxpayer has depreciable property that was not placed in service during the current tax year, they will have prior depreciation. As the note above states, property cannot be depreciated for an amount over its basis. In order to make sure that doesn't happen, we have to keep track of the prior depreciation. Sometimes it is easy because we have the prior year's return to go by, but many times the prior depreciation is not clearly stated on the taxpayer's prior return, or the taxpayer does not have their prior return. In this case, we will have to calculate the prior depreciation. Following is an example of depreciation and calculating the prior depreciation.

Illustration 13-4

Description of Property	Date Placed in Service	Cost or other Basis	Business/ Investment Use %	Business Basis (C x D)	Salvage/ Land Value	Section 179 Deduction or Bonus Depreciation	Depreciation Basis [E – (F + G)]	Method/ Convention	Recovery Period	Prior Depreciation	Depreciation Percentage	Depreciation Deduction (H x L)
A	B	C	D	E	F	G	H	I	J	K	L	M

Illustration 13-5

Description of Property	Date Placed in Service	Cost or other Basis	Business/ Investment Use %	Business Basis (C x D)	Salvage/ Land Value	Section 179 Deduction or Bonus Depreciation	Depreciation Basis [E – (F + G)]	Method/ Convention	Recovery Period	Prior Depreciation	Depreciation Percentage	Depreciation Deduction (H x L)
A	B	C	D	E	F	G	H	I	J	K	L	M
Desk Chair	04/02/14	$125	100%	$125			$125	200%DB HY	7 yrs		14.29%	$18

Example: Bob needs us to depreciate 4 different properties. His tax records were lost in a move from one house to another. All he can provide us with is the dates placed in service and the basis of the properties. Illustration 13-6 shows a depreciation worksheet.

Rental house – placed in service on June 6, 2008. He paid $56,000 for the entire property. The land was worth $10,000 when purchased.

Copy machine – placed in service on May 5, 2012. He purchased it for $363.

Computer – placed in service on October 16, 2011. He purchased it for $969.

Filing cabinet – placed in service on January 30, 2007. He purchased it for $313.

To calculate the prior depreciation, we have to figure out what the depreciation would have been for each year the property was eligible for depreciation.

	Year	Percentage	Depreciation
Rental house:	2008	1.970%	$ 906
	2009	3.636%	1,673
	2010	3.636%	1,673
	2011	3.636%	1,673
	2012	3.636%	1,673
	2013	3.636%	1,673
Copy machine	2012	20%	73
	2013	32%	116
Computer	2011	20%	194
	2012	32%	310
	2013	19.20%	186
Filing Cabinet	2007	14.29%	45
	2008	24.49%	77
	2009	17.49%	55
	2010	12.49%	39
	2011	8.93%	28
	2012	8.92%	28
	2013	8.93%	28

Notice that this is the last year the filing cabinet is going to be depreciated. The prior depreciation for it is $300. 2014's depreciation would be $13.95 which would be rounded up to $14. However, the basis of the filing cabinet is $313 and the total depreciation would total $314 (300 prior depreciation + 14 for this year's depreciation). Therefore an adjustment would be made for this year's depreciation and he would claim $13.

Illustration 13-6

Description of Property	Date Placed in Service	Cost or other Basis	Business/Investment Use %	Business Basis (C x D)	Salvage/Land Value	Section 179 Deduction or Bonus Depreciation	Depreciation Basis [E - (F + G)]	Method/Convention	Recovery Period	Prior Depreciation	Depreciation Percentage	Depreciation Deduction (H x L)
A	B	C	D	E	F	G	H	I	J	K	L	M
Rental House	06/06/08	$56,000	100%	$56,000	$10,000		$46,000	SL MM	27.5 yrs	$9,271	3.636%	$1,673
Copy Machine	05/05/12	363	100%	363			363	200%DB HY	5 yrs	189	19.20%	70
Computer	10/16/11	969	100%	969			969	200%DB HY	5 yrs	690	11.52%	112
Filing Cabinet	01/30/07	313	100%	313			313	200%DB HY	7 yrs	300	4.46%	13

Chapter Review

1) Is a filing cabinet personal property or real property?

2) Is an office building personal or real property?

3) Define tangible property.

4) What is the recovery period for a computer?

5) What is the recovery period for a taxi cab?

6) What is the recovery period for safe?

7) What is the recovery period for an office building?

8) Which table should be used to depreciate the computer if using the HY convention?

9) Which table should be used to depreciate the safe if the safe was purchased in February and the convention is MQ?

10) Which table should be used for the office building if it was purchased in January of 2004?

11) What is the percentage of depreciation for the office building in the previous question?

Exercise

Find this year's depreciation deduction for the following properties. Use the HY convention for personal property unless specifically stated otherwise. Also determine the prior year depreciation.

Rental house: Purchased for $27,500 ($10,000 for the land); placed in service in October of 2005.

Computer: Purchased for $1,309; placed in service on July 5, 2012.

Copy machine: Purchased for $599; placed in service on August 7, 2014.

Heavy General Purpose Truck: Purchased for $17,289; placed in service on March 19, 2013.

Sofa purchased for $921 for use in the rental house; placed in service on June 23, 2010.

Refrigerator purchased for $1,126 for use in the rental house; placed in service February 3, 2013.

Chapter 14 – Depreciation, Part II

We have learned how to calculate depreciation. In this chapter we will learn the different types of activities that may require the use of depreciation, the Section 179 deduction, and listed property. We will also learn the effects of depreciation on the sale of depreciable property.

Form 4562

A Form 4562 (Illustration 14-1) must be filed if any of the following are being claimed by the taxpayer:

- A section 179 deduction for the current year or a section 179 carryover from a prior year.
- Depreciation for property placed in service during the current year.
- Depreciation on any vehicle or other listed property, regardless of when it was placed in service.
- A deduction for any vehicle if the deduction is reported on a form other than Schedule C or Schedule C-EZ.
- Amortization of costs if the current year is the first year of the amortization period.
- Depreciation or amortization on any asset on a corporate income tax return (other than Form 1120S, U.S. Income Tax Return for an S Corporation) regardless of when it was placed in service.

If the taxpayer has more than one activity in which a Form 4562 is required, a separate Form 4562 must be used for each activity.

Part I – Election to Expense Certain Property Under Section 179

The taxpayer can elect to recover all or part of the cost of certain qualifying property, up to a limit, by deducting it in the year they place the property in service. This is the election to take a section 179 deduction. To qualify for the deduction the property must meet the following requirements:

- It must be eligible property,
- It must be acquired for business use,
- It must have been acquired by purchase, and
- It must not be property that does not qualify (defined later).

Illustration 14-1

Form **4562**

Department of the Treasury
Internal Revenue Service   (99)

Depreciation and Amortization
(Including Information on Listed Property)
▶ Attach to your tax return.
▶ Information about Form 4562 and its separate instructions is at *www.irs.gov/form4562.*

OMB No. 1545-0172

20**14**

Attachment
Sequence No. **179**

Name(s) shown on return	Business or activity to which this form relates	Identifying number

Part I   **Election To Expense Certain Property Under Section 179**
Note: *If you have any listed property, complete Part V before you complete Part I.*

1	Maximum amount (see instructions)	**1**
2	Total cost of section 179 property placed in service (see instructions)	**2**
3	Threshold cost of section 179 property before reduction in limitation (see instructions)	**3**
4	Reduction in limitation. Subtract line 3 from line 2. If zero or less, enter -0-	**4**
5	Dollar limitation for tax year. Subtract line 4 from line 1. If zero or less, enter -0-. If married filing separately, see instructions	**5**

6	(a) Description of property	(b) Cost (business use only)	(c) Elected cost

7	Listed property. Enter the amount from line 29	**7**	
8	Total elected cost of section 179 property. Add amounts in column (c), lines 6 and 7	**8**
9	Tentative deduction. Enter the **smaller** of line 5 or line 8	**9**
10	Carryover of disallowed deduction from line 13 of your 2013 Form 4562	**10**
11	Business income limitation. Enter the smaller of business income (not less than zero) or line 5 (see instructions)	**11**
12	Section 179 expense deduction. Add lines 9 and 10, but do not enter more than line 11	**12**
13	Carryover of disallowed deduction to 2015. Add lines 9 and 10, less line 12 ▶	**13**	

Note: *Do not use Part II or Part III below for listed property. Instead, use Part V.*

Part II   **Special Depreciation Allowance and Other Depreciation (Do not** include listed property.) (See instructions.)

14	Special depreciation allowance for qualified property (other than listed property) placed in service during the tax year (see instructions)	**14**
15	Property subject to section 168(f)(1) election	**15**
16	Other depreciation (including ACRS)	**16**

Part III   **MACRS Depreciation (Do not** include listed property.) (See instructions.)

Section A

17	MACRS deductions for assets placed in service in tax years beginning before 2014	**17**
18	If you are electing to group any assets placed in service during the tax year into one or more general asset accounts, check here . . . . ▶ ☐	

Section B—Assets Placed in Service During 2014 Tax Year Using the General Depreciation System

(a) Classification of property	(b) Month and year placed in service	(c) Basis for depreciation (business/investment use only—see instructions)	(d) Recovery period	(e) Convention	(f) Method	(g) Depreciation deduction
19a 3-year property						
b 5-year property						
c 7-year property						
d 10-year property						
e 15-year property						
f 20-year property						
g 25-year property			25 yrs.		S/L	
h Residential rental property			27.5 yrs.	MM	S/L	
			27.5 yrs.	MM	S/L	
i Nonresidential real property			39 yrs.	MM	S/L	
				MM	S/L	

Section C—Assets Placed in Service During 2014 Tax Year Using the Alternative Depreciation System

20a Class life					S/L	
b 12-year			12 yrs.		S/L	
c 40-year			40 yrs.	MM	S/L	

Part IV   **Summary** (See instructions.)

21	Listed property. Enter amount from line 28	**21**
22	**Total.** Add amounts from line 12, lines 14 through 17, lines 19 and 20 in column (g), and line 21. Enter here and on the appropriate lines of your return. Partnerships and S corporations—see instructions .	**22**
23	For assets shown above and placed in service during the current year, enter the portion of the basis attributable to section 263A costs	**23**	

For Paperwork Reduction Act Notice, see separate instructions.   Cat. No. 12906N   Form **4562** (2014)

Illustration 14-1 continued

Part V	Listed Property (Include automobiles, certain other vehicles, certain aircraft, certain computers, and property used for entertainment, recreation, or amusement.)

Note: *For any vehicle for which you are using the standard mileage rate or deducting lease expense, complete **only** 24a, 24b, columns (a) through (c) of Section A, all of Section B, and Section C if applicable.*

Section A—Depreciation and Other Information (Caution: *See the instructions for limits for passenger automobiles.*)

24a Do you have evidence to support the business/investment use claimed? ☐ Yes ☐ No **24b** If "Yes," is the evidence written? ☐ Yes ☐ No

(a) Type of property (list vehicles first)	(b) Date placed in service	(c) Business/ investment use percentage	(d) Cost or other basis	(e) Basis for depreciation (business/investment use only)	(f) Recovery period	(g) Method/ Convention	(h) Depreciation deduction	(i) Elected section 179 cost
25 Special depreciation allowance for qualified listed property placed in service during the tax year and used more than 50% in a qualified business use (see instructions) . **25**								
26 Property used more than 50% in a qualified business use:								
		%						
		%						
		%						
27 Property used 50% or less in a qualified business use:								
		%					S/L –	
		%					S/L –	
		%					S/L –	
28 Add amounts in column (h), lines 25 through 27. Enter here and on line 21, page 1 . **28**								
29 Add amounts in column (i), line 26. Enter here and on line 7, page 1 . . . . **29**								

Section B—Information on Use of Vehicles

Complete this section for vehicles used by a sole proprietor, partner, or other "more than 5% owner," or related person. If you provided vehicles to your employees, first answer the questions in Section C to see if you meet an exception to completing this section for those vehicles.

		(a) Vehicle 1		(b) Vehicle 2		(c) Vehicle 3		(d) Vehicle 4		(e) Vehicle 5		(f) Vehicle 6	
30	Total business/investment miles driven during the year (**do not** include commuting miles) .												
31	Total commuting miles driven during the year												
32	Total other personal (noncommuting) miles driven												
33	Total miles driven during the year. Add lines 30 through 32												
34	Was the vehicle available for personal use during off-duty hours?	Yes	No	Yes	No	Yes	No	Yes	No	Yes	No	Yes	No
35	Was the vehicle used primarily by a more than 5% owner or related person? . .												
36	Is another vehicle available for personal use?												

Section C—Questions for Employers Who Provide Vehicles for Use by Their Employees

Answer these questions to determine if you meet an exception to completing Section B for vehicles used by employees who **are not** more than 5% owners or related persons (see instructions).

		Yes	No
37	Do you maintain a written policy statement that prohibits all personal use of vehicles, including commuting, by your employees?		
38	Do you maintain a written policy statement that prohibits personal use of vehicles, except commuting, by your employees? See the instructions for vehicles used by corporate officers, directors, or 1% or more owners . .		
39	Do you treat all use of vehicles by employees as personal use?		
40	Do you provide more than five vehicles to your employees, obtain information from your employees about the use of the vehicles, and retain the information received?		
41	Do you meet the requirements concerning qualified automobile demonstration use? (See instructions.) . . .		

Note: *If your answer to 37, 38, 39, 40, or 41 is "Yes," do not complete Section B for the covered vehicles.*

Part VI	Amortization

(a) Description of costs	(b) Date amortization begins	(c) Amortizable amount	(d) Code section	(e) Amortization period or percentage	(f) Amortization for this year
42 Amortization of costs that begins during your 2014 tax year (see instructions):					
43 Amortization of costs that began before your 2014 tax year **43**					
44 **Total.** Add amounts in column (f). See the instructions for where to report **44**					

Form **4562** (2014)

Eligible Property

To be eligible property it must be one of the following types of property:

- Tangible personal property.
- Other tangible property (except buildings and their structural components) used as:
  - An integral part of manufacturing, production, or extraction or of furnishing transportation, communications, electricity, gas, water, or sewage disposal services,
  - A research facility used in connection with any of the activities in the above point, or
  - A facility used in connection with any of the same activities for the bulk storage of fungible commodities.
- Single purpose agricultural (livestock) or horticultural structures.
- Storage facilities (except buildings and their structural components) used in connection with distributing petroleum or any primary product of petroleum.
- Off-the-shelf computer software.
- Qualified real property.

Qualified real property: The following real property qualifies for the Section 179 deduction.

- Qualified leasehold improvement property,
- Qualified restaurant property, or
- Qualified retail improvement property.

Property Acquired for Business Use

To be eligible for the section 179 deduction, the property must have been purchased for business use. If the property was acquired only for the production of income, such as rental property or investment property, it does not qualify for the section 179 deduction.

Property Acquired by Purchase

The property must have been purchased by the person seeking the deduction to be eligible for the section 179 deduction. The property does not qualify if it was acquired by inheritance or gift.

Property That does not Qualify

If the property meets the previous requirements and is not listed in this section, it qualifies for the section 179 deduction. Property listed in this section does not qualify for the section 179 deduction:

- Certain leased property (see Pub. 946 for more information).
- Certain property used predominantly to furnish lodging or in connection with the furnishing of lodging (see Pub. 946 for more information).
- Air conditioning or heating units.
- Property used predominantly outside the United States.
- Property used by certain tax-exempt organizations, except property used in connection with the production of income subject to the tax on unrelated trade or business income.
- Property used by governmental units or foreign persons or entities, except property used under a lease with a term of less than 6 months.

Section 179 Limitations

General Limit

The section 179 deduction for most property is limited to $500,000. This is the most section 179 deduction that a taxpayer is allowed to use on their return. If the taxpayer has more than one property they would like to elect the section 179 deduction for, they may allocate the deduction to each property. The taxpayer does not have to claim a section 179 deduction for the entire cost of the property; they may only take the deduction for a portion of it and depreciate the remainder.

Cost of Property Exceeding $2,000,000.

If the cost of most qualifying section 179 deduction property placed into service during the tax year is more than $2,000,000, the general limit will be reduced. This includes the property that would be eligible for the section 179 deduction whether the election is made for that particular property or not. Once the cost of the property exceeds $2,000,000, the $500,000 limitation is reduced dollar for dollar of the excess. For example, if the taxpayer placed $2,075,000 worth of qualifying section 179 deduction properties into service during the tax year, the limit would be $425,000. If the cost of the qualifying property reaches or exceeds $2,500,000 a section 179 deduction is not allowed.

Note: Qualified real property that the taxpayer elects to treat as Section 179 real property is limited to $250,000 of the maximum deduction of $500,000 for 2014.

Business Income Limit

The section 179 deduction is further limited to the amount of taxable income from the active conduct of any trade or business by the taxpayer. For this purpose, taxable income is the total net income and losses from all trades and businesses, including the interest from working capital of the taxpayer's trade or business and wages, salaries, tips, or other pay earned as an employee. When figuring the taxable income, do not take into account any section 179 deduction.

Electing the Section 179 Deduction

To make the election to claim a section 179 deduction, the taxpayer must complete part I of Form 4562.

Example: Jonah Jacobs has total taxable income of $75,000. He placed a small trailer into service this year. He purchased the trailer in June for $2,500 and a desk in March for $350. He would like to take a section 179 deduction for the trailer but he would like to depreciate the desk. See Illustration 14-2.

Illustration 14-2

Form 4562

Department of the Treasury
Internal Revenue Service (99)

Depreciation and Amortization
(Including Information on Listed Property)
▶ Attach to your tax return.
▶ Information about Form 4562 and its separate instructions is at *www.irs.gov/form4562*.

OMB No. 1545-0172

2014

Attachment
Sequence No. **179**

Name(s) shown on return	Business or activity to which this form relates	Identifying number
John Jacobs	Lawn Care	111-11-1111

Part I Election To Expense Certain Property Under Section 179
Note: *If you have any listed property, complete Part V before you complete Part I.*

1 Maximum amount (see instructions)	1	500,000
2 Total cost of section 179 property placed in service (see instructions)	2	2,850
3 Threshold cost of section 179 property before reduction in limitation (see instructions)	3	2,000,000
4 Reduction in limitation. Subtract line 3 from line 2. If zero or less, enter -0-	4	0
5 Dollar limitation for tax year. Subtract line 4 from line 1. If zero or less, enter -0-. If married filing separately, see instructions	5	500,000

6	(a) Description of property	(b) Cost (business use only)	(c) Elected cost	
	Trailer	2,500	2,500	

7 Listed property. Enter the amount from line 29 ... 7		
8 Total elected cost of section 179 property. Add amounts in column (c), lines 6 and 7	8	2,500
9 Tentative deduction. Enter the **smaller** of line 5 or line 8	9	2,500
10 Carryover of disallowed deduction from line 13 of your 2013 Form 4562	10	
11 Business income limitation. Enter the smaller of business income (not less than zero) or line 5 (see instructions)	11	75,000
12 Section 179 expense deduction. Add lines 9 and 10, but do not enter more than line 11	12	2,500
13 Carryover of disallowed deduction to 2015. Add lines 9 and 10, less line 12 ▶	13	

Note: *Do not use Part II or Part III below for listed property. Instead, use Part V.*

Part II Special Depreciation Allowance and Other Depreciation (Do not include listed property.) (See instructions.)

14 Special depreciation allowance for qualified property (other than listed property) placed in service during the tax year (see instructions)	14	
15 Property subject to section 168(f)(1) election	15	
16 Other depreciation (including ACRS)	16	

Part III MACRS Depreciation (Do not include listed property.) (See instructions.)

Section A

17 MACRS deductions for assets placed in service in tax years beginning before 2014	17	
18 If you are electing to group any assets placed in service during the tax year into one or more general asset accounts, check here ▶ ☐		

Section B—Assets Placed in Service During 2014 Tax Year Using the General Depreciation System

(a) Classification of property	(b) Month and year placed in service	(c) Basis for depreciation (business/investment use only—see instructions)	(d) Recovery period	(e) Convention	(f) Method	(g) Depreciation deduction
19a 3-year property						
b 5-year property						
c 7-year property		350	7 yrs	HY	200% DB	50
d 10-year property						
e 15-year property						
f 20-year property						
g 25-year property			25 yrs.		S/L	
h Residential rental property			27.5 yrs.	MM	S/L	
			27.5 yrs.	MM	S/L	
i Nonresidential real property			39 yrs.	MM	S/L	
				MM	S/L	

Section C—Assets Placed in Service During 2014 Tax Year Using the Alternative Depreciation System

20a Class life					S/L	
b 12-year			12 yrs.		S/L	
c 40-year			40 yrs.	MM	S/L	

Part IV Summary (See instructions.)

21 Listed property. Enter amount from line 28	21	
22 **Total.** Add amounts from line 12, lines 14 through 17, lines 19 and 20 in column (g), and line 21. Enter here and on the appropriate lines of your return. Partnerships and S corporations—see instructions	22	2,550
23 For assets shown above and placed in service during the current year, enter the portion of the basis attributable to section 263A costs ...	23	

For Paperwork Reduction Act Notice, see separate instructions.   Cat. No. 12906N   Form **4562** (2014)

14-6

Part II – Special Depreciation Allowance...

For tax year 2014, the taxpayer may receive an additional 50% special depreciation allowance. This allowance is taken after any Section 179 deduction and before the regular depreciation is calculated. The property that qualifies for the special depreciation allowance is:

- Qualified reuse and recycling property.
- Second generation biofuel plant property.
- Certain qualified property placed in service after December 31, 2007.

If you encounter either of the first two items, additional research will be required.

Certain Qualified Property Acquired After December 31, 2007

The taxpayer can take a special depreciation deduction allowance of 50%, if applicable, for property that meets the following requirements:

- It is one of the following types of property:
  - Tangible property depreciated under MACRS with a recovery period of 20 years or less.
  - Water utility property
  - Computer software that is readily available for purchase by the general public, is subject to a nonexclusive license, and has not been substantially modified. (The cost of some computer software is treated as part of the cost of hardware and is depreciated under MACRS.)
  - Qualified leasehold improvement property
- The property must have been acquired by purchase after December 31, 2007, with no binding written contract for the acquisition of in effect before January 1, 2008.
- The original use of the property must begin with the taxpayer after December 31, 2007.
- The property must be placed in service for use in the trade or business or for the production of income before January 1, 2015.
- It is not excepted property.

Qualified property does not include any of the following (excepted property):

- Property placed in service and disposed of in the same tax year.
- Property converted from business use to personal use in the same tax year acquired. Property converted from personal use to business use in the same or later tax year may be qualified property.
- Property required to be depreciated under the Alternative Depreciation System. This includes listed property used 50% or less in a qualified business (explained later in the chapter).
- Qualified restaurant property.
- Qualified retail improvement property.
- Property for which the taxpayer elected not to claim any special depreciation allowance.

Electing Not to Claim an Allowance

The taxpayer can elect, for any classes of property, not to deduct any special allowances for all property in such class placed in service during the tax year. To make that election, attach a statement to the return indicating what election the taxpayer is making, and the class of property for which they are making the election.

Example: Bobby Schultz (122-45-9832) operates his own business as an insurance agent, with net business income of $63,251. On February 2, 2014, he bought and placed in service a new desk. He purchased the desk for $1,819 and He wants to take the special depreciation allowance. See Illustration 14-3.

Note: If the taxpayer took the special depreciation deduction allowance last year, remember to adjust the depreciable basis accordingly. Filling out the depreciation worksheet will help you remember.

The next item that appears in part II is property that is subject to section 168(f)(1) election. This is property that the taxpayer elects to depreciate under the unit-of-production method. This is beyond the scope of this course and will require additional research if encountered.

The last item in this section is any other depreciation. This line is for property that is not eligible for MACRS. If this is encountered, additional research will be required.

Illustration 14-3

Form **4562**

Department of the Treasury
Internal Revenue Service (99)

Depreciation and Amortization
(Including Information on Listed Property)
▶ Attach to your tax return.
▶ Information about Form 4562 and its separate instructions is at *www.irs.gov/form4562*.

OMB No. 1545-0172

2014

Attachment
Sequence No. **179**

Name(s) shown on return	Business or activity to which this form relates	Identifying number
Bobby Schultz	Insurance Agent	122-45-9832

Part I Election To Expense Certain Property Under Section 179
Note: *If you have any listed property, complete Part V before you complete Part I.*

1	Maximum amount (see instructions)	**1**	
2	Total cost of section 179 property placed in service (see instructions)	**2**	
3	Threshold cost of section 179 property before reduction in limitation (see instructions)	**3**	
4	Reduction in limitation. Subtract line 3 from line 2. If zero or less, enter -0-	**4**	
5	Dollar limitation for tax year. Subtract line 4 from line 1. If zero or less, enter -0-. If married filing separately, see instructions	**5**	

6	(a) Description of property	(b) Cost (business use only)	(c) Elected cost

7	Listed property. Enter the amount from line 29	**7**	
8	Total elected cost of section 179 property. Add amounts in column (c), lines 6 and 7	**8**	
9	Tentative deduction. Enter the **smaller** of line 5 or line 8	**9**	
10	Carryover of disallowed deduction from line 13 of your 2013 Form 4562	**10**	
11	Business income limitation. Enter the smaller of business income (not less than zero) or line 5 (see instructions)	**11**	
12	Section 179 expense deduction. Add lines 9 and 10, but do not enter more than line 11	**12**	
13	Carryover of disallowed deduction to 2015. Add lines 9 and 10, less line 12 ▶	**13**	

Note: *Do not use Part II or Part III below for listed property. Instead, use Part V.*

Part II Special Depreciation Allowance and Other Depreciation (Do not include listed property.) (See instructions.)

14	Special depreciation allowance for qualified property (other than listed property) placed in service during the tax year (see instructions)	**14**	910
15	Property subject to section 168(f)(1) election	**15**	
16	Other depreciation (including ACRS)	**16**	

Part III MACRS Depreciation (Do not include listed property.) (See instructions.)
Section A

17	MACRS deductions for assets placed in service in tax years beginning before 2014	**17**	
18	If you are electing to group any assets placed in service during the tax year into one or more general asset accounts, check here . . . . ▶ ☐		

Section B—Assets Placed in Service During 2014 Tax Year Using the General Depreciation System

(a) Classification of property	(b) Month and year placed in service	(c) Basis for depreciation (business/investment use only—see instructions)	(d) Recovery period	(e) Convention	(f) Method	(g) Depreciation deduction
19a 3-year property						
b 5-year property						
c 7-year property		909	7 yrs	HY	200% DB	130
d 10-year property						
e 15-year property						
f 20-year property						
g 25-year property			25 yrs.		S/L	
h Residential rental property			27.5 yrs.	MM	S/L	
			27.5 yrs.	MM	S/L	
i Nonresidential real property			39 yrs.	MM	S/L	
				MM	S/L	

Section C—Assets Placed in Service During 2014 Tax Year Using the Alternative Depreciation System

20a Class life					S/L	
b 12-year			12 yrs.		S/L	
c 40-year			40 yrs.	MM	S/L	

Part IV Summary (See instructions.)

21	Listed property. Enter amount from line 28	**21**	
22	**Total.** Add amounts from line 12, lines 14 through 17, lines 19 and 20 in column (g), and line 21. Enter here and on the appropriate lines of your return. Partnerships and S corporations—see instructions .	**22**	1,040
23	For assets shown above and placed in service during the current year, enter the portion of the basis attributable to section 263A costs	**23**		

For Paperwork Reduction Act Notice, see separate instructions.   Cat. No. 12906N   Form **4562** (2014)

Illustration 14-3

Description of Property	Date Placed in Service	Cost or other Basis	Business/ Investment Use %	Business Basis (C x D)	Salvage/ Land Value	Section 179 Deduction or Bonus Depreciation	Depreciation Basis [E – (F + G)]	Method/ Convention	Recovery Period	Prior Depreciation	Depreciation Percentage	Depreciation Deduction (H x L)
A	B	C	D	E	F	G	H	I	J	K	L	M
Desk	02/02/14	$1,819	100%	$1,819		$910	$909	200%DB HY	7 yrs		14.29%	130

Part III – MACRS Depreciation

Remember, if all the taxpayer has is property that was placed into service in a prior year, and they are still depreciating it, a Form 4562 is not required. However, if the taxpayer placed depreciable property in service during the current tax year, a Form 4562 is required. In this case, the current year depreciation deduction for all of the property placed into service in a prior year is entered on line 17. Then, the depreciation for any property that was placed in service during the current tax year will be entered on line 19, beside the correct classification listed in column b. If there is more than one property for a classification that was placed in service during the current tax year, they will be added together and entered on the correct line.

Example: John Jacobs (from a previous example) has a desk he has been depreciating for 2 years and the depreciation deduction on it this year is $87. He also placed another desk in service in March that he purchased for $350. He does not want to take the special depreciation allowance. See Illustration 14-4 for the completed Form 4562 including the section 179 deduction from the previous example.

Part V – Listed Property

Listed property is property that is subject to additional limits on depreciation. Listed property is any of the following:

- Passenger automobiles weighing 6,000 pounds or less.
- Any other property used for transportation, unless it is an excepted vehicle.
- Property generally used for entertainment, recreation, or amusement (including photographic, communication, and video-recording equipment).
- Computers and related peripheral equipment, unless used only at a regular business establishment and owned or leased by the person operating the establishment. A regular business establishment includes a portion of a dwelling unit that is used both regularly and exclusively for business.

Deductions for these properties are subject to the following special rules and limits:

- Deductions for employees: If the taxpayer's use of the property is not for the employer's convenience, or is not required as a condition of their employment, the taxpayer cannot deduct depreciation or rent expenses for the use of the property as an employee.
- Business use requirement: If the property is not used predominantly (more than 50%) for qualified business use, the taxpayer cannot claim the section 179 deduction or a special depreciation allowance. In addition, the taxpayer must figure the depreciation deduction under the Modified Accelerated Cost Recovery System (MACRS) using the straight line method over the ADS recovery period. The taxpayer may also have to recapture any excess depreciation claimed in previous years.

Illustration 14-4 continued

Form **4562**	**Depreciation and Amortization** **(Including Information on Listed Property)** ▶ Attach to your tax return. ▶ **Information about Form 4562 and its separate instructions is at** *www.irs.gov/form4562.*	OMB No. 1545-0172 20**14** Attachment Sequence No. **179**
Department of the Treasury Internal Revenue Service (99)		

Name(s) shown on return	Business or activity to which this form relates	Identifying number
John Jacobs	Lawn Care	111-11-1111

Part I   Election To Expense Certain Property Under Section 179
Note: *If you have any listed property, complete Part V before you complete Part I.*

1	Maximum amount (see instructions)	**1** 500,000
2	Total cost of section 179 property placed in service (see instructions)	**2** 2,850
3	Threshold cost of section 179 property before reduction in limitation (see instructions)	**3** 2,000,000
4	Reduction in limitation. Subtract line 3 from line 2. If zero or less, enter -0-	**4** 0
5	Dollar limitation for tax year. Subtract line 4 from line 1. If zero or less, enter -0-. If married filing separately, see instructions	**5** 500,000

6	(a) Description of property	(b) Cost (business use only)	(c) Elected cost	
	Trailer	2,500	2,500	

7	Listed property. Enter the amount from line 29 . . . . **7**	
8	Total elected cost of section 179 property. Add amounts in column (c), lines 6 and 7	**8** 2,500
9	Tentative deduction. Enter the **smaller** of line 5 or line 8	**9** 2,500
10	Carryover of disallowed deduction from line 13 of your 2013 Form 4562	**10**
11	Business income limitation. Enter the smaller of business income (not less than zero) or line 5 (see instructions)	**11** 75,000
12	Section 179 expense deduction. Add lines 9 and 10, but do not enter more than line 11	**12** 2,500
13	Carryover of disallowed deduction to 2015. Add lines 9 and 10, less line 12 ▶	**13**

Note: *Do not use Part II or Part III below for listed property. Instead, use Part V.*

Part II   Special Depreciation Allowance and Other Depreciation (Do not include listed property.) (See instructions.)

14	Special depreciation allowance for qualified property (other than listed property) placed in service during the tax year (see instructions)	**14**
15	Property subject to section 168(f)(1) election	**15**
16	Other depreciation (including ACRS)	**16**

Part III   MACRS Depreciation (Do not include listed property.) (See instructions.)

Section A

17	MACRS deductions for assets placed in service in tax years beginning before 2014	**17** 87
18	If you are electing to group any assets placed in service during the tax year into one or more general asset accounts, check here ▶ ☐	

Section B—Assets Placed in Service During 2014 Tax Year Using the General Depreciation System

(a) Classification of property	(b) Month and year placed in service	(c) Basis for depreciation (business/investment use only—see instructions)	(d) Recovery period	(e) Convention	(f) Method	(g) Depreciation deduction
19a 3-year property						
b 5-year property						
c 7-year property		350	7 yrs	HY	200% DB	50
d 10-year property						
e 15-year property						
f 20-year property						
g 25-year property			25 yrs.		S/L	
h Residential rental property			27.5 yrs.	MM	S/L	
			27.5 yrs.	MM	S/L	
i Nonresidential real property			39 yrs.	MM	S/L	
				MM	S/L	

Section C—Assets Placed in Service During 2014 Tax Year Using the Alternative Depreciation System

20a Class life					S/L	
b 12-year			12 yrs.		S/L	
c 40-year			40 yrs.	MM	S/L	

Part IV   Summary (See instructions.)

21	Listed property. Enter amount from line 28	**21**
22	**Total.** Add amounts from line 12, lines 14 through 17, lines 19 and 20 in column (g), and line 21. Enter here and on the appropriate lines of your return. Partnerships and S corporations—see instructions .	**22** 2,637
23	For assets shown above and placed in service during the current year, enter the portion of the basis attributable to section 263A costs **23**	

For Paperwork Reduction Act Notice, see separate instructions.   Cat. No. 12906N   Form **4562** (2014)

- Passenger automobile limits and rules: Annual limits apply to depreciation deductions (including section 179 deductions) for certain passenger automobiles. The taxpayer can continue to deduct depreciation for the unrecovered basis resulting from these limits after the end of the recovery period.

In summary, if the taxpayer is depreciating listed property and the business use of the property is 50% or less, no section 179 deduction is allowed and the property must be depreciated using MACRS alternative depreciation system. Any listed property that is depreciated must be reported on Form 4562, part V (Illustration 14-1).

Chapter 1 Revisited

As promised, now that we have covered depreciation, we will revisit how it will apply to unreimbursed employee expenses.

First, let's discuss the actual auto expense. Included in the deductible auto expenses under this method, will be depreciation, if the car belongs to the taxpayer. The taxpayer cannot deduct depreciation if they are deducting transportation expenses using the standard mileage rate. To take a depreciation deduction, the taxpayer must first calculate what percent of use of the vehicle was for business. The depreciation is then calculated but is subject to further limitations (Illustration 14-5). These limits are first multiplied by the percent of business use of the vehicle, then applied to the depreciation deduction.

Now, we'll discuss the business use of home. If the home is owned by the taxpayer (the taxpayer is considered to own it even if it's subject to a mortgage) it is eligible for depreciation. If the home office is eligible for depreciation but a deduction for depreciation is not taken, when sold the taxpayer will be required to recapture the depreciation whether it was deducted or not, unless the taxpayer used the Simplified Method.

Sale of Depreciable Property

This subject will be briefly discussed in the section, but if it is encountered, additional research will be required. When depreciable property is sold, the depreciation *allowed or allowable* must be recaptured. The seller will generally have to pay taxes on that depreciation Even if the taxpayer does not take the depreciation deduction. The depreciation the property was eligible for will have to be recaptured whether or not the taxpayer took the deduction.

Illustration 14-5

Maximum Depreciation Deduction
for Passenger Automobiles

Date Placed In Service	1st Year	2nd Year	3rd Year	4th & Later Years
2014	$11,160[1]	$5,100	$3,050	$1,875
2013	11,160[1]	5,100	3,050	1,875
2012	11,160[1]	5,100	3,050	1,875
2011	11,060[2]	4,900	2,950	1,775
2010	11,060[2]	4,900	2,950	1,775
2009	10,960[3]	4,800	2,850	1,775
2008	10,960[3]	4,800	2,850	1,775
2007	3,060	4,900	2,850	1,775
2006	2,960	4,800	2,850	1,775
2005	2,960	4,700	2,850	1,675
2004	10,610[4]	4,800	2,850	1,675

[1]If you elected **not** to claim any special depreciation allowance or the vehicle is **not** qualified property, the maximum deduction is $3,160.

[2]If you elected **not** to claim any special depreciation allowance or the vehicle is **not** qualified property, the maximum deduction is $3,060.

[3]If you elected **not** to claim any special depreciation allowance for the vehicle or the vehicle is **not** qualified property, the maximum deduction is $2,960.

[4]If you elected **not** to claim any special depreciation allowance for the vehicle, the vehicle is **not** qualified property, or the vehicle is qualified Liberty Zone property, the maximum deduction is $2,960.

Illustration 14-5 continued

Maximum Depreciation Deduction
For Trucks and Vans

Date Placed In Service	1st Year	2nd Year	3rd Year	4th & Later Years
2014	$11,460[1]	$5,500	$3,500	$1,975
2013	11,360[2]	5,400	3,250	1,975
2012	11,360[2]	5,300	3,150	1,875
2011	11,260[3]	5,200	3,150	1,875
2010	11,160[4]	5,100	3,050	1,875
2009	11,060[5]	4,900	2,950	1,775
2008	11,160[6]	5,100	3,050	1,875
2007	3,260	5,200	3,050	1,875
2006	3,260	5,200	3,150	1,875
2005	3,260	5,200	3,150	1,875
2004	10,910[7]	5,300	3,150	1,875

[1] If you elected **not** to claim any special depreciation allowance or the vehicle is **not** qualified property, the maximum deduction is $3,460.

[2] If you elected **not** to claim any special depreciation allowance or the vehicle is **not** qualified property, the maximum deduction is $3,360.

[3] If you elected **not** to claim any special depreciation allowance or the vehicle is **not** qualified property, the maximum deduction is $3,260.

[4] If you elected **not** to claim any special depreciation allowance or the vehicle is **not** qualified property, the maximum deduction is $3,160.

[5] If you elect **not** to claim any special depreciation allowance for the vehicle or the vehicle is **not** qualified property, the maximum deduction is $3,060.

[6] If you elected **not** to claim any special depreciation allowance for the vehicle or the vehicle is **not** qualified property, the maximum deduction is $3,160.

[7] If you elected **not** to claim any special depreciation allowance for the vehicle, the vehicle is not qualified property, or the vehicle is qualified Liberty Zone property, the maximum deduction is $3,260.

Chapter Review

1) What is the section 179 general limitation?

2) What part of Form 4562 is needed to take the section 179 deduction?

3) What are the four requirements property must meet to qualify for the section 179 deduction?

4) Which property is eligible for section 179: tangible or intangible?

5) What part of the Form 4562 is needed to depreciate listed property?

Exercise

Calculate the depreciation deduction for John McClain (857-55-3344). He operates a farm. He has a tractor he purchased in 2011 for $23,998. He placed it in service on June 4, 2011. He has two dairy cows he purchased on January 23, 2012 for $822 each. He has 3 breeding goats he purchased on August 9, 2012 for $355 each. He purchased a new tractor this year for $38,997 on February 15th. Use a depreciation worksheet and don't forget to fill out Form 4562. He would like to take the special depreciation allowance deduction if he's eligible.

Reminder: All farm property is depreciated using 150%DB as shown in Chapter 13.

Chapter 15 – Self Employment Income

Self Employed Taxpayers

A taxpayer is self employed if they carry on a trade or business as a sole proprietor or an independent contractor. A sole proprietor is the sole owner of a business. An independent contractor is generally someone who has the right to control or to direct only the result of the work and not how it will be done.

A self employed taxpayer must file a tax return if net earnings from self employment are $400 or more. Schedule C (Illustration 15-4) is used to report income and expenses and Schedule SE is also completed to pay self employment taxes on the income. The self employment tax consists of Medicare and Social Security tax.

There are many cases when the line between an employee and a self employed taxpayer is a bit blurry. To determine whether the taxpayer is an employee or is an independent contractor, many things must be considered. Generally, an employee will be told by the employer:

- When and where to do the work.
- What tools or equipment to use.
- What workers to hire or to assist with the work.
- Where to purchase supplies and services.
- What work must be performed by a specified individual.
- What order or sequence to follow.

Ultimately, as a tax preparer, the decision is already made when the taxpayer comes to us. If the taxpayer's income is reported on a Form W-2, they are considered an employee. If the taxpayer's income is reported on a Form 1099-MISC (Illustration 15-1) as nonemployee compensation (box 7), they are considered self employed. Also, if the taxpayer is paid cash for their work and it's not reported by the payer, they are still considered self employed and must file a tax return claiming their earnings. If the taxpayer believes they were an employee, but the employer reported their earnings on a Form 1099-MISC instead of a Form W-2, refer the taxpayer to IRS Pub. 1779 for more information.

There are many husband and wife teams that own and operate a business together. If one of them is the primary owner, they may file a Schedule C to report their income and expenses. If they own the business together and share in the profit or losses, they generally must file a partnership return. However, there are two exceptions to this rule. The first is for taxpayers that own and operate their business in a community property state. They may treat the business as a sole proprietorship or a partnership. The second exception is a "Qualified Joint Venture". If the taxpayer and spouse materially participate as the only owners of a jointly owned and operated business and they file a joint return, they may each divide the income and expenses in accordance with their respective interests. They will each file a separate Schedule C for their portion of the income and expenses.

If the taxpayer receives a Form W-2 that has the statutory box in box 13 of their Form W-2 marked, the income will be reported on line 7 of Form 1040, but they can use a Schedule C to report their expenses. The statutory box applies only to certain occupations, such as life insurance salespersons, certain agent or commission drivers, traveling salespersons, and certain home workers.

Filing Requirement for the Self Employed

If the taxpayer's net earnings from self employment were $400 or more, they are required to file a return. If the taxpayer's net earnings from self employment were less than $400 and they meet any of the other filing requirements from Chapter 2, they will still be required to file a tax return.

Schedule C

If the taxpayer has self employment income, a Schedule C will need to be filed. If the taxpayer owns more than one business, a separate Schedule C must be filed for each business.

Line A: The taxpayer's business or professional activity that provided the main source of income reported on the Schedule C is reported here. Enter the general field or activity and the type of product or service. If the taxpayer is in wholesale or retail trade or services connected with production services, also enter the type of customer or client the taxpayer targets.

Line B: The principal business or professional activity code is entered on this line. Illustration 15-2 is a sample of the table. The table in its entirety can be found in the appendix. Select the category that best describes the principal business and enter the six digit code. For example, someone whose principal business is Drywall installation will enter 238310 as their six digit code.

Line D: The taxpayer will need an employer ID number if they had a qualified retirement plan or were required to file an employment, excise, estate, trust, or alcohol, tobacco, and firearms tax return. If the taxpayer has an EIN it will be entered here. If the taxpayer does not, leave this line blank. Do not enter the SSN on this line.

Line E: Enter the address at which the business is located. If the business is located at the home address reported on the Form 1040, this line may be left blank.

Line F: The accounting method the taxpayer used in their business must be specified here.
> **Cash Method:** This is the most widely used method. The cash method of accounting requires the taxpayer to include income when it is actually or constructively received. The expenses are deducted when they are paid.
> **Accrual Method:** The accrual method requires the taxpayer to include income when it is earned and to deduct expenses when they are incurred. If the taxpayer has inventory, they must generally use the accrual method for the sales and purchases.
> **Hybrid Method:** The hybrid method is a combination of both accounting methods. It is especially used when the taxpayer has inventory and the taxpayer must use the accrual method of accounting for the inventory, but uses the cash method of accounting for everything else.

Line G: The question asks if the taxpayer materially participated in the business. If the taxpayer answers no and has a net loss from the business, it is deemed a passive loss and is subject to certain limits. The taxpayer materially participated in the business generally if they did any work regularly in connection with the business. If in doubt research material participation.

Line I: If the taxpayer pays anyone $600 or more for contract labor, a Form-MISC must be filed.

Part I – Income

Line 1: Enter the amount for gross income attributable to the business.
Note: If the taxpayer received merchant card payments (for example: Visa or Mastercard), or third party payments (for example: Paypal or Google Checkout), they should receive a Form 1099-K (Illustration 15-3).

Line 2: Returns and allowances are any cash and credit refunds, rebates, and other allowances given to the customer if they were included in line 1. If the amounts were not included in income, there is no need to report them. They are not deductible.

Line 4: Cost of Goods Sold
The taxpayer will only have an amount on this line if they keep inventory. Generally, a taxpayer will keep an inventory if they produce, purchase, or sell merchandise in the business. This amount will come from Schedule C, page 2, part III.

Line 35: On this line, enter the value of the inventory at the beginning of the tax year. If a Schedule C was filed for this business in the previous year, this amount should be the same as the ending inventory on last year's return. If the amount is different than the ending inventory from last year's return, a statement must be attached explaining why.

Line 36: If the taxpayer purchases items for sale, use the cost of what was purchased during the year. If the taxpayer manufactures or produces property for sale, the cost of raw materials or parts purchased to manufacture the finished product will be entered on this line.

Line 37: This is the cost of labor associated with the cost of goods sold. It only includes the labor cost allocable to the direct and indirect labor used in fabricating the raw material into a finished, saleable product. Generally, only manufacturing and mining businesses will have an amount to enter on this line.

Line 38: Only materials and supplies used in manufacturing goods are entered on this line.

Line 39: Other costs incurred in the manufacturing or mining process such as containers, freight, and overhead expenses directly related to the manufacturing of the product will be entered here.

Line 41: The value of the inventory at the close of the tax year is entered on this line.

Line 42: This is the cost of goods sold and is carried to Schedule C, page 1, line 4.

Line 6: This is where income from a source other than the regular operation of the business is located. This includes income such as interest on notes and accounts receivable, prizes and awards, and income from scrap sales.

Line 7: This is the gross income from the operation of the business.

Illustration 15-1

☐ CORRECTED (if checked)

PAYER'S name, street address, city or town, state or province, country, ZIP or foreign postal code, and telephone no.		**1** Rents $	OMB No. 1545-0115 **2014** Form **1099-MISC**	**Miscellaneous Income**
		2 Royalties $		
		3 Other income $	**4** Federal income tax withheld $	**Copy B For Recipient**
PAYER'S federal identification number	RECIPIENT'S identification number	**5** Fishing boat proceeds $	**6** Medical and health care payments $	
RECIPIENT'S name		**7** Nonemployee compensation $	**8** Substitute payments in lieu of dividends or interest $	This is important tax information and is being furnished to the Internal Revenue Service. If you are required to file a return, a negligence penalty or other sanction may be imposed on you if this income is taxable and the IRS determines that it has not been reported.
Street address (including apt. no.)		**9** Payer made direct sales of $5,000 or more of consumer products to a buyer (recipient) for resale ▶ ☐	**10** Crop insurance proceeds $	
City or town, state or province, country, and ZIP or foreign postal code		**11**	**12**	
Account number (see instructions)		**13** Excess golden parachute payments $	**14** Gross proceeds paid to an attorney $	
15a Section 409A deferrals $	**15b** Section 409A income $	**16** State tax withheld $ $	**17** State/Payer's state no.	**18** State income $ $

Form **1099-MISC**   (keep for your records)   www.irs.gov/form1099misc   Department of the Treasury - Internal Revenue Service

Illustration 15-2

561110	Office administrative services	**Specialty Trade Contractors**		621340	Offices of physical, occupational & speech therapists, & audiologists	325300	Pesticide, fertilizer, & other agricultural chemical mfg.
561420	Telephone call centers (including telephone answering services & telemarketing bureaus)	238310	Drywall & insulation contractors	621111	Offices of physicians (except mental health specialists)	325410	Pharmaceutical & medicine mfg.
		238210	Electrical contractors			325200	Resin, synthetic rubber, & artificial & synthetic fibers & filaments mfg.
561500	Travel arrangement & reservation services	238350	Finish carpentry contractors	621112	Offices of physicians, mental health specialists		
		238330	Flooring contractors				
561490	Other business support services (including repossession services, court reporting, & stenotype services)	238130	Framing carpentry contractors	621391	Offices of podiatrists	325600	Soap, cleaning compound, & toilet preparation mfg.
		238150	Glass & glazing contractors	621399	Offices of all other miscellaneous health practitioners	325900	Other chemical product & preparation mfg.
		238140	Masonry contractors				

Illustration15-3

☐ CORRECTED (if checked)

FILER'S name, street address, city or town, state or province, country, ZIP or foreign postal code, and telephone no.		FILER'S federal identification no.	OMB No. 1545-2205 **2014** Form **1099-K**	**Payment Card and Third Party Network Transactions**
		PAYEE'S taxpayer identification no.		
		1a Gross amount of payment card/third party network transactions $		
		1b Card Not Present transactions (optional) $	**2** Merchant category code	**Copy B For Payee**
Check to indicate if FILER is a (an): Payment settlement entity (PSE) ☐ Electronic Payment Facilitator (EPF)/Other third party ☐	Check to indicate transactions reported are: Payment card ☐ Third party network ☐	**3** Number of payment transactions	**4** Federal income tax withheld $	This is important tax information and is being furnished to the Internal Revenue Service. If you are required to file a return, a negligence penalty or other sanction may be imposed on you if taxable income results from this transaction and the IRS determines that it has not been reported.
PAYEE'S name		**5a** January $	**5b** February $	
Street address (including apt. no.)		**5c** March $	**5d** April $	
		5e May $	**5f** June $	
City or town, state or province, country, and ZIP or foreign postal code		**5g** July $	**5h** August $	
		5i September $	**5j** October $	
PSE'S name and telephone number		**5k** November $	**5l** December $	
Account number (see instructions)		**6** State	**7** State identification no.	**8** State income tax withheld $ $

Form **1099-K**   (Keep for your records)   www.irs.gov/form1099k   Department of the Treasury - Internal Revenue Service

Illustration 15-4

SCHEDULE C (Form 1040) Department of the Treasury Internal Revenue Service (99)	**Profit or Loss From Business** (Sole Proprietorship) ▶ Information about Schedule C and its separate instructions is at *www.irs.gov/schedulec.* ▶ **Attach to Form 1040, 1040NR, or 1041; partnerships generally must file Form 1065.**	OMB No. 1545-0074 20**14** Attachment Sequence No. **09**

Name of proprietor	Social security number (SSN)

A	Principal business or profession, including product or service (see instructions)	**B Enter code from instructions** ▶					

C	Business name. If no separate business name, leave blank.	**D Employer ID number (EIN),** (see instr.)

E Business address (including suite or room no.) ▶ _____
City, town or post office, state, and ZIP code

F Accounting method: **(1)** ☐ Cash **(2)** ☐ Accrual **(3)** ☐ Other (specify) ▶ _____

G Did you "materially participate" in the operation of this business during 2014? If "No," see instructions for limit on losses . ☐ Yes ☐ No

H If you started or acquired this business during 2014, check here . . . . ▶ ☐

I Did you make any payments in 2014 that would require you to file Form(s) 1099? (see instructions) . . . . ☐ Yes ☐ No

J If "Yes," did you or will you file required Forms 1099? . . . . ☐ Yes ☐ No

Part I Income

1	Gross receipts or sales. See instructions for line 1 and check the box if this income was reported to you on Form W-2 and the "Statutory employee" box on that form was checked . . . . ▶ ☐	1	
2	Returns and allowances	2	
3	Subtract line 2 from line 1	3	
4	Cost of goods sold (from line 42)	4	
5	**Gross profit.** Subtract line 4 from line 3	5	
6	Other income, including federal and state gasoline or fuel tax credit or refund (see instructions)	6	
7	**Gross income.** Add lines 5 and 6 . . . . ▶	7	

Part II Expenses. Enter expenses for business use of your home **only** on line 30.

8	Advertising	8			18	Office expense (see instructions)	18	
9	Car and truck expenses (see instructions)	9			19	Pension and profit-sharing plans .	19	
10	Commissions and fees .	10			20	Rent or lease (see instructions):		
11	Contract labor (see instructions)	11			a	Vehicles, machinery, and equipment	20a	
12	Depletion	12			b	Other business property . . .	20b	
13	Depreciation and section 179 expense deduction (not included in Part III) (see instructions)	13			21	Repairs and maintenance . . .	21	
					22	Supplies (not included in Part III) .	22	
					23	Taxes and licenses	23	
					24	Travel, meals, and entertainment:		
14	Employee benefit programs (other than on line 19) . .	14			a	Travel	24a	
15	Insurance (other than health)	15			b	Deductible meals and entertainment (see instructions) .	24b	
16	Interest:				25	Utilities	25	
a	Mortgage (paid to banks, etc.)	16a			26	Wages (less employment credits) .	26	
b	Other	16b			27a	Other expenses (from line 48) . .	27a	
17	Legal and professional services	17			b	**Reserved for future use** . . .	27b	

28	**Total expenses** before expenses for business use of home. Add lines 8 through 27a . . . . . . ▶	28	
29	Tentative profit or (loss). Subtract line 28 from line 7	29	
30	Expenses for business use of your home. Do not report these expenses elsewhere. Attach Form 8829 unless using the simplified method (see instructions). **Simplified method filers only:** enter the total square footage of: (a) your home: _____ and (b) the part of your home used for business: _____. Use the Simplified Method Worksheet in the instructions to figure the amount to enter on line 30	30	
31	**Net profit or (loss).** Subtract line 30 from line 29. • If a profit, enter on both **Form 1040, line 12** (or **Form 1040NR, line 13**) and on **Schedule SE, line 2.** (If you checked the box on line 1, see instructions). Estates and trusts, enter on **Form 1041, line 3.** • If a loss, you **must** go to line 32.	31	
32	If you have a loss, check the box that describes your investment in this activity (see instructions). • If you checked 32a, enter the loss on both **Form 1040, line 12,** (or **Form 1040NR, line 13**) and on **Schedule SE, line 2.** (If you checked the box on line 1, see the line 31 instructions). Estates and trusts, enter on **Form 1041, line 3.** • If you checked 32b, you **must** attach **Form 6198.** Your loss may be limited.	32a ☐ All investment is at risk. 32b ☐ Some investment is not at risk.
---	---	---

For Paperwork Reduction Act Notice, see the separate instructions. Cat. No. 11334P Schedule C (Form 1040) 2014

Illustration 15-4 continued

Part III	Cost of Goods Sold (see instructions)

33 Method(s) used to
value closing inventory: **a** ☐ Cost **b** ☐ Lower of cost or market **c** ☐ Other (attach explanation)

34 Was there any change in determining quantities, costs, or valuations between opening and closing inventory?
If "Yes," attach explanation . . . . ☐ Yes ☐ No

35	Inventory at beginning of year. If different from last year's closing inventory, attach explanation	35		
36	Purchases less cost of items withdrawn for personal use	36		
37	Cost of labor. Do not include any amounts paid to yourself	37		
38	Materials and supplies	38		
39	Other costs	39		
40	Add lines 35 through 39	40		
41	Inventory at end of year	41		
42	**Cost of goods sold.** Subtract line 41 from line 40. Enter the result here and on line 4	42		

Part IV	**Information on Your Vehicle.** Complete this part **only** if you are claiming car or truck expenses on line 9 and are not required to file Form 4562 for this business. See the instructions for line 13 to find out if you must file Form 4562.

43 When did you place your vehicle in service for business purposes? (month, day, year) ▶ _____ / ____ / _____

44 Of the total number of miles you drove your vehicle during 2014, enter the number of miles you used your vehicle for:

a Business _____ **b** Commuting (see instructions) _____ **c** Other _____

45 Was your vehicle available for personal use during off-duty hours? . . . . ☐ Yes ☐ No

46 Do you (or your spouse) have another vehicle available for personal use?. . . . . ☐ Yes ☐ No

47a Do you have evidence to support your deduction? . . . . ☐ Yes ☐ No

b If "Yes," is the evidence written? . . . . ☐ Yes ☐ No

Part V	**Other Expenses.** List below business expenses not included on lines 8–26 or line 30.

--	
--	
--	
--	
--	
--	
--	
--	
--	
48 **Total other expenses.** Enter here and on line 27a	48

Part II – Expenses: Lines 8 through 27 pertain to expenses from the operation of the business. In this section, we will only discuss the expenses that may need additional explanation.

Line 9: The car and truck expenses for the business use of the vehicle are reported here. The taxpayer may deduct actual expense or standard mileage subject to the requirements for each, as explained in Chapter 1. To claim car and truck expenses, Part IV of page 2 on the Schedule C must be filled out. The standard mileage will give the taxpayer a deduction of 56 cents per business mile driven in 2014. If the taxpayer claims actual auto expenses, enter the business expenses on line 9 and enter any depreciation taken for the vehicle on line 13 of the Schedule C.

Line 11: Enter the amounts paid for work done by persons the taxpayer does not consider employees on this line. If the taxpayer pays anyone $600 or more, the taxpayer must file a Form 1099-MISC with the IRS, as well as the payee.

Line 12: If the taxpayer has an economic interest in mineral property, they may be able to take a deduction for depletion. We will discuss this further, later in the course.

Line 13: We've discussed depreciation. If a Form 4562 is needed to be filed with the return, carry the amounts from that form to this line of the Schedule C. If no Form 4562 is needed, carry the amounts directly from the depreciation worksheet.

Line 14: Enter any amounts that were paid on behalf of the taxpayer's employees to benefit programs, other than pension and profit-sharing plans, on this line. This includes amounts paid for health and accident insurance, group term life insurance, and dependent care programs. Any amounts paid on behalf of the self-employed person are not included on this line.

Line 15: On this line any insurance premiums paid for the purpose of the business other than health insurance are entered. This includes liability insurance, insurance on the business property and assets, and worker's compensation insurance.

Line 16: Interest expense is entered on this line. Mortgage interest goes on line 16a and interest on any other business accounts is entered on line 16b.

Line 19: Enter any contributions to pension or profit-sharing plans for the employees on this line. Do not include any amounts paid on behalf of the self-employed person.

Line 22: Supplies that are not considered a part of the cost of goods sold are included on this line. The supplies that are a part of the cost of goods sold are entered on Schedule C, part III, line 38.

Line 23: The taxes and cost of licenses are included on this line. The taxes deductible on this line include:

- State income tax directly attributable to the business income.
- Employment taxes such as Social Security, Medicare, and federal unemployment taxes paid out of the employer's funds.
- Personal property tax imposed on personal property belonging to the business.
- Real estate taxes paid on the business property.

- Excise taxes that are ordinary and necessary expenses of carrying on the business.

Line 24: Travel expenses that are the ordinary and necessary expenses of traveling away from home for the business are deductible on this line. The deductible expenses are the same as what is covered in Chapter 1. Remember, in most cases, only 50% of the meals and entertainment expenses are deductible.

Line 26: Enter the total salaries and wages paid to employees on this line. Do not include amounts claimed for the Work Opportunity Credit, Empowerment Zone and Renewal Community Employment Credit, Indian Employment Credit, and Credit for Employer Differential Wage Payments.

Line 27a: This line is for the total other expenses as listed on page 2, part V. These expenses are ordinary and necessary expenses for operating the business that are not included on any of the other lines on Schedule C.

Line 30: Expenses for the business use of home are entered on this line. These expenses will be carried from Form 8829 (Illustration 15-5) or the Simplified Method Worksheet (Illustration 15-6). We will go over both next.

Line 31: This is the result of the gross income minus all of the expenses. If it is a positive amount, the business has a profit. If the result has a negative amount, the business has a loss. Any profit is carried to Form 1040, line 12, and the Schedule SE (Illustration 15-7). If the result is a loss, it is subject to the at-risk rules. The loss is only deductible up to the amount the taxpayer has at risk. The at risk amount is the actual cash and the adjusted basis of other property the taxpayer has invested in the business. The allowable loss is carried to the Form 1040, line 12.

Form 8829

The Form 8829 is very similar to the business use of home worksheet for the Form 2106. Generally, the business use of home expense is determined by what area of the house is used regularly and exclusively for business. There are two exceptions to this rule: First, if the home is used as a daycare facility, business use of home expenses can be deducted even though the area of the house that is used for daycare is also used for personal purposes. If the house is used as a daycare facility, instead of using the square footage of the house, the hours it is used as such are divided by the total hours in a year to arrive at the business percentage. Second, if the home is used to store inventory from the taxpayer's trade or business of selling products at retail or wholesale, the taxpayer can deduct the business use of home expenses. The home must be the only fixed location of the taxpayer's trade or business. This calculation is made on Part I of the Form 8829.

Simplified Method

The taxpayer may elect to use the simplified method to calculate the business use of home. In this case, the calculation is made on a Simplified Method Worksheet (Illustration 15-6), and carried to the Schedule C. Generally, the simplified method of calculating the business use of home method is multiplying the area used regularly and exclusively for business, regularly for daycare, or regularly for storage of inventory or product samples, by $5.00. The area used to figure the deduction cannot exceed 300 square feet. Once this method is chosen in a taxable year, it may not change for that year. However, it may change from using the simplified method in one year to using the actual expense method in the next year, or vice-versa.

All of the use requirements needed for the Form 8829 must also be met for the simplified method. If the taxpayer used the Form 8829 in a prior year and had a carryover to the next year, they cannot claim the carryover using the simplified method. They will be carried over to the next year the taxpayer files the Form 8829. Also, the depreciation of the home is not deducted using the simplified method. Therefore, the allowable depreciation deduction for any year the simplified method is used is deemed to be $0.

Note: Although depreciation is not deducted on the home, depreciation may still be claimed on other assets (for example: furniture or equipment) used in the qualified business use of the home.

Schedule SE

As stated earlier, self employment taxes are the social security and Medicare taxes the self employed taxpayer must pay on their business income. A Schedule SE (Illustration 15-7) must be filed if the taxpayer has net earnings of $400 or more, or if the taxpayer has church employee income and that income is $108.28 or more. There are two pages to the Schedule SE. The first page is the Short Schedule SE. Page 2 is the Long Schedule SE. The Long Schedule SE must be used if any of the following apply:

- The taxpayer received wages and other income subject to Social Security tax and the net earnings that are subject to Social Security tax is more than $113,700
- The taxpayer received tips subject to Social Security and Medicare tax that they did not report to their employer,
- The taxpayer reported any wages on Form 8919, Uncollected Social Security and Medicare tax on Wages,
- The taxpayer is a minister, member of a religious order, or Christian Science practitioner who received IRS approval not to be taxed on earnings from these sources, but the taxpayer owes self-employment tax on other earnings,
- The taxpayer is using an optional method to figure their net earnings (see page SE-4 of the 1040 Instructions), or
- The taxpayer received church employee income reported on Form W-2 of $108.28 or more.

Most taxpayers are only required to file page 1 which is the only one we will cover in this course. There is a flow chart on page 1 that will let the taxpayer know which one they will need to file.

Self Employment Adjustments

We have covered all of the adjustments on the Form 1040, page 1, except for three of them.

Line 27: In an employee's case their employer pays a portion of the social security and Medicare taxes, and the rest is withheld from the employee's wages. To even this out, the IRS allows a deduction for half of the self employment tax for a self employed taxpayer. This calculation is made on the Schedule SE.

Line 28: If the taxpayer makes any contributions to a self employed SEP, SIMPLE, or qualified plan on behalf of themselves, those amounts are deductible on this line.

Line 29: If the taxpayer pays premiums for health insurance for themselves or their families, the premiums may be deductible on this line. For the premiums to be deductible, they cannot be paid for any month which the self employed person is eligible to be covered under their employer's plan if they work as an employee in addition to being self employed, or any month which the self employed person is eligible to be covered under a spouse's health insurance plan. In either of these cases, it doesn't matter whether the self employed person is actually covered or not, only that they're eligible to be covered. To deduct self employed health insurance premiums the taxpayer:

- Must have been self employed and had a net profit for the year,
- Must have used one of the optional methods to figure their net earnings from self-employment on Schedule SE, or
- Must have received wages for the tax year from an S corporation in which the taxpayer was a more than 2% shareholder.

A worksheet to calculate the deduction is in the Form 1040 instructions.

Illustration 15-5

Form **8829**	**Expenses for Business Use of Your Home**		OMB No. 1545-0074
	▶ File only with Schedule C (Form 1040). Use a separate Form 8829 for each home you used for business during the year.		**2014**
Department of the Treasury Internal Revenue Service (99)	▶ Information about Form 8829 and its separate instructions is at *www.irs.gov/form8829*.		Attachment Sequence No. **176**
Name(s) of proprietor(s)			Your social security number

Part I   Part of Your Home Used for Business

1	Area used regularly and exclusively for business, regularly for daycare, or for storage of inventory or product samples (see instructions)	**1**	
2	Total area of home	**2**	
3	Divide line 1 by line 2. Enter the result as a percentage	**3**	%

For daycare facilities not used exclusively for business, go to line 4. All others, go to line 7.

4	Multiply days used for daycare during year by hours used per day	**4**		hr.
5	Total hours available for use during the year (365 days x 24 hours) (see instructions)	**5**	8,760	hr.
6	Divide line 4 by line 5. Enter the result as a decimal amount . . .	**6**	.	
7	Business percentage. For daycare facilities not used exclusively for business, multiply line 6 by line 3 (enter the result as a percentage). All others, enter the amount from line 3 . . . . . ▶	**7**		%

Part II   Figure Your Allowable Deduction

8	Enter the amount from Schedule C, line 29, **plus** any gain derived from the business use of your home, **minus** any loss from the trade or business not derived from the business use of your home (see instructions)		**8**	

See instructions for columns **(a)** and **(b)** before completing lines 9–21.

		(a) Direct expenses	**(b)** Indirect expenses		
9	Casualty losses (see instructions).	**9**			
10	Deductible mortgage interest (see instructions)	**10**			
11	Real estate taxes (see instructions)	**11**			
12	Add lines 9, 10, and 11	**12**			
13	Multiply line 12, column (b) by line 7		**13**		
14	Add line 12, column (a) and line 13			**14**	
15	Subtract line 14 from line 8. If zero or less, enter -0-			**15**	
16	Excess mortgage interest (see instructions) .	**16**			
17	Insurance	**17**			
18	Rent	**18**			
19	Repairs and maintenance	**19**			
20	Utilities	**20**			
21	Other expenses (see instructions).	**21**			
22	Add lines 16 through 21	**22**			
23	Multiply line 22, column (b) by line 7	**23**		
24	Carryover of prior year operating expenses (see instructions) . .	**24**		
25	Add line 22, column (a), line 23, and line 24		**25**	
26	Allowable operating expenses. Enter the **smaller** of line 15 or line 25		**26**	
27	Limit on excess casualty losses and depreciation. Subtract line 26 from line 15		**27**	
28	Excess casualty losses (see instructions)	**28**		
29	Depreciation of your home from line 41 below	**29**		
30	Carryover of prior year excess casualty losses and depreciation (see instructions)	**30**		
31	Add lines 28 through 30		**31**	
32	Allowable excess casualty losses and depreciation. Enter the **smaller** of line 27 or line 31 . .		**32**	
33	Add lines 14, 26, and 32.		**33**	
34	Casualty loss portion, if any, from lines 14 and 32. Carry amount to **Form 4684** (see instructions)		**34**	
35	**Allowable expenses for business use of your home.** Subtract line 34 from line 33. Enter here and on Schedule C, line 30. If your home was used for more than one business, see instructions ▶		**35**	

Part III   Depreciation of Your Home

36	Enter the **smaller** of your home's adjusted basis or its fair market value (see instructions) . .	**36**	
37	Value of land included on line 36	**37**	
38	Basis of building. Subtract line 37 from line 36	**38**	
39	Business basis of building. Multiply line 38 by line 7.	**39**	
40	Depreciation percentage (see instructions).	**40**	%
41	Depreciation allowable (see instructions). Multiply line 39 by line 40. Enter here and on line 29 above	**41**	

Part IV   Carryover of Unallowed Expenses to 2015

42	Operating expenses. Subtract line 26 from line 25. If less than zero, enter -0-	**42**	
43	Excess casualty losses and depreciation. Subtract line 32 from line 31. If less than zero, enter -0-	**43**	

For Paperwork Reduction Act Notice, see your tax return instructions.	Cat. No. 13232M	Form **8829** (2014)

Illustration 15-6

Simplified Method Worksheet

1. Enter the amount of the gross income limitation. See Instructions for the Simplified Method Worksheet . . . . 1. _____

2. Allowable square footage for the qualified business use. Do not enter more than 300 square feet. See Instructions for the Simplified Method Worksheet . . . . 2. _____

3. Simplified method amount
   a. Maximum allowable amount . . . . 3a. ____$5____

   b. For daycare facilities not used exclusively for business, enter the decimal amount from the Daycare Facility Worksheet; otherwise, enter 1.0 . . . . 3b. _____

   c. Multiply line 3a by line 3b and enter result to 2 decimal places . . . . 3c. _____

4. Multiply line 2 by line 3c . . . . 4. _____

5. **Allowable expenses using the simplified method.** Enter the smaller of line 1 or line 4 here and include that amount on Schedule C, line 30. If zero or less, enter -0- . . . . 5. _____

6. **Carryover of unallowed expenses from 2013 that are not allowed in 2014.**
   a. Operating expenses. Enter the amount from your 2013 Form 8829, line 42 . . . . 6a. _____

   b. Excess casualty losses and depreciation. Enter the amount from your 2013 Form 8829, line 43 . . . . 6b. _____

Illustration 15-7

SCHEDULE SE (Form 1040) Department of the Treasury Internal Revenue Service (99)	Self-Employment Tax ▶ Information about Schedule SE and its separate instructions is at *www.irs.gov/schedulese.* ▶ Attach to Form 1040 or Form 1040NR.	OMB No. 1545-0074 20**14** Attachment Sequence No. **17**

Name of person with **self-employment** income (as shown on Form 1040 or Form 1040NR)	Social security number of person with **self-employment** income ▶

Before you begin: To determine if you must file Schedule SE, see the instructions.

May I Use Short Schedule SE or Must I Use Long Schedule SE?

Note. Use this flowchart **only if** you must file Schedule SE. If unsure, see *Who Must File Schedule SE* in the instructions.

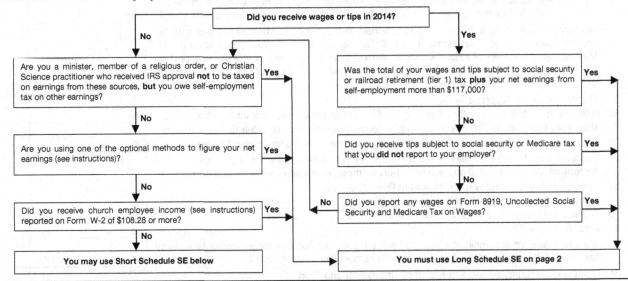

Section A—Short Schedule SE.   Caution. Read above to see if you can use Short Schedule SE.

1a	Net farm profit or (loss) from Schedule F, line 34, and farm partnerships, Schedule K-1 (Form 1065), box 14, code A	**1a**	
b	If you received social security retirement or disability benefits, enter the amount of Conservation Reserve Program payments included on Schedule F, line 4b, or listed on Schedule K-1 (Form 1065), box 20, code Z	**1b**	( )
2	Net profit or (loss) from Schedule C, line 31; Schedule C-EZ, line 3; Schedule K-1 (Form 1065), box 14, code A (other than farming); and Schedule K-1 (Form 1065-B), box 9, code J1. Ministers and members of religious orders, see instructions for types of income to report on this line. See instructions for other income to report	**2**	
3	Combine lines 1a, 1b, and 2	**3**	
4	Multiply line 3 by 92.35% (.9235). If less than $400, you do not owe self-employment tax; **do not** file this schedule unless you have an amount on line 1b . . . . ▶	**4**	
	Note. If line 4 is less than $400 due to Conservation Reserve Program payments on line 1b, see instructions.		
5	**Self-employment tax.** If the amount on line 4 is: • $117,000 or less, multiply line 4 by 15.3% (.153). Enter the result here and on **Form 1040, line 57,** or **Form 1040NR, line 55** • More than $117,000, multiply line 4 by 2.9% (.029). Then, add $14,508 to the result. Enter the total here and on **Form 1040, line 57,** or **Form 1040NR, line 55**	**5**	
6	**Deduction for one-half of self-employment tax.** Multiply line 5 by 50% (.50). Enter the result here and on **Form 1040, line 27,** or **Form 1040NR, line 27**	**6**	

For Paperwork Reduction Act Notice, see your tax return instructions.   Cat. No. 11358Z   Schedule SE (Form 1040) 2014

Illustration 15-7

Attachment Sequence No. **17**

Page **2**

Name of person with **self-employment** income (as shown on Form 1040 or Form 1040NR)	Social security number of person with **self-employment** income ▶	

Section B—Long Schedule SE

Part I   Self-Employment Tax

Note. If your only income subject to self-employment tax is **church employee income,** see instructions. Also see instructions for the definition of church employee income.

A   If you are a minister, member of a religious order, or Christian Science practitioner **and** you filed Form 4361, but you had $400 or more of **other** net earnings from self-employment, check here and continue with Part I . . . . ▶ ☐

1a	Net farm profit or (loss) from Schedule F, line 34, and farm partnerships, Schedule K-1 (Form 1065), box 14, code A. **Note.** Skip lines 1a and 1b if you use the farm optional method (see instructions)	**1a**		
b	If you received social security retirement or disability benefits, enter the amount of Conservation Reserve Program payments included on Schedule F, line 4b, or listed on Schedule K-1 (Form 1065), box 20, code Z	**1b**	(	)
2	Net profit or (loss) from Schedule C, line 31; Schedule C-EZ, line 3; Schedule K-1 (Form 1065), box 14, code A (other than farming); and Schedule K-1 (Form 1065-B), box 9, code J1. Ministers and members of religious orders, see instructions for types of income to report on this line. See instructions for other income to report. **Note.** Skip this line if you use the nonfarm optional method (see instructions)	**2**		
3	Combine lines 1a, 1b, and 2	**3**		
4a	If line 3 is more than zero, multiply line 3 by 92.35% (.9235). Otherwise, enter amount from line 3 **Note.** If line 4a is less than $400 due to Conservation Reserve Program payments on line 1b, see instructions.	**4a**		
b	If you elect one or both of the optional methods, enter the total of lines 15 and 17 here . .	**4b**		
c	Combine lines 4a and 4b. If less than $400, **stop;** you do not owe self-employment tax. **Exception.** If less than $400 and you had **church employee income,** enter -0- and continue ▶	**4c**		
5a	Enter your **church employee income** from Form W-2. See instructions for definition of church employee income . . .	**5a**			
b	Multiply line 5a by 92.35% (.9235). If less than $100, enter -0-	**5b**		
6	Add lines 4c and 5b	**6**		
7	Maximum amount of combined wages and self-employment earnings subject to social security tax or the 6.2% portion of the 7.65% railroad retirement (tier 1) tax for 2014	**7**	117,000	00
8a	Total social security wages and tips (total of boxes 3 and 7 on Form(s) W-2) and railroad retirement (tier 1) compensation. If $117,000 or more, skip lines 8b through 10, and go to line 11	**8a**			
b	Unreported tips subject to social security tax (from Form 4137, line 10)	**8b**			
c	Wages subject to social security tax (from Form 8919, line 10)	**8c**			
d	Add lines 8a, 8b, and 8c	**8d**		
9	Subtract line 8d from line 7. If zero or less, enter -0- here and on line 10 and go to line 11 ▶	**9**		
10	Multiply the **smaller** of line 6 or line 9 by 12.4% (.124)	**10**		
11	Multiply line 6 by 2.9% (.029)	**11**		
12	**Self-employment tax.** Add lines 10 and 11. Enter here and on **Form 1040, line 57,** or **Form 1040NR, line 55**	**12**		
13	**Deduction for one-half of self-employment tax.** Multiply line 12 by 50% (.50). Enter the result here and on **Form 1040, line 27,** or **Form 1040NR, line 27**	**13**		

Part II   Optional Methods To Figure Net Earnings   (see instructions)

Farm Optional Method. You may use this method **only if (a)** your gross farm income[1] was not more than $7,200, **or (b)** your net farm profits[2] were less than $5,198.

14	Maximum income for optional methods	**14**	4,800	00
15	Enter the **smaller** of: two-thirds (2/3) of gross farm income[1] (not less than zero) **or** $4,800. Also include this amount on line 4b above	**15**		

Nonfarm Optional Method. You may use this method **only if (a)** your net nonfarm profits[3] were less than $5,198 and also less than 72.189% of your gross nonfarm income,[4] **and (b)** you had net earnings from self-employment of at least $400 in 2 of the prior 3 years. **Caution.** You may use this method no more than five times.

16	Subtract line 15 from line 14	**16**		
17	Enter the **smaller** of: two-thirds (2/3) of gross nonfarm income[4] (not less than zero) **or** the amount on line 16. Also include this amount on line 4b above	**17**		

[1] From Sch. F, line 9, and Sch. K-1 (Form 1065), box 14, code B.
[2] From Sch. F, line 34, and Sch. K-1 (Form 1065), box 14, code A—minus the amount you would have entered on line 1b had you not used the optional method.

[3] From Sch. C, line 31; Sch. C-EZ, line 3; Sch. K-1 (Form 1065), box 14, code A; and Sch. K-1 (Form 1065-B), box 9, code J1.
[4] From Sch. C, line 7; Sch. C-EZ, line 1; Sch. K-1 (Form 1065), box 14, code C; and Sch. K-1 (Form 1065-B), box 9, code J2.

Schedule SE (Form 1040) 2014

Chapter Review

1) What is a sole proprietor?

2) What form is needed to report self employment income?

3) What is the filing requirement for a self employed taxpayer with no other income?

4) What is the business code for an electrical contractor?

5) What are the three methods of accounting?

6) What form must a taxpayer file if they pay a nonemployee $600 or more for work performed?

7) What two methods can be used for business use of home for a self employed taxpayer?

8) What does self employment tax consist of?

Exercise

Prepare a return for Keith and Karen Keys. Keith and Karen Keys are married. They have one son, Kyle. Keith is self employed and Karen is a nurse. Kyle is a full time student at Monarch University. Karen has insurance for all three of them through her employer. They had the insurance all year. Neither wants to designate $3 to the presidential election campaign fund.

Keith's SSN is 333-55-4322 and his birth date is November 18, 1971.

Karen's SSN is 888-55-3456 and her birth date is February 27, 1973.

Kyle's SSN is 333-54-6654 and his birth date is January 16, 1996.

Kyle is in his freshman year at college. His tuition and related fees were $4,543. His books were $788. Kyle has never been arrested.

Keith's business is the sale of comic books at Comic Book Heaven. Comic Book Heaven is located at 900 Comic Lane, Your City, Your State, your zip code. He uses the hybrid method of accounting. He's had his business for 15 years. He operates the business by himself. He has no employees. His inventory at the end of last year was worth $16,388. This was valued using the cost method. He purchased $32,776 of inventory during the year. His ending inventory was $26,399. He had gross receipts of $70,665. His other expenses were as follows:

Advertising	$ 4,665
Supplies	3,450
Rent	8,500
Repairs	1,232
Bookkeeping	2,311
Utilities	4,896
Liability Insurance	5,647

Keith also attended a couple of sales conventions out of town. His airline expenses were $944. His lodging was $533. His meals were $232.

☐ CORRECTED

FILER'S name, street address, city or town, state or province, country, ZIP or foreign postal code, and telephone number Monarch University 250 Grand Ave. Your City, Your State, Your Zip Code	1 Payments received for qualified tuition and related expenses $ 4,543.00	OMB No. 1545-1574 2014	Tuition Statement
	2 Amounts billed for qualified tuition and related expenses $	Form 1098-T	
FILER'S federal identification no. 63-5252333	STUDENT'S social security number 333-54-6654	3 If this box is checked, your educational institution has changed its reporting method for 2014 ☐	Copy B For Student
STUDENT'S name Kyle Keys	4 Adjustments made for a prior year $	5 Scholarships or grants $	This is important tax information and is being furnished to the Internal Revenue Service.
Street address (including apt. no.) 3343 Quaint Blvd.	6 Adjustments to scholarships or grants for a prior year $	7 Checked if the amount in box 1 or 2 includes amounts for an academic period beginning January - March 2015 ▶ ☐	
City or town, state or province, country, and ZIP or foreign postal code Your City, Your State, Your Zip Code			
Service Provider/Acct. No. (see instr.)	8 Check if at least half-time student ☐	9 Checked if a graduate student . . . . ☐	10 Ins. contract reimb./refund $

Form 1098-T   (keep for your records)   www.irs.gov/form1098t   Department of the Treasury - Internal Revenue Service

a Employee's social security number 888-55-4332		

OMB No. 1545-0008 | Safe, accurate, FAST! Use | IRS e-file | Visit the IRS website at www.irs.gov/efile

b Employer identification number (EIN)
85-9643789

1 Wages, tips, other compensation 42,999.00

2 Federal income tax withheld 4,342.00

c Employer's name, address, and ZIP code

First Aid Hospital
4500 Health Lane
Your City, Your State, Your Zip Code

3 Social security wages 42,999.00

4 Social security tax withheld 2,665.94

5 Medicare wages and tips 42,999.00

6 Medicare tax withheld 623.49

7 Social security tips

8 Allocated tips

d Control number

9

10 Dependent care benefits

e Employee's first name and initial   Last name   Suff.

11 Nonqualified plans

12a See instructions for box 12
Code DD   8,350.00

13 Statutory employee ☐ Retirement plan ☐ Third-party sick pay ☐

12b Code

Karen Keys
3343 Quaint Blvd.
Your City, Your State, Your Zip Code

14 Other

12c Code

12d Code

f Employee's address and ZIP code

15 State	Employer's state ID number	16 State wages, tips, etc.	17 State income tax	18 Local wages, tips, etc.	19 Local income tax	20 Locality name
YS	859643780	42,999.00	2,933.00			

Form **W-2** Wage and Tax Statement   **2014**   Department of the Treasury—Internal Revenue Service

Copy B—To Be Filed With Employee's FEDERAL Tax Return.
This information is being furnished to the Internal Revenue Service.

☐ CORRECTED (if checked)

RECIPIENT'S/LENDER'S name, address, city or town, state or province, country, ZIP or foreign postal code, and telephone number

Student Financial Services
5534 Helpful Way
Your City, Your State, Your Zip Code

OMB No. 1545-1576

2014

Form **1098-E**

Student Loan Interest Statement

RECIPIENT'S federal identification no. 44-6726262	BORROWER'S social security number 888-55-3456	1 Student loan interest received by lender $ 1,293.00

Copy B
For Borrower

BORROWER'S name

Karen Keys

Street address (including apt. no.)
3343 Quaint Blvd.

City or town, state or province, country, and ZIP or foreign postal code
Your City, Your State, Your Zip Code

This is important tax information and is being furnished to the Internal Revenue Service. If you are required to file a return, a negligence penalty or other sanction may be imposed on you if the IRS determines that an underpayment of tax results because you overstated a deduction for student loan interest.

Account number (see instructions)

2 If checked, box 1 does **not** include loan origination fees and/or capitalized interest for loans made before September 1, 2004 . . . . ☐

Form **1098-E**   (keep for your records)   www.irs.gov/form1098e   Department of the Treasury - Internal Revenue Service

Chapter 16 – Rental and Royalty Income

Rental Income

Rental Income is income the taxpayer receives for the use or occupation of their property. Net rental income is taxable. Net rental income is figured the same way as net business income: the gross rental income minus expenses.

Royalty Income

There are two different types of royalty income. The first is royalties from copyrights and patents from literary works, musical or artistic works, or inventions. Royalties are paid for the right to use these properties for a specified time period. The second is royalties from oil, gas, and mineral properties. Royalties are paid based on units sold.

Schedule E

Rental and royalty income and expenses are reported on a Schedule E (Illustration 16-1) and then carried to the Form 1040.

Line 1: This line is for the type and location of each property that the taxpayer is receiving rental or royalty income from.

Line 2: To calculate the number of fair rental days:
- Any day the unit is rented at fair rental price is considered rental use even if it is used for personal purposes on the same day.
- Any day the unit is available for rent is not considered rental use if it is not rented for fair rental price on that day.
- Any day the taxpayer or member of the family does maintenance or repairs full time is not considered personal use, even if it is used for personal purposes on the same day.

Fair rental price – The fair rental price of the property is the amount of rent that a person who is not related to the taxpayer is willing to pay. It is not the fair rental price if it is substantially less than rents charged for similar properties used for similar purposes located in the same area.
QJV – Qualified Joint Venture, as explained in Chapter 15.

Line 3: The total rents or royalties received are entered on this line. There are different types of income that must be included in this section if received.
Advance rent – Advanced rent is reported in the year received, regardless of what accounting method the taxpayer uses.
Security deposit – A security deposit received that the taxpayer intends to return to the tenant at the end of the lease is not included in income. However, if the tenant forfeits it

and the taxpayer keeps some or all of the security deposit, the taxpayer will include it in income in the year forfeited.

Lease cancellation – If the tenant pays an amount to cancel a lease, the payment is included as rental income when received.

Expenses paid by the tenant – If the tenant pays any of the taxpayer's expenses, the amount paid is considered rental income. If the expense is a deductible rental expense, the taxpayer may deduct the expense on the Schedule E.

Property or services – If the tenant provides property or services as rent, the fair market value of the property or services is included as rental income.

Royalty Income – Royalty income is generally paid on the basis of units extracted or sold. If royalties paid are more than $10 in a tax year, the taxpayer will receive a Form 1099-MISC (Illustration 16-2) with the royalty amount reported in box 2. If the taxpayer owns an operating oil, gas, or mineral interest or is in business as a self employed creator of original works, their income is reported on a Schedule C.

Lines 5 through 19: Expenses directly related to the rental or royalty income are deducted on these lines. Lines that may need additional explanation are as follows:

Repairs – Repairs are a deductible expense, but improvements made are depreciated as discussed in Chapter 12. The designation between repairs and improvements must be made. Repairs include painting, plumbing, repairing the roof, lawn care, and cleaning. Labor of the owner, or the unpaid labor of friends and relatives, is not deductible.

Insurance premiums – If the insurance is prepaid for a period of more than one year, only the premiums allocable to the current tax year are deductible on the current year's Schedule E.

Illustration 16-2

□ CORRECTED (if checked)		

PAYER'S name, street address, city or town, state or province, country, ZIP or foreign postal code, and telephone no.	1 Rents $	OMB No. 1545-0115
	2 Royalties $	**2014** Form **1099-MISC**
	3 Other income $	4 Federal income tax withheld $
PAYER'S federal identification number / RECIPIENT'S identification number	5 Fishing boat proceeds $	6 Medical and health care payments $
RECIPIENT'S name	7 Nonemployee compensation $	8 Substitute payments in lieu of dividends or interest $
Street address (including apt. no.)	9 Payer made direct sales of $5,000 or more of consumer products to a buyer (recipient) for resale ▶ □	10 Crop insurance proceeds $
City or town, state or province, country, and ZIP or foreign postal code	11	12
Account number (see instructions)	13 Excess golden parachute payments $	14 Gross proceeds paid to an attorney $
15a Section 409A deferrals $ / 15b Section 409A income $	16 State tax withheld $	17 State/Payer's state no. / 18 State income $

Miscellaneous Income

Copy B
For Recipient

This is important tax information and is being furnished to the Internal Revenue Service. If you are required to file a return, a negligence penalty or other sanction may be imposed on you if this income is taxable and the IRS determines that it has not been reported.

Form **1099-MISC**   (keep for your records)   www.irs.gov/form1099misc   Department of the Treasury - Internal Revenue Service

Illustration 16-1

SCHEDULE E (Form 1040)	Supplemental Income and Loss	OMB No. 1545-0074
Department of the Treasury Internal Revenue Service (99)	(From rental real estate, royalties, partnerships, S corporations, estates, trusts, REMICs, etc.) ▶ Attach to Form 1040, 1040NR, or Form 1041. ▶ Information about Schedule E and its separate instructions is at *www.irs.gov/schedulee*.	2014 Attachment Sequence No. 13

Name(s) shown on return   Your social security number

Part I   **Income or Loss From Rental Real Estate and Royalties** Note. If you are in the business of renting personal property, use **Schedule C** or **C-EZ** (see instructions). If you are an individual, report farm rental income or loss from **Form 4835** on page 2, line 40.

A Did you make any payments in 2014 that would require you to file Form(s) 1099? (see instructions)   ☐ Yes ☐ No

B If "Yes," did you or will you file required Forms 1099?   ☐ Yes ☐ No

1a Physical address of each property (street, city, state, ZIP code)

A
B
C

1b	Type of Property (from list below)	2	For each rental real estate property listed above, report the number of fair rental and personal use days. Check the QJV box only if you meet the requirements to file as a qualified joint venture. See instructions.		Fair Rental Days	Personal Use Days	QJV
A				A			☐
B				B			☐
C				C			☐

Type of Property:

1 Single Family Residence	3 Vacation/Short-Term Rental	5 Land	7 Self-Rental
2 Multi-Family Residence	4 Commercial	6 Royalties	8 Other (describe)

Income:	Properties:		A	B	C
3	Rents received	3			
4	Royalties received	4			
Expenses:					
5	Advertising	5			
6	Auto and travel (see instructions)	6			
7	Cleaning and maintenance	7			
8	Commissions.	8			
9	Insurance	9			
10	Legal and other professional fees	10			
11	Management fees	11			
12	Mortgage interest paid to banks, etc. (see instructions)	12			
13	Other interest.	13			
14	Repairs.	14			
15	Supplies	15			
16	Taxes	16			
17	Utilities.	17			
18	Depreciation expense or depletion	18			
19	Other (list) ▶ _____	19			
20	Total expenses. Add lines 5 through 19	20			
21	Subtract line 20 from line 3 (rents) and/or 4 (royalties). If result is a (loss), see instructions to find out if you must file **Form 6198**	21			
22	Deductible rental real estate loss after limitation, if any, on **Form 8582** (see instructions)	22	( )	( )	( )
23a	Total of all amounts reported on line 3 for all rental properties	23a			
b	Total of all amounts reported on line 4 for all royalty properties	23b			
c	Total of all amounts reported on line 12 for all properties	23c			
d	Total of all amounts reported on line 18 for all properties	23d			
e	Total of all amounts reported on line 20 for all properties	23e			
24	**Income.** Add positive amounts shown on line 21. **Do not** include any losses		24		
25	**Losses.** Add royalty losses from line 21 and rental real estate losses from line 22. Enter total losses here		25	(	)
26	**Total rental real estate and royalty income or (loss).** Combine lines 24 and 25. Enter the result here. If Parts II, III, IV, and line 40 on page 2 do not apply to you, also enter this amount on Form 1040, line 17, or Form 1040NR, line 18. Otherwise, include this amount in the total on line 41 on page 2		26		

For Paperwork Reduction Act Notice, see the separate instructions.   Cat. No. 11344L   Schedule E (Form 1040) 2014

Line 18: If the taxpayer owns the home or any of the furniture or appliances in the home, they should be depreciated. Also, if the taxpayer makes any improvements to the home that increase the value of the home, such as a new roof or putting in a new driveway, those improvements are depreciated.

Depletion refers to the recovery of cost of an economic interest is mineral deposits, oil or gas wells, or standing timber over the economic life of the property. There are two types of depletion:

> **Cost depletion** – Cost depletion is determined on the basis of the economic interest. Cost depletion cannot be taken once the basis of the property reaches $0. To determine the cost depletion deduction, divide the estimated total number of recoverable units (for example, barrels or tons) into the remaining adjusted basis of the property. The result is the unit rate. The unit rate is then multiplied by how many units that payment was received for during the year.

> **Percentage depletion** – To determine the percentage depletion, multiply the gross royalties from the mineral interest by the percentage specified for that mineral found in the IRS Pub. 535. Percentage depletion can be taken even after the basis of the property reaches $0. The deduction for percentage depletion, however, cannot exceed 50% of the taxable income from the property.

Gain – If the result of the Schedule E is a gain, the amount is carried to Form 1040, line 17.

Loss – Rental activity losses are subject to limitations. Generally, all rental activities are passive. A passive activity is an activity in which a taxpayer does not materially participate. Losses from passive activities usually can only be deducted against income from other passive activities. However, if the taxpayer actively participates in rental activities, they may be able to deduct up to $25,000 of losses against any other kind of income. For the taxpayer to meet the active participation rule, they must participate by collecting rent or making management decisions in the rental of the property. If the taxpayer's modified AGI is over $100,000, the deductible $25,000 loss is further limited. See IRS Pub. 925.

> **Exception for Real Estate Professionals** – If the taxpayer qualifies as a real estate professional by meeting both of the following requirements, any rental losses are not subject to the limitation:
> - More than half of the personal services performed in all trades or businesses during the tax year were performed in real property trades or businesses in which the taxpayer materially participated.
> - The taxpayer performed more than 750 hours of services during the tax year in real property trades or businesses in which the taxpayer materially participated.
>   - Real property trades or business include the following:
>   - Development or redevelopment,
>   - Construction or reconstruction,
>   - Acquiring the property,
>   - Converting the property,
>   - Renting or leasing the property,
>   - Operating or managing the property, or
>   - Brokering the property.

Rental Income Belonging on a Schedule C

If the taxpayer provides services for the tenants such as housekeeping services or meals, the rental income and expenses must be reported as business income on a Schedule C.

Personal Use of Rental Property

If the taxpayer uses part of the property for personal reasons and rents out part of it, the expenses must be allocated. For example, the taxpayer lives in a home they own, but rent the basement to a tenant. Any expenses that are solely for the rented basement will be deductible in full. However any expenses that are for the entire household must be allocated. Those expenses include mortgage interest, property tax, insurance, and utilities. If the expenses are normally deductible on a Schedule A, report the rental portion on the Schedule E and the personal portion of mortgage interest and property tax is reported on the Schedule A. To determine how much of the expenses are allocated to the rental portion of the property, use a reasonable method, such as the area of the home or the number of rooms.

Example: Benny rents out his basement and lives in the rest of the house. The area of the house is 2200 square feet and the basement is 250 square feet: 250 ÷ 2200 = 11.36%
11.36% of the expenses for the entire home are allocable to the rental income and reportable on the Schedule E.

Vacation Home

If a dwelling is used as a personal residence part of the time and rented out part of the time, the rent may be taxable and the expenses may be deductible depending on certain circumstances. If the dwelling is rented for less than 15 days the income is not taxable and the expenses are not deductible except expenses that are normally deductible on the Schedule A. If the dwelling is rented out for 15 days or more, the expenses will be prorated.

The dwelling is considered used as a personal residence for any days it is used for personal purposes by any owner that has an interest in the property or their family members unless the dwelling is rented out at fair rental price. Also include days the property was rented out for less than fair rental price and if the taxpayer has an agreement that lets the taxpayer use some other dwelling unit.

The unit is used as a main home if it is used for personal purposes for more than the greater of:

- 14 days, or
- 10% of total days the unit is rented to others at fair rental price.

If the dwelling is used as a main home, the expenses deducted cannot be more than the rental income from the property. If the dwelling is not used as a main home, the expenses deducted may be more than the rental income from the property, creating a loss.

Rental Not for Profit

If the taxpayer does not rent their property for the purpose of making a profit, the rental activity is considered to be a hobby and the rental income is hobby income. The rental income is reported on Form 1040, line 21. The expenses are deductible to the extent of the income on the Schedule A, line 23 which is subject to the 2% of AGI floor.

Other Income Reported on the Schedule E

There are a few other types of income that are reported on the Schedule E, page 2 (Illustration 16-3). We will briefly discuss these types of income, but if encountered additional research will be needed.

Partnerships

If the taxpayer is involved in a partnership any taxes that are required to be paid are paid with the taxpayer's individual tax return. A partnership is required to file an information return and provide each partner with a Schedule K-1 which provides the taxpayer with their share of income, loss, deductions, and credits. This information is carried from the Schedule K-1 to the Schedule E.

S Corporations

Most corporations are treated as separate entities. This means that the corporation files a tax return and pays any taxes owed. However, some small corporations may elect to be subchapter S corporations. S corporations are treated similarly to a partnership. They pay no taxes themselves, but pass them to the shareholders.

Estates and Trusts

Estates and trusts must provide each beneficiary with a Schedule K-1 informing them of their share of income and deductions. This information must be carried to the Schedule E.

Real Estate Mortgage Investment Conduit (REMIC)

If the taxpayer is a holder of a residual interest in a REMIC, they will be provided with a Schedule Q. The Schedule Q will have the information needed to complete the Schedule E.

Illustration 16-3

Attachment Sequence No. **13**

Page **2**

Name(s) shown on return. Do not enter name and social security number if shown on other side.

Your social security number

Caution. The IRS compares amounts reported on your tax return with amounts shown on Schedule(s) K-1.

Part II | **Income or Loss From Partnerships and S Corporations** | **Note.** If you report a loss from an at-risk activity for which **any** amount is **not** at risk, you **must** check the box in column **(e)** on line 28 and attach **Form 6198.** See instructions.

27   Are you reporting any loss not allowed in a prior year due to the at-risk, excess farm loss, or basis limitations, a prior year unallowed loss from a passive activity (if that loss was not reported on Form 8582), or unreimbursed partnership expenses? If you answered "Yes," see instructions before completing this section.   ☐ **Yes**   ☐ **No**

28	(a) Name	(b) Enter **P** for partnership; **S** for S corporation	(c) Check if foreign partnership	(d) Employer identification number	(e) Check if any amount is not at risk
A			☐		☐
B			☐		☐
C			☐		☐
D			☐		☐

	Passive Income and Loss		Nonpassive Income and Loss		
	(f) Passive loss allowed (attach **Form 8582** if required)	(g) Passive income from **Schedule K–1**	(h) Nonpassive loss from **Schedule K–1**	(i) Section 179 expense deduction from **Form 4562**	(j) Nonpassive income from **Schedule K–1**
A					
B					
C					
D					

29a	Totals					
b	Totals					

30	Add columns (g) and (j) of line 29a	30	
31	Add columns (f), (h), and (i) of line 29b	31	( )
32	**Total partnership and S corporation income or (loss).** Combine lines 30 and 31. Enter the result here and include in the total on line 41 below	32	

Part III | **Income or Loss From Estates and Trusts**

33	(a) Name	(b) Employer identification number
A		
B		

	Passive Income and Loss		Nonpassive Income and Loss	
	(c) Passive deduction or loss allowed (attach **Form 8582** if required)	(d) Passive income from **Schedule K–1**	(e) Deduction or loss from **Schedule K–1**	(f) Other income from **Schedule K–1**
A				
B				

34a	Totals				
b	Totals				

35	Add columns (d) and (f) of line 34a	35	
36	Add columns (c) and (e) of line 34b	36	( )
37	**Total estate and trust income or (loss).** Combine lines 35 and 36. Enter the result here and include in the total on line 41 below	37	

Part IV | **Income or Loss From Real Estate Mortgage Investment Conduits (REMICs)—Residual Holder**

38	(a) Name	(b) Employer identification number	(c) Excess inclusion from **Schedules Q,** line 2c (see instructions)	(d) Taxable income (net loss) from **Schedules Q,** line 1b	(e) Income from **Schedules Q,** line 3b

39	Combine columns (d) and (e) only. Enter the result here and include in the total on line 41 below	39	

Part V | **Summary**

40	Net farm rental income or (loss) from **Form 4835.** Also, complete line 42 below	40	
41	Total income or (loss). Combine lines 26, 32, 37, 39, and 40. Enter the result here and on Form 1040, line 17, or Form 1040NR, line 18 ▶	41	

42   **Reconciliation of farming and fishing income.** Enter your **gross** farming and fishing income reported on Form 4835, line 7; Schedule K-1 (Form 1065), box 14, code B; Schedule K-1 (Form 1120S), box 17, code V; and Schedule K-1 (Form 1041), box 14, code F (see instructions) . . | **42** | |

43   **Reconciliation for real estate professionals.** If you were a real estate professional (see instructions), enter the net income or (loss) you reported anywhere on Form 1040 or Form 1040NR from all rental real estate activities in which you materially participated under the passive activity loss rules . . | **43** | |

Chapter Review

1) What is rental income?

2) If the taxpayer receives royalty income of over $10, how will it be reported to the taxpayer?

3) Is a security deposit rental income?

4) If the tenant pays real estate taxes for the taxpayer of $850, how much is included in the taxpayer's rental income?

5) If the taxpayer prepays $3,600 of insurance premiums for a rental home for 3 calendar years of coverage, how much is a deductible expense for the current tax year?

6) What is fair rental price?

7) The taxpayer owns a house on the beach and lets a friend rent it for 1 week for $750 (fair rental price). He does not rent it to anyone else and uses it frequently for personal reasons. How much of the rental income is taxable to the taxpayer?

Exercise

Prepare a return for Nicole. Nicole Nugget (545-44-0332; birth date is Feb. 2, 1946) is retired and owns a rental house located at 450 Beautiful Blvd., Your City, Your State, your zip code. She purchased it in May of 2009 for $75,000 with $12,000 allocated to the value of the land. She began renting it immediately. She receives $1,244 of rent per month. It was rented for the entire year. Her expenses are as follows:

Mortgage Interest	$ 8,544
Real Estate Taxes	763
Repairs	778
Insurance	1,455
Management fees	899

Nicole also received social security benefits of $9,166.22. She was covered by Medicare the entire year.

☐ CORRECTED (if checked)		
PAYER'S name, street address, city or town, state or province, country, and ZIP or foreign postal code Provincial Retirement Planning 6664 Security Way Your City, Your State, Your Zip Code	**1** Gross distribution $ 32,533.27 **2a** Taxable amount $ 32,533.27	OMB No. 1545-0119 2014 Form **1099-R**	Distributions From Pensions, Annuities, Retirement or Profit-Sharing Plans, IRAs, Insurance Contracts, etc.
	2b Taxable amount not determined ☐	Total distribution ☐	**Copy B** **Report this** income on your federal tax return. If this form shows federal income tax withheld in box 4, attach this copy to your return.
PAYER'S federal identification number 65-8765441	RECIPIENT'S identification number 545-44-0332	**3** Capital gain (included in box 2a) $	**4** Federal income tax withheld $ 3,253.49
RECIPIENT'S name Nicole Nugget		**5** Employee contributions /Designated Roth contributions or insurance premiums $	**6** Net unrealized appreciation in employer's securities $
Street address (including apt. no.) 244 Niceville Rd.		**7** Distribution code(s) 7	IRA/ SEP/ SIMPLE ☐	**8** Other $ %	This information is being furnished to the Internal Revenue Service.
City or town, state or province, country, and ZIP or foreign postal code Your City, Your State, Your Zip Code		**9a** Your percentage of total distribution % 	**9b** Total employee contributions $
10 Amount allocable to IRR within 5 years $	**11** 1st year of desig. Roth contrib.	**12** State tax withheld $ $	**13** State/Payer's state no.	**14** State distribution $ $
Account number (see instructions)		**15** Local tax withheld $ $	**16** Name of locality	**17** Local distribution $ $

Form **1099-R** www.irs.gov/form1099r Department of the Treasury - Internal Revenue Service

Chapter 17 – Capital Gains and Losses

When capital assets are sold, it creates a gain or loss. The capital gains and losses are treated many different ways for tax purposes, depending on different factors. We will discuss the differences in this chapter.

Capital Assets

Generally, if property is owned by a taxpayer and used for personal, pleasure, or investment purposes, the property is a capital asset. The following are examples of capital assets:

- Stocks or bonds held in a personal account,
- A house owned and used by the taxpayer and their family,
- Household furnishings,
- A car used for pleasure or commuting,
- Coin or stamp collections,
- Gems and jewelry, and
- Gold, silver, or any other metal.

Because the variety of capital assets is so large, there is no definitive list of what qualifies as capital assets. Instead, the IRS has developed a list of what property is not a capital asset. The following are not capital assets:

- Property held mainly for sale to customers or property that will physically become a part of the merchandise that is for sale to customers.
- Depreciable property used in the taxpayer's trade or business, even if fully depreciated.
- Real property used in trade or business.
- A copyright, a literary, musical, or artistic composition, a letter or memorandum, or similar property...
    - Created by personal efforts,
    - Prepared or produced for the taxpayer (in the case of a letter, memorandum, or similar property), or
    - Acquired under circumstances (for example, by gift) entitling the taxpayer to the basis of the person who created the property or for whom it was prepared or produced.
- Accounts or notes receivable acquired in the ordinary course of a trade or business for services rendered or from the sale of inventory.
- Certain U.S. Government publications.
- Certain commodities derivative financial instruments held by commodities derivatives dealers.
- Hedging transactions.

- Supplies of a type regularly used or consumed in the ordinary course of a trade or business.

As stated before, capital assets can be held for personal, pleasure, or investment use. If the sale of personal use property results in a loss, the loss is not deductible.

Basis

After determining what type of property was sold, the basis of the property must be determined.

Cost Basis

The basis of property purchased is usually the cost. The cost is the amount the taxpayer paid in cash, debt obligations, other property, or services. The cost also includes any amounts paid for the following:

- Sales tax.
- Freight.
- Installation and testing.
- Excise taxes.
- Revenue stamps.
- Recording fees.
- Real estate taxes that are assumed by the seller.

The basis of stocks and bonds

The basis of stocks and bonds is usually the purchase price plus any expenses of the purchase, such as commissions and recording or transfer fees. Many times, the taxpayer receives stock dividends that are reinvested. This means that the reinvested dividends are used to purchase additional stock. These dividends are basis of the stock purchased.

The basis of real property

Sometimes, when purchasing real property, there are items paid that will add to the basis of that property. If the purchaser pays real estate taxes that the seller owed, and is not reimbursed for those taxes, they add to the basis of the property. Settlement fees can also be added to the basis of the property. (Do not include fees or costs of getting a loan on the property.) The following are settlement fees that can add to the basis of the property:

- Charges for installing utility services.
- Legal fees, including title search and preparation of the sales contract and deed.
- Recording fees.
- Surveys.
- Transfer taxes.
- Owner's title insurance.
- Any amounts that the purchaser pays that the seller owes, such as interest or recording and mortgage fees.

The following items do not add to the basis of the property: fire insurance premiums, rent for occupancy of the property before closing, or charges for utilities or other services related to occupancy of the property before closing.

Illustration 17-1

Examples of Increases and Decreases to Basis

Increases to Basis	Decreases to Basis
Capital improvements: • Putting an addition on your home • Replacing an entire roof • Paving your driveway • Installing central air conditioning • Rewiring your home Assessments for local improvements: • Water connections • Sidewalks • Roads Casualty losses: • Restoring damaged property Legal fees: • Cost of defending and perfecting a title Zoning costs	Exclusion from income of subsidies for energy conservation measures Casualty or theft loss deductions and insurance reimbursements Credit for qualified electric vehicles Section 179 deduction Deduction for clean-fuel vehicles and clean-fuel vehicle refueling property Depreciation Nontaxable corporate distributions

The Basis of Gifts

The basis of gift property received can be difficult to determine. The taxpayer must know the adjusted basis of the property to the donor, and the fair market value of the gift when it is received.

If the FMV of the gift is less than the donor's adjusted basis, the basis is determined by whether the taxpayer has a gain or loss when selling the property. If the taxpayer has a gain, the basis is the adjusted basis of the donor. If the taxpayer has a loss, the basis is the FMV when the gift is received.

If the donor's basis is used to figure a gain and you get a loss, and then use the FMV for figuring a loss then have a gain, you have neither a gain nor a loss on the sale or disposition of the property.

If the FMV of the property is equal to or greater than the Donor's adjusted basis, the taxpayer must use the adjusted basis of the donor as their basis. This is true regardless of whether the taxpayer has a gain or loss when selling the property.

The Basis of Inherited Property

The basis of inherited property is either the FMV on the date of the individual's death or the FMV on the alternate valuation date. The alternate valuation date can only be used if the deceased has an estate and the personal representative chooses to use the alternate valuation date.

Adjusted Basis

Now that we've determined what the starting basis is for the taxpayer, we must determine what the adjusted basis of it is at the time of sale. There are many items that may increase or decrease the property's basis. The table in Illustration 17-1 gives a summary of different increases and decreases that must be made to the basis of the property. Now, let's consider some examples of determining the adjusted basis of the property.

Example: You purchased some land about 10 years ago. You paid $10,000 for it when purchased and have pretty much ignored it since then. The basis of the land is $10,000.

Example: You purchased a house about 10 years ago for $25,000, and put on a new roof for $4,500, and a new driveway for $1,300. Your basis in the house is now $30,800.

Example: Your dad gave you some land as a gift. He purchased the land for $5,000. The FMV on the date he gave it to you was $15,000. Your basis is $5,000.

Example: Your dad gave you some land as a gift. He purchased the land for $15,000, but because of the value of property in that particular area, the FMV of the land when gifted to you was $5,000. Your basis in the property is determined by whether you sell the property as a gain or loss. If you sell it at a gain, the basis is $15,000. If you sell it at a loss, the basis is $5,000.

Example: Your mom is deceased and she left her house to you. She purchased it for $13,000, 20 years ago. When she died, the FMV was $97,000. Your basis in the house is $97,000.

Example: The same situation as the above example, except you had a new roof installed for $3,300, you repainted the house for $840, and you repaired some pot holes in the driveway for $120. The basis of the house now is $100,300. The repainting and fixing the driveway are repairs, and do not add to the value of the home.

Holding Period

The holding period for capital gains and losses determines how they are treated for tax purposes.

Long term

To qualify as long term, the property must have been held over one year, meaning one year and one day. To determine holding period, begin counting the day after the property is acquired. The day the property is disposed of is counted in determining the holding period.

Short term

If the property is held for one year or less, it is short term property.

Form 8949

The Form 8949 (Illustration 17-2) will assist us in learning more important factors in capital gains and losses. If the taxpayer has sold any capital assets, a Form 8949 and a Schedule D (Illustration 17-5) must be completed and filed with their tax return. Part I, of the Form 8949, is where short term sales are reported and Part II is for long term sales.

Part I

A separate Form 8949, Part I, must be completed for each of the following transactions:

- Short term transactions that were reported to the taxpayer on a Form 1099-B, (Illustration 17-5), with the cost or basis shown and the statement indicates that the basis was reported to the IRS.
- Short term transactions that were reported to the taxpayer on a Form 1099-B, on which it is indicated that the cost or basis is not reported to the IRS.
- Short term transactions for which the taxpayer did not receive a Form 1099-B.

Note: Columns b and g will be covered later in the Chapter.

Date Acquired: The date acquired is needed for determining the holding period. It is the taxpayer's responsibility to know the date they acquired the property they sold. If they use a brokerage firm or something similar, sometimes that information is provided for them. Many times, though, the taxpayer must know that information. If a block of stock was sold that was acquired at various dates, VARIOUS may be placed in the date acquired. If it is short term, it must be placed in Part I. If it is long term, place it in Part II.

Date Sold: Enter the date the property was sold. In many cases, this information will come from a Form 1099-B (Illustration 17-5).

Sales Price: If the taxpayer received a Form 1099-B, it will either have an amount for gross proceeds less commissions and option premiums or an amount for gross proceeds. Whichever it has, enter on this line.

Cost or other Basis: Enter the adjusted basis of the property in this column.

Gain or (Loss): If the sales price is more than the basis, the taxpayer will recognize a gain. If the sales price is less than the basis, the taxpayer will recognize a loss. Losses are shown in parenthesis: ().

Part II

A separate Form 8949, Part II, must be completed for each of the following transactions:

- Long term transactions that were reported to the taxpayer on a Form 1099-B, (Illustration 17-5), with the cost or basis shown and the statement indicates that the basis was reported to the IRS.
- Long term transactions that were reported to the taxpayer on a Form 1099-B, on which it is indicated that the cost or basis is not reported to the IRS.
- Long term transactions for which the taxpayer did not receive a Form 1099-B.

Note: If the taxpayer sold property they had inherited, it is long term property, regardless of how long the taxpayer held it before selling it. Enter INHERITED in the Date Acquired column.

Columns e and f

These columns should only be completed if the taxpayer encounters any of the situations shown in Illustration 17-3. If you encounter any of these situations, additional research may be required.

Schedule D

Once the Form 8949 is completed, a Schedule D must be completed.

Part I

Complete Rows 1, 2, and/or 3, as needed for each type of short term transaction the taxpayer has.

Line 6: We will cover capital loss carryovers a little later in the chapter.

Part II

Complete rows 8, 9, and/or 10, as needed for each type of long term transaction the taxpayer has.

Line 13: If the taxpayer receives capital gain distributions, those amounts are entered on this line. A capital gain distribution is a distribution paid by a mutual fund, another regulated investment trust, or a real estate investment trust. These distributions are treated as long term capital gains. Any capital gain distributions received will be reported in box 2a of Form 1099-DIV (Illustration 17-6).

Now, we know whether we have a short term gain or loss and a long term gain or loss. Next, we complete page 2 of the Schedule D to find out how they are reported.

Line 16: Any net long term gain or loss is combined with any net short term gain or loss to determine the net capital gain or loss. Let's look at the gains first and then we will come back to the losses.

Illustration 17-2

Form **8949**

Department of the Treasury
Internal Revenue Service

Sales and Other Dispositions of Capital Assets

▶ Information about Form 8949 and its separate instructions is at *www.irs.gov/form8949.*
▶ File with your Schedule D to list your transactions for lines 1b, 2, 3, 8b, 9, and 10 of Schedule D.

OMB No. 1545-0074

20**14**

Attachment
Sequence No. **12A**

Name(s) shown on return	Social security number or taxpayer identification number

Before you check Box A, B, or C below, see whether you received any Form(s) 1099-B or substitute statement(s) from your broker. A substitute statement will have the same information as Form 1099-B. Either may show your basis (usually your cost) even if your broker did not report it to the IRS. Brokers must report basis to the IRS for most stock you bought in 2011 or later (and for certain debt instruments you bought in 2014 or later).

Part I — **Short-Term.** Transactions involving capital assets you held 1 year or less are short term. For long-term transactions, see page 2.

Note. You may aggregate all short-term transactions reported on Form(s) 1099-B showing basis was reported to the IRS and for which no adjustments or codes are required. Enter the total directly on Schedule D, line 1a; you are not required to report these transactions on Form 8949 (see instructions).

You *must* check Box A, B, *or* C below. Check only one box. If more than one box applies for your short-term transactions, complete a separate Form 8949, page 1, for each applicable box. If you have more short-term transactions than will fit on this page for one or more of the boxes, complete as many forms with the same box checked as you need.

- ☐ **(A)** Short-term transactions reported on Form(s) 1099-B showing basis was reported to the IRS (see **Note** above)
- ☐ **(B)** Short-term transactions reported on Form(s) 1099-B showing basis was **not** reported to the IRS
- ☐ **(C)** Short-term transactions not reported to you on Form 1099-B

1 (a) Description of property (Example: 100 sh. XYZ Co.)	(b) Date acquired (Mo., day, yr.)	(c) Date sold or disposed (Mo., day, yr.)	(d) Proceeds (sales price) (see instructions)	(e) Cost or other basis. See the **Note** below and see *Column (e)* in the separate instructions	Adjustment, if any, to gain or loss. If you enter an amount in column (g), enter a code in column (f). **See the separate instructions.**		(h) Gain or (loss). Subtract column (e) from column (d) and combine the result with column (g)
					(f) Code(s) from instructions	**(g)** Amount of adjustment	
2 Totals. Add the amounts in columns (d), (e), (g), and (h) (subtract negative amounts). Enter each total here and include on your Schedule D, **line 1b** (if **Box A** above is checked), **line 2** (if **Box B** above is checked), or **line 3** (if **Box C** above is checked) ▶							

Note. If you checked Box A above but the basis reported to the IRS was incorrect, enter in column (e) the basis as reported to the IRS, and enter an adjustment in column (g) to correct the basis. See *Column (g)* in the separate instructions for how to figure the amount of the adjustment.

For Paperwork Reduction Act Notice, see your tax return instructions.   Cat. No. 37768Z   Form **8949** (2014)

Illustration 17-2 continued

Attachment Sequence No. **12A**   Page **2**

Name(s) shown on return. Name and SSN or taxpayer identification no. not required if shown on other side	Social security number or taxpayer identification number

Before you check Box D, E, or F below, see whether you received any Form(s) 1099-B or substitute statement(s) from your broker. A substitute statement will have the same information as Form 1099-B. Either may show your basis (usually your cost) even if your broker did not report it to the IRS. Brokers must report basis to the IRS for most stock you bought in 2011 or later (and for certain debt instruments you bought in 2014 or later).

Part II   **Long-Term.** Transactions involving capital assets you held more than 1 year are long term. For short-term transactions, see page 1.

Note. You may aggregate all long-term transactions reported on Form(s) 1099-B showing basis was reported to the IRS and for which no adjustments or codes are required. Enter the total directly on Schedule D, line 8a; you are not required to report these transactions on Form 8949 (see instructions).

You **must** check Box D, E, **or** F below. **Check only one box.** If more than one box applies for your long-term transactions, complete a separate Form 8949, page 2, for each applicable box. If you have more long-term transactions than will fit on this page for one or more of the boxes, complete as many forms with the same box checked as you need.

- ☐ **(D)** Long-term transactions reported on Form(s) 1099-B showing basis was reported to the IRS (see **Note** above)
- ☐ **(E)** Long-term transactions reported on Form(s) 1099-B showing basis was **not** reported to the IRS
- ☐ **(F)** Long-term transactions not reported to you on Form 1099-B

1 (a) Description of property (Example: 100 sh. XYZ Co.)	(b) Date acquired (Mo., day, yr.)	(c) Date sold or disposed (Mo., day, yr.)	(d) Proceeds (sales price) (see instructions)	(e) Cost or other basis. See the **Note** below and see *Column (e)* in the separate instructions	Adjustment, if any, to gain or loss. If you enter an amount in column (g), enter a code in column (f). **See the separate instructions.** (f) Code(s) from instructions	(g) Amount of adjustment	(h) Gain or (loss). Subtract column (e) from column (d) and combine the result with column (g)
2 Totals. Add the amounts in columns (d), (e), (g), and (h) (subtract negative amounts). Enter each total here and include on your Schedule D, **line 8b** (if **Box D** above is checked), **line 9** (if **Box E** above is checked), or **line 10** (if **Box F** above is checked) ▶							

Note. If you checked Box D above but the basis reported to the IRS was incorrect, enter in column (e) the basis as reported to the IRS, and enter an adjustment in column (g) to correct the basis. See *Column (g)* in the separate instructions for how to figure the amount of the adjustment.

Form **8949** (2014)

Illustration 17-3

IF . . .	THEN enter this code in column (f) . . .	AND. . .
You received a Form 1099-B (or substitute statement) and the basis shown in box 1e is incorrect	B	• If box B is checked at the top of Part I or if box E is checked at the top of Part II, enter the correct basis in column (e), and enter -0- in column (g). • If box A is checked at the top of Part I or if box D is checked at the top of Part II, enter the basis shown on Form 1099-B (or substitute statement) in column (e), even though that basis is incorrect. Correct the error by entering an adjustment in column (g). To figure the adjustment needed, see the *Worksheet for Basis Adjustments in Column (g)*. Also see *Example 4—adjustment for incorrect basis* in the instructions for column (h).
You received a Form 1099-B (or substitute statement) and the type of gain or loss (short-term or long-term) shown in box 2 is incorrect	T	Enter -0- in column (g). Report the gain or loss on the correct Part of Form 8949.
You received a Form 1099-B or 1099-S (or substitute statement) as a nominee for the actual owner of the property	N	Report the transaction on Form 8949 as you would if you were the actual owner, but also enter any resulting gain as a negative adjustment (in parentheses) in column (g) or any resulting loss as a positive adjustment in column (g). As a result of this adjustment, the amount in column (h) should be zero. However, if you received capital gain distributions as a nominee, report them instead as described under *Capital Gain Distributions* in the Instructions for Schedule D (Form 1040).
You sold or exchanged your main home at a gain, must report the sale or exchange on Part II of Form 8949 (as explained in *Sale of Your Home* in the Instructions for Schedule D (Form 1040)), and can exclude some or all of the gain	H	Report the sale or exchange on Form 8949 as you would if you were not taking the exclusion. Then enter the amount of excluded (nontaxable) gain as a negative number (in parentheses) in column (g). See the example in instructions for column (g).
You received a Form 1099-B showing accrued market discount in box 1g	D	Use the *Worksheet for Accrued Market Discount Adjustment in Column (g)*, later, to figure the amount to enter in column (g). However: • If you received a partial payment of principal on a bond, do not use the worksheet. Instead, enter the smaller of the accrued market discount or your proceeds in column (g). Also report it as interest on your tax return. • If you chose to include market discount in income currently, enter -0- in column (g). Before figuring your gain or loss, increase your basis in the bond by the market discount you have included in income for all years. See the instructions for code B, above. If the disposition of a market discount bond results in a loss subject to the wash sale rules, enter only "W" in column (f) and enter only the disallowed wash sale loss in column (g).
You sold or exchanged qualified small business stock and can exclude part of the gain	Q	Report the sale or exchange on Form 8949 as you would if you were not taking the exclusion and enter the amount of the exclusion as a negative number (in parentheses) in column (g). However, if the transaction is reported as an installment sale, see *Gain from an installment sale of QSB stock* in the Instructions for Schedule D (Form 1040).

Illustration 17-3 continued

IF . . .	THEN enter this code in column (f) . . .	AND. . .
You can exclude all or part of your gain under the rules explained in the Schedule D instructions for DC Zone assets or qualified community assets	X	Report the sale or exchange on Form 8949 as you would if you were not taking the exclusion. Then enter the amount of the exclusion as a negative number (in parentheses) in column (g).
You are electing to postpone all or part of your gain under the rules explained in the Schedule D instructions for any rollover of gain (for example, rollover of gain from QSB stock or publicly traded securities)	R	Report the sale or exchange on Form 8949 as you would if you were not making the election. Then enter the amount of postponed gain as a negative number (in parentheses) in column (g).
You have a nondeductible loss from a wash sale	W	Report the sale or exchange on Form 8949 and enter the amount of the nondeductible loss as a positive number in column (g). See the Schedule D instructions for more information about wash sales. If you received a Form 1099-B (or substitute statement) and the amount of nondeductible wash sale loss shown (box 1g with code W in box 1f of Form 1099-B) is incorrect, enter the correct amount of the nondeductible loss as a positive number in column (g). If the amount of the nondeductible loss is less than the amount shown on Form 1099-B (or substitute statement), attach a statement explaining the difference. If no part of the loss is a nondeductible loss from a wash sale transaction, enter -0- in column (g).
You have a nondeductible loss other than a loss indicated by code W	L	Report the sale or exchange on Form 8949 and enter the amount of the nondeductible loss as a positive number in column (g). See *Nondeductible Losses* in the Instructions for Schedule D (Form 1040).
You received a Form 1099-B or 1099-S (or substitute statement) for a transaction and there are selling expenses or option premiums that are not reflected on the form or statement by an adjustment to either the proceeds or basis shown	E	Enter in column (d) the proceeds shown on the form or statement you received. Enter in column (e) any cost or other basis shown on Form 1099-B (or substitute statement). In column (g), enter as a negative number (in parentheses) any selling expenses and option premium that you paid (and that are not reflected on the form or statement you received) and enter as a positive number any option premium that you received (and that is not reflected on the form or statement you received). For more information about option premiums, see *Gain or Loss From Options* in the Instructions for Schedule D (Form 1040).
You had a loss from the sale, exchange, or worthlessness of small business (section 1244) stock and the total loss is more than the maximum amount that can be treated as an ordinary loss	S	See *Small Business (Section 1244) Stock* in the Schedule D (Form 1040) instructions.
You disposed of collectibles (see the Schedule D instructions)	C	Enter -0- in column (g). Report the disposition on Form 8949 as you would report any sale or exchange.
You report multiple transactions on a single row as described in *Exception 2* or *Special provision for certain corporations, partnerships, securities dealers, and other qualified entities* under *Exceptions to reporting each transaction on a separate row*	M	See *Exception 2* and *Special provision for certain corporations, partnerships, securities dealers, and other qualified entities* under *Exceptions to reporting each transaction on a separate row*. Enter -0- in column (g) unless an adjustment is required because of another code.
You have an adjustment not explained earlier in this column	O	Enter the appropriate adjustment amount in column (g). See the instructions for column (g).
None of the other statements in this column apply	Leave columns (f) and (g) blank.	

Illustration 17-4

| SCHEDULE D
(Form 1040)

Department of the Treasury
Internal Revenue Service (99) | **Capital Gains and Losses**

▶ **Attach to Form 1040 or Form 1040NR.**
▶ **Information about Schedule D and its separate instructions is at *www.irs.gov/scheduled*.**
▶ **Use Form 8949 to list your transactions for lines 1b, 2, 3, 8b, 9, and 10.** | OMB No. 1545-0074

20**14**

Attachment
Sequence No. **12** |

Name(s) shown on return | Your social security number

Part I   Short-Term Capital Gains and Losses—Assets Held One Year or Less

See instructions for how to figure the amounts to enter on the lines below. This form may be easier to complete if you round off cents to whole dollars.	**(d)** Proceeds (sales price)	**(e)** Cost (or other basis)	**(g)** Adjustments to gain or loss from Form(s) 8949, Part I, line 2, column (g)	**(h) Gain or (loss)** Subtract column (e) from column (d) and combine the result with column (g)
1a Totals for all short-term transactions reported on Form 1099-B for which basis was reported to the IRS and for which you have no adjustments (see instructions). However, if you choose to report all these transactions on Form 8949, leave this line blank and go to line 1b .				
1b Totals for all transactions reported on Form(s) 8949 with **Box A** checked				
2 Totals for all transactions reported on Form(s) 8949 with **Box B** checked				
3 Totals for all transactions reported on Form(s) 8949 with **Box C** checked				

4 Short-term gain from Form 6252 and short-term gain or (loss) from Forms 4684, 6781, and 8824 .	**4**	
5 Net short-term gain or (loss) from partnerships, S corporations, estates, and trusts from Schedule(s) K-1	**5**	
6 Short-term capital loss carryover. Enter the amount, if any, from line 8 of your **Capital Loss Carryover Worksheet** in the instructions	**6**	( )
7 **Net short-term capital gain or (loss).** Combine lines 1a through 6 in column (h). If you have any long-term capital gains or losses, go to Part II below. Otherwise, go to Part III on the back	**7**	

Part II   Long-Term Capital Gains and Losses—Assets Held More Than One Year

See instructions for how to figure the amounts to enter on the lines below. This form may be easier to complete if you round off cents to whole dollars.	**(d)** Proceeds (sales price)	**(e)** Cost (or other basis)	**(g)** Adjustments to gain or loss from Form(s) 8949, Part II, line 2, column (g)	**(h) Gain or (loss)** Subtract column (e) from column (d) and combine the result with column (g)
8a Totals for all long-term transactions reported on Form 1099-B for which basis was reported to the IRS and for which you have no adjustments (see instructions). However, if you choose to report all these transactions on Form 8949, leave this line blank and go to line 8b .				
8b Totals for all transactions reported on Form(s) 8949 with **Box D** checked				
9 Totals for all transactions reported on Form(s) 8949 with **Box E** checked				
10 Totals for all transactions reported on Form(s) 8949 with **Box F** checked				

11 Gain from Form 4797, Part I; long-term gain from Forms 2439 and 6252; and long-term gain or (loss) from Forms 4684, 6781, and 8824	**11**	
12 Net long-term gain or (loss) from partnerships, S corporations, estates, and trusts from Schedule(s) K-1	**12**	
13 Capital gain distributions. See the instructions	**13**	
14 Long-term capital loss carryover. Enter the amount, if any, from line 13 of your **Capital Loss Carryover Worksheet** in the instructions	**14**	( )
15 **Net long-term capital gain or (loss).** Combine lines 8a through 14 in column (h). Then go to Part III on the back	**15**	

For Paperwork Reduction Act Notice, see your tax return instructions.   Cat. No. 11338H   Schedule D (Form 1040) 2014

Illustration 17-4 continued

Part III	**Summary**		

16   Combine lines 7 and 15 and enter the result **16**

     • If line 16 is a **gain,** enter the amount from line 16 on Form 1040, line 13, or Form 1040NR, line 14. Then go to line 17 below.

     • If line 16 is a **loss,** skip lines 17 through 20 below. Then go to line 21. Also be sure to complete line 22.

     • If line 16 is **zero,** skip lines 17 through 21 below and enter -0- on Form 1040, line 13, or Form 1040NR, line 14. Then go to line 22.

17   Are lines 15 and 16 **both** gains?
     ☐ **Yes.** Go to line 18.
     ☐ **No.** Skip lines 18 through 21, and go to line 22.

18   Enter the amount, if any, from line 7 of the **28% Rate Gain Worksheet** in the instructions . . ▶ **18**

19   Enter the amount, if any, from line 18 of the **Unrecaptured Section 1250 Gain Worksheet** in the instructions . . . . ▶ **19**

20   Are lines 18 and 19 **both** zero or blank?
     ☐ **Yes.** Complete the **Qualified Dividends and Capital Gain Tax Worksheet** in the instructions for Form 1040, line 44 (or in the instructions for Form 1040NR, line 42). **Do not** complete lines 21 and 22 below.

     ☐ **No.** Complete the **Schedule D Tax Worksheet** in the instructions. **Do not** complete lines 21 and 22 below.

21   If line 16 is a loss, enter here and on Form 1040, line 13, or Form 1040NR, line 14, the **smaller** of:

     • The loss on line 16 or
     • ($3,000), or if married filing separately, ($1,500)   . . . . **21** (   )

     Note. When figuring which amount is smaller, treat both amounts as positive numbers.

22   Do you have qualified dividends on Form 1040, line 9b, or Form 1040NR, line 10b?

     ☐ **Yes.** Complete the **Qualified Dividends and Capital Gain Tax Worksheet** in the instructions for Form 1040, line 44 (or in the instructions for Form 1040NR, line 42).

     ☐ **No.** Complete the rest of Form 1040 or Form 1040NR.

Illustration 17-5

☐ CORRECTED (if checked)

PAYER'S name, street address, city or town, state or province, country, ZIP or foreign postal code, and telephone no.	Applicable check box on Form 8949	OMB No. 1545-0715 2014 Form 1099-B	Proceeds From Broker and Barter Exchange Transactions
	1a Description of property (Example 100 sh. XYZ Co.)		
	1b Date acquired	**1c** Date sold or disposed	
PAYER'S federal identification number · RECIPIENT'S identification number	**1d** Proceeds $	**1e** Cost or other basis $	**Copy B** **For Recipient**
	1f Code, if any	**1g** Adjustments $	
RECIPIENT'S name	**2** Type of gain or loss: Short-term ☐ Long-term ☐	**3** If checked, basis reported to IRS ☐	This is important tax information and is being furnished to the Internal Revenue Service. If you are required to file a return, a negligence penalty or other sanction may be imposed on you if this income is taxable and the IRS determines that it has not been reported.
Street address (including apt. no.)	**4** Federal income tax withheld $	**5** If checked, noncovered security ☐	
City or town, state or province, country, and ZIP or foreign postal code	**6** Reported to IRS: Gross proceeds ☐ Net proceeds ☐	**7** If checked, loss is not allowed based on amount in 1d ☐	
	8 Profit or (loss) realized in 2014 on closed contracts $	**9** Unrealized profit or (loss) on open contracts—12/31/2013 $	
Account number (see instructions)			
CUSIP number	**10** Unrealized profit or (loss) on open contracts—12/31/2014	**11** Aggregate profit or (loss) on contracts	
14 State name · **15** State identification no. · **16** State tax withheld $ $	**12**	**13** Bartering $	

Form **1099-B**   www.irs.gov/form1099b   Department of the Treasury - Internal Revenue Service

Illustration 17-6

☐ CORRECTED (if checked)

PAYER'S name, street address, city or town, state or province, country, ZIP or foreign postal code, and telephone no.	**1a** Total ordinary dividends $	OMB No. 1545-0110	Dividends and Distributions
	1b Qualified dividends $	2014 Form 1099-DIV	
	2a Total capital gain distr. $	**2b** Unrecap. Sec. 1250 gain $	**Copy B** **For Recipient**
PAYER'S federal identification number · RECIPIENT'S identification number	**2c** Section 1202 gain $	**2d** Collectibles (28%) gain $	
RECIPIENT'S name	**3** Nondividend distributions $	**4** Federal income tax withheld $	This is important tax information and is being furnished to the Internal Revenue Service. If you are required to file a return, a negligence penalty or other sanction may be imposed on you if this income is taxable and the IRS determines that it has not been reported.
Street address (including apt. no.)		**5** Investment expenses $	
	6 Foreign tax paid $	**7** Foreign country or U.S. possession	
City or town, state or province, country, and ZIP or foreign postal code	**8** Cash liquidation distributions $	**9** Noncash liquidation distributions $	
	10 Exempt-interest dividends $	**11** Specified private activity bond interest dividends $	
Account number (see instructions)	**12** State · **13** State identification no.	**14** State tax withheld $ $	

Form **1099-DIV**   (keep for your records)   www.irs.gov/form1099div   Department of the Treasury - Internal Revenue Service

Capital Gains

Short term capital gains are treated as ordinary income. This means that they are taxed as the rest of the income is taxed. They receive no special treatment.

Long term capital gains are subject to a special capital gain tax rate. The tax rate they are subject to is determined by what kind of property it is and what tax rate the taxpayer is subject to with the rest of their income. There are special tax rates on the sale of qualified small business stock and section 1250 gain (part of the gain from the sale of real property that is from depreciation), but those are beyond the scope of this course. We will cover the tax rate on the sale of collectibles and the tax rate on the sale of regular property.

Collectibles are works of art, rugs, antiques, metal (such as gold, silver, and platinum), gems, stamps, or coins. If the sale of collectibles results in a long term gain, they are subject to a 28% maximum tax rate. The maximum tax rate means that if the taxpayer's other income is subject to a tax rate less than 28%, the gain from the sale of collectibles will be subject to the same tax rate as the other income. If the taxpayer's regular tax rate is over 28%, the gain from the sale of collectibles is subject to 28% tax rate. If the taxpayer has any gains from either of the two previous categories, they will need the Schedule D worksheet in the Schedule D instructions.

If the taxpayer had long term capital gains from property that has not already been listed above, the maximum tax rate of that property is 0% and 15%. If the taxpayer's tax rate is 15% or less, their long term capital gains are subject to the 0% tax rate. If the taxpayer's tax rate is 25%, 28%, 33%, or 35% their long term capital gains are subject to the 15% tax rate. If the taxpayer's tax rate is 39.6%, their long term capital gains are subject to the 20% tax rate.

Thankfully, the IRS provides us with a worksheet (Illustration 17-7) to make the calculations that are needed to determine the tax liabilities. We will do an example using the Schedule D tax worksheet a little later in the chapter.

Capital losses

The annual limit for a deductible capital loss is $3,000 ($1,500 for MFS). If the taxpayer's deductible capital loss is under this amount, it can all be deducted in the current year. However, if the taxpayer's deductible capital loss is over this amount, the deductible loss is limited and the excess can be carried over until next year. Remember, losses from personal use property are never deductible.

Illustration 17-7

Qualified Dividends and Capital Gain Tax Worksheet—Line 44

Keep for Your Records

Before you begin:
- ✓ See the earlier instructions for line 44 to see if you can use this worksheet to figure your tax.
- ✓ Before completing this worksheet, complete Form 1040 through line 43.
- ✓ If you do not have to file Schedule D and you received capital gain distributions, be sure you checked the box on line 13 of Form 1040.

1. Enter the amount from Form 1040, line 43. However, if you are filing Form 2555 or 2555-EZ (relating to foreign earned income), enter the amount from line 3 of the Foreign Earned Income Tax Worksheet .... 1. _____

2. Enter the amount from Form 1040, line 9b* .... 2. _____

3. Are you filing Schedule D?*
   ☐ **Yes.** Enter the **smaller** of line 15 or 16 of Schedule D. If either line 15 or line 16 is blank or a loss, enter -0-
   ☐ **No.** Enter the amount from Form 1040, line 13   } 3. _____

4. Add lines 2 and 3 .... 4. _____

5. If filing Form 4952 (used to figure investment interest expense deduction), enter any amount from line 4g of that form. Otherwise, enter -0- .... 5. _____

6. Subtract line 5 from line 4. If zero or less, enter -0- .... 6. _____

7. Subtract line 6 from line 1. If zero or less, enter -0- .... 7. _____

8. Enter:
   $36,900 if single or married filing separately,
   $73,800 if married filing jointly or qualifying widow(er),
   $49,400 if head of household. } .... 8. _____

9. Enter the smaller of line 1 or line 8 .... 9. _____

10. Enter the smaller of line 7 or line 9 .... 10. _____

11. Subtract line 10 from line 9. This amount is taxed at 0% .... 11. _____

12. Enter the smaller of line 1 or line 6 .... 12. _____

13. Enter the amount from line 11 .... 13. _____

14. Subtract line 13 from line 12 .... 14. _____

15. Enter:
    $406,750 if single,
    $228,800 if married filing separately,
    $457,600 if married filing jointly or qualifying widow(er),
    $432,200 if head of household. } .... 15. _____

16. Enter the smaller of line 1 or line 15 .... 16. _____

17. Add lines 7 and 11 .... 17. _____

18. Subtract line 17 from line 16. If zero or less, enter -0- .... 18. _____

19. Enter the smaller of line 14 or line 18 .... 19. _____

20. Multiply line 19 by 15% (.15) .... 20. _____

21. Add lines 11 and 19 .... 21. _____

22. Subtract line 21 from line 12 .... 22. _____

23. Multiply line 22 by 20% (.20) .... 23. _____

24. Figure the tax on the amount on line 7. If the amount on line 7 is less than $100,000, use the Tax Table to figure the tax. If the amount on line 7 is $100,000 or more, use the Tax Computation Worksheet .... 24. _____

25. Add lines 20, 23, and 24 .... 25. _____

26. Figure the tax on the amount on line 1. If the amount on line 1 is less than $100,000, use the Tax Table to figure the tax. If the amount on line 1 is $100,000 or more, use the Tax Computation Worksheet .... 26. _____

27. **Tax on all taxable income.** Enter the **smaller** of line 25 or line 26. Also include this amount on Form 1040, line 44. If you are filing Form 2555 or 2555-EZ, do not enter this amount on Form 1040, line 44. Instead, enter it on line 4 of the Foreign Earned Income Tax Worksheet .... 27. _____

If you are filing Form 2555 or 2555-EZ, see the footnote in the Foreign Earned Income Tax Worksheet before completing this line.

Sale of a Main Home

If the taxpayer sells their main home they may be able to exclude any gain from the sale. To be able to exclude up to $250,000 of the gain, the taxpayer must meet the following conditions:

- The ownership test
- The use test.
- Have not excluded a gain for a 2 year period ending on the date of the sale.

A married filing joint couple may be able to exclude up to $500,000 if they meet the following conditions:

- At least one spouse meets the ownership test.
- Both spouses meet the use test.
- Neither spouse has excluded a gain for a 2 year period ending on the date of the sale.

Ownership test

The taxpayer must have owned the home for at least 2 years during the 5 year period ending on the date of the sale.

Use test

The taxpayer must have lived in the home as their main home for at least 2 years during the 5 year period ending on the date of the sale.

The 2 years required for the ownership and use tests do not have to be consecutive. As long as the time can be added to equal 2 years and it all occurred during the 5 year period ending on the date of the sale, the 2 year period has been met.

There are times when the exclusion may be limited or reduced if all of the qualifications are not met. See Pub. 523 for more information.

Net Investment Income Tax

Taxpayers that meet the following modified adjusted gross income threshold and have investment income will be subject to an additional 3.9% in net investment income tax:

- $250,000 if Married Filing Jointly or Qualifying Widow(er),
- $125,000 if Married Filing Separate, or
- $200,000 if Single or Head of Household.

Investment income for this purpose includes taxable interest, ordinary dividends, Annuity distributions with a code "D" in box 7 of the Form 1099R, and certain gains and losses from the sale or disposition of property. The form 8960 (Illustration 17-8) is used to report the Net Investment Income Tax. If this is encountered, additional research is required.

Illustration 17-8

Form **8960**	**Net Investment Income Tax—**	OMB No. 1545-2227

Form **8960**

Department of the Treasury
Internal Revenue Service (99)

**Net Investment Income Tax—
Individuals, Estates, and Trusts**

▶ Attach to your tax return.
▶ **Information about Form 8960 and its separate instructions is at** *www.irs.gov/form8960.*

OMB No. 1545-2227

2014

Attachment
Sequence No. **72**

Name(s) shown on your tax return

Your social security number or EIN

Part I   Investment Income

☐ Section 6013(g) election (see instructions)
☐ Section 6013(h) election (see instructions)
☐ Regulations section 1.1411-10(g) election (see instructions)

1	Taxable interest (see instructions)	**1**	
2	Ordinary dividends (see instructions)	**2**	
3	Annuities (see instructions)	**3**	
4a	Rental real estate, royalties, partnerships, S corporations, trusts, etc. (see instructions) **4a**		
b	Adjustment for net income or loss derived in the ordinary course of a non-section 1411 trade or business (see instructions) **4b**		
c	Combine lines 4a and 4b	**4c**	
5a	Net gain or loss from disposition of property (see instructions) **5a**		
b	Net gain or loss from disposition of property that is not subject to net investment income tax (see instructions) **5b**		
c	Adjustment from disposition of partnership interest or S corporation stock (see instructions) **5c**		
d	Combine lines 5a through 5c	**5d**	
6	Adjustments to investment income for certain CFCs and PFICs (see instructions)	**6**	
7	Other modifications to investment income (see instructions)	**7**	
8	Total investment income. Combine lines 1, 2, 3, 4c, 5d, 6, and 7	**8**	

Part II   Investment Expenses Allocable to Investment Income and Modifications

9a	Investment interest expenses (see instructions) **9a**		
b	State, local, and foreign income tax (see instructions) **9b**		
c	Miscellaneous investment expenses (see instructions) **9c**		
d	Add lines 9a, 9b, and 9c	**9d**	
10	Additional modifications (see instructions)	**10**	
11	Total deductions and modifications. Add lines 9d and 10	**11**	

Part III   Tax Computation

12	Net investment income. Subtract Part II, line 11 from Part I, line 8. Individuals complete lines 13–17. Estates and trusts complete lines 18a–21. If zero or less, enter -0-	**12**	

Individuals:

13	Modified adjusted gross income (see instructions) **13**		
14	Threshold based on filing status (see instructions) **14**		
15	Subtract line 14 from line 13. If zero or less, enter -0- **15**		
16	Enter the smaller of line 12 or line 15	**16**	
17	Net investment income tax for individuals. Multiply line 16 by 3.8% (.038). **Enter here and include on your tax return** (see instructions)	**17**	

Estates and Trusts:

18a	Net investment income (line 12 above) **18a**		
b	Deductions for distributions of net investment income and deductions under section 642(c) (see instructions) **18b**		
c	Undistributed net investment income. Subtract line 18b from 18a (see instructions). If zero or less, enter -0- **18c**		
19a	Adjusted gross income (see instructions) **19a**		
b	Highest tax bracket for estates and trusts for the year (see instructions) **19b**		
c	Subtract line 19b from line 19a. If zero or less, enter -0- **19c**		
20	Enter the smaller of line 18c or line 19c	**20**	
21	Net investment income tax for estates and trusts. Multiply line 20 by 3.8% (.038). **Enter here and include on your tax return** (see instructions)	**21**	

For Paperwork Reduction Act Notice, see your tax return instructions.   Cat. No. 59474M   Form **8960** (2014)

Comprehensive Example

Colin Cuthbert sold several blocks of stock this year. We are going to prepare a Schedule D, capital gain tax worksheet, and the remainder of the Form 1040. All of the amounts on page 1 of the Form 1040 are already provided for convenience.

100 shares of ABC: purchased on 10/12/2013 for $1,290; sold on 4/3/2014 for $455

230 shares of XYZ: purchased on 1/6/2011 for $322; sold on 4/3/2014 for $3,266

332 shares of INC: purchased on 2/2/2006 for $555; sold on 4/3/2014 for $990.

Notice in the following return, if not for the special long term capital gain tax rate, Mr. Cuthbert would have paid $13,225 in taxes. However, because his capital gain is only taxed at a 15% rate, he only has to pay $12,970 in taxes.

Form **1040**

Department of the Treasury—Internal Revenue Service (99)

U.S. Individual Income Tax Return **2014**

OMB No. 1545-0074 | IRS Use Only—Do not write or staple in this space.

For the year Jan. 1–Dec. 31, 2014, or other tax year beginning _____ , 2014, ending _____ , 20 ____ | See separate instructions.

Your first name and initial	Last name	Your social security number
Colin	Cuthbert	3 3 3 3 3 3 3 3 3

If a joint return, spouse's first name and initial | Last name | Spouse's social security number

Home address (number and street). If you have a P.O. box, see instructions. | Apt. no.

100 First Ave.

▲ Make sure the SSN(s) above and on line 6c are correct.

City, town or post office, state, and ZIP code. If you have a foreign address, also complete spaces below (see instructions).

Your City, Your State, Your Zip Code

Foreign country name | Foreign province/state/county | Foreign postal code

Presidential Election Campaign
Check here if you, or your spouse if filing jointly, want $3 to go to this fund. Checking a box below will not change your tax or refund. ☐ You ☐ Spouse

Filing Status

Check only one box.

1. ☑ Single
2. ☐ Married filing jointly (even if only one had income)
3. ☐ Married filing separately. Enter spouse's SSN above and full name here. ▶
4. ☐ Head of household (with qualifying person). (See instructions.) If the qualifying person is a child but not your dependent, enter this child's name here. ▶
5. ☐ Qualifying widow(er) with dependent child

Exemptions

6a ☑ **Yourself.** If someone can claim you as a dependent, **do not** check box 6a . . . . .
b ☐ **Spouse** . . . .

Boxes checked on 6a and 6b	1

c **Dependents:**

(1) First name Last name	(2) Dependent's social security number	(3) Dependent's relationship to you	(4) ✓ if child under age 17 qualifying for child tax credit (see instructions)
			☐
			☐
			☐
			☐

If more than four dependents, see instructions and check here ▶ ☐

No. of children on 6c who:
• lived with you ____
• did not live with you due to divorce or separation (see instructions) ____
Dependents on 6c not entered above ____

d Total number of exemptions claimed . . . .

Add numbers on lines above ▶ | 1

Income

Attach Form(s) W-2 here. Also attach Forms W-2G and 1099-R if tax was withheld.

If you did not get a W-2, see instructions.

7	Wages, salaries, tips, etc. Attach Form(s) W-2	**7**	77,099 00
8a	**Taxable** interest. Attach Schedule B if required	**8a**	
b	**Tax-exempt** interest. **Do not** include on line 8a . . .	8b	
9a	Ordinary dividends. Attach Schedule B if required	**9a**	
b	Qualified dividends	9b	
10	Taxable refunds, credits, or offsets of state and local income taxes	**10**	
11	Alimony received	**11**	
12	Business income or (loss). Attach Schedule C or C-EZ	**12**	
13	Capital gain or (loss). Attach Schedule D if required. If not required, check here ▶ ☐	**13**	2,544 00
14	Other gains or (losses). Attach Form 4797	**14**	
15a	IRA distributions . 15a	b Taxable amount . . .	**15b**	
16a	Pensions and annuities 16a	b Taxable amount . . .	**16b**	
17	Rental real estate, royalties, partnerships, S corporations, trusts, etc. Attach Schedule E	**17**	
18	Farm income or (loss). Attach Schedule F	**18**	
19	Unemployment compensation	**19**	
20a	Social security benefits 20a	b Taxable amount . . .	**20b**	
21	Other income. List type and amount	**21**	
22	Combine the amounts in the far right column for lines 7 through 21. This is your **total income** ▶	**22**	79,643 00

Adjusted Gross Income

23	Educator expenses	23	
24	Certain business expenses of reservists, performing artists, and fee-basis government officials. Attach Form 2106 or 2106-EZ	24	
25	Health savings account deduction. Attach Form 8889 .	25	
26	Moving expenses. Attach Form 3903	26	
27	Deductible part of self-employment tax. Attach Schedule SE .	27	
28	Self-employed SEP, SIMPLE, and qualified plans . . .	28	
29	Self-employed health insurance deduction	29	
30	Penalty on early withdrawal of savings	30	
31a	Alimony paid b Recipient's SSN ▶	31a	
32	IRA deduction	32	
33	Student loan interest deduction	33	
34	Tuition and fees. Attach Form 8917	34	
35	Domestic production activities deduction. Attach Form 8903	35	
36	Add lines 23 through 35	36	
37	Subtract line 36 from line 22. This is your **adjusted gross income** . . . . . . ▶	37	79,643 00

For Disclosure, Privacy Act, and Paperwork Reduction Act Notice, see separate instructions.   Cat. No. 11320B   Form **1040** (2014)

Tax and Credits	38	Amount from line 37 (adjusted gross income)	38	79,643	00
	39a	Check if: ☐ **You** were born before January 2, 1950, ☐ Blind. ☐ **Spouse** was born before January 2, 1950, ☐ Blind. } **Total boxes** checked ▶ 39a			
	b	If your spouse itemizes on a separate return or you were a dual-status alien, check here ▶ 39b☐			
Standard Deduction for— • People who check any box on line 39a or 39b **or** who can be claimed as a dependent, see instructions. • All others: Single or Married filing separately, $6,200 Married filing jointly or Qualifying widow(er), $12,400 Head of household, $9,100	40	**Itemized deductions** (from Schedule A) **or** your **standard deduction** (see left margin) . .	40	6,200	00
	41	Subtract line 40 from line 38	41	73,443	00
	42	**Exemptions.** If line 38 is $152,525 or less, multiply $3,950 by the number on line 6d. Otherwise, see instructions	42	3,950	00
	43	**Taxable income.** Subtract line 42 from line 41. If line 42 is more than line 41, enter -0-	43	69,493	00
	44	**Tax** (see instructions). Check if any from: **a** ☐ Form(s) 8814 **b** ☐ Form 4972 **c** ☐	44	12,970	00
	45	**Alternative minimum tax** (see instructions). Attach Form 6251	45		
	46	Excess advance premium tax credit repayment. Attach Form 8962	46		
	47	Add lines 44, 45, and 46 . . . . ▶	47	12,970	00
	48	Foreign tax credit. Attach Form 1116 if required	48		
	49	Credit for child and dependent care expenses. Attach Form 2441	49		
	50	Education credits from Form 8863, line 19	50		
	51	Retirement savings contributions credit. Attach Form 8880	51		
	52	Child tax credit. Attach Schedule 8812, if required . . .	52		
	53	Residential energy credits. Attach Form 5695	53		
	54	Other credits from Form: **a** ☐ 3800 **b** ☐ 8801 **c** ☐	54		
	55	Add lines 48 through 54. These are your **total credits**	55		
	56	Subtract line 55 from line 47. If line 55 is more than line 47, enter -0- . . . . ▶	56	12,970	00
Other Taxes	57	Self-employment tax. Attach Schedule SE	57		
	58	Unreported social security and Medicare tax from Form: **a** ☐ 4137 **b** ☐ 8919 . .	58		
	59	Additional tax on IRAs, other qualified retirement plans, etc. Attach Form 5329 if required . .	59		
	60a	Household employment taxes from Schedule H	60a		
	b	First-time homebuyer credit repayment. Attach Form 5405 if required	60b		
	61	Health care: individual responsibility (see instructions) Full-year coverage ☑	61		
	62	Taxes from: **a** ☐ Form 8959 **b** ☐ Form 8960 **c** ☐ Instructions; enter code(s)	62		
	63	Add lines 56 through 62. This is your **total tax** . . . . ▶	63	12,970	00
Payments If you have a qualifying child, attach Schedule EIC.	64	Federal income tax withheld from Forms W-2 and 1099 . .	64	14,000	00
	65	2014 estimated tax payments and amount applied from 2013 return	65		
	66a	**Earned income credit (EIC)**	66a		
	b	Nontaxable combat pay election 66b			
	67	Additional child tax credit. Attach Schedule 8812	67		
	68	American opportunity credit from Form 8863, line 8 . . .	68		
	69	Net premium tax credit. Attach Form 8962	69		
	70	Amount paid with request for extension to file	70		
	71	Excess social security and tier 1 RRTA tax withheld . . .	71		
	72	Credit for federal tax on fuels. Attach Form 4136 . . .	72		
	73	Credits from Form: **a** ☐ 2439 **b** ☐ Reserved **c** ☐ Reserved **d** ☐	73		
	74	Add lines 64, 65, 66a, and 67 through 73. These are your **total payments** . . . . . ▶	74	14,000	00
Refund Direct deposit? ▶ See instructions.	75	If line 74 is more than line 63, subtract line 63 from line 74. This is the amount you **overpaid**	75	1,030	00
	76a	Amount of line 75 you want **refunded to you.** If Form 8888 is attached, check here . ▶ ☐	76a	1,030	00
	▶ b	Routing number			
	▶ c	Type: ☐ Checking ☐ Savings			
	▶ d	Account number			
	77	Amount of line 75 you want **applied to your 2015 estimated tax** ▶ 77			
Amount You Owe	78	**Amount you owe.** Subtract line 74 from line 63. For details on how to pay, see instructions ▶	78		
	79	Estimated tax penalty (see instructions) 79			

Third Party Designee	Do you want to allow another person to discuss this return with the IRS (see instructions)? ☐ **Yes.** Complete below. ☑ **No**
	Designee's name ▶ Phone no. ▶ Personal identification number (PIN) ▶

Sign Here Joint return? See instructions. Keep a copy for your records.	Under penalties of perjury, I declare that I have examined this return and accompanying schedules and statements, and to the best of my knowledge and belief, they are true, correct, and complete. Declaration of preparer (other than taxpayer) is based on all information of which preparer has any knowledge.		
	Your signature Date	Your occupation **Manager**	Daytime phone number **(555)555-5555**
	Spouse's signature. If a joint return, **both** must sign. Date	Spouse's occupation	If the IRS sent you an Identity Protection PIN, enter it here (see inst.)

Paid Preparer Use Only	Print/Type preparer's name Jane Doe	Preparer's signature	Date	Check ☐ if self employed	PTIN P00000000
	Firm's name ▶ **My Tax Service**			Firm's EIN ▶	**63-0000000**
	Firm's address ▶ **100 Main St., Your City, Your State, Your Zip Code**			Phone no.	**(555)555-1111**

SCHEDULE D
(Form 1040)

Department of the Treasury
Internal Revenue Service (99)

Capital Gains and Losses

▶ Attach to Form 1040 or Form 1040NR.
▶ Information about Schedule D and its separate instructions is at *www.irs.gov/scheduled*.
▶ Use Form 8949 to list your transactions for lines 1b, 2, 3, 8b, 9, and 10.

OMB No. 1545-0074

20**14**

Attachment
Sequence No. **12**

Name(s) shown on return

Colin Cuthbert

Your social security number

333-33-3333

Part I — Short-Term Capital Gains and Losses—Assets Held One Year or Less

See instructions for how to figure the amounts to enter on the lines below. This form may be easier to complete if you round off cents to whole dollars.	(d) Proceeds (sales price)	(e) Cost (or other basis)	(g) Adjustments to gain or loss from Form(s) 8949, Part I, line 2, column (g)	(h) Gain or (loss) Subtract column (e) from column (d) and combine the result with column (g)
1a Totals for all short-term transactions reported on Form 1099-B for which basis was reported to the IRS and for which you have no adjustments (see instructions). However, if you choose to report all these transactions on Form 8949, leave this line blank and go to line 1b .				
1b Totals for all transactions reported on Form(s) 8949 with **Box A** checked				
2 Totals for all transactions reported on Form(s) 8949 with **Box B** checked	455	1,290		(835)
3 Totals for all transactions reported on Form(s) 8949 with **Box C** checked				

4 Short-term gain from Form 6252 and short-term gain or (loss) from Forms 4684, 6781, and 8824 .	**4**	
5 Net short-term gain or (loss) from partnerships, S corporations, estates, and trusts from Schedule(s) K-1	**5**	
6 Short-term capital loss carryover. Enter the amount, if any, from line 8 of your **Capital Loss Carryover Worksheet** in the instructions	**6**	( )
7 **Net short-term capital gain or (loss).** Combine lines 1a through 6 in column (h). If you have any long-term capital gains or losses, go to Part II below. Otherwise, go to Part III on the back	**7**	(835)

Part II — Long-Term Capital Gains and Losses—Assets Held More Than One Year

See instructions for how to figure the amounts to enter on the lines below. This form may be easier to complete if you round off cents to whole dollars.	(d) Proceeds (sales price)	(e) Cost (or other basis)	(g) Adjustments to gain or loss from Form(s) 8949, Part II, line 2, column (g)	(h) Gain or (loss) Subtract column (e) from column (d) and combine the result with column (g)
8a Totals for all long-term transactions reported on Form 1099-B for which basis was reported to the IRS and for which you have no adjustments (see instructions). However, if you choose to report all these transactions on Form 8949, leave this line blank and go to line 8b .				
8b Totals for all transactions reported on Form(s) 8949 with **Box D** checked				
9 Totals for all transactions reported on Form(s) 8949 with **Box E** checked	4,256	877		3,379
10 Totals for all transactions reported on Form(s) 8949 with **Box F** checked.				

11 Gain from Form 4797, Part I; long-term gain from Forms 2439 and 6252; and long-term gain or (loss) from Forms 4684, 6781, and 8824	**11**	
12 Net long-term gain or (loss) from partnerships, S corporations, estates, and trusts from Schedule(s) K-1	**12**	
13 Capital gain distributions. See the instructions	**13**	
14 Long-term capital loss carryover. Enter the amount, if any, from line 13 of your **Capital Loss Carryover Worksheet** in the instructions	**14**	( )
15 **Net long-term capital gain or (loss).** Combine lines 8a through 14 in column (h). Then go to Part III on the back	**15**	3,379

For Paperwork Reduction Act Notice, see your tax return instructions.   Cat. No. 11338H   Schedule D (Form 1040) 2014

| **Part III** | **Summary** | |

16 Combine lines 7 and 15 and enter the result . . . . **16** | 2,544

- If line 16 is a **gain,** enter the amount from line 16 on Form 1040, line 13, or Form 1040NR, line 14. Then go to line 17 below.
- If line 16 is a **loss,** skip lines 17 through 20 below. Then go to line 21. Also be sure to complete line 22.
- If line 16 is **zero,** skip lines 17 through 21 below and enter -0- on Form 1040, line 13, or Form 1040NR, line 14. Then go to line 22.

17 Are lines 15 and 16 **both** gains?
- ☑ **Yes.** Go to line 18.
- ☐ **No.** Skip lines 18 through 21, and go to line 22.

18 Enter the amount, if any, from line 7 of the **28% Rate Gain Worksheet** in the instructions . . ▶ **18**

19 Enter the amount, if any, from line 18 of the **Unrecaptured Section 1250 Gain Worksheet** in the instructions . . . . ▶ **19**

20 Are lines 18 and 19 **both** zero or blank?
- ☑ **Yes.** Complete the **Qualified Dividends and Capital Gain Tax Worksheet** in the instructions for Form 1040, line 44 (or in the instructions for Form 1040NR, line 42). **Do not** complete lines 21 and 22 below.
- ☐ **No.** Complete the **Schedule D Tax Worksheet** in the instructions. **Do not** complete lines 21 and 22 below.

21 If line 16 is a loss, enter here and on Form 1040, line 13, or Form 1040NR, line 14, the **smaller** of:
- The loss on line 16 or
- ($3,000), or if married filing separately, ($1,500) . . . . **21** ( )

Note. When figuring which amount is smaller, treat both amounts as positive numbers.

22 Do you have qualified dividends on Form 1040, line 9b, or Form 1040NR, line 10b?

- ☐ **Yes.** Complete the **Qualified Dividends and Capital Gain Tax Worksheet** in the instructions for Form 1040, line 44 (or in the instructions for Form 1040NR, line 42).
- ☐ **No.** Complete the rest of Form 1040 or Form 1040NR.

Schedule D (Form 1040) 2014

Form **8949**

Department of the Treasury
Internal Revenue Service

Sales and Other Dispositions of Capital Assets

▶ Information about Form 8949 and its separate instructions is at *www.irs.gov/form8949.*

▶ File with your Schedule D to list your transactions for lines 1b, 2, 3, 8b, 9, and 10 of Schedule D.

OMB No. 1545-0074

2014

Attachment
Sequence No. **12A**

Name(s) shown on return	Social security number or taxpayer identification number
Colin Cuthbert	333-33-3333

Before you check Box A, B, or C below, see whether you received any Form(s) 1099-B or substitute statement(s) from your broker. A substitute statement will have the same information as Form 1099-B. Either may show your basis (usually your cost) even if your broker did not report it to the IRS. Brokers must report basis to the IRS for most stock you bought in 2011 or later (and for certain debt instruments you bought in 2014 or later).

Part I **Short-Term.** Transactions involving capital assets you held 1 year or less are short term. For long-term transactions, see page 2.

Note. You may aggregate all short-term transactions reported on Form(s) 1099-B showing basis was reported to the IRS and for which no adjustments or codes are required. Enter the total directly on Schedule D, line 1a; you are not required to report these transactions on Form 8949 (see instructions).

You *must* check Box A, B, *or* C below. Check only one box. If more than one box applies for your short-term transactions, complete a separate Form 8949, page 1, for each applicable box. If you have more short-term transactions than will fit on this page for one or more of the boxes, complete as many forms with the same box checked as you need.

- ☐ **(A)** Short-term transactions reported on Form(s) 1099-B showing basis was reported to the IRS (see **Note** above)
- ☑ **(B)** Short-term transactions reported on Form(s) 1099-B showing basis was **not** reported to the IRS
- ☐ **(C)** Short-term transactions not reported to you on Form 1099-B

1 (a) Description of property (Example: 100 sh. XYZ Co.)	(b) Date acquired (Mo., day, yr.)	(c) Date sold or disposed (Mo., day, yr.)	(d) Proceeds (sales price) (see instructions)	(e) Cost or other basis. See the **Note** below and see *Column (e)* in the separate instructions	Adjustment, if any, to gain or loss. If you enter an amount in column (g), enter a code in column (f). See the separate instructions.		(h) Gain or (loss). Subtract column (e) from column (d) and combine the result with column (g)
					(f) Code(s) from instructions	(g) Amount of adjustment	
100 sh ABC	10/12/13	04/03/14	455	1,290			(835)
2 Totals. Add the amounts in columns (d), (e), (g), and (h) (subtract negative amounts). Enter each total here and include on your Schedule D, **line 1b** (if **Box A** above is checked), **line 2** (if **Box B** above is checked), or **line 3** (if **Box C** above is checked) ▶			455	1,290			(835)

Note. If you checked Box A above but the basis reported to the IRS was incorrect, enter in column (e) the basis as reported to the IRS, and enter an adjustment in column (g) to correct the basis. See *Column (g)* in the separate instructions for how to figure the amount of the adjustment.

For Paperwork Reduction Act Notice, see your tax return instructions.   Cat. No. 37768Z   Form **8949** (2014)

Name(s) shown on return. Name and SSN or taxpayer identification no. not required if shown on other side	Social security number or taxpayer identification number
Colin Cuthbert	333-33-3333

Before you check Box D, E, or F below, see whether you received any Form(s) 1099-B or substitute statement(s) from your broker. A substitute statement will have the same information as Form 1099-B. Either may show your basis (usually your cost) even if your broker did not report it to the IRS. Brokers must report basis to the IRS for most stock you bought in 2011 or later (and for certain debt instruments you bought in 2014 or later).

Part II **Long-Term.** Transactions involving capital assets you held more than 1 year are long term. For short-term transactions, see page 1.

Note. You may aggregate all long-term transactions reported on Form(s) 1099-B showing basis was reported to the IRS and for which no adjustments or codes are required. Enter the total directly on Schedule D, line 8a; you are not required to report these transactions on Form 8949 (see instructions).

You **must** check Box D, E, **or** F below. **Check only one box.** If more than one box applies for your long-term transactions, complete a separate Form 8949, page 2, for each applicable box. If you have more long-term transactions than will fit on this page for one or more of the boxes, complete as many forms with the same box checked as you need.

- ☐ **(D)** Long-term transactions reported on Form(s) 1099-B showing basis was reported to the IRS (see **Note** above)
- ☑ **(E)** Long-term transactions reported on Form(s) 1099-B showing basis was **not** reported to the IRS
- ☐ **(F)** Long-term transactions not reported to you on Form 1099-B

1 (a) Description of property (Example: 100 sh. XYZ Co.)	(b) Date acquired (Mo., day, yr.)	(c) Date sold or disposed (Mo., day, yr.)	(d) Proceeds (sales price) (see instructions)	(e) Cost or other basis. See the **Note** below and see *Column (e)* in the separate instructions	(f) Code(s) from instructions	(g) Amount of adjustment	(h) Gain or (loss). Subtract column (e) from column (d) and combine the result with column (g)
230 sh XYZ	01/06/11	04/03/14	3,266	322			2,944
332 sh INC	02/02/06	04/03/14	990	555			435
2 Totals. Add the amounts in columns (d), (e), (g), and (h) (subtract negative amounts). Enter each total here and include on your Schedule D, **line 8b** (if **Box D** above is checked), **line 9** (if **Box E** above is checked), or **line 10** (if **Box F** above is checked) ▶			4,256	877			3,379

Note. If you checked Box D above but the basis reported to the IRS was incorrect, enter in column (e) the basis as reported to the IRS, and enter an adjustment in column (g) to correct the basis. See *Column (g)* in the separate instructions for how to figure the amount of the adjustment.

Form **0040** (2014)

Qualified Dividends and Capital Gain Tax Worksheet—Line 44

Keep for Your Records

Before you begin:	√ See the earlier instructions for line 44 to see if you can use this worksheet to figure your tax.	
	√ Before completing this worksheet, complete Form 1040 through line 43.	
	√ If you do not have to file Schedule D and you received capital gain distributions, be sure you checked the box on line 13 of Form 1040.	

1. Enter the amount from Form 1040, line 43. However, if you are filing Form 2555 or 2555-EZ (relating to foreign earned income), enter the amount from line 3 of the Foreign Earned Income Tax Worksheet **1.**   **69,493**

2. Enter the amount from Form 1040, line 9b* .... **2.** _____

3. Are you filing Schedule D?*

   ■ **Yes.** Enter the **smaller** of line 15 or 16 of Schedule D. If either line 15 or line 16 is blank or a loss, enter -0- } **3.**   **2,544**

   □ **No.** Enter the amount from Form 1040, line 13

4. Add lines 2 and 3 .... **4.**   **2,544**

5. If filing Form 4952 (used to figure investment interest expense deduction), enter any amount from line 4g of that form. Otherwise, enter -0- .... **5.**

6. Subtract line 5 from line 4. If zero or less, enter -0- **6.**   **2,544**

7. Subtract line 6 from line 1. If zero or less, enter -0- **7.**   **66,949**

8. Enter:
   $36,900 if single or married filing separately,
   $73,800 if married filing jointly or qualifying widow(er),
   $49,400 if head of household. } **8.**   **36,900**

9. Enter the smaller of line 1 or line 8 .... **9.**   **36,900**

10. Enter the smaller of line 7 or line 9 .... **10.**   **36,900**

11. Subtract line 10 from line 9. This amount is taxed at 0% **11.**   **0**

12. Enter the smaller of line 1 or line 6 .... **12.**   **2,544**

13. Enter the amount from line 11 .... **13.**   **0**

14. Subtract line 13 from line 12 .... **14.**   **2,544**

15. Enter:
    $406,750 if single,
    $228,800 if married filing separately,
    $457,600 if married filing jointly or qualifying widow(er),
    $432,200 if head of household. } **15.**   **406,750**

16. Enter the smaller of line 1 or line 15 .... **16.**   **69,493**

17. Add lines 7 and 11 .... **17.**   **66,949**

18. Subtract line 17 from line 16. If zero or less, enter -0- **18.**   **2,544**

19. Enter the smaller of line 14 or line 18 .... **19.**   **2,544**

20. Multiply line 19 by 15% (.15) **20.**   **382**

21. Add lines 11 and 19 .... **21.**   **2,544**

22. Subtract line 21 from line 12 .... **22.**   **0**

23. Multiply line 22 by 20% (.20) **23.**   **0**

24. Figure the tax on the amount on line 7. If the amount on line 7 is less than $100,000, use the Tax Table to figure the tax. If the amount on line 7 is $100,000 or more, use the Tax Computation Worksheet **24.**   **12,588**

25. Add lines 20, 23, and 24 .... **25.**   **12,970**

26. Figure the tax on the amount on line 1. If the amount on line 1 is less than $100,000, use the Tax Table to figure the tax. If the amount on line 1 is $100,000 or more, use the Tax Computation Worksheet **26.**   **13,225**

27. **Tax on all taxable income.** Enter the **smaller** of line 25 or line 26. Also include this amount on Form 1040, line 44. If you are filing Form 2555 or 2555-EZ, do not enter this amount on Form 1040, line 44. Instead, enter it on line 4 of the Foreign Earned Income Tax Worksheet **27.**   **12,970**

If you are filing Form 2555 or 2555-EZ, see the footnote in the Foreign Earned Income Tax Worksheet before completing this line.

Chapter Review

1) What is the basis of inherited property?

2) What is the automatic holding period of inherited property?

3) Do repairs add to the basis of the property?

4) Do improvements add to the basis of property?

5) How long does property have to be held to be considered long term property?

6) What is the benefit of selling long term property as opposed to short term?

7) What is the capital loss limit?

8) What is the maximum exclusion amount for the sale of a main home?

Exercise

Prepare a tax return for Gweneth George. She is single and an Event Coordinator. She does not want to designate $3 for the presidential campaign fund. She doesn't receive any type of Veteran's Affairs or Social Security benefits. Her birth date is April 3, 1982. She has health care coverage through her employer which began on March 1st, 2014. She sold some land she inherited along with some stock she had purchased. She inherited the land from her Mom on April 15, 2014 and she sold it on June 14, 2014. It cost her Mom $1,200 when she purchased it. It was worth $15,600 when Gweneth's mom passed away. Gweneth sold it for $16,000. She did not receive a Form 1099 for the sale of the land. The stock she sold are as follows:

5 shares of ABC purchased on 01/05/14 for $544; sold on 11/15/14 for $650.

67 shares of BBB purchased on 03/06/06 for $577; sold on 12/12/14 for $1,200.

These transactions were reported on a Form 1099B showing basis was not reported to the IRS.

a Employee's social security number 333-33-4454		OMB No. 1545-0008	Safe, accurate, FAST! Use	IRS e~file	Visit the IRS website at www.irs.gov/efile
b Employer identification number (EIN) 72-9643452		**1** Wages, tips, other compensation 44,566.22		**2** Federal income tax withheld 5,999.87	
c Employer's name, address, and ZIP code Geneva's Inn 243 Knott Dr. Your City, Your State, Your Zip Code		**3** Social security wages 44,566.22		**4** Social security tax withheld 2,763.11	
		5 Medicare wages and tips 44,566.22		**6** Medicare tax withheld 646.22	
		7 Social security tips		**8** Allocated tips	
d Control number		**9**		**10** Dependent care benefits	
e Employee's first name and initial Last name Suff.		**11** Nonqualified plans		**12a** See instructions for box 12 DD 6,059.23	
Gweneth George 250 First Ave. Your City, Your State, Your Zip Code		**13** Statutory employee ☐ Retirement plan ☐ Third-party sick pay ☐		**12b**	
		14 Other		**12c**	
				12d	
f Employee's address and ZIP code					

15 State	Employer's state ID number	16 State wages, tips, etc.	17 State income tax	18 Local wages, tips, etc.	19 Local income tax	20 Locality name
YS	72-9643457	44,566.22	1,782.65			

Form **W-2** Wage and Tax Statement **2014** Department of the Treasury—Internal Revenue Service

Copy B—To Be Filed With Employee's FEDERAL Tax Return.
This information is being furnished to the Internal Revenue Service.

Chapter 18 – AMT, Kiddie Tax, Underpayments, and Estimates

Alternative Minimum Tax (AMT)

Alternative minimum tax is a tax that was developed to limit certain tax benefits for taxpayer's with higher economic incomes. If a taxpayer makes above a certain amount of income and some of the income receives favorable treatment or they have certain deductions that can greatly reduce the tax they pay, AMT comes into play. AMT will limit the amounts these benefits can reduce the tax owed.

Alternative minimum tax can apply to taxpayers if their taxable income combined with certain adjustments and tax preference items is more than:

- $52,800 if Single or Head of Household.
- $82,100 if Married Filing Joint or Qualifying Widow(er).
- $41,050 if Married Filing Separately.

The certain adjustments and tax preference items that must be applied to the taxable income are:

- Addition of personal exemptions,
- Addition of standard deduction if claimed,
- Addition of itemized deductions claimed for state and local taxes, certain interest, most miscellaneous deductions, and part of medical expenses,
- Subtraction of any refund of state and local taxes included in gross income,
- Changes to accelerated depreciation for certain property,
- Difference between gain or loss on the sale of property reported for regular tax purposes and AMT purposes.
- Addition of certain income from incentive stock options,
- Change in certain passive activity loss deductions,
- Addition of certain depletion that is more than the adjusted basis of the property,
- Addition of part of the deduction for certain intangible drilling costs, and
- Addition of tax-exempt interest on certain private activity bonds.

As you can see, AMT can be a very complex subject. Illustration 18-1 shows the Form 6251 which must be filed if the taxpayer qualifies for the AMT.

Example: A tax return for Rodney and Rhonda Bowers follows. Rodney is in outside sales, and Rhonda is a manager. Rodney's W-2 wages are $98,221 with $8,983 federal taxes withheld and $2,053 state taxes withheld. Rhonda's W-2 wages are $36,322 with $4,203 federal taxes withheld and $1,012 state taxes withheld. Rodney put 55,950 total miles on his vehicle. 40,362 miles were for business. He had $11,998 in travel expenses and $5,233 in other business expenses. The Bowers paid $8,891 of mortgage interest, $2,521 of real estate taxes, $93 of personal property taxes, and $691 of charitable contributions. (Illustration 18-2)

Notice the AMT form (Form 6251); we take his taxable income before the exemptions have been deducted, and we add the taxes paid, along with the miscellaneous deductions that were claimed on the Schedule A, back into the taxable income. The taxpayers are filing Married Filing Jointly so their AMT exemption is $82,100. Their taxable income for AMT purposes is $42,861. This income is taxed at 26%. The tax that was already entered on the Form 1040 is then deducted to prevent double taxation. The taxpayers are left with $763 in Alternative Minimum Taxes. This amount is entered on the Form 1040, page 2, line 45.

We will not cover AMT any further in this course.

Illustration 18-1

Form 6251

Department of the Treasury
Internal Revenue Service (99)

Alternative Minimum Tax—Individuals

▶ Information about Form 6251 and its separate instructions is at *www.irs.gov/form6251.*
▶ Attach to Form 1040 or Form 1040NR.

OMB No. 1545-0074

2014

Attachment
Sequence No. **32**

Name(s) shown on Form 1040 or Form 1040NR

Your social security number

Part I   Alternative Minimum Taxable Income (See instructions for how to complete each line.)

1	If filing Schedule A (Form 1040), enter the amount from Form 1040, line 41, and go to line 2. Otherwise, enter the amount from Form 1040, line 38, and go to line 7. (If less than zero, enter as a negative amount.)	**1**
2	Medical and dental. If you or your spouse was 65 or older, enter the **smaller** of Schedule A (Form 1040), line 4, **or** 2.5% (.025) of Form 1040, line 38. If zero or less, enter -0-	**2**
3	Taxes from Schedule A (Form 1040), line 9	**3**
4	Enter the home mortgage interest adjustment, if any, from line 6 of the worksheet in the instructions for this line	**4**
5	Miscellaneous deductions from Schedule A (Form 1040), line 27.	**5**
6	If Form 1040, line 38, is $152,525 or less, enter -0-. Otherwise, see instructions	**6** ( )
7	Tax refund from Form 1040, line 10 or line 21	**7** ( )
8	Investment interest expense (difference between regular tax and AMT).	**8**
9	Depletion (difference between regular tax and AMT)	**9**
10	Net operating loss deduction from Form 1040, line 21. Enter as a positive amount	**10**
11	Alternative tax net operating loss deduction	**11** ( )
12	Interest from specified private activity bonds exempt from the regular tax	**12**
13	Qualified small business stock (7% of gain excluded under section 1202)	**13**
14	Exercise of incentive stock options (excess of AMT income over regular tax income)	**14**
15	Estates and trusts (amount from Schedule K-1 (Form 1041), box 12, code A)	**15**
16	Electing large partnerships (amount from Schedule K-1 (Form 1065-B), box 6)	**16**
17	Disposition of property (difference between AMT and regular tax gain or loss)	**17**
18	Depreciation on assets placed in service after 1986 (difference between regular tax and AMT)	**18**
19	Passive activities (difference between AMT and regular tax income or loss)	**19**
20	Loss limitations (difference between AMT and regular tax income or loss)	**20**
21	Circulation costs (difference between regular tax and AMT)	**21**
22	Long-term contracts (difference between AMT and regular tax income)	**22**
23	Mining costs (difference between regular tax and AMT)	**23**
24	Research and experimental costs (difference between regular tax and AMT)	**24**
25	Income from certain installment sales before January 1, 1987	**25** ( )
26	Intangible drilling costs preference	**26**
27	Other adjustments, including income-based related adjustments	**27**
28	**Alternative minimum taxable income.** Combine lines 1 through 27. (If married filing separately and line 28 is more than $242,450, see instructions.)	**28**

Part II   Alternative Minimum Tax (AMT)

29	Exemption. (If you were under age 24 at the end of 2014, see instructions.)	

IF your filing status is ...	AND line 28 is not over ...	THEN enter on line 29 ...	
Single or head of household	$117,300	$52,800	
Married filing jointly or qualifying widow(er)	156,500	82,100	
Married filing separately	78,250	41,050	**29**

If line 28 is **over** the amount shown above for your filing status, see instructions.

30	Subtract line 29 from line 28. If more than zero, go to line 31. If zero or less, enter -0- here and on lines 31, 33, and 35, and go to line 34	**30**
31	• If you are filing Form 2555 or 2555-EZ, see instructions for the amount to enter. • If you reported capital gain distributions directly on Form 1040, line 13; you reported qualified dividends on Form 1040, line 9b; **or** you had a gain on both lines 15 and 16 of Schedule D (Form 1040) (as refigured for the AMT, if necessary), complete Part III on the back and enter the amount from line 64 here. • **All others:** If line 30 is $182,500 or less ($91,250 or less if married filing separately), multiply line 30 by 26% (.26). Otherwise, multiply line 30 by 28% (.28) and subtract $3,650 ($1,825 if married filing separately) from the result.	**31**
32	Alternative minimum tax foreign tax credit (see instructions)	**32**
33	Tentative minimum tax. Subtract line 32 from line 31	**33**
34	Add Form 1040, line 44 (minus any tax from Form 4972), and Form 1040, line 46. Subtract from the result any foreign tax credit from Form 1040, line 48. If you used Schedule J to figure your tax on Form 1040, line 44, refigure that tax without using Schedule J before completing this line (see instructions)	**34**
35	**AMT.** Subtract line 34 from line 33. If zero or less, enter -0-. Enter here and on Form 1040, line 45	**35**

For Paperwork Reduction Act Notice, see your tax return instructions.   Cat. No. 13600G   Form **6251** (2014)

Illustration 18-2

Form **1040**

Department of the Treasury—Internal Revenue Service (99)

U.S. Individual Income Tax Return

2014 OMB No. 1545-0074 | IRS Use Only—Do not write or staple in this space.

For the year Jan. 1–Dec. 31, 2014, or other tax year beginning _____ , 2014, ending _____ , 20____ | See separate instructions.

Your first name and initial	Last name	Your social security number
Rodney	Bowers	3 9 4 3 2 1 3 8 7

If a joint return, spouse's first name and initial	Last name	Spouse's social security number
Rhonda	Bowers	2 2 1 9 3 6 7 2 9

Home address (number and street). If you have a P.O. box, see instructions. | Apt. no.

250 Meeher St.

▲ Make sure the SSN(s) above and on line 6c are correct.

City, town or post office, state, and ZIP code. If you have a foreign address, also complete spaces below (see instructions).

Mobile, AL 36608

Presidential Election Campaign

Check here if you, or your spouse if filing jointly, want $3 to go to this fund. Checking a box below will not change your tax or refund. ☐ You ☐ Spouse

Foreign country name	Foreign province/state/county	Foreign postal code

Filing Status

Check only one box.

1. ☐ Single
2. ☑ Married filing jointly (even if only one had income)
3. ☐ Married filing separately. Enter spouse's SSN above and full name here. ▶
4. ☐ Head of household (with qualifying person). (See instructions.) If the qualifying person is a child but not your dependent, enter this child's name here. ▶
5. ☐ Qualifying widow(er) with dependent child

Exemptions

6a ☑ **Yourself.** If someone can claim you as a dependent, **do not** check box 6a.
b ☑ **Spouse**

Boxes checked on 6a and 6b	2

c **Dependents:**

(1) First name Last name	(2) Dependent's social security number	(3) Dependent's relationship to you	(4) ✓ if child under age 17 qualifying for child tax credit (see instructions)
			☐
			☐
			☐
			☐

If more than four dependents, see instructions and check here ▶ ☐

No. of children on 6c who:
• lived with you
• did not live with you due to divorce or separation (see instructions)

Dependents on 6c not entered above

Add numbers on lines above ▶ | 2

d Total number of exemptions claimed

Income

Attach Form(s) W-2 here. Also attach Forms W-2G and 1099-R if tax was withheld.

If you did not get a W-2, see instructions.

7	Wages, salaries, tips, etc. Attach Form(s) W-2	7	134,543 00
8a	**Taxable** interest. Attach Schedule B if required	8a	
b	**Tax-exempt** interest. **Do not** include on line 8a	8b	
9a	Ordinary dividends. Attach Schedule B if required	9a	
b	Qualified dividends	9b	
10	Taxable refunds, credits, or offsets of state and local income taxes	10	
11	Alimony received	11	
12	Business income or (loss). Attach Schedule C or C-EZ	12	
13	Capital gain or (loss). Attach Schedule D if required. If not required, check here ▶ ☐	13	
14	Other gains or (losses). Attach Form 4797	14	
15a	IRA distributions 15a _____ b Taxable amount	15b	
16a	Pensions and annuities 16a _____ b Taxable amount	16b	
17	Rental real estate, royalties, partnerships, S corporations, trusts, etc. Attach Schedule E	17	
18	Farm income or (loss). Attach Schedule F	18	
19	Unemployment compensation	19	
20a	Social security benefits 20a _____ b Taxable amount	20b	
21	Other income. List type and amount	21	
22	Combine the amounts in the far right column for lines 7 through 21. This is your **total income** ▶	22	134,543 00

Adjusted Gross Income

23	Educator expenses	23	
24	Certain business expenses of reservists, performing artists, and fee-basis government officials. Attach Form 2106 or 2106-EZ	24	
25	Health savings account deduction. Attach Form 8889	25	
26	Moving expenses. Attach Form 3903	26	
27	Deductible part of self-employment tax. Attach Schedule SE	27	
28	Self-employed SEP, SIMPLE, and qualified plans	28	
29	Self-employed health insurance deduction	29	
30	Penalty on early withdrawal of savings	30	
31a	Alimony paid b Recipient's SSN ▶	31a	
32	IRA deduction	32	
33	Student loan interest deduction	33	
34	Tuition and fees. Attach Form 8917	34	
35	Domestic production activities deduction. Attach Form 8903	35	
36	Add lines 23 through 35	36	
37	Subtract line 36 from line 22. This is your **adjusted gross income** ▶	37	134,543 00

For Disclosure, Privacy Act, and Paperwork Reduction Act Notice, see separate instructions. Cat. No. 11320B Form **1040** (2014)

Illustration 18-2 continued

Form 1040 (2014)   Page **2**

Tax and Credits	38	Amount from line 37 (adjusted gross income)	38	134,543	00
	39a	Check if: ☐ **You** were born before January 2, 1950, ☐ Blind. } **Total boxes** ☐ **Spouse** was born before January 2, 1950, ☐ Blind. } checked ▶ 39a			
	b	If your spouse itemizes on a separate return or you were a dual-status alien, check here▶ 39b☐			
Standard Deduction for— ● People who check any box on line 39a or 39b **or** who can be claimed as a dependent, see instructions. ● All others: Single or Married filing separately, $6,200 Married filing jointly or Qualifying widow(er), $12,400 Head of household, $9,100	40	**Itemized deductions** (from Schedule A) **or** your **standard deduction** (see left margin) . .	40	51,954	00
	41	Subtract line 40 from line 38	41	82,589	00
	42	**Exemptions.** If line 38 is $152,525 or less, multiply $3,950 by the number on line 6d. Otherwise, see instructions	42	7,900	00
	43	**Taxable income.** Subtract line 42 from line 41. If line 42 is more than line 41, enter -0- . .	43	74,689	00
	44	**Tax** (see instructions). Check if any from: **a** ☐ Form(s) 8814 **b** ☐ Form 4972 **c** ☐ _____	44	10,381	00
	45	**Alternative minimum tax** (see instructions). Attach Form 6251	45	763	00
	46	Excess advance premium tax credit repayment. Attach Form 8962	46		
	47	Add lines 44, 45, and 46 . . . . ▶	47	11,144	00
	48	Foreign tax credit. Attach Form 1116 if required . . .	48		
	49	Credit for child and dependent care expenses. Attach Form 2441	49		
	50	Education credits from Form 8863, line 19 . . .	50		
	51	Retirement savings contributions credit. Attach Form 8880	51		
	52	Child tax credit. Attach Schedule 8812, if required . . .	52		
	53	Residential energy credits. Attach Form 5695	53		
	54	Other credits from Form: **a** ☐ 3800 **b** ☐ 8801 **c** ☐ _____	54		
	55	Add lines 48 through 54. These are your **total credits**	55		
	56	Subtract line 55 from line 47. If line 55 is more than line 47, enter -0- . . . . ▶	56	11,144	00
Other Taxes	57	Self-employment tax. Attach Schedule SE	57		
	58	Unreported social security and Medicare tax from Form: **a** ☐ 4137 **b** ☐ 8919 . .	58		
	59	Additional tax on IRAs, other qualified retirement plans, etc. Attach Form 5329 if required . .	59		
	60a	Household employment taxes from Schedule H	60a		
	b	First-time homebuyer credit repayment. Attach Form 5405 if required	60b		
	61	Health care: individual responsibility (see instructions) Full-year coverage ☑	61		
	62	Taxes from: **a** ☐ Form 8959 **b** ☐ Form 8960 **c** ☐ Instructions; enter code(s) _____	62		
	63	Add lines 56 through 62. This is your **total tax** . . . . ▶	63	11,144	00
Payments If you have a qualifying child, attach Schedule EIC.	64	Federal income tax withheld from Forms W-2 and 1099 . .	64	13,186	00
	65	2014 estimated tax payments and amount applied from 2013 return	65		
	66a	**Earned income credit (EIC)**	66a		
	b	Nontaxable combat pay election	66b		
	67	Additional child tax credit. Attach Schedule 8812	67		
	68	American opportunity credit from Form 8863, line 8 . . .	68		
	69	Net premium tax credit. Attach Form 8962	69		
	70	Amount paid with request for extension to file	70		
	71	Excess social security and tier 1 RRTA tax withheld . . .	71		
	72	Credit for federal tax on fuels. Attach Form 4136 . . .	72		
	73	Credits from Form: **a** ☐ 2439 **b** ▨ Reserved **c** ▨ Reserved **d** ☐ _____	73		
	74	Add lines 64, 65, 66a, and 67 through 73. These are your **total payments** . . . . . ▶	74	13,186	00
Refund Direct deposit? See instructions.	75	If line 74 is more than line 63, subtract line 63 from line 74. This is the amount you **overpaid**	75	2,042	00
	76a	Amount of line 75 you want **refunded to you.** If Form 8888 is attached, check here . ▶ ☐	76a	2,042	00
	▶ b	Routing number ☐☐☐☐☐☐☐☐☐ ▶ **c** Type: ☐ Checking ☐ Savings			
	▶ d	Account number ☐☐☐☐☐☐☐☐☐☐☐☐☐☐☐☐☐			
	77	Amount of line 75 you want **applied to your 2015 estimated tax** ▶ 77			
Amount You Owe	78	**Amount you owe.** Subtract line 74 from line 63. For details on how to pay, see instructions ▶	78		
	79	Estimated tax penalty (see instructions) 79			

Third Party Designee	Do you want to allow another person to discuss this return with the IRS (see instructions)? ☐ **Yes.** Complete below. ☑ **No**
	Designee's name ▶ _____ Phone no. ▶ _____ Personal identification number (PIN) ▶ ☐☐☐☐☐

Sign Here Joint return? See instructions. Keep a copy for your records.	Under penalties of perjury, I declare that I have examined this return and accompanying schedules and statements, and to the best of my knowledge and belief, they are true, correct, and complete. Declaration of preparer (other than taxpayer) is based on all information of which preparer has any knowledge.

Your signature	Date	Your occupation **Outside Sales**	Daytime phone number **(555)555-5555**
Spouse's signature. If a joint return, **both** must sign.	Date	Spouse's occupation **Manager**	If the IRS sent you an Identity Protection PIN, enter it here (see inst.) ☐☐☐☐☐☐

Paid Preparer Use Only	Print/Type preparer's name **Jane Doe**	Preparer's signature	Date	Check ☐ if self-employed	PTIN **P00000000**
	Firm's name ▶ **My Tax Service**			Firm's EIN ▶	**63-0000000**
	Firm's address ▶ **100 Main St., Your City, Your State, Your Zip Code**			Phone no.	**(555)555-1111**

www.irs.gov/form1040   Form **1040** (2014)

Illustration 18-2 continued

SCHEDULE A (Form 1040)		**Itemized Deductions**	OMB No. 1545-0074
Department of the Treasury Internal Revenue Service (99)		▶ Information about Schedule A and its separate instructions is at *www.irs.gov/schedulea*. ▶ **Attach to Form 1040.**	20**14** Attachment Sequence No. **07**

Name(s) shown on Form 1040 — Rodney and Rhonda Bowers

Your social security number — 394-32-1387

Caution. Do not include expenses reimbursed or paid by others.

Medical and Dental Expenses	1	Medical and dental expenses (see instructions)	1		
	2	Enter amount from Form 1040, line 38 **2**			
	3	Multiply line 2 by 10% (.10). But if either you or your spouse was born before January 2, 1950, multiply line 2 by 7.5% (.075) instead	3		
	4	Subtract line 3 from line 1. If line 3 is more than line 1, enter -0-		4	

Taxes You Paid	5	State and local (**check only one box**): a ☑ Income taxes, **or** b ☐ General sales taxes	5	3,065	00
	6	Real estate taxes (see instructions)	6	2,521	00
	7	Personal property taxes	7	93	00
	8	Other taxes. List type and amount ▶	8		
	9	Add lines 5 through 8	9	5,679	00

Interest You Paid **Note.** Your mortgage interest deduction may be limited (see instructions).	10	Home mortgage interest and points reported to you on Form 1098	10	8,891	00
	11	Home mortgage interest not reported to you on Form 1098. If paid to the person from whom you bought the home, see instructions and show that person's name, identifying no., and address ▶	11		
	12	Points not reported to you on Form 1098. See instructions for special rules	12		
	13	Mortgage insurance premiums (see instructions)	13		
	14	Investment interest. Attach Form 4952 if required. (See instructions.)	14		
	15	Add lines 10 through 14	15	8,891	00

Gifts to Charity If you made a gift and got a benefit for it, see instructions.	16	Gifts by cash or check. If you made any gift of $250 or more, see instructions	16	691	00
	17	Other than by cash or check. If any gift of $250 or more, see instructions. You **must** attach Form 8283 if over $500	17		
	18	Carryover from prior year	18		
	19	Add lines 16 through 18	19	691	00

Casualty and Theft Losses	20	Casualty or theft loss(es). Attach Form 4684. (See instructions.)	20		

Job Expenses and Certain Miscellaneous Deductions	21	Unreimbursed employee expenses—job travel, union dues, job education, etc. Attach Form 2106 or 2106-EZ if required. (See instructions.) ▶ Form 2106	21	39,384	00
	22	Tax preparation fees	22		
	23	Other expenses—investment, safe deposit box, etc. List type and amount ▶	23		
	24	Add lines 21 through 23	24		
	25	Enter amount from Form 1040, line 38 **25** 34,543 00			
	26	Multiply line 25 by 2% (.02)	26	2,691	00
	27	Subtract line 26 from line 24. If line 26 is more than line 24, enter -0-	27	36,693	00

Other Miscellaneous Deductions	28	Other—from list in instructions. List type and amount ▶	28		

Total Itemized Deductions	29	Is Form 1040, line 38, over $152,525? ☑ **No.** Your deduction is not limited. Add the amounts in the far right column for lines 4 through 28. Also, enter this amount on Form 1040, line 40. ☐ **Yes.** Your deduction may be limited. See the Itemized Deductions Worksheet in the instructions to figure the amount to enter.	29	51,954	00
	30	If you elect to itemize deductions even though they are less than your standard deduction, check here ▶ ☐			

For Paperwork Reduction Act Notice, see Form 1040 instructions.   Cat. No. 17145C   Schedule A (Form 1040) 2014

Illustration 18-2 continued

Form **6251**	**Alternative Minimum Tax—Individuals**	OMB No. 1545-0074

Department of the Treasury
Internal Revenue Service (99)

▶ Information about Form 6251 and its separate instructions is at *www.irs.gov/form6251.*
▶ **Attach to Form 1040 or Form 1040NR.**

2014
Attachment
Sequence No. **32**

Name(s) shown on Form 1040 or Form 1040NR	Your social security number
Rodney and Rhonda Bowers	394-32-1387

Part I Alternative Minimum Taxable Income (See instructions for how to complete each line.)

1	If filing Schedule A (Form 1040), enter the amount from Form 1040, line 41, and go to line 2. Otherwise, enter the amount from Form 1040, line 38, and go to line 7. (If less than zero, enter as a negative amount.)	**1**	82,589	00
2	Medical and dental. If you or your spouse was 65 or older, enter the **smaller** of Schedule A (Form 1040), line 4, **or** 2.5% (.025) of Form 1040, line 38. If zero or less, enter -0-	**2**		
3	Taxes from Schedule A (Form 1040), line 9	**3**	5,679	00
4	Enter the home mortgage interest adjustment, if any, from line 6 of the worksheet in the instructions for this line	**4**	0	00
5	Miscellaneous deductions from Schedule A (Form 1040), line 27.	**5**	36,693	00
6	If Form 1040, line 38, is $152,525 or less, enter -0-. Otherwise, see instructions	**6** (	0	00)
7	Tax refund from Form 1040, line 10 or line 21	**7** (		)
8	Investment interest expense (difference between regular tax and AMT).	**8**		
9	Depletion (difference between regular tax and AMT)	**9**		
10	Net operating loss deduction from Form 1040, line 21. Enter as a positive amount	**10**		
11	Alternative tax net operating loss deduction	**11** (		)
12	Interest from specified private activity bonds exempt from the regular tax	**12**		
13	Qualified small business stock (7% of gain excluded under section 1202)	**13**		
14	Exercise of incentive stock options (excess of AMT income over regular tax income)	**14**		
15	Estates and trusts (amount from Schedule K-1 (Form 1041), box 12, code A)	**15**		
16	Electing large partnerships (amount from Schedule K-1 (Form 1065-B), box 6)	**16**		
17	Disposition of property (difference between AMT and regular tax gain or loss)	**17**		
18	Depreciation on assets placed in service after 1986 (difference between regular tax and AMT)	**18**		
19	Passive activities (difference between AMT and regular tax income or loss)	**19**		
20	Loss limitations (difference between AMT and regular tax income or loss)	**20**		
21	Circulation costs (difference between regular tax and AMT)	**21**		
22	Long-term contracts (difference between AMT and regular tax income)	**22**		
23	Mining costs (difference between regular tax and AMT)	**23**		
24	Research and experimental costs (difference between regular tax and AMT)	**24**		
25	Income from certain installment sales before January 1, 1987	**25** (		)
26	Intangible drilling costs preference	**26**		
27	Other adjustments, including income-based related adjustments	**27**		
28	**Alternative minimum taxable income.** Combine lines 1 through 27. (If married filing separately and line 28 is more than $242,450, see instructions.)	**28**	124,961	00

Part II Alternative Minimum Tax (AMT)

29	Exemption. (If you were under age 24 at the end of 2014, see instructions.)			

IF your filing status is . . .	**AND line 28 is not over . . .**	**THEN enter on line 29 . . .**			
Single or head of household	$117,300	$52,800			
Married filing jointly or qualifying widow(er)	156,500	82,100	} . .		
Married filing separately.	78,250	41,050		**29**	82,100	00

If line 28 is **over** the amount shown above for your filing status, see instructions.

30	Subtract line 29 from line 28. If more than zero, go to line 31. If zero or less, enter -0- here and on lines 31, 33, and 35, and go to line 34	**30**	42,861	00
31	• If you are filing Form 2555 or 2555-EZ, see instructions for the amount to enter. • If you reported capital gain distributions directly on Form 1040, line 13; you reported qualified dividends on Form 1040, line 9b; **or** you had a gain on both lines 15 and 16 of Schedule D (Form 1040) (as refigured for the AMT, if necessary), complete Part III on the back and enter the amount from line 64 here. • **All others:** If line 30 is $182,500 or less ($91,250 or less if married filing separately), multiply line 30 by 26% (.26). Otherwise, multiply line 30 by 28% (.28) and subtract $3,650 ($1,825 if married filing separately) from the result.	**31**	11,144	00
32	Alternative minimum tax foreign tax credit (see instructions)	**32**		
33	Tentative minimum tax. Subtract line 32 from line 31	**33**	11,144	00
34	Add Form 1040, line 44 (minus any tax from Form 4972), and Form 1040, line 46. Subtract from the result any foreign tax credit from Form 1040, line 48. If you used Schedule J to figure your tax on Form 1040, line 44, refigure that tax without using Schedule J before completing this line (see instructions)	**34**	10,381	00
35	**AMT.** Subtract line 34 from line 33. If zero or less, enter -0-. Enter here and on Form 1040, line 45	**35**	763	00

For Paperwork Reduction Act Notice, see your tax return instructions. Cat. No. 13600G Form **6251** (2014)

Illustration 18-2 continued

Form **2106**

Department of the Treasury
Internal Revenue Service (99)

Employee Business Expenses

► Attach to Form 1040 or Form 1040NR.

► Information about Form 2106 and its separate instructions is available at *www.irs.gov/form2106.*

OMB No. 1545-0074

2014

Attachment
Sequence No. **129**

Your name	Occupation in which you incurred expenses	Social security number		
Rodney Bowers	Outside Sales	394	32	1387

Part I Employee Business Expenses and Reimbursements

Step 1 Enter Your Expenses

| | | Column A
Other Than Meals
and Entertainment | | Column B
Meals and
Entertainment | |
|---|---|---|---|---|---|
| 1 | Vehicle expense from line 22 or line 29. (Rural mail carriers: See instructions.) | **1** | 22,603 00 | | |
| 2 | Parking fees, tolls, and transportation, including train, bus, etc., that **did not** involve overnight travel or commuting to and from work | **2** | | | |
| 3 | Travel expense while away from home overnight, including lodging, airplane, car rental, etc. **Do not** include meals and entertainment | **3** | 11,998 00 | | |
| 4 | Business expenses not included on lines 1 through 3. **Do not** include meals and entertainment | **4** | 5,233 00 | | |
| 5 | Meals and entertainment expenses (see instructions) | **5** | | | |
| 6 | **Total expenses.** In Column A, add lines 1 through 4 and enter the result. In Column B, enter the amount from line 5 | **6** | 39,834 00 | | |

Note. *If you were not reimbursed for any expenses in Step 1, skip line 7 and enter the amount from line 6 on line 8.*

Step 2 Enter Reimbursements Received From Your Employer for Expenses Listed in Step 1

7	Enter reimbursements received from your employer that were **not** reported to you in box 1 of Form W-2. Include any reimbursements reported under code "L" in box 12 of your Form W-2 (see instructions).	**7**			

Step 3 Figure Expenses To Deduct on Schedule A (Form 1040 or Form 1040NR)

8	Subtract line 7 from line 6. If zero or less, enter -0-. However, if line 7 is greater than line 6 in Column A, report the excess as income on Form 1040, line 7 (or on Form 1040NR, line 8)	**8**	39,834 00		
	Note. *If both columns of line 8 are zero, you cannot deduct employee business expenses. Stop here and attach Form 2106 to your return.*				
9	In Column A, enter the amount from line 8. In Column B, multiply line 8 by 50% (.50). (Employees subject to Department of Transportation (DOT) hours of service limits: Multiply meal expenses incurred while away from home on business by 80% (.80) instead of 50%. For details, see instructions.)	**9**	39,834 00		
10	Add the amounts on line 9 of both columns and enter the total here. **Also, enter the total on Schedule A (Form 1040), line 21** (or on **Schedule A (Form 1040NR), line 7**). (Armed Forces reservists, qualified performing artists, fee-basis state or local government officials, and individuals with disabilities: See the instructions for special rules on where to enter the total.) ►	**10**		39,834	00

For Paperwork Reduction Act Notice, see your tax return instructions.

Cat. No. 11700N

Form **2106** (2014)

Illustration 18-2 continued

Part II   **Vehicle Expenses**

Section A—General Information (You must complete this section if you are claiming vehicle expenses.)

			(a) Vehicle 1	**(b)** Vehicle 2
11	Enter the date the vehicle was placed in service	11	02 / 02 / 05	/ /
12	Total miles the vehicle was driven during 2014	12	55,950 miles	miles
13	Business miles included on line 12	13	40,362 miles	miles
14	Percent of business use. Divide line 13 by line 12	14	72.14 %	%
15	Average daily roundtrip commuting distance	15	2 miles	miles
16	Commuting miles included on line 12	16	600 miles	miles
17	Other miles. Add lines 13 and 16 and subtract the total from line 12	17	14,988 miles	miles
18	Was your vehicle available for personal use during off-duty hours?		☑ Yes ☐ No	
19	Do you (or your spouse) have another vehicle available for personal use?		☑ Yes ☐ No	
20	Do you have evidence to support your deduction?		☑ Yes ☐ No	
21	If "Yes," is the evidence written?		☑ Yes ☐ No	

Section B—Standard Mileage Rate (See the instructions for Part II to find out whether to complete this section or Section C.)

22	Multiply line 13 by 56¢ (.56). Enter the result here and on line 1	22

Section C—Actual Expenses

			(a) Vehicle 1		**(b)** Vehicle 2	
23	Gasoline, oil, repairs, vehicle insurance, etc.	23				
24a	Vehicle rentals	24a				
b	Inclusion amount (see instructions)	24b				
c	Subtract line 24b from line 24a	24c				
25	Value of employer-provided vehicle (applies only if 100% of annual lease value was included on Form W-2—see instructions)	25				
26	Add lines 23, 24c, and 25	26				
27	Multiply line 26 by the percentage on line 14	27				
28	Depreciation (see instructions)	28				
29	Add lines 27 and 28. Enter total here and on line 1	29				

Section D—Depreciation of Vehicles (Use this section only if you owned the vehicle and are completing Section C for the vehicle.)

			(a) Vehicle 1		**(b)** Vehicle 2	
30	Enter cost or other basis (see instructions)	30				
31	Enter section 179 deduction (see instructions)	31				
32	Multiply line 30 by line 14 (see instructions if you claimed the section 179 deduction)	32				
33	Enter depreciation method and percentage (see instructions)	33				
34	Multiply line 32 by the percentage on line 33 (see instructions)	34				
35	Add lines 31 and 34	35				
36	Enter the applicable limit explained in the line 36 instructions	36				
37	Multiply line 36 by the percentage on line 14	37				
38	Enter the **smaller** of line 35 or line 37. If you skipped lines 36 and 37, enter the amount from line 35. Also enter this amount on line 28 above	38				

Form **2106** (2014)

Kiddie Tax

If a child under the age of 18 has investment income they may be taxed at their parent's tax rate. In the first half of the course, we covered filing requirements for dependents. We know that someone that can be claimed as a dependent on another's tax return must file if their unearned income is over $1,000, their earned income is over $6,200, or their gross income is over the greater of $1,000 or their earned income (up to $5,850) plus $350. Now, we will carry it one step further.

If the child meets the following conditions (whether or not they are claimed as a dependent), the child's investment income will be taxed at the parent's tax rate.

- The child was under the age of 18 at the end of the tax year and did not have earned income that was more than half of his or her support, or was a full-time student over age 18 and under age 24 at the end of the tax year and did not have earned income that was more than half of his or her support..
- The child's investment income was more than $2,000.
- The child does not file a joint return for the tax year.
- The child is required to file for the tax year.
- At least one of the child's parents was alive at the end of the tax year.

In most cases, the child may choose to file the investment income on their own return, or the parents may claim the investment income on their return. The parents may elect to claim the income on their own return if the following apply:

- The income is only from interest, dividends, or capital gain distributions.
- The gross income was less than $10,000.
- The child is required to file for the tax year unless this election is made.
- The child does not file a joint return for the tax year.
- No estimated payments were made under the child's social security number.
- No federal income tax was withheld from the child's pay.

If the child elects to file their own return, a Form 8615 (Illustration 18-3) must be filed with their return. If the parents make the election to include the income on their return, a Form 8814 (Illustration 18-4) must be filed with the parent's return.

Example: Robbie Jones, age 15, received $2,319 of interest income in 2014. His parents are going to file a return for him, claiming this income. Their taxable income is $32,521 and their tax liability is $3,971. They are Married Filing Jointly. Robbie's Forms 1040 and 8615 follow (Illustration 18-5).

Illustration 18-3

Form **8615**

Department of the Treasury
Internal Revenue Service (99)

Tax for Certain Children Who Have Unearned Income

▶ Attach only to the child's Form 1040, Form 1040A, or Form 1040NR.
▶ Information about Form 8615 and its separate instructions is at *www.irs.gov/form8615*.

OMB No. 1545-0074

2014

Attachment
Sequence No. **33**

Child's name shown on return	Child's social security number

Before you begin: If the child, the parent, or any of the parent's other children for whom Form 8615 must be filed must use the Schedule D Tax Worksheet or has income from farming or fishing, see **Pub. 929,** Tax Rules for Children and Dependents. It explains how to figure the child's tax using the **Schedule D Tax Worksheet** or **Schedule J** (Form 1040).

A Parent's name (first, initial, and last). **Caution:** *See instructions before completing.*

B Parent's social security number

C Parent's filing status (check one):

☐ Single   ☐ Married filing jointly   ☐ Married filing separately   ☐ Head of household   ☐ Qualifying widow(er)

Part I   Child's Net Unearned Income

1	Enter the child's unearned income (see instructions)	**1**	
2	If the child **did not** itemize deductions on **Schedule A** (Form 1040 or Form 1040NR), enter $2,000. Otherwise, see instructions	**2**	
3	Subtract line 2 from line 1. If zero or less, **stop;** do not complete the rest of this form but **do** attach it to the child's return	**3**	
4	Enter the child's **taxable income** from Form 1040, line 43; Form 1040A, line 27; or Form 1040NR, line 41. If the child files Form 2555 or 2555-EZ, see the instructions	**4**	
5	Enter the **smaller** of line 3 or line 4. If zero, **stop;** do not complete the rest of this form but **do** attach it to the child's return	**5**	

Part II   Tentative Tax Based on the Tax Rate of the Parent

6	Enter the parent's **taxable income** from Form 1040, line 43; Form 1040A, line 27; Form 1040EZ, line 6; Form 1040NR, line 41; or Form 1040NR-EZ, line 14. If zero or less, enter -0-. If the parent files Form 2555 or 2555-EZ, see the instructions	**6**	
7	Enter the total, if any, from Forms 8615, line 5, of **all other** children of the parent named above. **Do not** include the amount from line 5 above	**7**	
8	Add lines 5, 6, and 7 (see instructions)	**8**	
9	Enter the tax on the amount on line 8 based on the **parent's** filing status above (see instructions). If the Qualified Dividends and Capital Gain Tax Worksheet, Schedule D Tax Worksheet, or Schedule J (Form 1040) is used to figure the tax, check here . . . . ▶ ☐	**9**	
10	Enter the parent's tax from Form 1040, line 44; Form 1040A, line 28, minus any alternative minimum tax; Form 1040EZ, line 10; Form 1040NR, line 42; or Form 1040NR-EZ, line 15. **Do not** include any tax from **Form 4972 or 8814** or any tax from recapture of an education credit. If the parent files Form 2555 or 2555-EZ, see the instructions. If the Qualified Dividends and Capital Gain Tax Worksheet, Schedule D Tax Worksheet, or Schedule J (Form 1040) was used to figure the tax, check here . . . . ▶ ☐	**10**	
11	Subtract line 10 from line 9 and enter the result. If line 7 is blank, also enter this amount on line 13 and go to **Part III**	**11**	
12a	Add lines 5 and 7 . . . . **12a**		
b	Divide line 5 by line 12a. Enter the result as a decimal (rounded to at least three places)	**12b**	× .
13	Multiply line 11 by line 12b	**13**	

Part III   Child's Tax—If lines 4 and 5 above are the same, enter -0- on line 15 and go to line 16.

14	Subtract line 5 from line 4 . . . . **14**		
15	Enter the tax on the amount on line 14 based on the **child's** filing status (see instructions). If the Qualified Dividends and Capital Gain Tax Worksheet, Schedule D Tax Worksheet, or Schedule J (Form 1040) is used to figure the tax, check here . . . . ▶ ☐	**15**	
16	Add lines 13 and 15	**16**	
17	Enter the tax on the amount on line 4 based on the **child's** filing status (see instructions). If the Qualified Dividends and Capital Gain Tax Worksheet, Schedule D Tax Worksheet, or Schedule J (Form 1040) is used to figure the tax, check here . . . . ▶ ☐	**17**	
18	Enter the **larger** of line 16 or line 17 here and on the **child's** Form 1040, line 44; Form 1040A, line 28; or Form 1040NR, line 42. If the child files Form 2555 or 2555-EZ, see the instructions . .	**18**	

For Paperwork Reduction Act Notice, see your tax return instructions.   Cat. No. 64113U   Form **8615** (2014)

Illustration 18-4

Form **8814**	**Parents' Election To Report Child's Interest and Dividends**	OMB No. 1545-0074

Form 8814

Department of the Treasury
Internal Revenue Service (99)

Parents' Election To Report
Child's Interest and Dividends
▶ Information about Form 8814 and its instructions is at *www.irs.gov/form8814*.
▶ Attach to parents' Form 1040 or Form 1040NR.

OMB No. 1545-0074

20**14**

Attachment
Sequence No. **40**

Name(s) shown on your return | Your social security number

Caution. The federal income tax on your child's income, including qualified dividends and capital gain distributions, may be less if you file a separate tax return for the child instead of making this election. This is because you cannot take certain tax benefits that your child could take on his or her own return. For details, see **Tax benefits you cannot take** in the instructions.

A Child's name (first, initial, and last) | **B** Child's social security number

C If more than one Form 8814 is attached, check here . . . . ▶ ☐

Part I **Child's Interest and Dividends To Report on Your Return**

1a	Enter your child's **taxable** interest. If this amount is different from the amounts shown on the child's Forms 1099-INT and 1099-OID, see the instructions	**1a**		
b	Enter your child's **tax-exempt** interest. **Do not** include this amount on line 1a **1b**			
2a	Enter your child's ordinary dividends, including any Alaska Permanent Fund dividends. If your child received any ordinary dividends as a nominee, see the instructions	**2a**		
b	Enter your child's qualified dividends included on line 2a. See the instructions **2b**			
3	Enter your child's capital gain distributions. If your child received any capital gain distributions as a nominee, see the instructions	**3**		
4	Add lines 1a, 2a, and 3. If the total is $2,000 or less, skip lines 5 through 12 and go to line 13. If the total is $10,000 or more, **do not** file this form. Your child **must** file his or her own return to report the income	**4**		
5	Base amount	**5**	2,000	00
6	Subtract line 5 from line 4	**6**		
	If both lines 2b and 3 are zero or blank, skip lines 7 through 10, enter -0- on line 11, and go to line 12. Otherwise, go to line 7.			
7	Divide line 2b by line 4. Enter the result as a decimal (rounded to at least three places) . . . . . . **7** .			
8	Divide line 3 by line 4. Enter the result as a decimal (rounded to at least three places) . . . . . . **8** .			
9	Multiply line 6 by line 7. Enter the result here. See the instructions for where to report this amount on your return **9**			
10	Multiply line 6 by line 8. Enter the result here. See the instructions for where to report this amount on your return **10**			
11	Add lines 9 and 10	**11**		
12	Subtract line 11 from line 6. Include this amount in the total on Form 1040, line 21, or Form 1040NR, line 21. In the space next to line 21, enter "Form 8814" and show the amount. If you checked the box on line C above, see the instructions. Go to line 13 below	**12**		

Part II **Tax on the First $2,000 of Child's Interest and Dividends**

13	Amount not taxed	**13**	1,000	00
14	Subtract line 13 from line 4. If the result is zero or less, enter -0-	**14**		
15	**Tax.** Is the amount on line 14 less than $1,000?			
	☐ **No.** Enter $100 here and see the **Note** below.	**15**		
	☐ **Yes.** Multiply line 14 by 10% (.10). Enter the result here and see the **Note** below.			

Note. If you checked the box on line C above, see the instructions. Otherwise, include the amount from line 15 in the tax you enter on Form 1040, line 44, or Form 1040NR, line 42. Be sure to check box **a** on Form 1040, line 44, or Form 1040NR, line 42.

For Paperwork Reduction Act Notice, see your tax return instructions.　　Cat. No. 10750J　　Form **8814** (2014)

Illustration 18-5

Form 1040

Department of the Treasury—Internal Revenue Service (99)

U.S. Individual Income Tax Return **2014** OMB No. 1545-0074 | IRS Use Only—Do not write or staple in this space.

For the year Jan. 1–Dec. 31, 2014, or other tax year beginning _____, 2014, ending _____, 20___ | See separate instructions.

Your first name and initial	Last name	Your social security number
Robbie	Jones	2 3 3 9 3 4 3 2 3

If a joint return, spouse's first name and initial | Last name | Spouse's social security number

Home address (number and street). If you have a P.O. box, see instructions. | Apt. no.

153 Johnson Ct.

▲ Make sure the SSN(s) above and on line 6c are correct.

City, town or post office, state, and ZIP code. If you have a foreign address, also complete spaces below (see instructions).

Your City, Your State, Your Zip Code

Foreign country name | Foreign province/state/county | Foreign postal code

Presidential Election Campaign
Check here if you, or your spouse if filing jointly, want $3 to go to this fund. Checking a box below will not change your tax or refund. ☐ You ☐ Spouse

Filing Status

Check only one box.

1 ☑ Single
2 ☐ Married filing jointly (even if only one had income)
3 ☐ Married filing separately. Enter spouse's SSN above and full name here. ▶
4 ☐ Head of household (with qualifying person). (See instructions.) If the qualifying person is a child but not your dependent, enter this child's name here. ▶
5 ☐ Qualifying widow(er) with dependent child

Exemptions

6a ☐ **Yourself.** If someone can claim you as a dependent, **do not** check box 6a
b ☐ **Spouse**

Boxes checked on 6a and 6b ____

c **Dependents:**		(2) Dependent's social security number	(3) Dependent's relationship to you	(4) ✓ if child under age 17 qualifying for child tax credit (see instructions)
(1) First name	Last name			
				☐
				☐
				☐
				☐

No. of children on 6c who:
• lived with you ____
• did not live with you due to divorce or separation (see instructions) ____

If more than four dependents, see instructions and check here ▶ ☐

Dependents on 6c not entered above ____

d Total number of exemptions claimed

Add numbers on lines above ▶ ____

Income

Attach Form(s) W-2 here. Also attach Forms W-2G and 1099-R if tax was withheld.

If you did not get a W-2, see instructions.

7	Wages, salaries, tips, etc. Attach Form(s) W-2	7	
8a	**Taxable** interest. Attach Schedule B if required	8a	2,319 00
b	**Tax-exempt** interest. **Do not** include on line 8a	8b	
9a	Ordinary dividends. Attach Schedule B if required	9a	
b	Qualified dividends	9b	
10	Taxable refunds, credits, or offsets of state and local income taxes	10	
11	Alimony received	11	
12	Business income or (loss). Attach Schedule C or C-EZ	12	
13	Capital gain or (loss). Attach Schedule D if required. If not required, check here ▶ ☐	13	
14	Other gains or (losses). Attach Form 4797	14	
15a	IRA distributions 15a	b Taxable amount	15b	
16a	Pensions and annuities 16a	b Taxable amount	16b	
17	Rental real estate, royalties, partnerships, S corporations, trusts, etc. Attach Schedule E	17	
18	Farm income or (loss). Attach Schedule F	18	
19	Unemployment compensation	19	
20a	Social security benefits 20a	b Taxable amount	20b	
21	Other income. List type and amount	21	
22	Combine the amounts in the far right column for lines 7 through 21. This is your **total income** ▶	22	2,319 00

Adjusted Gross Income

23	Educator expenses	23	
24	Certain business expenses of reservists, performing artists, and fee-basis government officials. Attach Form 2106 or 2106-EZ	24	
25	Health savings account deduction. Attach Form 8889	25	
26	Moving expenses. Attach Form 3903	26	
27	Deductible part of self-employment tax. Attach Schedule SE	27	
28	Self-employed SEP, SIMPLE, and qualified plans	28	
29	Self-employed health insurance deduction	29	
30	Penalty on early withdrawal of savings	30	
31a	Alimony paid b Recipient's SSN ▶	31a	
32	IRA deduction	32	
33	Student loan interest deduction	33	
34	Tuition and fees. Attach Form 8917	34	
35	Domestic production activities deduction. Attach Form 8903	35	
36	Add lines 23 through 35	36	
37	Subtract line 36 from line 22. This is your **adjusted gross income** ▶	37	2,319 00

For Disclosure, Privacy Act, and Paperwork Reduction Act Notice, see separate instructions. | Cat. No. 11320B | Form **1040** (2014)

Illustration 18-5 continued

Form 1040 (2014)   Page **2**

Tax and Credits	38	Amount from line 37 (adjusted gross income)	38	2,319	00

39a	Check if: ☐ **You** were born before January 2, 1950, ☐ Blind. **Total boxes** ☐ **Spouse** was born before January 2, 1950, ☐ Blind. checked ▶ 39a	
b	If your spouse itemizes on a separate return or you were a dual-status alien, check here ▶ 39b ☐	

Standard Deduction for—

• People who check any box on line 39a or 39b **or** who can be claimed as a dependent, see instructions.

• All others:

Single or Married filing separately, $6,200

Married filing jointly or Qualifying widow(er), $12,400

Head of household, $9,100

40	**Itemized deductions** (from Schedule A) **or** your **standard deduction** (see left margin) . .	40	1,000	00
41	Subtract line 40 from line 38	41	1,319	00
42	**Exemptions.** If line 38 is $152,525 or less, multiply $3,950 by the number on line 6d. Otherwise, see instructions	42		
43	**Taxable income.** Subtract line 42 from line 41. If line 42 is more than line 41, enter -0- . .	43	1,319	00
44	**Tax** (see instructions). Check if any from: **a** ☐ Form(s) 8814 **b** ☐ Form 4972 **c** ☐	44	146	00
45	**Alternative minimum tax** (see instructions). Attach Form 6251	45		
46	Excess advance premium tax credit repayment. Attach Form 8962	46		
47	Add lines 44, 45, and 46 . . . . ▶	47	146	00

48	Foreign tax credit. Attach Form 1116 if required . . .	48		
49	Credit for child and dependent care expenses. Attach Form 2441	49		
50	Education credits from Form 8863, line 19	50		
51	Retirement savings contributions credit. Attach Form 8880	51		
52	Child tax credit. Attach Schedule 8812, if required . .	52		
53	Residential energy credits. Attach Form 5695 . . .	53		
54	Other credits from Form: **a** ☐ 3800 **b** ☐ 8801 **c** ☐	54		
55	Add lines 48 through 54. These are your **total credits**	55		
56	Subtract line 55 from line 47. If line 55 is more than line 47, enter -0- . . . . . . ▶	56	146	00

Other Taxes	57	Self-employment tax. Attach Schedule SE	57		
	58	Unreported social security and Medicare tax from Form: **a** ☐ 4137 **b** ☐ 8919 . .	58		
	59	Additional tax on IRAs, other qualified retirement plans, etc. Attach Form 5329 if required . .	59		
	60a	Household employment taxes from Schedule H	60a		
	b	First-time homebuyer credit repayment. Attach Form 5405 if required	60b		
	61	Health care: individual responsibility (see instructions) Full-year coverage ☐ . . .	61		
	62	Taxes from: **a** ☐ Form 8959 **b** ☐ Form 8960 **c** ☐ Instructions; enter code(s) _____	62		
	63	Add lines 56 through 62. This is your **total tax** . . . . ▶	63	146	00

Payments

If you have a qualifying child, attach Schedule EIC.

64	Federal income tax withheld from Forms W-2 and 1099 . .	64		
65	2014 estimated tax payments and amount applied from 2013 return	65		
66a	**Earned income credit (EIC)**	66a		
b	Nontaxable combat pay election	66b		
67	Additional child tax credit. Attach Schedule 8812	67		
68	American opportunity credit from Form 8863, line 8 . . .	68		
69	Net premium tax credit. Attach Form 8962	69		
70	Amount paid with request for extension to file	70		
71	Excess social security and tier 1 RRTA tax withheld . . .	71		
72	Credit for federal tax on fuels. Attach Form 4136 . . .	72		
73	Credits from Form: **a** ☐ 2439 **b** ☐ Reserved **c** ☐ Reserved **d** ☐	73		
74	Add lines 64, 65, 66a, and 67 through 73. These are your **total payments** . . . . . . ▶	74		

Refund	75	If line 74 is more than line 63, subtract line 63 from line 74. This is the amount you **overpaid**	75		
	76a	Amount of line 75 you want **refunded to you.** If Form 8888 is attached, check here . ▶ ☐	76a		

Direct deposit? See instructions.

▶ b	Routing number	▶ c Type: ☐ Checking ☐ Savings
▶ d	Account number	

77	Amount of line 75 you want **applied to your 2015 estimated tax** ▶	77	

Amount You Owe	78	**Amount you owe.** Subtract line 74 from line 63. For details on how to pay, see instructions ▶	78	146	00
	79	Estimated tax penalty (see instructions)	79		

Third Party Designee

Do you want to allow another person to discuss this return with the IRS (see instructions)? ☐ **Yes.** Complete below. ☑ **No**

Designee's name ▶	Phone no. ▶	Personal identification number (PIN) ▶

Sign Here

Joint return? See instructions. Keep a copy for your records.

Under penalties of perjury, I declare that I have examined this return and accompanying schedules and statements, and to the best of my knowledge and belief, they are true, correct, and complete. Declaration of preparer (other than taxpayer) is based on all information of which preparer has any knowledge.

Your signature	Date	Your occupation **Student**	Daytime phone number **(555)555-5555**
Spouse's signature. If a joint return, **both** must sign.	Date	Spouse's occupation	If the IRS sent you an Identity Protection PIN, enter it here (see inst.)

Paid Preparer Use Only

Print/Type preparer's name **Jane Doe**	Preparer's signature	Date	Check ☐ if self-employed	PTIN * **P00000000**
Firm's name ▶ **My Tax Service**			Firm's EIN ▶	**63-0000000**
Firm's address ▶ **100 Main St., Your City, Your State, Your Zip Code**			Phone no.	**(555)555-1111**

www.irs.gov/form1040   Form **1040** (2014)

Illustration 18-5 continued

SCHEDULE B **(Form 1040A or 1040)** Department of the Treasury Internal Revenue Service (99)		**Interest and Ordinary Dividends** ► Attach to Form 1040A or 1040. ►Information about Schedule B and its instructions is at *www.irs.gov/scheduleb*.		OMB No. 1545-0074 20**14** Attachment Sequence No. **08**	

Name(s) shown on return	Your social security number
Robbie Jones	233-93-4323

Part I Interest (See instructions on back and the instructions for Form 1040A, or Form 1040, line 8a.) **Note.** If you received a Form 1099-INT, Form 1099-OID, or substitute statement from a brokerage firm, list the firm's name as the payer and enter the total interest shown on that form.	**1**	List name of payer. If any interest is from a seller-financed mortgage and the buyer used the property as a personal residence, see instructions on back and list this interest first. Also, show that buyer's social security number and address ►		**Amount**
		First Bank	**1**	2,319	00
	2	Add the amounts on line 1	**2**	2,319	00
	3	Excludable interest on series EE and I U.S. savings bonds issued after 1989. Attach Form 8815	**3**		
	4	Subtract line 3 from line 2. Enter the result here and on Form 1040A, or Form 1040, line 8a . . . . ►	**4**	2,319	00

Note. If line 4 is over $1,500, you must complete Part III.

Part II Ordinary Dividends (See instructions on back and the instructions for Form 1040A, or Form 1040, line 9a.) **Note.** If you received a Form 1099-DIV or substitute statement from a brokerage firm, list the firm's name as the payer and enter the ordinary dividends shown on that form.	**5**	List name of payer ►		**Amount**
			5	
	6	Add the amounts on line 5. Enter the total here and on Form 1040A, or Form 1040, line 9a . . . . ►	**6**	

Note. If line 6 is over $1,500, you must complete Part III.

		You must complete this part if you **(a)** had over $1,500 of taxable interest or ordinary dividends; **(b)** had a foreign account; or **(c)** received a distribution from, or were a grantor of, or a transferor to, a foreign trust.	Yes	No
Part III **Foreign Accounts and Trusts** (See instructions on back.)	**7a**	At any time during 2014, did you have a financial interest in or signature authority over a financial account (such as a bank account, securities account, or brokerage account) located in a foreign country? See instructions		✓
		If "Yes," are you required to file FinCEN Form 114, Report of Foreign Bank and Financial Accounts (FBAR), to report that financial interest or signature authority? See FinCEN Form 114 and its instructions for filing requirements and exceptions to those requirements		
	b	If you are required to file FinCEN Form 114, enter the name of the foreign country where the financial account is located ►		
	8	During 2014, did you receive a distribution from, or were you the grantor of, or transferor to, a foreign trust? If "Yes," you may have to file Form 3520. See instructions on back		✓

For Paperwork Reduction Act Notice, see your tax return instructions.	Cat. No. 17146N	Schedule B (Form 1040A or 1040) 2014

Illustration 18-5 continued

Form **8615**	**Tax for Certain Children Who Have Unearned Income**	OMB No. 1545-0074

Department of the Treasury
Internal Revenue Service (99)

► Attach only to the child's Form 1040, Form 1040A, or Form 1040NR.
► Information about Form 8615 and its separate instructions is at *www.irs.gov/form8615*.

2014
Attachment Sequence No. **33**

Child's name shown on return	Child's social security number
Robbie Jones	233-93-4323

Before you begin: If the child, the parent, or any of the parent's other children for whom Form 8615 must be filed must use the Schedule D Tax Worksheet or has income from farming or fishing, see **Pub. 929,** Tax Rules for Children and Dependents. It explains how to figure the child's tax using the **Schedule D Tax Worksheet** or **Schedule J (Form 1040).**

A Parent's name (first, initial, and last). **Caution:** *See instructions before completing.*	**B** Parent's social security number
Martin and Rita Jones	433-23-9514

C Parent's filing status (check one):

☐ Single   ☑ Married filing jointly   ☐ Married filing separately   ☐ Head of household   ☐ Qualifying widow(er)

Part I	**Child's Net Unearned Income**			
1	Enter the child's unearned income (see instructions)	**1**	2,319	00
2	If the child **did not** itemize deductions on **Schedule A** (Form 1040 or Form 1040NR), enter $2,000. Otherwise, see instructions	**2**	2,000	00
3	Subtract line 2 from line 1. If zero or less, **stop;** do not complete the rest of this form but **do** attach it to the child's return	**3**	319	00
4	Enter the child's **taxable income** from Form 1040, line 43; Form 1040A, line 27; or Form 1040NR, line 41. If the child files Form 2555 or 2555-EZ, see the instructions	**4**	1,319	00
5	Enter the **smaller** of line 3 or line 4. If zero, **stop;** do not complete the rest of this form but **do** attach it to the child's return	**5**	319	00

Part II	**Tentative Tax Based on the Tax Rate of the Parent**			
6	Enter the parent's **taxable income** from Form 1040, line 43; Form 1040A, line 27; Form 1040EZ, line 6; Form 1040NR, line 41; or Form 1040NR-EZ, line 14. If zero or less, enter -0-. If the parent files Form 2555 or 2555-EZ, see the instructions	**6**	32,521	00
7	Enter the total, if any, from Forms 8615, line 5, of **all other** children of the parent named above. **Do not** include the amount from line 5 above	**7**		
8	Add lines 5, 6, and 7 (see instructions)	**8**	32,840	00
9	Enter the tax on the amount on line 8 based on the **parent's** filing status above (see instructions). If the Qualified Dividends and Capital Gain Tax Worksheet, Schedule D Tax Worksheet, or Schedule J (Form 1040) is used to figure the tax, check here ► ☐	**9**	4,016	00
10	Enter the parent's tax from Form 1040, line 44; Form 1040A, line 28, minus any alternative minimum tax; Form 1040EZ, line 10; Form 1040NR, line 42; or Form 1040NR-EZ, line 15. **Do not** include any tax from **Form 4972** or **8814** or any tax from recapture of an education credit. If the parent files Form 2555 or 2555-EZ, see the instructions. If the Qualified Dividends and Capital Gain Tax Worksheet, Schedule D Tax Worksheet, or Schedule J (Form 1040) was used to figure the tax, check here ► ☐	**10**	3,971	00
11	Subtract line 10 from line 9 and enter the result. If line 7 is blank, also enter this amount on line 13 and go to **Part III**	**11**	45	00
12a	Add lines 5 and 7 . . . . **12a**			
b	Divide line 5 by line 12a. Enter the result as a decimal (rounded to at least three places)	**12b**	× .	
13	Multiply line 11 by line 12b	**13**	45	00

Part III	**Child's Tax**—If lines 4 and 5 above are the same, enter -0- on line 15 and go to line 16.			
14	Subtract line 5 from line 4 . . . . **14** 1,000 00			
15	Enter the tax on the amount on line 14 based on the **child's** filing status (see instructions). If the Qualified Dividends and Capital Gain Tax Worksheet, Schedule D Tax Worksheet, or Schedule J (Form 1040) is used to figure the tax, check here ► ☐	**15**	101	00
16	Add lines 13 and 15	**16**	146	00
17	Enter the tax on the amount on line 4 based on the **child's** filing status (see instructions). If the Qualified Dividends and Capital Gain Tax Worksheet, Schedule D Tax Worksheet, or Schedule J (Form 1040) is used to figure the tax, check here ► ☐	**17**	131	00
18	Enter the **larger** of line 16 or line 17 here and on the **child's** Form 1040, line 44; Form 1040A, line 28; or Form 1040NR, line 42. If the child files Form 2555 or 2555-EZ, see the instructions	**18**	146	00

For Paperwork Reduction Act Notice, see your tax return instructions.   Cat. No. 64113U   Form **8615** (2014)

Underpayment Penalty

Paying taxes is a pay as you go concept. It is expected that the taxpayer pays the tax owed on their income as it is earned. To enforce this system the IRS assesses an underpayment penalty. If the taxpayer does not pay enough through withholding, they must pay estimated taxes.

The underpayment penalty applies to someone who owes taxes with the 2014 tax return unless one of the following applies:

- The total withholding and estimated tax payments was at least as much as the 2013 tax (or 110% of the 2013 if the AGI was more than $150,000 ($75,000 if MFS) and the taxpayer paid all required estimated tax payments on time.
- The tax balance due on the return is no more than 10% of the total 2014 tax, and the taxpayer paid all required estimated tax payments on time.
- The total 2014 tax minus withholding is less than $1,000.
- The taxpayer does not have a tax liability for 2013.
- The taxpayer did not have any withholding taxes and the current year tax less any household employment taxes is less than $1,000.

To determine what the penalty is, a Form 2210 (Illustration 18-6) can be filed. If the taxpayer does not want to figure it themselves, the IRS will, gladly, figure the penalty for them and send them a bill. However, the sooner the taxpayer pays the penalty, the less it will be. The penalty will accrue interest until it is paid.

Example: The taxpayer's AGI is $93,225 this year. He has a tax liability of $16,899. His total withholding for the year is $11,150, leaving him with a balance due of $5,749. This amount is over $1,000 and more than 10% of the total 2014 tax (10% is $1,690), which may make him subject to the underpayment penalty. His 2013 tax liability was $13,344. If his 2013 tax return showed a tax liability of $11,150 (his 2013 withholding) or under, he would have been exempt from the penalty. However, since his 2013 tax return showed a tax liability of over $11,150, he is subject to the underpayment penalty.

Form 2210

The first two pages of the Form 2210 are illustrated on the next two pages. The first page is completed to determine if the taxpayer owes a penalty. If the taxpayer would like to figure the penalty, page 2 will help with that. Page 2 of the Form 2210 determines the penalty using the short method. If the taxpayer must use the regular method (the requirements are listed on the top of page 2), page 3 and 4 (not illustrated) of the Form 2210 must be used.

Illustration 18-6

Form **2210**	**Underpayment of Estimated Tax by Individuals, Estates, and Trusts**	OMB No. 1545-0074
Department of the Treasury Internal Revenue Service	▶ **Information about Form 2210 and its separate instructions is at** *www.irs.gov/form2210.* ▶ **Attach to Form 1040, 1040A, 1040NR, 1040NR-EZ, or 1041.**	20**14** Attachment Sequence No. **06**

Name(s) shown on tax return	Identifying number

Do You Have To File Form 2210?

Complete lines 1 through 7 below. Is line 7 less than $1,000? **Yes** ▶ **Do not file Form 2210.** You do not owe a penalty.

No ↓

Complete lines 8 and 9 below. Is line 6 equal to or more than line 9? **Yes** ▶ You do not owe a penalty. **Do not file Form 2210** (but if box **E** in Part II applies, you must file page 1 of Form 2210).

No ↓

You may owe a penalty. Does any box in Part II below apply? **Yes** ▶ You **must** file Form 2210. Does box **B, C,** or **D** in Part II apply?

No ↓

        No   **Yes** ▶ You must figure your penalty.

Do not file Form 2210. You are not required to figure your penalty because the IRS will figure it and send you a bill for any unpaid amount. If you want to figure it, you may use Part III or Part IV as a worksheet and enter your penalty amount on your tax return, but **do not file Form 2210.**

You are **not** required to figure your penalty because the IRS will figure it and send you a bill for any unpaid amount. If you want to figure it, you may use Part III or Part IV as a worksheet and enter your penalty amount on your tax return, but **file only page 1 of Form 2210.**

Part I   Required Annual Payment

1	Enter your 2014 tax after credits from Form 1040, line 56 (see instructions if not filing Form 1040)	**1**	
2	Other taxes, including self-employment tax and, if applicable, Additional Medicare Tax and/or Net Investment Income Tax (see instructions)	**2**	
3	Refundable credits, including the premium tax credit (see instructions)	**3**	( )
4	Current year tax. Combine lines 1, 2, and 3. If less than $1,000, **stop;** you do not owe a penalty. **Do not** file Form 2210	**4**	
5	Multiply line 4 by 90% (.90) **5**		
6	Withholding taxes. **Do not** include estimated tax payments (see instructions)	**6**	
7	Subtract line 6 from line 4. If less than $1,000, **stop;** you do not owe a penalty. **Do not** file Form 2210	**7**	
8	Maximum required annual payment based on prior year's tax (see instructions)	**8**	
9	**Required annual payment.** Enter the **smaller** of line 5 or line 8	**9**	

Next: Is line 9 more than line 6?

☐ **No.** You **do not** owe a penalty. **Do not** file Form 2210 unless box **E** below applies.

☐ **Yes.** You may owe a penalty, but **do not** file Form 2210 unless one or more boxes in Part II below applies.

    • If box **B, C,** or **D** applies, you must figure your penalty and file Form 2210.

    • If box **A** or **E** applies (but not **B, C,** or **D**) file only page 1 of Form 2210. You are **not** required to figure your penalty; the IRS will figure it and send you a bill for any unpaid amount. If you want to figure your penalty, you may use Part III or IV as a worksheet and enter your penalty on your tax return, but **file only page 1 of Form 2210.**

Part II   Reasons for Filing. Check applicable boxes. If none apply, **do not** file Form 2210.

A ☐ You request a **waiver** (see instructions) of your entire penalty. You must check this box and file page 1 of Form 2210, but you are not required to figure your penalty.

B ☐ You request a **waiver** (see instructions) of part of your penalty. You must figure your penalty and waiver amount and file Form 2210.

C ☐ Your income varied during the year and your penalty is reduced or eliminated when figured using the **annualized income installment method.** You must figure the penalty using Schedule AI and file Form 2210.

D ☐ Your penalty is lower when figured by treating the federal income tax withheld from your income as paid on the dates it was actually withheld, instead of in equal amounts on the payment due dates. You must figure your penalty and file Form 2210.

E ☐ You filed or are filing a joint return for either 2013 or 2014, but not for both years, and line 8 above is smaller than line 5 above. You must file page 1 of Form 2210, but you are **not** required to figure your penalty (unless box **B, C,** or **D** applies).

For Paperwork Reduction Act Notice, see separate instructions.   Cat. No. 11744P   Form **2210** (2014)

Illustration 18-6 continued

Part III	Short Method

Can You Use the Short Method?	You can use the short method if: • You made no estimated tax payments (or your only payments were withheld federal income tax), **or** • You paid the same amount of estimated tax on each of the four payment due dates.
Must You Use the Regular Method?	You must use the regular method (Part IV) instead of the short method if: • You made any estimated tax payments late, • You checked box **C** or **D** in Part II, **or** • You are filing Form 1040NR or 1040NR-EZ and you did not receive wages as an employee subject to U.S. income tax withholding.

Note. *If any payment was made earlier than the due date, you can use the short method, but using it may cause you to pay a larger penalty than the regular method. If the payment was only a few days early, the difference is likely to be small.*

10 Enter the amount from Form 2210, line 9		**10**	
11 Enter the amount, if any, from Form 2210, line 6	**11**		
12 Enter the total amount, if any, of estimated tax payments you made .	**12**		
13 Add lines 11 and 12		**13**	
14 Total underpayment for year. Subtract line 13 from line 10. If zero or less, **stop;** you do not owe a penalty. **Do not file Form 2210 unless you checked box E in Part II**		**14**	
15 Multiply line 14 by .01995		**15**	

16 • If the amount on line 14 was paid **on or after** 4/15/15, enter -0-.
• If the amount on line 14 was paid **before** 4/15/15, make the following computation to find the amount to enter on line 16.
 	
       Amount on   Number of days paid
        line 14   ×   before 4/15/15   ×   .00008 . . . .
		16	

17 Penalty. Subtract line 16 from line 15. Enter the result here and on Form 1040, line 79; Form 1040A, line 51; Form 1040NR, line 76; Form 1040NR-EZ, line 26; or Form 1041, line 26. **Do not file Form 2210 unless you checked a box in Part II** . . . . ▶		**17**	

Form **2210** (2014)

Estimated Tax

If the taxpayer does not have enough or any taxes withheld from their income, they may pay estimated taxes to keep from owing an underpayment penalty. Paying estimated tax is a way to pay the tax owed over four quarterly installments during the tax year. Generally, the taxpayer must make estimated tax payments if both of the following apply:

- The taxpayer expects to owe at least $1,000 in tax for 2015, after subtracting the withholding and credits.
- The taxpayer expects the withholding and credits to be less than the smaller of:
  - 90% of the tax to be shown on the taxpayer's 2015 tax return, or
  - 100% of the tax shown on the taxpayer's 2014 tax return. The 2014 tax return must cover all 12 months.

Even if the taxpayer is not required to make estimated payments, they may if they are going to owe tax when they file their tax return.

Estimated tax payments are due on the 15th of the month following the close of each quarter:

- Jan 1 – March 31...........April 15
- April 1 – May 31.............June 15
- June 1 – August 31........September 15
- Sept 1 – Dec 31............January 15 of the next year.

If the due date falls on a Saturday, Sunday, or legal holiday, the due date is the next business day. The IRS has a worksheet (Illustration 18-7) to help calculate the amount of estimated tax the taxpayer should pay. The taxpayer will be required to mail in a voucher with the payment as shown in Illustration 18-8.

If the taxpayer made estimated payments for the current tax year, the total of those payments is entered on Form 1040, page 2, line 63.

Illsutration 18-7

2015 Estimated Tax Worksheet
Keep for Your Records

1	Adjusted gross income you expect in 2015 (see instructions)	**1**		
2	• If you plan to itemize deductions, enter the estimated total of your itemized deductions. **Caution:** *If line 1 is over $154,950 your deduction may be reduced. See Pub. 505 for details.*			
	• If you do not plan to itemize deductions, enter your standard deduction.	**2**		
3	Subtract line 2 from line 1.	**3**		
4	Exemptions. Multiply $4,000 by the number of personal exemptions. **Caution:** *See Worksheet 2-6 in Pub. 505 to figure the amount to enter if line 1 is over: $154,950*	**4**		
5	Subtract line 4 from line 3	**5**		
6	**Tax.** Figure your tax on the amount on line 5 by using the **2015 Tax Rate Schedules.** **Caution:** *If you will have qualified dividends or a net capital gain, or expect to exclude or deduct foreign earned income or housing, see Worksheets 2-7 and 2-8 in Pub. 505 to figure the tax.* . .	**6**		
7	Alternative minimum tax from **Form 6251** or included on **Form 1040A, line 28**	**7**		
8	Add lines 6 and 7. Add to this amount any other taxes you expect to include in the total on Form 1040, line 44	**8**		
9	Credits (see instructions). **Do not** include any income tax withholding on this line	**9**		
10	Subtract line 9 from line 8. If zero or less, enter -0-	**10**		
11	Self-employment tax (see instructions)	**11**		
12	Other taxes (see instructions)	**12**		
13a	Add lines 10 through 12	**13a**		
b	Earned income credit, additional child tax credit, fuel tax credit, net premium tax credit, and refundable American opportunity credit	**13b**		
c	**Total 2015 estimated tax.** Subtract line 13b from line 13a. If zero or less, enter -0- . . . ▶	**13c**		
14a	Multiply line 13c by 90% (66²/₃% for farmers and fishermen) **14a**			
b	Required annual payment based on prior year's tax (see instructions) . **14b**			
c	**Required annual payment to avoid a penalty.** Enter the **smaller** of line 14a or 14b . . . ▶	**14c**		
	Caution: *Generally, if you do not prepay (through income tax withholding and estimated tax payments) at least the amount on line 14c, you may owe a penalty for not paying enough estimated tax. To avoid a penalty, make sure your estimate on line 13c is as accurate as possible. Even if you pay the required annual payment, you may still owe tax when you file your return. If you prefer, you can pay the amount shown on line 13c. For details, see chapter 2 of Pub. 505.*			
15	Income tax withheld and estimated to be withheld during 2015 (including income tax withholding on pensions, annuities, certain deferred income, etc.)	**15**		
16a	Subtract line 15 from line 14c **16a**			
	Is the result zero or less?			
	☐ **Yes.** Stop here. You are not required to make estimated tax payments.			
	☐ **No.** Go to line 16b.			
b	Subtract line 15 from line 13c **16b**			
	Is the result less than $1,000?			
	☐ **Yes.** Stop here. You are not required to make estimated tax payments.			
	☐ **No.** Go to line 17 to figure your required payment.			
17	If the first payment you are required to make is due April 15, 2015, enter ¼ of line 16a (minus any 2014 overpayment that you are applying to this installment) here, and on your estimated tax payment voucher(s) if you are paying by check or money order	**17**		

Illustration 18-8

Form 1040-ES
Department of the Treasury
Internal Revenue Service

2015 Estimated Tax

Payment Voucher 3

OMB No. 1545-0074

Calendar year—Due Sept. 15, 2015

File only if you are making a payment of estimated tax by check or money order. Mail this voucher with your check or money order payable to "**United States Treasury.**" Write your social security number and "2015 Form 1040-ES" on your check or money order. Do not send cash. Enclose, but do not staple or attach, your payment with this voucher.

Amount of estimated tax you are paying by check or money order.

	Dollars	Cents

Print or type

Your first name and initial	Your last name	Your social security number

If joint payment, complete for spouse

Spouse's first name and initial	Spouse's last name	Spouse's social security number

Address (number, street, and apt. no.)		
City, state, and ZIP code. (If a foreign address, enter city, also complete spaces below.)		

Foreign country name	Foreign province/county	Foreign postal code

For Privacy Act and Paperwork Reduction Act Notice, see instructions.

- - - - - - - - - - - - - - - - Tear off here - - - - - - - - - - - - - - - -

Form 1040-ES
Department of the Treasury
Internal Revenue Service

2015 Estimated Tax

Payment Voucher 2

OMB No. 1545-0074

Calendar year—Due June 15, 2015

File only if you are making a payment of estimated tax by check or money order. Mail this voucher with your check or money order payable to "**United States Treasury.**" Write your social security number and "2015 Form 1040-ES" on your check or money order. Do not send cash. Enclose, but do not staple or attach, your payment with this voucher.

Amount of estimated tax you are paying by check or money order.

	Dollars	Cents

Print or type

Your first name and initial	Your last name	Your social security number

If joint payment, complete for spouse

Spouse's first name and initial	Spouse's last name	Spouse's social security number

Address (number, street, and apt. no.)		
City, state, and ZIP code. (If a foreign address, enter city, also complete spaces below.)		

Foreign country name	Foreign province/county	Foreign postal code

For Privacy Act and Paperwork Reduction Act Notice, see instructions.

- - - - - - - - - - - - - - - - Tear off here - - - - - - - - - - - - - - - -

Form 1040-ES
Department of the Treasury
Internal Revenue Service

2015 Estimated Tax

Payment Voucher 1

OMB No. 1545-0074

Calendar year—Due April 15, 2015

File only if you are making a payment of estimated tax by check or money order. Mail this voucher with your check or money order payable to "**United States Treasury.**" Write your social security number and "2015 Form 1040-ES" on your check or money order. Do not send cash. Enclose, but do not staple or attach, your payment with this voucher.

Amount of estimated tax you are paying by check or money order.

	Dollars	Cents

Print or type

Your first name and initial	Your last name	Your social security number

If joint payment, complete for spouse

Spouse's first name and initial	Spouse's last name	Spouse's social security number

Address (number, street, and apt. no.)		
City, state, and ZIP code. (If a foreign address, enter city, also complete spaces below.)		

Foreign country name	Foreign province/county	Foreign postal code

For Privacy Act and Paperwork Reduction Act Notice, see instructions.

Form 1040-ES (2015)

Chapter Review

1) How much investment income does a child have to make to be required to pay tax at the rate their parents are taxed at?

2) What form must be filed to calculate an underpayment penalty?

3) What can the taxpayer do to avoid paying the underpayment penalty?

4) What are the due dates for estimated tax payments?

5) What are the two requirements, one of which must be met, for the taxpayer not to be required to pay estimated taxes?

Exercise

Prepare a tax return. Samantha Snowden is single and lives in a house with her daughter, Sara. Samantha is a teacher at the elementary school her daughter attends. Samantha's SSN is 734-77-5444 and her birth date is August 23, 1987. Sara's SSN is 443-22-5643 and her birth date is April 22, 2008. Samantha wants to designate $3 to the presidential election campaign fund. They were both covered by health insurance all year. Their expenses are as follows:

Medical expenses	$1,333
Mortgage interest	3,499
Real estate tax	321
Personal property tax	31

Sara's grandmother opened an account in Sara's name when she was born. Sara received a 1099-INT (shown on the next page). Samantha wants to know if you can just add it to her return.

Note: Be sure to include the lesser of Form 8814, line 4 or 5 in the Modified AGI for purposes of the Premium Tax Credit.

☐ CORRECTED (if checked)

Form 1099-INT — Interest Income

PAYER'S name, street address, city or town, state or province, country, ZIP or foreign postal code, and telephone no.	Payer's RTN (optional)	OMB No. 1545-0112
Second National Bank 300 Gold Court Your City, Your State, Your Zip Code	**1** Interest income $ 2,876.00	20**14** Interest Income Form **1099-INT**

PAYER'S federal identification number	RECIPIENT'S identification number
45-1343242	443-22-5643

2 Early withdrawal penalty
$

3 Interest on U.S. Savings Bonds and Treas. obligations
$

Copy B

For Recipient

RECIPIENT'S name

Sara Snowden

4 Federal income tax withheld
$

5 Investment expenses
$

Street address (including apt. no.)

87 Lively Circle

6 Foreign tax paid
$

7 Foreign country or U.S. possession

City or town, state or province, country, and ZIP or foreign postal code

Your City, Your State, Your Zip Code

8 Tax-exempt interest
$

9 Specified private activity bond interest
$

This is important tax information and is being furnished to the Internal Revenue Service. If you are required to file a return, a negligence penalty or other sanction may be imposed on you if this income is taxable and the IRS determines that it has not been reported.

10 Market discount
$

11 Bond premium
$

Account number (see instructions)

12 Tax-exempt bond CUSIP no. | **13** State | **14** State identification no. | **15** State tax withheld
$
$

Form **1099-INT**   (keep for your records)   www.irs.gov/form1099int   Department of the Treasury - Internal Revenue Service

---

Form W-2 Wage and Tax Statement — 2014

a Employee's social security number 737-77-5444	OMB No. 1545-0008	Safe, accurate, FAST! Use	IRS e~file	Visit the IRS website at www.irs.gov/efile

b Employer identification number (EIN) 85-8743452	1 Wages, tips, other compensation 22,355.12	2 Federal income tax withheld 1,211.00
c Employer's name, address, and ZIP code Alphabet School 700 Learning Way Your City, Your State, Your Zip Code	3 Social security wages 22,355.12	4 Social security tax withheld 1,386.00
	5 Medicare wages and tips 22,355.12	6 Medicare tax withheld 324.15
	7 Social security tips	8 Allocated tips
d Control number	9	10 Dependent care benefits
e Employee's first name and initial Last name Suff.	11 Nonqualified plans	12a See instructions for box 12
	13 Statutory employee ☐ Retirement plan ☐ Third party sick pay ☐	12b
Samantha Snowden 87 Lively Circle Your City, Your State, Your Zip Code	14 Other	12c
		12d
f Employee's address and ZIP code		

15 State	Employer's state ID number	16 State wages, tips, etc.	17 State income tax	18 Local wages, tips, etc.	19 Local income tax	20 Locality name
YS	859643452	22,355.12	1,134.67			

Form **W-2** Wage and Tax Statement   2014   Department of the Treasury—Internal Revenue Service

Copy B—To Be Filed With Employee's FEDERAL Tax Return.
This information is being furnished to the Internal Revenue Service.

Form **1095-A**

Department of the Treasury
Internal Revenue Service

Health Insurance Marketplace Statement

▶ Information about Form 1095-A and its separate instructions is at *www.irs.gov/form1095a.*

☐ CORRECTED

OMB No. 1545-2232

2014

Part I   Recipient Information

1 Marketplace identifier	2 Marketplace-assigned policy number	3 Policy issuer's name
12-987456	11111	Trust Insurance

4 Recipient's name	5 Recipient's SSN	6 Recipient's date of birth
Samantha Snowden	767-77-5444	09/23/1987

7 Recipient's spouse's name	8 Recipient's spouse's SSN	9 Recipient's spouse's date of birth

10 Policy start date	11 Policy termination date	12 Street address (including apartment no.)
01/01/2014		87 Lively Circle

13 City or town	14 State or province	15 Country and ZIP or foreign postal code
Your City	Your State	Your Zip Code

Part II   Coverage Household

A. Covered Individual Name	B. Covered Individual SSN	C. Covered Individual Date of Birth	D. Covered Individual Start Date	E. Covered Individual Termination Date
16 Samanta Snowden	737-77-5444	08/23/1987	01/01/2014	
17 Sara Snowden	443-22-5643	04/22/2008	01/01/2014	
18				
19				
20				

Part III   Household Information

Month	A. Monthly Premium Amount	B. Monthly Premium Amount of Second Lowest Cost Silver Plan (SLCSP)	C. Monthly Advance Payment of Premium Tax Credit
21 January	331.22	340.53	263.22
22 February	331.22	340.53	263.22
23 March	331.22	340.53	263.22
24 April	331.22	340.53	263.22
25 May	331.22	340.53	263.22
26 June	331.22	340.53	263.22
27 July	331.22	340.53	263.22
28 August	331.22	340.53	263.22
29 September	331.22	340.53	263.22
30 October	331.22	340.53	263.22
31 November	331.22	340.53	263.22
32 December	331.22	340.53	263.22
33 **Annual Totals**	3,974.64	4,086.36	3,158.64

For Privacy Act and Paperwork Reduction Act Notice, see separate instructions.   Cat. No. 60703Q   Form **1095-A** (2014)

Chapter 19 – Other Tax Topics

Amendments

If the taxpayer files their tax return on time, then they find out that there was an error in the return or something was omitted, they must file an amended return. The amendment may result in them owing additional taxes or receiving a refund. The taxpayer may also file an amendment if they find a more advantageous way to file.

An amendment must be filed within three years after the original return was filed or within two years after the date the tax is paid, whichever is later. If the return was filed before the April 15th due date for the tax return, the return is treated as having been filed on the due date. If the taxpayer applied for an extension and received it, the file date is the date the return was filed if within the extension period. If the taxpayer filed after the extension period, the filing date is April 15th.

If the taxpayer and spouse filed MFJ they may not amend their return to the MFS filing status. When they file jointly, they are signing that they are jointly responsible that they both owe the tax, interest, and penalty on the return. See injured spouse and innocent spouse topics later in the chapter.

Form 1040X

To amend a tax return, a taxpayer must file a Form 1040X (Illustration 19-1).

Amended Return Filing Status: On this line, the filing status will be entered. This line must be completed even if the taxpayer's filing status is not being changed.

This Return is for Calendar Year: Mark the year for which the amendment is being filed.

Column A: Enter the amounts from the original return.

Column B: Enter the net increase or decrease for each line being changed.

Column C: Enter the corrected amounts in this column.

Note: When filing an amended return, be sure to use the tax laws for the year of the return that is being amended.

Every line that has changed should be explained on page 2, Part III. If any of the changes affect forms and schedules, ***make sure*** these forms and schedules are attached. If adding a Form W-2, attach it to the Form 1040X. Also, if Earned Income Credit is added or changed, attach the Earned Income Credit worksheets.

Example: Barbara Bangles is 24 and lives alone with her son, Edward. She pays all of the household bills. She filed her 2014 taxes on February 1, 2015. She did them herself. One of her friends found out she filed Single on her return and told her, correctly, that she could have filed Head of Household. Her original return and amended return follow (Illustration 19-2).

Illustration 19-1

Form **1040X**
(Rev. December 2014)

Department of the Treasury—Internal Revenue Service

Amended U.S. Individual Income Tax Return

▶ Information about Form 1040X and its separate instructions is at *www.irs.gov/form1040x*.

OMB No. 1545-0074

This return is for calendar year ☐ 2014 ☐ 2013 ☐ 2012 ☐ 2011
Other year. Enter one: calendar year _____ **or** fiscal year (month and year ended): _____

Your first name and initial	Last name	Your social security number
If a joint return, spouse's first name and initial	Last name	Spouse's social security number
Current home address (number and street). If you have a P.O. box, see instructions.	Apt. no.	Your phone number

City, town or post office, state, and ZIP code. If you have a foreign address, also complete spaces below (see instructions).

Foreign country name	Foreign province/state/county	Foreign postal code

Amended return filing status. You **must** check one box even if you are not changing your filing status. *Caution. In general, you cannot change your filing status from joint to separate returns after the due date.*

☐ Single
☐ Qualifying widow(er)
☐ Married filing jointly
☐ Married filing separately
☐ Head of household (If the qualifying person is a child but not your dependent, see instructions.)

Full-year coverage.
If all members of your household have full-year minimal essential health care coverage, check "Yes." Otherwise, check "No." (See instructions.)
☐ Yes ☐ No

Use Part III on the back to explain any changes

			A. Original amount or as previously adjusted (see instructions)	**B.** Net change— amount of increase or (decrease)— explain in Part III	**C.** Correct amount
Income and Deductions					
1	Adjusted gross income. If net operating loss (NOL) carryback is included, check here ▶ ☐	1			
2	Itemized deductions or standard deduction	2			
3	Subtract line 2 from line 1	3			
4	Exemptions. **If changing, complete Part I on page 2 and enter the amount from line 29**	4			
5	Taxable income. Subtract line 4 from line 3	5			
Tax Liability					
6	Tax. Enter method(s) used to figure tax (see instructions): _____	6			
7	Credits. If general business credit carryback is included, check here ▶ ☐	7			
8	Subtract line 7 from line 6. If the result is zero or less, enter -0-	8			
9	Health care: individual responsibility (see instructions)	9			
10	Other taxes	10			
11	Total tax. Add lines 8, 9, and 10	11			
Payments					
12	Federal income tax withheld and excess social security and tier 1 RRTA tax withheld (**if changing**, see instructions)	12			
13	Estimated tax payments, including amount applied from prior year's return	13			
14	Earned income credit (EIC)	14			
15	Refundable credits from: ☐ Schedule 8812 Form(s) ☐ 2439 ☐ 4136 ☐ 5405 ☐ 8801 ☐ 8812 (2011) ☐ 8839 ☐ 8863 ☐ 8885 ☐ 8962 or ☐ other (specify): _____	15			
16	Total amount paid with request for extension of time to file, tax paid with original return, and additional tax paid after return was filed	16			
17	Total payments. Add lines 12 through 16	17			
Refund or Amount You Owe (*Note. Allow up to 16 weeks for Form 1040X to be processed.*)					
18	Overpayment, if any, as shown on original return or as previously adjusted by the IRS	18			
19	Subtract line 18 from line 17 (If less than zero, see instructions)	19			
20	**Amount you owe.** If line 11, column C, is more than line 19, enter the difference	20			
21	If line 11, column C, is less than line 19, enter the difference. This is the amount **overpaid** on this return	21			
22	Amount of line 21 you want **refunded to you**	22			
23	Amount of line 21 you want **applied to your** (enter year): _____ estimated tax .	23			

Complete and sign this form on Page 2.

Illustration 19-1 continued

Part I	**Exemptions**

Complete this part **only** if you are increasing or decreasing the number of exemptions (personal and dependents) claimed on line 6d of the return you are amending.

		A. Original number of exemptions or amount reported or as previously adjusted	B. Net change	C. Correct number or amount
24	Yourself and spouse. *Caution. If someone can claim you as a dependent, you cannot claim an exemption for yourself* **24**			
25	Your dependent children who lived with you **25**			
26	Your dependent children who did not live with you due to divorce or separation **26**			
27	Other dependents **27**			
28	Total number of exemptions. Add lines 24 through 27 . . . . . . **28**			
29	Multiply the number of exemptions claimed on line 28 by the exemption amount shown in the instructions for line 29 for the year you are amending. Enter the result here and on line 4 on page 1 of this form. . **29**			

30 List **ALL** dependents (children and others) claimed on this amended return. If more than 4 dependents, see instructions.

(a) First name Last name	**(b)** Dependent's social security number	**(c)** Dependent's relationship to you	**(d)** Check box if qualifying child for child tax credit (see instructions)
			☐
			☐
			☐
			☐

Part II	**Presidential Election Campaign Fund**

Checking below will not increase your tax or reduce your refund.

☐   Check here if you did not previously want $3 to go to the fund, but now do.

☐   Check here if this is a joint return and your spouse did not previously want $3 to go to the fund, but now does.

Part III	**Explanation of changes.** In the space provided below, tell us why you are filing Form 1040X.

▶ Attach any supporting documents and new or changed forms and schedules.

Sign Here
Remember to keep a copy of this form for your records.

Under penalties of perjury, I declare that I have filed an original return and that I have examined this amended return, including accompanying schedules and statements, and to the best of my knowledge and belief, this amended return is true, correct, and complete. Declaration of preparer (other than taxpayer) is based on all information about which the preparer has any knowledge.

▶ _____   _____   ▶ _____   _____

Your signature   Date   Spouse's signature. If a joint return, **both** must sign.   Date

Paid Preparer Use Only

▶ _____   _____   _____

Preparer's signature   Date   Firm's name (or yours if self-employed)

_____   _____

Print/type preparer's name   Firm's address and ZIP code

                              ☐ Check if self-employed

PTIN _____   Phone number _____   EIN _____

For forms and publications, visit IRS.gov.   Form **1040X** (Rev. 12-2014)

Illustration 19-2

Form **1040**
Department of the Treasury—Internal Revenue Service (99)

U.S. Individual Income Tax Return 2014

OMB No. 1545-0074 | IRS Use Only—Do not write or staple in this space.

For the year Jan. 1–Dec. 31, 2014, or other tax year beginning _____ , 2014, ending _____ , 20 ___   **See separate instructions.**

Your first name and initial	Last name	Your social security number
Barbara	Bangles	1 2 2 2 2 1 1 1 1

If a joint return, spouse's first name and initial	Last name	Spouse's social security number

Home address (number and street). If you have a P.O. box, see instructions. | Apt. no.
10 My St.

▲ Make sure the SSN(s) above and on line 6c are correct.

City, town or post office, state, and ZIP code. If you have a foreign address, also complete spaces below (see instructions).
Your City, Your State, Your Zip Code

Presidential Election Campaign
Check here if you, or your spouse if filing jointly, want $3 to go to this fund. Checking a box below will not change your tax or refund. ☑ You ☐ Spouse

Foreign country name	Foreign province/state/county	Foreign postal code

Filing Status
Check only one box.

1. ☑ Single
2. ☐ Married filing jointly (even if only one had income)
3. ☐ Married filing separately. Enter spouse's SSN above and full name here. ▶
4. ☐ Head of household (with qualifying person). (See instructions.) If the qualifying person is a child but not your dependent, enter this child's name here. ▶
5. ☐ Qualifying widow(er) with dependent child

Exemptions

6a ☑ **Yourself.** If someone can claim you as a dependent, **do not** check box 6a . . . . . .
b ☐ **Spouse** . . . .

Boxes checked on 6a and 6b — **1**

c **Dependents:**

(1) First name Last name	(2) Dependent's social security number	(3) Dependent's relationship to you	(4) ✓ if child under age 17 qualifying for child tax credit (see instructions)
Edward Bangles	4 3 4 4 5 6 5 4 3	Son	☑
			☐
			☐
			☐

If more than four dependents, see instructions and check here ▶ ☐

No. of children on 6c who:
• lived with you — **1**
• did not live with you due to divorce or separation (see instructions)
Dependents on 6c not entered above

Add numbers on lines above ▶ **2**

d Total number of exemptions claimed . . . .

Income

Attach Form(s) W-2 here. Also attach Forms W-2G and 1099-R if tax was withheld.

If you did not get a W-2, see instructions.

7	Wages, salaries, tips, etc. Attach Form(s) W-2	7	40,000 00
8a	**Taxable** interest. Attach Schedule B if required	8a	
b	**Tax-exempt** interest. **Do not** include on line 8a . . .	8b	
9a	Ordinary dividends. Attach Schedule B if required	9a	
b	Qualified dividends	9b	
10	Taxable refunds, credits, or offsets of state and local income taxes	10	
11	Alimony received	11	
12	Business income or (loss). Attach Schedule C or C-EZ	12	
13	Capital gain or (loss). Attach Schedule D if required. If not required, check here ▶ ☐	13	
14	Other gains or (losses). Attach Form 4797	14	
15a	IRA distributions . 15a _____ b Taxable amount . . .	15b	
16a	Pensions and annuities 16a _____ b Taxable amount . . .	16b	
17	Rental real estate, royalties, partnerships, S corporations, trusts, etc. Attach Schedule E	17	
18	Farm income or (loss). Attach Schedule F	18	
19	Unemployment compensation	19	
20a	Social security benefits 20a _____ b Taxable amount . . .	20b	
21	Other income. List type and amount _____	21	
22	Combine the amounts in the far right column for lines 7 through 21. This is your **total income** ▶	22	40,000 00

Adjusted Gross Income

23	Educator expenses	23	
24	Certain business expenses of reservists, performing artists, and fee-basis government officials. Attach Form 2106 or 2106-EZ	24	
25	Health savings account deduction. Attach Form 8889 .	25	
26	Moving expenses. Attach Form 3903	26	
27	Deductible part of self-employment tax. Attach Schedule SE .	27	
28	Self-employed SEP, SIMPLE, and qualified plans .	28	
29	Self-employed health insurance deduction . .	29	
30	Penalty on early withdrawal of savings	30	
31a	Alimony paid b Recipient's SSN ▶ _____	31a	
32	IRA deduction	32	
33	Student loan interest deduction	33	
34	Tuition and fees. Attach Form 8917	34	
35	Domestic production activities deduction. Attach Form 8903	35	
36	Add lines 23 through 35	36	
37	Subtract line 36 from line 22. This is your **adjusted gross income** . . . . . ▶	37	40,000 00

For Disclosure, Privacy Act, and Paperwork Reduction Act Notice, see separate instructions.   Cat. No. 11320B   Form **1040** (2014)

Illustration 19-2 continued

Form 1040 (2014)
Page **2**

Tax and Credits	38	Amount from line 37 (adjusted gross income)	38	40,000	00
	39a	Check if: ☐ **You** were born before January 2, 1950, ☐ Blind. ☐ **Spouse** was born before January 2, 1950, ☐ Blind. } Total boxes checked ▶ 39a			
	b	If your spouse itemizes on a separate return or you were a dual-status alien, check here▶ 39b☐			
Standard Deduction for— • People who check any box on line 39a or 39b **or** who can be claimed as a dependent, see instructions. • All others: Single or Married filing separately, $6,200 Married filing jointly or Qualifying widow(er), $12,400 Head of household, $9,100	40	**Itemized deductions** (from Schedule A) **or** your **standard deduction** (see left margin)	40	6,200	00
	41	Subtract line 40 from line 38	41	33,800	00
	42	**Exemptions.** If line 38 is $152,525 or less, multiply $3,950 by the number on line 6d. Otherwise, see instructions	42	7,900	00
	43	**Taxable income.** Subtract line 42 from line 41. If line 42 is more than line 41, enter -0-	43	25,900	00
	44	**Tax** (see instructions). Check if any from: **a** ☐ Form(s) 8814 **b** ☐ Form 4972 **c** ☐	44	3,435	00
	45	**Alternative minimum tax** (see instructions). Attach Form 6251	45		
	46	Excess advance premium tax credit repayment. Attach Form 8962	46		
	47	Add lines 44, 45, and 46 ▶	47	3,435	00
	48	Foreign tax credit. Attach Form 1116 if required	48		
	49	Credit for child and dependent care expenses. Attach Form 2441	49		
	50	Education credits from Form 8863, line 19	50		
	51	Retirement savings contributions credit. Attach Form 8880	51		
	52	Child tax credit. Attach Schedule 8812, if required	52	1,000	00
	53	Residential energy credits. Attach Form 5695	53		
	54	Other credits from Form: **a** ☐ 3800 **b** ☐ 8801 **c** ☐	54		
	55	Add lines 48 through 54. These are your **total credits**	55	1,000	00
	56	Subtract line 55 from line 47. If line 55 is more than line 47, enter -0- ▶	56	2,435	00
Other Taxes	57	Self-employment tax. Attach Schedule SE	57		
	58	Unreported social security and Medicare tax from Form: **a** ☐ 4137 **b** ☐ 8919	58		
	59	Additional tax on IRAs, other qualified retirement plans, etc. Attach Form 5329 if required	59		
	60a	Household employment taxes from Schedule H	60a		
	b	First-time homebuyer credit repayment. Attach Form 5405 if required	60b		
	61	Health care: individual responsibility (see instructions) Full-year coverage ☑	61		
	62	Taxes from: **a** ☐ Form 8959 **b** ☐ Form 8960 **c** ☐ Instructions; enter code(s)	62		
	63	Add lines 56 through 62. This is your **total tax** ▶	63	2,435	00
Payments If you have a qualifying child, attach Schedule EIC.	64	Federal income tax withheld from Forms W-2 and 1099	64	4,000	00
	65	2014 estimated tax payments and amount applied from 2013 return	65		
	66a	**Earned income credit (EIC)**	66a		
	b	Nontaxable combat pay election	66b		
	67	Additional child tax credit. Attach Schedule 8812	67		
	68	American opportunity credit from Form 8863, line 8	68		
	69	Net premium tax credit. Attach Form 8962	69		
	70	Amount paid with request for extension to file	70		
	71	Excess social security and tier 1 RRTA tax withheld	71		
	72	Credit for federal tax on fuels. Attach Form 4136	72		
	73	Credits from Form: **a** ☐ 2439 **b** ☐ Reserved **c** ☐ Reserved **d** ☐	73		
	74	Add lines 64, 65, 66a, and 67 through 73. These are your **total payments** ▶	74	4,000	00
Refund Direct deposit? See instructions.	75	If line 74 is more than line 63, subtract line 63 from line 74. This is the amount you **overpaid**	75	1,565	00
	76a	Amount of line 75 you want **refunded to you.** If Form 8888 is attached, check here ▶☐	76a	1,565	00
	▶ b	Routing number			
		▶ c Type: ☐ Checking ☐ Savings			
	▶ d	Account number			
	77	Amount of line 75 you want **applied to your 2015 estimated tax** ▶ 77			
Amount You Owe	78	**Amount you owe.** Subtract line 74 from line 63. For details on how to pay, see instructions ▶	78		
	79	Estimated tax penalty (see instructions) 79			

Third Party Designee	Do you want to allow another person to discuss this return with the IRS (see instructions)? ☐ **Yes.** Complete below. ☐ **No**
	Designee's name ▶ Phone no. ▶ Personal identification number (PIN) ▶

Sign Here
Joint return? See instructions. Keep a copy for your records.

Under penalties of perjury, I declare that I have examined this return and accompanying schedules and statements, and to the best of my knowledge and belief, they are true, correct, and complete. Declaration of preparer (other than taxpayer) is based on all information of which preparer has any knowledge.

Your signature	Date	Your occupation Bank Teller	Daytime phone number (555)555-5555
Spouse's signature. If a joint return, **both** must sign.	Date	Spouse's occupation	If the IRS sent you an Identity Protection PIN, enter it here (see inst.)

Paid Preparer Use Only	Print/Type preparer's name Jane Doe	Preparer's signature	Date	Check ☐ if self-employed	PTIN P00000000
	Firm's name ▶ **My Tax Service**			Firm's EIN ▶	63-0000000
	Firm's address ▶ **100 Main St., Your City, Your State, Your Zip Code**			Phone no.	(555)555-1111

www.irs.gov/form1040
Form **1040** (2014)

19-5

Illustration 19-2 continued

Form **1040X** (Rev. December 2014)

Amended U.S. Individual Income Tax Return

Department of the Treasury   Internal Revenue Service

► Information about Form 1040X and its separate instructions is at *www.irs.gov/form1040x*.

OMB No. 1545-0074

This return is for calendar year   ☑ 2014   ☐ 2013   ☐ 2012   ☐ 2011

Other year. Enter one: calendar year _____ **or** fiscal year (month and year ended): _____

Your first name and initial	Last name	Your social security number
Barbara	Bangles	1 2 2 2 2 1 1 1 1
If a joint return, spouse's first name and initial	Last name	Spouse's social security number

Current home address (number and street). If you have a P.O. box, see instructions. | Apt. no. | Your phone number

10 My Street

City, town or post office, state, and ZIP code. If you have a foreign address, also complete spaces below (see instructions).

Your City, Your State, Your Zip Code

Foreign country name	Foreign province/state/county	Foreign postal code

Amended return filing status. You **must** check one box even if you are not changing your filing status. *Caution. In general, you cannot change your filing status from joint to separate returns after the due date.*

☐ Single
☐ Qualifying widow(er)
☐ Married filing jointly
☐ Married filing separately
☑ Head of household (If the qualifying person is a child but not your dependent, see instructions.)

Full-year coverage.
If all members of your household have full-year minimal essential health care coverage, check "Yes." Otherwise, check "No." (See instructions.)
☑ Yes   ☐ No

Use Part III on the back to explain any changes

	Income and Deductions		A. Original amount or as previously adjusted (see instructions)	B. Net change— amount of increase or (decrease)— explain in Part III	C. Correct amount
1	Adjusted gross income. If net operating loss (NOL) carryback is included, check here ►☐	1	40,000		40,000
2	Itemized deductions or standard deduction	2	6,200	2,900	9,100
3	Subtract line 2 from line 1	3	33,800	(2,900)	30,900
4	Exemptions. **If changing, complete Part I on page 2 and enter the amount from line 29**	4	7,900		7,900
5	Taxable income. Subtract line 4 from line 3	5	25,900	(2,900)	23,000
Tax Liability					
6	Tax. Enter method(s) used to figure tax (see instructions): Tax Table	6	3,435	(629)	2,806
7	Credits. If general business credit carryback is included, check here ►☐	7	1,000		1,000
8	Subtract line 7 from line 6. If the result is zero or less, enter -0-	8	2,435	(629)	1,806
9	Health care: individual responsibility (see instructions)	9			
10	Other taxes	10			
11	Total tax. Add lines 8, 9, and 10	11	2,435	(629)	1,806
Payments					
12	Federal income tax withheld and excess social security and tier 1 RRTA tax withheld (**if changing**, see instructions)	12	4,000		4,000
13	Estimated tax payments, including amount applied from prior year's return	13			
14	Earned income credit (EIC)	14			
15	Refundable credits from: ☐ Schedule 8812 Form(s) ☐ 2439 ☐ 4136 ☐ 5405 ☐ 8801 ☐ 8812 (2011) ☐ 8839 ☐ 8863 ☐ 8885 ☐ 8962 or ☐ other (specify): _____	15			

16	Total amount paid with request for extension of time to file, tax paid with original return, and additional tax paid after return was filed	16	4,000
17	Total payments. Add lines 12 through 16	17	4,000

Refund or Amount You Owe *(Note. Allow up to 16 weeks for Form 1040X to be processed.)*

18	Overpayment, if any, as shown on original return or as previously adjusted by the IRS	18	1,565
19	Subtract line 18 from line 17 (If less than zero, see instructions)	19	2,435
20	**Amount you owe.** If line 11, column C, is more than line 19, enter the difference	20	
21	If line 11, column C, is less than line 19, enter the difference. This is the amount **overpaid** on this return	21	629
22	Amount of line 21 you want **refunded to you**	22	629
23	Amount of line 21 you want **applied to your** (enter year): _____ estimated tax 23		

Complete and sign this form on Page 2.

For Paperwork Reduction Act Notice, see instructions.   Cat. No. 11360L   Form **1040X** (Rev. 12-2014)

Illustration 19-2 continued

Form 1040X (Rev. 12-2014)   Page **2**

Part I   Exemptions

Complete this part **only** if you are increasing or decreasing the number of exemptions (personal and dependents) claimed on line 6d of the return you are amending.

			A. Original number of exemptions or amount reported or as previously adjusted	B. Net change	C. Correct number or amount
See *Form 1040 or Form 1040A instructions and Form 1040X instructions.*					
24	Yourself and spouse. ***Caution.*** *If someone can claim you as a dependent, you cannot claim an exemption for yourself*	**24**			
25	Your dependent children who lived with you	**25**			
26	Your dependent children who did not live with you due to divorce or separation	**26**			
27	Other dependents	**27**			
28	Total number of exemptions. Add lines 24 through 27	**28**			
29	Multiply the number of exemptions claimed on line 28 by the exemption amount shown in the instructions for line 29 for the year you are amending. Enter the result here and on line 4 on page 1 of this form. .	**29**			

30   List **ALL** dependents (children and others) claimed on this amended return. If more than 4 dependents, see instructions.

(a) First name Last name	**(b)** Dependent's social security number	**(c)** Dependent's relationship to you	**(d)** Check box if qualifying child for child tax credit (see instructions)
			☐
			☐
			☐
			☐

Part II   Presidential Election Campaign Fund

Checking below will not increase your tax or reduce your refund.

☐   Check here if you did not previously want $3 to go to the fund, but now do.

☐   Check here if this is a joint return and your spouse did not previously want $3 to go to the fund, but now does.

Part III   Explanation of changes. In the space provided below, tell us why you are filing Form 1040X.

▶ Attach any supporting documents and new or changed forms and schedules.

The taxpayer used the single filing status on her original return. She qualifies to use the head of household filing status. The change in filing status decreased the taxable income by $2,900 as shown in lines 2 through 5. The tax has decreased by $629 on line 6 due to the decreased taxable income, and the lower tax rate given to the new filing status. The taxpayer is due an additional refund of $629.

Sign Here
Remember to keep a copy of this form for your records.

Under penalties of perjury, I declare that I have filed an original return and that I have examined this amended return, including accompanying schedules and statements, and to the best of my knowledge and belief, this amended return is true, correct, and complete. Declaration of preparer (other than taxpayer) is based on all information about which the preparer has any knowledge.

▶ _____   ▶ _____
Your signature   Date   Spouse's signature. If a joint return, **both** must sign.   Date

Paid Preparer Use Only

▶ _____

Preparer's signature   Date

Jane Doe
Print/type preparer's name

         P00000000
PTIN

☐ Check if self-employed

My Tax Service
Firm's name (or yours if self-employed)

100 Main St., Your City, Your State, Your Zip Code
Firm's address and ZIP code

(555)555-1111
Phone number

63-5555555
EIN

For forms and publications, visit IRS.gov.   Form **1040X** (Rev. 12-2014)

Injured Spouse

If the taxpayer and spouse are filing a Married Filing Joint tax return and the refund is expected to offset a debt that either the taxpayer or spouse (but not both) legally owes, an Injured Spouse Form can be filed. The debt can be from back taxes, delinquent child support, or a federal past debt such as a student loan. The injured spouse is the spouse that is not legally required to pay the past debt. There must be a refund on the return and the injured spouse must be entitled to a part of it. An Injured Spouse Form allows the one without the debt to receive their portion of the refund. Form 8379 (Illustration 19-3) can be filed with the return or if the return has already been filed, it can be mailed in by itself. It also can be filed with an amended return. To qualify as an injured spouse, all of the following must apply:

- The injured spouse is not legally obligated to pay the past due amount.
- The injured spouse had taxable income.
- The injured spouse made and reported payments such as federal income tax withheld from their wages or estimated tax payments, or they claimed a refundable tax credit such as earned income credit or additional child tax credit.

Innocent Spouse

If a taxpayer and spouse filed a Married Filing Joint return they are jointly and separately liable for any tax owed on that return. If one spouse incorrectly or fraudulently filed an incorrect tax return that the other spouse had no knowledge of, they may be able to file for some relief from the IRS. There are four types of relief they may file for:

- Innocent spouse relief,
- Separation of liability, which applies to joint filers who are divorced, widowed, legally separated, or have not lived together for the 12 months ending on the date election of this relief is filed,
- Equitable relief, or
- Relief from liability arising from community property law.

To file for any of these reliefs, a Form 8857 (Illustration 19-4) must be filed. Due to the length of the Form, only page 1 is provided in the Illustration.

Illustration 19-3

Form 8379

(Rev. February 2015)
Department of the Treasury
Internal Revenue Service

Injured Spouse Allocation

▶ Information about Form 8379 and its separate instructions is at *www.irs.gov/form8379*.

OMB No. 1545-0074

Attachment
Sequence No. **104**

Part I Should You File This Form? You must complete this part.

1 Enter the tax year for which you are filing this form. ▶ _____   Answer the following questions for that year.

2 Did you (or will you) file a joint return?
- ☐ **Yes.** Go to line 3.
- ☐ **No. Stop here.** Do not file this form. You are not an injured spouse.

3 Did (or will) the IRS use the joint overpayment to pay any of the following legally enforceable past-due debt(s) owed only by your spouse? (see instructions)
- • Federal tax • State income tax • State unemployment compensation • Child support • Spousal support
- • Federal nontax debt (such as a student loan)
- ☐ **Yes.** Go to line 4.
- ☐ **No. Stop here.** Do not file this form. You are not an injured spouse.

  Note. If the past-due amount is for a joint federal tax, you may qualify for innocent spouse relief for the year to which the overpayment was (or will be) applied. See *Innocent Spouse Relief,* in the instructions for more information.

4 Are you legally obligated to pay this past-due amount?
- ☐ **Yes. Stop here.** Do not file this form. You are not an injured spouse.

  Note. If the past-due amount is for a joint federal tax, you may qualify for innocent spouse relief for the year to which the overpayment was (or will be) applied. See *Innocent Spouse Relief,* in the instructions for more information.
- ☐ **No.** Go to line 5a.

5a Were you a resident of a community property state at any time during the tax year entered on line 1? (see instructions)
- ☐ **Yes.** Enter the name(s) of the community property state(s) _____.
  Go to line 5b.
- ☐ **No.** Skip line 5b and go to line 6.

b If you answered "Yes" on line 5a, was your marriage recognized under the laws of the community property state(s)? (see instructions)
- ☐ **Yes.** Skip lines 6 through 9. **Go to Part II** and complete the rest of this form.
- ☐ **No.** Go to line 6.

6 Did you make and report payments, such as federal income tax withholding or estimated tax payments?
- ☐ **Yes.** Skip lines 7 through 9 and **go to Part II** and complete the rest of this form.
- ☐ **No.** Go to line 7.

7 Did you have earned income, such as wages, salaries, or self-employment income?
- ☐ **Yes.** Go to line 8.
- ☐ **No.** Skip line 8 and go to line 9.

8 Did (or will) you claim the earned income credit or additional child tax credit?
- ☐ **Yes.** Skip line 9 and **go to Part II** and complete the rest of this form.
- ☐ **No.** Go to line 9.

9 Did (or will) you claim a refundable tax credit? (see instructions)
- ☐ **Yes. Go to Part II** and complete the rest of this form.
- ☐ **No. Stop here.** Do not file this form. You are not an injured spouse.

Part II Information About the Joint Tax Return for Which This Form Is Filed

10 Enter the following information exactly as it is shown on the tax return for which you are filing this form.
The spouse's name and social security number shown first on that tax return must also be shown first below.

First name, initial, and last name shown first on the return	Social security number shown first	If Injured Spouse, check here ▶ ☐
First name, initial, and last name shown second on the return	Social security number shown second	If Injured Spouse, check here ▶ ☐

11 Check this box only if you want your refund issued in both names. Otherwise, separate refunds will be issued for each spouse, if applicable. . . . . ☐

12 Do you want any injured spouse refund mailed to an address different from the one on your joint return? ☐ **Yes** ☐ **No**
If "Yes," enter the address.

Number and street	City, town, or post office, state, and ZIP code

For Paperwork Reduction Act Notice, see separate instructions.   Cat. No. 62474Q   Form **8379** (Rev. 2-2015)

Illustration 19-3 continued

Part III	**Allocation Between Spouses of Items on the Joint Tax Return** (See the separate Form 8379 instructions for Part III.)		
Allocated Items (Column **(a)** must equal columns **(b)** + **(c)**)	**(a)** Amount shown on joint return	**(b)** Allocated to injured spouse	**(c)** Allocated to other spouse
13 Income: **a.** Income reported on Form(s) W-2			
b. All other income			
14 Adjustments to income			
15 Standard deduction or Itemized deductions			
16 Number of exemptions			
17 Credits (**do not** include any earned income credit)			
18 Other taxes			
19 Federal income tax withheld			
20 Payments			

Part IV	**Signature.** Complete this part only if you are filing Form 8379 by itself and not with your tax return.

Under penalties of perjury, I declare that I have examined this form and any accompanying schedules or statements and to the best of my knowledge and belief, they are true, correct, and complete. Declaration of preparer (other than taxpayer) is based on all information of which preparer has any knowledge.

Keep a copy of this form for your records	Injured spouse's signature		Date		Phone number

Paid Preparer Use Only	Print/Type preparer's name	Preparer's signature	Date	Check ☐ if self-employed	PTIN
	Firm's name ▶			Firm's EIN ▶	
	Firm's address ▶			Phone no.	

Form **8379** (Rev. 2-2015)

Illustration 19-4

Form 8857
(Rev. January 2014)
Department of the Treasury
Internal Revenue Service (99)

Request for Innocent Spouse Relief

▶ Information about Form 8857 and its separate instructions is at *www.irs.gov/form8857*.

OMB No. 1545-1596

Important things you should know

- **Do not file this form with your tax return.** See *Where To File* in the instructions.
- Review and follow the instructions to complete this form. Instructions can be obtained at *www.irs.gov/form8857* or by calling 1-800-TAX-FORM (1-800-829-3676).
- While your request is being considered, the IRS generally cannot collect any tax from you for the year(s) you request relief. However, filing this form extends the amount of time the IRS has to collect the tax you owe, if any, for those years.
- The IRS is required by law to notify the person on line 5 that you requested this relief. That person will have the opportunity to participate in the process by completing a questionnaire about the tax years you enter on line 3. This will be done before the IRS issues preliminary and final determination letters.
- The IRS will not disclose the following information: your current name, address, phone numbers, or employer.

Part I	Should you file this form?

Generally, both you and your spouse are responsible, jointly and individually, for paying any tax, interest, or penalties from your joint return. If you believe your current or former spouse should be solely responsible for an erroneous item or an underpayment of tax from your joint tax return, you may be eligible for innocent spouse relief.

Innocent spouse relief may also be available if you were a resident of a community property state (see list of community property states in the instructions) and did not file a joint federal income tax return and you believe you should not be held responsible for the tax attributable to an item of community income.

1 **Do either of the paragraphs above describe your situation?**
- ☐ Yes. You should file this Form 8857. Go to question 2.
- ☐ No. Do not file this Form 8857, but go to question 2 to see if you need to file a different form.

2 **Did the IRS take your share of a joint refund from any tax year to pay any of the following past-due debt(s) owed ONLY by your spouse?** • Child support • Spousal support • Student loan (or other federal nontax debt) • Federal or state taxes
- ☐ Yes. You may be able to get back your share of the refund. See Form 8379, Injured Spouse Allocation, and the instructions to that form. Go to question 3 if you answered "Yes" to question 1.
- ☐ No. Go to question 3 if you answered "Yes" to question 1. If you answered "No" to question 1, do not file this form.

3 **If you determine you should file this form, enter each tax year you want innocent spouse relief.** It is important to enter the correct year. For example, if the IRS used your 2011 income tax refund to pay a 2009 joint tax liability, enter tax year 2009, not tax year 2011.

Tax Year _____ Tax Year _____ Tax Year _____

Tax Year _____ Tax Year _____ Tax Year _____

Part II	Tell us about yourself and your spouse for the tax years you want relief

4 Your current name (see instructions) | Your social security number

Address where you wish to be contacted. If this is a change of address, see instructions.

Number and street or P.O. box | Apt. no. | County

City, town or post office, state, and ZIP code. If a foreign address, see instructions. | Best or safest daytime phone number (between 6 a.m. and 5 p.m. Eastern Time)

5 **Who was your spouse for the tax years you want relief?** File a separate Form 8857 for tax years involving different spouses or former spouses.

That person's current name | Social security number (if known)

Current home address (number and street) (if known). If a P.O. box, see instructions. | Apt. no.

City, town or post office, state, and ZIP code. If a foreign address, see instructions. | Daytime phone number (between 6 a.m. and 5 p.m. Eastern Time)

For Privacy Act and Paperwork Reduction Act Notice, see instructions. | Cat. No. 24647V | Form **8857** (Rev. 1-2014)

Household Employment Taxes

A household employee is someone hired by the taxpayer to do household work that the taxpayer has control over. Some examples of household employees are babysitters, housekeepers, and private nurses. A Schedule H (Illustration 19-5) must be filed by the taxpayer if one of the following applies:

- The taxpayer paid any one employee cash wages of $1,900 or more in 2014,
- The taxpayer withheld any federal income tax during 2014 for any household employee, or
- The taxpayer paid total cash wages of $1,000 or more in any calendar quarter of 2013 or 2014 to all household employees.

The Schedule H will calculate the amount of Social Security taxes, Medicare taxes, and Federal Unemployment taxes (FUTA) the taxpayer will be required to pay on their employees' behalf. The taxes will be added to the taxpayer's tax liability on the Form 1040.

Extensions

Some taxpayers cannot get everything ready to file their taxes on time. The reason can be anything from a death in the family to not being able to get all of their paperwork ready. They may file for an automatic extension. An extension is an extension to file, _not_ an extension to pay. When the extension is filed, the taxpayer must estimate what their tax liability is and make a payment with the extension accordingly. If they file an extension but do not make a payment, they will be liable for late payment penalties and interest. A Form 4868 (Illustration 19-6) must be filed by the due date of the tax return.

An extension gives the taxpayer 6 additional months to file their tax return. If a Form 4868 is filed, the IRS will not notify the taxpayer that it is accepted. They will only notify the taxpayer if it is denied. The due date for the return after an extension has been filed is October 15th.

Illustration 19-5

SCHEDULE H (Form 1040)	Household Employment Taxes	OMB No. 1545-1971

SCHEDULE H
(Form 1040)

Department of the Treasury
Internal Revenue Service (99)

Household Employment Taxes

(For Social Security, Medicare, Withheld Income, and Federal Unemployment (FUTA) Taxes)

▶ **Attach to Form 1040, 1040NR, 1040-SS, or 1041.**

▶ Information about Schedule H and its separate instructions is at *www.irs.gov/scheduleh.*

OMB No. 1545-1971

2014

Attachment
Sequence No. **44**

Name of employer

Social security number

Employer identification number

Calendar year taxpayers having no household employees in 2014 do not have to complete this form for 2014.

A Did you pay **any one** household employee cash wages of $1,900 or more in 2014? (If any household employee was your spouse, your child under age 21, your parent, or anyone under age 18, see the line A instructions before you answer this question.)

☐ **Yes.** Skip lines B and C and go to line 1.
☐ **No.** Go to line B.

B Did you withhold federal income tax during 2014 for any household employee?

☐ **Yes.** Skip line C and go to line 7.
☐ **No.** Go to line C.

C Did you pay **total** cash wages of $1,000 or more in **any** calendar **quarter** of 2013 or 2014 to **all** household employees? (**Do not** count cash wages paid in 2013 or 2014 to your spouse, your child under age 21, or your parent.)

☐ **No. Stop.** Do not file this schedule.
☐ **Yes.** Skip lines 1-9 and go to line 10.

Part I — Social Security, Medicare, and Federal Income Taxes

1	Total cash wages subject to social security tax	**1**	
2	Social security tax. Multiply line 1 by 12.4% (.124)	**2**	
3	Total cash wages subject to Medicare tax	**3**	
4	Medicare tax. Multiply line 3 by 2.9% (.029)	**4**	
5	Total cash wages subject to Additional Medicare Tax withholding	**5**	
6	Additional Medicare Tax withholding. Multiply line 5 by 0.9% (.009)	**6**	
7	Federal income tax withheld, if any	**7**	
8	**Total social security, Medicare, and federal income taxes.** Add lines 2, 4, 6, and 7	**8**	

9 Did you pay **total** cash wages of $1,000 or more in **any** calendar **quarter** of 2013 or 2014 to **all** household employees? (**Do not** count cash wages paid in 2013 or 2014 to your spouse, your child under age 21, or your parent.)

☐ **No. Stop.** Include the amount from line 8 above on Form 1040, line 60a. If you are not required to file Form 1040, see the line 9 instructions.

☐ **Yes.** Go to line 10.

For Privacy Act and Paperwork Reduction Act Notice, see the instructions.   Cat. No. 12187K   Schedule H (Form 1040) 2014

Illustration 19-5 continued

Part II   Federal Unemployment (FUTA) Tax

		Yes	No
10	Did you pay unemployment contributions to only one state? (If you paid contributions to a credit reduction state, see instructions and check "No.") **10**		
11	Did you pay all state unemployment contributions for 2014 by April 15, 2015? Fiscal year filers see instructions **11**		
12	Were all wages that are taxable for FUTA tax also taxable for your state's unemployment tax? **12**		

Next: If you checked the **"Yes"** box on **all** the lines above, complete Section A.

If you checked the **"No"** box on **any** of the lines above, skip Section A and complete Section B.

Section A

13   Name of the state where you paid unemployment contributions ▶ ------------------------------------

14 Contributions paid to your state unemployment fund	**14**	
15 Total cash wages subject to FUTA tax	**15**	
16 **FUTA tax.** Multiply line 15 by .6% (.006). Enter the result here, skip Section B, and go to line 25	**16**	

Section B

17   Complete all columns below that apply (if you need more space, see instructions):

(a) Name of state	(b) Taxable wages (as defined in state act)	(c) State experience rate period		(d) State experience rate	(e) Multiply col. (b) by .054	(f) Multiply col. (b) by col. (d)	(g) Subtract col. (f) from col. (e). If zero or less, enter -0-.	(h) Contributions paid to state unemployment fund
		From	To					

18 Totals **18**		
19 Add columns (g) and (h) of line 18 . . . . **19**		
20 Total cash wages subject to FUTA tax (see the line 15 instructions)	**20**	
21 Multiply line 20 by 6.0% (.060)	**21**	
22 Multiply line 20 by 5.4% (.054) **22**		
23 Enter the **smaller** of line 19 or line 22		
(Employers in a credit reduction state must use the worksheet on page H-7 and check here) . ☐	**23**	
24 **FUTA tax.** Subtract line 23 from line 21. Enter the result here and go to line 25	**24**	

Part III   Total Household Employment Taxes

25 Enter the amount from line 8. If you checked the "Yes" box on line C of page 1, enter -0- . . .	**25**	
26 Add line 16 (or line 24) and line 25	**26**	

27   Are you required to file Form 1040?

☐ **Yes. Stop.** Include the amount from line 26 above on Form 1040, line 60a. **Do not** complete Part IV below.

☐ **No.** You may have to complete Part IV. See instructions for details.

Part IV   Address and Signature— Complete this part **only** if required. See the line 27 instructions.

Address (number and street) or P.O. box if mail is not delivered to street address   Apt., room, or suite no.

City, town or post office, state, and ZIP code

Under penalties of perjury, I declare that I have examined this schedule, including accompanying statements, and to the best of my knowledge and belief, it is true, correct, and complete. No part of any payment made to a state unemployment fund claimed as a credit was, or is to be, deducted from the payments to employees. Declaration of preparer (other than taxpayer) is based on all information of which preparer has any knowledge.

▶ _____   ▶ _____

   Employer's signature   Date

Paid Preparer Use Only	Print/Type preparer's name	Preparer's signature	Date	Check ☐ if self-employed	PTIN
	Firm's name ▶			Firm's EIN ▶	
	Firm's address ▶			Phone no.	

Illustration 19-6

Form **4868**

Department of the Treasury
Internal Revenue Service (99)

Application for Automatic Extension of Time To File U.S. Individual Income Tax Return

▶ Information about Form 4868 and its instructions is available at *www.irs.gov/form4868.*

OMB No. 1545-0074

2014

There are three ways to request an automatic extension of time to file a U.S. individual income tax return.

1. You can file Form 4868 and pay all or part of your estimated income tax due. See *How To Make a Payment,* on page 3.
2. You can file Form 4868 electronically by accessing IRS *e-file* using your home computer or by using a tax professional who uses *e-file.*
3. You can file a paper Form 4868.

It's Convenient, Safe, and Secure

IRS *e-file* is the IRS's electronic filing program. You can get an automatic extension of time to file your tax return by filing Form 4868 electronically. You will receive an electronic acknowledgment once you complete the transaction. Keep it with your records. Do not mail in Form 4868 if you file electronically, unless you are making a payment with a check or money order (see page 3).

Complete Form 4868 to use as a worksheet. If you think you may owe tax when you file your return, you will need to estimate your total tax liability and subtract how much you have already paid (lines 4, 5, and 6 below).

Several companies offer free e-filing of Form 4868 through the Free File program. For more details, go to IRS.gov and click on *freefile.*

 Pay Electronically

You **do not** need to submit a paper Form 4868 if you file it with a payment using our electronic payment options. Your extension will be automatically processed when you pay part or all of your estimated income tax electronically. You can pay online or by phone (see page 3).

 ***E-file* Using Your Personal Computer or Through a Tax Professional**

Refer to your tax software package or tax preparer for ways to file electronically. Be sure to have a copy of your 2013 tax return—you will be asked to provide information from the return for taxpayer verification. If you wish to make a payment, you can pay by electronic funds withdrawal or send your check or money order to the address shown in the middle column under *Where To File a Paper Form 4868* (see page 4).

 File a Paper Form 4868

If you wish to file on paper instead of electronically, fill in the Form 4868 below and mail it to the address shown on page 4.

For information on using a private delivery service, see page 4.

Note. If you are a fiscal year taxpayer, you must file a paper Form 4868.

General Instructions

Purpose of Form

Use Form 4868 to apply for 6 more months (4 if "out of the country" (defined on page 2) and a U.S. citizen or resident) to file Form 1040, 1040A, 1040EZ, 1040NR, 1040NR-EZ, 1040-PR, or 1040-SS.

Gift and generation–skipping transfer (GST) tax return (Form 709). An extension of time to file your 2014 calendar year income tax return also extends the time to file Form 709 for 2014. However, it does not extend the time to pay any gift and GST tax you may owe for 2014. To make a payment of gift and GST tax, see Form 8892. If you do not pay the amount due by the regular due date for Form 709, you will owe interest and may also be charged penalties. If the donor died during 2014, see the instructions for Forms 709 and 8892.

Qualifying for the Extension

To get the extra time you must:

1. Properly estimate your 2014 tax liability using the information available to you,
2. Enter your total tax liability on line 4 of Form 4868, and
3. File Form 4868 by the regular due date of your return.

 Although you are not required to make a payment of the tax you estimate as due, Form 4868 does not extend the time to pay taxes. If you do not pay the amount due by the regular due date, you will owe interest. You may also be charged penalties. For more details, see Interest and Late Payment Penalty on page 2. Any remittance you make with your application for extension will be treated as a payment of tax.

You do not have to explain why you are asking for the extension. We will contact you only if your request is denied.

Do not file Form 4868 if you want the IRS to figure your tax or you are under a court order to file your return by the regular due date.

▼ DETACH HERE ▼

Form **4868**

Department of the Treasury
Internal Revenue Service (99)

Application for Automatic Extension of Time To File U.S. Individual Income Tax Return

OMB No. 1545-0074

2014

For calendar year 2014, or other tax year beginning _____ **, 2014, ending** _____ **, 20** ____ .

Part I Identification	**Part II** Individual Income Tax
1 Your name(s) (see instructions)	**4** Estimate of total tax liability for 2014 . . . $ _____
	5 Total 2014 payments . . . . _____
Address (see instructions)	**6 Balance due.** Subtract line 5 from line 4 (see instructions) . . . . _____
	7 Amount you are paying (see instructions).... ▶ _____
City, town, or post office — State — ZIP Code	**8** Check here if you are "out of the country" and a U.S. citizen or resident (see instructions) . . . . . . ▶ ☐
2 Your social security number — **3** Spouse's social security number	**9** Check here if you file Form 1040NR or 1040NR-EZ and did not receive wages as an employee subject to U.S. income tax withholding . . . . ▶ ☐

For Privacy Act and Paperwork Reduction Act Notice, see page 4.   Cat. No. 13141W   Form **4868** (2014)

Tax Preparers

Many of us are or plan to become professional tax preparers. There are many good tax preparers, but there are some that do not follow the tax laws. When someone brings their information to a tax preparer, they trust that person to prepare their taxes correctly and not cost them any more money than necessary. Becoming a tax preparer is a huge responsibility.

We all want our clients to get big refunds or not have to pay any taxes. Realistically, however, that cannot happen. All we can do is give them every deduction that to which they are entitled and explain what they can do to make their situations better for the next year. It is ultimately the taxpayer's responsibility to keep their records to substantiate anything that is reported on their tax return.

The IRS is watching for the dishonest tax preparers. If they find that a tax preparer has been acting fraudulently, they will not only assess them with a harsh penalty, they also may make that tax preparer pay the taxes the client owes the IRS due to the fraudulent tax return.

Penalties

Filing Late

If the return is not filed by the due date including extensions, the taxpayer may have to pay a failure to file penalty. The penalty is 5% for each month or part of a month, but not more than 25%. If the return is over 60 days late the minimum penalty is the smaller of $135 or 100% of the unpaid tax.

Paying Tax Late

The failure to pay penalty is 0.50% of the unpaid taxes for each month or part of a month after the due date that the tax is not paid.

Accuracy related penalty

If the taxpayer underpays their taxes because:

- They show negligence or disregard of the rules or regulations, or
- They substantially understate their income tax.

Negligence – A failure to make a reasonable attempt to comply with the tax law or to exercise ordinary and reasonable care in preparing a return.

Disregard – Any careless, reckless, or intentional disregard.

Filing an erroneous claim for refund or credit

If the taxpayer files for an erroneous claim for refund or credit, they may have to pay a penalty of 20% of the disallowed amount of the claim, unless they can show a reasonable basis for the way they treated an item.

Frivolous tax submission

The penalty for a filing a frivolous tax return is $5,000. A frivolous tax return is one that does not include enough information to figure the correct tax or that contains information clearly showing that the tax they reported is substantially incorrect.

Fraud

If there is any underpayment of tax on the return due to fraud, a penalty of 75% of the underpayment due to fraud will be added to the tax.

Criminal Penalties

The IRS may subject a taxpayer to criminal prosecution for actions such as:

- Tax evasion,
- Willful failure to file a return, supply information or pay any tax due,
- Fraud and false statements, or
- Preparing and filing a fraudulent return.

Electronic Filing

Electronic filing is sending a tax return to the IRS through computers. Electronic filing the tax return has many benefits:

- The taxpayer will receive their refund faster.
- The return will be acknowledged by the IRS which gives proof of receipt.
- The return is received by the IRS as it has been input into the computer originally.

The returns that can be e-filed are current year tax returns. At this time, an amended or prior year tax return cannot be electronically filed.

As with tax returns filed by mail, an electronically filed tax return must be signed by the taxpayer as well as the preparer if applicable. The taxpayer must sign and date the Declaration of Taxpayer to authorize the origination of the electronic submission of the return to the IRS prior to the transmission of the return to the IRS. If the return is changed after it is signed and the amounts differ by more than either $50 to Total Income or AGI, or $14 to Total Tax, Federal Income Tax Withheld, Refund, or Amount You Owe, a new declaration must be signed.

There are two methods of signing the return. One method is the Self Select PIN. This method requires the taxpayer to provide their prior year Adjusted Gross Income (AGI) amount for use by the IRS to authenticate the taxpayers. When taxpayers sign, using this method, signature documents are not required.

The other method of signing the return is the Practitioner PIN. This method does not require the taxpayer to provide their prior year AGI amount. A signature authorization form (Form 8879 – Illustration 19-7) must be completed. The ERO (Electronic Return Originator) must retain Forms 8879 for three years from the return due date or the IRS received date, whichever is later. This form must not be sent to the IRS unless the IRS requests it.

Electronic Return Originator (ERO) – An authorized IRS e-file provider that originates the electronic submission of returns to the IRS.

If the taxpayer signs the return using either of the electronic signature methods, the ERO must also sign with a PIN. If the return is prepared by the ERO firm, the preparer is declaring under the penalties of perjury that the return was reviewed and is true, correct, and complete. For returns prepared by other than the ERO firm, the ERO attests that the return preparer signed the copy of the return and that the electronic return contains the tax information identical to that contained in the paper return. The paid preparer's identifying information must also be entered in the e-file return.

The ERO must retain, on paper or by electronic image, and make available to the IRS upon request, until the end of the calendar year in which a return was filed, the following material:

- A copy of signed Forms 8453 and any supporting documents that are not included in the electronic return data, and copies of Forms W-2, W-2G, and 1099-R;
- A copy of signed IRS e-file consent to disclose forms;
- A complete copy of the electronic portion of the return that can be readily and accurately converted into an electronic transmission that the IRS can process; and
- The acknowledgement file for IRS accepted returns.

The ERO must provide a complete copy of the return to the taxpayer.

The IRS electronically acknowledges the receipt of all transmissions. The return will either be accepted or rejected. A return can be rejected for specific reasons and is not considered filed. The acknowledgement of a rejected return will contain the reason the return was rejected. The return data can be corrected and retransmitted without new signatures or authorizations if the changes do not differ by more than $50 to Total Income or AGI, or more than $14 to Total Tax, Federal Income Tax Withheld, Refund, or Amount You Owe. If new signatures are required, they must be done before the tax return is resubmitted. Either way, the taxpayer must receive copies of the new electronic return data.

If the reject cannot be rectified, the ERO must take reasonable steps to inform the taxpayer of the rejection within 24 hours. If the taxpayer chooses not to have the electronic portion of the return corrected and transmitted, the taxpayer must file a paper return.

Form 8453

A Form 8453 (Illustration 19-8) is required if the taxpayer has any supporting documents that must be mailed to the IRS upon submission of the tax return. A list of what documents are required is on the Form 8453. The Form 8453 along with the supporting documents must be mailed within 3 business days of the acknowledgement that the IRS accepted the return.

Illustration 19-7

Form **8879**	**IRS *e-file* Signature Authorization**	OMB No. 1545-0074
Department of the Treasury Internal Revenue Service	▶ Do not send to the IRS. This is not a tax return. ▶ Keep this form for your records. ▶ Information about Form 8879 and its instructions is at *www.irs.gov/form8879*.	20**14**

Submission Identification Number (SID) ▶

Taxpayer's name	Social security number
Spouse's name	Spouse's social security number

Part I — Tax Return Information—Tax Year Ending December 31, 2014 (Whole Dollars Only)

1	Adjusted gross income (Form 1040, line 38; Form 1040A, line 22; Form 1040EZ, line 4)	**1**
2	Total tax (Form 1040, line 63; Form 1040A, line 39; Form 1040EZ, line 12)	**2**
3	Federal income tax withheld (Form 1040, line 64; Form 1040A, line 40; Form 1040EZ, line 7) . . .	**3**
4	Refund (Form 1040, line 76a; Form 1040A, line 48a; Form 1040EZ, line 13a; Form 1040-SS, Part I, line 13a)	**4**
5	Amount you owe (Form 1040, line 78; Form 1040A, line 50; Form 1040EZ, line 14)	**5**

Part II — Taxpayer Declaration and Signature Authorization (Be sure you get and keep a copy of your return)

Under penalties of perjury, I declare that I have examined a copy of my electronic individual income tax return and accompanying schedules and statements for the tax year ending December 31, 2014, and to the best of my knowledge and belief, it is true, correct, and complete. I further declare that the amounts in Part I above are the amounts from my electronic income tax return. I consent to allow my intermediate service provider, transmitter, or electronic return originator (ERO) to send my return to the IRS and to receive from the IRS **(a)** an acknowledgement of receipt or reason for rejection of the transmission, **(b)** the reason for any delay in processing the return or refund, and **(c)** the date of any refund. If applicable, I authorize the U.S. Treasury and its designated Financial Agent to initiate an ACH electronic funds withdrawal (direct debit) entry to the financial institution account indicated in the tax preparation software for payment of my federal taxes owed on this return and/or a payment of estimated tax, and the financial institution to debit the entry to this account. This authorization is to remain in full force and effect until I notify the U.S. Treasury Financial Agent to terminate the authorization. To revoke (cancel) a payment, I must contact the U.S. Treasury Financial Agent at 1-888-353-4537. Payment cancellation requests must be received no later than 2 business days prior to the payment (settlement) date. I also authorize the financial institutions involved in the processing of the electronic payment of taxes to receive confidential information necessary to answer inquiries and resolve issues related to the payment. I further acknowledge that the personal identification number (PIN) below is my signature for my electronic income tax return and, if applicable, my Electronic Funds Withdrawal Consent.

Taxpayer's PIN: check one box only

☐ I authorize _____ to enter or generate my PIN ⬚⬚⬚⬚⬚
                          ERO firm name   Enter five digits, but do
as my signature on my tax year 2014 electronically filed income tax return.   not enter all zeros

☐ I will enter my PIN as my signature on my tax year 2014 electronically filed income tax return. Check this box **only** if you are entering your own PIN **and** your return is filed using the Practitioner PIN method. The ERO must complete Part III below.

Your signature ▶ _____   Date ▶ _____

Spouse's PIN: check one box only

☐ I authorize _____ to enter or generate my PIN ⬚⬚⬚⬚⬚
                          ERO firm name   Enter five digits, but do
as my signature on my tax year 2014 electronically filed income tax return.   not enter all zeros

☐ I will enter my PIN as my signature on my tax year 2014 electronically filed income tax return. Check this box **only** if you are entering your own PIN **and** your return is filed using the Practitioner PIN method. The ERO must complete Part III below.

Spouse's signature ▶ _____   Date ▶ _____

Practitioner PIN Method Returns Only—continue below

Part III — Certification and Authentication—Practitioner PIN Method Only

ERO's EFIN/PIN. Enter your six-digit EFIN followed by your five-digit self-selected PIN.   ⬚⬚⬚⬚⬚⬚⬚⬚⬚⬚⬚
                                                Do not enter all zeros

I certify that the above numeric entry is my PIN, which is my signature for the tax year 2014 electronically filed income tax return for the taxpayer(s) indicated above. I confirm that I am submitting this return in accordance with the requirements of the Practitioner PIN method and **Publication 1345,** Handbook for Authorized IRS *e-file* Providers of Individual Income Tax Returns.

ERO's signature ▶ _____   Date ▶ _____

ERO Must Retain This Form — See Instructions
Do Not Submit This Form to the IRS Unless Requested To Do So

For Paperwork Reduction Act Notice, see your tax return instructions.   Cat. No. 32778X   Form **8879** (2014)

Illustration 19-8

Form **8453**	**U.S. Individual Income Tax Transmittal for an IRS e-file Return**	OMB No. 1545-0074

Department of the Treasury
Internal Revenue Service

For the year January 1–December 31, 2014
▶ See instructions on back.
▶ Information about Form 8453 and its instructions is available at *www.irs.gov/form8453*.

2014

Please print or type.

PRINT CLEARLY

Your first name and initial	Last name	Your social security number
If a joint return, spouse's first name and initial	Last name	Spouse's social security number
Home address (number and street). If you have a P.O. box, see instructions.	Apt. no.	▲ **Important!** ▲
City, town or post office, state, and ZIP code (If a foreign address, also complete spaces below.)		You **must** enter your SSN(s) above.
Foreign country name	Foreign province/state/county	Foreign postal code

---

FILE THIS FORM ONLY IF YOU ARE ATTACHING ONE OR MORE OF THE FOLLOWING FORMS OR SUPPORTING DOCUMENTS.

Check the applicable box(es) to identify the attachments.

☐ Form 1098-C, Contributions of Motor Vehicles, Boats, and Airplanes (or equivalent contemporaneous written acknowledgement)

☐ Form 2848, Power of Attorney and Declaration of Representative (or POA that states the agent is granted authority to sign the return)

☐ Form 3115, Application for Change in Accounting Method

☐ Form 3468 - attach a copy of the first page of NPS Form 10-168, Historic Preservation Certification Application (Part 2—Description of Rehabilitation), with an indication that it was received by the Department of the Interior or the State Historic Preservation Officer, together with proof that the building is a certified historic structure (or that such status has been requested)

☐ Form 4136 - attach the Certificate for Biodiesel and, if applicable, Statement of Biodiesel Reseller or a certificate from the provider identifying the product as renewable diesel and, if applicable, a statement from the reseller

☐ Form 5713, International Boycott Report

☐ Form 8283, Noncash Charitable Contributions, Section A (if any statement or qualified appraisal is required), or Section B, Donated Property, and any related attachments (including any qualified appraisal or partnership Form 8283)

☐ Form 8332, Release/Revocation of Release of Claim to Exemption for Child by Custodial Parent (or certain pages from a divorce decree or separation agreement, that went into effect after 1984 and before 2009) (see instructions)

☐ Form 8858, Information Return of U.S. Persons With Respect to Foreign Disregarded Entities

☐ Form 8864 - attach the Certificate for Biodiesel and, if applicable, Statement of Biodiesel Reseller or a certificate from the provider identifying the product as renewable diesel and, if applicable, a statement from the reseller

☐ Form 8949, Sales and Other Dispositions of Capital Assets (or a statement with the same information), if you elect not to report your transactions electronically on Form 8949

DO NOT SIGN THIS FORM.

For Paperwork Reduction Act Notice, see your tax return instructions.   Cat. No. 62766T   Form **8453** (2014)

Chapter Review

1) Within what time is an amended return required to be filed?

2) What form or schedule must be filed to amend a tax return?

3) If the taxpayer and spouse filed a joint return and the refund was kept for federal income taxes the taxpayer owed, what form may the spouse file to receive her part of the refund if all of the other requirements are met?

4) An extension is an extension to file, not to _____.

5) What is the due date for a return after an extension has been filed?

6) What are the two methods of signing an electronically filed return?

7) What is an ERO?

8) What is the signature authorization form for an electronically filed return?

Exercise

Prepare a tax return for Tammy and Tommy Carmichael. They have been married for 5 years and have one son, Timothy. Tammy is a bank teller and Tommy is an electrician. They both would like to designate $3 for the presidential election campaign fund. They had Minimum Essential Coverage all of 2014.

Tammy's SSN is 756-37-2345 and her birth date is December 12, 1980.

Tommy's SSN is 630-20-5493 and his birth date is July 30, 1981.

Timothy's SSN is 275-65-3245 and his birth date is February 3, 2013.

While Tammy and Tommy worked, Timothy attended First Steps daycare. Their EIN is 54-2958223 and address is 45 ABC Street, Your city, Your state, Your zip code. The Carmichaels paid them $2,322 for the year. Tammy also attended one class at State University. She paid $900 for the class and $46 for the books required. The address is 250 Grand Ave., Your City, Your State, Your Zip Code. She did not receive a Form 1098-T, but she did keep her receipts. She made it through her junior year of college in prior years.

☐ CORRECTED (if checked)		

RECIPIENT'S/LENDER'S name, address, city or town, state or province, country, ZIP or foreign postal code, and telephone number Student Financial Services 5534 Helpful Way Your City, Your State, Your Zip Code		OMB No. 1545-1576 20**14** Form **1098-E**	**Student Loan Interest Statement**
RECIPIENT'S federal identification no. 44-6726262	BORROWER'S social security number 630-20-5493	**1** Student loan interest received by lender $ 1,977.34	**Copy B** **For Borrower**
BORROWER'S name Tommy Carmichael Street address (including apt. no.) 89 Sunrise Circle City or town, state or province, country, and ZIP or foreign postal code Your City, Your State, Your Zip Code			This is important tax information and is being furnished to the Internal Revenue Service. If you are required to file a return, a negligence penalty or other sanction may be imposed on you if the IRS determines that an underpayment of tax results because you overstated a deduction for student loan interest.
Account number (see instructions)		**2** If checked, box 1 does **not** include loan origination fees and/or capitalized interest for loans made before September 1, 2004 . . . . ☐	

Form **1098-E**   (keep for your records)   www.irs.gov/form1098e   Department of the Treasury - Internal Revenue Service

Form W-2 (Top)

a Employee's social security number		
756-37-2345	OMB No. 1545-0008	Safe, accurate, FAST! Use IRS e-file

Visit the IRS website at www.irs.gov/efile

b Employer identification number (EIN)	1 Wages, tips, other compensation	2 Federal income tax withheld
85-8742535	31,998.00	3,454.88

c Employer's name, address, and ZIP code	3 Social security wages	4 Social security tax withheld
First Bank	33,798.00	2,095.48
67 Financial Blvd.	5 Medicare wages and tips	6 Medicare tax withheld
Your City, Your State, Your Zip Code	33,798.00	490.07
	7 Social security tips	8 Allocated tips

d Control number	9	10 Dependent care benefits

e Employee's first name and initial Last name Suff.	11 Nonqualified plans	12a See instructions for box 12
		Code D 1,800.00
	13 Statutory employee / Retirement plan / Third-party sick pay	12b
Tammy Carmichael		
89 Sunrise Circle	14 Other	12c
Your City, Your State, Your Zip Code		
		12d

f Employee's address and ZIP code

15 State	Employer's state ID number	16 State wages, tips, etc.	17 State income tax	18 Local wages, tips, etc.	19 Local income tax	20 Locality name
YS	85872534	33,798.00	1,544.98			

Form W-2 Wage and Tax Statement   **2014**   Department of the Treasury—Internal Revenue Service

Copy B—To Be Filed With Employee's FEDERAL Tax Return.
This information is being furnished to the Internal Revenue Service.

Form W-2 (Bottom)

a Employee's social security number		
630-20-5493	OMB No. 1545-0008	Safe, accurate, FAST! Use IRS e-file

Visit the IRS website at www.irs.gov/efile

b Employer identification number (EIN)	1 Wages, tips, other compensation	2 Federal income tax withheld
85-4562534	36,999.04	4,768.09

c Employer's name, address, and ZIP code	3 Social security wages	4 Social security tax withheld
Electricity Idol	36,999.04	2,293.94
900 Shock Ave.	5 Medicare wages and tips	6 Medicare tax withheld
Your City, Your State, Your Zip Code	36,999.04	536.49
	7 Social security tips	8 Allocated tips

d Control number	9	10 Dependent care benefits

e Employee's first name and initial Last name Suff.	11 Nonqualified plans	12a See instructions for box 12
		Code DD 7,923.15
	13 Statutory employee / Retirement plan / Third-party sick pay	12b
Tommy Carmichael		
89 Sunrise Circle	14 Other	12c
Your City, Your State, Your Zip Code		
		12d

f Employee's address and ZIP code

15 State	Employer's state ID number	16 State wages, tips, etc.	17 State income tax	18 Local wages, tips, etc.	19 Local income tax	20 Locality name
YS	854452534	36,999.04	1,879.35			

Form W-2 Wage and Tax Statement   **2014**   Department of the Treasury—Internal Revenue Service

Copy B—To Be Filed With Employee's FEDERAL Tax Return.
This information is being furnished to the Internal Revenue Service.

Appendix A – Tax Tables

2014 Tax Table

CAUTION

See the instructions for line 44 to see if you must use the Tax Table below to figure your tax.

Example. Mr. and Mrs. Brown are filing a joint return. Their taxable income on Form 1040, line 43, is $25,300. First, they find the $25,300-25,350 taxable income line. Next, they find the column for married filing jointly and read down the column. The amount shown where the taxable income line and filing status column meet is $2,891. This is the tax amount they should enter on Form 1040, line 44.

Sample Table

At Least	But Less Than	Single	Married filing jointly*	Married filing separately	Head of a household
			Your tax is—		
25,200	25,250	3,330	2,876	3,330	3,136
25,250	25,300	3,338	2,884	3,338	3,144
25,300	25,350	3,345	2,891	3,345	3,151
25,350	25,400	3,353	2,899	3,353	3,159

If line 43 (taxable income) is— At least	But less than	Single	Married filing jointly *	Married filing separately	Head of a household
			Your tax is—		
0	5	0	0	0	0
5	15	1	1	1	1
15	25	2	2	2	2
25	50	4	4	4	4
50	75	6	6	6	6
75	100	9	9	9	9
100	125	11	11	11	11
125	150	14	14	14	14
150	175	16	16	16	16
175	200	19	19	19	19
200	225	21	21	21	21
225	250	24	24	24	24
250	275	26	26	26	26
275	300	29	29	29	29
300	325	31	31	31	31
325	350	34	34	34	34
350	375	36	36	36	36
375	400	39	39	39	39
400	425	41	41	41	41
425	450	44	44	44	44
450	475	46	46	46	46
475	500	49	49	49	49
500	525	51	51	51	51
525	550	54	54	54	54
550	575	56	56	56	56
575	600	59	59	59	59
600	625	61	61	61	61
625	650	64	64	64	64
650	675	66	66	66	66
675	700	69	69	69	69
700	725	71	71	71	71
725	750	74	74	74	74
750	775	76	76	76	76
775	800	79	79	79	79
800	825	81	81	81	81
825	850	84	84	84	84
850	875	86	86	86	86
875	900	89	89	89	89
900	925	91	91	91	91
925	950	94	94	94	94
950	975	96	96	96	96
975	1,000	99	99	99	99

1,000

At least	But less than	Single	Married filing jointly *	Married filing separately	Head of a household
			Your tax is—		
1,000	1,025	101	101	101	101
1,025	1,050	104	104	104	104
1,050	1,075	106	106	106	106
1,075	1,100	109	109	109	109
1,100	1,125	111	111	111	111
1,125	1,150	114	114	114	114
1,150	1,175	116	116	116	116
1,175	1,200	119	119	119	119
1,200	1,225	121	121	121	121
1,225	1,250	124	124	124	124
1,250	1,275	126	126	126	126
1,275	1,300	129	129	129	129
1,300	1,325	131	131	131	131
1,325	1,350	134	134	134	134
1,350	1,375	136	136	136	136
1,375	1,400	139	139	139	139
1,400	1,425	141	141	141	141
1,425	1,450	144	144	144	144
1,450	1,475	146	146	146	146
1,475	1,500	149	149	149	149
1,500	1,525	151	151	151	151
1,525	1,550	154	154	154	154
1,550	1,575	156	156	156	156
1,575	1,600	159	159	159	159
1,600	1,625	161	161	161	161
1,625	1,650	164	164	164	164
1,650	1,675	166	166	166	166
1,675	1,700	169	169	169	169
1,700	1,725	171	171	171	171
1,725	1,750	174	174	174	174
1,750	1,775	176	176	176	176
1,775	1,800	179	179	179	179
1,800	1,825	181	181	181	181
1,825	1,850	184	184	184	184
1,850	1,875	186	186	186	186
1,875	1,900	189	189	189	189
1,900	1,925	191	191	191	191
1,925	1,950	194	194	194	194
1,950	1,975	196	196	196	196
1,975	2,000	199	199	199	199

2,000

At least	But less than	Single	Married filing jointly *	Married filing separately	Head of a household
			Your tax is—		
2,000	2,025	201	201	201	201
2,025	2,050	204	204	204	204
2,050	2,075	206	206	206	206
2,075	2,100	209	209	209	209
2,100	2,125	211	211	211	211
2,125	2,150	214	214	214	214
2,150	2,175	216	216	216	216
2,175	2,200	219	219	219	219
2,200	2,225	221	221	221	221
2,225	2,250	224	224	224	224
2,250	2,275	226	226	226	226
2,275	2,300	229	229	229	229
2,300	2,325	231	231	231	231
2,325	2,350	234	234	234	234
2,350	2,375	236	236	236	236
2,375	2,400	239	239	239	239
2,400	2,425	241	241	241	241
2,425	2,450	244	244	244	244
2,450	2,475	246	246	246	246
2,475	2,500	249	249	249	249
2,500	2,525	251	251	251	251
2,525	2,550	254	254	254	254
2,550	2,575	256	256	256	256
2,575	2,600	259	259	259	259
2,600	2,625	261	261	261	261
2,625	2,650	264	264	264	264
2,650	2,675	266	266	266	266
2,675	2,700	269	269	269	269
2,700	2,725	271	271	271	271
2,725	2,750	274	274	274	274
2,750	2,775	276	276	276	276
2,775	2,800	279	279	279	279
2,800	2,825	281	281	281	281
2,825	2,850	284	284	284	284
2,850	2,875	286	286	286	286
2,875	2,900	289	289	289	289
2,900	2,925	291	291	291	291
2,925	2,950	294	294	294	294
2,950	2,975	296	296	296	296
2,975	3,000	299	299	299	299

(Continued)

* This column must also be used by a qualifying widow(er).

If line 43 (taxable income) is—		And you are—				If line 43 (taxable income) is—		And you are—				If line 43 (taxable income) is—		And you are—			
At least	But less than	Single	Married filing jointly *	Married filing separately	Head of a household	At least	But less than	Single	Married filing jointly *	Married filing separately	Head of a household	At least	But less than	Single	Married filing jointly *	Married filing separately	Head of a household
		Your tax is—						Your tax is—						Your tax is—			
3,000						**6,000**						**9,000**					
3,000	3,050	303	303	303	303	6,000	6,050	603	603	603	603	9,000	9,050	903	903	903	903
3,050	3,100	308	308	308	308	6,050	6,100	608	608	608	608	9,050	9,100	908	908	908	908
3,100	3,150	313	313	313	313	6,100	6,150	613	613	613	613	9,100	9,150	915	913	915	913
3,150	3,200	318	318	318	318	6,150	6,200	618	618	618	618	9,150	9,200	923	918	923	918
3,200	3,250	323	323	323	323	6,200	6,250	623	623	623	623	9,200	9,250	930	923	930	923
3,250	3,300	328	328	328	328	6,250	6,300	628	628	628	628	9,250	9,300	938	928	938	928
3,300	3,350	333	333	333	333	6,300	6,350	633	633	633	633	9,300	9,350	945	933	945	933
3,350	3,400	338	338	338	338	6,350	6,400	638	638	638	638	9,350	9,400	953	938	953	938
3,400	3,450	343	343	343	343	6,400	6,450	643	643	643	643	9,400	9,450	960	943	960	943
3,450	3,500	348	348	348	348	6,450	6,500	648	648	648	648	9,450	9,500	968	948	968	948
3,500	3,550	353	353	353	353	6,500	6,550	653	653	653	653	9,500	9,550	975	953	975	953
3,550	3,600	358	358	358	358	6,550	6,600	658	658	658	658	9,550	9,600	983	958	983	958
3,600	3,650	363	363	363	363	6,600	6,650	663	663	663	663	9,600	9,650	990	963	990	963
3,650	3,700	368	368	368	368	6,650	6,700	668	668	668	668	9,650	9,700	998	968	998	968
3,700	3,750	373	373	373	373	6,700	6,750	673	673	673	673	9,700	9,750	1,005	973	1,005	973
3,750	3,800	378	378	378	378	6,750	6,800	678	678	678	678	9,750	9,800	1,013	978	1,013	978
3,800	3,850	383	383	383	383	6,800	6,850	683	683	683	683	9,800	9,850	1,020	983	1,020	983
3,850	3,900	388	388	388	388	6,850	6,900	688	688	688	688	9,850	9,900	1,028	988	1,028	988
3,900	3,950	393	393	393	393	6,900	6,950	693	693	693	693	9,900	9,950	1,035	993	1,035	993
3,950	4,000	398	398	398	398	6,950	7,000	698	698	698	698	9,950	10,000	1,043	998	1,043	998
4,000						**7,000**						**10,000**					
4,000	4,050	403	403	403	403	7,000	7,050	703	703	703	703	10,000	10,050	1,050	1,003	1,050	1,003
4,050	4,100	408	408	408	408	7,050	7,100	708	708	708	708	10,050	10,100	1,058	1,008	1,058	1,008
4,100	4,150	413	413	413	413	7,100	7,150	713	713	713	713	10,100	10,150	1,065	1,013	1,065	1,013
4,150	4,200	418	418	418	418	7,150	7,200	718	718	718	718	10,150	10,200	1,073	1,018	1,073	1,018
4,200	4,250	423	423	423	423	7,200	7,250	723	723	723	723	10,200	10,250	1,080	1,023	1,080	1,023
4,250	4,300	428	428	428	428	7,250	7,300	728	728	728	728	10,250	10,300	1,088	1,028	1,088	1,028
4,300	4,350	433	433	433	433	7,300	7,350	733	733	733	733	10,300	10,350	1,095	1,033	1,095	1,033
4,350	4,400	438	438	438	438	7,350	7,400	738	738	738	738	10,350	10,400	1,103	1,038	1,103	1,038
4,400	4,450	443	443	443	443	7,400	7,450	743	743	743	743	10,400	10,450	1,110	1,043	1,110	1,043
4,450	4,500	448	448	448	448	7,450	7,500	748	748	748	748	10,450	10,500	1,118	1,048	1,118	1,048
4,500	4,550	453	453	453	453	7,500	7,550	753	753	753	753	10,500	10,550	1,125	1,053	1,125	1,053
4,550	4,600	458	458	458	458	7,550	7,600	758	758	758	758	10,550	10,600	1,133	1,058	1,133	1,058
4,600	4,650	463	463	463	463	7,600	7,650	763	763	763	763	10,600	10,650	1,140	1,063	1,140	1,063
4,650	4,700	468	468	468	468	7,650	7,700	768	768	768	768	10,650	10,700	1,148	1,068	1,148	1,068
4,700	4,750	473	473	473	473	7,700	7,750	773	773	773	773	10,700	10,750	1,155	1,073	1,155	1,073
4,750	4,800	478	478	478	478	7,750	7,800	778	778	778	778	10,750	10,800	1,163	1,078	1,163	1,078
4,800	4,850	483	483	483	483	7,800	7,850	783	783	783	783	10,800	10,850	1,170	1,083	1,170	1,083
4,850	4,900	488	488	488	488	7,850	7,900	788	788	788	788	10,850	10,900	1,178	1,088	1,178	1,088
4,900	4,950	493	493	493	493	7,900	7,950	793	793	793	793	10,900	10,950	1,185	1,093	1,185	1,093
4,950	5,000	498	498	498	498	7,950	8,000	798	798	798	798	10,950	11,000	1,193	1,098	1,193	1,098
5,000						**8,000**						**11,000**					
5,000	5,050	503	503	503	503	8,000	8,050	803	803	803	803	11,000	11,050	1,200	1,103	1,200	1,103
5,050	5,100	508	508	508	508	8,050	8,100	808	808	808	808	11,050	11,100	1,208	1,108	1,208	1,108
5,100	5,150	513	513	513	513	8,100	8,150	813	813	813	813	11,100	11,150	1,215	1,113	1,215	1,113
5,150	5,200	518	518	518	518	8,150	8,200	818	818	818	818	11,150	11,200	1,223	1,118	1,223	1,118
5,200	5,250	523	523	523	523	8,200	8,250	823	823	823	823	11,200	11,250	1,230	1,123	1,230	1,123
5,250	5,300	528	528	528	528	8,250	8,300	828	828	828	828	11,250	11,300	1,238	1,128	1,238	1,128
5,300	5,350	533	533	533	533	8,300	8,350	833	833	833	833	11,300	11,350	1,245	1,133	1,245	1,133
5,350	5,400	538	538	538	538	8,350	8,400	838	838	838	838	11,350	11,400	1,253	1,138	1,253	1,138
5,400	5,450	543	543	543	543	8,400	8,450	843	843	843	843	11,400	11,450	1,260	1,143	1,260	1,143
5,450	5,500	548	548	548	548	8,450	8,500	848	848	848	848	11,450	11,500	1,268	1,148	1,268	1,148
5,500	5,550	553	553	553	553	8,500	8,550	853	853	853	853	11,500	11,550	1,275	1,153	1,275	1,153
5,550	5,600	558	558	558	558	8,550	8,600	858	858	858	858	11,550	11,600	1,283	1,158	1,283	1,158
5,600	5,650	563	563	563	563	8,600	8,650	863	863	863	863	11,600	11,650	1,290	1,163	1,290	1,163
5,650	5,700	568	568	568	568	8,650	8,700	868	868	868	868	11,650	11,700	1,298	1,168	1,298	1,168
5,700	5,750	573	573	573	573	8,700	8,750	873	873	873	873	11,700	11,750	1,305	1,173	1,305	1,173
5,750	5,800	578	578	578	578	8,750	8,800	878	878	878	878	11,750	11,800	1,313	1,178	1,313	1,178
5,800	5,850	583	583	583	583	8,800	8,850	883	883	883	883	11,800	11,850	1,320	1,183	1,320	1,183
5,850	5,900	588	588	588	588	8,850	8,900	888	888	888	888	11,850	11,900	1,328	1,188	1,328	1,188
5,900	5,950	593	593	593	593	8,900	8,950	893	893	893	893	11,900	11,950	1,335	1,193	1,335	1,193
5,950	6,000	598	598	598	598	8,950	9,000	898	898	898	898	11,950	12,000	1,343	1,198	1,343	1,198

(Continued)

* This column must also be used by a qualifying widow(er).

12,000

At least	But less than	Single	Married filing jointly *	Married filing separately	Head of a household
12,000	12,050	1,350	1,203	1,350	1,203
12,050	12,100	1,358	1,208	1,358	1,208
12,100	12,150	1,365	1,213	1,365	1,213
12,150	12,200	1,373	1,218	1,373	1,218
12,200	12,250	1,380	1,223	1,380	1,223
12,250	12,300	1,388	1,228	1,388	1,228
12,300	12,350	1,395	1,233	1,395	1,233
12,350	12,400	1,403	1,238	1,403	1,238
12,400	12,450	1,410	1,243	1,410	1,243
12,450	12,500	1,418	1,248	1,418	1,248
12,500	12,550	1,425	1,253	1,425	1,253
12,550	12,600	1,433	1,258	1,433	1,258
12,600	12,650	1,440	1,263	1,440	1,263
12,650	12,700	1,448	1,268	1,448	1,268
12,700	12,750	1,455	1,273	1,455	1,273
12,750	12,800	1,463	1,278	1,463	1,278
12,800	12,850	1,470	1,283	1,470	1,283
12,850	12,900	1,478	1,288	1,478	1,288
12,900	12,950	1,485	1,293	1,485	1,293
12,950	13,000	1,493	1,298	1,493	1,299

13,000

At least	But less than	Single	Married filing jointly *	Married filing separately	Head of a household
13,000	13,050	1,500	1,303	1,500	1,306
13,050	13,100	1,508	1,308	1,508	1,314
13,100	13,150	1,515	1,313	1,515	1,321
13,150	13,200	1,523	1,318	1,523	1,329
13,200	13,250	1,530	1,323	1,530	1,336
13,250	13,300	1,538	1,328	1,538	1,344
13,300	13,350	1,545	1,333	1,545	1,351
13,350	13,400	1,553	1,338	1,553	1,359
13,400	13,450	1,560	1,343	1,560	1,366
13,450	13,500	1,568	1,348	1,568	1,374
13,500	13,550	1,575	1,353	1,575	1,381
13,550	13,600	1,583	1,358	1,583	1,389
13,600	13,650	1,590	1,363	1,590	1,396
13,650	13,700	1,598	1,368	1,598	1,404
13,700	13,750	1,605	1,373	1,605	1,411
13,750	13,800	1,613	1,378	1,613	1,419
13,800	13,850	1,620	1,383	1,620	1,426
13,850	13,900	1,628	1,388	1,628	1,434
13,900	13,950	1,635	1,393	1,635	1,441
13,950	14,000	1,643	1,398	1,643	1,449

14,000

At least	But less than	Single	Married filing jointly *	Married filing separately	Head of a household
14,000	14,050	1,650	1,403	1,650	1,456
14,050	14,100	1,658	1,408	1,658	1,464
14,100	14,150	1,665	1,413	1,665	1,471
14,150	14,200	1,673	1,418	1,673	1,479
14,200	14,250	1,680	1,423	1,680	1,486
14,250	14,300	1,688	1,428	1,688	1,494
14,300	14,350	1,695	1,433	1,695	1,501
14,350	14,400	1,703	1,438	1,703	1,509
14,400	14,450	1,710	1,443	1,710	1,516
14,450	14,500	1,718	1,448	1,718	1,524
14,500	14,550	1,725	1,453	1,725	1,531
14,550	14,600	1,733	1,458	1,733	1,539
14,600	14,650	1,740	1,463	1,740	1,546
14,650	14,700	1,748	1,468	1,748	1,554
14,700	14,750	1,755	1,473	1,755	1,561
14,750	14,800	1,763	1,478	1,763	1,569
14,800	14,850	1,770	1,483	1,770	1,576
14,850	14,900	1,778	1,488	1,778	1,584
14,900	14,950	1,785	1,493	1,785	1,591
14,950	15,000	1,793	1,498	1,793	1,599

15,000

At least	But less than	Single	Married filing jointly *	Married filing separately	Head of a household
15,000	15,050	1,800	1,503	1,800	1,606
15,050	15,100	1,808	1,508	1,808	1,614
15,100	15,150	1,815	1,513	1,815	1,621
15,150	15,200	1,823	1,518	1,823	1,629
15,200	15,250	1,830	1,523	1,830	1,636
15,250	15,300	1,838	1,528	1,838	1,644
15,300	15,350	1,845	1,533	1,845	1,651
15,350	15,400	1,853	1,538	1,853	1,659
15,400	15,450	1,860	1,543	1,860	1,666
15,450	15,500	1,868	1,548	1,868	1,674
15,500	15,550	1,875	1,553	1,875	1,681
15,550	15,600	1,883	1,558	1,883	1,689
15,600	15,650	1,890	1,563	1,890	1,696
15,650	15,700	1,898	1,568	1,898	1,704
15,700	15,750	1,905	1,573	1,905	1,711
15,750	15,800	1,913	1,578	1,913	1,719
15,800	15,850	1,920	1,583	1,920	1,726
15,850	15,900	1,928	1,588	1,928	1,734
15,900	15,950	1,935	1,593	1,935	1,741
15,950	16,000	1,943	1,598	1,943	1,749

16,000

At least	But less than	Single	Married filing jointly *	Married filing separately	Head of a household
16,000	16,050	1,950	1,603	1,950	1,756
16,050	16,100	1,958	1,608	1,958	1,764
16,100	16,150	1,965	1,613	1,965	1,771
16,150	16,200	1,973	1,618	1,973	1,779
16,200	16,250	1,980	1,623	1,980	1,786
16,250	16,300	1,988	1,628	1,988	1,794
16,300	16,350	1,995	1,633	1,995	1,801
16,350	16,400	2,003	1,638	2,003	1,809
16,400	16,450	2,010	1,643	2,010	1,816
16,450	16,500	2,018	1,648	2,018	1,824
16,500	16,550	2,025	1,653	2,025	1,831
16,550	16,600	2,033	1,658	2,033	1,839
16,600	16,650	2,040	1,663	2,040	1,846
16,650	16,700	2,048	1,668	2,048	1,854
16,700	16,750	2,055	1,673	2,055	1,861
16,750	16,800	2,063	1,678	2,063	1,869
16,800	16,850	2,070	1,683	2,070	1,876
16,850	16,900	2,078	1,688	2,078	1,884
16,900	16,950	2,085	1,693	2,085	1,891
16,950	17,000	2,093	1,698	2,093	1,899

17,000

At least	But less than	Single	Married filing jointly *	Married filing separately	Head of a household
17,000	17,050	2,100	1,703	2,100	1,906
17,050	17,100	2,108	1,708	2,108	1,914
17,100	17,150	2,115	1,713	2,115	1,921
17,150	17,200	2,123	1,718	2,123	1,929
17,200	17,250	2,130	1,723	2,130	1,936
17,250	17,300	2,138	1,728	2,138	1,944
17,300	17,350	2,145	1,733	2,145	1,951
17,350	17,400	2,153	1,738	2,153	1,959
17,400	17,450	2,160	1,743	2,160	1,966
17,450	17,500	2,168	1,748	2,168	1,974
17,500	17,550	2,175	1,753	2,175	1,981
17,550	17,600	2,183	1,758	2,183	1,989
17,600	17,650	2,190	1,763	2,190	1,996
17,650	17,700	2,198	1,768	2,198	2,004
17,700	17,750	2,205	1,773	2,205	2,011
17,750	17,800	2,213	1,778	2,213	2,019
17,800	17,850	2,220	1,783	2,220	2,026
17,850	17,900	2,228	1,788	2,228	2,034
17,900	17,950	2,235	1,793	2,235	2,041
17,950	18,000	2,243	1,798	2,243	2,049

18,000

At least	But less than	Single	Married filing jointly *	Married filing separately	Head of a household
18,000	18,050	2,250	1,803	2,250	2,056
18,050	18,100	2,258	1,808	2,258	2,064
18,100	18,150	2,265	1,813	2,265	2,071
18,150	18,200	2,273	1,819	2,273	2,079
18,200	18,250	2,280	1,826	2,280	2,086
18,250	18,300	2,288	1,834	2,288	2,094
18,300	18,350	2,295	1,841	2,295	2,101
18,350	18,400	2,303	1,849	2,303	2,109
18,400	18,450	2,310	1,856	2,310	2,116
18,450	18,500	2,318	1,864	2,318	2,124
18,500	18,550	2,325	1,871	2,325	2,131
18,550	18,600	2,333	1,879	2,333	2,139
18,600	18,650	2,340	1,886	2,340	2,146
18,650	18,700	2,348	1,894	2,348	2,154
18,700	18,750	2,355	1,901	2,355	2,161
18,750	18,800	2,363	1,909	2,363	2,169
18,800	18,850	2,370	1,916	2,370	2,176
18,850	18,900	2,378	1,924	2,378	2,184
18,900	18,950	2,385	1,931	2,385	2,191
18,950	19,000	2,393	1,939	2,393	2,199

19,000

At least	But less than	Single	Married filing jointly *	Married filing separately	Head of a household
19,000	19,050	2,400	1,946	2,400	2,206
19,050	19,100	2,408	1,954	2,408	2,214
19,100	19,150	2,415	1,961	2,415	2,221
19,150	19,200	2,423	1,969	2,423	2,229
19,200	19,250	2,430	1,976	2,430	2,236
19,250	19,300	2,438	1,984	2,438	2,244
19,300	19,350	2,445	1,991	2,445	2,251
19,350	19,400	2,453	1,999	2,453	2,259
19,400	19,450	2,460	2,006	2,460	2,266
19,450	19,500	2,468	2,014	2,468	2,274
19,500	19,550	2,475	2,021	2,475	2,281
19,550	19,600	2,483	2,029	2,483	2,289
19,600	19,650	2,490	2,036	2,490	2,296
19,650	19,700	2,498	2,044	2,498	2,304
19,700	19,750	2,505	2,051	2,505	2,311
19,750	19,800	2,513	2,059	2,513	2,319
19,800	19,850	2,520	2,066	2,520	2,326
19,850	19,900	2,528	2,074	2,528	2,334
19,900	19,950	2,535	2,081	2,535	2,341
19,950	20,000	2,543	2,089	2,543	2,349

20,000

At least	But less than	Single	Married filing jointly *	Married filing separately	Head of a household
20,000	20,050	2,550	2,096	2,550	2,356
20,050	20,100	2,558	2,104	2,558	2,364
20,100	20,150	2,565	2,111	2,565	2,371
20,150	20,200	2,573	2,119	2,573	2,379
20,200	20,250	2,580	2,126	2,580	2,386
20,250	20,300	2,588	2,134	2,588	2,394
20,300	20,350	2,595	2,141	2,595	2,401
20,350	20,400	2,603	2,149	2,603	2,409
20,400	20,450	2,610	2,156	2,610	2,416
20,450	20,500	2,618	2,164	2,618	2,424
20,500	20,550	2,625	2,171	2,625	2,431
20,550	20,600	2,633	2,179	2,633	2,439
20,600	20,650	2,640	2,186	2,640	2,446
20,650	20,700	2,648	2,194	2,648	2,454
20,700	20,750	2,655	2,201	2,655	2,461
20,750	20,800	2,663	2,209	2,663	2,469
20,800	20,850	2,670	2,216	2,670	2,476
20,850	20,900	2,678	2,224	2,678	2,484
20,900	20,950	2,685	2,231	2,685	2,491
20,950	21,000	2,693	2,239	2,693	2,499

(Continued)

* This column must also be used by a qualifying widow(er).

If line 43 (taxable income) is—		And you are—			
At least	But less than	Single	Married filing jointly *	Married filing separately	Head of a household
		Your tax is—			

21,000

At least	But less than	Single	MFJ *	MFS	HoH
21,000	21,050	2,700	2,246	2,700	2,506
21,050	21,100	2,708	2,254	2,708	2,514
21,100	21,150	2,715	2,261	2,715	2,521
21,150	21,200	2,723	2,269	2,723	2,529
21,200	21,250	2,730	2,276	2,730	2,536
21,250	21,300	2,738	2,284	2,738	2,544
21,300	21,350	2,745	2,291	2,745	2,551
21,350	21,400	2,753	2,299	2,753	2,559
21,400	21,450	2,760	2,306	2,760	2,566
21,450	21,500	2,768	2,314	2,768	2,574
21,500	21,550	2,775	2,321	2,775	2,581
21,550	21,600	2,783	2,329	2,783	2,589
21,600	21,650	2,790	2,336	2,790	2,596
21,650	21,700	2,798	2,344	2,798	2,604
21,700	21,750	2,805	2,351	2,805	2,611
21,750	21,800	2,813	2,359	2,813	2,619
21,800	21,850	2,820	2,366	2,820	2,626
21,850	21,900	2,828	2,374	2,828	2,634
21,900	21,950	2,835	2,381	2,835	2,641
21,950	22,000	2,843	2,389	2,843	2,649

22,000

At least	But less than	Single	MFJ *	MFS	HoH
22,000	22,050	2,850	2,396	2,850	2,656
22,050	22,100	2,858	2,404	2,858	2,664
22,100	22,150	2,865	2,411	2,865	2,671
22,150	22,200	2,873	2,419	2,873	2,679
22,200	22,250	2,880	2,426	2,880	2,686
22,250	22,300	2,888	2,434	2,888	2,694
22,300	22,350	2,895	2,441	2,895	2,701
22,350	22,400	2,903	2,449	2,903	2,709
22,400	22,450	2,910	2,456	2,910	2,716
22,450	22,500	2,918	2,464	2,918	2,724
22,500	22,550	2,925	2,471	2,925	2,731
22,550	22,600	2,933	2,479	2,933	2,739
22,600	22,650	2,940	2,486	2,940	2,746
22,650	22,700	2,948	2,494	2,948	2,754
22,700	22,750	2,955	2,501	2,955	2,761
22,750	22,800	2,963	2,509	2,963	2,769
22,800	22,850	2,970	2,516	2,970	2,776
22,850	22,900	2,978	2,524	2,978	2,784
22,900	22,950	2,985	2,531	2,985	2,791
22,950	23,000	2,993	2,539	2,993	2,799

23,000

At least	But less than	Single	MFJ *	MFS	HoH
23,000	23,050	3,000	2,546	3,000	2,806
23,050	23,100	3,008	2,554	3,008	2,814
23,100	23,150	3,015	2,561	3,015	2,821
23,150	23,200	3,023	2,569	3,023	2,829
23,200	23,250	3,030	2,576	3,030	2,836
23,250	23,300	3,038	2,584	3,038	2,844
23,300	23,350	3,045	2,591	3,045	2,851
23,350	23,400	3,053	2,599	3,053	2,859
23,400	23,450	3,060	2,606	3,060	2,866
23,450	23,500	3,068	2,614	3,068	2,874
23,500	23,550	3,075	2,621	3,075	2,881
23,550	23,600	3,083	2,629	3,083	2,889
23,600	23,650	3,090	2,636	3,090	2,896
23,650	23,700	3,098	2,644	3,098	2,904
23,700	23,750	3,105	2,651	3,105	2,911
23,750	23,800	3,113	2,659	3,113	2,919
23,800	23,850	3,120	2,666	3,120	2,926
23,850	23,900	3,128	2,674	3,128	2,934
23,900	23,950	3,135	2,681	3,135	2,941
23,950	24,000	3,143	2,689	3,143	2,949

24,000

At least	But less than	Single	MFJ *	MFS	HoH
24,000	24,050	3,150	2,696	3,150	2,956
24,050	24,100	3,158	2,704	3,158	2,964
24,100	24,150	3,165	2,711	3,165	2,971
24,150	24,200	3,173	2,719	3,173	2,979
24,200	24,250	3,180	2,726	3,180	2,986
24,250	24,300	3,188	2,734	3,188	2,994
24,300	24,350	3,195	2,741	3,195	3,001
24,350	24,400	3,203	2,749	3,203	3,009
24,400	24,450	3,210	2,756	3,210	3,016
24,450	24,500	3,218	2,764	3,218	3,024
24,500	24,550	3,225	2,771	3,225	3,031
24,550	24,600	3,233	2,779	3,233	3,039
24,600	24,650	3,240	2,786	3,240	3,046
24,650	24,700	3,248	2,794	3,248	3,054
24,700	24,750	3,255	2,801	3,255	3,061
24,750	24,800	3,263	2,809	3,263	3,069
24,800	24,850	3,270	2,816	3,270	3,076
24,850	24,900	3,278	2,824	3,278	3,084
24,900	24,950	3,285	2,831	3,285	3,091
24,950	25,000	3,293	2,839	3,293	3,099

25,000

At least	But less than	Single	MFJ *	MFS	HoH
25,000	25,050	3,300	2,846	3,300	3,106
25,050	25,100	3,308	2,854	3,308	3,114
25,100	25,150	3,315	2,861	3,315	3,121
25,150	25,200	3,323	2,869	3,323	3,129
25,200	25,250	3,330	2,876	3,330	3,136
25,250	25,300	3,338	2,884	3,338	3,144
25,300	25,350	3,345	2,891	3,345	3,151
25,350	25,400	3,353	2,899	3,353	3,159
25,400	25,450	3,360	2,906	3,360	3,166
25,450	25,500	3,368	2,914	3,368	3,174
25,500	25,550	3,375	2,921	3,375	3,181
25,550	25,600	3,383	2,929	3,383	3,189
25,600	25,650	3,390	2,936	3,390	3,196
25,650	25,700	3,398	2,944	3,398	3,204
25,700	25,750	3,405	2,951	3,405	3,211
25,750	25,800	3,413	2,959	3,413	3,219
25,800	25,850	3,420	2,966	3,420	3,226
25,850	25,900	3,428	2,974	3,428	3,234
25,900	25,950	3,435	2,981	3,435	3,241
25,950	26,000	3,443	2,989	3,443	3,249

26,000

At least	But less than	Single	MFJ *	MFS	HoH
26,000	26,050	3,450	2,996	3,450	3,256
26,050	26,100	3,458	3,004	3,458	3,264
26,100	26,150	3,465	3,011	3,465	3,271
26,150	26,200	3,473	3,019	3,473	3,279
26,200	26,250	3,480	3,026	3,480	3,286
26,250	26,300	3,488	3,034	3,488	3,294
26,300	26,350	3,495	3,041	3,495	3,301
26,350	26,400	3,503	3,049	3,503	3,309
26,400	26,450	3,510	3,056	3,510	3,316
26,450	26,500	3,518	3,064	3,518	3,324
26,500	26,550	3,525	3,071	3,525	3,331
26,550	26,600	3,533	3,079	3,533	3,339
26,600	26,650	3,540	3,086	3,540	3,346
26,650	26,700	3,548	3,094	3,548	3,354
26,700	26,750	3,555	3,101	3,555	3,361
26,750	26,800	3,563	3,109	3,563	3,369
26,800	26,850	3,570	3,116	3,570	3,376
26,850	26,900	3,578	3,124	3,578	3,384
26,900	26,950	3,585	3,131	3,585	3,391
26,950	27,000	3,593	3,139	3,593	3,399

27,000

At least	But less than	Single	MFJ *	MFS	HoH
27,000	27,050	3,600	3,146	3,600	3,406
27,050	27,100	3,608	3,154	3,608	3,414
27,100	27,150	3,615	3,161	3,615	3,421
27,150	27,200	3,623	3,169	3,623	3,429
27,200	27,250	3,630	3,176	3,630	3,436
27,250	27,300	3,638	3,184	3,638	3,444
27,300	27,350	3,645	3,191	3,645	3,451
27,350	27,400	3,653	3,199	3,653	3,459
27,400	27,450	3,660	3,206	3,660	3,466
27,450	27,500	3,668	3,214	3,668	3,474
27,500	27,550	3,675	3,221	3,675	3,481
27,550	27,600	3,683	3,229	3,683	3,489
27,600	27,650	3,690	3,236	3,690	3,496
27,650	27,700	3,698	3,244	3,698	3,504
27,700	27,750	3,705	3,251	3,705	3,511
27,750	27,800	3,713	3,259	3,713	3,519
27,800	27,850	3,720	3,266	3,720	3,526
27,850	27,900	3,728	3,274	3,728	3,534
27,900	27,950	3,735	3,281	3,735	3,541
27,950	28,000	3,743	3,289	3,743	3,549

28,000

At least	But less than	Single	MFJ *	MFS	HoH
28,000	28,050	3,750	3,296	3,750	3,556
28,050	28,100	3,758	3,304	3,758	3,564
28,100	28,150	3,765	3,311	3,765	3,571
28,150	28,200	3,773	3,319	3,773	3,579
28,200	28,250	3,780	3,326	3,780	3,586
28,250	28,300	3,788	3,334	3,788	3,594
28,300	28,350	3,795	3,341	3,795	3,601
28,350	28,400	3,803	3,349	3,803	3,609
28,400	28,450	3,810	3,356	3,810	3,616
28,450	28,500	3,818	3,364	3,818	3,624
28,500	28,550	3,825	3,371	3,825	3,631
28,550	28,600	3,833	3,379	3,833	3,639
28,600	28,650	3,840	3,386	3,840	3,646
28,650	28,700	3,848	3,394	3,848	3,654
28,700	28,750	3,855	3,401	3,855	3,661
28,750	28,800	3,863	3,409	3,863	3,669
28,800	28,850	3,870	3,416	3,870	3,676
28,850	28,900	3,878	3,424	3,878	3,684
28,900	28,950	3,885	3,431	3,885	3,691
28,950	29,000	3,893	3,439	3,893	3,699

29,000

At least	But less than	Single	MFJ *	MFS	HoH
29,000	29,050	3,900	3,446	3,900	3,706
29,050	29,100	3,908	3,454	3,908	3,714
29,100	29,150	3,915	3,461	3,915	3,721
29,150	29,200	3,923	3,469	3,923	3,729
29,200	29,250	3,930	3,476	3,930	3,736
29,250	29,300	3,938	3,484	3,938	3,744
29,300	29,350	3,945	3,491	3,945	3,751
29,350	29,400	3,953	3,499	3,953	3,759
29,400	29,450	3,960	3,506	3,960	3,766
29,450	29,500	3,968	3,514	3,968	3,774
29,500	29,550	3,975	3,521	3,975	3,781
29,550	29,600	3,983	3,529	3,983	3,789
29,600	29,650	3,990	3,536	3,990	3,796
29,650	29,700	3,998	3,544	3,998	3,804
29,700	29,750	4,005	3,551	4,005	3,811
29,750	29,800	4,013	3,559	4,013	3,819
29,800	29,850	4,020	3,566	4,020	3,826
29,850	29,900	4,028	3,574	4,028	3,834
29,900	29,950	4,035	3,581	4,035	3,841
29,950	30,000	4,043	3,589	4,043	3,849

(Continued)

* This column must also be used by a qualifying widow(er).

If line 43 (taxable income) is—		And you are—			
At least	But less than	Single	Married filing jointly *	Married filing separately	Head of a household
		Your tax is—			

30,000

At least	But less than	Single	MFJ	MFS	HoH
30,000	30,050	4,050	3,596	4,050	3,856
30,050	30,100	4,058	3,604	4,058	3,864
30,100	30,150	4,065	3,611	4,065	3,871
30,150	30,200	4,073	3,619	4,073	3,879
30,200	30,250	4,080	3,626	4,080	3,886
30,250	30,300	4,088	3,634	4,088	3,894
30,300	30,350	4,095	3,641	4,095	3,901
30,350	30,400	4,103	3,649	4,103	3,909
30,400	30,450	4,110	3,656	4,110	3,916
30,450	30,500	4,118	3,664	4,118	3,924
30,500	30,550	4,125	3,671	4,125	3,931
30,550	30,600	4,133	3,679	4,133	3,939
30,600	30,650	4,140	3,686	4,140	3,946
30,650	30,700	4,148	3,694	4,148	3,954
30,700	30,750	4,155	3,701	4,155	3,961
30,750	30,800	4,163	3,709	4,163	3,969
30,800	30,850	4,170	3,716	4,170	3,976
30,850	30,900	4,178	3,724	4,178	3,984
30,900	30,950	4,185	3,731	4,185	3,991
30,950	31,000	4,193	3,739	4,193	3,999

31,000

At least	But less than	Single	MFJ	MFS	HoH
31,000	31,050	4,200	3,746	4,200	4,006
31,050	31,100	4,208	3,754	4,208	4,014
31,100	31,150	4,215	3,761	4,215	4,021
31,150	31,200	4,223	3,769	4,223	4,029
31,200	31,250	4,230	3,776	4,230	4,036
31,250	31,300	4,238	3,784	4,238	4,044
31,300	31,350	4,245	3,791	4,245	4,051
31,350	31,400	4,253	3,799	4,253	4,059
31,400	31,450	4,260	3,806	4,260	4,066
31,450	31,500	4,268	3,814	4,268	4,074
31,500	31,550	4,275	3,821	4,275	4,081
31,550	31,600	4,283	3,829	4,283	4,089
31,600	31,650	4,290	3,836	4,290	4,096
31,650	31,700	4,298	3,844	4,298	4,104
31,700	31,750	4,305	3,851	4,305	4,111
31,750	31,800	4,313	3,859	4,313	4,119
31,800	31,850	4,320	3,866	4,320	4,126
31,850	31,900	4,328	3,874	4,328	4,134
31,900	31,950	4,335	3,881	4,335	4,141
31,950	32,000	4,343	3,889	4,343	4,149

32,000

At least	But less than	Single	MFJ	MFS	HoH
32,000	32,050	4,350	3,896	4,350	4,156
32,050	32,100	4,358	3,904	4,358	4,164
32,100	32,150	4,365	3,911	4,365	4,171
32,150	32,200	4,373	3,919	4,373	4,179
32,200	32,250	4,380	3,926	4,380	4,186
32,250	32,300	4,388	3,934	4,388	4,194
32,300	32,350	4,395	3,941	4,395	4,201
32,350	32,400	4,403	3,949	4,403	4,209
32,400	32,450	4,410	3,956	4,410	4,216
32,450	32,500	4,418	3,964	4,418	4,224
32,500	32,550	4,425	3,971	4,425	4,231
32,550	32,600	4,433	3,979	4,433	4,239
32,600	32,650	4,440	3,986	4,440	4,246
32,650	32,700	4,448	3,994	4,448	4,254
32,700	32,750	4,455	4,001	4,455	4,261
32,750	32,800	4,463	4,009	4,463	4,269
32,800	32,850	4,470	4,016	4,470	4,276
32,850	32,900	4,478	4,024	4,478	4,284
32,900	32,950	4,485	4,031	4,485	4,291
32,950	33,000	4,493	4,039	4,493	4,299

33,000

At least	But less than	Single	MFJ	MFS	HoH
33,000	33,050	4,500	4,046	4,500	4,306
33,050	33,100	4,508	4,054	4,508	4,314
33,100	33,150	4,515	4,061	4,515	4,321
33,150	33,200	4,523	4,069	4,523	4,329
33,200	33,250	4,530	4,076	4,530	4,336
33,250	33,300	4,538	4,084	4,538	4,344
33,300	33,350	4,545	4,091	4,545	4,351
33,350	33,400	4,553	4,099	4,553	4,359
33,400	33,450	4,560	4,106	4,560	4,366
33,450	33,500	4,568	4,114	4,568	4,374
33,500	33,550	4,575	4,121	4,575	4,381
33,550	33,600	4,583	4,129	4,583	4,389
33,600	33,650	4,590	4,136	4,590	4,396
33,650	33,700	4,598	4,144	4,598	4,404
33,700	33,750	4,605	4,151	4,605	4,411
33,750	33,800	4,613	4,159	4,613	4,419
33,800	33,850	4,620	4,166	4,620	4,426
33,850	33,900	4,628	4,174	4,628	4,434
33,900	33,950	4,635	4,181	4,635	4,441
33,950	34,000	4,643	4,189	4,643	4,449

34,000

At least	But less than	Single	MFJ	MFS	HoH
34,000	34,050	4,650	4,196	4,650	4,456
34,050	34,100	4,658	4,204	4,658	4,464
34,100	34,150	4,665	4,211	4,665	4,471
34,150	34,200	4,673	4,219	4,673	4,479
34,200	34,250	4,680	4,226	4,680	4,486
34,250	34,300	4,688	4,234	4,688	4,494
34,300	34,350	4,695	4,241	4,695	4,501
34,350	34,400	4,703	4,249	4,703	4,509
34,400	34,450	4,710	4,256	4,710	4,516
34,450	34,500	4,718	4,264	4,718	4,524
34,500	34,550	4,725	4,271	4,725	4,531
34,550	34,600	4,733	4,279	4,733	4,539
34,600	34,650	4,740	4,286	4,740	4,546
34,650	34,700	4,748	4,294	4,748	4,554
34,700	34,750	4,755	4,301	4,755	4,561
34,750	34,800	4,763	4,309	4,763	4,569
34,800	34,850	4,770	4,316	4,770	4,576
34,850	34,900	4,778	4,324	4,778	4,584
34,900	34,950	4,785	4,331	4,785	4,591
34,950	35,000	4,793	4,339	4,793	4,599

35,000

At least	But less than	Single	MFJ	MFS	HoH
35,000	35,050	4,800	4,346	4,800	4,606
35,050	35,100	4,808	4,354	4,808	4,614
35,100	35,150	4,815	4,361	4,815	4,621
35,150	35,200	4,823	4,369	4,823	4,629
35,200	35,250	4,830	4,376	4,830	4,636
35,250	35,300	4,838	4,384	4,838	4,644
35,300	35,350	4,845	4,391	4,845	4,651
35,350	35,400	4,853	4,399	4,853	4,659
35,400	35,450	4,860	4,406	4,860	4,666
35,450	35,500	4,868	4,414	4,868	4,674
35,500	35,550	4,875	4,421	4,875	4,681
35,550	35,600	4,883	4,429	4,883	4,689
35,600	35,650	4,890	4,436	4,890	4,696
35,650	35,700	4,898	4,444	4,898	4,704
35,700	35,750	4,905	4,451	4,905	4,711
35,750	35,800	4,913	4,459	4,913	4,719
35,800	35,850	4,920	4,466	4,920	4,726
35,850	35,900	4,928	4,474	4,928	4,734
35,900	35,950	4,935	4,481	4,935	4,741
35,950	36,000	4,943	4,489	4,943	4,749

36,000

At least	But less than	Single	MFJ	MFS	HoH
36,000	36,050	4,950	4,496	4,950	4,756
36,050	36,100	4,958	4,504	4,958	4,764
36,100	36,150	4,965	4,511	4,965	4,771
36,150	36,200	4,973	4,519	4,973	4,779
36,200	36,250	4,980	4,526	4,980	4,786
36,250	36,300	4,988	4,534	4,988	4,794
36,300	36,350	4,995	4,541	4,995	4,801
36,350	36,400	5,003	4,549	5,003	4,809
36,400	36,450	5,010	4,556	5,010	4,816
36,450	36,500	5,018	4,564	5,018	4,824
36,500	36,550	5,025	4,571	5,025	4,831
36,550	36,600	5,033	4,579	5,033	4,839
36,600	36,650	5,040	4,586	5,040	4,846
36,650	36,700	5,048	4,594	5,048	4,854
36,700	36,750	5,055	4,601	5,055	4,861
36,750	36,800	5,063	4,609	5,063	4,869
36,800	36,850	5,070	4,616	5,070	4,876
36,850	36,900	5,078	4,624	5,078	4,884
36,900	36,950	5,088	4,631	5,088	4,891
36,950	37,000	5,100	4,639	5,100	4,899

37,000

At least	But less than	Single	MFJ	MFS	HoH
37,000	37,050	5,113	4,646	5,113	4,906
37,050	37,100	5,125	4,654	5,125	4,914
37,100	37,150	5,138	4,661	5,138	4,921
37,150	37,200	5,150	4,669	5,150	4,929
37,200	37,250	5,163	4,676	5,163	4,936
37,250	37,300	5,175	4,684	5,175	4,944
37,300	37,350	5,188	4,691	5,188	4,951
37,350	37,400	5,200	4,699	5,200	4,959
37,400	37,450	5,213	4,706	5,213	4,966
37,450	37,500	5,225	4,714	5,225	4,974
37,500	37,550	5,238	4,721	5,238	4,981
37,550	37,600	5,250	4,729	5,250	4,989
37,600	37,650	5,263	4,736	5,263	4,996
37,650	37,700	5,275	4,744	5,275	5,004
37,700	37,750	5,288	4,751	5,288	5,011
37,750	37,800	5,300	4,759	5,300	5,019
37,800	37,850	5,313	4,766	5,313	5,026
37,850	37,900	5,325	4,774	5,325	5,034
37,900	37,950	5,338	4,781	5,338	5,041
37,950	38,000	5,350	4,789	5,350	5,049

38,000

At least	But less than	Single	MFJ	MFS	HoH
38,000	38,050	5,363	4,796	5,363	5,056
38,050	38,100	5,375	4,804	5,375	5,064
38,100	38,150	5,388	4,811	5,388	5,071
38,150	38,200	5,400	4,819	5,400	5,079
38,200	38,250	5,413	4,826	5,413	5,086
38,250	38,300	5,425	4,834	5,425	5,094
38,300	38,350	5,438	4,841	5,438	5,101
38,350	38,400	5,450	4,849	5,450	5,109
38,400	38,450	5,463	4,856	5,463	5,116
38,450	38,500	5,475	4,864	5,475	5,124
38,500	38,550	5,488	4,871	5,488	5,131
38,550	38,600	5,500	4,879	5,500	5,139
38,600	38,650	5,513	4,886	5,513	5,146
38,650	38,700	5,525	4,894	5,525	5,154
38,700	38,750	5,538	4,901	5,538	5,161
38,750	38,800	5,550	4,909	5,550	5,169
38,800	38,850	5,563	4,916	5,563	5,176
38,850	38,900	5,575	4,924	5,575	5,184
38,900	38,950	5,588	4,931	5,588	5,191
38,950	39,000	5,600	4,939	5,600	5,199

(Continued)

* This column must also be used by a qualifying widow(er).

Table header (all sections):

If line 43 (taxable income) is— At least	But less than	And you are— Single	Married filing jointly *	Married filing separately	Head of a house-hold
		Your tax is—			

39,000

At least	But less than	Single	MFJ*	MFS	HoH
39,000	39,050	5,613	4,946	5,613	5,206
39,050	39,100	5,625	4,954	5,625	5,214
39,100	39,150	5,638	4,961	5,638	5,221
39,150	39,200	5,650	4,969	5,650	5,229
39,200	39,250	5,663	4,976	5,663	5,236
39,250	39,300	5,675	4,984	5,675	5,244
39,300	39,350	5,688	4,991	5,688	5,251
39,350	39,400	5,700	4,999	5,700	5,259
39,400	39,450	5,713	5,006	5,713	5,266
39,450	39,500	5,725	5,014	5,725	5,274
39,500	39,550	5,738	5,021	5,738	5,281
39,550	39,600	5,750	5,029	5,750	5,289
39,600	39,650	5,763	5,036	5,763	5,296
39,650	39,700	5,775	5,044	5,775	5,304
39,700	39,750	5,788	5,051	5,788	5,311
39,750	39,800	5,800	5,059	5,800	5,319
39,800	39,850	5,813	5,066	5,813	5,326
39,850	39,900	5,825	5,074	5,825	5,334
39,900	39,950	5,838	5,081	5,838	5,341
39,950	40,000	5,850	5,089	5,850	5,349

40,000

At least	But less than	Single	MFJ*	MFS	HoH
40,000	40,050	5,863	5,096	5,863	5,356
40,050	40,100	5,875	5,104	5,875	5,364
40,100	40,150	5,888	5,111	5,888	5,371
40,150	40,200	5,900	5,119	5,900	5,379
40,200	40,250	5,913	5,126	5,913	5,386
40,250	40,300	5,925	5,134	5,925	5,394
40,300	40,350	5,938	5,141	5,938	5,401
40,350	40,400	5,950	5,149	5,950	5,409
40,400	40,450	5,963	5,156	5,963	5,416
40,450	40,500	5,975	5,164	5,975	5,424
40,500	40,550	5,988	5,171	5,988	5,431
40,550	40,600	6,000	5,179	6,000	5,439
40,600	40,650	6,013	5,186	6,013	5,446
40,650	40,700	6,025	5,194	6,025	5,454
40,700	40,750	6,038	5,201	6,038	5,461
40,750	40,800	6,050	5,209	6,050	5,469
40,800	40,850	6,063	5,216	6,063	5,476
40,850	40,900	6,075	5,224	6,075	5,484
40,900	40,950	6,088	5,231	6,088	5,491
40,950	41,000	6,100	5,239	6,100	5,499

41,000

At least	But less than	Single	MFJ*	MFS	HoH
41,000	41,050	6,113	5,246	6,113	5,506
41,050	41,100	6,125	5,254	6,125	5,514
41,100	41,150	6,138	5,261	6,138	5,521
41,150	41,200	6,150	5,269	6,150	5,529
41,200	41,250	6,163	5,276	6,163	5,536
41,250	41,300	6,175	5,284	6,175	5,544
41,300	41,350	6,188	5,291	6,188	5,551
41,350	41,400	6,200	5,299	6,200	5,559
41,400	41,450	6,213	5,306	6,213	5,566
41,450	41,500	6,225	5,314	6,225	5,574
41,500	41,550	6,238	5,321	6,238	5,581
41,550	41,600	6,250	5,329	6,250	5,589
41,600	41,650	6,263	5,336	6,263	5,596
41,650	41,700	6,275	5,344	6,275	5,604
41,700	41,750	6,288	5,351	6,288	5,611
41,750	41,800	6,300	5,359	6,300	5,619
41,800	41,850	6,313	5,366	6,313	5,626
41,850	41,900	6,325	5,374	6,325	5,634
41,900	41,950	6,338	5,381	6,338	5,641
41,950	42,000	6,350	5,389	6,350	5,649

42,000

At least	But less than	Single	MFJ*	MFS	HoH
42,000	42,050	6,363	5,396	6,363	5,656
42,050	42,100	6,375	5,404	6,375	5,664
42,100	42,150	6,388	5,411	6,388	5,671
42,150	42,200	6,400	5,419	6,400	5,679
42,200	42,250	6,413	5,426	6,413	5,686
42,250	42,300	6,425	5,434	6,425	5,694
42,300	42,350	6,438	5,441	6,438	5,701
42,350	42,400	6,450	5,449	6,450	5,709
42,400	42,450	6,463	5,456	6,463	5,716
42,450	42,500	6,475	5,464	6,475	5,724
42,500	42,550	6,488	5,471	6,488	5,731
42,550	42,600	6,500	5,479	6,500	5,739
42,600	42,650	6,513	5,486	6,513	5,746
42,650	42,700	6,525	5,494	6,525	5,754
42,700	42,750	6,538	5,501	6,538	5,761
42,750	42,800	6,550	5,509	6,550	5,769
42,800	42,850	6,563	5,516	6,563	5,776
42,850	42,900	6,575	5,524	6,575	5,784
42,900	42,950	6,588	5,531	6,588	5,791
42,950	43,000	6,600	5,539	6,600	5,799

43,000

At least	But less than	Single	MFJ*	MFS	HoH
43,000	43,050	6,613	5,546	6,613	5,806
43,050	43,100	6,625	5,554	6,625	5,814
43,100	43,150	6,638	5,561	6,638	5,821
43,150	43,200	6,650	5,569	6,650	5,829
43,200	43,250	6,663	5,576	6,663	5,836
43,250	43,300	6,675	5,584	6,675	5,844
43,300	43,350	6,688	5,591	6,688	5,851
43,350	43,400	6,700	5,599	6,700	5,859
43,400	43,450	6,713	5,606	6,713	5,866
43,450	43,500	6,725	5,614	6,725	5,874
43,500	43,550	6,738	5,621	6,738	5,881
43,550	43,600	6,750	5,629	6,750	5,889
43,600	43,650	6,763	5,636	6,763	5,896
43,650	43,700	6,775	5,644	6,775	5,904
43,700	43,750	6,788	5,651	6,788	5,911
43,750	43,800	6,800	5,659	6,800	5,919
43,800	43,850	6,813	5,666	6,813	5,926
43,850	43,900	6,825	5,674	6,825	5,934
43,900	43,950	6,838	5,681	6,838	5,941
43,950	44,000	6,850	5,689	6,850	5,949

44,000

At least	But less than	Single	MFJ*	MFS	HoH
44,000	44,050	6,863	5,696	6,863	5,956
44,050	44,100	6,875	5,704	6,875	5,964
44,100	44,150	6,888	5,711	6,888	5,971
44,150	44,200	6,900	5,719	6,900	5,979
44,200	44,250	6,913	5,726	6,913	5,986
44,250	44,300	6,925	5,734	6,925	5,994
44,300	44,350	6,938	5,741	6,938	6,001
44,350	44,400	6,950	5,749	6,950	6,009
44,400	44,450	6,963	5,756	6,963	6,016
44,450	44,500	6,975	5,764	6,975	6,024
44,500	44,550	6,988	5,771	6,988	6,031
44,550	44,600	7,000	5,779	7,000	6,039
44,600	44,650	7,013	5,786	7,013	6,046
44,650	44,700	7,025	5,794	7,025	6,054
44,700	44,750	7,038	5,801	7,038	6,061
44,750	44,800	7,050	5,809	7,050	6,069
44,800	44,850	7,063	5,816	7,063	6,076
44,850	44,900	7,075	5,824	7,075	6,084
44,900	44,950	7,088	5,831	7,088	6,091
44,950	45,000	7,100	5,839	7,100	6,099

45,000

At least	But less than	Single	MFJ*	MFS	HoH
45,000	45,050	7,113	5,846	7,113	6,106
45,050	45,100	7,125	5,854	7,125	6,114
45,100	45,150	7,138	5,861	7,138	6,121
45,150	45,200	7,150	5,869	7,150	6,129
45,200	45,250	7,163	5,876	7,163	6,136
45,250	45,300	7,175	5,884	7,175	6,144
45,300	45,350	7,188	5,891	7,188	6,151
45,350	45,400	7,200	5,899	7,200	6,159
45,400	45,450	7,213	5,906	7,213	6,166
45,450	45,500	7,225	5,914	7,225	6,174
45,500	45,550	7,238	5,921	7,238	6,181
45,550	45,600	7,250	5,929	7,250	6,189
45,600	45,650	7,263	5,936	7,263	6,196
45,650	45,700	7,275	5,944	7,275	6,204
45,700	45,750	7,288	5,951	7,288	6,211
45,750	45,800	7,300	5,959	7,300	6,219
45,800	45,850	7,313	5,966	7,313	6,226
45,850	45,900	7,325	5,974	7,325	6,234
45,900	45,950	7,338	5,981	7,338	6,241
45,950	46,000	7,350	5,989	7,350	6,249

46,000

At least	But less than	Single	MFJ*	MFS	HoH
46,000	46,050	7,363	5,996	7,363	6,256
46,050	46,100	7,375	6,004	7,375	6,264
46,100	46,150	7,388	6,011	7,388	6,271
46,150	46,200	7,400	6,019	7,400	6,279
46,200	46,250	7,413	6,026	7,413	6,286
46,250	46,300	7,425	6,034	7,425	6,294
46,300	46,350	7,438	6,041	7,438	6,301
46,350	46,400	7,450	6,049	7,450	6,309
46,400	46,450	7,463	6,056	7,463	6,316
46,450	46,500	7,475	6,064	7,475	6,324
46,500	46,550	7,488	6,071	7,488	6,331
46,550	46,600	7,500	6,079	7,500	6,339
46,600	46,650	7,513	6,086	7,513	6,346
46,650	46,700	7,525	6,094	7,525	6,354
46,700	46,750	7,538	6,101	7,538	6,361
46,750	46,800	7,550	6,109	7,550	6,369
46,800	46,850	7,563	6,116	7,563	6,376
46,850	46,900	7,575	6,124	7,575	6,384
46,900	46,950	7,588	6,131	7,588	6,391
46,950	47,000	7,600	6,139	7,600	6,399

47,000

At least	But less than	Single	MFJ*	MFS	HoH
47,000	47,050	7,613	6,146	7,613	6,406
47,050	47,100	7,625	6,154	7,625	6,414
47,100	47,150	7,638	6,161	7,638	6,421
47,150	47,200	7,650	6,169	7,650	6,429
47,200	47,250	7,663	6,176	7,663	6,436
47,250	47,300	7,675	6,184	7,675	6,444
47,300	47,350	7,688	6,191	7,688	6,451
47,350	47,400	7,700	6,199	7,700	6,459
47,400	47,450	7,713	6,206	7,713	6,466
47,450	47,500	7,725	6,214	7,725	6,474
47,500	47,550	7,738	6,221	7,738	6,481
47,550	47,600	7,750	6,229	7,750	6,489
47,600	47,650	7,763	6,236	7,763	6,496
47,650	47,700	7,775	6,244	7,775	6,504
47,700	47,750	7,788	6,251	7,788	6,511
47,750	47,800	7,800	6,259	7,800	6,519
47,800	47,850	7,813	6,266	7,813	6,526
47,850	47,900	7,825	6,274	7,825	6,534
47,900	47,950	7,838	6,281	7,838	6,541
47,950	48,000	7,850	6,289	7,850	6,549

(Continued)

* This column must also be used by a qualifying widow(er).

If line 43 (taxable income) is—		And you are—			
At least	But less than	Single	Married filing jointly *	Married filing separately	Head of a household
		Your tax is—			

48,000

At least	But less than	Single	MFJ*	MFS	HoH
48,000	48,050	7,863	6,296	7,863	6,556
48,050	48,100	7,875	6,304	7,875	6,564
48,100	48,150	7,888	6,311	7,888	6,571
48,150	48,200	7,900	6,319	7,900	6,579
48,200	48,250	7,913	6,326	7,913	6,586
48,250	48,300	7,925	6,334	7,925	6,594
48,300	48,350	7,938	6,341	7,938	6,601
48,350	48,400	7,950	6,349	7,950	6,609
48,400	48,450	7,963	6,356	7,963	6,616
48,450	48,500	7,975	6,364	7,975	6,624
48,500	48,550	7,988	6,371	7,988	6,631
48,550	48,600	8,000	6,379	8,000	6,639
48,600	48,650	8,013	6,386	8,013	6,646
48,650	48,700	8,025	6,394	8,025	6,654
48,700	48,750	8,038	6,401	8,038	6,661
48,750	48,800	8,050	6,409	8,050	6,669
48,800	48,850	8,063	6,416	8,063	6,676
48,850	48,900	8,075	6,424	8,075	6,684
48,900	48,950	8,088	6,431	8,088	6,691
48,950	49,000	8,100	6,439	8,100	6,699

49,000

At least	But less than	Single	MFJ*	MFS	HoH
49,000	49,050	8,113	6,446	8,113	6,706
49,050	49,100	8,125	6,454	8,125	6,714
49,100	49,150	8,138	6,461	8,138	6,721
49,150	49,200	8,150	6,469	8,150	6,729
49,200	49,250	8,163	6,476	8,163	6,736
49,250	49,300	8,175	6,484	8,175	6,744
49,300	49,350	8,188	6,491	8,188	6,751
49,350	49,400	8,200	6,499	8,200	6,759
49,400	49,450	8,213	6,506	8,213	6,769
49,450	49,500	8,225	6,514	8,225	6,781
49,500	49,550	8,238	6,521	8,238	6,794
49,550	49,600	8,250	6,529	8,250	6,806
49,600	49,650	8,263	6,536	8,263	6,819
49,650	49,700	8,275	6,544	8,275	6,831
49,700	49,750	8,288	6,551	8,288	6,844
49,750	49,800	8,300	6,559	8,300	6,856
49,800	49,850	8,313	6,566	8,313	6,869
49,850	49,900	8,325	6,574	8,325	6,881
49,900	49,950	8,338	6,581	8,338	6,894
49,950	50,000	8,350	6,589	8,350	6,906

50,000

At least	But less than	Single	MFJ*	MFS	HoH
50,000	50,050	8,363	6,596	8,363	6,919
50,050	50,100	8,375	6,604	8,375	6,931
50,100	50,150	8,388	6,611	8,388	6,944
50,150	50,200	8,400	6,619	8,400	6,956
50,200	50,250	8,413	6,626	8,413	6,969
50,250	50,300	8,425	6,634	8,425	6,981
50,300	50,350	8,438	6,641	8,438	6,994
50,350	50,400	8,450	6,649	8,450	7,006
50,400	50,450	8,463	6,656	8,463	7,019
50,450	50,500	8,475	6,664	8,475	7,031
50,500	50,550	8,488	6,671	8,488	7,044
50,550	50,600	8,500	6,679	8,500	7,056
50,600	50,650	8,513	6,686	8,513	7,069
50,650	50,700	8,525	6,694	8,525	7,081
50,700	50,750	8,538	6,701	8,538	7,094
50,750	50,800	8,550	6,709	8,550	7,106
50,800	50,850	8,563	6,716	8,563	7,119
50,850	50,900	8,575	6,724	8,575	7,131
50,900	50,950	8,588	6,731	8,588	7,144
50,950	51,000	8,600	6,739	8,600	7,156

51,000

At least	But less than	Single	MFJ*	MFS	HoH
51,000	51,050	8,613	6,746	8,613	7,169
51,050	51,100	8,625	6,754	8,625	7,181
51,100	51,150	8,638	6,761	8,638	7,194
51,150	51,200	8,650	6,769	8,650	7,206
51,200	51,250	8,663	6,776	8,663	7,219
51,250	51,300	8,675	6,784	8,675	7,231
51,300	51,350	8,688	6,791	8,688	7,244
51,350	51,400	8,700	6,799	8,700	7,256
51,400	51,450	8,713	6,806	8,713	7,269
51,450	51,500	8,725	6,814	8,725	7,281
51,500	51,550	8,738	6,821	8,738	7,294
51,550	51,600	8,750	6,829	8,750	7,306
51,600	51,650	8,763	6,836	8,763	7,319
51,650	51,700	8,775	6,844	8,775	7,331
51,700	51,750	8,788	6,851	8,788	7,344
51,750	51,800	8,800	6,859	8,800	7,356
51,800	51,850	8,813	6,866	8,813	7,369
51,850	51,900	8,825	6,874	8,825	7,381
51,900	51,950	8,838	6,881	8,838	7,394
51,950	52,000	8,850	6,889	8,850	7,406

52,000

At least	But less than	Single	MFJ*	MFS	HoH
52,000	52,050	8,863	6,896	8,863	7,419
52,050	52,100	8,875	6,904	8,875	7,431
52,100	52,150	8,888	6,911	8,888	7,444
52,150	52,200	8,900	6,919	8,900	7,456
52,200	52,250	8,913	6,926	8,913	7,469
52,250	52,300	8,925	6,934	8,925	7,481
52,300	52,350	8,938	6,941	8,938	7,494
52,350	52,400	8,950	6,949	8,950	7,506
52,400	52,450	8,963	6,956	8,963	7,519
52,450	52,500	8,975	6,964	8,975	7,531
52,500	52,550	8,988	6,971	8,988	7,544
52,550	52,600	9,000	6,979	9,000	7,556
52,600	52,650	9,013	6,986	9,013	7,569
52,650	52,700	9,025	6,994	9,025	7,581
52,700	52,750	9,038	7,001	9,038	7,594
52,750	52,800	9,050	7,009	9,050	7,606
52,800	52,850	9,063	7,016	9,063	7,619
52,850	52,900	9,075	7,024	9,075	7,631
52,900	52,950	9,088	7,031	9,088	7,644
52,950	53,000	9,100	7,039	9,100	7,656

53,000

At least	But less than	Single	MFJ*	MFS	HoH
53,000	53,050	9,113	7,046	9,113	7,669
53,050	53,100	9,125	7,054	9,125	7,681
53,100	53,150	9,138	7,061	9,138	7,694
53,150	53,200	9,150	7,069	9,150	7,706
53,200	53,250	9,163	7,076	9,163	7,719
53,250	53,300	9,175	7,084	9,175	7,731
53,300	53,350	9,188	7,091	9,188	7,744
53,350	53,400	9,200	7,099	9,200	7,756
53,400	53,450	9,213	7,106	9,213	7,769
53,450	53,500	9,225	7,114	9,225	7,781
53,500	53,550	9,238	7,121	9,238	7,794
53,550	53,600	9,250	7,129	9,250	7,806
53,600	53,650	9,263	7,136	9,263	7,819
53,650	53,700	9,275	7,144	9,275	7,831
53,700	53,750	9,288	7,151	9,288	7,844
53,750	53,800	9,300	7,159	9,300	7,856
53,800	53,850	9,313	7,166	9,313	7,869
53,850	53,900	9,325	7,174	9,325	7,881
53,900	53,950	9,338	7,181	9,338	7,894
53,950	54,000	9,350	7,189	9,350	7,906

54,000

At least	But less than	Single	MFJ*	MFS	HoH
54,000	54,050	9,363	7,196	9,363	7,919
54,050	54,100	9,375	7,204	9,375	7,931
54,100	54,150	9,388	7,211	9,388	7,944
54,150	54,200	9,400	7,219	9,400	7,956
54,200	54,250	9,413	7,226	9,413	7,969
54,250	54,300	9,425	7,234	9,425	7,981
54,300	54,350	9,438	7,241	9,438	7,994
54,350	54,400	9,450	7,249	9,450	8,006
54,400	54,450	9,463	7,256	9,463	8,019
54,450	54,500	9,475	7,264	9,475	8,031
54,500	54,550	9,488	7,271	9,488	8,044
54,550	54,600	9,500	7,279	9,500	8,056
54,600	54,650	9,513	7,286	9,513	8,069
54,650	54,700	9,525	7,294	9,525	8,081
54,700	54,750	9,538	7,301	9,538	8,094
54,750	54,800	9,550	7,309	9,550	8,106
54,800	54,850	9,563	7,316	9,563	8,119
54,850	54,900	9,575	7,324	9,575	8,131
54,900	54,950	9,588	7,331	9,588	8,144
54,950	55,000	9,600	7,339	9,600	8,156

55,000

At least	But less than	Single	MFJ*	MFS	HoH
55,000	55,050	9,613	7,346	9,613	8,169
55,050	55,100	9,625	7,354	9,625	8,181
55,100	55,150	9,638	7,361	9,638	8,194
55,150	55,200	9,650	7,369	9,650	8,206
55,200	55,250	9,663	7,376	9,663	8,219
55,250	55,300	9,675	7,384	9,675	8,231
55,300	55,350	9,688	7,391	9,688	8,244
55,350	55,400	9,700	7,399	9,700	8,256
55,400	55,450	9,713	7,406	9,713	8,269
55,450	55,500	9,725	7,414	9,725	8,281
55,500	55,550	9,738	7,421	9,738	8,294
55,550	55,600	9,750	7,429	9,750	8,306
55,600	55,650	9,763	7,436	9,763	8,319
55,650	55,700	9,775	7,444	9,775	8,331
55,700	55,750	9,788	7,451	9,788	8,344
55,750	55,800	9,800	7,459	9,800	8,356
55,800	55,850	9,813	7,466	9,813	8,369
55,850	55,900	9,825	7,474	9,825	8,381
55,900	55,950	9,838	7,481	9,838	8,394
55,950	56,000	9,850	7,489	9,850	8,406

56,000

At least	But less than	Single	MFJ*	MFS	HoH
56,000	56,050	9,863	7,496	9,863	8,419
56,050	56,100	9,875	7,504	9,875	8,431
56,100	56,150	9,888	7,511	9,888	8,444
56,150	56,200	9,900	7,519	9,900	8,456
56,200	56,250	9,913	7,526	9,913	8,469
56,250	56,300	9,925	7,534	9,925	8,481
56,300	56,350	9,938	7,541	9,938	8,494
56,350	56,400	9,950	7,549	9,950	8,506
56,400	56,450	9,963	7,556	9,963	8,519
56,450	56,500	9,975	7,564	9,975	8,531
56,500	56,550	9,988	7,571	9,988	8,544
56,550	56,600	10,000	7,579	10,000	8,556
56,600	56,650	10,013	7,586	10,013	8,569
56,650	56,700	10,025	7,594	10,025	8,581
56,700	56,750	10,038	7,601	10,038	8,594
56,750	56,800	10,050	7,609	10,050	8,606
56,800	56,850	10,063	7,616	10,063	8,619
56,850	56,900	10,075	7,624	10,075	8,631
56,900	56,950	10,088	7,631	10,088	8,644
56,950	57,000	10,100	7,639	10,100	8,656

(Continued)

* This column must also be used by a qualifying widow(er).

If line 43 (taxable income) is—		And you are—			
At least	But less than	Single	Married filing jointly *	Married filing separately	Head of a household
		Your tax is—			

57,000

At least	But less than	Single	Married filing jointly *	Married filing separately	Head of a household
57,000	57,050	10,113	7,646	10,113	8,669
57,050	57,100	10,125	7,654	10,125	8,681
57,100	57,150	10,138	7,661	10,138	8,694
57,150	57,200	10,150	7,669	10,150	8,706
57,200	57,250	10,163	7,676	10,163	8,719
57,250	57,300	10,175	7,684	10,175	8,731
57,300	57,350	10,188	7,691	10,188	8,744
57,350	57,400	10,200	7,699	10,200	8,756
57,400	57,450	10,213	7,706	10,213	8,769
57,450	57,500	10,225	7,714	10,225	8,781
57,500	57,550	10,238	7,721	10,238	8,794
57,550	57,600	10,250	7,729	10,250	8,806
57,600	57,650	10,263	7,736	10,263	8,819
57,650	57,700	10,275	7,744	10,275	8,831
57,700	57,750	10,288	7,751	10,288	8,844
57,750	57,800	10,300	7,759	10,300	8,856
57,800	57,850	10,313	7,766	10,313	8,869
57,850	57,900	10,325	7,774	10,325	8,881
57,900	57,950	10,338	7,781	10,338	8,894
57,950	58,000	10,350	7,789	10,350	8,906

58,000

At least	But less than	Single	Married filing jointly *	Married filing separately	Head of a household
58,000	58,050	10,363	7,796	10,363	8,919
58,050	58,100	10,375	7,804	10,375	8,931
58,100	58,150	10,388	7,811	10,388	8,944
58,150	58,200	10,400	7,819	10,400	8,956
58,200	58,250	10,413	7,826	10,413	8,969
58,250	58,300	10,425	7,834	10,425	8,981
58,300	58,350	10,438	7,841	10,438	8,994
58,350	58,400	10,450	7,849	10,450	9,006
58,400	58,450	10,463	7,856	10,463	9,019
58,450	58,500	10,475	7,864	10,475	9,031
58,500	58,550	10,488	7,871	10,488	9,044
58,550	58,600	10,500	7,879	10,500	9,056
58,600	58,650	10,513	7,886	10,513	9,069
58,650	58,700	10,525	7,894	10,525	9,081
58,700	58,750	10,538	7,901	10,538	9,094
58,750	58,800	10,550	7,909	10,550	9,106
58,800	58,850	10,563	7,916	10,563	9,119
58,850	58,900	10,575	7,924	10,575	9,131
58,900	58,950	10,588	7,931	10,588	9,144
58,950	59,000	10,600	7,939	10,600	9,156

59,000

At least	But less than	Single	Married filing jointly *	Married filing separately	Head of a household
59,000	59,050	10,613	7,946	10,613	9,169
59,050	59,100	10,625	7,954	10,625	9,181
59,100	59,150	10,638	7,961	10,638	9,194
59,150	59,200	10,650	7,969	10,650	9,206
59,200	59,250	10,663	7,976	10,663	9,219
59,250	59,300	10,675	7,984	10,675	9,231
59,300	59,350	10,688	7,991	10,688	9,244
59,350	59,400	10,700	7,999	10,700	9,256
59,400	59,450	10,713	8,006	10,713	9,269
59,450	59,500	10,725	8,014	10,725	9,281
59,500	59,550	10,738	8,021	10,738	9,294
59,550	59,600	10,750	8,029	10,750	9,306
59,600	59,650	10,763	8,036	10,763	9,319
59,650	59,700	10,775	8,044	10,775	9,331
59,700	59,750	10,788	8,051	10,788	9,344
59,750	59,800	10,800	8,059	10,800	9,356
59,800	59,850	10,813	8,066	10,813	9,369
59,850	59,900	10,825	8,074	10,825	9,381
59,900	59,950	10,838	8,081	10,838	9,394
59,950	60,000	10,850	8,089	10,850	9,406

60,000

At least	But less than	Single	Married filing jointly *	Married filing separately	Head of a household
60,000	60,050	10,863	8,096	10,863	9,419
60,050	60,100	10,875	8,104	10,875	9,431
60,100	60,150	10,888	8,111	10,888	9,444
60,150	60,200	10,900	8,119	10,900	9,456
60,200	60,250	10,913	8,126	10,913	9,469
60,250	60,300	10,925	8,134	10,925	9,481
60,300	60,350	10,938	8,141	10,938	9,494
60,350	60,400	10,950	8,149	10,950	9,506
60,400	60,450	10,963	8,156	10,963	9,519
60,450	60,500	10,975	8,164	10,975	9,531
60,500	60,550	10,988	8,171	10,988	9,544
60,550	60,600	11,000	8,179	11,000	9,556
60,600	60,650	11,013	8,186	11,013	9,569
60,650	60,700	11,025	8,194	11,025	9,581
60,700	60,750	11,038	8,201	11,038	9,594
60,750	60,800	11,050	8,209	11,050	9,606
60,800	60,850	11,063	8,216	11,063	9,619
60,850	60,900	11,075	8,224	11,075	9,631
60,900	60,950	11,088	8,231	11,088	9,644
60,950	61,000	11,100	8,239	11,100	9,656

61,000

At least	But less than	Single	Married filing jointly *	Married filing separately	Head of a household
61,000	61,050	11,113	8,246	11,113	9,669
61,050	61,100	11,125	8,254	11,125	9,681
61,100	61,150	11,138	8,261	11,138	9,694
61,150	61,200	11,150	8,269	11,150	9,706
61,200	61,250	11,163	8,276	11,163	9,719
61,250	61,300	11,175	8,284	11,175	9,731
61,300	61,350	11,188	8,291	11,188	9,744
61,350	61,400	11,200	8,299	11,200	9,756
61,400	61,450	11,213	8,306	11,213	9,769
61,450	61,500	11,225	8,314	11,225	9,781
61,500	61,550	11,238	8,321	11,238	9,794
61,550	61,600	11,250	8,329	11,250	9,806
61,600	61,650	11,263	8,336	11,263	9,819
61,650	61,700	11,275	8,344	11,275	9,831
61,700	61,750	11,288	8,351	11,288	9,844
61,750	61,800	11,300	8,359	11,300	9,856
61,800	61,850	11,313	8,366	11,313	9,869
61,850	61,900	11,325	8,374	11,325	9,881
61,900	61,950	11,338	8,381	11,338	9,894
61,950	62,000	11,350	8,389	11,350	9,906

62,000

At least	But less than	Single	Married filing jointly *	Married filing separately	Head of a household
62,000	62,050	11,363	8,396	11,363	9,919
62,050	62,100	11,375	8,404	11,375	9,931
62,100	62,150	11,388	8,411	11,388	9,944
62,150	62,200	11,400	8,419	11,400	9,956
62,200	62,250	11,413	8,426	11,413	9,969
62,250	62,300	11,425	8,434	11,425	9,981
62,300	62,350	11,438	8,441	11,438	9,994
62,350	62,400	11,450	8,449	11,450	10,006
62,400	62,450	11,463	8,456	11,463	10,019
62,450	62,500	11,475	8,464	11,475	10,031
62,500	62,550	11,488	8,471	11,488	10,044
62,550	62,600	11,500	8,479	11,500	10,056
62,600	62,650	11,513	8,486	11,513	10,069
62,650	62,700	11,525	8,494	11,525	10,081
62,700	62,750	11,538	8,501	11,538	10,094
62,750	62,800	11,550	8,509	11,550	10,106
62,800	62,850	11,563	8,516	11,563	10,119
62,850	62,900	11,575	8,524	11,575	10,131
62,900	62,950	11,588	8,531	11,588	10,144
62,950	63,000	11,600	8,539	11,600	10,156

63,000

At least	But less than	Single	Married filing jointly *	Married filing separately	Head of a household
63,000	63,050	11,613	8,546	11,613	10,169
63,050	63,100	11,625	8,554	11,625	10,181
63,100	63,150	11,638	8,561	11,638	10,194
63,150	63,200	11,650	8,569	11,650	10,206
63,200	63,250	11,663	8,576	11,663	10,219
63,250	63,300	11,675	8,584	11,675	10,231
63,300	63,350	11,688	8,591	11,688	10,244
63,350	63,400	11,700	8,599	11,700	10,256
63,400	63,450	11,713	8,606	11,713	10,269
63,450	63,500	11,725	8,614	11,725	10,281
63,500	63,550	11,738	8,621	11,738	10,294
63,550	63,600	11,750	8,629	11,750	10,306
63,600	63,650	11,763	8,636	11,763	10,319
63,650	63,700	11,775	8,644	11,775	10,331
63,700	63,750	11,788	8,651	11,788	10,344
63,750	63,800	11,800	8,659	11,800	10,356
63,800	63,850	11,813	8,666	11,813	10,369
63,850	63,900	11,825	8,674	11,825	10,381
63,900	63,950	11,838	8,681	11,838	10,394
63,950	64,000	11,850	8,689	11,850	10,406

64,000

At least	But less than	Single	Married filing jointly *	Married filing separately	Head of a household
64,000	64,050	11,863	8,696	11,863	10,419
64,050	64,100	11,875	8,704	11,875	10,431
64,100	64,150	11,888	8,711	11,888	10,444
64,150	64,200	11,900	8,719	11,900	10,456
64,200	64,250	11,913	8,726	11,913	10,469
64,250	64,300	11,925	8,734	11,925	10,481
64,300	64,350	11,938	8,741	11,938	10,494
64,350	64,400	11,950	8,749	11,950	10,506
64,400	64,450	11,963	8,756	11,963	10,519
64,450	64,500	11,975	8,764	11,975	10,531
64,500	64,550	11,988	8,771	11,988	10,544
64,550	64,600	12,000	8,779	12,000	10,556
64,600	64,650	12,013	8,786	12,013	10,569
64,650	64,700	12,025	8,794	12,025	10,581
64,700	64,750	12,038	8,801	12,038	10,594
64,750	64,800	12,050	8,809	12,050	10,606
64,800	64,850	12,063	8,816	12,063	10,619
64,850	64,900	12,075	8,824	12,075	10,631
64,900	64,950	12,088	8,831	12,088	10,644
64,950	65,000	12,100	8,839	12,100	10,656

65,000

At least	But less than	Single	Married filing jointly *	Married filing separately	Head of a household
65,000	65,050	12,113	8,846	12,113	10,669
65,050	65,100	12,125	8,854	12,125	10,681
65,100	65,150	12,138	8,861	12,138	10,694
65,150	65,200	12,150	8,869	12,150	10,706
65,200	65,250	12,163	8,876	12,163	10,719
65,250	65,300	12,175	8,884	12,175	10,731
65,300	65,350	12,188	8,891	12,188	10,744
65,350	65,400	12,200	8,899	12,200	10,756
65,400	65,450	12,213	8,906	12,213	10,769
65,450	65,500	12,225	8,914	12,225	10,781
65,500	65,550	12,238	8,921	12,238	10,794
65,550	65,600	12,250	8,929	12,250	10,806
65,600	65,650	12,263	8,936	12,263	10,819
65,650	65,700	12,275	8,944	12,275	10,831
65,700	65,750	12,288	8,951	12,288	10,844
65,750	65,800	12,300	8,959	12,300	10,856
65,800	65,850	12,313	8,966	12,313	10,869
65,850	65,900	12,325	8,974	12,325	10,881
65,900	65,950	12,338	8,981	12,338	10,894
65,950	66,000	12,350	8,989	12,350	10,906

(Continued)

* This column must also be used by a qualifying widow(er).

If line 43 (taxable income) is— / And you are— / Your tax is—

Columns: At least | But less than | Single | Married filing jointly * | Married filing separately | Head of a household

66,000

At least	But less than	Single	Married filing jointly *	Married filing separately	Head of a household
66,000	66,050	12,363	8,996	12,363	10,919
66,050	66,100	12,375	9,004	12,375	10,931
66,100	66,150	12,388	9,011	12,388	10,944
66,150	66,200	12,400	9,019	12,400	10,956
66,200	66,250	12,413	9,026	12,413	10,969
66,250	66,300	12,425	9,034	12,425	10,981
66,300	66,350	12,438	9,041	12,438	10,994
66,350	66,400	12,450	9,049	12,450	11,006
66,400	66,450	12,463	9,056	12,463	11,019
66,450	66,500	12,475	9,064	12,475	11,031
66,500	66,550	12,488	9,071	12,488	11,044
66,550	66,600	12,500	9,079	12,500	11,056
66,600	66,650	12,513	9,086	12,513	11,069
66,650	66,700	12,525	9,094	12,525	11,081
66,700	66,750	12,538	9,101	12,538	11,094
66,750	66,800	12,550	9,109	12,550	11,106
66,800	66,850	12,563	9,116	12,563	11,119
66,850	66,900	12,575	9,124	12,575	11,131
66,900	66,950	12,588	9,131	12,588	11,144
66,950	67,000	12,600	9,139	12,600	11,156

67,000

At least	But less than	Single	Married filing jointly *	Married filing separately	Head of a household
67,000	67,050	12,613	9,146	12,613	11,169
67,050	67,100	12,625	9,154	12,625	11,181
67,100	67,150	12,638	9,161	12,638	11,194
67,150	67,200	12,650	9,169	12,650	11,206
67,200	67,250	12,663	9,176	12,663	11,219
67,250	67,300	12,675	9,184	12,675	11,231
67,300	67,350	12,688	9,191	12,688	11,244
67,350	67,400	12,700	9,199	12,700	11,256
67,400	67,450	12,713	9,206	12,713	11,269
67,450	67,500	12,725	9,214	12,725	11,281
67,500	67,550	12,738	9,221	12,738	11,294
67,550	67,600	12,750	9,229	12,750	11,306
67,600	67,650	12,763	9,236	12,763	11,319
67,650	67,700	12,775	9,244	12,775	11,331
67,700	67,750	12,788	9,251	12,788	11,344
67,750	67,800	12,800	9,259	12,800	11,356
67,800	67,850	12,813	9,266	12,813	11,369
67,850	67,900	12,825	9,274	12,825	11,381
67,900	67,950	12,838	9,281	12,838	11,394
67,950	68,000	12,850	9,289	12,850	11,406

68,000

At least	But less than	Single	Married filing jointly *	Married filing separately	Head of a household
68,000	68,050	12,863	9,296	12,863	11,419
68,050	68,100	12,875	9,304	12,875	11,431
68,100	68,150	12,888	9,311	12,888	11,444
68,150	68,200	12,900	9,319	12,900	11,456
68,200	68,250	12,913	9,326	12,913	11,469
68,250	68,300	12,925	9,334	12,925	11,481
68,300	68,350	12,938	9,341	12,938	11,494
68,350	68,400	12,950	9,349	12,950	11,506
68,400	68,450	12,963	9,356	12,963	11,519
68,450	68,500	12,975	9,364	12,975	11,531
68,500	68,550	12,988	9,371	12,988	11,544
68,550	68,600	13,000	9,379	13,000	11,556
68,600	68,650	13,013	9,386	13,013	11,569
68,650	68,700	13,025	9,394	13,025	11,581
68,700	68,750	13,038	9,401	13,038	11,594
68,750	68,800	13,050	9,409	13,050	11,606
68,800	68,850	13,063	9,416	13,063	11,619
68,850	68,900	13,075	9,424	13,075	11,631
68,900	68,950	13,088	9,431	13,088	11,644
68,950	69,000	13,100	9,439	13,100	11,656

69,000

At least	But less than	Single	Married filing jointly *	Married filing separately	Head of a household
69,000	69,050	13,113	9,446	13,113	11,669
69,050	69,100	13,125	9,454	13,125	11,681
69,100	69,150	13,138	9,461	13,138	11,694
69,150	69,200	13,150	9,469	13,150	11,706
69,200	69,250	13,163	9,476	13,163	11,719
69,250	69,300	13,175	9,484	13,175	11,731
69,300	69,350	13,188	9,491	13,188	11,744
69,350	69,400	13,200	9,499	13,200	11,756
69,400	69,450	13,213	9,506	13,213	11,769
69,450	69,500	13,225	9,514	13,225	11,781
69,500	69,550	13,238	9,521	13,238	11,794
69,550	69,600	13,250	9,529	13,250	11,806
69,600	69,650	13,263	9,536	13,263	11,819
69,650	69,700	13,275	9,544	13,275	11,831
69,700	69,750	13,288	9,551	13,288	11,844
69,750	69,800	13,300	9,559	13,300	11,856
69,800	69,850	13,313	9,566	13,313	11,869
69,850	69,900	13,325	9,574	13,325	11,881
69,900	69,950	13,338	9,581	13,338	11,894
69,950	70,000	13,350	9,589	13,350	11,906

70,000

At least	But less than	Single	Married filing jointly *	Married filing separately	Head of a household
70,000	70,050	13,363	9,596	13,363	11,919
70,050	70,100	13,375	9,604	13,375	11,931
70,100	70,150	13,388	9,611	13,388	11,944
70,150	70,200	13,400	9,619	13,400	11,956
70,200	70,250	13,413	9,626	13,413	11,969
70,250	70,300	13,425	9,634	13,425	11,981
70,300	70,350	13,438	9,641	13,438	11,994
70,350	70,400	13,450	9,649	13,450	12,006
70,400	70,450	13,463	9,656	13,463	12,019
70,450	70,500	13,475	9,664	13,475	12,031
70,500	70,550	13,488	9,671	13,488	12,044
70,550	70,600	13,500	9,679	13,500	12,056
70,600	70,650	13,513	9,686	13,513	12,069
70,650	70,700	13,525	9,694	13,525	12,081
70,700	70,750	13,538	9,701	13,538	12,094
70,750	70,800	13,550	9,709	13,550	12,106
70,800	70,850	13,563	9,716	13,563	12,119
70,850	70,900	13,575	9,724	13,575	12,131
70,900	70,950	13,588	9,731	13,588	12,144
70,950	71,000	13,600	9,739	13,600	12,156

71,000

At least	But less than	Single	Married filing jointly *	Married filing separately	Head of a household
71,000	71,050	13,613	9,746	13,613	12,169
71,050	71,100	13,625	9,754	13,625	12,181
71,100	71,150	13,638	9,761	13,638	12,194
71,150	71,200	13,650	9,769	13,650	12,206
71,200	71,250	13,663	9,776	13,663	12,219
71,250	71,300	13,675	9,784	13,675	12,231
71,300	71,350	13,688	9,791	13,688	12,244
71,350	71,400	13,700	9,799	13,700	12,256
71,400	71,450	13,713	9,806	13,713	12,269
71,450	71,500	13,725	9,814	13,725	12,281
71,500	71,550	13,738	9,821	13,738	12,294
71,550	71,600	13,750	9,829	13,750	12,306
71,600	71,650	13,763	9,836	13,763	12,319
71,650	71,700	13,775	9,844	13,775	12,331
71,700	71,750	13,788	9,851	13,788	12,344
71,750	71,800	13,800	9,859	13,800	12,356
71,800	71,850	13,813	9,866	13,813	12,369
71,850	71,900	13,825	9,874	13,825	12,381
71,900	71,950	13,838	9,881	13,838	12,394
71,950	72,000	13,850	9,889	13,850	12,406

72,000

At least	But less than	Single	Married filing jointly *	Married filing separately	Head of a household
72,000	72,050	13,863	9,896	13,863	12,419
72,050	72,100	13,875	9,904	13,875	12,431
72,100	72,150	13,888	9,911	13,888	12,444
72,150	72,200	13,900	9,919	13,900	12,456
72,200	72,250	13,913	9,926	13,913	12,469
72,250	72,300	13,925	9,934	13,925	12,481
72,300	72,350	13,938	9,941	13,938	12,494
72,350	72,400	13,950	9,949	13,950	12,506
72,400	72,450	13,963	9,956	13,963	12,519
72,450	72,500	13,975	9,964	13,975	12,531
72,500	72,550	13,988	9,971	13,988	12,544
72,550	72,600	14,000	9,979	14,000	12,556
72,600	72,650	14,013	9,986	14,013	12,569
72,650	72,700	14,025	9,994	14,025	12,581
72,700	72,750	14,038	10,001	14,038	12,594
72,750	72,800	14,050	10,009	14,050	12,606
72,800	72,850	14,063	10,016	14,063	12,619
72,850	72,900	14,075	10,024	14,075	12,631
72,900	72,950	14,088	10,031	14,088	12,644
72,950	73,000	14,100	10,039	14,100	12,656

73,000

At least	But less than	Single	Married filing jointly *	Married filing separately	Head of a household
73,000	73,050	14,113	10,046	14,113	12,669
73,050	73,100	14,125	10,054	14,125	12,681
73,100	73,150	14,138	10,061	14,138	12,694
73,150	73,200	14,150	10,069	14,150	12,706
73,200	73,250	14,163	10,076	14,163	12,719
73,250	73,300	14,175	10,084	14,175	12,731
73,300	73,350	14,188	10,091	14,188	12,744
73,350	73,400	14,200	10,099	14,200	12,756
73,400	73,450	14,213	10,106	14,213	12,769
73,450	73,500	14,225	10,114	14,225	12,781
73,500	73,550	14,238	10,121	14,238	12,794
73,550	73,600	14,250	10,129	14,250	12,806
73,600	73,650	14,263	10,136	14,263	12,819
73,650	73,700	14,275	10,144	14,275	12,831
73,700	73,750	14,288	10,151	14,288	12,844
73,750	73,800	14,300	10,159	14,300	12,856
73,800	73,850	14,313	10,169	14,313	12,869
73,850	73,900	14,325	10,181	14,325	12,881
73,900	73,950	14,338	10,194	14,338	12,894
73,950	74,000	14,350	10,206	14,350	12,906

74,000

At least	But less than	Single	Married filing jointly *	Married filing separately	Head of a household
74,000	74,050	14,363	10,219	14,363	12,919
74,050	74,100	14,375	10,231	14,375	12,931
74,100	74,150	14,388	10,244	14,388	12,944
74,150	74,200	14,400	10,256	14,400	12,956
74,200	74,250	14,413	10,269	14,413	12,969
74,250	74,300	14,425	10,281	14,425	12,981
74,300	74,350	14,438	10,294	14,438	12,994
74,350	74,400	14,450	10,306	14,450	13,006
74,400	74,450	14,463	10,319	14,463	13,019
74,450	74,500	14,475	10,331	14,477	13,031
74,500	74,550	14,488	10,344	14,491	13,044
74,550	74,600	14,500	10,356	14,505	13,056
74,600	74,650	14,513	10,369	14,519	13,069
74,650	74,700	14,525	10,381	14,533	13,081
74,700	74,750	14,538	10,394	14,547	13,094
74,750	74,800	14,550	10,406	14,561	13,106
74,800	74,850	14,563	10,419	14,575	13,119
74,850	74,900	14,575	10,431	14,589	13,131
74,900	74,950	14,588	10,444	14,603	13,144
74,950	75,000	14,600	10,456	14,617	13,156

(Continued)

* This column must also be used by a qualifying widow(er).

If line 43 (taxable income) is— At least	But less than	Single	Married filing jointly *	Married filing separately	Head of a household
75,000					
75,000	75,050	14,613	10,469	14,631	13,169
75,050	75,100	14,625	10,481	14,645	13,181
75,100	75,150	14,638	10,494	14,659	13,194
75,150	75,200	14,650	10,506	14,673	13,206
75,200	75,250	14,663	10,519	14,687	13,219
75,250	75,300	14,675	10,531	14,701	13,231
75,300	75,350	14,688	10,544	14,715	13,244
75,350	75,400	14,700	10,556	14,729	13,256
75,400	75,450	14,713	10,569	14,743	13,269
75,450	75,500	14,725	10,581	14,757	13,281
75,500	75,550	14,738	10,594	14,771	13,294
75,550	75,600	14,750	10,606	14,785	13,306
75,600	75,650	14,763	10,619	14,799	13,319
75,650	75,700	14,775	10,631	14,813	13,331
75,700	75,750	14,788	10,644	14,827	13,344
75,750	75,800	14,800	10,656	14,841	13,356
75,800	75,850	14,813	10,669	14,855	13,369
75,850	75,900	14,825	10,681	14,869	13,381
75,900	75,950	14,838	10,694	14,883	13,394
75,950	76,000	14,850	10,706	14,897	13,406
76,000					
76,000	76,050	14,863	10,719	14,911	13,419
76,050	76,100	14,875	10,731	14,925	13,431
76,100	76,150	14,888	10,744	14,939	13,444
76,150	76,200	14,900	10,756	14,953	13,456
76,200	76,250	14,913	10,769	14,967	13,469
76,250	76,300	14,925	10,781	14,981	13,481
76,300	76,350	14,938	10,794	14,995	13,494
76,350	76,400	14,950	10,806	15,009	13,506
76,400	76,450	14,963	10,819	15,023	13,519
76,450	76,500	14,975	10,831	15,037	13,531
76,500	76,550	14,988	10,844	15,051	13,544
76,550	76,600	15,000	10,856	15,065	13,556
76,600	76,650	15,013	10,869	15,079	13,569
76,650	76,700	15,025	10,881	15,093	13,581
76,700	76,750	15,038	10,894	15,107	13,594
76,750	76,800	15,050	10,906	15,121	13,606
76,800	76,850	15,063	10,919	15,135	13,619
76,850	76,900	15,075	10,931	15,149	13,631
76,900	76,950	15,088	10,944	15,163	13,644
76,950	77,000	15,100	10,956	15,177	13,656
77,000					
77,000	77,050	15,113	10,969	15,191	13,669
77,050	77,100	15,125	10,981	15,205	13,681
77,100	77,150	15,138	10,994	15,219	13,694
77,150	77,200	15,150	11,006	15,233	13,706
77,200	77,250	15,163	11,019	15,247	13,719
77,250	77,300	15,175	11,031	15,261	13,731
77,300	77,350	15,188	11,044	15,275	13,744
77,350	77,400	15,200	11,056	15,289	13,756
77,400	77,450	15,213	11,069	15,303	13,769
77,450	77,500	15,225	11,081	15,317	13,781
77,500	77,550	15,238	11,094	15,331	13,794
77,550	77,600	15,250	11,106	15,345	13,806
77,600	77,650	15,263	11,119	15,359	13,819
77,650	77,700	15,275	11,131	15,373	13,831
77,700	77,750	15,288	11,144	15,387	13,844
77,750	77,800	15,300	11,156	15,401	13,856
77,800	77,850	15,313	11,169	15,415	13,869
77,850	77,900	15,325	11,181	15,429	13,881
77,900	77,950	15,338	11,194	15,443	13,894
77,950	78,000	15,350	11,206	15,457	13,906
78,000					
78,000	78,050	15,363	11,219	15,471	13,919
78,050	78,100	15,375	11,231	15,485	13,931
78,100	78,150	15,388	11,244	15,499	13,944
78,150	78,200	15,400	11,256	15,513	13,956
78,200	78,250	15,413	11,269	15,527	13,969
78,250	78,300	15,425	11,281	15,541	13,981
78,300	78,350	15,438	11,294	15,555	13,994
78,350	78,400	15,450	11,306	15,569	14,006
78,400	78,450	15,463	11,319	15,583	14,019
78,450	78,500	15,475	11,331	15,597	14,031
78,500	78,550	15,488	11,344	15,611	14,044
78,550	78,600	15,500	11,356	15,625	14,056
78,600	78,650	15,513	11,369	15,639	14,069
78,650	78,700	15,525	11,381	15,653	14,081
78,700	78,750	15,538	11,394	15,667	14,094
78,750	78,800	15,550	11,406	15,681	14,106
78,800	78,850	15,563	11,419	15,695	14,119
78,850	78,900	15,575	11,431	15,709	14,131
78,900	78,950	15,588	11,444	15,723	14,144
78,950	79,000	15,600	11,456	15,737	14,156
79,000					
79,000	79,050	15,613	11,469	15,751	14,169
79,050	79,100	15,625	11,481	15,765	14,181
79,100	79,150	15,638	11,494	15,779	14,194
79,150	79,200	15,650	11,506	15,793	14,206
79,200	79,250	15,663	11,519	15,807	14,219
79,250	79,300	15,675	11,531	15,821	14,231
79,300	79,350	15,688	11,544	15,835	14,244
79,350	79,400	15,700	11,556	15,849	14,256
79,400	79,450	15,713	11,569	15,863	14,269
79,450	79,500	15,725	11,581	15,877	14,281
79,500	79,550	15,738	11,594	15,891	14,294
79,550	79,600	15,750	11,606	15,905	14,306
79,600	79,650	15,763	11,619	15,919	14,319
79,650	79,700	15,775	11,631	15,933	14,331
79,700	79,750	15,788	11,644	15,947	14,344
79,750	79,800	15,800	11,656	15,961	14,356
79,800	79,850	15,813	11,669	15,975	14,369
79,850	79,900	15,825	11,681	15,989	14,381
79,900	79,950	15,838	11,694	16,003	14,394
79,950	80,000	15,850	11,706	16,017	14,406
80,000					
80,000	80,050	15,863	11,719	16,031	14,419
80,050	80,100	15,875	11,731	16,045	14,431
80,100	80,150	15,888	11,744	16,059	14,444
80,150	80,200	15,900	11,756	16,073	14,456
80,200	80,250	15,913	11,769	16,087	14,469
80,250	80,300	15,925	11,781	16,101	14,481
80,300	80,350	15,938	11,794	16,115	14,494
80,350	80,400	15,950	11,806	16,129	14,506
80,400	80,450	15,963	11,819	16,143	14,519
80,450	80,500	15,975	11,831	16,157	14,531
80,500	80,550	15,988	11,844	16,171	14,544
80,550	80,600	16,000	11,856	16,185	14,556
80,600	80,650	16,013	11,869	16,199	14,569
80,650	80,700	16,025	11,881	16,213	14,581
80,700	80,750	16,038	11,894	16,227	14,594
80,750	80,800	16,050	11,906	16,241	14,606
80,800	80,850	16,063	11,919	16,255	14,619
80,850	80,900	16,075	11,931	16,269	14,631
80,900	80,950	16,088	11,944	16,283	14,644
80,950	81,000	16,100	11,956	16,297	14,656
81,000					
81,000	81,050	16,113	11,969	16,311	14,669
81,050	81,100	16,125	11,981	16,325	14,681
81,100	81,150	16,138	11,994	16,339	14,694
81,150	81,200	16,150	12,006	16,353	14,706
81,200	81,250	16,163	12,019	16,367	14,719
81,250	81,300	16,175	12,031	16,381	14,731
81,300	81,350	16,188	12,044	16,395	14,744
81,350	81,400	16,200	12,056	16,409	14,756
81,400	81,450	16,213	12,069	16,423	14,769
81,450	81,500	16,225	12,081	16,437	14,781
81,500	81,550	16,238	12,094	16,451	14,794
81,550	81,600	16,250	12,106	16,465	14,806
81,600	81,650	16,263	12,119	16,479	14,819
81,650	81,700	16,275	12,131	16,493	14,831
81,700	81,750	16,288	12,144	16,507	14,844
81,750	81,800	16,300	12,156	16,521	14,856
81,800	81,850	16,313	12,169	16,535	14,869
81,850	81,900	16,325	12,181	16,549	14,881
81,900	81,950	16,338	12,194	16,563	14,894
81,950	82,000	16,350	12,206	16,577	14,906
82,000					
82,000	82,050	16,363	12,219	16,591	14,919
82,050	82,100	16,375	12,231	16,605	14,931
82,100	82,150	16,388	12,244	16,619	14,944
82,150	82,200	16,400	12,256	16,633	14,956
82,200	82,250	16,413	12,269	16,647	14,969
82,250	82,300	16,425	12,281	16,661	14,981
82,300	82,350	16,438	12,294	16,675	14,994
82,350	82,400	16,450	12,306	16,689	15,006
82,400	82,450	16,463	12,319	16,703	15,019
82,450	82,500	16,475	12,331	16,717	15,031
82,500	82,550	16,488	12,344	16,731	15,044
82,550	82,600	16,500	12,356	16,745	15,056
82,600	82,650	16,513	12,369	16,759	15,069
82,650	82,700	16,525	12,381	16,773	15,081
82,700	82,750	16,538	12,394	16,787	15,094
82,750	82,800	16,550	12,406	16,801	15,106
82,800	82,850	16,563	12,419	16,815	15,119
82,850	82,900	16,575	12,431	16,829	15,131
82,900	82,950	16,588	12,444	16,843	15,144
82,950	83,000	16,600	12,456	16,857	15,156
83,000					
83,000	83,050	16,613	12,469	16,871	15,169
83,050	83,100	16,625	12,481	16,885	15,181
83,100	83,150	16,638	12,494	16,899	15,194
83,150	83,200	16,650	12,506	16,913	15,206
83,200	83,250	16,663	12,519	16,927	15,219
83,250	83,300	16,675	12,531	16,941	15,231
83,300	83,350	16,688	12,544	16,955	15,244
83,350	83,400	16,700	12,556	16,969	15,256
83,400	83,450	16,713	12,569	16,983	15,269
83,450	83,500	16,725	12,581	16,997	15,281
83,500	83,550	16,738	12,594	17,011	15,294
83,550	83,600	16,750	12,606	17,025	15,306
83,600	83,650	16,763	12,619	17,039	15,319
83,650	83,700	16,775	12,631	17,053	15,331
83,700	83,750	16,788	12,644	17,067	15,344
83,750	83,800	16,800	12,656	17,081	15,356
83,800	83,850	16,813	12,669	17,095	15,369
83,850	83,900	16,825	12,681	17,109	15,381
83,900	83,950	16,838	12,694	17,123	15,394
83,950	84,000	16,850	12,706	17,137	15,406

(Continued)

* This column must also be used by a qualifying widow(er).

84,000

If line 43 (taxable income) is— At least	But less than	Single	Married filing jointly *	Married filing separately	Head of a household
84,000	84,050	16,863	12,719	17,151	15,419
84,050	84,100	16,875	12,731	17,165	15,431
84,100	84,150	16,888	12,744	17,179	15,444
84,150	84,200	16,900	12,756	17,193	15,456
84,200	84,250	16,913	12,769	17,207	15,469
84,250	84,300	16,925	12,781	17,221	15,481
84,300	84,350	16,938	12,794	17,235	15,494
84,350	84,400	16,950	12,806	17,249	15,506
84,400	84,450	16,963	12,819	17,263	15,519
84,450	84,500	16,975	12,831	17,277	15,531
84,500	84,550	16,988	12,844	17,291	15,544
84,550	84,600	17,000	12,856	17,305	15,556
84,600	84,650	17,013	12,869	17,319	15,569
84,650	84,700	17,025	12,881	17,333	15,581
84,700	84,750	17,038	12,894	17,347	15,594
84,750	84,800	17,050	12,906	17,361	15,606
84,800	84,850	17,063	12,919	17,375	15,619
84,850	84,900	17,075	12,931	17,389	15,631
84,900	84,950	17,088	12,944	17,403	15,644
84,950	85,000	17,100	12,956	17,417	15,656

85,000

At least	But less than	Single	Married filing jointly *	Married filing separately	Head of a household
85,000	85,050	17,113	12,969	17,431	15,669
85,050	85,100	17,125	12,981	17,445	15,681
85,100	85,150	17,138	12,994	17,459	15,694
85,150	85,200	17,150	13,006	17,473	15,706
85,200	85,250	17,163	13,019	17,487	15,719
85,250	85,300	17,175	13,031	17,501	15,731
85,300	85,350	17,188	13,044	17,515	15,744
85,350	85,400	17,200	13,056	17,529	15,756
85,400	85,450	17,213	13,069	17,543	15,769
85,450	85,500	17,225	13,081	17,557	15,781
85,500	85,550	17,238	13,094	17,571	15,794
85,550	85,600	17,250	13,106	17,585	15,806
85,600	85,650	17,263	13,119	17,599	15,819
85,650	85,700	17,275	13,131	17,613	15,831
85,700	85,750	17,288	13,144	17,627	15,844
85,750	85,800	17,300	13,156	17,641	15,856
85,800	85,850	17,313	13,169	17,655	15,869
85,850	85,900	17,325	13,181	17,669	15,881
85,900	85,950	17,338	13,194	17,683	15,894
85,950	86,000	17,350	13,206	17,697	15,906

86,000

At least	But less than	Single	Married filing jointly *	Married filing separately	Head of a household
86,000	86,050	17,363	13,219	17,711	15,919
86,050	86,100	17,375	13,231	17,725	15,931
86,100	86,150	17,388	13,244	17,739	15,944
86,150	86,200	17,400	13,256	17,753	15,956
86,200	86,250	17,413	13,269	17,767	15,969
86,250	86,300	17,425	13,281	17,781	15,981
86,300	86,350	17,438	13,294	17,795	15,994
86,350	86,400	17,450	13,306	17,809	16,006
86,400	86,450	17,463	13,319	17,823	16,019
86,450	86,500	17,475	13,331	17,837	16,031
86,500	86,550	17,488	13,344	17,851	16,044
86,550	86,600	17,500	13,356	17,865	16,056
86,600	86,650	17,513	13,369	17,879	16,069
86,650	86,700	17,525	13,381	17,893	16,081
86,700	86,750	17,538	13,394	17,907	16,094
86,750	86,800	17,550	13,406	17,921	16,106
86,800	86,850	17,563	13,419	17,935	16,119
86,850	86,900	17,575	13,431	17,949	16,131
86,900	86,950	17,588	13,444	17,963	16,144
86,950	87,000	17,600	13,456	17,977	16,156

87,000

At least	But less than	Single	Married filing jointly *	Married filing separately	Head of a household
87,000	87,050	17,613	13,469	17,991	16,169
87,050	87,100	17,625	13,481	18,005	16,181
87,100	87,150	17,638	13,494	18,019	16,194
87,150	87,200	17,650	13,506	18,033	16,206
87,200	87,250	17,663	13,519	18,047	16,219
87,250	87,300	17,675	13,531	18,061	16,231
87,300	87,350	17,688	13,544	18,075	16,244
87,350	87,400	17,700	13,556	18,089	16,256
87,400	87,450	17,713	13,569	18,103	16,269
87,450	87,500	17,725	13,581	18,117	16,281
87,500	87,550	17,738	13,594	18,131	16,294
87,550	87,600	17,750	13,606	18,145	16,306
87,600	87,650	17,763	13,619	18,159	16,319
87,650	87,700	17,775	13,631	18,173	16,331
87,700	87,750	17,788	13,644	18,187	16,344
87,750	87,800	17,800	13,656	18,201	16,356
87,800	87,850	17,813	13,669	18,215	16,369
87,850	87,900	17,825	13,681	18,229	16,381
87,900	87,950	17,838	13,694	18,243	16,394
87,950	88,000	17,850	13,706	18,257	16,406

88,000

At least	But less than	Single	Married filing jointly *	Married filing separately	Head of a household
88,000	88,050	17,863	13,719	18,271	16,419
88,050	88,100	17,875	13,731	18,285	16,431
88,100	88,150	17,888	13,744	18,299	16,444
88,150	88,200	17,900	13,756	18,313	16,456
88,200	88,250	17,913	13,769	18,327	16,469
88,250	88,300	17,925	13,781	18,341	16,481
88,300	88,350	17,938	13,794	18,355	16,494
88,350	88,400	17,950	13,806	18,369	16,506
88,400	88,450	17,963	13,819	18,383	16,519
88,450	88,500	17,975	13,831	18,397	16,531
88,500	88,550	17,988	13,844	18,411	16,544
88,550	88,600	18,000	13,856	18,425	16,556
88,600	88,650	18,013	13,869	18,439	16,569
88,650	88,700	18,025	13,881	18,453	16,581
88,700	88,750	18,038	13,894	18,467	16,594
88,750	88,800	18,050	13,906	18,481	16,606
88,800	88,850	18,063	13,919	18,495	16,619
88,850	88,900	18,075	13,931	18,509	16,631
88,900	88,950	18,088	13,944	18,523	16,644
88,950	89,000	18,100	13,956	18,537	16,656

89,000

At least	But less than	Single	Married filing jointly *	Married filing separately	Head of a household
89,000	89,050	18,113	13,969	18,551	16,669
89,050	89,100	18,125	13,981	18,565	16,681
89,100	89,150	18,138	13,994	18,579	16,694
89,150	89,200	18,150	14,006	18,593	16,706
89,200	89,250	18,163	14,019	18,607	16,719
89,250	89,300	18,175	14,031	18,621	16,731
89,300	89,350	18,188	14,044	18,635	16,744
89,350	89,400	18,201	14,056	18,649	16,756
89,400	89,450	18,215	14,069	18,663	16,769
89,450	89,500	18,229	14,081	18,677	16,781
89,500	89,550	18,243	14,094	18,691	16,794
89,550	89,600	18,257	14,106	18,705	16,806
89,600	89,650	18,271	14,119	18,719	16,819
89,650	89,700	18,285	14,131	18,733	16,831
89,700	89,750	18,299	14,144	18,747	16,844
89,750	89,800	18,313	14,156	18,761	16,856
89,800	89,850	18,327	14,169	18,775	16,869
89,850	89,900	18,341	14,181	18,789	16,881
89,900	89,950	18,355	14,194	18,803	16,894
89,950	90,000	18,369	14,206	18,817	16,906

90,000

At least	But less than	Single	Married filing jointly *	Married filing separately	Head of a household
90,000	90,050	18,383	14,219	18,831	16,919
90,050	90,100	18,397	14,231	18,845	16,931
90,100	90,150	18,411	14,244	18,859	16,944
90,150	90,200	18,425	14,256	18,873	16,956
90,200	90,250	18,439	14,269	18,887	16,969
90,250	90,300	18,453	14,281	18,901	16,981
90,300	90,350	18,467	14,294	18,915	16,994
90,350	90,400	18,481	14,306	18,929	17,006
90,400	90,450	18,495	14,319	18,943	17,019
90,450	90,500	18,509	14,331	18,957	17,031
90,500	90,550	18,523	14,344	18,971	17,044
90,550	90,600	18,537	14,356	18,985	17,056
90,600	90,650	18,551	14,369	18,999	17,069
90,650	90,700	18,565	14,381	19,013	17,081
90,700	90,750	18,579	14,394	19,027	17,094
90,750	90,800	18,593	14,406	19,041	17,106
90,800	90,850	18,607	14,419	19,055	17,119
90,850	90,900	18,621	14,431	19,069	17,131
90,900	90,950	18,635	14,444	19,083	17,144
90,950	91,000	18,649	14,456	19,097	17,156

91,000

At least	But less than	Single	Married filing jointly *	Married filing separately	Head of a household
91,000	91,050	18,663	14,469	19,111	17,169
91,050	91,100	18,677	14,481	19,125	17,181
91,100	91,150	18,691	14,494	19,139	17,194
91,150	91,200	18,705	14,506	19,153	17,206
91,200	91,250	18,719	14,519	19,167	17,219
91,250	91,300	18,733	14,531	19,181	17,231
91,300	91,350	18,747	14,544	19,195	17,244
91,350	91,400	18,761	14,556	19,209	17,256
91,400	91,450	18,775	14,569	19,223	17,269
91,450	91,500	18,789	14,581	19,237	17,281
91,500	91,550	18,803	14,594	19,251	17,294
91,550	91,600	18,817	14,606	19,265	17,306
91,600	91,650	18,831	14,619	19,279	17,319
91,650	91,700	18,845	14,631	19,293	17,331
91,700	91,750	18,859	14,644	19,307	17,344
91,750	91,800	18,873	14,656	19,321	17,356
91,800	91,850	18,887	14,669	19,335	17,369
91,850	91,900	18,901	14,681	19,349	17,381
91,900	91,950	18,915	14,694	19,363	17,394
91,950	92,000	18,929	14,706	19,377	17,406

92,000

At least	But less than	Single	Married filing jointly *	Married filing separately	Head of a household
92,000	92,050	18,943	14,719	19,391	17,419
92,050	92,100	18,957	14,731	19,405	17,431
92,100	92,150	18,971	14,744	19,419	17,444
92,150	92,200	18,985	14,756	19,433	17,456
92,200	92,250	18,999	14,769	19,447	17,469
92,250	92,300	19,013	14,781	19,461	17,481
92,300	92,350	19,027	14,794	19,475	17,494
92,350	92,400	19,041	14,806	19,489	17,506
92,400	92,450	19,055	14,819	19,503	17,519
92,450	92,500	19,069	14,831	19,517	17,531
92,500	92,550	19,083	14,844	19,531	17,544
92,550	92,600	19,097	14,856	19,545	17,556
92,600	92,650	19,111	14,869	19,559	17,569
92,650	92,700	19,125	14,881	19,573	17,581
92,700	92,750	19,139	14,894	19,587	17,594
92,750	92,800	19,153	14,906	19,601	17,606
92,800	92,850	19,167	14,919	19,615	17,619
92,850	92,900	19,181	14,931	19,629	17,631
92,900	92,950	19,195	14,944	19,643	17,644
92,950	93,000	19,209	14,956	19,657	17,656

(Continued)

* This column must also be used by a qualifying widow(er).

If line 43 (taxable income) is—		And you are—			
At least	But less than	Single	Married filing jointly *	Married filing separately	Head of a house-hold
		Your tax is—			

93,000

At least	But less than	Single	MFJ *	MFS	HoH
93,000	93,050	19,223	14,969	19,671	17,669
93,050	93,100	19,237	14,981	19,685	17,681
93,100	93,150	19,251	14,994	19,699	17,694
93,150	93,200	19,265	15,006	19,713	17,706
93,200	93,250	19,279	15,019	19,727	17,719
93,250	93,300	19,293	15,031	19,741	17,731
93,300	93,350	19,307	15,044	19,755	17,744
93,350	93,400	19,321	15,056	19,769	17,756
93,400	93,450	19,335	15,069	19,783	17,769
93,450	93,500	19,349	15,081	19,797	17,781
93,500	93,550	19,363	15,094	19,811	17,794
93,550	93,600	19,377	15,106	19,825	17,806
93,600	93,650	19,391	15,119	19,839	17,819
93,650	93,700	19,405	15,131	19,853	17,831
93,700	93,750	19,419	15,144	19,867	17,844
93,750	93,800	19,433	15,156	19,881	17,856
93,800	93,850	19,447	15,169	19,895	17,869
93,850	93,900	19,461	15,181	19,909	17,881
93,900	93,950	19,475	15,194	19,923	17,894
93,950	94,000	19,489	15,206	19,937	17,906

94,000

At least	But less than	Single	MFJ *	MFS	HoH
94,000	94,050	19,503	15,219	19,951	17,919
94,050	94,100	19,517	15,231	19,965	17,931
94,100	94,150	19,531	15,244	19,979	17,944
94,150	94,200	19,545	15,256	19,993	17,956
94,200	94,250	19,559	15,269	20,007	17,969
94,250	94,300	19,573	15,281	20,021	17,981
94,300	94,350	19,587	15,294	20,035	17,994
94,350	94,400	19,601	15,306	20,049	18,006
94,400	94,450	19,615	15,319	20,063	18,019
94,450	94,500	19,629	15,331	20,077	18,031
94,500	94,550	19,643	15,344	20,091	18,044
94,550	94,600	19,657	15,356	20,105	18,056
94,600	94,650	19,671	15,369	20,119	18,069
94,650	94,700	19,685	15,381	20,133	18,081
94,700	94,750	19,699	15,394	20,147	18,094
94,750	94,800	19,713	15,406	20,161	18,106
94,800	94,850	19,727	15,419	20,175	18,119
94,850	94,900	19,741	15,431	20,189	18,131
94,900	94,950	19,755	15,444	20,203	18,144
94,950	95,000	19,769	15,456	20,217	18,156

95,000

At least	But less than	Single	MFJ *	MFS	HoH
95,000	95,050	19,783	15,469	20,231	18,169
95,050	95,100	19,797	15,481	20,245	18,181
95,100	95,150	19,811	15,494	20,259	18,194
95,150	95,200	19,825	15,500	20,273	18,206
95,200	95,250	19,839	15,519	20,287	18,219
95,250	95,300	19,853	15,531	20,301	18,231
95,300	95,350	19,867	15,544	20,315	18,244
95,350	95,400	19,881	15,556	20,329	18,256
95,400	95,450	19,895	15,569	20,343	18,269
95,450	95,500	19,909	15,581	20,357	18,281
95,500	95,550	19,923	15,594	20,371	18,294
95,550	95,600	19,937	15,606	20,385	18,306
95,600	95,650	19,951	15,619	20,399	18,319
95,650	95,700	19,965	15,631	20,413	18,331
95,700	95,750	19,979	15,644	20,427	18,344
95,750	95,800	19,993	15,656	20,441	18,356
95,800	95,850	20,007	15,669	20,455	18,369
95,850	95,900	20,021	15,681	20,469	18,381
95,900	95,950	20,035	15,694	20,483	18,394
95,950	96,000	20,049	15,706	20,497	18,406

96,000

At least	But less than	Single	MFJ *	MFS	HoH
96,000	96,050	20,063	15,719	20,511	18,419
96,050	96,100	20,077	15,731	20,525	18,431
96,100	96,150	20,091	15,744	20,539	18,444
96,150	96,200	20,105	15,756	20,553	18,456
96,200	96,250	20,119	15,769	20,567	18,469
96,250	96,300	20,133	15,781	20,581	18,481
96,300	96,350	20,147	15,794	20,595	18,494
96,350	96,400	20,161	15,806	20,609	18,506
96,400	96,450	20,175	15,819	20,623	18,519
96,450	96,500	20,189	15,831	20,637	18,531
96,500	96,550	20,203	15,844	20,651	18,544
96,550	96,600	20,217	15,856	20,665	18,556
96,600	96,650	20,231	15,869	20,679	18,569
96,650	96,700	20,245	15,881	20,693	18,581
96,700	96,750	20,259	15,894	20,707	18,594
96,750	96,800	20,273	15,906	20,721	18,606
96,800	96,850	20,287	15,919	20,735	18,619
96,850	96,900	20,301	15,931	20,749	18,631
96,900	96,950	20,315	15,944	20,763	18,644
96,950	97,000	20,329	15,956	20,777	18,656

97,000

At least	But less than	Single	MFJ *	MFS	HoH
97,000	97,050	20,343	15,969	20,791	18,669
97,050	97,100	20,357	15,981	20,805	18,681
97,100	97,150	20,371	15,994	20,819	18,694
97,150	97,200	20,385	16,006	20,833	18,706
97,200	97,250	20,399	16,019	20,847	18,719
97,250	97,300	20,413	16,031	20,861	18,731
97,300	97,350	20,427	16,044	20,875	18,744
97,350	97,400	20,441	16,056	20,889	18,756
97,400	97,450	20,455	16,069	20,903	18,769
97,450	97,500	20,469	16,081	20,917	18,781
97,500	97,550	20,483	16,094	20,931	18,794
97,550	97,600	20,497	16,106	20,945	18,806
97,600	97,650	20,511	16,119	20,959	18,819
97,650	97,700	20,525	16,131	20,973	18,831
97,700	97,750	20,539	16,144	20,987	18,844
97,750	97,800	20,553	16,156	21,001	18,856
97,800	97,850	20,567	16,169	21,015	18,869
97,850	97,900	20,581	16,181	21,029	18,881
97,900	97,950	20,595	16,194	21,043	18,894
97,950	98,000	20,609	16,206	21,057	18,906

98,000

At least	But less than	Single	MFJ *	MFS	HoH
98,000	98,050	20,623	16,219	21,071	18,919
98,050	98,100	20,637	16,231	21,085	18,931
98,100	98,150	20,651	16,244	21,099	18,944
98,150	98,200	20,665	16,256	21,113	18,956
98,200	98,250	20,679	16,269	21,127	18,969
98,250	98,300	20,693	16,281	21,141	18,981
98,300	98,350	20,707	16,294	21,155	18,994
98,350	98,400	20,721	16,306	21,169	19,006
98,400	98,450	20,735	16,319	21,183	19,019
98,450	98,500	20,749	16,331	21,197	19,031
98,500	98,550	20,763	16,344	21,211	19,044
98,550	98,600	20,777	16,356	21,225	19,056
98,600	98,650	20,791	16,369	21,239	19,069
98,650	98,700	20,805	16,381	21,253	19,081
98,700	98,750	20,819	16,394	21,267	19,094
98,750	98,800	20,833	16,406	21,281	19,106
98,800	98,850	20,847	16,419	21,295	19,119
98,850	98,900	20,861	16,431	21,309	19,131
98,900	98,950	20,875	16,444	21,323	19,144
98,950	99,000	20,889	16,456	21,337	19,156

99,000

At least	But less than	Single	MFJ *	MFS	HoH
99,000	99,050	20,903	16,469	21,351	19,169
99,050	99,100	20,917	16,481	21,365	19,181
99,100	99,150	20,931	16,494	21,379	19,194
99,150	99,200	20,945	16,506	21,393	19,206
99,200	99,250	20,959	16,519	21,407	19,219
99,250	99,300	20,973	16,531	21,421	19,231
99,300	99,350	20,987	16,544	21,435	19,244
99,350	99,400	21,001	16,556	21,449	19,256
99,400	99,450	21,015	16,569	21,463	19,269
99,450	99,500	21,029	16,581	21,477	19,281
99,500	99,550	21,043	16,594	21,491	19,294
99,550	99,600	21,057	16,606	21,505	19,306
99,600	99,650	21,071	16,619	21,519	19,319
99,650	99,700	21,085	16,631	21,533	19,331
99,700	99,750	21,099	16,644	21,547	19,344
99,750	99,800	21,113	16,656	21,561	19,356
99,800	99,850	21,127	16,669	21,575	19,369
99,850	99,900	21,141	16,681	21,589	19,381
99,900	99,950	21,155	16,694	21,603	19,394
99,950	100,000	21,169	16,706	21,617	19,406

$100,000 or over use the Tax Computation Worksheet

* This column must also be used by a qualifying widow(er).

2014 Tax Computation Worksheet—Line 44

See the instructions for line 44 to see if you must use the worksheet below to figure your tax.

Note. If you are required to use this worksheet to figure the tax on an amount from another form or worksheet, such as the Qualified Dividends and Capital Gain Tax Worksheet, the Schedule D Tax Worksheet, Schedule J, Form 8615, or the Foreign Earned Income Tax Worksheet, enter the amount from that form or worksheet in column (a) of the row that applies to the amount you are looking up. Enter the result on the appropriate line of the form or worksheet that you are completing.

Section A—Use if your filing status is **Single.** Complete the row below that applies to you.

Taxable income. If line 43 is—	(a) Enter the amount from line 43	(b) Multiplication amount	(c) Multiply (a) by (b)	(d) Subtraction amount	Tax. Subtract (d) from (c). Enter the result here and on Form 1040, line 44
At least $100,000 but not over $186,350	$	× 28% (.28)	$	$ 6,824.25	$
Over $186,350 but not over $405,100	$	× 33% (.33)	$	$ 16,141.75	$
Over $405,100 but not over $406,750	$	× 35% (.35)	$	$ 24,243.75	$
Over $406,750	$	× 39.6% (.396)	$	$ 42,954.25	$

Section B—Use if your filing status is **Married filing jointly** or **Qualifying widow(er).** Complete the row below that applies to you.

Taxable income. If line 43 is—	(a) Enter the amount from line 43	(b) Multiplication amount	(c) Multiply (a) by (b)	(d) Subtraction amount	Tax. Subtract (d) from (c). Enter the result here and on Form 1040, line 44
At least $100,000 but not over $148,850	$	× 25% (.25)	$	$ 8,287.50	$
Over $148,850 but not over $226,850	$	× 28% (.28)	$	$ 12,753.00	$
Over $226,850 but not over $405,100	$	× 33% (.33)	$	$ 24,095.50	$
Over $405,100 but not over $457,600	$	× 35% (.35)	$	$ 32,197.50	$
Over $457,600	$	× 39.6% (.396)	$	$ 53,247.10	$

Section C—Use if your filing status is **Married filing separately.** Complete the row below that applies to you.

Taxable income. If line 43 is—	(a) Enter the amount from line 43	(b) Multiplication amount	(c) Multiply (a) by (b)	(d) Subtraction amount	Tax. Subtract (d) from (c). Enter the result here and on Form 1040, line 44
At least $100,000 but not over $113,425	$	× 28% (.28)	$	$ 6,376.50	$
Over $113,425 but not over $202,550	$	× 33% (.33)	$	$ 12,047.75	$
Over $202,550 but not over $228,800	$	× 35% (.35)	$	$ 16,098.75	$
Over $228,800	$	× 39.6% (.396)	$	$ 26,623.55	$

Section D—Use if your filing status is **Head of household.** Complete the row below that applies to you.

Taxable income. If line 43 is—	(a) Enter the amount from line 43	(b) Multiplication amount	(c) Multiply (a) by (b)	(d) Subtraction amount	Tax. Subtract (d) from (c). Enter the result here and on Form 1040, line 44
At least $100,000 but not over $127,550	$	× 25% (.25)	$	$ 5,587.50	$
Over $127,550 but not over $206,600	$	× 28% (.28)	$	$ 9,414.00	$
Over $206,600 but not over $405,100	$	× 33% (.33)	$	$ 19,744.00	$
Over $405,100 but not over $432,200	$	× 35% (.35)	$	$ 27,846.00	$
Over $432,200	$	× 39.6% (.396)	$	$ 47,727.20	$

Appendix B –Earned Income Credit Tables

2014 Earned Income Credit (EIC) Table

Caution. This is not a tax table.

1. To find your credit, read down the "At least - But less than" columns and find the line that includes the amount you were told to look up from your EIC Worksheet.

2. Then, go to the column that includes your filing status and the number of qualifying children you have. Enter the credit from that column on your EIC Worksheet.

Example. If your filing status is single, you have one qualifying child, and the amount you are looking up from your EIC Worksheet is $2,455, you would enter $842.

If the amount you are looking up from the worksheet is—		And your filing status is— Single, head of household, or qualifying widow(er) and the number of children you have is—			
		0	1	2	3
At least	But less than	Your credit is—			
2,400	2,450	186	825	970	1,091
2,450	2,500	189	842	990	1,114

If the amount you are looking up from the worksheet is—		And your filing status is—							
		Single, head of household, or qualifying widow(er) and the number of children you have is—				Married filing jointly and the number of children you have is—			
		0	1	2	3	0	1	2	3
At least	But less than	Your credit is—				Your credit is—			
$1	$50	$2	$9	$10	$11	$2	$9	$10	$11
50	100	6	26	30	34	6	26	30	34
100	150	10	43	50	56	10	43	50	56
150	200	13	60	70	79	13	60	70	79
200	250	17	77	90	101	17	77	90	101
250	300	21	94	110	124	21	94	110	124
300	350	25	111	130	146	25	111	130	146
350	400	29	128	150	169	29	128	150	169
400	450	33	145	170	191	33	145	170	191
450	500	36	162	190	214	36	162	190	214
500	550	40	179	210	236	40	179	210	236
550	600	44	196	230	259	44	196	230	259
600	650	48	213	250	281	48	213	250	281
650	700	52	230	270	304	52	230	270	304
700	750	55	247	290	326	55	247	290	326
750	800	59	264	310	349	59	264	310	349
800	850	63	281	330	371	63	281	330	371
850	900	67	298	350	394	67	298	350	394
900	950	71	315	370	416	71	315	370	416
950	1,000	75	332	390	439	75	332	390	439
1,000	1,050	78	349	410	461	78	349	410	461
1,050	1,100	82	366	430	484	82	366	430	484
1,100	1,150	86	383	450	506	86	383	450	506
1,150	1,200	90	400	470	529	90	400	470	529
1,200	1,250	94	417	490	551	94	417	490	551
1,250	1,300	98	434	510	574	98	434	510	574
1,300	1,350	101	451	530	596	101	451	530	596
1,350	1,400	105	468	550	619	105	468	550	619
1,400	1,450	109	485	570	641	109	485	570	641
1,450	1,500	113	502	590	664	113	502	590	664
1,500	1,550	117	519	610	686	117	519	610	686
1,550	1,600	120	536	630	709	120	536	630	709
1,600	1,650	124	553	650	731	124	553	650	731
1,650	1,700	128	570	670	754	128	570	670	754
1,700	1,750	132	587	690	776	132	587	690	776
1,750	1,800	136	604	710	799	136	604	710	799
1,800	1,850	140	621	730	821	140	621	730	821
1,850	1,900	143	638	750	844	143	638	750	844
1,900	1,950	147	655	770	866	147	655	770	866
1,950	2,000	151	672	790	889	151	672	790	889
2,000	2,050	155	689	810	911	155	689	810	911
2,050	2,100	159	706	830	934	159	706	830	934
2,100	2,150	163	723	850	956	163	723	850	956
2,150	2,200	166	740	870	979	166	740	870	979
2,200	2,250	170	757	890	1,001	170	757	890	1,001
2,250	2,300	174	774	910	1,024	174	774	910	1,024
2,300	2,350	178	791	930	1,046	178	791	930	1,046
2,350	2,400	182	808	950	1,069	182	808	950	1,069
2,400	2,450	186	825	970	1,091	186	825	970	1,091
2,450	2,500	189	842	990	1,114	189	842	990	1,114
2,500	2,550	193	859	1,010	1,136	193	859	1,010	1,136
2,550	2,600	197	876	1,030	1,159	197	876	1,030	1,159
2,600	2,650	201	893	1,050	1,181	201	893	1,050	1,181
2,650	2,700	205	910	1,070	1,204	205	910	1,070	1,204
2,700	2,750	208	927	1,090	1,226	208	927	1,090	1,226
2,750	2,800	212	944	1,110	1,249	212	944	1,110	1,249

If the amount you are looking up from the worksheet is—		And your filing status is—							
		Single, head of household, or qualifying widow(er) and the number of children you have is—				Married filing jointly and the number of children you have is—			
		0	1	2	3	0	1	2	3
At least	But less than	Your credit is—				Your credit is—			
2,800	2,850	216	961	1,130	1,271	216	961	1,130	1,271
2,850	2,900	220	978	1,150	1,294	220	978	1,150	1,294
2,900	2,950	224	995	1,170	1,316	224	995	1,170	1,316
2,950	3,000	228	1,012	1,190	1,339	228	1,012	1,190	1,339
3,000	3,050	231	1,029	1,210	1,361	231	1,029	1,210	1,361
3,050	3,100	235	1,046	1,230	1,384	235	1,046	1,230	1,384
3,100	3,150	239	1,063	1,250	1,406	239	1,063	1,250	1,406
3,150	3,200	243	1,080	1,270	1,429	243	1,080	1,270	1,429
3,200	3,250	247	1,097	1,290	1,451	247	1,097	1,290	1,451
3,250	3,300	251	1,114	1,310	1,474	251	1,114	1,310	1,474
3,300	3,350	254	1,131	1,330	1,496	254	1,131	1,330	1,496
3,350	3,400	258	1,148	1,350	1,519	258	1,148	1,350	1,519
3,400	3,450	262	1,165	1,370	1,541	262	1,165	1,370	1,541
3,450	3,500	266	1,182	1,390	1,564	266	1,182	1,390	1,564
3,500	3,550	270	1,199	1,410	1,586	270	1,199	1,410	1,586
3,550	3,600	273	1,216	1,430	1,609	273	1,216	1,430	1,609
3,600	3,650	277	1,233	1,450	1,631	277	1,233	1,450	1,631
3,650	3,700	281	1,250	1,470	1,654	281	1,250	1,470	1,654
3,700	3,750	285	1,267	1,490	1,676	285	1,267	1,490	1,676
3,750	3,800	289	1,284	1,510	1,699	289	1,284	1,510	1,699
3,800	3,850	293	1,301	1,530	1,721	293	1,301	1,530	1,721
3,850	3,900	296	1,318	1,550	1,744	296	1,318	1,550	1,744
3,900	3,950	300	1,335	1,570	1,766	300	1,335	1,570	1,766
3,950	4,000	304	1,352	1,590	1,789	304	1,352	1,590	1,789
4,000	4,050	308	1,369	1,610	1,811	308	1,369	1,610	1,811
4,050	4,100	312	1,386	1,630	1,834	312	1,386	1,630	1,834
4,100	4,150	316	1,403	1,650	1,856	316	1,403	1,650	1,856
4,150	4,200	319	1,420	1,670	1,879	319	1,420	1,670	1,879
4,200	4,250	323	1,437	1,690	1,901	323	1,437	1,690	1,901
4,250	4,300	327	1,454	1,710	1,924	327	1,454	1,710	1,924
4,300	4,350	331	1,471	1,730	1,946	331	1,471	1,730	1,946
4,350	4,400	335	1,488	1,750	1,969	335	1,488	1,750	1,969
4,400	4,450	339	1,505	1,770	1,991	339	1,505	1,770	1,991
4,450	4,500	342	1,522	1,790	2,014	342	1,522	1,790	2,014
4,500	4,550	346	1,539	1,810	2,036	346	1,539	1,810	2,036
4,550	4,600	350	1,556	1,830	2,059	350	1,556	1,830	2,059
4,600	4,650	354	1,573	1,850	2,081	354	1,573	1,850	2,081
4,650	4,700	358	1,590	1,870	2,104	358	1,590	1,870	2,104
4,700	4,750	361	1,607	1,890	2,126	361	1,607	1,890	2,126
4,750	4,800	365	1,624	1,910	2,149	365	1,624	1,910	2,149
4,800	4,850	369	1,641	1,930	2,171	369	1,641	1,930	2,171
4,850	4,900	373	1,658	1,950	2,194	373	1,658	1,950	2,194
4,900	4,950	377	1,675	1,970	2,216	377	1,675	1,970	2,216
4,950	5,000	381	1,692	1,990	2,239	381	1,692	1,990	2,239
5,000	5,050	384	1,709	2,010	2,261	384	1,709	2,010	2,261
5,050	5,100	388	1,726	2,030	2,284	388	1,726	2,030	2,284
5,100	5,150	392	1,743	2,050	2,306	392	1,743	2,050	2,306
5,150	5,200	396	1,760	2,070	2,329	396	1,760	2,070	2,329
5,200	5,250	400	1,777	2,090	2,351	400	1,777	2,090	2,351
5,250	5,300	404	1,794	2,110	2,374	404	1,794	2,110	2,374
5,300	5,350	407	1,811	2,130	2,396	407	1,811	2,130	2,396
5,350	5,400	411	1,828	2,150	2,419	411	1,828	2,150	2,419
5,400	5,450	415	1,845	2,170	2,441	415	1,845	2,170	2,441
5,450	5,500	419	1,862	2,190	2,464	419	1,862	2,190	2,464
5,500	5,550	423	1,879	2,210	2,486	423	1,879	2,210	2,486
5,550	5,600	426	1,896	2,230	2,509	426	1,896	2,230	2,509

(Continued)

Earned Income Credit (EIC) Table - Continued

(**Caution.** This is **not** a tax table.)

If the amount you are looking up from the worksheet is— At least	But less than	Single, head of household, or qualifying widow(er) 0	1	2	3	Married filing jointly 0	1	2	3
5,600	5,650	430	1,913	2,250	2,531	430	1,913	2,250	2,531
5,650	5,700	434	1,930	2,270	2,554	434	1,930	2,270	2,554
5,700	5,750	438	1,947	2,290	2,576	438	1,947	2,290	2,576
5,750	5,800	442	1,964	2,310	2,599	442	1,964	2,310	2,599
5,800	5,850	446	1,981	2,330	2,621	446	1,981	2,330	2,621
5,850	5,900	449	1,998	2,350	2,644	449	1,998	2,350	2,644
5,900	5,950	453	2,015	2,370	2,666	453	2,015	2,370	2,666
5,950	6,000	457	2,032	2,390	2,689	457	2,032	2,390	2,689
6,000	6,050	461	2,049	2,410	2,711	461	2,049	2,410	2,711
6,050	6,100	465	2,066	2,430	2,734	465	2,066	2,430	2,734
6,100	6,150	469	2,083	2,450	2,756	469	2,083	2,450	2,756
6,150	6,200	472	2,100	2,470	2,779	472	2,100	2,470	2,779
6,200	6,250	476	2,117	2,490	2,801	476	2,117	2,490	2,801
6,250	6,300	480	2,134	2,510	2,824	480	2,134	2,510	2,824
6,300	6,350	484	2,151	2,530	2,846	484	2,151	2,530	2,846
6,350	6,400	488	2,168	2,550	2,869	488	2,168	2,550	2,869
6,400	6,450	492	2,185	2,570	2,891	492	2,185	2,570	2,891
6,450	6,500	496	2,202	2,590	2,914	496	2,202	2,590	2,914
6,500	6,550	496	2,219	2,610	2,936	496	2,219	2,610	2,936
6,550	6,600	496	2,236	2,630	2,959	496	2,236	2,630	2,959
6,600	6,650	496	2,253	2,650	2,981	496	2,253	2,650	2,981
6,650	6,700	496	2,270	2,670	3,004	496	2,270	2,670	3,004
6,700	6,750	496	2,287	2,690	3,026	496	2,287	2,690	3,026
6,750	6,800	496	2,304	2,710	3,049	496	2,304	2,710	3,049
6,800	6,850	496	2,321	2,730	3,071	496	2,321	2,730	3,071
6,850	6,900	496	2,338	2,750	3,094	496	2,338	2,750	3,094
6,900	6,950	496	2,355	2,770	3,116	496	2,355	2,770	3,116
6,950	7,000	496	2,372	2,790	3,139	496	2,372	2,790	3,139
7,000	7,050	496	2,389	2,810	3,161	496	2,389	2,810	3,161
7,050	7,100	496	2,406	2,830	3,184	496	2,406	2,830	3,184
7,100	7,150	496	2,423	2,850	3,206	496	2,423	2,850	3,206
7,150	7,200	496	2,440	2,870	3,229	496	2,440	2,870	3,229
7,200	7,250	496	2,457	2,890	3,251	496	2,457	2,890	3,251
7,250	7,300	496	2,474	2,910	3,274	496	2,474	2,910	3,274
7,300	7,350	496	2,491	2,930	3,296	496	2,491	2,930	3,296
7,350	7,400	496	2,508	2,950	3,319	496	2,508	2,950	3,319
7,400	7,450	496	2,525	2,970	3,341	496	2,525	2,970	3,341
7,450	7,500	496	2,542	2,990	3,364	496	2,542	2,990	3,364
7,500	7,550	496	2,559	3,010	3,386	496	2,559	3,010	3,386
7,550	7,600	496	2,576	3,030	3,409	496	2,576	3,030	3,409
7,600	7,650	496	2,593	3,050	3,431	496	2,593	3,050	3,431
7,650	7,700	496	2,610	3,070	3,454	496	2,610	3,070	3,454
7,700	7,750	496	2,627	3,090	3,476	496	2,627	3,090	3,476
7,750	7,800	496	2,644	3,110	3,499	496	2,644	3,110	3,499
7,800	7,850	496	2,661	3,130	3,521	496	2,661	3,130	3,521
7,850	7,900	496	2,678	3,150	3,544	496	2,678	3,150	3,544
7,900	7,950	496	2,695	3,170	3,566	496	2,695	3,170	3,566
7,950	8,000	496	2,712	3,190	3,589	496	2,712	3,190	3,589
8,000	8,050	496	2,729	3,210	3,611	496	2,729	3,210	3,611
8,050	8,100	496	2,746	3,230	3,634	496	2,746	3,230	3,634
8,100	8,150	496	2,763	3,250	3,656	496	2,763	3,250	3,656
8,150	8,200	491	2,780	3,270	3,679	496	2,780	3,270	3,679
8,200	8,250	487	2,797	3,290	3,701	496	2,797	3,290	3,701
8,250	8,300	483	2,814	3,310	3,724	496	2,814	3,310	3,724
8,300	8,350	479	2,831	3,330	3,746	496	2,831	3,330	3,746
8,350	8,400	475	2,848	3,350	3,769	496	2,848	3,350	3,769
8,400	8,450	472	2,865	3,370	3,791	496	2,865	3,370	3,791
8,450	8,500	468	2,882	3,390	3,814	496	2,882	3,390	3,814
8,500	8,550	464	2,899	3,410	3,836	496	2,899	3,410	3,836
8,550	8,600	460	2,916	3,430	3,859	496	2,916	3,430	3,859
8,600	8,650	456	2,933	3,450	3,881	496	2,933	3,450	3,881
8,650	8,700	452	2,950	3,470	3,904	496	2,950	3,470	3,904
8,700	8,750	449	2,967	3,490	3,926	496	2,967	3,490	3,926
8,750	8,800	445	2,984	3,510	3,949	496	2,984	3,510	3,949
8,800	8,850	441	3,001	3,530	3,971	496	3,001	3,530	3,971
8,850	8,900	437	3,018	3,550	3,994	496	3,018	3,550	3,994
8,900	8,950	433	3,035	3,570	4,016	496	3,035	3,570	4,016
8,950	9,000	430	3,052	3,590	4,039	496	3,052	3,590	4,039
9,000	9,050	426	3,069	3,610	4,061	496	3,069	3,610	4,061
9,050	9,100	422	3,086	3,630	4,084	496	3,086	3,630	4,084
9,100	9,150	418	3,103	3,650	4,106	496	3,103	3,650	4,106
9,150	9,200	414	3,120	3,670	4,129	496	3,120	3,670	4,129
9,200	9,250	410	3,137	3,690	4,151	496	3,137	3,690	4,151
9,250	9,300	407	3,154	3,710	4,174	496	3,154	3,710	4,174
9,300	9,350	403	3,171	3,730	4,196	496	3,171	3,730	4,196
9,350	9,400	399	3,188	3,750	4,219	496	3,188	3,750	4,219
9,400	9,450	395	3,205	3,770	4,241	496	3,205	3,770	4,241
9,450	9,500	391	3,222	3,790	4,264	496	3,222	3,790	4,264
9,500	9,550	387	3,239	3,810	4,286	496	3,239	3,810	4,286
9,550	9,600	384	3,256	3,830	4,309	496	3,256	3,830	4,309
9,600	9,650	380	3,273	3,850	4,331	496	3,273	3,850	4,331
9,650	9,700	376	3,290	3,870	4,354	408	3,290	3,870	4,354
9,700	9,750	372	3,305	3,890	4,376	496	3,305	3,890	4,376
9,750	9,800	368	3,305	3,910	4,399	496	3,305	3,910	4,399
9,800	9,850	365	3,305	3,930	4,421	496	3,305	3,930	4,421
9,850	9,900	361	3,305	3,950	4,444	496	3,305	3,950	4,444
9,900	9,950	357	3,305	3,970	4,466	496	3,305	3,970	4,466
9,950	10,000	353	3,305	3,990	4,489	496	3,305	3,990	4,489
10,000	10,050	349	3,305	4,010	4,511	496	3,305	4,010	4,511
10,050	10,100	345	3,305	4,030	4,534	496	3,305	4,030	4,534
10,100	10,150	342	3,305	4,050	4,556	496	3,305	4,050	4,556
10,150	10,200	338	3,305	4,070	4,579	496	3,305	4,070	4,579
10,200	10,250	334	3,305	4,090	4,601	496	3,305	4,090	4,601
10,250	10,300	330	3,305	4,110	4,624	496	3,305	4,110	4,624
10,300	10,350	326	3,305	4,130	4,646	496	3,305	4,130	4,646
10,350	10,400	322	3,305	4,150	4,669	496	3,305	4,150	4,669
10,400	10,450	319	3,305	4,170	4,691	496	3,305	4,170	4,691
10,450	10,500	315	3,305	4,190	4,714	496	3,305	4,190	4,714
10,500	10,550	311	3,305	4,210	4,736	496	3,305	4,210	4,736
10,550	10,600	307	3,305	4,230	4,759	496	3,305	4,230	4,759
10,600	10,650	303	3,305	4,250	4,781	496	3,305	4,250	4,781
10,650	10,700	299	3,305	4,270	4,804	496	3,305	4,270	4,804
10,700	10,750	296	3,305	4,290	4,826	496	3,305	4,290	4,826
10,750	10,800	292	3,305	4,310	4,849	496	3,305	4,310	4,849
10,800	10,850	288	3,305	4,330	4,871	496	3,305	4,330	4,871
10,850	10,900	284	3,305	4,350	4,894	496	3,305	4,350	4,894
10,900	10,950	280	3,305	4,370	4,916	496	3,305	4,370	4,916
10,950	11,000	277	3,305	4,390	4,939	496	3,305	4,390	4,939
11,000	11,050	273	3,305	4,410	4,961	496	3,305	4,410	4,961
11,050	11,100	269	3,305	4,430	4,984	496	3,305	4,430	4,984
11,100	11,150	265	3,305	4,450	5,006	496	3,305	4,450	5,006
11,150	11,200	261	3,305	4,470	5,029	496	3,305	4,470	5,029
11,200	11,250	257	3,305	4,490	5,051	496	3,305	4,490	5,051
11,250	11,300	254	3,305	4,510	5,074	496	3,305	4,510	5,074
11,300	11,350	250	3,305	4,530	5,096	496	3,305	4,530	5,096
11,350	11,400	246	3,305	4,550	5,119	496	3,305	4,550	5,119
11,400	11,450	242	3,305	4,570	5,141	496	3,305	4,570	5,141
11,450	11,500	238	3,305	4,590	5,164	496	3,305	4,590	5,164
11,500	11,550	234	3,305	4,610	5,186	496	3,305	4,610	5,186
11,550	11,600	231	3,305	4,630	5,209	496	3,305	4,630	5,209
11,600	11,650	227	3,305	4,650	5,231	496	3,305	4,650	5,231
11,650	11,700	223	3,305	4,670	5,254	496	3,305	4,670	5,254
11,700	11,750	219	3,305	4,690	5,276	496	3,305	4,690	5,276
11,750	11,800	215	3,305	4,710	5,299	496	3,305	4,710	5,299
11,800	11,850	212	3,305	4,730	5,321	496	3,305	4,730	5,321
11,850	11,900	208	3,305	4,750	5,344	496	3,305	4,750	5,344
11,900	11,950	204	3,305	4,770	5,366	496	3,305	4,770	5,366
11,950	12,000	200	3,305	4,790	5,389	496	3,305	4,790	5,389
12,000	12,050	196	3,305	4,810	5,411	496	3,305	4,810	5,411
12,050	12,100	192	3,305	4,830	5,434	496	3,305	4,830	5,434
12,100	12,150	189	3,305	4,850	5,456	496	3,305	4,850	5,456
12,150	12,200	185	3,305	4,870	5,479	496	3,305	4,870	5,479
12,200	12,250	181	3,305	4,890	5,501	496	3,305	4,890	5,501
12,250	12,300	177	3,305	4,910	5,524	496	3,305	4,910	5,524
12,300	12,350	173	3,305	4,930	5,546	496	3,305	4,930	5,546
12,350	12,400	169	3,305	4,950	5,569	496	3,305	4,950	5,569
12,400	12,450	166	3,305	4,970	5,591	496	3,305	4,970	5,591
12,450	12,500	162	3,305	4,990	5,614	496	3,305	4,990	5,614
12,500	12,550	158	3,305	5,010	5,636	496	3,305	5,010	5,636
12,550	12,600	154	3,305	5,030	5,659	496	3,305	5,030	5,659
12,600	12,650	150	3,305	5,050	5,681	496	3,305	5,050	5,681
12,650	12,700	146	3,305	5,070	5,704	496	3,305	5,070	5,704
12,700	12,750	143	3,305	5,090	5,726	496	3,305	5,090	5,726
12,750	12,800	139	3,305	5,110	5,749	496	3,305	5,110	5,749

(Continued)

Earned Income Credit (EIC) Table - *Continued*

(**Caution.** This is **not** a tax table.)

If the amount you are looking up from the worksheet is—		Single, head of household, or qualifying widow(er) and the number of children you have is—				Married filing jointly and the number of children you have is—			
At least	But less than	0	1	2	3	0	1	2	3
		Your credit is—				Your credit is—			
12,800	12,850	135	3,305	5,130	5,771	496	3,305	5,130	5,771
12,850	12,900	131	3,305	5,150	5,794	496	3,305	5,150	5,794
12,900	12,950	127	3,305	5,170	5,816	496	3,305	5,170	5,816
12,950	13,000	124	3,305	5,190	5,839	496	3,305	5,190	5,839
13,000	13,050	120	3,305	5,210	5,861	496	3,305	5,210	5,861
13,050	13,100	116	3,305	5,230	5,884	496	3,305	5,230	5,884
13,100	13,150	112	3,305	5,250	5,906	496	3,305	5,250	5,906
13,150	13,200	108	3,305	5,270	5,929	496	3,305	5,270	5,929
13,200	13,250	104	3,305	5,290	5,951	496	3,305	5,290	5,951
13,250	13,300	101	3,305	5,310	5,974	496	3,305	5,310	5,974
13,300	13,350	97	3,305	5,330	5,996	496	3,305	5,330	5,996
13,350	13,400	93	3,305	5,350	6,019	496	3,305	5,350	6,019
13,400	13,450	89	3,305	5,370	6,041	496	3,305	5,370	6,041
13,450	13,500	85	3,305	5,390	6,064	496	3,305	5,390	6,064
13,500	13,550	81	3,305	5,410	6,086	496	3,305	5,410	6,086
13,550	13,600	78	3,305	5,430	6,109	493	3,305	5,430	6,109
13,600	13,650	74	3,305	5,450	6,131	489	3,305	5,450	6,131
13,650	13,700	70	3,305	5,460	6,143	485	3,305	5,460	6,143
13,700	13,750	66	3,305	5,460	6,143	482	3,305	5,460	6,143
13,750	13,800	62	3,305	5,460	6,143	478	3,305	5,460	6,143
13,800	13,850	59	3,305	5,460	6,143	474	3,305	5,460	6,143
13,850	13,900	55	3,305	5,460	6,143	470	3,305	5,460	6,143
13,900	13,950	51	3,305	5,460	6,143	466	3,305	5,460	6,143
13,950	14,000	47	3,305	5,460	6,143	462	3,305	5,460	6,143
14,000	14,050	43	3,305	5,460	6,143	459	3,305	5,460	6,143
14,050	14,100	39	3,305	5,460	6,143	455	3,305	5,460	6,143
14,100	14,150	36	3,305	5,460	6,143	451	3,305	5,460	6,143
14,150	14,200	32	3,305	5,460	6,143	447	3,305	5,460	6,143
14,200	14,250	28	3,305	5,460	6,143	443	3,305	5,460	6,143
14,250	14,300	24	3,305	5,460	6,143	439	3,305	5,460	6,143
14,300	14,350	20	3,305	5,460	6,143	436	3,305	5,460	6,143
14,350	14,400	16	3,305	5,460	6,143	432	3,305	5,460	6,143
14,400	14,450	13	3,305	5,460	6,143	428	3,305	5,460	6,143
14,450	14,500	9	3,305	5,460	6,143	424	3,305	5,460	6,143
14,500	14,550	5	3,305	5,460	6,143	420	3,305	5,460	6,143
14,550	14,600	*	3,305	5,460	6,143	417	3,305	5,460	6,143
14,600	14,650	0	3,305	5,460	6,143	413	3,305	5,460	6,143
14,650	14,700	0	3,305	5,460	6,143	409	3,305	5,460	6,143
14,700	14,750	0	3,305	5,460	6,143	405	3,305	5,460	6,143
14,750	14,800	0	3,305	5,460	6,143	401	3,305	5,460	6,143
14,800	14,850	0	3,305	5,460	6,143	397	3,305	5,460	6,143
14,850	14,900	0	3,305	5,460	6,143	394	3,305	5,460	6,143
14,900	14,950	0	3,305	5,460	6,143	390	3,305	5,460	6,143
14,950	15,000	0	3,305	5,460	6,143	386	3,305	5,460	6,143
15,000	15,050	0	3,305	5,460	6,143	382	3,305	5,460	6,143
15,050	15,100	0	3,305	5,460	6,143	378	3,305	5,460	6,143
15,100	15,150	0	3,305	5,460	6,143	374	3,305	5,460	6,143
15,150	15,200	0	3,305	5,460	6,143	371	3,305	5,460	6,143
15,200	15,250	0	3,305	5,460	6,143	367	3,305	5,460	6,143
15,250	15,300	0	3,305	5,460	6,143	363	3,305	5,460	6,143
15,300	15,350	0	3,305	5,460	6,143	359	3,305	5,460	6,143
15,350	15,400	0	3,305	5,460	6,143	355	3,305	5,460	6,143
15,400	15,450	0	3,305	5,460	6,143	352	3,305	5,460	6,143
15,450	15,500	0	3,305	5,460	6,143	348	3,305	5,460	6,143
15,500	15,550	0	3,305	5,460	6,143	344	3,305	5,460	6,143
15,550	15,600	0	3,305	5,460	6,143	340	3,305	5,460	6,143
15,600	15,650	0	3,305	5,460	6,143	336	3,305	5,460	6,143
15,650	15,700	0	3,305	5,460	6,143	332	3,305	5,460	6,143
15,700	15,750	0	3,305	5,460	6,143	329	3,305	5,460	6,143
15,750	15,800	0	3,305	5,460	6,143	325	3,305	5,460	6,143
15,800	15,850	0	3,305	5,460	6,143	321	3,305	5,460	6,143
15,850	15,900	0	3,305	5,460	6,143	317	3,305	5,460	6,143
15,900	15,950	0	3,305	5,460	6,143	313	3,305	5,460	6,143
15,950	16,000	0	3,305	5,460	6,143	309	3,305	5,460	6,143

If the amount you are looking up from the worksheet is—		Single, head of household, or qualifying widow(er) and the number of children you have is—				Married filing jointly and the number of children you have is—			
At least	But less than	0	1	2	3	0	1	2	3
		Your credit is—				Your credit is—			
16,000	16,050	0	3,305	5,460	6,143	306	3,305	5,460	6,143
16,050	16,100	0	3,305	5,460	6,143	302	3,305	5,460	6,143
16,100	16,150	0	3,305	5,460	6,143	298	3,305	5,460	6,143
16,150	16,200	0	3,305	5,460	6,143	294	3,305	5,460	6,143
16,200	16,250	0	3,305	5,460	6,143	290	3,305	5,460	6,143
16,250	16,300	0	3,305	5,460	6,143	286	3,305	5,460	6,143
16,300	16,350	0	3,305	5,460	6,143	283	3,305	5,460	6,143
16,350	16,400	0	3,305	5,460	6,143	279	3,305	5,460	6,143
16,400	16,450	0	3,305	5,460	6,143	275	3,305	5,460	6,143
16,450	16,500	0	3,305	5,460	6,143	271	3,305	5,460	6,143
16,500	16,550	0	3,305	5,460	6,143	267	3,305	5,460	6,143
16,550	16,600	0	3,305	5,460	6,143	264	3,305	5,460	6,143
16,600	16,650	0	3,305	5,460	6,143	260	3,305	5,460	6,143
16,650	16,700	0	3,305	5,460	6,143	256	3,305	5,460	6,143
16,700	16,750	0	3,305	5,460	6,143	252	3,305	5,460	6,143
16,750	16,800	0	3,305	5,460	6,143	248	3,305	5,460	6,143
16,800	16,850	0	3,305	5,460	6,143	244	3,305	5,460	6,143
16,850	16,900	0	3,305	5,460	6,143	241	3,305	5,460	6,143
16,900	16,950	0	3,305	5,460	6,143	237	3,305	5,460	6,143
16,950	17,000	0	3,305	5,460	6,143	233	3,305	5,460	6,143
17,000	17,050	0	3,305	5,460	6,143	229	3,305	5,460	6,143
17,050	17,100	0	3,305	5,460	6,143	225	3,305	5,460	6,143
17,100	17,150	0	3,305	5,460	6,143	221	3,305	5,460	6,143
17,150	17,200	0	3,305	5,460	6,143	218	3,305	5,460	6,143
17,200	17,250	0	3,305	5,460	6,143	214	3,305	5,460	6,143
17,250	17,300	0	3,305	5,460	6,143	210	3,305	5,460	6,143
17,300	17,350	0	3,305	5,460	6,143	206	3,305	5,460	6,143
17,350	17,400	0	3,305	5,460	6,143	202	3,305	5,460	6,143
17,400	17,450	0	3,305	5,460	6,143	199	3,305	5,460	6,143
17,450	17,500	0	3,305	5,460	6,143	195	3,305	5,460	6,143
17,500	17,550	0	3,305	5,460	6,143	191	3,305	5,460	6,143
17,550	17,600	0	3,305	5,460	6,143	187	3,305	5,460	6,143
17,600	17,650	0	3,305	5,460	6,143	183	3,305	5,460	6,143
17,650	17,700	0	3,305	5,460	6,143	179	3,305	5,460	6,143
17,700	17,750	0	3,305	5,460	6,143	176	3,305	5,460	6,143
17,750	17,800	0	3,305	5,460	6,143	172	3,305	5,460	6,143
17,800	17,850	0	3,305	5,460	6,143	168	3,305	5,460	6,143
17,850	17,900	0	3,298	5,451	6,133	164	3,305	5,460	6,143
17,900	17,950	0	3,290	5,440	6,122	160	3,305	5,460	6,143
17,950	18,000	0	3,282	5,429	6,112	156	3,305	5,460	6,143
18,000	18,050	0	3,274	5,419	6,101	153	3,305	5,460	6,143
18,050	18,100	0	3,266	5,408	6,091	149	3,305	5,460	6,143
18,100	18,150	0	3,258	5,398	6,080	145	3,305	5,460	6,143
18,150	18,200	0	3,250	5,387	6,070	141	3,305	5,460	6,143
18,200	18,250	0	3,242	5,377	6,059	137	3,305	5,460	6,143
18,250	18,300	0	3,234	5,366	6,049	133	3,305	5,460	6,143
18,300	18,350	0	3,226	5,356	6,038	130	3,305	5,460	6,143
18,350	18,400	0	3,218	5,345	6,028	126	3,305	5,460	6,143
18,400	18,450	0	3,210	5,335	6,017	122	3,305	5,460	6,143
18,450	18,500	0	3,202	5,324	6,007	118	3,305	5,460	6,143
18,500	18,550	0	3,194	5,314	5,996	114	3,305	5,460	6,143
18,550	18,600	0	3,186	5,303	5,986	111	3,305	5,460	6,143
18,600	18,650	0	3,178	5,293	5,975	107	3,305	5,460	6,143
18,650	18,700	0	3,170	5,282	5,965	103	3,305	5,460	6,143
18,700	18,750	0	3,162	5,272	5,954	99	3,305	5,460	6,143
18,750	18,800	0	3,154	5,261	5,943	95	3,305	5,460	6,143
18,800	18,850	0	3,146	5,250	5,933	91	3,305	5,460	6,143
18,850	18,900	0	3,138	5,240	5,922	88	3,305	5,460	6,143
18,900	18,950	0	3,130	5,229	5,912	84	3,305	5,460	6,143
18,950	19,000	0	3,122	5,219	5,901	80	3,305	5,460	6,143
19,000	19,050	0	3,114	5,208	5,891	76	3,305	5,460	6,143
19,050	19,100	0	3,106	5,198	5,880	72	3,305	5,460	6,143
19,100	19,150	0	3,098	5,187	5,870	68	3,305	5,460	6,143
19,150	19,200	0	3,090	5,177	5,859	65	3,305	5,460	6,143

* If the amount you are looking up from the worksheet is at least $14,550 but less than $14,590, and you have no qualifying children, your credit is $2. If the amount you are looking up from the worksheet is $14,590 or more, and you have no qualifying children, you cannot take the credit.

(Continued)

Earned Income Credit (EIC) Table - *Continued*

(**Caution.** This is **not** a tax table.)

If the amount you are looking up from the worksheet is–		And your filing status is– Single, head of household, or qualifying widow(er) and the number of children you have is–				Married filing jointly and the number of children you have is–			
		0	1	2	3	0	1	2	3
At least	But less than	Your credit is–				Your credit is–			
19,200	19,250	0	3,082	5,166	5,849	61	3,305	5,460	6,143
19,250	19,300	0	3,074	5,156	5,838	57	3,305	5,460	6,143
19,300	19,350	0	3,066	5,145	5,828	53	3,305	5,460	6,143
19,350	19,400	0	3,058	5,135	5,817	49	3,305	5,460	6,143
19,400	19,450	0	3,050	5,124	5,807	46	3,305	5,460	6,143
19,450	19,500	0	3,042	5,114	5,796	42	3,305	5,460	6,143
19,500	19,550	0	3,034	5,103	5,786	38	3,305	5,460	6,143
19,550	19,600	0	3,026	5,093	5,775	34	3,305	5,460	6,143
19,600	19,650	0	3,018	5,082	5,764	30	3,305	5,460	6,143
19,650	19,700	0	3,010	5,071	5,754	26	3,305	5,460	6,143
19,700	19,750	0	3,002	5,061	5,743	23	3,305	5,460	6,143
19,750	19,800	0	2,994	5,050	5,733	19	3,305	5,460	6,143
19,800	19,850	0	2,986	5,040	5,722	15	3,305	5,460	6,143
19,850	19,900	0	2,978	5,029	5,712	11	3,305	5,460	6,143
19,900	19,950	0	2,970	5,019	5,701	7	3,305	5,460	6,143
19,950	20,000	0	2,962	5,008	5,691	3	3,305	5,460	6,143
20,000	20,050	0	2,954	4,998	5,680	*	3,305	5,460	6,143
20,050	20,100	0	2,946	4,987	5,670	0	3,305	5,460	6,143
20,100	20,150	0	2,938	4,977	5,659	0	3,305	5,460	6,143
20,150	20,200	0	2,930	4,966	5,649	0	3,305	5,460	6,143
20,200	20,250	0	2,922	4,956	5,638	0	3,305	5,460	6,143
20,250	20,300	0	2,914	4,945	5,628	0	3,305	5,460	6,143
20,300	20,350	0	2,906	4,935	5,617	0	3,305	5,460	6,143
20,350	20,400	0	2,898	4,924	5,607	0	3,305	5,460	6,143
20,400	20,450	0	2,890	4,913	5,596	0	3,305	5,460	6,143
20,450	20,500	0	2,882	4,903	5,585	0	3,305	5,460	6,143
20,500	20,550	0	2,874	4,892	5,575	0	3,305	5,460	6,143
20,550	20,600	0	2,866	4,882	5,564	0	3,305	5,460	6,143
20,600	20,650	0	2,858	4,871	5,554	0	3,305	5,460	6,143
20,650	20,700	0	2,850	4,861	5,543	0	3,305	5,460	6,143
20,700	20,750	0	2,842	4,850	5,533	0	3,305	5,460	6,143
20,750	20,800	0	2,834	4,840	5,522	0	3,305	5,460	6,143
20,800	20,850	0	2,826	4,829	5,512	0	3,305	5,460	6,143
20,850	20,900	0	2,818	4,819	5,501	0	3,305	5,460	6,143
20,900	20,950	0	2,810	4,808	5,491	0	3,305	5,460	6,143
20,950	21,000	0	2,802	4,798	5,480	0	3,305	5,460	6,143
21,000	21,050	0	2,794	4,787	5,470	0	3,305	5,460	6,143
21,050	21,100	0	2,786	4,777	5,459	0	3,305	5,460	6,143
21,100	21,150	0	2,778	4,766	5,449	0	3,305	5,460	6,143
21,150	21,200	0	2,770	4,756	5,438	0	3,305	5,460	6,143
21,200	21,250	0	2,762	4,745	5,428	0	3,305	5,460	6,143
21,250	21,300	0	2,754	4,734	5,417	0	3,305	5,460	6,143
21,300	21,350	0	2,746	4,724	5,406	0	3,305	5,460	6,143
21,350	21,400	0	2,738	4,713	5,396	0	3,305	5,460	6,143
21,400	21,450	0	2,730	4,703	5,385	0	3,305	5,460	6,143
21,450	21,500	0	2,722	4,692	5,375	0	3,305	5,460	6,143
21,500	21,550	0	2,714	4,682	5,364	0	3,305	5,460	6,143
21,550	21,600	0	2,706	4,671	5,354	0	3,305	5,460	6,143
21,600	21,650	0	2,698	4,661	5,343	0	3,305	5,460	6,143
21,650	21,700	0	2,690	4,650	5,333	0	3,305	5,460	6,143
21,700	21,750	0	2,682	4,640	5,322	0	3,305	5,460	6,143
21,750	21,800	0	2,674	4,629	5,312	0	3,305	5,460	6,143
21,800	21,850	0	2,666	4,619	5,301	0	3,305	5,460	6,143
21,850	21,900	0	2,658	4,608	5,291	0	3,305	5,460	6,143
21,900	21,950	0	2,650	4,598	5,280	0	3,305	5,460	6,143
21,950	22,000	0	2,642	4,587	5,270	0	3,305	5,460	6,143
22,000	22,050	0	2,634	4,577	5,259	0	3,305	5,460	6,143
22,050	22,100	0	2,626	4,566	5,249	0	3,305	5,460	6,143
22,100	22,150	0	2,618	4,555	5,238	0	3,305	5,460	6,143
22,150	22,200	0	2,610	4,545	5,227	0	3,305	5,460	6,143
22,200	22,250	0	2,602	4,534	5,217	0	3,305	5,460	6,143
22,250	22,300	0	2,594	4,524	5,206	0	3,305	5,460	6,143
22,300	22,350	0	2,586	4,513	5,196	0	3,305	5,460	6,143
22,350	22,400	0	2,579	4,503	5,185	0	3,305	5,460	6,143

If the amount you are looking up from the worksheet is–		And your filing status is– Single, head of household, or qualifying widow(er) and the number of children you have is–				Married filing jointly and the number of children you have is–			
		0	1	2	3	0	1	2	3
At least	But less than	Your credit is–				Your credit is–			
22,400	22,450	0	2,571	4,492	5,175	0	3,305	5,460	6,143
22,450	22,500	0	2,563	4,482	5,164	0	3,305	5,460	6,143
22,500	22,550	0	2,555	4,471	5,154	0	3,305	5,460	6,143
22,550	22,600	0	2,547	4,461	5,143	0	3,305	5,460	6,143
22,600	22,650	0	2,539	4,450	5,133	0	3,305	5,460	6,143
22,650	22,700	0	2,531	4,440	5,122	0	3,305	5,460	6,143
22,700	22,750	0	2,523	4,429	5,112	0	3,305	5,460	6,143
22,750	22,800	0	2,515	4,419	5,101	0	3,305	5,460	6,143
22,800	22,850	0	2,507	4,408	5,091	0	3,305	5,460	6,143
22,850	22,900	0	2,499	4,398	5,080	0	3,305	5,460	6,143
22,900	22,950	0	2,491	4,387	5,069	0	3,305	5,460	6,143
22,950	23,000	0	2,483	4,376	5,059	0	3,305	5,460	6,143
23,000	23,050	0	2,475	4,366	5,048	0	3,305	5,460	6,143
23,050	23,100	0	2,467	4,355	5,038	0	3,305	5,460	6,143
23,100	23,150	0	2,459	4,345	5,027	0	3,305	5,460	6,143
23,150	23,200	0	2,451	4,334	5,017	0	3,305	5,460	6,143
23,200	23,250	0	2,443	4,324	5,006	0	3,305	5,460	6,143
23,250	23,300	0	2,435	4,313	4,996	0	3,305	5,460	6,143
23,300	23,350	0	2,427	4,303	4,985	0	3,294	5,446	6,129
23,350	23,400	0	2,419	4,292	4,975	0	3,286	5,436	6,118
23,400	23,450	0	2,411	4,282	4,964	0	3,278	5,425	6,108
23,450	23,500	0	2,403	4,271	4,954	0	3,270	5,415	6,097
23,500	23,550	0	2,395	4,261	4,943	0	3,262	5,404	6,087
23,550	23,600	0	2,387	4,250	4,933	0	3,254	5,394	6,076
23,600	23,650	0	2,379	4,240	4,922	0	3,246	5,383	6,066
23,650	23,700	0	2,371	4,229	4,912	0	3,238	5,373	6,055
23,700	23,750	0	2,363	4,219	4,901	0	3,230	5,362	6,045
23,750	23,800	0	2,355	4,208	4,890	0	3,223	5,352	6,034
23,800	23,850	0	2,347	4,197	4,880	0	3,215	5,341	6,024
23,850	23,900	0	2,339	4,187	4,869	0	3,207	5,330	6,013
23,900	23,950	0	2,331	4,176	4,859	0	3,199	5,320	6,002
23,950	24,000	0	2,323	4,166	4,848	0	3,191	5,309	5,992
24,000	24,050	0	2,315	4,155	4,838	0	3,183	5,299	5,981
24,050	24,100	0	2,307	4,145	4,827	0	3,175	5,288	5,971
24,100	24,150	0	2,299	4,134	4,817	0	3,167	5,278	5,960
24,150	24,200	0	2,291	4,124	4,806	0	3,159	5,267	5,950
24,200	24,250	0	2,283	4,113	4,796	0	3,151	5,257	5,939
24,250	24,300	0	2,275	4,103	4,785	0	3,143	5,246	5,929
24,300	24,350	0	2,267	4,092	4,775	0	3,135	5,236	5,918
24,350	24,400	0	2,259	4,082	4,764	0	3,127	5,225	5,908
24,400	24,450	0	2,251	4,071	4,754	0	3,119	5,215	5,897
24,450	24,500	0	2,243	4,061	4,743	0	3,111	5,204	5,887
24,500	24,550	0	2,235	4,050	4,733	0	3,103	5,194	5,876
24,550	24,600	0	2,227	4,040	4,722	0	3,095	5,183	5,866
24,600	24,650	0	2,219	4,029	4,711	0	3,087	5,173	5,855
24,650	24,700	0	2,211	4,018	4,701	0	3,079	5,162	5,845
24,700	24,750	0	2,203	4,008	4,690	0	3,071	5,151	5,834
24,750	24,800	0	2,195	3,997	4,680	0	3,063	5,141	5,823
24,800	24,850	0	2,187	3,987	4,669	0	3,055	5,130	5,813
24,850	24,900	0	2,179	3,976	4,659	0	3,047	5,120	5,802
24,900	24,950	0	2,171	3,966	4,648	0	3,039	5,109	5,792
24,950	25,000	0	2,163	3,955	4,638	0	3,031	5,099	5,781
25,000	25,050	0	2,155	3,945	4,627	0	3,023	5,088	5,771
25,050	25,100	0	2,147	3,934	4,617	0	3,015	5,078	5,760
25,100	25,150	0	2,139	3,924	4,606	0	3,007	5,067	5,750
25,150	25,200	0	2,131	3,913	4,596	0	2,999	5,057	5,739
25,200	25,250	0	2,123	3,903	4,585	0	2,991	5,046	5,729
25,250	25,300	0	2,115	3,892	4,575	0	2,983	5,036	5,718
25,300	25,350	0	2,107	3,882	4,564	0	2,975	5,025	5,708
25,350	25,400	0	2,099	3,871	4,554	0	2,967	5,015	5,697
25,400	25,450	0	2,091	3,860	4,543	0	2,959	5,004	5,687
25,450	25,500	0	2,083	3,850	4,532	0	2,951	4,994	5,676
25,500	25,550	0	2,075	3,839	4,522	0	2,943	4,983	5,665
25,550	25,600	0	2,067	3,829	4,511	0	2,935	4,972	5,655

* If the amount you are looking up from the worksheet is at least $20,000 but less than $20,020, and you have no qualifying children, your credit is $1.
If the amount you are looking up from the worksheet is $20,020 or more, and you have no qualifying children, you cannot take the credit.

(Continued)

Earned Income Credit (EIC) Table - Continued

If the amount you are looking up from the worksheet is–		Single, head of household, or qualifying widow(er) and the number of children you have is–				Married filing jointly and the number of children you have is–			
At least	But less than	0	1	2	3	0	1	2	3
		Your credit is–				Your credit is–			
25,600	25,650	0	2,059	3,818	4,501	0	2,927	4,962	5,644
25,650	25,700	0	2,051	3,808	4,490	0	2,919	4,951	5,634
25,700	25,750	0	2,043	3,797	4,480	0	2,911	4,941	5,623
25,750	25,800	0	2,035	3,787	4,469	0	2,903	4,930	5,613
25,800	25,850	0	2,027	3,776	4,459	0	2,895	4,920	5,602
25,850	25,900	0	2,019	3,766	4,448	0	2,887	4,909	5,592
25,900	25,950	0	2,011	3,755	4,438	0	2,879	4,899	5,581
25,950	26,000	0	2,003	3,745	4,427	0	2,871	4,888	5,571
26,000	26,050	0	1,995	3,734	4,417	0	2,863	4,878	5,560
26,050	26,100	0	1,987	3,724	4,406	0	2,855	4,867	5,550
26,100	26,150	0	1,979	3,713	4,396	0	2,847	4,857	5,539
26,150	26,200	0	1,971	3,703	4,385	0	2,839	4,846	5,529
26,200	26,250	0	1,963	3,692	4,375	0	2,831	4,836	5,518
26,250	26,300	0	1,955	3,681	4,364	0	2,823	4,825	5,508
26,300	26,350	0	1,947	3,671	4,353	0	2,815	4,815	5,497
26,350	26,400	0	1,939	3,660	4,343	0	2,807	4,804	5,486
26,400	26,450	0	1,931	3,650	4,332	0	2,799	4,793	5,476
26,450	26,500	0	1,923	3,639	4,322	0	2,791	4,783	5,465
26,500	26,550	0	1,915	3,629	4,311	0	2,783	4,772	5,455
26,550	26,600	0	1,907	3,618	4,301	0	2,775	4,762	5,444
26,600	26,650	0	1,899	3,608	4,290	0	2,767	4,751	5,434
26,650	26,700	0	1,891	3,597	4,280	0	2,759	4,741	5,423
26,700	26,750	0	1,883	3,587	4,269	0	2,751	4,730	5,413
26,750	26,800	0	1,875	3,576	4,259	0	2,743	4,720	5,402
26,800	26,850	0	1,867	3,566	4,248	0	2,735	4,709	5,392
26,850	26,900	0	1,859	3,555	4,238	0	2,727	4,699	5,381
26,900	26,950	0	1,851	3,545	4,227	0	2,719	4,688	5,371
26,950	27,000	0	1,843	3,534	4,217	0	2,711	4,678	5,360
27,000	27,050	0	1,835	3,524	4,206	0	2,703	4,667	5,350
27,050	27,100	0	1,827	3,513	4,196	0	2,695	4,657	5,339
27,100	27,150	0	1,819	3,502	4,185	0	2,687	4,646	5,329
27,150	27,200	0	1,811	3,492	4,174	0	2,679	4,636	5,318
27,200	27,250	0	1,803	3,481	4,164	0	2,671	4,625	5,307
27,250	27,300	0	1,795	3,471	4,153	0	2,663	4,614	5,297
27,300	27,350	0	1,787	3,460	4,143	0	2,655	4,604	5,286
27,350	27,400	0	1,780	3,450	4,132	0	2,647	4,593	5,276
27,400	27,450	0	1,772	3,439	4,122	0	2,639	4,583	5,265
27,450	27,500	0	1,764	3,429	4,111	0	2,631	4,572	5,255
27,500	27,550	0	1,756	3,418	4,101	0	2,623	4,562	5,244
27,550	27,600	0	1,748	3,408	4,090	0	2,615	4,551	5,234
27,600	27,650	0	1,740	3,397	4,080	0	2,607	4,541	5,223
27,650	27,700	0	1,732	3,387	4,069	0	2,599	4,530	5,213
27,700	27,750	0	1,724	3,376	4,059	0	2,591	4,520	5,202
27,750	27,800	0	1,716	3,366	4,048	0	2,583	4,509	5,192
27,800	27,850	0	1,708	3,355	4,038	0	2,575	4,499	5,181
27,850	27,900	0	1,700	3,345	4,027	0	2,567	4,488	5,171
27,900	27,950	0	1,692	3,334	4,016	0	2,559	4,478	5,160
27,950	28,000	0	1,684	3,323	4,006	0	2,551	4,467	5,150
28,000	28,050	0	1,676	3,313	3,995	0	2,543	4,456	5,139
28,050	28,100	0	1,668	3,302	3,985	0	2,535	4,446	5,128
28,100	28,150	0	1,660	3,292	3,974	0	2,527	4,435	5,118
28,150	28,200	0	1,652	3,281	3,964	0	2,519	4,425	5,107
28,200	28,250	0	1,644	3,271	3,953	0	2,511	4,414	5,097
28,250	28,300	0	1,636	3,260	3,943	0	2,503	4,404	5,086
28,300	28,350	0	1,628	3,250	3,932	0	2,495	4,393	5,076
28,350	28,400	0	1,620	3,239	3,922	0	2,487	4,383	5,065
28,400	28,450	0	1,612	3,229	3,911	0	2,479	4,372	5,055
28,450	28,500	0	1,604	3,218	3,901	0	2,471	4,362	5,044
28,500	28,550	0	1,596	3,208	3,890	0	2,463	4,351	5,034
28,550	28,600	0	1,588	3,197	3,880	0	2,455	4,341	5,023
28,600	28,650	0	1,580	3,187	3,869	0	2,447	4,330	5,013
28,650	28,700	0	1,572	3,176	3,859	0	2,439	4,320	5,002
28,700	28,750	0	1,564	3,166	3,848	0	2,431	4,309	4,992
28,750	28,800	0	1,556	3,155	3,837	0	2,424	4,299	4,981
28,800	28,850	0	1,548	3,144	3,827	0	2,416	4,288	4,971
28,850	28,900	0	1,540	3,134	3,816	0	2,408	4,277	4,960
28,900	28,950	0	1,532	3,123	3,806	0	2,400	4,267	4,949
28,950	29,000	0	1,524	3,113	3,795	0	2,392	4,256	4,939
29,000	29,050	0	1,516	3,102	3,785	0	2,384	4,246	4,928
29,050	29,100	0	1,508	3,092	3,774	0	2,376	4,235	4,918
29,100	29,150	0	1,500	3,081	3,764	0	2,368	4,225	4,907
29,150	29,200	0	1,492	3,071	3,753	0	2,360	4,214	4,897
29,200	29,250	0	1,484	3,060	3,743	0	2,352	4,204	4,886
29,250	29,300	0	1,476	3,050	3,732	0	2,344	4,193	4,876
29,300	29,350	0	1,468	3,039	3,722	0	2,336	4,183	4,865
29,350	29,400	0	1,460	3,029	3,711	0	2,328	4,172	4,855
29,400	29,450	0	1,452	3,018	3,701	0	2,320	4,162	4,844
29,450	29,500	0	1,444	3,008	3,690	0	2,312	4,151	4,834
29,500	29,550	0	1,436	2,997	3,680	0	2,304	4,141	4,823
29,550	29,600	0	1,428	2,987	3,669	0	2,296	4,130	4,813
29,600	29,650	0	1,420	2,976	3,658	0	2,288	4,120	4,802
29,650	29,700	0	1,412	2,965	3,648	0	2,280	4,109	4,792
29,700	29,750	0	1,404	2,955	3,637	0	2,272	4,098	4,781
29,750	29,800	0	1,396	2,944	3,627	0	2,264	4,088	4,770
29,800	29,850	0	1,388	2,934	3,616	0	2,256	4,077	4,760
29,850	29,900	0	1,380	2,923	3,606	0	2,248	4,067	4,749
29,900	29,950	0	1,372	2,913	3,595	0	2,240	4,056	4,739
29,950	30,000	0	1,364	2,902	3,585	0	2,232	4,046	4,728
30,000	30,050	0	1,356	2,892	3,574	0	2,224	4,035	4,718
30,050	30,100	0	1,348	2,881	3,564	0	2,216	4,025	4,707
30,100	30,150	0	1,340	2,871	3,553	0	2,208	4,014	4,697
30,150	30,200	0	1,332	2,860	3,543	0	2,200	4,004	4,686
30,200	30,250	0	1,324	2,850	3,532	0	2,192	3,993	4,676
30,250	30,300	0	1,316	2,839	3,522	0	2,184	3,983	4,665
30,300	30,350	0	1,308	2,829	3,511	0	2,176	3,972	4,655
30,350	30,400	0	1,300	2,818	3,501	0	2,168	3,962	4,644
30,400	30,450	0	1,292	2,807	3,490	0	2,160	3,951	4,634
30,450	30,500	0	1,284	2,797	3,479	0	2,152	3,941	4,623
30,500	30,550	0	1,276	2,786	3,469	0	2,144	3,930	4,612
30,550	30,600	0	1,268	2,776	3,458	0	2,136	3,919	4,602
30,600	30,650	0	1,260	2,765	3,448	0	2,128	3,909	4,591
30,650	30,700	0	1,252	2,755	3,437	0	2,120	3,898	4,581
30,700	30,750	0	1,244	2,744	3,427	0	2,112	3,888	4,570
30,750	30,800	0	1,236	2,734	3,416	0	2,104	3,877	4,560
30,800	30,850	0	1,228	2,723	3,406	0	2,096	3,867	4,549
30,850	30,900	0	1,220	2,713	3,395	0	2,088	3,856	4,539
30,900	30,950	0	1,212	2,702	3,385	0	2,080	3,846	4,528
30,950	31,000	0	1,204	2,692	3,374	0	2,072	3,835	4,518
31,000	31,050	0	1,196	2,681	3,364	0	2,064	3,825	4,507
31,050	31,100	0	1,188	2,671	3,353	0	2,056	3,814	4,497
31,100	31,150	0	1,180	2,660	3,343	0	2,048	3,804	4,486
31,150	31,200	0	1,172	2,650	3,332	0	2,040	3,793	4,476
31,200	31,250	0	1,164	2,639	3,322	0	2,032	3,783	4,465
31,250	31,300	0	1,156	2,628	3,311	0	2,024	3,772	4,455
31,300	31,350	0	1,148	2,616	3,300	0	2,016	3,762	4,444
31,350	31,400	0	1,140	2,607	3,290	0	2,008	3,751	4,433
31,400	31,450	0	1,132	2,597	3,279	0	2,000	3,740	4,423
31,450	31,500	0	1,124	2,586	3,269	0	1,992	3,730	4,412
31,500	31,550	0	1,116	2,576	3,258	0	1,984	3,719	4,402
31,550	31,600	0	1,108	2,565	3,248	0	1,976	3,709	4,391
31,600	31,650	0	1,100	2,555	3,237	0	1,968	3,698	4,381
31,650	31,700	0	1,092	2,544	3,227	0	1,960	3,688	4,370
31,700	31,750	0	1,084	2,534	3,216	0	1,952	3,677	4,360
31,750	31,800	0	1,076	2,523	3,206	0	1,944	3,667	4,349
31,800	31,850	0	1,068	2,513	3,195	0	1,936	3,656	4,339
31,850	31,900	0	1,060	2,502	3,185	0	1,928	3,646	4,328
31,900	31,950	0	1,052	2,492	3,174	0	1,920	3,635	4,318
31,950	32,000	0	1,044	2,481	3,164	0	1,912	3,625	4,307
32,000	32,050	0	1,036	2,471	3,153	0	1,904	3,614	4,297
32,050	32,100	0	1,028	2,460	3,143	0	1,896	3,604	4,286
32,100	32,150	0	1,020	2,449	3,132	0	1,888	3,593	4,276
32,150	32,200	0	1,012	2,439	3,121	0	1,880	3,583	4,265
32,200	32,250	0	1,004	2,428	3,111	0	1,872	3,572	4,254
32,250	32,300	0	996	2,418	3,100	0	1,864	3,561	4,244
32,300	32,350	0	988	2,407	3,090	0	1,856	3,551	4,233
32,350	32,400	0	981	2,397	3,079	0	1,848	3,540	4,223
32,400	32,450	0	973	2,386	3,069	0	1,840	3,530	4,212
32,450	32,500	0	965	2,376	3,058	0	1,832	3,519	4,202
32,500	32,550	0	957	2,365	3,048	0	1,824	3,509	4,191
32,550	32,600	0	949	2,355	3,037	0	1,816	3,498	4,181
32,600	32,650	0	941	2,344	3,027	0	1,808	3,488	4,170
32,650	32,700	0	933	2,334	3,016	0	1,800	3,477	4,160
32,700	32,750	0	925	2,323	3,006	0	1,792	3,467	4,149
32,750	32,800	0	917	2,313	2,995	0	1,784	3,456	4,139

(Continued)

Earned Income Credit (EIC) Table - *Continued*

(Caution. This is not a tax table.)

If the amount you are looking up from the worksheet is—		Single, head of household, or qualifying widow(er) and the number of children you have is—				Married filing jointly and the number of children you have is—			
At least	But less than	0	1	2	3	0	1	2	3
		Your credit is—				Your credit is—			
32,800	32,850	0	909	2,302	2,985	0	1,776	3,446	4,128
32,850	32,900	0	901	2,292	2,974	0	1,768	3,435	4,118
32,900	32,950	0	893	2,281	2,963	0	1,760	3,425	4,107
32,950	33,000	0	885	2,270	2,953	0	1,752	3,414	4,097
33,000	33,050	0	877	2,260	2,942	0	1,744	3,403	4,086
33,050	33,100	0	869	2,249	2,932	0	1,736	3,393	4,075
33,100	33,150	0	861	2,239	2,921	0	1,728	3,382	4,065
33,150	33,200	0	853	2,228	2,911	0	1,720	3,372	4,054
33,200	33,250	0	845	2,218	2,900	0	1,712	3,361	4,044
33,250	33,300	0	837	2,207	2,890	0	1,704	3,351	4,033
33,300	33,350	0	829	2,197	2,879	0	1,696	3,340	4,023
33,350	33,400	0	821	2,186	2,869	0	1,688	3,330	4,012
33,400	33,450	0	813	2,176	2,858	0	1,680	3,319	4,002
33,450	33,500	0	805	2,165	2,848	0	1,672	3,309	3,991
33,500	33,550	0	797	2,155	2,837	0	1,664	3,298	3,981
33,550	33,600	0	789	2,144	2,827	0	1,656	3,288	3,970
33,600	33,650	0	781	2,134	2,816	0	1,648	3,277	3,960
33,650	33,700	0	773	2,123	2,806	0	1,640	3,267	3,949
33,700	33,750	0	765	2,113	2,795	0	1,632	3,256	3,939
33,750	33,800	0	757	2,102	2,784	0	1,625	3,246	3,928
33,800	33,850	0	749	2,091	2,774	0	1,617	3,235	3,918
33,850	33,900	0	741	2,081	2,763	0	1,609	3,224	3,907
33,900	33,950	0	733	2,070	2,753	0	1,601	3,214	3,896
33,950	34,000	0	725	2,060	2,742	0	1,593	3,203	3,886
34,000	34,050	0	717	2,049	2,732	0	1,585	3,193	3,875
34,050	34,100	0	709	2,039	2,721	0	1,577	3,182	3,865
34,100	34,150	0	701	2,028	2,711	0	1,569	3,172	3,854
34,150	34,200	0	693	2,018	2,700	0	1,561	3,161	3,844
34,200	34,250	0	685	2,007	2,690	0	1,553	3,151	3,833
34,250	34,300	0	677	1,997	2,679	0	1,545	3,140	3,823
34,300	34,350	0	669	1,986	2,669	0	1,537	3,130	3,812
34,350	34,400	0	661	1,976	2,658	0	1,529	3,119	3,802
34,400	34,450	0	653	1,965	2,648	0	1,521	3,109	3,791
34,450	34,500	0	645	1,955	2,637	0	1,513	3,098	3,781
34,500	34,550	0	637	1,944	2,627	0	1,505	3,088	3,770
34,550	34,600	0	629	1,934	2,616	0	1,497	3,077	3,760
34,600	34,650	0	621	1,923	2,605	0	1,489	3,067	3,749
34,650	34,700	0	613	1,912	2,595	0	1,481	3,056	3,739
34,700	34,750	0	605	1,902	2,584	0	1,473	3,045	3,728
34,750	34,800	0	597	1,891	2,574	0	1,465	3,035	3,717
34,800	34,850	0	589	1,881	2,563	0	1,457	3,024	3,707
34,850	34,900	0	581	1,870	2,553	0	1,449	3,014	3,696
34,900	34,950	0	573	1,860	2,542	0	1,441	3,003	3,686
34,950	35,000	0	565	1,849	2,532	0	1,433	2,993	3,675
35,000	35,050	0	557	1,839	2,521	0	1,425	2,982	3,665
35,050	35,100	0	549	1,828	2,511	0	1,417	2,972	3,654
35,100	35,150	0	541	1,818	2,500	0	1,409	2,961	3,644
35,150	35,200	0	533	1,807	2,490	0	1,401	2,951	3,633
35,200	35,250	0	525	1,797	2,479	0	1,393	2,940	3,623
35,250	35,300	0	517	1,786	2,469	0	1,385	2,930	3,612
35,300	35,350	0	509	1,776	2,458	0	1,377	2,919	3,602
35,350	35,400	0	501	1,765	2,448	0	1,369	2,909	3,591
35,400	35,450	0	493	1,754	2,437	0	1,361	2,898	3,581
35,450	35,500	0	485	1,744	2,426	0	1,353	2,888	3,570
35,500	35,550	0	477	1,733	2,416	0	1,345	2,877	3,559
35,550	35,600	0	469	1,723	2,405	0	1,337	2,866	3,549
35,600	35,650	0	461	1,712	2,395	0	1,329	2,856	3,538
35,650	35,700	0	453	1,702	2,384	0	1,321	2,845	3,528
35,700	35,750	0	445	1,691	2,374	0	1,313	2,835	3,517
35,750	35,800	0	437	1,681	2,363	0	1,305	2,824	3,507
35,800	35,850	0	429	1,670	2,353	0	1,297	2,814	3,496
35,850	35,900	0	421	1,660	2,342	0	1,289	2,803	3,486
35,900	35,950	0	413	1,649	2,332	0	1,281	2,793	3,475
35,950	36,000	0	405	1,639	2,321	0	1,273	2,782	3,465

If the amount you are looking up from the worksheet is—		Single, head of household, or qualifying widow(er) and the number of children you have is—				Married filing jointly and the number of children you have is—			
At least	But less than	0	1	2	3	0	1	2	3
		Your credit is—				Your credit is—			
36,000	36,050	0	397	1,628	2,311	0	1,265	2,772	3,454
36,050	36,100	0	389	1,618	2,300	0	1,257	2,761	3,444
36,100	36,150	0	381	1,607	2,290	0	1,249	2,751	3,433
36,150	36,200	0	373	1,597	2,279	0	1,241	2,740	3,423
36,200	36,250	0	365	1,586	2,269	0	1,233	2,730	3,412
36,250	36,300	0	357	1,575	2,258	0	1,225	2,719	3,402
36,300	36,350	0	349	1,565	2,247	0	1,217	2,709	3,391
36,350	36,400	0	341	1,554	2,237	0	1,209	2,698	3,380
36,400	36,450	0	333	1,544	2,226	0	1,201	2,687	3,370
36,450	36,500	0	325	1,533	2,216	0	1,193	2,677	3,359
36,500	36,550	0	317	1,523	2,205	0	1,185	2,666	3,349
36,550	36,600	0	309	1,512	2,195	0	1,177	2,656	3,338
36,600	36,650	0	301	1,502	2,184	0	1,169	2,645	3,328
36,650	36,700	0	293	1,491	2,174	0	1,161	2,635	3,317
36,700	36,750	0	285	1,481	2,163	0	1,153	2,624	3,307
36,750	36,800	0	277	1,470	2,153	0	1,145	2,614	3,296
36,800	36,850	0	269	1,460	2,142	0	1,137	2,603	3,286
36,850	36,900	0	261	1,449	2,132	0	1,129	2,593	3,275
36,900	36,950	0	253	1,439	2,121	0	1,121	2,582	3,265
36,950	37,000	0	245	1,428	2,111	0	1,113	2,572	3,254
37,000	37,050	0	237	1,418	2,100	0	1,105	2,561	3,244
37,050	37,100	0	229	1,407	2,090	0	1,097	2,551	3,233
37,100	37,150	0	221	1,396	2,079	0	1,089	2,540	3,223
37,150	37,200	0	213	1,386	2,068	0	1,081	2,530	3,212
37,200	37,250	0	205	1,375	2,058	0	1,073	2,519	3,201
37,250	37,300	0	197	1,365	2,047	0	1,065	2,508	3,191
37,300	37,350	0	189	1,354	2,037	0	1,057	2,498	3,180
37,350	37,400	0	182	1,344	2,026	0	1,049	2,487	3,170
37,400	37,450	0	174	1,333	2,016	0	1,041	2,477	3,159
37,450	37,500	0	166	1,323	2,005	0	1,033	2,466	3,149
37,500	37,550	0	158	1,312	1,995	0	1,025	2,456	3,138
37,550	37,600	0	150	1,302	1,984	0	1,017	2,445	3,128
37,600	37,650	0	142	1,291	1,974	0	1,009	2,435	3,117
37,650	37,700	0	134	1,281	1,963	0	1,001	2,424	3,107
37,700	37,750	0	126	1,270	1,953	0	993	2,414	3,096
37,750	37,800	0	118	1,260	1,942	0	985	2,403	3,086
37,800	37,850	0	110	1,249	1,932	0	977	2,393	3,075
37,850	37,900	0	102	1,239	1,921	0	969	2,382	3,065
37,900	37,950	0	94	1,228	1,910	0	961	2,372	3,054
37,950	38,000	0	86	1,217	1,900	0	953	2,361	3,044
38,000	38,050	0	78	1,207	1,889	0	945	2,350	3,033
38,050	38,100	0	70	1,196	1,879	0	937	2,340	3,022
38,100	38,150	0	62	1,186	1,868	0	929	2,329	3,012
38,150	38,200	0	54	1,175	1,858	0	921	2,319	3,001
38,200	38,250	0	46	1,165	1,847	0	913	2,308	2,991
38,250	38,300	0	38	1,154	1,837	0	905	2,298	2,980
38,300	38,350	0	30	1,144	1,826	0	897	2,287	2,970
38,350	38,400	0	22	1,133	1,816	0	889	2,277	2,959
38,400	38,450	0	14	1,123	1,805	0	881	2,266	2,949
38,450	38,500	0	6	1,112	1,795	0	873	2,256	2,938
38,500	38,550	0	*	1,102	1,784	0	866	2,245	2,928
38,550	38,600	0	0	1,091	1,774	0	857	2,235	2,917
38,600	38,650	0	0	1,081	1,763	0	849	2,224	2,907
38,650	38,700	0	0	1,070	1,753	0	841	2,214	2,896
38,700	38,750	0	0	1,060	1,742	0	833	2,203	2,886
38,750	38,800	0	0	1,049	1,731	0	826	2,193	2,875
38,800	38,850	0	0	1,038	1,721	0	818	2,182	2,865
38,850	38,900	0	0	1,028	1,710	0	810	2,171	2,854
38,900	38,950	0	0	1,017	1,700	0	802	2,161	2,843
38,950	39,000	0	0	1,007	1,689	0	794	2,150	2,833
39,000	39,050	0	0	996	1,679	0	786	2,140	2,822
39,050	39,100	0	0	986	1,668	0	778	2,129	2,812
39,100	39,150	0	0	975	1,658	0	770	2,119	2,801
39,150	39,200	0	0	965	1,647	0	762	2,108	2,791

* If the amount you are looking up from the worksheet is at least $38,500 but less than $38,511, and you have one qualifying child, your credit is $1. If the amount you are looking up from the worksheet is $38,511 or more, and you have one qualifying child, you cannot take the credit.

(Continued)

Earned Income Credit (EIC) Table - *Continued*

(**Caution.** This is **not** a tax table.)

If the amount you are looking up from the worksheet is–		And your filing status is–							
		Single, head of household, or qualifying widow(er) and the number of children you have is–				Married filing jointly and the number of children you have is–			
At least	But less than	0	1	2	3	0	1	2	3
		Your credit is–				Your credit is–			
39,200	39,250	0	0	954	1,637	0	754	2,098	2,780
39,250	39,300	0	0	944	1,626	0	746	2,087	2,770
39,300	39,350	0	0	933	1,616	0	738	2,077	2,759
39,350	39,400	0	0	923	1,605	0	730	2,066	2,749
39,400	39,450	0	0	912	1,595	0	722	2,056	2,738
39,450	39,500	0	0	902	1,584	0	714	2,045	2,728
39,500	39,550	0	0	891	1,574	0	706	2,035	2,717
39,550	39,600	0	0	881	1,563	0	698	2,024	2,707
39,600	39,650	0	0	870	1,552	0	690	2,014	2,696
39,650	39,700	0	0	859	1,542	0	682	2,003	2,686
39,700	39,750	0	0	849	1,531	0	674	1,992	2,675
39,750	39,800	0	0	838	1,521	0	666	1,982	2,664
39,800	39,850	0	0	828	1,510	0	658	1,971	2,654
39,850	39,900	0	0	817	1,500	0	650	1,961	2,643
39,900	39,950	0	0	807	1,489	0	642	1,950	2,633
39,950	40,000	0	0	796	1,479	0	634	1,940	2,622
40,000	40,050	0	0	786	1,468	0	626	1,929	2,612
40,050	40,100	0	0	775	1,458	0	618	1,919	2,601
40,100	40,150	0	0	765	1,447	0	610	1,908	2,591
40,150	40,200	0	0	754	1,437	0	602	1,898	2,580
40,200	40,250	0	0	744	1,426	0	594	1,887	2,570
40,250	40,300	0	0	733	1,416	0	586	1,877	2,559
40,300	40,350	0	0	723	1,405	0	578	1,866	2,549
40,350	40,400	0	0	712	1,395	0	570	1,856	2,538
40,400	40,450	0	0	701	1,384	0	562	1,845	2,528
40,450	40,500	0	0	691	1,373	0	554	1,835	2,517
40,500	40,550	0	0	680	1,363	0	546	1,824	2,506
40,550	40,600	0	0	670	1,352	0	538	1,813	2,496
40,600	40,650	0	0	659	1,342	0	530	1,803	2,485
40,650	40,700	0	0	649	1,331	0	522	1,792	2,475
40,700	40,750	0	0	638	1,321	0	514	1,782	2,464
40,750	40,800	0	0	628	1,310	0	506	1,771	2,454
40,800	40,850	0	0	617	1,300	0	498	1,761	2,443
40,850	40,900	0	0	607	1,289	0	490	1,750	2,433
40,900	40,950	0	0	596	1,279	0	482	1,740	2,422
40,950	41,000	0	0	586	1,268	0	474	1,729	2,412
41,000	41,050	0	0	575	1,258	0	466	1,719	2,401
41,050	41,100	0	0	565	1,247	0	458	1,708	2,391
41,100	41,150	0	0	554	1,237	0	450	1,698	2,380
41,150	41,200	0	0	544	1,226	0	442	1,687	2,370
41,200	41,250	0	0	533	1,216	0	434	1,677	2,359
41,250	41,300	0	0	522	1,205	0	426	1,666	2,349
41,300	41,350	0	0	512	1,194	0	418	1,656	2,338
41,350	41,400	0	0	501	1,184	0	410	1,645	2,327
41,400	41,450	0	0	491	1,173	0	402	1,634	2,317
41,450	41,500	0	0	480	1,163	0	394	1,624	2,306
41,500	41,550	0	0	470	1,152	0	386	1,613	2,296
41,550	41,600	0	0	459	1,142	0	378	1,603	2,285
41,600	41,650	0	0	449	1,131	0	370	1,592	2,275
41,650	41,700	0	0	438	1,121	0	362	1,582	2,264
41,700	41,750	0	0	428	1,110	0	354	1,571	2,254
41,750	41,800	0	0	417	1,100	0	346	1,561	2,243
41,800	41,850	0	0	407	1,089	0	338	1,550	2,233
41,850	41,900	0	0	396	1,079	0	330	1,540	2,222
41,900	41,950	0	0	386	1,068	0	322	1,529	2,212
41,950	42,000	0	0	375	1,058	0	314	1,519	2,201
42,000	42,050	0	0	365	1,047	0	306	1,508	2,191
42,050	42,100	0	0	354	1,037	0	298	1,498	2,180
42,100	42,150	0	0	343	1,026	0	290	1,487	2,170
42,150	42,200	0	0	333	1,015	0	282	1,477	2,159
42,200	42,250	0	0	322	1,005	0	274	1,466	2,148
42,250	42,300	0	0	312	994	0	266	1,455	2,138
42,300	42,350	0	0	301	984	0	258	1,445	2,127
42,350	42,400	0	0	291	973	0	250	1,434	2,117
42,400	42,450	0	0	280	963	0	242	1,424	2,106
42,450	42,500	0	0	270	952	0	234	1,413	2,096
42,500	42,550	0	0	259	942	0	226	1,403	2,085
42,550	42,600	0	0	249	931	0	218	1,392	2,075
42,600	42,650	0	0	238	921	0	210	1,382	2,064
42,650	42,700	0	0	228	910	0	202	1,371	2,054
42,700	42,750	0	0	217	900	0	194	1,361	2,043
42,750	42,800	0	0	207	889	0	186	1,350	2,033
42,800	42,850	0	0	196	879	0	178	1,340	2,022
42,850	42,900	0	0	186	868	0	170	1,329	2,012
42,900	42,950	0	0	175	857	0	162	1,319	2,001
42,950	43,000	0	0	164	847	0	154	1,308	1,991
43,000	43,050	0	0	154	836	0	146	1,297	1,980
43,050	43,100	0	0	143	826	0	138	1,287	1,969
43,100	43,150	0	0	133	815	0	130	1,276	1,959
43,150	43,200	0	0	122	805	0	122	1,266	1,948
43,200	43,250	0	0	112	794	0	114	1,255	1,938
43,250	43,300	0	0	101	784	0	106	1,245	1,927
43,300	43,350	0	0	91	773	0	98	1,234	1,917
43,350	43,400	0	0	80	763	0	90	1,224	1,906
43,400	43,450	0	0	70	752	0	82	1,213	1,896
43,450	43,500	0	0	59	742	0	74	1,203	1,885
43,500	43,550	0	0	49	731	0	66	1,192	1,875
43,550	43,600	0	0	38	721	0	58	1,182	1,864
43,600	43,650	0	0	28	710	0	50	1,171	1,854
43,650	43,700	0	0	17	700	0	42	1,161	1,843
43,700	43,750	0	0	7	689	0	34	1,150	1,833
43,750	43,800	0	0	*	678	0	27	1,140	1,822
43,800	43,850	0	0	0	668	0	19	1,129	1,812
43,850	43,900	0	0	0	657	0	11	1,118	1,801
43,900	43,950	0	0	0	647	0	**	1,108	1,790
43,950	44,000	0	0	0	636	0	0	1,097	1,780
44,000	44,050	0	0	0	626	0	0	1,087	1,769
44,050	44,100	0	0	0	615	0	0	1,076	1,759
44,100	44,150	0	0	0	605	0	0	1,066	1,748
44,150	44,200	0	0	0	594	0	0	1,055	1,738
44,200	44,250	0	0	0	584	0	0	1,045	1,727
44,250	44,300	0	0	0	573	0	0	1,034	1,717
44,300	44,350	0	0	0	563	0	0	1,024	1,706
44,350	44,400	0	0	0	552	0	0	1,013	1,696
44,400	44,450	0	0	0	542	0	0	1,003	1,685
44,450	44,500	0	0	0	531	0	0	992	1,675
44,500	44,550	0	0	0	521	0	0	982	1,664
44,550	44,600	0	0	0	510	0	0	971	1,654
44,600	44,650	0	0	0	499	0	0	961	1,643
44,650	44,700	0	0	0	489	0	0	950	1,633
44,700	44,750	0	0	0	478	0	0	939	1,622
44,750	44,800	0	0	0	468	0	0	929	1,611
44,800	44,850	0	0	0	457	0	0	918	1,601
44,850	44,900	0	0	0	447	0	0	908	1,590
44,900	44,950	0	0	0	436	0	0	897	1,580
44,950	45,000	0	0	0	426	0	0	887	1,569
45,000	45,050	0	0	0	415	0	0	876	1,559
45,050	45,100	0	0	0	405	0	0	866	1,548
45,100	45,150	0	0	0	394	0	0	855	1,538
45,150	45,200	0	0	0	384	0	0	845	1,527
45,200	45,250	0	0	0	373	0	0	834	1,517
45,250	45,300	0	0	0	363	0	0	824	1,506
45,300	45,350	0	0	0	352	0	0	813	1,496
45,350	45,400	0	0	0	342	0	0	803	1,485
45,400	45,450	0	0	0	331	0	0	792	1,475
45,450	45,500	0	0	0	320	0	0	782	1,464
45,500	45,550	0	0	0	310	0	0	771	1,453
45,550	45,600	0	0	0	299	0	0	760	1,443

* If the amount you are looking up from the worksheet is at least $43,750 but less than $43,756, and you have two qualifying children, your credit is $1.
If the amount you are looking up from the worksheet is $43,756 or more, and you have two qualifying children, you cannot take the credit.

** If the amount you are looking up from the worksheet is at least $43,900 but less than $43,941, and you have one qualifying child, your credit is $3.
If the amount you are looking up from the worksheet is $43,941 or more, and you have one qualifying child, you cannot take the credit.

(Continued)

Earned Income Credit (EIC) Table - *Continued*

(Caution. This is **not** a tax table.**)**

If the amount you are looking up from the worksheet is–		And your filing status is–							
		Single, head of household, or qualifying widow(er) and the number of children you have is–				Married filing jointly and the number of children you have is–			
		0	1	2	3	0	1	2	3
At least	But less than	Your credit is–				Your credit is–			
45,600	45,650	0	0	0	289	0	0	750	1,432
45,650	45,700	0	0	0	278	0	0	739	1,422
45,700	45,750	0	0	0	268	0	0	729	1,411
45,750	45,800	0	0	0	257	0	0	718	1,401
45,800	45,850	0	0	0	247	0	0	708	1,390
45,850	45,900	0	0	0	236	0	0	697	1,380
45,900	45,950	0	0	0	226	0	0	687	1,369
45,950	46,000	0	0	0	215	0	0	676	1,359
46,000	46,050	0	0	0	205	0	0	666	1,348
46,050	46,100	0	0	0	194	0	0	655	1,338
46,100	46,150	0	0	0	184	0	0	645	1,327
46,150	46,200	0	0	0	173	0	0	634	1,317
46,200	46,250	0	0	0	163	0	0	624	1,306
46,250	46,300	0	0	0	152	0	0	613	1,296
46,300	46,350	0	0	0	141	0	0	603	1,285
46,350	46,400	0	0	0	131	0	0	592	1,274
46,400	46,450	0	0	0	120	0	0	581	1,264
46,450	46,500	0	0	0	110	0	0	571	1,253
46,500	46,550	0	0	0	99	0	0	560	1,243
46,550	46,600	0	0	0	89	0	0	550	1,232
46,600	46,650	0	0	0	78	0	0	539	1,222
46,650	46,700	0	0	0	68	0	0	529	1,211
46,700	46,750	0	0	0	57	0	0	518	1,201
46,750	46,800	0	0	0	47	0	0	508	1,190
46,800	46,850	0	0	0	36	0	0	497	1,180
46,850	46,900	0	0	0	26	0	0	487	1,169
46,900	46,950	0	0	0	15	0	0	476	1,159
46,950	47,000	0	0	0	*	0	0	466	1,148
47,000	47,050	0	0	0	0	0	0	455	1,138
47,050	47,100	0	0	0	0	0	0	445	1,127
47,100	47,150	0	0	0	0	0	0	434	1,117
47,150	47,200	0	0	0	0	0	0	424	1,106
47,200	47,250	0	0	0	0	0	0	413	1,095
47,250	47,300	0	0	0	0	0	0	402	1,085
47,300	47,350	0	0	0	0	0	0	392	1,074
47,350	47,400	0	0	0	0	0	0	381	1,064
47,400	47,450	0	0	0	0	0	0	371	1,053
47,450	47,500	0	0	0	0	0	0	360	1,043
47,500	47,550	0	0	0	0	0	0	350	1,032
47,550	47,600	0	0	0	0	0	0	339	1,022
47,600	47,650	0	0	0	0	0	0	329	1,011
47,650	47,700	0	0	0	0	0	0	318	1,001
47,700	47,750	0	0	0	0	0	0	308	990
47,750	47,800	0	0	0	0	0	0	297	980
47,800	47,850	0	0	0	0	0	0	287	969
47,850	47,900	0	0	0	0	0	0	276	959
47,900	47,950	0	0	0	0	0	0	266	948
47,950	48,000	0	0	0	0	0	0	255	938
48,000	48,050	0	0	0	0	0	0	244	927
48,050	48,100	0	0	0	0	0	0	234	916
48,100	48,150	0	0	0	0	0	0	223	906
48,150	48,200	0	0	0	0	0	0	213	895
48,200	48,250	0	0	0	0	0	0	202	885
48,250	48,300	0	0	0	0	0	0	192	874
48,300	48,350	0	0	0	0	0	0	181	864
48,350	48,400	0	0	0	0	0	0	171	853
48,400	48,450	0	0	0	0	0	0	160	843
48,450	48,500	0	0	0	0	0	0	150	832
48,500	48,550	0	0	0	0	0	0	139	822
48,550	48,600	0	0	0	0	0	0	129	811
48,600	48,650	0	0	0	0	0	0	118	801
48,650	48,700	0	0	0	0	0	0	108	790
48,700	48,750	0	0	0	0	0	0	97	780
48,750	48,800	0	0	0	0	0	0	87	769

If the amount you are looking up from the worksheet is–		And your filing status is–							
		Single, head of household, or qualifying widow(er) and the number of children you have is–				Married filing jointly and the number of children you have is–			
		0	1	2	3	0	1	2	3
At least	But less than	Your credit is–				Your credit is–			
48,800	48,850	0	0	0	0	0	0	76	759
48,850	48,900	0	0	0	0	0	0	65	748
48,900	48,950	0	0	0	0	0	0	55	737
48,950	49,000	0	0	0	0	0	0	44	727
49,000	49,050	0	0	0	0	0	0	34	716
49,050	49,100	0	0	0	0	0	0	23	706
49,100	49,150	0	0	0	0	0	0	13	695
49,150	49,200	0	0	0	0	0	0	**	685
49,200	49,250	0	0	0	0	0	0	0	674
49,250	49,300	0	0	0	0	0	0	0	664
49,300	49,350	0	0	0	0	0	0	0	653
49,350	49,400	0	0	0	0	0	0	0	643
49,400	49,450	0	0	0	0	0	0	0	632
49,450	49,500	0	0	0	0	0	0	0	622
49,500	49,550	0	0	0	0	0	0	0	611
49,550	49,600	0	0	0	0	0	0	0	601
49,600	49,650	0	0	0	0	0	0	0	590
49,650	49,700	0	0	0	0	0	0	0	580
49,700	49,750	0	0	0	0	0	0	0	569
49,750	49,800	0	0	0	0	0	0	0	558
49,800	49,850	0	0	0	0	0	0	0	548
49,850	49,900	0	0	0	0	0	0	0	537
49,900	49,950	0	0	0	0	0	0	0	527
49,950	50,000	0	0	0	0	0	0	0	516
50,000	50,050	0	0	0	0	0	0	0	506
50,050	50,100	0	0	0	0	0	0	0	495
50,100	50,150	0	0	0	0	0	0	0	485
50,150	50,200	0	0	0	0	0	0	0	474
50,200	50,250	0	0	0	0	0	0	0	464
50,250	50,300	0	0	0	0	0	0	0	453
50,300	50,350	0	0	0	0	0	0	0	443
50,350	50,400	0	0	0	0	0	0	0	432
50,400	50,450	0	0	0	0	0	0	0	422
50,450	50,500	0	0	0	0	0	0	0	411
50,500	50,550	0	0	0	0	0	0	0	400
50,550	50,600	0	0	0	0	0	0	0	390
50,600	50,650	0	0	0	0	0	0	0	379
50,650	50,700	0	0	0	0	0	0	0	369
50,700	50,750	0	0	0	0	0	0	0	358
50,750	50,800	0	0	0	0	0	0	0	348
50,800	50,850	0	0	0	0	0	0	0	337
50,850	50,900	0	0	0	0	0	0	0	327
50,900	50,950	0	0	0	0	0	0	0	316
50,950	51,000	0	0	0	0	0	0	0	306
51,000	51,050	0	0	0	0	0	0	0	295
51,050	51,100	0	0	0	0	0	0	0	285
51,100	51,150	0	0	0	0	0	0	0	274
51,150	51,200	0	0	0	0	0	0	0	264
51,200	51,250	0	0	0	0	0	0	0	253
51,250	51,300	0	0	0	0	0	0	0	243
51,300	51,350	0	0	0	0	0	0	0	232
51,350	51,400	0	0	0	0	0	0	0	221
51,400	51,450	0	0	0	0	0	0	0	211
51,450	51,500	0	0	0	0	0	0	0	200
51,500	51,550	0	0	0	0	0	0	0	190
51,550	51,600	0	0	0	0	0	0	0	179
51,600	51,650	0	0	0	0	0	0	0	169
51,650	51,700	0	0	0	0	0	0	0	158
51,700	51,750	0	0	0	0	0	0	0	148
51,750	51,800	0	0	0	0	0	0	0	137
51,800	51,850	0	0	0	0	0	0	0	127
51,850	51,900	0	0	0	0	0	0	0	116
51,900	51,950	0	0	0	0	0	0	0	106
51,950	52,000	0	0	0	0	0	0	0	95

* If the amount you are looking up from the worksheet is at least $46,950 but less than $46,997, and you have three qualifying children, your credit is $5.
If the amount you are looking up from the worksheet is $46,997 or more, and you have three qualifying children, you cannot take the credit.

** If the amount you are looking up from the worksheet is at least $49,150 but less than $49,186, and you have two qualifying children, your credit is $4.
If the amount you are looking up from the worksheet is $49,186 or more, and you have two qualifying children, you cannot take the credit.

(Continued)

Earned Income Credit (EIC) Table - *Continued*

(Caution. This is **not** a tax table.)

If the amount you are looking up from the worksheet is–		Single, head of household, or qualifying widow(er) and the number of children you have is–				Married filing jointly and the number of children you have is–				If the amount you are looking up from the worksheet is–		Single, head of household, or qualifying widow(er) and the number of children you have is–				Married filing jointly and the number of children you have is–			
		0	1	2	3	0	1	2	3			0	1	2	3	0	1	2	3
At least	But less than	Your credit is–				Your credit is–				At least	But less than	Your credit is–				Your credit is–			
52,000	52,050	0	0	0	0	0	0	0	85	52,400	52,427	0	0	0	0	0	0	0	3
52,050	52,100	0	0	0	0	0	0	0	74										
52,100	52,150	0	0	0	0	0	0	0	64										
52,150	52,200	0	0	0	0	0	0	0	53										
52,200	52,250	0	0	0	0	0	0	0	42										
52,250	52,300	0	0	0	0	0	0	0	32										
52,300	52,350	0	0	0	0	0	0	0	21										
52,350	52,400	0	0	0	0	0	0	0	11										

Appendix C – Optional Sales Tax Tables

2014 Optional State Sales Tax Tables *(State Sales Tax Rate Shown Next to State Name)*

Income		Exemptions						Exemptions						Exemptions						Exemptions					
At least	But less than	1	2	3	4	5	Over 5	1	2	3	4	5	Over 5	1	2	3	4	5	Over 5	1	2	3	4	5	Over 5
		Alabama			1	**4.0000%**		**Arizona**			2	**5.6000%**		**Arkansas**			2	**6.5000%**		**California**			3	**7.5000%**	
$0	$20,000	223	263	290	310	328	352	214	237	251	262	271	283	283	315	335	350	363	380	267	292	308	321	330	344
$20,000	$30,000	329	387	426	456	481	517	364	403	428	446	462	482	460	513	546	572	592	620	446	488	515	536	552	574
$30,000	$40,000	384	451	496	531	560	601	448	496	527	550	569	595	558	621	662	693	718	753	546	598	631	656	676	703
$40,000	$50,000	431	505	556	595	628	673	524	580	616	644	666	696	644	718	765	801	830	869	635	695	734	763	787	818
$50,000	$60,000	473	554	609	652	687	737	594	658	699	730	755	789	722	805	859	899	931	976	716	785	829	861	888	924
$60,000	$70,000	510	598	657	703	741	795	658	729	775	809	837	875	794	886	945	989	1025	1074	792	867	916	952	981	1021
$70,000	$80,000	545	638	701	750	790	847	719	797	847	884	915	956	862	961	1025	1073	1112	1165	862	945	998	1037	1069	1112
$80,000	$90,000	577	675	742	793	836	896	777	861	915	955	988	1033	925	1032	1100	1152	1194	1251	929	1018	1075	1117	1152	1198
$90,000	$100,000	607	710	780	834	879	942	832	922	979	1023	1058	1106	985	1099	1172	1227	1272	1333	992	1088	1148	1194	1230	1280
$100,000	$120,000	647	757	831	888	936	1003	906	1004	1067	1115	1153	1206	1066	1189	1269	1328	1377	1443	1078	1182	1248	1297	1337	1391
$120,000	$140,000	699	817	896	958	1010	1082	1005	1114	1184	1237	1279	1338	1173	1309	1396	1462	1515	1588	1192	1306	1379	1434	1478	1538
$140,000	$160,000	747	873	957	1023	1078	1155	1099	1218	1295	1353	1399	1464	1274	1421	1516	1588	1646	1726	1299	1424	1504	1564	1612	1677
$160,000	$180,000	792	924	1013	1083	1141	1222	1187	1316	1399	1462	1512	1582	1368	1526	1628	1705	1768	1853	1400	1535	1621	1685	1737	1808
$180,000	$200,000	833	972	1066	1139	1200	1285	1272	1411	1499	1566	1621	1695	1457	1627	1736	1818	1884	1976	1497	1641	1733	1802	1857	1933
$200,000	$225,000	877	1023	1121	1198	1261	1351	1362	1510	1605	1677	1735	1815	1552	1732	1848	1936	2007	2104	1599	1753	1851	1924	1984	2064
$225,000	$250,000	924	1077	1180	1260	1327	1421	1460	1618	1721	1798	1860	1945	1654	1847	1970	2064	2140	2244	1709	1874	1979	2058	2121	2207
$250,000	$275,000	968	1127	1235	1319	1389	1487	1553	1722	1831	1913	1979	2070	1751	1955	2087	2186	2266	2376	1815	1990	2101	2185	2252	2344
$275,000	$300,000	1009	1176	1288	1375	1448	1550	1643	1822	1937	2024	2094	2191	1845	2060	2198	2303	2387	2504	1917	2102	2219	2307	2379	2476
$300,000	or more	1256	1461	1598	1705	1794	1919	2199	2439	2594	2711	2805	2935	2413	2696	2878	3015	3126	3279	2540	2785	2942	3059	3153	3282
Income		**Colorado**			2	**2.9000%**		**Connecticut**			4	**6.3500%**		**District of Columbia**			4	**5.7500%**		**Florida**			1	**6.0000%**	
$0	$20,000	111	124	133	139	144	151	263	289	305	317	327	340	168	181	189	195	200	207	238	261	276	287	296	308
$20,000	$30,000	174	194	207	217	225	236	432	475	502	522	539	561	284	307	322	332	341	353	396	434	459	478	493	513
$30,000	$40,000	208	232	247	259	268	281	526	578	611	636	656	683	350	379	397	410	421	436	483	531	561	584	602	627
$40,000	$50,000	237	264	282	295	306	320	609	670	708	737	760	792	409	443	464	480	493	510	561	616	651	678	699	729
$50,000	$60,000	264	294	313	328	339	356	685	753	797	829	856	891	464	502	526	544	559	579	632	695	734	764	789	822
$60,000	$70,000	288	320	341	357	370	388	755	830	878	914	943	983	514	556	583	604	620	642	698	767	811	844	871	907
$70,000	$80,000	310	345	368	385	399	418	820	902	955	994	1025	1068	561	608	638	660	678	702	759	834	882	918	948	988
$80,000	$90,000	331	368	392	410	425	446	882	970	1027	1069	1103	1149	606	657	689	713	732	759	817	898	950	989	1020	1063
$90,000	$100,000	350	390	415	435	450	472	940	1035	1095	1140	1176	1226	649	704	738	764	784	813	873	959	1014	1056	1090	1136
$100,000	$120,000	377	419	447	467	484	507	1019	1122	1187	1236	1276	1329	708	767	804	833	855	886	947	1041	1101	1147	1183	1233
$120,000	$140,000	411	457	487	510	528	553	1124	1237	1309	1363	1407	1466	785	851	893	924	949	984	1046	1150	1216	1266	1307	1362
$140,000	$160,000	444	493	525	550	569	596	1222	1346	1425	1484	1531	1596	858	931	977	1011	1039	1077	1139	1253	1325	1380	1424	1484
$160,000	$180,000	474	526	561	586	607	636	1315	1448	1533	1596	1647	1717	928	1006	1056	1093	1123	1164	1227	1349	1427	1486	1533	1599
$180,000	$200,000	502	558	594	621	644	674	1403	1545	1636	1704	1758	1833	994	1078	1132	1172	1204	1248	1310	1441	1525	1588	1639	1708
$200,000	$225,000	532	591	629	658	682	714	1496	1648	1745	1817	1875	1955	1064	1155	1212	1255	1290	1337	1399	1538	1628	1695	1749	1824
$225,000	$250,000	564	626	667	698	722	757	1597	1759	1863	1940	2002	2087	1141	1238	1300	1346	1383	1434	1494	1644	1739	1811	1869	1949
$250,000	$275,000	594	660	703	735	761	797	1693	1865	1975	2057	2123	2213	1214	1318	1384	1433	1473	1527	1586	1744	1846	1922	1984	2068
$275,000	$300,000	623	692	737	771	798	836	1785	1967	2083	2170	2240	2335	1285	1395	1465	1517	1559	1617	1674	1841	1949	2029	2094	2184
$300,000	or more	798	885	942	985	1020	1068	2350	2591	2744	2859	2951	3078	1721	1870	1965	2036	2093	2171	2211	2434	2576	2683	2770	2889
Income		**Georgia**			2	**4.0000%**		**Hawaii**			1,7	**4.0000%**		**Idaho**			1	**6.0000%**		**Illinois**			2	**6.2500%**	
$0	$20,000	151	168	179	187	194	203	220	255	279	297	312	333	337	396	436	467	493	529	251	281	301	316	329	346
$20,000	$30,000	241	267	284	297	308	322	356	414	452	482	507	542	501	588	647	692	730	783	389	434	465	488	507	533
$30,000	$40,000	289	321	341	357	369	387	430	501	548	584	614	656	586	687	756	809	852	914	462	516	551	578	601	632
$40,000	$50,000	332	368	391	409	423	443	496	578	632	674	708	757	660	773	849	908	957	1026	525	586	626	657	682	718
$50,000	$60,000	370	411	437	456	472	494	556	647	708	755	794	849	725	849	932	997	1051	1126	582	649	694	728	756	795
$60,000	$70,000	405	449	478	499	517	541	611	711	779	830	873	933	784	917	1007	1077	1135	1216	634	707	755	792	822	864
$70,000	$80,000	438	486	516	540	558	584	662	771	844	900	947	1012	838	980	1076	1150	1212	1298	681	760	812	851	884	929
$80,000	$90,000	468	519	552	577	597	625	711	828	906	966	1016	1086	888	1038	1140	1218	1283	1375	726	809	864	907	941	989
$90,000	$100,000	497	551	586	613	634	663	756	881	964	1029	1082	1156	935	1093	1199	1282	1351	1447	768	856	914	959	995	1046
$100,000	$120,000	536	594	632	660	683	715	818	953	1043	1113	1170	1250	998	1166	1279	1367	1440	1542	824	919	981	1028	1067	1122
$120,000	$140,000	587	651	692	723	748	783	899	1047	1147	1223	1287	1375	1080	1260	1382	1477	1556	1666	898	1000	1068	1119	1162	1221
$140,000	$160,000	635	704	748	782	809	846	975	1136	1244	1328	1396	1493	1155	1348	1478	1579	1663	1781	967	1076	1149	1204	1250	1313
$160,000	$180,000	680	753	801	836	865	905	1047	1220	1335	1425	1499	1602	1225	1429	1567	1673	1762	1886	1030	1147	1224	1283	1331	1398
$180,000	$200,000	722	800	850	888	919	961	1115	1299	1422	1518	1597	1707	1291	1506	1650	1762	1855	1986	1091	1214	1295	1357	1409	1480
$200,000	$225,000	766	849	903	943	975	1020	1186	1383	1514	1616	1699	1817	1360	1585	1737	1855	1952	2090	1154	1284	1369	1435	1489	1564
$225,000	$250,000	814	902	959	1002	1036	1084	1263	1473	1613	1721	1811	1936	1433	1670	1830	1953	2056	2200	1221	1359	1449	1519	1576	1655
$250,000	$275,000	860	952	1012	1057	1094	1144	1337	1559	1707	1822	1916	2049	1503	1750	1917	2046	2154	2305	1285	1429	1525	1598	1658	1741
$275,000	$300,000	903	1001	1064	1111	1149	1202	1407	1641	1798	1918	2018	2158	1569	1826	2000	2135	2247	2404	1347	1497	1597	1673	1736	1823
$300,000	or more	1166	1292	1372	1433	1482	1550	1836	2142	2347	2505	2636	2819	1959	2277	2492	2658	2796	2990	1713	1902	2028	2124	2203	2312
Income		**Indiana**			4	**7.0000%**		**Iowa**			1	**6.0000%**		**Kansas**			1	**6.1500%**		**Kentucky**			4	**6.0000%**	
$0	$20,000	288	322	343	360	373	391	246	273	291	304	315	330	354	413	453	483	509	545	235	262	279	293	303	318
$20,000	$30,000	448	500	533	558	579	607	407	453	483	506	524	549	546	637	698	746	785	840	371	414	441	462	479	502
$30,000	$40,000	533	595	634	664	688	721	497	554	590	618	640	671	648	756	828	884	931	996	445	496	529	553	573	601
$40,000	$50,000	607	677	722	756	783	821	577	644	686	718	744	780	736	859	941	1005	1057	1131	509	567	605	633	656	688
$50,000	$60,000	674	751	801	839	869	911	651	726	774	810	840	880	815	951	1042	1113	1171	1253	568	632	674	705	731	766
$60,000	$70,000	734	818	873	914	947	992	718	801	855	895	927	972	887	1035	1134	1211	1274	1363	621	691	736	771	799	837
$70,000	$80,000	790	881	939	983	1019	1068	782	872	930	974	1010	1059	953	1112	1219	1301	1369	1465	670	746	795	832	862	903
$80,000	$90,000	842	939	1001	1048	1086	1138	842	939	1002	1049	1088	1140	1015	1184	1298	1386	1458	1560	716	797	850	889	921	965
$90,000	$100,000	891	994	1060	1109	1149	1205	899	1003	1070	1121	1162	1218	1074	1252	1372	1465	1542	1649	760	846	901	943	977	1024
$100,000	$120,000	957	1067	1138	1191	1234	1293	976	1089	1162	1217	1262	1323	1152	1343	1472	1571	1654	1769	818	911	970	1015	1052	1103
$120,000	$140,000	1043	1163	1240	1298	1345	1409	1078	1203	1284	1345	1395	1463	1253	1462	1602	1710	1800	1925	895	996	1061	1110	1150	1205
$140,000	$160,000	1123	1252	1335	1398	1448	1518	1175	1312	1400	1467	1521	1595	1348	1573	1723	1839	1936	2071	967	1076	1146	1199	1243	1302
$160,000	$180,000	1198	1335	1424	1490	1544	1618	1265	1413	1508	1580	1638	1719	1436	1675	1835	1959	2062	2205	1034	1150	1226	1282	1328	1392
$180,000	$200,000	1269	1414	1508	1578	1635	1714	1352	1510	1612	1689	1751	1837	1520	1772	1942	2073	2181	2333	1098	1221	1301	1361	1410	1477
$200,000	$225,000	1342	1496	1595	1670	1730	1813	1443	1612	1722	1804	1871	1962	1607	1873	2053	2191	2306	2466	1165	1295	1380	1443	1495	1566
$225,000	$250,000	1422	1585	1689	1768	1832	1920	1542	1724	1840	1928	2000	2098	1700	1982	2172	2318	2440	2610	1237	1375	1464	1532	1587	1662
$250,000	$275,000	1497	1668	1779	1862	1929	2021	1637	1830	1954	2047	2123	2228	1788	2085	2284	2439	2566	2745	1305	1451	1545	1616	1674	1754
$275,000	$300,000	1569	1748	1864	1951	2022	2118	1728	1932	2063	2162	2243	2353	1873	2184	2392	2554	2687	2874	1371	1523	1622	1697	1758	1841
$300,000	or more	1998	2226	2373	2484	2574	2697	2288	2559	2734	2866	2973	3120	2376	2770	3034	3239	3408	3645	1764	1960	2086	2182	2260	2367

(Continued)

2014 Optional State Sales Tax Tables *(Continued)*

Income		Louisiana			2	4.0000%		Maine			4	5.5000%		Maryland			4	6.0000%		Massachusetts			4	6.2500%	
$0	$20,000	161	175	184	191	196	204	146	159	167	173	178	184	208	229	244	255	264	276	201	219	230	239	246	255
$20,000	$30,000	267	291	306	318	327	339	246	267	281	291	299	310	343	380	404	422	437	458	317	345	363	376	387	402
$30,000	$40,000	326	356	374	388	399	415	302	328	345	358	368	381	419	464	493	515	533	559	379	413	434	450	463	481
$40,000	$50,000	379	413	435	451	464	482	352	383	402	417	429	445	486	538	572	598	619	648	434	472	496	514	529	549
$50,000	$60,000	427	466	490	509	523	544	398	433	455	472	485	503	547	606	644	673	697	731	483	525	552	573	589	611
$60,000	$70,000	471	514	541	562	578	600	441	479	504	522	537	557	604	668	711	743	770	806	528	574	603	626	643	668
$70,000	$80,000	513	560	589	612	629	654	480	523	550	570	586	608	656	727	773	808	837	877	569	619	651	675	694	720
$80,000	$90,000	552	603	635	659	678	704	518	564	593	615	632	656	706	782	832	870	901	944	608	661	695	721	741	769
$90,000	$100,000	590	644	678	703	724	752	554	603	634	657	676	701	754	835	888	929	962	1008	645	701	737	764	786	815
$100,000	$120,000	640	699	736	764	786	817	603	656	690	715	736	763	818	906	964	1008	1044	1093	694	755	793	822	846	877
$120,000	$140,000	707	772	813	844	868	902	668	727	764	792	815	845	902	1000	1064	1112	1152	1207	759	825	867	899	924	959
$140,000	$160,000	771	841	886	919	946	983	729	793	834	865	889	923	982	1088	1158	1211	1254	1314	819	891	936	970	997	1035
$160,000	$180,000	830	906	954	990	1020	1059	786	856	900	933	960	996	1057	1171	1247	1304	1350	1415	875	952	1000	1036	1066	1106
$180,000	$200,000	887	968	1020	1058	1090	1132	842	916	963	999	1027	1066	1129	1251	1331	1392	1442	1511	929	1009	1061	1099	1130	1173
$200,000	$225,000	946	1033	1089	1130	1163	1209	900	980	1030	1068	1099	1140	1204	1335	1420	1486	1539	1613	985	1070	1125	1165	1198	1243
$225,000	$250,000	1011	1104	1164	1208	1243	1292	963	1049	1103	1143	1176	1220	1286	1426	1517	1587	1644	1723	1045	1136	1193	1236	1271	1319
$250,000	$275,000	1073	1172	1235	1282	1320	1371	1024	1114	1172	1215	1250	1297	1364	1512	1609	1683	1744	1828	1102	1197	1258	1304	1341	1391
$275,000	$300,000	1133	1237	1304	1353	1393	1448	1082	1178	1239	1285	1321	1371	1439	1596	1698	1776	1840	1929	1157	1257	1321	1368	1407	1460
$300,000	or more	1498	1637	1725	1791	1844	1917	1440	1569	1650	1711	1760	1827	1898	2105	2241	2345	2429	2546	1485	1613	1695	1756	1805	1872

Income		Michigan			4	6.0000%		Minnesota			1	6.8750%		Mississippi			1	7.0000%		Missouri			2	4.2250%	
$0	$20,000	226	251	266	278	288	301	235	254	265	274	281	291	414	476	518	550	576	613	172	195	211	223	233	247
$20,000	$30,000	357	395	419	437	452	473	394	426	446	461	473	489	642	739	803	853	893	950	272	309	334	353	368	390
$30,000	$40,000	427	472	501	523	541	565	483	522	547	566	581	601	763	878	955	1014	1062	1129	325	370	400	422	441	466
$40,000	$50,000	488	540	573	598	618	646	562	609	638	660	677	701	868	1000	1087	1154	1209	1285	373	424	457	483	504	534
$50,000	$60,000	543	601	638	665	688	719	636	688	722	746	766	793	963	1109	1205	1279	1340	1425	415	472	509	538	562	594
$60,000	$70,000	594	656	697	727	751	785	703	762	799	826	848	878	1048	1207	1313	1393	1460	1552	454	516	557	588	614	650
$70,000	$80,000	641	708	751	784	810	847	767	831	871	901	925	958	1128	1299	1412	1499	1570	1670	490	557	601	635	663	701
$80,000	$90,000	685	757	803	837	866	904	827	896	940	972	998	1034	1202	1384	1505	1598	1674	1780	524	595	643	679	708	749
$90,000	$100,000	726	802	851	888	918	959	885	959	1005	1040	1068	1106	1272	1465	1593	1690	1771	1883	556	632	682	720	751	794
$100,000	$120,000	782	863	916	956	988	1032	962	1043	1094	1132	1162	1204	1366	1573	1710	1815	1901	2021	599	680	734	775	809	855
$120,000	$140,000	854	944	1001	1044	1079	1127	1065	1155	1212	1254	1288	1333	1488	1713	1862	1977	2071	2202	655	744	803	847	884	935
$140,000	$160,000	923	1019	1081	1127	1165	1217	1163	1262	1324	1370	1407	1457	1602	1845	2005	2129	2230	2371	708	804	867	915	955	1010
$160,000	$180,000	986	1089	1155	1204	1245	1300	1255	1361	1428	1478	1518	1572	1708	1966	2138	2269	2377	2527	757	859	927	979	1021	1080
$180,000	$200,000	1047	1155	1225	1278	1320	1379	1343	1457	1529	1583	1625	1684	1808	2082	2263	2402	2517	2676	804	912	984	1039	1083	1146
$200,000	$225,000	1110	1225	1299	1355	1400	1462	1436	1559	1636	1693	1739	1801	1913	2202	2394	2541	2662	2831	853	968	1043	1101	1149	1215
$225,000	$250,000	1178	1300	1378	1437	1485	1551	1537	1669	1751	1813	1862	1929	2025	2332	2535	2691	2819	2997	905	1027	1108	1169	1220	1290
$250,000	$275,000	1242	1371	1453	1516	1566	1635	1634	1774	1862	1927	1980	2051	2132	2454	2668	2832	2967	3155	955	1084	1169	1233	1287	1360
$275,000	$300,000	1304	1439	1526	1591	1644	1716	1728	1876	1969	2038	2094	2169	2234	2572	2796	2968	3109	3305	1003	1138	1227	1295	1351	1428
$300,000	or more	1676	1848	1959	2042	2109	2202	2303	2502	2627	2720	2795	2896	2842	3272	3557	3775	3955	4205	1292	1464	1578	1665	1737	1836

Income		Nebraska			1	5.5000%		Nevada			5	6.8500%		New Jersey			4,6	7.0000%		New Mexico			1	5.1250%	
$0	$20,000	223	247	262	273	282	294	265	293	311	324	335	350	248	266	278	286	293	302	195	217	231	241	250	262
$20,000	$30,000	371	410	436	455	470	491	412	455	482	503	520	543	413	443	463	477	489	505	337	375	400	419	434	455
$30,000	$40,000	453	502	533	556	575	601	490	541	574	598	618	646	504	542	566	584	599	618	419	467	498	522	541	567
$40,000	$50,000	527	583	619	647	669	699	558	616	653	681	704	735	586	631	659	680	696	719	492	550	587	614	637	668
$50,000	$60,000	594	658	699	730	755	789	619	683	725	755	780	815	661	712	743	767	786	812	561	626	669	701	727	762
$60,000	$70,000	656	727	772	806	834	872	675	745	789	823	850	888	730	786	822	848	869	898	625	698	745	781	810	850
$70,000	$80,000	714	792	841	878	908	949	727	802	850	886	915	955	795	856	895	924	947	978	685	766	818	857	889	933
$80,000	$90,000	769	853	906	946	979	1023	775	855	906	944	975	1018	857	923	964	995	1020	1054	743	831	887	930	965	1013
$90,000	$100,000	822	911	968	1011	1046	1093	821	905	959	999	1032	1077	915	986	1030	1063	1090	1126	798	892	954	1000	1037	1089
$100,000	$120,000	892	990	1052	1098	1136	1188	881	972	1030	1073	1108	1157	994	1071	1119	1155	1184	1224	873	977	1044	1094	1136	1192
$120,000	$140,000	986	1094	1163	1214	1256	1314	961	1059	1122	1170	1208	1260	1098	1184	1238	1278	1310	1353	973	1089	1165	1221	1267	1331
$140,000	$160,000	1075	1193	1268	1324	1370	1433	1036	1141	1209	1260	1301	1357	1197	1291	1349	1393	1428	1476	1069	1197	1280	1343	1393	1463
$160,000	$180,000	1158	1285	1366	1427	1477	1544	1105	1217	1289	1343	1387	1447	1290	1391	1454	1502	1540	1591	1159	1299	1389	1457	1512	1588
$180,000	$200,000	1238	1374	1461	1526	1579	1651	1171	1289	1365	1423	1469	1533	1379	1487	1555	1606	1646	1702	1247	1397	1494	1568	1627	1709
$200,000	$225,000	1322	1467	1560	1630	1687	1764	1239	1365	1445	1506	1555	1622	1473	1588	1661	1716	1759	1818	1340	1502	1606	1685	1750	1838
$225,000	$250,000	1414	1569	1669	1744	1804	1887	1313	1446	1531	1595	1647	1718	1575	1698	1776	1835	1881	1945	1441	1616	1729	1814	1883	1978
$250,000	$275,000	1501	1666	1772	1852	1916	2004	1383	1522	1612	1679	1734	1808	1672	1803	1887	1948	1998	2066	1538	1725	1846	1937	2012	2113
$275,000	$300,000	1585	1760	1872	1956	2024	2117	1450	1596	1690	1760	1817	1895	1766	1905	1993	2058	2111	2182	1633	1832	1960	2057	2136	2245
$300,000	or more	2100	2334	2483	2596	2686	2811	1850	2035	2154	2243	2315	2414	2340	2526	2644	2731	2802	2897	2222	2496	2672	2806	2915	3064

Income		New York			2	4.0000%		North Carolina			2	4.7500%		North Dakota			1	5.0000%		Ohio			1	5.7500%	
$0	$20,000	144	154	161	166	170	175	221	250	270	285	297	314	188	210	225	237	246	259	225	245	258	268	275	286
$20,000	$30,000	238	256	268	276	283	292	350	398	429	452	472	498	295	330	353	370	385	405	371	404	426	442	455	472
$30,000	$40,000	291	313	327	338	346	357	420	477	514	543	566	598	352	394	421	442	459	483	452	493	519	538	554	576
$40,000	$50,000	338	364	380	392	402	415	481	547	589	622	648	685	402	449	481	505	524	552	523	571	601	624	642	667
$50,000	$60,000	382	411	429	443	454	468	536	609	657	693	723	764	447	500	534	561	583	613	589	642	677	702	723	751
$60,000	$70,000	421	453	474	489	501	518	587	667	719	759	791	836	488	545	583	612	636	669	649	708	746	774	797	828
$70,000	$80,000	459	494	516	532	546	564	634	720	777	819	855	903	527	588	628	660	685	721	705	770	811	841	866	900
$80,000	$90,000	494	532	556	573	588	607	678	770	830	876	914	966	562	628	671	704	731	769	758	828	872	905	932	968
$90,000	$100,000	527	568	593	613	628	649	719	817	881	930	970	1025	596	665	711	746	775	815	809	883	930	965	994	1033
$100,000	$120,000	572	617	645	665	682	705	775	881	950	1002	1045	1104	641	715	764	802	833	876	877	958	1009	1047	1078	1120
$120,000	$140,000	632	681	712	735	754	779	848	964	1039	1097	1144	1209	700	781	835	876	909	956	967	1056	1112	1155	1189	1235
$140,000	$160,000	689	743	776	802	822	849	917	1042	1124	1186	1236	1307	755	842	900	944	981	1031	1052	1149	1210	1256	1294	1344
$160,000	$180,000	742	800	837	864	886	915	981	1114	1202	1268	1323	1398	806	899	961	1008	1047	1101	1132	1236	1302	1352	1392	1446
$180,000	$200,000	793	855	894	923	947	978	1041	1183	1276	1347	1404	1484	855	954	1019	1069	1110	1167	1208	1319	1390	1443	1485	1544
$200,000	$225,000	847	913	955	986	1011	1045	1105	1256	1354	1429	1490	1575	906	1010	1079	1132	1176	1236	1288	1407	1482	1539	1584	1646
$225,000	$250,000	905	976	1021	1054	1081	1117	1174	1334	1438	1518	1583	1673	961	1071	1144	1201	1247	1311	1375	1501	1582	1642	1691	1758
$250,000	$275,000	961	1036	1084	1119	1148	1186	1239	1407	1518	1602	1671	1766	1013	1129	1206	1265	1314	1381	1457	1592	1677	1741	1793	1864
$275,000	$300,000	1014	1094	1144	1182	1212	1253	1301	1478	1594	1683	1755	1855	1063	1185	1265	1327	1378	1448	1537	1679	1769	1837	1891	1966
$300,000	or more	1342	1449	1516	1566	1607	1661	1676	1905	2054	2168	2261	2390	1362	1517	1619	1698	1763	1853	2023	2210	2330	2419	2491	2589

(Continued)

2014 Optional State Sales Tax Tables *(Continued)*

Income		Oklahoma			1	4.5000%		Pennsylvania			1	6.0000%		Rhode Island			4	7.0000%		South Carolina			2	6.0000%	
$0	$20,000	243	279	303	322	338	359	194	210	220	228	234	243	255	278	293	304	313	325	234	257	272	284	293	305
$20,000	$30,000	379	435	473	502	526	560	319	346	363	376	386	400	397	433	455	472	486	504	386	425	450	469	484	505
$30,000	$40,000	452	519	564	598	627	667	388	421	442	458	471	488	472	515	541	562	578	600	470	519	549	572	591	616
$40,000	$50,000	515	591	642	682	714	760	449	488	512	530	545	566	537	586	616	639	658	683	545	601	637	664	685	715
$50,000	$60,000	572	657	713	757	793	844	505	548	576	597	614	637	596	650	684	709	730	758	614	677	718	748	772	805
$60,000	$70,000	624	716	778	826	865	920	557	605	635	658	677	702	650	708	745	773	795	825	677	747	792	825	852	888
$70,000	$80,000	672	771	838	889	931	990	605	657	690	715	736	763	699	762	802	832	855	888	736	812	861	897	926	966
$80,000	$90,000	717	823	894	948	993	1056	650	707	743	770	791	821	745	812	855	886	912	947	792	874	926	965	997	1040
$90,000	$100,000	760	871	946	1004	1052	1119	693	754	792	821	844	876	789	860	905	938	965	1002	845	933	988	1030	1064	1110
$100,000	$120,000	817	936	1017	1079	1130	1202	752	817	859	890	916	950	847	923	971	1007	1036	1076	917	1012	1072	1118	1154	1204
$120,000	$140,000	891	1022	1109	1177	1233	1311	829	901	947	982	1010	1048	923	1006	1059	1098	1130	1173	1011	1117	1183	1233	1274	1329
$140,000	$160,000	960	1101	1195	1268	1328	1412	901	980	1031	1068	1099	1141	994	1084	1140	1182	1216	1263	1101	1216	1288	1343	1387	1447
$160,000	$180,000	1025	1175	1275	1353	1417	1507	969	1054	1109	1150	1182	1228	1060	1155	1216	1261	1297	1346	1185	1308	1387	1445	1493	1557
$180,000	$200,000	1086	1245	1351	1433	1501	1596	1034	1125	1183	1227	1262	1311	1123	1224	1287	1335	1374	1426	1265	1397	1481	1544	1594	1663
$200,000	$225,000	1150	1318	1431	1518	1589	1690	1103	1200	1262	1309	1346	1398	1188	1295	1362	1413	1453	1509	1350	1490	1580	1647	1701	1775
$225,000	$250,000	1219	1397	1516	1608	1684	1790	1177	1281	1347	1397	1438	1493	1258	1371	1443	1496	1539	1598	1441	1592	1687	1759	1817	1896
$250,000	$275,000	1284	1471	1597	1694	1774	1886	1248	1358	1429	1482	1524	1583	1325	1444	1519	1575	1620	1682	1528	1688	1790	1866	1927	2011
$275,000	$300,000	1347	1543	1674	1776	1860	1977	1316	1432	1507	1563	1608	1670	1388	1513	1592	1651	1698	1763	1613	1781	1889	1969	2034	2122
$300,000	or more	1721	1970	2137	2266	2373	2522	1731	1886	1985	2059	2119	2201	1768	1926	2027	2102	2162	2245	2127	2350	2492	2599	2684	2801

Income		South Dakota			1	4.0000%		Tennessee			2	7.0000%		Texas			1	6.2500%		Utah			2	4.7000%	
$0	$20,000	235	271	296	314	330	351	366	416	450	475	496	525	254	283	301	315	326	342	236	267	288	304	317	335
$20,000	$30,000	366	423	461	490	514	548	579	658	711	751	784	830	419	466	497	520	539	565	376	426	459	484	504	533
$30,000	$40,000	437	505	550	584	613	653	693	789	852	900	940	995	510	568	606	634	657	688	452	512	551	581	606	640
$40,000	$50,000	498	575	627	666	699	744	793	903	975	1030	1075	1138	591	658	702	735	762	799	518	587	632	666	695	734
$50,000	$60,000	553	639	696	740	776	827	884	1006	1086	1147	1198	1268	664	741	790	828	858	899	578	655	705	743	775	819
$60,000	$70,000	603	697	759	807	846	901	967	1099	1187	1254	1309	1386	732	817	872	913	946	992	633	717	772	814	848	896
$70,000	$80,000	649	750	817	869	911	971	1043	1187	1281	1354	1413	1495	796	888	948	993	1029	1079	684	774	834	879	917	968
$80,000	$90,000	693	800	872	927	972	1035	1115	1268	1369	1447	1510	1598	856	956	1020	1068	1107	1161	732	829	892	941	981	1036
$90,000	$100,000	733	848	923	982	1030	1097	1183	1345	1453	1535	1602	1695	913	1020	1088	1140	1181	1239	777	880	947	999	1041	1100
$100,000	$120,000	788	911	992	1055	1106	1178	1274	1449	1564	1652	1725	1825	991	1106	1180	1236	1282	1344	838	948	1021	1077	1123	1186
$120,000	$140,000	860	993	1082	1151	1207	1285	1393	1584	1710	1807	1886	1996	1092	1220	1302	1364	1414	1483	917	1039	1118	1179	1229	1299
$140,000	$160,000	927	1071	1167	1240	1301	1385	1505	1712	1848	1952	2037	2156	1189	1328	1417	1485	1540	1615	992	1123	1210	1276	1330	1404
$160,000	$180,000	989	1143	1245	1323	1388	1478	1609	1830	1975	2086	2178	2305	1279	1429	1525	1598	1657	1739	1062	1202	1294	1365	1423	1503
$180,000	$200,000	1048	1211	1319	1402	1471	1566	1708	1942	2096	2214	2311	2446	1365	1525	1629	1707	1770	1857	1128	1277	1375	1450	1511	1596
$200,000	$225,000	1109	1282	1396	1485	1567	1658	1812	2060	2223	2348	2451	2594	1456	1627	1738	1821	1888	1981	1197	1356	1460	1539	1604	1695
$225,000	$250,000	1175	1358	1480	1573	1650	1757	1923	2186	2360	2493	2602	2753	1555	1738	1856	1945	2017	2116	1272	1440	1551	1635	1705	1800
$250,000	$275,000	1238	1431	1559	1657	1738	1851	2029	2307	2490	2630	2745	2904	1649	1843	1968	2063	2139	2245	1343	1521	1638	1727	1800	1901
$275,000	$300,000	1298	1500	1634	1737	1822	1941	2131	2422	2614	2761	2882	3049	1739	1944	2077	2177	2258	2369	1412	1598	1721	1814	1891	1997
$300,000	or more	1657	1915	2086	2218	2326	2478	2740	3114	3361	3550	3705	3920	2292	2564	2740	2872	2979	3127	1822	2063	2221	2342	2441	2578

Income		Vermont			1	6.0000%		Virginia			2	4.3000%		Washington			1	6.5000%		West Virginia			2	6.0000%	
$0	$20,000	163	174	181	186	190	195	178	203	218	230	240	254	260	287	304	316	327	341	250	279	297	311	323	338
$20,000	$30,000	253	270	281	288	294	303	274	310	334	352	367	388	431	476	504	526	543	567	413	461	492	516	535	561
$30,000	$40,000	301	321	334	343	350	360	324	367	395	417	434	459	526	581	616	642	663	693	503	563	601	630	653	686
$40,000	$50,000	343	366	380	390	399	410	368	416	448	472	492	520	611	674	715	746	770	804	584	653	697	731	758	796
$50,000	$60,000	380	406	422	433	442	455	407	460	495	522	544	574	688	760	806	840	868	907	657	735	786	824	855	897
$60,000	$70,000	415	442	459	472	482	496	442	500	538	567	591	624	760	839	889	928	959	1001	725	811	867	909	943	991
$70,000	$80,000	446	476	494	508	519	533	475	537	578	609	634	670	826	912	968	1009	1043	1090	789	883	943	989	1027	1078
$80,000	$90,000	476	507	527	541	553	569	506	572	615	648	675	712	890	982	1042	1087	1123	1173	849	950	1016	1065	1105	1161
$90,000	$100,000	503	537	558	573	585	602	534	604	650	685	713	753	950	1049	1112	1160	1199	1252	906	1014	1084	1137	1180	1239
$100,000	$120,000	540	576	599	615	628	646	573	647	696	733	764	806	1030	1138	1207	1259	1302	1360	983	1101	1177	1234	1281	1345
$120,000	$140,000	589	628	652	670	685	704	623	704	757	797	830	876	1138	1257	1333	1391	1437	1502	1085	1215	1299	1363	1415	1486
$140,000	$160,000	634	677	703	722	738	758	670	757	813	857	892	941	1239	1369	1452	1515	1566	1636	1181	1323	1415	1485	1541	1619
$160,000	$180,000	676	721	749	770	786	809	714	805	866	912	949	1001	1334	1474	1563	1631	1686	1762	1271	1425	1524	1599	1660	1744
$180,000	$200,000	716	764	793	815	833	856	755	852	915	964	1003	1058	1424	1574	1670	1743	1801	1882	1358	1522	1628	1708	1773	1863
$200,000	$225,000	758	808	840	863	881	906	798	900	967	1018	1060	1118	1520	1680	1783	1860	1923	2009	1449	1624	1738	1823	1893	1989
$225,000	$250,000	803	856	889	914	933	959	844	952	1022	1076	1121	1182	1624	1795	1905	1987	2055	2147	1548	1735	1857	1948	2023	2125
$250,000	$275,000	845	901	936	962	982	1010	887	1001	1075	1132	1178	1242	1723	1904	2021	2109	2180	2278	1642	1841	1970	2068	2147	2256
$275,000	$300,000	886	944	981	1008	1029	1059	929	1047	1125	1184	1233	1300	1818	2010	2133	2226	2301	2405	1733	1944	2080	2183	2266	2381
$300,000	or more	1128	1203	1249	1283	1311	1348	1178	1326	1424	1498	1559	1643	2401	2655	2819	2942	3042	3179	2289	2569	2750	2886	2998	3151

Income		Wisconsin			1	5.0000%		Wyoming			1	4.0000%	
$0	$20,000	212	233	247	257	266	277	160	175	184	191	197	204
$20,000	$30,000	347	382	405	422	436	455	266	290	305	317	326	339
$30,000	$40,000	421	465	493	513	530	553	324	354	372	387	398	414
$40,000	$50,000	487	538	570	594	614	640	376	410	432	449	462	480
$50,000	$60,000	547	604	641	668	690	720	423	462	487	506	520	541
$60,000	$70,000	603	666	706	736	760	793	467	510	537	558	574	597
$70,000	$80,000	654	723	767	799	826	862	508	555	585	607	625	649
$80,000	$90,000	703	777	824	859	888	927	547	597	629	653	673	699
$90,000	$100,000	750	828	878	916	946	988	583	637	671	697	718	746
$100,000	$120,000	812	898	952	993	1026	1071	633	691	729	757	779	810
$120,000	$140,000	895	989	1049	1094	1130	1180	698	763	804	835	860	894
$140,000	$160,000	973	1075	1141	1190	1229	1283	760	831	876	909	937	974
$160,000	$180,000	1046	1156	1226	1279	1322	1380	818	894	943	979	1008	1048
$180,000	$200,000	1115	1233	1308	1365	1410	1472	874	955	1007	1046	1077	1119
$200,000	$225,000	1189	1314	1395	1455	1503	1570	932	1019	1074	1116	1149	1195
$225,000	$250,000	1268	1402	1488	1552	1604	1675	996	1089	1148	1192	1227	1276
$250,000	$275,000	1344	1486	1577	1645	1700	1776	1056	1155	1217	1264	1302	1354
$275,000	$300,000	1416	1567	1663	1735	1793	1872	1114	1219	1285	1334	1374	1429
$300,000	or more	1860	2059	2186	2281	2357	2462	1470	1608	1696	1762	1815	1887

Note. Residents of **Alaska** do not have a state sales tax, but should follow the instructions on the next pages to determine their local sales tax amount.

1. Use the Ratio Method to determine your local sales tax deduction, then add that to the appropriate amount in the state table. Your state sales tax rate is provided next to the state name.

2. Follow the instructions on the next pages to determine your local sales tax deduction, then add that to the appropriate amount in the state table.

3. The California table includes the 1.25% uniform local sales tax rate in addition to the 6.25% state sales tax rate for a total of 7.50%. Some California localities impose a larger local sales tax. Taxpayers who reside in those jurisdictions should use the Ratio Method to determine their local sales tax deduction, then add that to the appropriate amount in the state table. The denominator of the correct ratio is 7.50%, and the numerator is the total sales tax rate minus the 7.50% tax rate.

4. This state does not have a local general sales tax, so the amount in the state table is the only amount to be deducted.

5. The Nevada table includes the 2.25% uniform local sales tax rate in addition to the 4.6000% state sales tax rate for a total of 6.85%. Some Nevada localities impose a larger local sales tax. Taypayers who reside in those jurisdictions should use the Ratio Method to determine their local sales tax deduction, then add that to the appropriate amount in the state table. The denominator of the correct ratio is 6.85%, and the numerator is the total sales tax rate minus the 6.85% tax rate.

6. Residents of Salem County, New Jersey should deduct only half of the amount in the state table.

7. The 4.0% rate for Hawaii is actually an excise tax but is treated as a sales tax for purpose of this deduction.

Which Optional Local Sales Tax Table Should I Use?

IF you live in the state of...	AND you live in...	THEN use Local Table...
Alaska	Any locality	C
Arizona	Chandler, Glendale, Gilbert, Mesa, Peoria, Phoenix, Scottsdale, Tempe, Tucson, Yuma, or any other locality	B
Arkansas	Any locality	B
Colorado	Adams County, Arapahoe County, Boulder County, Centennial, Colorado Springs, Denver City/Denver County, El Paso County, Larimer County, Pueblo County, or any other locality	A
	Greeley, Jefferson County, Lakewood, Longmont or Pueblo City	B
	Arvada, Boulder, Fort Collins, Thornton, or Westminster	C
Georgia	Any locality	B
Illinois	City of Aurora	B
	Any other locality	A
Louisiana	Ascension Parish, Bossier Parish, Caddo Parish, Calcasieu Parish, East Baton Rouge Parish, Iberia Parish, Jefferson Parish, Lafayette Parish, Lafourche Parish, Livingston Parish, Orleans Parish, Ouachita Parish, Rapides Parish, St. Bernard Parish, St. Landry Parish, St. Tammany Parish, Tangipahoa Parish, or Terrebonne Parish	C
Missouri	Any other locality	B
	Any locality	B
New York	Counties: Albany, Allegany, Broome, Cattaraugus, Cayuga, Chautauqua, Chemung, Chenango, Clinton, Columbia, Cortland, Delaware, Dutchess, Erie, Essex, Franklin, Fulton, Genesee, Greene, Hamilton, Herkimer, Jefferson, Lewis, Livingston, Madison, Monroe, Montgomery, Nassau, Niagara, Oneida, Onondaga, Ontario, Orange, Orleans, Oswego, Otsego, Putnam, Rensselaer, Rockland, St. Lawrence, Saratoga, Schenectady, Schoharie, Schuyler, Seneca, Steuben, Suffolk, Sullivan, Tioga, Tompkins, Ulster, Warren, Washington, Wayne, Westchester, Wyoming, or Yates	B
	New York City or Norwich City	D*
	Any other locality	A
North Carolina	Any locality	A
South Carolina	Aiken County, Horry County, Lexington County, Newberry County, Orangeburg County, York County, or Myrtle Beach	B
	Bamberg County, Charleston County, Cherokee County, Chesterfield County, Darlington County, Dillon County, Florence County, Hampton County, Jasper County, Lee County, Marion County, Marlboro County, or any other locality	B
Tennessee	Any locality	A
Utah	Any locality	B
Virginia	Any locality	B
West Virginia	Any locality	

*Note. Local Table D is 25% of the NY State table.

2014 Optional Local Sales Tax Tables for Certain Local Jurisdictions

Income At least	But less than	| Exemptions 1 (A)	2	3	4	5	Over 5	| Exemptions 1 (B)	2	3	4	5	Over 5
		Local Table A						**Local Table B**					
$0	$20,000	38	43	46	48	50	52	47	53	58	62	64	68
20,000	30,000	60	66	71	74	77	81	71	82	89	94	99	105
30,000	40,000	71	79	84	88	91	96	84	97	105	111	117	124
40,000	50,000	81	90	96	100	104	109	96	110	119	126	132	140
50,000	60,000	89	99	106	111	115	121	106	122	132	140	146	155
60,000	70,000	97	108	115	121	125	131	115	132	143	152	159	169
70,000	80,000	105	117	124	130	135	141	124	142	154	163	170	181
80,000	90,000	112	124	132	139	144	150	132	151	164	173	181	192
90,000	100,000	118	131	140	147	152	159	139	159	173	183	192	203
100,000	120,000	127	141	150	157	163	171	149	171	185	196	205	218
120,000	140,000	138	154	164	171	178	186	162	186	201	213	223	237
140,000	160,000	149	166	176	184	191	200	175	200	216	229	240	254
160,000	180,000	159	176	188	197	204	213	186	212	230	244	255	271
180,000	200,000	168	187	199	208	216	226	196	225	243	258	270	286
200,000	225,000	178	198	210	220	228	239	208	237	257	272	285	302
225,000	250,000	189	209	223	233	241	253	220	251	272	288	301	319
250,000	275,000	199	220	234	245	254	266	231	264	286	303	316	336
275,000	300,000	208	231	246	257	266	279	242	276	299	317	331	351
300,000	or more	265	294	313	327	338	354	306	349	378	400	418	444
		Local Table C						**Local Table D**					
$0	$20,000	56	64	69	73	77	81	36	39	40	42	43	44
20,000	30,000	87	100	108	114	120	127	60	64	67	69	71	73
30,000	40,000	104	119	129	136	143	151	73	78	82	85	87	89
40,000	50,000	119	136	147	156	163	173	85	91	95	98	101	104
50,000	60,000	132	151	163	173	181	192	96	103	107	111	114	117
60,000	70,000	144	164	178	189	197	209	105	113	119	122	125	130
70,000	80,000	155	177	192	203	212	225	115	124	129	133	137	141
80,000	90,000	165	189	205	217	227	240	124	133	139	143	147	152
90,000	100,000	175	200	217	230	240	255	132	142	148	153	157	162
100,000	120,000	188	215	233	247	258	274	143	154	161	166	171	176
120,000	140,000	205	235	254	269	282	299	158	170	178	184	189	195
140,000	160,000	221	253	274	290	304	322	172	186	194	201	206	212
160,000	180,000	236	270	293	310	324	344	186	200	209	216	222	229
180,000	200,000	250	286	310	328	343	364	198	214	224	231	237	245
200,000	225,000	265	303	329	348	364	386	212	228	239	247	253	261
225,000	250,000	281	322	348	369	385	409	226	244	255	264	270	279
250,000	275,000	296	339	367	388	406	431	240	259	271	280	287	297
275,000	300,000	311	355	385	407	426	452	254	274	286	296	303	313
300,000	or more	397	454	492	520	544	577	336	362	379	392	402	415

Appendix D – Depreciation Tables

Table B-1. **Table of Class Lives and Recovery Periods**

Asset class	Description of assets included	Class Life (in years)	Recovery Periods (in years) GDS (MACRS)	ADS
SPECIFIC DEPRECIABLE ASSETS USED IN ALL BUSINESS ACTIVITIES, EXCEPT AS NOTED:				
00.11	**Office Furniture, Fixtures, and Equipment:** Includes furniture and fixtures that are not a structural component of a building. Includes such assets as desks, files, safes, and communications equipment. Does not include communications equipment that is included in other classes.	10	7	10
00.12	**Information Systems:** Includes computers and their peripheral equipment used in administering normal business transactions and the maintenance of business records, their retrieval and analysis. Information systems are defined as: 1) Computers: A computer is a programmable electronically activated device capable of accepting information, applying prescribed processes to the information, and supplying the results of these processes with or without human intervention. It usually consists of a central processing unit containing extensive storage, logic, arithmetic, and control capabilities. Excluded from this category are adding machines, electronic desk calculators, etc., and other equipment described in class 00.13. 2) Peripheral equipment consists of the auxiliary machines which are designed to be placed under control of the central processing unit. Nonlimiting examples are: Card readers, card punches, magnetic tape feeds, high speed printers, optical character readers, tape cassettes, mass storage units, paper tape equipment, keypunches, data entry devices, teleprinters, terminals, tape drives, disc drives, disc files, disc packs, visual image projector tubes, card sorters, plotters, and collators. Peripheral equipment may be used on-line or off-line. Does not incude equipment that is an integral part of other capital equipment that is included in other classes of economic activity, i.e., computers used primarily for process or production control, switching, channeling, and automating distributive trades and services such as point of sale (POS) computer systems. Also, does not include equipment of a kind used primarily for amusement or entertainment of the user.	6	5	5
00.13	**Data Handling Equipment; except Computers:** Includes only typewriters, calculators, adding and accounting machines, copiers, and duplicating equipment.	6	5	6
00.21	**Airplanes (airframes and engines), except those used in commercial or contract carrying of passengers or freight, and all helicopters (airframes and engines)**	6	5	6
00.22	**Automobiles, Taxis**	3	5	5
00.23	**Buses**	9	5	9
00.241	**Light General Purpose Trucks:** Includes trucks for use over the road (actual weight less than 13,000 pounds)	4	5	5
00.242	**Heavy General Purpose Trucks:** Includes heavy general purpose trucks, concrete ready mix-trucks, and ore trucks, for use over the road (actual unloaded weight 13,000 pounds or more)	6	5	6
00.25	**Railroad Cars and Locomotives, except those owned by railroad transportation companies**	15	7	15
00.26	**Tractor Units for Use Over-The-Road**	4	3	4
00.27	**Trailers and Trailer-Mounted Containers**	6	5	6
00.28	**Vessels, Barges, Tugs, and Similar Water Transportation Equipment, except those used in marine construction**	18	10	18
00.3	**Land Improvements:** Includes improvements directly to or added to land, whether such improvements are section 1245 property or section 1250 property, provided such improvements are depreciable. Examples of such assets might include sidewalks, roads, canals, waterways, drainage facilities, sewers (not including municipal sewers in Class 51), wharves and docks, bridges, fences, landscaping shrubbery, or radio and television transmitting towers. Does not include land improvements that are explicitly included in any other class, and buildings and structural components as defined in section 1.48-1(e) of the regulations. Excludes public utility initial clearing and grading land improvements as specified in Rev. Rul. 72-403, 1972-2 C.B. 102.	20	15	20
00.4	**Industrial Steam and Electric Generation and/or Distribution Systems:** Includes assets, whether such assets are section 1245 property or 1250 property, providing such assets are depreciable, used in the production and/or distribution of electricity with rated total capacity in excess of 500 Kilowatts and/or assets used in the production and/or distribution of steam with rated total capacity in excess of 12,500 pounds per hour for use by the taxpayer in its industrial manufacturing process or plant activity and not ordinarily available for sale to others. Does not include buildings and structural components as defined in section 1.48-1(e) of the regulations. Assets used to generate and/or distribute electricity or steam of the type described above, but of lesser rated capacity, are not included, but are included in the appropriate manufacturing equipment classes elsewhere specified. Also includes electric generating and steam distribution assets, which may utilize steam produced by a waste reduction and resource recovery plant, used by the taxpayer in its industrial manufacturing process or plant activity. Steam and chemical recovery boiler systems used for the recovery and regeneration of chemicals used in manufacturing, with rated capacity in excess of that described above, with specifically related distribution and return systems are not included but are included in appropriate manufacturing equipment classes elsewhere specified. An example of an excluded steam and chemical recovery boiler system is that used in the pulp and paper manufacturing equipment classes elsewhere specified. An example of an excluded steam and chemical recovery boiler system is that used in the pulp and paper manufacturing industry.	22	15	22

Table B-2. **Table of Class Lives and Recovery Periods**

Asset class	Description of assets included	Class Life (in years)	GDS (MACRS)	ADS
			Recovery Periods (in years)	
DEPRECIABLE ASSETS USED IN THE FOLLOWING ACTIVITIES:				
01.1	**Agriculture:** Includes machinery and equipment, grain bins, and fences but no other land improvements, that are used in the production of crops or plants, vines, and trees; livestock; the operation of farm dairies, nurseries, greenhouses, sod farms, mushroom cellars, cranberry bogs, apiaries, and fur farms; the performance of agriculture, animal husbandry, and horticultural services.	10	7	10
01.11	**Cotton Ginning Assets**	12	7	12
01.21	**Cattle, Breeding or Dairy**	7	5	7
01.221	**Any breeding or work horse that is 12 years old or less at the time it is placed in service****	10	7	10
01.222	**Any breeding or work horse that is more than 12 years old at the time it is placed in service****	10	3	10
01.223	**Any race horse that is more than 2 years old at the time it is placed in service****	*	3	12
01.224	**Any horse that is more than 12 years old at the time it is placed in service and that is neither a race horse nor a horse described in class 01.222****	*	3	12
01.225	**Any horse not described in classes 01.221, 01.222, 01.223, or 01.224**	*	7	12
01.23	**Hogs, Breeding**	3	3	3
01.24	**Sheep and Goats, Breeding**	5	5	5
01.3	**Farm buildings except structures included in Class 01.4**	25	20	25
01.4	**Single purpose agricultural or horticultural structures (within the meaning of section 168(i)(13) of the Code)**	15	10***	15
10.0	**Mining:** Includes assets used in the mining and quarrying of metallic and nonmetallic minerals (including sand, gravel, stone, and clay) and the milling, beneficiation and other primary preparation of such materials.	10	7	10
13.0	**Offshore Drilling:** Includes assets used in offshore drilling for oil and gas such as floating, self-propelled and other drilling vessels, barges, platforms, and drilling equipment and support vessels such as tenders, barges, towboats and crewboats. Excludes oil and gas production assets.	7.5	5	7.5
13.1	**Drilling of Oil and Gas Wells:** Includes assets used in the drilling of onshore oil and gas wells and the provision of geophysical and other exploration services; and the provision of such oil and gas field services as chemical treatment, plugging and abandoning of wells and cementing or perforating well casings. Does not include assets used in the performance of any of these activities and services by integrated petroleum and natural gas producers for their own account.	6	5	6
13.2	**Exploration for and Production of Petroleum and Natural Gas Deposits:** Includes assets used by petroleum and natural gas producers for drilling of wells and production of petroleum and natural gas, including gathering pipelines and related storage facilities. Also includes petroleum and natural gas offshore transportation facilities used by producers and others consisting of platforms (other than drilling platforms classified in Class 13.0), compression or pumping equipment, and gathering and transmission lines to the first onshore transshipment facility. The assets used in the first onshore transshipment facility are also included and consist of separation equipment (used for separation of natural gas, liquids, and in Class 49.23), and liquid holding or storage facilities (other than those classified in Class 49.25). Does not include support vessels.	14	7	14
13.3	**Petroleum Refining:** Includes assets used for the distillation, fractionation, and catalytic cracking of crude petroleum into gasoline and its other components.	16	10	16
15.0	**Construction:** Includes assets used in construction by general building, special trade, heavy and marine construction contractors, operative and investment builders, real estate subdividers and developers, and others except railroads.	6	5	6
20.1	**Manufacture of Grain and Grain Mill Products:** Includes assets used in the production of flours, cereals, livestock feeds, and other grain and grain mill products.	17	10	17
20.2	**Manufacture of Sugar and Sugar Products:** Includes assets used in the production of raw sugar, syrup, or finished sugar from sugar cane or sugar beets.	18	10	18
20.3	**Manufacture of Vegetable Oils and Vegetable Oil Products:** Includes assets used in the production of oil from vegetable materials and the manufacture of related vegetable oil products.	18	10	18
20.4	**Manufacture of Other Food and Kindred Products:** Includes assets used in the production of foods and beverages not included in classes 20.1, 20.2 and 20.3.	12	7	12
20.5	**Manufacture of Food and Beverages—Special Handling Devices:** Includes assets defined as specialized materials handling devices such as returnable pallets, palletized containers, and fish processing equipment including boxes, baskets, carts, and flaking trays used in activities as defined in classes 20.1, 20.2, 20.3 and 20.4. Does not include general purpose small tools such as wrenches and drills, both hand and power-driven, and other general purpose equipment such as conveyors, transfer equipment, and materials handling devices.	4	3	4

* Property described in asset classes 01.223, 01.224, and 01.225 are assigned recovery periods but have no class lives.
** A horse is more than 2 (or 12) years old after the day that is 24 (or 144) months after its actual birthdate.
*** 7 if property was placed in service before 1989.

Table B-2. **Table of Class Lives and Recovery Periods**

Asset class	Description of assets included	Class Life (in years)	Recovery Periods (in years) GDS (MACRS)	ADS
21.0	**Manufacture of Tobacco and Tobacco Products:** Includes assets used in the production of cigarettes, cigars, smoking and chewing tobacco, snuff, and other tobacco products.	15	7	15
22.1	**Manufacture of Knitted Goods:** Includes assets used in the production of knitted and netted fabrics and lace. Assets used in yarn preparation, bleaching, dyeing, printing, and other similar finishing processes, texturing, and packaging, are elsewhere classified.	7.5	5	7.5
22.2	**Manufacture of Yarn, Thread, and Woven Fabric:** Includes assets used in the production of spun yarns including the preparing, blending, spinning, and twisting of fibers into yarns and threads, the preparation of yarns such as twisting, warping, and winding, the production of covered elastic yarn and thread, cordage, woven fabric, tire fabric, braided fabric, twisted jute for packaging, mattresses, pads, sheets, and industrial belts, and the processing of textile mill waste to recover fibers, flocks, and shoddies. Assets used to manufacture carpets, man-made fibers, and nonwovens, and assets used in texturing, bleaching, dyeing, printing, and other similar finishing processes, are elsewhere classified.	11	7	11
22.3	**Manufacture of Carpets and Dyeing, Finishing, and Packaging of Textile Products and Manufacture of Medical and Dental Supplies:** Includes assets used in the production of carpets, rugs, mats, woven carpet backing, chenille, and other tufted products, and assets used in the joining together of backing with carpet yarn or fabric. Includes assets used in washing, scouring, bleaching, dyeing, printing, drying, and similar finishing processes applied to textile fabrics, yarns, threads, and other textile goods. Includes assets used in the production and packaging of textile products, other than apparel, by creasing, forming, trimming, cutting, and sewing, such as the preparation of carpet and fabric samples, or similar joining together processes (other than the production of scrim reinforced paper products and laminated paper products) such as the sewing and folding of hosiery and panty hose, and the creasing, folding, trimming, and cutting of fabrics to produce nonwoven products, such as disposable diapers and sanitary products. Also includes assets used in the production of medical and dental supplies other than drugs and medicines. Assets used in the manufacture of nonwoven carpet backing, and hard surface floor covering such as tile, rubber, and cork, are elsewhere classified.	9	5	9
22.4	**Manufacture of Textile Yarns:** Includes assets used in the processing of yarns to impart bulk and/or stretch properties to the yarn. The principal machines involved are falsetwist, draw, beam-to-beam, and stuffer box texturing equipment and related highspeed twisters and winders. Assets, as described above, which are used to further process man-made fibers are elsewhere classified when located in the same plant in an integrated operation with man-made fiber producing assets. Assets used to manufacture man-made fibers and assets used in bleaching, dyeing, printing, and other similar finishing processes, are elsewhere classified.	8	5	8
22.5	**Manufacture of Nonwoven Fabrics:** Includes assets used in the production of nonwoven fabrics, felt goods including felt hats, padding, batting, wadding, oakum, and fillings, from new materials and from textile mill waste. Nonwoven fabrics are defined as fabrics (other than reinforced and laminated composites consisting of nonwovens and other products) manufactured by bonding natural and/or synthetic fibers and/or filaments by means of induced mechanical interlocking, fluid entanglement, chemical adhesion, thermal or solvent reaction, or by combination thereof other than natural hydration bonding as occurs with natural cellulose fibers. Such means include resin bonding, web bonding, and melt bonding. Specifically includes assets used to make flocked and needle punched products other than carpets and rugs. Assets, as described above, which are used to manufacture nonwovens are elsewhere classified when located in the same plant in an integrated operation with man-made fiber producing assets. Assets used to manufacture man-made fibers and assets used in bleaching, dyeing, printing, and other similar finishing processes, are elsewhere classified.	10	7	10
23.0	**Manufacture of Apparel and Other Finished Products:** Includes assets used in the production of clothing and fabricated textile products by the cutting and sewing of woven fabrics, other textile products, and furs; but does not include assets used in the manufacture of apparel from rubber and leather.	9	5	9
24.1	**Cutting of Timber:** Includes logging machinery and equipment and roadbuilding equipment used by logging and sawmill operators and pulp manufacturers for their own account.	6	5	6
24.2	**Sawing of Dimensional Stock from Logs:** Includes machinery and equipment installed in permanent or well established sawmills.	10	7	10
24.3	**Sawing of Dimensional Stock from Logs:** Includes machinery and equipment in sawmills characterized by temporary foundations and a lack, or minimum amount, of lumberhandling, drying, and residue disposal equipment and facilities.	6	5	6
24.4	**Manufacture of Wood Products, and Furniture:** Includes assets used in the production of plywood, hardboard, flooring, veneers, furniture, and other wood products, including the treatment of poles and timber.	10	7	10
26.1	**Manufacture of Pulp and Paper:** Includes assets for pulp materials handling and storage, pulp mill processing, bleach processing, paper and paperboard manufacturing, and on-line finishing. Includes pollution control assets and all land improvements associated with the factory site or production process such as effluent ponds and canals, provided such improvements are depreciable but does not include buildings and structural components as defined in section 1.48-1(e)(1) of the regulations. Includes steam and chemical recovery boiler systems, with any rated capacity, used for the recovery and regeneration of chemicals used in manufacturing. Does not include assets used either in pulpwood logging, or in the manufacture of hardboard.	13	7	13

Table B-2. **Table of Class Lives and Recovery Periods**

Asset class	Description of assets included	Class Life (in years)	GDS (MACRS)	ADS
			Recovery Periods (in years)	
26.2	**Manufacture of Converted Paper, Paperboard, and Pulp Products:** Includes assets used for modification, or remanufacture of paper and pulp into converted products, such as paper coated off the paper machine, paper bags, paper boxes, cartons and envelopes. Does not include assets used for manufacture of nonwovens that are elsewhere classified.	10	7	10
27.0	**Printing, Publishing, and Allied Industries:** Includes assets used in printing by one or more processes, such as letter-press, lithography, gravure, or screen; the performance of services for the printing trade, such as bookbinding, typesetting, engraving, photo-engraving, and electrotyping; and the publication of newspapers, books, and periodicals.	11	7	11
28.0	**Manufacture of Chemicals and Allied Products:** Includes assets used to manufacture basic organic and inorganic chemicals; chemical products to be used in further manufacture, such as synthetic fibers and plastics materials; and finished chemical products. Includes assets used to further process man-made fibers, to manufacture plastic film, and to manufacture nonwoven fabrics, when such assets are located in the same plant in an integrated operation with chemical products producing assets. Also includes assets used to manufacture photographic supplies, such as film, photographic paper, sensitized photographic paper, and developing chemicals. Includes all land improvements associated with plant site or production processes, such as effluent ponds and canals, provided such land improvements are depreciable but does not include buildings and structural components as defined in section 1.48-1(e) of the regulations. Does not include assets used in the manufacture of finished rubber and plastic products or in the production of natural gas products, butane, propane, and by-products of natural gas production plants.	9.5	5	9.5
30.1	**Manufacture of Rubber Products:** Includes assets used for the production of products from natural, synthetic, or reclaimed rubber, gutta percha, balata, or gutta siak, such as tires, tubes, rubber footwear, mechanical rubber goods, heels and soles, flooring, and rubber sundries; and in the recapping, retreading, and rebuilding of tires.	14	7	14
30.11	**Manufacture of Rubber Products—Special Tools and Devices:** Includes assets defined as special tools, such as jigs, dies, mandrels, molds, lasts, patterns, specialty containers, pallets, shells; and tire molds, and accessory parts such as rings and insert plates used in activities as defined in class 30.1. Does not include tire building drums and accessory parts and general purpose small tools such as wrenches and drills, both power and hand-driven, and other general purpose equipment such as conveyors and transfer equipment.	4	3	4
30.2	**Manufacture of Finished Plastic Products:** Includes assets used in the manufacture of plastics products and the molding of primary plastics for the trade. Does not include assets used in the manufacture of basic plastics materials nor the manufacture of phonograph records.	11	7	11
30.21	**Manufacture of Finished Plastic Products—Special Tools:** Includes assets defined as special tools, such as jigs, dies, fixtures, molds, patterns, gauges, and specialty transfer and shipping devices, used in activities as defined in class 30.2. Special tools are specifically designed for the production or processing of particular parts and have no significant utilitarian value and cannot be adapted to further or different use after changes or improvements are made in the model design of the particular part produced by the special tools. Does not include general purpose small tools such as wrenches and drills, both hand and power-driven, and other general purpose equipment such as conveyors, transfer equipment, and materials handling devices.	3.5	3	3.5
31.0	**Manufacture of Leather and Leather Products:** Includes assets used in the tanning, currying, and finishing of hides and skins; the processing of fur pelts; and the manufacture of finished leather products, such as footwear, belting, apparel, and luggage.	11	7	11
32.1	**Manufacture of Glass Products:** Includes assets used in the production of flat, blown, or pressed products of glass, such as float and window glass, glass containers, glassware and fiberglass. Does not include assets used in the manufacture of lenses.	14	7	14
32.11	**Manufacture of Glass Products—Special Tools:** Includes assets defined as special tools such as molds, patterns, pallets, and specialty transfer and shipping devices such as steel racks to transport automotive glass, used in activities as defined in class 32.1. Special tools are specifically designed for the production or processing of particular parts and have no significant utilitarian value and cannot be adapted to further or different use after changes or improvements are made in the model design of the particular part produced by the special tools. Does not include general purpose small tools such as wrenches and drills, both hand and power-driven, and other general purpose equipment such as conveyors, transfer equipment, and materials handling devices.	2.5	3	2.5
32.2	**Manufacture of Cement:** Includes assets used in the production of cement, but does not include assets used in the manufacture of concrete and concrete products nor in any mining or extraction process.	20	15	20
32.3	**Manufacture of Other Stone and Clay Products:** Includes assets used in the manufacture of products from materials in the form of clay and stone, such as brick, tile, and pipe; pottery and related products, such as vitreous-china, plumbing fixtures, earthenware and ceramic insulating materials; and also includes assets used in manufacture of concrete and concrete products. Does not include assets used in any mining or extraction processes.	15	7	15

Table B-2. **Table of Class Lives and Recovery Periods**

Asset class	Description of assets included	Class Life (in years)	Recovery Periods (in years) GDS (MACRS)	ADS
33.2	**Manufacture of Primary Nonferrous Metals:** Includes assets used in the smelting, refining, and electrolysis of nonferrous metals from ore, pig, or scrap, the rolling, drawing, and alloying of nonferrous metals; the manufacture of castings, forgings, and other basic products of nonferrous metals; and the manufacture of nails, spikes, structural shapes, tubing, wire, and cable.	14	7	14
33.21	**Manufacture of Primary Nonferrous Metals—Special Tools:** Includes assets defined as special tools such as dies, jigs, molds, patterns, fixtures, gauges, and drawings concerning such special tools used in the activities as defined in class 33.2, Manufacture of Primary Nonferrous Metals. Special tools are specifically designed for the production or processing of particular products or parts and have no significant utilitarian value and cannot be adapted to further or different use after changes or improvements are made in the model design of the particular part produced by the special tools. Does not include general purpose small tools such as wrenches and drills, both hand and power-driven, and other general purpose equipment such as conveyors, transfer equipment, and materials handling devices. Rolls, mandrels and refractories are not included in class 33.21 but are included in class 33.2.	6.5	5	6.5
33.3	**Manufacture of Foundry Products:** Includes assets used in the casting of iron and steel, including related operations such as molding and coremaking. Also includes assets used in the finishing of castings and patternmaking when performed at the foundry, all special tools and related land improvements.	14	7	14
33.4	**Manufacture of Primary Steel Mill Products:** Includes assets used in the smelting, reduction, and refining of iron and steel from ore, pig, or scrap; the rolling, drawing and alloying of steel; the manufacture of nails, spikes, structural shapes, tubing, wire, and cable. Includes assets used by steel service centers, ferrous metal forges, and assets used in coke production, regardless of ownership. Also includes related land improvements and all special tools used in the above activities.	15	7	15
34.0	**Manufacture of Fabricated Metal Products:** Includes assets used in the production of metal cans, tinware, fabricated structural metal products, metal stampings, and other ferrous and nonferrous metal and wire products not elsewhere classified. Does not include assets used to manufacture non-electric heating apparatus.	12	7	12
34.01	**Manufacture of Fabricated Metal Products—Special Tools:** Includes assets defined as special tools such as dies, jigs, molds, patterns, fixtures, gauges, and returnable containers and drawings concerning such special tools used in the activities as defined in class 34.0. Special tools are specifically designed for the production or processing of particular machine components, products, or parts, and have no significant utilitarian value and cannot be adapted to further or different use after changes or improvements are made in the model design of the particular part produced by the special tools. Does not include general small tools such as wrenches and drills, both hand and power-driven, and other general purpose equipment such as conveyors, transfer equipment, and materials handling devices.	3	3	3
35.0	**Manufacture of Electrical and Non-Electrical Machinery and Other Mechanical Products:** Includes assets used to manufacture or rebuild finished machinery and equipment and replacement parts thereof such as machine tools, general industrial and special industry machinery, electrical power generation, transmission, and distribution systems, space heating, cooling, and refrigeration systems, commercial and home appliances, farm and garden machinery, construction machinery, mining and oil field machinery, internal combustion engines (except those elsewhere classified), turbines (except those that power airborne vehicles), batteries, lamps and lighting fixtures, carbon and graphite products, and electromechanical and mechanical products including business machines, instruments, watches and clocks, vending and amusement machines, photographic equipment, medical and dental equipment and appliances, and ophthalmic goods. Includes assets used by manufacturers or rebuilders of such finished machinery and equipment in activities elsewhere classified such as the manufacture of castings, forgings, rubber and plastic products, electronic subassemblies or other manufacturing activities if the interim products are used by the same manufacturer primarily in the manufacture, assembly, or rebuilding of such finished machinery and equipment. Does not include assets used in mining, assets used in the manufacture of primary ferrous and nonferrous metals, assets included in class 00.11 through 00.4 and assets elsewhere classified.	10	7	10
36.0	**Manufacture of Electronic Components, Products, and Systems:** Includes assets used in the manufacture of electronic communication, computation, instrumentation and control system, including airborne applications; also includes assets used in the manufacture of electronic products such as frequency and amplitude modulated transmitters and receivers, electronic switching stations, television cameras, video recorders, record players and tape recorders, computers and computer peripheral machines, and electronic instruments, watches, and clocks; also includes assets used in the manufacture of components, provided their primary use is products and systems defined above such as electron tubes, capacitors, coils, resistors, printed circuit substrates, switches, harness cables, lasers, fiber optic devices, and magnetic media devices. Specifically excludes assets used to manufacture electronic products and components, photocopiers, typewriters, postage meters and other electromechanical and mechanical business machines and instruments that are elsewhere classified. Does not include semiconductor manufacturing equipment included in class 36.1.	6	5	6
36.1	**Any Semiconductor Manufacturing Equipment**	5	5	5

Table B-2. **Table of Class Lives and Recovery Periods**

Asset class	Description of assets included	Class Life (in years)	GDS (MACRS)	ADS
			Recovery Periods (in years)	
37.11	**Manufacture of Motor Vehicles:** Includes assets used in the manufacture and assembly of finished automobiles, trucks, trailers, motor homes, and buses. Does not include assets used in mining, printing and publishing, production of primary metals, electricity, or steam, or the manufacture of glass, industrial chemicals, batteries, or rubber products, which are classified elsewhere. Includes assets used in manufacturing activities elsewhere classified other than those excluded above, where such activities are incidental to and an integral part of the manufacture and assembly of finished motor vehicles such as the manufacture of parts and subassemblies of fabricated metal products, electrical equipment, textiles, plastics, leather, and foundry and forging operations. Does not include any assets not classified in manufacturing activity classes, e.g., does not include any assets classified in asset guideline classes 00.11 through 00.4. Activities will be considered incidental to the manufacture and assembly of finished motor vehicles only if 75 percent or more of the value of the products produced under one roof are used for the manufacture and assembly of finished motor vehicles. Parts that are produced as a normal replacement stock complement in connection with the manufacture and assembly of finished motor vehicles are considered used for the manufacture assembly of finished motor vehicles. Does not include assets used in the manufacture of component parts if these assets are used by taxpayers not engaged in the assembly of finished motor vehicles.	12	7	12
37.12	**Manufacture of Motor Vehicles—Special Tools:** Includes assets defined as special tools, such as jigs, dies, fixtures, molds, patterns, gauges, and specialty transfer and shipping devices, owned by manufacturers of finished motor vehicles and used in qualified activities as defined in class 37.11. Special tools are specifically designed for the production or processing of particular motor vehicle components and have no significant utilitarian value, and cannot be adapted to further or different use, after changes or improvements are made in the model design of the particular part produced by the special tools. Does not include general purpose small tools such as wrenches and drills, both hand and powerdriven, and other general purpose equipment such as conveyors, transfer equipment, and materials handling devices.	3	3	3
37.2	**Manufacture of Aerospace Products:** Includes assets used in the manufacture and assembly of airborne vehicles and their component parts including hydraulic, pneumatic, electrical, and mechanical systems. Does not include assets used in the production of electronic airborne detection, guidance, control, radiation, computation, test, navigation, and communication equipment or the components thereof.	10	7	10
37.31	**Ship and Boat Building Machinery and Equipment:** Includes assets used in the manufacture and repair of ships, boats, caissons, marine drilling rigs, and special fabrications not included in asset classes 37.32 and 37.33. Specifically includes all manufacturing and repairing machinery and equipment, including machinery and equipment used in the operation of assets included in asset class 37.32. Excludes buildings and their structural components.	12	7	12
37.32	**Ship and Boat Building Dry Docks and Land Improvements:** Includes assets used in the manufacture and repair of ships, boats, caissons, marine drilling rigs, and special fabrications not included in asset classes 37.31 and 37.33. Specifically includes floating and fixed dry docks, ship basins, graving docks, shipways, piers, and all other land improvements such as water, sewer, and electric systems. Excludes buildings and their structural components.	16	10	16
37.33	**Ship and Boat Building—Special Tools:** Includes assets defined as special tools such as dies, jigs, molds, patterns, fixtures, gauges, and drawings concerning such special tools used in the activities defined in classes 37.31 and 37.32. Special tools are specifically designed for the production or processing of particular machine components, products, or parts, and have no significant utilitarian value and cannot be adapted to further or different use after changes or improvements are made in the model design of the particular part produced by the special tools. Does not include general purpose small tools such as wrenches and drills, both hand and power-driven, and other general purpose equipment such as conveyors, transfer equipment, and materials handling devices.	6.5	5	6.5
37.41	**Manufacture of Locomotives:** Includes assets used in building or rebuilding railroad locomotives (including mining and industrial locomotives). Does not include assets of railroad transportation companies or assets of companies which manufacture components of locomotives but do not manufacture finished locomotives.	11.5	7	11.5
37.42	**Manufacture of Railroad Cars:** Includes assets used in building or rebuilding railroad freight or passenger cars (including rail transit cars). Does not include assets of railroad transportation companies or assets of companies which manufacture components of railroad cars but do not manufacture finished railroad cars.	12	7	12
39.0	**Manufacture of Athletic, Jewelry, and Other Goods:** Includes assets used in the production of jewelry; musical instruments; toys and sporting goods; motion picture and television films and tapes; and pens, pencils, office and art supplies, brooms, brushes, caskets, etc. **Railroad Transportation:** Classes with the prefix 40 include the assets identified below that are used in the commercial and contract carrying of passengers and freight by rail. Assets of electrified railroads will be classified in a manner corresponding to that set forth below for railroads not independently operated as electric lines. Excludes the assets included in classes with the prefix beginning 00.1 and 00.2 above, and also excludes any non-depreciable assets included in Interstate Commerce Commission accounts enumerated for this class.	12	7	12

Table B-2. **Table of Class Lives and Recovery Periods**

Asset class	Description of assets included	Class Life (in years)	Recovery Periods (in years) GDS (MACRS)	ADS
40.1	**Railroad Machinery and Equipment:** Includes assets classified in the following Interstate Commerce Commission accounts: **Roadway accounts:** (16) Station and office buildings (freight handling machinery and equipment only) (25) TOFC/COFC terminals (freight handling machinery and equipment only) (26) Communication systems (27) Signals and interlockers (37) Roadway machines (44) Shop machinery **Equipment accounts:** (52) Locomotives (53) Freight train cars (54) Passenger train cars (57) Work equipment	14	7	14
40.2	**Railroad Structures and Similar Improvements:** Includes assets classified in the following Interstate Commerce Commission road accounts: (6) Bridges, trestles, and culverts (7) Elevated structures (13) Fences, snowsheds, and signs (16) Station and office buildings (stations and other operating structures only) (17) Roadway buildings (18) Water stations (19) Fuel stations (20) Shops and enginehouses (25) TOFC/COFC terminals (operating structures only) (31) Power transmission systems (35) Miscellaneous structures (39) Public improvements construction	30	20	30
40.3	**Railroad Wharves and Docks:** Includes assets classified in the following Interstate Commission Commerce accounts: (23) Wharves and docks (24) Coal and ore wharves	20	15	20
40.4	**Railroad Track**	10	7	10
40.51	**Railroad Hydraulic Electric Generating Equipment**	50	20	50
40.52	**Railroad Nuclear Electric Generating Equipment**	20	15	20
40.53	**Railroad Steam Electric Generating Equipment**	28	20	28
40.54	**Railroad Steam, Compressed Air, and Other Power Plan Equipment**	28	20	28
41.0	**Motor Transport—Passengers:** Includes assets used in the urban and interurban commercial and contract carrying of passengers by road, except the transportation assets included in classes with the prefix 00.2.	8	5	8
42.0	**Motor Transport—Freight:** Includes assets used in the commercial and contract carrying of freight by road, except the transportation assets included in classes with the prefix 00.2.	8	5	8
44.0	**Water Transportation:** Includes assets used in the commercial and contract carrying of freight and passengers by water except the transportation assets included in classes with the prefix 00.2. Includes all related land improvements.	20	15	20
45.0	**Air Transport:** Includes assets (except helicopters) used in commercial and contract carrying of passengers and freight by air. For purposes of section 1.167(a)-11(d)(2)(iv)(a) of the regulations, expenditures for "repair, maintenance, rehabilitation, or improvement," shall consist of direct maintenance expenses (irrespective of airworthiness provisions or charges) as defined by Civil Aeronautics Board uniform accounts 5200, maintenance burden (exclusive of expenses pertaining to maintenance buildings and improvements) as defined by Civil Aeronautics Board accounts 5300, and expenditures which are not "excluded additions" as defined in section 1.167(a)-11(d)(2)(vi) of the regulations and which would be charged to property and equipment accounts in the Civil Aeronautics Board uniform system of accounts.	12	7	12
45.1	**Air Transport (restricted):** Includes each asset described in the description of class 45.0 which was held by the taxpayer on April 15, 1976, or is acquired by the taxpayer pursuant to a contract which was, on April 15, 1976, and at all times thereafter, binding on the taxpayer. This criterion of classification based on binding contract concept is to be applied in the same manner as under the general rules expressed in section 49(b)(1), (4), (5) and (8) of the Code (as in effect prior to its repeal by the Revenue Act of 1978, section 312(c)(1), (d), 1978-3 C.B. 1, 60).	6	5	6
46.0	**Pipeline Transportation:** Includes assets used in the private, commercial, and contract carrying of petroleum, gas and other products by means of pipes and conveyors. The trunk lines and related storage facilities of integrated petroleum and natural gas producers are included in this class. Excludes initial clearing and grading land improvements as specified in Rev. Rul. 72-403, 1972-2; C.B. 102, but includes all other related land improvements.	22	15	22

Table B-2. **Table of Class Lives and Recovery Periods**

Asset class	Description of assets included	Class Life (in years)	Recovery Periods (in years) GDS (MACRS)	ADS
48.11	**Telephone Communications:** Includes the assets classified below and that are used in the provision of commercial and contract telephonic services such as: **Telephone Central Office Buildings:** Includes assets intended to house central office equipment, as defined in Federal Communications Commission Part 31 Account No. 212 whether section 1245 or section 1250 property.	45	20	45
48.12	**Telephone Central Office Equipment:** Includes central office switching and related equipment as defined in Federal Communications Commission Part 31 Account No. 221. Does not include computer-based telephone central office switching equipment included in class 48.121. Does not include private branch exchange (PBX) equipment.	18	10	18
48.121	**Computer-based Telephone Central Office Switching Equipment:** Includes equipment whose functions are those of a computer or peripheral equipment (as defined in section 168(i)(2)(B) of the Code) used in its capacity as telephone central office equipment. Does not include private exchange (PBX) equipment.	9.5	5	9.5
48.13	**Telephone Station Equipment:** Includes such station apparatus and connections as teletypewriters, telephones, booths, private exchanges, and comparable equipment as defined in Federal Communications Commission Part 31 Account Nos. 231, 232, and 234.	10	7*	10*
48.14	**Telephone Distribution Plant:** Includes such assets as pole lines, cable, aerial wire, underground conduits, and comparable equipment, and related land improvements as defined in Federal Communications Commission Part 31 Account Nos. 241, 242.1, 242.2, 242.3, 242.4, 243, and 244.	24	15	24
48.2	**Radio and Television Broadcastings:** Includes assets used in radio and television broadcasting, except transmitting towers. **Telegraph, Ocean Cable, and Satellite Communications (TOCSC)** includes communications-related assets used to provide domestic and international radio-telegraph, wire-telegraph, ocean-cable, and satellite communications services; also includes related land improvements. If property described in Classes 48.31–48.45 is comparable to telephone distribution plant described in Class 48.14 and used for 2-way exchange of voice and data communication which is the equivalent of telephone communication, such property is assigned a class life of 24 years under this revenue procedure. Comparable equipment does not include cable television equipment used primarily for 1-way communication.	6	5	6
48.31	**TOCSC—Electric Power Generating and Distribution Systems:** Includes assets used in the provision of electric power by generation, modulation, rectification, channelization, control, and distribution. Does not include these assets when they are installed on customers premises.	19	10	19
48.32	**TOCSC—High Frequency Radio and Microwave Systems:** Includes assets such as transmitters and receivers, antenna supporting structures, antennas, transmission lines from equipment to antenna, transmitter cooling systems, and control and amplification equipment. Does not include cable and long-line systems.	13	7	13
48.33	**TOCSC—Cable and Long-line Systems:** Includes assets such as transmission lines, pole lines, ocean cables, buried cable and conduit, repeaters, repeater stations, and other related assets. Does not include high frequency radio or microwave systems.	26.5	20	26.5
48.34	**TOCSC—Central Office Control Equipment:** Includes assets for general control, switching, and monitoring of communications signals including electromechanical switching and channeling apparatus, multiplexing equipment patching and monitoring facilities, in-house cabling, teleprinter equipment, and associated site improvements.	16.5	10	16.5
48.35	**TOCSC—Computerized Switching, Channeling, and Associated Control Equipment:** Includes central office switching computers, interfacing computers, other associated specialized control equipment, and site improvements.	10.5	7	10.5
48.36	**TOCSC—Satellite Ground Segment Property:** Includes assets such as fixed earth station equipment, antennas, satellite communications equipment, and interface equipment used in satellite communications. Does not include general purpose equipment or equipment used in satellite space segment property.	10	7	10
48.37	**TOCSC—Satellite Space Segment Property:** Includes satellites and equipment used for telemetry, tracking, control, and monitoring when used in satellite communications.	8	5	8
48.38	**TOCSC—Equipment Installed on Customer's Premises:** Includes assets installed on customer's premises, such as computers, terminal equipment, power generation and distribution systems, private switching center, teleprinters, facsimile equipment and other associated and related equipment.	10	7	10
48.39	**TOCSC—Support and Service Equipment:** Includes assets used to support but not engage in communications. Includes store, warehouse and shop tools, and test and laboratory assets. **Cable Television (CATV):** Includes communications-related assets used to provide cable television community antenna television services. Does not include assets used to provide subscribers with two-way communications services.	13.5	7	13.5

* Property described in asset guideline class 48.13 which is qualified technological equipment as defined in section 168(i)(2) is assigned a 5-year recovery period.

Table B-2. **Table of Class Lives and Recovery Periods**

Asset class	Description of assets included	Class Life (in years)	Recovery Periods (in years) GDS (MACRS)	ADS
48.41	**CATV—Headend:** Includes assets such as towers, antennas, preamplifiers, converters, modulation equipment, and program non-duplication systems. Does not include headend buildings and program origination assets.	11	7	11
48.42	**CATV—Subscriber Connection and Distribution Systems:** Includes assets such as trunk and feeder cable, connecting hardware, amplifiers, power equipment, passive devices, directional taps, pedestals, pressure taps, drop cables, matching transformers, multiple set connector equipment, and convertors.	10	7	10
48.43	**CATV—Program Origination:** Includes assets such as cameras, film chains, video tape recorders, lighting, and remote location equipment excluding vehicles. Does not include buildings and their structural components.	9	5	9
48.44	**CATV—Service and Test:** Includes assets such as oscilloscopes, field strength meters, spectrum analyzers, and cable testing equipment, but does not include vehicles.	8.5	5	8.5
48.45	**CATV—Microwave Systems:** Inlcudes assets such as towers, antennas, transmitting and receiving equipment, and broad band microwave assets is used in the provision of cable television services. Does not include assets used in the provision of common carrier services.	9.5	5	9.5
49.11	**Electric, Gas, Water and Steam, Utility Services:** Includes assets used in the production, transmission and distribution of electricity, gas, steam, or water for sale including related land improvements. **Electric Utility Hydraulic Production Plant:** Includes assets used in the hydraulic power production of electricity for sale, including related land improvements, such as dams, flumes, canals, and waterways.	50	20	50
49.12	**Electric Utility Nuclear Production Plant:** Includes assets used in the nuclear power production and electricity for sale and related land improvements. Does not include nuclear fuel assemblies.	20	15	20
49.121	**Electric Utility Nuclear Fuel Assemblies:** Includes initial core and replacement core nuclear fuel assemblies (i.e., the composite of fabricated nuclear fuel and container) when used in a boiling water, pressurized water, or high temperature gas reactor used in the production of electricity. Does not include nuclear fuel assemblies used in breader reactors.	5	5	5
49.13	**Electric Utility Steam Production Plant:** Includes assets used in the steam power production of electricity for sale, combusion turbines operated in a combined cycle with a conventional steam unit and related land improvements. Also includes package boilers, electric generators and related assets such as electricity and steam distribution systems as used by a waste reduction and resource recovery plant if the steam or electricity is normally for sale to others.	28	20	28
49.14	**Electric Utility Transmission and Distribution Plant:** Includes assets used in the transmission and distribution of electricity for sale and related land improvements. Excludes initial clearing and grading land improvements as specified in Rev. Rul. 72-403, 1972-2 C.B. 102.	30	20	30
49.15	**Electric Utility Combustion Turbine Production Plant:** Includes assets used in the production of electricity for sale by the use of such prime movers as jet engines, combustion turbines, diesel engines, gasoline engines, and other internal combustion engines, their associated power turbines and/or generators, and related land improvements. Does not include combustion turbines operated in a combined cycle with a conventional steam unit.	20	15	20
49.21	**Gas Utility Distribution Facilities:** Includes gas water heaters and gas conversion equipment installed by utility on customers' premises on a rental basis.	35	20	35
49.221	**Gas Utility Manufactured Gas Production Plants:** Includes assets used in the manufacture of gas having chemical and/or physical properties which do not permit complete interchangeability with domestic natural gas. Does not include gas-producing systems and related systems used in waste reduction and resource recovery plants which are elsewhere classified.	30	20	30
49.222	**Gas Utility Substitute Natural Gas (SNG) Production Plant (naphtha or lighter hydrocarbon feedstocks):** Includes assets used in the catalytic conversion of feedstocks or naphtha or lighter hydrocarbons to a gaseous fuel which is completely interchangeable with domestic natural gas.	14	7	14
49.223	**Substitute Natural Gas—Coal Gasification:** Includes assets used in the manufacture and production of pipeline quality gas from coal using the basic Lurgi process with advanced methanation. Includes all process plant equipment and structures used in this coal gasification process and all utility assets such as cooling systems, water supply and treatment facilities, and assets used in the production and distribution of electricity and steam for use by the taxpayer in a gasification plant and attendant coal mining site processes but not for assets used in the production and distribution of electricity and steam for sale to others. Also includes all other related land improvements. Does not include assets used in the direct mining and treatment of coal prior to the gasification process itself.	18	10	18
49.23	**Natural Gas Production Plant**	14	7	14
49.24	**Gas Utility Trunk Pipelines and Related Storage Facilities:** Excluding initial clearing and grading land improvements as specified in Rev. Rul. 72-40.	22	15	22
49.25	**Liquefied Natural Gas Plant:** Includes assets used in the liquefaction, storage, and regasification of natural gas including loading and unloading connections, instrumentation equipment and controls, pumps, vaporizers and odorizers, tanks, and related land improvements. Also includes pipeline interconnections with gas transmission lines and distribution systems and marine terminal facilities.	22	15	22

Table B-2. **Table of Class Lives and Recovery Periods**

Asset class	Description of assets included	Class Life (in years)	Recovery Periods (in years) GDS (MACRS)	ADS
49.3	**Water Utilities:** Includes assets used in the gathering, treatment, and commercial distribution of water.	50	20***	50
49.4	**Central Steam Utility Production and Distribution:** Includes assets used in the production and distribution of steam for sale. Does not include assets used in waste reduction and resource recovery plants which are elsewhere classified.	28	20	28
49.5	**Waste Reduction and Resource Recovery Plants:** Includes assets used in the conversion of refuse or other solid waste or biomass to heat or to a solid, liquid, or gaseous fuel. Also includes all process plant equipment and structures at the site used to receive, handle, collect, and process refuse or other solid waste or biomass in a waterwall, combustion system, oil or gas pyrolysis system, or refuse derived fuel system to create hot water, gas, steam and electricity. Includes material recovery and support assets used in refuse or solid refuse or solid waste receiving, collecting, handling, sorting, shredding, classifying, and separation systems. Does not include any package boilers, or electric generators and related assets such as electricity, hot water, steam and manufactured gas production plants classified in classes 00.4, 49.13, 49.221, and 49.4. Does include, however, all other utilities such as water supply and treatment facilities, ash handling and other related land improvements of a waste reduction and resource recovery plant.	10	7	10
50.	**Municipal Wastewater Treatment Plant**	24	15	24
51.	**Municipal Sewer**	50	20***	50
57.0	**Distributive Trades and Services:** Includes assets used in wholesale and retail trade, and personal and professional services. Includes section 1245 assets used in marketing petroleum and petroleum products.	9	5	9*
57.1	**Distributive Trades and Services—Billboard, Service Station Buildings and Petroleum Marketing Land Improvements:** Includes section 1250 assets, including service station buildings and depreciable land improvements, whether section 1245 property or section 1250 property, used in the marketing of petroleum and petroleum products, but not including any of these facilities related to petroleum and natural gas trunk pipelines. Includes car wash buildings and related land improvements. Includes billboards, whether such assets are section 1245 property or section 1250 property. Excludes all other land improvements, buildings and structural components as defined in section 1.48-1(e) of the regulations. See *Gas station convenience stores* in chapter 3.	20	15	20
79.0	**Recreation:** Includes assets used in the provision of entertainment services on payment of a fee or admission charge, as in the operation of bowling alleys, billiard and pool establishments, theaters, concert halls, and miniature golf courses. Does not include amusement and theme parks and assets which consist primarily of specialized land improvements or structures, such as golf courses, sports stadia, race tracks, ski slopes, and buildings which house the assets used in entertainment services.	10	7	10
80.0	**Theme and Amusement Parks:** Includes assets used in the provision of rides, attractions, and amusements in activities defined as theme and amusement parks, and includes appurtenances associated with a ride, attraction, amusement or theme setting within the park such as ticket booths, facades, shop interiors, and props, special purpose structures, and buildings other than warehouses, administration buildings, hotels, and motels. Includes all land improvements for or in support of park activities (e.g., parking lots, sidewalks, waterways, bridges, fences, landscaping, etc.), and support functions (e.g., food and beverage retailing, souvenir vending and other nonlodging accommodations) if owned by the park and provided exclusively for the benefit of park patrons. Theme and amusement parks are defined as combinations of amusements, rides, and attractions which are permanently situated on park land and open to the public for the price of admission. This guideline class is a composite of all assets used in this industry except transportation equipment (general purpose trucks, cars, airplanes, etc.), which are included in asset guideline classes with the prefix 00.2), assets used in the provision of administrative services (asset classes with the prefix 00.1) and warehouses, administration buildings, hotels and motels.	12.5	7	12.5
	Certain Property for Which Recovery Periods Assigned A. Personal Property With No Class Life Section 1245 Real Property With No Class Life		7 7	12 40
	B. Qualified Technological Equipment, as defined in section 168(i)(2).	**	5	5
	C. Property Used in Connection with Research and Experimentation referred to in section 168(e)(3)(B).	**	5	class life if no class life—12
	D. Alternative energy property described in sections 48(l)(3)(A)(ix) (as in effect on the day before the date of enactment (11/5/90) of the Revenue Reconciliation Act of 1990).	**	5	class life if no class life—12
	E. Biomass property described in section 48(l)(15) (as in effect on the day before the date of enactment (11/5/90) of the Revenue Reconciliation Act of 1990) and is a qualifying small production facility within the meaning of section 3(17)(c) of the Federal Power Act (16 U.S.C. 796(17)(C)), as in effect on September 1, 1986.	**	5	class life if no class life—12
	F. Energy property described in section 48(a)(3)(A) (or would be described if "solar or wind energy" were substituted for "solar energy" in section 48(a)(3)(A)(i)).	**	5	class life if no class life—12

*   Any high technology medical equipment as defined in section 168(i)(2)(C) which is described in asset guideline class 57.0 is assigned a 5-year recovery period for the alternate MACRS method.

**   The class life (if any) of property described in classes B, C, D, E, or F is determined by reference to the asset guideline classes. If an item of property described in paragraphs B, C, D, E, or F is not described in any asset guideline class, such item of property has no class life.

*** Use straight line over 25 years if placed in service after June 12, 1996, unless placed in service under a binding contract in effect before June 10, 1996, and at all times until placed in service.

Table A-1.   3-, 5-, 7-, 10-, 15-, and 20-Year Property
             Half-Year Convention

Year	Depreciation rate for recovery period					
	3-year	5-year	7-year	10-year	15-year	20-year
1	33.33%	20.00%	14.29%	10.00%	5.00%	3.750%
2	44.45	32.00	24.49	18.00	9.50	7.219
3	14.81	19.20	17.49	14.40	8.55	6.677
4	7.41	11.52	12.49	11.52	7.70	6.177
5		11.52	8.93	9.22	6.93	5.713
6		5.76	8.92	7.37	6.23	5.285
7			8.93	6.55	5.90	4.888
8			4.46	6.55	5.90	4.522
9				6.56	5.91	4.462
10				6.55	5.90	4.461
11				3.28	5.91	4.462
12					5.90	4.461
13					5.91	4.462
14					5.90	4.461
15					5.91	4.462
16					2.95	4.461
17						4.462
18						4.461
19						4.462
20						4.461
21						2.231

Table A-2.   3-, 5-, 7-, 10-, 15-, and 20-Year Property
             Mid-Quarter Convention
             Placed in Service in First Quarter

Year	Depreciation rate for recovery period					
	3-year	5-year	7-year	10-year	15-year	20-year
1	58.33%	35.00%	25.00%	17.50%	8.75%	6.563%
2	27.78	26.00	21.43	16.50	9.13	7.000
3	12.35	15.60	15.31	13.20	8.21	6.482
4	1.54	11.01	10.93	10.56	7.39	5.996
5		11.01	8.75	8.45	6.65	5.546
6		1.38	8.74	6.76	5.99	5.130
7			8.75	6.55	5.90	4.746
8			1.09	6.55	5.91	4.459
9				6.56	5.90	4.459
10				6.55	5.91	4.459
11				0.82	5.90	4.459
12					5.91	4.460
13					5.90	4.459
14					5.91	4.460
15					5.90	4.459
16					0.74	4.460
17						4.459
18						4.460
19						4.459
20						4.460
21						0.565

Table A-3. 3-, 5-, 7-, 10-, 15-, and 20-Year Property
Mid-Quarter Convention
Placed in Service in Second Quarter

Year	Depreciation rate for recovery period					
	3-year	5-year	7-year	10-year	15-year	20-year
1	41.67%	25.00%	17.85%	12.50%	6.25%	4.688%
2	38.89	30.00	23.47	17.50	9.38	7.148
3	14.14	18.00	16.76	14.00	8.44	6.612
4	5.30	11.37	11.97	11.20	7.59	6.116
5		11.37	8.87	8.96	6.83	5.658
6		4.26	8.87	7.17	6.15	5.233
7			8.87	6.55	5.91	4.841
8			3.34	6.55	5.90	4.478
9				6.56	5.91	4.463
10				6.55	5.90	4.463
11				2.46	5.91	4.463
12					5.90	4.463
13					5.91	4.463
14					5.90	4.463
15					5.91	4.462
16					2.21	4.463
17						4.462
18						4.463
19						4.462
20						4.463
21						1.673

Table A-4. 3-, 5-, 7-, 10-, 15-, and 20-Year Property
Mid-Quarter Convention
Placed in Service in Third Quarter

Year	Depreciation rate for recovery period					
	3-year	5-year	7-year	10-year	15-year	20-year
1	25.00%	15.00%	10.71%	7.50%	3.75%	2.813%
2	50.00	34.00	25.51	18.50	9.63	7.289
3	16.67	20.40	18.22	14.80	8.66	6.742
4	8.33	12.24	13.02	11.84	7.80	6.237
5		11.30	9.30	9.47	7.02	5.769
6		7.06	8.85	7.58	6.31	5.336
7			8.86	6.55	5.90	4.936
8			5.53	6.55	5.90	4.566
9				6.56	5.91	4.460
10				6.55	5.90	4.460
11				4.10	5.91	4.460
12					5.90	4.460
13					5.91	4.461
14					5.90	4.460
15					5.91	4.461
16					3.69	4.460
17						4.461
18						4.460
19						4.461
20						4.460
21						2.788

Table A-5. **3-, 5-, 7-, 10-, 15-, and 20-Year Property**
Mid-Quarter Convention
Placed in Service in Fourth Quarter

Year	Depreciation rate for recovery period					
	3-year	5-year	7-year	10-year	15-year	20-year
1	8.33%	5.00%	3.57%	2.50%	1.25%	0.938%
2	61.11	38.00	27.55	19.50	9.88	7.430
3	20.37	22.80	19.68	15.60	8.89	6.872
4	10.19	13.68	14.06	12.48	8.00	6.357
5		10.94	10.04	9.98	7.20	5.880
6		9.58	8.73	7.99	6.48	5.439
7			8.73	6.55	5.90	5.031
8			7.64	6.55	5.90	4.654
9				6.56	5.90	4.458
10				6.55	5.91	4.458
11				5.74	5.90	4.458
12					5.91	4.458
13					5.90	4.458
14					5.91	4.458
15					5.90	4.458
16					5.17	4.458
17						4.458
18						4.459
19						4.458
20						4.459
21						3.901

Table A-6. **Residential Rental Property**
Mid-Month Convention
Straight Line—27.5 Years

Year	Month property placed in service											
	1	2	3	4	5	6	7	8	9	10	11	12
1	3.485%	3.182%	2.879%	2.576%	2.273%	1.970%	1.667%	1.364%	1.061%	0.758%	0.455%	0.152%
2–9	3.636	3.636	3.636	3.636	3.636	3.636	3.636	3.636	3.636	3.636	3.636	3.636
10	3.637	3.637	3.637	3.637	3.637	3.637	3.636	3.636	3.636	3.636	3.636	3.636
11	3.636	3.636	3.636	3.636	3.636	3.636	3.637	3.637	3.637	3.637	3.637	3.637
12	3.637	3.637	3.637	3.637	3.637	3.637	3.636	3.636	3.636	3.636	3.636	3.636
13	3.636	3.636	3.636	3.636	3.636	3.636	3.637	3.637	3.637	3.637	3.637	3.637
14	3.637	3.637	3.637	3.637	3.637	3.637	3.636	3.636	3.636	3.636	3.636	3.636
15	3.636	3.636	3.636	3.636	3.636	3.636	3.637	3.637	3.637	3.637	3.637	3.637
16	3.637	3.637	3.637	3.637	3.637	3.637	3.636	3.636	3.636	3.636	3.636	3.636
17	3.636	3.636	3.636	3.636	3.636	3.636	3.637	3.637	3.637	3.637	3.637	3.637
18	3.637	3.637	3.637	3.637	3.637	3.637	3.636	3.636	3.636	3.636	3.636	3.636
19	3.636	3.636	3.636	3.636	3.636	3.636	3.637	3.637	3.637	3.637	3.637	3.637
20	3.637	3.637	3.637	3.637	3.637	3.637	3.636	3.636	3.636	3.636	3.636	3.636
21	3.636	3.636	3.636	3.636	3.636	3.636	3.637	3.637	3.637	3.637	3.637	3.637
22	3.637	3.637	3.637	3.637	3.637	3.637	3.636	3.636	3.636	3.636	3.636	3.636
23	3.636	3.636	3.636	3.636	3.636	3.636	3.637	3.637	3.637	3.637	3.637	3.637
24	3.637	3.637	3.637	3.637	3.637	3.637	3.636	3.636	3.636	3.636	3.636	3.636
25	3.636	3.636	3.636	3.636	3.636	3.636	3.637	3.637	3.637	3.637	3.637	3.637
26	3.637	3.637	3.637	3.637	3.637	3.637	3.636	3.636	3.636	3.636	3.636	3.636
27	3.636	3.636	3.636	3.636	3.636	3.636	3.637	3.637	3.637	3.637	3.637	3.637
28	1.97	2.273	2.576	2.879	3.182	3.485	3.636	3.636	3.636	3.636	3.636	3.636
29							0.152	0.455	0.758	1.061	1.364	1.667

Table A-7. **Nonresidential Real Property**
Mid-Month Convention
Straight Line—31.5 Years

Year	Month property placed in service											
	1	2	3	4	5	6	7	8	9	10	11	12
1	3.042%	2.778%	2.513%	2.249%	1.984%	1.720%	1.455%	1.190%	0.926%	0.661%	0.397%	0.132%
2–7	3.175	3.175	3.175	3.175	3.175	3.175	3.175	3.175	3.175	3.175	3.175	3.175
8	3.175	3.174	3.175	3.174	3.175	3.174	3.175	3.175	3.175	3.175	3.175	3.175
9	3.174	3.175	3.174	3.175	3.174	3.175	3.174	3.175	3.174	3.175	3.174	3.175
10	3.175	3.174	3.175	3.174	3.175	3.174	3.175	3.174	3.175	3.174	3.175	3.174
11	3.174	3.175	3.174	3.175	3.174	3.175	3.174	3.175	3.174	3.175	3.174	3.175
12	3.175	3.174	3.175	3.174	3.175	3.174	3.175	3.174	3.175	3.174	3.175	3.174
13	3.174	3.175	3.174	3.175	3.174	3.175	3.174	3.175	3.174	3.175	3.174	3.175
14	3.175	3.174	3.175	3.174	3.175	3.174	3.175	3.174	3.175	3.174	3.175	3.174
15	3.174	3.175	3.174	3.175	3.174	3.175	3.174	3.175	3.174	3.175	3.174	3.175
16	3.175	3.174	3.175	3.174	3.175	3.174	3.175	3.174	3.175	3.174	3.175	3.174
17	3.174	3.175	3.174	3.175	3.174	3.175	3.174	3.175	3.174	3.175	3.174	3.175
18	3.175	3.174	3.175	3.174	3.175	3.174	3.175	3.174	3.175	3.174	3.175	3.174
19	3.174	3.175	3.174	3.175	3.174	3.175	3.174	3.175	3.174	3.175	3.174	3.175
20	3.175	3.174	3.175	3.174	3.175	3.174	3.175	3.174	3.175	3.174	3.175	3.174
21	3.174	3.175	3.174	3.175	3.174	3.175	3.174	3.175	3.174	3.175	3.174	3.175
22	3.175	3.174	3.175	3.174	3.175	3.174	3.175	3.174	3.175	3.174	3.175	3.174
23	3.174	3.175	3.174	3.175	3.174	3.175	3.174	3.175	3.174	3.175	3.174	3.175
24	3.175	3.174	3.175	3.174	3.175	3.174	3.175	3.174	3.175	3.174	3.175	3.174
25	3.174	3.175	3.174	3.175	3.174	3.175	3.174	3.175	3.174	3.175	3.174	3.175
26	3.175	3.174	3.175	3.174	3.175	3.174	3.175	3.174	3.175	3.174	3.175	3.174
27	3.174	3.175	3.174	3.175	3.174	3.175	3.174	3.175	3.174	3.175	3.174	3.175
28	3.175	3.174	3.175	3.174	3.175	3.174	3.175	3.174	3.175	3.174	3.175	3.174
29	3.174	3.175	3.174	3.175	3.174	3.175	3.174	3.175	3.174	3.175	3.174	3.175
30	3.175	3.174	3.175	3.174	3.175	3.174	3.175	3.174	3.175	3.174	3.175	3.174
31	3.174	3.175	3.174	3.175	3.174	3.175	3.174	3.175	3.174	3.175	3.174	3.175
32	1.720	1.984	2.249	2.513	2.778	3.042	3.175	3.174	3.175	3.174	3.175	3.174
33							0.132	0.397	0.661	0.926	1.190	1.455

Table A-7a. **Nonresidential Real Property**
Mid-Month Convention
Straight Line—39 Years

Year	Month property placed in service											
	1	2	3	4	5	6	7	8	9	10	11	12
1	2.461%	2.247%	2.033%	1.819%	1.605%	1.391%	1.177%	0.963%	0.749%	0.535%	0.321%	0.107%
2–39	2.564	2.564	2.564	2.564	2.564	2.564	2.564	2.564	2.564	2.564	2.564	2.564
40	0.107	0.321	0.535	0.749	0.963	1.177	1.391	1.605	1.819	2.033	2.247	2.461

Appendix E – Schedule C Business Codes

Principal Business or Professional Activity Codes

These codes for the Principal Business or Professional Activity classify sole proprietorships by the type of activity they are engaged in to facilitate the administration of the Internal Revenue Code. These six-digit codes are based on the North American Industry Classification System (NAICS).

Select the category that best describes your primary business activity (for example, Real Estate). Then select the activity that best identifies the principal source of your sales or receipts (for example, real estate agent). Now find the six-digit code assigned to this activity (for example, 531210, the code for offices of real estate agents and brokers) and enter it on Schedule C or C-EZ, line B.

Note. If your principal source of income is from farming activities, you should file Schedule F.

Accommodation, Food Services, & Drinking Places

Accommodation
721310 Rooming & boarding houses
721210 RV (recreational vehicle) parks & recreational camps
721100 Traveler accommodation (including hotels, motels, & bed & breakfast inns)

Food Services & Drinking Places
722514 Cafeterias & buffets
722410 Drinking places (alcoholic beverages)
722511 Full-service restaurants
722513 Limited-service restaurants
722515 Snack & non-alcoholic beverage bars
722300 Special food services (including food service contractors & caterers)

Administrative & Support and Waste Management & Remediation Services

Administrative & Support Services
561430 Business service centers (including private mail centers & copy shops)
561740 Carpet & upholstery cleaning services
561440 Collection agencies
561450 Credit bureaus
561410 Document preparation services
561300 Employment services
561710 Exterminating & pest control services
561210 Facilities support (management) services
561600 Investigation & security services
561720 Janitorial services
561730 Landscaping services
561110 Office administrative services
561420 Telephone call centers (including telephone answering services & telemarketing bureaus)
561500 Travel arrangement & reservation services
561490 Other business support services (including repossession services, court reporting, & stenotype services)
561790 Other services to buildings & dwellings
561900 Other support services (including packaging & labeling services, & convention & trade show organizers)

Waste Management & Remediation Services
562000 Waste management & remediation services

Agriculture, Forestry, Hunting, & Fishing

112900 Animal production (including breeding of cats and dogs)
114110 Fishing
113000 Forestry & logging (including forest nurseries & timber tracts)
114210 Hunting & trapping

Support Activities for Agriculture & Forestry
115210 Support activities for animal production (including farriers)
115110 Support activities for crop production (including cotton ginning, soil preparation, planting, & cultivating)

115310 Support activities for forestry

Arts, Entertainment, & Recreation

Amusement, Gambling, & Recreation Industries
713100 Amusement parks & arcades
713200 Gambling industries
713900 Other amusement & recreation services (including golf courses, skiing facilities, marinas, fitness centers, bowling centers, skating rinks, miniature golf courses)

Museums, Historical Sites, & Similar Institutions
712100 Museums, historical sites, & similar institutions

Performing Arts, Spectator Sports, & Related Industries
711410 Agents & managers for artists, athletes, entertainers, & other public figures
711510 Independent artists, writers, & performers
711100 Performing arts companies
711300 Promoters of performing arts, sports, & similar events
711210 Spectator sports (including professional sports clubs & racetrack operations)

Construction of Buildings

236200 Nonresidential building construction
236100 Residential building construction

Heavy and Civil Engineering Construction
237310 Highway, street, & bridge construction
237210 Land subdivision
237100 Utility system construction
237990 Other heavy & civil engineering construction

Specialty Trade Contractors
238310 Drywall & insulation contractors
238210 Electrical contractors
238350 Finish carpentry contractors
238330 Flooring contractors
238130 Framing carpentry contractors
238150 Glass & glazing contractors
238140 Masonry contractors
238320 Painting & wall covering contractors
238220 Plumbing, heating & air-conditioning contractors
238110 Poured concrete foundation & structure contractors
238160 Roofing contractors
238170 Siding contractors
238910 Site preparation contractors
238120 Structural steel & precast concrete construction contractors
238340 Tile & terrazzo contractors
238290 Other building equipment contractors
238390 Other building finishing contractors
238190 Other foundation, structure, & building exterior contractors
238990 All other specialty trade contractors

Educational Services

611000 Educational services (including schools, colleges, & universities)

Finance & Insurance

Credit Intermediation & Related Activities
522100 Depository credit intermediation (including commercial banking, savings institutions, & credit unions)
522200 Nondepository credit intermediation (including sales financing & consumer lending)
522300 Activities related to credit intermediation (including loan brokers)

Insurance Agents, Brokers, & Related Activities
524210 Insurance agencies & brokerages
524290 Other insurance related activities

Securities, Commodity Contracts, & Other Financial Investments & Related Activities
523140 Commodity contracts brokers
523130 Commodity contracts dealers
523110 Investment bankers & securities dealers
523210 Securities & commodity exchanges
523120 Securities brokers
523900 Other financial investment activities (including investment advice)

Health Care & Social Assistance

Ambulatory Health Care Services
621610 Home health care services
621510 Medical & diagnostic laboratories
621310 Offices of chiropractors
621210 Offices of dentists
621330 Offices of mental health practitioners (except physicians)
621320 Offices of optometrists
621340 Offices of physical, occupational & speech therapists, & audiologists
621111 Offices of physicians (except mental health specialists)
621112 Offices of physicians, mental health specialists
621391 Offices of podiatrists
621399 Offices of all other miscellaneous health practitioners
621400 Outpatient care centers
621900 Other ambulatory health care services (including ambulance services, blood, & organ banks)

Hospitals
622000 Hospitals

Nursing & Residential Care Facilities
623000 Nursing & residential care facilities

Social Assistance
624410 Child day care services
624200 Community food & housing, & emergency & other relief services
624100 Individual & family services
624310 Vocational rehabilitation services

Information

511000 Publishing industries (except Internet)

Broadcasting (except Internet) & Telecommunications
515000 Broadcasting (except Internet)

517000 Telecommunications & Internet service providers

Data Processing Services
518210 Data processing, hosting, & related services
519100 Other information services (including news syndicates & libraries, Internet publishing & broadcasting)

Motion Picture & Sound Recording
512100 Motion picture & video industries (except video rental)
512200 Sound recording industries

Manufacturing

315000 Apparel mfg.
312000 Beverage & tobacco product mfg.
334000 Computer & electronic product mfg.
335000 Electrical equipment, appliance, & component mfg.
332000 Fabricated metal product mfg.
337000 Furniture & related product mfg.
333000 Machinery mfg.
339110 Medical equipment & supplies mfg.
322000 Paper mfg.
324100 Petroleum & coal products mfg.
326000 Plastics & rubber products mfg.
331000 Primary metal mfg.
323100 Printing & related support activities
313000 Textile mills
314000 Textile product mills
336000 Transportation equipment mfg.
321000 Wood product mfg.
339900 Other miscellaneous mfg.

Chemical Manufacturing
325100 Basic chemical mfg.
325500 Paint, coating, & adhesive mfg.
325300 Pesticide, fertilizer, & other agricultural chemical mfg.
325410 Pharmaceutical & medicine mfg.
325200 Resin, synthetic rubber, & artificial & synthetic fibers & filaments mfg.
325600 Soap, cleaning compound, & toilet preparation mfg.
325900 Other chemical product & preparation mfg.

Food Manufacturing
311110 Animal food mfg.
311800 Bakeries, tortilla, & dry pasta mfg.
311500 Dairy product mfg.
311400 Fruit & vegetable preserving & speciality food mfg.
311200 Grain & oilseed milling
311610 Animal slaughtering & processing
311710 Seafood product preparation & packaging
311300 Sugar & confectionery product mfg.
311900 Other food mfg. (including coffee, tea, flavorings, & seasonings)

Leather & Allied Product Manufacturing
316210 Footwear mfg. (including leather, rubber, & plastics)
316110 Leather & hide tanning & finishing
316990 Other leather & allied product mfg.

Nonmetallic Mineral Product Manufacturing
327300 Cement & concrete product mfg.
327100 Clay product & refractory mfg.
327210 Glass & glass product mfg.
327400 Lime & gypsum product mfg.
327900 Other nonmetallic mineral product mfg.

Mining
212110 Coal mining
212200 Metal ore mining
212300 Nonmetallic mineral mining & quarrying
211110 Oil & gas extraction
213110 Support activities for mining

Other Services

Personal & Laundry Services
812111 Barber shops
812112 Beauty salons
812220 Cemeteries & crematories
812310 Coin-operated laundries & drycleaners
812320 Drycleaning & laundry services (except coin-operated) (including laundry & drycleaning drop-off & pickup sites)
812210 Funeral homes & funeral services
812330 Linen & uniform supply
812113 Nail salons
812930 Parking lots & garages
812910 Pet care (except veterinary) services
812920 Photofinishing
812190 Other personal care services (including diet & weight reducing centers)
812990 All other personal services

Repair & Maintenance
811120 Automotive body, paint, interior, & glass repair
811110 Automotive mechanical & electrical repair & maintenance
811190 Other automotive repair & maintenance (including oil change & lubrication shops & car washes)
811310 Commercial & industrial machinery & equipment (except automotive & electronic) repair & maintenance
811210 Electronic & precision equipment repair & maintenance
811430 Footwear & leather goods repair
811410 Home & garden equipment & appliance repair & maintenance
811420 Reupholstery & furniture repair
811490 Other personal & household goods repair & maintenance

Professional, Scientific, & Technical Services
541100 Legal services
541211 Offices of certified public accountants
541214 Payroll services
541213 Tax preparation services
541219 Other accounting services

Architectural, Engineering, & Related Services
541310 Architectural services
541350 Building inspection services
541340 Drafting services
541330 Engineering services
541360 Geophysical surveying & mapping services
541320 Landscape architecture services
541370 Surveying & mapping (except geophysical) services

541380 Testing laboratories

Computer Systems Design & Related Services
541510 Computer systems design & related services

Specialized Design Services
541400 Specialized design services (including interior, industrial, graphic, & fashion design)

Other Professional, Scientific, & Technical Services
541800 Advertising & related services
541600 Management, scientific, & technical consulting services
541910 Market research & public opinion polling
541920 Photographic services
541700 Scientific research & development services
541930 Translation & interpretation services
541940 Veterinary services
541990 All other professional, scientific, & technical services

Real Estate & Rental & Leasing

Real Estate
531100 Lessors of real estate (including miniwarehouses & self-storage units)
531210 Offices of real estate agents & brokers
531320 Offices of real estate appraisers
531310 Real estate property managers
531390 Other activities related to real estate

Rental & Leasing Services
532100 Automotive equipment rental & leasing
532400 Commercial & industrial machinery & equipment rental & leasing
532210 Consumer electronics & appliances rental
532220 Formal wear & costume rental
532310 General rental centers
532230 Video tape & disc rental
532290 Other consumer goods rental

Religious, Grantmaking, Civic, Professional, & Similar Organizations
813000 Religious, grantmaking, civic, professional, & similar organizations

Retail Trade

Building Material & Garden Equipment & Supplies Dealers
444130 Hardware stores
444110 Home centers
444200 Lawn & garden equipment & supplies stores
444120 Paint & wallpaper stores
444190 Other building materials dealers

Clothing & Accessories Stores
448130 Children's & infants' clothing stores
448150 Clothing accessories stores
448140 Family clothing stores
448310 Jewelry stores
448320 Luggage & leather goods stores
448110 Men's clothing stores
448210 Shoe stores
448120 Women's clothing stores
448190 Other clothing stores

Electronic & Appliance Stores
443142 Electronics stores (including audio, video, computer, & camera stores)
443141 Household appliance stores

Food & Beverage Stores
445310 Beer, wine, & liquor stores
445220 Fish & seafood markets
445230 Fruit & vegetable markets
445100 Grocery stores (including supermarkets & convenience stores without gas)
445210 Meat markets
445290 Other specialty food stores

Furniture & Home Furnishing Stores
442110 Furniture stores
442200 Home furnishings stores

Gasoline Stations
447100 Gasoline stations (including convenience stores with gas)

General Merchandise Stores
452000 General merchandise stores

Health & Personal Care Stores
446120 Cosmetics, beauty supplies, & perfume stores
446130 Optical goods stores
446110 Pharmacies & drug stores
446190 Other health & personal care stores

Motor Vehicle & Parts Dealers
441300 Automotive parts, accessories, & tire stores
441222 Boat dealers
441228 Motorcycle, ATV, & all other motor vehicle dealers
441110 New car dealers
441210 Recreational vehicle dealers (including motor home & travel trailer dealers)
441120 Used car dealers

Sporting Goods, Hobby, Book, & Music Stores
451211 Book stores
451120 Hobby, toy, & game stores
451140 Musical instrument & supplies stores
451212 News dealers & newsstands
451130 Sewing, needlework, & piece goods stores
451110 Sporting goods stores

Miscellaneous Store Retailers
453920 Art dealers
453110 Florists
453220 Gift, novelty, & souvenir stores
453930 Manufactured (mobile) home dealers
453210 Office supplies & stationery stores
453910 Pet & pet supplies stores
453310 Used merchandise stores
453990 All other miscellaneous store retailers (including tobacco, candle, & trophy shops)

Nonstore Retailers
454112 Electronic auctions
454111 Electronic shopping
454310 Fuel dealers (including heating oil & liquefied petroleum)
454113 Mail-order houses
454210 Vending machine operators
454390 Other direct selling establishments (including door-to-door retailing, frozen food plan providers, party plan merchandisers, & coffee-break service providers)

Transportation & Warehousing
481000 Air transportation
485510 Charter bus industry
484110 General freight trucking, local
484120 General freight trucking, long distance
485210 Interurban & rural bus transportation

486000 Pipeline transportation
482110 Rail transportation
487000 Scenic & sightseeing transportation
485410 School & employee bus transportation
484200 Specialized freight trucking (including household moving vans)
485300 Taxi & limousine service
485110 Urban transit systems
483000 Water transportation
485990 Other transit & ground passenger transportation
488000 Support activities for transportation (including motor vehicle towing)

Couriers & Messengers
492000 Couriers & messengers

Warehousing & Storage Facilities
493100 Warehousing & storage (except leases of miniwarehouses & self-storage units)

Utilities
221000 Utilities

Wholesale Trade

Merchant Wholesalers, Durable Goods
423200 Furniture & home furnishing
423700 Hardware, & plumbing & heating equipment & supplies
423600 Household appliances & electrical & electronic goods
423940 Jewelry, watch, precious stone, & precious metals
423300 Lumber & other construction materials
423800 Machinery, equipment, & supplies
423500 Metal & mineral (except petroleum)
423100 Motor vehicle & motor vehicle parts & supplies
423400 Professional & commercial equipment & supplies
423930 Recyclable materials
423910 Sporting & recreational goods & supplies
423920 Toy & hobby goods & supplies
423990 Other miscellaneous durable goods

Merchant Wholesalers, Nondurable Goods
424300 Apparel, piece goods, & notions
424800 Beer, wine, & distilled alcoholic beverage
424920 Books, periodicals, & newspapers
424600 Chemical & allied products
424210 Drugs & druggists' sundries
424500 Farm product raw materials
424910 Farm supplies
424930 Flower, nursery stock, & florists' supplies
424400 Grocery & related products
424950 Paint, varnish, & supplies
424100 Paper & paper products
424700 Petroleum & petroleum products
424940 Tobacco & tobacco products
424990 Other miscellaneous nondurable goods

Wholesale Electronic Markets and Agents & Brokers
425110 Business to business electronic markets
425120 Wholesale trade agents & brokers

999999 **Unclassified establishments (unable to classify)**

Appendix F - Answer Guide

Chapter 1 Review

(1)   What are the three main tax forms?

Forms 1040, 1040EZ, and 1040A

(2)   What four pieces of information are in the heading of the tax return?

The name of the taxpayer (and spouse if Married Filing Joint), the address of the taxpayer (and spouse if Married Filing Jointly), the taxpayer's (and spouse's if Married Filing Jointly) social security number, and the Presidential Election Campaign Fund.

(3)   When assembling the tax return, the Form 1040 is first. The other forms and schedules are assembled how?

The other forms and schedules are attached using sequence numbers, always shown in the top right corner, behind the Form 1040.

(4)   What are the 2 accounting periods?

Calendar year – this is the 12 month period from January 1st through December 31st. This is the period used by most taxpayers.

Fiscal year – A 12 month period that ends on the last day of any month other than December.

(5)   What are the 2 accounting methods?

Cash method – Counting income when it is constructively received and expenses when paid. Constructive receipt is when it becomes available to the taxpayer whether it is actually in their hand or not.

Accrual method – Counting income when earned and expenses when accrued.

(6)   What is the due date of a calendar year return?

The due date for filing a calendar year tax return is April 15th of the following year. The due date for filing a fiscal year return is the 15th day of the 4th month after the close of the fiscal year. If the due date is a Saturday, Sunday, or holiday, the due date will be the first business day after.

(7)   When preparing a return for a married couple, what should you double check?

When dealing with a married couple, always check to make sure the wife has changed her name with the Social Security Administration.

(8)   How long does the Third party designee last?

   The authorization will last until the due date of the <u>next</u> tax return. For the 2014 tax return, the Third Party Designee will expire on April 15th, 2016.

(9)   What is the penalty for a tax preparer that does not sign or provide an identification number on the tax return?

   The fine for not signing or providing an identification number on a tax return is $50 per return, up to $25,000.

Chapter 2 Review

(1) What are the five filing statuses?

- **Single**
- **Married Filing Joint**
- **Qualifying Widow(er)**
- **Head of Household**
- **Married Filing Separately**

(2) On what day of the year is the marital status determined?

The marital status of the taxpayer is determined on the last day of the tax year (December 31st for most taxpayers).

(3) When can a Married Filing Separate taxpayer claim an exemption for his or her spouse?

A taxpayer filing Married Filing Separately can claim their spouse's exemption on their tax return if the spouse had no income for the tax year and no one else can claim the spouse as a dependent.

(4) What are the four qualifications for married but unmarried for tax purposes?

A taxpayer may be considered unmarried for tax purposes if:

- **They are filing separately from their spouse.**
- **They paid more than half the cost of keeping up the home for the tax year.**
- **The spouse did not live in the home during the last six months of the year.**
- **The home is the main home for his child, stepchild, or eligible foster child for more than half the year and the child can be claimed as a dependent.**

*Exception: This test can be met if the only reason the taxpayer cannot claim the child as a dependent is if the noncustodial parent can claim the child under the rules for Children of Divorced or Separated Parents.

(5) What are the two reasons a taxpayer may get an additional standard deduction for tax year 2014?

Some taxpayers (and their spouses if MFJ) may be eligible for an additional Standard Deduction amount if:

- **the taxpayer (and/or spouse if MFJ) is age 65 or older at the end of the tax year (They are considered 65 on the day before their 65th birthday.), or**
- **the taxpayer (and/or spouse if MFJ) is totally or partly blind on the last day of the tax year.**

(6) What is the standard deduction for a dependent?

The Standard Deduction for someone that can be claimed as a dependent on someone else's tax return is the greater of:

- **their earned income plus $350 not to exceed the Single Standard Deduction of $6,200 or**
- **$1,000.**

(7) What is the exemption amount for 2014?

The amount of each exemption is $3,950 for 2014.

(8) What are the three tests that apply for both the qualifying child and the qualifying relative?

- **Dependent Taxpayer Test**
- **Joint Return Test**
- **Citizen or Resident Test**

(9) What are the five qualifying child tests?

- **Relationship**
- **Age**
- **Residency**
- **Support**
- **Special test for qualifying child of more than one person**

(10) What is a Custodial parent?

The custodial parent is the parent with whom the child lived for the greater part of the year.

(11) What is a noncustodial parent?

The noncustodial parent is the other parent (not the custodial parent).

(12) What are the four qualifying relative test?

- **Not a qualifying child test**
- **Member of the household or relationship test**
- **Gross income test**
- **Support test**

Dependency Support Worksheet

Household Expenses		Funds belonging to the person supported	
1. Rent paid or fair rental value	10200	17. Income received during the year (taxable and nontaxable)	8000
2. Food consumed in the home	5100	18. Amounts borrowed by the person supported during the year	
3. Utilities	4140	19. Amount in savings and other account at the beginning of the year	
4. Repairs on the house	350	20. If home belongs to the person supported, enter the fair rental value of the home here.	
5. Total household expense, add lines 1 through 4.	19790	21. Add lines 17 through 20	8000
6. Number of people living in the house	2	22. Amount in savings and other accounts at the end of the year	0
7. Divide line 5 by line 6. This is the amount of household expenses for each person in the house.	9895	23. Subtract line 22 from line 21. This is the amount the person supported provided toward their own support.	8000
Expenses for the person supported		**Qualifying child support test**	
8. Amount from line 7 above	9895	24. Enter the amount from line 16.	22015
9. Clothing	850	25. Multiply line 24 by 50%.	11008
10. Education	3345	26. Enter the amount from line 23.	8000
11. Out of pocket medical and dental expenses		27. Is line 26 less than line 25? If yes, they meet the support test to be a qualifying child.	yes
12. Travel and recreation	3430	**Qualifying relative support test**	
13. Transportation	3720	28. Enter the amount from line 23.	
14. Capital expenditures, for example: tv's, cars, furniture, etc		29. Enter the amount provided by anyone other than the taxpayer.	
15. Other expenses	775	30. Add lines 28 and 29.	
16. Add lines 8 through 16. These are the total expenses for the person supported.	22015	31. Is line 30 less than line 25? If yes, they meet the support test to be a qualifying relative.	

Chapter 3 Review

1) What is employee compensation?

   Employee compensation is what you receive in payment for personal services performed for an employer.

2) On what line of the tax return is the amount in Box 1 of the W-2's entered?

   Form 1040, line 7

3) On what line of the tax return is the amount in Box 2 of the W-2's entered?

   Form 1040, line 64

4) How many copies are there of the Form W-2?

   There are five copies of the W-2.

5) Is alimony received taxable?

   Alimony received is taxable in the year it is received.

6) Is child support received taxable?

   Child support is never taxable to the recipient.

7) On what line of the Form 1040 is taxable unemployment compensation entered?

   Form 1040, line 19

8) What is reported on Form 1099-INT?

   Interest income of $10 or more is reported on Form 1099-INT.

9) What is reported on Form 1099-DIV?

   Dividend income is reported on Form 1099-DIV.

Form **1040**	Department of the Treasury—Internal Revenue Service (99) **U.S. Individual Income Tax Return**	20**14**	OMB No. 1545-0074	IRS Use Only—Do not write or staple in this space.

For the year Jan. 1–Dec. 31, 2014, or other tax year beginning	, 2014, ending	, 20	See separate instructions.

Your first name and initial	Last name		Your social security number
Mark	Jones		0 9 8	7 6	5 4 3 2

If a joint return, spouse's first name and initial	Last name		Spouse's social security number
Beverly	Jones		0 2 3	4 5	9 8 7 6

Home address (number and street). If you have a P.O. box, see instructions. | Apt. no.

▲ Make sure the SSN(s) above and on line 6c are correct.

877 Oak Ave.

City, town or post office, state, and ZIP code. If you have a foreign address, also complete spaces below (see instructions).

Your City, Your State, Your Zip Code

Presidential Election Campaign
Check here if you, or your spouse if filing jointly, want $3 to go to this fund. Checking a box below will not change your tax or refund. ☐ You ☐ Spouse

Foreign country name	Foreign province/state/county	Foreign postal code

Filing Status

Check only one box.

1. ☐ Single
2. ☑ Married filing jointly (even if only one had income)
3. ☐ Married filing separately. Enter spouse's SSN above and full name here. ▶
4. ☐ Head of household (with qualifying person). (See instructions.) If the qualifying person is a child but not your dependent, enter this child's name here. ▶
5. ☐ Qualifying widow(er) with dependent child

Exemptions

6a ☑ **Yourself.** If someone can claim you as a dependent, **do not** check box 6a . . . . .
b ☑ **Spouse** . . . .

c **Dependents:**

(1) First name Last name	(2) Dependent's social security number	(3) Dependent's relationship to you	(4) ✓ if child under age 17 qualifying for child tax credit (see instructions)
Catherine Smith	3 4 5 6 7 4 3 2 1	Daughter	☐
			☐
			☐
			☐

If more than four dependents, see instructions and check here ▶ ☐

Boxes checked on 6a and 6b	2
No. of children on 6c who: • lived with you	1
• did not live with you due to divorce or separation (see instructions)	
Dependents on 6c not entered above	
Add numbers on lines above ▶	3

d Total number of exemptions claimed . . . .

Income

Attach Form(s) W-2 here. Also attach Forms W-2G and 1099-R if tax was withheld.

If you did not get a W-2, see instructions.

7	Wages, salaries, tips, etc. Attach Form(s) W-2	7	83,563	00
8a	**Taxable** interest. Attach Schedule B if required	8a		
b	**Tax-exempt** interest. **Do not** include on line 8a . . .	8b		
9a	Ordinary dividends. Attach Schedule B if required . . .	9a		
b	Qualified dividends	9b		
10	Taxable refunds, credits, or offsets of state and local income taxes	10		
11	Alimony received	11		
12	Business income or (loss). Attach Schedule C or C-EZ	12		
13	Capital gain or (loss). Attach Schedule D if required. If not required, check here ▶ ☐	13		
14	Other gains or (losses). Attach Form 4797	14		
15a	IRA distributions .	15a		b Taxable amount . . .	15b		
16a	Pensions and annuities	16a		b Taxable amount . . .	16b		
17	Rental real estate, royalties, partnerships, S corporations, trusts, etc. Attach Schedule E	17		
18	Farm income or (loss). Attach Schedule F	18		
19	Unemployment compensation	19		
20a	Social security benefits	20a		b Taxable amount . . .	20b		
21	Other income. List type and amount _____	21		
22	Combine the amounts in the far right column for lines 7 through 21. This is your **total income** ▶	22	83,563	00

Adjusted Gross Income

23	Educator expenses	23		
24	Certain business expenses of reservists, performing artists, and fee-basis government officials. Attach Form 2106 or 2106-EZ	24		
25	Health savings account deduction. Attach Form 8889 .	25		
26	Moving expenses. Attach Form 3903	26		
27	Deductible part of self-employment tax. Attach Schedule SE .	27		
28	Self-employed SEP, SIMPLE, and qualified plans . . .	28		
29	Self-employed health insurance deduction	29		
30	Penalty on early withdrawal of savings	30		
31a	Alimony paid b Recipient's SSN ▶	31a		
32	IRA deduction	32		
33	Student loan interest deduction	33		
34	Tuition and fees. Attach Form 8917	34		
35	Domestic production activities deduction. Attach Form 8903	35		
36	Add lines 23 through 35	36		
37	Subtract line 36 from line 22. This is your **adjusted gross income** . . . . . ▶	37	83,563	00

For Disclosure, Privacy Act, and Paperwork Reduction Act Notice, see separate instructions. | Cat. No. 11320B | Form **1040** (2014)

Chapter 3 Exercise

Form 1040 (2014)

Page **2**

Tax and Credits	38	Amount from line 37 (adjusted gross income)	38	83,563 00
	39a	Check if: ☐ **You** were born before January 2, 1950, ☐ Blind. ☐ **Spouse** was born before January 2, 1950, ☐ Blind. } Total boxes checked ► 39a		
	b	If your spouse itemizes on a separate return or you were a dual-status alien, check here ► 39b ☐		
Standard Deduction for— • People who check any box on line 39a or 39b **or** who can be claimed as a dependent, see instructions. • All others: Single or Married filing separately, $6,200 Married filing jointly or Qualifying widow(er), $12,400 Head of household, $9,100	40	**Itemized deductions** (from Schedule A) **or** your **standard deduction** (see left margin)	40	12,400 00
	41	Subtract line 40 from line 38	41	61,163 00
	42	**Exemptions.** If line 38 is $152,525 or less, multiply $3,950 by the number on line 6d. Otherwise, see instructions	42	11,850 00
	43	**Taxable income.** Subtract line 42 from line 41. If line 42 is more than line 41, enter -0- . .	43	59,313 00
	44	**Tax** (see instructions). Check if any from: **a** ☐ Form(s) 8814 **b** ☐ Form 4972 **c** ☐	44	7,991 00
	45	**Alternative minimum tax** (see instructions). Attach Form 6251	45	
	46	Excess advance premium tax credit repayment. Attach Form 8962	46	
	47	Add lines 44, 45, and 46 . . . . ►	47	7,991 00
	48	Foreign tax credit. Attach Form 1116 if required	48		
	49	Credit for child and dependent care expenses. Attach Form 2441	49		
	50	Education credits from Form 8863, line 19	50		
	51	Retirement savings contributions credit. Attach Form 8880	51		
	52	Child tax credit. Attach Schedule 8812, if required . .	52		
	53	Residential energy credits. Attach Form 5695	53		
	54	Other credits from Form: **a** ☐ 3800 **b** ☐ 8801 **c** ☐	54		
	55	Add lines 48 through 54. These are your **total credits**	55	
	56	Subtract line 55 from line 47. If line 55 is more than line 47, enter -0- . . . . . ►	56	7,991 00
Other Taxes	57	Self-employment tax. Attach Schedule SE	57	
	58	Unreported social security and Medicare tax from Form: **a** ☐ 4137 **b** ☐ 8919 . .	58	
	59	Additional tax on IRAs, other qualified retirement plans, etc. Attach Form 5329 if required . .	59	
	60a	Household employment taxes from Schedule H	60a	
	b	First-time homebuyer credit repayment. Attach Form 5405 if required . . .	60b	
	61	Health care: individual responsibility (see instructions) Full-year coverage ☐ . . .	61	
	62	Taxes from: **a** ☐ Form 8959 **b** ☐ Form 8960 **c** ☐ Instructions; enter code(s)	62	
	63	Add lines 56 through 62. This is your **total tax** . . . . . . ►	63	7,991 00
Payments If you have a qualifying child, attach Schedule EIC.	64	Federal income tax withheld from Forms W-2 and 1099 . .	64	9,343 00	
	65	2014 estimated tax payments and amount applied from 2013 return	65		
	66a	**Earned income credit (EIC)**	66a		
	b	Nontaxable combat pay election	66b		
	67	Additional child tax credit. Attach Schedule 8812	67		
	68	American opportunity credit from Form 8863, line 8 . . .	68		
	69	Net premium tax credit. Attach Form 8962	69		
	70	Amount paid with request for extension to file	70		
	71	Excess social security and tier 1 RRTA tax withheld . . .	71		
	72	Credit for federal tax on fuels. Attach Form 4136	72		
	73	Credits from Form: **a** ☐ 2439 **b** ☐ Reserved **c** ☐ Reserved **d** ☐	73		
	74	Add lines 64, 65, 66a, and 67 through 73. These are your **total payments** . . . . . ►	74	9,343 00
Refund Direct deposit? See instructions.	75	If line 74 is more than line 63, subtract line 63 from line 74. This is the amount you **overpaid**	75	1,352 00
	76a	Amount of line 75 you want **refunded to you.** If Form 8888 is attached, check here . . ► ☐	76a	1,352 00
	b	Routing number ► c Type: ☐ Checking ☐ Savings		
	d	Account number		
	77	Amount of line 75 you want **applied to your 2015 estimated tax** ►	77	
Amount You Owe	78	**Amount you owe.** Subtract line 74 from line 63. For details on how to pay, see instructions ►	78	
	79	Estimated tax penalty (see instructions)	79	

Third Party Designee	Do you want to allow another person to discuss this return with the IRS (see instructions)? ☐ **Yes.** Complete below. ☑ **No**		
	Designee's name ►	Phone no. ►	Personal identification number (PIN) ►

Sign Here
Joint return? See instructions. Keep a copy for your records.

Under penalties of perjury, I declare that I have examined this return and accompanying schedules and statements, and to the best of my knowledge and belief, they are true, correct, and complete. Declaration of preparer (other than taxpayer) is based on all information of which preparer has any knowledge.

Your signature	Date	Your occupation	Daytime phone number
		Supervisor	**(555)555-5555**
Spouse's signature. If a joint return, **both** must sign.	Date	Spouse's occupation	If the IRS sent you an Identity Protection PIN, enter it here (see inst.)
		Teacher	

Paid Preparer Use Only	Print/Type preparer's name Jane Doe	Preparer's signature	Date	Check ☐ if self-employed	PTIN P000000000
	Firm's name ► **My Tax Service**			Firm's EIN ►	63-0000000
	Firm's address ► **100 Main St., Your City, Your State, Your Zip Code**			Phone no.	**(555)555-1111**

www.irs.gov/form1040

Form **1040** (2014)

F-9

Chapter 4 Review

1) How much tip income may a taxpayer make per month without having to report it to the employer?

   The employee is required to report tips to the employer if they received $20 or over in any month.

2) What is the penalty for a taxpayer who was required to report the tip income to their employer but did not?

   The taxpayer may be penalized 50% of the Medicare and social security tax due on those tips.

3) In what situations is a Schedule B required to be filed?

   A Schedule B is required if the taxpayer received over $1,500 of taxable interest, has a seller-financed mortgage, Nominee interest, Accrued interest, Original Issue Discount, Amortizable Bond Premiums, if the taxpayer is claiming the exclusion of interest from a series EE or I U.S. savings bonds issued after 1989 used for education purposes, if the taxpayer has over $1,500 of ordinary dividends, or if the taxpayer received nominee dividends.

4) What requirements must the taxpayer meet to be able to exclude series EE and I U.S. savings bond interest?

   Part or all of the interest earned on Series EE and I bonds may be excludable if used to pay higher education expenses.

5) What is the difference between ordinary dividends and qualified dividends?

   Ordinary dividends are the most common type of dividend distribution. Ordinary dividends paid are taxed as ordinary income. Qualified dividends are dividends that are subject to the capital gains tax rate.

6) What is a nondividend distribution and how is it taxed?

   A nondividend distribution is a return of capital or investment. The distribution is not taxable, but reduces the taxpayer's investment (basis) in the stock. When the taxpayer's investment is completely recovered, the distributions become taxable.

7) Name three types of taxable "other income".

- **Gambling winnings,**
- **Gifts and Inheritances,**
- **Bribes,**
- **Illegal Income,**
- **Kickbacks,**
- **Prizes and awards,**
- **Jury Duty,**
- **Activity Not for Profit, or**
- **Compensatory Damages.**

8) Are scholarships and fellowships taxable?

Some scholarships and fellowships are not taxable if certain requirements are met. These requirements are:
- **The student must be a degree candidate.**
- **The funds must be used to pay the tuition and fees to enroll at or attend an educational institution, or**
- **Fees, books, supplies, and equipment required for courses at the educational institution.**

Amounts used for room and board are not excludable from income and are taxable to the recipient.

Chapter 4 Exercise

| Form **1040** | Department of the Treasury—Internal Revenue Service (99) **U.S. Individual Income Tax Return** | 2014 | OMB No. 1545-0074 | IRS Use Only—Do not write or staple in this space |

For the year Jan. 1–Dec. 31, 2014, or other tax year beginning , 2014, ending , 20 — **See separate instructions.**

Your first name and initial	Last name		Your social security number
Hank	Lee		7 6 7 8 9 1 2 1 2
If a joint return, spouse's first name and initial	Last name		Spouse's social security number
Hilary	Lee		4 3 4 5 5 3 3 2 2

Home address (number and street). If you have a P.O. box, see instructions. — Apt. no.

99 Juice St.

▲ Make sure the SSN(s) above and on line 6c are correct.

City, town or post office, state, and ZIP code. If you have a foreign address, also complete spaces below (see instructions).

Your City, Your State, Your Zip Code

| Foreign country name | Foreign province/state/county | Foreign postal code |

Presidential Election Campaign
Check here if you, or your spouse if filing jointly, want $3 to go to this fund. Checking a box below will not change your tax or refund. ☑ You ☑ Spouse

Filing Status

Check only one box.

1. ☐ Single
2. ☑ Married filing jointly (even if only one had income)
3. ☐ Married filing separately. Enter spouse's SSN above and full name here. ▶
4. ☐ Head of household (with qualifying person). (See instructions.) If the qualifying person is a child but not your dependent, enter this child's name here. ▶
5. ☐ Qualifying widow(er) with dependent child

Exemptions

If more than four dependents, see instructions and check here ▶ ☐

6a ☑ **Yourself.** If someone can claim you as a dependent, **do not** check box 6a . . . . .
b ☑ **Spouse** . . . .

c	Dependents:	(2) Dependent's social security number	(3) Dependent's relationship to you	(4) ✓ if child under age 17 qualifying for child tax credit (see instructions)
(1) First name Last name				☐
				☐
				☐
				☐

Boxes checked on 6a and 6b	2
No. of children on 6c who:	
• lived with you	
• did not live with you due to divorce or separation (see instructions)	
Dependents on 6c not entered above	
Add numbers on lines above ▶	2

d Total number of exemptions claimed . . . .

Income

Attach Form(s) W-2 here. Also attach Forms W-2G and 1099-R if tax was withheld.

If you did not get a W-2, see instructions.

7	Wages, salaries, tips, etc. Attach Form(s) W-2	7	49,111	00
8a	**Taxable** interest. Attach Schedule B if required	8a	1,676	00
b	**Tax-exempt** interest. **Do not** include on line 8a	8b		
9a	Ordinary dividends. Attach Schedule B if required	9a	2,898	00
b	Qualified dividends	9b		
10	Taxable refunds, credits, or offsets of state and local income taxes	10		
11	Alimony received	11		
12	Business income or (loss). Attach Schedule C or C-EZ	12		
13	Capital gain or (loss). Attach Schedule D if required. If not required, check here ▶ ☐	13		
14	Other gains or (losses). Attach Form 4797	14		
15a	IRA distributions . 15a	b Taxable amount	15b		
16a	Pensions and annuities 16a	b Taxable amount	16b		
17	Rental real estate, royalties, partnerships, S corporations, trusts, etc. Attach Schedule E	17		
18	Farm income or (loss). Attach Schedule F	18		
19	Unemployment compensation	19	2,893	00
20a	Social security benefits 20a	b Taxable amount	20b		
21	Other income. List type and amount	21		
22	Combine the amounts in the far right column for lines 7 through 21. This is your **total income** ▶	22	56,578	00

Adjusted Gross Income

23	Educator expenses	23		
24	Certain business expenses of reservists, performing artists, and fee-basis government officials. Attach Form 2106 or 2106-EZ	24		
25	Health savings account deduction. Attach Form 8889	25		
26	Moving expenses. Attach Form 3903	26		
27	Deductible part of self-employment tax. Attach Schedule SE	27		
28	Self-employed SEP, SIMPLE, and qualified plans	28		
29	Self-employed health insurance deduction	29		
30	Penalty on early withdrawal of savings	30		
31a	Alimony paid b Recipient's SSN ▶	31a		
32	IRA deduction	32		
33	Student loan interest deduction	33		
34	Tuition and fees. Attach Form 8917	34		
35	Domestic production activities deduction. Attach Form 8903	35		
36	Add lines 23 through 35	36		
37	Subtract line 36 from line 22. This is your **adjusted gross income** ▶	37	56,578	00

For Disclosure, Privacy Act, and Paperwork Reduction Act Notice, see separate instructions. Cat. No. 11320B Form **1040** (2014)

Chapter 4 Exercise

Tax and Credits	38	Amount from line 37 (adjusted gross income)	38	56,578	00
	39a	Check if: ☐ **You** were born before January 2, 1950, ☐ Blind. **Total boxes** ☐ **Spouse** was born before January 2, 1950, ☐ Blind. **checked ▶ 39a**			
	b	If your spouse itemizes on a separate return or you were a dual-status alien, check here▶ 39b☐			
Standard Deduction for— • People who check any box on line 39a or 39b **or** who can be claimed as a dependent, see instructions. • All others: Single or Married filing separately, $6,200 Married filing jointly or Qualifying widow(er), $12,400 Head of household, $9,100	40	**Itemized deductions** (from Schedule A) **or** your **standard deduction** (see left margin) . .	40	12,400	00
	41	Subtract line 40 from line 38	41	44,178	00
	42	**Exemptions.** If line 38 is $152,525 or less, multiply $3,950 by the number on line 6d. Otherwise, see instructions	42	7,900	00
	43	**Taxable income.** Subtract line 42 from line 41. If line 42 is more than line 41, enter -0- . .	43	36,278	00
	44	Tax (see instructions). Check if any from: **a** ☐ Form(s) 8814 **b** ☐ Form 4972 **c** ☐ ____	44	4,534	00
	45	**Alternative minimum tax** (see instructions). Attach Form 6251	45		
	46	Excess advance premium tax credit repayment. Attach Form 8962	46		
	47	Add lines 44, 45, and 46 . . . . ▶	47	4,534	00
	48	Foreign tax credit. Attach Form 1116 if required . . .	48			
	49	Credit for child and dependent care expenses. Attach Form 2441	49			
	50	Education credits from Form 8863, line 19	50			
	51	Retirement savings contributions credit. Attach Form 8880	51			
	52	Child tax credit. Attach Schedule 8812, if required . . .	52			
	53	Residential energy credits. Attach Form 5695	53			
	54	Other credits from Form: **a** ☐ 3800 **b** ☐ 8801 **c** ☐ ____	54			
	55	Add lines 48 through 54. These are your **total credits**	55		
	56	Subtract line 55 from line 47. If line 55 is more than line 47, enter -0- . . . . ▶	56	4,534	00
Other Taxes	57	Self-employment tax. Attach Schedule SE	57		
	58	Unreported social security and Medicare tax from Form: **a** ☑ 4137 **b** ☐ 8919 . .	58	6	00
	59	Additional tax on IRAs, other qualified retirement plans, etc. Attach Form 5329 if required .	59		
	60a	Household employment taxes from Schedule H	60a		
	b	First-time homebuyer credit repayment. Attach Form 5405 if required	60b		
	61	Health care: individual responsibility (see instructions) Full-year coverage ☐	61		
	62	Taxes from: **a** ☐ Form 8959 **b** ☐ Form 8960 **c** ☐ Instructions; enter code(s) ____	62		
	63	Add lines 56 through 62. This is your **total tax** . . . . ▶	63	4,540	00
Payments If you have a qualifying child, attach Schedule EIC.	64	Federal income tax withheld from Forms W-2 and 1099 . .	64	5,376	00	
	65	2014 estimated tax payments and amount applied from 2013 return	65			
	66a	**Earned income credit (EIC)**	66a			
	b	Nontaxable combat pay election	66b			
	67	Additional child tax credit. Attach Schedule 8812	67			
	68	American opportunity credit from Form 8863, line 8 . . .	68			
	69	Net premium tax credit. Attach Form 8962	69			
	70	Amount paid with request for extension to file	70			
	71	Excess social security and tier 1 RRTA tax withheld . . .	71			
	72	Credit for federal tax on fuels. Attach Form 4136 . . .	72			
	73	Credits from Form: **a** ☐ 2439 **b** ☐ Reserved **c** ☐ Reserved **d** ☐	73			
	74	Add lines 64, 65, 66a, and 67 through 73. These are your **total payments** . . . . . ▶	74	5,376	00
Refund Direct deposit? ▶ See instructions.	75	If line 74 is more than line 63, subtract line 63 from line 74. This is the amount you **overpaid**	75	836	00
	76a	Amount of line 75 you want **refunded to you**. If Form 8888 is attached, check here . . ▶ ☐	76a	836	00
	▶ b	Routing number	▶ **c** Type: ☐ Checking ☐ Savings		
	▶ d	Account number			
	77	Amount of line 75 you want **applied to your 2015 estimated tax ▶**	77			
Amount You Owe	78	**Amount you owe.** Subtract line 74 from line 63. For details on how to pay, see instructions ▶	78		
	79	Estimated tax penalty (see instructions)	79			

Third Party Designee	Do you want to allow another person to discuss this return with the IRS (see instructions)? ☐ **Yes.** Complete below. ☐ **No**
	Designee's name ▶ Phone no. ▶ Personal identification number (PIN) ▶ ☐☐☐☐☐

Sign Here Joint return? See instructions. Keep a copy for your records.	Under penalties of perjury, I declare that I have examined this return and accompanying schedules and statements, and to the best of my knowledge and belief, they are true, correct, and complete. Declaration of preparer (other than taxpayer) is based on all information of which preparer has any knowledge.
	Your signature Date Your occupation **Manager** Daytime phone number **(555)555-5555**
	Spouse's signature. If a joint return, **both** must sign. Date Spouse's occupation **Server** If the IRS sent you an Identity Protection PIN, enter it here (see inst.)

Paid Preparer Use Only	Print/Type preparer's name **Jane Doe** Preparer's signature Date Check ☐ if self-employed PTIN **P00000000**
	Firm's name ▶ **My Tax Service** Firm's EIN ▶ **63-0000000**
	Firm's address ▶ **100 Main St., Your City, Your State, Your Zip Code** Phone no. **(555)555-1111**

SCHEDULE B (Form 1040A or 1040) Department of the Treasury Internal Revenue Service (99)	**Interest and Ordinary Dividends** ▶ Attach to Form 1040A or 1040. ▶ Information about Schedule B and its instructions is at *www.irs.gov/scheduleb*.	OMB No. 1545-0074 20**14** Attachment Sequence No. **08**

Name(s) shown on return	Your social security number
Hank and Hilary Lee	767-89-1212

Part I **Interest** (See instructions on back and the instructions for Form 1040A, or Form 1040, line 8a.) **Note.** If you received a Form 1099-INT, Form 1099-OID, or substitute statement from a brokerage firm, list the firm's name as the payer and enter the total interest shown on that form.	**1**	List name of payer. If any interest is from a seller-financed mortgage and the buyer used the property as a personal residence, see instructions on back and list this interest first. Also, show that buyer's social security number and address ▶		**Amount**	
		First National Bank	**1**	1,676	00
	2	Add the amounts on line 1	**2**	1,676	00
	3	Excludable interest on series EE and I U.S. savings bonds issued after 1989. Attach Form 8815	**3**		
	4	Subtract line 3 from line 2. Enter the result here and on Form 1040A, or Form 1040, line 8a . . . . ▶	**4**	1,676	00

Note. If line 4 is over $1,500, you must complete Part III.

Part II **Ordinary Dividends** (See instructions on back and the instructions for Form 1040A, or Form 1040, line 9a.) **Note.** If you received a Form 1099-DIV or substitute statement from a brokerage firm, list the firm's name as the payer and enter the ordinary dividends shown on that form.	**5**	List name of payer ▶ Brighton Financial Services		**Amount**	
			5	2,898	00
	6	Add the amounts on line 5. Enter the total here and on Form 1040A, or Form 1040, line 9a . . . . ▶	**6**	2,898	00

Note. If line 6 is over $1,500, you must complete Part III.

	You must complete this part if you **(a)** had over $1,500 of taxable interest or ordinary dividends; **(b)** had a foreign account; or **(c)** received a distribution from, or were a grantor of, or a transferor to, a foreign trust.	**Yes**	**No**
Part III **Foreign Accounts and Trusts** (See instructions on back.)	**7a** At any time during 2014, did you have a financial interest in or signature authority over a financial account (such as a bank account, securities account, or brokerage account) located in a foreign country? See instructions		✓
	If "Yes," are you required to file FinCEN Form 114, Report of Foreign Bank and Financial Accounts (FBAR), to report that financial interest or signature authority? See FinCEN Form 114 and its instructions for filing requirements and exceptions to those requirements		
	b If you are required to file FinCEN Form 114, enter the name of the foreign country where the financial account is located ▶		
	8 During 2014, did you receive a distribution from, or were you the grantor of, or transferor to, a foreign trust? If "Yes," you may have to file Form 3520. See instructions on back		✓

For Paperwork Reduction Act Notice, see your tax return instructions.   Cat. No. 17146N   Schedule B (Form 1040A or 1040) 2014

Form **4137**

Department of the Treasury
Internal Revenue Service (99)

Social Security and Medicare Tax
on Unreported Tip Income

▶ Information about Form 4137 and its instructions is at *www.irs.gov/form4137*.
▶ **Attach to Form 1040, Form 1040NR, Form 1040NR-EZ, Form 1040-SS, or Form 1040-PR.**

OMB No. 1545-0074

2014

Attachment
Sequence No. **24**

Name of person who received tips. If married, complete a separate Form 4137 for each spouse with unreported tips.	Social security number
Hilary Lee	434-55-3322

1	(a) Name of employer to whom you were required to, but did not report all your tips (see instructions)	(b) Employer identification number (see instructions)	(c) Total cash and charge tips you received (including unreported tips) (see instructions)		(d) Total cash and charge tips you reported to your employer	
A	Mom's Home Cooking	63-8853766	2,416	00	2,315	00
B						
C						
D						
E						

2	Total cash and charge tips you **received** in 2014. Add the amounts from line 1, column (c)	**2**	2,416	00	
3	Total cash and charge tips you **reported** to your employer(s) in 2014. Add the amounts from line 1, column (d)	**3**	2,315	00	
4	Subtract line 3 from line 2. This amount is income you **must** include in the total on Form 1040, line 7; Form 1040NR, line 8; or Form 1040NR-EZ, line 3	**4**	101	00	
5	Cash and charge tips you received but did not report to your employer because the total was less than $20 in a calendar month (see instructions)	**5**	14	00	
6	Unreported tips subject to Medicare tax. Subtract line 5 from line 4	**6**	87	00	
7	Maximum amount of wages (including tips) subject to social security tax	**7**	117,000	00	
8	Total social security wages and social security tips (total of boxes 3 and 7 shown on your Form(s) W-2) and railroad retirement (RRTA) compensation (subject to 6.2% rate) (see instructions).	**8**	16,780	00	
9	Subtract line 8 from line 7. If line 8 is more than line 7, enter -0-	**9**	100,220	00	
10	Unreported tips subject to social security tax. Enter the **smaller** of line 6 or line 9. If you received tips as a federal, state, or local government employee (see instructions)	**10**	87	00	
11	Multiply line 10 by .062 (social security tax rate)	**11**	5	00	
12	Multiply line 6 by .0145 (Medicare tax rate).	**12**	1	00	
13	Add lines 11 and 12. Enter the result here and on Form 1040, line 58; Form 1040NR, line 56; or Form 1040NR-EZ, line 16 (Form 1040-SS and 1040-PR filers, see instructions.) . . .	**13**	6	00	

General Instructions

Future Developments

For the latest information about developments related to Form 4137 and its instructions, such as legislation enacted after they were published, go to *www.irs.gov/form4137*.

What's New

For 2014, the maximum wages and tips subject to social security tax increased to $117,000. The social security tax rate an employee must pay on tips remains at 6.2% (.062).

Reminder

A 0.9% Additional Medicare Tax applies to Medicare wages, Railroad Retirement Tax Act compensation, and self-employment income over a threshold amount based on your filing status. Use Form 8959, Additional Medicare Tax, to figure this tax. For more information on Additional Medicare Tax, go to *www.IRS.gov* and enter "Additional Medicare Tax" in the search box.

Purpose of form. Use Form 4137 **only** to figure the social security and Medicare tax owed on tips you did not report to your employer, including any allocated tips shown on your Form(s) W-2 that you must report as income. You must also report the income on Form 1040, line 7; Form 1040NR, line 8; or

Form 1040NR-EZ, line 3. By filing this form, your social security and Medicare tips will be credited to your social security record (used to figure your benefits).

 If you believe you are an employee and you received Form 1099-MISC, Miscellaneous Income, instead of Form W-2, Wage and Tax Statement, because your employer did not consider you an employee, do not use this form to report the social security and Medicare tax on that income. Instead, use Form 8919, Uncollected Social Security and Medicare Tax on Wages.

For Paperwork Reduction Act Notice, see your tax return instructions.

Cat. No. 12626C

Form **4137** (2014)

Chapter 5 Review

1) What is a nonrefundable credit?

   A nonrefundable credit cannot reduce the tax liability below zero.

2) What is a refundable credit?

   A refundable credit is added to the tax payments made. If the total is more than the tax liability, then the excess is refunded to the taxpayer.

3) Ed and Erma are Married Filing Jointly. They have a son, Ethan. Ethan is 14 and lived with them all year. What is the most adjusted gross income they can have and still be eligible for the Earned Income Credit?

   Their AGI must be less than $43,941.

4) Mike and Julie are divorced. Steven, their son, lives with Mike all year. Julie gets to claim Steven's dependency exemption as stated in the divorce decree. If all other requirements are met, who will receive the EIC for Steven? The Child Tax Credit?

   Mike will claim the EIC because he is the custodial parent. However, Julie will claim the Child Tax Credit.

5) What is earned income?

   Earned income includes the following types of income: wages, salaries, tips, and other taxable employee pay; net earnings from self-employment; and gross income received as a statutory employee.

6) What is the significance of earned income for the EIC?

   The taxpayer must have earned income. Unearned income will not qualify for EIC. The amount of EIC the taxpayer receives is determined by the amount of their earned income.

7) What is the penalty for a tax preparer that does not meet the due diligence requirements?

   If the tax preparer does not meet the due diligence requirements, they will be penalized $500 per instance by the IRS.

8) What form (or equivalent of it) must a preparer complete and file with the return in order to follow the due diligence requirements?

Form 8867

9) What is Form 8862 and when must it be filed?

If the taxpayer claimed EIC for any year after 1996 and the EIC was disallowed or reduced for any reason other than a math or clerical error, they will have to file a Form 8862.

10) Is Child Tax Credit refundable or nonrefundable? What about Additional Child Tax Credit?

Child Tax Credit is a nonrefundable credit while Additional Child Tax Credit is a refundable credit.

Form 1040
Department of the Treasury—Internal Revenue Service (99)

U.S. Individual Income Tax Return 2014

OMB No. 1545-0074 | IRS Use Only—Do not write or staple in this space.

For the year Jan. 1–Dec. 31, 2014, or other tax year beginning _____, 2014, ending _____, 20____

See separate instructions.

Your first name and initial **Jordan**	Last name **Smith**	Your social security number **5 5 5 4 4 3 3 3 3**
If a joint return, spouse's first name and initial **Judith**	Last name **Smith**	Spouse's social security number **8 8 8 7 7 6 6 6 6**

Home address (number and street). If you have a P.O. box, see instructions. **64 Miracle Blvd.** | Apt. no. |

▲ Make sure the SSN(s) above and on line 6c are correct.

City, town or post office, state, and ZIP code. If you have a foreign address, also complete spaces below (see instructions). **Your City, Your State, Your Zip Code**

Foreign country name | Foreign province/state/county | Foreign postal code

Presidential Election Campaign
Check here if you, or your spouse if filing jointly, want $3 to go to this fund. Checking a box below will not change your tax or refund. ☐ You ☐ Spouse

Filing Status

Check only one box.

1. ☐ Single
2. ☑ Married filing jointly (even if only one had income)
3. ☐ Married filing separately. Enter spouse's SSN above and full name here. ▶
4. ☐ Head of household (with qualifying person). (See instructions.) If the qualifying person is a child but not your dependent, enter this child's name here. ▶
5. ☐ Qualifying widow(er) with dependent child

Exemptions

6a ☑ **Yourself.** If someone can claim you as a dependent, **do not** check box 6a . . . . .
b ☑ **Spouse** . . . .

c **Dependents:**

(1) First name Last name	(2) Dependent's social security number	(3) Dependent's relationship to you	(4) ✓ if child under age 17 qualifying for child tax credit (see instructions)
Joanne Smith	2 2 3 3 2 2 2 3 2	Daughter	☑
			☐
			☐
			☐

If more than four dependents, see instructions and check here ▶ ☐

d Total number of exemptions claimed . . . .

Boxes checked on 6a and 6b **2**
No. of children on 6c who:
• lived with you **1**
• did not live with you due to divorce or separation (see instructions)
Dependents on 6c not entered above
Add numbers on lines above ▶ **3**

Income

Attach Form(s) W-2 here. Also attach Forms W-2G and 1099-R if tax was withheld.

If you did not get a W-2, see instructions.

7	Wages, salaries, tips, etc. Attach Form(s) W-2	7	28,510 00
8a	**Taxable** interest. Attach Schedule B if required	8a	
b	**Tax-exempt** interest. **Do not** include on line 8a 8b		
9a	Ordinary dividends. Attach Schedule B if required	9a	
b	Qualified dividends 9b		
10	Taxable refunds, credits, or offsets of state and local income taxes	10	
11	Alimony received	11	
12	Business income or (loss). Attach Schedule C or C-EZ	12	
13	Capital gain or (loss). Attach Schedule D if required. If not required, check here ▶ ☐	13	
14	Other gains or (losses). Attach Form 4797	14	
15a	IRA distributions 15a	b Taxable amount	15b	
16a	Pensions and annuities 16a	b Taxable amount	16b	
17	Rental real estate, royalties, partnerships, S corporations, trusts, etc. Attach Schedule E	17	
18	Farm income or (loss). Attach Schedule F	18	
19	Unemployment compensation	19	
20a	Social security benefits 20a	b Taxable amount	20b	
21	Other income. List type and amount _____	21	
22	Combine the amounts in the far right column for lines 7 through 21. This is your **total income** ▶	22	28,510 00

Adjusted Gross Income

23	Educator expenses	23	
24	Certain business expenses of reservists, performing artists, and fee-basis government officials. Attach Form 2106 or 2106-EZ	24	
25	Health savings account deduction. Attach Form 8889	25	
26	Moving expenses. Attach Form 3903	26	
27	Deductible part of self-employment tax. Attach Schedule SE	27	
28	Self-employed SEP, SIMPLE, and qualified plans	28	
29	Self-employed health insurance deduction	29	
30	Penalty on early withdrawal of savings	30	
31a	Alimony paid b Recipient's SSN ▶	31a	
32	IRA deduction	32	
33	Student loan interest deduction	33	
34	Tuition and fees. Attach Form 8917	34	
35	Domestic production activities deduction. Attach Form 8903	35	
36	Add lines 23 through 35	36	
37	Subtract line 36 from line 22. This is your **adjusted gross income** ▶	37	28,510 00

For Disclosure, Privacy Act, and Paperwork Reduction Act Notice, see separate instructions. | Cat. No. 11320B | Form **1040** (2014)

Chapter 5 Exercise

Form 1040 (2014) Page **2**

Tax and Credits	38	Amount from line 37 (adjusted gross income)	38	28,510 00
	39a	Check if: ☐ **You** were born before January 2, 1950, ☐ Blind. ☐ **Spouse** was born before January 2, 1950, ☐ Blind. **Total boxes checked ▶ 39a**		
	b	If your spouse itemizes on a separate return or you were a dual-status alien, check here▶ 39b☐		
Standard Deduction for—	40	**Itemized deductions** (from Schedule A) **or** your **standard deduction** (see left margin) . .	40	12,400 00
• People who check any box on line 39a or 39b **or** who can be claimed as a dependent, see instructions.	41	Subtract line 40 from line 38	41	16,110 00
	42	**Exemptions.** If line 38 is $152,525 or less, multiply $3,950 by the number on line 6d. Otherwise, see instructions	42	11,850 00
	43	**Taxable income.** Subtract line 42 from line 41. If line 42 is more than line 41, enter -0- . .	43	4,260 00
	44	**Tax** (see instructions). Check if any from: **a** ☐ Form(s) 8814 **b** ☐ Form 4972 **c** ☐ ____	44	428 00
	45	**Alternative minimum tax** (see instructions). Attach Form 6251	45	
• All others: Single or Married filing separately, $6,200	46	Excess advance premium tax credit repayment. Attach Form 8962	46	
	47	Add lines 44, 45, and 46 . . . . ▶	47	428 00
Married filing jointly or Qualifying widow(er), $12,400	48	Foreign tax credit. Attach Form 1116 if required . . .	48		
	49	Credit for child and dependent care expenses. Attach Form 2441	49		
	50	Education credits from Form 8863, line 19	50		
Head of household, $9,100	51	Retirement savings contributions credit. Attach Form 8880	51		
	52	Child tax credit. Attach Schedule 8812, if required . . .	52	428 00	
	53	Residential energy credits. Attach Form 5695	53		
	54	Other credits from Form: **a** ☐ 3800 **b** ☐ 8801 **c** ☐	54		
	55	Add lines 48 through 54. These are your **total credits**	55	428 00
	56	Subtract line 55 from line 47. If line 55 is more than line 47, enter -0- . . . . . ▶	56	0 00
Other Taxes	57	Self-employment tax. Attach Schedule SE	57	
	58	Unreported social security and Medicare tax from Form: **a** ☐ 4137 **b** ☐ 8919	58	
	59	Additional tax on IRAs, other qualified retirement plans, etc. Attach Form 5329 if required . .	59	
	60a	Household employment taxes from Schedule H	60a	
	b	First-time homebuyer credit repayment. Attach Form 5405 if required	60b	
	61	Health care: individual responsibility (see instructions) Full-year coverage ☐ . . .	61	
	62	Taxes from: **a** ☐ Form 8959 **b** ☐ Form 8960 **c** ☐ Instructions; enter code(s) ____	62	
	63	Add lines 56 through 62. This is your **total tax** . . . . ▶	63	0 00
Payments	64	Federal income tax withheld from Forms W-2 and 1099 . .	64	3,053 00	
If you have a qualifying child, attach Schedule EIC.	65	2014 estimated tax payments and amount applied from 2013 return	65		
	66a	**Earned income credit (EIC)**	66a	2,463 00	
	b	Nontaxable combat pay election	66b		
	67	Additional child tax credit. Attach Schedule 8812	67	572 00	
	68	American opportunity credit from Form 8863, line 8 . . .	68		
	69	Net premium tax credit. Attach Form 8962	69		
	70	Amount paid with request for extension to file	70		
	71	Excess social security and tier 1 RRTA tax withheld . . .	71		
	72	Credit for federal tax on fuels. Attach Form 4136 . . .	72		
	73	Credits from Form: **a** ☐ 2439 **b** ☐ Reserved **c** ☐ Reserved **d** ☐	73		
	74	Add lines 64, 65, 66a, and 67 through 73. These are your **total payments** . . . . . ▶	74	6,088 00
Refund	75	If line 74 is more than line 63, subtract line 63 from line 74. This is the amount you **overpaid**	75	6,088 00
	76a	Amount of line 75 you want **refunded to you.** If Form 8888 is attached, check here . ▶☐	76a	6,088 00
Direct deposit? See instructions.	▶ b	Routing number [ ] ▶**c** Type: ☐ Checking ☐ Savings		
	▶ d	Account number [ ]		
	77	Amount of line 75 you want **applied to your 2015 estimated tax** ▶	77		
Amount You Owe	78	**Amount you owe.** Subtract line 74 from line 63. For details on how to pay, see instructions ▶	78	
	79	Estimated tax penalty (see instructions)	79		

Third Party Designee
Do you want to allow another person to discuss this return with the IRS (see instructions)? ☐ **Yes.** Complete below. ☑ **No**
Designee's name ▶ | Phone no. ▶ | Personal identification number (PIN) ▶ [   ]

Sign Here
Joint return? See instructions. Keep a copy for your records.
Under penalties of perjury, I declare that I have examined this return and accompanying schedules and statements, and to the best of my knowledge and belief, they are true, correct, and complete. Declaration of preparer (other than taxpayer) is based on all information of which preparer has any knowledge.

Your signature	Date	Your occupation Mechanic	Daytime phone number (555)555-5555
Spouse's signature. If a joint return, **both** must sign.	Date	Spouse's occupation Homemaker	If the IRS sent you an Identity Protection PIN, enter it here (see inst.) [ ]

Paid Preparer Use Only
Print/Type preparer's name Jane Doe	Preparer's signature	Date	Check ☐ if self-employed	PTIN P00000000
Firm's name ▶ My Tax Service			Firm's EIN ▶	63-0000000
Firm's address ▶ 100 Main St., Your City, Your State, Your Zip Code			Phone no.	(555)555-1111

www.irs.gov/form1040

Form **1040** (2014)

F-19

SCHEDULE EIC	**Earned Income Credit**
(Form 1040A or 1040)	Qualifying Child Information

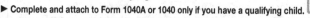

OMB No. 1545-0074

2014

► Complete and attach to Form 1040A or 1040 only if you have a qualifying child.

Department of the Treasury
Internal Revenue Service (99)

► Information about Schedule EIC (Form 1040A or 1040) and its instructions is at *www.irs.gov/scheduleeic*.

Attachment Sequence No. **43**

Name(s) shown on return

Jordan & Judith Smith

Your social security number

555-44-3333

Before you begin:

- See the instructions for Form 1040A, lines 42a and 42b, or Form 1040, lines 66a and 66b, to make sure that **(a)** you can take the EIC, and **(b)** you have a qualifying child.
- Be sure the child's name on line 1 and social security number (SSN) on line 2 agree with the child's social security card. Otherwise, at the time we process your return, we may reduce or disallow your EIC. If the name or SSN on the child's social security card is not correct, call the Social Security Administration at 1-800-772-1213.

- *If you take the EIC even though you are not eligible, you may not be allowed to take the credit for up to 10 years. See the instructions for details.*
- *It will take us longer to process your return and issue your refund if you do not fill in all lines that apply for each qualifying child.*

Qualifying Child Information	Child 1	Child 2	Child 3
1 Child's name If you have more than three qualifying children, you have to list only three to get the maximum credit.	First name Last name Joanne Smith	First name Last name	First name Last name
2 Child's SSN The child must have an SSN as defined in the instructions for Form 1040A, lines 42a and 42b, or Form 1040, lines 66a and 66b, unless the child was born and died in 2014. If your child was born and died in 2014 and did not have an SSN, enter "Died" on this line and attach a copy of the child's birth certificate, death certificate, or hospital medical records.	223-32-2232		
3 Child's year of birth	Year 2 0 1 3 *If born after 1995 **and** the child is younger than you (or your spouse, if filing jointly), skip lines 4a and 4b; go to line 5.*	Year ___ ___ ___ ___ *If born after 1995 **and** the child is younger than you (or your spouse, if filing jointly), skip lines 4a and 4b; go to line 5.*	Year ___ ___ ___ ___ *If born after 1995 **and** the child is younger than you (or your spouse, if filing jointly), skip lines 4a and 4b; go to line 5.*
4 a Was the child under age 24 at the end of 2014, a student, and younger than you (or your spouse, if filing jointly)?	✓ Yes. ☐ No. *Go to line 5.* *Go to line 4b.*	☐ Yes. ☐ No. *Go to line 5.* *Go to line 4b.*	☐ Yes. ☐ No. *Go to line 5.* *Go to line 4b.*
b Was the child permanently and totally disabled during any part of 2014?	☐ Yes. ☐ No. *Go to line 5.* The child is not a qualifying child.	☐ Yes. ☐ No. *Go to line 5.* The child is not a qualifying child.	☐ Yes. ☐ No. *Go to line 5.* The child is not a qualifying child.
5 Child's relationship to you (for example, son, daughter, grandchild, niece, nephew, foster child, etc.)	Daughter		
6 Number of months child lived with you in the United States during 2014 • If the child lived with you for more than half of 2014 but less than 7 months, enter "7." • If the child was born or died in 2014 and your home was the child's home for more than half the time he or she was alive during 2014, enter "12."	12 months *Do not enter more than 12 months.*	___ months *Do not enter more than 12 months.*	___ months *Do not enter more than 12 months.*

For Paperwork Reduction Act Notice, see your tax return instructions.

Cat. No. 13339M

Schedule EIC (Form 1040A or 1040) 2014

SCHEDULE 8812 (Form 1040A or 1040)	**Child Tax Credit**		OMB No. 1545-0074 20**14**
Department of the Treasury Internal Revenue Service (99)	▶ Attach to Form 1040, Form 1040A, or Form 1040NR. ▶ Information about Schedule 8812 and its separate instructions is at *www.irs.gov/schedule8812.*		Attachment Sequence No. 47

Name(s) shown on return	Your social security number
Jordan & Judith Smith	555-44-3333

Part I   **Filers Who Have Certain Child Dependent(s) with an ITIN (Individual Taxpayer Identification Number)**

 Complete this part only for each dependent who has an ITIN and for whom you are claiming the child tax credit.
If your dependent is not a qualifying child for the credit, you cannot include that dependent in the calculation of this credit.

Answer the following questions for each dependent listed on Form 1040, line 6c; Form 1040A, line 6c; or Form 1040NR, line 7c, who has an ITIN (Individual Taxpayer Identification Number) and that you indicated is a qualifying child for the child tax credit by checking column (4) for that dependent.

A   For the first dependent identified with an ITIN and listed as a qualifying child for the child tax credit, did this child meet the substantial presence test? See separate instructions.

     ☐ Yes   ☐ No

B   For the second dependent identified with an ITIN and listed as a qualifying child for the child tax credit, did this child meet the substantial presence test? See separate instructions.

     ☐ Yes   ☐ No

C   For the third dependent identified with an ITIN and listed as a qualifying child for the child tax credit, did this child meet the substantial presence test? See separate instructions.

     ☐ Yes   ☐ No

D   For the fourth dependent identified with an ITIN and listed as a qualifying child for the child tax credit, did this child meet the substantial presence test? See separate instructions.

     ☐ Yes   ☐ No

Note. If you have more than four dependents identified with an ITIN and listed as a qualifying child for the child tax credit, see the instructions and check here . . . . ▶ ☐

Part II   **Additional Child Tax Credit Filers**

1	**1040 filers:**	Enter the amount from line 6 of your Child Tax Credit Worksheet (see the Instructions for Form 1040, line 52).		
	1040A filers:	Enter the amount from line 6 of your Child Tax Credit Worksheet (see the Instructions for Form 1040A, line 35).	1	1,000 00
	1040NR filers:	Enter the amount from line 6 of your Child Tax Credit Worksheet (see the Instructions for Form 1040NR, line 49).		
		If you used Pub. 972, enter the amount from line 8 of the Child Tax Credit Worksheet in the publication.		

2	Enter the amount from Form 1040, line 52; Form 1040A, line 35; or Form 1040NR, line 49	2	428 00
3	Subtract line 2 from line 1. If zero, **stop;** you cannot take this credit	3	572 00

4a	Earned income (see separate instructions)	4a	28,510 00		
b	Nontaxable combat pay (see separate instructions)	4b			

5	Is the amount on line 4a more than $3,000?			
	☐ **No.** Leave line 5 blank and enter -0- on line 6.			
	☑ **Yes.** Subtract $3,000 from the amount on line 4a. Enter the result . . .	5	25,510 00	

6	Multiply the amount on line 5 by 15% (.15) and enter the result	6	3,827 00

     Next. Do you have three or more qualifying children?

     ☑ **No.** If line 6 is zero, stop; you cannot take this credit. Otherwise, skip Part III and enter the **smaller** of line 3 or line 6 on line 13.

     ☐ **Yes.** If line 6 is equal to or more than line 3, skip Part III and enter the amount from line 3 on line 13. Otherwise, go to line 7.

For Paperwork Reduction Act Notice, see your tax return instructions.   Cat. No. 59761M   Schedule 8812 (Form 1040A or 1040) 2014

Chapter 5 Exercise

Part III   Certain Filers Who Have Three or More Qualifying Children

7   Withheld social security, Medicare, and Additional Medicare taxes from Form(s) W-2, boxes 4 and 6. If married filing jointly, include your spouse's amounts with yours. If your employer withheld or you paid Additional Medicare Tax or tier 1 RRTA taxes, see separate instructions **7**

8   **1040 filers:**   Enter the total of the amounts from Form 1040, lines 27 and 58, plus any taxes that you identified using code "UT" and entered on line 62.

       1040A filers: Enter -0-.   **8**

       1040NR filers: Enter the total of the amounts from Form 1040NR, lines 27 and 56, plus any taxes that you identified using code "UT" and entered on line 60.

9   Add lines 7 and 8 . . . . **9**

10   **1040 filers:**   Enter the total of the amounts from Form 1040, lines 66a and 71.

       1040A filers: Enter the total of the amount from Form 1040A, line 42a, plus any excess social security and tier 1 RRTA taxes withheld that you entered to the left of line 46 (see separate instructions).   **10**

       1040NR filers: Enter the amount from Form 1040NR, line 67.

11   Subtract line 10 from line 9. If zero or less, enter -0- **11**

12   Enter the **larger** of line 6 or line 11 . . . . **12**

     Next, enter the **smaller** of line 3 or line 12 on line 13.

Part IV   Additional Child Tax Credit

13   **This is your additional child tax credit** **13**   572   00

1040
1040A
1040NR

Enter this amount on Form 1040, line 67, Form 1040A, line 43, or Form 1040NR, line 64.

Form **8867**

Department of the Treasury
Internal Revenue Service

Paid Preparer's Earned Income Credit Checklist

▶ To be completed by preparer and filed with Form 1040, 1040A, or 1040EZ.

▶ Information about Form 8867 and its separate instructions is at *www.irs.gov/form8867*.

OMB No. 1545-1629

2014

Attachment
Sequence No. **177**

Taxpayer name(s) shown on return	Taxpayer's social security number
Jordan & Judith Smith	555-44-3333

For the definitions of **Qualifying Child** and **Earned Income**, see **Pub. 596**.

Part I	**All Taxpayers**		

1 Enter preparer's name and PTIN ▶ Jane Doe P00000000
----

2 Is the taxpayer's filing status married filing separately? . . . . ☐ Yes ☑ No

▶ If you checked **"Yes"** on line 2, **stop;** the taxpayer **cannot** take the EIC. Otherwise, continue.

3 Does the taxpayer (and the taxpayer's spouse if filing jointly) have a social security number (SSN) that allows him or her to work and is valid for EIC purposes? See the instructions before answering . . . . ☑ Yes ☐ No

▶ If you checked **"No"** on line 3, **stop;** the taxpayer **cannot** take the EIC. Otherwise, continue.

4 Is the taxpayer (or the taxpayer's spouse if filing jointly) filing Form 2555 or 2555-EZ (relating to the exclusion of foreign earned income)? . . . . ☐ Yes ☑ No

▶ If you checked **"Yes"** on line 4, **stop;** the taxpayer **cannot** take the EIC. Otherwise, continue.

5a Was the taxpayer (or the taxpayer's spouse) a nonresident alien for any part of 2014? . . . . . ☐ Yes ☑ No

▶ If you checked **"Yes"** on line 5a, go to line 5b. Otherwise, skip line 5b and go to line 6.

b Is the taxpayer's filing status married filing jointly? . . . . ☐ Yes ☑ No

▶ If you checked **"Yes"** on line 5a and **"No"** on line 5b, **stop;** the taxpayer **cannot** take the EIC. Otherwise, continue.

6 Is the taxpayer's **investment income** more than $3,350? See the instructions before answering. ☐ Yes ☑ No

▶ If you checked **"Yes"** on line 6, **stop;** the taxpayer **cannot** take the EIC. Otherwise, continue.

7 Could the taxpayer be a **qualifying child** of another person for 2014? If the taxpayer's filing status is married filing jointly, check **"No."** Otherwise, see instructions before answering . . . . ☐ Yes ☑ No

▶ If you checked **"Yes"** on line 7, **stop;** the taxpayer **cannot** take the EIC. Otherwise, go to Part II or Part III, whichever applies.

For Paperwork Reduction Act Notice, see separate instructions.   Cat. No. 26142H   Form **8867** (2014)

Part II	Taxpayers With a Child			
	Caution. If there is more than one child, complete lines 8 through 14 for one child before going to the next column.	**Child 1**	**Child 2**	**Child 3**
8	Child's name	Joanne		
9	Is the child the taxpayer's son, daughter, stepchild, foster child, brother, sister, stepbrother, stepsister, half brother, half sister, or a descendant of any of them?	☑ Yes ☐ No	☐ Yes ☐ No	☐ Yes ☐ No
10	Was the child unmarried at the end of 2014? If the child was married at the end of 2014, see the instructions before answering	☑ Yes ☐ No	☐ Yes ☐ No	☐ Yes ☐ No
11	Did the child live with the taxpayer in the United States for over half of 2014? See the instructions before answering	☑ Yes ☐ No	☐ Yes ☐ No	☐ Yes ☐ No
12	Was the child (at the end of 2014)— • Under age 19 and younger than the taxpayer (or the taxpayer's spouse, if the taxpayer files jointly), • Under age 24, a student (defined in the instructions), and younger than the taxpayer (or the taxpayer's spouse, if the taxpayer files jointly), or • Any age and permanently and totally disabled? . . . . ▶ If you checked **"Yes"** on lines 9, 10, 11, **and** 12, the child is the taxpayer's qualifying child; go to line 13a. If you checked **"No"** on line 9, 10, 11, **or** 12, the child is not the taxpayer's qualifying child; see the instructions for line 12.	☑ Yes ☐ No	☐ Yes ☐ No	☐ Yes ☐ No
13a	Do you or the taxpayer know of another person who could check **"Yes"** on lines 9, 10, 11, **and** 12 for the child? (If the only other person is the taxpayer's spouse, see the instructions before answering.) . . . . ▶ If you checked **"No"** on line 13a, go to line 14. Otherwise, go to line 13b.	☐ Yes ☑ No	☐ Yes ☐ No	☐ Yes ☐ No
b	Enter the child's relationship to the other person(s)			
c	Under the tiebreaker rules, is the child treated as the taxpayer's qualifying child? See the instructions before answering . . . . ▶ If you checked **"Yes"** on line 13c, go to line 14. If you checked **"No,"** the taxpayer **cannot** take the EIC based on this child and cannot take the EIC for taxpayers who do not have a qualifying child. If there is more than one child, see the **Note** at the bottom of this page. If you checked **"Don't know,"** explain to the taxpayer that, under the tiebreaker rules, the taxpayer's EIC and other tax benefits may be disallowed. Then, if the taxpayer wants to take the EIC based on this child, complete lines 14 and 15. If not, and there are no other qualifying children, the taxpayer cannot take the EIC, including the EIC for taxpayers without a qualifying child; do not complete Part III. If there is more than one child, see the **Note** at the bottom of this page.	☐ Yes ☐ No ☐ Don't know	☐ Yes ☐ No ☐ Don't know	☐ Yes ☐ No ☐ Don't know
14	Does the qualifying child have an SSN that allows him or her to work and is valid for EIC purposes? See the instructions before answering . . . . ▶ If you checked **"No"** on line 14, the taxpayer **cannot** take the EIC based on this child and cannot take the EIC available to taxpayers without a qualifying child. If there is more than one child, see the **Note** at the bottom of this page. If you checked "Yes" on line 14, continue.	☑ Yes ☐ No	☐ Yes ☐ No	☐ Yes ☐ No
15	Are the taxpayer's **earned income** and **adjusted gross income** each less than the limit that applies to the taxpayer for 2014? See instructions . . ▶ If you checked **"No"** on line 15, **stop;** the taxpayer **cannot** take the EIC. If you checked **"Yes"** on line 15, the taxpayer can take the EIC. Complete **Schedule EIC** and attach it to the taxpayer's return. If there are two or three qualifying children with valid SSNs, list them on Schedule EIC in the same order as they are listed here. If the taxpayer's EIC was reduced or disallowed for a year after 1996, see Pub. 596 to see if Form 8862 must be filed. Go to line 20.	☑ Yes ☐ No		

Note. If there is more than one child, complete lines 8 through 14 for the other child(ren) (but for no more than three qualifying children).

Chapter 5 Exercise

Part III Taxpayers Without a Qualifying Child

16 Was the taxpayer's main home, and the main home of the taxpayer's spouse if filing jointly, in the United States for more than half the year? (Military personnel on extended active duty outside the United States are considered to be living in the United States during that duty period.) See the instructions before answering. ☐ Yes ☐ No

▶ If you checked **"No"** on line 16, **stop**; the taxpayer **cannot** take the EIC. Otherwise, continue.

17 Was the taxpayer, or the taxpayer's spouse if filing jointly, at least age 25 but under age 65 at the end of 2014? See the instructions before answering . . . . ☐ Yes ☐ No

▶ If you checked **"No"** on line 17, **stop**; the taxpayer **cannot** take the EIC. Otherwise, continue.

18 Is the taxpayer eligible to be claimed as a dependent on anyone else's federal income tax return for 2014? If the taxpayer's filing status is married filing jointly, check **"No"**. . . . . ☐ Yes ☐ No

▶ If you checked **"Yes"** on line 18, **stop**; the taxpayer **cannot** take the EIC. Otherwise, continue.

19 Are the taxpayer's **earned income** and **adjusted gross income** each less than the limit that applies to the taxpayer for 2014? See instructions . . . . ☐ Yes ☐ No

▶ If you checked **"No"** on line 19, **stop**; the taxpayer **cannot** take the EIC. If you checked **"Yes"** on line 19, the taxpayer can take the EIC. If the taxpayer's EIC was reduced or disallowed for a year after 1996, see Pub. 596 to find out if **Form 8862** must be filed. Go to line 20.

Part IV Due Diligence Requirements

20 Did you complete Form 8867 based on current information provided by the taxpayer or reasonably obtained by you? . . . . ☑ Yes ☐ No

21 Did you complete the EIC worksheet found in the Form 1040, 1040A, or 1040EZ instructions (or your own worksheet that provides the same information as the 1040, 1040A, or 1040EZ worksheet)? . . ☑ Yes ☐ No

22 If any qualifying child was not the taxpayer's son or daughter, do you know or did you ask why the parents were not claiming the child? . . . . ☐ Yes ☐ No ☑ Does not apply

23 If the answer to question 13a is **"Yes"** (indicating that the child lived for more than half the year with someone else who could claim the child for the EIC), did you explain the tiebreaker rules and possible consequences of another person claiming your client's qualifying child? . . . . ☐ Yes ☐ No ☑ Does not apply

24 Did you ask this taxpayer any additional questions that are necessary to meet your knowledge requirement? See the instructions before answering . . . . ☑ Yes ☐ No ☐ Does not apply

To comply with the EIC knowledge requirement, you must not know or have reason to know that any information you used to determine the taxpayer's eligibility for, and the amount of, the EIC is incorrect. You may not ignore the implications of information furnished to you or known by you, and you must make reasonable inquiries if the information furnished to you appears to be incorrect, inconsistent, or incomplete. At the time you make these inquiries, you must document in your files the inquiries you made and the taxpayer's responses.

25 Did you document (a) the taxpayer's answer to question 22 (if applicable), (b) whether you explained the tiebreaker rules to the taxpayer and any additional information you got from the taxpayer as a result, and (c) any additional questions you asked and the taxpayer's answers? . . . . ☐ Yes ☐ No ☑ Does not apply

▶ You have complied with all the due diligence requirements if you:
1. Completed the actions described on lines 20 and 21 and checked **"Yes"** on those lines,
2. Completed the actions described on lines 22, 23, 24, and 25 (if they apply) and checked **"Yes"** (or **"Does not apply"**) on those lines,
3. Submit Form 8867 in the manner required, **and**
4. Keep all five of the following records for 3 years from the latest of the dates specified in the instructions under *Document Retention*:

    a. Form 8867,
    b. The EIC worksheet(s) or your own worksheet(s),
    c. Copies of any taxpayer documents you relied on to determine eligibility for or amount of EIC,
    d. A record of how, when, and from whom the information used to prepare the form and worksheet(s) was obtained, and
    e. A record of any additional questions you asked and your client's answers.

▶ You have not complied with all the due diligence requirements if you checked **"No"** on line 20, 21, 22, 23, 24, or 25. You may have to pay a $500 penalty for each failure to comply.

Form **8867** (2014)

Chapter 5 Exercise

Part V	Documents Provided to You

26   Identify below any document that the taxpayer provided to you and that you relied on to determine the taxpayer's EIC eligibility. Check all that apply. **Keep a copy of any documents you relied on.** See the instructions before answering. If there is no qualifying child, check box a. If there is no disabled child, check box o.

Residency of Qualifying Child(ren)

☐ a	No qualifying child	☐ i	Place of worship statement
☐ b	School records or statement	☐ j	Indian tribal official statement
☐ c	Landlord or property management statement	☐ k	Employer statement
☐ d	Health care provider statement	☐ l	Other (specify) ▼
☐ e	Medical records		
☐ f	Child care provider records		
☐ g	Placement agency statement		
☐ h	Social service records or statement	☑ m	Did not rely on any documents, but made notes in file
		☐ n	Did not rely on any documents

Disability of Qualifying Child(ren)

☑ o	No disabled child	☐ s	Other (specify) ▼
☐ p	Doctor statement		
☐ q	Other health care provider statement		
☐ r	Social services agency or program statement	☐ t	Did not rely on any documents, but made notes in file
		☐ u	Did not rely on any documents

27   If a Schedule C is included with this return, identify below the information that the taxpayer provided to you and that you relied on to prepare the Schedule C. Check all that apply. **Keep a copy of any documents you relied on.** See the instructions before answering. If there is no Schedule C, check box a.

Documents or Other Information

☑ a	No Schedule C	☐ h	Bank statements
☐ b	Business license	☐ i	Reconstruction of income and expenses
☐ c	Forms 1099	☐ j	Other (specify) ▼
☐ d	Records of gross receipts provided by taxpayer		
☐ e	Taxpayer summary of income		
☐ f	Records of expenses provided by taxpayer	☐ k	Did not rely on any documents, but made notes in file
☐ g	Taxpayer summary of expenses	☐ l	Did not rely on any documents

2014 Child Tax Credit Worksheet—Line 52

Keep for Your Records

CAUTION

1. To be a qualifying child for the child tax credit, the child must be your dependent, **under age 17** at the end of 2014, and meet all the conditions in Steps 1 through 3 in the instructions for line 6c. Make sure you checked the box on Form 1040, line 6c, column (4), for each qualifying child.
2. If you do not have a qualifying child, you cannot claim the child tax credit.
3. If your qualifying child has an ITIN instead of an SSN, file Schedule 8812.
4. Do **not** use this worksheet, but use Pub. 972 instead, if:
   a. You are claiming the adoption credit, mortgage interest credit, District of Columbia first-time homebuyer credit, or residential energy efficient property credit,
   b. You are excluding income from Puerto Rico, or
   c. You are filing Form 2555, 2555-EZ, or 4563.

Part 1

1. Number of qualifying children: ____1____ × $1,000. Enter the result. | **1** | 1,000

2. Enter the amount from Form 1040, line 38. | **2** | 28,510

3. Enter the amount shown below for your filing status.
   - Married filing jointly — $110,000
   - Single, head of household, or qualifying widow(er) — $75,000
   - Married filing separately — $55,000
   | **3** | 110,000

4. Is the amount on line 2 more than the amount on line 3?

   ■ **No.** Leave line 4 blank. Enter -0- on line 5, and go to line 6.

   ☐ **Yes.** Subtract line 3 from line 2.
   If the result is not a multiple of $1,000, increase it to the next multiple of $1,000. For example, increase $425 to $1,000, increase $1,025 to $2,000, etc.
   | **4** |

5. Multiply the amount on line 4 by 5% (.05). Enter the result. | **5** | 0

6. Is the amount on line 1 more than the amount on line 5?

   ☐ **No.** (STOP)
   You cannot take the child tax credit on Form 1040, line 52. You also cannot take the additional child tax credit on Form 1040, line 67. Complete the rest of your Form 1040.

   ■ **Yes.** Subtract line 5 from line 1. Enter the result.
   Go to Part 2.
   | **6** | 1,000

2014 Child Tax Credit Worksheet—*Continued*

Keep for Your Records

Before you begin Part 2: √ Figure the amount of any credits you are claiming on Form 5695, Part II; Form 8910; Form 8936; or Schedule R.

Part 2

7. Enter the amount from Form 1040, line 47.

| 7 | 428 |

8. Add any amounts from:

Form 1040, line 48 _____

Form 1040, line 49 + _____

Form 1040, line 50 + _____

Form 1040, line 51 + _____

Form 5695, line 30 + _____

Form 8910, line 15 + _____

Form 8936, line 23 + _____

Schedule R, line 22 + _____

Enter the total.

| 8 | |

9. Are the amounts on lines 7 and 8 the same?

☐ **Yes.** (STOP)
You cannot take this credit because there is no tax to reduce. However, you may be able to take the **additional child tax credit.** See the **TIP** below.

■ **No.** Subtract line 8 from line 7.

| 9 | 428 |

10. Is the amount on line 6 more than the amount on line 9?

■ **Yes.** Enter the amount from line 9.
Also, you may be able to take the **additional child tax credit.** See the **TIP** below.

☐ **No.** Enter the amount from line 6.

} **This is your child tax credit.**

| 10 | 428 |

Enter this amount on Form 1040, line 52.

1040

TIP

You may be able to take the **additional child tax credit** on Form 1040, line 67, if you answered "Yes" on line 9 **or** line 10 above.

● First, complete your Form 1040 through lines 66a and 66b.

● Then, use Schedule 8812 to figure any additional child tax credit.

Earned Income Credit Worksheet

1.	Enter the amount from Form 1040, Line 7.	1. 28,510
2.	Taxable Scholarship or Fellowship grant not reported on a W-2, if included on line 7, Form 10.................................. _____	
3.	Amount received for work performed while an inmate in a penal institution (enter "PRI" and the amount subtracted on the dotted line next to Form 1040, line 7), if included on line 7.. _____	
4.	Amount received as a pension or annuity from a nonqualified deferred compensation plan or a nongovernmental Sec. 457 plan. (Enter "DFC" and amount subtracted on the dotted line next to Form 1040, line 7), if included on line 7.................. _____	
5.	Add lines 2, 3, and 4.	5. 0
6.	Subtract line 5 from line 1.	6. 28,510
7.	Nontaxable Combat pay if the election is made to use it. You will have to complete two worksheets: one with the combat pay and one without. Use the one that will result in the most EIC.	7.
8.	Add lines 6 and 7.	8. 28,510
9.	If the taxpayer had any income from self-employment or was a statutory employee, complete lines 10 –18. If not skip lines 10 –18 and go to line 19.	
10.	If the taxpayer is filing a Schedule SE, enter the amount from Schedule SE, Section A, line 3 or Section B, line 3, whichever applies. If the taxpayer is not filing a Schedule SE, skip lines 10 –14 and go to line 15. If the taxpayer is a statutory employee, go to line 18.	10.
11.	Enter any amounts from Schedule SE, Section B, line 4b, and line 5a.	11.
12.	Combine lines 10 and 11.	12.
13.	Enter the amount from Schedule SE, Section A, line 6 or Section B, line 13.	13.
14.	Subtract line 13 from line 12. If lines 15 and 18 do not apply, enter this amount on line 17 and go to line 19.	14.
15.	If the taxpayer is not required to file a Schedule SE because the net earnings were less than $400, enter amount from Schedule F, line 36, and from farm partnerships, Schedule K-1 (Form 1065), box 14, code A.	15.
16.	Enter any net profit or (loss) from Schedule C, line 31; Schedule C-EZ, line 3, Schedule K-1, box 14, code A (other than farming); and Schedule K-1, box 9, code J1.	16.
17.	Combine lines 14, 15, and 16.	17.
18.	If the taxpayer is a statutory employee, enter the amount from Schedule C, line 1, or Schedule C-EZ, line 1 that the taxpayer is filing as a statutory employee.	18.
19.	Add lines 8, 17, and 18. This is the earned income.	19. 28,510
20.	Look up the amount on line 19 above in the EIC Table to find the credit. If the amount is 0, stop. The taxpayer does not qualify for the credit.	20. 2,463
21.	Enter the amount from Form 1040, line 38. If the amount on line 21 is the same as the amount on line 19, stop and enter the amount from line 20 on line 64a of the Form 1040. This is the taxpayer's Earned Income Credit. If not, go to line 22.	21. 28,510
22.	Is the amount on line 21 less than: • $8,150 ($13,550 if MFJ) if the taxpayer has no qualifying children? • $17,850 ($23,300 if MFJ) if the taxpayer has one or more qualifying children? If the answer is yes, stop and enter the amount from line 21 on the Form 1040, line 66a. If the answer is no, look up the amount from line 21 in the EIC Table to find the credit and go to line 23.	22.
23.	Look at the amounts on line 20 and 22. Enter the smaller amount here and on Form 1040, line 66a.	23.

Chapter 6 Review

1) What age must a child be under to be a qualifying person for the credit for child and dependent care expenses?

   The taxpayer's qualifying child who is their dependent and who was under age 13 when the care was provided.

2) If the noncustodial parent is eligible to claim the exemption for a child, who is eligible to claim the credit for child and dependent care expenses?

   If the qualifying child is a child of divorced or separated parents or parents living apart and the noncustodial parent is able to claim the dependency exemption, that parent cannot claim the dependent care credit. However, the custodial parent can claim the credit if they meet all of the other requirements, even if not claiming the dependency exemption.

3) How much earned income would be shown on the Form 2441, line 5 for a spouse that was a full-time student for 7 months of the year? The spouse earned no other income.

   $1,750; $250 for each month multiplied by 7 months.

4) What information must the taxpayer have from the child care provider to claim child and dependent care credit?

   In order to claim the dependent care credit the taxpayer must include the name, address, and identification number on the tax return.

5) What filing status is not eligible for the education credits?

   A taxpayer filing using the Married Filing Separately filing status is not eligible to claim the education credits.

6) What are the two types of education credits?

   The two types of education credits are the American Opportunity Credit and the Lifetime Learning Credit.

7) Betty paid $3,200 for tuition at State University for the year. She also paid $750 for room and board and she bought books from the University book store even though she was not required to. The books were $445 for the year. What amount are qualified education expenses if she takes the American Opportunity Credit? The Lifetime learning credit?

Her qualified education expenses for the American Opportunity Credit are $3,645. Her qualified education expenses for The Lifetime Learning Credit are $3,200.

8) June finished her freshman year of college and started her sophomore year in 2014. If she meets all other requirements, which education credit may she claim?

She may claim either The American Opportunity Credit or the Lifetime Learning Credit.

9) Elizabeth is 20 and a full-time student. She only made $3,200 in 2014. She is filing a tax return to get back the taxes she paid in. Her parents are claiming her on their tax return. Who will receive the education credit for which she is eligible?

Elizabeth's parents will receive the education credit because they are claiming her exemption.

10) What are the maximum social security wages for 2014?

The maximum social security wages for 2014 are $117,000.

Form **2441**

Child and Dependent Care Expenses

▶ Attach to Form 1040, Form 1040A, or Form 1040NR.

▶ Information about Form 2441 and its separate instructions is at *www.irs.gov/form2441*.

Department of the Treasury
Internal Revenue Service (99)

OMB No. 1545-0074

2014

Attachment
Sequence No. 21

Name(s) shown on return	Your social security number
Matt & Mary Marrott	166-33-4444

Part I — Persons or Organizations Who Provided the Care—You **must** complete this part.
(If you have more than two care providers, see the instructions.)

1	(a) Care provider's name	(b) Address (number, street, apt. no., city, state, and ZIP code)	(c) Identifying number (SSN or EIN)	(d) Amount paid (see instructions)
	ABC Daycare	544 Young One Lane Your City, Your State, Your Zip Code	45-6654431	3,800 00

Did you receive **dependent care benefits?** — No ——▶ Complete only Part II below.
— Yes ——▶ Complete Part III on the back next.

Caution. If the care was provided in your home, you may owe employment taxes. If you do, you cannot file Form 1040A. For details, see the instructions for Form 1040, line 60a, or Form 1040NR, line 59a.

Part II — Credit for Child and Dependent Care Expenses

2 Information about your **qualifying person(s).** If you have more than two qualifying persons, see the instructions.

(a) Qualifying person's name		(b) Qualifying person's social security number	(c) Qualified expenses you incurred and paid in 2014 for the person listed in column (a)
First	Last		
Miranda	Marrott	321-54-9876	3,800 00

3	Add the amounts in column (c) of line 2. **Do not** enter more than $3,000 for one qualifying person or $6,000 for two or more persons. If you completed Part III, enter the amount from line 31		3	3,000 00
4	Enter your **earned income.** See instructions		4	26,465 00
5	If married filing jointly, enter your spouse's earned income (if you or your spouse was a student or was disabled, see the instructions); **all others**, enter the amount from line 4		5	12,200 00
6	Enter the **smallest** of line 3, 4, or 5		6	3,000 00
7	Enter the amount from Form 1040, line 38; Form 1040A, line 22; or Form 1040NR, line 37.	7	38,665 00	

8 Enter on line 8 the decimal amount shown below that applies to the amount on line 7

If line 7 is:				If line 7 is:		
Over	**But not over**	**Decimal amount is**		**Over**	**But not over**	**Decimal amount is**
$0—15,000		.35		$29,000—31,000		.27
15,000—17,000		.34		31,000—33,000		.26
17,000—19,000		.33		33,000—35,000		.25
19,000—21,000		.32		35,000—37,000		.24
21,000—23,000		.31		37,000—39,000		.23
23,000—25,000		.30		39,000—41,000		.22
25,000—27,000		.29		41,000—43,000		.21
27,000—29,000		.28		43,000—No limit		.20

8 X . 23

9	Multiply line 6 by the decimal amount on line 8. If you paid 2013 expenses in 2014, see the instructions	9	690 00
10	Tax liability limit. Enter the amount from the Credit Limit Worksheet in the instructions.	10	1,443 00
11	**Credit for child and dependent care expenses.** Enter the **smaller** of line 9 or line 10 here and on Form 1040, line 49; Form 1040A, line 31; or Form 1040NR, line 47	11	690 00

For Paperwork Reduction Act Notice, see your tax return instructions.   Cat. No. 11862M   Form **2441** (2014)

Form 8863

Department of the Treasury
Internal Revenue Service (99)

Education Credits
(American Opportunity and Lifetime Learning Credits)

▶ Attach to Form 1040 or Form 1040A.
▶ Information about Form 8863 and its separate instructions is at *www.irs.gov/form8863*.

OMB No. 1545-0074

2014

Attachment
Sequence No. **50**

Name(s) shown on return

Matt & Mary Marrott

Your social security number		
166	33	4444

⚠ CAUTION

Complete a separate Part III on page 2 for each student for whom you are claiming either credit before you complete Parts I and II.

Part I   Refundable American Opportunity Credit

1	After completing Part III for each student, enter the total of all amounts from all Parts III, line 30 .	**1**		
2	Enter: $180,000 if married filing jointly; $90,000 if single, head of household, or qualifying widow(er) **2**			
3	Enter the amount from Form 1040, line 38, or Form 1040A, line 22. If you are filing Form 2555, 2555-EZ, or 4563, or you are excluding income from Puerto Rico, see Pub. 970 for the amount to enter **3**			
4	Subtract line 3 from line 2. If zero or less, **stop;** you cannot take any education credit **4**			
5	Enter: $20,000 if married filing jointly; $10,000 if single, head of household, or qualifying widow(er) **5**			
6	If line 4 is: • Equal to or more than line 5, enter 1.000 on line 6 . . . . • Less than line 5, divide line 4 by line 5. Enter the result as a decimal (rounded to at least three places)	**6**	.	
7	Multiply line 1 by line 6. **Caution:** If you were under age 24 at the end of the year **and** meet the conditions described in the instructions, you **cannot** take the refundable American opportunity credit; skip line 8, enter the amount from line 7 on line 9, and check this box . . . . ▶ ☐	**7**		
8	**Refundable American opportunity credit.** Multiply line 7 by 40% (.40). Enter the amount here and on Form 1040, line 68, or Form 1040A, line 44. Then go to line 9 below.	**8**		

Part II   Nonrefundable Education Credits

9	Subtract line 8 from line 7. Enter here and on line 2 of the Credit Limit Worksheet (see instructions)			**9**		
10	After completing Part III for each student, enter the total of all amounts from all Parts III, line 31. If zero, skip lines 11 through 17, enter -0- on line 18, and go to line 19			**10**	2,335	00
11	Enter the smaller of line 10 or $10,000			**11**	2,335	00
12	Multiply line 11 by 20% (.20)			**12**	467	00
13	Enter: $128,000 if married filing jointly; $64,000 if single, head of household, or qualifying widow(er)	**13**	28,000 00			
14	Enter the amount from Form 1040, line 38, or Form 1040A, line 22. If you are filing Form 2555, 2555-EZ, or 4563, or you are excluding income from Puerto Rico, see Pub. 970 for the amount to enter	**14**	38,665 00			
15	Subtract line 14 from line 13. If zero or less, skip lines 16 and 17, enter -0- on line 18, and go to line 19	**15**	89,335 00			
16	Enter: $20,000 if married filing jointly; $10,000 if single, head of household, or qualifying widow(er)	**16**	20,000 00			
17	If line 15 is: • Equal to or more than line 16, enter 1.000 on line 17 and go to line 18 • Less than line 16, divide line 15 by line 16. Enter the result as a decimal (rounded to at least three places)			**17**	1 . 000	
18	Multiply line 12 by line 17. Enter here and on line 1 of the Credit Limit Worksheet (see instructions) ▶			**18**	467	00
19	**Nonrefundable education credits.** Enter the amount from line 7 of the Credit Limit Worksheet (see instructions) here and on Form 1040, line 50, or Form 1040A, line 33			**19**	467	00

For Paperwork Reduction Act Notice, see your tax return instructions.   Cat. No. 25379M   Form **8863** (2014)

Chapter 6 Exercise

Name(s) shown on return	Your social security number		
Matt & Mary Marrott	166	33	4444

⚠ CAUTION *Complete Part III for each student for whom you are claiming either the American opportunity credit or lifetime learning credit. Use additional copies of Page 2 as needed for each student.*

Part III **Student and Educational Institution Information**
See instructions.

20 Student name (as shown on page 1 of your tax return)	21 Student social security number (as shown on page 1 of your tax return)		
Mary Marrott	322	66	4444

22 Educational institution information (see instructions)

a. Name of first educational institution	**b.** Name of second educational institution (if any)
State University	
(1) Address. Number and street (or P.O. box). City, town or post office, state, and ZIP code. If a foreign address, see instructions.	**(1)** Address. Number and street (or P.O. box). City, town or post office, state, and ZIP code. If a foreign address, see instructions.
150 Grand Ave., Your City, Your State, Your Zip Code	
(2) Did the student receive Form 1098-T from this institution for 2014? ☑ Yes ☐ No	**(2)** Did the student receive Form 1098-T from this institution for 2014? ☐ Yes ☐ No
(3) Did the student receive Form 1098-T from this institution for 2013 with Box 2 filled in and Box 7 checked? ☐ Yes ☑ No	**(3)** Did the student receive Form 1098-T from this institution for 2013 with Box 2 filled in and Box 7 checked? ☐ Yes ☐ No
If you checked "No" in **both (2) and (3)**, skip **(4)**.	If you checked "No" in **both (2) and (3)**, skip **(4)**.
(4) If you checked "Yes" in **(2) or (3)**, enter the institution's federal identification number (from Form 1098-T). 6 3 – 3 3 2 1 9 8 9	**(4)** If you checked "Yes" in **(2) or (3)**, enter the institution's federal identification number (from Form 1098-T). __ __ – __ __ __ __ __ __ __

23 Has the Hope Scholarship Credit or American opportunity credit been claimed for this student for any 4 tax years before 2014? — ☐ Yes — **Stop!** Go to line 31 for this student. ☑ No — Go to line 24.

24 Was the student enrolled at least half-time for at least one academic period that began or is treated as having begun in 2014 at an eligible educational institution in a program leading towards a postsecondary degree, certificate, or other recognized postsecondary educational credential? (see instructions) — ☐ Yes — Go to line 25. ☑ No — **Stop!** Go to line 31 for this student.

25 Did the student complete the first 4 years of post-secondary education before 2014? — ☐ Yes — **Stop!** Go to line 31 for this student. ☐ No — Go to line 26.

26 Was the student convicted, before the end of 2014, of a felony for possession or distribution of a controlled substance? — ☐ Yes — **Stop!** Go to line 31 for this student. ☐ No — Complete lines 27 through 30 for this student.

⚠ CAUTION *You cannot take the American opportunity credit and the lifetime learning credit for the same student in the same year. If you complete lines 27 through 30 for this student, do not complete line 31.*

American Opportunity Credit

27	Adjusted qualified education expenses (see instructions). **Do not enter more than $4,000**	**27**	
28	Subtract $2,000 from line 27. If zero or less, enter -0-.	**28**	
29	Multiply line 28 by 25% (.25)	**29**	
30	If line 28 is zero, enter the amount from line 27. Otherwise, add $2,000 to the amount on line 29 and enter the result. Skip line 31. Include the total of all amounts from all Parts III, line 30 on Part I, line 1 .	**30**	

Lifetime Learning Credit

31	Adjusted qualified education expenses (see instructions). Include the total of all amounts from all Parts III, line 31, on Part II, line 10	**31**	2,335

Line 10

Credit Limit Worksheet

Complete this worksheet to figure the amount to enter on line 10.

1. Enter the amount from Form 1040, line 47; Form 1040A, line 28; or Form 1040NR, line 45 . . . . **1.** <u>1,443</u>

2. Enter the amount from Form 1040, line 48; or Form 1040NR, line 46; Form 1040A filers enter -0- . . . . . **2.** _____

3. Subtract line 2 from line 1. Also enter this amount on Form 2441, line 10. But if zero or less, **stop**; you cannot take the credit . . . . **3.** <u>1,443</u>

Adjusted Qualified Education Expenses Worksheet

See *Qualified Education Expenses*, earlier, before completing.

Complete a separate worksheet for each student for each academic period beginning or treated as beginning (see below) in 2014 for which you paid (or are treated as having paid) qualified education expenses in 2014.

1. Total qualified education expenses paid for or on behalf of the student in 2014 for the academic period . . . . <u>4,335</u>

2. Less adjustments:
   a. Tax-free educational assistance received in 2014 allocable to the academic period . . . . <u>2,000</u>
   b. Tax-free educational assistance received in 2015 (and before you file your 2014 tax return) allocable to the academic period . . . _____
   c. Refunds of qualified education expenses paid in 2014 if the refund is received in 2014 or in 2015 before you file your 2014 tax return . . . . _____

3. Total adjustments (add lines 2a, 2b, and 2c) . . . . <u>2,000</u>

4. Adjusted qualified education expenses. Subtract line 3 from line 1. If zero or less, enter -0- . . . . <u>2,335</u>

Credit Limit Worksheet

Complete this worksheet to figure the amount to enter on line 19.

1. Enter the amount from Form 8863, line 18 . . . . **1.** <u>467</u>

2. Enter the amount from Form 8863, line 9 . . . . **2.** _____

3. Add lines 1 and 2 . . . . **3.** <u>467</u>

4. Enter the amount from: Form 1040, line 47; or Form 1040A, line 30 . . . . **4.** <u>1,443</u>

5. Enter the total of your credits from either: Form 1040, lines 48 and 49, and Schedule R, line 22; or Form 1040A, lines 31 and 32 . . . . . . **5.** <u>690</u>

6. Subtract line 5 from line 4 . . . . **6.** <u>753</u>

7. Enter the smaller of line 3 or line 6 here and on Form 8863, line 19 . . . . **7.** <u>467</u>

Chapter 7 Review

1) What is a contribution?

   A contribution is when a taxpayer puts money into something.

2) What is a distribution?

   A distribution is when a taxpayer withdraws money out of an account.

3) When is a deductible contribution to a traditional IRA limited?

   A deductible contribution may be limited if the taxpayer (or spouse if MFJ) is covered by a retirement plan at work.

4) What is the contribution limit for a traditional IRA?

   The contribution limit is the smaller of the following amounts:

   - **$5,500 ($6,500 if age 50 or older), or**
   - **The taxable compensation for the year.**

5) What is modified adjusted gross income for traditional IRA purposes?

   The Modified Adjusted Gross Income is the total income from line 22 of the Form 1040 plus

   - **Any foreign earned income exclusion.**
   - **Any foreign housing exclusion or deduction.**
   - **Exclusion of qualified savings bond interest shown on Form 8815, for filers with qualified higher education expenses.**
   - **Exclusion of employer-provided adoption benefits.**

   Minus any adjustments taken on the Form 1040, lines 23 through 31a.

6) How are excess contributions penalized?

   The taxpayer must pay 6% tax on the excess contribution and any earnings on that amount. This tax will be assessed every year the excess contribution remains in the account.

7) When are traditional IRA distributions taxable?

   Generally, all traditional IRA distributions are taxable in the year received.

8) When are Roth IRA contributions limited?

   The contributions are limited if their modified AGI is more than $114,000 if Single, Head of Household, or Married Filing Separately and the taxpayer did not live with the spouse at any time during the year; $181,000 if Married Filing Jointly or Qualifying Widow(er); or $0 if Married Filing Separately and the taxpayer lived with the spouse at any time during the year.

9) What is the contribution limit for a Roth IRA?

The contribution limit for Roth IRA is generally the smaller of the following amounts:

- **$5,500($6,500 if age 50 or older) or**
- **The taxable compensation.**

10) At what age are you required to make minimum distributions from a traditional IRA?

The taxpayer must begin receiving distributions when they reach age 70½.

11) At what age are you required to make minimum distributions from a Roth IRA?

The taxpayer is not ever required to make minimum distributions from a Roth IRA.

12) What is the additional tax penalty on early distributions?

The taxpayer may have to pay a 10% additional tax on early distributions.

Form 1040 Department of the Treasury—Internal Revenue Service (99)
U.S. Individual Income Tax Return **2014** OMB No. 1545-0074 | IRS Use Only—Do not write or staple in this space.

For the year Jan. 1–Dec. 31, 2014, or other tax year beginning	, 2014, ending	, 20	See separate instructions.

Your first name and initial	Last name	Your social security number
Marian	Monglow	3 2 1 5 4 9 8 7 6

If a joint return, spouse's first name and initial | Last name | Spouse's social security number

Home address (number and street). If you have a P.O. box, see instructions. | Apt. no.
556 Willow Lane

▲ Make sure the SSN(s) above and on line 6c are correct.

City, town or post office, state, and ZIP code. If you have a foreign address, also complete spaces below (see instructions).
Your City, Your State, Your Zip Code

Presidential Election Campaign
Check here if you, or your spouse if filing jointly, want $3 to go to this fund. Checking a box below will not change your tax or refund. ☐ You ☐ Spouse

Foreign country name | Foreign province/state/county | Foreign postal code

Filing Status
Check only one box.

1. ☑ Single
2. ☐ Married filing jointly (even if only one had income)
3. ☐ Married filing separately. Enter spouse's SSN above and full name here. ▶
4. ☐ Head of household (with qualifying person). (See instructions.) If the qualifying person is a child but not your dependent, enter this child's name here. ▶
5. ☐ Qualifying widow(er) with dependent child

Exemptions

6a ☑ **Yourself.** If someone can claim you as a dependent, **do not** check box 6a . . . . .
b ☐ **Spouse** . . . .

Boxes checked on 6a and 6b: **1**

c **Dependents:**

(1) First name Last name	(2) Dependent's social security number	(3) Dependent's relationship to you	(4) ✓ if child under age 17 qualifying for child tax credit (see instructions)
			☐
			☐
			☐
			☐

No. of children on 6c who:
• lived with you
• did not live with you due to divorce or separation (see instructions)
Dependents on 6c not entered above

If more than four dependents, see instructions and check here ▶ ☐

d Total number of exemptions claimed . . . .

Add numbers on lines above ▶ **1**

Income

Attach Form(s) W-2 here. Also attach Forms W-2G and 1099-R if tax was withheld.

If you did not get a W-2, see instructions.

7	Wages, salaries, tips, etc. Attach Form(s) W-2	7	62,534 00
8a	**Taxable** interest. Attach Schedule B if required	8a	44 00
b	**Tax-exempt** interest. **Do not** include on line 8a	8b	
9a	Ordinary dividends. Attach Schedule B if required	9a	67 00
b	Qualified dividends	9b	
10	Taxable refunds, credits, or offsets of state and local income taxes	10	
11	Alimony received	11	
12	Business income or (loss). Attach Schedule C or C-EZ	12	
13	Capital gain or (loss). Attach Schedule D if required. If not required, check here ▶ ☐	13	
14	Other gains or (losses). Attach Form 4797	14	
15a	IRA distributions . 15a	b Taxable amount	15b	
16a	Pensions and annuities 16a	b Taxable amount	16b	
17	Rental real estate, royalties, partnerships, S corporations, trusts, etc. Attach Schedule E	17	
18	Farm income or (loss). Attach Schedule F	18	
19	Unemployment compensation	19	
20a	Social security benefits 20a	b Taxable amount	20b	
21	Other income. List type and amount	21	
22	Combine the amounts in the far right column for lines 7 through 21. This is your **total income** ▶	22	62,645 00

Adjusted Gross Income

23	Educator expenses	23	
24	Certain business expenses of reservists, performing artists, and fee-basis government officials. Attach Form 2106 or 2106-EZ	24	
25	Health savings account deduction. Attach Form 8889	25	
26	Moving expenses. Attach Form 3903	26	
27	Deductible part of self-employment tax. Attach Schedule SE	27	
28	Self-employed SEP, SIMPLE, and qualified plans	28	
29	Self-employed health insurance deduction	29	
30	Penalty on early withdrawal of savings	30	
31a	Alimony paid b Recipient's SSN ▶	31a	
32	IRA deduction	32	5,500 00
33	Student loan interest deduction	33	
34	Tuition and fees. Attach Form 8917	34	
35	Domestic production activities deduction. Attach Form 8903	35	
36	Add lines 23 through 35	36	5,500 00
37	Subtract line 36 from line 22. This is your **adjusted gross income** ▶	37	57,145 00

For Disclosure, Privacy Act, and Paperwork Reduction Act Notice, see separate instructions. | Cat. No. 11320B | Form **1040** (2014)

Chapter 7 Exercise

Form 1040 (2014)

Page **2**

Tax and Credits	38	Amount from line 37 (adjusted gross income)	38	57,145	00
	39a	Check if: ☐ **You** were born before January 2, 1950, ☐ Blind. ☐ **Spouse** was born before January 2, 1950, ☐ Blind. } Total boxes checked ▶ 39a			
	b	If your spouse itemizes on a separate return or you were a dual-status alien, check here▶ 39b☐			
Standard Deduction for—	40	**Itemized deductions** (from Schedule A) **or** your **standard deduction** (see left margin)	40	6,200	00
• People who check any box on line 39a or 39b **or** who can be claimed as a dependent, see instructions.	41	Subtract line 40 from line 38	41	50,945	00
	42	**Exemptions.** If line 38 is $152,525 or less, multiply $3,950 by the number on line 6d. Otherwise, see instructions	42	3,950	00
	43	**Taxable income.** Subtract line 42 from line 41. If line 42 is more than line 41, enter -0-	43	46,995	00
	44	**Tax** (see instructions). Check if any from: a ☐ Form(s) 8814 b ☐ Form 4972 c ☐	44	7,600	00
• All others:	45	**Alternative minimum tax** (see instructions). Attach Form 6251	45		
Single or Married filing separately, $6,200	46	Excess advance premium tax credit repayment. Attach Form 8962	46		
	47	Add lines 44, 45, and 46 ▶	47	7,600	00
Married filing jointly or Qualifying widow(er), $12,400	48	Foreign tax credit. Attach Form 1116 if required . 48			
	49	Credit for child and dependent care expenses. Attach Form 2441 49			
Head of household, $9,100	50	Education credits from Form 8863, line 19 . 50			
	51	Retirement savings contributions credit. Attach Form 8880 51			
	52	Child tax credit. Attach Schedule 8812, if required . 52			
	53	Residential energy credits. Attach Form 5695 . 53			
	54	Other credits from Form: a ☐ 3800 b ☐ 8801 c ☐ 54			
	55	Add lines 48 through 54. These are your **total credits**	55		
	56	Subtract line 55 from line 47. If line 55 is more than line 47, enter -0- ▶	56	7,600	00
Other Taxes	57	Self-employment tax. Attach Schedule SE	57		
	58	Unreported social security and Medicare tax from Form: a ☐ 4137 b ☐ 8919	58		
	59	Additional tax on IRAs, other qualified retirement plans, etc. Attach Form 5329 if required	59		
	60a	Household employment taxes from Schedule H	60a		
	b	First-time homebuyer credit repayment. Attach Form 5405 if required	60b		
	61	Health care: individual responsibility (see instructions) Full-year coverage ☐	61		
	62	Taxes from: a ☐ Form 8959 b ☐ Form 8960 c ☐ Instructions; enter code(s)	62		
	63	Add lines 56 through 62. This is your **total tax** ▶	63	7,600	00
Payments	64	Federal income tax withheld from Forms W-2 and 1099 . 64	7,731	00	
	65	2014 estimated tax payments and amount applied from 2013 return 65			
If you have a qualifying child, attach Schedule EIC.	66a	**Earned income credit (EIC)** . 66a			
	b	Nontaxable combat pay election 66b			
	67	Additional child tax credit. Attach Schedule 8812 . 67			
	68	American opportunity credit from Form 8863, line 8 . 68			
	69	Net premium tax credit. Attach Form 8962 . 69			
	70	Amount paid with request for extension to file . 70			
	71	Excess social security and tier 1 RRTA tax withheld . 71			
	72	Credit for federal tax on fuels. Attach Form 4136 . 72			
	73	Credits from Form: a ☐ 2439 b ☐ Reserved c ☐ Reserved d ☐ 73			
	74	Add lines 64, 65, 66a, and 67 through 73. These are your **total payments** ▶	74	7,731	00
Refund	75	If line 74 is more than line 63, subtract line 63 from line 74. This is the amount you **overpaid**	75	131	00
	76a	Amount of line 75 you want **refunded to you.** If Form 8888 is attached, check here . ▶☐	76a	131	00
Direct deposit? See instructions.	b	Routing number ▶c Type: ☐ Checking ☐ Savings			
	d	Account number			
	77	Amount of line 75 you want **applied to your 2015 estimated tax** ▶ 77			
Amount You Owe	78	**Amount you owe.** Subtract line 74 from line 63. For details on how to pay, see instructions ▶	78		
	79	Estimated tax penalty (see instructions) . 79			

Third Party Designee
Do you want to allow another person to discuss this return with the IRS (see instructions)? ☐ **Yes.** Complete below. ☐ **No**

Designee's name ▶
Phone no. ▶
Personal identification number (PIN) ▶

Sign Here
Under penalties of perjury, I declare that I have examined this return and accompanying schedules and statements, and to the best of my knowledge and belief, they are true, correct, and complete. Declaration of preparer (other than taxpayer) is based on all information of which preparer has any knowledge.

Joint return? See instructions. Keep a copy for your records.

Your signature	Date	Your occupation **Accounts Manager**	Daytime phone number **(555)555-5555**
Spouse's signature. If a joint return, **both** must sign.	Date	Spouse's occupation	If the IRS sent you an Identity Protection PIN, enter it here (see inst.)

Paid Preparer Use Only

Print/Type preparer's name **Jane Doe**	Preparer's signature	Date	Check ☐ if self-employed	PTIN **P00000000**
Firm's name ▶ **My Tax Service**			Firm's EIN ▶	**63-0000000**
Firm's address▶ **100 Main St., Your City, Your State, Your Zip Code**			Phone no.	**(555)555-1111**

www.irs.gov/form1040

Form **1040** (2014)

Chapter 7 Exercise

Modified AGI

1.	Enter the amount from Form 1040, line 22.	1.	62,645
2.	Enter any amounts from Form 2555, lines 45 and 50, and Form 2555-EZ, line 18.	2.	
3.	Enter any amounts from Form 8815, line 14.	3.	
4.	Enter any amounts from Form 8839, line 26.	4.	
5.	Add lines 1 through 5 and enter the total here.	5.	
6.	Enter the sum of any amounts on Form 1040, lines 23 through 31a.	6.	
7.	Subtract line 6 from line 5. **This is the modified AGI.**	7.	62,645

Traditional IRA Worksheet

		Taxpayer	Spouse
1.	Enter the total of the taxpayer's (and spouse's if MFJ) wages, salaries, tips, etc.; alimony and separate maintenance payments, and nontaxable combat pay.	1. 62,534	
2.	Enter any earned income the taxpayer (and spouse if MFJ) received as a self-employed individual or partner minus any deductions on Form 1040, lines 27 and 28.	2.	
3.	Add lines 1 and 2. If MFJ, enter the result in both columns. If the result is 0, stop here, the taxpayer may not make any IRA contributions	3. 62,534	3.
4.	• If the taxpayer (**and** spouse if MFJ) was not covered by a retirement plan at work and line 3 is over $5,500 ($6,500 If age 50 or older, they may take a full deduction. Enter $5,500($6,500 if age 50 or older) on line 7 and go to line 8. If line 3 is not over $5,500 ($6,500 if age 50 or older) enter the amount from line 3 on line 7 and go to line 8. • If the taxpayer is covered by a retirement plan at work and their filing status is S, HH, or MFS and the taxpayer did not live with spouse at all during the year, enter $70,000. • If MFJ and only one is covered by a retirement plan at work, enter $116,000 in the column of the one covered and $191,000 in the other column. • If MFJ and both are covered by a retirement plan at work, enter $116,000 in both columns. • If QW and the taxpayer is covered by a retirement plan at work, enter $116,000. • If MFS and lived with spouse at any time during the year, enter $10,000.	4.	4.
5.	Enter the amount from line7 in the Modified AGI worksheet above.	5.	5.
6.	Subtract line 5 from line 4. If 0 or less, the taxpayer cannot deduct any IRA contributions. If the taxpayer wants to contribute to a Roth IRA or make nondeductible traditional IRA contributions, go to the applicable worksheet on the next page. If this amount is $10,000 or more ($20,000 if MFJ or QW), enter $5,500 ($6,500 if age 50 or over) on line 7 and go to line 8.	6.	6.
7.	Multiply line 6 by the percentage below that applies to the taxpayer. If the result is not a multiple of $10, round it to the next highest multiple of $10. If the amount is less than $200, enter $200. • MFJ or QW and covered by a retirement plan at work, multiply by 27.5% (32.5% if age 50 or over). • All others, multiply by 55% (65% if age 50 or over).	7. 5,500	7.
8.	Enter the amount from line 3.	8. 62,534	8.
9.	Enter the contributions made or to be made. Not more than $5,500 ($6,500 if age 50 or over).	9. 5,500	9.
10.	Enter the smaller of lines 7, 8, and 9 here and on Form 1040, line 32. If line 9 is more than this amount, and the taxpayer will withdraw the excess and does not choose to make a Roth IRA or nondeductible contribution, stop here.	10. 5,500	10.

Chapter 8 Review

1) Pensions and annuities are reported to the taxpayer on what form?

   Pensions and annuities are reported to the taxpayer on a Form 1099-R

2) If the taxpayer has no cost in the pension plan will the distributions be taxable, nontaxable, or partly taxable?

   If the taxpayer has no cost in the plan, the distributions will be fully taxable.

3) If the taxpayer starts receiving partly taxable distributions from a qualified employee plan this year, what method will be used to determine the taxable amount?

   The taxpayer will use the Simplified Method to determine the taxable amount.

4) What are periodic payments?

   Periodic payments are amounts paid at regular intervals for greater than one year.

5) What is a lump-sum distribution?

   A lump-sum distribution is the distribution or payment in a single tax year of a plan participant's entire balance from all of the employer's qualified plans of one kind.

6) What may the taxpayer do with a lump-sum distribution to totally defer the tax?

   The plan may be rolled over from a qualified retirement plan into another qualified retirement plan or a traditional IRA. This allows the taxpayer to defer tax on the distribution until withdrawn from the recipient account.

7) What is the maximum amount of social security distributions that may be taxable?

   Up to 85% of the social security benefits may be taxable.

Form 1040 Department of the Treasury—Internal Revenue Service (99)
U.S. Individual Income Tax Return **2014** OMB No. 1545-0074 IRS Use Only—Do not write or staple in this space.

For the year Jan. 1–Dec. 31, 2014, or other tax year beginning _____ , 2014, ending _____ , 20 ___   See separate instructions.

Your first name and initial	Last name	Your social security number
John	Megginson	5 6 4 5 6 3 6 7 6

If a joint return, spouse's first name and initial | Last name | Spouse's social security number

Home address (number and street). If you have a P.O. box, see instructions. | Apt. no.
7778 Happiness Circle

▲ Make sure the SSN(s) above and on line 6c are correct.

City, town or post office, state, and ZIP code. If you have a foreign address, also complete spaces below (see instructions).
Your City, Your State, Your Zip Code

Presidential Election Campaign
Check here if you, or your spouse if filing jointly, want $3 to go to this fund. Checking a box below will not change your tax or refund. ✓ You ☐ Spouse

Foreign country name | Foreign province/state/county | Foreign postal code

Filing Status

Check only one box.

1 ✓ Single
2 ☐ Married filing jointly (even if only one had income)
3 ☐ Married filing separately. Enter spouse's SSN above and full name here. ▶
4 ☐ Head of household (with qualifying person). (See instructions.) If the qualifying person is a child but not your dependent, enter this child's name here. ▶
5 ☐ Qualifying widow(er) with dependent child

Exemptions

6a ✓ **Yourself.** If someone can claim you as a dependent, **do not** check box 6a . . . . . .
b ☐ **Spouse** . . . .

c **Dependents:**		(2) Dependent's social security number	(3) Dependent's relationship to you	(4) ✓ if child under age 17 qualifying for child tax credit (see instructions)
(1) First name	Last name			☐
				☐
				☐
				☐

If more than four dependents, see instructions and check here ▶ ☐

d Total number of exemptions claimed

Boxes checked on 6a and 6b   **1**
No. of children on 6c who:
• lived with you
• did not live with you due to divorce or separation (see instructions)
Dependents on 6c not entered above
Add numbers on lines above ▶   **1**

Income

Attach Form(s) W-2 here. Also attach Forms W-2G and 1099-R if tax was withheld.

If you did not get a W-2, see instructions.

7	Wages, salaries, tips, etc. Attach Form(s) W-2	7	3,588	00
8a	**Taxable** interest. Attach Schedule B if required	8a		
b	**Tax-exempt** interest. **Do not** include on line 8a . .	8b		
9a	Ordinary dividends. Attach Schedule B if required	9a		
b	Qualified dividends	9b		
10	Taxable refunds, credits, or offsets of state and local income taxes	10		
11	Alimony received	11		
12	Business income or (loss). Attach Schedule C or C-EZ	12		
13	Capital gain or (loss). Attach Schedule D if required. If not required, check here ▶ ☐	13		
14	Other gains or (losses). Attach Form 4797	14		
15a	IRA distributions .	15a		b Taxable amount . . .	15b		
16a	Pensions and annuities	16a	32,778	00	b Taxable amount . . .	16b	29,665	00
17	Rental real estate, royalties, partnerships, S corporations, trusts, etc. Attach Schedule E	17		
18	Farm income or (loss). Attach Schedule F	18		
19	Unemployment compensation	19		
20a	Social security benefits	20a	16,221	00	b Taxable amount . . .	20b	10,759	00
21	Other income. List type and amount _____	21		
22	Combine the amounts in the far right column for lines 7 through 21. This is your **total income** ▶	22	44,012	00

Adjusted Gross Income

23	Educator expenses	23		
24	Certain business expenses of reservists, performing artists, and fee-basis government officials. Attach Form 2106 or 2106-EZ	24		
25	Health savings account deduction. Attach Form 8889 .	25		
26	Moving expenses. Attach Form 3903	26		
27	Deductible part of self-employment tax. Attach Schedule SE .	27		
28	Self-employed SEP, SIMPLE, and qualified plans . .	28		
29	Self-employed health insurance deduction	29		
30	Penalty on early withdrawal of savings	30		
31a	Alimony paid b Recipient's SSN ▶ _____	31a		
32	IRA deduction	32		
33	Student loan interest deduction	33		
34	Tuition and fees. Attach Form 8917	34		
35	Domestic production activities deduction. Attach Form 8903	35		
36	Add lines 23 through 35	36		
37	Subtract line 36 from line 22. This is your **adjusted gross income** . . . . . . ▶	37	44,012	00

For Disclosure, Privacy Act, and Paperwork Reduction Act Notice, see separate instructions.   Cat. No. 11320B   Form **1040** (2014)

Chapter 8 Exercise

Tax and Credits	38	Amount from line 37 (adjusted gross income)	38	44,012	00
	39a	Check if: ☐ **You** were born before January 2, 1950, ☐ Blind. / ☐ **Spouse** was born before January 2, 1950, ☐ Blind. } Total boxes checked ▶ 39a			
	b	If your spouse itemizes on a separate return or you were a dual-status alien, check here ▶ 39b ☐			

Standard Deduction for—

• People who check any box on line 39a or 39b **or** who can be claimed as a dependent, see instructions.

• All others:

Single or Married filing separately, $6,200

Married filing jointly or Qualifying widow(er), $12,400

Head of household, $9,100

40	Itemized deductions (from Schedule A) **or** your **standard deduction** (see left margin) . .	40	7,750	00
41	Subtract line 40 from line 38	41	36,262	00
42	**Exemptions.** If line 38 is $152,525 or less, multiply $3,950 by the number on line 6d. Otherwise, see instructions	42	3,950	00
43	**Taxable income.** Subtract line 42 from line 41. If line 42 is more than line 41, enter -0-	43	32,312	00
44	**Tax** (see instructions). Check if any from: **a** ☐ Form(s) 8814 **b** ☐ Form 4972 **c** ☐ ____	44	4,395	00
45	**Alternative minimum tax** (see instructions). Attach Form 6251	45		
46	Excess advance premium tax credit repayment. Attach Form 8962	46		
47	Add lines 44, 45, and 46 . . . . ▶	47	4,395	00
48	Foreign tax credit. Attach Form 1116 if required . .	48		
49	Credit for child and dependent care expenses. Attach Form 2441	49		
50	Education credits from Form 8863, line 19	50		
51	Retirement savings contributions credit. Attach Form 8880	51		
52	Child tax credit. Attach Schedule 8812, if required. . .	52		
53	Residential energy credits. Attach Form 5695 . . .	53		
54	Other credits from Form: **a** ☐ 3800 **b** ☐ 8801 **c** ☐	54		
55	Add lines 48 through 54. These are your **total credits**	55		
56	Subtract line 55 from line 47. If line 55 is more than line 47, enter -0- . . . . ▶	56	4,395	00

Other Taxes					
	57	Self-employment tax. Attach Schedule SE	57		
	58	Unreported social security and Medicare tax from Form: **a** ☐ 4137 **b** ☐ 8919 . .	58		
	59	Additional tax on IRAs, other qualified retirement plans, etc. Attach Form 5329 if required . .	59		
	60a	Household employment taxes from Schedule H	60a		
	b	First-time homebuyer credit repayment. Attach Form 5405 if required	60b		
	61	Health care: individual responsibility (see instructions) Full-year coverage ☐	61		
	62	Taxes from: **a** ☐ Form 8959 **b** ☐ Form 8960 **c** ☐ Instructions; enter code(s) ____	62		
	63	Add lines 56 through 62. This is your **total tax** . . . . ▶	63	4,395	00

Payments					
	64	Federal income tax withheld from Forms W-2 and 1099 . .	64	3,745	00	
	65	2014 estimated tax payments and amount applied from 2013 return	65		
If you have a qualifying child, attach Schedule EIC.	66a	**Earned income credit (EIC)**	66a		
	b	Nontaxable combat pay election	66b		
	67	Additional child tax credit. Attach Schedule 8812	67		
	68	American opportunity credit from Form 8863, line 8 . . .	68		
	69	Net premium tax credit. Attach Form 8962	69		
	70	Amount paid with request for extension to file	70		
	71	Excess social security and tier 1 RRTA tax withheld . . .	71		
	72	Credit for federal tax on fuels. Attach Form 4136	72		
	73	Credits from Form: **a** ☐ 2439 **b** ☐ Reserved **c** ☐ Reserved **d** ☐	73		
	74	Add lines 64, 65, 66a, and 67 through 73. These are your **total payments** . . . . . ▶	74	3,745	00

Refund					
	75	If line 74 is more than line 63, subtract line 63 from line 74. This is the amount you **overpaid**	75		
	76a	Amount of line 75 you want **refunded to you.** If Form 8888 is attached, check here . ▶ ☐	76a		
Direct deposit? See instructions.	▶ b	Routing number [ ][ ][ ][ ][ ][ ][ ][ ][ ] ▶ c Type: ☐ Checking ☐ Savings			
	▶ d	Account number [ ][ ][ ][ ][ ][ ][ ][ ][ ][ ][ ][ ][ ][ ][ ][ ][ ]			
	77	Amount of line 75 you want **applied to your 2015 estimated tax** ▶ 77			

Amount You Owe	78	**Amount you owe.** Subtract line 74 from line 63. For details on how to pay, see instructions ▶	78	650	00
	79	Estimated tax penalty (see instructions) 79			

Third Party Designee	Do you want to allow another person to discuss this return with the IRS (see instructions)? ☐ **Yes.** Complete below. ☐ **No**
	Designee's name ▶ Phone no. ▶ Personal identification number (PIN) ▶ [ ][ ][ ][ ][ ]

Sign Here

Joint return? See instructions. Keep a copy for your records.

Under penalties of perjury, I declare that I have examined this return and accompanying schedules and statements, and to the best of my knowledge and belief, they are true, correct, and complete. Declaration of preparer (other than taxpayer) is based on all information of which preparer has any knowledge.

Your signature	Date	Your occupation Retire	Daytime phone number **(555)555-5555**
Spouse's signature. If a joint return, **both** must sign.	Date	Spouse's occupation	If the IRS sent you an Identity Protection PIN, enter it here (see inst.)

Paid Preparer Use Only	Print/Type preparer's name Jane Doe	Preparer's signature	Date	Check ☐ if self-employed	PTIN P00000000
	Firm's name ▶ **My Tax Service**			Firm's EIN ▶	63-0000000
	Firm's address ▶ **100 Main St., Your City, Your State, Your Zip Code**			Phone no.	**(555)555-1111**

Social Security Benefits Worksheet—Lines 20a and 20b

Keep for Your Records

Before you begin:
- ✓ Complete Form 1040, lines 21 and 23 through 32, if they apply to you.
- ✓ Figure any write-in adjustments to be entered on the dotted line next to line 36 (see the instructions for line 36).
- ✓ If you are married filing separately and you lived apart from your spouse for all of 2014, enter "D" to the right of the word "benefits" on line 20a. If you do not, you may get a math error notice from the IRS.
- ✓ Be sure you have read the **Exception** in the line 20a and 20b instructions to see if you can use this worksheet instead of a publication to find out if any of your benefits are taxable.

1.	Enter the total amount from **box 5** of **all** your **Forms SSA-1099** and **Forms RRB-1099.** Also, enter this amount on Form 1040, line 20a	1.	16,221
2.	Enter one-half of line 1	2.	8,111
3.	Combine the amounts from Form 1040, lines 7, 8a, 9a, 10 through 14, 15b, 16b, 17 through 19, and 21	3.	33,253
4.	Enter the amount, if any, from Form 1040, line 8b	4.	
5.	Combine lines 2, 3, and 4	5.	41,364
6.	Enter the total of the amounts from Form 1040, lines 23 through 32, plus any write-in adjustments you entered on the dotted line next to line 36	6.	
7.	Is the amount on line 6 less than the amount on line 5?		

☐ **No.** 🛑 None of your social security benefits are taxable. Enter -0- on Form 1040, line 20b.

	☑ **Yes.** Subtract line 6 from line 5	7.	41,364
8.	If you are:		

- • Married filing jointly, enter $32,000
- • Single, head of household, qualifying widow(er), or married filing separately and you **lived apart** from your spouse for all of 2014, enter $25,000
- • Married filing separately and you lived with your spouse at any time in 2014, skip lines 8 through 15; multiply line 7 by 85% (.85) and enter the result on line 16. Then go to line 17

	....	8.	25,000
9.	Is the amount on line 8 less than the amount on line 7?		

☐ **No.** 🛑 None of your social security benefits are taxable. Enter -0- on Form 1040, line 20b. If you are married filing separately and you **lived apart** from your spouse for all of 2014, be sure you entered "D" to the right of the word "benefits" on line 20a.

	☑ **Yes.** Subtract line 8 from line 7	9.	16,364
10.	Enter: $12,000 if married filing jointly; $9,000 if single, head of household, qualifying widow(er), or married filing separately and you **lived apart** from your spouse for all of 2014	10.	9,000
11.	Subtract line 10 from line 9. If zero or less, enter -0-	11.	7,364
12.	Enter the **smaller** of line 9 or line 10	12.	9,000
13.	Enter one-half of line 12	13.	4,500
14.	Enter the **smaller** of line 2 or line 13	14.	4,500
15.	Multiply line 11 by 85% (.85). If line 11 is zero, enter -0-	15.	6,259
16.	Add lines 14 and 15	16.	10,759
17.	Multiply line 1 by 85% (.85)	17.	13,788
18.	**Taxable social security benefits.** Enter the **smaller** of line 16 or line 17. Also enter this amount on Form 1040, line 20b	18.	10,759

TIP *If any of your benefits are taxable for 2014 and they include a lump-sum benefit payment that was for an earlier year, you may be able to reduce the taxable amount. See Lump-Sum Election in Pub. 915 for details.*

Chapter 9 Review

1) What is the maximum amount allowed for the educator expense deduction?

   Eligible educators may deduct up to $250 of qualified expenses they paid in 2014.

2) What kind of health plan must the taxpayer be covered under to be eligible to contribute to a HSA?

   In order to contribute to an HSA, the taxpayer must be covered under a high deductible health plan (HDHP).

3) How much further must the taxpayer's new principal workplace be from the old home to qualify for the moving expense deduction?

   The new principal workplace must be at least 50 miles farther from the old home than the old workplace was.

4) What is the time requirement for an employee to qualify for the moving expense deduction?

   If the taxpayer is an employee, they must work full time in the general area of the new workplace for at least 39 weeks during the first 12 months after moving. If the taxpayer is self-employed, they must work full time in the general area of the new workplace for at least 39 weeks during the first 12 months and a total of at least 78 weeks during the first 24 months after moving.

5) Where will you find the amount of penalty on early withdrawal of savings?

   The amount of the penalty on early withdrawal of savings be reported in Box 2 of the Form 1099-INT.

6) What information is required to deduct alimony paid?

   To deduct these payments, the social security number of the recipient must be reported as well as the amount.

7) For whom can the student loan interest deduction be claimed?

A qualified student loan is any loan that was taken out to pay the qualified higher education expenses for any of the following individuals:
- **The taxpayer or spouse,**
- **Any person who was a dependent when the loan was taken out,**
- **Any person the taxpayer could have claimed as a dependent for the year the loan was taken out except that:**
  - **The person filed a joint return,**
  - **The person had gross income that was equal to or more than the exemption amount for the year,**
  - **The taxpayer, or spouse if filing jointly, could be claimed as a dependent on someone else's return.**

8) Must the eligible person for the tuition and fees deduction have a high school diploma?

The qualifying person must have either a high school diploma or a General Educational Development (GED) credential.

Form **1040**

Department of the Treasury—Internal Revenue Service (99)

U.S. Individual Income Tax Return **2014**

OMB No. 1545-0074 | IRS Use Only—Do not write or staple in this space.

For the year Jan. 1–Dec. 31, 2014, or other tax year beginning _____ , 2014, ending _____ , 20 ___ | See separate instructions.

Your first name and initial	Last name	Your social security number
Byron	Burrows	0 9 4 5 7 3 5 7 0
If a joint return, spouse's first name and initial	Last name	Spouse's social security number
Belinda	Burrows	3 5 4 5 7 3 7 4 4

Home address (number and street). If you have a P.O. box, see instructions. | Apt. no.

55 Mammoth Ct.

▲ Make sure the SSN(s) above and on line 6c are correct.

City, town or post office, state, and ZIP code. If you have a foreign address, also complete spaces below (see instructions).

Your City, Your State, Your Zip Code

Presidential Election Campaign

Check here if you, or your spouse if filing jointly, want $3 to go to this fund. Checking a box below will not change your tax or refund. ☐ You ☐ Spouse

Foreign country name | Foreign province/state/county | Foreign postal code

Filing Status

Check only one box.

1. ☐ Single
2. ☑ Married filing jointly (even if only one had income)
3. ☐ Married filing separately. Enter spouse's SSN above and full name here. ▶
4. ☐ Head of household (with qualifying person). (See instructions.) If the qualifying person is a child but not your dependent, enter this child's name here. ▶
5. ☐ Qualifying widow(er) with dependent child

Exemptions

6a ☑ **Yourself.** If someone can claim you as a dependent, **do not** check box 6a . . . . .
b ☑ **Spouse** . . . .

Boxes checked on 6a and 6b | **2**

c Dependents:	(2) Dependent's social security number	(3) Dependent's relationship to you	(4) ✓ if child under age 17 qualifying for child tax credit (see instructions)
(1) First name Last name			
Beth Burrows	6 6 2 5 4 8 2 3 2	Daughter	✓
Brian Burrows	4 3 6 2 4 9 4 3 3	Son	✓
			☐
			☐

No. of children on 6c who:
• lived with you | **2**
• did not live with you due to divorce or separation (see instructions)
Dependents on 6c not entered above

If more than four dependents, see instructions and check here ▶ ☐

d Total number of exemptions claimed . . . .

Add numbers on lines above ▶ | **4**

Income

Attach Form(s) W-2 here. Also attach Forms W-2G and 1099-R if tax was withheld.

If you did not get a W-2, see instructions.

7	Wages, salaries, tips, etc. Attach Form(s) W-2	7	46,557 00
8a	**Taxable** interest. Attach Schedule B if required	8a	1,443 00
b	**Tax-exempt** interest. **Do not** include on line 8a . . .	8b	
9a	Ordinary dividends. Attach Schedule B if required	9a	
b	Qualified dividends	9b	
10	Taxable refunds, credits, or offsets of state and local income taxes . .	10	
11	Alimony received	11	
12	Business income or (loss). Attach Schedule C or C-EZ	12	
13	Capital gain or (loss). Attach Schedule D if required. If not required, check here ▶ ☐	13	
14	Other gains or (losses). Attach Form 4797	14	
15a	IRA distributions . 15a _____ b Taxable amount . . .	15b	
16a	Pensions and annuities 16a _____ b Taxable amount . . .	16b	
17	Rental real estate, royalties, partnerships, S corporations, trusts, etc. Attach Schedule E	17	
18	Farm income or (loss). Attach Schedule F	18	
19	Unemployment compensation	19	
20a	Social security benefits 20a _____ b Taxable amount . . .	20b	
21	Other income. List type and amount _____	21	
22	Combine the amounts in the far right column for lines 7 through 21. This is your **total income** ▶	22	48,000 00

Adjusted Gross Income

23	Educator expenses	23	
24	Certain business expenses of reservists, performing artists, and fee-basis government officials. Attach Form 2106 or 2106-EZ	24	
25	Health savings account deduction. Attach Form 8889 .	25	
26	Moving expenses. Attach Form 3903	26	
27	Deductible part of self-employment tax. Attach Schedule SE .	27	
28	Self-employed SEP, SIMPLE, and qualified plans . . .	28	
29	Self-employed health insurance deduction	29	
30	Penalty on early withdrawal of savings	30	24 00
31a	Alimony paid b Recipient's SSN ▶ _____	31a	
32	IRA deduction	32	
33	Student loan interest deduction	33	2,331 00
34	Tuition and fees. Attach Form 8917	34	
35	Domestic production activities deduction. Attach Form 8903	35	
36	Add lines 23 through 35	36	2,355 00
37	Subtract line 36 from line 22. This is your **adjusted gross income** . . . . ▶	37	45,645 00

For Disclosure, Privacy Act, and Paperwork Reduction Act Notice, see separate instructions. Cat. No. 11320B Form **1040** (2014)

Chapter 9 Exercise

Tax and Credits	38	Amount from line 37 (adjusted gross income)	38	45,645	00
	39a	Check if: ☐ **You** were born before January 2, 1950, ☐ Blind. ☐ **Spouse** was born before January 2, 1950, ☐ Blind. **Total boxes** checked ▶ 39a			
	b	If your spouse itemizes on a separate return or you were a dual-status alien, check here ▶ 39b ☐			
Standard Deduction for— • People who check any box on line 39a or 39b **or** who can be claimed as a dependent, see instructions. • All others: Single or Married filing separately, $6,200 Married filing jointly or Qualifying widow(er), $12,400 Head of household, $9,100	40	**Itemized deductions** (from Schedule A) **or** your **standard deduction** (see left margin)	40	12,400	00
	41	Subtract line 40 from line 38	41	33,245	00
	42	**Exemptions.** If line 38 is $152,525 or less, multiply $3,950 by the number on line 6d. Otherwise, see instructions	42	15,800	00
	43	**Taxable income.** Subtract line 42 from line 41. If line 42 is more than line 41, enter -0-	43	17,445	00
	44	**Tax** (see instructions). Check if any from: **a** ☐ Form(s) 8814 **b** ☐ Form 4972 **c** ☐	44	1,743	00
	45	**Alternative minimum tax** (see instructions). Attach Form 6251	45		
	46	Excess advance premium tax credit repayment. Attach Form 8962	46		
	47	Add lines 44, 45, and 46 ▶	47	1,743	00
	48	Foreign tax credit. Attach Form 1116 if required	48		
	49	Credit for child and dependent care expenses. Attach Form 2441	49		
	50	Education credits from Form 8863, line 19	50	1,468 00	
	51	Retirement savings contributions credit. Attach Form 8880	51		
	52	Child tax credit. Attach Schedule 8812, if required	52	275 00	
	53	Residential energy credits. Attach Form 5695	53		
	54	Other credits from Form: **a** ☐ 3800 **b** ☐ 8801 **c** ☐	54		
	55	Add lines 48 through 54. These are your **total credits**	55	1,743	00
	56	Subtract line 55 from line 47. If line 55 is more than line 47, enter -0- ▶	56	0	00
Other Taxes	57	Self-employment tax. Attach Schedule SE	57		
	58	Unreported social security and Medicare tax from Form: **a** ☐ 4137 **b** ☐ 8919	58		
	59	Additional tax on IRAs, other qualified retirement plans, etc. Attach Form 5329 if required	59		
	60a	Household employment taxes from Schedule H	60a		
	b	First-time homebuyer credit repayment. Attach Form 5405 if required	60b		
	61	Health care: individual responsibility (see instructions) Full-year coverage ☐	61		
	62	Taxes from: **a** ☐ Form 8959 **b** ☐ Form 8960 **c** ☐ Instructions; enter code(s)	62		
	63	Add lines 56 through 62. This is your **total tax** ▶	63	0	00
Payments If you have a qualifying child, attach Schedule EIC.	64	Federal income tax withheld from Forms W-2 and 1099	64	4,444 00	
	65	2014 estimated tax payments and amount applied from 2013 return	65		
	66a	**Earned income credit (EIC)**	66a	550 00	
	b	Nontaxable combat pay election	66b		
	67	Additional child tax credit. Attach Schedule 8812	67	1,725 00	
	68	American opportunity credit from Form 8863, line 8	68	979 00	
	69	Net premium tax credit. Attach Form 8962	69		
	70	Amount paid with request for extension to file	70		
	71	Excess social security and tier 1 RRTA tax withheld	71		
	72	Credit for federal tax on fuels. Attach Form 4136	72		
	73	Credits from Form: **a** ☐ 2439 **b** ☐ Reserved **c** ☐ Reserved **d** ☐	73		
	74	Add lines 64, 65, 66a, and 67 through 73. These are your **total payments** ▶	74	7,698	00
Refund Direct deposit? See instructions.	75	If line 74 is more than line 63, subtract line 63 from line 74. This is the amount you **overpaid**	75	7,698	00
	76a	Amount of line 75 you want **refunded to you.** If Form 8888 is attached, check here ▶ ☐	76a	7,698	00
	b	Routing number ▶ c Type: ☐ Checking ☐ Savings			
	d	Account number			
	77	Amount of line 75 you want **applied to your 2015 estimated tax** ▶ 77			
Amount You Owe	78	**Amount you owe.** Subtract line 74 from line 63. For details on how to pay, see instructions ▶	78		
	79	Estimated tax penalty (see instructions) 79			

Third Party Designee

Do you want to allow another person to discuss this return with the IRS (see instructions)? ☐ **Yes.** Complete below. ☐ **No**

Designee's name ▶   Phone no. ▶   Personal identification number (PIN) ▶

Sign Here

Joint return? See instructions. Keep a copy for your records.

Under penalties of perjury, I declare that I have examined this return and accompanying schedules and statements, and to the best of my knowledge and belief, they are true, correct, and complete. Declaration of preparer (other than taxpayer) is based on all information of which preparer has any knowledge.

Your signature	Date	Your occupation	Daytime phone number
		Sales Associate	(555)555-5555
Spouse's signature. If a joint return, **both** must sign.	Date	Spouse's occupation	If the IRS sent you an Identity Protection PIN, enter it here (see inst.)
		Student	

Paid Preparer Use Only

Print/Type preparer's name	Preparer's signature	Date	Check ☐ if self-employed	PTIN
Jane Doe				P00000000

Firm's name ▶ My Tax Service   Firm's EIN ▶ 63-0000000

Firm's address ▶ 100 Main St., Your City, Your State, Your Zip Code   Phone no. (555)555-1111

SCHEDULE EIC (Form 1040A or 1040)	**Earned Income Credit** Qualifying Child Information ▶ Complete and attach to Form 1040A or 1040 only if you have a qualifying child.	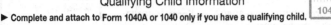	OMB No. 1545-0074 20**14**
Department of the Treasury Internal Revenue Service (99)	▶ Information about Schedule EIC (Form 1040A or 1040) and its instructions is at *www.irs.gov/scheduleeic*.		Attachment Sequence No. **43**

Name(s) shown on return	Your social security number
Byron & Belinda Burrows	094-57-3570

Before you begin:
- See the instructions for Form 1040A, lines 42a and 42b, or Form 1040, lines 66a and 66b, to make sure that **(a)** you can take the EIC, and **(b)** you have a qualifying child.
- Be sure the child's name on line 1 and social security number (SSN) on line 2 agree with the child's social security card. Otherwise, at the time we process your return, we may reduce or disallow your EIC. If the name or SSN on the child's social security card is not correct, call the Social Security Administration at 1-800-772-1213.

⚠ **CAUTION**
- *If you take the EIC even though you are not eligible, you may not be allowed to take the credit for up to 10 years. See the instructions for details.*
- *It will take us longer to process your return and issue your refund if you do not fill in all lines that apply for each qualifying child.*

Qualifying Child Information

		Child 1	**Child 2**	**Child 3**
1	**Child's name** If you have more than three qualifying children, you have to list only three to get the maximum credit.	First name / Last name Beth Burrows	First name / Last name Brian Burrows	First name / Last name
2	**Child's SSN** The child must have an SSN as defined in the instructions for Form 1040A, lines 42a and 42b, or Form 1040, lines 66a and 66b, unless the child was born and died in 2014. If your child was born and died in 2014 and did not have an SSN, enter "Died" on this line and attach a copy of the child's birth certificate, death certificate, or hospital medical records.	662-54-8232	436-24-9433	
3	**Child's year of birth**	Year **1 9 9 9** *If born after 1995 and the child is younger than you (or your spouse, if filing jointly), skip lines 4a and 4b; go to line 5.*	Year **2 0 0 6** *If born after 1995 and the child is younger than you (or your spouse, if filing jointly), skip lines 4a and 4b; go to line 5.*	Year ___ ___ ___ ___ *If born after 1995 and the child is younger than you (or your spouse, if filing jointly), skip lines 4a and 4b; go to line 5.*
4 a	Was the child under age 24 at the end of 2014, a student, and younger than you (or your spouse, if filing jointly)?	☑ **Yes.** ☐ **No.** *Go to line 5.* *Go to line 4b.*	☑ **Yes.** ☐ **No.** *Go to line 5.* *Go to line 4b.*	☐ **Yes.** ☐ **No.** *Go to line 5.* *Go to line 4b.*
b	Was the child permanently and totally disabled during any part of 2014?	☐ **Yes.** ☐ **No.** *Go to line 5.* The child is not a qualifying child.	☐ **Yes.** ☐ **No.** *Go to line 5.* The child is not a qualifying child.	☐ **Yes.** ☐ **No.** *Go to line 5.* The child is not a qualifying child.
5	**Child's relationship to you** (for example, son, daughter, grandchild, niece, nephew, foster child, etc.)	Daughter	Son	
6	**Number of months child lived with you in the United States during 2014** • If the child lived with you for more than half of 2014 but less than 7 months, enter "7." • If the child was born or died in 2014 and your home was the child's home for more than half the time he or she was alive during 2014, enter "12."	**12** months *Do not enter more than 12 months.*	**12** months *Do not enter more than 12 months.*	____ months *Do not enter more than 12 months.*

For Paperwork Reduction Act Notice, see your tax return instructions.　　Cat. No. 13339M　　Schedule EIC (Form 1040A or 1040) 2014

SCHEDULE 8812 (Form 1040A or 1040)	**Child Tax Credit**		OMB No. 1545-0074

SCHEDULE 8812
(Form 1040A or 1040)

Child Tax Credit

▶ Attach to Form 1040, Form 1040A, or Form 1040NR.
▶ Information about Schedule 8812 and its separate instructions is at
www.irs.gov/schedule8812.

Department of the Treasury
Internal Revenue Service (99)

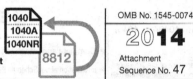

OMB No. 1545-0074

2014

Attachment
Sequence No. 47

Name(s) shown on return

Byron and Belinda Burrows

Your social security number

094-57-3570

Part I   **Filers Who Have Certain Child Dependent(s) with an ITIN (Individual Taxpayer Identification Number)**

⚠ **CAUTION**
Complete this part only for each dependent who has an ITIN and for whom you are claiming the child tax credit.
If your dependent is not a qualifying child for the credit, you cannot include that dependent in the calculation of this credit.

Answer the following questions for each dependent listed on Form 1040, line 6c; Form 1040A, line 6c; or Form 1040NR, line 7c, who has an ITIN (Individual Taxpayer Identification Number) and that you indicated is a qualifying child for the child tax credit by checking column (4) for that dependent.

A   For the first dependent identified with an ITIN and listed as a qualifying child for the child tax credit, did this child meet the substantial presence test? See separate instructions.

☐ Yes   ☐ No

B   For the second dependent identified with an ITIN and listed as a qualifying child for the child tax credit, did this child meet the substantial presence test? See separate instructions.

☐ Yes   ☐ No

C   For the third dependent identified with an ITIN and listed as a qualifying child for the child tax credit, did this child meet the substantial presence test? See separate instructions.

☐ Yes   ☐ No

D   For the fourth dependent identified with an ITIN and listed as a qualifying child for the child tax credit, did this child meet the substantial presence test? See separate instructions.

☐ Yes   ☐ No

Note. If you have more than four dependents identified with an ITIN and listed as a qualifying child for the child tax credit, see the instructions and check here . . . . ▶ ☐

Part II   **Additional Child Tax Credit Filers**

1	**1040 filers:**	Enter the amount from line 6 of your Child Tax Credit Worksheet (see the Instructions for Form 1040, line 52).		
	1040A filers:	Enter the amount from line 6 of your Child Tax Credit Worksheet (see the Instructions for Form 1040A, line 35).	**1**	2,000 00
	1040NR filers:	Enter the amount from line 6 of your Child Tax Credit Worksheet (see the Instructions for Form 1040NR, line 49).		
		If you used Pub. 972, enter the amount from line 8 of the Child Tax Credit Worksheet in the publication.		
2	Enter the amount from Form 1040, line 52; Form 1040A, line 35; or Form 1040NR, line 49	**2**	275 00
3	Subtract line 2 from line 1. If zero, **stop;** you cannot take this credit	**3**	1,725 00
4a	Earned income (see separate instructions) **4a** 46,557 00		
b	Nontaxable combat pay (see separate instructions) **4b**		
5	Is the amount on line 4a more than $3,000?		
	☐ **No.** Leave line 5 blank and enter -0- on line 6.		
	☑ **Yes.** Subtract $3,000 from the amount on line 4a. Enter the result . . . **5** 43,557 00		
6	Multiply the amount on line 5 by 15% (.15) and enter the result	**6**	6,534 00
	Next. Do you have three or more qualifying children?		
	☑ **No.** If line 6 is zero, stop; you cannot take this credit. Otherwise, skip Part III and enter the **smaller** of line 3 or line 6 on line 13.		
	☐ **Yes.** If line 6 is equal to or more than line 3, skip Part III and enter the amount from line 3 on line 13. Otherwise, go to line 7.		

For Paperwork Reduction Act Notice, see your tax return instructions.   Cat. No. 59761M   **Schedule 8812 (Form 1040A or 1040) 2014**

Chapter 9 Exercise

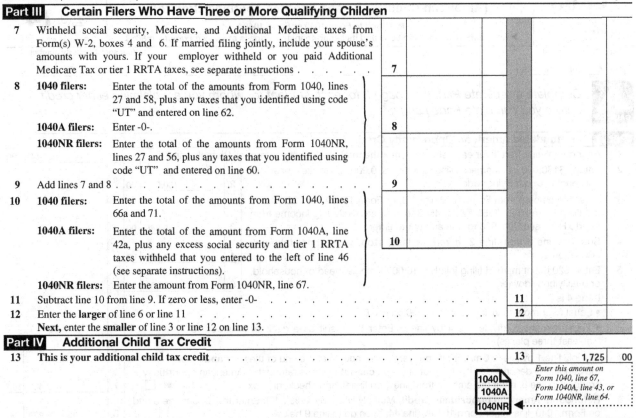

Part III   **Certain Filers Who Have Three or More Qualifying Children**

7   Withheld social security, Medicare, and Additional Medicare taxes from Form(s) W-2, boxes 4 and 6. If married filing jointly, include your spouse's amounts with yours. If your employer withheld or you paid Additional Medicare Tax or tier 1 RRTA taxes, see separate instructions **7**

8   **1040 filers:**   Enter the total of the amounts from Form 1040, lines 27 and 58, plus any taxes that you identified using code "UT" and entered on line 62.

    1040A filers: Enter -0-.   **8**

    1040NR filers: Enter the total of the amounts from Form 1040NR, lines 27 and 56, plus any taxes that you identified using code "UT" and entered on line 60.

9   Add lines 7 and 8 . . . .   **9**

10   **1040 filers:**   Enter the total of the amounts from Form 1040, lines 66a and 71.

    1040A filers: Enter the total of the amount from Form 1040A, line 42a, plus any excess social security and tier 1 RRTA taxes withheld that you entered to the left of line 46 (see separate instructions).   **10**

    1040NR filers: Enter the amount from Form 1040NR, line 67.

11   Subtract line 10 from line 9. If zero or less, enter -0- **11**

12   Enter the **larger** of line 6 or line 11 . . . .   **12**

    Next, enter the **smaller** of line 3 or line 12 on line 13.

Part IV   **Additional Child Tax Credit**

13   **This is your additional child tax credit** **13**   1,725   00

    1040   1040A   1040NR   *Enter this amount on Form 1040, line 67, Form 1040A, line 43, or Form 1040NR, line 64.*

Schedule 8812 (Form 1040A or 1040) 2014

F-51

Form **8863**	**Education Credits**	OMB No. 1545-0074
Department of the Treasury Internal Revenue Service (99)	**(American Opportunity and Lifetime Learning Credits)** ▶ Attach to Form 1040 or Form 1040A. ▶ Information about Form 8863 and its separate instructions is at *www.irs.gov/form8863*.	2014 Attachment Sequence No. **50**

Name(s) shown on return	Your social security number
Byron & Belinda Burrows	094 57 3570

 ! CAUTION | *Complete a separate Part III on page 2 for each student for whom you are claiming either credit before you complete Parts I and II.*

Part I   Refundable American Opportunity Credit

1	After completing Part III for each student, enter the total of all amounts from all Parts III, line 30 .		**1**	2,447 00
2	Enter: $180,000 if married filing jointly; $90,000 if single, head of household, or qualifying widow(er)	**2** 180,000 00		
3	Enter the amount from Form 1040, line 38, or Form 1040A, line 22. If you are filing Form 2555, 2555-EZ, or 4563, or you are excluding income from Puerto Rico, see Pub. 970 for the amount to enter	**3** 45,645 00		
4	Subtract line 3 from line 2. If zero or less, **stop**; you cannot take any education credit	**4** 134,355 00		
5	Enter: $20,000 if married filing jointly; $10,000 if single, head of household, or qualifying widow(er)	**5** 20,000 00		
6	If line 4 is: • Equal to or more than line 5, enter 1.000 on line 6 . . . . . . • Less than line 5, divide line 4 by line 5. Enter the result as a decimal (rounded to at least three places)		**6** 1 . 000	
7	Multiply line 1 by line 6. **Caution:** If you were under age 24 at the end of the year **and** meet the conditions described in the instructions, you **cannot** take the refundable American opportunity credit; skip line 8, enter the amount from line 7 on line 9, and check this box . . . . ▶ ☐		**7**	2,447 00
8	**Refundable American opportunity credit.** Multiply line 7 by 40% (.40). Enter the amount here and on Form 1040, line 68, or Form 1040A, line 44. Then go to line 9 below.		**8**	979 00

Part II   Nonrefundable Education Credits

9	Subtract line 8 from line 7. Enter here and on line 2 of the Credit Limit Worksheet (see instructions)		**9**	1,468 00
10	After completing Part III for each student, enter the total of all amounts from all Parts III, line 31. If zero, skip lines 11 through 17, enter -0- on line 18, and go to line 19		**10**	
11	Enter the smaller of line 10 or $10,000		**11**	
12	Multiply line 11 by 20% (.20)		**12**	
13	Enter: $128,000 if married filing jointly; $64,000 if single, head of household, or qualifying widow(er)	**13**		
14	Enter the amount from Form 1040, line 38, or Form 1040A, line 22. If you are filing Form 2555, 2555-EZ, or 4563, or you are excluding income from Puerto Rico, see Pub. 970 for the amount to enter	**14**		
15	Subtract line 14 from line 13. If zero or less, skip lines 16 and 17, enter -0- on line 18, and go to line 19	**15**		
16	Enter: $20,000 if married filing jointly; $10,000 if single, head of household, or qualifying widow(er)	**16**		
17	If line 15 is: • Equal to or more than line 16, enter 1.000 on line 17 and go to line 18 • Less than line 16, divide line 15 by line 16. Enter the result as a decimal (rounded to at least three places)		**17** .	
18	Multiply line 12 by line 17. Enter here and on line 1 of the Credit Limit Worksheet (see instructions) ▶		**18**	0 00
19	**Nonrefundable education credits.** Enter the amount from line 7 of the Credit Limit Worksheet (see instructions) here and on Form 1040, line 50, or Form 1040A, line 33		**19**	1,468 00

For Paperwork Reduction Act Notice, see your tax return instructions.   Cat. No. 25379M   Form **8863** (2014)

Chapter 9 Exercise

Name(s) shown on return	Your social security number
Byron & Belinda Burrows	094 | 57 | 3570

⚠ **CAUTION**

Complete Part III for each student for whom you are claiming either the American opportunity credit or lifetime learning credit. Use additional copies of Page 2 as needed for each student.

Part III **Student and Educational Institution Information**
See instructions.

20 Student name (as shown on page 1 of your tax return)	21 Student social security number (as shown on page 1 of your tax return)
Belinda Burrows	354 | 57 | 3744

22   Educational institution information (see instructions)

a. Name of first educational institution	**b.** Name of second educational institution (if any)
Sunny University	
(1) Address. Number and street (or P.O. box). City, town or post office, state, and ZIP code. If a foreign address, see instructions.	**(1)** Address. Number and street (or P.O. box). City, town or post office, state, and ZIP code. If a foreign address, see instructions.
300 Sunshine Lane, Your City, Your State, Your Zip Code	
(2) Did the student receive Form 1098-T from this institution for 2014? ☑ Yes ☐ No	**(2)** Did the student receive Form 1098-T from this institution for 2014? ☐ Yes ☐ No
(3) Did the student receive Form 1098-T from this institution for 2013 with Box 2 filled in and Box 7 checked? ☐ Yes ☑ No	**(3)** Did the student receive Form 1098-T from this institution for 2013 with Box 2 filled in and Box 7 checked? ☐ Yes ☐ No
If you checked "No" in **both (2) and (3)**, skip **(4)**.	If you checked "No" in **both (2) and (3)**, skip **(4)**.
(4) If you checked "Yes" in **(2) or (3)**, enter the institution's federal identification number (from Form 1098-T). 6 7 - 7 6 5 4 8 9 1	**(4)** If you checked "Yes" in **(2) or (3)**, enter the institution's federal identification number (from Form 1098-T). __ __ - __ __ __ __ __ __ __

23	Has the Hope Scholarship Credit or American opportunity credit been claimed for this student for any 4 tax years before 2014?	☐ Yes — **Stop!** Go to line 31 for this student.	☑ No — Go to line 24.
24	Was the student enrolled at least half-time for at least one academic period that began or is treated as having begun in 2014 at an eligible educational institution in a program leading towards a postsecondary degree, certificate, or other recognized postsecondary educational credential? (see instructions)	☐ Yes — Go to line 25.	☑ No — **Stop!** Go to line 31 for this student.
25	Did the student complete the first 4 years of post-secondary education before 2014?	☐ Yes — **Stop!** Go to line 31 for this student.	☐ No — Go to line 26.
26	Was the student convicted, before the end of 2014, of a felony for possession or distribution of a controlled substance?	☐ Yes — **Stop!** Go to line 31 for this student.	☐ No — Complete lines 27 through 30 for this student.

⚠ **CAUTION**   *You **cannot** take the American opportunity credit and the lifetime learning credit for the **same student** in the same year. If you complete lines 27 through 30 for this student, do not complete line 31.*

American Opportunity Credit

27	Adjusted qualified education expenses (see instructions). **Do not enter more than $4,000**	27	3,786
28	Subtract $2,000 from line 27. If zero or less, enter -0-.	28	1,786
29	Multiply line 28 by 25% (.25)	29	447
30	If line 28 is zero, enter the amount from line 27. Otherwise, add $2,000 to the amount on line 29 and enter the result. Skip line 31. Include the total of all amounts from all Parts III, line 30 on Part I, line 1 .	30	2,447

Lifetime Learning Credit

31	Adjusted qualified education expenses (see instructions). Include the total of all amounts from all Parts III, line 31, on Part II, line 10	31	

Chapter 9 Exercise

Form 8867

Department of the Treasury
Internal Revenue Service

Paid Preparer's Earned Income Credit Checklist

▶ To be completed by preparer and filed with Form 1040, 1040A, or 1040EZ.
▶ Information about Form 8867 and its separate instructions is at *www.irs.gov/form8867*.

OMB No. 1545-1629

20**14**

Attachment
Sequence No. **177**

Taxpayer name(s) shown on return	Taxpayer's social security number
Byron & Belinda Burrows	094-57-3570

For the definitions of **Qualifying Child** and **Earned Income**, see **Pub. 596**.

Part I   All Taxpayers

1 Enter preparer's name and PTIN ▶ Jane Doe

2 Is the taxpayer's filing status married filing separately? . . . . □ Yes ☑ No

▶ If you checked **"Yes"** on line 2, **stop;** the taxpayer **cannot** take the EIC. Otherwise, continue.

3 Does the taxpayer (and the taxpayer's spouse if filing jointly) have a social security number (SSN) that allows him or her to work and is valid for EIC purposes? See the instructions before answering . . . . . . ☑ Yes □ No

▶ If you checked **"No"** on line 3, **stop;** the taxpayer **cannot** take the EIC. Otherwise, continue.

4 Is the taxpayer (or the taxpayer's spouse if filing jointly) filing Form 2555 or 2555-EZ (relating to the exclusion of foreign earned income)? . . . . □ Yes ☑ No

▶ If you checked **"Yes"** on line 4, **stop;** the taxpayer **cannot** take the EIC. Otherwise, continue.

5a Was the taxpayer (or the taxpayer's spouse) a nonresident alien for any part of 2014? . . . . □ Yes ☑ No

▶ If you checked **"Yes"** on line 5a, go to line 5b. Otherwise, skip line 5b and go to line 6.

b Is the taxpayer's filing status married filing jointly? . . . . ☑ Yes □ No

▶ If you checked **"Yes"** on line 5a and **"No"** on line 5b, **stop;** the taxpayer **cannot** take the EIC. Otherwise, continue.

6 Is the taxpayer's **investment income** more than $3,350? See the instructions before answering. □ Yes ☑ No

▶ If you checked **"Yes"** on line 6, **stop;** the taxpayer **cannot** take the EIC. Otherwise, continue.

7 Could the taxpayer be a **qualifying child** of another person for 2014? If the taxpayer's filing status is married filing jointly, check **"No."** Otherwise, see instructions before answering . . . . □ Yes ☑ No

▶ If you checked **"Yes"** on line 7, **stop;** the taxpayer **cannot** take the EIC. Otherwise, go to Part II or Part III, whichever applies.

For Paperwork Reduction Act Notice, see separate instructions.   Cat. No. 26142H   Form **8867** (2014)

Chapter 9 Exercise

Part II	Taxpayers With a Child			

		Child 1	Child 2	Child 3
	Caution. If there is more than one child, complete lines 8 through 14 for one child before going to the next column.			
8	Child's name	Beth	Brian	
9	Is the child the taxpayer's son, daughter, stepchild, foster child, brother, sister, stepbrother, stepsister, half brother, half sister, or a descendant of any of them?	☑Yes ☐No	☑Yes ☐No	☐Yes ☐No
10	Was the child unmarried at the end of 2014? If the child was married at the end of 2014, see the instructions before answering	☑Yes ☐No	☑Yes ☐No	☐Yes ☐No
11	Did the child live with the taxpayer in the United States for over half of 2014? See the instructions before answering	☑Yes ☐No	☑Yes ☐No	☐Yes ☐No
12	Was the child (at the end of 2014)— • Under age 19 and younger than the taxpayer (or the taxpayer's spouse, if the taxpayer files jointly), • Under age 24, a student (defined in the instructions), and younger than the taxpayer (or the taxpayer's spouse, if the taxpayer files jointly), or • Any age and permanently and totally disabled? . . . . ▶ If you checked **"Yes"** on lines 9, 10, 11, **and** 12, the child is the taxpayer's qualifying child; go to line 13a. If you checked **"No"** on line 9, 10, 11, **or** 12, the child is not the taxpayer's qualifying child; see the instructions for line 12.	☑Yes ☐No	☑Yes ☐No	☐Yes ☐No
13a	Do you or the taxpayer know of another person who could check **"Yes"** on lines 9, 10, 11, **and** 12 for the child? (If the only other person is the taxpayer's spouse, see the instructions before answering.) . . . . ▶ If you checked **"No"** on line 13a, go to line 14. Otherwise, go to line 13b.	☐Yes ☑No	☐Yes ☑No	☐Yes ☐No
b	Enter the child's relationship to the other person(s)			
c	Under the tiebreaker rules, is the child treated as the taxpayer's qualifying child? See the instructions before answering . . . . ▶ If you checked **"Yes"** on line 13c, go to line 14. If you checked **"No,"** the taxpayer **cannot** take the EIC based on this child and cannot take the EIC for taxpayers who do not have a qualifying child. If there is more than one child, see the **Note** at the bottom of this page. If you checked **"Don't know,"** explain to the taxpayer that, under the tiebreaker rules, the taxpayer's EIC and other tax benefits may be disallowed. Then, if the taxpayer wants to take the EIC based on this child, complete lines 14 and 15. If not, and there are no other qualifying children, the taxpayer cannot take the EIC, including the EIC for taxpayers without a qualifying child; do not complete Part III. If there is more than one child, see the **Note** at the bottom of this page.	☐Yes ☐No ☐Don't know	☐Yes ☐No ☐Don't know	☐Yes ☐No ☐Don't know
14	Does the qualifying child have an SSN that allows him or her to work and is valid for EIC purposes? See the instructions before answering . . . . ▶ If you checked **"No"** on line 14, the taxpayer **cannot** take the EIC based on this child and cannot take the EIC available to taxpayers without a qualifying child. If there is more than one child, see the **Note** at the bottom of this page. If you checked "Yes" on line 14, continue.	☑Yes ☐No	☑Yes ☐No	☐Yes ☐No
15	Are the taxpayer's **earned income** and **adjusted gross income** each less than the limit that applies to the taxpayer for 2014? See instructions . . ▶ If you checked **"No"** on line 15, **stop;** the taxpayer **cannot** take the EIC. If you checked **"Yes"** on line 15, the taxpayer can take the EIC. Complete **Schedule EIC** and attach it to the taxpayer's return. If there are two or three qualifying children with valid SSNs, list them on Schedule EIC in the same order as they are listed here. If the taxpayer's EIC was reduced or disallowed for a year after 1996, see Pub. 596 to see if **Form 8862** must be filed. Go to line 20.			☑Yes ☐No

Note. If there is more than one child, complete lines 8 through 14 for the other child(ren) (but for no more than three qualifying children).

Form **8867** (2014)

Form 8867 (2014)   Page **3**

Part III	**Taxpayers Without a Qualifying Child**		

16 Was the taxpayer's main home, and the main home of the taxpayer's spouse if filing jointly, in the United States for more than half the year? (Military personnel on extended active duty outside the United States are considered to be living in the United States during that duty period.) See the instructions before answering. ☐ Yes ☐ No

▶ If you checked **"No"** on line 16, **stop;** the taxpayer **cannot** take the EIC. Otherwise, continue.

17 Was the taxpayer, or the taxpayer's spouse if filing jointly, at least age 25 but under age 65 at the end of 2014? See the instructions before answering . . . . ☐ Yes ☐ No

▶ If you checked **"No"** on line 17, **stop;** the taxpayer **cannot** take the EIC. Otherwise, continue.

18 Is the taxpayer eligible to be claimed as a dependent on anyone else's federal income tax return for 2014? If the taxpayer's filing status is married filing jointly, check **"No"**. . . . . . . ☐ Yes ☐ No

▶ If you checked **"Yes"** on line 18, **stop;** the taxpayer **cannot** take the EIC. Otherwise, continue.

19 Are the taxpayer's **earned income** and **adjusted gross income** each less than the limit that applies to the taxpayer for 2014? See instructions . . . . ☐ Yes ☐ No

▶ If you checked **"No"** on line 19, **stop;** the taxpayer **cannot** take the EIC. If you checked **"Yes"** on line 19, the taxpayer can take the EIC. If the taxpayer's EIC was reduced or disallowed for a year after 1996, see Pub. 596 to find out if **Form 8862** must be filed. Go to line 20.

Part IV	**Due Diligence Requirements**		

20 Did you complete Form 8867 based on current information provided by the taxpayer or reasonably obtained by you? . . . . ☑ Yes ☐ No

21 Did you complete the EIC worksheet found in the Form 1040, 1040A, or 1040EZ instructions (or your own worksheet that provides the same information as the 1040, 1040A, or 1040EZ worksheet)? . . ☑ Yes ☐ No

22 If any qualifying child was not the taxpayer's son or daughter, do you know or did you ask why the parents were not claiming the child? . . . . ☐ Yes ☐ No ☑ Does not apply

23 If the answer to question 13a is **"Yes"** (indicating that the child lived for more than half the year with someone else who could claim the child for the EIC), did you explain the tiebreaker rules and possible consequences of another person claiming your client's qualifying child? . . . . . ☐ Yes ☐ No ☑ Does not apply

24 Did you ask this taxpayer any additional questions that are necessary to meet your knowledge requirement? See the instructions before answering . . . . ☑ Yes ☐ No ☐ Does not apply

To comply with the EIC knowledge requirement, you must not know or have reason to know that any information you used to determine the taxpayer's eligibility for, and the amount of, the EIC is incorrect. You may not ignore the implications of information furnished to you or known by you, and you must make reasonable inquiries if the information furnished to you appears to be incorrect, inconsistent, or incomplete. At the time you make these inquiries, you must document in your files the inquiries you made and the taxpayer's responses.

25 Did you document (a) the taxpayer's answer to question 22 (if applicable), (b) whether you explained the tiebreaker rules to the taxpayer and any additional information you got from the taxpayer as a result, and (c) any additional questions you asked and the taxpayer's answers? . . . . ☐ Yes ☐ No ☑ Does not apply

▶ You have complied with all the due diligence requirements if you:

    1. Completed the actions described on lines 20 and 21 and checked **"Yes"** on those lines,

    2. Completed the actions described on lines 22, 23, 24, and 25 (if they apply) and checked **"Yes"** (or **"Does not apply"**) on those lines,

    3. Submit Form 8867 in the manner required, **and**

    4. Keep all five of the following records for 3 years from the latest of the dates specified in the instructions under *Document Retention*:

      a. Form 8867,

      b. The EIC worksheet(s) or your own worksheet(s),

      c. Copies of any taxpayer documents you relied on to determine eligibility for or amount of EIC,

      d. A record of how, when, and from whom the information used to prepare the form and worksheet(s) was obtained, and

      e. A record of any additional questions you asked and your client's answers.

▶ You have not complied with all the due diligence requirements if you checked **"No"** on line 20, 21, 22, 23, 24, or 25. You may have to pay a $500 penalty for each failure to comply.

Form **8867** (2014)

Chapter 9 Exercise

Part V	Documents Provided to You

26 Identify below any document that the taxpayer provided to you and that you relied on to determine the taxpayer's EIC eligibility. Check all that apply. **Keep a copy of any documents you relied on.** See the instructions before answering. If there is no qualifying child, check box a. If there is no disabled child, check box o.

Residency of Qualifying Child(ren)

- ☐ **a** No qualifying child
- ☐ **b** School records or statement
- ☐ **c** Landlord or property management statement
- ☐ **d** Health care provider statement
- ☐ **e** Medical records
- ☐ **f** Child care provider records
- ☐ **g** Placement agency statement
- ☐ **h** Social service records or statement

- ☐ **i** Place of worship statement
- ☐ **j** Indian tribal official statement
- ☐ **k** Employer statement
- ☐ **l** Other (specify) ▼
- ☑ **m** Did not rely on any documents, but made notes in file
- ☐ **n** Did not rely on any documents

Disability of Qualifying Child(ren)

- ☐ **o** No disabled child
- ☐ **p** Doctor statement
- ☐ **q** Other health care provider statement
- ☐ **r** Social services agency or program statement

- ☐ **s** Other (specify) ▼
- ☐ **t** Did not rely on any documents, but made notes in file
- ☐ **u** Did not rely on any documents

27 If a Schedule C is included with this return, identify below the information that the taxpayer provided to you and that you relied on to prepare the Schedule C. Check all that apply. **Keep a copy of any documents you relied on.** See the instructions before answering. If there is no Schedule C, check box a.

Documents or Other Information

- ☐ **a** No Schedule C
- ☐ **b** Business license
- ☐ **c** Forms 1099
- ☐ **d** Records of gross receipts provided by taxpayer
- ☐ **e** Taxpayer summary of income
- ☐ **f** Records of expenses provided by taxpayer
- ☐ **g** Taxpayer summary of expenses

- ☐ **h** Bank statements
- ☐ **i** Reconstruction of income and expenses
- ☐ **j** Other (specify) ▼
- ☐ **k** Did not rely on any documents, but made notes in file
- ☐ **l** Did not rely on any documents

Form **8867** (2014)

Chapter 9 Exercise

Student Loan Interest Deduction Worksheet—Line 33

Keep for Your Records

Before you begin: ✓ Figure any write-in adjustments to be entered on the dotted line next to line 36 (see the instructions for line 36).
✓ Be sure you have read the **Exception** in the instructions for this line to see if you can use this worksheet instead of Pub. 970 to figure your deduction.

1. Enter the total interest you paid in 2014 on qualified student loans (see the instructions for line 33). **Do not** enter more than $2,500 . . . . **1.** 2,331

2. Enter the amount from Form 1040, line 22 . . . . **2.** 48,000

3. Enter the total of the amounts from Form 1040, lines 23 through 32, plus any write-in adjustments you entered on the dotted line next to line 36 . . . . **3.** 24

4. Subtract line 3 from line 2 . . . . **4.** 47,976

5. Enter the amount shown below for your filing status.
   - Single, head of household, or qualifying widow(er)—$65,000
   - Married filing jointly—$130,000   } **5.** 130,000

6. Is the amount on line 4 more than the amount on line 5?
   - [ ] **No.** Skip lines 6 and 7, enter -0- on line 8, and go to line 9.
   - [ ] **Yes.** Subtract line 5 from line 4 . . . . **6.**

7. Divide line 6 by $15,000 ($30,000 if married filing jointly). Enter the result as a decimal (rounded to at least three places). If the result is 1.000 or more, enter 1.000 . . . . **7.** .

8. Multiply line 1 by line 7 . . . . **8.** 0

9. **Student loan interest deduction.** Subtract line 8 from line 1. Enter the result here and on Form 1040, line 33. **Do not** include this amount in figuring any other deduction on your return (such as on Schedule A, C, E, etc.) **9.** 2,331

F-58

2014 Child Tax Credit Worksheet—Line 52

Keep for Your Records

1. To be a qualifying child for the child tax credit, the child must be your dependent, **under age 17** at the end of 2014, and meet all the conditions in Steps 1 through 3 in the instructions for line 6c. Make sure you checked the box on Form 1040, line 6c, column (4), for each qualifying child.
2. If you do not have a qualifying child, you cannot claim the child tax credit.
3. If your qualifying child has an ITIN instead of an SSN, file Schedule 8812.
4. Do **not** use this worksheet, but use Pub. 972 instead, if:
   a. You are claiming the adoption credit, mortgage interest credit, District of Columbia first-time homebuyer credit, or residential energy efficient property credit,
   b. You are excluding income from Puerto Rico, or
   c. You are filing Form 2555, 2555-EZ, or 4563.

Part 1

1. Number of qualifying children: ___2___ × $1,000. Enter the result. | **1** | 2,000

2. Enter the amount from Form 1040, line 38. | **2** | 45,645

3. Enter the amount shown below for your filing status.
   - Married filing jointly — $110,000
   - Single, head of household, or qualifying widow(er) — $75,000
   - Married filing separately — $55,000

   | **3** | 110,000

4. Is the amount on line 2 more than the amount on line 3?

   ■ **No.** Leave line 4 blank. Enter -0- on line 5, and go to line 6.

   ☐ **Yes.** Subtract line 3 from line 2.
   If the result is not a multiple of $1,000, increase it to the next multiple of $1,000. For example, increase $425 to $1,000, increase $1,025 to $2,000, etc.

   | **4** |

5. Multiply the amount on line 4 by 5% (.05). Enter the result. | **5** | 0

6. Is the amount on line 1 more than the amount on line 5?

   ☐ **No.** (STOP)
   You cannot take the child tax credit on Form 1040, line 52. You also cannot take the additional child tax credit on Form 1040, line 67. Complete the rest of your Form 1040.

   ■ **Yes.** Subtract line 5 from line 1. Enter the result. | **6** | 2,000
   Go to Part 2.

2014 Child Tax Credit Worksheet—*Continued*

 Keep for Your Records

Before you begin Part 2: √ Figure the amount of any credits you are claiming on Form 5695, Part II; Form 8910; Form 8936; or Schedule R.

Part 2

7. Enter the amount from Form 1040, line 47.

| 7 | 1,743 |

8. Add any amounts from:

Form 1040, line 48 _____

Form 1040, line 49 + _____

Form 1040, line 50 + _____ 1,468

Form 1040, line 51 + _____

Form 5695, line 30 + _____

Form 8910, line 15 + _____

Form 8936, line 23 + _____

Schedule R, line 22 + _____

Enter the total.

| 8 | 1,468 |

9. Are the amounts on lines 7 and 8 the same?

☐ **Yes.** (STOP)
You cannot take this credit because there is no tax to reduce. However, you may be able to take the **additional child tax credit.** See the **TIP** below.

■ **No.** Subtract line 8 from line 7.

| 9 | 275 |

10. Is the amount on line 6 more than the amount on line 9?

■ **Yes.** Enter the amount from line 9. Also, you may be able to take the **additional child tax credit.** See the **TIP** below.

☐ **No.** Enter the amount from line 6.

} **This is your child tax credit.**

| 10 | 275 |

Enter this amount on Form 1040, line 52.

1040

 TIP

You may be able to take the **additional child tax credit** on Form 1040, line 67, if you answered "Yes" on line 9 **or** line 10 above.

● First, complete your Form 1040 through lines 66a and 66b.

● Then, use Schedule 8812 to figure any additional child tax credit.

Earned Income Credit Worksheet

1.	Enter the amount from Form 1040, Line 7.	1.	46,557
2.	Taxable Scholarship or Fellowship grant not reported on a W-2, if included on line 7, Form 10..................................... _____		
3.	Amount received for work performed while an inmate in a penal institution (enter "PRI" and the amount subtracted on the dotted line next to Form 1040, line 7), if included on line 7.. _____		
4.	Amount received as a pension or annuity from a nonqualified deferred compensation plan or a nongovernmental Sec. 457 plan. (Enter "DFC" and amount subtracted on the dotted line next to Form 1040, line 7), if included on line 7................... _____		
5.	Add lines 2, 3, and 4.	5.	0
6.	Subtract line 5 from line 1.	6.	46,557
7.	Nontaxable Combat pay if the election is made to use it. You will have to complete two worksheets: one with the combat pay and one without. Use the one that will result in the most EIC.	7.	
8.	Add lines 6 and 7.	8.	46,557
9.	If the taxpayer had any income from self-employment or was a statutory employee, complete lines 10 –18. If not skip lines 10 –18 and go to line 19.		
10.	If the taxpayer is filing a Schedule SE, enter the amount from Schedule SE, Section A, line 3 or Section B, line 3, whichever applies. If the taxpayer is not filing a Schedule SE, skip lines 10 –14 and go to line 15. If the taxpayer is a statutory employee, go to line 18.	10.	
11.	Enter any amounts from Schedule SE, Section B, line 4b, and line 5a.	11.	
12.	Combine lines 10 and 11.	12.	
13.	Enter the amount from Schedule SE, Section A, line 6 or Section B, line 13.	13.	
14.	Subtract line 13 from line 12. If lines 15 and 18 do not apply, enter this amount on line 17 and go to line 19.	14.	
15.	If the taxpayer is not required to file a Schedule SE because the net earnings were less than $400, enter amount from Schedule F, line 36, and from farm partnerships, Schedule K-1 (Form 1065), box 14, code A.	15.	
16.	Enter any net profit or (loss) from Schedule C, line 31; Schedule C-EZ, line 3, Schedule K-1, box 14, code A (other than farming); and Schedule K-1, box 9, code J1.	16.	
17.	Combine lines 14, 15, and 16.	17.	
18.	If the taxpayer is a statutory employee, enter the amount from Schedule C, line 1, or Schedule C-EZ, line 1 that the taxpayer is filing as a statutory employee.	18.	
19.	Add lines 8, 17, and 18. This is the earned income.	19.	46,557
20.	Look up the amount on line 19 above in the EIC Table to find the credit. If the amount is 0, stop. The taxpayer does not qualify for the credit.	20.	550
21.	Enter the amount from Form 1040, line 38. If the amount on line 21 is the same as the amount on line 19, stop and enter the amount from line 20 on line 64a of the Form 1040. This is the taxpayer's Earned Income Credit. If not, go to line 22.	21.	45,645
22.	Is the amount on line 21 less than: • $8,150 ($13,550 if MFJ) if the taxpayer has no qualifying children? • $17,850 ($23,300 if MFJ) if the taxpayer has one or more qualifying children? If the answer is yes, stop and enter the amount from line 21 on the Form 1040, line 66a. If the answer is no, look up the amount from line 21 in the EIC Table to find the credit and go to line 23.	22.	750
23.	Look at the amounts on line 20 and 22. Enter the smaller amount here and on Form 1040, line 66a.	23.	550

Adjusted Qualified Education Expenses Worksheet

See *Qualified Education Expenses*, earlier, before completing.

Complete a separate worksheet for each student for each academic period beginning or treated as beginning (see below) in 2014 for which you paid (or are treated as having paid) qualified education expenses in 2014.

1.	Total qualified education expenses paid for or on behalf of the student in 2014 for the academic period	3,786
2.	Less adjustments:	
a.	Tax-free educational assistance received in 2014 allocable to the academic period	
b.	Tax-free educational assistance received in 2015 (and before you file your 2014 tax return) allocable to the academic period . . .	
c.	Refunds of qualified education expenses paid in 2014 if the refund is received in 2014 or in 2015 before you file your 2014 tax return	
3.	Total adjustments (add lines 2a, 2b, and 2c)	
4.	Adjusted qualified education expenses. Subtract line 3 from line 1. If zero or less, enter -0-	3,768

Credit Limit Worksheet

Complete this worksheet to figure the amount to enter on line 19.

1.	Enter the amount from Form 8863, line 18 . . . . 1.	0
2.	Enter the amount from Form 8863, line 9 . . . . 2.	1,468
3.	Add lines 1 and 2 . . . . 3.	1,468
4.	Enter the amount from: Form 1040, line 47; or Form 1040A, line 30 . . . . 4.	1,743
5.	Enter the total of your credits from either: Form 1040, lines 48 and 49, and Schedule R, line 22; or Form 1040A, lines 31 and 32 . . . . . . 5.	0
6.	Subtract line 5 from line 4 . . . . 6.	1,743
7.	Enter the smaller of line 3 or line 6 here and on Form 8863, line 19 . . . . 7.	1,468

Chapter 10 Review

1) If the taxpayer doesn't have Minimum Essential Coverage, what are the consequences?

   The taxpayer must pay the Individual Shared Responsibility Payment.

2) In order for the taxpayer to be considered as having Minimum Essential Coverage for an entire month, they must have been covered for **at least one day during the month**.

3) What form will the taxpayer file to claim an exemption to the Shared Responsibility Payment?

   Form 8965 must be filed to claim an exemption from the Individual Shared Responsibility Payment.

4) A gap in coverage of less than three months is what?

   A short term coverage gap is a gap in coverage of less than three consecutive months.

5) The Individual Shared Responsibility Payment is capped at the national average premium for what plan?

   The Individual Shared Responsibility Payment is capped at the national average premium for a bronze level health plan.

6) Is the Premium Tax Credit refundable or nonrefundable?

   The Premium Tax Credit is a refundable credit.

7) The taxpayer is required to file a return if they qualify for the **Premium Tax Credit**.

8) Individuals and families qualify for the Premium Tax Credit if their income is between 100% and 400% of what?

   Individuals and families qualify for the Premium Tax Credit if their income is between 100% and 400% of the Federal Poverty Line.

9) What changes in circumstances should be reported to the Marketplace?

The following changes could affect the amount of the taxpayer's allowable Premium Tax Credit:
- **Increases or decreases in household income.**
- **Marriage.**
- **Divorce.**
- **Birth or adoption of a child.**
- **Other changes to their household composition.**
- **Gaining or losing eligibility for government sponsored or employer sponsored health care coverage.**

10) The taxpayer is not eligible for Premium Tax Credit if filing Married Filing Separately, unless what?

If the taxpayer files a Married Filing Separate return, they are not eligible for the Premium Tax Credit unless they are a victim of domestic abuse or abandonment.

11) Employers subject to the shared responsibility provisions sponsoring self-insured group health plans will be required to file what form?

Employers subject to the shared responsibility provisions sponsoring self-insured group health plans will be required to file Form 1095C beginning in 2016.

12) Health Coverage Exemptions can be claimed using what form?

Health Coverage Exemptions can be claimed by filing Form 8965.

13) What are the three hardship exemptions the taxpayer can obtain through the IRS?

The three hardship exemptions the taxpayer can obtain through the IRS are the following:
- **Their gross income is below the filing threshold.**
- **Two or more family members' aggregate cost of self-only employer-sponsored coverage exceeds 8% of household income, as does the cost of any available employer-sponsored coverage for the entire family.**
- **The taxpayer purchased insurance through the Marketplace during the initial enrollment period but have a coverage gap at the beginning of 2014.**

14) Name the five different levels of coverage available through the Marketplace.

The five different levels of coverage available through the Marketplace are Bronze, Silver, Gold, Platinum, and Catastrophic.

15) Using the answers to the previous question, what percentage of healthcare costs does each level pay?

- **Bronze – Pays about 60% of healthcare costs**
- **Silver – Pays about 70% of healthcare costs**
- **Gold – Pays about 80% of healthcare costs**
- **Platinum – Pays about 90% of healthcare costs**
- **Catastrophic – Available only to people under 30 or people with a hardship exemption. This plan will pay less than 60% of healthcare costs and is designed to protect the individual from very high medical costs.**

Shared Responsibility Payment Worksheet

If you or another member of your tax household had neither minimum essential coverage nor a coverage exemption for any month during 2014, use the Shared Responsibility Payment Worksheet, below, to figure your shared responsibility payment. You will enter the amount from line 14 of the worksheet on Form 1040, line 61; Form 1040A, line 38; or Form 1040EZ, line 11.

Complete the monthly columns by placing "X's" in each month in which you or another member of your tax household had neither minimum essential coverage nor a coverage exemption.

Name	Jan	Feb	Mar	Apr	May	Jun	Jul	Aug	Sep	Oct	Nov	Dec
Clark				✓	✓	✓	✓	✓	✓	✓	✓	✓
Catherine	✓	✓	✓	✓	✓	✓	✓	✓	✓	✓	✓	✓

	Jan	Feb	Mar	Apr	May	Jun	Jul	Aug	Sep	Oct	Nov	Dec
1. Total number of X's in a month. If 5 or more, enter 5	1	1	1	2	2	2	2	2	2	2	2	2
2. Total number of X's in a month for individuals 18 or over*	1	1	1	2	2	2	2	2	2	2	2	2
3. One-half the number of X's in a month for individuals under 18*												
4. Add lines 2 and 3 for each month ...	1	1	1	2	2	2	2	2	2	2	2	2
5. Multiply line 4 by $95 for each month. If $285 or more, enter $285	95	95	95	190	190	190	190	190	190	190	190	190

6. Sum of the monthly amounts entered on line 1	21
7. Enter your household income (see *Household income*, earlier)	54,322
8. Enter your filing threshold (see *Filing Thresholds For Most People*, later)	20,300
9. Subtract line 8 from line 7	34,022
10. Multiply line 9 by 1% (.01)	340.22
11. Is line 10 more than $285? ☑ **Yes.** Multiply line 10 by the number of months for which line 1 is more than zero ☐ **No.** Enter the amount from line 14 of the Flat Dollar Amount Worksheet	4,082.64
12. Divide line 11 by 12.0	340.22
13. Multiply line 6 by $204**	4,284
14. Enter the smaller of line 12 or line 13 here and on Form 1040, line 61; Form 1040A, line 38; or Form 1040EZ, line 11. This is your shared responsibility payment	340

*For purposes of figuring the shared responsibility payment, an individual is considered under 18 for an entire month if he or she did not turn 18 before the first day of the month. An individual turns 18 on the anniversary of the day the individual was born. For example, someone born on March 1, 1999, is considered age 18 on March 1, 2017, and, therefore, is not considered age 18 for purposes of the shared responsibility payment until April 2017.

**$204 is the 2014 national average premium for a bronze level health plan available through the Marketplace for one individual and should not be changed.

Chapter 11 Review

1) What floor are the medical expenses subject to?

   Only the part of the medical and dental expenses that exceed 10% of the adjusted gross income are deductible (7.5% if age 65 or over at the end of the tax year).

2) What is the standard rate for medical mileage?

   The standard rate for medical mileage is 23.5 cents per mile for 2014.

3) Joanne renews her car tag in November. She paid $78 in taxes and a tag fee of $29. What is her personal property tax deduction?

   Joanne's personal property tax deduction is $78.

4) For how many houses may the taxpayer deduct mortgage interest?

   Deductible mortgage interest can be on a main home and/ or a second home.

5) Are loan origination fees deductible?

   Loan origination fees are deductible.

6) What is the standard mileage rate for volunteer mileage?

   The standard mileage rate for volunteer mileage is 14 cents per mile.

7) When is a Form 8283 needed?

   If the taxpayer is deducting more than $500 of other than cash or check contributions, a Form 8283 must be filed with the tax return.

8) Are gambling losses deductible?

   Gambling losses to the extent of winnings reported on Form 1040, line 21, are deductible.

9) What are the differences for claiming a casualty and theft loss in a federally declared disaster area?

If the casualty and theft loss is in a Presidential declared disaster area, the taxpayer can elect to deduct the loss in the tax year immediately prior to the tax year in which the disaster occurred, or in the year of the disaster.

| SCHEDULE A
(Form 1040)

Department of the Treasury
Internal Revenue Service (99) | Itemized Deductions

► Information about Schedule A and its separate instructions is at *www.irs.gov/schedulea*.
► Attach to Form 1040. | OMB No. 1545-0074
2014
Attachment
Sequence No. 07 |

Name(s) shown on Form 1040 — Lloyd and Lynn Landon

Your social security number — 555-44-6666

Medical and Dental Expenses

Caution. Do not include expenses reimbursed or paid by others.

1	Medical and dental expenses (see instructions)	**1** 1,619 00
2	Enter amount from Form 1040, line 38 **2** 309,000 00	
3	Multiply line 2 by 10% (.10). But if either you or your spouse was born before January 2, 1950, multiply line 2 by 7.5% (.075) instead	**3** 30,900 00
4	Subtract line 3 from line 1. If line 3 is more than line 1, enter -0-	**4** 0 00

Taxes You Paid

5	State and local (check only one box): a ☑ Income taxes, or b ☐ General sales taxes	**5** 4,566 00
6	Real estate taxes (see instructions)	**6** 544 00
7	Personal property taxes	**7**
8	Other taxes. List type and amount ► _____	**8**
9	Add lines 5 through 8	**9** 5,110 00

Interest You Paid

Note. Your mortgage interest deduction may be limited (see instructions).

10	Home mortgage interest and points reported to you on Form 1098	**10** 9,987 00
11	Home mortgage interest not reported to you on Form 1098. If paid to the person from whom you bought the home, see instructions and show that person's name, identifying no., and address ►	**11**
12	Points not reported to you on Form 1098. See instructions for special rules	**12**
13	Mortgage insurance premiums (see instructions)	**13**
14	Investment interest. Attach Form 4952 if required. (See instructions.)	**14**
15	Add lines 10 through 14	**15** 9,987 00

Gifts to Charity

If you made a gift and got a benefit for it, see instructions.

16	Gifts by cash or check. If you made any gift of $250 or more, see instructions	**16** 2,329 00
17	Other than by cash or check. If any gift of $250 or more, see instructions. You **must** attach Form 8283 if over $500	**17**
18	Carryover from prior year	**18**
19	Add lines 16 through 18	**19** 2,329 00

Casualty and Theft Losses

20	Casualty or theft loss(es). Attach Form 4684. (See instructions.)	**20**

Job Expenses and Certain Miscellaneous Deductions

21	Unreimbursed employee expenses—job travel, union dues, job education, etc. Attach Form 2106 or 2106-EZ if required. (See instructions.) ►	**21**
22	Tax preparation fees	**22**
23	Other expenses—investment, safe deposit box, etc. List type and amount ►	**23**
24	Add lines 21 through 23	**24**
25	Enter amount from Form 1040, line 38 **25**	
26	Multiply line 25 by 2% (.02)	**26**
27	Subtract line 26 from line 24. If line 26 is more than line 24, enter -0-	**27**

Other Miscellaneous Deductions

28	Other—from list in instructions. List type and amount ► _____	**28**

Total Itemized Deductions

29	Is Form 1040, line 38, over $152,525? ☐ No. Your deduction is not limited. Add the amounts in the far right column for lines 4 through 28. Also, enter this amount on Form 1040, line 40. ☑ Yes. Your deduction may be limited. See the Itemized Deductions Worksheet in the instructions to figure the amount to enter.	**29** 17,307 00
30	If you elect to itemize deductions even though they are less than your standard deduction, check here ► ☐	

For Paperwork Reduction Act Notice, see Form 1040 instructions.   Cat. No. 17145C   Schedule A (Form 1040) 2014

Itemized Deductions Worksheet—Line 29

1.	Enter the total of the amounts from Schedule A, lines 4, 9, 15, 19, 20, 27, and 28	**1.** 17,426
2.	Enter the total of the amount from Schedule A, lines 4, 14, and 20, plus any gambling and casualty or theft losses included on line 28	**2.** 0

> ⚠️ **CAUTION** Be sure your total gambling and casualty or theft losses are clearly identified on the dotted lines next to line 28.

3. Is the amount on line 2 less than the amount on line 1?

   ☐ **No.** 🛑 Your deduction is not limited. Enter the amount from line 1 of this worksheet on Schedule A, line 29. **Do not** complete the rest of this worksheet.

   ☑ **Yes.** Subtract line 2 from line 1 . . . . **3.** 17,426

4.	Multiply line 3 by 80% (.80)	**4.** 13,941
5.	Enter the amount from Form 1040, line 38	**5.** 309,000
6.	Enter $305,050 if married filing jointly or qualifying widow(er); $279,650 if head of household; $254,200 if single; or $152,525 if married filing separately	**6.** 305,050

7. Is the amount on line 6 less than the amount on line 5?

   ☐ **No.** 🛑 Your deduction is not limited. Enter the amount from line 1 of this worksheet on Schedule A, line 29. **Do not** complete the rest of this worksheet.

   ☑ **Yes.** Subtract line 6 from line 5 . . . . **7.** 3,950

8.	Multiply line 7 by 3% (.03)	**8.** 119
9.	Enter the **smaller** of line 4 or line 8	**9.** 119
10.	**Total itemized deductions.** Subtract line 9 from line 1. Enter the result here and on Schedule A, line 29	**10.** 17,307

Chapter 11 Review

1) What employee business expenses require the use of a Form 2106?

   If the taxpayer is claiming any travel, transportation, meal, or entertainment expenses or receives a reimbursement, a Form 2106 must be filed.

2) How long does a temporary assignment last?

   A temporary assignment is one that is realistically expected to last (and does last) for one year or less.

3) Define bona fide business purpose.

   A bona fide business purpose exists if the taxpayer can prove a real business purpose for the individual's presence.

4) What is the limitation on deductible meals?

   The deduction for meals is limited to 50% of the cost or standard meal allowance. If the taxpayer is subject to the Department of Transportation's "hours of service" limits, the deduction is limited to 80%.

5) What is the federal meal and incidental expense allowance?

   The federal M&IE rate is $46 per day for travel within the United States for 2014.

6) How much of the federal allowance is for incidental expense?

   The standard amount for incidental expense is $5 per day.

7) What is the limitation for business gifts?

   The taxpayer may deduct up to $25 for business gifts given to each person during the tax year.

8) What is the standard mileage rate?

   For tax year 2014, the standard mileage rate is 56 cents per mile.

SCHEDULE A (Form 1040)	Itemized Deductions	OMB No. 1545-0074
Department of the Treasury Internal Revenue Service (99)	▶ Information about Schedule A and its separate instructions is at *www.irs.gov/schedulea*. ▶ Attach to Form 1040.	2014 Attachment Sequence No. 07

Name(s) shown on Form 1040
Harry Henderson

Your social security number
243-52-1656

Medical and Dental Expenses		**Caution.** Do not include expenses reimbursed or paid by others.		
	1	Medical and dental expenses (see instructions)	**1**	
	2	Enter amount from Form 1040, line 38 **2**		
	3	Multiply line 2 by 10% (.10). But if either you or your spouse was born before January 2, 1950, multiply line 2 by 7.5% (.075) instead	**3**	
	4	Subtract line 3 from line 1. If line 3 is more than line 1, enter -0-	**4**	
Taxes You Paid	5	State and local (check only one box):		
		a ☑ Income taxes, **or**	**5**	1,553 00
		b ☐ General sales taxes		
	6	Real estate taxes (see instructions)	**6**	
	7	Personal property taxes	**7**	23 00
	8	Other taxes. List type and amount ▶ _____	**8**	
	9	Add lines 5 through 8	**9**	1,576 00
Interest You Paid	10	Home mortgage interest and points reported to you on Form 1098	**10**	
	11	Home mortgage interest not reported to you on Form 1098. If paid to the person from whom you bought the home, see instructions and show that person's name, identifying no., and address ▶ _____	**11**	
Note. Your mortgage interest deduction may be limited (see instructions).	12	Points not reported to you on Form 1098. See instructions for special rules	**12**	
	13	Mortgage insurance premiums (see instructions)	**13**	
	14	Investment interest. Attach Form 4952 if required. (See instructions.)	**14**	
	15	Add lines 10 through 14	**15**	
Gifts to Charity	16	Gifts by cash or check. If you made any gift of $250 or more, see instructions	**16**	2,550 00
If you made a gift and got a benefit for it, see instructions.	17	Other than by cash or check. If any gift of $250 or more, see instructions. You **must** attach Form 8283 if over $500 . . .	**17**	
	18	Carryover from prior year	**18**	
	19	Add lines 16 through 18	**19**	2,550 00
Casualty and Theft Losses	20	Casualty or theft loss(es). Attach Form 4684. (See instructions.)	**20**	
Job Expenses and Certain Miscellaneous Deductions	21	Unreimbursed employee expenses—job travel, union dues, job education, etc. Attach Form 2106 or 2106-EZ if required. (See instructions.) ▶ Form 2106	**21**	14,102 00
	22	Tax preparation fees	**22**	
	23	Other expenses—investment, safe deposit box, etc. List type and amount ▶ _____	**23**	
	24	Add lines 21 through 23	**24**	14,102 00
	25	Enter amount from Form 1040, line 38 **25** 35,300 00		
	26	Multiply line 25 by 2% (.02)	**26**	706 00
	27	Subtract line 26 from line 24. If line 26 is more than line 24, enter -0-	**27**	13,396 00
Other Miscellaneous Deductions	28	Other—from list in instructions. List type and amount ▶ _____	**28**	
Total Itemized Deductions	29	Is Form 1040, line 38, over $152,525?		
		☑ **No.** Your deduction is not limited. Add the amounts in the far right column for lines 4 through 28. Also, enter this amount on Form 1040, line 40.	**29**	17,522 00
		☐ **Yes.** Your deduction may be limited. See the Itemized Deductions Worksheet in the instructions to figure the amount to enter.		
	30	If you elect to itemize deductions even though they are less than your standard deduction, check here . . . . ▶ ☐		

For Paperwork Reduction Act Notice, see Form 1040 instructions.   Cat. No. 17145C   Schedule A (Form 1040) 2014

Form **2106**	**Employee Business Expenses**	OMB No. 1545-0074
Department of the Treasury Internal Revenue Service (99)	▶ Attach to Form 1040 or Form 1040NR. ▶ Information about Form 2106 and its separate instructions is available at *www.irs.gov/form2106*.	20**14** Attachment Sequence No. **129**

Your name	Occupation in which you incurred expenses	Social security number
Harry Henderson	Sales	243 : 52 : 1656

Part I   **Employee Business Expenses and Reimbursements**

Step 1   Enter Your Expenses

		Column A Other Than Meals and Entertainment		Column B Meals and Entertainment	
1	Vehicle expense from line 22 or line 29. (Rural mail carriers: See instructions.)	**1**	11,816	00		
2	Parking fees, tolls, and transportation, including train, bus, etc., that **did not** involve overnight travel or commuting to and from work .	**2**	291	00		
3	Travel expense while away from home overnight, including lodging, airplane, car rental, etc. **Do not** include meals and entertainment .	**3**	1,313	00		
4	Business expenses not included on lines 1 through 3. **Do not** include meals and entertainment	**4**	560	00		
5	Meals and entertainment expenses (see instructions)	**5**			243	00
6	**Total expenses.** In Column A, add lines 1 through 4 and enter the result. In Column B, enter the amount from line 5	**6**	13,980	00	243	00

    Note. *If you were not reimbursed for any expenses in Step 1, skip line 7 and enter the amount from line 6 on line 8.*

Step 2   Enter Reimbursements Received From Your Employer for Expenses Listed in Step 1

7	Enter reimbursements received from your employer that were **not** reported to you in box 1 of Form W-2. Include any reimbursements reported under code "L" in box 12 of your Form W-2 (see instructions).	**7**				

Step 3   Figure Expenses To Deduct on Schedule A (Form 1040 or Form 1040NR)

8	Subtract line 7 from line 6. If zero or less, enter -0-. However, if line 7 is greater than line 6 in Column A, report the excess as income on Form 1040, line 7 (or on Form 1040NR, line 8)	**8**	13,980	00	243	00
	Note. *If **both columns** of line 8 are zero, you cannot deduct employee business expenses. Stop here and attach Form 2106 to your return.*					
9	In Column A, enter the amount from line 8. In Column B, multiply line 8 by 50% (.50). (Employees subject to Department of Transportation (DOT) hours of service limits: Multiply meal expenses incurred while away from home on business by 80% (.80) instead of 50%. For details, see instructions.)	**9**	13,980	00	122	00
10	Add the amounts on line 9 of both columns and enter the total here. **Also, enter the total on Schedule A (Form 1040), line 21** (or on **Schedule A (Form 1040NR), line 7**). (Armed Forces reservists, qualified performing artists, fee-basis state or local government officials, and individuals with disabilities: See the instructions for special rules on where to enter the total.) . . . . . . ▶	**10**			14,102	00

For Paperwork Reduction Act Notice, see your tax return instructions.   Cat. No. 11700N   Form **2106** (2014)

Chapter 12 Exercise

Part II Vehicle Expenses

Section A—General Information (You must complete this section if you are claiming vehicle expenses.)

			(a) Vehicle 1	(b) Vehicle 2
11	Enter the date the vehicle was placed in service	11	03 / 01 / 2014	/ /
12	Total miles the vehicle was driven during 2014	12	26,540 miles	miles
13	Business miles included on line 12	13	21,100 miles	miles
14	Percent of business use. Divide line 13 by line 12	14	79.50 %	%
15	Average daily roundtrip commuting distance	15	4 miles	miles
16	Commuting miles included on line 12	16	1,120 miles	miles
17	Other miles. Add lines 13 and 16 and subtract the total from line 12	17	4,320 miles	miles
18	Was your vehicle available for personal use during off-duty hours?		☑ Yes ☐ No	
19	Do you (or your spouse) have another vehicle available for personal use?		☐ Yes ☑ No	
20	Do you have evidence to support your deduction?		☑ Yes ☐ No	
21	If "Yes," is the evidence written?		☑ Yes ☐ No	

Section B—Standard Mileage Rate (See the instructions for Part II to find out whether to complete this section or Section C.)

22	Multiply line 13 by 56¢ (.56). Enter the result here and on line 1	22	11,816 00

Section C—Actual Expenses

			(a) Vehicle 1	(b) Vehicle 2
23	Gasoline, oil, repairs, vehicle insurance, etc.	23		
24a	Vehicle rentals	24a		
b	Inclusion amount (see instructions)	24b		
c	Subtract line 24b from line 24a	24c		
25	Value of employer-provided vehicle (applies only if 100% of annual lease value was included on Form W-2—see instructions)	25		
26	Add lines 23, 24c, and 25	26		
27	Multiply line 26 by the percentage on line 14	27		
28	Depreciation (see instructions)	28		
29	Add lines 27 and 28. Enter total here and on line 1	29		

Section D—Depreciation of Vehicles (Use this section only if you owned the vehicle and are completing Section C for the vehicle.)

			(a) Vehicle 1	(b) Vehicle 2
30	Enter cost or other basis (see instructions)	30		
31	Enter section 179 deduction (see instructions)	31		
32	Multiply line 30 by line 14 (see instructions if you claimed the section 179 deduction)	32		
33	Enter depreciation method and percentage (see instructions)	33		
34	Multiply line 32 by the percentage on line 33 (see instructions)	34		
35	Add lines 31 and 34	35		
36	Enter the applicable limit explained in the line 36 instructions	36		
37	Multiply line 36 by the percentage on line 14	37		
38	Enter the **smaller** of line 35 or line 37. If you skipped lines 36 and 37, enter the amount from line 35. Also enter this amount on line 28 above	38		

Form **2106** (2014)

Worksheet To Figure the Deduction for Business Use of Your Home

PART 1—Part of Your Home Used for Business:

1) Area of home used for business .... 1) ___112___
2) Total area of home .... 2) __1,600__
3) Percentage of home used for business (divide line 1 by line 2 and show result as percentage) ..... 3) ___7___ %

PART 2—Figure Your Allowable Deduction

4) Gross income from business (see instructions) .... 4) __35,300__

	(a) Direct Expenses	(b) Indirect Expenses	
5) Casualty losses	5)		**Enter lines**
6) Deductible mortgage interest and qualified mortgage insurance premiums	6)		**5-7 in full here and**
7) Real estate taxes	7)		**on**
8) Total of lines 5 through 7	8)		**Schedule A.**

9) Multiply line 8, column (b), by line 3 .... 9) _____
10) Add line 8, column (a), and line 9 .... 10) _____
11) Business expenses not from business use of home (see instructions) .... 11) __13,542__
12) Add lines 10 and 11 .... 12) __13,542__
13) Deduction limit. Subtract line 12 from line 4 .... 13) __21,758__

	(a) Direct Expenses	(b) Indirect Expenses
14) Excess mortgage interest and qualified mortgage insurance premiums	14)	
15) Insurance	15)	1,200
16) Rent	16)	4,800
17) Repairs and maintenance	17) 48	
18) Utilities	18)	1,280
19) Other expenses	19)	
20) Add lines 14 through 19	20) 48	7,280

21) Multiply line 20, column (b) by line 3 .... 21) 510
22) Carryover of operating expenses from prior year (see instructions) .... 22) _____
23) Add line 20, column (a), line 21, and line 22 .... 23) __558__
24) Allowable operating expenses. Enter the **smaller** of line 13 or line 23 .... 24) __558__
25) Limit on excess casualty losses and depreciation. Subtract line 24 from line 13 .... 25) _____
26) Excess casualty losses (see instructions) .... 26) _____
27) Depreciation of your home from line 39 below .... 27) _____
28) Carryover of excess casualty losses and depreciation from prior year (see instructions) .... 28) _____
29) Add lines 26 through 28 .... 29) __0__
30) Allowable excess casualty losses and depreciation. Enter the **smaller** of line 25 or line 29 .... 30) __0__
31) Add lines 24 and 30 .... 31) __558__
32) Casualty losses included on lines 10 and 30 (see instructions) .... 32) _____
33) Allowable expenses for business use of your home. (Subtract line 32 from line 31.) See instructions for where to enter on your return .... 33) __558__

PART 3—Depreciation of Your Home

34) Smaller of adjusted basis or fair market value of home (see instructions) .... 34) _____
35) Basis of land .... 35) _____
36) Basis of building (subtract line 35 from line 34) .... 36) _____
37) Business basis of building (multiply line 36 by line 3) .... 37) _____
38) Depreciation percentage (from applicable table or method) .... 38) _____ %
39) Depreciation allowable (multiply line 37 by line 38) .... 39) _____

PART 4—Carryover of Unallowed Expenses to Next Year

40) Operating expenses. Subtract line 24 from line 23. If less than zero, enter -0- .... 40) _____
41) Excess casualty losses and depreciation. Subtract line 30 from line 29. If less than zero, enter -0- .... 41) _____

Simplified Method Worksheet

1.	Enter the amount of the gross income limitation. See Instructions for the Simplified Method Worksheet .... 1.	21,758
2.	Allowable square footage for the qualified business use. Do not enter more than 300 square feet. See Instructions for the Simplified Method Worksheet .... 2.	112
3.	Simplified method amount	
	a. Maximum allowable amount .... 3a.	$5
	b. For daycare facilities not used exclusively for business, enter the decimal amount from the Daycare Facility Worksheet; otherwise, enter 1.0 .... 3b.	1.0
	c. Multiply line 3a by line 3b and enter result to 2 decimal places .... 3c.	5.00
4.	Multiply line 2 by line 3c .... 4.	560
5.	**Allowable expenses using the simplified method.** Enter the smaller of line 1 or line 4. If zero or less, enter -0-. See _Where To Deduct_, earlier, for where to enter this amount on your return .... 5.	560
6.	**Carryover of unallowed expenses from 2013 that are not allowed in 2014.**	
	a. Operating expenses. Enter the amount, if any, from your 2013 Worksheet To Figure the Deduction for Business Use of Your Home, line 40 .... 6a.	
	b. Excess casualty losses and depreciation. Enter the amount, if any, from your 2013 Worksheet To Figure the Deduction for Business Use of Your Home, line 41 .... 6b.	

Chapter 13 Review

1) Is a filing cabinet personal property or real property?

   A filing cabinet is personal property.

2) Is an office building personal or real property?

   An office building is real property.

3) Define tangible property.

   Tangible property has physical substance and its value is intrinsic.

4) What is the recovery period for a computer?

   The recovery period for a computer is 5 years.

5) What is the recovery period for a taxi cab?

   The recovery period for a taxi cab is 5 years.

6) What is the recovery period for safe?

   The recovery period for a safe is 7 years.

7) What is the recovery period for an office building?

   The recovery period for an office building is 39 years.

8) Which table should be used to depreciate the computer if using the HY convention?

   Table A should be used to depreciate the computer.

9) Which table should be used to depreciate the safe if the safe was purchased in February and the convention is MQ?

   Table D should be used to depreciate the safe.

10) Which table should be used for the office building if it was purchased in January of 2004?

Table I should be used for the office building.

11) What is the percentage of depreciation for the office building in the previous question?

The percentage of depreciation for the office building is 2.564%

Description of Property	Date Placed in Service	Cost or other Basis	Business/ Investment Use %	Business Basis (C x D)	Salvage/ Land Value	Section 179 Deduction or Bonus Depreciation	Depreciation Basis [E − (F + G)]	Method/ Convention	Recovery Period	Prior Depreciation	Depreciation Percentage	Depreciation Deduction (H x L)
A	B	C	D	E	F	G	H	I	J	K	L	M
Rental House	10/2005	$27,500	100%	$27,500	$10,000		$17,500	SL MM	27.5 yrs	$5,221	3.636%	$636
Computer	07/05/12	1,309	100%	1,309			1,309	200%DB HY	5 yrs	681	19.20%	251
Copy Machine	08/07/14	599	100%	599			599	200%DB HY	5 yrs	0	20%	120
Heavy Gen. Purp. Truck	03/19/13	17,289	100%	17,289			17,289	200%DB HY	5 yrs	3,458	32%	5,532
Sofa	06/23/10	921	100%	921			921	200%DB HY	5 yrs	762	11.52%	106
Refrigerator	02/03/13	1,126	100%	1,126			1,126	200%DB HY	5 yrs	225	32%	360

Chapter 14 Review

1) What is the section 179 general limitation?

   The section 179 deduction is limited to $500,000.

2) What part of Form 4562 is needed to take the section 179 deduction?

   Part I of the Form 4562 will be used to take the section 179 deduction.

3) What are the four requirements property must meet to qualify for the section 179 deduction?

   To qualify for the deduction the property must meet the following requirements:

   - **It must be eligible property,**
   - **It must be acquired for business use,**
   - **It must have been acquired by purchase, and**
   - **It must not be property that does not qualify**

4) Which property is eligible for section 179: tangible or intangible?

   Tangible property is eligible for section 179.

5) What part of the Form 4562 is needed to depreciate listed property?

   Part V of the Form 4562 is needed to depreciate listed property.

Form **4562**

Department of the Treasury
Internal Revenue Service (99)

Depreciation and Amortization
(Including Information on Listed Property)
▶ Attach to your tax return.
▶ Information about Form 4562 and its separate instructions is at *www.irs.gov/form4562.*

OMB No. 1545-0172

20**14**

Attachment
Sequence No. **179**

Name(s) shown on return	Business or activity to which this form relates	Identifying number
John McClain	Farming	857-55-3344

Part I Election To Expense Certain Property Under Section 179
Note: *If you have any listed property, complete Part V before you complete Part I.*

1	Maximum amount (see instructions)	**1**	
2	Total cost of section 179 property placed in service (see instructions)	**2**	
3	Threshold cost of section 179 property before reduction in limitation (see instructions)	**3**	
4	Reduction in limitation. Subtract line 3 from line 2. If zero or less, enter -0-	**4**	
5	Dollar limitation for tax year. Subtract line 4 from line 1. If zero or less, enter -0-. If married filing separately, see instructions	**5**	

6	(a) Description of property	(b) Cost (business use only)	(c) Elected cost

7	Listed property. Enter the amount from line 29	**7**	
8	Total elected cost of section 179 property. Add amounts in column (c), lines 6 and 7	**8**	
9	Tentative deduction. Enter the **smaller** of line 5 or line 8	**9**	
10	Carryover of disallowed deduction from line 13 of your 2013 Form 4562	**10**	
11	Business income limitation. Enter the smaller of business income (not less than zero) or line 5 (see instructions)	**11**	
12	Section 179 expense deduction. Add lines 9 and 10, but do not enter more than line 11	**12**	
13	Carryover of disallowed deduction to 2015. Add lines 9 and 10, less line 12 ▶	**13**	

Note: *Do not use Part II or Part III below for listed property. Instead, use Part V.*

Part II Special Depreciation Allowance and Other Depreciation (Do not include listed property.) (See instructions.)

14	Special depreciation allowance for qualified property (other than listed property) placed in service during the tax year (see instructions)	**14**	19,499
15	Property subject to section 168(f)(1) election	**15**	
16	Other depreciation (including ACRS)	**16**	

Part III MACRS Depreciation (Do not include listed property.) (See instructions.)

Section A

17	MACRS deductions for assets placed in service in tax years beginning before 2014	**17**	3,423
18	If you are electing to group any assets placed in service during the tax year into one or more general asset accounts, check here . . . . ▶ ☐		

Section B—Assets Placed in Service During 2014 Tax Year Using the General Depreciation System

(a) Classification of property	(b) Month and year placed in service	(c) Basis for depreciation (business/investment use only—see instructions)	(d) Recovery period	(e) Convention	(f) Method	(g) Depreciation deduction
19a 3-year property						
b 5-year property						
c 7-year property		19,498	7 yrs.	HY	150% DB	2,088
d 10-year property						
e 15-year property						
f 20-year property						
g 25-year property			25 yrs.		S/L	
h Residential rental property			27.5 yrs.	MM	S/L	
			27.5 yrs.	MM	S/L	
i Nonresidential real property			39 yrs.	MM	S/L	
				MM	S/L	

Section C—Assets Placed in Service During 2014 Tax Year Using the Alternative Depreciation System

20a Class life					S/L	
b 12-year			12 yrs.		S/L	
c 40-year			40 yrs.	MM	S/L	

Part IV Summary (See instructions.)

21	Listed property. Enter amount from line 28	**21**	
22	**Total.** Add amounts from line 12, lines 14 through 17, lines 19 and 20 in column (g), and line 21. Enter here and on the appropriate lines of your return. Partnerships and S corporations—see instructions	**22**	25,010
23	For assets shown above and placed in service during the current year, enter the portion of the basis attributable to section 263A costs	**23**	

For Paperwork Reduction Act Notice, see separate instructions.   Cat. No. 12906N   Form **4562** (2014)

Description of Property	Date Placed in Service	Cost or other Basis	Business/ Investment Use %	Business Basis (C x D)	Salvage/ Land Value	Section 179 Deduction or Bonus Depreciation	Depreciation Basis [E - (F + G)]	Method/ Convention	Recovery Period	Prior Depreciation	Depreciation Percentage	Depreciation Deduction (H x L)
A	B	C	D	E	F	G	H	I	J	K	L	M
Tractor	06/04/11	23,998	100%	23,998			23,998	150% DB HY	7 yrs	10,811	12.25	2,940
Dairy Cow	01/23/12	822	100%	822			822	150% DB HY	5 yrs	333	17.85	147
Dairy Cow	01/23/12	822	100%	822			822	150% DB HY	5 yrs	333	17.85	147
Breeding Goat	08/09/12	355	100%	355			355	150% DB HY	5 yrs	144	17.85	63
Breeding Goat	08/09/12	355	100%	355			355	150% DB HY	5 yrs	144	17.85	63
Breeding Goat	08/09/12	355	100%	355			355	150% DB HY	5 yrs	144	17.85	63
Tractor	02/15/14	38,997	100%	38,997		19,499	19,498	150% DB HY	7 yrs		10.71	2,088

Chapter 15 Review

1) What is a sole proprietor?

   A sole proprietor is the sole owner of a business.

2) What form is needed to report self employment income?

   Schedule C is used to report self employment income.

3) What is the filing requirement for a self employed taxpayer with no other income?

   If the taxpayer's net earnings from self employment were $400 or more, they are required to file a return.

4) What is the business code for an electrical contractor?

   The business code for an electrical contractor is 238210.

5) What are the three methods of accounting?

   The three methods of accounting are the cash method, the accrual method, and the hybrid method.

6) What form must a taxpayer file if they pay a nonemployee $600 or more for work performed?

   If the taxpayer pays a nonemployee $600 or more for work performed, they must file a form 1099-MISC.

7) What two methods can be used for business use of home for a self employed taxpayer?

   The taxpayer can file the Form 8829 or use the Simplified Method to deduct business use of home expenses.

8) What does self employment tax consist of?

   Self employment taxes are the social security and Medicare taxes the self employed taxpayer must pay on their business income.

Form **1040**	Department of the Treasury—Internal Revenue Service (99)				

U.S. Individual Income Tax Return 20**14** OMB No. 1545-0074 | IRS Use Only—Do not write or staple in this space.

For the year Jan. 1–Dec. 31, 2014, or other tax year beginning , 2014, ending , 20 | See separate instructions.

Your first name and initial	Last name	Your social security number
Keith	Keys	3 3 3 55 5 4 3 2 2

If a joint return, spouse's first name and initial	Last name	Spouse's social security number
Karen	Keys	8 8 8 55 5 3 4 5 6

Home address (number and street). If you have a P.O. box, see instructions. | Apt. no.

3343 Quaint Blvd.

▲ Make sure the SSN(s) above and on line 6c are correct.

City, town or post office, state, and ZIP code. If you have a foreign address, also complete spaces below (see instructions).

Your City, Your State, Your Zip Code

Presidential Election Campaign
Check here if you, or your spouse if filing jointly, want $3 to go to this fund. Checking a box below will not change your tax or refund. ☐ You ☐ Spouse

Foreign country name	Foreign province/state/county	Foreign postal code

Filing Status

Check only one box.

1. ☐ Single
2. ☑ Married filing jointly (even if only one had income)
3. ☐ Married filing separately. Enter spouse's SSN above and full name here. ▶
4. ☐ Head of household (with qualifying person). (See instructions.) If the qualifying person is a child but not your dependent, enter this child's name here. ▶
5. ☐ Qualifying widow(er) with dependent child

Exemptions

6a ☑ **Yourself.** If someone can claim you as a dependent, **do not** check box 6a . . . . .
b ☑ **Spouse** . . . .

Boxes checked on 6a and 6b	2

c **Dependents:**

(1) First name Last name	(2) Dependent's social security number	(3) Dependent's relationship to you	(4) ✓ if child under age 17 qualifying for child tax credit (see instructions)
Kyle Keys	3 3 3 54 4 6 6 5 4	Son	☐
			☐
			☐
			☐

If more than four dependents, see instructions and check here ▶ ☐

No. of children on 6c who:
• lived with you **1**
• did not live with you due to divorce or separation (see instructions)

Dependents on 6c not entered above

d Total number of exemptions claimed

Add numbers on lines above ▶	3

Income

Attach Form(s) W-2 here. Also attach Forms W-2G and 1099-R if tax was withheld.

If you did not get a W-2, see instructions.

7	Wages, salaries, tips, etc. Attach Form(s) W-2	7	42,999	00
8a	**Taxable** interest. Attach Schedule B if required	8a		
b	**Tax-exempt** interest. **Do not** include on line 8a . . ☐ 8b			
9a	Ordinary dividends. Attach Schedule B if required	9a		
b	Qualified dividends . . . . ☐ 9b			
10	Taxable refunds, credits, or offsets of state and local income taxes	10		
11	Alimony received	11		
12	Business income or (loss). Attach Schedule C or C-EZ	12	15,606	00
13	Capital gain or (loss). Attach Schedule D if required. If not required, check here ▶ ☐	13		
14	Other gains or (losses). Attach Form 4797	14		
15a	IRA distributions . ☐ 15a	b Taxable amount . .	15b		
16a	Pensions and annuities ☐ 16a	b Taxable amount . . .	16b		
17	Rental real estate, royalties, partnerships, S corporations, trusts, etc. Attach Schedule E	17		
18	Farm income or (loss). Attach Schedule F	18		
19	Unemployment compensation	19		
20a	Social security benefits ☐ 20a	b Taxable amount . . .	20b		
21	Other income. List type and amount _____	21		
22	Combine the amounts in the far right column for lines 7 through 21. This is your **total income** ▶	22	58,605	00

Adjusted Gross Income

23	Educator expenses 23			
24	Certain business expenses of reservists, performing artists, and fee-basis government officials. Attach Form 2106 or 2106-EZ 24			
25	Health savings account deduction. Attach Form 8889 . 25			
26	Moving expenses. Attach Form 3903 . . . 26			
27	Deductible part of self-employment tax. Attach Schedule SE . 27	1,103	00	
28	Self-employed SEP, SIMPLE, and qualified plans . . 28			
29	Self-employed health insurance deduction . . . 29			
30	Penalty on early withdrawal of savings 30			
31a	Alimony paid b Recipient's SSN ▶ _____ 31a			
32	IRA deduction 32			
33	Student loan interest deduction 33	1,293	00	
34	Tuition and fees. Attach Form 8917 34			
35	Domestic production activities deduction. Attach Form 8903 35			
36	Add lines 23 through 35 . . . . ▶	36	2,396	00
37	Subtract line 36 from line 22. This is your **adjusted gross income** . . . . ▶	37	56,209	00

For Disclosure, Privacy Act, and Paperwork Reduction Act Notice, see separate instructions. Cat. No. 11320B Form **1040** (2014)

Chapter 15 Exercise

Tax and Credits	38	Amount from line 37 (adjusted gross income)	38	56,209	00
	39a	Check if: ☐ **You** were born before January 2, 1950, ☐ Blind. ☐ **Spouse** was born before January 2, 1950, ☐ Blind. } Total boxes checked ▶ 39a			
	b	If your spouse itemizes on a separate return or you were a dual-status alien, check here ▶ 39b ☐			
Standard Deduction for— • People who check any box on line 39a or 39b **or** who can be claimed as a dependent, see instructions. • All others: Single or Married filing separately, $6,200 Married filing jointly or Qualifying widow(er), $12,400 Head of household, $9,100	40	**Itemized deductions** (from Schedule A) **or** your **standard deduction** (see left margin) . .	40	12,400	00
	41	Subtract line 40 from line 38	41	43,809	00
	42	**Exemptions.** If line 38 is $152,525 or less, multiply $3,950 by the number on line 6d. Otherwise, see instructions	42	11,850	00
	43	**Taxable income.** Subtract line 42 from line 41. If line 42 is more than line 41, enter -0- . .	43	31,959	00
	44	**Tax** (see instructions). Check if any from: **a** ☐ Form(s) 8814 **b** ☐ Form 4972 **c** ☐ ___	44	3,889	00
	45	**Alternative minimum tax** (see instructions). Attach Form 6251	45		
	46	Excess advance premium tax credit repayment. Attach Form 8962	46		
	47	Add lines 44, 45, and 46 . . . . ▶	47	3,889	00
	48	Foreign tax credit. Attach Form 1116 if required	48		
	49	Credit for child and dependent care expenses. Attach Form 2441	49		
	50	Education credits from Form 8863, line 19	50 1,500 00		
	51	Retirement savings contributions credit. Attach Form 8880	51		
	52	Child tax credit. Attach Schedule 8812, if required . . .	52		
	53	Residential energy credits. Attach Form 5695	53		
	54	Other credits from Form: **a** ☐ 3800 **b** ☐ 8801 **c** ☐	54		
	55	Add lines 48 through 54. These are your **total credits**	55	1,500	00
	56	Subtract line 55 from line 47. If line 55 is more than line 47, enter -0- . . . . . ▶	56	2,389	00
Other Taxes	57	Self-employment tax. Attach Schedule SE	57	2,205	00
	58	Unreported social security and Medicare tax from Form: **a** ☐ 4137 **b** ☐ 8919 . .	58		
	59	Additional tax on IRAs, other qualified retirement plans, etc. Attach Form 5329 if required . .	59		
	60a	Household employment taxes from Schedule H	60a		
	b	First-time homebuyer credit repayment. Attach Form 5405 if required	60b		
	61	Health care: individual responsibility (see instructions) Full-year coverage ☑	61		
	62	Taxes from: **a** ☐ Form 8959 **b** ☐ Form 8960 **c** ☐ Instructions; enter code(s) ___	62		
	63	Add lines 56 through 62. This is your **total tax** . . . . ▶	63	4,594	00
Payments If you have a qualifying child, attach Schedule EIC.	64	Federal income tax withheld from Forms W-2 and 1099 . .	64 4,342 00		
	65	2014 estimated tax payments and amount applied from 2013 return	65		
	66a	**Earned income credit (EIC)**	66a		
	b	Nontaxable combat pay election 66b ___			
	67	Additional child tax credit. Attach Schedule 8812	67		
	68	American opportunity credit from Form 8863, line 8 . . .	68 1,000 00		
	69	Net premium tax credit. Attach Form 8962	69		
	70	Amount paid with request for extension to file	70		
	71	Excess social security and tier 1 RRTA tax withheld . . .	71		
	72	Credit for federal tax on fuels. Attach Form 4136 . . .	72		
	73	Credits from Form: **a** ☐ 2439 **b** ☐ Reserved **c** ☐ Reserved **d** ☐	73		
	74	Add lines 64, 65, 66a, and 67 through 73. These are your **total payments** . . . . . ▶	74	5,342	00
Refund Direct deposit? ▶ See instructions.	75	If line 74 is more than line 63, subtract line 63 from line 74. This is the amount you **overpaid**	75	748	00
	76a	Amount of line 75 you want **refunded to you.** If Form 8888 is attached, check here ▶ ☐	76a	748	00
	b	Routing number ___ ▶ **c** Type: ☐ Checking ☐ Savings			
	d	Account number ___			
	77	Amount of line 75 you want **applied to your 2015 estimated tax** ▶ 77			
Amount You Owe	78	**Amount you owe.** Subtract line 74 from line 63. For details on how to pay, see instructions ▶	78		
	79	Estimated tax penalty (see instructions) 79			

Third Party Designee	Do you want to allow another person to discuss this return with the IRS (see instructions)? ☐ **Yes.** Complete below. ☐ **No** Designee's name ▶ ___ Phone no. ▶ ___ Personal identification number (PIN) ▶ ___

Sign Here Joint return? See instructions. Keep a copy for your records.	Under penalties of perjury, I declare that I have examined this return and accompanying schedules and statements, and to the best of my knowledge and belief, they are true, correct, and complete. Declaration of preparer (other than taxpayer) is based on all information of which preparer has any knowledge.

Your signature	Date	Your occupation **Self Employed**	Daytime phone number **(555)555-5555**
Spouse's signature. If a joint return, **both** must sign.	Date	Spouse's occupation **Nurse**	If the IRS sent you an Identity Protection PIN, enter it here (see inst.)

Paid Preparer Use Only	Print/Type preparer's name Jane Doe	Preparer's signature	Date	Check ☐ if self-employed	PTIN P00000000
	Firm's name ▶ My Tax Service			Firm's EIN ▶	63-0000000
	Firm's address ▶ 100 Main St., Your City, Your State, Your Zip Code			Phone no.	(555)555-1111

SCHEDULE C (Form 1040)

Department of the Treasury
Internal Revenue Service (99)

Profit or Loss From Business
(Sole Proprietorship)

▶ Information about Schedule C and its separate instructions is at www.irs.gov/schedulec.
▶ Attach to Form 1040, 1040NR, or 1041; partnerships generally must file Form 1065.

OMB No. 1545-0074

2014

Attachment Sequence No. **09**

Name of proprietor: **Keith Keys**

Social security number (SSN): **333-55-4322**

A Principal business or profession, including product or service (see instructions): **Comic Book Sales**

B Enter code from instructions ▶ 4 5 1 2 1 1

C Business name. If no separate business name, leave blank: **Comic Book Heaven**

D Employer ID number (EIN), (see instr.)

E Business address (including suite or room no.) ▶ 900 Comic Lane
City, town or post office, state, and ZIP code: Your City, Your State, Your Zip Code

F Accounting method: (1) ☑ Cash (2) ☐ Accrual (3) ☐ Other (specify) ▶

G Did you "materially participate" in the operation of this business during 2014? If "No," see instructions for limit on losses . ☑ Yes ☐ No

H If you started or acquired this business during 2014, check here ▶ ☐

I Did you make any payments in 2014 that would require you to file Form(s) 1099? (see instructions) . ☐ Yes ☑ No

J If "Yes," did you or will you file required Forms 1099? . ☐ Yes ☐ No

Part I Income

1	Gross receipts or sales. See instructions for line 1 and check the box if this income was reported to you on Form W-2 and the "Statutory employee" box on that form was checked ▶ ☐	1	70,665 00
2	Returns and allowances	2	
3	Subtract line 2 from line 1	3	70,665 00
4	Cost of goods sold (from line 42)	4	22,765 00
5	**Gross profit.** Subtract line 4 from line 3	5	47,900 00
6	Other income, including federal and state gasoline or fuel tax credit or refund (see instructions)	6	
7	**Gross income.** Add lines 5 and 6 ▶	7	47,900 00

Part II Expenses. Enter expenses for business use of your home **only** on line 30.

8	Advertising	8	4,665 00	18	Office expense (see instructions)	18	
9	Car and truck expenses (see instructions)	9		19	Pension and profit-sharing plans	19	
10	Commissions and fees	10		20	Rent or lease (see instructions):		
11	Contract labor (see instructions)	11		a	Vehicles, machinery, and equipment	20a	
12	Depletion	12		b	Other business property	20b	8,500 00
13	Depreciation and section 179 expense deduction (not included in Part III) (see instructions)	13		21	Repairs and maintenance	21	1,232 00
				22	Supplies (not included in Part III)	22	3,450 00
				23	Taxes and licenses	23	
				24	Travel, meals, and entertainment:		
14	Employee benefit programs (other than on line 19)	14		a	Travel	24a	1,477 00
15	Insurance (other than health)	15	5,647 00	b	Deductible meals and entertainment (see instructions)	24b	116 00
16	Interest:			25	Utilities	25	4,896 00
a	Mortgage (paid to banks, etc.)	16a		26	Wages (less employment credits)	26	
b	Other	16b		27a	Other expenses (from line 48)	27a	
17	Legal and professional services	17	2,311 00	b	**Reserved for future use**	27b	

28	**Total expenses** before expenses for business use of home. Add lines 8 through 27a ▶	28	32,294 00
29	Tentative profit or (loss). Subtract line 28 from line 7	29	15,606 00
30	Expenses for business use of your home. Do not report these expenses elsewhere. Attach Form 8829 unless using the simplified method (see instructions). **Simplified method filers only:** enter the total square footage of: (a) your home: _____ and (b) the part of your home used for business: _____ . Use the Simplified Method Worksheet in the instructions to figure the amount to enter on line 30	30	
31	**Net profit or (loss).** Subtract line 30 from line 29.
• If a profit, enter on both **Form 1040, line 12** (or **Form 1040NR, line 13**) and on **Schedule SE, line 2.** (If you checked the box on line 1, see instructions). Estates and trusts, enter on **Form 1041, line 3.**
• If a loss, you **must** go to line 32.	31	15,606 00
32	If you have a loss, check the box that describes your investment in this activity (see instructions).
• If you checked 32a, enter the loss on both **Form 1040, line 12,** (or **Form 1040NR, line 13**) and on **Schedule SE, line 2.** (If you checked the box on line 1, see the line 31 instructions). Estates and trusts, enter on **Form 1041, line 3.**
• If you checked 32b, you **must** attach **Form 6198.** Your loss may be limited.	32a ☑ All investment is at risk.
32b ☐ Some investment is not at risk.	

For Paperwork Reduction Act Notice, see the separate instructions.   Cat. No. 11334P   Schedule C (Form 1040) 2014

Chapter 15 Exercise

Part III   **Cost of Goods Sold** (see instructions)

33   Method(s) used to
     value closing inventory: **a** ☑ Cost   **b** ☐ Lower of cost or market   **c** ☐ Other (attach explanation)

34   Was there any change in determining quantities, costs, or valuations between opening and closing inventory?
     If "Yes," attach explanation . . . . ☐ Yes   ☑ No

35	Inventory at beginning of year. If different from last year's closing inventory, attach explanation	35	16,388	00
36	Purchases less cost of items withdrawn for personal use	36	32,776	00
37	Cost of labor. Do not include any amounts paid to yourself	37		
38	Materials and supplies	38		
39	Other costs	39		
40	Add lines 35 through 39	40	49,164	00
41	Inventory at end of year	41	26,399	00
42	**Cost of goods sold.** Subtract line 41 from line 40. Enter the result here and on line 4	42	22,765	00

Part IV   **Information on Your Vehicle.** Complete this part **only** if you are claiming car or truck expenses on line 9 and are not required to file Form 4562 for this business. See the instructions for line 13 to find out if you must file Form 4562.

43   When did you place your vehicle in service for business purposes? (month, day, year)   ▶ _____ / _____ / _____

44   Of the total number of miles you drove your vehicle during 2014, enter the number of miles you used your vehicle for:

  a Business _____   **b** Commuting (see instructions) _____   **c** Other _____

45   Was your vehicle available for personal use during off-duty hours? . . . . ☐ Yes   ☐ No

46   Do you (or your spouse) have another vehicle available for personal use? . . . . ☐ Yes   ☐ No

47a Do you have evidence to support your deduction? . . . . ☐ Yes   ☐ No

  b If "Yes," is the evidence written? . . . . ☐ Yes   ☐ No

Part V   **Other Expenses.** List below business expenses not included on lines 8–26 or line 30.

_____		
_____		
_____		
_____		
_____		
_____		
_____		
_____		
48 **Total other expenses.** Enter here and on line 27a	48	

SCHEDULE SE (Form 1040) Department of the Treasury Internal Revenue Service (99)	**Self-Employment Tax** ▶ Information about Schedule SE and its separate instructions is at *www.irs.gov/schedulese.* ▶ **Attach to Form 1040 or Form 1040NR.**	OMB No. 1545-0074 20**14** Attachment Sequence No. **17**

Name of person with **self-employment** income (as shown on Form 1040 or Form 1040NR) Keith Keys	Social security number of person with **self-employment** income ▶ 333-55-4322

Before you begin: To determine if you must file Schedule SE, see the instructions.

May I Use Short Schedule SE or Must I Use Long Schedule SE?

Note. Use this flowchart **only if** you must file Schedule SE. If unsure, see *Who Must File Schedule SE* in the instructions.

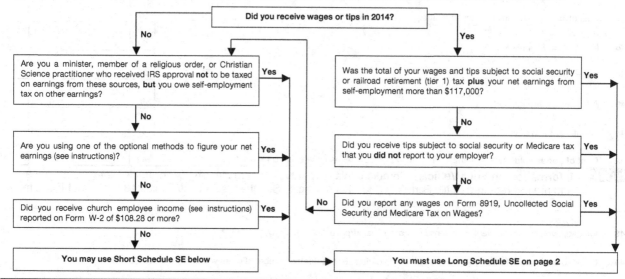

Section A—Short Schedule SE. Caution. Read above to see if you can use Short Schedule SE.

1a	Net farm profit or (loss) from Schedule F, line 34, and farm partnerships, Schedule K-1 (Form 1065), box 14, code A	**1a**	
b	If you received social security retirement or disability benefits, enter the amount of Conservation Reserve Program payments included on Schedule F, line 4b, or listed on Schedule K-1 (Form 1065), box 20, code Z	**1b** (	)
2	Net profit or (loss) from Schedule C, line 31; Schedule C-EZ, line 3; Schedule K-1 (Form 1065), box 14, code A (other than farming); and Schedule K-1 (Form 1065-B), box 9, code J1. Ministers and members of religious orders, see instructions for types of income to report on this line. See instructions for other income to report	**2**	15,606 | 00
3	Combine lines 1a, 1b, and 2	**3**	15,606 | 00
4	Multiply line 3 by 92.35% (.9235). If less than $400, you do not owe self-employment tax; **do not** file this schedule unless you have an amount on line 1b . . . . ▶	**4**	14,412 | 00
	Note. If line 4 is less than $400 due to Conservation Reserve Program payments on line 1b, see instructions.		
5	**Self-employment tax.** If the amount on line 4 is: • $117,000 or less, multiply line 4 by 15.3% (.153). Enter the result here and on **Form 1040, line 57,** or **Form 1040NR, line 55** • More than $117,000, multiply line 4 by 2.9% (.029). Then, add $14,508 to the result. Enter the total here and on **Form 1040, line 57,** or **Form 1040NR, line 55**	**5**	2,205 | 00
6	**Deduction for one-half of self-employment tax.** Multiply line 5 by 50% (.50). Enter the result here and on **Form 1040, line 27,** or **Form 1040NR, line 27** . . . . | **6** | 1,103 | 00		

For Paperwork Reduction Act Notice, see your tax return instructions.   Cat. No. 11358Z   Schedule SE (Form 1040) 2014

Form 8863

Department of the Treasury
Internal Revenue Service (99)

Education Credits
(American Opportunity and Lifetime Learning Credits)

▶ Attach to Form 1040 or Form 1040A.
▶ Information about Form 8863 and its separate instructions is at *www.irs.gov/form8863.*

OMB No. 1545-0074

2014

Attachment
Sequence No. **50**

Name(s) shown on return	Your social security number
Keith and Karen Keys	333 55 4322

⚠ **CAUTION** *Complete a separate Part III on page 2 for each student for whom you are claiming either credit before you complete Parts I and II.*

Part I   Refundable American Opportunity Credit

#	Description			Amount	
1	After completing Part III for each student, enter the total of all amounts from all Parts III, line 30 .		**1**	2,500	00
2	Enter: $180,000 if married filing jointly; $90,000 if single, head of household, or qualifying widow(er)	**2**	180,000 00		
3	Enter the amount from Form 1040, line 38, or Form 1040A, line 22. If you are filing Form 2555, 2555-EZ, or 4563, or you are excluding income from Puerto Rico, see Pub. 970 for the amount to enter	**3**	56,209 00		
4	Subtract line 3 from line 2. If zero or less, **stop**; you cannot take any education credit	**4**	123,791 00		
5	Enter: $20,000 if married filing jointly; $10,000 if single, head of household, or qualifying widow(er)	**5**	20,000 00		
6	If line 4 is: • Equal to or more than line 5, enter 1.000 on line 6 . . . . • Less than line 5, divide line 4 by line 5. Enter the result as a decimal (rounded to at least three places)		**6**	1 . 000	
7	Multiply line 1 by line 6. **Caution:** If you were under age 24 at the end of the year **and** meet the conditions described in the instructions, you **cannot** take the refundable American opportunity credit; skip line 8, enter the amount from line 7 on line 9, and check this box . . . . . ▶ ☐		**7**	2,500	00
8	**Refundable American opportunity credit.** Multiply line 7 by 40% (.40). Enter the amount here and on Form 1040, line 68, or Form 1040A, line 44. Then go to line 9 below.		**8**	1,000	00

Part II   Nonrefundable Education Credits

#	Description			Amount	
9	Subtract line 8 from line 7. Enter here and on line 2 of the Credit Limit Worksheet (see instructions)		**9**	1,500	00
10	After completing Part III for each student, enter the total of all amounts from all Parts III, line 31. If zero, skip lines 11 through 17, enter -0- on line 18, and go to line 19		**10**		
11	Enter the smaller of line 10 or $10,000		**11**	0	00
12	Multiply line 11 by 20% (.20)		**12**	0	00
13	Enter: $128,000 if married filing jointly; $64,000 if single, head of household, or qualifying widow(er)	**13**	128,000 00		
14	Enter the amount from Form 1040, line 38, or Form 1040A, line 22. If you are filing Form 2555, 2555-EZ, or 4563, or you are excluding income from Puerto Rico, see Pub. 970 for the amount to enter	**14**	56,209 00		
15	Subtract line 14 from line 13. If zero or less, skip lines 16 and 17, enter -0- on line 18, and go to line 19	**15**	71,791 00		
16	Enter: $20,000 if married filing jointly; $10,000 if single, head of household, or qualifying widow(er)	**16**	20,000 00		
17	If line 15 is: • Equal to or more than line 16, enter 1.000 on line 17 and go to line 18 • Less than line 16, divide line 15 by line 16. Enter the result as a decimal (rounded to at least three places)		**17**	1 . 000	
18	Multiply line 12 by line 17. Enter here and on line 1 of the Credit Limit Worksheet (see instructions) ▶		**18**	0	00
19	**Nonrefundable education credits.** Enter the amount from line 7 of the Credit Limit Worksheet (see instructions) here and on Form 1040, line 50, or Form 1040A, line 33		**19**	1,500	00

For Paperwork Reduction Act Notice, see your tax return instructions.   Cat. No. 25379M   Form **8863** (2014)

Form 8863 (2014)   Page **2**

Name(s) shown on return	Your social security number
Keith and Karen Keys	363 | 55 | 4322

> ⚠ **CAUTION**
> **Complete Part III for each student for whom you are claiming either the American opportunity credit or lifetime learning credit. Use additional copies of Page 2 as needed for each student.**

Part III   **Student and Educational Institution Information**
See instructions.

20 Student name (as shown on page 1 of your tax return)	**21** Student social security number (as shown on page 1 of your tax return)
Kyle Keys	333 | 54 | 6654

22   Educational institution information (see instructions)

a. Name of first educational institution	**b.** Name of second educational institution (if any)
Monarch University	
(1) Address. Number and street (or P.O. box). City, town or post office, state, and ZIP code. If a foreign address, see instructions. 250 Grand Ave., Your City, Your State, Your Zip Code	**(1)** Address. Number and street (or P.O. box). City, town or post office, state, and ZIP code. If a foreign address, see instructions.
(2) Did the student receive Form 1098-T from this institution for 2014? ☑ Yes ☐ No	**(2)** Did the student receive Form 1098-T from this institution for 2014? ☐ Yes ☐ No
(3) Did the student receive Form 1098-T from this institution for 2013 with Box 2 filled in and Box 7 checked? ☐ Yes ☑ No	**(3)** Did the student receive Form 1098-T from this institution for 2013 with Box 2 filled in and Box 7 checked? ☐ Yes ☐ No
If you checked "No" in **both (2) and (3)**, skip **(4)**.	If you checked "No" in **both (2) and (3)**, skip **(4)**.
(4) If you checked "Yes" in **(2) or (3)**, enter the institution's federal identification number (from Form 1098-T). 6 3 — 5 2 5 2 3 3 3	**(4)** If you checked "Yes" in **(2) or (3)**, enter the institution's federal identification number (from Form 1098-T).

23	Has the Hope Scholarship Credit or American opportunity credit been claimed for this student for any 4 tax years before 2014?	☐ Yes — **Stop!** Go to line 31 for this student. ☑ No — Go to line 24.
24	Was the student enrolled at least half-time for at least one academic period that began or is treated as having begun in 2014 at an eligible educational institution in a program leading towards a postsecondary degree, certificate, or other recognized postsecondary educational credential? (see instructions)	☑ Yes — Go to line 25. ☐ No — **Stop!** Go to line 31 for this student.
25	Did the student complete the first 4 years of post-secondary education before 2014?	☐ Yes — **Stop!** Go to line 31 for this student. ☑ No — Go to line 26.
26	Was the student convicted, before the end of 2014, of a felony for possession or distribution of a controlled substance?	☐ Yes — **Stop!** Go to line 31 for this student. ☑ No — Complete lines 27 through 30 for this student.

> ⚠ **CAUTION**
> You **cannot** take the American opportunity credit and the lifetime learning credit for the **same student** in the same year. If you complete lines 27 through 30 for this student, do not complete line 31.

American Opportunity Credit

27	Adjusted qualified education expenses (see instructions). **Do not enter more than $4,000**	**27**	4,000
28	Subtract $2,000 from line 27. If zero or less, enter -0-.	**28**	2,000
29	Multiply line 28 by 25% (.25)	**29**	500
30	If line 28 is zero, enter the amount from line 27. Otherwise, add $2,000 to the amount on line 29 and enter the result. Skip line 31. Include the total of all amounts from all Parts III, line 30 on Part I, line 1 .	**30**	2,500

Lifetime Learning Credit

31	Adjusted qualified education expenses (see instructions). Include the total of all amounts from all Parts III, line 31, on Part II, line 10	**31**	

Form **8863** (2014)

Student Loan Interest Deduction Worksheet—Line 33

Keep for Your Records

> ***Before you begin:*** ✓ Figure any write-in adjustments to be entered on the dotted line next to line 36 (see the instructions for line 36).
> ✓ Be sure you have read the **Exception** in the instructions for this line to see if you can use this worksheet instead of Pub. 970 to figure your deduction.

1.	Enter the total interest you paid in 2014 on qualified student loans (see the instructions for line 33). **Do not** enter more than $2,500	**1.**	1,293
2.	Enter the amount from Form 1040, line 22 .... **2.** 58,605		
3.	Enter the total of the amounts from Form 1040, lines 23 through 32, plus any write-in adjustments you entered on the dotted line next to line 36 .... **3.** 2,205		
4.	Subtract line 3 from line 2 .... **4.** 56,400		
5.	Enter the amount shown below for your filing status.		
	• Single, head of household, or qualifying widow(er)—$65,000 • Married filing jointly—$130,000	**5.** 130,000	
6.	Is the amount on line 4 more than the amount on line 5?		
	■ **No.** Skip lines 6 and 7, enter -0- on line 8, and go to line 9.		
	☐ **Yes.** Subtract line 5 from line 4 .... **6.**		
7.	Divide line 6 by $15,000 ($30,000 if married filing jointly). Enter the result as a decimal (rounded to at least three places). If the result is 1.000 or more, enter 1.000 .... **7.** .		
8.	Multiply line 1 by line 7 .... **8.**		0
9.	**Student loan interest deduction.** Subtract line 8 from line 1. Enter the result here and on Form 1040, line 33. **Do not** include this amount in figuring any other deduction on your return (such as on Schedule A, C, E, etc.) .... **9.**		1,293

Credit Limit Worksheet

Complete this worksheet to figure the amount to enter on line 19.

1. Enter the amount from Form 8863, line 18	**1.**	0
2. Enter the amount from Form 8863, line 9	**2.**	1,500
3. Add lines 1 and 2	**3.**	1,500
4. Enter the amount from: Form 1040, line 47; or Form 1040A, line 30	**4.**	3,889
5. Enter the total of your credits from either: Form 1040, lines 48 and 49, and Schedule R, line 22; or Form 1040A, lines 31 and 32	**5.**	0
6. Subtract line 5 from line 4	**6.**	3,889
7. Enter the smaller of line 3 or line 6 here and on Form 8863, line 19	**7.**	1,500

Chapter 16 Review

1) What is rental income?

Rental Income is income the taxpayer receives for the use or occupation of their property.

2) If the taxpayer receives royalty income of over $10, how will it be reported to the taxpayer?

If royalties paid are more than $10 in a tax year, the taxpayer will receive a Form 1099-MISC.

3) Is a security deposit rental income?

A security deposit received that the taxpayer intends to return to the tenant at the end of the lease is not included in income. However, if the tenant forfeits it and the taxpayer keeps some or all of the security deposit, the taxpayer will include it in income in the year forfeited.

4) If the tenant pays real estate taxes for the taxpayer of $850, how much is included in the taxpayer's rental income?

The taxpayer will include the full $850 in their rental income.

5) If the taxpayer prepays $3,600 of insurance premiums for a rental home for 3 years of coverage, how much is a deductible expense for the current tax year?

$1,200 is deductible as an insurance expense for the current tax year.

6) What is fair rental price?

The fair rental price of the property is the amount of rent that a person who is not related to the taxpayer is willing to pay.

7) The taxpayer owns a house on the beach and lets a friend rent it for 1 week for $750 (fair rental price). He does not rent it to anyone else and uses it frequently for personal reasons. How much of the rental income is taxable to the taxpayer?

Because the home was rented out for less than 15 days, none of the rental income is taxable.

Form 1040

Department of the Treasury—Internal Revenue Service (99)

U.S. Individual Income Tax Return

2014 OMB No. 1545-0074 IRS Use Only—Do not write or staple in this space.

For the year Jan. 1–Dec. 31, 2014, or other tax year beginning , 2014, ending , 20 | See separate instructions.

Your first name and initial	Last name	Your social security number
Nicole	Nugget	5 4 5 4 4 0 3 3 2

If a joint return, spouse's first name and initial | Last name | Spouse's social security number

Home address (number and street). If you have a P.O. box, see instructions. | Apt. no.

244 Niceville Rd.

▲ Make sure the SSN(s) above and on line 6c are correct.

City, town or post office, state, and ZIP code. If you have a foreign address, also complete spaces below (see instructions).

Your City, Your State, Your Zip Code

Presidential Election Campaign

Foreign country name | Foreign province/state/county | Foreign postal code

Check here if you, or your spouse if filing jointly, want $3 to go to this fund. Checking a box below will not change your tax or refund. ☐ You ☐ Spouse

Filing Status

Check only one box.

1 ☑ Single
2 ☐ Married filing jointly (even if only one had income)
3 ☐ Married filing separately. Enter spouse's SSN above and full name here. ▶
4 ☐ Head of household (with qualifying person). (See instructions.) If the qualifying person is a child but not your dependent, enter this child's name here. ▶
5 ☐ Qualifying widow(er) with dependent child

Exemptions

6a ☑ **Yourself.** If someone can claim you as a dependent, **do not** check box 6a
b ☐ **Spouse**

Boxes checked on 6a and 6b | 1

c **Dependents:**

(1) First name Last name	(2) Dependent's social security number	(3) Dependent's relationship to you	(4) ✓ if child under age 17 qualifying for child tax credit (see instructions)
			☐
			☐
			☐
			☐

No. of children on 6c who:
• lived with you
• did not live with you due to divorce or separation (see instructions)
Dependents on 6c not entered above

If more than four dependents, see instructions and check here ▶ ☐

d Total number of exemptions claimed

Add numbers on lines above ▶ | 1

Income

Attach Form(s) W-2 here. Also attach Forms W-2G and 1099-R if tax was withheld.

If you did not get a W-2, see instructions.

7	Wages, salaries, tips, etc. Attach Form(s) W-2	7		
8a	**Taxable** interest. Attach Schedule B if required	8a		
b	**Tax-exempt** interest. **Do not** include on line 8a	8b		
9a	Ordinary dividends. Attach Schedule B if required	9a		
b	Qualified dividends	9b		
10	Taxable refunds, credits, or offsets of state and local income taxes	10		
11	Alimony received	11		
12	Business income or (loss). Attach Schedule C or C-EZ	12		
13	Capital gain or (loss). Attach Schedule D if required. If not required, check here ▶ ☐	13		
14	Other gains or (losses). Attach Form 4797	14		
15a	IRA distributions 15a	b Taxable amount	15b		
16a	Pensions and annuities 16a	b Taxable amount	16b	32,533	00
17	Rental real estate, royalties, partnerships, S corporations, trusts, etc. Attach Schedule E	17	198	00
18	Farm income or (loss). Attach Schedule F	18		
19	Unemployment compensation	19		
20a	Social security benefits 20a 9,166 00	b Taxable amount	20b	7,317	00
21	Other income. List type and amount	21		
22	Combine the amounts in the far right column for lines 7 through 21. This is your **total income** ▶	22	40,048	00

Adjusted Gross Income

23	Educator expenses	23		
24	Certain business expenses of reservists, performing artists, and fee-basis government officials. Attach Form 2106 or 2106-EZ	24		
25	Health savings account deduction. Attach Form 8889	25		
26	Moving expenses. Attach Form 3903	26		
27	Deductible part of self-employment tax. Attach Schedule SE	27		
28	Self-employed SEP, SIMPLE, and qualified plans	28		
29	Self-employed health insurance deduction	29		
30	Penalty on early withdrawal of savings	30		
31a	Alimony paid b Recipient's SSN ▶	31a		
32	IRA deduction	32		
33	Student loan interest deduction	33		
34	Tuition and fees. Attach Form 8917	34		
35	Domestic production activities deduction. Attach Form 8903	35		
36	Add lines 23 through 35	36		
37	Subtract line 36 from line 22. This is your **adjusted gross income** ▶	37	40,048	00

For Disclosure, Privacy Act, and Paperwork Reduction Act Notice, see separate instructions. Cat. No. 11320B Form **1040** (2014)

Chapter 16 Exercise

Tax and Credits	38	Amount from line 37 (adjusted gross income)	38	40,048	00
	39a	Check if: ☑ **You** were born before January 2, 1950, ☐ Blind. **Total boxes** checked ▶ 39a			
		☐ **Spouse** was born before January 2, 1950, ☐ Blind.			
	b	If your spouse itemizes on a separate return or you were a dual-status alien, check here ▶ 39b ☐			
Standard Deduction for—	40	**Itemized deductions** (from Schedule A) **or** your **standard deduction** (see left margin) . .	40	7,700	00
• People who check any box on line 39a or 39b **or** who can be claimed as a dependent, see instructions.	41	Subtract line 40 from line 38	41	32,348	00
	42	**Exemptions.** If line 38 is $152,525 or less, multiply $3,950 by the number on line 6d. Otherwise, see instructions	42	3,950	00
	43	**Taxable income.** Subtract line 42 from line 41. If line 42 is more than line 41, enter -0-	43	28,398	00
	44	**Tax** (see instructions). Check if any from: **a** ☐ Form(s) 8814 **b** ☐ Form 4972 **c** ☐ _____	44	3,803	00
• All others:	45	**Alternative minimum tax** (see instructions). Attach Form 6251	45		
Single or Married filing separately, $6,200	46	Excess advance premium tax credit repayment. Attach Form 8962	46		
Married filing jointly or Qualifying widow(er), $12,400	47	Add lines 44, 45, and 46 . . . . ▶	47	3,803	00
	48	Foreign tax credit. Attach Form 1116 if required . . .	48		
Head of household, $9,100	49	Credit for child and dependent care expenses. Attach Form 2441	49		
	50	Education credits from Form 8863, line 19	50		
	51	Retirement savings contributions credit. Attach Form 8880	51		
	52	Child tax credit. Attach Schedule 8812, if required . . .	52		
	53	Residential energy credits. Attach Form 5695 . . .	53		
	54	Other credits from Form: **a** ☐ 3800 **b** ☐ 8801 **c** ☐	54		
	55	Add lines 48 through 54. These are your **total credits**	55		
	56	Subtract line 55 from line 47. If line 55 is more than line 47, enter -0- . . . . . ▶	56	3,803	00
Other Taxes	57	Self-employment tax. Attach Schedule SE	57		
	58	Unreported social security and Medicare tax from Form: **a** ☐ 4137 **b** ☐ 8919 . .	58		
	59	Additional tax on IRAs, other qualified retirement plans, etc. Attach Form 5329 if required . .	59		
	60a	Household employment taxes from Schedule H	60a		
	b	First-time homebuyer credit repayment. Attach Form 5405 if required	60b		
	61	Health care: individual responsibility (see instructions) Full-year coverage ☑	61		
	62	Taxes from: **a** ☐ Form 8959 **b** ☐ Form 8960 **c** ☐ Instructions; enter code(s) _____	62		
	63	Add lines 56 through 62. This is your **total tax** . . . . ▶	63	3,803	00
Payments	64	Federal income tax withheld from Forms W-2 and 1099 . .	64	3,253	00
	65	2014 estimated tax payments and amount applied from 2013 return	65		
If you have a qualifying child, attach Schedule EIC.	66a	**Earned income credit (EIC)**	66a		
	b	Nontaxable combat pay election	66b		
	67	Additional child tax credit. Attach Schedule 8812	67		
	68	American opportunity credit from Form 8863, line 8 . . .	68		
	69	Net premium tax credit. Attach Form 8962	69		
	70	Amount paid with request for extension to file	70		
	71	Excess social security and tier 1 RRTA tax withheld . . .	71		
	72	Credit for federal tax on fuels. Attach Form 4136	72		
	73	Credits from Form: **a** ☐ 2439 **b** ☐ Reserved **c** ☐ Reserved **d** ☐	73		
	74	Add lines 64, 65, 66a, and 67 through 73. These are your **total payments** . . . . . . ▶	74	3,253	00
Refund	75	If line 74 is more than line 63, subtract line 63 from line 74. This is the amount you **overpaid**	75		
	76a	Amount of line 75 you want **refunded to you.** If Form 8888 is attached, check here . ▶ ☐	76a		
Direct deposit? ▶ See instructions.	b	Routing number |_|_|_|_|_|_|_|_|_| ▶ **c** Type: ☐ Checking ☐ Savings			
	d	Account number |_|_|_|_|_|_|_|_|_|_|_|_|			
	77	Amount of line 75 you want **applied to your 2015 estimated tax** ▶ 77			
Amount You Owe	78	**Amount you owe.** Subtract line 74 from line 63. For details on how to pay, see instructions ▶	78	550	00
	79	Estimated tax penalty (see instructions) 79			

Third Party Designee	Do you want to allow another person to discuss this return with the IRS (see instructions)? ☐ **Yes.** Complete below. ☑ **No**
	Designee's name ▶ _____ Phone no. ▶ _____ Personal identification number (PIN) ▶ |_|_|_|_|_|

Sign Here Joint return? See instructions. Keep a copy for your records.	Under penalties of perjury, I declare that I have examined this return and accompanying schedules and statements, and to the best of my knowledge and belief, they are true, correct, and complete. Declaration of preparer (other than taxpayer) is based on all information of which preparer has any knowledge.

Your signature	Date	Your occupation	Daytime phone number
		Retired	(555)555-5555
Spouse's signature. If a joint return, **both** must sign.	Date	Spouse's occupation	If the IRS sent you an Identity Protection PIN, enter it here (see inst.)

Paid Preparer Use Only	Print/Type preparer's name	Preparer's signature	Date	Check ☐ if self-employed	PTIN
	Jane Doe				P00000000
	Firm's name ▶ My Tax Service			Firm's EIN ▶	63-0000000
	Firm's address ▶ 100 Main St., Your City, Your State, Your Zip Code			Phone no.	(555)555-1111

SCHEDULE E (Form 1040) Department of the Treasury Internal Revenue Service (99)	**Supplemental Income and Loss** (From rental real estate, royalties, partnerships, S corporations, estates, trusts, REMICs, etc.) ▶ Attach to Form 1040, 1040NR, or Form 1041. ▶ Information about Schedule E and its separate instructions is at *www.irs.gov/schedulee*	OMB No. 1545-0074 20**14** Attachment Sequence No. **13**

Name(s) shown on return	Your social security number
Nicole Nugget	545-44-0332

Part I   **Income or Loss From Rental Real Estate and Royalties**   **Note.** If you are in the business of renting personal property, use **Schedule C** or **C-EZ** (see instructions). If you are an individual, report farm rental income or loss from **Form 4835** on page 2, line 40.

		Yes	No
A	Did you make any payments in 2014 that would require you to file Form(s) 1099? (see instructions)	☐	☑
B	If "Yes," did you or will you file required Forms 1099?	☐	☐

1a	Physical address of each property (street, city, state, ZIP code)
A	450 Beautiful Blvd., Your City, Your State, Your Zip Code
B	
C	

1b	Type of Property (from list below)	2	For each rental real estate property listed above, report the number of fair rental and personal use days. Check the **QJV** box only if you meet the requirements to file as a qualified joint venture. See instructions.		Fair Rental Days	Personal Use Days	QJV
A	1			A	365		☐
B				B			☐
C				C			☐

Type of Property:

1 Single Family Residence   3 Vacation/Short-Term Rental   5 Land   7 Self-Rental
2 Multi-Family Residence   4 Commercial   6 Royalties   8 Other (describe)

Income:	Properties:		A		B	C
3	Rents received	3	14,928	00		
4	Royalties received	4				
Expenses:						
5	Advertising	5				
6	Auto and travel (see instructions)	6				
7	Cleaning and maintenance	7				
8	Commissions	8				
9	Insurance	9	1,455	00		
10	Legal and other professional fees	10				
11	Management fees	11	899	00		
12	Mortgage interest paid to banks, etc. (see instructions)	12	8,544	00		
13	Other interest	13				
14	Repairs	14	778	00		
15	Supplies	15				
16	Taxes	16	763	00		
17	Utilities	17				
18	Depreciation expense or depletion	18	2,291	00		
19	Other (list) ▶	19				
20	Total expenses. Add lines 5 through 19	20	14,730	00		
21	Subtract line 20 from line 3 (rents) and/or 4 (royalties). If result is a (loss), see instructions to find out if you must file **Form 6198**	21	198	00		
22	Deductible rental real estate loss after limitation, if any, on **Form 8582** (see instructions)	22	(	)(	)(	)

23a	Total of all amounts reported on line 3 for all rental properties	23a	14,928	00	
b	Total of all amounts reported on line 4 for all royalty properties	23b			
c	Total of all amounts reported on line 12 for all properties	23c	8,544	00	
d	Total of all amounts reported on line 18 for all properties	23d	2,291	00	
e	Total of all amounts reported on line 20 for all properties	23e	14,730	00	

24	**Income.** Add positive amounts shown on line 21. **Do not** include any losses	24	198	00
25	**Losses.** Add royalty losses from line 21 and rental real estate losses from line 22. Enter total losses here	25	(	)
26	**Total rental real estate and royalty income or (loss).** Combine lines 24 and 25. Enter the result here. If Parts II, III, IV, and line 40 on page 2 do not apply to you, also enter this amount on Form 1040, line 17, or Form 1040NR, line 18. Otherwise, include this amount in the total on line 41 on page 2	26	198	00

For Paperwork Reduction Act Notice, see the separate instructions.   Cat. No. 11344L   Schedule E (Form 1040) 2014

Description of Property	Date Placed in Service	Cost or other Basis	Business/ Investment Use %	Business Basis (C x D)	Salvage/ Land Value	Section 179 Deduction or Bonus Depreciation	Depreciation Basis [E − (F + G)]	Method/ Convention	Recovery Period	Prior Depreciation	Depreciation Percentage	Depreciation Deduction (H x L)
A	B	C	D	E	F	G	H	I	J	K	L	M
Rental House	05/2009	75,000	100	75,000	12,000		63,000	MM SL	27.5	10,596	3.636	2,291

Social Security Benefits Worksheet—Lines 20a and 20b

Keep for Your Records

Before you begin: ✓ Complete Form 1040, lines 21 and 23 through 32, if they apply to you.
✓ Figure any write-in adjustments to be entered on the dotted line next to line 36 (see the instructions for line 36).
✓ If you are married filing separately and you lived apart from your spouse for all of 2014, enter "D" to the right of the word "benefits" on line 20a. If you do not, you may get a math error notice from the IRS.
✓ Be sure you have read the **Exception** in the line 20a and 20b instructions to see if you can use this worksheet instead of a publication to find out if any of your benefits are taxable.

1.	Enter the total amount from **box 5** of **all** your **Forms SSA-1099** and **Forms RRB-1099.** Also, enter this amount on Form 1040, line 20a	1.	9,166
2.	Enter one-half of line 1	2.	4,583
3.	Combine the amounts from Form 1040, lines 7, 8a, 9a, 10 through 14, 15b, 16b, 17 through 19, and 21	3.	32,731
4.	Enter the amount, if any, from Form 1040, line 8b	4.	
5.	Combine lines 2, 3, and 4	5.	37,314
6.	Enter the total of the amounts from Form 1040, lines 23 through 32, plus any write-in adjustments you entered on the dotted line next to line 36	6.	0
7.	Is the amount on line 6 less than the amount on line 5?		

7. Is the amount on line 6 less than the amount on line 5?

    ☐ **No.** (STOP) None of your social security benefits are taxable. Enter -0- on Form 1040, line 20b.

    ■ **Yes.** Subtract line 6 from line 5 .... **7.**   37,314

8. If you are:
    • Married filing jointly, enter $32,000
    • Single, head of household, qualifying widow(er), or married filing separately and you **lived apart** from your spouse for all of 2014, enter $25,000
    • Married filing separately and you lived with your spouse at any time in 2014, skip lines 8 through 15; multiply line 7 by 85% (.85) and enter the result on line 16. Then go to line 17   **8.**   25,000

9. Is the amount on line 8 less than the amount on line 7?

    ☐ **No.** (STOP) None of your social security benefits are taxable. Enter -0- on Form 1040, line 20b. If you are married filing separately and you **lived apart** from your spouse for all of 2014, be sure you entered "D" to the right of the word "benefits" on line 20a.

    ■ **Yes.** Subtract line 8 from line 7 .... **9.**   12,314

10.	Enter: $12,000 if married filing jointly; $9,000 if single, head of household, qualifying widow(er), or married filing separately and you **lived apart** from your spouse for all of 2014	10.	9,000
11.	Subtract line 10 from line 9. If zero or less, enter -0-	11.	3,314
12.	Enter the **smaller** of line 9 or line 10	12.	9,000
13.	Enter one-half of line 12	13.	4,500
14.	Enter the **smaller** of line 2 or line 13	14.	4,500
15.	Multiply line 11 by 85% (.85). If line 11 is zero, enter -0-	15.	2,817
16.	Add lines 14 and 15	16.	7,317
17.	Multiply line 1 by 85% (.85)	17.	7,791
18.	**Taxable social security benefits.** Enter the **smaller** of line 16 or line 17. Also enter this amount on Form 1040, line 20b	18.	7,317

(TIP) *If any of your benefits are taxable for 2014 **and** they include a lump-sum benefit payment that was for an earlier year, you may be able to reduce the taxable amount. See Lump-Sum Election in Pub. 915 for details.*

Chapter 17 Review

1) What is the basis of inherited property?

   The basis of inherited property is either the FMV on the date of the individual's death or the FMV on the alternate valuation date.

2) What is the automatic holding period of inherited property?

   The automatic holding period of inherited property is long term.

3) Do repairs add to the basis of the property?

   Repairs do not add to the basis of the property.

4) Do improvements add to the basis of property?

   Improvements do add to the basis of property.

5) How long does property have to be held to be considered long term property?

   To qualify as long term, the property must have been held over one year, meaning one year and one day.

6) What is the benefit of selling long term property as opposed to short term?

   Short term capital gains are treated as ordinary income. This means that they are taxed as the rest of the income is taxed. They receive no special treatment. Long term capital gains are subject to a special capital gain tax rate.

7) What is the capital loss limit?

   The annual limit for a deductible capital loss is $3,000 ($1,500 for MFS).

8) What is the maximum exclusion amount for the sale of a main home?

   The taxpayer may be able to exclude up to $250,000 ($500,000 if MFJ) of the gain.

Form **1040** Department of the Treasury - Internal Revenue Service (99)
U.S. Individual Income Tax Return 20**14** OMB No. 1545-0074 | IRS Use Only—Do not write or staple in this space.

For the year Jan. 1–Dec. 31, 2014, or other tax year beginning _____ , 2014, ending _____ , 20 ___ | See separate instructions.

Your first name and initial	Last name		Your social security number
Gweneth	George		3 3 3 3 3 4 4 5 4

If a joint return, spouse's first name and initial | Last name | | Spouse's social security number

Home address (number and street). If you have a P.O. box, see instructions. | Apt. no. | ▲ Make sure the SSN(s) above and on line 6c are correct.

250 First Ave.

City, town or post office, state, and ZIP code. If you have a foreign address, also complete spaces below (see instructions).

Your City, Your State, Your Zip Code

Presidential Election Campaign
Check here if you, or your spouse if filing jointly, want $3 to go to this fund. Checking a box below will not change your tax or refund. ☐ You ☐ Spouse

Foreign country name | Foreign province/state/county | Foreign postal code

Filing Status

Check only one box.

1 ☑ Single
2 ☐ Married filing jointly (even if only one had income)
3 ☐ Married filing separately. Enter spouse's SSN above and full name here. ▶
4 ☐ Head of household (with qualifying person). (See instructions.) If the qualifying person is a child but not your dependent, enter this child's name here. ▶
5 ☐ Qualifying widow(er) with dependent child

Exemptions

6a ☑ **Yourself.** If someone can claim you as a dependent, **do not** check box 6a . . . . .
b ☐ **Spouse** . . . .

Boxes checked on 6a and 6b **1**

c **Dependents:**

(1) First name Last name	(2) Dependent's social security number	(3) Dependent's relationship to you	(4) ✓ if child under age 17 qualifying for child tax credit (see instructions)
			☐
			☐
			☐
			☐

If more than four dependents, see instructions and check here ▶ ☐

No. of children on 6c who:
• lived with you
• did not live with you due to divorce or separation (see instructions)
Dependents on 6c not entered above

Add numbers on lines above ▶ **1**

d Total number of exemptions claimed . . . .

Income

Attach Form(s) W-2 here. Also attach Forms W-2G and 1099-R if tax was withheld.

If you did not get a W-2, see instructions.

7	Wages, salaries, tips, etc. Attach Form(s) W-2	7	44,566 00
8a	**Taxable** interest. Attach Schedule B if required	8a	
b	**Tax-exempt** interest. **Do not** include on line 8a . . .	8b	
9a	Ordinary dividends. Attach Schedule B if required	9a	
b	Qualified dividends	9b	
10	Taxable refunds, credits, or offsets of state and local income taxes	10	
11	Alimony received	11	
12	Business income or (loss). Attach Schedule C or C-EZ	12	
13	Capital gain or (loss). Attach Schedule D if required. If not required, check here ▶ ☐	13	1,129 00
14	Other gains or (losses). Attach Form 4797	14	
15a	IRA distributions . 15a _____	b Taxable amount . . .	15b	
16a	Pensions and annuities 16a _____	b Taxable amount . . .	16b	
17	Rental real estate, royalties, partnerships, S corporations, trusts, etc. Attach Schedule E	17	
18	Farm income or (loss). Attach Schedule F	18	
19	Unemployment compensation	19	
20a	Social security benefits 20a _____	b Taxable amount . . .	20b	
21	Other income. List type and amount _____	21	
22	Combine the amounts in the far right column for lines 7 through 21. This is your **total income** ▶	22	45,695 00

Adjusted Gross Income

23	Educator expenses	23	
24	Certain business expenses of reservists, performing artists, and fee-basis government officials. Attach Form 2106 or 2106-EZ	24	
25	Health savings account deduction. Attach Form 8889 .	25	
26	Moving expenses. Attach Form 3903	26	
27	Deductible part of self-employment tax. Attach Schedule SE .	27	
28	Self-employed SEP, SIMPLE, and qualified plans . .	28	
29	Self-employed health insurance deduction . .	29	
30	Penalty on early withdrawal of savings	30	
31a	Alimony paid b Recipient's SSN ▶ _____	31a	
32	IRA deduction	32	
33	Student loan interest deduction	33	
34	Tuition and fees. Attach Form 8917	34	
35	Domestic production activities deduction. Attach Form 8903	35	
36	Add lines 23 through 35	36	
37	Subtract line 36 from line 22. This is your **adjusted gross income** . . . . . ▶	37	45,695 00

For Disclosure, Privacy Act, and Paperwork Reduction Act Notice, see separate instructions. Cat. No. 11320B Form **1040** (2014)

Chapter 17 Exercise

Tax and Credits	38	Amount from line 37 (adjusted gross income)	38	45,695	00
	39a	Check if: ☐ **You** were born before January 2, 1950, ☐ Blind. ☐ **Spouse** was born before January 2, 1950, ☐ Blind. } Total boxes checked ▶ 39a			
	b	If your spouse itemizes on a separate return or you were a dual-status alien, check here ▶ 39b ☐			

Standard Deduction for—
- **People who check any box on line 39a or 39b or who can be claimed as a dependent, see instructions.**
- **All others:**
Single or Married filing separately, $6,200
Married filing jointly or Qualifying widow(er), $12,400
Head of household, $9,100

40	**Itemized deductions** (from Schedule A) **or** your **standard deduction** (see left margin) . .	40	6,200	00
41	Subtract line 40 from line 38	41	39,495	00
42	**Exemptions.** If line 38 is $152,525 or less, multiply $3,950 by the number on line 6d. Otherwise, see instructions	42	3,950	00
43	**Taxable income.** Subtract line 42 from line 41. If line 42 is more than line 41, enter -0- . . .	43	35,545	00
44	Tax (see instructions). Check if any from: **a** ☐ Form(s) 8814 **b** ☐ Form 4972 **c** ☐ _____	44	4,725	00
45	**Alternative minimum tax** (see instructions). Attach Form 6251	45		
46	Excess advance premium tax credit repayment. Attach Form 8962	46		
47	Add lines 44, 45, and 46 . . . . ▶	47	4,725	00

48	Foreign tax credit. Attach Form 1116 if required	48		
49	Credit for child and dependent care expenses. Attach Form 2441	49		
50	Education credits from Form 8863, line 19	50		
51	Retirement savings contributions credit. Attach Form 8880	51		
52	Child tax credit. Attach Schedule 8812, if required . . .	52		
53	Residential energy credits. Attach Form 5695	53		
54	Other credits from Form: **a** ☐ 3800 **b** ☐ 8801 **c** ☐	54		
55	Add lines 48 through 54. These are your **total credits**	55		
56	Subtract line 55 from line 47. If line 55 is more than line 47, enter -0- . . . . ▶	56	4,725	00

Other Taxes					
	57	Self-employment tax. Attach Schedule SE	57		
	58	Unreported social security and Medicare tax from Form: **a** ☐ 4137 **b** ☐ 8919 . .	58		
	59	Additional tax on IRAs, other qualified retirement plans, etc. Attach Form 5329 if required . .	59		
	60a	Household employment taxes from Schedule H	60a		
	b	First-time homebuyer credit repayment. Attach Form 5405 if required	60b		
	61	Health care: individual responsibility (see instructions) Full-year coverage ☐ . . .	61		
	62	Taxes from: **a** ☐ Form 8959 **b** ☐ Form 8960 **c** ☐ Instructions; enter code(s) _____	62		
	63	Add lines 56 through 62. This is your **total tax** . . . . ▶	63	4,725	00

Payments					
If you have a qualifying child, attach Schedule EIC.	64	Federal income tax withheld from Forms W-2 and 1099 . .	64	6,000	00
	65	2014 estimated tax payments and amount applied from 2013 return	65		
	66a	**Earned income credit (EIC)**	66a		
	b	Nontaxable combat pay election 66b			
	67	Additional child tax credit. Attach Schedule 8812	67		
	68	American opportunity credit from Form 8863, line 8 . . .	68		
	69	Net premium tax credit. Attach Form 8962	69		
	70	Amount paid with request for extension to file	70		
	71	Excess social security and tier 1 RRTA tax withheld	71		
	72	Credit for federal tax on fuels. Attach Form 4136	72		
	73	Credits from Form: **a** ☐ 2439 **b** ☐ Reserved **c** ☐ Reserved **d** ☐	73		
	74	Add lines 64, 65, 66a, and 67 through 73. These are your **total payments** . . . . ▶	74	6,000	00

Refund					
	75	If line 74 is more than line 63, subtract line 63 from line 74. This is the amount you **overpaid**	75	1,275	00
	76a	Amount of line 75 you want **refunded to you.** If Form 8888 is attached, check here . ▶ ☐	76a	1,275	00
Direct deposit? ▶ See instructions.	b	Routing number [ ][ ][ ][ ][ ][ ][ ][ ][ ] ▶ c Type: ☐ Checking ☐ Savings			
	d	Account number [ ][ ][ ][ ][ ][ ][ ][ ][ ][ ][ ][ ][ ][ ][ ][ ][ ]			
	77	Amount of line 75 you want **applied to your 2015 estimated tax** ▶ 77			

Amount You Owe	78	**Amount you owe.** Subtract line 74 from line 63. For details on how to pay, see instructions ▶	78		
	79	Estimated tax penalty (see instructions) 79			

Third Party Designee	Do you want to allow another person to discuss this return with the IRS (see instructions)? ☐ **Yes.** Complete below. ☑ **No**		
	Designee's name ▶	Phone no. ▶	Personal identification number (PIN) ▶ [ ][ ][ ][ ][ ]

Sign Here
Joint return? See instructions.
Keep a copy for your records.

Under penalties of perjury, I declare that I have examined this return and accompanying schedules and statements, and to the best of my knowledge and belief, they are true, correct, and complete. Declaration of preparer (other than taxpayer) is based on all information of which preparer has any knowledge.

Your signature	Date	Your occupation Events Coordinator	Daytime phone number (555)555-5555
▶ Spouse's signature. If a joint return, **both** must sign.	Date	Spouse's occupation	If the IRS sent you an Identity Protection PIN, enter it here (see inst.) [ ][ ][ ][ ][ ][ ]

Paid Preparer Use Only	Print/Type preparer's name Jane Doe	Preparer's signature	Date	Check ☐ if self-employed	PTIN P00000000
	Firm's name ▶ My Tax Service			Firm's EIN ▶	63-0000000
	Firm's address ▶ 100 Main St., Your City, Your State, Your Zip Code			Phone no.	(555)555-1111

SCHEDULE D (Form 1040) Department of the Treasury Internal Revenue Service (99)	**Capital Gains and Losses** ▶ Attach to Form 1040 or Form 1040NR. ▶ Information about Schedule D and its separate instructions is at *www.irs.gov/scheduled*. ▶ Use Form 8949 to list your transactions for lines 1b, 2, 3, 8b, 9, and 10.	OMB No. 1545-0074 2014 Attachment Sequence No. 12

Name(s) shown on return Gweneth George	Your social security number 333-33-4454

Part I   Short-Term Capital Gains and Losses—Assets Held One Year or Less

See instructions for how to figure the amounts to enter on the lines below. This form may be easier to complete if you round off cents to whole dollars.	(d) Proceeds (sales price)	(e) Cost (or other basis)	(g) Adjustments to gain or loss from Form(s) 8949, Part I, line 2, column (g)	(h) Gain or (loss) Subtract column (e) from column (d) and combine the result with column (g)
1a Totals for all short-term transactions reported on Form 1099-B for which basis was reported to the IRS and for which you have no adjustments (see instructions). However, if you choose to report all these transactions on Form 8949, leave this line blank and go to line 1b .				
1b Totals for all transactions reported on Form(s) 8949 with **Box A** checked				
2 Totals for all transactions reported on Form(s) 8949 with **Box B** checked	650	544		106
3 Totals for all transactions reported on Form(s) 8949 with **Box C** checked				

4 Short-term gain from Form 6252 and short-term gain or (loss) from Forms 4684, 6781, and 8824 .	**4**	
5 Net short-term gain or (loss) from partnerships, S corporations, estates, and trusts from Schedule(s) K-1	**5**	
6 Short-term capital loss carryover. Enter the amount, if any, from line 8 of your **Capital Loss Carryover Worksheet** in the instructions	**6**	( )
7 **Net short-term capital gain or (loss).** Combine lines 1a through 6 in column (h). If you have any long-term capital gains or losses, go to Part II below. Otherwise, go to Part III on the back	**7**	106

Part II   Long-Term Capital Gains and Losses—Assets Held More Than One Year

See instructions for how to figure the amounts to enter on the lines below. This form may be easier to complete if you round off cents to whole dollars.	(d) Proceeds (sales price)	(e) Cost (or other basis)	(g) Adjustments to gain or loss from Form(s) 8949, Part II, line 2, column (g)	(h) Gain or (loss) Subtract column (e) from column (d) and combine the result with column (g)
8a Totals for all long-term transactions reported on Form 1099-B for which basis was reported to the IRS and for which you have no adjustments (see instructions). However, if you choose to report all these transactions on Form 8949, leave this line blank and go to line 8b .				
8b Totals for all transactions reported on Form(s) 8949 with **Box D** checked				
9 Totals for all transactions reported on Form(s) 8949 with **Box E** checked	1,200	577		623
10 Totals for all transactions reported on Form(s) 8949 with **Box F** checked.	16,000	15,600		400

11 Gain from Form 4797, Part I; long-term gain from Forms 2439 and 6252; and long-term gain or (loss) from Forms 4684, 6781, and 8824	**11**	
12 Net long-term gain or (loss) from partnerships, S corporations, estates, and trusts from Schedule(s) K-1	**12**	
13 Capital gain distributions. See the instructions	**13**	
14 Long-term capital loss carryover. Enter the amount, if any, from line 13 of your **Capital Loss Carryover Worksheet** in the instructions	**14**	( )
15 **Net long-term capital gain or (loss).** Combine lines 8a through 14 in column (h). Then go to Part III on the back	**15**	1,023

For Paperwork Reduction Act Notice, see your tax return instructions.   Cat. No. 11338H   Schedule D (Form 1040) 2014

Chapter 17 Exercise

Part III **Summary**

16	Combine lines 7 and 15 and enter the result	**16**	1,129

- If line 16 is a **gain,** enter the amount from line 16 on Form 1040, line 13, or Form 1040NR, line 14. Then go to line 17 below.
- If line 16 is a **loss,** skip lines 17 through 20 below. Then go to line 21. Also be sure to complete line 22.
- If line 16 is **zero,** skip lines 17 through 21 below and enter -0- on Form 1040, line 13, or Form 1040NR, line 14. Then go to line 22.

17 Are lines 15 and 16 **both** gains?
☑ **Yes.** Go to line 18.
☐ **No.** Skip lines 18 through 21, and go to line 22.

18 Enter the amount, if any, from line 7 of the **28% Rate Gain Worksheet** in the instructions . . ▶ **18**

19 Enter the amount, if any, from line 18 of the **Unrecaptured Section 1250 Gain Worksheet** in the instructions . . . . ▶ **19**

20 Are lines 18 and 19 **both** zero or blank?
☑ **Yes.** Complete the **Qualified Dividends and Capital Gain Tax Worksheet** in the instructions for Form 1040, line 44 (or in the instructions for Form 1040NR, line 42). **Do not** complete lines 21 and 22 below.

☐ **No.** Complete the **Schedule D Tax Worksheet** in the instructions. **Do not** complete lines 21 and 22 below.

21 If line 16 is a loss, enter here and on Form 1040, line 13, or Form 1040NR, line 14, the **smaller** of:

- The loss on line 16 or
- ($3,000), or if married filing separately, ($1,500) } . . . . **21** ( )

Note. When figuring which amount is smaller, treat both amounts as positive numbers.

22 Do you have qualified dividends on Form 1040, line 9b, or Form 1040NR, line 10b?

☐ **Yes.** Complete the **Qualified Dividends and Capital Gain Tax Worksheet** in the instructions for Form 1040, line 44 (or in the instructions for Form 1040NR, line 42).

☐ **No.** Complete the rest of Form 1040 or Form 1040NR.

Form **8949**

Department of the Treasury
Internal Revenue Service

Sales and Other Dispositions of Capital Assets

▶ Information about Form 0940 and its separate instructions is at *www.irs.gov/form8949.*
▶ File with your Schedule D to list your transactions for lines 1b, 2, 3, 8b, 9, and 10 of Schedule D.

OMB No. 1545-0074

20**14**

Attachment
Sequence No. **12A**

Name(s) shown on return	Social security number or taxpayer identification number
Gweneth George	333-33-4454

Before you check Box A, B, or C below, see whether you received any Form(s) 1099-B or substitute statement(s) from your broker. A substitute statement will have the same information as Form 1099-B. Either may show your basis (usually your cost) even if your broker did not report it to the IRS. Brokers must report basis to the IRS for most stock you bought in 2011 or later (and for certain debt instruments you bought in 2014 or later).

Part I   **Short-Term.** Transactions involving capital assets you held 1 year or less are short term. For long-term transactions, see page 2.

Note. You may aggregate all short-term transactions reported on Form(s) 1099-B showing basis was reported to the IRS and for which no adjustments or codes are required. Enter the total directly on Schedule D, line 1a; you are not required to report these transactions on Form 8949 (see instructions).

You *must* check Box A, B, *or* C below. **Check only one box.** If more than one box applies for your short-term transactions, complete a separate Form 8949, page 1, for each applicable box. If you have more short-term transactions than will fit on this page for one or more of the boxes, complete as many forms with the same box checked as you need.

☐ **(A)** Short-term transactions reported on Form(s) 1099-B showing basis was reported to the IRS (see **Note** above)
☑ **(B)** Short-term transactions reported on Form(s) 1099-B showing basis was **not** reported to the IRS
☐ **(C)** Short-term transactions not reported to you on Form 1099-B

1 (a) Description of property (Example: 100 sh. XYZ Co.)	(b) Date acquired (Mo., day, yr.)	(c) Date sold or disposed (Mo., day, yr.)	(d) Proceeds (sales price) (see instructions)	(e) Cost or other basis. See the **Note** below and see *Column (e)* in the separate instructions	Adjustment, if any, to gain or loss. If you enter an amount in column (g), enter a code in column (f). See the separate instructions. (f) Code(s) from instructions	(g) Amount of adjustment	(h) Gain or (loss). Subtract column (e) from column (d) and combine the result with column (g)
5 sh ABC	01/05/14	11/15/14	650	544			106
2 Totals. Add the amounts in columns (d), (e), (g), and (h) (subtract negative amounts). Enter each total here and include on your Schedule D, **line 1b** (if **Box A** above is checked), **line 2** (if **Box B** above is checked), or **line 3** (if **Box C** above is checked) ▶			650	544			106

Note. If you checked Box A above but the basis reported to the IRS was incorrect, enter in column (e) the basis as reported to the IRS, and enter an adjustment in column (g) to correct the basis. See *Column (g)* in the separate instructions for how to figure the amount of the adjustment.

For Paperwork Reduction Act Notice, see your tax return instructions.   Cat. No. 37768Z   Form **8949** (2014)

Chapter 17 Exercise

Attachment Sequence No. **12A**   Page **2**

Name(s) shown on return. Name and SSN or taxpayer identification no. not required if shown on other side	Social security number or taxpayer identification number
Gweneth George	333-33-4454

Before you check Box D, E, or F below, see whether you received any Form(s) 1099-B or substitute statement(s) from your broker. A substitute statement will have the same information as Form 1099-B. Either may show your basis (usually your cost) even if your broker did not report it to the IRS. Brokers must report basis to the IRS for most stock you bought in 2011 or later (and for certain debt instruments you bought in 2014 or later).

Part II   **Long-Term.** Transactions involving capital assets you held more than 1 year are long term. For short-term transactions, see page 1.

Note. You may aggregate all long-term transactions reported on Form(s) 1099-B showing basis was reported to the IRS and for which no adjustments or codes are required. Enter the total directly on Schedule D, line 8a; you are not required to report these transactions on Form 8949 (see instructions).

You **must** check Box D, E, **or** F below. **Check only one box.** If more than one box applies for your long-term transactions, complete a separate Form 8949, page 2, for each applicable box. If you have more long-term transactions than will fit on this page for one or more of the boxes, complete as many forms with the same box checked as you need.

- ☐ **(D)** Long-term transactions reported on Form(s) 1099-B showing basis was reported to the IRS (see **Note** above)
- ☑ **(E)** Long-term transactions reported on Form(s) 1099-B showing basis was **not** reported to the IRS
- ☐ **(F)** Long-term transactions not reported to you on Form 1099-B

1 **(a)** Description of property (Example: 100 sh. XYZ Co.)	**(b)** Date acquired (Mo., day, yr.)	**(c)** Date sold or disposed (Mo., day, yr.)	**(d)** Proceeds (sales price) (see instructions)	**(e)** Cost or other basis. See the **Note** below and see *Column (e)* in the separate instructions	**(f)** Code(s) from instructions	**(g)** Amount of adjustment	**(h)** Gain or (loss). Subtract column (e) from column (d) and combine the result with column (g)
67 sh BBB	03/06/05	12/12/14	1,200	577			623
2 Totals. Add the amounts in columns (d), (e), (g), and (h) (subtract negative amounts). Enter each total here and include on your Schedule D, **line 8b** (if **Box D** above is checked), **line 9** (if **Box E** above is checked), or **line 10** (if **Box F** above is checked) ▶			1,200	577			623

Note. If you checked Box D above but the basis reported to the IRS was incorrect, enter in column (e) the basis as reported to the IRS, and enter an adjustment in column (g) to correct the basis. See *Column (g)* in the separate instructions for how to figure the amount of the adjustment.

Form **8949** (2014)

Form 8949 (2014)   Attachment Sequence No. **12A**   Page **2**

Name(s) shown on return. Name and SSN or taxpayer identification no. not required if shown on other side	Social security number or taxpayer identification number
Gweneth George	333-33-4454

Before you check Box D, E, or F below, see whether you received any Form(s) 1099-B or substitute statement(s) from your broker. A substitute statement will have the same information as Form 1099-B. Either may show your basis (usually your cost) even if your broker did not report it to the IRS. Brokers must report basis to the IRS for most stock you bought in 2011 or later (and for certain debt instruments you bought in 2014 or later).

Part II   **Long-Term.** Transactions involving capital assets you held more than 1 year are long term. For short-term transactions, see page 1.

      Note. You may aggregate all long-term transactions reported on Form(s) 1099-B showing basis was reported to the IRS and for which no adjustments or codes are required. Enter the total directly on Schedule D, line 8a; you are not required to report these transactions on Form 8949 (see instructions).

You *must* check Box D, E, *or* F below. **Check only one box.** If more than one box applies for your long-term transactions, complete a separate Form 8949, page 2, for each applicable box. If you have more long-term transactions than will fit on this page for one or more of the boxes, complete as many forms with the same box checked as you need.

- ☐ **(D)** Long-term transactions reported on Form(s) 1099-B showing basis was reported to the IRS (see **Note** above)
- ☐ **(E)** Long-term transactions reported on Form(s) 1099-B showing basis was **not** reported to the IRS
- ☑ **(F)** Long-term transactions not reported to you on Form 1099-B

1

(a) Description of property (Example: 100 sh. XYZ Co.)	(b) Date acquired (Mo., day, yr.)	(c) Date sold or disposed (Mo., day, yr.)	(d) Proceeds (sales price) (see instructions)	(e) Cost or other basis. See the **Note** below and see *Column (e)* in the separate instructions	(f) Code(s) from instructions	(g) Amount of adjustment	(h) Gain or (loss). Subtract column (e) from column (d) and combine the result with column (g)
Land	Inherited	06/04/14	16,000	15,600			400
2 Totals. Add the amounts in columns (d), (e), (g), and (h) (subtract negative amounts). Enter each total here and include on your Schedule D, **line 8b** (if **Box D** above is checked), **line 9** (if **Box E** above is checked), or **line 10** (if **Box F** above is checked) ▶			16,000	15,600			400

Note. If you checked Box D above but the basis reported to the IRS was incorrect, enter in column (e) the basis as reported to the IRS, and enter an adjustment in column (g) to correct the basis. See *Column (g)* in the separate instructions for how to figure the amount of the adjustment.

Form **8949** (2014)

Chapter 17 Exercise

Form **8965**	**Health Coverage Exemptions**	OMB No. 1545-0074
Department of the Treasury Internal Revenue Service	▶ Attach to Form 1040, Form 1040A, or Form 1040EZ. ▶ **Information about Form 8965 and its separate instructions is at** *www.irs.gov/form8965.*	**2014** Attachment Sequence No. **75**

Name as shown on return	Your social security number
Gweneth George	333-33-4454

Complete this form if you have a Marketplace-granted coverage exemption or you are claiming a coverage exemption on your return.

Part I — **Marketplace-Granted Coverage Exemptions for Individuals:** If you and/or a member of your tax household have an exemption granted by the Marketplace, complete Part I.

	a Name of Individual	b SSN	c Exemption Certificate Number
1			
2			
3			
4			
5			
6			

Part II — **Coverage Exemptions for Your Household Claimed on Your Return:**

7a Are you claiming an exemption because your household income is below the filing threshold? . . . . . . ☐ Yes ☑ No

b Are you claiming a hardship exemption because your gross income is below the filing threshold? . . . . . ☐ Yes ☑ No

Part III — **Coverage Exemptions for Individuals Claimed on Your Return:** If you and/or a member of your tax household are claiming an exemption on your return, complete Part III.

	a Name of Individual	b SSN	c Exemption Type	d Full Year	e Jan	f Feb	g Mar	h Apr	i May	j June	k July	l Aug	m Sept	n Oct	o Nov	p Dec
8	Gweneth George	333-33-4454	B		X	X										
9																
10																
11																
12																
13																

For Privacy Act and Paperwork Reduction Act Notice, see your tax return instructions.　　　Cat. No. 37787G　　　Form **8965** (2014)

Qualified Dividends and Capital Gain Tax Worksheet—Line 44

Keep for Your Records

Before you begin: ✓ See the earlier instructions for line 44 to see if you can use this worksheet to figure your tax.
✓ Before completing this worksheet, complete Form 1040 through line 43.
✓ If you do not have to file Schedule D and you received capital gain distributions, be sure you checked the box on line 13 of Form 1040.

1.	Enter the amount from Form 1040, line 43. However, if you are filing Form 2555 or 2555-EZ (relating to foreign earned income), enter the amount from line 3 of the Foreign Earned Income Tax Worksheet	1.	35,545
2.	Enter the amount from Form 1040, line 9b* .... 2.		
3.	Are you filing Schedule D?*		
	■ **Yes.** Enter the **smaller** of line 15 or 16 of Schedule D. If either line 15 or line 16 is blank or a loss, enter -0-	3.	1,023
	☐ **No.** Enter the amount from Form 1040, line 13		
4.	Add lines 2 and 3	4.	1,023
5.	If filing Form 4952 (used to figure investment interest expense deduction), enter any amount from line 4g of that form. Otherwise, enter -0-	5.	0
6.	Subtract line 5 from line 4. If zero or less, enter -0-	6.	1,023
7.	Subtract line 6 from line 1. If zero or less, enter -0-	7.	34,522
8.	Enter: $36,900 if single or married filing separately, $73,800 if married filing jointly or qualifying widow(er), $49,400 if head of household.	8.	36,900
9.	Enter the smaller of line 1 or line 8	9.	35,545
10.	Enter the smaller of line 7 or line 9	10.	34,522
11.	Subtract line 10 from line 9. This amount is taxed at 0%	11.	1,023
12.	Enter the smaller of line 1 or line 6	12.	1,023
13.	Enter the amount from line 11	13.	1,023
14.	Subtract line 13 from line 12	14.	0
15.	Enter: $406,750 if single, $228,800 if married filing separately, $457,600 if married filing jointly or qualifying widow(er), $432,200 if head of household.	15.	406,750
16.	Enter the smaller of line 1 or line 15	16.	35,545
17.	Add lines 7 and 11	17.	35,545
18.	Subtract line 17 from line 16. If zero or less, enter -0-	18.	0
19.	Enter the smaller of line 14 or line 18	19.	0
20.	Multiply line 19 by 15% (.15)	20.	0
21.	Add lines 11 and 19	21.	1,023
22.	Subtract line 21 from line 12	22.	0
23.	Multiply line 22 by 20% (.20)	23.	0
24.	Figure the tax on the amount on line 7. If the amount on line 7 is less than $100,000, use the Tax Table to figure the tax. If the amount on line 7 is $100,000 or more, use the Tax Computation Worksheet	24.	4,725
25.	Add lines 20, 23, and 24	25.	4,725
26.	Figure the tax on the amount on line 1. If the amount on line 1 is less than $100,000, use the Tax Table to figure the tax. If the amount on line 1 is $100,000 or more, use the Tax Computation Worksheet	26.	4,875
27.	**Tax on all taxable income.** Enter the **smaller** of line 25 or line 26. Also include this amount on Form 1040, line 44. If you are filing Form 2555 or 2555-EZ, do not enter this amount on Form 1040, line 44. Instead, enter it on line 4 of the Foreign Earned Income Tax Worksheet	27.	4,725

If you are filing Form 2555 or 2555-EZ, see the footnote in the Foreign Earned Income Tax Worksheet before completing this line.

Chapter 18 Review

1) How much investment income does a child have to make to be required to pay tax at the rate their parents are taxed at?

   If the child has investment income of more than $2,000, they will be taxed at their parent's tax rate.

2) What form must be filed to calculate an underpayment penalty?

   Form 2210 is used to calculate an underpayment penalty.

3) What can the taxpayer do to avoid paying the underpayment penalty?

   The taxpayer can have enough taxes withheld or pay estimated taxes to avoid paying the underpayment penalty.

4) What are the due dates for estimated tax payments?

   Estimated tax payments are due on the 15th of the month following the close of each quarter:
   - **Jan 1 – March 31...........April 15**
   - **April 1 – May 31.............June 15**
   - **June 1 – August 31........September 15**
   - **Sept 1 – Dec 31............January 15 of the next year.**

   If the due date falls on a Saturday, Sunday, or legal holiday, the due date is the next business day.

5) What are the two requirements, one of which must be met, for the taxpayer not to be required to pay estimated taxes?

   The taxpayer is not required to pay estimated taxes if their withholding and credits are less than:

   - **90% of the tax to be shown on their 2015 tax return, or**
   - **100% of the tax shown on the taxpayer's 2014 tax return. The 2014 tax return must cover all 12 months.**

Form 1040 — U.S. Individual Income Tax Return (99) 2014

Department of the Treasury—Internal Revenue Service

OMB No. 1545-0074 | IRS Use Only—Do not write or staple in this space.

For the year Jan. 1–Dec. 31, 2014, or other tax year beginning _____ , 2014, ending _____ , 20 ___

See separate instructions.

Your first name and initial	Last name	Your social security number
Samantha	Snowden	7 3 7 7 7 5 4 4 4

If a joint return, spouse's first name and initial | Last name | Spouse's social security number

Home address (number and street). If you have a P.O. box, see instructions. | Apt. no.

87 Lively Circle

▲ Make sure the SSN(s) above and on line 6c are correct.

City, town or post office, state, and ZIP code. If you have a foreign address, also complete spaces below (see instructions).

Your City, Your State, Your Zip Code

Foreign country name | Foreign province/state/county | Foreign postal code

Presidential Election Campaign
Check here if you, or your spouse if filing jointly, want $3 to go to this fund. Checking a box below will not change your tax or refund. ☑ You ☐ Spouse

Filing Status

Check only one box.

1. ☐ Single
2. ☐ Married filing jointly (even if only one had income)
3. ☐ Married filing separately. Enter spouse's SSN above and full name here. ▶
4. ☑ Head of household (with qualifying person). (See instructions.) If the qualifying person is a child but not your dependent, enter this child's name here. ▶
5. ☐ Qualifying widow(er) with dependent child

Exemptions

6a ☑ **Yourself.** If someone can claim you as a dependent, **do not** check box 6a . . . . . .
b ☐ **Spouse**

Boxes checked on 6a and 6b **1**

c **Dependents:**

(1) First name Last name	(2) Dependent's social security number	(3) Dependent's relationship to you	(4) ✓ if child under age 17 qualifying for child tax credit (see instructions)
Sara Snowden	4 4 3 2 2 5 6 4 3	Daughter	☑
			☐
			☐
			☐

No. of children on 6c who:
• lived with you **1**
• did not live with you due to divorce or separation (see instructions)

Dependents on 6c not entered above

If more than four dependents, see instructions and check here ▶ ☐

d Total number of exemptions claimed . . . . . .

Add numbers on lines above ▶ **2**

Income

Attach Form(s) W-2 here. Also attach Forms W-2G and 1099-R if tax was withheld.

If you did not get a W-2, see instructions.

7	Wages, salaries, tips, etc. Attach Form(s) W-2	7	22,355 00
8a	**Taxable** interest. Attach Schedule B if required	8a	
b	**Tax-exempt** interest. **Do not** include on line 8a 8b		
9a	Ordinary dividends. Attach Schedule B if required	9a	
b	Qualified dividends 9b		
10	Taxable refunds, credits, or offsets of state and local income taxes	10	
11	Alimony received	11	
12	Business income or (loss). Attach Schedule C or C-EZ	12	
13	Capital gain or (loss). Attach Schedule D if required. If not required, check here ▶ ☐	13	
14	Other gains or (losses). Attach Form 4797	14	
15a	IRA distributions 15a	b Taxable amount	15b
16a	Pensions and annuities 16a	b Taxable amount	16b
17	Rental real estate, royalties, partnerships, S corporations, trusts, etc. Attach Schedule E	17	
18	Farm income or (loss). Attach Schedule F	18	
19	Unemployment compensation	19	
20a	Social security benefits 20a	b Taxable amount	20b
21	Other income. List type and amount Form 8814	21	876 00
22	Combine the amounts in the far right column for lines 7 through 21. This is your **total income** ▶	22	23,231 00

Adjusted Gross Income

23	Educator expenses	23	
24	Certain business expenses of reservists, performing artists, and fee-basis government officials. Attach Form 2106 or 2106-EZ	24	
25	Health savings account deduction. Attach Form 8889	25	
26	Moving expenses. Attach Form 3903	26	
27	Deductible part of self-employment tax. Attach Schedule SE	27	
28	Self-employed SEP, SIMPLE, and qualified plans	28	
29	Self-employed health insurance deduction	29	
30	Penalty on early withdrawal of savings	30	
31a	Alimony paid b Recipient's SSN ▶	31a	
32	IRA deduction	32	
33	Student loan interest deduction	33	
34	Tuition and fees. Attach Form 8917	34	
35	Domestic production activities deduction. Attach Form 8903	35	
36	Add lines 23 through 35	36	
37	Subtract line 36 from line 22. This is your **adjusted gross income** ▶	37	23,231 00

For Disclosure, Privacy Act, and Paperwork Reduction Act Notice, see separate instructions.   Cat. No. 11320B   Form **1040** (2014)

Form 1040 (2014)   Page **2**

Tax and Credits	38	Amount from line 37 (adjusted gross income)		38	23,231 00
	39a	Check if: ☐ **You** were born before January 2, 1950, ☐ Blind. ☐ **Spouse** was born before January 2, 1950, ☐ Blind. } Total boxes checked ▶ 39a			
	b	If your spouse itemizes on a separate return or you were a dual-status alien, check here▶ 39b☐			
Standard Deduction for—	40	**Itemized deductions** (from Schedule A) **or** your **standard deduction** (see left margin)		40	9,100 00
	41	Subtract line 40 from line 38		41	14,131 00
• People who check any box on line 39a or 39b **or** who can be claimed as a dependent, see instructions.	42	**Exemptions.** If line 38 is $152,525 or less, multiply $3,950 by the number on line 6d. Otherwise, see instructions		42	7,900 00
	43	**Taxable income.** Subtract line 42 from line 41. If line 42 is more than line 41, enter -0-		43	6,231 00
	44	Tax (see instructions). Check if any from: **a** ☐ Form(s) 8814 **b** ☐ Form 4972 **c** ☐		44	723 00
• All others: Single or Married filing separately, $6,200	45	**Alternative minimum tax** (see instructions). Attach Form 6251		45	
	46	Excess advance premium tax credit repayment. Attach Form 8962		46	234 00
Married filing jointly or Qualifying widow(er), $12,400	47	Add lines 44, 45, and 46 ▶		47	957 00
	48	Foreign tax credit. Attach Form 1116 if required	48		
	49	Credit for child and dependent care expenses. Attach Form 2441	49		
Head of household, $9,100	50	Education credits from Form 8863, line 19	50		
	51	Retirement savings contributions credit. Attach Form 8880	51		
	52	Child tax credit. Attach Schedule 8812, if required	52	957 00	
	53	Residential energy credits. Attach Form 5695	53		
	54	Other credits from Form: **a** ☐ 3800 **b** ☐ 8801 **c** ☐	54		
	55	Add lines 48 through 54. These are your **total credits**		55	957 00
	56	Subtract line 55 from line 47. If line 55 is more than line 47, enter -0- ▶		56	0 00
Other Taxes	57	Self-employment tax. Attach Schedule SE		57	
	58	Unreported social security and Medicare tax from Form: **a** ☐ 4137 **b** ☐ 8919		58	
	59	Additional tax on IRAs, other qualified retirement plans, etc. Attach Form 5329 if required		59	
	60a	Household employment taxes from Schedule H		60a	
	b	First-time homebuyer credit repayment. Attach Form 5405 if required		60b	
	61	Health care: individual responsibility (see instructions) Full-year coverage ☐		61	
	62	Taxes from: **a** ☐ Form 8959 **b** ☐ Form 8960 **c** ☐ Instructions; enter code(s)		62	
	63	Add lines 56 through 62. This is your **total tax** ▶		63	0 00
Payments	64	Federal income tax withheld from Forms W-2 and 1099	64	1,211 00	
	65	2014 estimated tax payments and amount applied from 2013 return	65		
If you have a qualifying child, attach Schedule EIC.	66a	**Earned income credit (EIC)**	66a	2,443 00	
	b	Nontaxable combat pay election 66b			
	67	Additional child tax credit. Attach Schedule 8812	67	43 00	
	68	American opportunity credit from Form 8863, line 8	68		
	69	Net premium tax credit. Attach Form 8962	69		
	70	Amount paid with request for extension to file	70		
	71	Excess social security and tier 1 RRTA tax withheld	71		
	72	Credit for federal tax on fuels. Attach Form 4136	72		
	73	Credits from Form: **a** ☐ 2439 **b** ☐ Reserved **c** ☐ Reserved **d** ☐	73		
	74	Add lines 64, 65, 66a, and 67 through 73. These are your **total payments** ▶		74	3,697 00
Refund	75	If line 74 is more than line 63, subtract line 63 from line 74. This is the amount you **overpaid**		75	3,697 00
	76a	Amount of line 75 you want **refunded to you.** If Form 8888 is attached, check here ▶☐		76a	3,697 00
Direct deposit? See instructions.	▶ b	Routing number	▶ c Type: ☐ Checking ☐ Savings		
	▶ d	Account number			
	77	Amount of line 75 you want **applied to your 2015 estimated tax** ▶ 77			
Amount You Owe	78	**Amount you owe.** Subtract line 74 from line 63. For details on how to pay, see instructions ▶		78	
	79	Estimated tax penalty (see instructions) 79			

Third Party Designee Do you want to allow another person to discuss this return with the IRS (see instructions)? ☐ **Yes.** Complete below. ☑ **No**
Designee's name ▶   Phone no. ▶   Personal identification number (PIN) ▶

Sign Here Under penalties of perjury, I declare that I have examined this return and accompanying schedules and statements, and to the best of my knowledge and belief, they are true, correct, and complete. Declaration of preparer (other than taxpayer) is based on all information of which preparer has any knowledge.
Joint return? See instructions. Keep a copy for your records.
Your signature | Date | Your occupation: Teacher | Daytime phone number (555)555-5555
Spouse's signature. If a joint return, **both** must sign. | Date | Spouse's occupation | If the IRS sent you an Identity Protection PIN, enter it here (see inst.)

Paid Preparer Use Only Print/Type preparer's name: Jane Doe | Preparer's signature | Date | Check ☐ if self-employed | PTIN P00000000
Firm's name ▶ My Tax Service | Firm's EIN ▶ 63-0000000
Firm's address ▶ 100 Main St., Your City, Your State, Your Zip Code | Phone no. (555)555-1111

www.irs.gov/form1040   Form **1040** (2014)

Form **8814**	**Parents' Election To Report Child's Interest and Dividends**	OMB No. 1545-0074
Department of the Treasury Internal Revenue Service (99)	▶ Information about Form 8814 and its Instructions is at *www.irs.gov/form8814*. ▶ Attach to parents' Form 1040 or Form 1040NR.	20**14** Attachment Sequence No. **40**

Name(s) shown on your return	Your social security number
Samantha Snowden	737-77-5444

Caution. The federal income tax on your child's income, including qualified dividends and capital gain distributions, may be less if you file a separate tax return for the child instead of making this election. This is because you cannot take certain tax benefits that your child could take on his or her own return. For details, see **Tax benefits you cannot take** in the instructions.

A Child's name (first, initial, and last)	B Child's social security number
Sara Snowden	443-22-5643

C If more than one Form 8814 is attached, check here . . . . ▶ ☐

Part I Child's Interest and Dividends To Report on Your Return

1a	Enter your child's **taxable** interest. If this amount is different from the amounts shown on the child's Forms 1099-INT and 1099-OID, see the instructions	**1a**	2,876 00
b	Enter your child's **tax-exempt** interest. **Do not** include this amount on line 1a **1b**		
2a	Enter your child's ordinary dividends, including any Alaska Permanent Fund dividends. If your child received any ordinary dividends as a nominee, see the instructions	**2a**	
b	Enter your child's qualified dividends included on line 2a. See the instructions **2b**		
3	Enter your child's capital gain distributions. If your child received any capital gain distributions as a nominee, see the instructions	**3**	
4	Add lines 1a, 2a, and 3. If the total is $2,000 or less, skip lines 5 through 12 and go to line 13. If the total is $10,000 or more, **do not** file this form. Your child **must** file his or her own return to report the income	**4**	2,876 00
5	Base amount	**5**	2,000 00
6	Subtract line 5 from line 4	**6**	876 00
	If both lines 2b and 3 are zero or blank, skip lines 7 through 10, enter -0- on line 11, and go to line 12. Otherwise, go to line 7.		
7	Divide line 2b by line 4. Enter the result as a decimal (rounded to at least three places) . . . . **7** .		
8	Divide line 3 by line 4. Enter the result as a decimal (rounded to at least three places) . . . . **8** .		
9	Multiply line 6 by line 7. Enter the result here. See the instructions for where to report this amount on your return **9**		
10	Multiply line 6 by line 8. Enter the result here. See the instructions for where to report this amount on your return **10**		
11	Add lines 9 and 10	**11**	0 00
12	Subtract line 11 from line 6. Include this amount in the total on Form 1040, line 21, or Form 1040NR, line 21. In the space next to line 21, enter "Form 8814" and show the amount. If you checked the box on line C above, see the instructions. Go to line 13 below	**12**	876 00

Part II Tax on the First $2,000 of Child's Interest and Dividends

13	Amount not taxed	**13**	1,000 00
14	Subtract line 13 from line 4. If the result is zero or less, enter -0-	**14**	1,876 00
15	**Tax.** Is the amount on line 14 less than $1,000? ☑ **No.** Enter $100 here and see the **Note** below. ☐ **Yes.** Multiply line 14 by 10% (.10). Enter the result here and see the **Note** below.	**15**	100 00

Note. If you checked the box on line C above, see the instructions. Otherwise, include the amount from line 15 in the tax you enter on Form 1040, line 44, or Form 1040NR, line 42. Be sure to check box **a** on Form 1040, line 44, or Form 1040NR, line 42.

For Paperwork Reduction Act Notice, see your tax return instructions.   Cat. No. 10750J   Form **8814** (2014)

SCHEDULE EIC (Form 1040A or 1040) Department of the Treasury Internal Revenue Service (99)	**Earned Income Credit** Qualifying Child Information ► Complete and attach to Form 1040A or 1040 only if you have a qualifying child. ► Information about Schedule EIC (Form 1040A or 1040) and its instructions is at *www.irs.gov/scheduleeic*.	OMB No. 1545-0074 20**14** Attachment Sequence No. **43**

Name(s) shown on return Samantha Snowden	Your social security number 737-77-5444

Before you begin:
- See the instructions for Form 1040A, lines 42a and 42b, or Form 1040, lines 66a and 66b, to make sure that (a) you can take the EIC, and (b) you have a qualifying child.
- Be sure the child's name on line 1 and social security number (SSN) on line 2 agree with the child's social security card. Otherwise, at the time we process your return, we may reduce or disallow your EIC. If the name or SSN on the child's social security card is not correct, call the Social Security Administration at 1-800-772-1213.

- *If you take the EIC even though you are not eligible, you may not be allowed to take the credit for up to 10 years. See the instructions for details.*
- *It will take us longer to process your return and issue your refund if you do not fill in all lines that apply for each qualifying child.*

Qualifying Child Information	Child 1	Child 2	Child 3
1 Child's name If you have more than three qualifying children, you have to list only three to get the maximum credit.	First name / Last name Sara Snowden	First name / Last name	First name / Last name
2 Child's SSN The child must have an SSN as defined in the instructions for Form 1040A, lines 42a and 42b, or Form 1040, lines 66a and 66b, unless the child was born and died in 2014. If your child was born and died in 2014 and did not have an SSN, enter "Died" on this line and attach a copy of the child's birth certificate, death certificate, or hospital medical records.	443-22-5643		
3 Child's year of birth	Year __2_ _0_ _0_ _8__ *If born after 1995 and the child is younger than you (or your spouse, if filing jointly), skip lines 4a and 4b; go to line 5.*	Year ___ ___ ___ ___ *If born after 1995 and the child is younger than you (or your spouse, if filing jointly), skip lines 4a and 4b; go to line 5.*	Year ___ ___ ___ ___ *If born after 1995 and the child is younger than you (or your spouse, if filing jointly), skip lines 4a and 4b; go to line 5.*
4 a Was the child under age 24 at the end of 2014, a student, and younger than you (or your spouse, if filing jointly)?	☐ **Yes.** ☐ **No.** *Go to line 5.* / *Go to line 4b.*	☐ **Yes.** ☐ **No.** *Go to line 5.* / *Go to line 4b.*	☐ **Yes.** ☐ **No.** *Go to line 5.* / *Go to line 4b.*
b Was the child permanently and totally disabled during any part of 2014?	☐ **Yes.** ☐ **No.** *Go to line 5.* / The child is not a qualifying child.	☐ **Yes.** ☐ **No.** *Go to line 5.* / The child is not a qualifying child.	☐ **Yes.** ☐ **No.** *Go to line 5.* / The child is not a qualifying child.
5 Child's relationship to you (for example, son, daughter, grandchild, niece, nephew, foster child, etc.)	Daughter		
6 Number of months child lived with you in the United States during 2014 • If the child lived with you for more than half of 2014 but less than 7 months, enter "7." • If the child was born or died in 2014 and your home was the child's home for more than half the time he or she was alive during 2014, enter "12."	___12___ months *Do not enter more than 12 months.*	_____ months *Do not enter more than 12 months.*	_____ months *Do not enter more than 12 months.*

For Paperwork Reduction Act Notice, see your tax return instructions.	Cat. No. 13339M	Schedule EIC (Form 1040A or 1040) 2014

SCHEDULE 8812 (Form 1040A or 1040) Department of the Treasury Internal Revenue Service (99)	**Child Tax Credit** ▶ Attach to Form 1040, Form 1040A, or Form 1040NR. ▶ Information about Schedule 8812 and its separate instructions is at *www.irs.gov/schedule8812.*	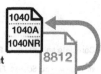	OMB No. 1545-0074 20**14** Attachment Sequence No. 47

Name(s) shown on return	Your social security number
Samantha Snowden	443-22-5643

Part I — Filers Who Have Certain Child Dependent(s) with an ITIN (Individual Taxpayer Identification Number)

⚠️ **CAUTION**
Complete this part only for each dependent who has an ITIN and for whom you are claiming the child tax credit.
If your dependent is not a qualifying child for the credit, you cannot include that dependent in the calculation of this credit.

Answer the following questions for each dependent listed on Form 1040, line 6c; Form 1040A, line 6c; or Form 1040NR, line 7c, who has an ITIN (Individual Taxpayer Identification Number) and that you indicated is a qualifying child for the child tax credit by checking column (4) for that dependent.

A For the first dependent identified with an ITIN and listed as a qualifying child for the child tax credit, did this child meet the substantial presence test? See separate instructions.

☐ Yes   ☐ No

B For the second dependent identified with an ITIN and listed as a qualifying child for the child tax credit, did this child meet the substantial presence test? See separate instructions.

☐ Yes   ☐ No

C For the third dependent identified with an ITIN and listed as a qualifying child for the child tax credit, did this child meet the substantial presence test? See separate instructions.

☐ Yes   ☐ No

D For the fourth dependent identified with an ITIN and listed as a qualifying child for the child tax credit, did this child meet the substantial presence test? See separate instructions.

☐ Yes   ☐ No

Note. If you have more than four dependents identified with an ITIN and listed as a qualifying child for the child tax credit, see the instructions and check here . . . . ▶ ☐

Part II — Additional Child Tax Credit Filers

1	**1040 filers:** Enter the amount from line 6 of your Child Tax Credit Worksheet (see the Instructions for Form 1040, line 52).			
	1040A filers: Enter the amount from line 6 of your Child Tax Credit Worksheet (see the Instructions for Form 1040A, line 35).	**1**	1,000	00
	1040NR filers: Enter the amount from line 6 of your Child Tax Credit Worksheet (see the Instructions for Form 1040NR, line 49).			
	If you used Pub. 972, enter the amount from line 8 of the Child Tax Credit Worksheet in the publication.			
2	Enter the amount from Form 1040, line 52; Form 1040A, line 35; or Form 1040NR, line 49	**2**	957	00
3	Subtract line 2 from line 1. If zero, **stop;** you cannot take this credit	**3**	43	00
4a	Earned income (see separate instructions) **4a** 22,355 00			
b	Nontaxable combat pay (see separate instructions) **4b**			
5	Is the amount on line 4a more than $3,000? ☐ **No.** Leave line 5 blank and enter -0- on line 6. ☑ **Yes.** Subtract $3,000 from the amount on line 4a. Enter the result . . . **5** 19,355 00			
6	Multiply the amount on line 5 by 15% (.15) and enter the result	**6**	2,903	00
	Next. Do you have three or more qualifying children? ☑ **No.** If line 6 is zero, stop; you cannot take this credit. Otherwise, skip Part III and enter the **smaller** of line 3 or line 6 on line 13. ☐ **Yes.** If line 6 is equal to or more than line 3, skip Part III and enter the amount from line 3 on line 13. Otherwise, go to line 7.			

For Paperwork Reduction Act Notice, see your tax return instructions.   Cat. No. 59761M   **Schedule 8812 (Form 1040A or 1040) 2014**

Chapter 18 Exercise

Part III   Certain Filers Who Have Three or More Qualifying Children

7   Withheld social security, Medicare, and Additional Medicare taxes from Form(s) W-2, boxes 4 and 6. If married filing jointly, include your spouse's amounts with yours. If your employer withheld or you paid Additional Medicare Tax or tier 1 RRTA taxes, see separate instructions **7**

8   **1040 filers:**   Enter the total of the amounts from Form 1040, lines 27 and 58, plus any taxes that you identified using code "UT" and entered on line 62.

      1040A filers: Enter -0-.   **8**

      1040NR filers: Enter the total of the amounts from Form 1040NR, lines 27 and 56, plus any taxes that you identified using code "UT" and entered on line 60.

9   Add lines 7 and 8 . . . .   **9**

10   **1040 filers:**   Enter the total of the amounts from Form 1040, lines 66a and 71.

      1040A filers: Enter the total of the amount from Form 1040A, line 42a, plus any excess social security and tier 1 RRTA taxes withheld that you entered to the left of line 46 (see separate instructions).   **10**

      1040NR filers: Enter the amount from Form 1040NR, line 67.

11   Subtract line 10 from line 9. If zero or less, enter -0- **11**

12   Enter the **larger** of line 6 or line 11 . . . .   **12**

      Next, enter the **smaller** of line 3 or line 12 on line 13.

Part IV   Additional Child Tax Credit

13   **This is your additional child tax credit** . . . .   **13**   43 | 00

1040
1040A
1040NR ◄   *Enter this amount on Form 1040, line 67, Form 1040A, line 43, or Form 1040NR, line 64.*

Form **8962**	**Premium Tax Credit (PTC)**	OMB No. 1545-0074
Department of the Treasury Internal Revenue Service	▶ Attach to Form 1040, 1040A, or 1040NR. ▶ Information about Form 8962 and its separate instructions is at *www.irs.gov/form8962*.	20**14** Attachment Sequence No. **73**

Name shown on your return	Your social security number	Relief (see instructions) ☐
Samantha Snowden	443-22-5643	

Part 1: Annual and Monthly Contribution Amount

1	Family Size: Enter the number of exemptions from Form 1040 or Form 1040A, line 6d, or Form 1040NR, line 7d .	**1**	2

2a Modified AGI: Enter your modified AGI (see instructions) . . . . . **2a** 25,231   **b** Enter total of your dependents' modified AGI (see instructions) **2b** 0

3	Household Income: Add the amounts on lines 2a and 2b	**3**	25,231

4 Federal Poverty Line: Enter the federal poverty amount as determined by the family size on line 1 and the federal poverty table for your state of residence during the tax year (see instructions). Check the appropriate box for the federal poverty table used.   **a** ☐ Alaska   **b** ☐ Hawaii   **c** ☑ Other 48 states and DC | **4** | 15,510

5 Household Income as a Percentage of Federal Poverty Line: Divide line 3 by line 4. Enter the result rounded to a whole percentage. (For example, for 1.542 enter the result as 154, for 1.549 enter as 155.) (See instructions for special rules.) | **5** | 163 %

6 Is the result entered on line 5 less than or equal to 400%? (See instructions if the result is less than 100%.)

   ☑ **Yes. Continue to line 7.**

   ☐ **No.** You are not eligible to receive PTC. If you received advance payment of PTC, see the instructions for how to report your Excess Advance PTC Repayment amount.

7	Applicable Figure: Using your line 5 percentage, locate your "applicable figure" on the table in the instructions . .	**7**	0.0460

8a Annual Contribution for Health Care: Multiply line 3 by line 7 . . . . . **8a** 1,161   **b** Monthly Contribution for Health Care: Divide line 8a by 12. Round to whole dollar amount | **8b** | 97

Part 2: Premium Tax Credit Claim and Reconciliation of Advance Payment of Premium Tax Credit

9 Did you share a policy with another taxpayer or get married during the year and want to use the alternative calculation? (see instructions)

   ☐ **Yes.** Skip to Part 4, Shared Policy Allocation, or Part 5, Alternative Calculation for Year of Marriage.   ☑ **No. Continue to line 10.**

10 Do all Forms 1095-A for your tax household include coverage for January through December with no changes in monthly amounts shown on lines 21–32, columns A and B?

   ☑ **Yes. Continue to line 11.** Compute your annual PTC. Skip lines 12–23 and continue to line 24.   ☐ **No. Continue to lines 12–23.** Compute your monthly PTC and continue to line 24.

Annual Calculation	**A.** Premium Amount (Form(s) 1095-A, line 33A)	**B.** Annual Premium Amount of SLCSP (Form(s) 1095-A, line 33B)	**C.** Annual Contribution Amount (Line 8a)	**D.** Annual Maximum Premium Assistance (Subtract C from B)	**E.** Annual Premium Tax Credit Allowed (Smaller of A or D)	**F.** Annual Advance Payment of PTC (Form(s) 1095-A, line 33C)
11 Annual Totals	3,975	4,086	1,161	2,925	2,925	3,159

Monthly Calculation	**A.** Monthly Premium Amount (Form(s) 1095-A, lines 21–32, column A)	**B.** Monthly Premium Amount of SLCSP (Form(s) 1095-A, lines 21–32, column B)	**C.** Monthly Contribution Amount (Amount from line 8b or alternative marriage monthly contribution)	**D.** Monthly Maximum Premium Assistance (Subtract C from B)	**E.** Monthly Premium Tax Credit Allowed (Smaller of A or D)	**F.** Monthly Advance Payment of PTC (Form(s) 1095-A, lines 21–32, column C)
12 January						
13 February						
14 March						
15 April						
16 May						
17 June						
18 July						
19 August						
20 September						
21 October						
22 November						
23 December						

24	Total Premium Tax Credit: Enter the amount from line 11E or add lines 12E through 23E and enter the total here .	**24**	2,925
25	Advance Payment of PTC: Enter the amount from line 11F or add lines 12F through 23F and enter the total here .	**25**	3,159
26	Net Premium Tax Credit: If line 24 is greater than line 25, subtract line 25 from line 24. Enter the difference here and on Form 1040, line 69; Form 1040A, line 45; or Form 1040NR, line 65. If you elected the alternative calculation for marriage, enter zero. If line 24 equals line 25, enter zero. Stop here. If line 25 is greater than line 24, leave this line blank and continue to line 27 .	**26**	

Part 3: Repayment of Excess Advance Payment of the Premium Tax Credit

27	Excess Advance Payment of PTC: If line 25 is greater than line 24, subtract line 24 from line 25. Enter the difference here	**27**	234
28	Repayment Limitation: Using the percentage on line 5 and your filing status, locate the repayment limitation amount in the instructions. Enter the amount here	**28**	600
29	Excess Advance Premium Tax Credit Repayment: Enter the smaller of line 27 or line 28 here and on Form 1040, line 46; Form 1040A, line 29; or Form 1040NR, line 44	**29**	234

For Paperwork Reduction Act Notice, see your tax return instructions.   Cat. No. 37784Z   Form **8962** (2014)

Form 8867

Department of the Treasury
Internal Revenue Service

Paid Preparer's Earned Income Credit Checklist

▶ To be completed by preparer and filed with Form 1040, 1040A, or 1040EZ.
▶ Information about Form 8867 and its separate instructions is at *www.irs.gov/form8867*.

OMB No. 1545-1629

2014

Attachment
Sequence No. **177**

Taxpayer name(s) shown on return	Taxpayer's social security number
Samantha Snowden	737-77-5444

For the definitions of **Qualifying Child** and **Earned Income**, see **Pub. 596**.

Part I	**All Taxpayers**

1   Enter preparer's name and PTIN ▶ Jane Doe P00000000

2   Is the taxpayer's filing status married filing separately? . . . .   ☐ Yes ☑ No

   ▶ If you checked **"Yes"** on line 2, **stop;** the taxpayer **cannot** take the EIC. Otherwise, continue.

3   Does the taxpayer (and the taxpayer's spouse if filing jointly) have a social security number (SSN) that allows him or her to work and is valid for EIC purposes? See the instructions before answering   . . . .   ☑ Yes ☐ No

   ▶ If you checked **"No"** on line 3, **stop;** the taxpayer **cannot** take the EIC. Otherwise, continue.

4   Is the taxpayer (or the taxpayer's spouse if filing jointly) filing Form 2555 or 2555-EZ (relating to the exclusion of foreign earned income)? . . . .   ☐ Yes ☑ No

   ▶ If you checked **"Yes"** on line 4, **stop;** the taxpayer **cannot** take the EIC. Otherwise, continue.

5a   Was the taxpayer (or the taxpayer's spouse) a nonresident alien for any part of 2014?   . . . .   ☐ Yes ☑ No

   ▶ If you checked **"Yes"** on line 5a, go to line 5b. Otherwise, skip line 5b and go to line 6.

 b   Is the taxpayer's filing status married filing jointly? . . . .   ☐ Yes ☑ No

   ▶ If you checked **"Yes"** on line 5a and **"No"** on line 5b, **stop;** the taxpayer **cannot** take the EIC. Otherwise, continue.

6   Is the taxpayer's **investment income** more than $3,350? See the instructions before answering.   ☐ Yes ☑ No

   ▶ If you checked **"Yes"** on line 6, **stop;** the taxpayer **cannot** take the EIC. Otherwise, continue.

7   Could the taxpayer be a **qualifying child** of another person for 2014? If the taxpayer's filing status is married filing jointly, check **"No."** Otherwise, see instructions before answering . . . .   ☐ Yes ☑ No

   ▶ If you checked **"Yes"** on line 7, **stop;** the taxpayer **cannot** take the EIC. Otherwise, go to Part II or Part III, whichever applies.

For Paperwork Reduction Act Notice, see separate instructions.   Cat. No. 26142H   Form **8867** (2014)

Part II — Taxpayers With a Child

Caution. If there is more than one child, complete lines 8 through 14 for one child before going to the next column.

	Child 1	Child 2	Child 3

8   Child's name . . . .
   Child 1: Sara

9   Is the child the taxpayer's son, daughter, stepchild, foster child, brother, sister, stepbrother, stepsister, half brother, half sister, or a descendant of any of them?
   Child 1: ☑ Yes ☐ No   Child 2: ☐ Yes ☐ No   Child 3: ☐ Yes ☐ No

10   Was the child unmarried at the end of 2014?
If the child was married at the end of 2014, see the instructions before answering . . . .
   Child 1: ☑ Yes ☐ No   Child 2: ☐ Yes ☐ No   Child 3: ☐ Yes ☐ No

11   Did the child live with the taxpayer in the United States for over half of 2014? See the instructions before answering . . . .
   Child 1: ☑ Yes ☐ No   Child 2: ☐ Yes ☐ No   Child 3: ☐ Yes ☐ No

12   Was the child (at the end of 2014)—
- Under age 19 and younger than the taxpayer (or the taxpayer's spouse, if the taxpayer files jointly),
- Under age 24, a student (defined in the instructions), and younger than the taxpayer (or the taxpayer's spouse, if the taxpayer files jointly), or
- Any age and permanently and totally disabled? . . . .
   Child 1: ☑ Yes ☐ No   Child 2: ☐ Yes ☐ No   Child 3: ☐ Yes ☐ No

▶ If you checked **"Yes"** on lines 9, 10, 11, **and** 12, the child is the taxpayer's qualifying child; go to line 13a. If you checked **"No"** on line 9, 10, 11, **or** 12, the child is not the taxpayer's qualifying child; see the instructions for line 12.

13a   Do you or the taxpayer know of another person who could check **"Yes"** on lines 9, 10, 11, **and** 12 for the child? (If the only other person is the taxpayer's spouse, see the instructions before answering.) . . . .
   Child 1: ☐ Yes ☑ No   Child 2: ☐ Yes ☐ No   Child 3: ☐ Yes ☐ No

▶ If you checked **"No"** on line 13a, go to line 14. Otherwise, go to line 13b.

   b   Enter the child's relationship to the other person(s) . . . .

   c   Under the tiebreaker rules, is the child treated as the taxpayer's qualifying child? See the instructions before answering . . . .
   Child 1: ☐ Yes ☐ No ☐ Don't know   Child 2: ☐ Yes ☐ No ☐ Don't know   Child 3: ☐ Yes ☐ No ☐ Don't know

▶ If you checked **"Yes"** on line 13c, go to line 14. If you checked **"No,"** the taxpayer **cannot** take the EIC based on this child and cannot take the EIC for taxpayers who do not have a qualifying child. If there is more than one child, see the **Note** at the bottom of this page. If you checked **"Don't know,"** explain to the taxpayer that, under the tiebreaker rules, the taxpayer's EIC and other tax benefits may be disallowed. Then, if the taxpayer wants to take the EIC based on this child, complete lines 14 and 15. If not, and there are no other qualifying children, the taxpayer cannot take the EIC, including the EIC for taxpayers without a qualifying child; do not complete Part III. If there is more than one child, see the **Note** at the bottom of this page.

14   Does the qualifying child have an SSN that allows him or her to work and is valid for EIC purposes? See the instructions before answering . . . .
   Child 1: ☑ Yes ☐ No   Child 2: ☐ Yes ☐ No   Child 3: ☐ Yes ☐ No

▶ If you checked **"No"** on line 14, the taxpayer **cannot** take the EIC based on this child and cannot take the EIC available to taxpayers without a qualifying child. If there is more than one child, see the **Note** at the bottom of this page. If you checked "Yes" on line 14, continue.

15   Are the taxpayer's **earned income** and **adjusted gross income** each less than the limit that applies to the taxpayer for 2014? See instructions . .
   ☑ Yes ☐ No

▶ If you checked **"No"** on line 15, **stop;** the taxpayer **cannot** take the EIC. If you checked **"Yes"** on line 15, the taxpayer can take the EIC. Complete **Schedule EIC** and attach it to the taxpayer's return. If there are two or three qualifying children with valid SSNs, list them on Schedule EIC in the same order as they are listed here. If the taxpayer's EIC was reduced or disallowed for a year after 1996, see Pub. 596 to see if **Form 8862** must be filed. Go to line 20.

Note. If there is more than one child, complete lines 8 through 14 for the other child(ren) (but for no more than three qualifying children).

Chapter 18 Exercise

Part III	**Taxpayers Without a Qualifying Child**		

16 Was the taxpayer's main home, and the main home of the taxpayer's spouse if filing jointly, in the United States for more than half the year? (Military personnel on extended active duty outside the United States are considered to be living in the United States during that duty period.) See the instructions before answering. ☐ Yes ☐ No

▶ If you checked **"No"** on line 16, **stop;** the taxpayer **cannot** take the EIC. Otherwise, continue.

17 Was the taxpayer, or the taxpayer's spouse if filing jointly, at least age 25 but under age 65 at the end of 2014? See the instructions before answering . . . . ☐ Yes ☐ No

▶ If you checked **"No"** on line 17, **stop;** the taxpayer **cannot** take the EIC. Otherwise, continue.

18 Is the taxpayer eligible to be claimed as a dependent on anyone else's federal income tax return for 2014? If the taxpayer's filing status is married filing jointly, check **"No"**. . . . . ☐ Yes ☐ No

▶ If you checked **"Yes"** on line 18, **stop;** the taxpayer **cannot** take the EIC. Otherwise, continue.

19 Are the taxpayer's **earned income** and **adjusted gross income** each less than the limit that applies to the taxpayer for 2014? See instructions . . . . ☐ Yes ☐ No

▶ If you checked **"No"** on line 19, **stop;** the taxpayer **cannot** take the EIC. If you checked **"Yes"** on line 19, the taxpayer can take the EIC. If the taxpayer's EIC was reduced or disallowed for a year after 1996, see Pub. 596 to find out if **Form 8862** must be filed. Go to line 20.

Part IV	**Due Diligence Requirements**		

20 Did you complete Form 8867 based on current information provided by the taxpayer or reasonably obtained by you? . . . . ☑ Yes ☐ No

21 Did you complete the EIC worksheet found in the Form 1040, 1040A, or 1040EZ instructions (or your own worksheet that provides the same information as the 1040, 1040A, or 1040EZ worksheet)? . . ☑ Yes ☐ No

22 If any qualifying child was not the taxpayer's son or daughter, do you know or did you ask why the parents were not claiming the child? . . . . ☐ Yes ☐ No
☑ Does not apply

23 If the answer to question 13a is **"Yes"** (indicating that the child lived for more than half the year with someone else who could claim the child for the EIC), did you explain the tiebreaker rules and possible consequences of another person claiming your client's qualifying child? . . . . ☐ Yes ☐ No
☑ Does not apply

24 Did you ask this taxpayer any additional questions that are necessary to meet your knowledge requirement? See the instructions before answering . . . . ☑ Yes ☐ No
☐ Does not apply

To comply with the EIC knowledge requirement, you must not know or have reason to know that any information you used to determine the taxpayer's eligibility for, and the amount of, the EIC is incorrect. You may not ignore the implications of information furnished to you or known by you, and you must make reasonable inquiries if the information furnished to you appears to be incorrect, inconsistent, or incomplete. At the time you make these inquiries, you must document in your files the inquiries you made and the taxpayer's responses.

25 Did you document (a) the taxpayer's answer to question 22 (if applicable), (b) whether you explained the tiebreaker rules to the taxpayer and any additional information you got from the taxpayer as a result, and (c) any additional questions you asked and the taxpayer's answers? . . . . ☑ Yes ☐ No
☐ Does not apply

▶ You have complied with all the due diligence requirements if you:

1. Completed the actions described on lines 20 and 21 and checked **"Yes"** on those lines,
2. Completed the actions described on lines 22, 23, 24, and 25 (if they apply) and checked **"Yes"** (or **"Does not apply"**) on those lines,
3. Submit Form 8867 in the manner required, **and**
4. Keep all five of the following records for 3 years from the latest of the dates specified in the instructions under *Document Retention*:

   a. Form 8867,
   b. The EIC worksheet(s) or your own worksheet(s),
   c. Copies of any taxpayer documents you relied on to determine eligibility for or amount of EIC,
   d. A record of how, when, and from whom the information used to prepare the form and worksheet(s) was obtained, and
   e. A record of any additional questions you asked and your client's answers.

▶ You have not complied with all the due diligence requirements if you checked **"No"** on line 20, 21, 22, 23, 24, or 25. You may have to pay a $500 penalty for each failure to comply.

Form **8867** (2014)

Chapter 18 Exercise

Part V	Documents Provided to You

26 Identify below any document that the taxpayer provided to you and that you relied on to determine the taxpayer's EIC eligibility. Check all that apply. **Keep a copy of any documents you relied on.** See the instructions before answering. If there is no qualifying child, check box a. If there is no disabled child, check box o.

Residency of Qualifying Child(ren)

☐ a No qualifying child	☐ i	Place of worship statement
☐ b School records or statement	☐ j	Indian tribal official statement
☐ c Landlord or property management statement	☐ k	Employer statement
☐ d Health care provider statement	☐ l	Other (specify) ▼
☐ e Medical records		
☐ f Child care provider records		
☐ g Placement agency statement		
☐ h Social service records or statement	☑ m	Did not rely on any documents, but made notes in file
	☐ n	Did not rely on any documents

Disability of Qualifying Child(ren)

☑ o No disabled child	☐ s	Other (specify) ▼
☐ p Doctor statement		
☐ q Other health care provider statement		
☐ r Social services agency or program statement	☐ t	Did not rely on any documents, but made notes in file
	☐ u	Did not rely on any documents

27 If a Schedule C is included with this return, identify below the information that the taxpayer provided to you and that you relied on to prepare the Schedule C. Check all that apply. **Keep a copy of any documents you relied on.** See the instructions before answering. If there is no Schedule C, check box a.

Documents or Other Information

☑ a No Schedule C	☐ h	Bank statements
☐ b Business license	☐ i	Reconstruction of income and expenses
☐ c Forms 1099	☐ j	Other (specify) ▼
☐ d Records of gross receipts provided by taxpayer		
☐ e Taxpayer summary of income		
☐ f Records of expenses provided by taxpayer	☐ k	Did not rely on any documents, but made notes in file
☐ g Taxpayer summary of expenses	☐ l	Did not rely on any documents

Form **8867** (2014)

Earned Income Credit Worksheet

1.	Enter the amount from Form 1040, Line 7.	1.	22,355
2.	Taxable Scholarship or Fellowship grant not reported on a W-2, if included on line 7, Form 10...................................... _____		
3.	Amount received for work performed while an inmate in a penal institution (enter "PRI" and the amount subtracted on the dotted line next to Form 1040, line 7), if included on line 7.. _____		
4.	Amount received as a pension or annuity from a nonqualified deferred compensation plan or a nongovernmental Sec. 457 plan. (Enter "DFC" and amount subtracted on the dotted line next to Form 1040, line 7), if included on line 7.................. _____		
5.	Add lines 2, 3, and 4.	5.	0
6.	Subtract line 5 from line 1.	6.	22,355
7.	Nontaxable Combat pay if the election is made to use it. You will have to complete two worksheets: one with the combat pay and one without. Use the one that will result in the most EIC.	7.	0
8.	Add lines 6 and 7.	8.	22,355
9.	If the taxpayer had any income from self-employment or was a statutory employee, complete lines 10 –18. If not skip lines 10 –18 and go to line 19.		
10.	If the taxpayer is filing a Schedule SE, enter the amount from Schedule SE, Section A, line 3 or Section B, line 3, whichever applies. If the taxpayer is not filing a Schedule SE, skip lines 10 –14 and go to line 15. If the taxpayer is a statutory employee, go to line 18.	10.	
11.	Enter any amounts from Schedule SE, Section B, line 4b, and line 5a.	11.	
12.	Combine lines 10 and 11.	12.	
13.	Enter the amount from Schedule SE, Section A, line 6 or Section B, line 13.	13.	
14.	Subtract line 13 from line 12. If lines 15 and 18 do not apply, enter this amount on line 17 and go to line 19.	14.	
15.	If the taxpayer is not required to file a Schedule SE because the net earnings were less than $400, enter amount from Schedule F, line 36, and from farm partnerships, Schedule K-1 (Form 1065), box 14, code A.	15.	
16.	Enter any net profit or (loss) from Schedule C, line 31; Schedule C-EZ, line 3, Schedule K-1, box 14, code A (other than farming); and Schedule K-1, box 9, code J1.	16.	
17.	Combine lines 14, 15, and 16.	17.	
18.	If the taxpayer is a statutory employee, enter the amount from Schedule C, line 1, or Schedule C-EZ, line 1 that the taxpayer is filing as a statutory employee.	18.	
19.	Add lines 8, 17, and 18. This is the earned income.	19.	22,355
20.	Look up the amount on line 19 above in the EIC Table to find the credit. If the amount is 0, stop. The taxpayer does not qualify for the credit.	20.	2,579
21.	Enter the amount from Form 1040, line 38. If the amount on line 21 is the same as the amount on line 19, stop and enter the amount from line 20 on line 64a of the Form 1040. This is the taxpayer's Earned Income Credit. If not, go to line 22.	21.	23,231
22.	Is the amount on line 21 less than: • $8,150 ($13,550 if MFJ) if the taxpayer has no qualifying children? • $17,850 ($23,300 if MFJ) if the taxpayer has one or more qualifying children? If the answer is yes, stop and enter the amount from line 21 on the Form 1040, line 66a. If the answer is no, look up the amount from line 21 in the EIC Table to find the credit and go to line 23.	22.	2,443
23.	Look at the amounts on line 20 and 22. Enter the smaller amount here and on Form 1040, line 66a.	23.	2,443

2014 Child Tax Credit Worksheet—Line 52

Keep for Your Records

CAUTION

1. To be a qualifying child for the child tax credit, the child must be your dependent, **under age 17** at the end of 2014, and meet all the conditions in Steps 1 through 3 in the instructions for line 6c. Make sure you checked the box on Form 1040, line 6c, column (4), for each qualifying child.

2. If you do not have a qualifying child, you cannot claim the child tax credit.

3. If your qualifying child has an ITIN instead of an SSN, file Schedule 8812.

4. Do **not** use this worksheet, but use Pub. 972 instead, if:

   a. You are claiming the adoption credit, mortgage interest credit, District of Columbia first-time homebuyer credit, or residential energy efficient property credit,

   b. You are excluding income from Puerto Rico, or

   c. You are filing Form 2555, 2555-EZ, or 4563.

Part 1

1. Number of qualifying children: ___1___ × $1,000. Enter the result.

   | 1 | 1,000 |

2. Enter the amount from Form 1040, line 38.

   | 2 | 23,231 |

3. Enter the amount shown below for your filing status.

   - Married filing jointly — $110,000
   - Single, head of household, or qualifying widow(er) — $75,000
   - Married filing separately — $55,000

   | 3 | 75,000 |

4. Is the amount on line 2 more than the amount on line 3?

   ■ **No.** Leave line 4 blank. Enter -0- on line 5, and go to line 6.

   ☐ **Yes.** Subtract line 3 from line 2. If the result is not a multiple of $1,000, increase it to the next multiple of $1,000. For example, increase $425 to $1,000, increase $1,025 to $2,000, etc.

   | 4 | |

5. Multiply the amount on line 4 by 5% (.05). Enter the result.

   | 5 | 0 |

6. Is the amount on line 1 more than the amount on line 5?

   ☐ **No.** (STOP) You cannot take the child tax credit on Form 1040, line 52. You also cannot take the additional child tax credit on Form 1040, line 67. Complete the rest of your Form 1040.

   ■ **Yes.** Subtract line 5 from line 1. Enter the result. *Go to Part 2.*

   | 6 | 1,000 |

2014 Form 1040—Line 52

2014 Child Tax Credit Worksheet—*Continued*   *Keep for Your Records*

Before you begin Part 2: √ Figure the amount of any credits you are claiming on Form 5695, Part II; Form 8910; Form 8936; or Schedule R.

Part 2	7.	Enter the amount from Form 1040, line 47.	**7** 957

8. Add any amounts from:

    Form 1040, line 48   _____

    Form 1040, line 49 + _____

    Form 1040, line 50 + _____

    Form 1040, line 51 + _____

    Form 5695, line 30 + _____

    Form 8910, line 15 + _____

    Form 8936, line 23 + _____

    Schedule R, line 22 + _____

    Enter the total. **8**

9. Are the amounts on lines 7 and 8 the same?

    ☐ **Yes.** (STOP)

        You cannot take this credit because there is no tax to reduce. However, you may be able to take the **additional child tax credit.** See the **TIP** below.

    ■ **No.** Subtract line 8 from line 7.   **9** 957

10. Is the amount on line 6 more than the amount on line 9?

    ■ **Yes.** Enter the amount from line 9.   ⎫
        Also, you may be able to take the   ⎬ **This is your child tax credit.**   **10** 957
        additional child tax credit. See the   ⎭
        TIP below.

    ☐ **No.** Enter the amount from line 6.

Enter this amount on Form 1040, line 52.

1040 ◄····

TIP You may be able to take the **additional child tax credit** on Form 1040, line 67, if you answered "Yes" on line 9 **or** line 10 above.

    ● First, complete your Form 1040 through lines 66a and 66b.

    ● Then, use Schedule 8812 to figure any additional child tax credit.

Chapter 19 Review

1) Within what time is an amended return required to be filed?

   An amendment must be filed within three years after the original return was filed or within two years after the date the tax is paid, whichever is later. If the return was filed before the April 15th due date for the tax return, the return is treated as having been filed on the due date.

2) What form or schedule must be filed to amend a tax return?

   To amend a tax return, a taxpayer must file a Form 1040X.

3) If the taxpayer and spouse filed a joint return and the refund was kept for federal income taxes the taxpayer owed, what form may the spouse file to receive her part of the refund if all of the other requirements are met?

   If the taxpayer and spouse are filing a Married Filing Joint tax return and the refund is expected to offset a debt that either the taxpayer or spouse (but not both) legally owes, an Injured Spouse Form (Form 8379) can be filed.

4) An extension is an extension to file, not to **pay**.

5) What is the due date for a return after an extension has been filed?

   The due date of a return after an extension has been filed is October 15th.

6) What are the two methods of signing an electronically filed return?

   There are two methods of signing the return. One method is the Self Select PIN and the other is the Practitioner PIN method.

7) What is an ERO?

   An ERO is an Electronic Return Originator – An authorized IRS e-file provider that originates the electronic submission of returns to the IRS.

8) What is the signature authorization form for an electronically filed return?

   The signature authorization form is Form 8879.

Form 1040 — Department of the Treasury—Internal Revenue Service (99)
U.S. Individual Income Tax Return **2014** OMB No. 1545-0074 IRS Use Only—Do not write or staple in this space.

For the year Jan. 1–Dec. 31, 2014, or other tax year beginning , 2014, ending , 20 — See separate instructions.

Your first name and initial: Tommy	Last name: Carmichael
Your social security number: 630 20 5493	
Spouse's first name and initial: Tammy	Last name: Carmichael
Spouse's social security number: 756 37 2345	

Home address (number and street): 89 Sunrise Circle Apt. no.

▲ Make sure the SSN(s) above and on line 6c are correct.

City, town or post office, state, and ZIP code: Your City, Your State, Your Zip Code

Presidential Election Campaign — Check here if you, or your spouse if filing jointly, want $3 to go to this fund. ☑ You ☑ Spouse

Filing Status — Check only one box.
1 ☐ Single
2 ☑ Married filing jointly (even if only one had income)
3 ☐ Married filing separately. Enter spouse's SSN above and full name here. ▶
4 ☐ Head of household (with qualifying person).
5 ☐ Qualifying widow(er) with dependent child

Exemptions
6a ☑ Yourself.
b ☑ Spouse

c Dependents: (1) First name / Last name	(2) Dependent's SSN	(3) Relationship to you	(4) ✓ if child under 17
Timothy Carmichael	275 65 3245	Son	☑

Boxes checked on 6a and 6b: 2
No. of children on 6c who lived with you: 1
Add numbers on lines above ▶ 3
d Total number of exemptions claimed

Income
7 Wages, salaries, tips, etc. Attach Form(s) W-2	7	68,997 00
8a Taxable interest	8a	
b Tax-exempt interest	8b	
9a Ordinary dividends	9a	
b Qualified dividends	9b	
10 Taxable refunds	10	
11 Alimony received	11	
12 Business income or (loss)	12	
13 Capital gain or (loss) ☐	13	
14 Other gains or (losses)	14	
15a IRA distributions	15b	
16a Pensions and annuities	16b	
17 Rental real estate, royalties, partnerships	17	
18 Farm income or (loss)	18	
19 Unemployment compensation	19	
20a Social security benefits	20b	
21 Other income	21	
22 Combine the amounts... total income ▶	22	68,997 00

Adjusted Gross Income
23 Educator expenses	23	
24 Certain business expenses	24	
25 Health savings account deduction	25	
26 Moving expenses	26	
27 Deductible part of self-employment tax	27	
28 Self-employed SEP, SIMPLE	28	
29 Self-employed health insurance deduction	29	
30 Penalty on early withdrawal of savings	30	
31a Alimony paid	31a	
32 IRA deduction	32	
33 Student loan interest deduction	33	1,977 00
34 Tuition and fees	34	
35 Domestic production activities deduction	35	
36 Add lines 23 through 35	36	1,977 00
37 Subtract line 36 from line 22. This is your adjusted gross income ▶	37	67,020 00

For Disclosure, Privacy Act, and Paperwork Reduction Act Notice, see separate instructions. Cat. No. 11320B Form 1040 (2014)

Form 1040 (2014)   Page **2**

Tax and Credits	38	Amount from line 37 (adjusted gross income)	38	67,020	00

	39a	Check if: ☐ **You** were born before January 2, 1950, ☐ **Spouse** was born before January 2, 1950, ☐ Blind. ☐ Blind. } Total boxes checked ► 39a			
	b	If your spouse itemizes on a separate return or you were a dual-status alien, check here ► 39b ☐			

Standard Deduction for—

- People who check any box on line 39a or 39b **or** who can be claimed as a dependent, see instructions.
- All others:

Single or Married filing separately, $6,200

Married filing jointly or Qualifying widow(er), $12,400

Head of household, $9,100

40	**Itemized deductions** (from Schedule A) **or** your **standard deduction** (see left margin) . .	40	12,400	00
41	Subtract line 40 from line 38	41	54,620	00
42	**Exemptions.** If line 38 is $152,525 or less, multiply $3,950 by the number on line 6d. Otherwise, see instructions	42	11,850	00
43	**Taxable income.** Subtract line 42 from line 41. If line 42 is more than line 41, enter -0- . .	43	42,770	00
44	**Tax** (see instructions). Check if any from: **a** ☐ Form(s) 8814 **b** ☐ Form 4972 **c** ☐ _____	44	5,509	00
45	**Alternative minimum tax** (see instructions). Attach Form 6251	45		
46	Excess advance premium tax credit repayment. Attach Form 8962	46		
47	Add lines 44, 45, and 46 . . . . ►	47	5,509	00

48	Foreign tax credit. Attach Form 1116 if required	48			
49	Credit for child and dependent care expenses. Attach Form 2441	49	464	0	
50	Education credits from Form 8863, line 19	50	180	00	
51	Retirement savings contributions credit. Attach Form 8880	51			
52	Child tax credit. Attach Schedule 8812, if required . . .	52	1,000	00	
53	Residential energy credits. Attach Form 5695	53			
54	Other credits from Form: **a** ☐ 3800 **b** ☐ 8801 **c** ☐	54			

55	Add lines 48 through 54. These are your **total credits**	55	1,644	00
56	Subtract line 55 from line 47. If line 55 is more than line 47, enter -0- . . . . . ►	56	3,865	00

Other Taxes	57	Self-employment tax. Attach Schedule SE	57		
	58	Unreported social security and Medicare tax from Form: **a** ☐ 4137 **b** ☐ 8919 . .	58		
	59	Additional tax on IRAs, other qualified retirement plans, etc. Attach Form 5329 if required . .	59		
	60a	Household employment taxes from Schedule H	60a		
	b	First-time homebuyer credit repayment. Attach Form 5405 if required	60b		
	61	Health care: individual responsibility (see instructions) Full-year coverage ☑ . . .	61		
	62	Taxes from: **a** ☐ Form 8959 **b** ☐ Form 8960 **c** ☐ Instructions; enter code(s) _____	62		
	63	Add lines 56 through 62. This is your **total tax** . . . . ►	63	3,865	00

Payments	64	Federal income tax withheld from Forms W-2 and 1099 . .	64	8,223	00	
If you have a qualifying child, attach Schedule EIC.	65	2014 estimated tax payments and amount applied from 2013 return	65			
	66a	**Earned income credit (EIC)**	66a			
	b	Nontaxable combat pay election	66b			
	67	Additional child tax credit. Attach Schedule 8812	67			
	68	American opportunity credit from Form 8863, line 8 . . .	68			
	69	Net premium tax credit. Attach Form 8962	69			
	70	Amount paid with request for extension to file	70			
	71	Excess social security and tier 1 RRTA tax withheld . . .	71			
	72	Credit for federal tax on fuels. Attach Form 4136	72			
	73	Credits from Form: **a** ☐ 2439 **b** ☐ Reserved **c** ☐ Reserved **d** ☐	73			
	74	Add lines 64, 65, 66a, and 67 through 73. These are your **total payments** . . . . . ►	74	8,223	00

Refund	75	If line 74 is more than line 63, subtract line 63 from line 74. This is the amount you **overpaid**	75	4,358	00
Direct deposit? See instructions.	76a	Amount of line 75 you want **refunded to you.** If Form 8888 is attached, check here . ► ☐	76a	4,358	00
	► b	Routing number _____ ► **c** Type: ☐ Checking ☐ Savings			
	► d	Account number _____			
	77	Amount of line 75 you want **applied to your 2015 estimated tax** ►	77		

Amount You Owe	78	**Amount you owe.** Subtract line 74 from line 63. For details on how to pay, see instructions ►	78	
	79	Estimated tax penalty (see instructions)	79	

Third Party Designee

Do you want to allow another person to discuss this return with the IRS (see instructions)? ☐ **Yes.** Complete below. ☐ **No**

Designee's name ►	Phone no. ►	Personal identification number (PIN) ►

Sign Here

Joint return? See instructions. Keep a copy for your records.

Under penalties of perjury, I declare that I have examined this return and accompanying schedules and statements, and to the best of my knowledge and belief, they are true, correct, and complete. Declaration of preparer (other than taxpayer) is based on all information of which preparer has any knowledge.

Your signature	Date	Your occupation	Daytime phone number
		Electrician	**(555)555-5555**
Spouse's signature. If a joint return, **both** must sign.	Date	Spouse's occupation	If the IRS sent you an Identity Protection PIN, enter it here (see inst.)
		Bank Teller	

Paid Preparer Use Only

Print/Type preparer's name	Preparer's signature	Date	Check ☐ if self-employed	PTIN
Jane Doe				P00000000
Firm's name ► My Tax Service			Firm's EIN ►	63-0000000
Firm's address ► 100 Main St., Your City, Your State, Your Zip Code			Phone no.	(555)555-1111

Form **2441**	**Child and Dependent Care Expenses**		OMB No. 1545-0074

Form **2441**

Child and Dependent Care Expenses

► Attach to Form 1040, Form 1040A, or Form 1040NR.

► Information about Form 2441 and its separate instructions is at *www.irs.gov/form2441*.

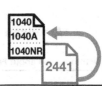

OMB No. 1545-0074

20**14**

Department of the Treasury
Internal Revenue Service (99)

Attachment Sequence No. **21**

Name(s) shown on return	Your social security number
Tommy and Tammy Carmichael	630-20-5493

Part I — **Persons or Organizations Who Provided the Care**—You **must** complete this part.
(If you have more than two care providers, see the instructions.)

1 (a) Care provider's name	(b) Address (number, street, apt. no., city, state, and ZIP code)	(c) Identifying number (SSN or EIN)	(d) Amount paid (see instructions)	
First Steps Daycare	45 ABC St. Your City, Your State, Your Zip Code	54-2958223	2,322	00

Did you receive **dependent care benefits?** — No → Complete only Part II below.
— Yes → Complete Part III on the back next.

Caution. If the care was provided in your home, you may owe employment taxes. If you do, you cannot file Form 1040A. For details, see the instructions for Form 1040, line 60a, or Form 1040NR, line 59a.

Part II — **Credit for Child and Dependent Care Expenses**

2 Information about your **qualifying person(s)**. If you have more than two qualifying persons, see the instructions.

(a) Qualifying person's name First / Last	(b) Qualifying person's social security number	(c) Qualified expenses you incurred and paid in 2014 for the person listed in column (a)	
Timothy Carmichael	275-65-3245	2,322	00

3	Add the amounts in column (c) of line 2. **Do not** enter more than $3,000 for one qualifying person or $6,000 for two or more persons. If you completed Part III, enter the amount from line 31	**3**	2,322	00
4	Enter your **earned income.** See instructions	**4**	36,999	00
5	If married filing jointly, enter your spouse's earned income (if you or your spouse was a student or was disabled, see the instructions); **all others**, enter the amount from line 4	**5**	31,998	00
6	Enter the **smallest** of line 3, 4, or 5	**6**	2,322	00
7	Enter the amount from Form 1040, line 38; Form 1040A, line 22; or Form 1040NR, line 37. . . . . **7**	67,020	00		

8 Enter on line 8 the decimal amount shown below that applies to the amount on line 7

If line 7 is: Over / But not over	Decimal amount is	If line 7 is: Over / But not over	Decimal amount is
$0—15,000	.35	$29,000—31,000	.27
15,000—17,000	.34	31,000—33,000	.26
17,000—19,000	.33	33,000—35,000	.25
19,000—21,000	.32	35,000—37,000	.24
21,000—23,000	.31	37,000—39,000	.23
23,000—25,000	.30	39,000—41,000	.22
25,000—27,000	.29	41,000—43,000	.21
27,000—29,000	.28	43,000—No limit	.20

		8	X.	20
9	Multiply line 6 by the decimal amount on line 8. If you paid 2013 expenses in 2014, see the instructions	**9**	464	00
10	Tax liability limit. Enter the amount from the Credit Limit Worksheet in the instructions. **10**	5,509	00	
11	**Credit for child and dependent care expenses.** Enter the **smaller** of line 9 or line 10 here and on Form 1040, line 49; Form 1040A, line 31; or Form 1040NR, line 47	**11**	464	00

For Paperwork Reduction Act Notice, see your tax return instructions.   Cat. No. 11862M   Form **2441** (2014)

Form **8863**	**Education Credits** **(American Opportunity and Lifetime Learning Credits)** ► Attach to Form 1040 or Form 1040A. ► Information about Form 8863 and its separate Instructions Is at *www.irs.gov/form8863*.	OMB No. 1545-0074 **20 14** Attachment Sequence No. **50**
Department of the Treasury Internal Revenue Service (99)		

Name(s) shown on return	Your social security number
Tommy and Tammy Carmichael	630 · 20 · 5493

> ⚠ **CAUTION** *Complete a separate Part III on page 2 for each student for whom you are claiming either credit before you complete Parts I and II.*

Part I   Refundable American Opportunity Credit

1	After completing Part III for each student, enter the total of all amounts from all Parts III, line 30	**1**		
2	Enter: $180,000 if married filing jointly; $90,000 if single, head of household, or qualifying widow(er)	**2**		
3	Enter the amount from Form 1040, line 38, or Form 1040A, line 22. If you are filing Form 2555, 2555-EZ, or 4563, or you are excluding income from Puerto Rico, see Pub. 970 for the amount to enter	**3**		
4	Subtract line 3 from line 2. If zero or less, **stop**; you cannot take any education credit	**4**		
5	Enter: $20,000 if married filing jointly; $10,000 if single, head of household, or qualifying widow(er)	**5**		
6	If line 4 is: • Equal to or more than line 5, enter 1.000 on line 6 . . . . • Less than line 5, divide line 4 by line 5. Enter the result as a decimal (rounded to at least three places)		**6**	.
7	Multiply line 1 by line 6. **Caution:** If you were under age 24 at the end of the year **and** meet the conditions described in the instructions, you **cannot** take the refundable American opportunity credit; skip line 8, enter the amount from line 7 on line 9, and check this box . . . . ► ☐	**7**		
8	**Refundable American opportunity credit.** Multiply line 7 by 40% (.40). Enter the amount here and on Form 1040, line 68, or Form 1040A, line 44. Then go to line 9 below.	**8**		

Part II   Nonrefundable Education Credits

9	Subtract line 8 from line 7. Enter here and on line 2 of the Credit Limit Worksheet (see instructions)		**9**		
10	After completing Part III for each student, enter the total of all amounts from all Parts III, line 31. If zero, skip lines 11 through 17, enter -0- on line 18, and go to line 19		**10**	900	00
11	Enter the smaller of line 10 or $10,000		**11**	900	00
12	Multiply line 11 by 20% (.20)		**12**	180	00
13	Enter: $128,000 if married filing jointly; $64,000 if single, head of household, or qualifying widow(er)	**13** 128,000 00			
14	Enter the amount from Form 1040, line 38, or Form 1040A, line 22. If you are filing Form 2555, 2555-EZ, or 4563, or you are excluding income from Puerto Rico, see Pub. 970 for the amount to enter	**14** 67,020 00			
15	Subtract line 14 from line 13. If zero or less, skip lines 16 and 17, enter -0- on line 18, and go to line 19	**15** 60,980 00			
16	Enter: $20,000 if married filing jointly; $10,000 if single, head of household, or qualifying widow(er)	**16** 20,000 00			
17	If line 15 is: • Equal to or more than line 16, enter 1.000 on line 17 and go to line 18 • Less than line 16, divide line 15 by line 16. Enter the result as a decimal (rounded to at least three places)		**17**	1 . 000	
18	Multiply line 12 by line 17. Enter here and on line 1 of the Credit Limit Worksheet (see instructions) ►		**18**	180	00
19	**Nonrefundable education credits.** Enter the amount from line 7 of the Credit Limit Worksheet (see instructions) here and on Form 1040, line 50, or Form 1040A, line 33		**19**	180	00

For Paperwork Reduction Act Notice, see your tax return instructions. Cat. No. 25379M Form **8863** (2014)

Chapter 19 Exercise

Form 8863 (2014)   Page **2**

Name(s) shown on return	Your social security number		
Tommy and Tammy Carmichael	630	20	5493

> ⚠️ **CAUTION** *Complete Part III for each student for whom you are claiming either the American opportunity credit or lifetime learning credit. Use additional copies of Page 2 as needed for each student.*

Part III	**Student and Educational Institution Information**
	See instructions.

20 Student name (as shown on page 1 of your tax return)	**21** Student social security number (as shown on page 1 of your tax return)
Tammy Carmichael	

22 Educational institution information (see instructions)

a. Name of first educational institution	**b.** Name of second educational institution (if any)
State University	
(1) Address. Number and street (or P.O. box). City, town or post office, state, and ZIP code. If a foreign address, see instructions.	**(1)** Address. Number and street (or P.O. box). City, town or post office, state, and ZIP code. If a foreign address, see instructions.
250 Grand Ave., Your City, Your State, Your Zip Code	
(2) Did the student receive Form 1098-T from this institution for 2014? ☐ Yes ☑ No	**(2)** Did the student receive Form 1098-T from this institution for 2014? ☐ Yes ☐ No
(3) Did the student receive Form 1098-T from this institution for 2013 with Box 2 filled in and Box 7 checked? ☐ Yes ☑ No	**(3)** Did the student receive Form 1098-T from this institution for 2013 with Box 2 filled in and Box 7 checked? ☐ Yes ☐ No
If you checked "No" in **both (2) and (3)**, skip **(4)**.	If you checked "No" in **both (2) and (3)**, skip **(4)**.
(4) If you checked "Yes" in **(2)** or **(3)**, enter the institution's federal identification number (from Form 1098-T). ___ ___ - ___ ___ ___ ___ ___ ___	**(4)** If you checked "Yes" in **(2)** or **(3)**, enter the institution's federal identification number (from Form 1098-T). ___ ___ - ___ ___ ___ ___ ___ ___

23	Has the Hope Scholarship Credit or American opportunity credit been claimed for this student for any 4 tax years before 2014?	☐ Yes — **Stop!** Go to line 31 for this student. ☑ No — Go to line 24.
24	Was the student enrolled at least half-time for at least one academic period that began or is treated as having begun in 2014 at an eligible educational institution in a program leading towards a postsecondary degree, certificate, or other recognized postsecondary educational credential? (see instructions)	☐ Yes — Go to line 25. ☑ No — **Stop!** Go to line 31 for this student.
25	Did the student complete the first 4 years of post-secondary education before 2014?	☐ Yes — **Stop!** Go to line 31 for this student. ☐ No — Go to line 26.
26	Was the student convicted, before the end of 2014, of a felony for possession or distribution of a controlled substance?	☐ Yes — **Stop!** Go to line 31 for this student. ☐ No — Complete lines 27 through 30 for this student.

> ⚠️ **CAUTION** *You **cannot** take the American opportunity credit and the lifetime learning credit for the **same student** in the same year. If you complete lines 27 through 30 for this student, do not complete line 31.*

American Opportunity Credit

27	Adjusted qualified education expenses (see instructions). **Do not enter more than $4,000**	**27**	
28	Subtract $2,000 from line 27. If zero or less, enter -0-.	**28**	
29	Multiply line 28 by 25% (.25)	**29**	
30	If line 28 is zero, enter the amount from line 27. Otherwise, add $2,000 to the amount on line 29 and enter the result. Skip line 31. Include the total of all amounts from all Parts III, line 30 on Part I, line 1 .	**30**	

Lifetime Learning Credit

31	Adjusted qualified education expenses (see instructions). Include the total of all amounts from all Parts III, line 31, on Part II, line 10	**31**	900

Form **8863** (2014)

F-129

2014 Child Tax Credit Worksheet—Line 52

Keep for Your Records

1. To be a qualifying child for the child tax credit, the child must be your dependent, **under age 17** at the end of 2014, and meet all the conditions in Steps 1 through 3 in the instructions for line 6c. Make sure you checked the box on Form 1040, line 6c, column (4), for each qualifying child.
2. If you do not have a qualifying child, you cannot claim the child tax credit.
3. If your qualifying child has an ITIN instead of an SSN, file Schedule 8812.
4. Do **not** use this worksheet, but use Pub. 972 instead, if:
   a. You are claiming the adoption credit, mortgage interest credit, District of Columbia first-time homebuyer credit, or residential energy efficient property credit,
   b. You are excluding income from Puerto Rico, or
   c. You are filing Form 2555, 2555-EZ, or 4563.

Part 1

1. Number of qualifying children: ___1___ × $1,000. Enter the result. | **1** | 1,000

2. Enter the amount from Form 1040, line 38. | **2** | 67,020

3. Enter the amount shown below for your filing status.
   - Married filing jointly — $110,000
   - Single, head of household, or qualifying widow(er) — $75,000
   - Married filing separately — $55,000
   | **3** | 110,000

4. Is the amount on line 2 more than the amount on line 3?
   ■ **No.** Leave line 4 blank. Enter -0- on line 5, and go to line 6.
   ☐ **Yes.** Subtract line 3 from line 2.
   If the result is not a multiple of $1,000, increase it to the next multiple of $1,000. For example, increase $425 to $1,000, increase $1,025 to $2,000, etc.
   | **4** |

5. Multiply the amount on line 4 by 5% (.05). Enter the result. | **5** | 0

6. Is the amount on line 1 more than the amount on line 5?
   ☐ **No.** (STOP)
   You cannot take the child tax credit on Form 1040, line 52. You also cannot take the additional child tax credit on Form 1040, line 67. Complete the rest of your Form 1040.
   ■ **Yes.** Subtract line 5 from line 1. Enter the result. *Go to Part 2.*
   | **6** | 1,000

2014 Child Tax Credit Worksheet—*Continued*   *Keep for Your Records*

Before you begin Part 2: √ Figure the amount of any credits you are claiming on Form 5695, Part II; Form 8910; Form 8936; or Schedule R.

Part 2

7. Enter the amount from Form 1040, line 47. **7** | 5,509

8. Add any amounts from:

Form 1040, line 48 _____

Form 1040, line 49 + ___464___

Form 1040, line 50 + ___180___

Form 1040, line 51 + _____

Form 5695, line 30 + _____

Form 8910, line 15 + _____

Form 8936, line 23 + _____

Schedule R, line 22 + _____

Enter the total. **8** | 644

9. Are the amounts on lines 7 and 8 the same?

☐ **Yes.** (STOP) You cannot take this credit because there is no tax to reduce. However, you may be able to take the **additional child tax credit.** See the **TIP** below.

■ **No.** Subtract line 8 from line 7.   **9** | 4,865

10. Is the amount on line 6 more than the amount on line 9?

☐ **Yes.** Enter the amount from line 9. Also, you may be able to take the **additional child tax credit.** See the **TIP** below.

■ **No.** Enter the amount from line 6.

This is your child tax credit.

10 | 1,000

Enter this amount on Form 1040, line 52.

1040

TIP You may be able to take the **additional child tax credit** on Form 1040, line 67, if you answered "Yes" on line 9 **or** line 10 above.

● First, complete your Form 1040 through lines 66a and 66b.

● Then, use Schedule 8812 to figure any additional child tax credit.

Student Loan Interest Deduction Worksheet—Line 33

Keep for Your Records

Before you begin:
  √ Figure any write-in adjustments to be entered on the dotted line next to line 36 (see the instructions for line 36).
  √ Be sure you have read the **Exception** in the instructions for this line to see if you can use this worksheet instead of Pub. 970 to figure your deduction.

1.	Enter the total interest you paid in 2014 on qualified student loans (see the instructions for line 33). **Do not** enter more than $2,500 . . . . **1.**	1,977
2.	Enter the amount from Form 1040, line 22 . . . . **2.**	68,997
3.	Enter the total of the amounts from Form 1040, lines 23 through 32, plus any write-in adjustments you entered on the dotted line next to line 36 . . . . **3.**	
4.	Subtract line 3 from line 2 . . . . **4.**	68,997

5.	Enter the amount shown below for your filing status.
	
	  • Single, head of household, or qualifying widow(er)—$65,000
	  • Married filing jointly—$130,000 } . . . . **5.**
		130,000

6.	Is the amount on line 4 more than the amount on line 5?
	
	  ■ **No.** Skip lines 6 and 7, enter -0- on line 8, and go to line 9.
	
	  ☐ **Yes.** Subtract line 5 from line 4 . . . . **6.**	

7.	Divide line 6 by $15,000 ($30,000 if married filing jointly). Enter the result as a decimal (rounded to at least three places). If the result is 1.000 or more, enter 1.000 . . . . **7.**	.
8.	Multiply line 1 by line 7 . . . . **8.**	0
9.	**Student loan interest deduction.** Subtract line 8 from line 1. Enter the result here and on Form 1040, line 33. **Do not** include this amount in figuring any other deduction on your return (such as on Schedule A, C, E, etc.) . . . . **9.**	1,977

Line 10

Credit Limit Worksheet

Complete this worksheet to figure the amount to enter on line 10.

1. Enter the amount from Form 1040, line 47; Form 1040A, line 28; or Form 1040NR, line 45 . . . . **1.** _5,509_

2. Enter the amount from Form 1040, line 48; or Form 1040NR, line 46; Form 1040A filers enter -0- . . . . . **2.** _0_

3. Subtract line 2 from line 1. Also enter this amount on Form 2441, line 10. But if zero or less, **stop**; you cannot take the credit . . . . **3.** _5,509_

Credit Limit Worksheet

Complete this worksheet to figure the amount to enter on line 19.

1. Enter the amount from Form 8863, line 18 . . . . **1.** _180_

2. Enter the amount from Form 8863, line 9 . . . . **2.** _____

3. Add lines 1 and 2 . . . . **3.** _180_

4. Enter the amount from:
   Form 1040, line 47; or
   Form 1040A, line 30 . . . . **4.** _5,509_

5. Enter the total of your credits from either:
   Form 1040, lines 48 and 49,
   and Schedule R, line 22; or
   Form 1040A, lines 31 and 32 . . . . . . **5.** _464_

6. Subtract line 5 from line 4 . . . . **6.** _5,045_

7. Enter the smaller of line 3 or line 6 here and on Form 8863, line 19 . . . . **7.** _180_

Adjusted Qualified Education Expenses Worksheet

See *Qualified Education Expenses*, earlier, before completing.

Complete a separate worksheet for each student for each academic period beginning or treated as beginning (see below) in 2014 for which you paid (or are treated as having paid) qualified education expenses in 2014.

1. Total qualified education expenses paid for or on behalf of the student in 2014 for the academic period . . . . _900_

2. Less adjustments:
   a. Tax-free educational assistance received in 2014 allocable to the academic period . . . . _____
   b. Tax-free educational assistance received in 2015 (and before you file your 2014 tax return) allocable to the academic period . . . _____
   c. Refunds of qualified education expenses paid in 2014 if the refund is received in 2014 or in 2015 before you file your 2014 tax return . . . . _____

3. Total adjustments (add lines 2a, 2b, and 2c) . . . . _____

4. Adjusted qualified education expenses. Subtract line 3 from line 1. If zero or less, enter -0- . . . . _900_

Printed in the United States
By Bookmasters